microeconomics

theory with applications sixth edition

b. curtis eaton | diane f. eaton | douglas w. allen

University of Calgary

Simon Fraser University

Toronto

National Library of Canada Cataloguing in Publication

Eaton, B. Curtis, 1943–
Microeconomics / B. Curtis Eaton, Diane F. Eaton, Douglas W. Allen. — 6th ed.

Includes bibliographical references and index.
ISBN 0-13-121790-9

1. Microeconomics. I. Eaton, Diane F. II. Allen, Douglas W. (Douglas Ward), 1960– III. Title.

HB172.E38 2005338.5 2003-905398-9

0-13-121790-9

Vice-President, Editorial Director: Michael J. Young
Acquisitions Editor: Gary Bennett
Marketing Manager: Steve McGill
Developmental Editor: Pam Voves
Production Editor: Cheryl Jackson
Copy Editor: Karen Bennett
Proofreader: Bonnie DiMalta
Production Coordinator: Janette Lush
Page Layout: Carol Anderson
Permissions Manager: Susan Wallace-Cox
Art Director: Julia Hall
Cover and Interior Design: Miguel Acevedo
Cover Image: PhotoDisc/Paul Edmondson

3 4 5 09 08 07 06 05

Printed and bound in Canada.

Contents

Chapter 12 The Distribution of Income 411

Chapter 13 Competitive General Equilibrium 440

Preface

To the Student

We are all curious about the world around us, and we want to understand it. Unfortunately, the world is a complicated place and not always easy to understand. Economics provides a systematic way of understanding the human behaviour that we see every day, from mundane things such as how traffic behaves to less obvious things such as why some religious groups require commitments of time or money as a condition of membership. Economics does this by developing a model of behaviour. If the word *model* seems intimidating, let's think of a model as a well-articulated story that leads to specific conclusions. The nice thing about the economic model we are going to develop is that it is widely applicable, and so it saves a great deal of time in analyzing problems. Once you understand the basic mechanics of supply and demand, you will be able to shift easily from thinking about tariffs for corn to considering shortages of tickets for a Rolling Stones "final" tour concert. We have made an effort in this book to apply the model constantly as we develop it. We would encourage you to apply the economic ideas to your own life as you read along. As with anything you wish to master, the best way is to practise, practise, practise.

As authors we are not content to simply teach you a large body of theory, presented in a vacuum. For us economic theory is of little use if it cannot explain real-world puzzles. Our view has strongly influenced the way we have written this book. In every chapter we carefully go through the standard economic theory found in most economics textbooks. However, along the way we provide numerous applications — some big, some small — that show how the theory can be used.

The use of in-chapter problems is meant to promote active reading in two ways: by encouraging you to check your understanding of material that you have just read and, sometimes, by challenging you to extend what you have learned one step farther. (We provide answers to all the in-chapter problems at the back of the book.) Our philosophy is that the only real way to learn microeconomics is to *do* it — every step of the way.

Of course, microeconomics is a field that is changing rapidly — and that is its real challenge. We not only cover the standard topics, but also provide an overview of current research and trends in many important areas. We bring you right up to the frontiers of modern microeconomic research — and also let you see just how much exciting work in microeconomics remains to be done. In the end we hope you will not only develop your economic modelling skills, but that your economic intuition will develop as well.

The Book

The sixth edition of *Microeconomics* continues the major changes found in the last two editions. The organization of the book has remained the same in this edition … mostly because our consumers have said they like it the way it is. Generally in this edition we have added to our strengths: new applications, more problems, and general updating of material. The most significant change is the elimination of the chapter on product differentiation and its replacement by a chapter on game theory. Game theory is a body of ideas that help us understand behaviour in situations where the interactions between people are important. There have been many applications of game theory to economics, and so it is appropriate for it to be dealt with in an intermediate text.

The text remains organized in 20 chapters, grouped into 7 parts. In turn, the seven parts form three large sections. The first section (consisting of Chapters 1–13, grouped together as Parts I–V) presents basic intermediate neoclassical theory. The second section (consisting of Chapters 14–16, forming Part VI) presents advanced neoclassical topics. The third section (consisting of Chapters 17–20, grouped together as Part VII) presents what might be called "modern microeconomics." The idea behind this organization was to move from easy material to more difficult material *within a model framework*. Too often textbooks present a chapter on neoclassical choice theory, followed by a chapter on choice under uncertainty, followed in turn by chapters on neoclassical production. Such a sequence requires users to "change gears" in midstream in terms of the fundamental model. The problem is made worse when theories of the firm are presented before a discussion of cost and output. In our new edition, the fundamental neoclassical assumptions are maintained until Chapter 17, and then a full break is made.

Features

We have retained and enhanced the effective features of the previous edition to facilitate learning and offer flexibility in the use of this book:

Key terms are boldfaced where they are defined in the text, and they are restated in the margins.

Important **assumptions** and **results** are set off by coloured rules for easy identification.

Every chapter contains a number of **applications**. These applications vary from the everyday variety to the exotic, from the very easy to the more difficult. The major applications are given their own subsections, separate from the theory.

Boxed Problems are interspersed throughout the chapters to enable users to test their understanding of the material. Full answers to these problems are provided at the back of the book.

Calculus material is set off from the rest of the text in footnotes and in chapter appendices.

A **Summary** is given for each chapter.

A set of **Exercises** at the end of each chapter offers the opportunity to apply the material to a variety of situations. Exercises that require calculus are identified by an asterisk.

References at the end of each chapter will help guide users to further readings.

A **Glossary** of important terms is found at the back of the book.

To the Instructor

The major focus of our book is to try to teach students how to think like economists. We almost always start with an interesting question and ask, "How would an economist try to answer this particular question?" Then we construct the solution — an economic model — from the ground up. We have been careful to choose applications that are interesting and not too difficult — applications that are well within students' grasp — and then to present them in clear, consistent, step-by-step discussions. We then show how the model can be generalized to apply to other similar problems. In this way, students are actively engaged in developing the standard tools of microeconomic analysis. More importantly, they see how economists create those tools and get a chance to do economics for themselves. The benefit of this approach is that students learn that abstract economic thinking (that is, economic model building) is essentially about very real and familiar problems.

This problem-solving approach is reinforced by many in-chapter problems and end-of-chapter exercises. The point of the in-chapter problems — a feature that we introduced to the intermediate microeconomics market in the first edition of *Microeconomics* — is to draw students into the material and to keep them actively engaged in their reading. Full answers to all the in-chapter problems are given at the back of the book to guarantee that students will not be frustrated if they fail to hit on solutions quickly. At the end of each chapter, a complete set of exercises (consisting of a mixture of intuitive, arithmetic, and calculus exercises) reinforces students' learning. Many of the exercises are relatively straightforward, but a few are quite challenging.

Because our whole approach is applied — we almost always work from the specific application to more general theory — our book is full of lively and interesting examples. The applications in each chapter have been designed to move from the easy and obvious to the difficult and more subtle. But our objective throughout is to use these applications as a means of developing economic theory in as precise and rigorous a way as possible. Our major aim is to give students a thorough grounding in microeconomic theory.

This book is analytically rigorous but still widely accessible to undergraduate students. The analysis is presented in a readable style, and each topic flows naturally from what came before it and leads smoothly into what follows.

We also provide a balance between traditional economic theory and modern developments in microeconomics. Our treatment of the standard topics of microeconomics is careful and comprehensive. Students using our book will acquire a thorough understanding of the traditional tools of the microeconomic theorist. However, we have also made efforts to introduce current research topics at the intermediate level.

For the most part, these more advanced topics are presented in the last section of the book in Parts VI and VII. Unlike most other authors, we have divided the study of monopoly into two chapters. In the first (Chapter 10) we deal with the standard monopoly model and applications. In the second (Chapter 14) we pick up where Chapter 10 left off and examine several monopoly pricing practices. These include not only the standard analysis of price discrimination, but also two-part pricing, tie-in sales, all-or-nothing pricing, and more. In Chapters 15 and 16 we provide an introduction to game theory with applications to oligopoly and market structure. In these chapters we introduce a new method of analyzing problems that we later apply to externalities and public goods. Perhaps the most innovative part of the book is Part VII (Chapters 17–20), in which we present an integrated analysis of uncertainty and asymmetric information. Here we rigorously analyze the role of transaction costs and property rights, and relate these concepts to asymmetric information. We have organized the individual chapters in Part VII around specific applications.

Course Designs

We have prepared the book so that it can be adapted for various types of courses. The entire book is intended for a two-semester course in microeconomic theory. The first semester would cover Parts I–V, and the second semester would cover Parts VI–VII.

A number of different one-semester courses can be taught from this book to suit the needs of various instructors. The chapters that form the core of a standard one-semester microeconomics course are Chapters 1–3 and Chapters 6–8. Since the remaining chapters are written almost as stand-alone units, they can be used in any combination. Hence a number of specialized courses — for example, courses that emphasize comparative institutional analysis, labour economics, industrial organization, or uncertainty and information — can easily be built on this core by assigning the relevant additional chapters.

To afford further flexibility, the calculus material has been grouped together separately in footnotes and in chapter appendices. In addition, the exercises that require calculus are identified by an asterisk (*). In the main text itself we rely on carefully explained graphic and algebraic techniques rather than calculus.

Supplements

The **Instructor's Resource CD-ROM** contains the following resources:

An **Instructor's Manual** that provides answers to the end-of-chapter exercises, as well as suggestions for lectures and a series of easy-to-administer classroom experiments.

Pearson TestGen, a computerized test item file that enables instructors to view and edit the existing questions, add questions, generate tests, and print the tests in a variety of formats. Powerful search and sort functions make it easy to locate questions and arrange them in any order desired. TestGen also enables instructors to administer tests on a local area network, have the tests graded electronically, and have the results prepared in electronic or printed reports. The Pearson TestGen is compatible with IBM or Macintosh systems.

PowerPoint Presentations provide lecture notes and the figures from the text.

The following items have been carefully prepared to supplement the new edition:

A **Study Guide**, entitled *Problem Solving in Microeconomics,* provides further study material for students. In addition to chapter summaries, case studies, lists of key words, multiple-choice questions, and true-false questions, this guide offers many additional fascinating real-world problems.

A **Companion Website**, at www.pearsoned.ca/eaton, includes student self-tests and additional resources for instructors.

Acknowledgments

We are grateful for the useful suggestions and encouragement given to us by the reviewers of the fifth edition and those who reviewed the manuscript for the new edition, including

Shari Corrigan, Camosun College
Al Slivinski, University of Western Ontario
Weiqiu Yu, University of New Brunswick
Bruce Cater, Trent University
Irwin Lipnowski, University of Manitoba

We would like to acknowledge all those at Pearson Education Canada who worked on this edition of the text, including Gary Bennett, Pam Voves, Cheryl Jackson, Janette Lush, Karen Bennett, Lawrence Lynch, Edie Franks, Miguel Acevedo, and Carol Anderson.

B. Curtis Eaton
Diane F. Eaton
Douglas W. Allen

Both Curtis Eaton and Doug Allen are available by email for comments and questions at **eaton@ucalgary.ca** or **allen@sfu.ca**.

A Great Way to Learn and Instruct Online

The Pearson Education Canada Companion Website is easy to navigate and is organized to correspond to the chapters in this textbook. Whether you are a student in the classroom or a distance learner you will discover helpful resources for in-depth study and research that empower you in your quest for greater knowledge and maximize your potential for success in the course.

[www.pearsoned.ca/eaton]

PEARSON Prentice Hall

Jump to... http://www.pearsoned.ca/eaton

Home Search Help Profile

Companion Website

Home >

PH Companion Website

Microeconomics, Sixth Edition, by Eaton, Eaton, and Allen

Student Resources

The modules in this section provide students with tools for learning course material. These modules include:

- Chapter Summary
- Destinations
- Quizzes
- Applications
- Power Point Presentations
- Glossary

In the quiz modules students can send answers to the grader and receive instant feedback on their progress through the Results Reporter. Coaching comments and references to the textbook may be available to ensure that students take advantage of all available resources to enhance their learning experience.

Instructor Resources

A link to the protected Instructor's Central site provides instructors with additional teaching tools. Downloadable PowerPoint Presentations, and an Instructor's Manual are just some of the materials that may be available in this section. Where appropriate, this section will be password protected. To get a password, simply contact your Pearson Education Canada Representative or call Faculty Sales and Services at 1-800-850-5813.

Part I

An Introduction to Microeconomics

Chapter 1 is your introduction to the world of economic thinking. We begin with a sampler of interesting microeconomic questions and show you how economists go about building specific economic models to answer these questions. We then use these examples to present a more systematic discussion of the subject matter and method of economics. We describe an economy, explore the equilibrium method that economists use to analyze economic problems, define positive and normative economics, and consider Pareto optimality and cost-benefit analysis. This introduction concludes with a brief discussion of a market economy and an outline of the remainder of the book.

CHAPTER 1

Microeconomics: A Working Methodology

Why do you sometimes find two or three gas stations at the same intersection? Why does the value of a new car plummet the instant you drive it off the lot? Why do people have to spend so much time searching for an apartment in rent-controlled areas? Why do amusement parks often charge a whopping admission price to the park and almost nothing for the rides? Why does McDonald's break down the job of making hamburgers into so many little tasks and hire different workers to do each one? Why does IBM produce a whole spectrum of products? Why are some markets (like the market for local telephone services) monopolized and others (like the market for carpet cleaning services) highly competitive? Why do only children tend to be spoiled? Why did so many pioneers rush to the American and Canadian Western frontiers, only to half starve while they waited for civilization to catch up to them? Why did the divorce rate jump up in the 1970s and remain high after decades of low divorce rates? Why do some people get paid in wages, while others get a salary or commission? Why are there braille letters on drive-through cash machines?

As you work your way through this book, you will discover answers to these and many other questions. But more importantly, you will discover that microeconomics is not a list of specific questions and answers. The real economic environment poses so many complex questions that we cannot expect to list and memorize answers to them all. The only way to understand economic behaviour is to find a method for setting out and then solving microeconomic problems. This methodology consists of a relatively small set of ideas that are applicable to vast numbers of situations. Throughout the book, you will be introduced to the ideas of economic analysis and shown how to use them to answer many economic questions.

Chapter 1 is an introduction to the working methodology of microeconomics. We begin the chapter with two short, nonrigorous explorations of different microeconomic problems. Are the seasonal water shortages that afflict so many communities inevitable, or do they sometimes result from the structure of the market? Once a government decides to support the price of an agricultural product, what is the best way to do it?

Our aim is to show you how economists typically approach such questions. In the concluding sections of the chapter, we use these problems as examples as we provide a more systematic discussion of the subject matter and method of economics. We show how to describe an economy, we look at the equilibrium method economists use to explore economic problems, and we consider two kinds of questions addressed by economists: positive and normative questions. We conclude with a brief discussion of a market economy and an outline of the book.

1.1 The Water Shortage Problem

One puzzling feature in the world around us is the existence of shortages. When there is a long hot summer it is quite common for communities to face water shortages and restrictions. Water shortages happen not only in desert locations, but even in places like Vancouver where the city is known for its abundance of rain. Thinking about shortages for a moment can help us discover a number of aspects of economic thinking.

One of the first steps in thinking economically is to simplify what in reality is a multitude of complex problems. Let's explore the water shortage problem in the context of a simple public water system on an imaginary island in the Pacific Ocean. (This imaginary story, however, is based on a real gulf island off of Vancouver, British Columbia.) We'll imagine that the island was subdivided into the 100-home Village Point Estates, and that the water for these homes comes from a series of wells owned by the Village Point Water District at a cost of $50 000 per year.

To generate the $50 000 required to cover its costs, the Village Point Water District levies a fixed annual fee of $500 per householder. Notice that the water district does *not* charge each of the 100 householders on the basis of amount of water used. Instead, *every household pays a fixed fee of $500 a year, regardless of how much or how little water it uses*. We will call this arrangement a *non-metered scheme.*

To grasp the essence of the problem, let's ignore the differences in yearly rainfall and in water usage among householders and think in terms of a *representative householder* in a representative year. That is, we will suppose that as far as water consumption is concerned, *all the Village Point householders are identical* and that this representative householder uses 80 000 litres of water over the crucial two-month summer period. He or she uses 60 000 litres in July, and — if the water were available — he or she would use 60 000 litres in August as well. But in August, water is not always available. Some days there is water in the wells and the water district can supply water to Village Point. Other days the wells are completely dry and the water district's pipes are empty. All told, in August the representative Village Point householder is able to use just 20 000 litres of water. To summarize: the householder currently has what we can call the *unbalanced water use profile* consisting of 60 000 litres of water in July and only 20 000 litres in August.

Interestingly, this householder would actually prefer to spread his or her water use evenly across the two-month period, using 40 000 litres of water in July and 40 000 litres in August, rather than 60 000 litres in July and only 20 000 litres in August. That is, the householder prefers what we can call the *balanced water use profile*, consisting of 40 000 litres per month, to the current unbalanced water use profile. However, under the current scheme, there is no way that the householder can achieve the preferred balanced water use profile by his or her own efforts — *even though the total amount of water in the two profiles is identical*.

To see why, imagine what would happen if just one householder in Village Point Estates reduced personal water use from 60 000 litres to 40 000 litres in July, thereby leaving 20 000 additional litres of water available for use in August. In August, this water-conserving householder would not get to use the full 20 000 litres saved in July. Instead, every one of the 100 householders served by the Village Point Water District would draw on the extra water supply, increasing their August water use by 200 litres each (20 000 litres divided by 100 householders). In other words, by reducing personal water use by 20 000 litres in July, the single water-conserving householder increases personal water use in August by *only* 200 litres.

In Figure 1.1 we have shown all the water use profiles that this householder can attain personally under the non-metered scheme. Litres of water used in July are measured on the horizontal axis and litres of water in August on the vertical axis. The householder is initially at point U, with an unbalanced water use profile composed of 60 000 litres in July and 20 000 litres in August. As we saw above, starting from the unbalanced water use profile, this householder can attain point C by conserving 20 000 litres in July. At point C, the householder uses 40 000 litres in July and 20 200 litres in August. Starting again from the unbalanced water use profile, this householder can attain point D by reducing personal water use in July to nothing. At point D, he or she uses no water in July and 20 600 litres in August. In other words, if this householder reduces personal water use in July by 60 000 litres, the result is an increase in personal water use in August of just 600 litres because the 60 000 additional litres now available in August are evenly split among all 100 Village Point householders who draw water from the system. Notice that the slope of the line DCU is −1/100. This slope reflects the fact that when this householder decreases July water use by one litre, he or she gets to use only a hundredth of that litre in August.

What is the best, or most preferred, profile on the line DCU from the individual householder's point of view? We know two facts relevant to this question: (1) All householders actually choose the unbalanced consumption profile at point U in each year, and (2) The line DCU describes the water use profiles that the householder can attain by his or her own actions. It seems natural to assume that, from the water use profiles on line DCU, the householder actually chooses the profile that is most preferred.

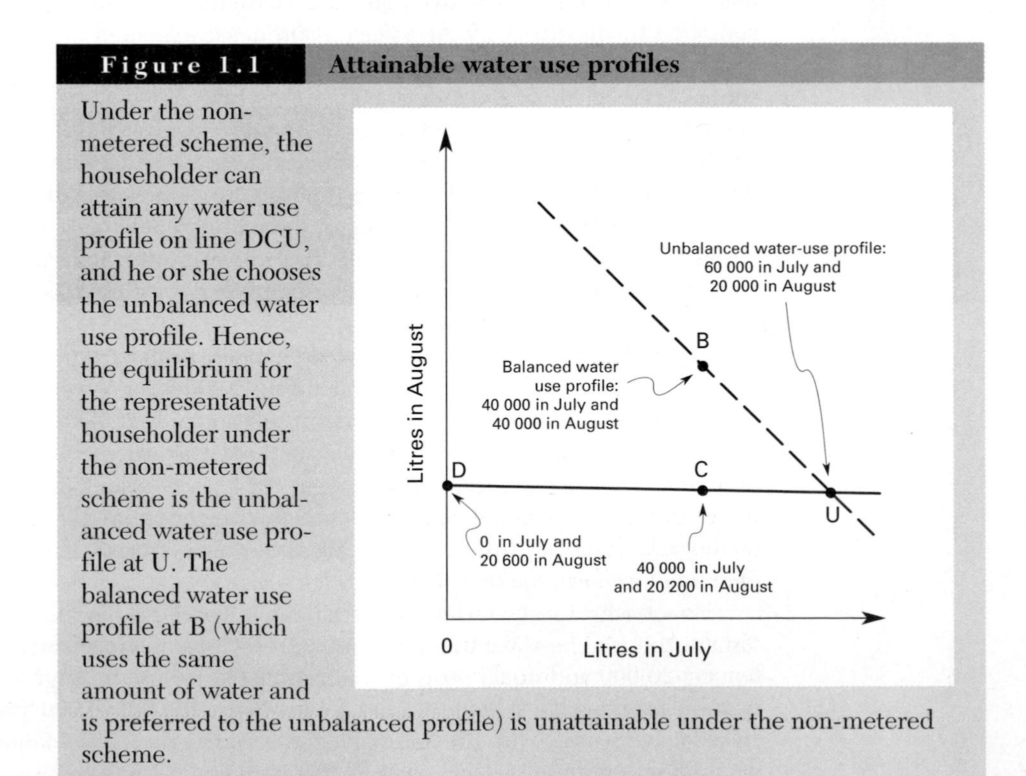

Figure 1.1 **Attainable water use profiles**

Under the non-metered scheme, the householder can attain any water use profile on line DCU, and he or she chooses the unbalanced water use profile. Hence, the equilibrium for the representative householder under the non-metered scheme is the unbalanced water use profile at U. The balanced water use profile at B (which uses the same amount of water and is preferred to the unbalanced profile) is unattainable under the non-metered scheme.

Given this assumption, we conclude that the unbalanced water consumption profile U is the most preferred profile on line DCU.

Because all 100 householders in Village Point Estates see the problem in exactly the same way, they find themselves in an *equilibrium* in which every householder has the unbalanced water use profile containing 60 000 litres of water in July and only 20 000 litres in August. This situation is an equilibrium because there is nothing any individual householder can do to attain a more preferred water use profile. In other words, among the water use profiles that the householder can attain by his or her own actions, the unbalanced profile is most preferred.

Yet this equilibrium is unattractive because every householder would actually prefer to reallocate 20 000 litres of water from July to August. That is, every householder prefers the balanced profile at point B in Figure 1.1 to the unbalanced profile at point U. Notice that because the total amount of water in the balanced and unbalanced water use profiles is identical, every single householder could be made *better off* if only a way could be found to induce *every* Village Point householder to save 20 000 litres of water in July for use in August.

PROBLEM 1.1

Under the non-metered scheme, what happens to an individual householder's private incentive to conserve water in July for use in August as the number of householders decreases?

Is there any way to make everyone in the Village Point Water District better off by giving each householder an incentive to use 40 000 litres each month? An economist might suggest trying a *metered scheme*. Suppose that the water district decided to install meters to monitor every householder's water use and charge a *price per litre* for water used during July and August. As you know from introductory economics, consumption of a good rises or falls depending on the price of that good. We could reasonably expect that a high price per litre would dramatically reduce water use while a more moderate price would lead to a less dramatic reduction. We can imagine that the water district might experiment with different prices to find the price that results in each Village Point householder using just 40 000 litres per month. Let us suppose that this price is $0.005 per litre. The representative householder's water bill would then be $200 per month for a total bill of $400 over the two-month period.

This price succeeds in achieving the desired reallocation of water use, but does it make each householder better off? The answer depends on how much it costs to monitor the amount of water used by each householder. Suppose for the moment that monitoring water use is costless. The water district could then use the $400 collected from each householder to reduce the fixed yearly fee of $500 per householder to a fixed yearly fee of just $100. Each householder still pays the water district a total of $500 per year since the householder uses 80 000 litres of water over the two-month period, but because the price-per-litre charge brings about the desired reallocation of water use, each householder is better off.

How does the metered scheme work? As we saw, under the non-metered scheme, the Village Point householder has no incentive to limit water use in July: if this householder reduces personal water use by one litre in July, he or she gets only an additional 1/100 of a litre in August. Clearly, it is not in this householder's self-interest to conserve water in July for use in August. Consequently, the non-metered scheme produces an equilibrium in which too much water is used in July, and too little in August.

By imposing a *price* on water use, however, the metered scheme provides householders with an *incentive to conserve water*. The higher the price, the larger the incentive. When the water district chooses the \$0.005 per litre price, the Village Point householders use 40 000 litres per month, and the metered scheme generates the balanced water use profile preferred by the householder. Since we have assumed that it costs nothing to monitor householders' water use, all the revenue generated by the per-litre price for water can be used to reduce the householders' fixed yearly fee. We see, then, that in this very simple model, *price serves only to allocate water use* across the two summer months. A clever choice of price produces the optimal allocation.

Of course, it is not costless to monitor water use. Meters have to be bought and installed, someone has to be paid to read the meters, and water bills have to be prepared and mailed. Once these *monitoring costs* enter the picture, how can we determine if the metered scheme is better or worse than the non-metered scheme? Let \$$C$ be the sum of all these monitoring costs, expressed as a yearly cost per householder. In other words, \$$C$ is the *cost* to each householder of the metered scheme. What is the *benefit* to the householder of having the balanced water use profile? Let \$$R$ represent the highest price that the householder is willing to pay for the balanced water use profile — given that the alternative is the unbalanced water use profile. This sum, \$$R$, is a measure of the benefit to the Village Point householder of the metered scheme. If \$$R$ is larger than \$$C$, then the metered scheme is preferred to the non-metered scheme. But if \$$R$ is smaller than \$$C$, then the opposite is true.

Common Property Problems

common property problem

This water shortage problem is one example of a what's called a **common property problem**. The two schemes produce different equilibriums because the property rights are different. With the non-metered scheme the water in the district's wells is property *held in common* by the 100 householders of Village Point Estates. As a result, the individual householder is able to use in August only 1/100 of any water personally saved in July. In other words, because the water is common property, the individual householder has insufficient incentive to conserve water in July. With the metered scheme the water in the wells becomes private property, which is sold to the individual users. The two different property rights systems create different incentives and different equilibrium outcomes. Which one is better depends on the cost of monitoring.

A similar common property problem bedeviled the oil industry in both the US and Canada in the early part of the twentieth century. To understand this problem we need to know something about the geology of oil and something about the legal institution that allows someone to establish a property right to oil.

Two things are important here about the geology of oil. First, oil occurs in very large subterranean reservoirs. Second, the total amount of oil that is recovered from a reservoir depends on the rate at which oil is extracted from it. If the oil is extracted too rapidly, there is an inverse relationship between the rate of extraction and the total amount of oil recovered from a reservoir: the faster oil is pumped out of a reservoir, the smaller is the total amount of oil recovered. In extreme cases of very rapid extraction, the amount of oil actually extracted is only one-fifth of the maximum amount that could have been extracted.

rule of capture

The legal institution governing property rights in oil extraction is the **rule of capture**. Surface landowners hold the right to drill for oil on their land (as well as other mineral rights). But to establish a property right to any oil beneath the surface, the owner must actually capture the oil; that is, the owner must drill one or more wells and pump the oil out of the ground. Notice that under the rule of capture, oil in any reservoir is the common property of everyone who owns drilling rights to land located above the reservoir. And because oil reservoirs typically are very large, there are many such landowners.

In the associated equilibrium, many landowners drill wells to tap the reservoir, and each well is pumped at or near maximum capacity. This equilibrium is unattractive for two reasons. Too many wells are drilled, and oil is pumped out so rapidly that the total quantity of oil actually extracted is only a fraction of the quantity that could have been extracted from the reservoir. Indeed, all those who pump oil from the reservoir would be better off if a way could be found to reduce the number of wells and/or the rate of extraction.

unitization

Notice that if only *one* person or organization managed the drilling rights to a whole oil field, oil in the reservoir would cease to be common property, and the incentive to drill too many wells and to extract oil too quickly would disappear. This institutional solution to the common property problem is called **unitization** since it results in the entire reservoir being managed as a unit. Beginning in the mid-1940s, most of the major oil-producing jurisdictions adopted laws that compel unitization if a majority of producers agree to a sharing formula.

Common property problems occur in many different forms in open ocean fisheries. Here, too, the source of the problem is the law of capture. To establish a property right to fish in the ocean, a fisherman must actually harvest the fish. As a result, too many resources (boats, labour, fishing gear) are used to harvest the fish that are caught. Furthermore, too many fish are caught because individual fishermen have only a limited incentive to leave fish in the ocean to reproduce. This, of course, can lead to the extinction of the fishery.

Put yourself in the place of a whaler who has the chance to harvest the last pair of whales of some species. If you did not care about the extinction of the species, almost certainly you would choose to harvest the whales, and the species would become extinct. If you did decide to harvest the whales, you would then sell them at their current market value. On the other hand, if you decided to leave them alive, someone else might harvest them. In this case, you would get nothing and the species would still become extinct. Even if the whales managed to survive and reproduce, chances are small that you would have the opportunity to harvest and sell their offspring. If you placed no direct value on the survival of the species, this line of reasoning would lead you to harvest the whales yourself.

In the following problem you can explore a simple game that captures the essence of common property problems.

PROBLEM 1.2

This game involves a host and four players in separate rooms. The host gives each player $90 and an envelope. Each player must choose either to keep the $90 or to put it into the envelope. Then the players assemble in a common room where the host collects the four envelopes, takes the money out, and puts it all into a common pool. For every $90 from an envelope, the host adds $120 to the common pool. The common pool is then divided equally among the four players. Before the players make their choice about keeping the $90 or putting it into the envelope, the host describes the entire sequence of events to each player.

1. Would a player motivated only by private gain choose to keep the $90 or put it into the envelope?
2. Suppose that all the players are forced to make the same choice and that the choice is determined by a vote. How will a player motivated only by private gain choose to vote?

Common property problems don't just exist in public works, oil fields, and ocean fisheries. If you think about your own daily experience you'll recognize common property problems everywhere. When you drive on the highway during rush hour, you're experiencing common property. Every licensed driver has access to the highway and imposes costs on all other drivers ... costs that a driver doesn't directly pay for. If the individual drivers had to pay a toll to enter the highway, there would be fewer drivers and less congestion. As you walk around campus, eat lunch in the cafeteria, or argue with your roommate over why the bathroom is so dirty, you're again experiencing common property. One of the important features of thinking like an economist is to recognize how one idea manifests over and over in different applications.

1.2 Agricultural Price Support Programs

For the last 50 years, farmers' groups have successfully lobbied governments in Europe, North America, Australia, and elsewhere to support prices for a whole range of agricultural products — including wheat, corn, butter, wine, and wool — at high levels. As you will see in later chapters, there are good economic reasons to oppose price supports. However, given that a political decision has been made to institute an agricultural price support program, what is the best way to do it? Let us create a simple model to explore and compare two possible price support programs.

Imagine that a government agency known as the Agricultural Price Support Authority (APSA) is about to institute one of two programs to support the price of a particular agricultural good. Under what we will call the *buy-and-store program*, APSA would offer to buy the good at a designated support price, and then it would store whatever quantity it ultimately bought. By contrast, under what we will call the *price subsidy program*, APSA would not buy the agricultural good; instead, it would pay farmers a subsidy per unit produced equal to the difference between the designated support price and the price the good actually sold for in the marketplace. Is there any reason to prefer one program to the other?

Tackling this question would be impossible without the context provided by the economic theory of markets. (You will have the opportunity to explore this theory in detail in Chapter 8.) In many agricultural markets, neither buyers nor sellers have any real control over the price of the good because the amount that any single buyer (seller) offers to buy (sell) is small relative to the total quantity transacted. In other words, in large agricultural markets characterized by many buyers and sellers, prices are taken as given. Economists refer to such markets as **perfectly competitive markets**.

perfectly competitive markets

Since neither buyers nor sellers in perfectly competitive markets can choose the price at which they either buy or sell the good in question, they decide only what *quantity* to buy or sell. In the following treatment of demand and supply, we will use the market for butter as our example; however, this discussion is applicable to any perfectly competitive market.

On the demand side of the market for butter, a consumer's behaviour can be described by the quantity of butter purchased at any given price. This relationship between quantity demanded and price is called the individual's demand curve. For example, one particular consumer might buy one and a half kilograms of butter per week at $1 per kilogram, one kilogram per week at $3 per kilogram, and just half a kilogram per week at $6 per kilogram. These are three points on that person's individual demand curve for butter.

market demand curve

We can add up the demand curves for every single consumer in an economy to get a **market demand curve**, labelled *DD* in Figure 1.2a. It tells us how much butter all individual demanders will buy at any given price in any given week. If, for example, the price of butter is $4 per kilogram, then 90 million kilograms will be demanded. If the price is higher, for example $6, then only 60 million kilograms will be demanded. Demand curves are downward-sloping: the higher the price, the smaller the quantity demanded.

market supply curve

On the supply side of the market, an individual producer's behaviour can be described by the quantity of butter supplied at any price. Once again, we can add up the supply curves for every single producer in an economy to get a **market supply curve**, labelled *SS* in Figure 1.2b. It tells how much butter all producers will supply at any given price. If, for example, the price of butter is $6 per kilogram, then 105 million kilograms will be supplied. If the price is lower, for example $4 per kilogram, then only 45 million kilograms will be supplied. Supply curves are usually upward-sloping: the higher the price, the larger the quantity supplied.

Competitive Equilibrium Price and Quantity

competitive equilibrium price

competitive equilibrium quantity

The **competitive equilibrium price** is the price at which quantity demanded is equal to quantity supplied. We can identify the competitive equilibrium price and the **competitive equilibrium quantity** by combining the demand and supply sides of the butter market into a single figure. As you can see from Figure 1.3, the equilibrium price is $5 and the equilibrium quantity is 75 million kilograms.

Figure 1.2 Demand and supply

The market demand curve *DD* specifies the quantity of butter demanded at any given price, and the market supply curve *SS* specifies the quantity of butter supplied at any given price. For example, when butter is $6 per kilogram, 60 million kilograms are demanded and 105 million kilograms are supplied.

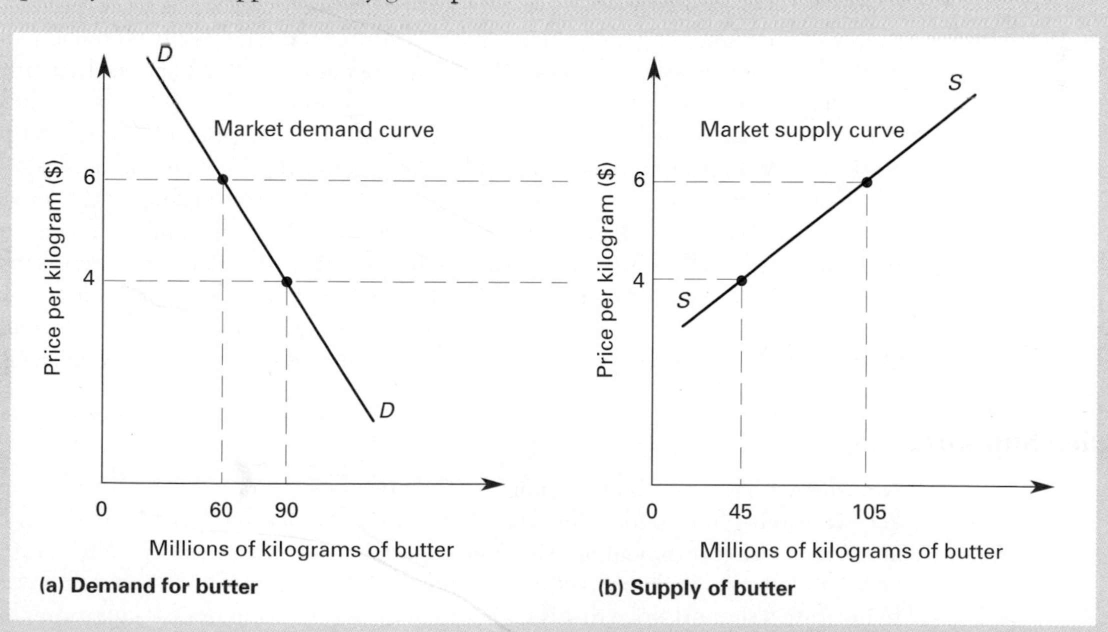

Figure 1.3 Competitive equilibrium

In a competitive equilibrium, price is such that quantity demanded equals quantity supplied. The competitive equilibrium price is $5 per kilogram, and 75 million kilograms of butter are supplied and demanded at this price.

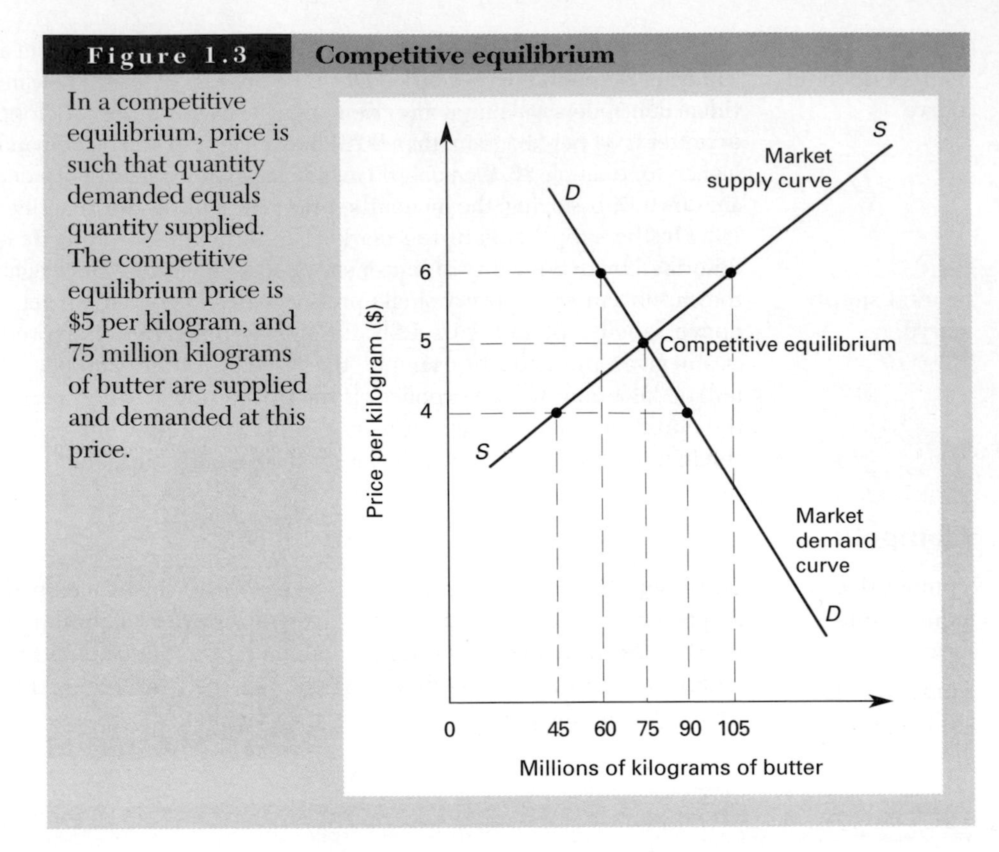

At prices higher than the $5 equilibrium price, butter is in excess supply: not all the butter supplied can be sold. As a result, the price will tend to drop towards the equilibrium price of $5 per kilogram. For example, when the price is $6 per kilogram, producers supply 105 million kilograms of butter, but consumers demand only 60 million kilograms, so there is an excess supply of 45 million kilograms of butter. Conversely, at prices lower than the $5 equilibrium price, butter is in excess demand: more butter is demanded than is available. (How large is the excess demand when the price of butter is $4 per kilogram?) As a result, the price will tend to rise towards the $5 equilibrium price.

Notice how *price* serves to coordinate economic decision making in this model: *Producers and consumers base their supply and demand decisions on price*. If their decisions are not mutually consistent — that is, if there is either excess demand or excess supply — the resulting pressure in the marketplace will tend to push the price either up or down. Only at the equilibrium price are the decisions of producers and consumers mutually consistent, and, therefore, only at this price is there no pressure for price to change.

Price Supports

Now that we have some understanding of how price is determined in a competitive market, we can begin to understand the implications of price support programs. In the absence of any government intervention, we would expect to see an equilibrium price of $5 per kilogram in the marketplace for butter. Let us suppose then that APSA wants to institute a support price that is higher than the equilibrium price — for example, a support price of $6 per kilogram.

What happens if APSA opts for the buy-and-store program, offering to buy butter at the $6 support price and then storing all the butter it buys, thereby removing it from the market? Given the support authority's offer to buy butter at $6 per kilogram, butter producers will accept nothing less in the marketplace. As a result, consumers of butter will also have to pay a market price of $6 per kilogram. As you can see from Figure 1.4, when the price of butter is $6, 105 million kilograms of butter will be supplied each week. Notice, however, that only 60 million kilograms will be sold in the marketplace at the $6 price. The support authority will therefore have to buy and store an amount equal to the difference between the quantity supplied and the quantity demanded, or 45 million kilograms of butter. This means, of course, that if the support authority opts for the buy-and-store program, it will have to spend $270 million per week to achieve the $6 support price. In addition, it will have to pay the costs of storing the butter.

What happens if the support authority decides instead to implement the price subsidy program, where it pays producers a subsidy per unit produced equal to the difference between the $6 support price and the market price? Under the price subsidy program, butter producers first sell their butter in the marketplace for whatever price they can get, and then the support authority pays them a subsidy per kilogram of butter sold equal to the difference between the $6 support price and the market price. As you can see from Figure 1.4, because producers once again get a total of $6 per kilogram for their butter, they will once again supply 105 million kilograms of butter. However, under the price subsidy program, all 105 million kilograms of butter will be sold in the marketplace at a price of $3 per kilogram. The support authority will there-

Figure 1.4 **Price support programs**

Because under both programs the producer gets $6 per kilogram of butter, 105 million kilograms are supplied. Under the buy-and-store program, 60 million kilograms are sold to consumers at $6 per kilogram, and APSA buys and stores the remaining 45 million kilograms. Under the price subsidy program, all 105 million kilograms are sold to consumers at $3 per kilogram, and APSA pays producers a subsidy equal to $3 per kilogram.

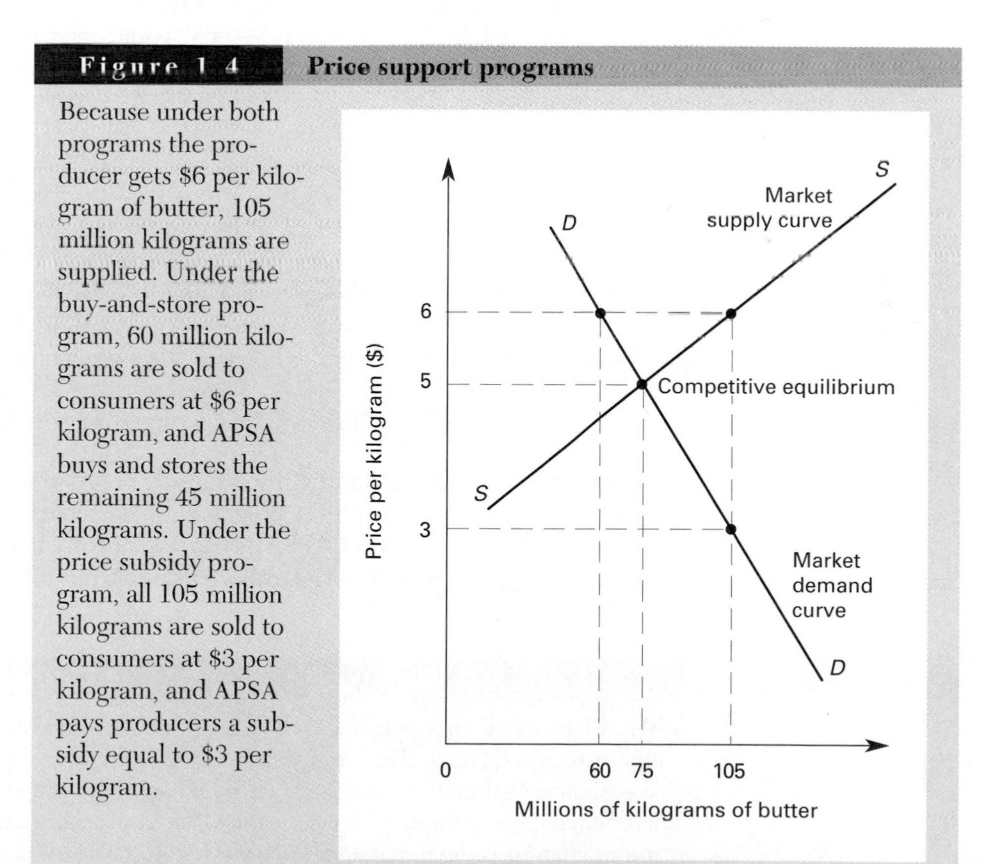

fore have to pay butter producers a subsidy of \$3 per kilogram, equal to the difference between the \$6 support price and the \$3 market price. This means that if the support authority opts for the price subsidy program, it will have to spend \$315 million per week to achieve the \$6 support price.

What can we say about which of these programs is preferred? First, look at the question from the point of view of the sellers in this market. Butter producers are indifferent between the buy-and-store and the price subsidy programs, since both programs result in the same \$6 support price. What about the buyers in this market? Consumers prefer the price subsidy program, where they pay just \$3 per kilogram for butter, to the buy-and-store program, where they pay \$6 per kilogram. Of course, as taxpayers, producers and consumers collectively will have to pay the costs incurred by APSA. Those costs are \$315 million under the price subsidy program, and \$270 million plus storage costs under the buy-and-store program.

We can easily establish the following results: If storage costs are larger than \$45 million (\$315 million minus \$270 million), then the price subsidy program is preferred. Producers are indifferent between the two programs; consumers prefer the price subsidy program; but, collectively as taxpayers, both producers and consumers prefer the cheaper price subsidy program. However, if costs of storage are less than \$45 million, the situation is more complex because the price subsidy program is then more expensive than the buy-and-store program. To compare programs in this case, we need to know just how much consumers as a group value the lower market price for butter that emerges under the price subsidy program.

How could we measure the aggregate benefit that consumers as a group place on the privilege of buying butter at a market price of \$3 compared with buying it at \$6 per kilogram? First, we could determine the largest amount each consumer would pay for this privilege for one week. Then, we simply add up all these amounts to get a measure of what we will call the *aggregate consumers' benefit* per week of the lower market price for butter under the price subsidy program. Let $\$ACB$ denote aggregate consumers' benefit. We want to compare $\$ACB$ with what we will call the *aggregate taxpayers' cost* of the price subsidy program relative to the buy-and-store program. Let $\$ATC$ denote aggregate taxpayers' costs. We know from above that the price subsidy program costs taxpayers \$315 million per week and that the buy-and-store program costs taxpayers \$270 million plus storage costs. Therefore, aggregate taxpayers' costs of the price subsidy program relative to the buy-and-store program are:

$$\$ATC = \$315 \text{ million} - (\$270 \text{ million} + \text{storage costs})$$

From this calculation we know that the price subsidy program is preferred if $\$ACB$ exceeds $\$ATC$, and that the buy-and-store program is preferred if $\$ATC$ exceeds $\$ACB$.

One important determinant of APSA's costs is the responsiveness of quantity demanded to a change in price. You can explore just how this affects costs in the following problem.

PROBLEM 1.3

We will continue to suppose that the market demand curve is linear and that it passes through the competitive equilibrium point in Figure 1.4. We want to explore the implications of a change in the slope of the market demand curve. Specifically, how do APSA's costs under the two programs change as the demand curve gets steeper?

1.3 Describing an Economy

The point of working through the above applications on water shortages and agricultural subsidy policies is to provide us with two concrete examples of how an economist thinks about behavioural problems. Over the next few sections, as we break down the basic components of this method of thinking, we'll refer back to these examples.

goods

resources

The purpose of *economic activity* is to transform resources into goods and services. Goods and services — or **goods**, for short — are what individuals value. They include the obvious: T-shirts, haircuts, artichokes, 18 holes of golf, and the not so obvious: relationships, fame, peace, and so on. **Resources** are what are used to produce such goods. Land in the Okanagan Valley of British Columbia, for example, is a resource because it can be used to produce peaches (or apples or a shopping mall or a golf course). Using the concepts of goods and resources, we can provide an informal but revealing definition of **economics**: *the study of the allocation of scarce resources to the production of alternative goods*.

economics

There is a lot more to this definition than meets the eye. First, consider the word "allocation." When people allocate goods they are behaving in a certain way. Marriage, education, career choice, and fightin' on Saturday night are all types of allocation related to specific types of behaviour. Economics is about how people behave when they allocate. Second, consider the word "scarce." A resource is scarce if, at a price of zero, more would be demanded than is available. If a good sells for a positive price, it is scarce. Oxygen, at least most of the time, is not scarce because there's so much available. Smallpox, on the other hand, is rare but not scarce, because no one wants it at any positive price. Third, consider the word "alternative." It is hard to imagine a resource with only one possible use. You are a resource. Think about the practically limitless ways you can occupy your time. This fact means you have a choice in how your resources are to be used. So, economics is the study of how people behave in placing their valuable resources in the right activity when there are many choices to be made.

This informal definition of economics is useful but limited. To develop a deeper understanding of what economics is all about, we first need to know just what an economy is. We can describe an **economy** by breaking it down into four basic building blocks: *resource endowment, technology, preferences of individuals*, and *institutions*.

economy

A Resource Endowment

resource endowment

A **resource endowment** consists of all the resources available to an economy. For example, the Canadian economy's resource endowment could be described by cataloguing the quantities of all available resources: X million litres of water in the Great Lakes, the labour of Y million people, Z million barrels of oil in the Alberta Tar Sands oil fields, Q million board metres of lumber in the forests of British Columbia, U million hectares of Class A farm land in Manitoba, V million tonnes of coal in Cape Breton, and so on. In essence, then, a resource endowment is simply a listing of everything in an economy that can be used to produce goods. In the two general applications that we examined, the resource endowments included things such as the amount of water available in each month and the number of cows producing butter.

Notice that — as we have said — these resources are in limited or scarce supply: There is only a certain amount available for use in an economy. A major source of this limitation is knowledge. If we have no knowledge of the existence of a resource or no knowledge of how to use it, then the resource is not available, and this increases scarcity. The flip side of this is that increased knowledge can reduce scarcity problems. It has always been popular to note that the world is finite and, therefore, exhaustible. But failure to recognize the role of knowledge can lead to great exaggerations. Even the famous economist Keynes failed to recognize this when he wrote:

> By 1914 the domestic requirements of the United States for wheat were approaching their production limit, and the date was evidently near when there would be an exportable surplus only in years of exceptionally favorable harvest ... (pp. 24–25, 1920)

Little did Keynes realize that the introduction of the tractor and pull combine was about to revolutionize the American Midwest and allow the United States to dominate wheat exports throughout the century. Scarcity hinges critically on knowledge.

A Technology

technology

An economy's **technology** specifies how those resources can be used to produce goods. International travellers often comment on the many ways that firms from different parts of the world do the same job. A striking example comes from the shrimp-packing industries situated on either side of the Mexico–United States border along the Gulf of Mexico. Shrimp-packers in Texas use many special-purpose labour-saving machines and relatively few workers, while shrimp-packers in Mexico use many workers and very few machines to do the same job. In India, you may see large water-diversion systems and canals dug by hand and the dirt carried away in baskets by dozens of labourers, while in North America and Europe the same job is done using huge earth-moving machines and relatively few workers. Likewise, the grass around the Taj Mahal is cut by many people using hand sickles, while in North America lawnmowers are ubiquitous.

To an economist, these observations pose a question: How can these marked differences in the choice of a production technique be explained? The economist's explanation is this: Among all the techniques that can be used to accomplish a particular task, the firm chooses the technique that is least costly. As a result, in countries where machines are relatively more expensive than labour, firms use fewer machines and more workers. And in countries where labour is relatively more expensive than machines, the reverse is true. In India labour is relatively cheaper than machines, so labour-intensive techniques are used to construct water works, while in North America and Europe, machinery is relatively cheaper, so machine-intensive techniques are used.

Problem 1.4

You may have noticed that the materials used to package consumer products sometimes change. For example, steel cans are sometimes substituted for aluminum cans and plastic bottles for glass bottles. How would you begin to explain these changes in packaging materials?

Figuratively speaking, a technology is the economy's cookbook because it tells us all the different combinations of resources that can be used to produce a good. For example, suppose that we were thinking about producing 10 tonnes of frozen shrimp for New Year's Eve in Toronto. The economy's technology would tell us all the different combinations of resources that could do the job: all the labour-intensive techniques and all the capital-intensive techniques for catching shrimp, the various techniques for freezing shrimp, and the various techniques for transporting frozen shrimp to Toronto. Notice that our technological cookbook provides not just one but potentially a very large number of resource combinations that will all achieve a given result.

Preferences of Individuals

preferences of individuals

preference ordering

Very loosely, which goods are actually produced in an economy depends upon what people would like to buy — that is, it depends upon the **preferences of individuals**. In principle, describing any person's preferences requires us to construct that individual's **preference ordering**. In Chapter 2 we will provide a full treatment of the concept of a preference ordering. Here we will simply give you an example of a very limited and specific preference ordering from the water shortage problem of Section 1.1.

From the Village Point householder's point of view, what matters is the amount of water used in each of the two summer months and, of course, the amount of money paid to the water district (since money paid to the water district is not available to buy other goods). A consumption profile can then be described as follows: (litres used in July, litres used in August, dollars spent on water). In this notation, the unbalanced profile produced by the non-metered scheme is (60 000 litres, 20 000 litres, $500), and the balanced profile produced by the metered scheme is (40 000 litres, 40 000 litres, $500). A preference ordering in this very limited context is a complete listing of all conceivable water use profiles for the Village Point householder in descending order of desirability. For example, we know that in this householder's preference ordering, the balanced water use profile (40 000 litres, 40 000 litres, $500) is higher than the unbalanced water use profile (60 000 litres, 20 000 litres, $500).

But many other water use profiles are also conceivable and will therefore appear in this preference ordering. For example, that preference ordering would tell how this householder ranks the following water use profiles: (44 000 litres, 42 000 litres, $300), (28 000 litres, 58 000 litres, $495), and (20 000 litres, 12 000 litres, $1500). A preference ordering for the Village Point householder is a complete ranking of these and every other conceivable profile in descending order of desirability. To check your understanding of this concept, try writing down your own preference ordering in another very limited context in the following problem.

PROBLEM 1.5

Write down your own preference ordering for the following bundles of bills.

a. (three $100 bills, ten $20 bills, seventeen $5 bills)
b. (two $100 bills, thirteen $20 bills, four $5 bills)
c. (four $100 bills, one $20 bill, fourteen $5 bills)
d. (one $100 bill, thirty $20 bills, one $5 bill)

Self-Interest and Making Choices

The preferences of individuals are the keystone of the economist's vision of the economy because preferences provide the motivation for all economic activity. In this sense economists often speak of the consumer as sovereign. Put briefly, the economist's theory of behaviour is this: In *any choice situation, the individual makes the choices that allow him or her to attain the highest possible ranking in his or her preference ordering.* This theory of making choices — often called the **theory of self-interest** — is at the core of all economic analysis.

theory of self-interest

We have already used the theory of self-interested choice making several times. We used it in the water shortage problem when we argued that under the non-metered scheme, the unbalanced profile (60 000 litres, 20 000 litres, $500) was an equilibrium. First we identified all the water use profiles the householder could achieve by his or her own actions. These were the profiles on the line DCU in Figure 1.1. Then we argued that the Village Point householder stayed with the unbalanced profile because he or she could not personally attain a more preferred profile. Obviously, this argument was based on the notion of self-interested choice making by the Village Point householder.

We've mentioned that shrimp packing uses different types of technology. In other words, the self-interest of individuals lies behind a firm's decisions. A firm chooses the production technique that costs the least. Why? Because the least costly production technique maximizes the firm's profits. But a firm is just the agent for its owners, and a firm's profit is just income for its owners. Therefore, when a firm maximizes its profit, it is maximizing the income of its owners. And as the income of an individual owner increases, the set of consumption choices available to that individual expands. Or, in the language of self-interest, as personal income increases, the individual can attain a higher ranking in his or her preference ordering. Thus, the self-interested choice making of individuals is also at the core of the profit-maximizing activities of firms.

Institutions

institutions

Notice that all three of the building blocks we have so far considered — an economy's resource endowment, its technology, and the preferences of individuals — are not easily changed over short periods of time. Indeed, in most economic theory, these building blocks are assumed to be unchangeable.[1] By contrast, **institutions** — the fourth building block — can be changed in important ways. You have already encountered a number of institutions. For example, in the water shortage problem, you looked at two different institutions for regulating water allocation — a metered scheme and a non-metered scheme. In the common property oil extraction problem, you encountered two legal institutions for regulating oil extraction — the rule of capture and unitization. And in the agricultural price support problem, you compared two institutions designed to support the price of butter — the buy-and-store program and the price subsidy program.

In almost any newspaper you can find articles about changes to major economic institutions. The Maastricht Treaty between member nations of the European Union (EU) and the North American Free Trade Agreement (NAFTA) between Canada, Mexico, and the United States are two recent examples of changes in national institutions. More recently there have been discussions of a common currency for New Zealand and Australia, and possibly one for North America. Newspapers are full of stories about provincial governments making changes to the way that health care, education, and social assistance programs are funded and provided. The Ontario and Quebec governments have even taken several institutions known as cities and regrouped them into different cities. New laws regulating who can marry (e.g. homosexuals), evolving social norms, and new types of firms are just a few examples of other changing institutions.

1. In an intertemporal framework, technology changes from period to period. Furthermore, it is possible to promote technological change by appropriate policy measures. Nuclear power is just one example of a policy-promoted technology.

Because institutions are changeable, they play an especially interesting role in economics. If we think of economic activity as a game in which the objective of each participant is to reach the highest possible ranking in his or her own preference ordering, then economic institutions are the *rules* by which the game in a particular economy must be played. For example, what we called the rule of capture established the rules for exploiting two different resources — oil and fish. Under the rule of capture, an owner can only establish a property right to oil in the ground by pumping it out of the ground. And a fisherman can only establish a property right to fish in the sea by hauling them out of the sea. An oil producer who chooses not to pump oil today has, under the rule of capture, no legal right to that oil tomorrow. A whaler who chooses not to catch a particular whale today, under the rule of capture has no legal right to that whale (or its offspring) tomorrow. Thus, these institutions define the rules of the economic game and affect the behaviour of individuals in important ways. If an institution is changed, we would expect to see individual participants change their actions in response to that institutional change. For example, the water consumption of Village Point householders was different under the metered and the non-metered schemes. Institutions are thus a powerful force for organizing and directing economic activity.

Many institutions are formally codified in law. For example, property law formally specifies how ownership of property may be acquired and transferred. Other important legal institutions that regulate economic behaviour include tax laws, antitrust laws, labour laws, minimum-wage laws, rent-control laws, and agricultural price-support laws.

PROBLEM 1.6

Governments often require retailers to collect a 10-cent deposit on pop bottles from their customers. What is the purpose of this institution and how does it work?

Less obvious but nevertheless important are the many private and often informal institutions that regulate everyday economic activity. For example, private rental deposit arrangements of various kinds are very much like the public institution you considered in Problem 1.6. If you want to rent certain kinds of merchandise like VCRs, ski equipment, furniture, or power tools, you will probably be asked to leave a sizable deposit to guarantee the return of the merchandise. If you rent an apartment, you will probably be asked to pay a damage deposit — a similar institution. And if you fly into certain airports, you will have to deposit four quarters in a coin box before you can take a baggage cart from a specially designed lock-up device. The clever twist is that you can get your money back if you return your cart (or any other cart) to the lock-up device. What is the special function of this refund-for-cart-return institution? These informal institutions, like more public and formal institutions, also organize and direct the actions of individuals.

1.4 The Equilibrium Method

Economists study real economies by selecting certain segments of an economy and then constructing *economic models* of those segments. For example, there are many different kinds of water systems in any modern economy. None of these real systems is identical to the hypothetical Village Point Water District described in the water shortage problem of Section 1.1. Real water systems are vastly more complex. Yet our simple economic model of the Village Point Water District captures important features of many real water systems.

The four features captured by the model of the hypothetical water district in Section 1.1 correspond to the four building blocks of an economy. First, there is a *scarce resource*: the water district has only 8 000 000 litres of water for the two-month summer season. Second, there is a specific *technology* for water distribution in which the water district's costs depend only on the total amount of water pumped through the system. Third, there are the *preferences of individuals:* each householder prefers the balanced to the unbalanced water use profile. And fourth, there are two possible *institutions* — a metered scheme and a non-metered scheme — that establish the rules of the economic "game" in which each of 100 Village Point householders chooses how much water to use in each month.

social state

As we said, the driving forces in any economic model are the choices made by individuals. Collectively, these choices give rise to what we will call a **social state**. In the water shortage model of Section 1.1, for example, a social state is described by the amount of water each of the 100 householders uses in each month and the amount each householder pays for water. The social state that arose from the choices of the Village Point householders under the metered scheme was the one in which each of 100 householders used 40 000 litres in each month, and paid $500 for water. In contrast, the social state that arose from the choices of the Village Point householders under the non-metered scheme was the one in which each of 100 householders used 60 000 litres in July and 20 000 litres in August, and paid $500 for water.

method of equilibrium

equilibrium

The economist's aim is to explain or predict the social state that will arise from the choices of the individual economic participants. The method used to make these predictions is the **method of equilibrium**. At the heart of this method is the concept of an **equilibrium**. It can be defined this way: *an equilibrium consists of a set of choices for the individuals and a corresponding social state such that no individual can make himself or herself better off by making some other choice.*

This concept of equilibrium is, of course, built squarely on the economist's theory of self-interest: an economy, or a model of it, is in equilibrium only when no individual participant can reach a higher ranking in his or her preference ordering by making a different choice.

comparative statics analysis

An important part of the method of equilibrium is a technique known as **comparative statics analysis**. Notice that in these simple models, we have sometimes substituted one institution for another and compared the resulting equilibria. For example, in the water shortage model, we compared the equilibrium arising from the non-metered scheme with the equilibrium under the metered scheme. And in the agricultural price support problem, we compared the equilibrium arising from the buy-and-store program with the equilibrium arising from the price subsidy program. These are just two examples of comparative statics analysis. *Comparative statics analysis is the method of analyzing the impact of a change in a model by comparing the equilibrium that results from the change with the original equilibrium.*

1.5 Positive and Normative Economics

Economics, as we have been discussing, is characterized by a certain way of thinking. Self-interested behaviour, fixed endowments, equilibrium, and comparative statics analysis are critical and necessary parts of the economist's tool kit. As economists we use these tools much as a plumber uses a monkey wrench — they are part of our trade. In this sense, economics is *normative*, like all other disciplines, since every field has its own set of assumptions that distinguishes it from others. One other characteristic of economics is that within this framework factual questions are addressed. This concern over factual matters is often called **positive economics**. Here we are using the word *positive* not in the popular sense of *good*, nor in the mathematical sense of *greater than zero,* but in the sense of *factual*. Positive economics is concerned with the social states that actually arise in different economic settings. For example, in the water shortage problem, we were posing a positive question in asking how patterns of water consumption might change when a metered scheme was substituted for a non-metered scheme. Similarly, in the agricultural price support problem, we were posing a positive question in asking how the price consumers pay for butter changes when a price subsidy program is substituted for a buy-and-store program.

positive economics

Positive economics involves questions about the *facts* of economic activity. Therefore, answers to positive questions are always supported (or refuted) by factual observations. Making careful empirical observations of the facts of the real world — however difficult collecting and interpreting those facts may sometimes be — is a way of testing the predictions of economic models. Do shrimp-packing operations actually switch from labour-intensive to machine-intensive techniques when the price of labour rises relative to the price of machines? Is the amount of oil pumped from a reservoir under unitization actually larger than under the rule of capture?

normative economics

On the other hand, **normative economics** involves value judgments and therefore cannot be answered by reference to factual observations alone. Answers to normative questions also depend on our commitment to certain values or *norms* that are outside the scope of positive economics. Should government try to aid butter producers? Should it attempt to protect and preserve particular species of fish or specific types of forests or designated watersheds? Answers to questions like these are necessarily based on normative judgments that go beyond the economic framework we have discussed, and therefore, cannot be answered by economic models alone.

Policy making often involves a subtle interplay between normative and positive economics. Normative considerations tell us what are and are not desirable social states, while positive theoretical and empirical analysis tells us what are (and are not) sensible ways of trying to achieve a particular desirable social state. Setting social and economic goals is clearly in the realm of normative economics. However, once certain social and economic goals are accepted, implementing those goals — and, indeed, discovering whether those goals can actually be achieved — is in the realm of positive economics.

The Pareto Criterion

Pareto criterion

Given the importance of normative evaluations in policy making, it would be useful to have a normative yardstick for comparing different social states. One such yardstick — the one most widely used by economists — is the **Pareto criterion**. It takes its name from Vilfredo Pareto, the nineteenth-century Italian economist who first developed it. The Pareto criterion can be defined this way: *In comparing any two social states—say, state I and state J — state I is Pareto-preferred to state J if no one is worse off in state I than in state J, and if at least one person is better off in state I than in state J.*

Now let us apply the Pareto criterion to the water shortage problem. Recall that we looked at just two social states. We will call the state in which all 100 householders have the balanced water use profile (40 000 litres, 40 000 litres, $500) state *I*, and the state in which all 100 householders have the unbalanced water use profile (60 000 litres, 20 000 litres, $500) state J. As you know, everyone in Village Point is better off in state I than in state J because everyone prefers the balanced water use profile to the unbalanced water use profile. Using the Pareto criterion, we can say, then, that state I is *Pareto-preferred* to state J. Although the Pareto criterion *is* a value judgment, it is not a very difficult one to accept. Moreover, it plays a central role in economic analysis, and we will be using it throughout the book.

Another concept that also plays a central role in economic analysis — and one that we will also be using throughout the book — follows directly from the Pareto criterion. It is called **Pareto optimality**, and it can be defined this way: *A social state is Pareto-optimal if no other attainable social state is Pareto-preferred to it.* To an economist, Pareto optimality is synonymous with economic **efficiency**, and we will therefore be using the terms *Pareto optimal* and *efficient* interchangeably.

Pareto optimality

efficiency

At this point you should pause for a moment to reflect upon this notion of efficiency because it is not the common meaning of the word. The ordinary meaning of efficiency relates to absolute levels of output and often even implies the use of advanced technology. Hence engineers say that a diesel electric locomotive is more efficient than a steam locomotive because it converts a given amount of energy into more power. Likewise, we think of a chainsaw as more efficient than an axe. However, being technically efficient is not the same as economically efficient. For example, if diesel fuel became extremely expensive, everyone might be better off using steam power. For different scales of production, different methods of production are economically efficient. A gardener might find a hatchet the most economical method of chopping wood, while a logger will certainly use a chainsaw. Do notice, however, that the concept of Pareto optimality (or efficiency) does *not* identify a single best possible social state. Consider the following problem.

PROBLEM 1.7

Two gluttons must split a pecan pie. A social state in this context is simply a particular division of the pie: $X\%$ to one glutton and $(100 - X)\%$ to the other. What values of X are Pareto-optimal or efficient?

The Pareto criterion is problematical for policy makers because it says that one state is preferred to another *only* if no one is worse off in one state than in the other. It is the business of policy makers to make judgments about the relative desirability of different policies. Yet few policies, if any, are free of adverse consequences for at least *some* individuals. In other words, any change in policy is almost bound to make at least one person worse off, even though it might make many other people better off. Guided only by the Pareto criterion, then, policy makers might always decide against a policy change and stick with the status quo.

Cost-Benefit Analysis

cost-benefit criterion

There is another, less widely accepted criterion — called the **cost-benefit criterion** — that can be used to compare social states. It differs from the Pareto criterion in that it *does* incorporate tradeoffs between making some individuals worse off and making other individuals better off. The cost-benefit criterion is attractive to many policy makers because it will rank social states where the Pareto criterion will not.

To see how cost-benefit analysis is done, let us consider a move from any social state to any other; say, from state I to state J. We begin by calculating the social benefits from this move. First we will identify the "winners" — all those who benefit as a result of the move from state I to state J. Then we compute a dollar measure of each winner's personal benefit. Finally, we add up all the measures of individual benefit to arrive at the **gross social benefit**. Now let us calculate the social costs from this move. First we identify the "losers" — all those who are made worse off as a result of the move from state I to state J. Then we compute a dollar measure of each loser's personal cost. Finally, we add up all the measures of individual cost to arrive at the **gross social cost**. (You will learn more about how to make these calculations in Chapter 4.)

gross social benefit

gross social cost

If we then subtract the gross social cost from the gross social benefit, we have the **net social benefit**. We can use net social benefit to define the cost-benefit criterion: *In the move from social state I to social state J, if net social benefit is positive, then the cost-benefit criterion ranks state J as preferred to state I. On the other hand, if net social benefit is negative, then the cost-benefit criterion ranks state I as preferred to state J.*

net social benefit

We used the cost-benefit criterion in Section 1.2 to compare the buy-and-store program for supporting the price of butter with the price support scheme. We organized our data by looking at how individuals in three groups — producers, consumers, and taxpayers — were affected by a move from the social state with the buy-and-sell program to the social state with the price subsidy program. Producers as producers were indifferent between the institutions because the support price was \$6 per kilogram under both institutions. Consumers as consumers clearly preferred the price subsidy program because butter was \$3 per kilogram under this program and \$6 per kilogram under the buy-and-store program. Collectively, producers and consumers as taxpayers preferred the buy-and-store program if the storage costs were less than \$45 million per week, and they preferred the price subsidy program if the storage costs were more than \$45 million per week. To compare programs, we first computed the aggregate consumers' benefit $\$ACB$ and the aggregate taxpayers' cost $\$ATC$ in a move from the buy-and-store to the price subsidy program. We then used the cost-benefit criterion to rank the two programs. The price subsidy (buy-and-store) program was preferred if $\$ACB$ was larger (smaller) than $\$ATC$.

The normative assumption of cost-benefit analysis is that a dollar of cost to one person can always be offset by a dollar of benefit to any other person. Which individuals enjoy greater benefits or suffer greater costs is *not* an issue in cost-benefit analysis. This assumption, like the Pareto criterion, is clearly a value judgment. Many economists do not accept it and therefore will not use the cost-benefit criterion.

PROBLEM 1.8

To see that the cost-benefit criterion does in fact trade off gains for some individuals against losses for others, imagine a situation in which aggregate taxpayers' costs are larger for the price subsidy scheme than for the buy-and-store scheme, and yet, according to the cost-benefit criterion, the price subsidy scheme is preferred. Which individuals will be made worse off and which individuals will be made better off by the move from the buy-and-store program to the price subsidy program? (*Hint*: Not everyone buys butter and not everyone pays taxes.)

1.6 The Market Economy

A quick glance at economies around the world is enough to remind us how much real economies vary from place to place. In making comparisons between different economic institutions, it is often convenient to use a specific set of institutions as a reference point. We will use a hypothetical **pure-market economy** as our baseline model of an economy. The only institutions regulating economic activity in this pure-market economy are the institutions of private property. These pure-market institutions create property rights and promote unrestricted voluntary exchange as the primary mode of economic interaction. The only role government plays in this hypothetical model is to enact and enforce private property laws.

pure-market economy

The hypothetical pure-market economy allows us to pose many interesting questions about alternative institutions that we see in real economies. These are a few of the questions you will encounter in later chapters: Relative to the pure-market economy, what are the implications of a minimum-wage law? Of a rent-control law? Of a price subsidy for agricultural goods? Of a negative income tax? In addition, the institutions of a pure-market economy are interesting because a good portion of economic activity in countries like Australia, Great Britain, France, Germany, Canada, and the United States *is* coordinated through markets. Understanding a pure-market economy is therefore useful in interpreting much of the economic activity we see around us.

The Circular Flow of Economic Activity

The circular-flow diagram in Figure 1.5 is a useful way of visualizing a market economy. In this diagram, two sets of participants play crucial economic roles: *individuals* and *firms*. From an economist's perspective, every individual on the left in Figure 1.5 can be described by his or her preferences and by the resources he or she owns. In a pure-market economy, all resources — including resources nominally owned by firms — are ultimately owned by individuals because firms are owned by individual people. Every firm on the right in Figure 1.5 can be described by its technology (the terms on which it can transform resources into goods) and by its organizational structure (the set of internal institutions used to organize the firm).

These individuals and firms interact in two sets of markets: *resource markets* and *goods markets*. In the resource markets at the bottom of Figure 1.5, individuals are the suppliers of labour and other resources, and firms are the demanders. In the goods markets at the top of Figure 1.5, firms are the suppliers of goods, and individuals are the demanders. In equilibrium, there is a price and a quantity in every resource market and in every goods market.

The Plan of This Book

Figure 1.5 provides a handy reference point for previewing the rest of this book. In Part II, Individual Choice, we concentrate on the individuals on the left side of our circular-flow diagram. In Chapter 2, we set out the standard economic theory of individual preferences. In Chapter 3, we analyze the individual's choice-making behaviour. In the process, we derive demand curves for goods and supply curves for resources, thereby filling in the demand side of the markets for goods at the top and the supply side of the markets for resources at the bottom of Figure 1.5. In Chapter 4, we expand

Figure 1.5 **The circular-flow diagram of an economy**

Individuals, who can be described by their preferences and the resources they own, supply resources to firms and demand goods from firms. Firms, which can be described by their technology and their organizational structure, demand resources from individuals and supply goods to them. Firms and individuals interact in resource markets and in goods markets, in both of which prices and quantities are determined.

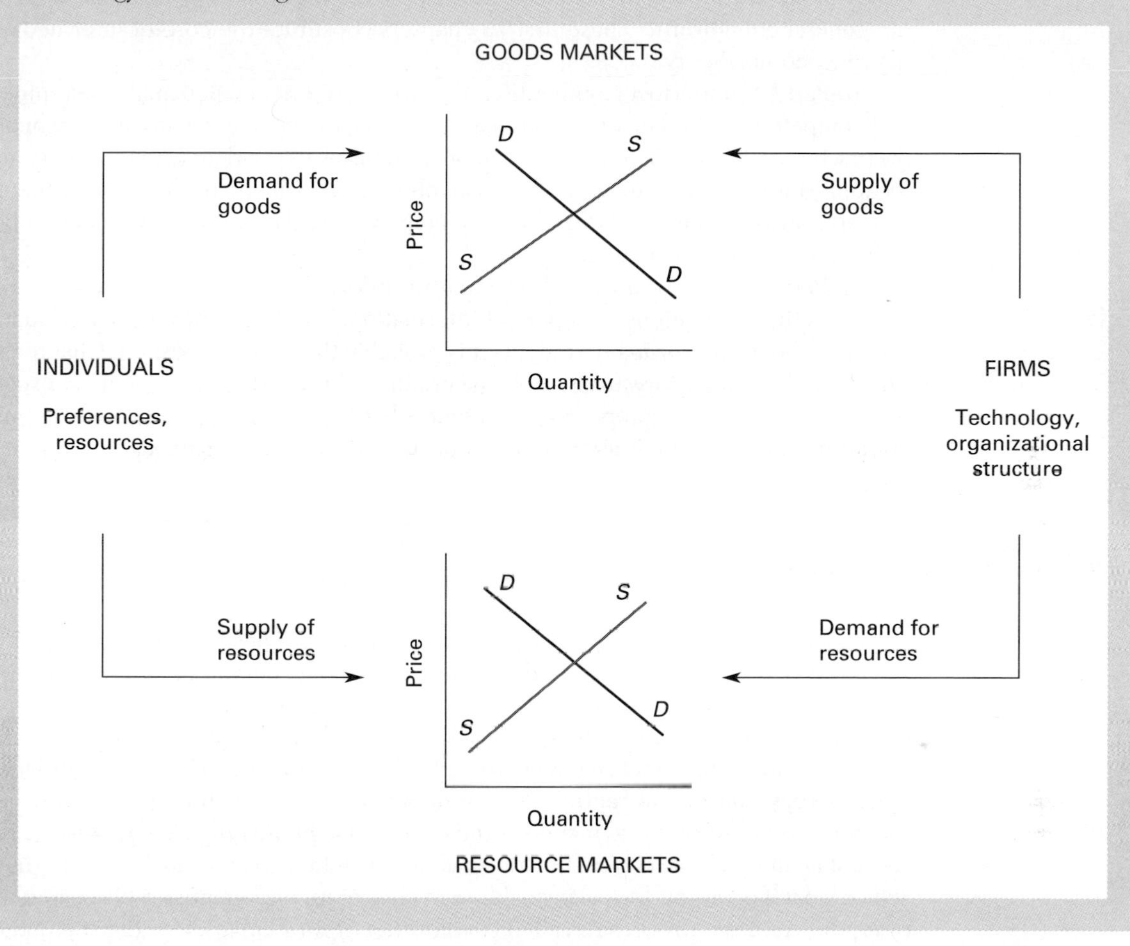

and explore in more detail the theory of demand, and examine a range of applications drawn from everyday life. In Chapter 5, we extend the theory of preferences to include choices made over time.

In Part III, Production and Cost, we turn our attention to the firms on the right side of our circular flow diagram. In Chapters 6 and 7, we introduce the idea of a production function and then use it to derive a number of cost relationships for a firm in the short run and the long run. We use these cost functions to derive the market supply curve. We also use them to understand the effect of changing institutions (e.g., a tax) on the output choices of a single firm.

In Part IV, Markets for Goods, we consider the forces that determine both the prices of the goods and inputs available in the goods and resource markets at the top and bottom of our circular flow diagram and the quantities in which they are produced and supplied. In Chapter 8, we look at perfectly competitive markets, and in Chapter 9 we consider a number of applications of this model. In Chapter 10, we examine the simple model of monopoly.

In Part V, Resource Markets and General Equilibrium, we consider the markets that go into production, and the entire circular flow diagram. In Chapter 11, we examine input markets; that is, the markets for labour and capital. Chapter 12 takes up the distribution of income and examines the conflict between economic efficiency and equity in the distribution of income. And Chapter 13 puts everything together to examine general equilibrium. These first 13 chapters constitute the core of intermediate microeconomic theory.

In Part VI, Imperfect Competition, we turn to a more detailed analysis of imperfect competition. Chapter 14 explores issues of price discrimination and other monopoly practices. Chapter 15, new to this edition, introduces the student to game theory and its application to economic problems. Chapter 16 takes many of these game theory concepts and examines undifferentiated oligopoly, a market in which a small number of firms sell an identical good.

In Part VII, Uncertainty and Asymmetric Information, we set out a model that considers the implications of imperfect information. This is the most advanced material in the book, but for many students it is probably the most interesting. Chapter 17 examines the straightforward issue of uncertainty where individuals live in an exogenously risky world. Chapters 18–20 examine what happens to consumers, firms, and equilibrium when there is asymmetric information between individuals.

SUMMARY

We began the chapter with two simple economic models. These served as examples in the more systematic discussion of the subject matter of economics that followed. Any economy can be described by breaking it down into four building blocks: the *resource endowment*, the *technology*, the *preferences of individuals*, and its *institutions*.

Economists study real economies by selecting certain segments of them and then constructing models that capture the essential features of the chosen segments. The method used to study these models is the *method of equilibrium*. An *equilibrium* is a social state in which the choices of individuals are such that no individual can make himself or herself better off by making a different choice. An important part of the method of equilibrium is a procedure called *comparative statics analysis* — the method of analyzing the impact of a change in a model by comparing the equilibrium that results from the change with the original equilibrium.

Three of an economy's building blocks — the resource endowment, the technology, and individual preferences — are assumed to be unchanging, or fixed, in most economic analyses. Only the fourth building block — *institutions* — is changeable, which makes institutions particularly interesting. Many comparative statics questions concern changes in institutions: What happens when we substitute one institution for another? To answer such questions consistently, however, we need a point of comparison. That is, we need a baseline set of institutions as a reference point. In this book, the baseline is the set of institutions defining a *pure-market (or free-enterprise) economy*.

The *preferences of individuals* play a crucial role in economic theory. First, preferences play a key role in positive economics, since the economist's *theory of self-interested choice making* is that every individual will choose to undertake the course of economic action that makes him or her as well off as possible. *Positive economics* provides predictions about what that course of action will be. Those predictions are supported or refuted by careful empirical observations of the relevant facts of economic life.

Preferences also play a key role in *normative economics*, because preferences give meaning to the expressions *better than* and *worse than* in characterizing the well-being of individual members of society. Economists use two different normative criteria to compare social states. The most widely accepted is the *Pareto criterion*. In comparing any two social states, say I and J, the Pareto criterion says that state I is Pareto-preferred to state J if no one is worse off and if at least one person is better off in state I than in state J. A social state is *Pareto-optimal* if no other attainable social state is Pareto-preferred to it. To an economist, *Pareto optimality* and *efficiency* are synonymous. Some economists also use the more controversial *cost-benefit criterion* to compare social states. In comparing any two social states, say I and J, the cost-benefit criterion says that if a move from state I to state J results in a positive (negative) net social benefit, then state J (state I) is preferred.

EXERCISES

1. "In economics any equilibrium is always optimal; in fact, the terms equilibrium and optimum are synonymous." Discuss.

2. Consider the following supply and demand functions:

$$x_D = 30 - p \qquad \text{(demand)}$$
$$x_S = p - 6 \qquad \text{(supply)}$$

   a. Find the competitive equilibrium price and quantity.
   b. Now suppose that consumers' incomes increase, shifting the demand curve up and to the right as follows:

$$x_D = 32 - p \qquad \text{(demand)}$$

   Find the new equilibrium price and quantity. Show both equilibria on a carefully constructed diagram.

3. One of the social problems associated with the use of illegal drugs is street crime. Drug addicts sometimes become muggers and thieves as they seek to raise money to support their addiction. If the police manage to restrict the supply of illegal drugs, what will be the effect on the price of illegal drugs? On the level of street crime?

4. Prices are not always used to allocate goods. What mechanism is used in the following situations?
   a. attendance at a "free concert" by the Rolling Stones
   b. allocating household chores
   c. student enrolment in this class
   d. obtaining a driver's licence
   e. obtaining a court decision

5. In the case of the water shortage, using prices to allocate water was better if the costs of monitoring were low enough. Speculate on the reasons why price is not used in the five cases just mentioned in Exercise 4. That is, what is the cost of the price mechanism in these cases? (We return to this issue in the last section of the book.)

6. At a recent meeting of the board of directors of the West Van Municipal Library, a director moved that the library eliminate fines for late books. In support of the motion, the director argued that the fines served no real purpose because very few people returned their books late. If you were a user of this library, would you support or oppose this motion? As a user of this library, do you think you would be better off or worse off if fines were eliminated? Justify your answers.

7. The disposal of household refuse is now a major problem in many parts of the world. In many cities, refuse disposal is provided by the city free of charge. (The cost of disposal is financed by tax revenue in these cities.) However, some cities use a refuse disposal fee, charging the household, for example, \$2 per bag of trash. Under which system will the quantity of trash hauled to the official trash dump be larger? Under which sys-

tem will the quantity of trash illegally dumped by the roadside be larger? Under which system will a bag of trash be heavier?

8. By volume, paper is the single largest source of household refuse, accounting for 40 percent of the total volume of trash by some estimates. Newspapers alone account for 15 percent of the total volume.
   a. For purposes of argument, suppose that the total cost of disposal is 1/10 of a cent per page of newspaper. What would be the effect of a law requiring newspapers to pay a refuse disposal tax equal to 1/10 of a cent per page printed on the price and quantity of newspapers? On the size of newspapers? On the format of newspapers? On the size of magazines? On the demand for radio and television ads?
   b. More generally, what would be the effects of such a disposal tax levied on the sale of all paper products?
   c. What sorts of institutions would encourage recycling of paper?

*9. This game involves a host and N players in separate rooms. The host gives each player \$$X$ and an envelope. Each player must choose either to keep the \$$X$ or to put it into the envelope. Then the players assemble in a common room where the host collects the envelopes, takes the money out, and puts it all into a common pool. For every \$$X$ from an envelope, the host adds \$$Y$ to the common pool. The common pool is then divided equally among the N players. Before the players make their choice about keeping the \$$X$ or putting it into the envelope, the host describes the entire sequence of events to each player.
   a. To focus on the decision of a *representative player*, let M denote the number of other players who choose to put their \$$X$ in the envelope. Then construct two payoff functions, one that tells you the payoff of a representative player who puts his or her \$$X$ in the envelope, and another that tells you the payoff of a representative player who keeps \$$X$. The payoff functions will involve the variables N, M, X, and Y.
   b. Then, compare the two functions to determine which choice yields the larger payoff. Under what circumstances would a player motivated only by private gain choose to keep the \$$X$, and under what circumstances would such a player choose to put \$$X$ into the envelope?
   c. Compute the partial derivatives of the payoff functions with respect to M, N, X, and Y. Does an increase in N make it more or less likely that a player motivated only by private gain will keep the \$$X$? How does an increase in \$$X$ affect this choice? How does an increase in \$$Y$ affect this choice? How does an increase in M affect this choice?
   d. Now suppose that the players are all forced to make the same choice, and that the choice is determined by a vote. How will a player motivated only by private gain choose to vote?

1A

Appendix: Model Building

We have explored several different economic models in this chapter, but we paid very little attention to how these models were constructed. In this appendix, we will show you how an economist builds a model by looking in some detail at one very useful model: the *Hotelling model of minimum differentiation*.

Choosing a Question

We will begin the process of model building with a casual observation from our own experience. We noticed that Bay-Bloor Radio has about 24 different portable radios in stock, and asked ourselves *why* a retailer would offer so many different radios for sale. Any attempt to answer that question is an **economic model**, or theory, although not necessarily a carefully formulated, accurate, or even conscious one. Suppose we answered the question this way: Not everybody wants the same kind of radio, so it pays a retailer to carry a selection of models. But this "answer" is not really a statement of fact. Rather, it is a tentative theory based on a series of implicit **assumptions** from which we have derived a conclusion or prediction. For example, we have implicitly assumed that different people have different preferences, that portable radios are significantly different, and that retailers are motivated by profit.

economic model

assumption

From implicit assumptions like these, we have made a very loose **deduction**: the retailer will offer a wide range of models because it can then sell more radios and thus make more profit. Our deduction is also a **prediction** about what we would discover if we attempted to verify our casual observation by making systematic empirical observations of many audio retailers. That is, we have predicted that audio retailers in general will offer a range of models for sale. But is this tentative theory well-founded?

deduction

prediction

The basic method of thinking through an economic model is by using deductive reasoning, in which conclusions are drawn from carefully selected and clearly defined assumptions. First, we explicitly choose and state the assumptions that we think are relevant. Then we draw deductions from those assumptions. These deductions (like deductions in geometry) must satisfy the rules of logic by following from the assumptions. They are also the predictions of our model; they are the statements about what we would actually expect to find in the world. We can test the accuracy of our model's predictions by conducting careful empirical investigations that will tend either to support or to refute them.

Now let us begin to build an economic model from the ground up. We will start by asking some other intriguing questions based on casual observation. Why do two, three, or even four gas stations sometimes locate at the same intersection? Why do large grocery stores seem so similar in terms of the range and quality of goods they offer us? Why do supposedly different brands of premium beer or tennis rackets or economics textbooks seem almost indistinguishable? Our challenge is to create a model or theory that helps us to understand the phenomenon of clustering, or **minimum differentiation**. However, you need to remember that any particular model is not the final or "right" one in any absolute sense. Your role is to think through this model for yourself rather than to simply accept it.

minimum differentiation

Choosing Assumptions

Because the multitude of economic "facts" relevant to any economic question is overwhelming, we need to reduce the question to a manageable size. That is, we need to choose a few simple assumptions that seem to approximate the key elements of the complex reality we are attempting to understand. Let us begin this process of abstraction by thinking about the different ways in which products can cluster, or be minimally differentiated, and then select the simplest kind of product differentiation. Firms can cluster in *geographic space* by locating their stores together, or they can cluster in *characteristics space* by producing products that have similar mixes of characteristics. Gas stations located at the same intersection are clustered in geographic space. Different brands of tennis rackets that are similar in weight, balance, size, and strength are clustered in characteristics space. Because choosing a location in geographic space is easier to visualize than choosing a point, or location, in characteristics space, let us ask where in a particular geographic market firms will choose to establish their businesses.

Our next step is to reduce the vast number of firms and of goods sold to the simplest possible case. At a minimum, we need two competing firms. We can also reduce the vast array of products these two firms might sell to identical goods. We will assume that both firms offer exactly the same good, which we will call groceries, for sale. We will also assume that no price competition exists between the two firms and that both sell groceries at the same *fixed price*, denoted by P. We will assume, too, that the cost of each unit of groceries, denoted by C, is exactly the same for both firms, and that the price P is greater than the cost C. We can combine these restrictions in our first assumption.

ASSUMPTION 1

There are two firms selling an identical good, groceries, at a fixed price P per unit. The firm's cost of groceries is C per unit, and P is greater than C.

Where firms choose to locate obviously has a great deal to do with where their potential customers are located. Our model must therefore include a geographic space that locates potential buyers in a particular pattern. Because we need to reduce the actual geographic space to something manageable, let us imagine that all the customers live along a single street called Main Street. We can then represent the geographic space where these customers live by a straight line that, for simplicity, we will assume is one kilometre long. This brings us to the second simplifying abstraction in our model.

ASSUMPTION 2

The geographic space is a street, Main Street, that is one kilometre long.

In Figure 1A.1, we have represented Main Street by a line segment extending from 0 to 1. We can then think of numbers between 0 and 1 as *addresses* on Main Street. For example, 1/2 is the address at the midpoint or middle of Main Street.

What assumptions should we make about the number and distribution of these buyers? We know, of course, that population density differs from place to place and even from block to block. For instance, a thousand people may be living in a high-rise development on one block but only a hundred people may be living in large, single-family houses on the next block. Nevertheless, to assume that the customers are spaced evenly, or *uniformly*, along Main Street is a useful simplification. Imagine, then, that a specific number of customers, N, are uniformly distributed along Main Street.

Figure 1A.1 **Main Street**

The geographic space is a street, Main Street, one kilometre long.

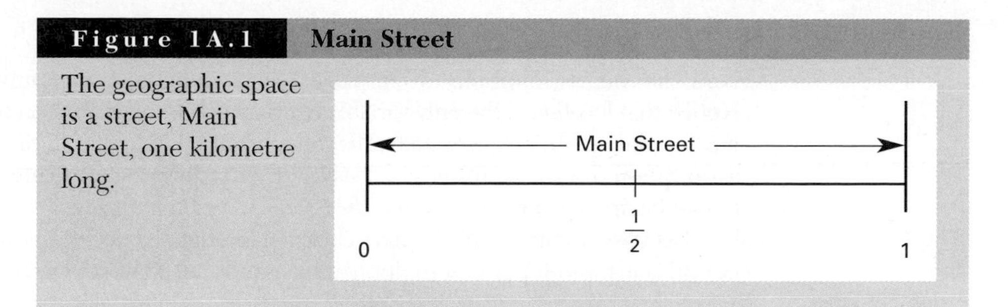

ASSUMPTION 3

There are N customers uniformly distributed along Main Street.

PROBLEM 1A.1

Suppose that N is equal to 128. How many customers live between addresses 1/2 and 3/4? Between addresses 1/4 and 1? Between addresses 0 and 1/8?

Although in reality customers buy groceries at different times and places and in different amounts, we can simplify this analysis by making a fourth assumption: each customer buys one unit of groceries at the fixed price P from one of the two firms described in assumption 1.

ASSUMPTION 4

In each period, each customer buys one unit of groceries at the fixed price P.

We will also assume that getting to the store and back is expensive for the customer and that the farther it is to the store, the more expensive it is to make the trip back and forth.

ASSUMPTION 5

Travel to either store is costly for the customer, and the customer's cost of travel increases with the distance travelled.

Finally, we need to identify the basis on which firms and customers make their respective decisions. What motivates a firm in choosing its location, and customers in choosing the store where they shop? As you know, the economist's answer to questions about individual motivation is *self-interest*. Our final assumption is that consumers and firms alike make the economic choices that are in their own self-interest.

ASSUMPTION 6

Both firms and customers are motivated by self-interest.

The precise meaning of the term self-interest varies from model to model. In this model, it is in the *firms' self-interest to make the largest possible profit*. Since both firms offer groceries at the same price, it is in *customers' self-interest to minimize travel costs*.

Finding the Equilibrium

Now that our assumptions are in place, what predictions can we derive from them? Notice that *location* is the only variable firms can choose because our other assumptions have equalized prices, products offered, and other relevant variables. According to assumption 6, our two firms — let us call them All-Valu and Bestway — *will attempt to maximize their profits through the locations of their stores.*

Let us concentrate on All-Valu's choice of location. Notice that All-Valu's profit in any period is just profit per unit multiplied by number of units sold in the period; that is,

$$\text{All-Valu's profit} = (\text{profit per unit})(\text{units sold})$$

Profit per unit is just $P - C$ since All-Valu pays C for a unit of groceries and sells it for P. Because each customer buys exactly one unit, the number of units sold is equal to the number of customers whom the store attracts; therefore,

$$\text{All-Valu's profit} = (P - C)(\text{number of All-Valu's customers})$$

To discover the number of customers who choose to shop at All-Valu, we need to look at the locations of the two stores. In Figure 1A.2, the line from address 0 on the left to address 1 on the right represents Main Street. We will refer to addresses 0 and 1 as the *market boundaries* of Main Street. Let us arbitrarily locate Bestway at point b, somewhere to the right of the halfway point on Main Street ($b > 1/2$). Now let us arbitrarily locate All-Valu's store at point a, somewhere to the left of Bestway's store ($a < b$). Given the locations represented in Figure 1A.2, how many customers will shop at All-Valu?

To answer this question, we need to derive a prediction about how individual customers will choose the stores where they shop. According to assumption 6, the customers — like the firms — are motivated by their own self-interest. Because the firms' prices are identical and because travel to the store is costly, self-interest will lead customers to buy their groceries at the closer store. We can now state the first prediction of our model:

Customers will patronize the closer store.

---

method of equilibrium

Notice how we used the **method of equilibrium** to derive this prediction. By definition, a model is in equilibrium when no individual economic participant can reach a higher ranking in his or her preference ordering by making a different choice. To get this prediction, we fixed the locations, or addresses, of the two firms at points a and b in Figure 1A.2, thereby creating a new model in which the only choices to be determined

Figure 1A.2 **Firms' locations**

All-Valu's location, or address, is a and Bestway's address is b.

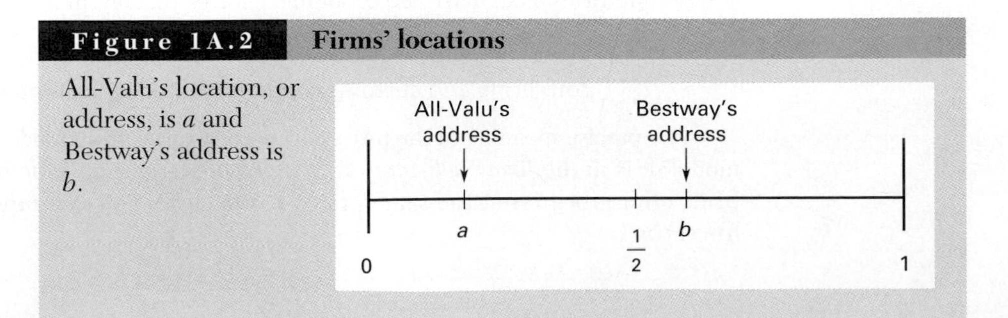

are the customers' choices of where to shop. This new model is, in a sense, a sub-model of the complete model. The point is that we used the method of equilibrium in this sub-model to derive the prediction that customers will shop at the closer store.

Knowing that customers will choose the closer store, we can calculate the number of customers who will shop at All-Valu. Let us begin by identifying the address of the customer who is indifferent between the two stores. Notice that in Figure 1A.3, the address $(a + b)/2$ is *midway* between points a and b, or equidistant from All-Valu and Bestway. The customer at address $(a + b)/2$ is therefore *indifferent* between shopping at All-Valu or at Bestway. However, customers to the left of this point prefer All-Valu because it is closer. Customers to the right of this point prefer Bestway for the same reason. We will call the address $(a + b)/2$ the *point of market segmentation* since it divides the total market into All-Valu's and Bestway's market segments. All-Valu's market segment extends from 0 to $(a + b)/2$, and Bestway's market segment extends from $(a + b)/2$ to 1. Because the N customers are uniformly distributed from 0 to 1, the number of All-Valu's customers is equal to the length of its market segment, $(a + b)/2$, multiplied by the total number of customers in the market, N; that is,

$$\text{number of All-Valu's customers} = N(a + b)/2$$

Combining this expression with the previous expression for All-Valu's profit, we have

$$\text{All-Valu's profit} = (P - C)[N(a + b)/2] \qquad \text{when } a < b$$

PROBLEM 1A.2

Suppose that N is 128, b is 3/4, and $P - C$ is 1. When a is 0, what is the point of market segmentation? How many customers shop at All-Valu? What is All-Valu's profit? When a is 1/4? When a is 1/2? Does the number of All-Valu's customers increase or decrease as a increases?

Given that the only decision All-Valu can make that affects its profit is where to locate, which value of a maximizes All-Valu's profit? As you saw in Problem 1A.2, as a increases, the point of market segmentation, $(a + b)/2$, moves to the right, and All-Valu's market segment increases. Because All-Valu's profit is *directly proportional* to its market segment, its profit increases as a increases.[2] Thus, our model predicts that when

Figure 1A.3 **Firms' markets**

All-Valu's market segment extends from 0 to $(a + b)/2$, and Bestway's market segment extends from $(a + b)/2$ to 1.

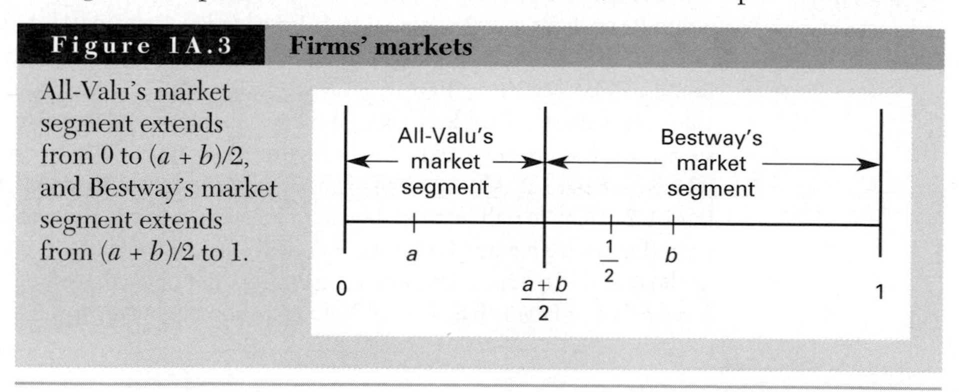

2. In this exercise, All-Valu is choosing its location a to maximize its profit. The partial derivative of this profit function with respect to a is $[(P - C)N]/2$, which is positive. All-Valu's profit is thus an increasing function of a. All-Valu will therefore locate as near to b as possible.

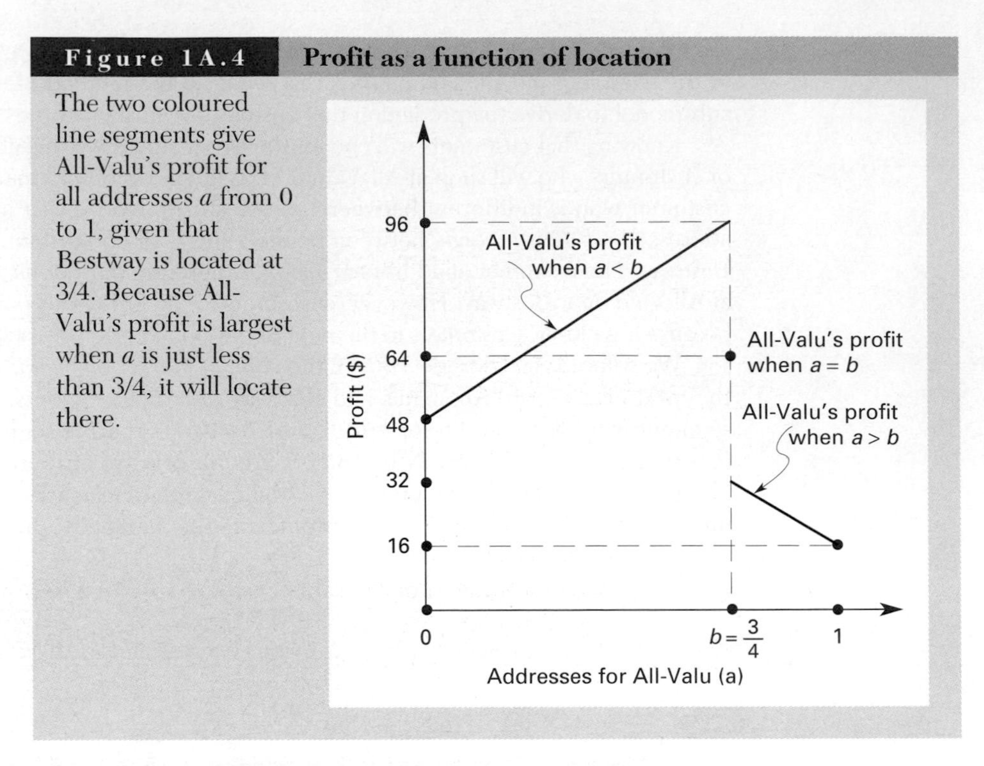

Figure 1A.4 **Profit as a function of location**

The two coloured line segments give All-Valu's profit for all addresses a from 0 to 1, given that Bestway is located at 3/4. Because All-Valu's profit is largest when a is just less than 3/4, it will locate there.

$a < b$, All-Valu will locate as close to b as possible; that is, a will be just less than b.

Of course, All-Valu is also free to locate anywhere to the *right* of Bestway; that is, to choose $a > b$. If it does so, All-Valu's market segment extends from $(a + b)/2$ to 1, and its profit is therefore

$$\text{All-Valu's profit} = (P - C)\, N\, [1 - (a + b)/2] \qquad \text{when } a > b$$

When All-Valu locates to the right of Bestway $a > b$, it is clear that as it relocates farther and farther to the right, it loses customers to Bestway, and its profit drops. Thus, when $a > b$, All-Valu's profit is largest when a is just to the right of b.

In Figure 1A.4, we have used the two algebraic expressions for All-Valu's profit to graph its profit as a varies from 0 to 1. Possible locations for All-Valu along Main Street are on the horizontal axis, and its profit is on the vertical axis. So that you can verify the details, in constructing Figure 1A.4 we have supposed that N, b, and $P - C$ are the values specified in Problem 1A.2. We have also assumed that when a is equal to b, the stores split the market evenly. From Figure 1A.4, we see that, because we have assumed that b exceeds 1/2, All-Valu will locate just to the left of Bestway. However, if b is less than 1/2, All-Valu will instead decide to locate just to the right of b. The general inference that we have made is that All-Valu will locate adjacent to its competitor on one side or the other. Whether it chooses to be on the right or on the left will depend on whether b is smaller or larger than 1/2. All-Valu will choose whichever side gives it the larger segment of the market. Of course, Bestway will choose its location in exactly the same way. As a result, we have our second prediction:

When a store is relocating, it will always choose to establish itself adjacent to its competitor on the side farther from a market boundary (points 0 and 1).

In deriving this prediction, once again we used the method of equilibrium. The second prediction tells us what will happen when one firm's address is fixed. Notice that when we fix one firm's address, we are creating a sub-model in which the choices to be determined are the other firm's choice of an address and each customer's choice of which store to patronize. In the equilibrium of this sub-model, the firm that is picking an address chooses to establish itself adjacent to its competitor on the side farther from a market boundary, and (consistent with our first prediction) customers choose to patronize the closer store.

This second prediction begins to make sense of our earlier observations about how gas stations tend to cluster at the same intersection. Using this prediction we can deduce the equilibrium of locations in the complete model. We can find the equilibrium by discovering what would happen if both stores were to locate to one side of the midpoint (1/2) of Main Street.

In Figure 1A.5, Bestway is initially located at b_1. Because it is closer than its competitor to the midpoint and therefore commands the larger share of the market, it will stay put. However, because All-Valu is initially located at a_1, it will "leapfrog" its competitor and relocate adjacent to its competitor on the side closer to the midpoint at a_2. As a result of All-Valu's move, Bestway's share of the market will drop. It will then leapfrog All-Valu to recapture its market advantage. This process will continue until both grocery stores are finally located together at the centre of Main Street. Of course, this leapfrogging is not something we would actually expect to see, but rather something these two firms would play out in their minds before choosing their equilibrium locations at the centre of the market. We have reached our third prediction:

Both stores will locate together at the centre of the market.

Figure 1A.5 **The equilibrium of locations**

The firms are initially located at a_1 and b_1. All-Valu relocates at a_2, inducing Bestway to relocate at b_2. This process of relocation by leapfrogging stops only when the firms are both located at the midpoint of the market; that is, $a = b = 1/2$ is the equilibrium pair of locations.

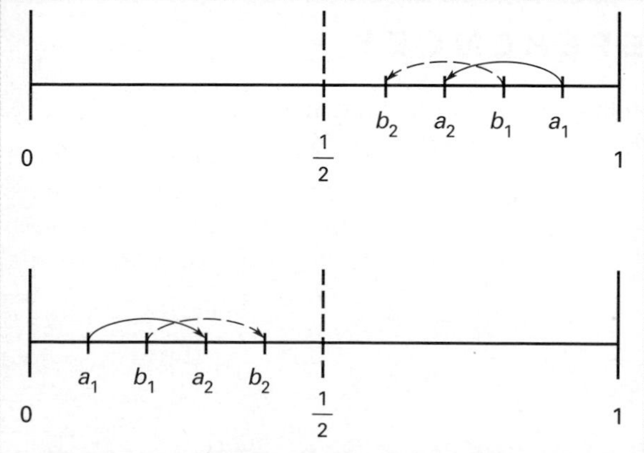

This third prediction concerns not a sub-model but the *complete model* in which the choices to be determined are Bestway's and All-Valu's choice of an address and also each customer's choice of where to buy groceries. In the equilibrium of the complete model, the stores are located together at the centre of the market and customers patronize either firm since both firms are the same distance away from any one customer.

PROBLEM 1A.3

In finding the equilibrium of this duopoly model, we assumed that the two grocers could change their locations at no cost. Consider the opposite extreme: assume that once they have chosen a location, the grocers cannot relocate their stores. Let All-Valu choose its location first and assume that it understands that once its location is chosen, Bestway will choose the location that maximizes its own profit. Which locations will the firms choose?

Summary

The objective of this appendix has been to illustrate the working methodology of the economic theorist. Because economic theory attempts to explain economic reality, what often sparks the theorist's interest is an intriguing observation from ordinary life coupled with the question, "Why?" For example, "Why do two, three, or even four gas stations sometimes locate at the same intersection?"

The theorist then builds a model (or theory) to explain the observation. This model building is the process of judiciously selecting a set of assumptions that capture the essential features of that economic reality and then deriving conclusions, or predictions, from those assumptions. The method used to derive those predictions is the method of equilibrium. An equilibrium consists of a set of choices for individuals and a corresponding social state such that no individual can make himself or herself better off by making some other choice. Thus, the force that drives this deductive process is the *self-interest* of individual economic agents. Indeed, the systematic application of this method of analysis distinguishes economics from other social sciences.

REFERENCES

Hotelling, H. 1929. "Stability in Competition," *The Economic Journal*, 39:41–57.

Keynes, J. M. 1920. *The Economic Consequences of the Peace*. New York: Harcourt, Brace.

PART II

Individual Choice

In Part II, we concentrate on the behaviour of individuals as economic agents as we see how consumers decide which goods to buy in the goods market. In Chapter 2, we set out the most widely used economic theory of individual preferences, we examine an individual's willingness to make tradeoffs among goods, and we show how to construct utility functions from data about individual preferences. We also see how the theory of preferences can be used to explore several intriguing observations from ordinary life.

In Chapter 3, we consider how a consumer allocates a limited income across consumption goods to maximize utility. The solution to this problem is a set of demand functions specifying how much of each good a consumer buys, given the consumer's income and any set of prices for consumption goods.

In Chapter 4, we apply the techniques of Chapter 3 to a wide range of day-to-day problems. We explain, for example, why people in different religions devote different amounts of income and time to their church; why squash courts are often booked solid on campus but not in private clubs; and why nice homes tend to be built on nice lots. Our intention is to let you see just how widely applicable the theory of choice actually is.

CHAPTER 2

A Theory of Preferences

All social sciences — including political science, sociology, psychology, and economics — are concerned with human behaviour. Yet each discipline in the social sciences views human nature from a different vantage point, and often makes different assumptions regarding the nature of people. In this respect, different social sciences often "compete" with each other in an effort to explain the same behaviour. If one were to ask a sociologist, a psychologist, and an economist why, for example, many corporations spend millions of dollars on seemingly useless and clearly uninformative TV advertisements, three distinct answers would be forthcoming. These different responses reflect the different assumptions of human behaviour that underlie each discipline. What distinguishes the economist's approach to the study of human behaviour is the universal application of the hypothesis of the pursuit of *self-interest*. For an economist, self-interest means that an individual maximizes over a set of preferences subject to constraints. This is a complicated way of saying individuals do the best they can given their circumstances. Economists see self-interest at work everywhere in life — it is what makes them so sought after at cocktail parties!

In Chapter 1, we introduced you to the concept of self-interest, and we saw that self-interest motivates all economic activity, including the profit-maximizing activities of firms. We also saw that — for economists — self-interest means that individuals make the choices that allow them to attain the highest possible ranking in their own preference orderings. In this chapter, we will set out the foundations of this approach in some detail as we explore the theory of preferences. This theory is based on three fairly simple ideas:

1. Individuals have consistent preferences.
2. Individuals seek to maximize their preference ranking.
3. Individuals are willing to make tradeoffs between different goods.

We begin the chapter by considering precisely what it means to say that individual preferences are consistent, and then we explore an individual's willingness to make tradeoffs — that is, his or her willingness to give up one thing to get another.

We go on to describe a useful measure of an individual's willingness to make tradeoffs called the *marginal rate of substitution*, and we introduce an additional and widely used assumption known as a *diminishing marginal rate of substitution*. Then we introduce *utility functions*, which are simply mathematical representations of preferences, and we show how to construct a utility function from preference data. Finally, we look at several applications of the theory of preferences.

2.1 Completeness and Consistency of Preferences

preferences

Clearly, what people like and what economic choices they make are directly linked: people's **preferences**, or personal tastes, dictate their economic decisions. But preferences may cover more territory than you might at first imagine. Individuals clearly have preferences over goods and services such as CDs, running shoes, paperback books, house cleaning, car washing, and banking. These are the kinds of economic goods that ordinarily come to mind when we think about individuals making economic choices.

However, people also have preferences about a whole range of other, less tangible economic goods. These include preferences about how to spend time (working, studying, watching TV, shopping), possible occupations (construction work, dentistry, massage therapy, accounting), locations (living in their home town or travelling the world), social relations (choice of spouse, number of children), different environmental settings (large cosmopolitan cities or remote wilderness areas), and charitable activities (donating to a food bank or volunteering for a charity fund drive). Notice that "self-interest" can include charitable actions of all kinds, as well as actions that are strictly "selfish." The theory of preferences developed in this chapter applies not only to ordinary consumption goods and services like golf balls and haircuts, but to these other kinds of goods. In short, if something is valued, it is an economic good and the theory of preferences applies.

In order to develop a model of preferences it is necessary to start with some assumptions about them. As we introduce these assumptions we will argue for why they are reasonable and why they accurately reflect true preferences. Ultimately, however, our model will be judged by how well it explains behaviour, and not by its assumptions. Making assumptions is essential, and yet economists are often criticized for it. One of the oldest jokes in the profession tells of an economist, an engineer, and a labourer stranded on a beach, arguing over how to open a can of beans without a can opener. "Let's crush it with a rock," suggests the labourer. "No," replies the engineer, " let's magnify the sun's rays with my glasses and heat the can until it explodes." The economist calmly holds up his hand and states, "I have the solution. First, assume we have a can opener … " Every discipline, whether it is literary criticism or physics, requires assumptions. The assumptions in this chapter are a little more useful than "assuming there is a can opener," but like our friend on the beach, we're going to be explicit in stating them.

The Two-Good Case

To keep the analysis of individual preferences simple, we will assume that there are just two goods. Here, the person is faced with choices among different combinations (or bundles) containing varying amounts of these two goods. We will use the terms *good* 1 and *good* 2 to represent the goods themselves. For example, good 1 might be T-shirts and good 2 hot dogs. We will use the symbols x_1 and x_2 to denote corresponding quantities of good 1 and good 2. For example, $x_1 = 2$ means two T-shirts and $x_2 = 5$ means five hot dogs. A **consumption bundle** is *a combination of a specific quantity of each good.* We will denote a consumption bundle by (x_1, x_2). For example, the consumption bundle (2,5) contains 2 units of good 1 (T-shirts) and 5 units of good 2 (hot dogs). The consumption bundle (62,17) contains 62 units of good 1 and 17 units of good 2, and so on.

consumption bundle

With only two goods we can represent every conceivable consumption bundle in a first quadrant graph. Figure 2.1 has good 1 on the horizontal axis and good 2 on the vertical axis. Although every point in this space represents a consumption bundle, only five bundles are shown in the graph.

A Preference Ordering

preference statements

Notice that implicit in choosing one consumption bundle or another is a person's ability to make one of two **preference statements** — the ability to say either "I like this bundle better than that one," or to say "I like both equally well: I'm indifferent between them." We can make use of a person's statements of preference and indifference to compare the relative attractiveness of two particular consumption bundles. By making a whole series of such comparisons, we may be able to construct a preference ordering for that person — a ranking from top to bottom, from most-preferred to least-preferred — of all consumption bundles. More precisely, we can use these preference statements to construct a complete **preference ordering** if two conditions are satisfied: 1. *a person is always able to make such preference statements,* and 2. *his or her preference statements are consistent.*

preference ordering

Our first challenge, then, is to find a set of assumptions that imply these two conditions. To begin, let us imagine that a particular person named Eleanor has made the following three preference statements about four consumption bundles containing good 1 (T-shirts) and good 2 (hot dogs): a. she prefers bundle (20,17) to bundle (4,12); b. she is indifferent between bundle (4,12) and bundle (10,5); and c. she prefers bundle (10,5) to bundle (2,3). Now let us try to rank, or order, Eleanor's preferences over these four consumption bundles. This seems to be the obvious ordering:

First:	bundle (20,17)
Second:	bundles (4,12) and (10,5)
Third:	bundle (2,3)

But this is just a tentative beginning in our attempt to create a preference ordering for Eleanor. First, do we know that her preference ordering is *complete*? Eleanor was able to make preference statements about these four bundles, but do we know that she can do so for every pair of consumption bundles? If she cannot make such preference statements about *all possible pairs of consumption bundles,* then we cannot construct a complete preference ordering for her. We therefore need the following assumption about the **completeness** of an individual's preferences:

completeness

COMPLETENESS ASSUMPTION

Given any two consumption bundles, one of the following statements is true:

Bundle 1 is preferred to bundle 2

Bundle 2 is preferred to bundle 1

Bundle 1 is indifferent to bundle 2

If we refer to Figure 2.1, this means Eleanor can compare any two points in the space. This seems to be a perfectly straightforward assumption, but you should be aware that it is also a strong one. For example, the completeness assumption implies that a person is familiar with every good in the consumption bundles. Yet someone who has never eaten, say, a papaya, cannot be expected to satisfy this assumption if papayas are included in those bundles. The completeness assumption also means that an individual can compare bundles with trivial differences — for example, whether there are four grains of sugar in a cup of tea or only three. The completeness assumption there-

FIGURE 2.1 **Possible consumption bundles**

Each point in the T-shirt/hot dog space represents a different consumption bundle. Five consumption bundles are actually shown in the picture.

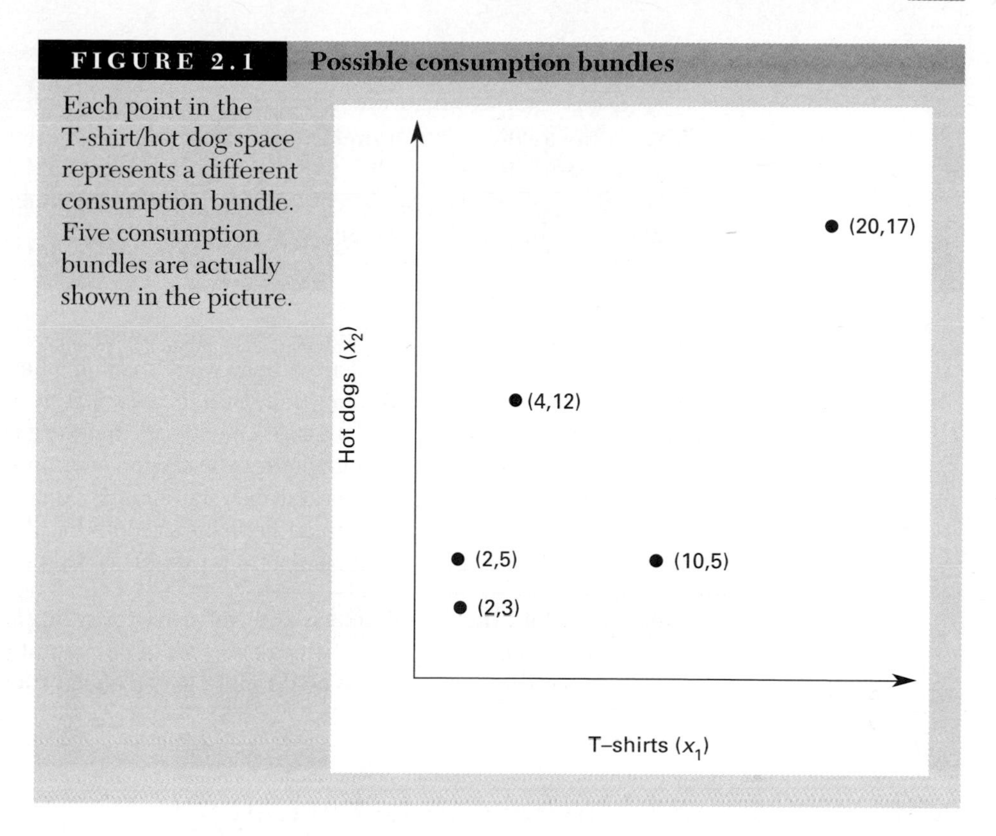

fore rules out interesting economic issues about how individuals explore, or find out about, their own preferences.

Second, do we know that Eleanor's preferences over these four bundles and all other bundles are *consistent*? For example, we placed bundle (20,17) first in her preference ordering and bundle (2,3) third. But can we be sure that if we asked Eleanor to compare these two bundles, she would say that she prefers bundle (20,17) to bundle (2,3)? What if she tells us instead that she prefers bundle (2,3) to bundle (20,17)? Or that she is indifferent between them? Then Eleanor's preferences are not consistent, and we cannot construct a complete preference ordering for her. We therefore need to make an assumption about the *consistency* of an individual's preferences.[1]

transitivity

The consistency assumption is known as **transitivity**. It guarantees, for example, that if Eleanor says that she prefers (20,17) to (4,12) and that she prefers (4,12) to (2,3), she will also say that she prefers (20,17) to (2,3).

TRANSITIVITY ASSUMPTION

Given any three consumption bundles:

If bundle 1 is at least as good as bundle 2 and bundle 2 is at least as good as bundle 3, then bundle 1 is at least as good as bundle 3.

In other words, if $1 \geq 2$, and $2 \geq 3$, then $1 \geq 3$. To check your understanding of the transitivity assumption, try the following problem.

1. Consistency not only requires the transitivity assumption above, it also requires that *only* one of the completeness statements be true.

PROBLEM 2.1

Does the following set of preference statements violate the transitivity assumption? Bundle (11,17) is indifferent to bundle (14,21); bundle (10,19) is preferred to bundle (14,21); bundle (14,21) is preferred to bundle (15,8); bundle (15,8) is preferred to bundle (11,17).

These two assumptions — completeness and transitivity — are basic or *core assumptions* about preferences, and are usually what is meant when economists speak of "rational" decision making. Taken together they tell us precisely what it means to say that an individual has consistent preferences. The first assumption guarantees that a person can always make preferences statements. The second assumption guarantees that a person will not make inconsistent preference statements. To help understand their significance, try to imagine what human behaviour would be like if people did not behave as if they had complete and consistent preferences. In summary:

Taken together, the completeness and transitivity assumptions guarantee that an individual can consistently rank any set of consumption bundles, or that the individual has a complete preference ordering.

2.2 Nonsatiation and Maximizing Behaviour

nonsatiation

Along with the existence of complete and consistent preferences, economists assume that individuals are generally nonsatiated — that a consumer always prefers a consumption bundle with more of both goods to a bundle with less. This assumption is known as the **nonsatiation** assumption. Nonsatiation means, for example, that Eleanor would rather have bundle (17,51) — that is, 17 T-shirts and 51 hot dogs — than bundle (4,5) — that is, 4 T-shirts and 5 hot dogs. The nonsatiation assumption can be stated as follows:

NONSATIATION ASSUMPTION

Given any two consumption bundles, if bundle 1 contains more of one good than bundle 2, and if it does not contain less of the other good, then bundle 1 is preferred to bundle 2.

To check your understanding of the nonsatiation assumption, try the following problem.

PROBLEM 2.2

Which of the following preference statements violate the nonsatiation assumption? Bundle (12,35) is preferred to bundle (10,30); bundle (17,98) is preferred to bundle (17,97); bundle (10,9) is preferred to bundle (10,10); bundle (42,67) is preferred to bundle (42,60); bundle (6,9) is preferred to bundle (7,8); bundle (99,43) is preferred to bundle (101,45).

It is quite possible that the nonsatiation assumption does not hold for a given good. For some commodities it is easy to imagine that, at some point, enough is enough. For example, Eleanor might decide that 912 T-shirts was enough, and she therefore might say that a consumption bundle containing 913 T-shirts and 6 hot dogs was not really preferable to a bundle containing 912 T-shirts and 6 hot dogs. In other cases, the nonsatiation assumption is not applicable at all. For example, in cases where consumption bundles contain what are sometimes called economic "bads" like garbage or nuclear waste, less — not more — is better. We will consider some economic bads in the applications of Section 2.5.

Nevertheless, economists generally assume that individuals are never satiated over all goods. That is, no matter what an individual has, there is always *some good* that they would prefer more of. If you find this questionable, consider the case of money. Dollars, though they bring no pleasure on their own, can be used to purchase just about anything, and so dollars are a convenient way of representing all goods. When was the last time you heard someone say he or she had enough money and would turn down a lottery prize? The world is full of wealthy people and, for better or worse, their behaviour suggests that there are many goods that they still want more of.

maximize

It is one thing to assume individuals prefer more goods to less, but economists go one step further and assert that people *act* to **maximize** over their preference ordering. That is, people are assumed to choose a bundle of goods that they most prefer. This returns us to the notion of self-interest. Not only do people have consistent preferences, but they make all of their choices in an effort to reach the highest level of preference possible. The **maximization assumption** is important because it is the motivation that drives all agents in an economic model.

maximization assumption

MAXIMIZATION ASSUMPTION

Individuals always make choices that make them better off.

The maximization assumption has three important implications. First, it restricts the type of argument that an economist can make to explain behaviour. This book is ultimately concerned with explaining why people do the things they do. In every one of our explanations, the individuals involved will be assumed to be maximizing; that is, making decisions that improve their preference ranking. For example, it is common in England for individuals to use cloth napkins at the table, while in North America paper napkins are mostly used. Why would there be this difference in behaviour? In search of an answer, economists avoid explanations based on customs, ignorance, or irrationality. It does not do to say that in England people have always used cloth or that they are unaware of paper napkins. An economic argument starts with the assumption that the English are better off using cloth, while at the same time North Americans are better off with paper. What do you think the answer is?[2]

scarcity

A second implication of maximization and the assumption of nonsatiation is **scarcity**. Given that we live in a finite world, and that individuals always prefer to have more rather than less, it follows that we never have enough. Scarcity is simply the result of wanting more than what we have freely available. Note that scarcity is the result of two things

2. Travel can reveal large differences in social behaviour. Though many North Americans travelling abroad are shocked when they discover differences like having to use water rather than toilet paper in a public washroom, for economists these differences are mysteries that beg for an explanation. The maximization assumption, along with consistent preferences, is always the starting place for the answer.

that are unlikely to change: a finite world and a greedy human disposition. As a result, scarcity will always be with us, and one is wise to be skeptical of anyone who promises to eliminate scarcity. Note also that *scarce* is not the same thing as limited or rare. Smallpox is rare, but it is not scarce. In order for something to be scarce people must want it, and they must want more than is freely available to them.

A society facing scarcity faces another problem: how to allocate a fixed amount of goods among a group of people who all want more. This is essentially the central concern of economics, and in this book we mostly focus on the role prices and markets play in allocating resources. However, in Part VI of the book we examine many non-price mechanisms that are used as well.

Finally, maximization implies that people fully exploit any opportunities that are presented to them. For example, when individuals trade, they trade until the gains from trade are maximized. If they did not do this, they would not be behaving according to the maximization assumption. Consider, for example, your trip home this evening. If you drive home along a highway with several lanes, which lane should you take? To keep things simple, suppose there are only two lanes. Of course, you will take the fast one, but wait … what are the other drivers doing? They are taking the fast lane as well, and this slows it down. If it slows down enough and the other lane gets faster, you might consider switching into the other lane. But the very act of switching slows down the lane you are moving to and speeds up the one you just left! Since all other drivers are behaving the same way, it doesn't matter which lane you use tonight. The maximization assumption implies that both lanes will be moving at approximately the same speed, because if they were not, maximizing drivers would change lanes until this was so.

This is a remarkable result, and one that we will see over and over again because it is at the heart of what economists call *equilibrium*. As we discussed in Chapter 1, equilibrium consists of a set of choices for the individual and a corresponding social state such that no individual can make himself or herself better off by making some other choices. In other words, an equilibrium is a set of choices that results from a maximization process from which there is no incentive to depart. It must be the case that all of the gains from trade are maximized in equilibrium. Otherwise, individuals would alter their choices and hence by definition there would not have been an equilibrium. To confirm that you follow this reasoning, consider the following problem.

PROBLEM 2.3

Imagine a city that has two suburbs. One of the suburbs is close, but the road to the city is quite congested. The other suburb is farther away, but the road is relatively uncongested. Suppose a new larger road is built for the first suburb.

a. What do you think will happen to congestion in the immediate future?
b. What do you think will happen to congestion in five years after people have had an opportunity to move?
c. Los Angeles has vast and expansive highways compared with those of New York City or Toronto. Explain why LA is just as congested.

2.3 Tradeoffs and Indifference Curves

The idea that individuals maximize over consistent preferences is one key concept in the economist's theory of human behaviour. The idea that individuals are willing to make tradeoffs is another. In lay terms, a willingness to make tradeoffs is like saying "everyone has a price." That is, if you are being asked to sacrifice some amount of a good, there is always some amount of another good that could compensate you enough to agree to the sacrifice. Let us consider precisely what economists mean by the term *tradeoffs* and see how tradeoffs and *indifference curves* are inextricably linked.

Recall the tentative preference ordering we constructed for Eleanor. By definition, the bundles among which she is indifferent will occupy the same position in her preference ordering. For example, because she is indifferent between bundle (4,12) and bundle (10,5), we know that these two bundles occupy the same position in her preference ordering. The list of all bundles occupying the same position in a preference ordering is called an **indifference curve**. An indifference curve for Eleanor, labelled I, is presented in Figure 2.2. We know that any two consumption bundles on this indifference curve must satisfy the indifference statement. For example, we know that Eleanor is also indifferent between bundle (10,5) and bundle (5,10) and that she is indifferent between bundle (4,12) and bundle (5,10).

indifference curve

Now let us look at the relationship between indifference curves and the willingness to make tradeoffs. Suppose that Eleanor is initially at bundle (4,12) in Figure 2.2, where she has a consumption bundle containing 4 T-shirts and 12 hot dogs. We know

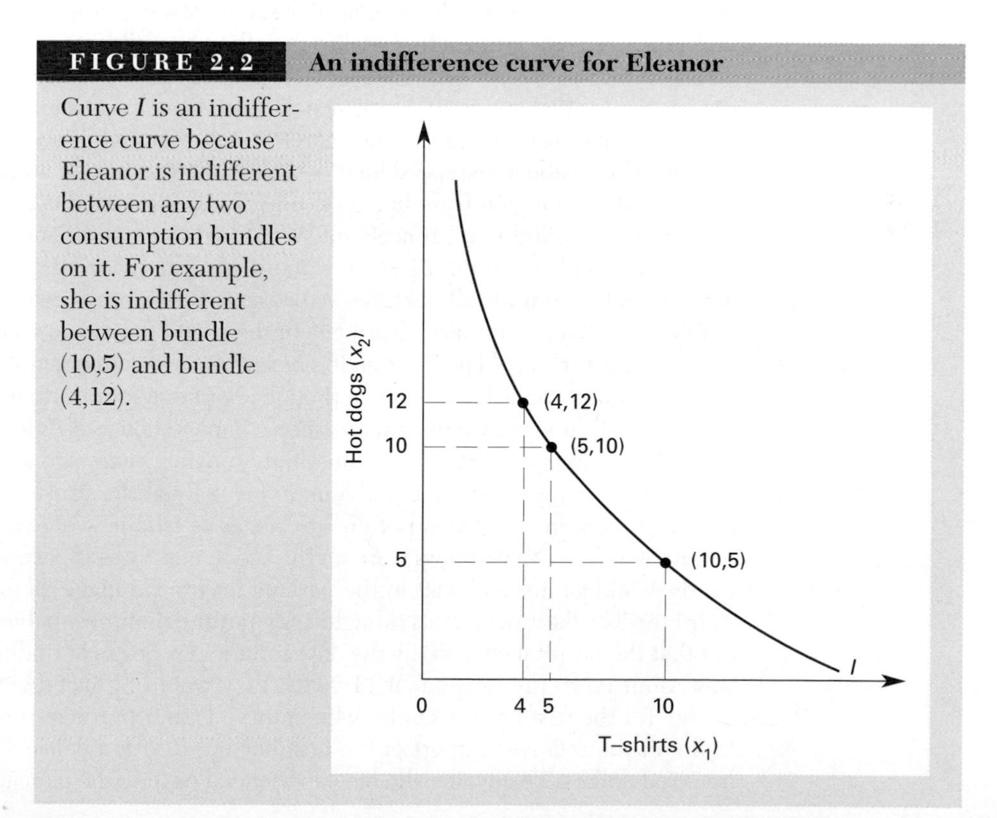

FIGURE 2.2 An indifference curve for Eleanor

Curve I is an indifference curve because Eleanor is indifferent between any two consumption bundles on it. For example, she is indifferent between bundle (10,5) and bundle (4,12).

that she is willing to give up 2 hot dogs in order to get 1 more T-shirt because the consumption bundle (5,10) is on the same indifference curve. Beginning at bundle (4, 12), we also know that she is willing to give up 7 hot dogs to get 6 T-shirts because the bundle (10,5) is also on the same indifference curve. As you can see, tradeoffs concern movements along indifference curves. Given an initial bundle, as we move along the associated indifference curve, we encounter all of the tradeoffs that a particular person is willing to make from the initial bundle.

As with the other assumptions made thus far, the willingness to make tradeoffs is more subtle than first appears. For example, the willingness to sacrifice one good in order to obtain more of another implies that there is no "priority of wants." Quite often people talk as if there is a priority in the goods we consume: "First I'll buy food, then clothing, then shelter, etc." The willingness to make tradeoffs, however, suggests that different combinations of food and clothing can yield the same level of satisfaction and that there is no priority. It is a little like the logger who was arrested for killing and eating a seagull. He pleaded that he'd only done it because he was starving; he'd never killed a bird before and never would again. Taking his hard luck story into account, the judge gave him only a small fine, then asked what seagull tasted like. "Not bad," came the reply, "it was like a cross between a spotted owl and a bald eagle." Like the logger, we all generate satisfaction from different combinations of goods, and we are constantly trading one off for another to improve our preference ordering. A corollary to this is that economists shun the word "need." Since different combinations of goods can lead to the same level of satisfaction, generally no one "needs" any particular good.

Although most people agree individuals make tradeoffs in their lives, economists assume that there is virtually nothing a person is unwilling to trade — if the compensation is high enough. By contrast non-economists often find this extreme position objectionable. Therefore, let us consider some extreme examples. What about your life? Are you willing to trade your life for other goods? First consider the risks you take that jeopardize your life and shorten it. Perhaps you enjoy smoking, even with the knowledge that you raise the chance of death from lung cancer. A smoker is someone who trades off one good — a cigarette — for another — a period of life. Have you ever driven above the speed limit because you were late for an appointment? If so, you traded off the gain from being on time for an increased chance that you might get injured or killed in a car accident. Would you accept a dangerous job for more pay? If you think about it for just a few moments, you realize that you make tradeoffs with respect to your life all the time. We observe this in other people as well. A survey of Olympic athletes revealed that many of them said they were willing to take a drug that would ensure a gold medal even if it meant they would die in five years. People continue to climb Mount Everest, even though about one in four do not make it back.

The really remarkable thing is how little compensation it takes for us to make a large tradeoff for things we claim we value highly. A few years ago a private hospital in Seattle was having a desperate problem. Every night at the stroke of midnight, up to a dozen women, in various and often late stages of labour, were rushing through the emergency door. News crews were on the scene nightly as the women and their husbands would gather and wait in the parking lot for the magic hour. These were not weird thrill-seekers or parents thoughtlessly putting their new babies at risk. It turned out that the hospital charged by the day, and the day began at midnight. If the couple was admitted to the hospital at 11:00 PM they would be faced with an entire day's charge for the first hour. Couples who entered labour in the evening were willing to trade off the relative comfort of the hospital and to risk a delivery outside for a few hundred dollars. To anyone who has experienced or seen the pain and stress of labour and delivery, this is a striking example of how individuals willingly make tradeoffs or substitute one good for another.[3]

The fact that individuals constantly make tradeoffs is an important fact of life for any government or regulatory agency. When a government, for example, attempts to improve the safety features of a product, it induces changes in the way the product is used. These changes may diminish or even reverse the effects intended by the product safety regulations. Or, if a government decides that it wants to help unemployed people and raises unemployment payments, it also creates an incentive for people to become unemployed. A remarkable example of unintended consequences resulting from substitution comes from efforts to reduce toxic chemicals in the water system. The province of British Columbia has a series of taxes and charges on the purchase of chemicals and pesticides, as well as disposal fees for harmful substances, all in an effort to discourage their use and pay for their cleanup. At the same time, water testing in the Fraser Valley outside the city of Vancouver has shown a rise in these chemicals in the water system, including chemicals like DDT which have been banned for years. It appears a plausible explanation that in an effort to avoid the large taxes and disposal fees, farmers and rural landowners have turned to black market sources for chemicals, which are flushed directly into the soil to avoid detection.

PROBLEM 2.4

1. Describe a good for which you would be unwilling to sacrifice *any amount*, no matter how large the compensation.
2. Do you know of or have you knowledge of anyone who has made the very tradeoff you described above?
3. List some of the ways your parents exploited your willingness to make tradeoffs in order to improve your behaviour while you were growing up (e.g., to induce you to eat your vegetables or to obey curfews).

Continuity of Preferences

Returning to Eleanor, recall that there were a number of bundles she found equally acceptable. The indifference curve in Figure 2.2 reflects the fact that she was willing to trade off one good against the other. Is it conceivable that there are consumption bundles for which a particular person finds *no* acceptable substitutes? If so, what will the resulting indifference curve look like? Try the following problem to find out.

PROBLEM 2.5

Clem is obsessed with good 1. Given any two bundles with unequal quantities of good 1, Clem prefers the bundle with the larger quantity of good 1. Given any two bundles with equal quantities of good 1, Clem prefers the bundle with the larger quantity of good 2. Consider bundle (2,3), and show that there is no other bundle, say bundle B, for which Clem will say that he is indifferent between bundle (2,3) and bundle B. Now, consider an arbitrary consumption bundle and show that it, too, is a single-point indifference curve.

3. The hospital eventually started to charge by the hour for deliveries and the problem cleared up.

As you discovered, Clem's indifference curves are simply points and are shown in Figure 2.3. In Figure 2.3 three bundles are shown, and Clem is not indifferent between any of them. This reflects the fact that Clem is completely *unwilling* to make tradeoffs of one good for another: there is no amount of good 2 large enough to persuade him to give up even a very small amount of good 1. However, few people's preferences are like Clem's. Most individuals are willing to make tradeoffs among goods. To ensure that individuals are willing to make tradeoffs, we need an additional assumption known as the **continuity of preferences**.

continuity of preferences

CONTINUITY OF PREFERENCES ASSUMPTION

Through any consumption bundle in which the quantity of at least one good is positive, there is a continuous indifference curve.

To see what the continuity assumption means in graphic terms, place your pencil on any consumption bundle in Figure 2.2. The continuity assumption means that you can draw the indifference curve from any bundle on the curve through all the others without lifting your pencil from the paper — that is, the indifference curve is continuous. In the following problem, you can try your hand at constructing indifference curves for a particularly simple preference ordering.

PROBLEM 2.6

Anna likes eating fish, but she only eats two kinds: trout (good 1) and salmon (good 2). Her preferences are such that, given a choice between two bundles containing trout and salmon, she always prefers the bundle that weighs more. Let x_1 and x_2 denote pounds of trout and salmon respectively.

a. What is Anna's preference ordering over the following six bundles: (10,15), (20,30), (25,0), (15,15), (20,15), (40,10)?
b. On one diagram draw the indifference curves defined by each of the following bundles: (10,15), (20,30), (20,15), (40,0).

FIGURE 2.3 **Clem's indifference curves**

Clem prefers the bundle (2,5) to (2,3) because it has the same amount of good 1, but more of good 2. Likewise Clem prefers the bundle (10,5) because it has more of good 1. Therefore, there are no two bundles for which Clem is indifferent.

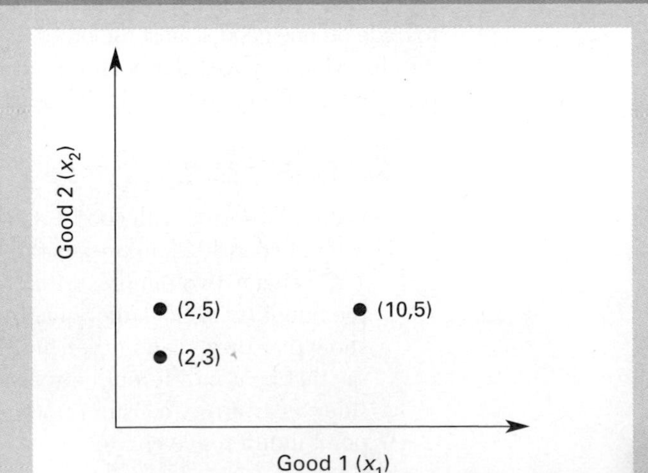

The Slope of Indifference Curves

In Figure 2.4, we have drawn an indifference curve and, for convenience, we have labelled it $I(2,2)$ since it passes through consumption bundle (2,2). Notice that its slope is negative. When the nonsatiation assumption is satisfied, the slope of *any* indifference curve is negative. To see why, notice that any bundle in the blue area of Figure 2.4 is preferred to bundle (2,2) because bundles in that area contain at least 2 units of both goods and more than 2 units of either good 1 or good 2. Similarly, bundle (2,2) is preferred to any bundle in the grey area, because those bundles contain less of at least one good and no more of the other good than consumption bundle (2,2). If we now imagine any indifference curve through bundle (2,2), it cannot enter the blue (more preferred) area or the grey (less preferred) area. The indifference curve $I(2,2)$ in Figure 2.4 must therefore slope downward and to the right:

The nonsatiation assumption implies that indifference curves have a negative slope.

The Indifference Map

There is another important observation to make about indifference curves. Because the preference ordering is a complete ordering, we know that there is an indifference curve through *every* bundle. Thus, the (x_1, x_2) plane is filled with indifference curves like those in Figure 2.3. Because of the nonsatiation assumption, bundles with more of both goods are preferred to those with less. As we move upward and to the right from indifference curve $I(2,2)$ to $I(3,3)$ to $I(4,4)$ to $I(5,5)$ in Figure 2.5, we encounter indif-

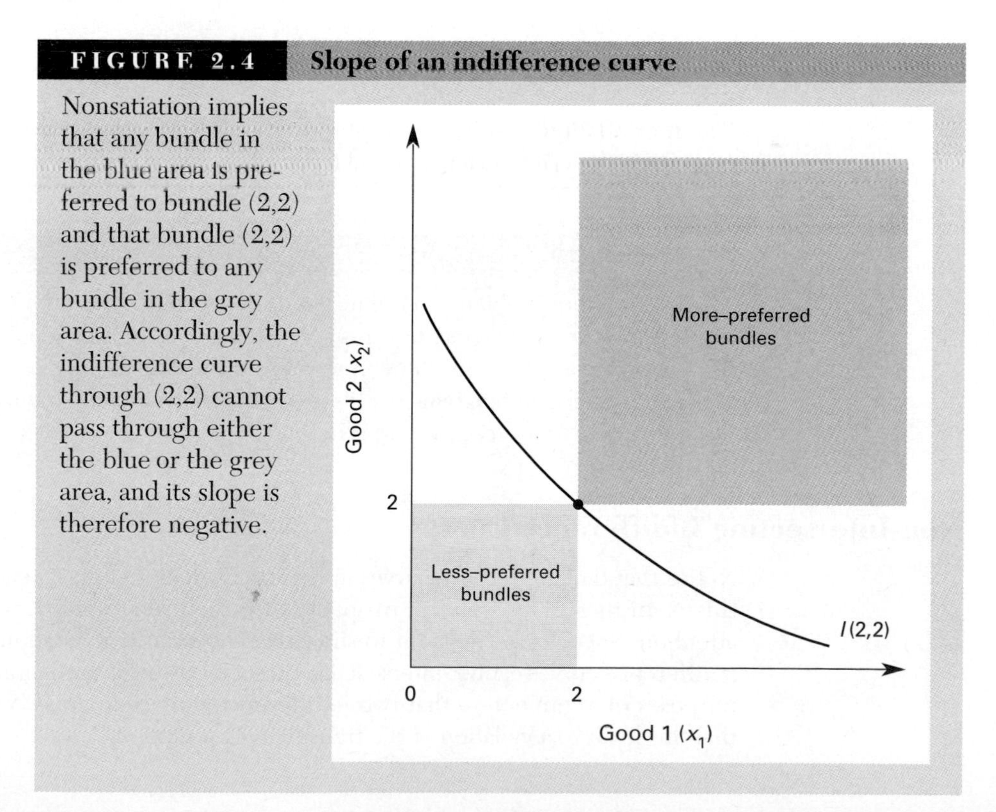

FIGURE 2.4 **Slope of an indifference curve**

Nonsatiation implies that any bundle in the blue area is preferred to bundle (2,2) and that bundle (2,2) is preferred to any bundle in the grey area. Accordingly, the indifference curve through (2,2) cannot pass through either the blue or the grey area, and its slope is therefore negative.

FIGURE 2.5 **An indifference map**

The space of consumption bundles is filled with indifference curves. Four indifference curves are shown here. Any bundle on $I(5,5)$ is preferred to any bundle on $I(4,4)$, any bundle on $I(4,4)$ is preferred to any bundle on $I(3,3)$, and any bundle on $I(3,3)$ is preferred to any bundle on $I(2,2)$.

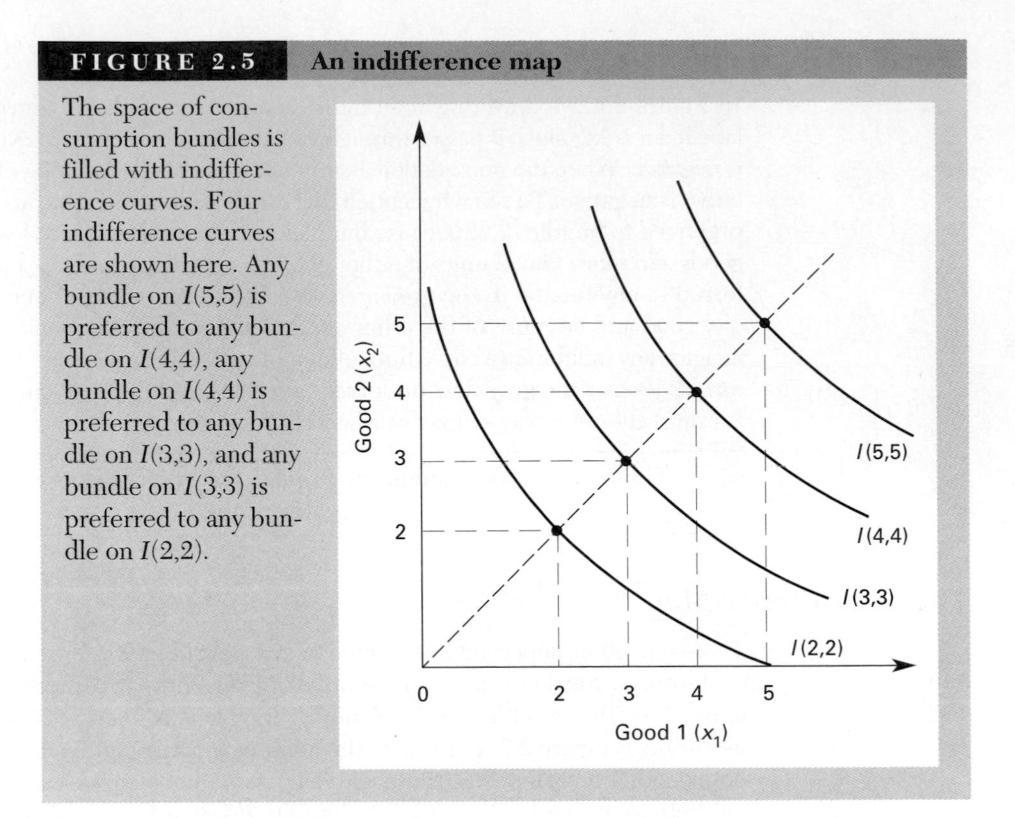

ference curves containing more-preferred consumption bundles. For example, any bundle on $I(3,3)$ is preferred to any bundle on $I(2,2)$. In summary:

The nonsatiation assumption implies that bundles on indifference curves farther from the origin are preferred to bundles on curves closer to the origin.

PROBLEM 2.7

Anna from Problem 2.6 is indifferent between two consumption bundles if the combined weight of trout (good 1) and salmon (good 2) in the two bundles is identical. Show that there is an indifference curve through every consumption bundle (x_1, x_2). (*Hint*: Pick an arbitrary bundle and construct her indifference curve.)

Non-Intersecting Indifference Curves

Notice that the indifference curves in Figure 2.5 do not intersect each other. Because this is an important general property of indifference maps, it deserves closer attention. Specifically, we want to show that the transitivity assumption implies that indifference curves cannot intersect. To do so, let us begin by assuming — strictly for purposes of argument — that two indifference curves *do* cross. We will then show that this leads to a violation of the transitivity assumption.

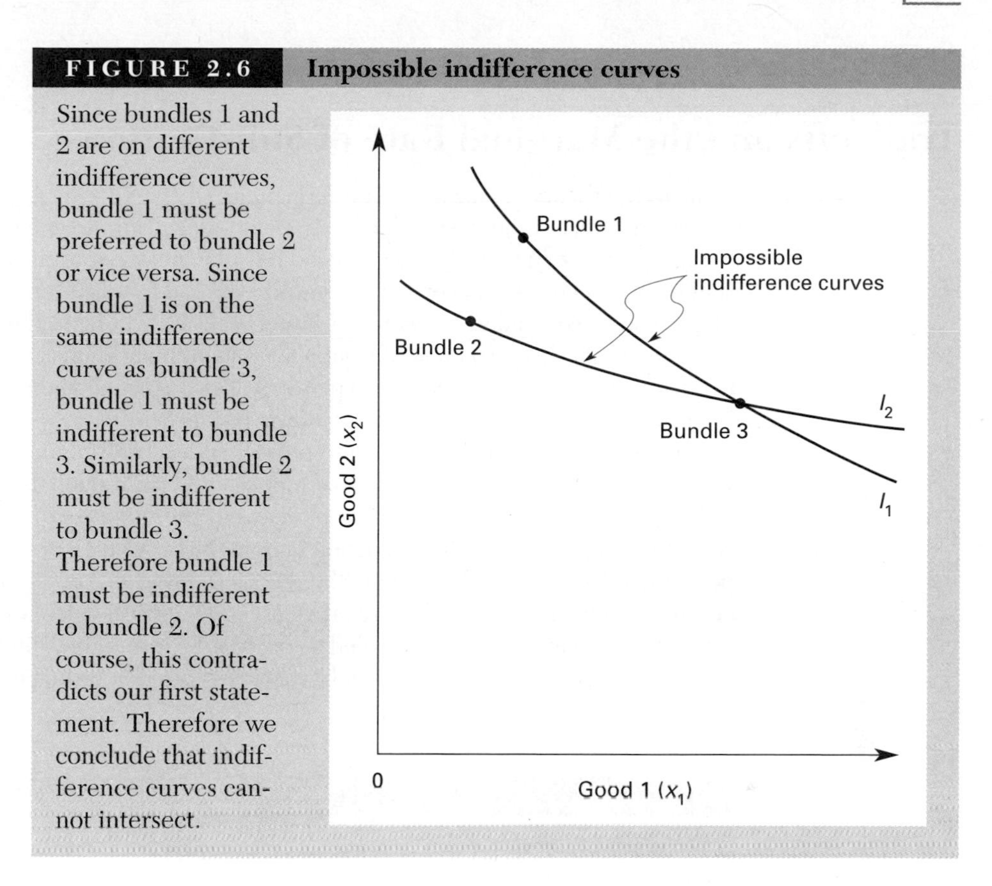

FIGURE 2.6 **Impossible indifference curves**

Since bundles 1 and 2 are on different indifference curves, bundle 1 must be preferred to bundle 2 or vice versa. Since bundle 1 is on the same indifference curve as bundle 3, bundle 1 must be indifferent to bundle 3. Similarly, bundle 2 must be indifferent to bundle 3. Therefore bundle 1 must be indifferent to bundle 2. Of course, this contradicts our first statement. Therefore we conclude that indifference curves cannot intersect.

Let us assume, then, that two indifference curves do intersect as shown in Figure 2.6. Now pick a bundle other than bundle 3 from each indifference curve — say, bundle 1 from indifference curve I_1 and bundle 2 from indifference curve I_2.

Since bundles 1 and 2 are on different indifference curves, one bundle must be preferred to the other. Suppose bundle 1 is the preferred bundle; then we have preference statement a: bundle 1 is preferred to bundle 2. In addition, since bundles 2 and 3 are on indifference curve I_2, we have preference statement b: bundle 2 is indifferent to bundle 3. Similarly, since bundles 1 and 3 are on indifference curve I_1, we have preference statement c: bundle 1 is indifferent to bundle 3. Notice, however, that these three preference statements violate part 2 of the transitivity assumption, which states that if statements a. and b. are true, then bundle 1 must be preferred to bundle 3. Therefore, it cannot be the case that indifference curves intersect and that preferences also satisfy the transitivity assumption. In other words, intersecting indifference curves for a single consumer and transitive preferences are contradictory notions.

The transitivity assumption implies that indifference curves cannot intersect.

2.4 Tradeoffs and the Marginal Rate of Substitution

Basic to the theory of consumer choice making, which we will discuss in Chapter 3, is the *rate* at which someone is willing to trade off, or substitute, one good for another — the rate at which the quantity of one good must be increased as the quantity of another is decreased in order to keep a consumer on the same indifference curve. For example, as you discovered in Problem 2.7, Anna is always willing to trade off or *substitute* a pound of salmon for a pound of trout. Our goal in this section is to develop a measure to quantify the amount of one good a person will give up to obtain more of another good. That measure is known as the *marginal rate of substitution*.

To begin, let us suppose that the person whose preferences are represented in Figure 2.7 is initially at bundle A. Now suppose that we reduce the quantity of good 1 in bundle A, denoted by Δx_1. What increase in the quantity of good 2, denoted by Δx_2, will compensate for that reduction in quantity of good 1? For example, what happens if good 1 is reduced by 9 units (i.e., $\Delta x_1 = 9$)? As you can see from Figure 2.7, to get this person back to indifference curve I, good 2 must be increased by 15 units (i.e., $\Delta x_2 = 15$). The ratio $\Delta x_2/\Delta x_1$ is called a *rate of substitution* because it tells us the rate at which the quantity of good 2 must be increased per unit reduction in the quantity of

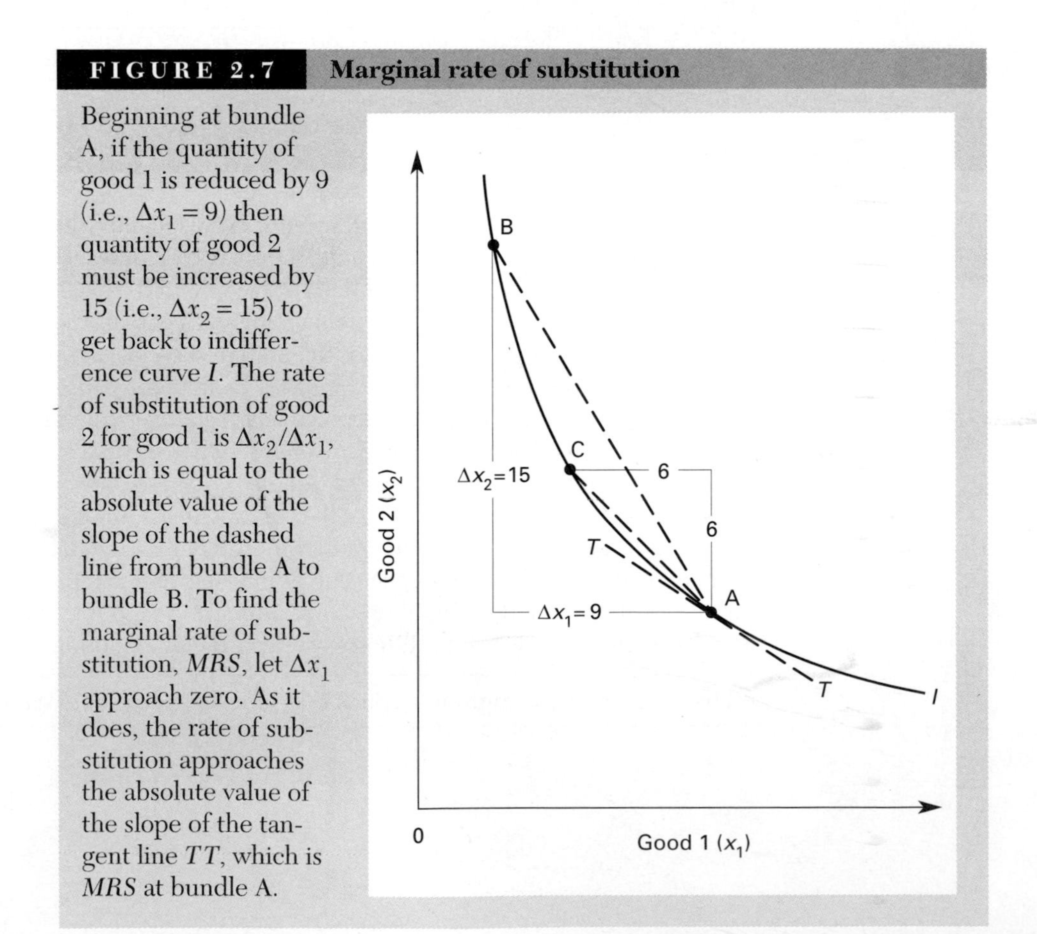

FIGURE 2.7 Marginal rate of substitution

Beginning at bundle A, if the quantity of good 1 is reduced by 9 (i.e., $\Delta x_1 = 9$) then quantity of good 2 must be increased by 15 (i.e., $\Delta x_2 = 15$) to get back to indifference curve I. The rate of substitution of good 2 for good 1 is $\Delta x_2/\Delta x_1$, which is equal to the absolute value of the slope of the dashed line from bundle A to bundle B. To find the marginal rate of substitution, *MRS*, let Δx_1 approach zero. As it does, the rate of substitution approaches the absolute value of the slope of the tangent line *TT*, which is *MRS* at bundle A.

good 1. In this case, the rate of substitution is 15/9, or approximately 1.67, which is equal to the absolute value of the slope of the dashed line AB in Figure 2.7.

marginal change

The rate of substitution that we just calculated is termed a *nonmarginal rate of substitution* because the initial 9-unit reduction in quantity of good 1 is clearly a *measurable* change. By contrast, a **marginal change** is immeasurably small, or *infinitesimal*. We will look more carefully at the marginal rate of substitution in a moment. But first, let us see why the nonmarginal rate of substitution is problematical.

The difficulty with the nonmarginal rate of substitution is that its *value* changes as the initial reduction in quantity of good 1 changes. For example, starting at bundle A in Figure 2.7, we initially reduced the quantity of good 1 by 9 units to get a nonmarginal rate of substitution of 15/9, or approximately 1.67. However, if instead we had reduced the quantity of good 1 by only 6 units, then we would have had to increase the quantity of good 2 by 6 units to get this person back to indifference curve *I*. In this case, the nonmarginal rate of substitution is 6/6, or 1, which is equal to the absolute value of the slope of dashed line AC in Figure 2.7. There is an ambiguity here. Is the rate of substitution of good 2 for good 1 equal to 1.67, or is it equal to 1?

marginal rate of substitution

To resolve this ambiguity, economists use the **marginal rate of substitution**, *MRS*. *MRS* is the rate of substitution associated with a *marginal* reduction in quantity of good 1. To find *MRS*, just imagine what happens to the nonmarginal rate of substitution as Δx_1 gets smaller and smaller, eventually approaching zero. For $\Delta x_1 = 9$, the nonmarginal rate of substitution is determined by the slope of the dashed line segment AB. For $\Delta x_1 = 6$, it is determined by the slope of the dashed line segment AC. Notice that as Δx_1 approaches zero, the dashed line segment approaches the line labelled *TT* that is tangent to indifference curve *I* at bundle A. Therefore, the marginal rate of substitution is the absolute value of the slope of *TT*. That is, the marginal rate of substitution *MRS* of good 2 for good 1 at bundle A is the absolute value of the slope of the indifference curve at bundle A. More generally, *the marginal rate of substitution of good 2 for good 1 at any point* (x_1, x_2), *denoted by* $MRS(x_1, x_2)$, *is the absolute value of the slope of the indifference curve at that point.*

Notice that if we had picked some bundle other than bundle A in Figure 2.7, we would have found a *different* value for *MRS* because the slope of indifference curve *I* varies from point to point. For instance, because the indifference curve is steeper at bundle C than at bundle A, *MRS* is larger at bundle C than at bundle A. And *MRS* is larger still at bundle B. In other words, $MRS(x_1, x_2)$ ordinarily takes on different values at different bundles, and is therefore a *function*, and not simply a number.

In the following problem, you can explore one case in which *MRS* is the same at all bundles. Notice the unusual shape of the indifference curves.

PROBLEM 2.8

1. Anna is indifferent between any two bundles in which the combined weight of trout and salmon is 10 kilograms. The indifference curve for such bundles is $10 = x_1 + x_2$, where x_1 is kilograms of trout and x_2 is kilograms of salmon. What is Anna's *MRS* for any bundle on this indifference curve?
2. Anna's cousin Arno likes eating fish, too, but his preferences are different from Anna's. He is interested only in the nutritional value of the fish he eats, and he believes that a kilogram of salmon is twice as nutritious as a kilogram of trout. Find an indifference curve for Arno, and then show that Arno's *MRS* of salmon for trout is 1/2.

Marginal Rate of Substitution and Marginal Value

A character in an Oscar Wilde play defined a cynic as "a man who knows the price of everything and the value of nothing." The comment could be extended to the general public, which often seems to lack a clear understanding of the meaning of economic value. We hear statements like, "Costs determine prices," "Prices could never go that high—nobody could afford them," or "I value the item at $20 000, but I'm just not willing to pay that much." Such commonplace statements demonstrate confused and imprecise notions of economic value.

value

marginal value

In the next chapter we discuss in detail the economic meaning of value, but we introduce it here because it is so important. The **value** of a good is the *maximum amount one is willing to sacrifice* to obtain it. If money (which we might use to represent all other goods) is being sacrificed, then we say that value is the maximum willingness to pay. When the amount of good being acquired is infinitesimal, then we have what is called **marginal value** (*MV*). If you have been reading carefully, you will recognize that marginal value is simply another name for the *MRS*. Hence the *MRS* is a very important concept because it provides an unambiguous and observable measure of value.

The $MRS(x_1, x_2)$ is the marginal value of good 1 measured in terms of good 2.

Diminishing Marginal Rate of Substitution

diminishing marginal rate of substitution

Notice that in Figure 2.7, *MRS* (or *MV*) declines or *diminishes* in a move down the indifference curve. This means that the person whose preferences are represented in Figure 2.7 is less willing to substitute good 2 for good 1 at point B than at point A. This seems reasonable since — relative to good 1 — good 2 is more abundant at point B than it is at point A. Economists generally make the assumption of a **diminishing marginal rate of substitution** because in many circumstances it seems to capture the reality of people's preferences.

Just imagine your own willingness to substitute food (good 2) for clothing (good 1). If you now have a consumption bundle in which food is plentiful relative to clothes, you might be reluctant to give up still more clothes to get additional food. On the other hand, if you have a bundle in which food is scarce relative to clothes, you might be quite willing to give up clothes to get additional food. If these speculations about your willingness to substitute food for clothes are right, then — in terms of food and clothing — your preferences satisfy the assumption of a diminishing marginal rate of substitution: in moving down an indifference curve, the marginal rate of substitution diminishes. As you will see in the applications of Section 2.5, a diminishing marginal rate of substitution can be used to explain some familiar observations from ordinary experience.

PROBLEM 2.9

Suppose that Mary's preferences satisfy the assumption of diminishing *MRS* (*MV*). Show that she cannot be indifferent between the following bundles.

	Meat	Fruit
A	100	200
B	120	160
C	110	180

2.5 Utility Functions

utility function
utility number

Economists have developed a mathematical tool for representing an individual's preference ordering. That tool is called a utility function. Although the term utility function may be a bit intimidating, the basic concept is simple and in the end you will find utility functions easier to work with than preference orderings. A **utility function** assigns a number — called a **utility number** — to every consumption bundle in a person's preference ordering in accordance with two rules. *First, if someone is indifferent between two bundles, the utility function assigns the same utility number to both bundles. Second, if he or she prefers one bundle to another, the utility function assigns a larger utility number to the preferred bundle.* We will use the notation $U(x_1, x_2)$ to represent a utility function.

To see for yourself just what utility functions and utility numbers are and what they do, pay careful attention to the following important problem.

PROBLEM 2.10

Let us return to Anna. Recall that she eats only trout (good 1) and salmon (good 2), and that her preferences are such that — given a choice between two bundles — she always prefers the bundle that weighs more. Let x_1 and x_2 denote kilograms of trout and salmon respectively. We want to show that the following function is a utility function for Anna:

$$U(x_1, x_2) = x_1 + x_2$$

a. What utility numbers does this function assign to the following six bundles: (10,15), (20,30), (25,0), (15,15), (20,15), (40,10)? Do these utility numbers accurately reflect her preference ordering over these bundles?

b. More generally, show that this function is a utility function for Anna. To do so, show that the answer to each of the following questions is "yes." Question 1: Does this function assign the same utility number to two bundles whenever Anna is indifferent between them? Question 2: Does this function assign a larger utility number to the preferred bundle when Anna prefers one bundle to another? Question 3: Does this function assign a utility number to all consumption bundles that contain trout and salmon?

Constructing a Utility Function

Now we want to generalize what you learned in this problem by establishing a rule for assigning utility numbers to consumption bundles that will allow us, in principle at least, to construct a utility function for any set of individual preferences that satisfy these four assumptions: completeness, transitivity, continuity, and nonsatiation. Notice that now we are *not* dealing with specific preferences like Anna's preferences for trout and salmon, but rather with *any preferences* that satisfy these four assumptions. Therefore, our objective is not to find a particular utility function such as the utility function $U(x_1, x_2) = x_1 + x_2$, but to show that *some utility function exists for any preferences that satisfy these four assumptions.*

In Figure 2.8, we have constructed a ray through the origin (the line $x_2 = x_1/2$). We will be using this ray in setting out the following rule for assigning utility numbers. For any bundle on the ray $x_2 = x_1/2$, first identify the associated indifference curve. Then, note the quantity of good 1 in the bundle on the ray, and use this quantity as the utility number for every bundle on the indifference curve. For example, consider bundle (2,1) on the ray in Figure 2.8. The associated indifference curve is $I(2,1)$, and the number 2 is therefore the utility number for every bundle on $I(2,1)$. Now consider a different bundle on the ray, bundle (4,2). The associated indifference curve is $I(4,2)$, and the number 4 is therefore the utility number for every bundle on $I(4,2)$. Because we are using the nonsatiation assumption, the indifference curves in Figure 2.8 are negatively sloped.

By considering the same questions you looked at in Problem 2.10, we can show that this rule does allow us to construct a utility function for any set of preferences that satisfy the four assumptions. We need to show that the answer to the following three questions is "yes." Question 1: Does this rule assign the same utility number to two bundles whenever the individual is indifferent between them? Question 2: Does this rule assign a larger utility number to the preferred bundle whenever the individual prefers one bundle to another? Question 3: Does this rule assign a utility number to all consumption bundles?

The answer to the first question is clearly yes. Because indifference curves are negatively sloped and because the ray is positively sloped, any indifference curve will

FIGURE 2.8 Constructing a utility function

To construct a utility function, for every bundle on the ray $x_2 = x_1/2$, identify the associated indifference curve, and assign the quantity of good 1 in the bundle as a utility number to all bundles on the indifference curve. This rule assigns utility number 2 to all bundles on $I(2,1)$, utility number 4 to all bundles on $I(4,2)$, and utility number 6 to all bundles on $I(6,3)$.

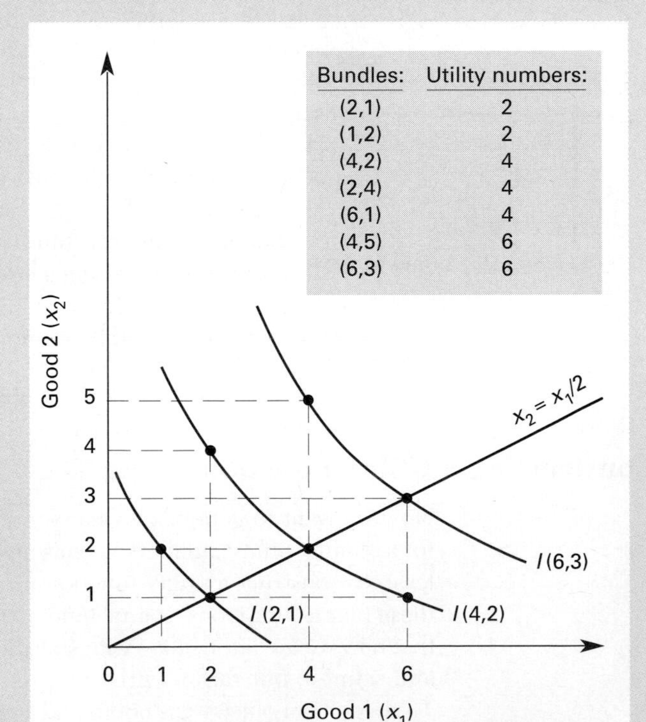

intersect the ray once and only once. Therefore, we know that this rule does assign the same utility number to all bundles on the same indifference curve.

Let us turn to the second question and consider two bundles in Figure 2.8 that are *not* on the same indifference curve, say bundles (6,1) and (1,2). Which is the preferred bundle? The answer is bundle (6,1) because it is on the indifference curve farther from the origin. Does this rule assign a larger number to bundle (6,1) than to bundle (1,2)? Yes; the utility number for bundle (6,1) is 4 and the utility number for bundle (1,2) is 2. That is, for this particular pair of bundles, the rule does assign a higher utility number to the more preferred bundle. Now consider any pair of bundles on distinct indifference curves. The nonsatiation assumption implies that the preferred bundle is on the indifference curve that is farther from the origin. The point of intersection of the more distant indifference curve and the ray through the origin is farther from the origin than is the point of intersection of the nearer indifference curve and the ray. Therefore, given our rule for assigning utility numbers, the bundle on the more distant indifference curve will be assigned a larger utility number than the bundle on the nearer indifference curve.

Now let us turn to the third question and consider some consumption bundle in Figure 2.8 that is not on the ray $x_2 = x_1/2$; say, for example, bundle (4,5). The continuity assumption implies that there is a continuous indifference curve, labelled $I(4,5)$, that passes through this bundle. Furthermore, the indifference curve $I(4,5)$ must intersect the ray through the origin because it is negatively sloped and the ray is positively sloped. Because $I(4,5)$ intersects the ray at (6,3) in Figure 2.8, the rule assigns utility number 6 to consumption bundle (4,5). In other words, our rule for assigning utility numbers does in fact assign a utility number to every consumption bundle.[4]

---

4. In Section 2.5, we show how to represent preferences by a utility function, $U(x_1, x_2)$. Using the implicit function theorem we can express *MRS* in terms of the partial derivatives of the utility function. An indifference curve can be written as

$$u^0 = U(x_1, x_2)$$

where u^0 is fixed and x_1 and x_2 are free to vary. Since the indifference curve defines x_2 as an implicit function of x_1, we can use the implicit function theorem to express this indifference curve as

$$x_2 = g(x_1)$$

MRS is, of course, just $-g'(x_1)$, where $g'(x_1)$ is the derivative of $g(x_1)$. Combining these equations, we have the following identity:

$$u^0 \equiv U[x_1, g(x_1)]$$

Differentiating the identity with respect to x_1 gives us

$$\partial U[x_1, g(x_1)]/\partial x_1 + g'(x_1)\{\partial U[x_1, g(x_1)]/\partial x_2\} = 0$$

The partial derivative $\partial U(x_1, x_2)/\partial x_i$ is called the *marginal utility* of good i. Rearranging this equation, we get

$$-g'(x_1) = \frac{\partial U(x_1, x_2)/\partial x_1}{\partial U(x_1, x_2)/\partial x_2}$$

But the left side of this equation is just *MRS*; hence

$$MRS(x_1, x_2) = \frac{\partial U(x_1, x_2)/\partial x_1}{\partial U(x_1, x_2)/\partial x_2}$$

Thus, for example, for the utility function $U(x_1, x_2) = x_1 x_2$, $MRS(x_1, x_2) = x_2/x_1$.

If preferences satisfy the four stated assumptions about preferences (namely, completeness, transitivity, continuity, and nonsatiation), there is a utility function that represents those preferences.

Many Utility Functions

Now we want to argue that, given preferences satisfying these assumptions, *any number of utility functions* can be constructed that represent these preferences. But first, try the following problem.

PROBLEM 2.11

This problem is also about Anna's preferences. In the preceding problem, you showed that the following function is a utility function for Anna:

$$U(x_1, x_2) = x_1 + x_2$$

Using the approach from that problem, show that the following are also utility functions for Anna:

1. $U(x_1, x_2) = 1000(x_1 + x_2)$
2. $U(x_1, x_2) = (x_1 + x_2)^2$
3. $U(x_1, x_2) = \log(x_1 + x_2 + 1)$
4. $U(x_1, x_2) = 5073 + x_1 + x_2$

In Problem 2.11 you discovered that many different functions will represent the same preference ordering. This is important because it helps us to see what utility numbers do and do not mean. It is therefore worth examining more carefully. Consider some utility function $U(x_1, x_2)$ that represents Ashok's preferences for goods 1 and 2, and two consumption bundles, (17,9) and (15,10). Ashok prefers bundle (17,9) to bundle (15,10). Since $U(x_1, x_2)$ is a utility function for Ashok, it is therefore true that the utility number $U(17,9)$ exceeds the utility number $U(15,10)$. Keep in mind that $U(17,9)$ and $U(15,10)$ are just the utility numbers that emerge when the utility function is evaluated first at (17,9) and then at (15,10). Now let us form a new function by multiplying the utility number associated with any bundle by some constant c. The new function, which we will call $V(x_1, x_2)$, is simply

$$V(x_1, x_2) = cU(x_1, x_2)$$

Is $V(x_1, x_2)$ also a utility function for Ashok? It is, if it always assigns a larger utility number to the preferred bundle. In particular, does $V(17,9)$ exceed $V(15,10)$? Or, equivalently, does $cU(17,9)$ exceed $cU(15,10)$? If c is positive, it does. Therefore, when c is positive, $V(x_1, x_2)$ is also a utility function for Ashok.

The point is this: if we have one utility function, we can generate others that represent the same preference ordering by multiplying the original utility function by a positive constant, just as we multiplied Anna's original utility function by the positive constant 16 to get another utility function for her. Clearly, this is not the only way to construct a new utility function. For example, adding a positive or negative constant to a utility function will generate another function that represents the same preference ordering as the original utility function.[5]

The Meaning of Utility Numbers

ordinal utility

These observations should make it clear that the economist's theory of utility is a theory of **ordinal utility**, not cardinal utility. Utility numbers reveal only the *relative* ordering of consumption bundles (first, second, or third) and nothing about the distance between bundles in terms of desirability (twice as desirable or one-third as desirable). In comparing two bundles, utility numbers tell us one of three things: the first bundle is preferred to the second, the second bundle is preferred to the first, or the individual is indifferent between the two bundles — and *nothing more*. In particular, we *cannot* use utility numbers to make comparisons among individuals. The notion of preference — not utility— is the primitive, or irreducible, concept at the heart of our analysis.[6]

Shapes of Indifference Curves

Let's summarize what we've learned thus far. Economists assume every individual has preferences, and that these preferences are complete, transitive, and nonsatiated. Furthermore, these preferences are characterized by diminishing marginal rates of substitution, which means they have a convex shape towards the origin. Preferences can be represented by a utility function that assigns numbers to any given consumption bundle, such that more preferred bundles have higher numbers and equally preferred bundles have equal numbers. It seems that all of these conditions suggest every indifference curve has the same shape, but this conjecture would be incorrect. Within the assumptions economists make about preferences, there are many different types of allowable preferences. In this section we'll consider a few of them.

First, consider the three indifference curves drawn in Figure 2.9. Each graph has T-bone steaks on the vertical axis and eggplant on the horizontal. Each graph shows a representative indifference curve for a different individual. Part (a) shows the indifference curve for a strict vegetarian. This person has a complete preference for eggplant and is unwilling to give up any in exchange for an unlimited amount of T-bone steak.

---

5. In general, we can form a new function $V(x_1, x_2)$ from $U(x_1, x_2)$ by feeding utility numbers into another function, which we will call f. Symbolically, the new function is

$$V(x_1, x_2) = f[U(x_1, x_2)]$$

If f has the property that the larger the number you feed into it, the larger the number that comes out, then $V(x)$ is also a utility function. (Any function f that has this property is said to be a *monotonically increasing function*.) Suppose that f is monotonically increasing. Then 1. when $U(B_1) > U(B_2)$, $V(B_1) > V(B_2)$, and 2. when $U(B_1) = U(B_2)$, $V(B_1) = V(B_2)$. In other words, the functions $V(x_1, x_2)$ and $U(x_1, x_2)$ represent the same preference ordering. Thus, given a utility function, we can create others by operating on it with any monotonically increasing function.

6. The derivative of the utility function $U(x_1, x_2)$ with respect to good 1 is called the marginal utility of good 1, and is written as $\partial U(x_1, x_2)/\partial x_1$. There is a similar marginal utility for good 2, which is written $\partial U(x_1, x_2)/\partial x_2$. Do not confuse marginal utilities with the *MRS* or *MV*, which is the *ratio* of the two marginal utilities. The *MRS* is observable since it is defined in terms of the amounts of goods being traded off. On the other hand, the marginal utility is simply defined in terms of unobservable ordinal utility numbers. The important assumption for economic behaviour is diminishing marginal rates of substitution. Diminishing *MRS does not imply, nor is it implied by* diminishing marginal utility.

Such an example seems ridiculous, but the point is that such a preference would not violate any of the assumptions we've had to make so far. In part (b) we have the indifference curve of someone who has no strong preference for either good. In part (c) the person has a relative preference for T-bone steak. The person in part (c) values both goods, but it takes a lot of eggplants to compensate for reductions in the amount of steak. Hence, different individuals can have different preferences for the same goods and not violate any of the conditions laid out in this chapter.

PROBLEM 2.12

Suppose the two goods are right shoes and left shoes. Then, if we begin at any point where the number of right shoes is equal to the number of left shoes, it seems sensible to suppose that we stay on the same indifference curve if either

a. we hold the number of left shoes constant and increase the number of right shoes, or if
b. we hold the number of right shoes constant and increase the number of left shoes. Draw an indifference curve, and identify the kink in it. What is *MRS* to the right of the kink? Above the kink? At the kink?

Second, consider the two indifference curves drawn in Figure 2.10. In part (a) the two goods are essentially the same. One dime always equals two nickels. As a result the indifference curve does not experience diminishing marginal rates of substitution. Each indifference curve has a slope of –2 because this person always trades off at the

FIGURE 2.9 Different preferences and different indifference curves

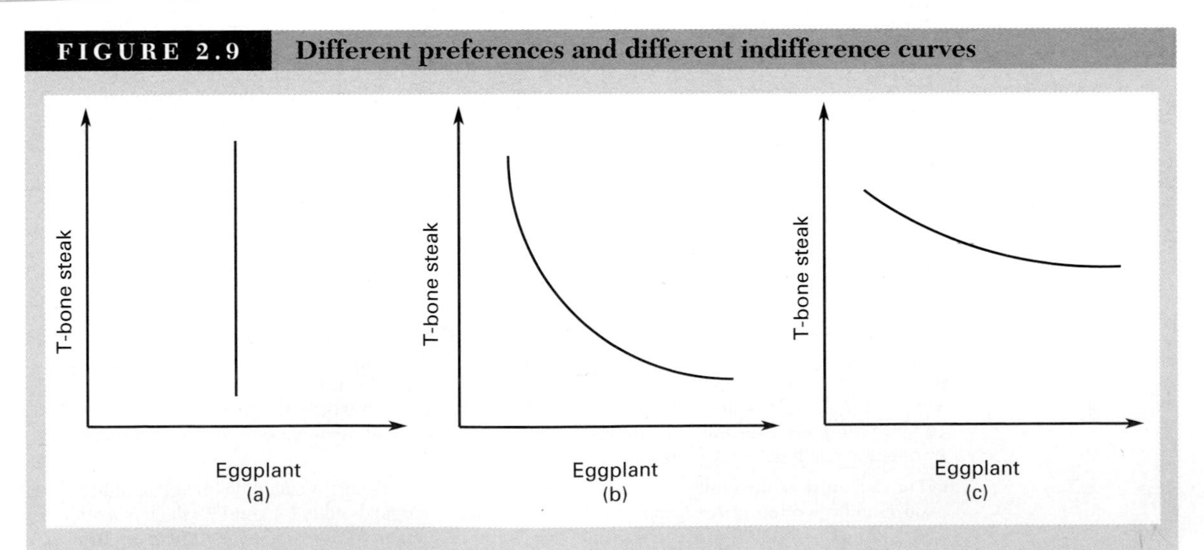

Each graph shows a single indifference curve for an individual. Part (a) shows the case of a vegetarian who will not give up any eggplant for any amount of steak. Part (b) shows an individual who has no strong preference. Part (c) shows an individual who prefers steak to eggplant.

FIGURE 2.10 **Perfect substitutes and perfect complements**

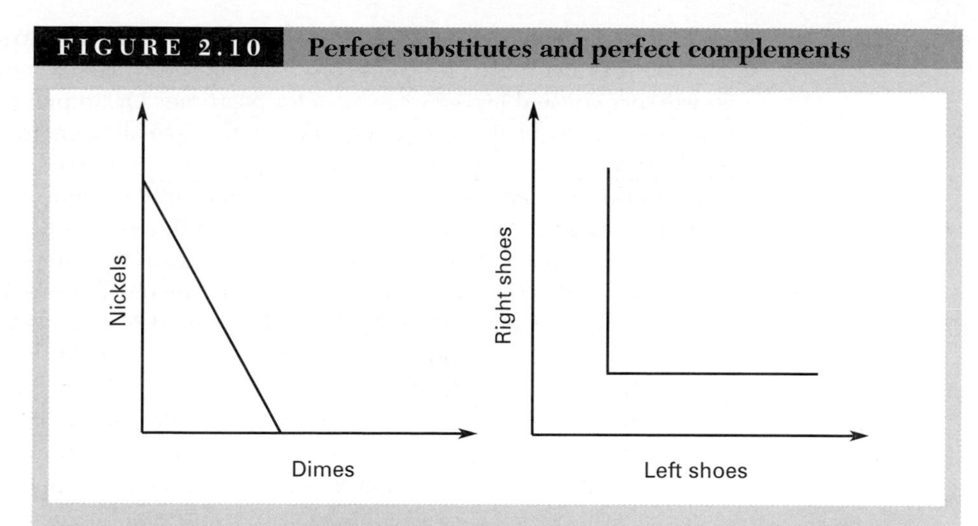

Part (a) shows the case of perfect substitutes where individuals make constant tradeoffs of nickels for dimes. Part (b) shows the case of perfect complements where the individual is unwilling to substitute right shoes for left shoes.

perfect substitutes

perfect complements

same rate. Goods in part (a) would be called **perfect substitutes**. In panel (b) the two goods are called **perfect complements** because there is zero ability to substitute between them. In the graph it requires one left shoe and one right shoe to make a pair of shoes, and the individual only cares about pairs of shoes. Hence having one right shoe but 20 left ones still leaves the individual with just one pair of shoes. These two examples are extreme cases of substitutability, and although neither is particularly realistic, often they are useful for making analytical points.

PROBLEM 2.13

Draw a graph of an indifference curve with oranges on the vertical axis and water torture on the horizontal. Assume that water torture is bad, and that the more you are tortured, the more you dislike it. Identify the shape of the indifference curve.

To show you just how powerful and wide-ranging the theory of preferences is, let us use it to analyze four problems from everyday life. First, we can use it to explain why we so often see higher wage rates — "time-and-a-half" or "double time" — for overtime work. Second, we can use it to explain why people spread their income over time even though they get paid in lump sums. Third, we can use it to create a measure of the harm done by air pollution. Finally, we can use it to explain why shopping carts have increased in size over the past few decades.

Application: Overtime Pay

Collective agreements between firms and their employees typically have provisions specifying a base work day, a base wage rate, and an overtime wage rate — often 1.5 times the base wage rate. For example, a collective agreement might have a provision establishing an eight-hour base work day, a $10 per hour base wage rate, and a $15 per hour overtime wage rate. These provisions for overtime pay raise a question: Why do workers demand higher wage rates for overtime? Or, to put it another way, why don't workers negotiate a single wage rate applying to all hours of work?

First, we need to represent the particular preferences relevant to this problem. The goods in this case are clearly not ordinary consumption goods like T-shirts and hot dogs. How can we characterize the two rather different "goods" in these particular consumption bundles? Because people work to make money to spend on consumption goods, one good in this case is *income* or expenditure on all goods. What is the second good in these consumption bundles? It could be hours of work. (You are asked to take this approach in Exercise 5(f) at the end of the chapter.) Traditionally, however, economists have approached the problem in a slightly different, but equivalent, way. They think of the 24 hours in a day as being divided into work time and leisure time. Because people trade off income (or work time) against leisure time, they use hours of *leisure* as the second "good" in these bundles. These particular consumption bundles are then of the following sort: (L,I) where L is hours of leisure and I is dollars of income. Bundle (16,80), for example, is the bundle containing 16 hours of leisure (and therefore 8 hours of work) and $80 of income per day (8 hours at a wage rate of $10 per hour).

If we apply the assumptions of complete, consistent, transitive, and continuous preferences, and if we assume that individuals prefer more income to less and more leisure to less, then employee indifference curves are continuous and downward sloping. If we add the assumption of diminishing marginal rate of substitution (that is, that the less leisure time an employee has, the less willing he or she is to give up additional leisure time to get additional income) then we can represent the employee preferences by the downward sloping indifference curve in (L,I) space in Figure 2.11. Notice that MRS at bundle B (equal to the absolute value of the slope of tangent line TT) exceeds MRS at bundle A (equal to the absolute value of the slope of tangent line $T'T'$). In other words, the rate at which an employee's income must be increased to compensate for a marginal decrease in leisure is larger at bundle B (where the employee has only 16 hours of leisure a day) than it is at bundle A (where the employee has 20 hours of leisure a day).

More generally, diminishing MRS implies that an employee becomes less and less willing to trade off leisure for income as work time increases and leisure time decreases. This provides an answer to the question about higher pay for overtime:

Employees demand more money for overtime work because the more hours they are working, the less willing they are to trade off leisure time for income.

Application: Pay Day versus Consumption

Most individuals who work get paid twice a month even though they work every day. Regarding income over a two-week period, such individuals would receive zero income on thirteen of the days and a relatively large paycheque only on the fourteenth day. However, regarding consumption over the same two-week period, these individuals would be consuming a little each day. This pattern conforms to our own experience. We spread out our own income, not only from payday to payday, but from high income periods to low income periods. For example, students who work in the summer save most of that income for consumption throughout the year. Another example concerns lifetime earnings and consumption. Most people have an income that increases until they

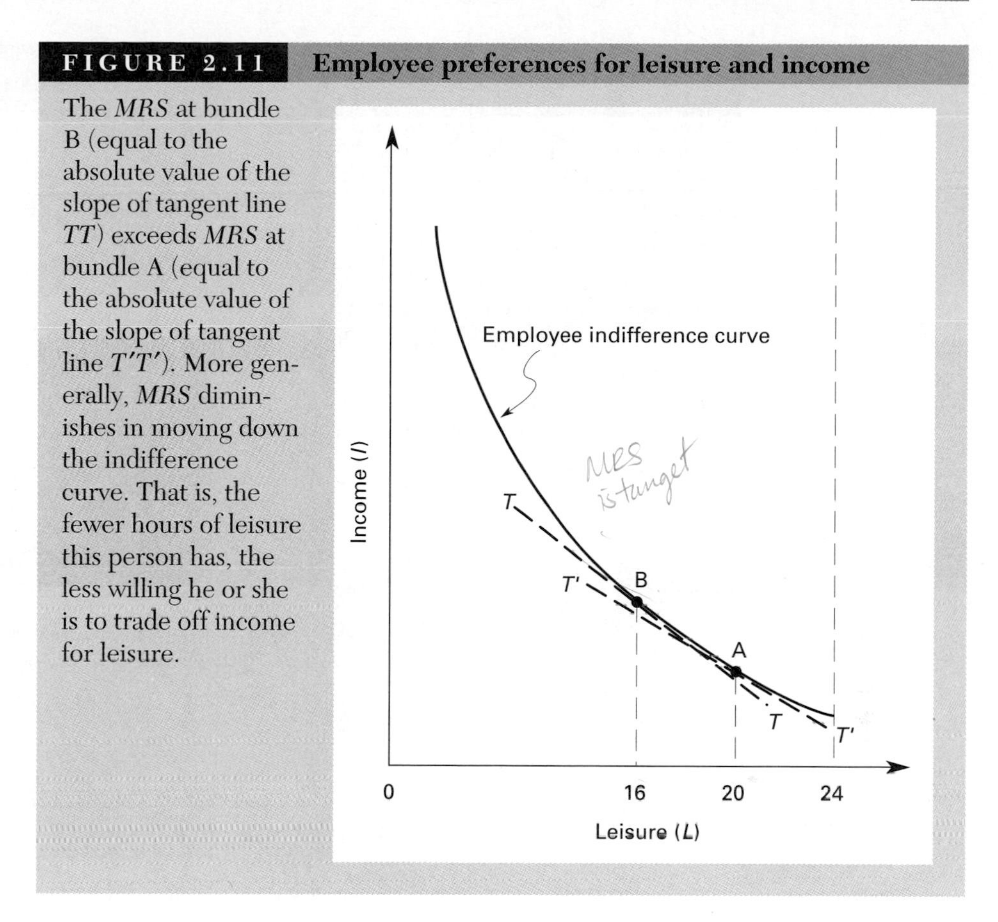

FIGURE 2.11 Employee preferences for leisure and income

The *MRS* at bundle B (equal to the absolute value of the slope of tangent line *TT*) exceeds *MRS* at bundle A (equal to the absolute value of the slope of tangent line *T′T′*). More generally, *MRS* diminishes in moving down the indifference curve. That is, the fewer hours of leisure this person has, the less willing he or she is to trade off income for leisure.

are 40 or 50 years old, but they tend to smooth out their consumption over the years by borrowing early in life and saving later on. Can you see how this behaviour is implied by diminishing marginal rates of substitution?

For simplicity, let us assume that there are only two days in our life: today and tomorrow. Suppose we get paid \$100 today and nothing tomorrow. Under these circumstances, let us consider consumption bundles of the sort (N, T) where N is the dollars we spend today and T is the dollars we spend tomorrow. For instance, at bundle A in Figure 2.12, we spend all of the \$100 today, leaving \$0 to spend tomorrow. If we assume a diminishing *MRS*, then A will lie on a continuous, downward sloping and convex indifference curve, shown as I_1 in Figure 2.12. At point A, the marginal value for consumption today is very low, and the marginal value for consumption tomorrow is very high. This means that if we reduce consumption today by, say, \$10 and increase consumption tomorrow by the same amount, the level of utility must rise. In effect, the income is more productive in generating utility in the period in which it has the higher marginal value. This is shown in the move from point A to point B. Clearly the individual is better off from "spreading" out consumption across the two periods. We leave it to Chapter 5 to discuss the optimal amount to save for consumption tomorrow. For now we emphasize that smoothing consumption even a little bit can increase one's utility.

FIGURE 2.12 **Preferences for current and future consumption**

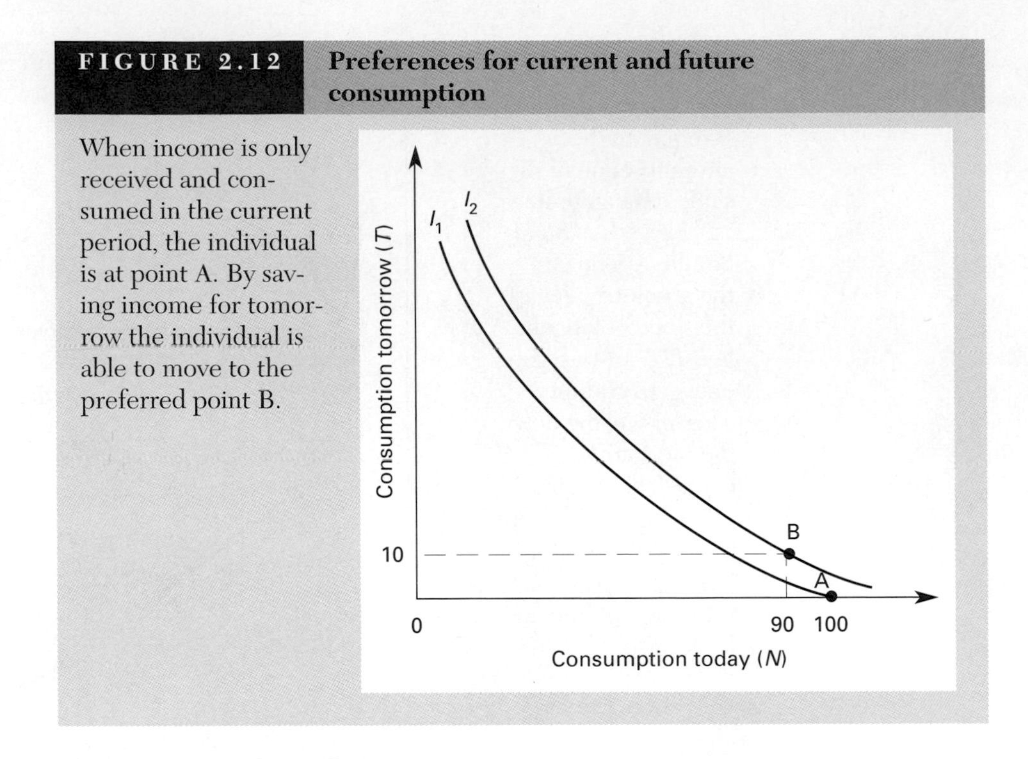

When income is only received and consumed in the current period, the individual is at point A. By saving income for tomorrow the individual is able to move to the preferred point B.

People smooth out their consumption over time in order to raise their level of utility.

PROBLEM 2.14

If an indifference map were concave to the origin (bowed out rather than in) we would say there was increasing *MRS*. To more fully appreciate the role of diminishing *MRS* in both our discussion of premium wages for overtime pay and our discussion of consumption smoothing, assume that the indifference curves in these applications exhibit an increasing *MRS*. Will workers demand a premium wage rate for overtime work? Will individuals smooth consumption?

Application: Pollution

Because air pollution is something that most of us would prefer to avoid, we classify it as a "bad," not a good. Let us develop a model of preferences that incorporates the economic bad of air pollution and then use that model to create *an economic measure of the cost of air pollution* to a particular person. Once again, notice that these consumption bundles clearly do not contain ordinary consumption goods. Instead, these bundles will necessarily contain a *measure of pollution* and expenditure on all other goods, or *income*. They are of the kind (P,I) where P is a measure of pollution and I is dollars of income.

Let us now use our understanding of an individual's willingness to trade off income against pollution to create an economic measure of the cost of air pollution to that person. For example, many city dwellers choose to put up with the polluted air of large urban areas because they can make more money working in cities than in less-polluted rural communities. That is, they are trading off higher levels of pollution for higher incomes.

Recall that nonsatiation implied that indifference curves have a negative slope when considering only goods. In the case of pollution and income, however, what will be the slope of indifference curves? Notice that the indifference curves shown in Figure 2.13 — which contain a "bad" (pollution) and a "good" (income) — are upward sloping in the (P,I) space. Let us see why. Beginning at bundle A on indifference curve 1, suppose that the level of air pollution rises by ΔP. Because pollution is a bad, this rise in air pollution (holding income constant) will put the person whose preferences are represented in Figure 2.13 at bundle C, on the less preferred indifference curve 2. What change in income is needed to get this person back onto indifference curve 1? The answer is an increase in income of ΔI, which puts the individual back onto indifference curve 1 at bundle B. Notice that bundle B is necessarily *above* and *to the right* of bundle A. Therefore, the indifference curve connecting bundles A and B is necessarily upward sloping. More generally:

When consumption bundles contain a bad and a good, the indifference curves are upward sloping.

Now we can use this model of preferences over pollution and income to create a measure of the personal cost of pollution. We can do so by exploring the tradeoffs that

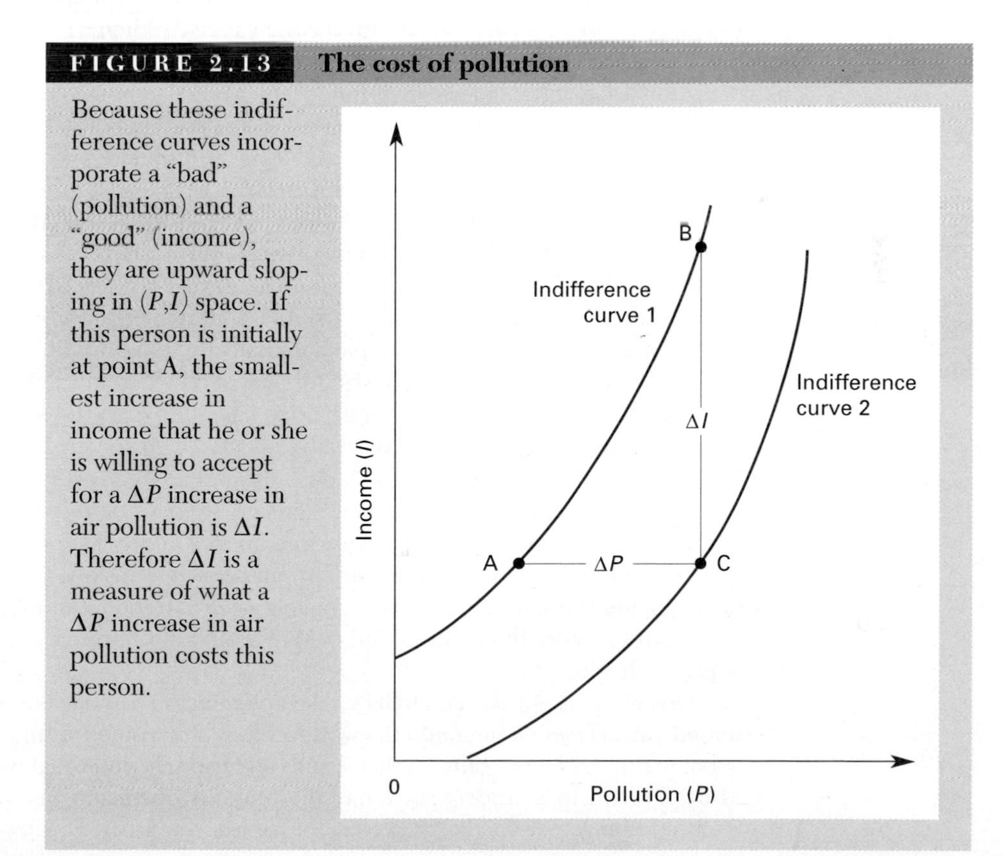

FIGURE 2.13 **The cost of pollution**

Because these indifference curves incorporate a "bad" (pollution) and a "good" (income), they are upward sloping in (P,I) space. If this person is initially at point A, the smallest increase in income that he or she is willing to accept for a ΔP increase in air pollution is ΔI. Therefore ΔI is a measure of what a ΔP increase in air pollution costs this person.

an individual is willing to make between pollution and income. Let us imagine that the person in Figure 2.13 is initially at bundle A and let us ask, "What does an increase in air pollution of ΔP cost this person?" Or, to put it another way, "What increase in income will compensate this person for an increase in air pollution of ΔP?" From Figure 2.13 we can see that *ΔI is the smallest increase in income such that he or she would voluntarily accept for the increase in pollution of ΔP*. Therefore, ΔI is one useful measure of what ΔP costs this person.

Notice that the slope of the indifference curve gives us the rate at which income must be increased to compensate for a marginal increase in pollution. Therefore, we can interpret the slope of an indifference curve at any point in Figure 2.13 as the *MRS* of income for pollution. *MRS* can then be interpreted as the *marginal cost of pollution* to this person. Notice that in constructing Figure 2.13, we have assumed that the *MRS* increases as we move from left to right along an indifference curve (for example, as we move from point A to point B along indifference curve 1). That is, we have assumed that the higher the initial level of pollution, the higher the marginal cost of air pollution.

Application: The Shopping Cart Puzzle

Most of the students reading this book never went grocery shopping in the 1960s or 1970s. If you could transport yourself back in time to your local Safeway store in 1970, aside from noticing that weights were in pounds and ounces, you would see that shopping carts were much smaller. In fact, shopping carts are on average three times larger than they were just thirty years ago. One of the authors lives close to a farmer's market where the owner has resurrected some of these old carts and his youngest child always refers to the place as the "store with the baby carts." When carts are put side by side the difference between an old cart and a new cart is quite dramatic, even though most of us don't notice the change over time. Why would shopping carts grow over time?

This is a good opportunity to test your economic thinking. If you've been paying attention and understand the argument thus far you should be considering that somehow the increased carts improved the situations of the customers and therefore the store owners. If you're thinking that store owners just increased the size of carts to fool customers into making larger purchases, then you are off track. Customers might get fooled once, but eventually they would learn that larger carts are bad things, and would only visit stores with small carts. As a budding economist, you want to avoid lines of reasoning that suggest people habitually do things that make them worse off. The carts have been increasing in size for almost 30 years, after all.

One explanation of the rise in cart size has to do with the amount and value of time spent shopping. Smaller carts really reflected a customer demand for small volumes of purchases (no one wants to push around a large cart just for the fun of it). However, small volumes of purchases at a grocery store meant that several trips per week had to be made. More trips per week meant that more time was spent shopping. Hence, one way to view the shopping cart puzzle is in terms of a change in the amount of time spent shopping. In the 1970s, people made a frequent number of smaller trips to the grocery store than they do today. Why would this improve the preference rankings of individuals?

One of the major changes to have taken place in the past 50 years has been the continued entrance of women into the workforce. When women were more likely to stay at home they had more time on their hands and had schedules that were more flexible. Multiple trips to a grocery store had the benefits of fresher produce and reduced required storage space at home in terms of pantries and freezers. However, the cost was that it involved large amounts of time. As women continued to work outside the home, their time became more scarce and a substitution took place: fewer but larger trips to the local grocery store. Larger shopping carts are not a marketing tool of exploitation, but just another example of substitution taking place.

PROBLEM 2.15

Microwaves became commonplace in the 1980s and now exist in most homes. Can you think of some examples of substitution that took place in terms of the types of food people now eat that resulted from the introduction of microwaves?

SUMMARY

The economist's approach to human behaviour is founded on three simple ideas. First, individuals have consistent preferences. Second, they make choices that maximize their preference ordering. And third, they are willing to make tradeoffs. As we saw in Section 2.1, an individual's preferences are consistent if they satisfy two assumptions: *the completeness assumption* — the individual can compare any two consumption bundles — and *the transitivity assumption* — the individual's preferences are consistent over any three bundles. In Section 2.2 we saw that preferences are usually assumed to be nonsatiated, which means that there is at least one good for which more is preferred to less. More importantly we also saw that individuals are assumed to make choices that maximize their preference ordering. In Section 2.3 we saw that individuals are willing to make tradeoffs if the *continuity assumption* is satisfied.

We also explored the important concept of the *marginal rate of substitution, MRS*. *MRS* is a measure of the willingness of a person to trade off an increase in the quantity of one good for a decrease in the quantity of another. The *MRS* of good 2 for good 1 is the rate at which the consumption of good 2 must be decreased as the consumption of good 1 is increased in order to keep an individual on the same indifference curve. As such we noted that the *MRS* is an observable measure of value, and is often called the marginal value (*MV*). At any point, *MRS* is equal to the absolute value of the slope of the indifference curve through that point. We then introduced an important empirical assumption concerning the shape of indifference curves — the *assumption of a diminishing MRS*.

We showed how to construct a *utility function* to represent any individual preference ordering. You discovered that *utility numbers* are ordinal, not cardinal, and that, given individual preferences that satisfy these assumptions, any number of utility functions can be constructed to represent those preferences.

Finally we used this theory of preferences to tackle some interesting questions. Why do employees often demand premium rates of pay for overtime work, and why do people spread their income over time? Because their indifference curves satisfy the hypothesis of diminishing *MRS*. How can we measure the cost of air pollution to a particular person? By looking at that person's willingness to substitute income for pollution — or that person's *MRS* of income for pollution. Why did shopping carts increase in size over the past 30 years? Because rising time costs for women (the ones who traditionally did the grocery shopping) increased, leading to a substitution away from many small trips to fewer larger ones.

One of the most important lessons you can grasp from these applications is that economics is about applying the same principles over and over again. There is no difference in analysis between the overtime and payday examples. Only the names on the graph and the context of the example change. Once you recognize this and start to practise it on your own, you will have a very powerful tool at your disposal.

EXERCISES

1. "When Mother Teresa used her $190 000 Nobel Peace Prize to build a leprosarium in Calcutta, she was violating the maximization assumption." True or false?

2. If two stocks are identical, with the exception that one pays dividends and the other does not, what does the maximization assumption imply about the relative capital gains that should be expected between the two?

3. Is anything worth doing, worth doing well?

4. Given a choice between two bundles containing good 1 and good 2, Dizzy says that (i) he prefers the bundle with the larger quantity of good 1 and (ii) if the quantity of good 1 is the same in the two bundles, he is indifferent between them.
   a. Draw one of Dizzy's indifference curves.
   b. Construct three utility functions that represent Dizzy's preferences.
   c. Can you find two goods such that your preferences are like Dizzy's?

5. Construct a representative indifference curve for each of the following situations. In so doing, you are creating a model of preferences for each situation much as we did in the applications section of this chapter. Keep in mind that a good theory is one that you can defend.
   a. The two goods are nickels (5¢) and quarters (25¢).
   b. The two goods are right gloves and left gloves, and the consumer has two hands; the consumer has only one hand.
   c. The two goods are money and cocaine, and the more cocaine the individual consumes, the more money he or she is willing to give up to get even more cocaine.
   d. The two goods are money and lobster tails, and eating more than a certain number of lobster tails makes the consumer sick. (Assuming that the consumer can dispose of unwanted lobster tails at no cost, how do the indifference curves change?)
   e. The two goods are Coke and Pepsi, and the consumer perceives no difference between the two soft drinks.
   f. There is one bad — water torture — and one good — chocolate chip cookies.
   g. There are two bads: water torture and garbage.

6. Consider the following utility functions:
   (i) $U(x_1, x_2) = x_1 x_2$
   (ii) $U(x_1, x_2) = 10x_1 x_2$
   (iii) $U(x_1, x_2) = (x_1 x_2)^2$
   a. Construct an indifference curve for each of these functions. For (i), use utility number 20; for (ii), use utility number 200; for (iii), use utility number 400.
   b. Do these utility functions represent different preference orderings?

7. Althea's preferences are captured in the following utility function:
   $$U(x_1, x_2) = \min(2x_1, 7x_2)$$
   a. Draw an indifference curve for Althea.
   b. Which of the assumptions in Chapter 2 do not apply to Althea?

8. Consider the following utility function:
   $$U(x_1, x_2) = x_2 + x_1^{1/2}$$
   a. Very carefully draw the indifference curves associated with utility numbers 64, 49, and 36. For all three indifference curves, find the quantity of x_2 when x_1 is 0, 1, 4, 9, 16, 25, and 36.
   b. How does *MRS* change as you move from one indifference curve to another along the *vertical line* $x_1 = 4$? Or $x_1 = 16$? Or any vertical line?

9. Consider the following statements and comment.
   a. "Air and water are not scarce because you don't have to pay for them."
   b. "Michael Jackson doesn't face any scarcity because he's rich."
   c. "Smallpox is scarce."

10. It is a "well-known fact" that the correlation between investor return and education level of stockbrokers is negative — better brokers usually have less education. Is this consistent with the maximization assumption or a refutation of it? That is, do you think those brokers who went on to college would have been better brokers by not going?

11. Jacques' preferences over goods 1 and 2 can be described as follows: bundle (x_1', x_2') is preferred to bundle (x_1'', x_2'') if the maximum of x_1' and x_2' is larger than the maximum of x_1'' and x_2''; if the maximums are equal, he is indifferent between the bundles.
    a. Show that Jacques is indifferent between (10,8) and (2,10). Draw the entire indifference curve through these two bundles.
    b. Find a utility function to represent these preferences.

12. When terrorists hijack an airplane, they are usually outnumbered (perhaps 100 to 1). As a result, the people on the airplane could easily overpower them. How do the terrorists exploit the maximization assumption and keep control of the plane?

13. Along the same lines as question 12, when army troops are advancing they tend to advance in a horizontal line together, rather than in a single column with one soldier behind the other. How is this the result of the maximization assumption?

14. In virtually every war of the twentieth century it has been discovered that soldiers are reluctant to fire their weapons. Some studies have found that as many as 80 percent of soldiers in a given battle return without a single shot fired. Some people claim this is a result of the human abhorrence of violence. How could it be explained with the maximization assumption? (*Hint*: What type of reaction comes from firing your weapon?)

15. Given the assumption of diminishing marginal rates of substitution, which types of families would you expect would be more likely to have a third child: families where the first two children are of the same sex (i.e., both boys or both girls), or families where there is one of each?

16. Friedman's Law for Finding Men's Washrooms states: "Men's rooms are adjacent, in one of the three dimensions, to ladies' rooms." Why is this a trivial application of the maximization assumption?

17. Leanne is concerned about her husband Carl's drinking. On their way to a wedding one Saturday she says to him "Tonight I want you to have no more than three drinks, and I don't want any drinking after 10 o'clock." Suppose she is able to monitor these conditions perfectly. What types of substitutions will Carl make to maximize his utility?

18. A poster with a picture of the leaning tower of Pisa has the caption "Mediocrity: it takes a lot less time and most people won't notice the difference until it's too late." Explain this in terms of the economic principles of the chapter.

19. "We should have the death penalty for armed robbery, then we'd have fewer of them." Is this consistent with the principles of this chapter? If this was the case, what would you have more of?

*20. Consider the following utility function:

$$U(x_1, x_2) = (x_1)^{1/3}(x_2)^{2/3}$$

   a. Find the two marginal utility functions; that is, the function that gives the marginal utility of good 1, and the function that gives the marginal utility of good 2.
   b. Find the marginal rate of substitution function.
   c. What happens to the marginal rate of substitution as x_1 gets arbitrarily large relative to x_2? As x_2 get arbitrarily large relative to x_1? As x_1/x_2 increases?
   d. Is the diminishing marginal rate of substitution assumption satisfied?

*21. Return to the utility functions in Exercise 6.
   a. Compute and compare the marginal rate of substitution functions for these utility func-

tions. What does your comparison suggest about the marginal rates of substitution for different utility functions that represent the same preference ordering?

b. Now compute and compare the marginal utility of good 1 functions for these utility functions. Observe that even though these functions represent the same preference ordering, the marginal utility functions are different. Explain this curious result.

*22. For the utility function in Exercise 8, compute the marginal rate of substitution function. Notice that it depends on x_1 but not on x_2. Given this property, if you had a perfect drawing of one indifference curve, how could you draw others?

*23. Consider the following utility function:

$U(x_1, x_2) = 0$ if $x_1 \leq 10$ or $x_2 \leq 20$
$U(x_1, x_2) = (x_1 - 10)(x_2 - 20)$ if $x_1 > 10$ and $x_2 > 20$

a. This utility function indicates that the subsistence levels of the two goods are 10 units of good 1 and 20 units of good 2. Do you agree or disagree with this interpretation? Explain.
b. Supposing that $x_1 > 10$ and $x_2 > 20$, find the marginal rate of substitution function.
c. Supposing that $x_1 \leq 10$ or $x_2 \leq 20$, what can you say about the marginal rate of substitution?
d. Carefully construct a diagram in which you indicate the consumption bundles that yield utility 0, those that yield utility 1, and those that yield utility 4.

*24. Cheryl likes to eat "trail mix" that she makes by mixing raisins and nuts. Her preferences between raisins and nuts are described by the utility function $U(r,n) = r + n$, where r and n are the quantity (in grams) of raisins and nuts respectively. However, if there are more than twice as many nuts as raisins she throws away the extra nuts, and if there are more than twice as many raisins as nuts, she throws away the extra raisins. Given these preferences,

a. Explain her preference between the following (r,n) bundles:
(i.) bundle (5,9) and bundle (7,8)
(ii.) bundle (4,10) and bundle (9,4)
(iii.) bundle (3,4) and bundle (2,20)
b. Draw a graph of Cheryl's indifference curves.

*25. Hayley's marginal rate of substitution of good 2 for good 1 is $MRS = 5X_2/2X_1$.

a. Is her marginal rate of substitution diminishing?
b. If Hayley is currently consuming 20 units of X_1 and 4 units of X_2, would she accept an offer of 4 units of X_1 (no more and no less) for 2 units of X_2? Explain.

CHAPTER 3

Demand Theory

In the nineteenth century, the English poet William Wordsworth lamented what he saw as a society obsessed with "getting and spending." Nothing has changed since Wordsworth's time and, lamentable or not, making choices regarding spending is still an inevitable part of our lives. Some choices are relatively unimportant: Should I spend the evening watching television? Should I buy new running shoes? Some are more significant: Should I spend the next eight years of my life studying to be a doctor? As we will see in this chapter, all economic decisions, large or small, have certain elementary but important factors in common. In this chapter, we develop a set of graphic tools to analyze a whole range of consumer-choice problems.

3.1 Choices and Constraints

In the theory of economic choice making, the word *constrained* is crucial. Constraints are basic to all choices. These constraints include limits on income, time, and human resources. Furthermore, constraints also include social customs, laws, and threats of violence. Implicit in the word *choice* is the notion that we must make choices among competing alternatives. That is, our choices are limited, or constrained: we cannot "have it all." *Income* is one constraint. For example, if I choose to buy a new house, I have implicitly decided to give up other consumption possibilities — perhaps buying a new car or having weekly dinners at a favourite restaurant. I cannot afford all three choices because my income — my command over goods — will not stretch that far.

Time is another constraint. By deciding to spend the evening watching television, I am implicitly giving up other activities that compete for my time — say, playing squash or reading. In fact, the most fundamental economic choice we all face is what to do with the one lifespan we have. By deciding to become a doctor, for example, I give up the chance to become a carpenter, a writer, an accountant, or a computer scientist.

Our endowment of *human resources* also constrains our choices. For example, someone who tips the scales at 45 kilograms cannot choose to become a heavyweight boxer. Of course, we can choose to augment the human resources we do have — for example, by obtaining further schooling — but in making this choice, we forgo other opportunities such as getting work experience or travelling. Because our limited endowments of income, time, and human resources necessarily restrict the possibilities open to us, we *must* make choices among competing alternatives.

Making choices is a complicated procedure. To even begin to understand consumer choice making, we need to reduce the bewildering complexity of choice problems to a few basic elements. In this chapter, we explore a relatively simple choice problem in which a particular consumer — knowing his or her budget and the price of all goods — chooses a consumption bundle in some period (this week, for instance) based on the utility function discussed in Chapter 2. Clearly, this simple choice problem is unlike the real problems consumers actually face, but despite its simplicity it has proven very useful in understanding a great amount of behaviour.

This choice problem assumes that consumers have already decided to spend a particular sum of money — what we have called the consumer's budget — on consumption goods *in a given period*. This problem also involves *perfect information* because we are assuming that this consumer knows all relevant prices. In later chapters, we will see how to analyze both intertemporal choice making and choice making under imperfect information.

3.2 The Budget Constraint

attainable consumption bundle

We will begin our exploration of the consumer's choice problem by examining the consumer's budget constraint and identifying the consumer's **attainable consumption bundles** — that is, the bundles that this consumer can actually afford to buy. Our choices are constrained by our budgets and by the prices of the goods we want to buy. An *attainable consumption bundle* is one that is affordable, given the consumer's budget constraint.

Attainable Consumption Bundles

Some notation will allow us to define attainable bundles more precisely. We will call the two goods in the consumption bundles good 1 and good 2, and we will denote their respective prices by p_1 and p_2. In addition, we will denote the consumer's budget (or income) by M. The total cost of bundle (x_1, x_2) is just the sum of prices multiplied by quantities, $p_1x_1 + p_2x_2$, and attainable bundles are just bundles whose total cost does not exceed M. Thus, an attainable consumption bundle is any bundle that satisfies the following inequality:

$$p_1x_1 + p_2x_2 \leq M$$

budget constraint

The inequality itself is called the **budget constraint**.

In Figure 3.1, the set of attainable bundles is indicated by the shaded area. The attainable bundles on the line $p_1x_1 + p_2x_2 = M$ use up all of the consumer's budget, whereas attainable bundles below the line do not. The line itself is commonly called the **budget line**. Because it important to understand what a budget line is, give the following problem careful attention.

budget line

PROBLEM 3.1

Why does the budget line intersect the x_1 axis at M/p_1 and the x_2 axis at M/p_2? What is the slope of the budget line? On the budget line, how many units of good 2 must the consumer give up to get an additional unit of good 1? What happens to the budget line as p_1 approaches zero? As p_2 approaches zero?

FIGURE 3.1 Attainable consumption bundles

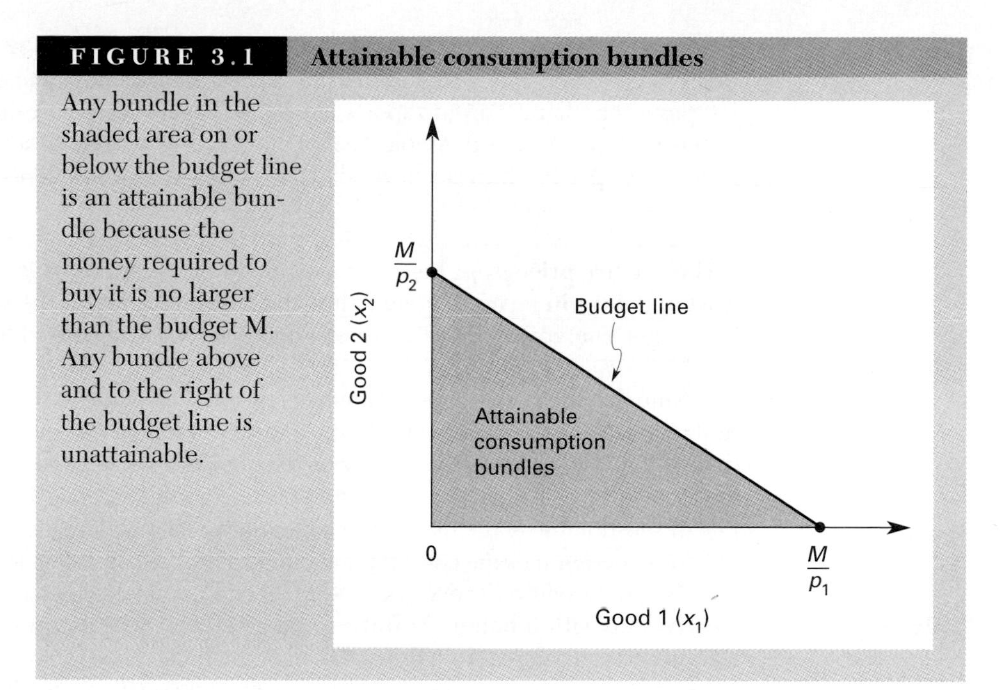

Any bundle in the shaded area on or below the budget line is an attainable bundle because the money required to buy it is no larger than the budget M. Any bundle above and to the right of the budget line is unattainable.

Opportunity Cost, Real Income, and Relative Prices

It is useful to rewrite the budget constraint by solving for x_2 (and dropping the inequality). If we do so we obtain

$$x_2 = M/p_2 - (p_1/p_2)x_1.$$

This equation is now in the famous point-slope form familiar to every grade 9 algebra student, where M/p_2 is the vertical intercept and $(-p_1/p_2)$ is the slope of the budget line. The economic interpretation, however, is much more important. This equation tells us that the two important parameters for budget constraints are **real income** (M/p_2) and **relative prices** (p_1/p_2). In other words, what matters for economic behaviour is not the nominal prices, p_1 and p_2, or the nominal income, M, but the prices and incomes in terms of real goods. In Problem 3.1, you discovered that, along the budget line, the consumer must give up p_1/p_2 units of good 2 to get an additional unit of good 1. That is, the relative price tells us the **opportunity cost** of good 1 is p_1/p_2 units of good 2. Conversely, the opportunity cost of good 2 is p_2/p_1 units of good 1.

real income

relative prices

opportunity cost

Imagine that you live in Toronto and that good 1 is tickets to Toronto Maple Leafs hockey games and good 2 is tickets to Toronto Raptors basketball games. If the ticket price of a Maple Leafs hockey game (p_1) is \$150 and the ticket price of a Raptors basketball game (p_2) is \$75, then the relative price is 150/75 = 2; that is, the *opportunity cost* of buying a ticket to one Maple Leafs game is not buying tickets to two Raptors games. If instead the ticket prices were identical, the opportunity cost of one ticket to a Maple Leafs game would be one ticket to a Raptors game. Thus, the absolute value of the slope of the budget line — the relative price — has an important economic interpretation: it is the opportunity cost of good 1 in terms of good 2.

It is useful to interpret opportunity cost in a slightly different way. The opportunity cost of good 1 in terms of good 2 is the rate at which the individual *can* substitute good 2 for good 1 in a market. Suppose again that the ticket price of a Maple Leafs game (good 1) is $40 and the ticket price of a Raptors game (good 2) is $20. Suppose, too, that a Toronto sports fan wants to substitute more tickets to Raptors games for fewer tickets to Maple Leafs games. Giving up one ticket to a Maple Leafs game frees up $40, which can be used to buy two ($40/$20) additional tickets to Raptors games. To summarize:

The relative price p_1/p_2 has the following interpretations: it is the opportunity cost of good 1 in terms of good 2; it is the absolute value of the slope of the budget line; it is the rate at which good 2 can be substituted for good 1.

Note that the relative price is the rate one is *able* to trade in the market, not necessarily the rate one is *willing* to trade at. As we saw in the last chapter, the willingness to trade is the *MRS* or *MV*. As you will soon see, the interplay between opportunity cost — the rate at which an individual is *able* to substitute good 2 for good 1 — and the marginal rate of substitution — the rate at which the individual is *willing* to substitute good 2 for good 1 — determines the consumption bundle that the consumer actually chooses.

The important difference between real and nominal prices and incomes is most clearly seen with inflation. **Inflation** is a general rise in the price level, including income. As you can see from the equation of the budget constraint, if p_1, p_2, and M all increase by the same amount, say 10 percent, the equation remains unchanged and the budget line does not move. That is, those bundles that were either attainable or unattainable remain so. Increasing all prices and incomes by the same amount is called a **pure inflation**. The problem with inflation is that it is not usually pure; all prices and incomes do not move together. If p_1 increases by 15 percent, p_2 by 11 percent, and M by 7 percent, then there is a change in relative prices and a change in real income. During the 1970s when Canada was experiencing double-digit inflation, there were large changes in relative prices and real incomes caused by inflation. For example, the wealth of individuals who held cash balances tended to decrease, while the wealth of those who held real estate tended to increase.

inflation

pure inflation

The result that, if all prices and income increase proportionately, then the budget constraint remains the same, is known as the **no money illusion**. It reflects two facts: when we double both prices, the opportunity cost of one good in terms of the other does not change; when prices and income double, the consumer's purchasing power does not change. As we will see in the rest of the chapter, because budget lines are unaffected by a pure inflation, the optimal utility maximizing choices remain the same.

no money illusion

PROBLEM 3.2

Take a piece of graph paper, and on four separate graphs, graph the budget line when $M = 100$, $p_1 = 5$, and $p_2 = 2$.

a. On the first graph, draw another budget line where $M = 200$, $p_1 = 5$, and $p_2 = 2$.
b. On the second graph, draw another budget line where $M = 100$, $p_1 = 10$, and $p_2 = 2$.
c. On the third graph draw another budget line where $M = 100$, $p_1 = 5$, and $p_2 = 1$.
d. On the fourth graph draw another budget line where $M = 200$, $p_1 = 10$, and $p_2 = 2$. How does this relate to the graph in (c)?

▶ Application: A Connecticut Yankee in King Arthur's Court

A humorous example of money illusion and real income is found in Mark Twain's classic story where the hero attempts in vain to convince a group of workers of the difference between real and nominal values.

"In your country, brother, what is the wage of a master bailiff, master hind, carter, shepherd, swineherd?"

The smith's face beamed with joy. He said:

"With us they are allowed the double of it! And what may a mechanic get — carpenter, dauber, mason, painter, blacksmith, wheelwright, and the like?"

"On the average, fifty milrays: half a cent a day."

"Ho-ho! With us they are allowed a hundred! With us any good mechanic is allowed a cent a day! I count out the tailor, but not the others — they are all allowed a cent a day, and in driving times they get more — yes, up to a hundred and ten and even fifteen milrays a day."

And his face shone upon the company like a sunburst. But I didn't scare at all. I rigged up my pile-driver, and allowed myself fifteen minutes to drive him into the earth — drive him ALL in — drive him in till not even the curve of his skull should show above ground. Here is the way I started in on him. I asked:

"What do you pay a pound for salt?"

"A hundred milrays."

"We pay 40. What do you pay for beef and mutton — when you buy it?" That was a neat hit; it made the color come.

"It varieth somewhat, but not much; one may say 75 milrays the pound."

"WE pay 33. What do you pay for eggs?"

"Fifty milrays the dozen."

"We pay 20. What do you pay for beer?"

"It costeth us 8½ milrays the pint."

"We get it for 4; 25 bottles for a cent. What do you pay for wheat?"

"At the rate of 900 milrays the bushel."

"We pay 400. What do you pay for a man's tow-linen suit?"

"Thirteen cents."

"We pay 6. What do you pay for a stuff gown for the wife of the laborer or the mechanic?"

"We pay 8.4.0."

"Well, observe the difference: you pay eight cents and four mills, we pay only four cents." I prepared, now, to sock it to him. I said, "Look here, dear friend, WHAT'S BECOME OF YOUR HIGH WAGES YOU WERE BRAGGING SO ABOUT, A FEW MINUTES AGO?" — and I looked around on the company with placid satisfaction, for I had slipped up on him gradually and tied him hand and foot, you see, without his ever noticing that he was being tied at all. "What's become of those noble high wages of yours? I seem to have knocked the stuffing all out of them, it appears to me."

But if you will believe me, he merely looked surprised, that is all! He didn't grasp the situation at all; didn't know he had walked into a trap, didn't discover that he was IN a trap. I could have shot him, from sheer vexation. With cloudy eye and a struggling intellect, he fetched this out:

"Marry, I seem not to understand. It is PROVED that our wages be double thine; how then may it be that thou'st knocked therefrom the stuffing? An I miscall not the wonderly word, this being the first time under grace and providence of God it hath been granted me to hear it."

Well, I was stunned; partly with this unlooked-for stupidity on his part, and partly because his fellows so manifestly sided with him and were of his mind — if you might call it mind. My position was simple enough, plain enough; how could it ever be simplified more? However, I must try:

"Why look here, brother Dowley, don't you see? Your wages are merely higher than ours in NAME, not in FACT."

"Hear him! They are the DOUBLE — ye have confessed it yourself."

"Yes, yes, I don't deny that at all. But that's got nothing to do with it; the AMOUNT of the wages in mere coins, with meaningless names attached to them to know them by, has got nothing to do with it. The thing is, how much can you BUY with your wages? — that's the idea. While it is true that with you a good mechanic is allowed about three dollars and a half a year, and with us only about a dollar and seventy-five—"

"There — ye're confessing it again, ye're confessing it again!"

"Confound it, I've never denied it I tell you! What I say is this. With us, HALF a dollar buys more than a DOLLAR buys with you — and THEREFORE it stands to reason and the commonest kind of common sense, that our wages are HIGHER than yours."

He looked dazed, and said, despairingly:

"Verily I cannot make it out. Ye've just said ours are the higher, and with the same breath ye take it back."

"Oh, great Scott, isn't it possible to get such a simple thing through your head? Now look here — let me illustrate. We pay four cents for a woman's stuff gown, you pay 8.4.0., which is four mills more than DOUBLE. What do you allow a laboring woman who works on a farm?"

"Two mills a day."

"Very good; we allow but half as much; we pay her only a tenth of a cent a day; and—"

"Again ye're conf—"

"Wait! Now, you see, the thing is very simple; this time you'll understand it. For instance, it takes your woman 42 days to earn her gown, at 2 mills a day — 7 weeks' work; but ours earns hers in 40 days — two days SHORT of 7 weeks. Your woman has a gown, and her whole 7 weeks' wages are gone; ours has a gown, and two day's wages left, to buy something else with. There — NOW you understand it!"

He looked — well he merely looked dubious, it's the most I can say; so did the others. I waited — to let the thing work. Dowley spoke at last — and betrayed the fact that he actually hadn't gotten away from his rooted and grounded superstitions yet. He said, with a trifle of hesitancy:

"But — but — ye cannot fail to grant that two mills a day is better than one."

"Shucks! Well, of course I hated to give it up. … But alas, it didn't crush. No, I had to give it up. What those people valued was HIGH WAGES; it didn't seem to be a matter of any consequence to them whether the high wages would buy anything or not."

Endowments Rather than Money

Thus far we have presented budget constraints where the individual has an amount of money, M. For many problems that we analyze in this book, this is sufficient. However, in some situations it is more appropriate to assume the individual is endowed with goods rather than cash. Consider the case of labour. As we saw in Chapter 2, deciding how much to work involves trading off consumption goods and leisure based on the wage rate. However, the wage rate obviously determines your income since everyone is endowed with labour. If we did not take this into account we would incorrectly analyze such problems.

To keep things simple, suppose Sally owns some apples, denoted x_1^0, and she also owns some eggs, denoted x_2^0. For example, Sally may own 100 apples ($x_1^0 = 100$) and 12 dozen eggs ($x_2^0 = 12$). The value of Sally's endowment is simply the sum of $p_1x_1^0 + p_2x_2^0$. If Sally wishes to consume eggs and apples, the amount she spends must be less than the value of her endowment. Hence her budget constraint is given by:

$$p_1x_1 + p_2x_2 \leq p_1x_1^0 + p_2x_2^0$$

This looks more intimidating than the last budget constraint, but it really isn't. Figure 3.2 shows that the graph for this budget constraint looks the same as the earlier one. If we solve for x_2 as before we have

$$x_2 = (p_1x_1^0 + p_2x_2^0)/p_2 - (p_1/p_2)x_1.$$

We see once again that the budget constraint depends on relative prices and the real income (as measured by the value of the endowment). Make sure you try the following problem before proceeding.

PROBLEM 3.3

Let $x_1^0 = 10$, $x_2^0 = 15$, $p_1 = 5$, and $p_2 = 5$. Using two separate graphs, graph the budget line on each.

a. Now, assuming everything else remains the same, graph a new budget line on the first graph when p_1 changes to 1.

b. Assuming everything else remains the same, graph a new budget line on the second graph when x_1^0 changes to 20.

FIGURE 3.2 **The budget line with endowments**

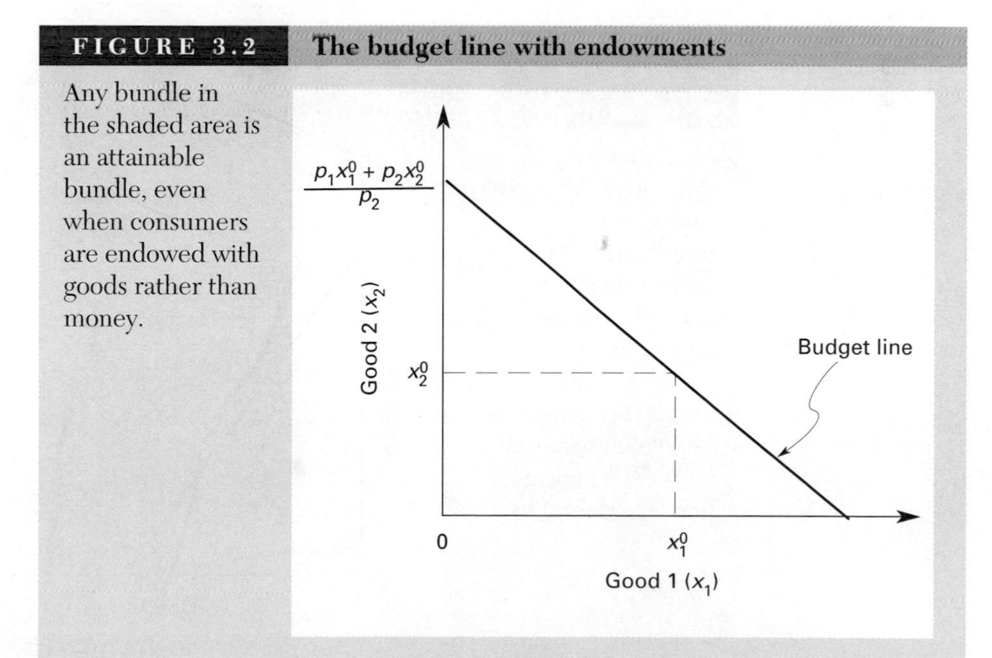

Any bundle in the shaded area is an attainable bundle, even when consumers are endowed with goods rather than money.

As you could see from the last problem, the budget constraint still shifts when income (the endowment) is changed. Also, when a price changes, the slope of the budget constraint changes, and the slope still equals the relative price ($-p_1/p_2$). The only difference is that now the budget constraint rotates through the endowment point rather than through a point on one of the axes.

3.3 The Consumer's Choice Problem

Consumer theory is built on the assumption that individual consumers make the most of their opportunities in light of their preferences. Because higher indifference curves are preferred to lower indifference curves, a consumer's problem is to reach the highest indifference curve permitted by his or her budget constraint. We can use the consumer's utility function $U(x_1, x_2)$ to reformulate the consumer's problem by thinking of the consumer as choosing the quantities of the two goods that maximize utility, subject to the budget constraint. We will call the consumption bundle that the consumer chooses the utility-maximizing bundle, denoted by (x_1^*, x_2^*).

We can infer one important characteristic of the utility-maximizing consumption bundle: it must lie *on* the budget line. To see why, consider the bundle at point A in Figure 3.3, which lies inside the budget line. This cannot be the utility-maximizing bundle (x_1^*, x_2^*) because the nonsatiation assumption implies that any of the bundles on segment CD of the budget line — every one of which contains more of both goods — is preferred to the bundle at point A. In other words, the nonsatiation assumption implies that a consumer will always pick a consumption bundle on the budget line:

The nonsatiation assumption implies that the utility-maximizing consumption bundle (x_1^*, x_2^*) lies on the budget line.

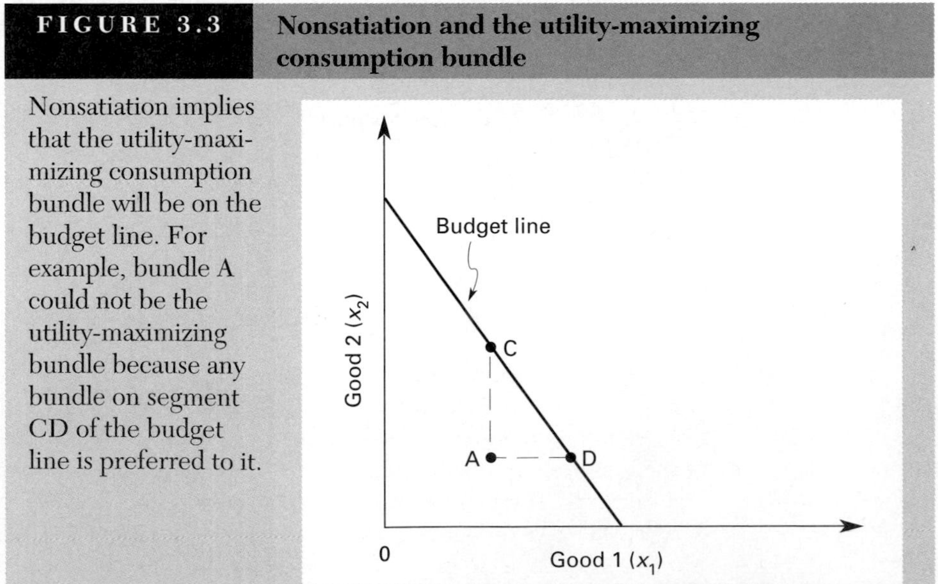

FIGURE 3.3 Nonsatiation and the utility-maximizing consumption bundle

Nonsatiation implies that the utility-maximizing consumption bundle will be on the budget line. For example, bundle A could not be the utility-maximizing bundle because any bundle on segment CD of the budget line is preferred to it.

The Choice Problem

We can use this result to write the consumer's choice problem as follows:

$$\text{maximize } U(x_1, x_2) \text{ by choice of } x_1 \text{ and } x_2$$
$$\text{subject to the constraint } p_1x_1 + p_2x_2 = M$$

This expression is a compact way of writing out the consumer's choice problem. It tells what the consumer's objective is — maximizing utility. It tells what the consumer is choosing — a consumption bundle. And it tells what constraint the consumer faces — the budget line.

Just what is the solution to a consumer's choice problem? It is very much like the solution to that recurring problem: What should I wear today? In the Maritimes, for example, fall weather is notoriously unpredictable. One day may be warm and sunny, the next cold and dry, the next very rainy, and the next snowy. Before choosing what clothing to venture out in, the sensible Maritimer looks out the window to see what the weather is like.

endogenous variables

exogenous variables

We could describe the solution to the Maritimer's choice problem by a series of rules of thumb. If it's warm and sunny, wear a light windbreaker. If it's raining, wear rain gear. If it's cold and dry, wear a down jacket. The items of clothing that we choose to wear are **endogenous variables** because we do the choosing. But the particular items we choose on any day are determined by the **exogenous variables** that we collectively call weather, over which we have no control. That is, according to the Maritimer's rules for choosing what to wear, the endogenous variables (items of clothing) are determined by the exogenous variables (weather).

The Solution: Demand Functions

The solution to the consumer choice problem in this chapter has the same form. Here, too, the endogenous variables are determined by the exogenous variables. Of course, in the consumer's utility-maximizing problem, the endogenous variables are the quantities of the two goods to be chosen: x_1 and x_2. The exogenous variables are the two prices p_1 and p_2 and the budget M; these are the givens, the constraints within which an individual consumer must operate. In the solution to this choice problem, then, the utility-maximizing values of x_1 and x_2 (the endogenous variables) are determined by p_1, p_2, and M (the exogenous variables).

Before taking up this general choice problem, it may be helpful to actually solve a specific choice problem — that is, to find (x_1^*, x_2^*) for a specific utility function. We will use the following utility function, which captures the preferences of Anna from the problems in Chapter 2:

$$U(x_1, x_2) = x_1 + x_2$$

Here, x_1 is kilograms of trout and x_2 is kilograms of salmon. Given a choice between any two bundles, Anna prefers the bundle that weighs more, and she is indifferent between the bundles if they weigh the same. Therefore, this function — which gives us the total weight of any consumption bundle — is a utility function for Anna.

For Anna, trout and salmon are *perfect substitutes* because an additional kilogram of either fish is equally attractive. In effect, Anna sees no real difference between the two kinds of fish. Therefore, she maximizes her utility by spending her whole budget on the cheaper fish; that is,

$$x_1^* = M/p_1 \quad \text{and} \quad x_2^* = 0 \qquad \text{if } p_1 < p_2$$
$$x_1^* = 0 \quad \text{and} \quad x_2^* = M/p_2 \qquad \text{if } p_1 > p_2$$

If the prices are identical, *any* bundle on the budget line is utility-maximizing since the budget line is then coincident with an indifference curve.

Notice how similar the solution of Anna's problem is to the solution to the Maritimer's what-to-wear problem. Both solutions have essentially the same form: the variables that are to be chosen (the endogenous variables) are determined by the variables that are given (the exogenous variables). If it is raining, wear rain gear (and leave the down parka in the closet). If $p_1 < p_2$, spend M/p_1 on good 1 and nothing on good 2.

In fact, the solution to *any* consumer choice problem has this form. We will therefore write the solution to the general two-good choice problem in the following symbolic way:

$$x_1^* = D_1(p_1, p_2, M)$$
$$x_2^* = D_2(p_1, p_2, M)$$

demand functions

The functions D_1 and D_2 are **demand functions**[1]. The first says that the utility-maximizing quantity of good 1 (denoted by x_1^*) is some function D_1 of the exogenous vari-

---

1. One method for solving the consumer's choice problem when the utility function is differentiable and the solution is interior is the *method of Lagrange multipliers*, developed in most basic calculus texts. The mechanics of the method are simple. First, combine the utility function and the budget line by introducing a Lagrange multiplier (to form what is called the Lagrangian function) as follows:

$$L(x_1, x_2, \lambda) = U(x_1, x_2) + \lambda(M - p_1x_1 - p_2x_2)$$

Now, differentiating with respect to x_1, x_2, and λ and set these derivatives equal to zero to obtain

$$\partial U(x_1, x_2)/\partial x_1 - \lambda p_1 = 0$$
$$\partial U(x_1, x_2)/\partial x_2 - \lambda p_2 = 0$$
$$M - p_1x_1 - p_2x_2 = 0$$

These three equations are called first order conditions. We now have a system of three simultaneous equations in three unknown endogenous variables, x_1, x_2, and λ. Solving for these unknown endogenous variables in terms of the three exogenous variables, p_1, p_2, and M, yields two demand functions, x_1^* and x_2^* and a function that determines an optimal value for λ^*. For example, if

$$U(x_1, x_2) = x_1x_2$$

then

$$L(x_1, x_2, \lambda) = x_1x_2 + \lambda(M - p_1x_1 - p_2x_2)$$

and the first order conditions are:

$$x_2 - \lambda p_1 = 0$$
$$x_1 - \lambda p_2 = 0$$
$$M - p_1x_1 - p_2x_2 = 0$$

When we solve these three equations for the three unknown variables we obtain

$$x_1^* = \frac{M}{2p_1}$$
$$x_2^* = \frac{M}{2p_2}$$
$$\lambda^* = \frac{M}{2p_1p_2}$$

The first two equations are the demand functions for x_1 and x_2.

ables p_1, p_2, and M. This equation is simply a symbolic way of saying that the choice of x_1^* is determined by (or depends on) the prices of all items in the consumption bundle and the budget to be devoted to the whole bundle.

system of demand functions

A single demand function describes the functional relationship between the quantity of a good demanded and all the factors that influence demand: the price of that good, the prices of other goods, and the size of the individual consumer's budget. A **system of demand functions**, D_1 and D_2, tells us how much of both goods will be chosen, given the exogenous variables. In the following problem, you are asked to solve another relatively simple utility-maximization problem, thereby generating the demand functions for another specific utility function.

PROBLEM 3.4

Consider the following utility function:

$$U(x_1, x_2) = \min(x_1, x_2)$$

Show that the demand functions are

$$x_1^* = M/(p_1 + p_2)$$
$$x_2^* = M/(p_1 + p_2)$$

(*Hint*: First draw an indifference curve and observe that it has a right-angled kink where it intersects the line $x_2 = x_1$. Then show that the utility-maximizing bundle lies on the line $x_2 = x_1$. Finally, use this information in combination with the budget line to derive the demand functions.)

3.4 Graphic Analysis of Utility Maximization

In this section, we will use graphic techniques to describe the solution to the utility-maximizing problem when indifference curves are *smooth* and *strictly convex*. We will distinguish two types of solutions to the problem — interior and corner solutions — and two kinds of goods — essential and inessential goods. An **interior solution** to the utility-maximizing problem is one in which the quantities of both goods are positive. A **corner solution** is one in which the quantity of one good is positive and the quantity of the other good is zero. An **essential good** is indispensable, such as water or air. Regardless of how high the price of an essential good may be, the consumer will still decide to buy some of it. In contrast, an **inessential good** is like fresh raspberries in January or cut flowers for the kitchen table: if the price of an inessential good is high enough, the consumer will decide not to buy any of it.

interior solution

corner solution

essential good

inessential good

Interior Solutions

As you already know, the maximization assumption implies that the solution to the utility-maximizing problem will lie on the budget line. This is one of the two statements that describe, or characterize, an interior solution:[2]

$$p_1 x_1^* + p_2 x_2^* \equiv M$$

2. Note that the above statement uses an identity sign ≡ indicating that the two sides of the statement are equivalent by definition.

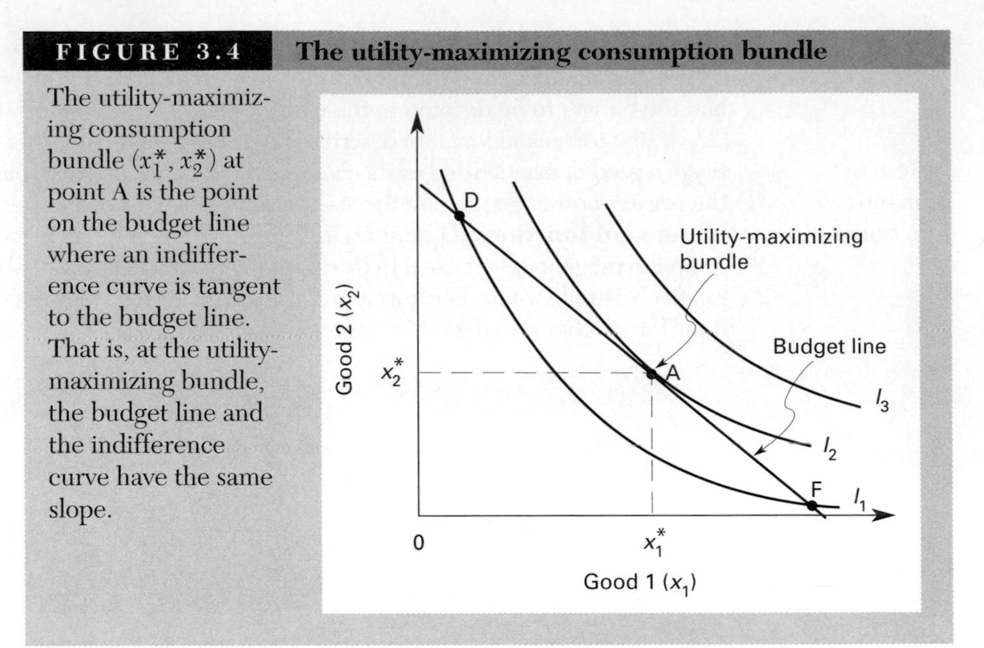

FIGURE 3.4 The utility-maximizing consumption bundle

The utility-maximizing consumption bundle (x_1^*, x_2^*) at point A is the point on the budget line where an indifference curve is tangent to the budget line. That is, at the utility-maximizing bundle, the budget line and the indifference curve have the same slope.

For example, the utility-maximizing bundle in Figure 3.4 lies on the budget line at bundle A.

The second statement tells us just which bundle on the budget line maximizes utility. Notice that at the utility-maximizing bundle in Figure 3.4, the indifference curve I_2 is *tangent* to the budget line. As long as indifference curves are smooth and the solution is an interior rather than a corner solution, this tangency result always holds: an indifference curve is tangent to the budget line at the utility-maximizing bundle. Why? The indifference curve through any bundle on the budget line will 1. intersect the budget line from above, 2. intersect it from below, or 3. be tangent to it. The first case is shown at bundle D in Figure 3.4. Because bundles along the budget line to the right of D (and to the left of F) are preferred to it, D cannot be the utility-maximizing bundle. The second case is shown at bundle F in Figure 3.4. Because bundles along the budget line to the left of F (and to the right of D) are preferred to it, F cannot be the utility-maximizing bundle. This means that the third case, where the indifference curve is tangent to the budget line, must be the utility-maximizing bundle.

As you learned in Problem 3.1, the absolute value of the slope of the budget line is p_1/p_2 and, as you learned in Chapter 2, the absolute value of the slope of an indifference curve at any bundle (x_1, x_2) is $MRS(x_1, x_2)$. Because the budget line and the indifference curve are tangent at bundle A, their slopes must be identical at this point. In other words,

$$MRS(x_1^*, x_2^*) \equiv p_1/p_2.$$

This is the second statement that characterizes an interior solution.[3]

But what does this tangency condition really mean? Suppose that the consumer is thinking about choosing some bundle on the budget line where *MRS* is less than p_1/p_2 — say, bundle *F* in Figure 3.4. As we argued in Chapter 2, *MRS* is the rate at which the consumer is *willing* to substitute good 2 for good 1; that is, the marginal value of good 1. On the other hand, as we saw in our discussion of opportunity cost, p_1/p_2 is the relative price at which the consumer *can* substitute good 2 for good 1. At bundle *F*, *MRS* is less than p_1/p_2 — that is, marginal value for good 1 is less than the relative price for good 1. Therefore, the consumer will be better off as he or she substitutes good 2 for good 1. Accordingly, the consumer will move to the left from F along the budget line, substituting good 2 for good 1. A corresponding argument tells us that if the consumer is considering some bundle on the budget line where *MRS* exceeds p_1/p_2 — say, bundle D in Figure 3.4 — he or she will move to the right along the budget line, substituting good 1 for good 2.

We can summarize these results in the following way: When indifference curves are smooth, an interior solution is characterized by two conditions:

$$p_1x_1^* + p_2x_2^* \equiv M$$

and

$$MRS(x_1^*, x_2^*) \equiv p_1/p_2$$

We can repeat these statements in plain English:

When indifference curves are smooth and when the quantities demanded of both goods are positive, the utility-maximizing bundle is on the budget line at the point where the relative price is equal to the marginal rate of substitution.

---

3. Let us derive this characterization of the utility-maximizing solution by using the method of Lagrange multipliers introduced in the first footnote. The Lagrangian function is

$$L(x_1, x_2, \lambda) = U(x_1, x_2) + \lambda(M - p_1x_1 - p_2x_2)$$

Differentiating with respect to x_1, x_2, and λ and setting the results equal to zero, we obtain

$$\partial U(x_1, x_2)/\partial x_1 - \lambda p_1 = 0$$
$$\partial U(x_1, x_2)/\partial x_2 - \lambda p_2 = 0$$
$$M - p_1x_1 - p_2x_2 = 0$$

The last condition is familiar — the utility-maximizing bundle is on the budget line. It is the first statement characterizing an interior solution. Eliminating the lambdas (by combining the first two conditions), we get

$$\frac{\partial U(x_1, x_2)/\partial x_1}{\partial U(x_1, x_2)/\partial x_2} = \frac{p_1}{p_2}.$$

But, as we saw in Chapter 2, the left side of this expression is just $MRS(x_1^* x_2^*)$. Hence, we have

$$MRS(x_1^* x_2^*) = \frac{p_1}{p_2}$$

which is the second statement characterizing an interior solution. This second statement says that in equilibrium, the relative price must equal the marginal rate of substitution.

Corner Solutions

The characterization above presumes that the consumer decides to buy some of both goods. It is called an *interior solution* because graphically it always lies somewhere in the space between the two axes. But this characterization does *not* apply if the consumer decides not to buy even the smallest amount of a particular good. This case is called a *corner solution*, because graphically it lies, not in the interior between the two axes, but at a corner where the budget line intersects one of the two axes.

In fact, deciding not to buy a particular good is not an unusual or perverse choice. Imagine taking a walk through several large stores that offer various kinds of merchandise — hardware, groceries, clothing, electronic equipment, books, records, cosmetics — and tabulating the number of goods that you will never buy out of all the items for sale. Chances are that your list will be very long. Of the vast array of available goods, most of us choose not to buy most of them.

With two goods, two kinds of corner solutions are possible. We will focus on the case in which this consumer decides not to buy any of good 1 and instead chooses to spend the entire budget on good 2. In this corner solution, the utility-maximizing bundle is bundle ($x_1^* = 0$, $x_2^* = M/p_2$) — the bundle where the budget line intersects the x_2 axis. (Using the budget line from Problem 3.3, you can explore the corner solution in which the consumer spends the entire budget on good 1.)

What types of indifference curves give rise to corner solutions, and what types do not? If indifference curves *do not* intersect the x_2 axis, then we will *never* see a corner solution. In other words, no matter how expensive good 1 becomes, the consumer will persist in buying a positive quantity of it. This case is shown in Figure 3.5. Even when the price is relatively high, as in Figure 3.5b — the steep slope of the budget line is a telltale sign that good 1 is expensive relative to good 2 — the consumer still buys some of good 1. By definition, then, it must be an essential good.

On the other hand, if the indifference curves *do* intersect the x_2 axis, then a corner solution *is* possible. This case is shown in Figure 3.6. When the price of good 1 is moderate, as in Figure 3.6a, the consumer will decide to buy some of both goods. However, in Figure 3.6b, where good 1 is relatively expensive, the consumer decides not to buy any of good 1. That is, in Figure 3.6b, this consumer's utility-maximizing solution is this: $x_1^* = 0$ and $x_2^* = M/p_2$. In this circumstance, the consumer chooses to spend the whole budget on good 2. In the case shown in Figure 3.6, good 1 is an inessential good. If its price is too high, the consumer decides not to buy any.

When good 1 is an inessential good, what determines whether the result is an interior or a corner solution? The determining factor is the relationship between the relative price of good 1, p_1/p_2, and *MRS* at the point where the budget line intersects the x_2 axis. If $MRS(x_1, x_2)$ at the point $x_1 = 0$ and $x_2 = M/p_2$ is greater than p_1/p_2, as in Figure 3.6a, the result is an interior solution. If it is less than p_1/p_2, as in Figure 3.6b, the result is a corner solution.

FIGURE 3.5 Essential goods

If indifference curves do not intersect the x_2 axis, then x_1^* is always positive, and good 1 is therefore an essential good. In both (a), where p_1 is moderate, and (b), where p_1 is high, x_1^* is positive.

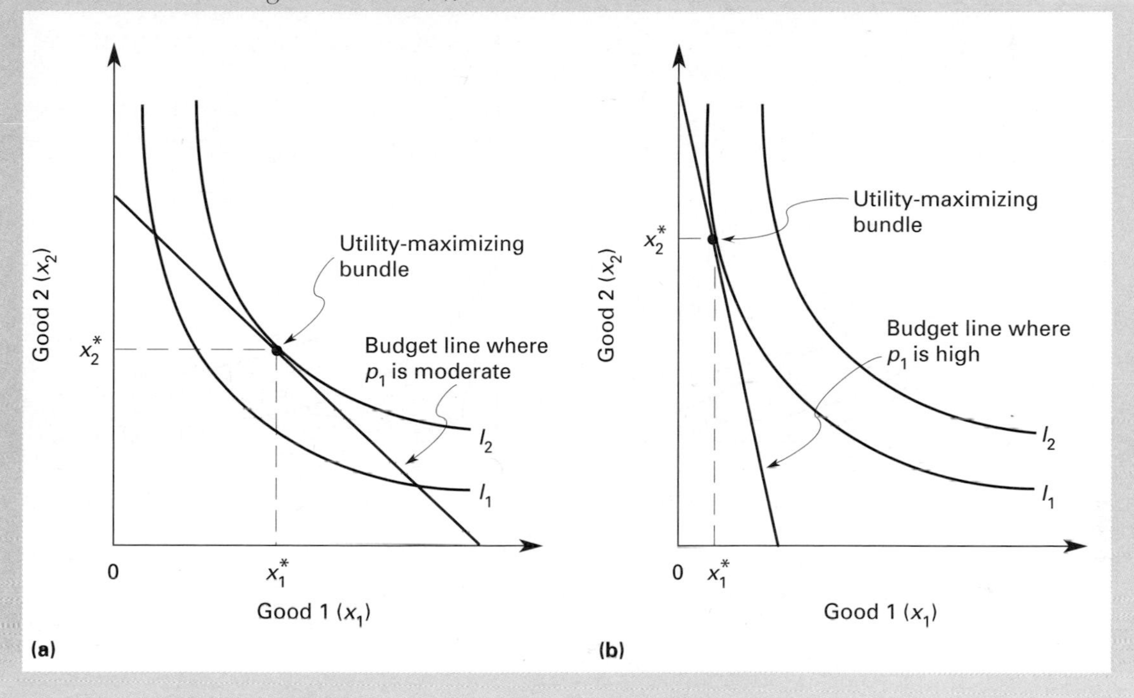

We can summarize these results as follows: If $MRS(x_1, x_2)$ at the point $x_1 = 0$ and $x_2 = M/p_2$ is less than p_1/p_2, the result is a corner solution in which the consumer buys only good 2:[4]

$$x_1^* = 0 \text{ and } x_2^* = M/p_2$$

4. We can use calculus techniques to see when we have a corner solution. We know from Chapter 2 that

$$MRS(x_1, x_2) = \frac{\partial U(x_1, x_2)/\partial x_1}{\partial U(x_1, x_2)/\partial x_2}$$

Hence, we have a corner solution if

$$\frac{\partial U(0, M/p_2)/\partial x_1}{\partial U(0, M/p_2)/\partial x_2} < \frac{p_1}{p_2}$$

For example, suppose that $U(x_1,x_2) = x_2 + x_1x_2$. Then

$$\frac{\partial U(0, M/p_2)/\partial x_1}{\partial U(0, M/p_2)/\partial x_2} = \frac{M}{p_2}$$

Hence $\quad x_1^* = 0 \text{ and } x_2^* = M/p_2 \quad \text{if } M < p_1$

As you may want to verify, $\quad x_1^* = \dfrac{(M - p_1)}{2p_1} \quad \text{and} \quad x_2^* = \dfrac{(M + p_1)}{2p_2} \quad \text{if } M \geq p_1.$

FIGURE 3.6 Inessential goods

If indifference curves intersect the x_2 axis, then there is always a p_1 large enough that $x_1^* = 0$, and good 1 is therefore an inessential good. In (b), for example, p_1 is so large that $x_1^* = 0$. In (a), p_1 is low enough that x_1^* is positive.

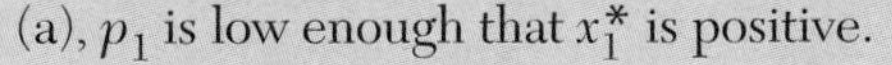

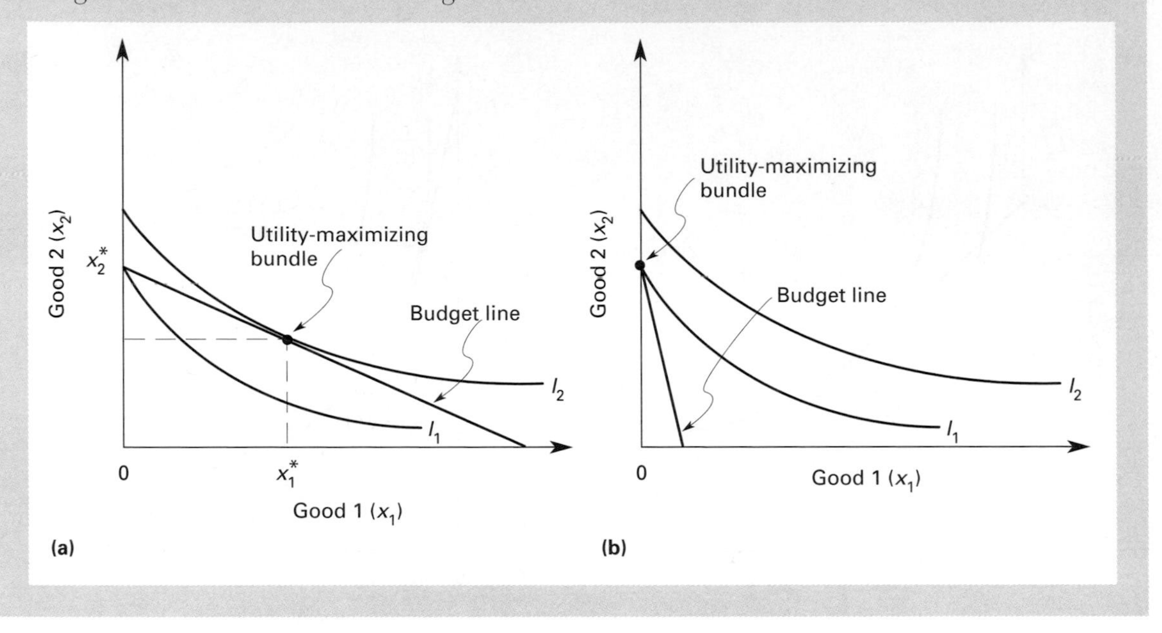

We can repeat these results in plain English:

If, at the point where the budget line intersects the x_2 axis, the budget line is steeper than the indifference curve, the consumer buys only good 2.

If we now look at a large group of people with heterogeneous preferences, we get an interesting prediction regarding the percentage of the group who consume an inessential good. Given any arbitrary price p_1 that is neither too high nor too low, some people will find themselves in the situation shown in Figure 3.6a and will buy a positive amount of good 1 while others will find themselves in the situation shown in Figure 3.6b and will buy any of it. Then, if we increase p_1 (the price of the inessential good) some people who were initially in the situation in Figure 3.6a will find themselves, after the price increase, in the situation in Figure 3.6b. In other words, we have derived the following prediction:

If the price of an inessential good increases, the percentage of the group who consume a positive amount of the good will decrease.

In the following problem, you can explore the case in which good 2 is an inessential good.

PROBLEM 3.5

Suppose that indifference curves intersect the x_1 axis but not the x_2 axis. Draw a figure in which the consumer chooses to buy only good 1, and describe the conditions that give rise to this corner solution.

Although we have discussed the consumer choice problem in the simple context of choosing bundles of goods, the model of utility maximization has very broad applications. Consider the case of taxation and wealth transfers. Given that governments are going to dip their hands into private pockets to pay for public services, what sort of taxation scheme would the taxpayer prefer? In other words, given that someone must pay a particular sum of money to the government, what sort of tax would leave him or her better off? On the other hand, if the government was to hand over money to an individual, would that individual be better off having cash, or goods in kind?

Application: Excise Tax versus Lump-Sum Tax

excise tax

lump-sum tax

We will compare two taxes: an excise tax and a lump-sum tax. An **excise tax** is one in which a given tax surcharge is added to the price of each unit of a particular good. Excise taxes on gasoline, liquor, and perfume are common examples. By contrast, a **lump-sum tax** is a fixed tax. Under this scheme, a government simply demands that an individual remit a certain sum. For example, the Conservative government in Britain first introduced and then was forced to review a highly controversial tax that has many of the features of a lump-sum tax — the Community Service Tax.

Imagine, then, that a government wants to raise a specified sum of money by imposing either a lump-sum tax or an excise tax on some good — gasoline, for example. From the taxpayer's point of view, which is preferable? The first thing to notice is that an excise tax increases the *relative price* of the taxed good to the consumer. By contrast, a lump-sum tax alters the *budget* available to the individual.

composite commodity

Let us suppose that good 1 is gasoline and that an excise tax on gasoline has been imposed. Good 2 will be the expenditure on all other goods. (Good 2 is what is called a **composite commodity**, and is discussed in the appendix.) Since good 2 is an expenditure, it is measured in dollars and its price is therefore $1.

Let us begin by considering a consumer — Tammy — before any tax is imposed. Her pretax budget line is the dashed line ACG in Figure 3.7, where x_1 is quantity of gasoline and x_2 is quantity of the composite good.

Now let us impose an excise tax t per unit of gasoline so that its price becomes p_1+t per unit rather than just p_1, where p_1 is the price not including the tax. Tammy's budget line is now the solid line ADH. We know that the new budget line is represented graphically by a line rotated downward from the point at which the pretax budget line intersects the x_2 axis. In other words, the same budget is still available (indicated by the intersection of both budget lines at the same point on the x_2 axis), but the price (inclusive of the excise tax) of gasoline is higher once an excise tax is in effect (indicated by the steeper pitch of the new budget line).

Once the excise tax is in place, Tammy chooses the consumption bundle at point D in Figure 3.7. The tax take, or the amount of tax the government collects, is just tx_1^* because x_1^* is the amount of gasoline Tammy buys and t is the tax per unit of gasoline. Let us identify the tax take graphically. In the absence of the excise tax, Tammy could have bought the bundle at point C on the pretax budget line. The tax take is therefore equal to the distance DC.

Now, what about the alternative scheme, in which a lump-sum tax yields the same revenue, distance DC in Figure 3.7? Once the lump-sum tax is imposed, Tammy's budget constraint is the solid line BDEF in Figure 3.7. The new budget line is below, but parallel to, the pretax budget line since Tammy's income — but not the prices she pays — has changed. Notice that the lump-sum tax budget line passes through point D.

FIGURE 3.7 **Excise versus lump-sum taxes**

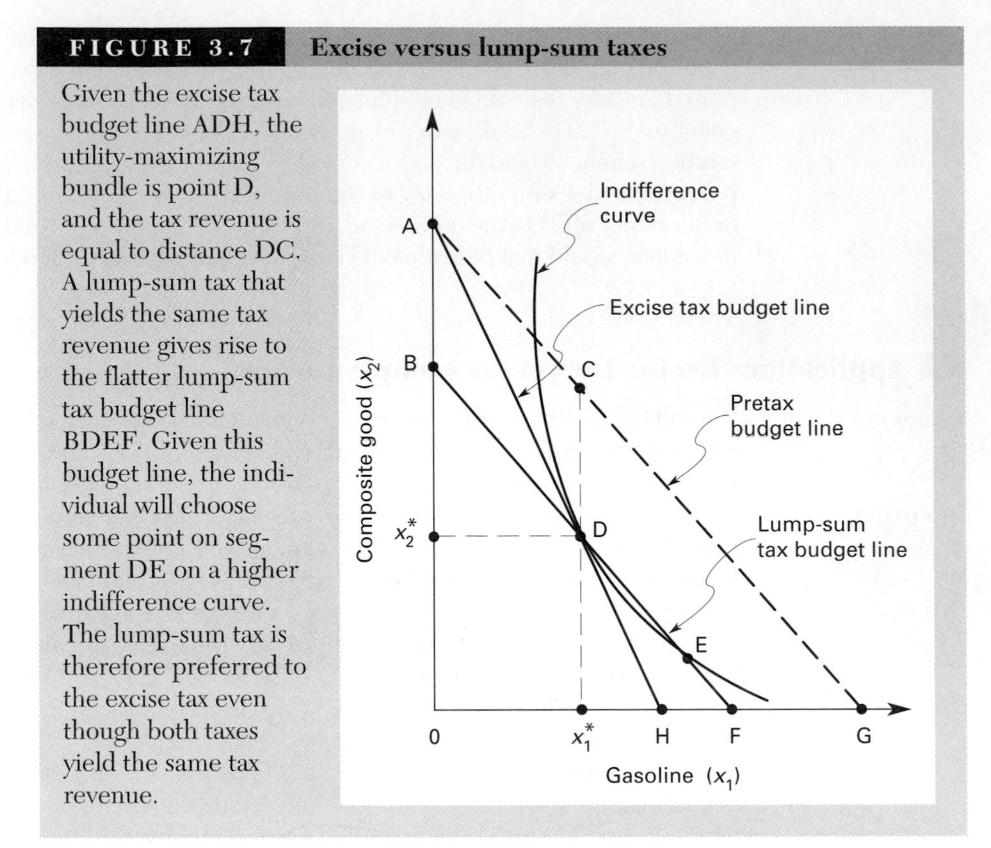

Given the excise tax budget line ADH, the utility-maximizing bundle is point D, and the tax revenue is equal to distance DC. A lump-sum tax that yields the same tax revenue gives rise to the flatter lump-sum tax budget line BDEF. Given this budget line, the individual will choose some point on segment DE on a higher indifference curve. The lump-sum tax is therefore preferred to the excise tax even though both taxes yield the same tax revenue.

Why? In the absence of any tax, the bundle at point C is attainable and, since the lump-sum tax is equal to distance DC, the bundle at D is attainable after the lump-sum tax has been deducted from her income.

Although Tammy could buy the bundle at D, she will choose instead some bundle on segment DE of the lump-sum budget line because this segment lies above and to the right of the indifference curve in Figure 3.7. By nonsatiation, any point on segment DE is preferred to the bundle at D. Of course, this means that Tammy is better off with the lump-sum tax than she is with the excise tax. In other words, a lump-sum tax is the preferable form of taxation:

Given a choice between a lump-sum tax and an excise tax that raise the same revenue, the consumer will choose the lump-sum tax.[5]

5. At the outset of this section, we were careful to discuss the question of the preferred form of taxation in the context of a single person, Tammy. To extend the result directly to a larger group of taxpayers in a municipality, province, state, or nation, however, we would have to assume that the group is composed of taxpayers whose individual preferences and income are all *identical*. Yet taxpayers in any particular jurisdiction are not so much alike. We therefore must be cautious in applying these principles of taxation to real situations. Imagine, for example, the choice between a lump-sum tax and an excise tax on cigarettes that raise the same revenue in a jurisdiction where half the taxpayers are smokers and half are nonsmokers. The heavy smokers will clearly prefer the lump-sum tax and the nonsmokers will prefer the excise tax.

Application: Membership Fees as Lump-Sum Taxes

representative consumer

If we randomly pick two Canadians, their preferences will probably be quite different. However, in some situations the assumption of a **representative consumer** — the assumption that the preferences and income of an individual randomly selected from the group will be characteristic of each person in that group — is likely to be nearly true. Private clubs, for example, cater primarily to people who seek the same amenities and can all afford the membership fee. Because club members can, in a rough way, be viewed as self-selecting according to certain preferences and income levels, any individual club member we select is likely to be representative of the whole membership.

Let us broaden the meaning of taxation to apply to any circumstances in which sums are taken out of someone's pocket and used to fund some project of a group to which that person belongs. If the project is a private club, then what is the preferred way for such a club to assess its membership fees? The maximization assumption says that the club will charge in the manner most preferable to its members. In fact, many private clubs actually sell a membership fee that just covers their overhead and then sell their services at marginal cost. That membership fee is analogous to a lump-sum tax.

Application: Cash versus In-kind Payments

Although governments produce many goods and services, an extremely large part of any government budget involves transfers to individuals. Many times these transfers are simple cash grants that shift the budget constraints of the recipients, but often, especially with transfers to low income households, the payments have restrictions placed on them. In the United States, food stamps are a common transfer to the poor. These stamps can only be used for the purchase of food, and are not the same as cash. In Canada, there are a number of such in-kind transfers that vary from province to province including housing, food allowances, eyeware, and medical services.

Let's see how our utility analysis of choice handles cases of in-kind transfers. Like the case of lump-sum and excise taxes you will see that the model is very general and easily handles variations on choice constraints.

Suppose we have two people, Carla and Murray, who are both eligible to receive food vouchers. These vouchers provide \$300 of food per month and cannot be sold to purchase other goods. Suppose both Carla and Murray have identical initial incomes of \$500 per month, but that their preferences are different: Carla prefers food relative to Murray. Figure 3.8 shows the initial situation before the vouchers are received, assuming the price of both goods is 1. Carla maximizes her utility at point A while Murray does the same at point B. Given their different preferences, Carla consumes more food and less of the composite good than does Murray.

When a voucher is handed out it increases the opportunities to consume more of both goods, but in a special way. Given that both have an income of \$500 and that the vouchers cannot be used on the composite good, after the vouchers are received they can still only purchase 500 units of the composite good. The new budget line shifts out, but is truncated at the top.

For Carla this truncation is irrelevant. She prefers food and her new tangency is nowhere near the kink in the budget line. Notice, however, that Carla still increases her consumption of both goods. For Murray, though, the situation is much different. He maximizes his utility at point D, where the budget line is kinked. If a cash transfer of \$300 had been made, Murray would have maximized his utility at point E, but under the voucher system Murray is unable to do this. The voucher is forcing Murray to consume more food than he otherwise would.

FIGURE 3.8 Cash transfer versus in-kind transfers

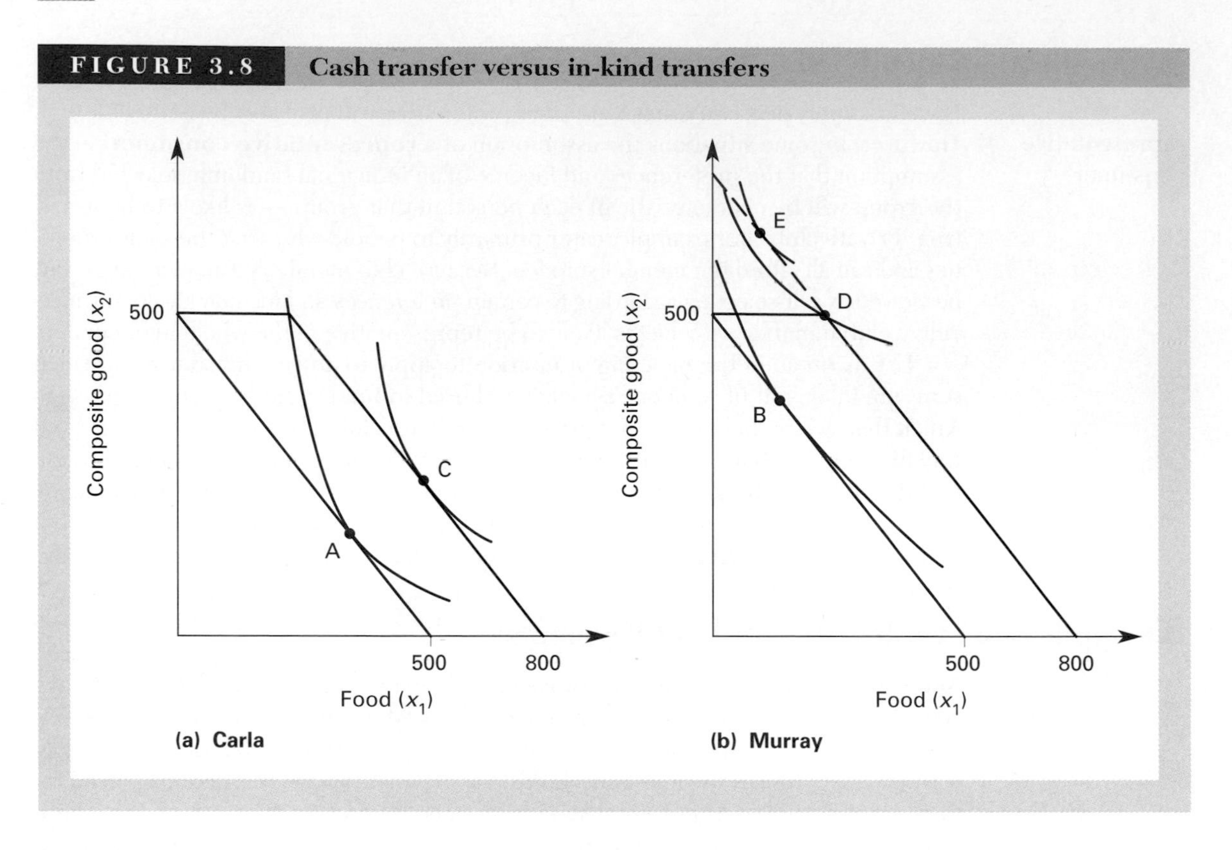

Hence a cash transfer would always be preferred *by the recipient*, rather than a gift in kind. A cash transfer shifts out the budget constraint as a simple income effect and allows individuals the freedom to choose the consumption bundle that maximizes utility. Of course, this raises the immediate question: why do we observe in-kind transfers and restrictions on choices? There would appear to be many reasons, depending on the transfer in question. Governments may transfer food and shelter because they want to prevent freedom of choice. That is, they may want to prevent the consumption of goods that they deem may injure individuals (like alcohol and cigarettes). On the other hand, restrictions on transfers may encourage other types of behaviour. Our universities pay part of our salaries in terms of nice office space. Some faculty may prefer to be paid more income and buy office space on campus, but the university no doubt suspects that most faculty would buy little space on campus. By restricting our consumption choices they encourage us to spend more time on campus and be more available to students. There are other instances where the recipient seems to prefer in-kind transfers. If you don't believe this, try giving your boyfriend or girlfriend a cheque on his or her next birthday and see what the reaction is. These are the most puzzling cases and require more economics than our current model can handle. We return to issues like these in the last chapters of the book.

Application: The Welfare Paradox of Housing Prices

The largest single purchase for most people is their home. Houses often account for one-third of most asset portfolios held by private individuals. Almost everyone who owns a home pays some attention to its market value. They seem pleased when its price goes up, and less happy when its price goes down. Imagine you just bought your own house, and after the purchase was complete the price of the house fell. Would you be better off or worse off? Let's suppose nothing else changes but the price of houses. On the one hand the value of your house went down (a bad thing), but on the other hand you now face lower prices (a good thing). Perhaps the effect is ambiguous?

Now suppose instead of the house price falling, the price increases after you make your purchase. On the one hand you've made a capital gain on your purchase, but again, prices are higher and this is a bad thing. Are you better or worse off? The amazing, counter-intuitive, answer is: you are better off in both circumstances!

Consider Figure 3.9, which has the square metres of housing purchased on the horizontal axis and the expenditure of all other goods on the vertical axis. The initial budget constraint is given by the solid line P_0, and at this price you consume the bundle (a) and have a level of utility equal to I_1. This point (a) is an endowment of housing and other goods. When the relative price of housing falls, the budget line rotates through the endowment point to become the dotted line marked P_L. At this lower relative price you demand more housing square metres and less of other goods. This substitution puts you on the higher indifference curve I_2, and you consume bundle (c). Notice that you've made it to a higher level of utility. In other words, the fall in housing prices has made you better off. When the relative price of housing increases, the budget line again rotates through the endowment point and becomes the dotted line marked P_H. At this higher relative price you substitute out of housing and into other goods. This process leads you to consume bundle (b) and reach the level of utility I_3. Again, you are better off.

The paradox of improving welfare regardless of the change in price results from the ability to substitute. When the relative price of housing increases, it means the relative price of other goods falls. As you move out of the expensive housing and into the cheaper other goods, you make yourself better off. The same reasoning applies when the relative price of housing falls. In effect, owning a large asset and consuming the amount you own acts as a form of insurance against changes in price. This no doubt explains the strong desire for most people to want to own their own home.

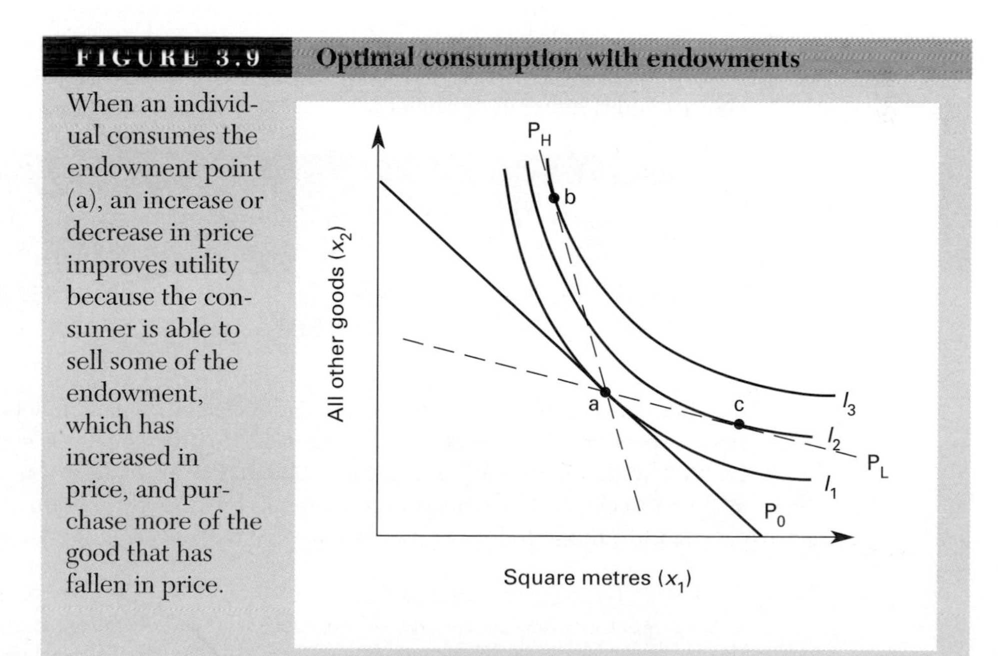

FIGURE 3.9 **Optimal consumption with endowments**

When an individual consumes the endowment point (a), an increase or decrease in price improves utility because the consumer is able to sell some of the endowment, which has increased in price, and purchase more of the good that has fallen in price.

3.5 Comparative Statics Analysis of Demand

When we differentiated between essential and inessential goods, we were creating a *classification* or *taxonomy* based on the kind of consumption response a consumer makes to a change in the price of a good. The response in the case of an inessential good is to give it up if the price goes too high; in the case of an essential good, to continue to buy some amount regardless of price. If consumer demand theory is to be useful, it must provide a framework for asking and answering questions like these about how a consumer responds to such changes: How does an increase in a consumer's income affect his or her consumption decisions? How does an increase in the price level affect consumption decisions? What happens if the price of one good goes up and all other prices remain the same? Will consumer demand for that good necessarily decline? Will demand for all other goods necessarily increase?

We can generate a great number of such questions. There are, however, three fundamental questions about consumption responses.

1. How will a consumer's demand for some good — say, good 1 — change in response to an increase (or decrease) in income (M)?
2. How will a consumer's demand for good 1 change in response to an increase (or decrease) in the price of good 2 (p_2)?
3. How will a consumer's demand for good 1 change in response to an increase (or decrease) in the price of good 1 (p_1)?

Notice that all three questions are about a consumer's response to a change in the value of an exogenous variable in a demand function. By altering the values of exogenous variables, we can compare solutions to the utility-maximization problem before and after the change. You were first introduced to this procedure, called comparative statics analysis, in Chapter 1. It is termed *statics analysis* because it is concerned with static equilibrium points rather than with the dynamic adjustments between these points. And it is termed *comparative* because it allows us to compare consumer choices in different circumstances.[6]

PROBLEM 3.6

Consider the following demand function — one that you first encountered in Problem 3.4: $x_1^* = M/(p_1 + p_2)$. Suppose that initially $M = \$120$, $p_1 = \$1$, and $p_2 = \$1$. How does x_1^* respond to a \$1 increase in p_1? To a \$1 increase in p_2? To a \$2 increase in M?

Because in Problem 3.4 you had in hand a specific demand function — one derived from a specific utility function — you were able to provide *precise answers* to the comparative statics questions posed in the problem. For example, given p_1 and p_2 equal to \$1, you discovered that whenever M increases by \$2, consumption of good 1 increases by one unit. In the following sections, we will be concerned with more general ques-

6. These qualitative comparative statics questions are simply questions about the signs of partial derivatives of demand functions. For example, is the partial derivative of the demand function for good 1 with respect to M always positive?

tions that presume only that a consumer maximizes his or her utility. As a result, we will not look for precise answers to comparative statics questions, but instead for *qualitative answers* that indicate the *direction* but not the magnitude of the demand response. For instance, we will ask: Does utility maximization imply that a consumer will buy less of a particular good when its price rises?

3.6 Consumption Response to a Change in Income

What will happen to the demand for good 1 as income M changes? More precisely: If the prices of both goods are held constant and if income rises, will a consumer buy more, less, or just the same amount of good 1?

Normal Goods and Inferior Goods

The answer depends on just what that good is. Casual observation suggests that as consumers become wealthier, they buy less of some goods and more of others. For example, many students eat lots of relatively inexpensive pasta for dinner before they graduate, but switch to relatively more expensive meat once they leave school and find well-paid, full-time employment. This observation provides us with a taxonomy: a good is a **normal good** if consumption of the good *increases* as income increases. It is an **inferior good** if consumption *decreases* as income increases.

normal good

inferior good

In Figure 3.10a, good 1 is a normal good. We have constructed three dashed budget lines corresponding to income levels \$100, \$150, and \$200. Notice that the budget

FIGURE 3.10 **Normal and inferior goods**

In (a), as income increases, so does quantity demanded of good 1; good 1 is therefore a normal good. In (b), as income increases, quantity demanded of good 1 decreases; good 1 is therefore an inferior good.

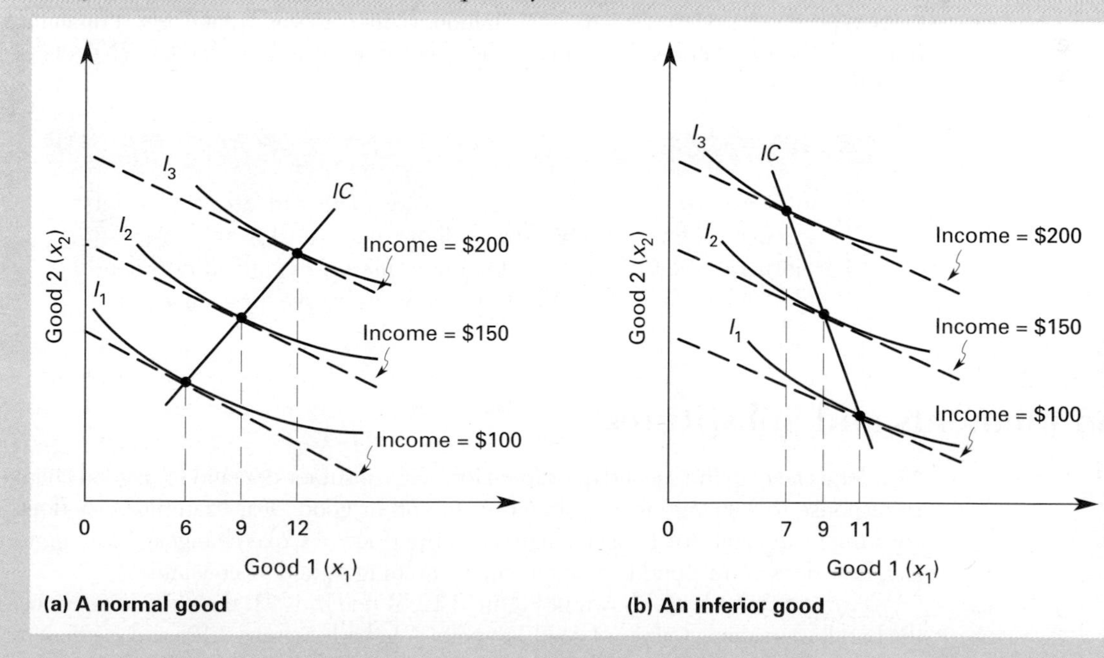

lines have the same slope (and are therefore parallel) since prices are held constant. Only income changes. Notice, too, that as this consumer's income increases from \$100 to \$150 to \$200, his or her consumption of good 1 increases from 6 to 9 to 12 units. We know, then, that for this consumer, good 1 is a normal good. The line labelled *IC* in Figure 3.10a, which passes through the utility-maximizing bundles that are generated as this consumer's income increases, is called an **income-consumption path**. In Figure 3.10a, its slope is positive because both good 1 and good 2 are normal goods. (Can you confirm that good 2 is also a normal good?)

income-consumption path

In Figure 3.10b, good 1 is an inferior good. As this consumer's income increases from \$100 to \$150 to \$200, his or her consumption of good 1 decreases from 11 to 9 to 7 units. Notice that the slope of the income-consumption path *IC* is negative in this case. (Is good 2 a normal or inferior good in Figure 3.10b?)

PROBLEM 3.7

Are the following statements true or false?

1. When *IC* is negatively sloped, good 1 is invariably inferior.
2. When *IC* is negatively sloped, one good is inferior and the other is normal.
3. Both goods cannot be inferior.
4. Both goods cannot be normal.

Engel Curves

In Figure 3.11, we have used the information from each of the cases in Figure 3.10 to construct a relationship between income and the utility-maximizing quantity of good 1. This relationship is named an **Engel curve** after the nineteenth-century Prussian statistician Ernst Engel. In effect, we have plotted the demand function for good 1 when income is allowed to vary and prices are held constant. For a normal good, the Engel curve is positively sloped because, by definition, x_1^* increases as M increases. For an inferior good, the Engel curve is negatively sloped because, again by definition, x_1^* decreases as M increases.

Engel curve

PROBLEM 3.8

Suppose that *MRS* depends only on x_1. Then *MRS* is identical at all points on any vertical line in (x_1, x_2) space. Show that good 1 is neither inferior nor normal — that is, show that the utility-maximizing quantity of good 1 is independent of income. Illustrate the Engel curve for such a good.

3.7 Complements and Substitutes

Now let us take up the second question: How will consumer demand for a good change in response to a change in the price of some other good? For example, how does a consumer's demand for Pepsi change when the price of Coke changes? More generally, how does x_1^* respond to a change in p_2, holding p_1 and M constant?

Two possibilities are shown in Figure 3.12. When p_2 is \$1, the consumer chooses the bundle containing 6 units of good 1 at point A in both Figures 3.12a and 3.12b. Now,

FIGURE 3.11 Engel curves

An Engel curve is a graph of a demand function, holding all prices constant and allowing income to vary. Income is plotted on the horizontal axis and quantity demanded on the vertical axis. In (a), the Engel curve for a normal good is positively sloped. In (b), the Engel curve for an inferior good is negatively sloped.

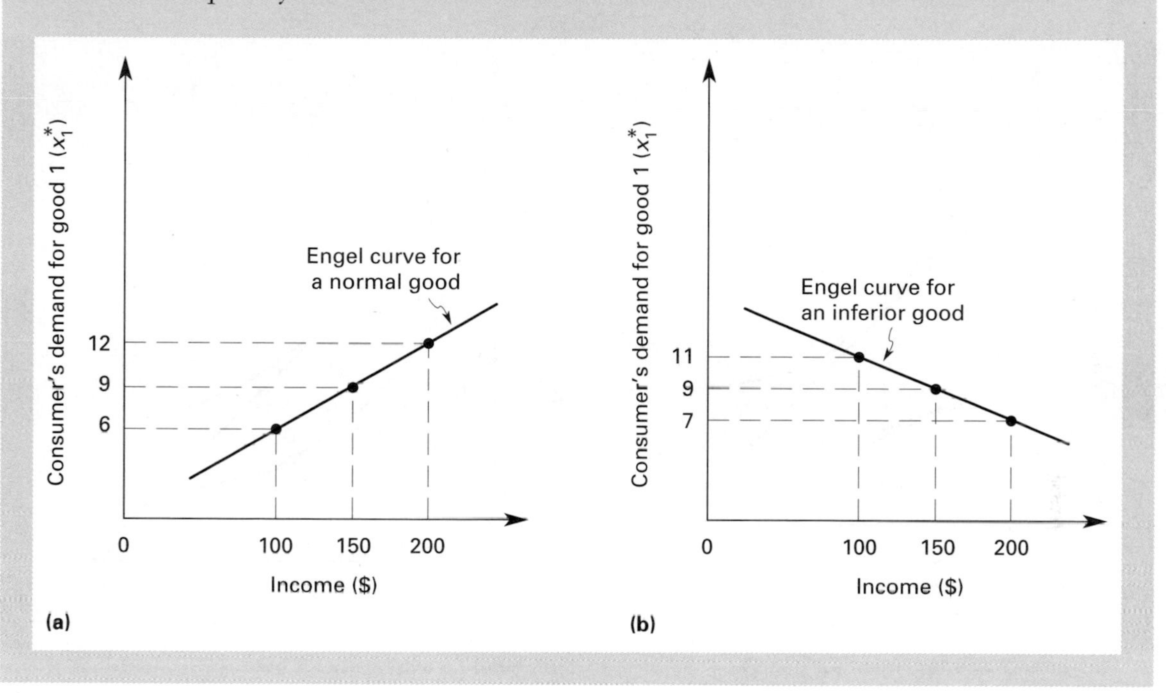

what happens when p_2 rises to $2? The higher price for good 2 causes the budget line to pivot around point F, shifting it from GAF to HCF. Because of the increase in p_2, the quantity demanded of good 1 *decreases* to 4 in Figure 3.12a, but it *increases* to 8 in Figure 3.12b. In other words, the consumer's response depends on the consumer's preferences. When p_2 increases, the consumer may decide to buy either more or less of good 1. Both possibilities are consistent with utility-maximizing behaviour

What have we learned? Although our theory gives us no qualitative result, it does provide us with a useful taxonomy. If x_1^* decreases in response to an increase in p_2 as in Figure 3.12a, we say that good 2 is a **complement** for good 1. Movies and popcorn, computers and software, and tennis balls and tennis rackets are all examples of complements. When the price of a movie goes up, a consumer might decide to go to fewer movies and therefore buy less popcorn. The utility function $U(x_1, x_2) = \min(x_1, x_2)$ — a function you explored in Problems 3.4 and 3.6 — illustrates the case of *perfect complementarity*. Right skis and left skis, for instance, are perfect complements since you do not decide to buy one ski without buying the other.

complement

On the other hand, if x_1^* increases in response to an increase in p_2, as in Figure 3.12b, we say that good 2 is a **substitute** for good 1. Coke and Pepsi, coffee and tea, or Volvos and BMWs might be thought of as substitutes. The utility function $U(x_1, x_2) = x_1 + x_2$ — the function we used in Chapter 2 to capture Anna's preferences — illustrates the case of *perfect substitutability*. As you know, when p_1 is equal to p_2,

substitute

FIGURE 3.12 The consumption response to a change in the price of another good

In (a), the quantity demanded of good 1 decreases from 6 to 4 as the price of good 2 increases from \$1 to \$2. In this case, good 2 is said to be a complement for good 1. In (b), the quantity demanded of good 1 increases from 6 to 8 as the price of good 2 increases from \$1 to \$2. In this case, good 2 is said to be a substitute for good 1.

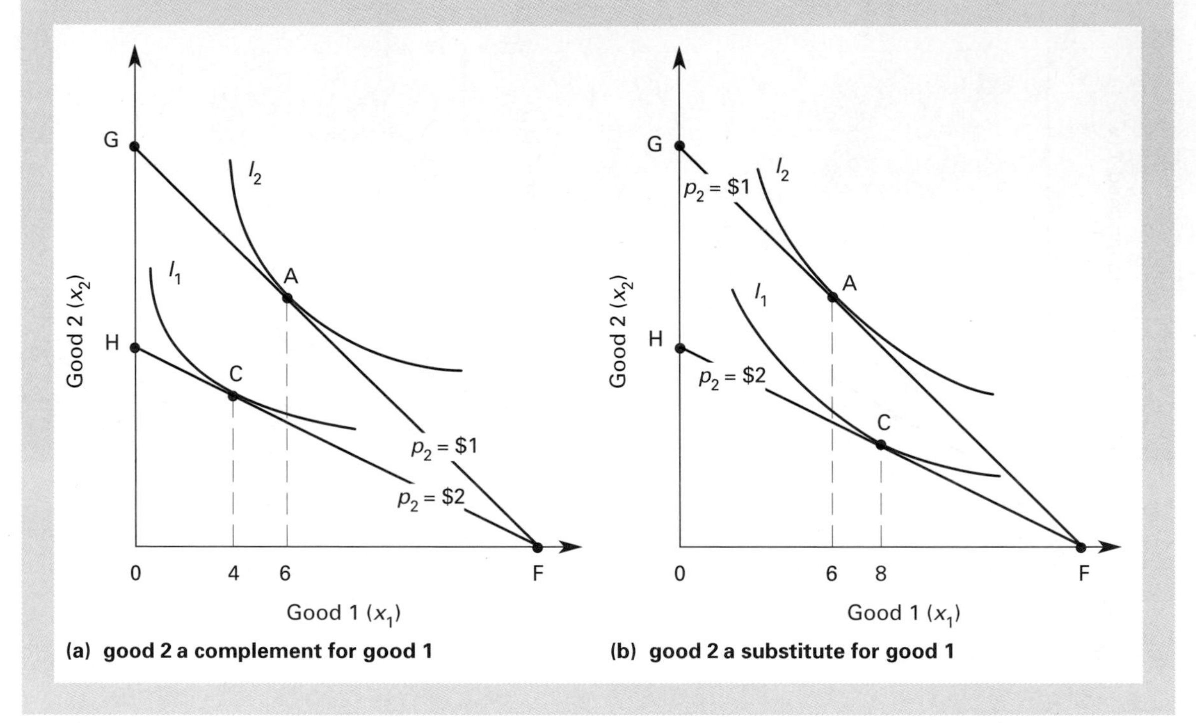

(a) good 2 a complement for good 1

(b) good 2 a substitute for good 1

these preferences imply that any bundle on the budget line is a utility-maximizing bundle. However, if p_2 decreases ever so slightly, the consumption of good 1 goes to zero. For example, if the price of one brand of soft drink rises by just a bit, a consumer will switch to a substitute brand — if they are perfect substitutes and if the consumer is initially indifferent between them.

3.8 Consumption Response to a Change in Price

Now let us turn to the last and most important comparative statics question: What will happen to the demand for a good — say, good 1 — as its own price changes, holding the price of the other good p_2 and income M constant? What happens to a particular consumer's demand for Darjeeling tea, for instance, as its price rises or falls?

In Figure 3.13a, we have drawn three budget lines and indicated the three resulting utility-maximizing bundles at points E, F, and G. (Notice that we have not included the corresponding indifference curves, which are tangent to the three budget lines at these three points.) In constructing this figure, we have held p_2 constant at \$2 and M constant at \$60. And we have used three different values for p_1: p_1 is \$4 on the lowest budget line, \$3 on the intermediate budget line, and \$2 on the highest budget line.

The Price-Consumption Path

price-consumption path

The line labelled *PC* in Figure 3.13a is called a **price-consumption path**. It connects the utility-maximizing bundles that arise as p_1 is successively decreased from $4 to $3 to $2. The price-consumption path is analogous to the income-consumption path, with this difference: in the income-consumption path, only income varied; here, only the price of good 1 varies.

The Demand Curve

ordinary demand curve

law of demand

We can use the price-consumption path to construct a relationship between the price of good 1 and the quantity demanded in much the same way that we used the income-consumption path to construct an Engel curve. This relationship — which we will call the consumer's **ordinary demand curve** for good 1 — is shown in Figure 3.13b. The three points E′, F′, and G′ on the demand curve correspond to the utility-maximizing points E, F, and G in Figure 3.13a. The demand curve is a graph of the demand function when p_1 is varied and p_2 and M are held constant. Just as common sense suggests, price and quantity demanded are negatively related in Figure 3.13b. As price increases from $2 to $3 to $4, the quantity demanded decreases from 19 to 12 to 8.[7] Although we will qualify this inverse relationship between price and quantity in the next chapter, the **law of demand**, as it is called, is one of the most powerful and subtle ideas in all social science.

▶ Application: Ingenious Advertising and the Demand Curve

Not long ago, a well-known grocery store, Tradewell, launched an advertising campaign against a rival store, Safeway. In the ad an interviewer approaches a customer coming out of the Tradewell store and inspects the groceries purchased. The interviewer then says "Let's go over to Safeway and *buy the exact same bundle,* and see if the total bill is higher." Sure enough, the next clip shows the customer coming out of Safeway with the same bundle of goods and the bill is higher. No matter who came out of the store the result was always the same and the commercial always ended with the interviewer saying "and there you have it, folks; Tradewell, where you always trade well for the lowest prices."

A skeptic might think that the entire affair was simply staged. However, the experiment is actually a clever exploitation of the theory of choice and the law of demand that we have developed thus far. When consumers go to Tradewell they face a host of different products and prices. Given their preferences and budget constraint they maximize their utility — they cannot do any better. This maximization process involves tradeoffs. If cream cheese is on sale at Tradewell, the consumer substitutes into cream cheese, and away from goods that have higher prices. Hence, when the customer comes out of Tradewell, the bundle of groceries is biased towards goods that were low in price at Tradewell. Assuming that the prices of identical goods at Safeway and Tradewell are not identical (because of in-store specials and the like), if you force a customer to buy the Tradewell bundle at Safeway *it must cost more.*

Let's consider this case a little more carefully. Suppose that the two stores each carry the same items and each have the same regular prices, with the only difference being

7. It is customary in plotting this type of relationship to put the exogenous variable on the horizontal axis and the endogenous variable on the vertical axis. Although we followed this custom when we plotted the Engel curve, tradition dictates that we violate it when we plot the demand curve. The demand curve has quantity demanded (the endogenous variable) on the horizontal axis and price (the exogenous variable) on the vertical axis.

FIGURE 3.13 **The price-consumption path and the demand function**

In (a), the price-consumption path *PC* passes through the utility-maximizing consumption bundles that are generated as the price of good 1 changes, holding income and all other prices constant. In (b), the ordinary demand curve is the graph of the demand for good 1 as its price changes.

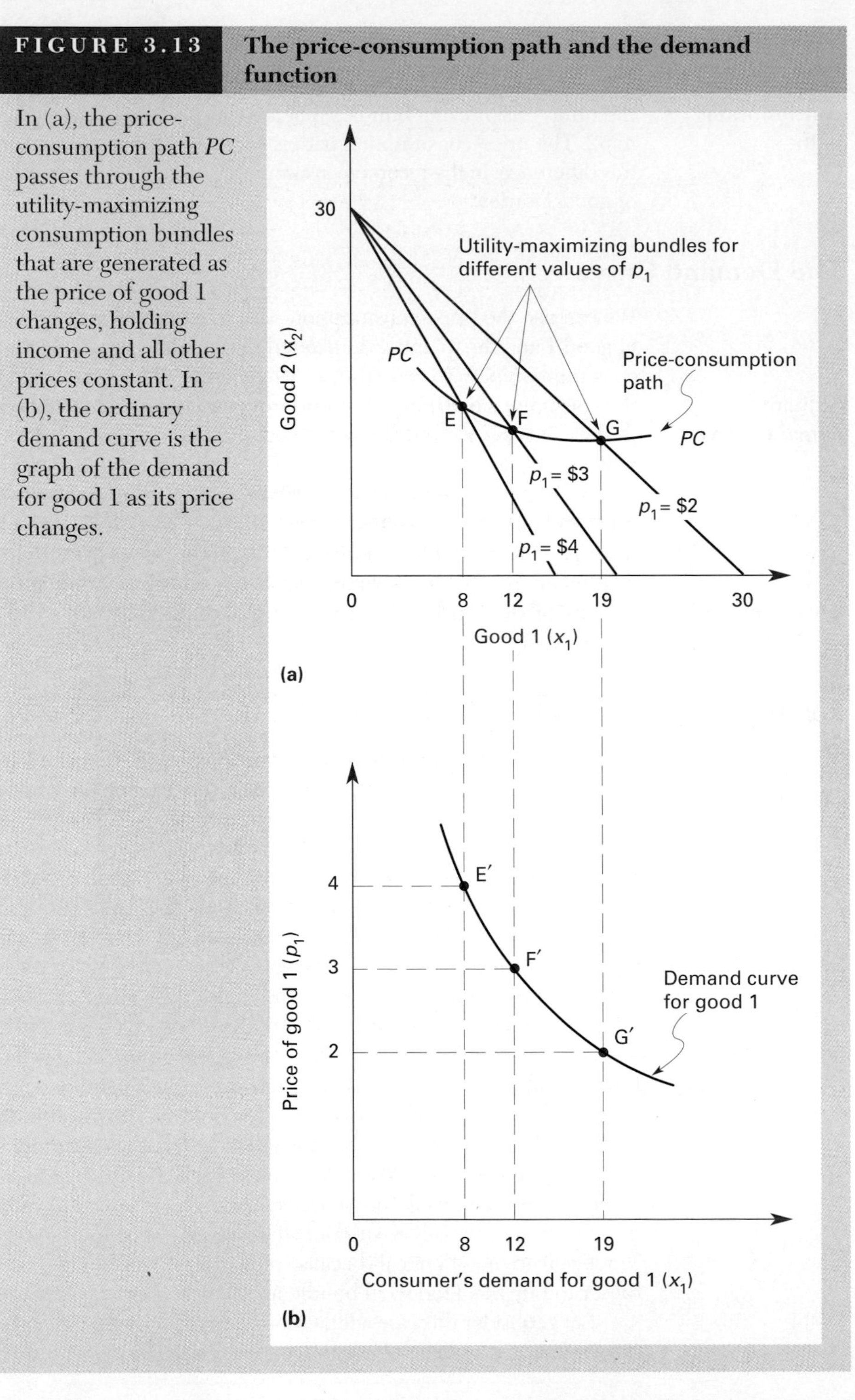

that different items are on sale throughout the week. For example, both Tradewell and Safeway might carry corn flakes for \$5 a box, but for one week Tradewell might have it on sale for \$3. To make the example trivial, suppose the consumer buys only corn flakes and, at \$3, buys five boxes for a total cost of \$15. Clearly if the consumer is now forced to buy five boxes at Safeway it will cost $25. When more than one good is purchased the same result holds because consumers always buy more of the cheaper goods and fewer of the more expensive ones. The irony of this whole affair is that doing the same thing with customers leaving Safeway would have shown that total expenditures were always lower at Safeway. Obviously this is not a wise procedure for determining which store has the lower prices (more on this in the next chapter). To make sure you understand this application, do the following problem.

PROBLEM 3.9

Suppose there are only three goods at both Safeway and Tradewell: meat, fruit, and canned goods. To make matters even simpler, suppose that all three goods have the following demand function: $x = 11 - p$, where x is the quantity demanded of either meat, fruit, or canned goods and p is the respective price. The regular prices at both stores are $10 for all goods, however, due to store specials the current prices at Tradewell are $p_m = 10$, $p_f = 8$, and $p_{cg} = 10$, while the current prices at Safeway are $p_m = 8$, $p_f = 10$, and $p_{cg} = 8$.

a. What is the optimal quantity of each good bought at Tradewell? What is the total expenditure?

b. Using the same *quantities* from (a), but the *prices* from Safeway, calculate the new total expenditure.

c. Now repeat (a) and (b), but start with an optimal bundle from Safeway.

3.9 Elasticity

We have seen how the quantity demanded of a particular good responds to a change in an exogenous variable; however, how do we compare *measures of responsiveness*? To make meaningful comparisons we need a *unit-free* measure — one that is not based on a particular measure like gallons or litres. In this section we will develop a general unit-free measure of responsiveness that can be used in a variety of contexts.

To see why the measure must be unit-free, let us look at two hypothetical Engel curves in Figure 3.14. A hypothetical Engel curve for gasoline is shown in Figure 3.14a. Notice that the unit of measure for gasoline is the litre. A hypothetical Engel curve for electricity is shown in Figure 3.14b. Notice that the unit of measure for electricity is the kilowatt-hour. In both cases income is measured in dollars.

In which of these two cases is the response of quantity demanded to a $1 increase in income greater? A glance at the two figures suggests that the right answer is gasoline because the Engel curve for gasoline is more steeply pitched than the Engel curve for electricity. However, if the unit of measure for gasoline is changed from the litre to the gallon, we get the much flatter, dashed Engel curve $E'E'$ in Figure 3.14, suggesting that the right answer is electricity.

The point is that we cannot compare demand responsiveness meaningfully by comparing the slopes of the Engel curves in Figure 3.14 because the units of measurement are not the same. Furthermore, we cannot make the comparison meaningful by choosing the same unit of measurement for each, because gasoline cannot be measured in kilowatt-hours or electricity in litres or gallons. What we need is a *unit-free measure of responsiveness*.

FIGURE 3.14 The need for a unit-free measure of responsiveness

Because the Engel curve in (a) is steeper than the Engel curve in (b), the demand for gasoline appears to be more responsive to changes in income than the demand for electricity. But the appearance is deceiving. For example, when we measure gasoline in gallons instead of litres, the Engel curve for gasoline in the line E′E′, and the demand for gasoline appears to be less responsive. Meaningful comparisons require a unit-free measure of responsiveness.

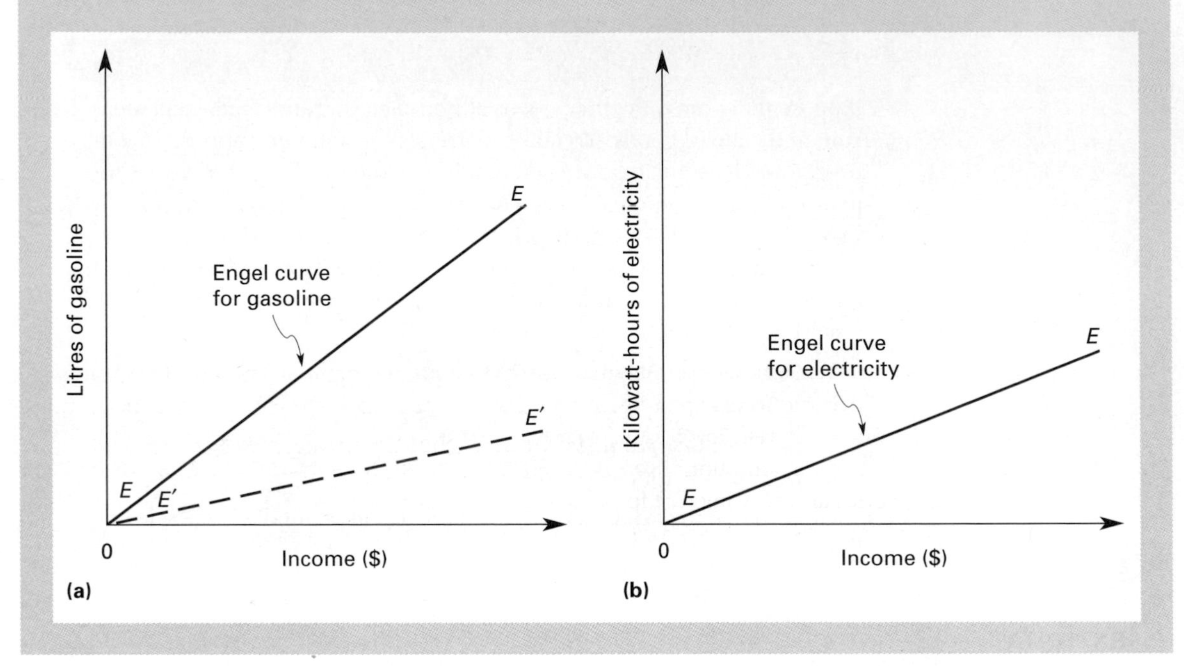

Economists use a number called an elasticity to measure the responsiveness of the quantity demanded of one good to a change in one of the exogenous variables: prices or income. For example, we may be interested in how the quantity of chocolate bars responds to the price of chocolate bars. Or we may be interested in how the quantity of chocolate bars responds to the price of peanuts, or changes in the income of consumers. Depending on which exogenous variable changes, we get a different elasticity measure. Hence, if we are interested in how the amount of one good changes when its own price changes, we call this the **own-price elasticity**. If we let the good be called x_1, and its price be p_1, then the own-price elasticity is denoted as E_{11} and is defined as:

own-price elasticity

$$E_{11} = \text{Percentage change in } x_1 \div \text{Percentage change in } P_1 = \frac{(\Delta x_1/x_1)}{(\Delta p_1/p_1)}$$

This can be written as

$$E_{11} = (\Delta x_1/\Delta p_1)(p_1/x_1)$$

where Δp_1 is the old price of good 1 minus the new price, and Δx_1 is the quantity demanded at the old price minus the quantity demanded at the new price. Notice that the simplified version of the own-price elasticity in the last equation has two components: the first is the inverse of the slope of the demand curve $(\Delta x_1/\Delta p_1)$; the second is a weight determined by the location along the demand curve (p_1/x_1). Supposing that the law of demand holds, or that the ordinary demand curve is downward sloping, then Δx_1 and Δp_1 have the opposite signs, and E_{11} will be negative. The value of the elasticity number measures the degree to which one good can be substituted for another. Large absolute numbers indicate the existence of good substitutes, while small absolute numbers indicate the lack of good substitutes. For example, the own-price elasticity for Molson's beer is quite high, because other beers are close substitutes. On the other hand, the own-price elasticity for all beers taken together is considerably lower. In general, the more broadly defined the good, the lower the own-price elasticity.

arc elasticity

E is called the **arc elasticity** because it measures the discrete change in x_1 when there is a discrete, measurable change in either p_1, p_2, or M.[8] If we allow the changes in the exogenous variables to approach zero we obtain a **marginal** or **point elasticity**. When we discuss elasticities, we will always be talking about point elasticities. To keep the terminology simple, however, we will drop the adjective *point* and refer simply to the *elasticity* of one variable with respect to another.[9]

marginal or point elasticity

Some Own-Price Elasticities of Demand

The price elasticity of demand for cigarettes has received a great deal of attention in recent years. One strategy that governments have used to reduce cigarette consumption is to raise the excise tax on cigarettes, thereby raising the price of cigarettes and — to the extent that consumption is responsive to price — decreasing consumption of cigarettes. Cigarettes are a commodity for which preferences vary a great deal. Many people dislike them and would only consume them if paid large sums of money. Others cannot get through a day without smoking several packs. In between lie consumers with less extreme preferences. Our theory of demand predicts that as the price of cigarettes increases (decreases) the percentage of the population who choose to smoke will decrease (increase). Is this prediction borne out by experience? And if it is, just how responsive is smoking behaviour to a change in the price of cigarettes? For example, would a $1 increase in the price of a pack result in a substantial reduction in the percentage of people who smoke?

price elasticity of demand

We can use aggregate data to compute a price elasticity of demand for the average consumer. The **price elasticity of demand** for a good is the elasticity of quantity consumed per capita with respect to the price of the good. There have been many studies of the demand for cigarettes over the years. Lewit and Coate (1982) estimate the price elasticity in the United States to be –0.42. Wasserman (1988) calculates the price elasticity to be –0.23, and Hersch (2000) finds an elasticity for women to be –0.55 and for men –0.44. Over a 20-year period, these elasticities seem remarkably stable. They mean that a 10 percent increase in price would lead to a fall in quantity demanded between 2.3 percent and 5.5 percent. Notice that the demand for cigarettes is **inelastic**. This makes sense given its addictive character.

inelastic

If you choose a good, you can almost bet someone has estimated its own-price elasticity. Just as some examples, McCarthy (1996) estimated the own-price elasticity of

8. Arc elasticity has one disadvantage over point elasticity: there is an ambiguity in its value resulting from what numbers to use for p_1 and x_1. Should the starting price and quantity be used? The terminal price and quantity? Or some intermediate values? There is no correct answer, and individuals that use arc elasticities simply choose one, although it is quite common to choose the average price and quantity.

9. When we are calculating the own-price elasticity we use the formula

$$E_{11} = [dx_1(p_1)/dp_1][p_1/x_1]$$

demand for new vehicles in the US and found it to be –0.87. As with the demand for cigarettes, the demand for new cars is inelastic. On the other hand, many goods have own-price elasticities which are **elastic**. Mocan et al. (2000) found the own-price elasticity of health care in China to be –1.03. Tauras and Chaloupka (2001) found the own-price elasiticity of nicotine replacement products (like "the patch") to be between –1.13 and –1.51 depending on the product. Finally, Devoretz and Salvanes (1993) find the demand for fresh salmon is responsive, or elastic with respect to price. They calculate the price elasticity of demand for fresh salmon to be –2.47. According to this estimate, a 1 percent increase in the price of salmon will decrease per capita consumption by 2.47 percent.

elastic

An interesting example of demand elasticities concerns the increased consumption of poultry compared to red meat over time. In 1970, the per capita consumption of red meat was four times the per capita consumption of poultry (chicken and turkey). By the 1990s, consumption had fallen to only two times. One explanation is that consumers' preferences have changed over time due to health concerns about red meat. However, a better explanation is found in changing prices. Due to increases in factory farming for chickens, the real price of chicken has fallen by almost 75 percent since 1950 — much more than red meat. Because the price of chicken has fallen relative to red meat, the quantity demanded has increased. Putnam and Allshouse (1992) have estimated that the own-price elasticity for chicken is –1.67.

The recent increases in gasoline prices across North America have led to all types of calls for government intervention on the grounds that individuals cannot substitute out of gasoline. Chris Nicol (2000) of the University of Regina has estimated the own-price elasticity of gasoline across Canada for different types of households. He finds that there is very little difference across the country. Whether in Nova Scotia or British Columbia the price elasticity hovers around –0.5. That is, for a 1 percent change in price there is about a half of one percent fall in demand. The demand is inelastic, but it is not perfectly inelastic as some would say. One of the interesting things found by Nicol is that families who rent their homes are more sensitive to gasoline prices than families who own their homes. Renters may find it easier to move closer to their places of work or school. Renters may also be poorer and more willing to substitute into public transit.

PROBLEM 3.10

The demand for your product is $x = 12 - p$, where x is the quantity demanded and p is its price. The table below lists several points along this demand curve.

P	*Q*	*Elasticity*	*Total Revenue*
11	1		
9	3		
7	5		
5	7		
3	9		
1	11		

a. Calculate the elasticities over the segments indicated in the table and the total revenue at those points.

b. What is the relationship between total revenue and elasticity?

c. Assume the demand curve shifts to the right with two more units sold at every price. Recalculate the elasticities. Is the new demand curve more or less elastic?

Some Income Elasticities of Demand

When income changes we can measure an income elasticity of demand in a fashion similar to the own-price elasticity. The income elasticity is given by

$$E_{1m}=(\Delta x_1/\Delta M)(M/x_1),$$

where ΔM is the old income minus the new income, and Δx_1 is the quantity demanded at the old income minus the quantity demanded at the new income. Strictly speaking, we cannot say that a particular good — for example, fresh salmon — is a normal good or an inferior good without also specifying the particular consumer whose preferences we are considering. It is possible, even likely, that one person — say Janet — may respond to an increase in her income by buying more fresh salmon while another person — say Craig — may respond to an increase in his income by buying less of it. For Janet fresh salmon is a normal good, while for Craig it is an inferior good.

income elasticity of demand

Nevertheless, we can get a good idea of whether, for the average consumer, a particular good is normal or inferior by using aggregate data to compute an average income elasticity of demand. The **income elasticity of demand** is the elasticity of quantity consumed per capita with respect to per capita income. In empirical studies of income elasticity of demand for a good, aggregate data is used to compute an average demand function. Then, this average demand function is used to compute various average elasticities, including the income elasticity of demand.

Empirical evidence suggests that for the average consumer, fresh salmon is a normal good. Using data for North America and Europe, DeVoretz and Salvanes (1993) estimate the income elasticity of demand for fresh salmon to be 2.14. The fact that the elasticity is positive indicates that fresh salmon is a normal good. As per capita income increases, so does per capita consumption of fresh salmon. The *magnitude* of the response is also of interest. An income elasticity of demand of 2.14 indicates that a 1 percent increase in per capita income would result in a 2.14 percent increase in per capita consumption of fresh salmon. Notice just how responsive consumption of salmon is to changes in income: holding the price of salmon and other relevant variables constant, we see that per capita consumption of salmon tends to increase at more than twice the rate at which per capita income increases.

luxury

A normal good is said to be a **luxury** if consumption increases at a rate larger than the rate at which per capita income increases — if the income elasticity of demand for the good exceeds 1. Clearly, fresh salmon is a luxury. Houthakker (1951) estimated the income elasticity of demand for electricity to be 1.17. This means that in Britain in the 1940s, electricity was a luxury. McCarthy (1996) estimates the income elasticity for new cars to be 1.70, which means new cars are also a luxury.

necessity

On the other hand, a normal good is said to be a **necessity** if the income elasticity of demand for the good is between 0 and 1. Baltagi and Griffin (1983) report a range of income elasticities for gasoline. A typical elasticity for gasoline is 0.8, indicating that a 1 percent increase in per capita income results in an increase in per capita consumption of gasoline equal to 0.8 percent. Therefore, gasoline is a necessity.

Of course, the income elasticity of demand for an inferior good is negative, since quantity demanded of an inferior good decreases as income increases. Wasserman (1988) finds that the income elasticity of demand for cigarettes has been declining in recent years. Up to about 1980, his estimates of the income elasticity of demand for cigarettes for American adults are positive but small. These estimates indicate that cigarettes were a necessity prior to 1980. After 1980, however, Wasserman estimates a small negative income elasticity of demand in the range of –0.02 to –0.2. These estimates indicate that after 1980, cigarettes were an inferior good for adults. Interestingly, when he calculates the elasticity of per capita consumption of cigarettes for teenagers with respect to average family income, he gets an estimate of –0.44, indicating that a 1 percent increase in family income is associated with a 0.44 percent decrease in cigarette consumption by teenagers. These results are supported in Hersch's (2000) more recent study. She also finds a slightly negative income elasticity of –0.04.

Some Cross-Price Elasticities of Demand

cross-price elasticity of demand

If we want to measure the response in quantity demanded of one good with respect to a change in the price of another good, we can calculate a cross-price elasticity of demand. The **cross-price elasticity of demand** for good 1 with respect to the price of good 2 is the elasticity of per-capita consumption of good 1 with respect to p_2, and is given by the formula:

$$E_{12} = (\Delta x_1/\Delta p_2)(p_2/x_1)$$

Where Δp_2 is the old price of good 2 minus the new price, and Δx_1 is the quantity demanded at the old price minus the quantity demanded at the new price. Using aggregate data for North America and Europe, DeVoretz and Salvanes (1993) calculate the cross-price elasticity of demand for fresh salmon with respect to the price of frozen salmon to be 1.12. The fact that this elasticity is positive means that frozen salmon is a substitute for fresh salmon: the higher the price of frozen salmon, the larger the quantity demanded of fresh salmon. Furthermore, a 1 percent increase in the price of frozen salmon will result in a 1.12 percent increase in the per capita demand for fresh salmon.

Tauras and Chaloupka (2001), in looking at the demands for several nicotine replacement therapies, find the cross-price elasticities of Nicoderm and Nicorette with cigarettes to be 0.68 and 0.81. This means the replacement therapies and cigarettes are substitutes. When the price of cigarettes increases, people substitute into therapies to help them stop smoking. From time to time, cross-price elasticities of demand have played a role in anti-monopoly court cases. For example, in the 1950s Du Pont was charged with monopolizing the market for cellophane production in the United States. Du Pont countered the charge by arguing that the relevant market was not the narrowly defined market for cellophane (where it was a monopolist) but the more broadly defined market for so-called flexible packaging materials (where its market share was roughly 18 percent). In support of its argument it pointed to a very high cross-price elasticity of demand between cellophane and other flexible packaging materials such as waxed paper. The Supreme Court ruled in favour of Du Pont, saying that "it seems to us that Du Pont should not be found to monopolize cellophane when that product has the competition and interchangeability with other wrappings… ." (*U.S. Reports*, 1956, in Steltzer, 1961). Similarly in the recent Microsoft antitrust case where Microsoft was being sued for offering its Internet Explorer software free with its operating system, issues of cross elasticity were relevant. A necessary condition for Netscape to make its case was to first show that the two softwares were indeed substitutes.

SUMMARY

We began this chapter by considering the *constraints* — wealth, time, and human resources — on individual decision making. We also noted how complex rational decision making can be, because decisions are inherently intertemporal and because they inevitably involve imperfect information. To analyze decision making in this complex world, we created an ideal case; we defined a choice problem involving just *one period*, *perfect information*, and *two goods*.

We then looked at the consumer's *constrained-choice problem* in this static framework. Given the prices of consumption goods and the consumer's income, the solution — a *system of demand functions* — yields the utility-maximizing quantities of those goods.

We then graphically solved a range of choice problems, beginning with the demand for *essential* and *inessential goods*. A consumer will always buy some amount of an essential good, regardless of how high its price is. By contrast, a consumer will not necessarily buy a positive amount of an inessential good; if the price is high enough, he or she will choose not to buy any. This distinction helps us to understand why most individuals choose not to buy many — perhaps most — of the goods available in advanced economies. Next we applied this model of choice to the problem of taxation, and showed that for a given amount of money to be raised, consumers would prefer to have a lump-sum tax rather than an excise tax.

Next, we characterized *normal* and *inferior goods* in terms of the consumer's demand response to a change in income. As income goes up, the consumption of a normal good also increases, but the consumption of an inferior good declines. Next we looked at how demand for one good changes in response to a change in the price of some other good. We called goods *complements* when consumption moves up or down in tandem (right shoes and left shoes) and *substitutes* when an increase in consumption of one good is paired with a decline in consumption of another (chocolate mousse and lemon meringue pie). We then explored the relationship between a good's own price and the quantity demanded of that good, which we called the (ordinary) *demand curve*. In all of these comparative statics applications, we saw how to use the concept of *elasticity* to measure and compare the response of quantity demanded to changes in the values of exogenous variables in the demand function.

A major thrust of this chapter has been to create a set of useful analytical tools for exploring consumer choice problems. In the next chapter, we will continue to build on these ideas and put them to work in analyzing a number of varied and interesting problems.

EXERCISES

1. The government wants to raise $50 a month from Joe Blow. A $1 sales tax per package of cigarettes will raise the required revenue, as will a lump-sum tax of $50 per month. Which tax would Joe prefer? Will he smoke more cigarettes under the sales tax or the lump-sum tax?

2. Rashid is a frequent flyer with a major airline. His fare is reduced 25 percent after he flies 30 000 miles a year, and then is reduced to 50 percent after he flies 60 000 miles. Graph the budget line that Rashid faces.

3. Consumption bundles (10,20) and (15,40) are both on the income-consumption path. What, if anything, can you say about the *MRS* at these two bundles? Illustrate your answer.

4. Suppose that the government has decided to transfer income to a particular person. Draw a graph analogous to the one in Figure 3.7 and compare the implications of a program that subsidizes the consumption of some good — food, for example — with the implications of a lump-sum transfer of cash.

a. Show that if the two programs involve an equal expenditure of public revenues, the recipient will never prefer the first program.
b. Supposing that the two programs involve an equal expenditure of public revenues, illustrate the case in which the recipient would be indifferent between them.

5. Nancy spends all her income on good 1 and good 2, and her income-consumption path is downward sloping. Is it possible that both goods are normal? That both are inferior? That good 1 is normal? That good 1 is inferior? That one of these goods is inferior and the other normal?

6. Smiling Jack's utility function is
$$U(x_1, x_2) = x_2(1 + x_1)$$
   a. Carefully plot the indifference curve that passes through the bundle (2,1).
   b. Is good 1 essential or inessential? What about good 2?

7. Ted lives in a two-good world. He always spends 40 percent of his income on good 1 and 60 percent on good 2.
   a. What are his demand functions?
   b. Suppose that both prices are $1, and construct Ted's income-consumption path and the Engel curves for both goods.

8. A student went one night to Jimmy's Bar, where beer and whiskies both cost $1.00, and he drank six beers and four whiskies. The next night, on the eve of a final exam, the student went to the Eagle Bar, where beers cost $0.50 and whiskies $1.50, and drank two beers and six whiskies. Was this student behaving rationally?

9. Nancy spends all her income on good 1 and good 2. As p_1 increases while p_2 remains fixed, Nancy's price-consumption path is horizontal.
   a. How does Nancy's expenditure on good 1 respond to changes in p_1?
   b. Show that Nancy's demand for good 1 is proportional to $1/p_1$.
   c. Is good 1 a complement or a substitute for good 2?
   d. What is Nancy's price elasticity of demand for good 1?

10. It is sometimes argued that demand for medical services is perfectly inelastic with respect to the price of medical services. By considering the limitations imposed by a finite income, show that no demand curve can be perfectly inelastic for all prices.

11. Ronald spends all his income on good 1 and good 2, and good 1 is a normal good. As p_1 increases while p_2 remains fixed, Ronald's price-consumption path is downward sloping.
   a. What can you say about the price elasticity of demand for good 1?
   b. Is good 1 a complement or a substitute for good 2?

12. Norma spends all her income on good 1 and good 2 and her income-consumption path is upward sloping. What, if anything, can you say about the demand response for good 1 and good 2 to an increase in income?

13. Mr. Lucky intends to spend a recent inheritance of $1000 over the next two periods. He has no other source of income. Let x_1 and x_2 be two composite commodities: expenditure on consumption in this period and in the next period. Suppose that the rate of interest that Mr. Lucky can get on his savings is 25 percent; that is, for every $1 invested in this period, he will have $1.25 in the next period. What is Mr. Lucky's budget line? That is, what combinations of x_1 and x_2 does his inheritance allow him to have? What is the opportunity cost of consumption in the first (second) period in terms of forgone consumption in the second (first) period?

14. Mr. Lucky's cousin Not-So is broke, but his grandmother has left him an inheritance of $1250 in trust. Let x_1 and x_2 be two composite commodities: expenditure on consumption in this period and the next period. The terms of the trust specify that he cannot have the money until the next period, but his banker will lend him money at a 25 percent interest rate (thereby frustrating his grandmother's intentions). For every $1 borrowed today, Not-So must pay back $1.25 tomorrow. What is Not-So's budget line? How does it compare with Mr. Lucky's?

15. Forestry economists have been estimating various elasticities for wood for years. They have found the following: softwood short-run demands are very price-inelastic; the cross-price

elasticity for British Columbian softwoods with respect to softwoods from other parts of the world is quite high; and the cross-price elasticity of softwoods with respect to other woods is positive, but not as high.

a. Does this make sense?
b. British Columbia and the Pacific Northwest happen to be very productive in producing high-quality softwood timber (old growth, clear wood). This means that for a given hectare of land, more timber is produced than in a given hectare of, say, the Amazon rainforest. Recently the province of BC has started to set land aside from logging. This reduction in the supply of softwood should raise the price. Given the elasticities, what should happen to the amount of wood consumed from other countries, and to the amount of land cleared elsewhere in the world?
c. In what sense are the "friends of BC forests" also the "enemies of the Amazon rainforest?"

16. Suppose that the indifference curves between x_1 and x_2 are concave (as opposed to convex) to the origin. Show that the point on the budget line where $MRS(x_1, x_2)$ is equal to p_1/p_2 is not a solution to the utility-maximizing problem. What points on the budget line are preferred to this point? Show that utility maximization implies that the consumer will spend all of his or her income on good 1 or good 2.

17. Show that a utility-maximizing consumer will never choose a consumption bundle (in which both quantities are positive) on a nonconvex portion of an indifference curve.

18. The following utility function, in which F is kilograms of food and T is metres of textiles, is an example of *hierarchical preferences*:

$$U(F,T) = \begin{cases} F & \text{if } F \leq 100 \\ T & \text{if } F > 100 \end{cases}$$

a. Suppose income M is \$100 and the price of textiles p_T is \$1. Find the demand functions for both goods as the price of food p_F varies. (*Hint:* Show that when p_F is larger than \$1, this consumer will buy only food, and that when p_F is less than \$1, he or she will buy exactly 100 kilograms of food.)
b. Find the two demand functions for arbitrary values of M, p_F, and p_T.

19. In the analysis on taxation, we implicitly assumed that Tammy's indifference curves were convex and smooth and that she buys a positive amount of gasoline. Is the lump-sum tax still preferred when the utility function is $U(x_1, x_2) = \min(x_1, x_2)$?

20. Suppose that a private dining club, composed of 100 members with identical preferences, incurs an overhead cost of \$100 000 each year and that the cost of each meal is \$50. (If the club sells one meal in a year, for example, its total costs are \$100 050; if it sells five meals, its total costs are \$100 250.) The club is considering two possible fee structures designed to generate just enough revenue to cover its costs. Its first option is to charge members a fixed price p_1 per meal. Let x_1^* denote the number of meals per year that each member buys at price p_1. If the club is to cover costs, it must choose p_1 so that $100x_1^*(p_1 - 50) = \$100\,000$ or so that $x_1^*(p_1 - 50) = \$1000$. The club's second option is to charge each person a membership fee equal to \$1000 and then to sell meals at a price of \$50 per meal. Show that from the point of view of the club members, the second option is preferred to the first if indifference curves are smooth and convex. (*Hint*: $p_1 - \$50$ is analogous to an excise tax on club meals, and the \$1000 membership fee is analogous to a lump-sum tax.)

21. Let us generalize the basic insight regarding lump-sum versus excise taxes. Suppose that Laura's indifference curves are smooth and convex and that both good 1 and good 2 are essential. Consider her choice between (1) a system of excise taxes, composed of separate excise taxes t_1 and t_2 on goods 1 and 2, or (2) a lump-sum tax, and suppose that both raise equal tax revenue.

a. Show that she is never better off with the system of excise taxes.
b. When will she be indifferent to the two tax regimes?
c. How would your answer to (b) change if her indifference curves were not smooth?
d. How would your answer to (b) change if good 1 were inessential?

22. Suppose that the government is considering a welfare scheme and has to decide whether or not it should give the recipients cash or goods in kind. Suppose that the only two goods avail-

able to consume are fish and fruit, and suppose that a gift in kind is not resalable.

a. Draw the budget constraint for both types of welfare, assuming that the recipient has some initial income.
b. Under which scheme is the recipient better off?
c. If cash grants improve welfare, why do you think we observe gifts in kind? What is missing from this analysis? Does your answer explain why we don't give our loved ones cash for birthday presents?

*23. Suppose that income is M = \$102, and prices are p_1 = \$2 and p_2 = \$5, and consider the following utility function:

$$U(x_1, x_2) = (x_1 + 2)(x_2 + 1)$$

a. Write out the Lagrangian function.
b. Find the utility-maximizing quantities of x_1 and x_2.

*24. Now consider the generalization of the problem you solved in 23. Prices are now arbitrary, p_1 and p_2, and so is income M. The utility function is once again

$$U(x_1, x_2) = (x_1 + 2)(x_2 + 1)$$

a. Write out the Lagrangian function.
b. Find the utility-maximizing quantities of x_1 and x_2 as functions of p_1, p_2, and M. That is, find the two ordinary demand functions.
c. Use these demand functions to verify the answers you found in (b) of the previous problem.

*25. Gulshun's income is \$120 per month, and her utility function is

$$U(x_1, x_2) = x_1(x_2)^2$$

a. Write out the Lagrangian function.
b. Find her ordinary demand functions.
c. Is good 1 normal, or inferior? Is good 2 normal, or inferior?
d. What is the price elasticity of demand for good 1? For good 2?
e. Supposing that p_2 is \$1, draw the price consumption path for good 1. Explain the shape of the price consumption path in terms of the price elasticity of demand.

*26. Consider the following utility function:

$$U(x_1, x_2) = x_2 + 120x_1 - (x_1)^2/2$$

a. Given an arbitrary price for good 1, p_1, and given p_2 = \$1, and income of \$1000, find the demand function for good 1.
b. Compute the price elasticity of demand for good 1 for the following values of p_1: \$100, \$80, \$60, \$40, \$20.

*27. Consider the following Cobb-Douglas utility function:

$$U(x_1, x_2) = (x_1)^a(x_2)^b$$

where a and b are parameters that are strictly positive: $a > 0$ and $b > 0$.

a. Show that utility maximization implies that the fraction $a/(a + b)$ of the total budget will be spent on good 1, and the fraction $b/(a + b)$ will be spent on good 2.
b. What can you say about the price elasticity of demand for goods 1 and 2?

*28. Angelica's endowment is composed of 20 units of good 1 and 50 units of good 2, and the prices of goods 1 and 2 are p_1 and p_2. She has no income, and her utility function is:

$$U(x_1, x_2) = (x_1 - 2)(x_2 - 5).$$

a. What is Angelica's budget constraint?
b. Write out the Lagrangian for her utility maximization problem.
c. Find her ordinary demand functions.

*29. Suppose a consumer has a utility function $U = x_2 + \ln x_1$ and has a budget constraint $M = p_1x_1 + p_2x_2$.

a. Write out the Lagrangian equation. What are the choice variables and parameters in this problem? Find the first-order conditions.
b. Find the demand functions. Does the law of demand hold? Is there anything unique or unusual about these demand functions?
c. Calculate the cross-price elasticity of demand for good 1.

*30. Suppose a consumer has a utility function $U = -1/x_1 - 1/x_2$ and has a budget constraint $M = p_1x_1 + p_2x_2$.

a. Write out the Lagrangian equation, and find the first-order conditions.

b. Find the demand functions. Does the law of demand hold for these functions?
c. Is x_1 a normal or inferior good? Are these goods substitutes or complements? Explain using the information you generated from (b).

31. Sarah buys candy from a store that sells only two types, red and orange. She has $6 to spend. For each of the following questions, draw Sarah's budget line.
    a. The price of red candy is $0.25 and the price of orange candy is $0.50.
    b. Prices are the same but the store gives one free red candy for every two red candies that she buys.
    c. Prices are the same but the store gives one free orange candy for every three red candies that she buys.
    d. Prices are the same but the store also offers an "orange lovers" card that costs $1 and allows the bearer to buy as many orange candies as they want for $0.25.

32. Scotty consumes two goods, X_1 and X_2, and his marginal rate of substitution of good 2 for good 1 is $MRS = X_2/(X_1 + 20)$.
    a. Suppose Scotty has an endowment of 20 units of each good and he consumes this endowment. Would he accept a trade of 1 unit of X_1 for 1 unit of X_2?
    b. Suppose instead that Scotty has an income of $200 and faces prices $P_1 = \$2$ and $P_2 = \$1$. What is Scotty's equilibrium consumption of X_1 and X_2?
    c. Is Scotty's income elasticity greater than, less than or equal to 1?

33. Use graphs to answer the following questions.
    a. Can all goods be inferior?
    b. Is it possible for a good to be normal for low and high levels of income yet be inferior in between? If so, graph an income consumption path consistent with this.

34. A newspaper article states, "Rising tuition over the past decade has not affected enrollment at universities or colleges." The article goes on to state that a 75 percent increase in tuition has led to less than a 1 percent fall in applications to university. Why would an elasticity measure of 1/75 be a biased estimate of the elasticity of demand for university education? (*Hint:* What major cost is not being accounted for?)

3A Appendix: Composite Commodities

Throughout this chapter, we have focused on consumer choice problems in which there are just *two goods*. As you have undoubtedly realized, very few real choice problems involve just two goods. In the course of a day, each of us uses dozens of different goods, and in the course of a year we buy and use hundreds or even thousands of different goods. How can the analysis of this chapter shed light on these real choice problems?

Perhaps surprisingly, for many problems the analytical tools we have developed for the two-good choice case are sufficient for analyzing much more complex choice problems. To see why, let us focus on a particular consumer's demand for just one good — Lisette's demand for gasoline. Lisette buys gasoline for her car, which she uses to get around town. Of course, to use the car she has to buy other complementary products, such as lubricating oil and tires. Her car is not, however, Lisette's only available means of transportation. She often takes the bus and, less frequently, a taxi. To use the analytical tools from the two-good choice problem to analyze Lisette's demand for gasoline, we will lump together all goods other than gasoline into a *composite commodity*. Lubricating oil, tires, bus and taxi rides, and all the goods other than gasoline that Lisette buys are contained in this composite commodity. To analyze her demand for gasoline, we will then look at her choice of a consumption bundle composed of two goods: gasoline (good 1) and this composite commodity (good 2).

We can measure the quantity of gasoline in these consumption bundles in litres. Since the composite commodity is just the amount Lisette spends on all goods other than gasoline, we can measure the quantity of the composite commodity — Lisette's expenditure on all other goods — in dollars. A consumption bundle is then just (x_1, x_2), where x_1 is litres of gasoline and x_2 is expenditure on all other goods. Lisette's budget line is

$$p_1x_1 + x_2 = M$$

Here M is Lisette's income and p_1 is the price of gasoline. Because the composite commodity is measured in dollars, its price is just \$1 per unit. We see that, as far the budget line is concerned, the only new twist in this analysis is that the price of good 2— the composite commodity — is 1.

Similarly, as far as Lisette's consumption preferences are concerned, there is also just one new twist. As you will see, however, this new element is more subtle. If Lisette's preferences for these bundles composed of litres of gasoline and expenditure on all other goods satisfy the completeness, transitivity, and continuity assumptions, then we know from Chapter 2 that Lisette has a well-defined preference ordering for such bundles. She has continuous indifference curves in the (x_1, x_2) space; and her preference ordering can be represented by a utility function $U(x_1, x_2)$. Clearly, then, we can use the tools developed in this chapter to analyze Lisette's choice of how much gasoline to buy (that is, her demand for gasoline) and how much to spend on all other goods. The new element in this analysis concerns the prices of the goods included in the composite commodity. Because Lisette's preference ordering for these bundles changes as the prices of the goods in the composite commodity change, these prices must be held constant.

To see why prices of these goods affect Lisette's preference ordering, let us try a simple thought experiment. First, imagine that on Sunday evening we ask Lisette to reveal her preference ordering for consumption bundles containing litres of gasoline and expenditure on all other goods. Suppose that Lisette tells us that she prefers bundle (50,1000) containing 50 litres of gasoline and $1000 to spend on all other goods, to bundle (10,1200) containing 10 litres of gasoline and $1200 to spend on all other goods. Now imagine that on Monday morning a series of unanticipated and radical price changes hit the headlines. The prices of lubricating oil and tires have jumped by 1900%; the price of a bus ride has fallen from $2.00 to $0; and the price of a taxi ride has dropped from $10 to $0.50. After Lisette has read about these price changes on Monday evening, we once again ask her to reveal her preference ordering for bundles containing gasoline and dollars spent on all other goods. Will she still prefer bundle (50,1000) to bundle (10,1200)? More generally, will Monday evening's preference ordering be the same as Sunday evening's? Almost certainly not. After these radical price changes, it is very likely that she will prefer bundle (10,1200) to bundle (50,1000). After all, the prices of the goods that are complementary to gasoline (lubricating oil and tires) have skyrocketed and the prices of substitute means of transportation (buses and taxis) have plummeted. Therefore it is no longer attractive for Lisette to use her car to get around town relative to taking a bus or a taxi. In fact, she may choose not to drive her car at all and rely instead on buses and taxis for transportation. If she does give up driving her car, gasoline is of no use to her, and on Monday evening she will definitely prefer bundle (10,1200) to bundle (50,1000).

We see that we can legitimately use a composite commodity to reduce complex choice problems to relatively simple problems that can be solved graphically using the tools developed in this chapter for the two-good case. Indeed, we will do so repeatedly in the following chapters. We must recognize, however, that when we use a composite commodity, we are implicitly assuming that the prices of all the goods included in the composite commodity are held constant.

REFERENCES

Baltagi, B. H. and J. M. Griffin. 1983. "Gasoline Demand in the OECD," *European Economic Review*, 22:117–37.

DeVoretz, D. J. and K. G. Salvanes. 1993. "Market Structure for Farmed Salmon," *American Journal of Agricultural Economics*, 75:227–33.

Hersch, J. 2000. "Gender, Income Levels, and the Demand for Cigarettes," *Journal of Risk and Uncertainty*, 21:263–82.

Houthakker, H. S. 1951. "Some Calculations on Electricity Consumption in Great Britain," *Journal of the Royal Statistical Society*, Series A, No. 114 Pt. III, 351–71.

Lewit, E. M. and D. Coate 1982. "The Potential for Using Excise Taxes to Reduce Smoking," *Journal of Health Economics*, 1:545–70.

McCarthy, P. 1996. "Market Price and Income Elasticities of New Vehicle Demands," *Review of Economics and Statistics*, 78:543–47.

Mocan, H.N., E. Tekin, and J. Zax. 2000. "The Demand for Medical Care in Urban China," NBER Working Paper No. 7673.

Nicol, C. 2000. "Elasticities of Demand for Gasoline in Canada and the United States," Working paper, University of Regina.

Putnam, J. and J. Allshouse (1992). "Food Consumption, Prices, and Expenditure, 1970–1990, SB-840, Economic Research Service, USDA.

Steltzer, I. 1961. Selected Antitrust Cases: Landmark Decisions in Federal Antitrust. Homewood, IL: Richard D. Irwin, 59.

Tauras, J. and F. Chaloupka. 2001. "The Demand for Nicotine Replacement Therapies," NBER Working Paper No. 8332.

Wasserman, J. 1988. *Excise Taxes, Regulation, and the Demand for Cigarettes,* Santa Monica, California: The Rand Corporation.

CHAPTER 4

More Demand Theory

In Chapter 3, we first defined the choice-making problem from the consumer's perspective and then modelled how consumers would solve that problem. Although we examined some applications, they were fairly narrow. As we try our hand at exploring demand theory in this chapter, the central question is just how much territory we can cover — that is, how wide-ranging will our theory of consumer choice prove to be?

4.1 The Law of Demand

In Chapter 3 we analyzed the comparative static question: What happens to the choice of good x_1 when its own price p_1 changes? In this chapter we explore this question in greater detail. Here we will discover the exact requirements necessary for an inverse relationship to exist between the quantity demanded of a good and its own price. Economists of all stripes believe that demand curves are generally downward sloping, and many believe that they always are. George Stigler, a Nobel-prize-winning economist, once quipped that the proof that all demand curves were downward sloping is that the finder of the opposite case would win a Nobel prize; since there were no finders, there were no upward-sloping demand curves. Though there is no proof of downward-sloping demand curves that follow from the assumptions made in Chapter 2, the general empirical regularity of this inverse relationship is often called the **law of demand**. The law of demand is a subtle and powerful idea. Before we consider some of the finer points in the theory of demand, let's examine a number of applications to improve our understanding and our ability to think like an economist.

law of demand

Relative Prices, Speculation, and Shipping the Good Apples Out

Simple examples of the law of demand are all around us. Vegetables are cheaper in the summer because in order for individuals to want to consume the larger summer supply, the price must be lowered to reflect the lower marginal value of increased consumption. The announcement for price specials at Zellers says, "Attention Zellers shoppers: all items on aisle 4 *reduced* by 30 percent" because in order to induce increased consumption, the price of the product must fall. And lineups at the U.S. border were longer before the Free Trade Agreement, when Canadian tariffs meant that many products could be bought more cheaply in the U.S. than in Canada. But there are many subtle examples of the law of demand as well.

The famous attempt of the Hunt brothers to corner the silver market is an interesting case. In the summer of 1979, the price of silver was $8 per ounce. Throughout the

1970s, a wealthy Dallas oil man, Nelson Bunker Hunt, and his brother William Herbert had been accumulating silver, and by the summer of 1979 they had control of 42 million ounces. In the fall of that year, the price of silver began to rise sharply, and by January 1980 the price of silver was an unprecedented $50 per ounce. The Hunt brothers, by this time, had gained control of 280 million ounces of silver — equivalent to the annual world silver production. On the surface, the Hunt brothers look like an exception to the law of demand — as the price increased, the quantity of silver they demanded increased. In fact, the Hunt brothers were just an example of behaviour commonly known as speculation. Is speculation a counter-example to the law of demand?

It turns out that speculation is a nice example of downward-sloping demand curves. Recall that demand depends on the relative price (p_1/p_2), not the nominal price. With speculation the two prices that matter are the price today and the *expected* price tomorrow of the good in question. In the case of the Hunt brothers, they were not so much concerned with the price of silver on a given day but with what they thought the price would be in the coming weeks. We might think of the relative price as: $p_{today}/p^{e}_{tomorrow}$. If the price of silver today is $8, and you expect the price tomorrow to be $8, then the relative price is 1, and a certain amount of silver is demanded today. But if the expected price of silver tomorrow is $50, then the relative price today is 8/50 = 0.16. Silver is an absolute bargain today and the quantity demanded today increases. A speculator is by definition someone who thinks the price tomorrow will be higher than the price today. Thus, when the price of silver rises today, but the investor thinks it will rise *even more* tomorrow, then the relative price today actually falls! Given the law of demand, the speculator should buy more today. Rather than being a counter-example to the law of demand, the Hunt brothers are actually a testimony to it.

Speculation is an example of the law of demand because the price today relative to the expected price tomorrow is lower.

Alchian-Allen theorem

An even more subtle example of the law of demand is called the **Alchian-Allen theorem**, after the two economists who first articulated it. Suppose there is a commodity called leather sandals made in Spain, which can be broken down into two goods: high-quality sandals and low-quality sandals. In Spain the high-quality sandals sell for $10, while the low-quality ones sell for $5. In other words, the relative price in Spain of high-quality sandals is 2 pairs of low quality sandals. Further suppose that in order to ship the sandals to North America it costs $10/pair *independent* of the quality. The relative price in North America is now 20/15 = 1.33. Now the relative price of high-quality sandals is down from 2 to 1.33. The law of demand predicts that there will be a higher proportion of good sandals relative to bad sandals consumed in North America than in Spain. Furthermore, since both types of sandals are more expensive in North America relative to other goods, North Americans should consume fewer Spanish sandals than people in Spain.

This is a remarkable result and holds for all goods that are traded over large distances. In fact, the Alchian-Allen theorem is often called “shipping the good apples out” because of the observation that the better apples grown in the Pacific Northwest find their way to distant parts of North America that do not grow apples. In general, the foreign place consumes less of the good, but a higher fraction of their consumption is of high quality. Examples of this relative price effect abound: Alaskans eat less beef than Texans, but more of it is deboned; Canadians drink less French wine than the French, but the proportion of expensive wine is higher; New Yorkers consume fewer grapes than Californians, but they consume a higher proportion of high-quality grapes; and on and on. Essentially what is happening here is that consumers are substituting into the relatively cheaper commodity, even though both goods are becoming more expensive. The critical lesson here is that moving up and down a demand curve involves substitution. We will see very shortly that it also involves an income effect, but for the moment we are setting this aside.

This result of a change in relative prices goes beyond transportation charges. Whenever there is a fixed charge added to two separate prices, it lowers the relative price of the high quality good. Hence couples with children go out less often, but to more expensive events, than similar couples without children because they must pay for a babysitter, and the babysitting fee is independent of where they go. For example, suppose there is a discount movie house that charges only $1 per show, and a first-run movie theatre that charges $10 per show. Before a couple has children, the relative price of the expensive theatre is 10. That is, the couple sacrifices ten old movies for every current movie they see. Once the couple has a child they must pay a babysitting fee, which is independent of the type of movie they attend. If the babysitter charges $25 for the evening, then the relative price of the two types of entertainment becomes 35/26 = 1.3. Now the relative price of the expensive movie falls a great deal. Instead of giving up ten cheap movies, they give up less than one-and-a-half. Faced with this choice, the couple will substitute into the more expensive form of entertainment. Because both prices have gone up, however, the couple will demand fewer movies overall.

The number of examples you can imagine that involve fixed charges is limited only by your imagination. For example, nice homes are built on expensive lots rather than cheap ones because the fixed lot cost lowers the relative price of the expensive home; gold bindings only go on hardback books, not paperbacks, because the fixed printing cost lowers the relative price of the hardback book; and tailored suits use more expensive cloth than suits sold off the rack because the fixed tailor fee lowers the relative cost of the expensive cloth. All are examples of changes in relative prices brought about by fixed charges, and how these bear on the law of demand.

A fixed charge applied to a high- and low-quality good lowers the relative price of the high-quality good and results in a higher relative consumption of the high-quality good.

PROBLEM 4.1

Suppose that a large company owns an underground parking lot that has spaces currently worth $200/month. Initially the company provides the parking for free to its employees with the condition that they are not allowed to sublet the spaces. After a change in management, the company removes the free parking privileges and charges the employees $200/month for the space. If there are only two types of cars (good cars that rent for $1000/month and bad cars that rent for $500/month), what would you predict would happen to the average quality of car parked in the lot after the increase in fee?

You might be wondering, if the high-quality items tend to be shipped out, why do you have to go to Maine to get a great lobster, or Vancouver to get a great salmon? The answer, of course, is just the law of demand once again. It doesn't really matter if the salmon gets shipped to you, or you get shipped to the salmon — there is still a fixed transportation charge. Let's suppose that you are travelling from Montreal to Vancouver for the sole purpose of sitting down at the Pan-Pacific Hotel dining room and eating the best salmon in the house. Suppose there are two salmon prices on the menu: high quality, costing $50, and low quality, costing $25. Suppose also your travel costs are $1000. The relative price for you of the good salmon is $1050/1025 \approx 1$. The relative price for a local Vancoverite is 2. Since your relative price is extremely close to 1, you are much more likely to buy the expensive salmon than the local Vancouverite is. Now you know why travellers often return home boasting about the food on their adventures.[1]

Objections to the Law of Demand

Two objections to the law of demand should be mentioned. People are often heard to say, "If the price goes up, I'll still have to buy the same amount because x_1 is a necessity." All the law of demand is stating is that the quantity demanded falls when the price increases. It is only referring to marginal changes, not to all-or-nothing changes, and it says nothing about how small the change in quantity demanded is. As we saw in Chapter 3, a demand curve could have a very small elasticity, meaning that for large changes in price there is a relatively small change in quantity demanded. This small change, however, is still moving in the opposite direction of the price.

A similar objection is raised over situations where it just doesn't seem plausible that an individual would substitute. For example, would the number of suicides respond to changes in price? It hardly seems reasonable. Yet the number of suicides decreases with income and increases with age — suggesting that those with more to lose commit fewer suicides. In order for a life insurance policy to be valid for a suicide, a grace period must elapse. The two standard grace periods are 12 and 24 months. An economist is not surprised to find that most suicides happen in the 13th and 25th months of a policy, while the fewest happen in the 11th and 23rd. The law of demand appears to hold. When the cost of a suicide increases, the number of suicides falls.

Likewise, economists have long claimed that seat belt legislation, because it lowers the cost of an accident to the driver, should increase the number of accidents. This prediction has been mocked by several noneconomists on the grounds that no one decides to have an accident on purpose. However, it is not a question of deliberate actions, but one of substitution. Rather than cite studies showing that pedestrians, bike riders, and passengers have an increased chance of being injured when seat belt laws are in place, let us ask a question first posed by Gordon Tullock: How safely would you drive if, rather than an air bag and seat belt, you had a six-inch dagger coming at you from the steering column? Enough said. Let us now turn to a more rigorous study of the law of demand and see under what conditions it holds.

PROBLEM 4.2

In part, the cost of driving at any speed is the risk of an accident, with the higher the speed the greater the risk of an accident. As ABS braking systems become more common, what do you think will happen to the speed at which we drive? Use the law of demand in your answer.

---

1. Bertonazzi, et al., in one of the few formal tests of this proposition, show that individuals who travelled farther to college football games purchased the better seats.

4.2
Income and Substitution Effects

Our intuition strongly suggests that the quantity demanded of any good is *negatively* related to that good's price. In other words, it seems reasonable to suppose that as the price of a good continues to drop, the consumer decides to buy more and more of it. Graphically, the consumer's demand curve would then be downward sloping. As Figure 4.1 reveals, however, it is possible *in theory* for the quantity demanded to be *positively* related to price. As p_1 increases from \$2 to \$3 in Figure 4.1, the quantity demanded of good 1 increases from 12 to 14. When price and quantity demanded of a good are positively related, the good is called a **Giffen good**.

Giffen good

To understand this surprising theoretical possibility, let us look at the consumer's response to a change in the price of good 1 in more detail. We will perform a hypothetical exercise that allows us to decompose the overall response into two components, a **substitution effect** and an **income effect**. Then, using this decomposition, we can say something more definite about the consumer's response.

substitution effect

income effect

A change in p_1 (holding p_2 constant) changes the relative price of good 1 in terms of good 2. If p_1 rises, good 1 is relatively more expensive and, if it drops, good 1 is relatively less expensive. The *substitution effect* of a change in p_1 is associated with the *change in the relative price* of good 1.

In addition, a change in p_1 (holding p_2 and M constant) results in an equilibrium for the consumer on a different indifference curve. If p_1 goes up, the set of attainable bundles shrinks and the consumer ends up on a lower indifference curve. Therefore,

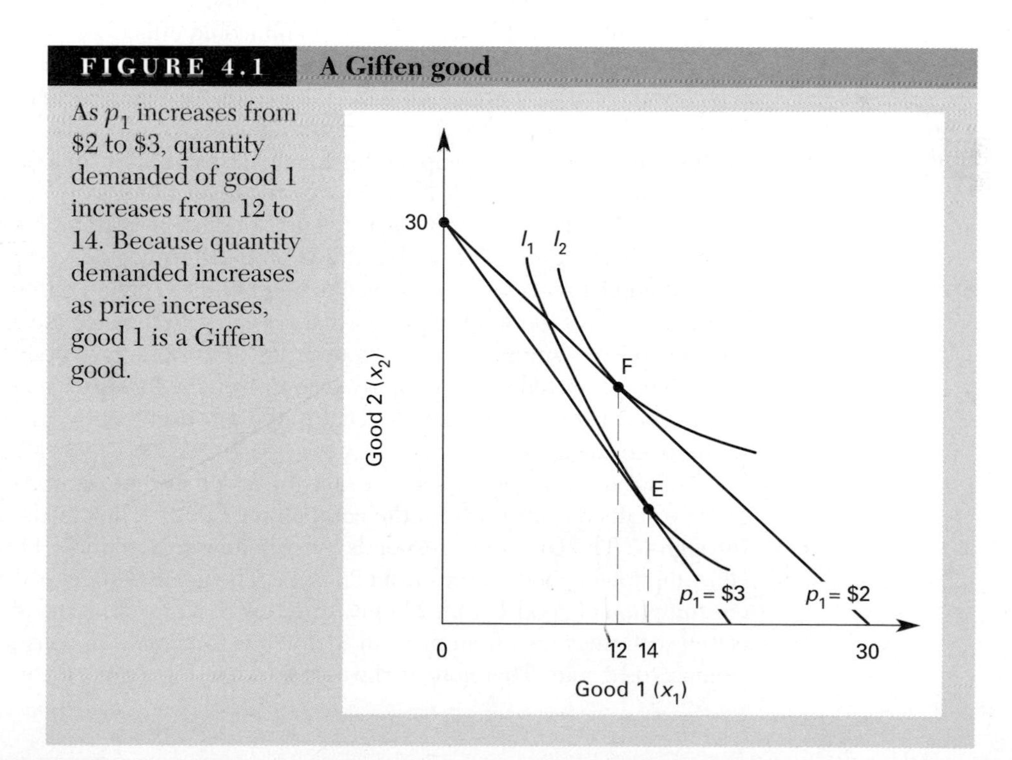

FIGURE 4.1 A Giffen good

As p_1 increases from \$2 to \$3, quantity demanded of good 1 increases from 12 to 14. Because quantity demanded increases as price increases, good 1 is a Giffen good.

we say that the increase in p_1 results in a decrease in the consumer's *real income*. Similarly, if p_1 goes down, the set of attainable consumption bundles expands and the consumer ends up on a higher indifference curve. Therefore, we say that a decrease in p_1 results in an increase in the consumer's real income. The *income effect* of a change in p_1 is associated with the *change in real income*.

Imagine, for example, the reaction of an avid New York baseball fan with $1200 per season to spend on major-league ballgame tickets to a drop in the price of admission to Yankee games from $20 to $10 (holding the price of admission to Mets games constant at $20). The opportunity cost of watching a Yankee game has suddenly changed from one Mets game to half a Mets game. In addition, the fan's real income has increased because he or she can now attend more of both sports events. For example, if the fan initially chose to buy tickets to 30 Yankee games and 30 Met games, after the price reduction for Yankee games, he or she can now afford to buy tickets to 40 Yankee games and 40 Met games. The substitution effect is associated with the change in the *relative price* of a Yankee game, and the income effect is associated with the fact that the fan's *real income* has increased.

Income and Substitution Effects for a Price Increase

Let us look at income and substitution effects graphically. In Figure 4.2, M is held constant at $60, and p_2 is held constant at $1. When the price of good 1 is $1, the utility-maximizing bundle is bundle A — containing 30 units of good 1 — on indifference curve I_2. When the price of good 1 rises to $3, the consumer switches to bundle C — containing 12 units of good 1 — on indifference curve I_1. This consumer's response to an increase in the price of good 1 from $1 to $3 is to reduce consumption of good 1 by 18 units.

Now let us decompose this quantity response — the drop from 30 to 12 units of good 1 — into a substitution effect and an income effect. Beginning at bundle C in Figure 4.2, to isolate the substitution effect we eliminate the income effect by giving the consumer just enough additional income to allow him or her to get back to the original indifference curve, I_2. The resulting budget line is called the **compensated budget line** because it compensates for the loss in real income associated with the increase in p_1 from $1 to $3. The compensated budget line is the dashed line in Figure 4.2. It is parallel to the budget line through C because in both instances p_1 is $3. Given the compensated budget line, bundle D on indifference curve I_2 — containing 22 units of good 1 — is the utility-maximizing bundle. Having eliminated the income effect, we see that the substitution effect associated with this increase in the price of good 1 is a drop in consumption of that good from 30 to 22 units. Notice that the substitution effect associated with this *increase* in p_1 from $1 to $3 is a *decrease* in consumption of good 1 from 30 to 22 units. That is, the substitution effect is *negatively related* to the price change.

compensated budget line

To isolate the income effect, we take the added income away. As a result, the budget line shifts downward from the compensated budget line to the solid budget line through C. The consumer responds by switching from bundle D to bundle C, and consumption of good 1 drops from 22 to 12. The income effect is then a reduction in consumption of good 1 from 22 units to 12 units. Notice that the income effect associated with this *increase* in p_1 from $1 to $3 is a *decrease* in consumption of good 1 from 22 to 12 units. Therefore, in the case shown in Figure 4.2, the income effect is also

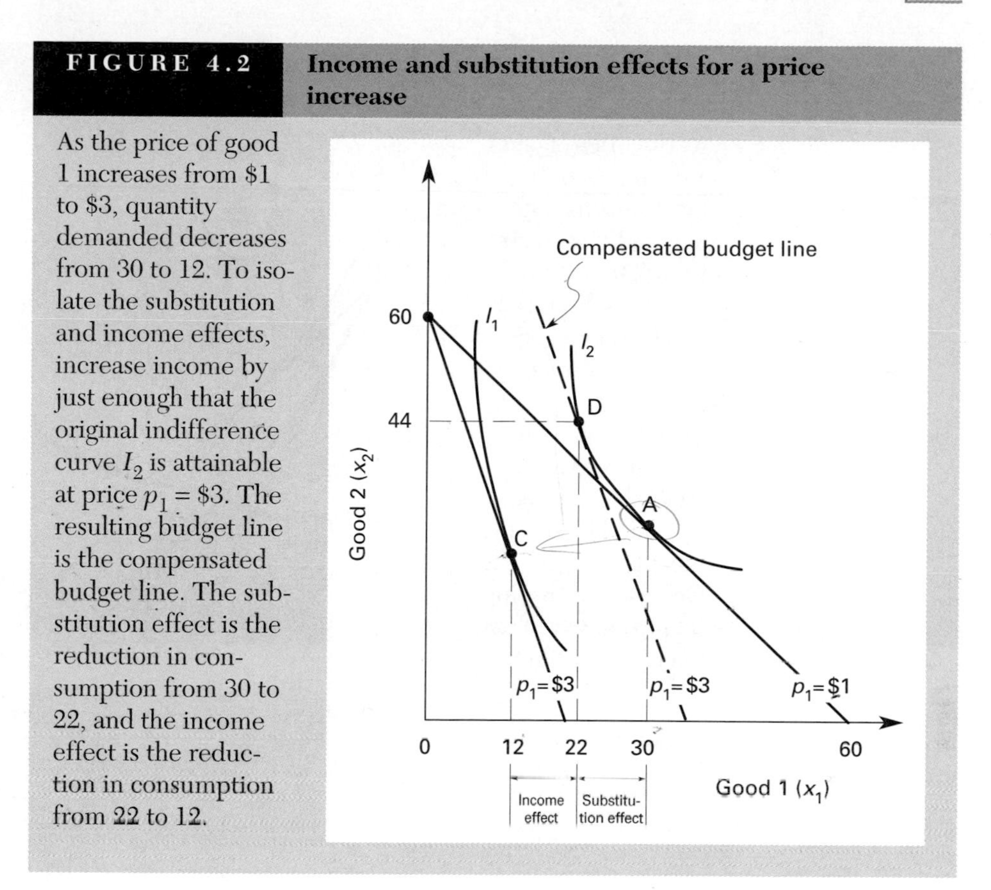

FIGURE 4.2 **Income and substitution effects for a price increase**

As the price of good 1 increases from \$1 to \$3, quantity demanded decreases from 30 to 12. To isolate the substitution and income effects, increase income by just enough that the original indifference curve I_2 is attainable at price $p_1 = \$3$. The resulting budget line is the compensated budget line. The substitution effect is the reduction in consumption from 30 to 22, and the income effect is the reduction in consumption from 22 to 12.

negatively related to the price change. This reflects the fact that good 1 is a normal good. (We know that good 1 is normal, because when income decreases, the consumer buys less of it.)

PROBLEM 4.3

Using the information embodied in Figure 4.2, find an algebraic expression for the compensated budget line. What is the *added income* associated with the compensated budget line?

Income and Substitution Effects for a Price Decrease

Now let us perform the same sort of decomposition for a price reduction instead of a price rise. In Figure 4.3, when p_1 is \$2, the utility-maximizing bundle is bundle A — containing 3 units of good 1 — on indifference I_1. When p_1 then drops from \$2 to \$1, the consumer switches to bundle C — containing 9 units of good 1 — on indifference curve I_2. The consumer responds to the decrease in the price of good 1 from \$2 to \$1 by increasing consumption of good 1 from 3 to 9 units. Once again price and quantity demanded are negatively related. How can we decompose this increase in consumption into a substitution effect and an income effect?

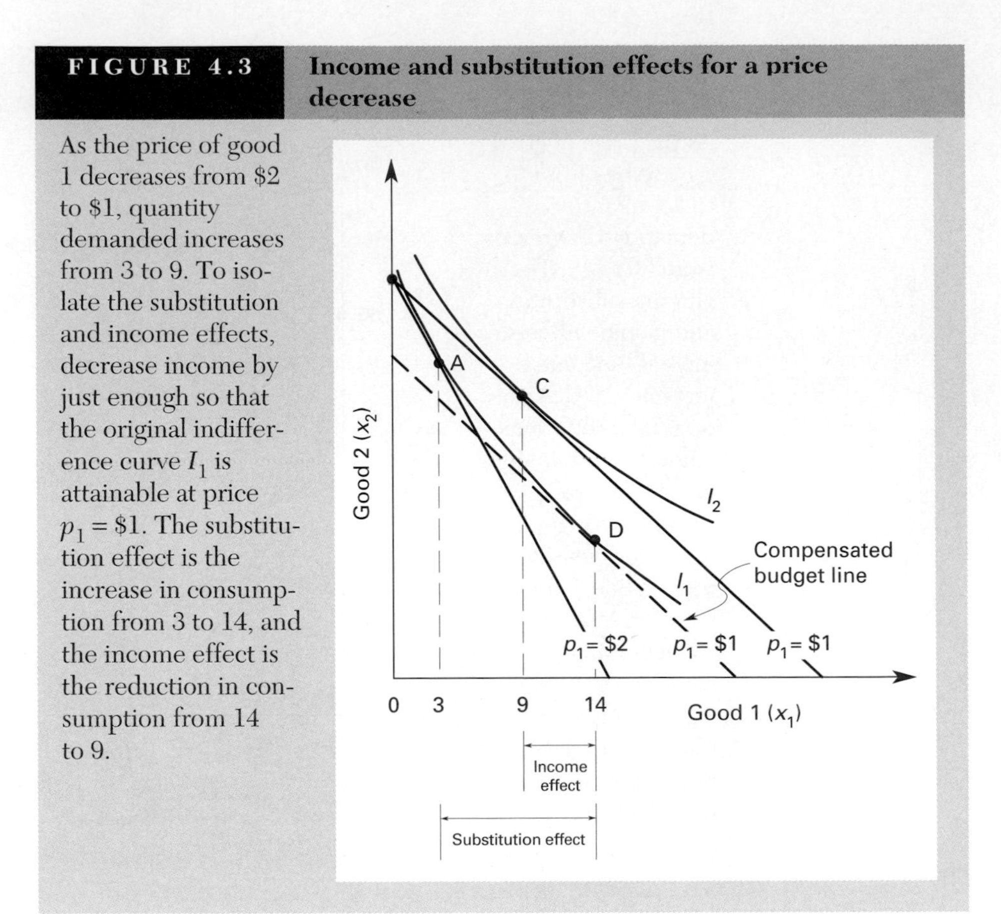

FIGURE 4.3 **Income and substitution effects for a price decrease**

As the price of good 1 decreases from \$2 to \$1, quantity demanded increases from 3 to 9. To isolate the substitution and income effects, decrease income by just enough so that the original indifference curve I_1 is attainable at price $p_1 = \$1$. The substitution effect is the increase in consumption from 3 to 14, and the income effect is the reduction in consumption from 14 to 9.

First, we need to isolate the substitution effect. Beginning at bundle C in Figure 4.3, we can eliminate the income effect by changing the consumer's income just enough so that he or she can attain the initial indifference curve, I_1. Because the price of good 1 has dropped, this time we have to take income away from the consumer. The dashed line in Figure 4.3 is the compensated budget line, and the utility-maximizing bundle is bundle D, which contains 14 units of good 1. Thus, the substitution effect associated with a decrease in the price of good 1 from \$2 to \$1 is an increase in quantity of good 1 from 3 to 14 units. Notice, the substitution effect associated with this *decrease* in p_1 is an *increase* in consumption of good 1. Here, as in the previous case, the substitution effect is *negatively related* to the price change.

Now, beginning at bundle D, to isolate the income effect we restore the income that we just took away. The solid line through C is the resulting budget line, and the consumer chooses bundle C, which contains 9 units of good 1. The income effect associated with this *decrease* in the price of good 1 from \$2 to \$1 is then a *decrease* in consumption of good 1 from 14 units to 9. In this case, the income effect is *positively* related to the price change. This positive relationship reflects the fact that good 1 in Figure 4.3 is an inferior good. We know this because in response to an increase in income, the consumer buys less of it.

In Figure 4.3 the income and substitution effects work in opposite directions. Because the substitution effect is larger than the income effect, however, the *total effect* is negatively related to the price change. In the following problem, you will discover that when good 1 is an inferior good, the income effect may be larger than the substitution effect. When it is, the good is a Giffen good.

PROBLEM 4.4

Consider again Figure 4.1, in which the price and quantity demanded of good 1 are positively related. Suppose that initially the price of good 1 is $3 and that it subsequently drops to $2. First, decompose the change in quantity of good 1 demanded into income and substitution effects. Then notice that the substitution effect is negatively related to the price change, that the income effect is positively related to the price change, that good 1 is an inferior good, and that the income effect is larger than the substitution effect.

The Negative Substitution Effect

In all of these decompositions, the substitution effect is negatively related to the price change. In Figure 4.2, when the price rose, the substitution effect generated a decline in the consumption of good 1. In Figure 4.3 and in your analysis of Figure 4.1, when the price dropped, the substitution effect generated an increase in consumption. The negative relationship between the substitution effect and the price change is *always* true when indifference curves are convex and smooth and when the consumer buys a positive amount of both goods.

It is easy to see why. In isolating the substitution effect we identified two points on the same indifference curve. The first was a point of tangency of the indifference curve with the original budget line — the points labelled A in Figures 4.2 and 4.3. The second was a point of tangency of the indifference curve with the compensated budget line — the points labelled D in Figures 4.2 and 4.3. If the indifference curve is convex and smooth, *MRS* diminishes from left to right along the indifference curve. Therefore, the point of tangency with the budget line that reflects the lower price of good 1 will be to the right of the other point of tangency. The result is a negative relationship between the change in price and the change in quantity demanded of good 1.

If indifference curves are smooth and convex and if the consumer buys a positive quantity of both goods, then the substitution effect is always negatively related to the price change.

The Ambiguous Income Effect

Unlike the substitution effect, however, the income effect of a price change may be either negatively or positively related to the price change.

For a normal good, the income effect is negatively related to the price change; for an inferior good, the income effect is positively related to the price change.

The Slope of the Demand Curve

We can now fit these various pieces together to develop a deeper understanding of the slope of the demand curve, or the qualitative relationship between the price and the quantity demanded of a good. If the good is normal, the substitution and income effects of a price change are both negatively related to the price change and are therefore complementary.

If a good is normal, then its demand curve is always downward sloping: price and quantity demanded are negatively related.

If the good is inferior, the income effect of a price change is positively related and the substitution effect is negatively related to the price change; the slope of the demand curve then depends on the relative strengths of the two effects.

If a good is inferior and if the substitution effect is larger than the income effect, then its demand curve is downward sloping: price and quantity demanded are negatively related. If a good is inferior and if the income effect is larger than the substitution effect, then its demand curve is upward sloping: price and quantity demanded are positively related.

The last result describes the Giffen good case. Although Giffen goods are theoretically possible, they are rare. No single case has ever been documented.[2] For this reason, we will set Giffen goods aside in the rest of this book and simply assume that demand curves are downward sloping.

4.3 The Compensated Demand Curve

We used the assumptions that indifference curves are smooth and convex to derive the result that the substitution effect is negatively related to the price change. In this section, we drop the assumptions of smoothness and convexity and instead use only minimal assumptions to show that the *substitution effect* is never *positively related to the price change*. We also introduce the *compensated demand curve*, which reflects only the substitution effect. Unlike the ordinary demand curve, the compensated demand curve cannot be upward sloping.

The Substitution Effect Revisited

compensatory income

Recall that when we identified the substitution effect, we identified the *minimum income* that allowed the consumer to attain the original indifference curve. Let us call this minimum income the **compensatory income**. The associated budget line is, of course, the compensated budget line.

2. The Giffen good is named after Colonel Robert Giffen, despite the fact that there is no historical evidence that he ever mentioned it. The account, first related by Alfred Marshall and later popularized by Paul Samuelson, relates to the Irish potato famine of 1845–49. According to Marshall's version, the blight reduced the supply of potatoes, the price rose, and more potatoes were consumed. The story is highly suspect for several reasons. First, if the demand was upward sloping, a fall in supply would lead to a fall in price. Second, how could the Irish, as a group, consume more potatoes when there were fewer potatoes to be had? Third, it seems highly unlikely that potatoes would be inferior goods among starving peasants.

FIGURE 4.4 **The nonpositive substitution effect**

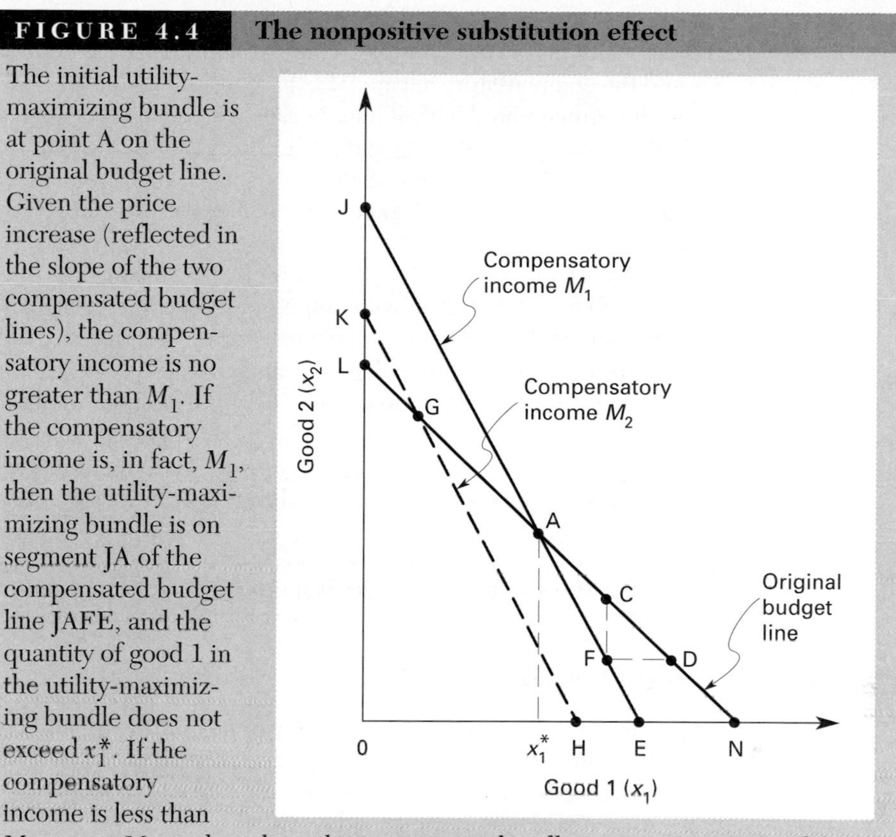

The initial utility-maximizing bundle is at point A on the original budget line. Given the price increase (reflected in the slope of the two compensated budget lines), the compensatory income is no greater than M_1. If the compensatory income is, in fact, M_1, then the utility-maximizing bundle is on segment JA of the compensated budget line JAFE, and the quantity of good 1 in the utility-maximizing bundle does not exceed x_1^*. If the compensatory income is less than M_1 — say, M_2 — then the utility-maximizing bundle is on segment KG of the compensated budget line KGH, and the quantity of good 1 in the bundle is less than x_1^*. In either case, the substitution effect is nonpositively related to the price change.

In Figure 4.4, the indifference curves have been omitted because their shapes now play no role in the analysis. In the initial situation, given the lower value of p_1 — reflected by the flatter budget line LGACDN — this consumer chose the utility-maximizing bundle at A. Now suppose that p_1 goes up and let M_1 be the level of income such that the consumer could buy the original consumption bundle, given the higher price of good 1. The budget line associated with the higher price of good 1 and income M_1 is JAFE. Clearly, the compensatory income — because it is the minimum income that allows the consumer to attain the original indifference curve — can be no greater than M_1.

Suppose for the moment that the compensatory income is M_1. (It is unlikely to be this large; however, as you will see in Problem 4.5, it can be.) The compensated budget line is then JAFE in Figure 4.4. Notice that on segment AFE of the compensated budget line, only bundle A can be on the original indifference curve. Why? If another bundle on AFE were on the original indifference curve — say, the bundle at F — then, by nonsatiation, any bundle on segment CD of the original budget line would be preferred to bundle A. But this is impossible because bundle A is the original utility-maximizing bundle. Thus, we know that given the higher price of good 1 and the compensatory income M_1, this consumer will choose a bundle on segment JA of the compensated budget line. Because the quantity of good 1 in these bundles *does not exceed* x_1^*, we also know that the substitution effect in this instance is *nonpositively related* to the price change. In other words, given the compensated budget line, the quantity demanded of good 1 will not increase. Instead, it will either remain the same or decrease.

Now let us suppose that the compensatory income is something less than M_1, say M_2 in Figure 4.4. This lower compensatory income gives rise to the lower compensated budget line KGH. By simply revising the argument above, we can establish that — given the higher price of good 1 and compensatory income M_2 — the consumer will now pick a bundle on segment KG of the compensated budget line. Because the quantity of good 1 in all these bundles is *strictly less than* x_1^*, we know that the substitution effect in this instance is *negatively* related to the price change.

In sum, we now know that the substitution effect cannot be positively related to the price change.

The substitution effect is nonpositively related to the price change.

The Compensated Demand Function

In the preceding analysis, we held p_2 constant while allowing p_1 to vary. We also adjusted the consumer's income up or down so that he or she remained on the same indifference curve. And for each value of p_1, we identified the quantity of good 1 in the consumer's utility-maximizing bundle. If we now plot these price-quantity pairs, we have what is called a **compensated demand curve**. The adjective *compensated* indicates that the consumer has been given the compensatory income needed to keep him or her on the original indifference curve.

compensated demand curve

In Figure 4.5a, we have held p_2 constant at \$2 and considered three different values of p_1 — \$1, \$2, and \$4. This lets us identify the corresponding points of tangency between the three compensated budget lines and the indifference curve *I*. These points are labelled A, B, and C in Figure 4.5a, and the corresponding points A′, B′, and C′ on the compensated demand curve are plotted in Figure 4.5b. For instance, when p_1 is \$1 in Figure 4.5a, the compensated budget line is tangent to the indifference curve *I* at bundle A, which contains 16 units of good 1. Therefore, point A′ in Figure 4.5b is one point on the compensated demand curve. Similarly, when p_1 is \$2 (or \$4), the compensated budget line is tangent to *I* at bundle B (or bundle C), which gives rise to point B′ (or C′) on the compensated demand curve.

Since the compensated demand curve reflects *only* the substitution effect, it cannot be upward sloping. That is, when p_1 increases, quantity demanded on the compensated demand curve will ordinarily decrease, and it cannot increase. Thus, our

FIGURE 4.5 The compensated demand curve

In (a), the three compensated budget lines, which are associated with three prices for good 1, are tangent to indifference curve I at points A, B, and C. These points of tangency are used to construct the compensated demand curve in (b). For example, when p_1 is \$4, the compensated budget line is tangent at bundle C, which contains 8 units of good 1; therefore, one point on the compensated demand curve is point C′, where 8 units are demanded at price $p_1 = \$4$.

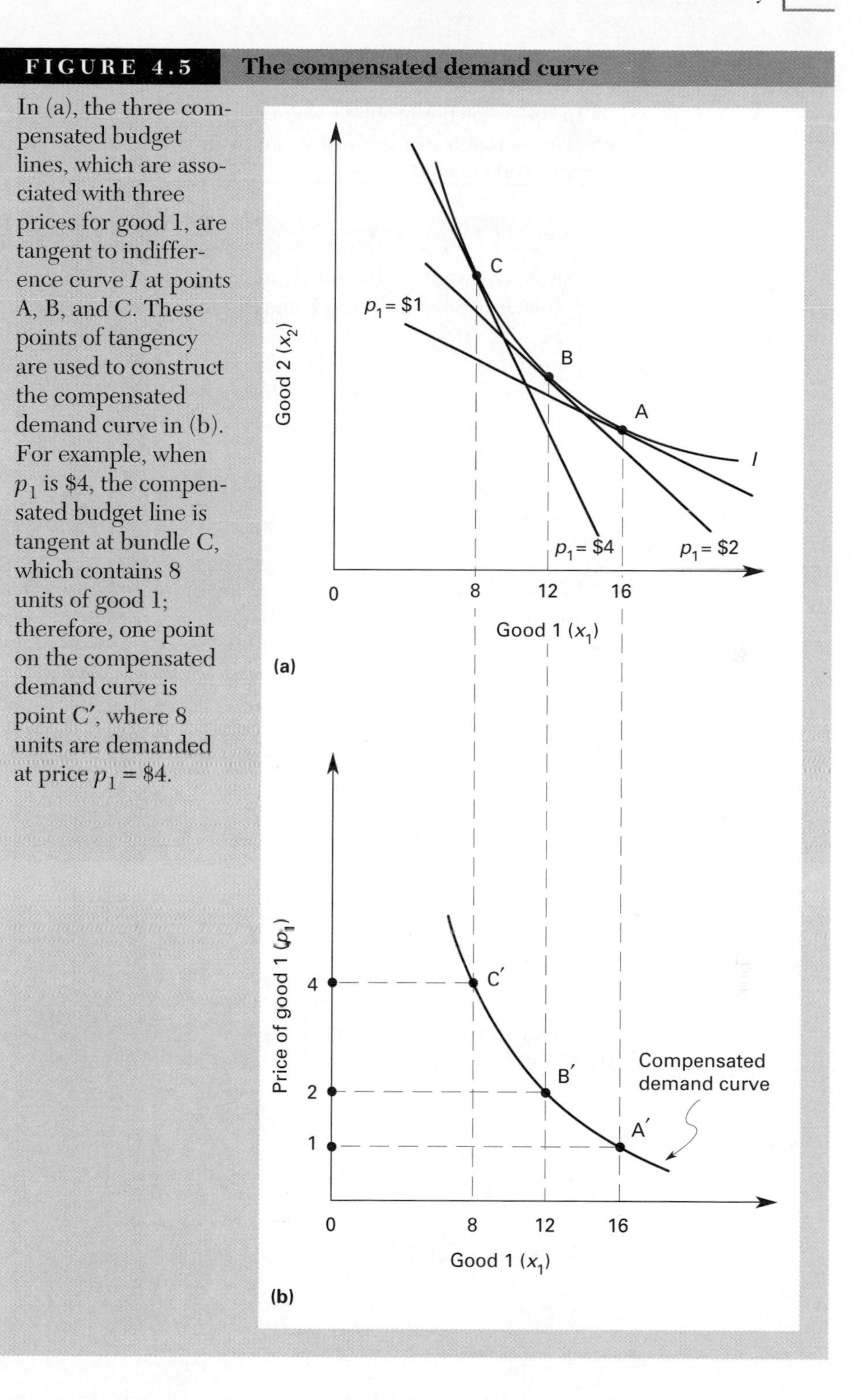

intuition that demand functions are downward sloping is correct for compensated demand functions.[3]

In the following problem, you will see that the substitution effect is not always negative — that it can be zero — and you will have the opportunity to construct a compensated demand curve.

PROBLEM 4.5

Suppose we have the following utility function: $U(x_1, x_2) = \min(x_1, x_2)$. Initially, both prices are \$1, and income is \$30. Find the utility-maximizing bundle. (*Hint*: First show that $x_1 = x_2$ in the utility maximizing bundle, and use this result to find the bundle.) Now let p_1 increase to \$2. What is the compensatory income? Show that the substitution effect is zero. Construct the compensated demand curve for good 1. Now use your answer to Problem 3.4 to find the ordinary demand curve for good 1, given $p_2 = \$1$ and $M = \$30$, and plot both demand curves on the same diagram.

We now have two demand curves: the ordinary demand curve, which arises from the consumer's real choice problem, and the compensated demand curve, which arises from the choice problem in which the consumer is given a different income — the compensatory income — every time the good's price changes. In the remainder of the book, when we use the term *demand curve*, we will mean the ordinary demand curve. When we talk about the compensated demand curve, we will always add the adjective *compensated*.

3. Notice that to find the compensated demand function, in essence, we solved an expenditure-minimization problem by minimizing the cost of attaining a specified indifference curve; that is, we implicitly solved

$$\text{minimize } (p_1x_2 + p_2x_2) \text{ by choice of } x_1 \text{ and } x_2$$
$$\text{subject to the constraint } U(x_1, x_2) = u$$

where u is a fixed utility number. (The Lagrange multiplier method can be used to solve this problem.) The solution gives us x_1^H and x_2^H as functions of p_1, p_2, and u. Symbolically,

$$x_1^H = H_1(p_1, p_2, u)$$
$$x_2^H = H_2(p_1, p_2, u)$$

The functions H_1 and H_2 are the compensated demand functions. We have shown that the partial derivative of $H(p_1, p_2, u)$ with respect to p_1 is nonpositive. For example, suppose the utility function was $U(x_1, x_2) = x_1x_2$. Then

$$L(x_1, x_2, \lambda) = x_1p_1 + x_2p_2 + \lambda(U^0 x_1 - x_2),$$

and the first order conditions are:

$$p_1 - \lambda x_2 = 0$$
$$p_2 - \lambda x_1 = 0$$
$$U^0 - x_1x_2 = 0.$$

Solving these three equations for the two compensated demand curves gives:

$$x_1^H = (U^0p_2/p_1)^{1/2}$$
$$x_2^H = (U^0p_1/p_2)^{1/2}$$

Application: COLA Clauses and Consuming an Endowment

Although the compensated demand curve may appear to be complete fiction, there are instances when natural compensations occur. Costs of living adjustments (COLA clauses), common features of many labour contracts and pension plans, attempt to protect people from the effects of inflation. The idea behind a COLA clause is to continually adjust income so that the original consumption bundle can be purchased. If there is a pure inflation of 10 percent, then income is adjusted upward by 10 percent. The more interesting case of an impure inflation is illustrated in Figure 4.6.

Figure 4.6 shows an original budget line AA with E the optimal bundle chosen. After an inflation in which relative prices also change, the new budget line is BB, which lies below the original due to the fall in real income. Notice that the slope of BB is different because it is assumed that the inflation is not pure. When income is adjusted to compensate for the inflation the final budget constraint CC passes through the original bundle E. However, due to the change in the relative prices, these workers now substitute into the cheaper good (in this case x_1) and have an optimal bundle at point F. In effect, the COLA clause acts as a compensation mechanism and leaves only a substitution effect.[4]

FIGURE 4.6 **COLA clauses**

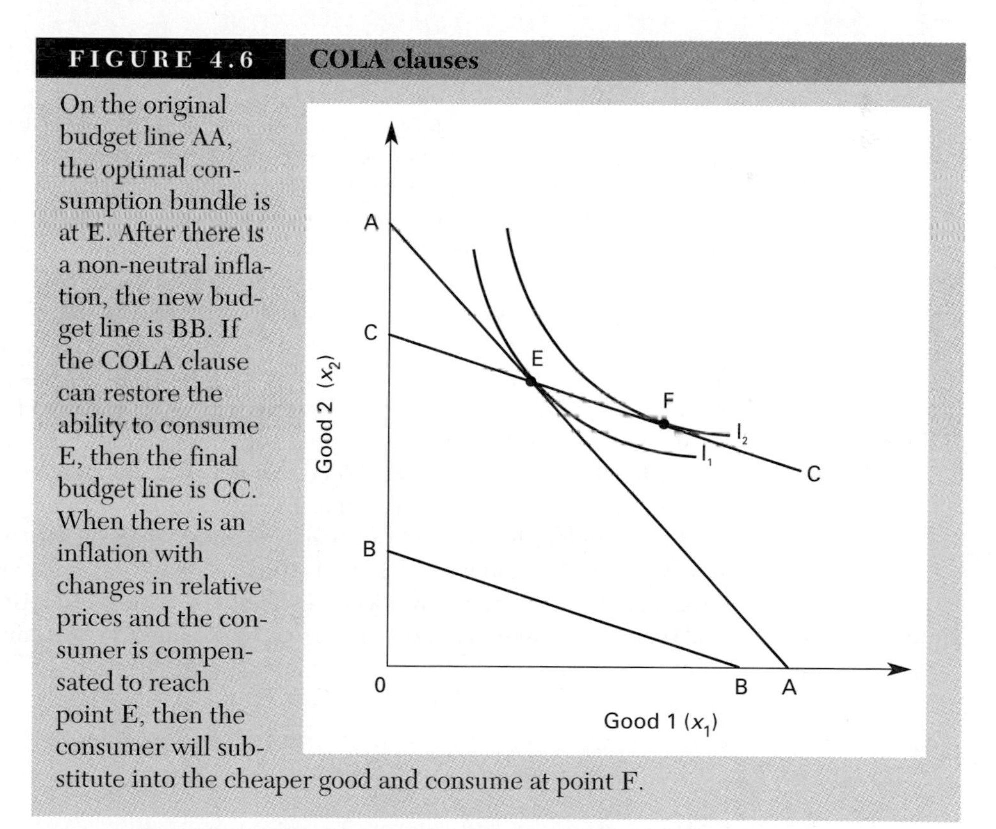

On the original budget line AA, the optimal consumption bundle is at E. After there is a non-neutral inflation, the new budget line is BB. If the COLA clause can restore the ability to consume E, then the final budget line is CC. When there is an inflation with changes in relative prices and the consumer is compensated to reach point E, then the consumer will substitute into the cheaper good and consume at point F.

4. We say "in effect" because for large changes in relative prices there still remains an income effect. In Figure 4.6 notice that the individual is actually better off than in the initial situation because although he or she can buy the original bundle E, the change in relative prices leads the individual to choose instead the bundle F, which contains more of the relatively cheaper good 1. This type of compensation is actually called a Slutsky compensation. In practice, it is the only one that can take place because true compensations of income would require knowledge of the utility function.

Another example of a natural compensation results when people are endowed with goods rather than money. We saw in Chapter 3 that, rather than money, consumers could be endowed with goods like labour or housing. Recall that in this case the budget line rotated through the endowment point, because no matter what the relative price, you always owned your endowment. This provides another interesting natural compensation. Going back to Figure 4.6, reinterpret point E as both the endowment *and* the optimal consumption bundle at prices AA. That is, suppose the individual consumes just his or her endowment. Now, when a relative price changes, there is another compensated substitution effect into the cheaper good, and again consumption moves to point F.

The most important example of this is individual home ownership.[5] Most North Americans own their own home, and very few have more than one. In other words, most people consume their endowment of housing. When the price of housing goes up in a neighbourhood, homeowners substitute out of housing. They subdivide their lots, rent out the basement or spare room, perhaps sell and buy a smaller house in the same neighbourhood or a larger one out of town. When the price of housing falls, the opposite happens. There is no ambiguous income effect here because the endowment acts as a natural compensation.[6]

4.4 Time and Money Prices

Until now, we have considered the price of a good strictly in terms of its dollar price. Usually, though, consumption of goods requires time, and time has a cost, given that individuals have the option of working. A moment's consideration reveals that the time component of consumption can be substantial. A round of golf may cost $40, but usually takes four hours to complete. Not only does it take time to shop for clothes, see a movie, or buy and use a personal computer, but different goods vary in their time intensity. As a student at your university, you've no doubt paid a substantial amount of money in tuition, but consider the value of the time you are sacrificing. The time component in the cost of your education is likely 10 times the dollar component. These observations led Gary Becker (1965) to formulate the consumer choice problem in an enlightening way by including both a *time price* and a *money price* in the **full price** of a good. Fortunately, time is easily added to the model, and does not alter the results of demand theory we have examined thus far.

full price

Let us explore Becker's formulation by considering the case in which consumption requires both time and money. Let T be time available in some period, h be hours of work, and l be hours of leisure. Because the hours of work and leisure must add up to total time, the **time constraint** (analogous to the budget constraint) is

time constraint

$$h + l = T$$

5. This example comes from Barzel (1982); he provides many more.

6. This is an important case that provides one reason why Giffen goods may be so difficult to find. In order for there to be a Giffen good, the good must have a large negative income effect *and* consume a large fraction of the household budget. Houses and automobiles are usually the largest items people consume, but people also tend to consume their endowments of these goods. As we have just seen, when you consume an endowment the income effect is compensated for and the substitution effect always dominates. Hence we would not expect a Giffen result regardless of the income effect. For smaller ticket items, the substitution effect will tend to dominate because the item has so little effect on income. For example, when bubble gum doubles in price, it has little impact on real incomes.

How we choose to divide our time between work and leisure obviously determines our work-generated income; that is, the time at work multiplied by the wage rate determines earned income. Here we are assuming (somewhat unrealistically) that a particular person — say, Jan — can choose her hours of work. Letting w be the wage rate at which Jan can sell her labour and assuming that she has A dollars of income from other sources, we can write Jan's income as $A + wh$. We will assume that Jan spends her income on goods, x_1 and x_2. Let p_1 and p_2 be money prices and z_1 and z_2 be time prices for goods 1 and 2. Consuming one unit of good 1, for example, requires p_1 units of money and z_1 units of time. Now the consumer's choice problem involves two constraints: the budget constraint,

$$p_1x_1 + p_2x_2 = A + wh$$

and the time constraint,

$$z_1x_1 + z_2x_2 + h = T$$

We can combine the two constraints. We have $h = T - z_1x_1 - z_2x_2$ from the time constraint. The time devoted to work is simply the total time available T minus the time devoted to consumption. When we combine this with the budget constraint, we have

$$p_1x_1 + p_2x_2 = A + wT - wz_1x_1 - wz_2x_2$$

We can rearrange this combined constraint to get

$$(p_1 + wz_1)x_1 + (p_2 + wz_2)x_2 = A + wT$$

full income

Here we can interpret $A + wT$ as potential or **full income**, and — this is the crucial point — we can interpret $p_1 + wz_1$ as the full price of good 1 and $p_2 + wz_2$ as the full price of good 2. We can easily see that the full price of a good has two parts: the money component p_1, and the time component wz_1. Notice that the time component is further broken down into the wage rate and the time intensity of the good. All else equal, individuals with high wages have high time costs. For these people, goods that take a great deal of time are relatively expensive and they tend to avoid or minimize them. For example, there is an old saying that "North Americans waste food, but keep appointments." To the extent that it is true, it reflects the high time costs that North Americans have. When time is valuable at the margin, it is treated carefully, and appointments are kept. In countries and locations where time costs are low, a missed appointment involves a minimal loss and is not a matter of concern.

In fact, recognizing that consumption of different goods requires money and time in different proportions, and that people have different time costs, explains a great deal of behaviour. For example, because many women and men have the opportunity to work outside the home at high wage rates, the two-income family is now quite common. Interestingly, in such families the norm is to have only two children, who are relatively close together. The explanation is that the full price of a child in such a family is high, because children are time-intensive and time is more valuable in two-income families. By having fewer children, spaced closer together, working parents substitute at both margins.

PROBLEM 4.6

Compared to even 50 years ago, the average home has many more time-saving features: gas rather than wood fireplaces, microwave ovens, built-in vacuum cleaners, prepared foods, automatic washing machines, etc. Furthermore, cellular phones, faxes, and e-mail help to save time as well. Why, despite all of these time-saving devices, do we live such rushed lives?

Application: Religious Behaviour

Over the past 40 years the scope of application of economic reasoning has increased dramatically. Economists now study phenomena that were formerly thought to be outside the scope of economics. Marriage, child rearing, racial discrimination, criminal activity, and even religion have attracted the attention of economists. These phenomena are not exclusively economic, but economic reasoning can nevertheless shed light on them. To help you assess for yourself the proper scope of application of economics, we will discuss a number of these applications, beginning with religion.

Religion is an important activity for many people, and several economists have spent most of their careers examining the economics of religion. From an economic perspective, religious activity is similar to many other activities where scarce time and money are allocated to produce goods and services. One thing that has been discovered is that one of the most important factors in determining church attendance and church giving is income. As an individual's income increases, church attendance falls but dollar giving increases. The economic explanation of this behaviour rests on the observation that high-income individuals have high time costs, making it more costly to sit through a church service or participate in other church activities. Not only is this true in comparing individuals, but it is also true in considering the same individual over time. Incomes are small for young people, rise and peak during middle age, and then fall during the latter part of life. Consistent with the law of demand, the young and seniors spend more time at church, but give less money. Finally, it is also true across the sexes. On average women still earn less than men, and on average women attend church more often than men.

Iannaccone, et al. (1995) have uncovered a particularly interesting example of time costs and church attendance. From the inception of the Church of Jesus Christ and the Latter-Day Saints in the 1830s, Mormons have always stressed the importance of education. Brigham Young University in Provo, Utah is, in fact, one of the largest universities in the world. This stress on education, among other things, has led to a high average income among Mormons. In contrast, the Jehovah's Witnesses actively discourage the education of its members, and few have a post-secondary degree. Jehovah's Witnesses have relatively low incomes compared to other religious groups.

Can you predict which group gives more in time and money? Iannaccone, et al. found that Mormons give more dollars per capita than any other Christian group, while the Jehovah's Witnesses are second from the bottom in terms of financial giving. On the other hand, the Mormons had low attendance rates compared to other churches, while the Jehovah's Witnesses were first in attendance and participation by a long shot.

Application: Rationing by Waiting in Squash

Quite often the dollar price of a scarce good is zero. In these circumstances, the good is often allocated by time, and people have to line up.[7] Lineups are quite common, and here we examine in some detail the allocation of squash court time by waiting. At community centres, private clubs, and universities around the world, squash court time is often allocated on a first-come-first-served basis. When there are more courts available than are demanded, there is no wait. When the quantity demanded exceeds the number of courts, then people must "wait" by signing up first on a list, or getting up early to book a court by phone. What can we learn about the implications of this allocation mechanism by applying the tools we have developed?

Let us imagine a situation in which 200 avid players have common access to a university squash facility that will accommodate 3000 one-hour bookings per month. The facility can therefore accommodate up to 15 bookings per player per month ($15 \times 200 = 3000$). We will suppose that these players have identical preferences and that they value their time at $10 per hour. The time price of playing squash is then $10 per booking. Suppose, too, that the players have free access to the courts — they need not pay a fee for booking court time, so that the money price is zero.

If x_1 is the number of bookings the player makes per month and x_2 a composite good, the player's choice problem is to maximize $U(x_1, x_2)$, by choice of x_1 and x_2, subject to the constraint,

$$10x_1 + x_2 = 10T.$$

The full price of each booking is the value of an hour of time, $10. The constraint then says that the value of the time spent on the court each period, $10x_1$, added to the value of the composite good, x_2, must add up to full income, $10T$.

In the solution to this problem, if each player, at the dollar price of zero, demands a relatively small number of bookings, say 10, then the total number of bookings demanded each month, $2000 = 10 \times 200$, will be less than the facility's capacity, 3000, and everyone can be accommodated without difficulty. But what happens when the demand for court time is greater than the facility's capacity? What happens, for example, when each player demands 20 bookings per month, so that total demand, $4000 = 20 \times 200$, exceeds capacity, 3000?

What happens depends on the information people have about everyone's preferences, how fast people are processed, and the type of booking scheme in place. Let's consider a couple of cases. Suppose that everyone knows that the courts are booked on a first-come basis, they know that everyone else has the same preferences they do, and they also know that it takes no time whatsoever for the university gym to process their booking. If you have to show up in person to book, the excess demand implies that lineups will form before the gym opens. Anyone who decides to wait and show up on time will only find that all the courts have been booked. If the marginal value of the 20th booking is $10, then this means that everyone must wait one hour to book the court. Everyone wants to wait less — just like consumers want to pay less for all goods — but competition to get the courts forces individuals to wait for one hour. Can you now see what the equilibrium will look like? Everyone shows up one hour before the gym opens and books their court. At a waiting time of one hour, the players only book 15 bookings per month.

---

7. Can you think of other ways goods are allocated besides by time or money?

Now, let's complicate this a little more. Suppose it takes the gentleman at the squash counter 10 minutes to process all of the squash bookings for the next hour. What happens to the amount of time everyone waits? You might think the squash players wait less, but the answer is you wait exactly the same amount of time. Now the players show up 50 minutes before the courts open, and simply wait another 10 minutes to be processed. In equilibrium the players must wait an hour, and it doesn't matter how that waiting time is allocated.

Under either booking procedure access to bookings is not really free even though the university does not charge for the use of its courts. The time required to make a booking — which we can regard as the time price of making a booking — will increase until the excess demand is eliminated; that is, until the total number of bookings demanded is just 3000, or until each player demands exactly 15 bookings per month (since $15 \times 200 = 3000$).

Let q represent the time necessary to make a booking. The total time spent per booking is then $(1 + q)$, since the game itself takes an hour to play and it takes q hours to make a booking. The total time price per booking is then $\$10(1 + q)$, and the revised constraint for the player's choice problem is then:

$$10(1 + q)x_1 + x_2 = 10T$$

In Figure 4.7, we have illustrated the solution to the player's choice problem when q is large enough that each player demands 15 bookings. The total number of bookings

FIGURE 4.7 **Squash and the time spent waiting in line**

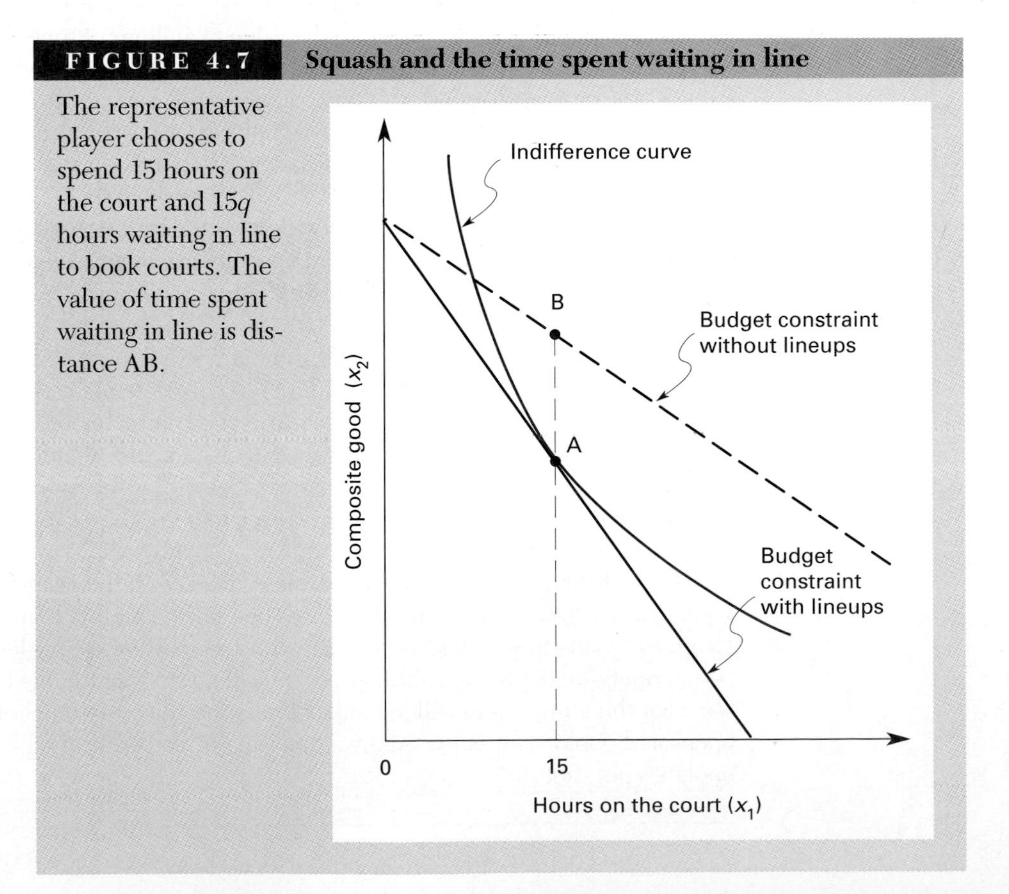

The representative player chooses to spend 15 hours on the court and $15q$ hours waiting in line to book courts. The value of time spent waiting in line is distance AB.

demanded is therefore 3000, and the excess demand has been eliminated. The player's equilibrium is at point A on the indifference curve. To identify graphically the value to the individual player of the time spent acquiring a booking, we have also included the constraint that would arise if q were equal to zero — the dashed line in Figure 4.7. The value of the time spent in the lineup each month is then the distance AB, since the price of x_2 is one.

PROBLEM 4.7

Suppose that 'N Sync is coming to Saskatoon, and every 13-year-old girl in the city wants to watch the all-boy singing group do their stuff at the ticket price of \$60. Unfortunately, there are 20 000 thirteen-year-old girls in the city and the concert hall only seats 5000. When tickets go on sale a huge line develops. What will happen to the number of people in the line if each girl is limited to buying one ticket compared to the case where each girl can buy two tickets? What would the line look like if the preferences for 'N Sync were not identical across all the 13-year-old girls? That is, suppose there is a continuum of preferences with some at one end who would "kill" for a ticket, while those at the other end would only be willing to pay \$10 to go see them? (Assume that the tickets are still handed out instantaneously.)

PROBLEM 4.8

The School District of Langley has several alternative schools that are quite popular; so popular in fact that parents often line up for days to register their children to attend. At first parents had to simply stand outside the school waiting for it to open. The school board, over a series of years, made the wait more comfortable. First they allowed chairs, then tents, then campers. Eventually they opened up the fields and parking lots for RVs. They then allowed the washrooms and water services of the school to be used by those waiting. And on and on. What do you think happened to the length of line given that the number of students the school could accept is fixed? Did the efforts to make the line more comfortable make the parents better off?

Notice that when there is excess demand, it is time in the lineup that discourages players from attempting to use the facility so frequently and thereby establishes an equilibrium between demand and supply. Yet, as we know, time is a valuable resource. The time spent in the lineup uses up this valuable resource. Spending time to acquire bookings is avoidable; it is the consequence of the first-come-first-served allocation mechanism.

If there is no value to having a line, then there *are* other institutional arrangements that are clearly better. For instance, imagine substituting a money price for the time price. Specifically, suppose that the university charged a dollar price equal to $10q$ for each booking. Then the player's constraint would still be $10(1+q)x_1 + x_2 = 10T$ (since we have just substituted an equivalent money price for a time price) and the player's equilibrium would still be at point A in Figure 4.7. Notice that there would then be no excess demand for bookings, since each player again demands 15 per month. This price institution produces an equilibrium in which the player is just as well off, the university generates some income, and it completely avoids the waste of time that occurs with the first-come-first-served institution.

Application: Homesteading

When allocating goods by waiting is wasteful, it is usually avoided by using prices to allocate goods. However, allocating goods on a first-come-first-served basis often provides side benefits that make it worthwhile. Consider the case of homesteading on the Great Plains of the US and on the Canadian Prairies.

During the first half of the nineteenth century a small, debt-ridden, loosely-held-together, sparsely populated new country called the United States had a difficult problem to solve. On paper it claimed ownership of vast tracks of land to the west, yet this land was occupied by native Indians, Mexicans, British trappers, and a host of other minor interests. How were they to actually take possession?

At the very beginning of the century the US government sold public lands in the areas of Ohio, Kentucky, and Tennessee, but they quickly switched over to a system of first-come-first-served called homesteading. A homestead was 160 acres that could be had by the first person to claim it, pay a small registration fee of $10 and improve the land for five years. The advantage homesteading had over land sales was that the settler had to occupy the land. Occupation was important because the government did not have the resources to defend the land against others claiming it.

As in the case with squash bookings, homesteading forced individual settlers to show up early and claim the land. Someone purchasing land could buy it and not show up to farm for many years when it is optimal to show up. A homesteader who waited to show up would find his plot had long been taken by someone who got there earlier.

When it came time for Canada to settle its western frontier, the new country faced a similar problem, only this time the threat was not Mexicans or the Aboriginal peoples; rather it was Americans moving north. Selling the land to private interests would not improve the Canadian claim to sovereignty on the prairies if there were no guns to back it up. Thus the Canadian government adopted the identical homesteading laws the US had used to settle their frontier. By providing an incentive to settlers to "rush" to the Prairies and stay to improve the land, the area was populated by Canadians who quite naturally kept the Americans out.

Homesteading was not free. Suppose the optimal time to arrive in say, Lone Spruce, Saskatchewan, in order to start farming was 1920. The problem for a young family living in Ontario in 1900 was that if they waited until 1920, the homestead would be gone, and so the settlers would plan to move out west a year early. Other potential farmers would think the same way and would plan on moving two years early. This process continued until it was just barely worth moving at all. By allocating the frontier this way, both governments forced settlers to move too soon and wait for development to catch up. This meant that many settlers waited years for railways, schools, and the rest of civilization. As one settler put it, "There ain't no such thing as free land."

4.5 Measuring Benefits and Costs

As we indicated in Section 1.6, cost-benefit analysis is a very important tool in any economic policy maker's tool kit. But how can we measure the benefits and costs to individuals arising from a particular policy or institution? In Chapter 3 we saw the incorrect way to measure low prices in the Tradewell/Safeway case. How could we more accurately measure which store had the lowest prices? If we can devise adequate benefit measures for this specific problem, we can then adapt those measures to a range of similar benefit questions. We will begin by asking a specific question: What value does Mr. Polo, a potential member of an exclusive dining club, place on the right to be a member of the club? More precisely, what is the value to him of the right to buy meals in the club at some specified price p_1?

We will make the realistic assumption that "meals at the club" is an inessential good and begin the analysis by identifying Mr. Polo's equilibrium in two circumstances. In the first situation, he is not a member and therefore does not buy meals at the club. In the second situation, he is a club member and can buy meals at price p_1. In Figure 4.8, x_1 is the number of meals he eats at the club and x_2 is his expenditure on all other goods. Because in the first situation Mr. Polo is not a member, he spends his entire income $\$M$ on the composite good. The initial equilibrium is therefore M units up the vertical axis at E_0 on indifference curve I_0. In the second situation, however, he can buy club meals at price p_1, and his budget line is the solid line E_0E_1 in Figure 4.8. The subsequent equilibrium is at E_1 on indifference curve I_1. In essence, our problem is to measure the value that Mr. Polo places on the move from indifference curve I_0 to indifference curve I_1. Furthermore, we want to measure this value in dollars or, equivalently, in units of the composite good.

Equivalent Variation for a New Good

equivalent variation

By taking the subsequent indifference curve I_1 as our point of reference, we get a measure called the **equivalent variation** and labelled EV in Figure 4.8. This measure answers the following question: What is the *variation* in income that is *equivalent* to the right to buy club meals at price p_1? The answer is distance EV in Figure 4.8. Why? Because if Mr. Polo had $\$EV$ of additional income instead of a club membership, he would still be on the subsequent indifference curve I_1. In other words, that additional income is *equivalent* to the right to buy club meals.

Compensating Variation for a New Good

compensating variation

On the other hand, by taking the initial indifference curve I_0 as our point of reference, we get a measure called the **compensating variation,** labelled CV in Figure 4.8. This measure answers the following question: What *variation* in income *compensates* for the right to buy club meals at price p_1? The answer is distance CV. Why? Because if Mr. Polo had a club membership but his income had been reduced by $\$CV$, he would still be on the initial indifference I_0 at point E_3. In other words, the reduction in income exactly *compensates* for the right to buy club meals.

Another interpretation of CV is useful. Since $\$CV$ exactly compensates for the right to buy meals in the club, it is the *maximum price* that Mr. Polo will pay for meal priv-

FIGURE 4.8 Measuring the benefit of a new good

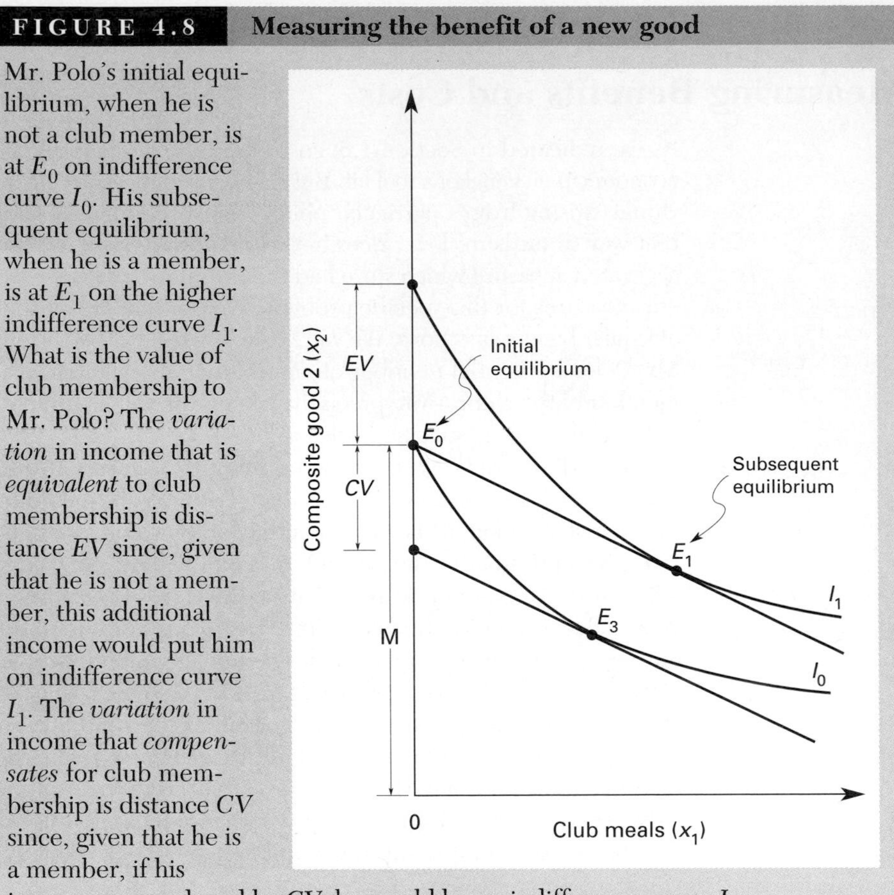

Mr. Polo's initial equilibrium, when he is not a club member, is at E_0 on indifference curve I_0. His subsequent equilibrium, when he is a member, is at E_1 on the higher indifference curve I_1. What is the value of club membership to Mr. Polo? The *variation* in income that is *equivalent* to club membership is distance *EV* since, given that he is not a member, this additional income would put him on indifference curve I_1. The *variation* in income that *compensates* for club membership is distance *CV* since, given that he is a member, if his income were reduced by *CV*, he would be on indifference curve I_0.

ileges. Therefore, if he is offered meal privileges for any price less than $\$CV$, he will buy them — and end up on an indifference curve higher than I_0. We will use this interpretation in Section 5.2, where we consider the demand for consumer capital.

PROBLEM 4.9

Show that as p_1 increases, *CV* for a new good decreases. In other words, show that the larger is p_1, the smaller is the maximum amount a consumer will pay for the right to buy good 1 at price p_1. Identify the values of p_1 such that *CV* is \$0.

So far, we have been focusing on measures of the benefit associated with the introduction of a specific new good, meals at a private club. These measures are obviously applicable to other new goods. For example, what value would someone in the town of Lethbridge place on the privilege of being able to listen to a symphony orchestra based in Lethbridge? These measures are also applicable to the costs associated with the disappearance of goods. For example, what value would a Vancouverite place on the loss of the Vancouver Grizzly basketball team to Memphis? We could easily adapt these concepts to measure the resulting costs borne by a Vancouver resident as well as the benefits enjoyed by a Memphis resident.

Many interesting policies and institutions, however, involve not the introduction of a new good, but a change in the price of some existing good. For example, every time the government raises the excise tax on cigarettes, a smoker faces a higher price for smoking. Every time your university increases tuition fees, you face a higher price for your education. Let us adapt the equivalent and compensating variations to measure the costs and benefits of such price changes.

Let us begin with a price increase, and again suppose that good 2 is a composite good. In Figure 4.9, p_1 is initially \$1 and the initial equilibrium is at E_0 on indifference curve I_0. The price of good 1 then rises to \$2, and the subsequent equilibrium is at E_1 on indifference curve I_1.

Equivalent Variation for a Price Change

To identify the equivalent variation of this price change, we will use the subsequent indifference curve I_1 as a point of reference and ask: What variation in income is equivalent

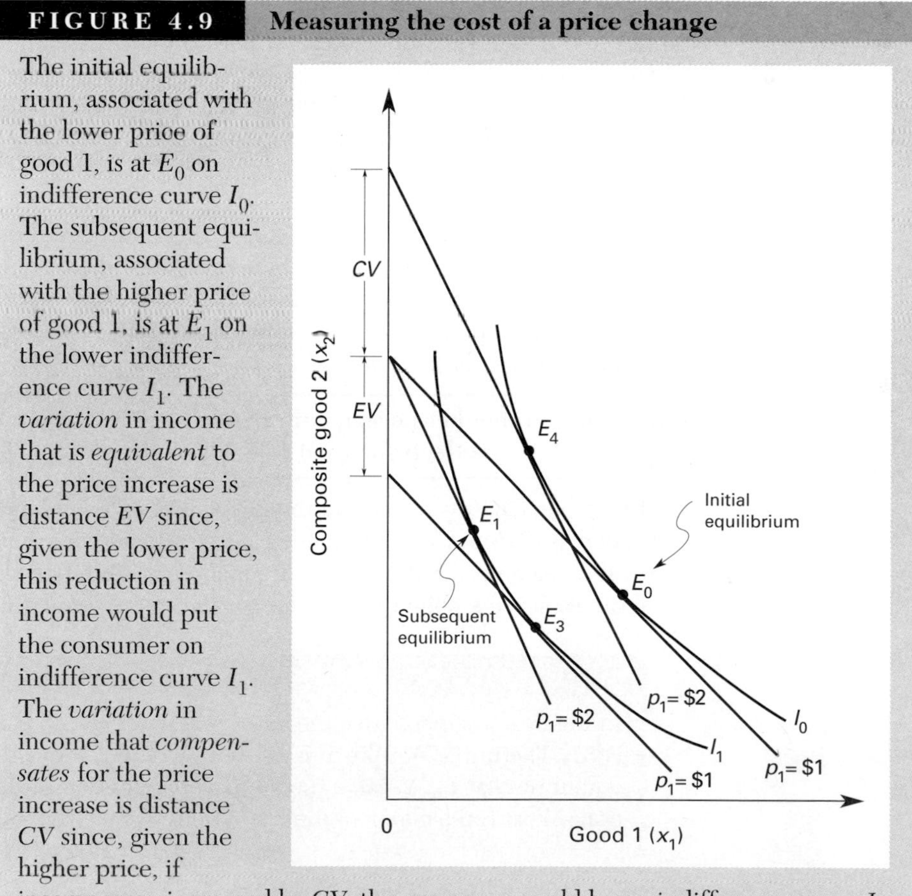

FIGURE 4.9 **Measuring the cost of a price change**

The initial equilibrium, associated with the lower price of good 1, is at E_0 on indifference curve I_0. The subsequent equilibrium, associated with the higher price of good 1, is at E_1 on the lower indifference curve I_1. The *variation* in income that is *equivalent* to the price increase is distance EV since, given the lower price, this reduction in income would put the consumer on indifference curve I_1. The *variation* in income that *compensates* for the price increase is distance CV since, given the higher price, if income were increased by CV, the consumer would be on indifference curve I_0.

to the price increase? In other words, holding p_1 constant at its initial value of \$1, what variation in income is equivalent to the price increase? The answer is distance EV in Figure 4.9. If this consumer has to give up \$$EV$ of income but can still buy good 1 at the initial price of \$1, he or she will remain on indifference curve I_1. In other words, a decrease in income of \$$EV$ is equivalent to a price increase from \$1 to \$2.

Compensating Variation for a Price Change

To identify the compensating variation of this price change, we will use the initial indifference curve I_0 as a point of reference and ask: What variation in income compensates for the price increase? In other words, holding p_1 constant at its subsequent value of \$2, what variation in income compensates for the price increase? The answer is distance CV in Figure 4.9. Even though the price of good 1 has increased from \$1 to \$2, if this consumer's income is increased by \$$CV$, he or she will remain on indifference curve I_0 at E_4. In other words, a \$$CV$ increase in income compensates for the price increase.

Comparing Equivalent Variation and Compensating Variation

Curiously, in Figure 4.9 the equivalent variation associated with the price increase is smaller than the compensating variation. This raises an important question: Are these two measures *ever* the same? They are when the good in question is neither normal nor inferior and the quantity demanded is therefore independent of income. In Figure 4.10 we have repeated the exercise from Figure 4.9. The difference is that good 1 in Figure 4.10 is neither normal nor inferior. As a result, the vertical distance between the two indifference curves is constant. Therefore, distance E_3E_0 is equal to distance E_1E_4. But distance E_3E_0 is equal to EV and distance E_1E_4 is equal to CV. We see, then, that EV is equal to CV in Figure 4.10.

There is another way to look at Figure 4.10. Since the indifference curves are vertically parallel, MRS is constant along any vertical line in this figure. But this implies that the quantity demanded of good 1 is independent of income. When quantity demanded of good 1 is independent of income, we say that there are *no income effects* for good 1. We can summarize these results:

When good 1 is neither normal nor inferior — that is, when there are no income effects for good 1 — EV is identical to CV.

In Problem 4.10 you can find the equivalent and compensating variations for a price decrease. (*Hints*: The indifference curve attained in the subsequent situation is the point of reference for the equivalent variation; the indifference curve attained in the initial situation is the point of reference for the compensating variation.)

PROBLEM 4.10

In Figure 4.9, suppose that the initial price is \$2 and the subsequent price is \$1. The initial equilibrium is therefore at E_1 and the subsequent equilibrium at E_0. What is the equivalent variation of this price reduction? What is the compensating variation?

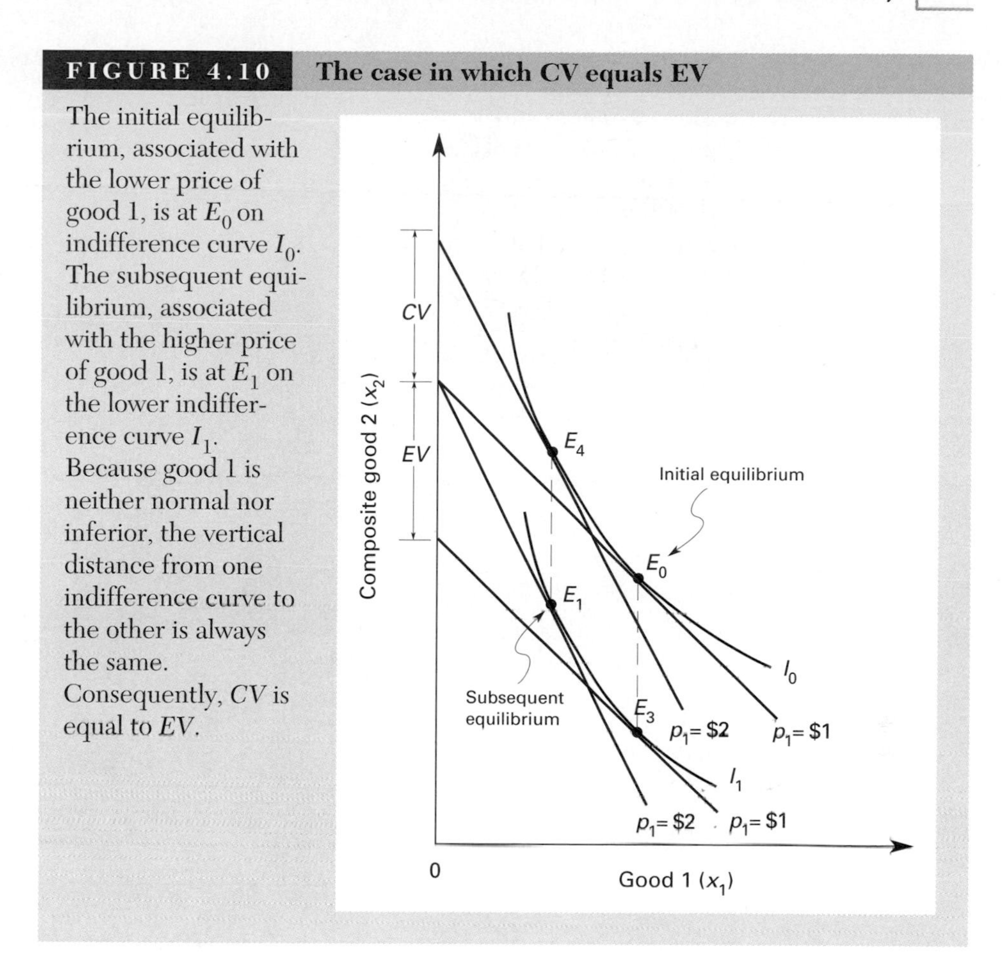

FIGURE 4.10 **The case in which CV equals EV**

The initial equilibrium, associated with the lower price of good 1, is at E_0 on indifference curve I_0. The subsequent equilibrium, associated with the higher price of good 1, is at E_1 on the lower indifference curve I_1. Because good 1 is neither normal nor inferior, the vertical distance from one indifference curve to the other is always the same. Consequently, *CV* is equal to *EV*.

Consumer's Surplus

consumer's surplus

The *CV* and *EV* benefit measures share one major drawback: to use either of them, we must know a consumer's preferences. A more practical measure of benefit, known as **consumer's surplus** (*CS*), can be calculated simply by observing what consumers actually buy and then estimating their demand functions from their consumption behaviour.

How can we use *CS* to measure the value to Mr. Polo of the privilege of buying meals at price p_1 at his private club? Mr. Polo's demand curve for club meals is shown in Figure 4.11. At price p_1, the price at which meals are actually sold in the club, Mr. Polo buys six meals per period. Now suppose that we interpret the prices along this demand curve as the value Mr. Polo places on successive meals. He values the first meal at $300, the second at $280, and so on. Notice that even though Mr. Polo values the first meal at $300, he pays only p_1 for it. He therefore receives a surplus of ($300 – p_1) on that first meal. His surplus on the second meal is ($280 – p_1), and so on. Mr. Polo's total surplus on the six meals that he actually buys at p_1 — his *CS* — is therefore the shaded area in Figure 4.11.

We can also use *CS* to measure the benefit of a price reduction or the cost of a price increase. In Figure 4.12, for example, the shaded area can be interpreted either as the benefit to the consumer of a price reduction from $15 to $10 or as the cost borne by the consumer of a price increase from $10 to $15.

FIGURE 4.11 Consumer's surplus for a new good

The consumer's surplus (CS) measure of the benefit of the right to buy good 1 at price p_1, instead of being unable to buy it at any price, is the shaded area.

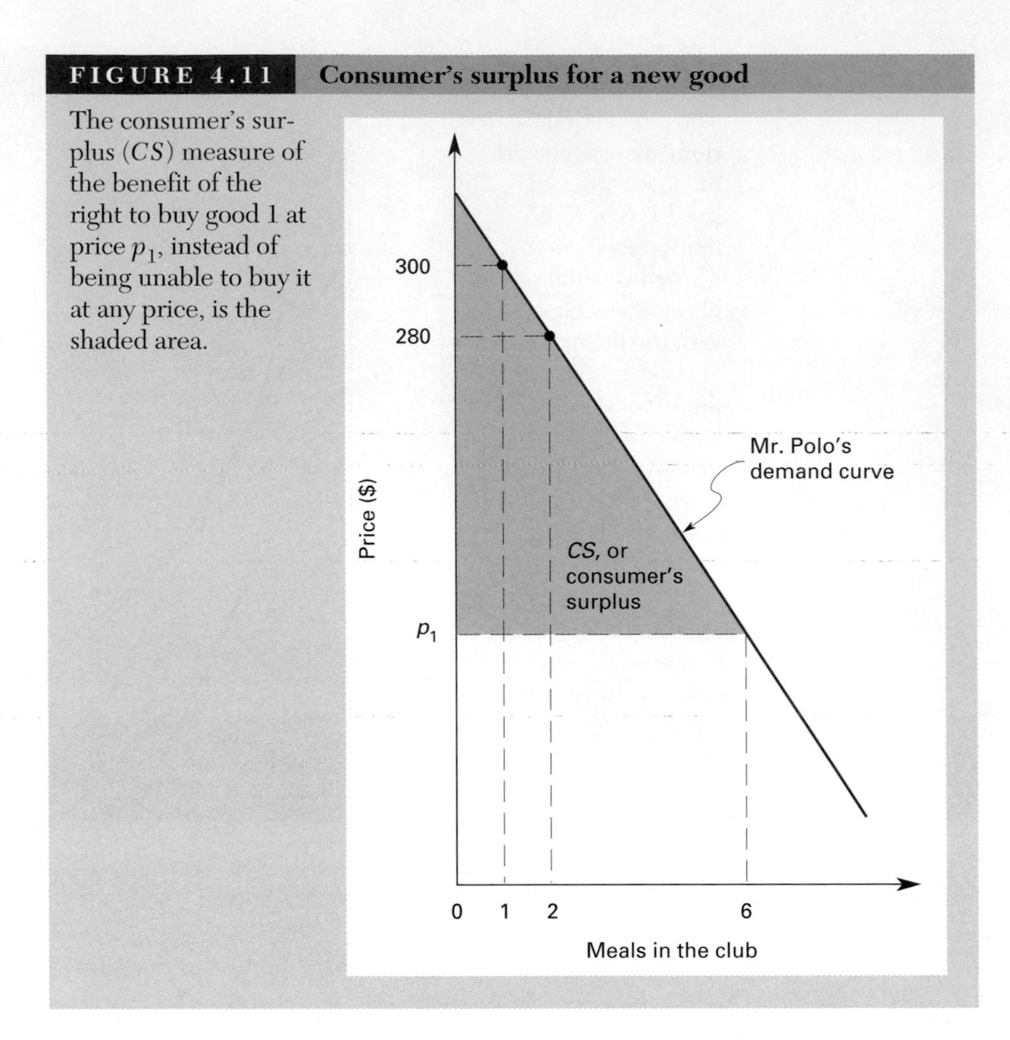

Because the only information needed to calculate CS is an individual's demand curve for the good in question, CS is more practical as a benefit measure. But is it a good measure compared with CV and EV, which have more solid theoretical foundations? Interestingly:

When good 1 is neither normal nor inferior, or when there are no income effects for good 1, then

$$EV = CV = CS$$

When we use the consumer's surplus measure at various points in the following chapters, we will assume that demand for the good in question is independent of income or, equivalently, that the good is neither normal nor inferior.[8]

8. Although preferences do not always, or even usually, display this very convenient property, Willig (1976) provides a convincing argument that even when they do not, CS remains a useful measure of individual benefit when the portion of income spent on the good in question is small.

FIGURE 4.12 Consumer's surplus for a price reduction

The consumer's surplus (CS) measure of the benefit of the right to buy good 1 at price $p_1 = \$10$, instead of price $p_1 = \$15$, is the shaded area.

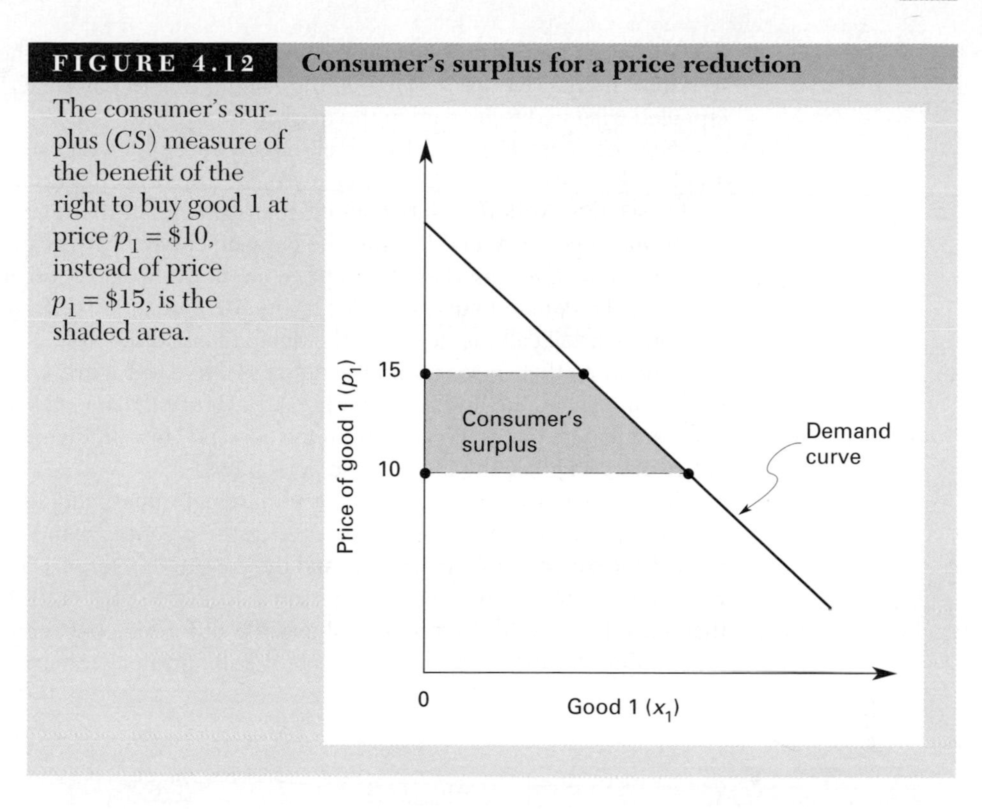

PROBLEM 4.11

Suppose that for Ms J the demand for good 1 is independent of income and is given by the following demand curve:

$$p_1 = 100 - 2x_1$$

What is the benefit to her of a decrease in the price of good 1 from \$60 to \$40? If good 1 is initially unavailable, what is the benefit to Ms J if it is subsequently available at $p_1 = \$50$?

PROBLEM 4.12

In Chapter 3 we considered the case of Tradewell and Safeway. As you will recall, each store had three goods: meat, fruit, and canned goods. The consumer's demand for each good was $x = 11 - p$, and the sale prices in Tradewell were $p_m = 10$, $p_f = 8$, $p_{cg} = 10$, while the sale prices in Safeway were $p_m = 8$, $p_f = 10$, and $p_{cg} = 8$. Calculate the total consumer's surplus at each store. Which store has the lowest prices?

Application: Total Value versus Marginal Value

In Chapters 2 and 3 considerable attention was given to the concept of the *MRS*, which is also called the marginal value. If we don't mind being a little inaccurate, the *MV* is the maximum willingness to pay for an additional unit of x_1. Recall also that one of the conditions for determining the optimal choice of x_1 was that the *MRS*, or *MV*, had to equal the relative price. That is, the willingness to pay for x_1 at the margin just equalled what had to be paid in the market.

Now consider Figure 4.13, which closely resembles Figure 3.13. Here we have graphically derived another demand curve, D, from a set of preferences and two budget constraints. At both points A and B the *MRS* equals the relative price. But just as important, at points A′ and B′ along the demand curve the *MRS* still equals the relative price, since we have put the relative price on the vertical axis. So, in Figure 4.13b, the *height* of the demand curve is equal to the *MRS* or the *MV*. In order to follow conventions, we will call the height of the demand curve the *MV*.

One thing that is clear from the demand curve in Figure 4.13 is that the more x_1 the individual has, the lower is his or her *MV*. Hence the *MV* at A′ is greater than at B′. A second feature that is less clear from the demand curve in Figure 4.13 is that the **total value** of x_1 is higher the more x_1 the person has.

total value

Total value is just the sum of all the marginal values, and, assuming there are no income effects, is graphically represented as the *area under* the demand curve. Total value is the sum of total expenditure and the consumer's surplus. The total value of, say $x_1 = 10$, is the maximum amount a person is willing to pay for all 10 units of x_1 rather than have none at all. Figure 4.14 shows the difference between marginal and total values. For 15 units of x_1 the individual is willing to pay a maximum of $120 rather

FIGURE 4.13 Marginal values and marginal rates of substitution

At point A in part (a), the *MRS* is equal to the relative price of 1.5. At A′ in part (b), the height of the demand curve is also equal to 1.5. Similarly, at point B in part (a), the slope of the indifference curve, the *MRS*, is equal to the relative price of 1. At point B′, in part (b), the height of the demand curve is also equal to 1. The height of the demand curve is called the marginal value and is always equal to the *MRS*. As the quantity of x_1 increases, the marginal value falls.

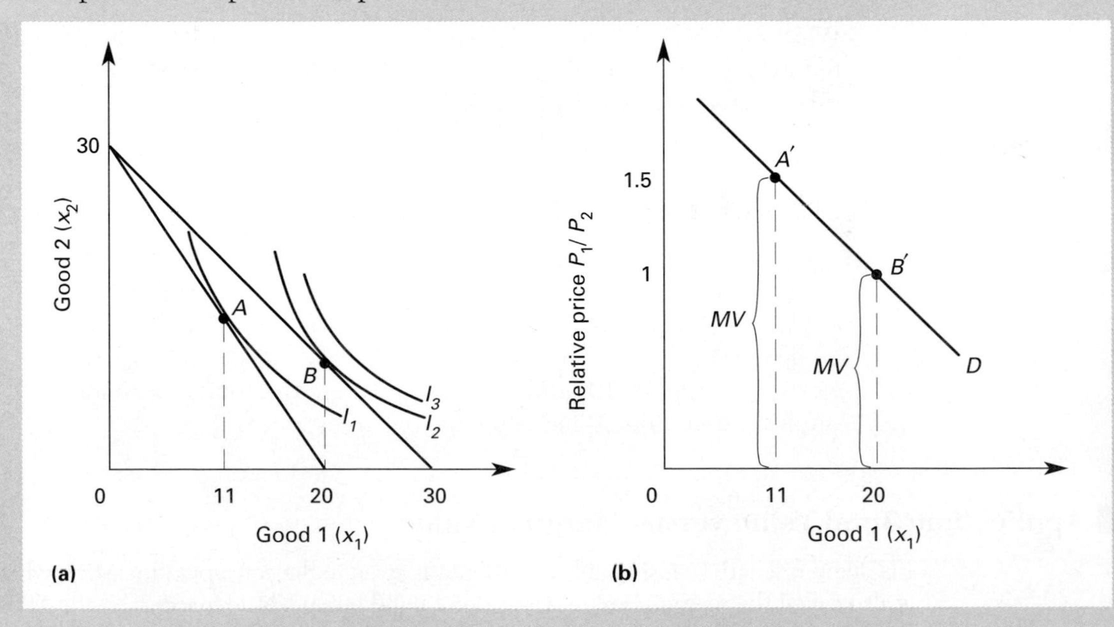

FIGURE 4.14 **Total value and marginal value**

The total value (TV) is the area under the demand curve. The marginal value (MV) is the height.

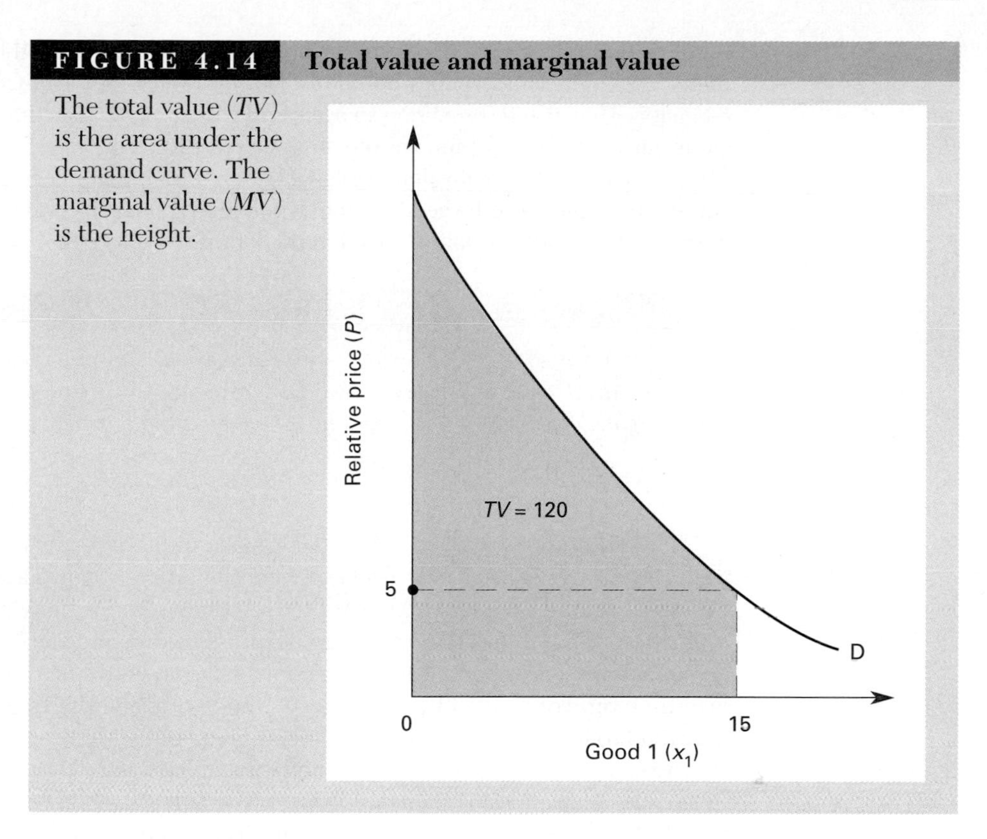

than have no x_1 — this is the total value or TV. For the 15th unit of x_1, however, the individual is only willing to pay \$5. If we increased the amount of x_1 to 20 the TV would clearly increase, but the MV would fall.[9]

The difference between marginal and total value explains a number of paradoxes that arise in life over the ambiguous use of the word *value*. For example, a nineteenth-century paradox of value arose from the observation that falling grain prices always accompanied a bumper grain harvest. If more grain is always better, why did the price fall, indicating that consumers valued the grain less? The answer, of course, is that more grain increases the total value, but lowers the marginal value. Since prices equal marginal values, not total values, the prices also fall. This is commonly known as the **water–diamond paradox**, after a well-known example. Water is necessary for life while diamonds are of only minor importance, yet water is generally very inexpensive and diamonds are pricey.[10] The water-diamond paradox is very common, and if you pay attention to what goes on around you, a week will seldom go by that you do not observe an example of it.

water–diamond paradox

9. Since demand curves are drawn assuming p_2 is constant, we can assume $p_2 = 1$, in which case the relative price equals $p_1/1 = p_1$. We also follow the convention of dropping the $p_2 = 1$ on the vertical axis. Keep in mind, however, that it is still the relative price on the axis and not the nominal price.

10. Water and diamonds are not very good examples of the paradox of value because the units of measure are different, and as a result it is not always true that water is cheaper than diamonds. There is some volume of water that is more expensive than some small low-quality diamond.

For example, in the mid-1980s, when gasoline prices dipped below $1/gallon in many US cities, a newspaper columnist pointed out that Coca-Cola was selling for $4/gallon. How could something so useless as Coke sell for four times the price of precious gasoline? Once again, we see an abuse of the term *value*. Gas has a high total value and a low marginal value, while Coke has a high marginal value and a low total value. If people were forced to choose between giving up either gasoline or Coke entirely, they would certainly abandon the latter.

PROBLEM 4.13

"Water is so precious for life, and without it everything dies. Therefore, we must treat it with care and look after it. Unfortunately, we abuse water. We waste it watering our lawns, flushing our toilets, and washing our cars." If water is so valuable, why are we so frivolous with it?

The difference between *MV* and *TV* has a number of personal applications as well. Have you ever had a near-fatal experience? Perhaps you had a serious car accident or a close friend or relative almost died. At those times many people sense a re-evaluation of the things they value, and express sentiments like "It really makes you appreciate what is important in life." People make vows to spend more time together, take time off work, smell the roses, etc … and yet when the tragic moment passes, they tend to live as they always did. What is going on?

A famous example of this happened on August 24, 2001, when Captain Robert Piche was flying an Air Transat Airbus from Toronto to Lisbon with 304 passengers on board. With 1000 miles to go, the captain discovered he was out of fuel, a problem that was later discovered to be caused by a crack in a fuel line. For over 100 miles the pilot flew the plane without power, and announced to the passengers they would likely end up in the Atlantic. Passengers universally told reporters later that they were confident no one would make it out of the crash alive. With it still dark outside, the plane's interior was completely black as passengers removed their shoes, and held back vomiting as the plane descended quickly. Miraculously, Piche was able to land the plane on the Azore island of Terceira. Hitting the ground at over twice the normal speed, all landing gear burst into flames. Within minutes passengers were evacuating the plane, and no one was seriously injured. Passengers were euphoric. One passenger was reported to shout over and over, "I'm alive! I'm alive!"

Now put yourself in that plane. You're on vacation, looking forward to a few weeks of sun in southern Europe, and suddenly you're staring death in the face. What are you going to think about? Are you going to think about what colour the bathroom should be? Whether or not you should take sociology or history next term? No, you're thinking about how much your parents mean to you, and what a jerk you've been lately. Suddenly, miracle of miracles, the plane lands. What do you shout? "I'm alive! I'm going to call my parents and tell them I love them." But you were alive two hours earlier; why didn't you shout and call before? The sad truth is that within hours of landing, passengers weren't following these sentiments … they were signing up for a class-action lawsuit. What happened to the earlier emotion?

The answer to both questions lies in the difference between *MV* and *TV*. Most of our lives are spent at the margin. We divide our time and income up and we choose to spend an hour here, a dollar there. Thus it is natural for us to often think about values in terms of marginal values because in choosing optimal quantities we set *MV*s equal to prices. In tragic moments, though, when a child suddenly disappears or life flashes before your eyes when your plane is about to crash, you are faced with an all-or-nothing situation. Now you have to make decisions based on total values, not marginal ones. Things that had high total valuations and low marginal ones become much more important than they were before. When life returns to normal, we again go about our days making marginal decisions.

The last point to be made about marginal values is that they tend to equalize across people and goods when prices are equal. Figure 4.15 shows the demand curves for original *Star Trek* and *The Bachelor* episodes for one of the authors. Both shows take an hour to watch and are often on at approximately the same time of day, so, for the sake of argument, the price in terms of hours is equal across the two shows. Clearly this individual has a higher total value for *Star Trek*, but notice that the marginal values are equal. As long as the *MV* of a *Star Trek* episode is greater than its price, the author is better off consuming an additional hour. The same is also true for *The Bachelor*. The optimal amount to watch is determined when $P = MV$. Since the price is the same for both shows, the *MV* for each show is equal, which means that at the margin, the author is indifferent between the two shows. This equalizing across the two margins is the result of maximizing behaviour and occurs for the same reason that the speed of traffic across the lanes on a highway tends to equalize. Can you see why?

FIGURE 4.15 Equal marginal values

When two goods have the same price, they are consumed until the marginal values are equal. Note that the total values (the coloured area) will in general not be equal.

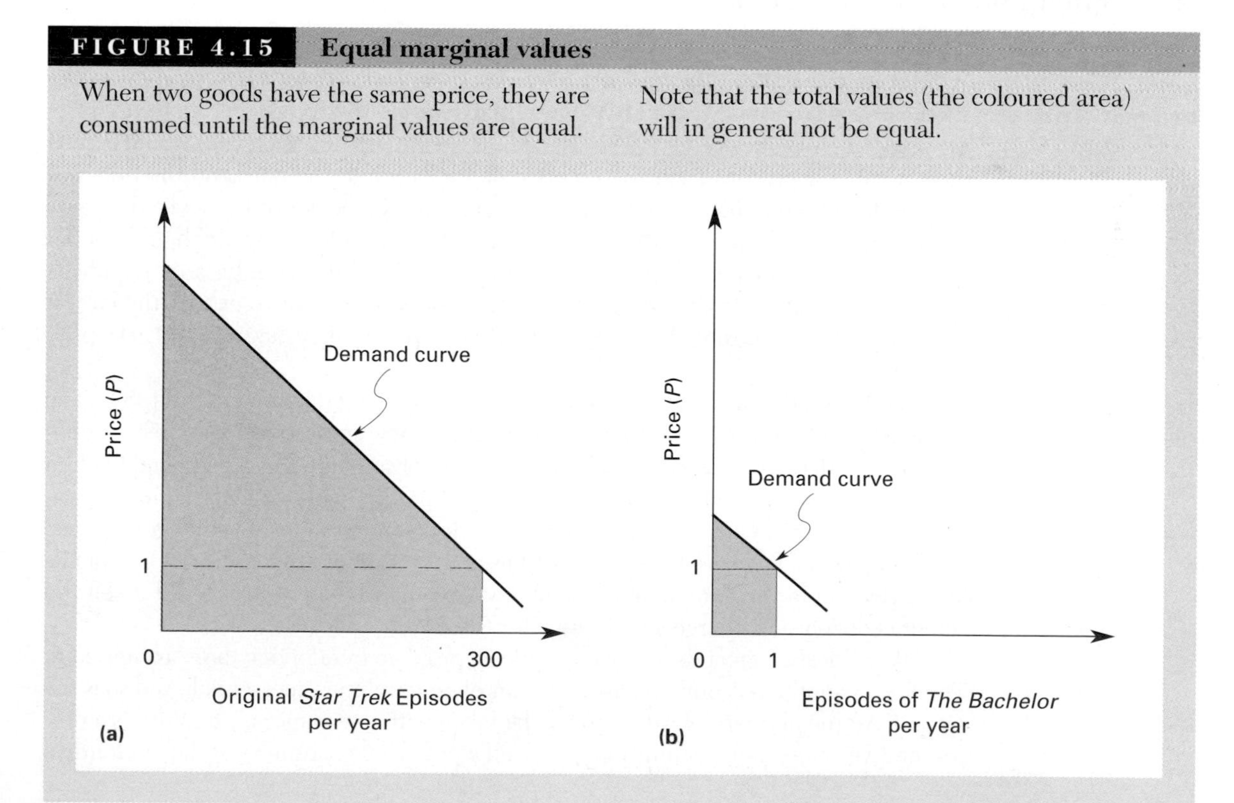

PROBLEM 4.14

Children are fond of asking parents "What's your favourite ... [colour, television show, cereal, etc.]? What notion of value are they implicitly using? If you ask children, however, to name their favourite toy, friend, or parent(!), they often say, "All of them are my favourite." What notion of value are they using in this answer and why would they give this answer? (*Hint*: Here is your chance to really start thinking like an economist. Don't take the easy way out and say "Kids don't like to choose," or "Kids don't want to offend." Anyone who has watched kids pick teams in a playground knows this is not true.)

PROBLEM 4.15

Recently the football player Curt Warner signed a contract for $47 million ($47 million! ... to play football!). Tiger Woods is predicted to be the first athlete to earn a billion dollars for hitting a little white ball fewer times than other golfers. These sums are enormous and seem out of line compared to salaries for doctors, nurses, firefighters, and others that we consider crucial. How is it that society can value sports figures more than life-saving occupations?

Application: Two-Part Tariffs

two-part tariff

Knowing something about demand curves and consumer's surplus can help us understand something about the way some goods are priced. Walter Oi, a pioneer in the study of what are usually called **two-part tariff** questions, was curious about this pricing problem. Specifically, Oi (1971) asked how executives of Disneyland would exploit their monopoly power in setting the price of admission to the park and the prices of each of the amusements inside the gates. If you were the owner of Disneyland, should you charge high lump-sum admission fees and give the rides away, or should you let people into the amusement park for nothing and stick them with high monopolistic prices for the rides? Insofar as the Disneyland executives want to extract the largest possible profit in choosing the two sets of tariffs, or prices, they face a fairly tricky pricing problem.

The Polaroid Land Corporation faced a similar pricing dilemma in the 1950s. The introduction of the Polaroid camera gave birth to a new commodity, the "instant photograph." At that time, the corporation had a monopoly on both the camera and the film it used. Because the demand for its camera and its film were so clearly interdependent, the Polaroid Corporation's pricing predicament was closely analogous to the pricing dilemma faced by the owners of Disneyland. Should the corporation attach a high price tag to the camera and essentially give the film away, or should it sell the camera cheaply and charge a high price for the film?

We can learn a great deal about this pricing problem by adopting three assumptions. The first assumption is quite realistic: Instant photographs are inessential. And so is the second: All the photographs desired can be taken with one camera. The third is a representative-consumer assumption: Polaroid's potential customers all have identical preferences and income. This last assumption allows us to focus on Polaroid's profit from just one consumer, Juli.

What combination of the price of the camera, p_c, and the price of film, p_1, will maximize the profit Polaroid Corporation can extract from Juli? Specifically, let us suppose that Polaroid's cost of producing a camera is $5 and its cost of producing a unit of film is $1. Polaroid's profit from Juli can then be written in the following way:

$$\text{profit} = x_1^*(p_1 - 1) + n^*(p_c - 5)$$

Here, n^* is Juli's demand for cameras (0 or 1), and x_1^* is her demand for film, given the two prices p_1 and p_c. Because the firm will choose p_1 and p_c so that n^* is 1, we can rewrite the profit function as

$$\text{profit} = x_1^*(p_1 - 1) + (p_c - 5)$$

If we assume for simplicity that Juli's demand for instant photos is independent of her income, we can then solve this profit-maximization problem easily. Juli's demand curve for instant photos is presented in Figure 4.16. Let us start by supposing that Polaroid charges $3 for its film. Given this price, if Juli had a camera, she would buy 5 units of film. Polaroid's profit on the film would be $10 = 5($3 – $1), or the grey area in Figure 4.16. Given p_1 = $3, Polaroid will clearly decide to price its camera at Juli's reservation price. Yet we know that because Juli's demand for instant photos is independent of her income,

FIGURE 4.16 **The Polaroid pricing problem**

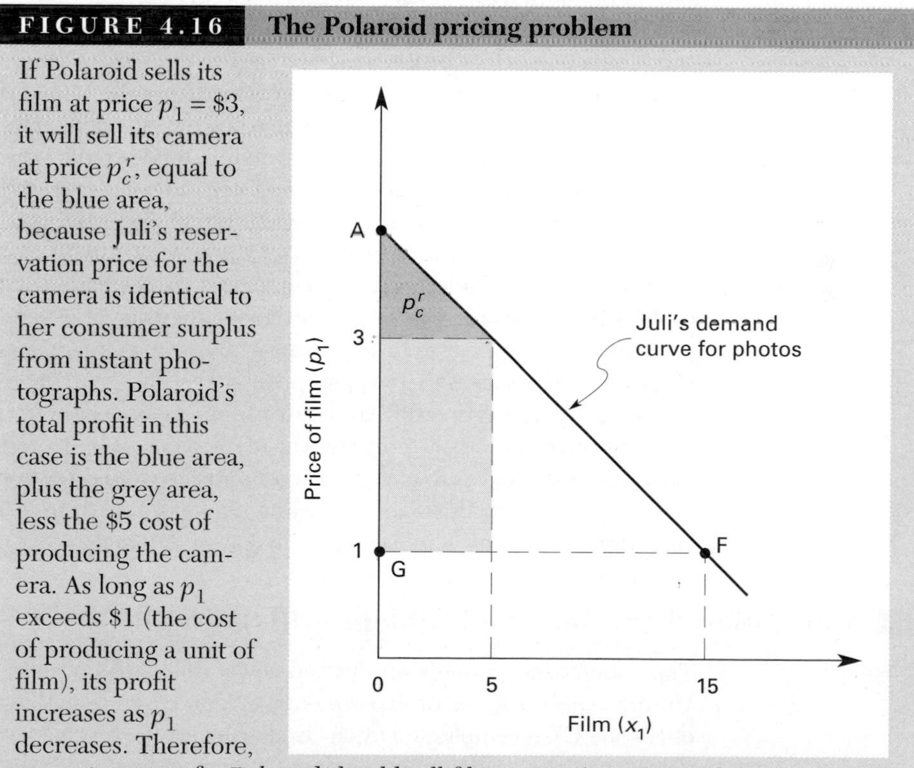

If Polaroid sells its film at price p_1 = $3, it will sell its camera at price p_c^r, equal to the blue area, because Juli's reservation price for the camera is identical to her consumer surplus from instant photographs. Polaroid's total profit in this case is the blue area, plus the grey area, less the $5 cost of producing the camera. As long as p_1 exceeds $1 (the cost of producing a unit of film), its profit increases as p_1 decreases. Therefore, to maximize profit, Polaroid should sell film at cost (p_1 = $1) and the camera at a price equal to the triangular area *GAF*.

her reservation price for the camera is simply the consumer surplus associated with $p_1 = \$3$. If Polaroid decides to sell its film at \$3, it will then sell its camera at price p_c^r, represented by the blue area in Figure 4.16. Its profit will then be equal to the sum of the two shaded areas in Figure 4.16, minus the cost of producing the camera, \$5.

But Polaroid can do better than that. As you can easily verify, as long as the price of film exceeds \$1 — the cost of producing a unit of film — Polaroid can increase its profit by decreasing the price of its film and correspondingly increasing the price of its camera to reflect Juli's increasing reservation price. When p_1 is equal to \$1, Polaroid's profit from its film is zero [15(\$1 – \$1)], but the profit from its camera is the area of triangle *GAF* in Figure 4.16 minus the \$5 cost of producing the camera. In Problem 4.16, you will see that Polaroid's profit decreases as it lowers the price of film below \$1.

The firm's profit-maximizing strategy is to sell film at cost and to charge the corresponding reservation price for the camera.

PROBLEM 4.16

Consider any p_1 less than \$1, and the associated reservation price for the camera. Show that the profit is smaller than it is when Polaroid sells its film at \$1 and its camera at area *GAF*.

Casual observation would suggest that many firms use two-part pricing. Disneyland and other amusement parks charge a large entry fee, but then set the price per ride at zero. It is arguable that the cost of letting an additional person use the ride is close to zero, and so this looks like profit-maximizing pricing. Costco, the wholesale discounter, charges a membership fee to face lower inside prices; many night clubs and country clubs charge entry fees to be members; and one buys coupon books for a fixed fee in order to obtain the lower couponed price. Even telephone companies, cable TV companies, and utility companies use similar pricing structures: a hook-up fee and a separate fee based on use. (If you have rented an apartment and paid for your own utilities, you have probably encountered this sort of strategy.) Unlike Polaroid, Disneyland, and Costco, telephone, cable, and utility companies are regulated, and their ability to extract profit is therefore constrained. Nevertheless, they do choose to use two-part tariffs.

There does appear to be one strange anomaly. Why is popcorn so darn expensive in theatres? All theatres use two-part pricing: they charge an entry fee to get in, and then charge a separate price for candy, drinks, and popcorn. On the surface it appears that the refreshments are priced way above cost. Why would this be if the profit-maximizing strategy is to charge a larger entry fee and offer popcorn at cost? We will let you think about this one for a while, and will return to it later in the book. Not everything is a *simple* application of the law of demand!

Application: Experimental Problems with EV and CV

The notion of consumer's surplus and how it relates to EV and CV is extremely useful. Unfortunately a series of experimental evidence suggests that the actual calculation of EV and CV is complicated by an "Endowment Effect." That is, whether or not an individual owns the good in question or not influences how much they are willing to pay for it. In the analysis so far, an individual's choice among goods and willingness to sacrifice other things to obtain them or to keep them are assumed to be independent of whether or not the person owns or possesses the good.

In one economic experiment, three groups of Canadian undergraduate students indicated their relative preferences for a 400-g chocolate bar and an embossed coffee mug. Individuals in one group were asked to choose which of the two goods they wished to receive; those in a second group were first given a mug and then asked if they would prefer to give back the mug and receive a chocolate bar in exchange; and the individuals in the third group were first given a chocolate bar and then asked if they would like to give back the chocolate bar and receive a mug. As the individuals in each group have the same opportunity to take away either good and as the variations in the means of expressing their preferences is assumed to have no impact on people's valuations, economic theory strongly predicts roughly the same proportions in all three groups will prefer to have mugs and chocolate bars. The results, however, were very different. Given a simple choice, 56 percent of the first group indicated they valued a mug more than a chocolate bar. Required to give up their mug to gain a chocolate bar, 89 percent of the second group showed a preference for a mug. When giving up a chocolate bar was required to obtain a mug, only 10 percent of the third group preferred a mug. For most participants, a mug was more valuable than a chocolate bar when the mug had to be given up, but less valuable when the chocolate had to be given up. Contrary to the assumptions of economic theory, the loss of a good is more important than the gain of the same good.

In another experiment involving actual exchanges of money and mugs, individuals in one group were asked the maximum amount of money they would pay for a mug; those in a second group were asked the minimum sum they would require to give up an identical coffee mug; and people in a third group were asked to choose between receiving a mug or money and indicated the smallest sum they would take rather than accept a mug. Again, economic theory predicts individuals in each group should value the mugs the same, as their valuations should be independent of the means to elicit them. The results were sharply different: participants were willing to pay an average of $2 to gain a mug, the compensation required to give up a mug was $7, and the sum equivalent to gaining a mug was $3.50. The valuations were not, as theory assumes, independent of entitlement! They were very dependent on the context of the valuation — a mug was worth over three times more in the context of a loss than in the context of a gain.

In recent years, professional journals and other publications have reported consistent findings from various carefully controlled real exchange economic experiments and consumer surveys. Research attention is now shifting from the accumulation of further empirical verification of such anomalies, to attempting to understand why this happens. One solution is that preferences change depending on the endowment of the good. Another is that perhaps an endowment influences the information one has over the good and this affects what you are willing to pay for something. This is because when you own something you learn more about the good than when you don't own it. You might think you'd like good x and value it at $4, but when you own it you discover you'd only be willing to pay $2 for it. In any event, these experiments point out that there is still much work to be done in understanding behaviour.[11]

[11]See Kahneman et al. (1990) for a discussion of the endowment effect.

4.6 Index Numbers

We are continually bombarded by index numbers. We may be told, for example, that in the third quarter of some year, real disposable income grew at x percent per year or that the consumer price index has increased at y percent per year. The first statement is about a **quantity index** — an indicator of the amount of real disposable income available to consumers. Ordinarily, an increase in real disposable income is interpreted as an increase in the average consumer's economic welfare, since he or she can buy more. The second statement is about a **price index** — an indicator of the price level that consumers face in the marketplace. If a consumer's income is unchanged, then an increase in the consumer price index is ordinarily interpreted as a decline in the average consumer's economic welfare, since he or she can buy less with the same income.

quantity index

price index

In this section, we will see precisely what quantity and price indexes are, and we will learn two important things about these indexes. First, given the same data, two different quantity (or price) indexes can send different qualitative messages — for example, one index may suggest that disposable income is increasing and the other that it is decreasing. Second, when two different indexes do send different messages, it may be impossible to determine which message is correct. The setting we will use to develop an understanding of index numbers is deceptively simple, but the understanding itself is profound.

Let us begin by imagining that we can observe the consumption decisions of a particular person named Norm in two different periods. Let us also assume that Norm's preferences are identical in both periods. A question naturally arises: In which period was Norm better off? If we can answer this question, a second question then arises: By how much was he better off?

Quantity Indexes

There can be no direct answer to the second question. Even if we knew Norm's utility function, we could not say how much better off he was in one period than another, because a direct answer requires cardinal information. As we saw in Chapter 2, a utility function contains only ordinal information. Nevertheless, we may be able to use the information at hand to construct an indirect answer: a quantity index that will give us some indication of how the aggregate quantity of the goods Norm consumed has changed from period to period.

Analogous questions arise at the macroeconomic level. Were Canadian citizens better off in 2001 than in 2000? If so, by how much was the average person better off? If we again adopt the assumption of a representative consumer, we can reinterpret this microeconomic exercise — which focuses on a single person, Norm — in a macroeconomic context. If we assume that the economy is composed of individuals with preferences identical to Norm's, we can then interpret the indexes discussed below as indexes of real national income per capita.

We can see the types of problems that arise with any index number by using the two-good case. The notation is necessarily a little clumsy: subscripts denote goods, and superscripts denote time periods. Thus, in period 0, Norm buys the bundle $B^0 = (x_1^0, x_2^0)$ at prices (p_1^0, p_2^0). From these quantities and prices, we can compute his income in period 0: $M^0 = p_1^0 x_1^0 + p_2^0 x_2^0$. In period 1, he buys the bundle $B^1 = (x_1^1, x_2^1)$ at prices (p_1^1, p_2^1), and his income is $M^1 = p_1^1 x_1^1 + p_2^1 x_2^1$.

If this information on prices and quantities is available, it obviously reveals something about Norm's preferences and therefore something about his well-being.[12] But exactly what does it tell us? The first step is to answer the following question: In what circumstances can we infer either that B^0 is preferred to B^1 or that B^1 is preferred to B^0? If we can infer that one or the other of these statements is true, we can develop a quantity index indicating the extent to which aggregate quantity consumed in one period exceeds aggregate quantity consumed in the other.

Let us begin by looking at the case in which Norm is definitely better off in period 1. Suppose that B^0 is inside Norm's period-1 budget constraint, as in Figure 4.17. That is, suppose that

$$p_1^1x_1^0 + p_2^1x_2^0 < p_1^1x_1^1 + p_2^1x_2^1 \qquad (= M^1)$$

The left-hand side of this inequality is the expenditure required to buy B^0 at period-1 prices, and the right-hand side is Norm's actual expenditure in period 1. Because bundle B^1 is revealed by Norm's choice to be the utility-maximizing bundle in period 1 and because bundle B^0 is attainable in period 1, we infer that B^1 is preferred to B^0.

If $p_1^1x_1^0 + p_2^1x_2^0 < p_1^1x_1^1 + p_2^1x_2^1$ $(= M^1)$, then B^1 is preferred to B^0.

Paasche quantity index

The inequality that allows us to make this inference suggests a quantity index known as the **Paasche quantity index.** If we divide Norm's actual expenditure in period 1 by the expenditure required to buy B^0 in period 1, we have an index of the extent to which Norm's aggregate consumption in period 1 exceeds his aggregate consumption in period 0. The Paasche quantity index P is defined as follows:

$$P = [p_1^1x_1^1 + p_2^1x_2^1]/[p_1^1x_1^0 + p_2^1x_2^0]$$

We can then restate the proposition above.

If the Paasche quantity index exceeds 1, then B^1 is preferred to B^0.

As we will see, if this index is less than 1, we cannot be sure that Norm is worse off in period 1. As a result, this quantity index is not always an accurate indicator of Norm's well-being.

Laspeyres quantity index

Notice that the Paasche quantity index uses period-1 prices for aggregating quantities in both periods. By substituting period-0 prices for aggregating quantities in both periods, we have another quantity index, known as the **Laspeyres quantity index**, denoted by L:

$$L = [p_1^0x_1^1 + p_2^0x_2^1]/[p_1^0x_1^0 + p_2^0x_2^0]$$

By simply reversing the argument of the previous paragraph, we arrive at an analogous proposition.

---

12. We can be more precise about the assumption that Norm's preferences are identical in the two periods. His utility function has four arguments — $x_1^0, x_2^0, x_1^1, x_2^1$ — because a good today and the same good tomorrow must be regarded as different goods. We are assuming, then, that Norm's utility function can be written in the following way:

$$U(x_1^0, x_2^0, x_1^1, x_2^1) = V'(x_1^0, x_2^0) + V'(x_1^1, x_2^1)$$

The function $V'(x_1, x_2)$ is then Norm's utility function in each period.

FIGURE 4.17 **The Paasche quantity index**

Norm bought bundle B^0 in period 0 and B^1 in period 1. He could have bought bundle B^0 in period 1 since it lies below the period-1 budget line. Therefore, we can infer that B^1 is preferred to B^0.

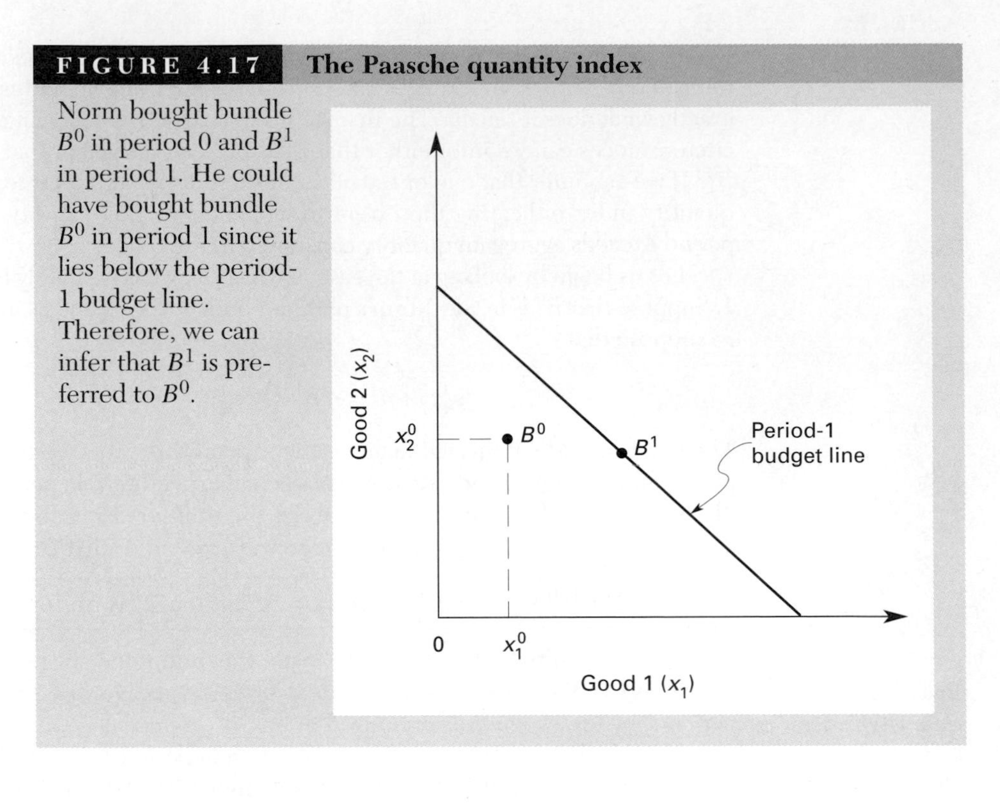

If the Laspeyres quantity index is less than 1, then B^0 is preferred to B^1.

In other words, if L is less than 1, Norm was better off in period 0 because he could have bought B^1 in period 0 but chose instead to buy B^0.

As you will discover in the following problem, P can be less than 1 and L greater than 1 at the same time. In this case, which is shown in Figure 4.18, the two indexes send conflicting messages. P indicates that Norm's consumption has fallen and L that it has risen. Furthermore, neither of these two propositions is applicable, and without more information on Norm's preferences, we cannot know in which period Norm was better off.

PROBLEM 4.17

Given the information in Figure 4.18, show that P is less than 1 and that L is greater than 1. In addition, draw one indifference map in Figure 4.18 such that B^1 is preferred to B^0 and another such that B^0 is preferred to B^1.

Price Indexes

We used fixed sets of prices (period-0 prices or period-1 prices) above to define two quantity indexes. In this section, we will reverse the procedure and use fixed sets of quantities to define price indexes. Price indexes are supposed to measure the extent to which the *price level* — as opposed to the prices of individual goods — changes from one period to another. We will discover that the commonly used price indexes, like the commonly used quantity indexes, are not entirely satisfactory.

FIGURE 4.18 An index-number puzzle

Norm bought bundle B^0 in period 0 and B^1 in period 1. In this case, P is less than 1 and L is greater than 1, and it is impossible to tell in which period Norm was better off.

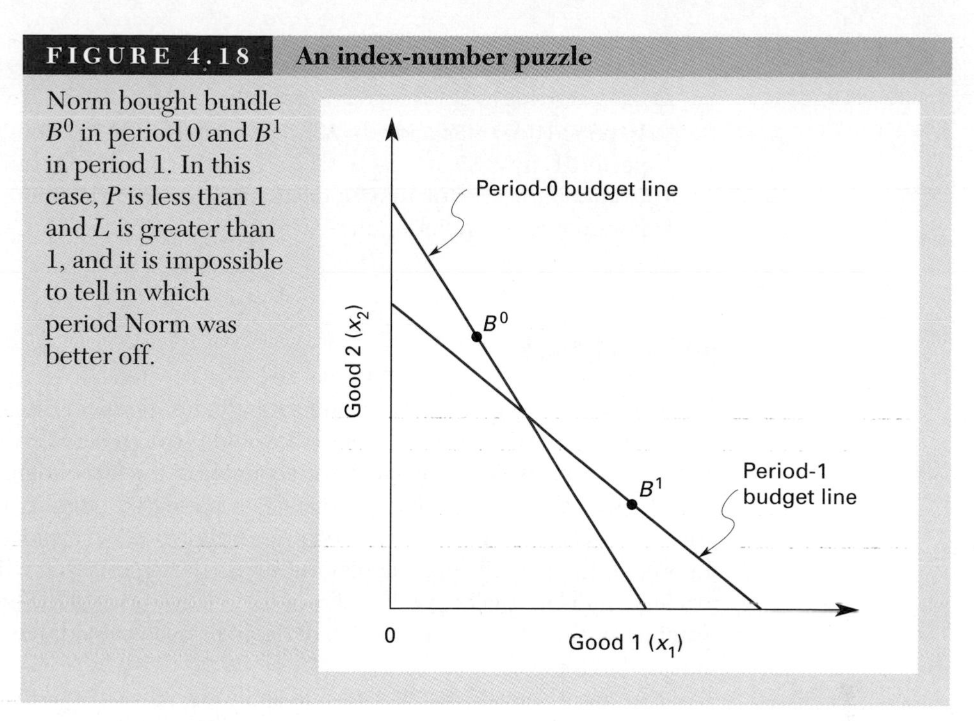

Paasche price index

The **Paasche price index,** denoted by P', uses period-1 quantities:

$$P' = [p_1^1 x_1^1 + p_2^1 x_2^1]/[p_1^0 x_1^1 + p_2^0 x_2^1]$$

If P' is 2, for example, it takes twice as many dollars to buy B^1 at period-1 prices than at period-0 prices.

Laspeyres price index

The **Laspeyres price index,** denoted by L', uses period-0 quantities:

$$L' = [p_1^1 x_1^0 + p_2^1 x_2^0]/[p_1^0 x_1^0 + p_2^0 x_2^0]$$

If L' is 2, for instance, it would cost twice as much to buy B^0 at period-1 prices than at period-0 prices.

It is useful to look at the case in which Norm has the same income in both periods. We can then use these price indices to restate the conditions under which we know for certain that Norm is better off in one period than in the other:

When L' is less than 1, then P' is also less than 1, and Norm is better off in period 1; when P' is greater than 1, then L' is also greater than 1, and Norm is better off in period 0.

The difficulty is that the situation is not always so clear-cut. It is entirely possible that L' is greater than 1 and, at the same time, that P' is less than 1. When this happens, the two indices convey different messages. L' indicates that the price level has risen and P' that it has fallen. Which message is correct? There is no way of knowing, given only the information we have at hand.

PROBLEM 4.18

In period 0, $p_1 = \$4$ and $p_2 = \$3$, and Norm bought the bundle (15,20). In period 1, $p_1 = \$5$ and $p_2 = \$2$, and Norm bought the bundle (10,35). Compute the two quantity indexes and the two price indexes. In which period was Norm better off?

SUMMARY

In this chapter, we extended our understanding of demand theory and saw just how widely applicable the tools of Chapter 3 would prove to be. We showed, for example, that speculation, while it appears to run counter to the law of demand, in fact demonstrates this law. The speculator demands an increased quantity of a good when the price today is lower than the expected price tomorrow. We explored the Alchian-Allen theorem ("shipping the good apples out"), which suggests that a fixed charge applied to a high- and low-quality good will lower the relative price of the high-quality good and result in higher relative consumption of the high-quality good (but less consumption of the good in total).

The law of demand can be shown to apply even to activities that are not purely economic, such as participation in religion. We showed that to see the workings of the law of demand more clearly, we must extend our notion of price to include the *full* price of a good: that is, the price in time (opportunity cost) as well as money.

One of the most important lessons to draw from this chapter is the power of the non-zero substitution effect. As was shown, the law of demand is the result of a substitution effect that either works with or dominates the income effect. In theory, when the income effect is stronger, a Giffen good may result: one for which demand will increase as the price increases. In practice, Giffen goods have never been found. Income and substitution effects can be considered separately. A compensated budget line can be used to decompose the two effects, holding real income constant in order to observe the substitution effect alone. In fact, a cost of living allowance acts in much the same way—or would, if inflation were pure.

It was the substitution effect that made consumers prefer lump-sum to per-unit taxes, and leads to two-tariff pricing, such as a high entrance fee to an amusement park or a private club, coupled with the sale of subsequent services at or near cost. It is also the substitution effect that created the puzzle with index numbers. The Paasche and Laspeyres price and quantity indexes are used to determine whether a consumer is better off in one period or another. Paasche indexes use period-1 prices or quantities to compare aggregates from both periods; Laspeyres indexes use period-0 prices or quantities to compare aggregates from both periods. Unfortunately, these indexes are not conclusive; sometimes comparing both indexes will suggest that the consumer is both better and worse off in the second period.

More importantly, the substitution effect, as it manifests itself in the law of demand, is a powerful tool in explaining a broad range of human behaviour.

We examined in more detail the concepts of marginal and total value. Because prices always equal marginal value — the value we attach to additional units of the good — rather than total value, it is common to find goods of importance with low prices. This finding is sometimes known as the water–diamond paradox.

A second feature you should notice from this chapter is how we were able to reduce very complex problems to manageable ones by employing the useful fiction of a *representative consumer*. We simplified the real diversity of individual tastes and incomes to those of a representative individual and then analyzed only this person's choice problem. This abstraction is an extremely useful one, as long as we recognize the need to reintroduce diversity when confronting real situations. The most general conclusion we can draw is that these tools can yield insights into a wide range of economic problems from everyday experience.

EXERCISES

1. Why do the British tend to use cloth napkins, while North Americans generally use paper ones?

2. In Problem 4.1 the employees had not been allowed to sublet the parking spaces. How would the answer have changed if employees could sublet? (*Hint*: What is the cost of using a space when you are allowed to sublet?)

3. Johnny Doe has just learned about the effect of a fixed charge on relative prices, and he's now sitting in the school cafeteria pondering it all. As he sits there he begins to watch coffee drinkers, and counts the number that have coffee to go in large cups versus small cups, and then he repeats this for the people consuming coffee within the cafeteria. He thinks that those people having coffee to go will consume the larger cups, relative to those remaining, because they have the "fixed charge" of walking. What's wrong with Johnny's test?

4. The 50 students in Dunnell's Boardinghouse have formed a club to buy a coffee vending machine that costs $500. They currently pay $0.75 per cup at the café next door, and they figure that coffee from the machine will cost them just $0.25 per cup. The problem is that no one except Marya has $10 to pay his or her share of the $500. Marya has agreed either (i) to lend each of the other students $10, in which case they can get coffee at $0.25 per cup immediately; or (ii) to buy the machine herself and charge $0.75 per cup until she recovers the $490. Only then will the price drop to $0.25 per cup. Which option would you recommend to these students?

5. When a professor visits another university to give a talk, the faculty of the hosting department often take the speaker out to dinner. Suppose that faculty at the history department pay for their own dinners, but the department of economics subsidizes the dinners by a flat amount, $15 per meal. What difference would you expect in the number of dinners attended by faculty from the respective departments? In the quality of the dinners?

6. Juli has an old camera that produces instant photographs. The film for this camera costs $2 per exposure. A new camera model on the market is identical to Juli's camera in every way but one: the film for the new model costs only $1 per exposure. Let p_c' denote the price of the new camera and p_c'' the price at which Juli could sell her old camera.

   a. Use a graphic argument based on indifference curves to determine the price differential $p_c' - p_c''$ at which Juli will be indifferent between keeping her old camera and selling it so that she can buy the new model.
   b. Now suppose that her demand for instant photographs is independent of her income, and use a graphic argument based on her demand curve for instant photographs to determine the same price differential.

7. Jay's income elasticity of demand for garlic is zero, and his demand curve for garlic is

   $$p = 150 - 2x_1$$

   a. What is the maximum sum that Jay will pay in order to have 50 units of garlic rather than none?
   b. If he currently cannot buy garlic at any price, what is the maximum amount that he will pay for the opportunity to buy it at a price of $30 per unit?

c. What is the maximum amount that he is willing to pay for the opportunity to buy garlic at a price of \$10 rather than \$30 per unit?

8. Each of the 100 kids in Ess Cee has the following demand for rides on Walt's Magic Merry-Go-Round:

$$p = 10 - x$$

where x is the number of rides per week and p is the price per ride. Demand is independent of income. What is magical about Walt's Merry-Go-Round is that it costs nothing to run and has unlimited capacity. What two-part tariff maximizes Walt's profit? How much profit does Walt earn? How many rides does each kid take in a week?

9. Alison's father has told her a number of times, "Please don't bring food and drinks into the car." This past weekend, Alison spilled some hot chocolate on her lap and the car seat, and had to listen to another lecture from her father. At the end she said, "I think you love your car more than you love me!" How is Alison confusing marginal and total values?

10. At many universities, students are admitted free to football and basketball games. Because seating is on a first-come-first-served basis and because the number of good seats is limited, the good seats are often taken 1 to 2 hours before game time. What would happen if more good seats were made available to students? If the average quality of the seats in the student section were improved? What is true about the average value of the seats when they are allocated this way compared to when they are allocated by price?

11. Buford buys consumption bundle (4,8) when the prices of good 1 and good 2 are both \$1, and he buys bundle (8,2) when the price of good 1 is \$1 and the price of good 2 is \$2. Is it possible to infer from this information which of the two bundles Buford prefers?

12. Juan's income was \$10 500 in both periods 0 and 1. For which of the following three cases was Juan better off in period 1? For which was he worse off in period 1? For which cases are you uncertain?

a. Both P' and L' exceed 1.
b. Both P' and L' are less than 1.
c. L' exceeds 1 and P' is less than 1.
d. Construct a diagram consistent with case (a) in which you indicate Juan's budget line and consumption bundle for both periods. Do the same for case (c).

13. When we used Norm's consumption decisions to develop quantity indexes for him, we supposed that we knew nothing about his preferences. Suppose now that his preferences in both periods are captured by the following perfect-complements utility function:

$$U(x_1, x_2) = \min(x_1, x_2)$$

Supposing that Norm always chooses the utility-maximizing bundle, show that (i) if one quantity index is less than 1, then so is the other; (ii) if one quantity index is greater than 1, then so is the other; and (iii) if one quantity index is equal to 1, then so is the other. Explain these curious results. (*Hint*: Ask yourself why the situation shown in Figure 4.18 cannot arise with this utility function.)

14. I buy gasoline only when my tank is virtually empty, and I always fill it up because it takes 10 minutes of my valuable time to buy 30 litres, 60 litres, or the full 80 litres. Show that my behaviour is utility-maximizing. (*Hint*: Using Becker's full-income apparatus, consider my budget lines between gasoline and a composite good when I buy 30 litres at a time, 60 litres at a time, 80 litres at a time.)

15. One day, Thomas (who was an economics major) was waiting in a line for almost an hour. When the person in front of him got to the head of the line he had to fill out a form which took about five minutes. The person complained that the time spent in line would be much less if the office gave the forms to those in line before they reached the window so they could fill them out while waiting. The clerk thought this was a good idea, and was about to tell the supervisor the plan when Thomas said, "Excuse me, but I don't think it will make any difference." Why wouldn't it? (*Hint*: Suppose Thomas and the others are waiting in line because some good is underpriced. Suppose the value of what is being given

away is $10 and that waiting costs are $10 per hour for everyone. Hence 1 hour is the equilibrium price.)

16. A murder has been committed. The only clue is a grocery receipt left at the scene by the murderer. The receipt shows that 20 bags of chips selling for $2 a bag and 10 six-packs of pop selling for $6 per six-pack were bought that day. There are two suspects: Colonel Mustard and Miss Scarlet. On searching their apartments, you find each suspect's grocery bill for the previous week. Last week chips were $3 a bag and pop was $5 a six-pack. Colonel Mustard bought 35 bags of chips and 4 packs of pop at those prices. Miss Scarlet bought 30 bags of chips and 7 packs of pop at those prices. Supposing that these people have well-behaved preferences, can you tell who the murderer is not?

17. Suppose you are endowed with two goods: apples and eggs. Furthermore, suppose your utility-maximizing consumption bundle is equal to your endowment. What happens to the level of your utility if the price of apples goes down? What happens to the level of your utility if the price of apples goes up? How can you explain this puzzle?

18. Prior to unleaded gasoline all cars used leaded gas, with the more expensive gas containing more lead. It turned out that lead was a major pollutant and in the 1960s, in an effort to mitigate pollution, a tax of $ 0.10/gallon was placed on all gas in the hope that it would reduce the level of gas consumption and lower the amount of pollution. Can it be said, unambiguously, that such a tax would lower pollution from leaded gasoline?

19. When dining out in a group of size N, it is often the case that at the end of the meal each person in the group pays $1/N$ of the total bill. Building on insight from our treatment of common property (Chapter 1), suggest a reason why individuals might choose higher-quality meals in this circumstance.

20. This chapter discussed the disadvantages of using time to allocate goods. However, we observe time being used all of the time. Consider two cases. First, we often line up at check-out stands in the grocery and other stores. Second, concerts of famous rock bands are often so underpriced that some people line up for days to purchase tickets. Think up economic explanations for why prices do not increase in these cases to avoid the lines.

21. A province in Canada recently passed labour legislation that effectively prevented children from working on farms (picking berries in particular). The minister in charge noted a couple of years later that "the total value of crops has increased and so there was no harm done by the law." Suppose that the market value of the crops has increased. Is the conclusion correct?

22. When the price of salmon is $4 per kilo, a certain consumer decides to eat no salmon. If the price falls to $1.50 per kilo, he purchases 10 kilos of salmon per week.
    a. How much would this consumer pay per week for the right to purchase salmon at $1.50 rather than face the $4 price? Assume a linear demand curve.
    b. Suppose there is a "Salmon Price Club" that sells salmon for $1.50 when the price in the store is $3. How much will this person pay to join this club?

23. Curtis and Doug both purchase cowboy shirts and hats at their friendly stampede and tack store. The two wild and crazy professors have different tastes for these two goods, different incomes, and they end up purchasing different quantities. Nevertheless, they have the same marginal rate of substitution of cowboy shirts for hats. How is this possible?

24. Quite often a firm will sell "seconds," damaged goods, at a considerably lower price than the undamaged merchandise. Why are seconds always sold close to the point of production?

25. Suppose a university charges students by the semester; that is, students pay a fixed amount for a given semester, independent of the number of credits taken. What would happen to the expected number of credits taken if the semester fee increased?

26. Dogs are more time-intensive pets than cats. They require more attention, more exercise, and

daily maintenance. Since 1980, labour force participation rates and per capita incomes have increased in both the US and Canada. What would you predict has happened to the relative ownership of dogs and cats in the past 20 years?

*27. In Exercise 29 of Chapter 3, you derived demand functions for the following utility functions: $U = x_2 + \ln x_1$ and has a budget constraint $M = p_1x_1 + p_2x_2$. Using those demand functions, answer the following.

a. Assuming $p_2 = 1$, graph x_1^*, putting the relative price on the vertical axis. Interpret the height and area under the demand curve.

b. Without doing any calculations and using a new graph, draw x_1^* and x_1^u (the compensated demand curve).

c. On another new graph, put x_1 on the horizontal axis, x_2 on the vertical one and draw three indifference curves. (Exact numbers are not important, concentrate on the exact shapes).

*28. Henrietta sleeps exactly 8 hours per day, and she devotes the remaining 16 hours of time to work and golf. She can work as many hours as she wants at a wage rate of $\$w$ per hour. She spends her money on a composite commodity, with price equal to \$1, and golf. The money price of a round of golf is p_2, and the time price is four hours. Her utility function is

$$U(x_1, x_2) = x_1x_2$$

where x_1 is quantity of the composite commodity and x_2 is rounds of golf.

a. Find the utility-maximizing values of x_1 and x_2 as functions of w and p_2.

b. What is the derivative of her demand for golf with respect to w? With respect to p_2?

c. Compute the elasticity of her demand for golf with respect to w. With respect to p_2. With respect to the *full price* of golf.

*29. Consider the following utility function:

$$U(x_1, x_2) = x_2 + 120x_1 - (x_1)^2/2$$

a. Find the ordinary demand function for good 1. Is quantity demanded dependent on income?

b. Find the compensated demand function for good 1.

c. Compare the two demand functions, and explain the result in terms of the absence of income effects on the demand for good 1.

*30. Using the demand function for good 1 from Exercise 29, compute the total and marginal values of 10 units of good 1, 20 units of good 1, 80 units of good 1, and 115 units of good 1.

*31. Emma consumes two goods and her preferences between these goods is described by the utility function $U(X_1, X_2) = (X_1)^{0.5}(X_2)^{0.5}$

a. Derive her ordinary and compensated demand functions.

b. If $P_1 = 1$ and $P_2 = 2$ and she has an income of \$160, how much would she demand of X_1 and X_2? What would her utility be if she consumed this bundle?

c. If the price of good 1 increases to \$2, how much additional income would she need so that her level of utility would be unaffected?

d. What are the income and substitution effects of this price change?

32. Vegetarian Mike eats only two kinds of food, tofu and lima beans. His preferences are described by $U = X_1 + 2X_2$, where X_1 and X_2 are quantities of tofu and lima beans respectively.

a. If his income is \$32 and $P_1 = P_2 = \$4$, how much of each food will he consume?

b. If the price of tofu drops to \$1, calculate his compensating and equivalent variations.

REFERENCES

Barzel, Y. 1982. "The Testability of the Law of Demand," in W. Sharpe and C. Cootner (eds.), *Financial Economics: Essays in Honor of Paul Cootner*. Englewood Cliffs, NJ: Prentice-Hall, 223–45.

Becker, G. 1965. "A Theory of the Allocation of Time," *The Economic Journal*, 75:493–517.

Bertonazzi, E., M. Maloney, and R. McCormick. 1993. "Some Evidence on the Alchian and Allen Theorem: the Third Law of Demand?" *Economic Inquiry*, 31:383–93.

Iannaccone, L., D. Olson, and R. Stark. 1995. "Religious Resources and Church Growth," *Social Forces*, 74(2):705–31.

Kahneman, D., J. L. Knetsch, and R. H. Thaler. 1990. "Experimental Tests of the Endowment Effect and the Coase Theorem," *Journal of Political Economy*, 98:1325–48.

Oi, W. 1971. "A Disneyland Dilemma: Two-Part Tariffs for a Mickey Mouse Monopoly," *Quarterly Journal of Economics*, 85:77–96.

Willig, R. 1976. "Consumer's Surplus Without Apology," *American Economic Review*, 66:589–97.

CHAPTER 5

Intertemporal Decision Making and Capital Values

intertemporal resource allocation

In exploring the model of consumer choice in the last three chapters, we used a static model in which time played no role. Yet many interesting and important allocation problems are inherently problems about **intertemporal resource allocation** — about the allocation of resources to present and future uses. Your decisions with respect to education and occupational choice are unavoidably intertemporal. When you decide to spend money today instead of saving it for a future use, you are making an intertemporal decision. An oil company's decision to pump and sell oil today, or to wait for tomorrow, is an intertemporal decision. All investment decisions are intertemporal.

Inevitably, intertemporal choices involve comparisons of sums of money at different times. Think, for example, about the intertemporal resource problem that arises in choosing between becoming a doctor or a carpenter. Medicine involves a long period of training during which the medical student earns little income, but it promises a very high annual income once training is completed. In contrast, carpentry involves a much shorter training period, but the annual income of a journeyman carpenter is small relative to that of a practising doctor. A person who faces the choice between these occupations needs to compare the two income streams. But how does an eighteen-year-old student trying to choose an occupation go about comparing the stream of earnings for a doctor, with its high annual income but very long training period, to the stream of earnings for a carpenter, with its shorter training period but smaller annual income?

interest rate

The key to making such comparisons is the ability to borrow and lend money, and the price that drives these comparisons is the **interest rate** at which borrowing and lending take place. This one very important price governs all decisions about the intertemporal allocation of resources.

Interest rates sound mysterious and complicated, but they are simply prices. Quite often one hears the remark that "interest is the price of money." This is not true. The price of one dollar is one dollar, not a number like 10 percent. The interest rate is the *price of borrowing money*. In fact, money doesn't even need to exist for there to be interest. Interest is the price paid for early consumption of one good in terms of another. In other words, it is just a relative price. We speak of comparing sums of money at different times simply as a matter of convenience.

In the first part of this chapter, we examine present values in order to compare values over time. We then see how the price of assets depends on interest rates and look at a number of examples. In the rest of the chapter we see how the interest rate affects a number of important intertemporal decisions, including the major economic decisions that individuals must make over their life cycle. In this chapter we see a further demonstration of the power of the model developed in Chapter 2. With minimal modifications we can apply our model of choice to problems over time.

5.1 Intertemporal Value Comparisons

market for loanable funds

The fact that people can borrow and lend money in what is called the **market for loanable funds** implies that they can compare different sums of money at different times. Your local banker, from whom you can borrow money and to whom you can lend money, works in this market. The rate of interest at which you can borrow money from your local bank is called the **borrowing rate**, and is denoted by i_b. We usually do not think about lending money to the bank, but when you deposit money in a savings account, for example, you are in fact lending money to the bank. The rate of interest you earn on money deposited in the bank is called the **deposit rate**, and is denoted by i_d.

borrowing rate

deposit rate

Typically, i_b exceeds i_d; that is, the borrowing rate of interest exceeds the deposit rate of interest. Why? Fundamentally, a bank is a business which borrows money from some people — at the deposit rate of interest i_d — and lends to other people — at the borrowing rate of interest i_b. If the bank is to cover its costs — salaries, overhead, etc. — then i_b must exceed i_d.

Now let us see how to compare \$1000 today with \$1100 one year from today. Imagine that you have been given the choice between two windfall gains: \$1000 to be paid to you today or \$1100 to be paid to you one year from today. Which should you choose? Since the two windfall gains are separated by exactly one year, we can think of the interest rates i_b and i_d as annual rates.

Suppose you want to save this money for some future purpose — say a trip to Argentina after you graduate. The sensible way to make the comparison is to compute a **future value** FV for \$1000 received today, and then compare this future value with \$1100 received one year in the future. If you deposited \$1000 in your bank today (perhaps in a one-year Guaranteed Investment Certificate) at interest rate i_d, one year from today you would have $FV = \$1000(1 + i_d)$, the original \$1000 plus interest equal to \$1000 times i_d. In other words, $\$1000(1 + i_d)$ is the *future value* (one period in the future) of \$1000 received today. Notice that FV is greater than or less than \$1100 as i_d is greater than or less than 10 percent. In comparing future values, then, we can use the following rule to make the choice:

future value

Future Value Choice Rule: (i) choose \$1000 received today if i_d exceeds 10 percent; (ii) choose \$1100 to be received in one year if i_d is less than 10 percent; (iii) choose either if i_d is equal to 10 percent.

present value

Now suppose you want to spend this windfall gain today for a new mountain bike. In this case the sensible thing to do is to compute a **present value** PV for the \$1100 to be received in one year, and then compare this present value with the \$1000 to be received today. The present value of \$1100 one year from today is the amount you could borrow from your banker in exchange for a payment of \$1100 in one year. Since for each dollar you borrow today at interest rate i_b you must pay back $1 + i_b$ dollars one year from today, we see that $PV(1 + i_b) = \$1100$, or that $PV = \$1100/(1 + i_b)$. In other words, $\$1100/(1 + i_b)$ is the *present value* of \$1100 to be received one year from today. Notice that PV is greater than or less than \$1000 as i_b is less than or greater than 10 percent. In comparing present values, then, you can use the following rule to make your choice:

Present Value Choice Rule: (i) choose $1000 payable today if i_b exceeds 10 percent; (ii) choose $1100 payable in one year if i_b is less than 10 percent; (iii) choose either if i_b is equal to 10 percent.

These choice rules are almost identical. The only difference is that i_d — the interest rate you earn on money deposited in the bank — is the relevant rate for the future value choice rule, while i_b — the interest rate at which you can borrow money from your bank — is the relevant rate for the present value choice rule. If both rates exceed 10 percent, or if both are less than 10 percent, we know what you should do: choose $1000 payable today if both rates exceed 10 percent, and choose $1100 payable in a year if both rates are less than 10 percent.

If i_b is greater than 10 percent and i_d is less than 10 percent, however, the two rules lead us to different choices. To determine what you should do, we need to know when you intend to spend the money; that is, we need to know something about your preferences. If you want to spend this windfall gain on a new bicycle today, then the present value rule should guide your choice to maximize the amount of money available today. In contrast, if you want to save the windfall gain for future consumption, the future value rule is the relevant rule. If you want to spend some of it today and some of it in the future, we need to know more about your preferences to determine your best choice.

A Perfect Market for Loanable Funds

In certain circumstances, your choice of which windfall to pick can be separated from the way in which you intend to spend the money — that is, from your preferences. If the two rates of interest are identical, we can *always* achieve this separation. For this reason, we will assume throughout the chapter that the borrowing and lending rates are identical, and we will denote that single interest rate by i. When this assumption is satisfied, the market for loanable funds is said to be *perfect*.

Empirically, the market for loanable funds is never perfect, but this assumption greatly simplifies and clarifies the principles of choice in situations where time matters.

The Separation Theorem

Let us generalize what we learned from the windfall example. Given a perfect market for loanable funds, we can separate the choice of income streams over time from the choice of consumption expenditures over time. The ability to neatly separate decisions in this way is called the **separation theorem**:

separation theorem

1. **Individuals will choose among different income streams by choosing the income stream with the largest present value.**
2. **They will choose consumption expenditures over time to maximize utility, given the constraint that the present value of income not exceed the present value of consumption expenditures.**

Notice that the criterion for choosing among different income streams is couched in terms of present value. However, given a perfect market for loanable funds, an equivalent criterion is to choose the income stream with the largest future value (at some future time). For example, in choosing between the two windfall gains, we saw that when the two rates of interest are identical, the windfall gain with the larger present value is also the one with the larger future value. Though the two criteria are equivalent, it is conventional to use the present-value criterion.

PROBLEM 5.1

In recent years investment houses have offered investors mutual funds, which invest in companies that supposedly act in a "moral" fashion by not polluting, not investing in military weapons, and the like. Are these "ethical funds" consistent or inconsistent with our assumption of the separation theorem?

Present Values

We saw in the previous section that \$1 will grow to a future value of $\$1(1 + i)$ at the end of the specified period. Likewise, the present value of \$1 in the next period is $\$1/(1 + i)$. For example, \$1 a year from now is only worth approximately 90.9¢ today if the interest rate is 10 percent. But how do we calculate present values if there is a stream of future amounts to be discounted?

Suppose we have the following income stream: $(M_0, M_1, M_2, \ldots, M_T)$. Income M_0 is received today, income M_1 is received one period in the future, and so on. First let us calculate the present value of M_t — income that is received t periods in the future. The key to this calculation is the following definition: the present value of M_t is a sum of money PV such that, if we were to invest it today at interest rate i, it would be worth M_t in t periods.

Suppose, for example, that you deposit \$1 in your savings account at interest rate i. At the end of one period, your balance will be the original dollar plus interest i on that dollar, or $\$(1 + i)$. At the end of two periods, your balance in dollars will be

$$(1 + i)^2 = (1 + i) + i(1 + i)$$

The first expression on the right, $(1 + i)$, is the balance at the end of the first period, and the second expression on the right, $i(1 + i)$, is the interest earned in the second period. As you can easily verify, at the end of t periods, the balance will be $(1 + i)^t$. Therefore, \$1 invested today at interest rate i will be worth $(1 + i)^t$ in t periods.

Now we can use this result to find the present value of M_t. If you deposit PV in your savings account, at the end of t periods you will have $PV(1 + i)^t$. But this sum must be equal to M_t, since PV is the present value of M_t. By solving the following equation for PV, we have the present value of M_t.

$$PV(1 + i)^t = M_t$$

Solving for PV we have,

$$PV = \frac{M_t}{(1 + i)^t}$$

As you know, if today you invested PV at interest rate i, you would have M_t in t periods. Alternatively, the maximum sum your banker would lend you today in exchange for a payment of M_t in t periods is PV. In these *two* senses, then, PV today is *equivalent to* M_t in period t.

With the help of this formula, we can calculate the present value of income stream $(M_0, M_1, M_2, \ldots, M_T)$.[1]

$$PV = M_0 + \frac{M_1}{(1+i)} + \frac{M_2}{(1+i)^2} + \ldots + \frac{M_T}{(1+i)^T}$$

annuity
perpetuity
consol

An income stream with equal payments is called an **annuity**. If the annuity lasts forever it is called a **perpetuity** or a **consol**. When a perpetuity that pays \$$M$ per period is discounted at a constant rate of interest, an incredibly simple and useful present value formula results:[2]

$$PV = \frac{M}{i}$$

This simple formula closely approximates the *PV* of an annuity, especially when the annuity lasts for more than twenty years and the interest rate is above 10 percent.

PROBLEM 5.2

The first income stream consists of \$0 today, \$5000 one year from today, and \$12 100 two years from today. The second income stream consists of \$10 000 today, \$5000 one year from today, and \$0 two years from today. Which income stream has the larger present value when the annual rate of interest is 0 percent? When it is 5 percent? When it is 10 percent? When it is 15 percent? When it is 20 percent? There is a pattern in these results. What is it? Can you explain it?

Application: You're a Millionaire! (almost)

Many lotteries in the US boldly announce that the winner will walk away with a substantial prize, followed by a brief statement that payments are made annually for a period like twenty years. If you were told that you had won \$1 000 000, but you would receive this in twenty installments of \$50 000 over twenty years starting one year from now, would you have won a million dollars?

If the interest rate was more than zero, the answer is no. What the lottery is offering you is a \$50 000 annuity, not a \$1 million lump-sum payment. In order to convert the annuity to current dollars we need to calculate its present value. Suppose the interest rate was 10 percent. The present value of the first payment is \$45 454 = 50 000/1.1. The value of the last payment in twenty years is only \$7400 in current dollars! If we calculate the present value of the entire annuity, it amounts to \$425 500 — not quite half the value of the stated prize.

---

1. Interest rates often change from period to period. Letting i_t denote the interest rate in period t, the present value of income stream $(\$M_0, \$M_1, \$M_2, \ldots, \$M_T)$ is

$$\$PV = \$M_0 + \frac{\$M_1}{1+i_1} + \frac{\$M_2}{(1+i_1)(1+i_2)} + \ldots + \frac{\$M_T}{(1+i_1)(1+i_2)\ldots(1+i_T)}$$

2. This formula results when the first payment begins one year in the future. If the payment begins today, then the simple formula becomes

$$PV = \frac{M(1+i)}{i}.$$

Calculating the value of an annuity by hand is quite painful, and in fact most calculators do the job in seconds. However, suppose we used the simple perpetuity formula to get an approximate value, how well would it do? In this case we would have come up with $500 000 = 50 000/0.1, which is quite close and easy enough to do in your head. The higher the interest rate and the longer the annuity, the more accurate this formula becomes. Remember this when you want to impress your new boss with how good you are with figures.

Rates of Return

rate of return

Suppose a gold bar is currently selling for $1000 and is expected to sell for $1200 one year from now. What is the expected **rate of return** on the gold bar? The rate of return is given by the difference in the two prices divided by the current price, or:

$$R = \frac{(p_1 - p_0)}{p_0}$$

where the subscripts represent the two periods. In the case of the gold bar, the rate of return is 20 percent = (1200 – 1000)/1000.

The more important question is, what rate of return would we expect on an asset like a gold bar in equilibrium? In answering this question, let us ignore any aspect of risk and assume that all investments have equal risks, and let us further assume that there is no utility found in holding gold bars *per se.* That is, they are valued strictly for their financial rate of return.

Under such conditions the rate of return on the gold bar must equal the rate of interest. Suppose that it did not, and that the rate of interest was only 10 percent. Given that gold bars yield a return of 20 percent, people will begin to invest in gold bars, and in so doing they will drive the price today up. This takes place until the current price is $1091. At this price the rate of return is equal to $R = (1200 - 1091)/1091 = 10$ percent. If the current interest rate had been 30 percent rather than 10 percent, then individuals would have sold gold bars and driven down the current price until the rate of return again equalled the interest rate. This equalization of rates of return across assets is another application of the principle of maximization, and in principle is no different than our example of traffic moving at the same speed across different lanes, or the example of equal *MV*s for old *Star Trek* and *The Bachelor* episodes. In equilibrium one asset cannot systematically be yielding a higher rate of return than other assets.

Application: Old Equipment and Stock Investments

The television show *60 Minutes* once ran an episode on some decrepit manufacturing plants in England. The show mostly consisted of visiting various plants that were using very old machines for producing clothing, porcelain, and the like. Some of the machines in use dated back to the industrial revolution. The driving theme of the show was that these ancient techniques were inefficient, and without a massive injection of capital, England would cease to exist as an industrial power. Ignoring the melodramatic conclusion, the show still raised an interesting question: How can firms use old machines, trucks, computers, and the like and still stay in business?

The answer is that the prices for these used pieces of equipment adjust until the rates of return are equal to those on the newer equipment. If you were starting a business and you had to decide between two computers to purchase, the price you would be willing to pay would be the present value of the stream of income each machine would generate. The more productive the computer, the larger the income stream it yields, and the more you are willing to pay. In this way, the differences in productivity are **capitalized** into the price of the computers and, as a result, their rates of return are equal. Firms that use old equipment pay less for the equipment. These lower costs just compensate for the lower productivity. Firms that use newer equipment pay more for it and these higher costs are just compensated for by the higher productivity. The rates of return must be the same in both cases.

capitalized

As another example, suppose you own two stocks: A and B. Stock A has had a great previous week, increasing by 50 percent in value. Unfortunately stock B has done very poorly, and has fallen in value by 30 percent over the last week. If you want to sell one of the stocks, and if you are only concerned with the rate of return, which stock should you sell? The answer is that you should be indifferent!

The stock prices were adjusting to reflect the future streams of income of each company. For company A there must have been good news regarding the future profits of the firm. With this news the current price of the stock increased until these future profits were capitalized into the price. For company B the news must have been bad, and this bad news was capitalized into its stock price. As we have seen, the prices adjust until the rates of return are the same, and so as an investor, you should be indifferent between them.

The preceding discussion is important enough to consider more carefully. Our assumption of maximization, when applied to rates of return on different assets, predicts that past movements in prices have no bearing on future price movements. All information about interest rates and future expected incomes are capitalized into the current price and the past prices are irrelevant. A great example of this is found in the movie *Wall Street*, starring Michael Douglas and Charlie Sheen. The Sheen character impresses his boss, Michael Douglas, by passing on some inside information that allows him to make some money on a stock deal. Sheen then stays up night after night tracking stock prices in an effort to repeat his insightful advice — all to no avail. In the end he discovers that the only way to make an above-normal return is to engage in illegal activity. Keep this in mind the next time you get a hot tip on a stock based on its past market performance.

If the preceding is true, why are the returns to many assets so obviously different? One reason is that assets have different risks involved, and more risky assets must pay a premium in order for individuals to invest in them. However, it is not difficult to find assets with similar risk yet with very different rates of return. At your university, for example, more students apply for admission into the accounting program than the philosophy department because the financial rate of return is higher for accountants. Degrees in dentistry, medicine, law, and engineering all give higher financial rates of return than do degrees in drama, history, education, and political science. How is this so?

Part of the answer is that many assets yield utility as well as income, and it is the *total* rate of return that must be equal across assets, not just the financial rate of return. For example, suppose there are two assets: gold bars that yield a financial return of 10 percent and yield no utility; and a painting that yields a financial return of 10 percent and a utility return of 3 percent. Could this be an equilibrium? No, because at a return of 13 percent the painting is too good a deal. The price of the painting must rise until its financial rate of return is 7 percent and its total rate of return is 10 percent. The opposite is true for an asset that yields disutility. If holding an asset is dangerous, distasteful, or painful, then its financial return must be higher in order to compensate. So take heart that dentists get paid so much … it is simply the price of boredom, smelling bad breath, and knowing that no one wants to come visit you.

5.2
The Demand for Consumer Capital and Complementary Goods

capital

human capital

consumer capital

The word **capital** conjures up a great number of images. We think of the distinction between labour and capital, of machines and buildings, and perhaps even notions of capitalist exploitation. Capital, though, is just a name given to anything that yields services over time. A fresh strawberry is not capital, but a computer or a person is. Economists often refer to human inputs in production as **human capital** to stress the fact that our human endowments yield services and income over time. There is another class of goods called **consumer capital** — goods that are valued not for themselves, but for the services they provide over time. We buy chairs, beds, and television sets for what they allow us to do: sit, sleep in comfort, and watch TV. We buy refrigerators to get refrigeration, telephones to get telephone service, and personal computers to do word processing and play video games.

Notice that the items themselves have only *indirect value*. Few of us find a refrigerator intrinsically appealing; we simply use it to keep our meat and milk cold. Consumer capital, then, is valued only *indirectly*, as a necessary means of producing a valued service or good. Notice, too, that producing a desired service from consumer capital often means buying *complementary*, or interdependent, goods. We buy both cars and gasoline to get transportation; both televisions and electricity to get TV programming; both a printer and computer paper to get computer printouts; and both skis and lift tickets to go skiing. In this section, we want to apply what we know about demand theory and present values to analyze the demand for consumer capital.

Imagine that an economist is trying to derive the demand for cameras. The economist might begin with two observations. First, cameras are items of consumer capital because the buyer values not cameras but photographs. Second, producing photographs involves a complementarity because the photographer must buy both a camera and some film.

To keep matters simple, we will make a number of assumptions. First, recall from Chapter 4 that our potential purchaser, Juli, directly values photographs, but not film or cameras. Second, assume that one unit of film produces one photograph. Third, assume that Juli can produce all of the photographs she wants with just one camera and that she cannot rent a camera. Finally, assume that there are no income effects so that our measures CV and EV are equal to consumer's surplus. Our problem is to discover how much Juli is willing to pay for a camera.

Suppose for the moment that a camera only lasts one period and then it falls apart. Alternatively, we can imagine that it is possible to rent a camera for one period. How much would Juli be willing to pay? Figure 5.1 shows us the answer. If film costs p_1 and the demand for film is D_1, then x_1 units of film are demanded and the consumer's surplus is equal to the shaded area. As we saw in Chapter 4 with two-part tariffs, the maximum Juli is willing to pay for the camera, given that the price of film is equal to p_1, is the shaded area of consumer's surplus. For the sake of argument, suppose this area is equal to \$25.

Cameras, however, last for a number of years and are therefore capital goods. In every year, if we assume the demand and price for film remains the same, Juli would earn a surplus of \$25. If a camera was expected to last 10 years, would the price of the camera be \$250? By now you should know that the camera would be worth less than

FIGURE 5.1 The demand for film

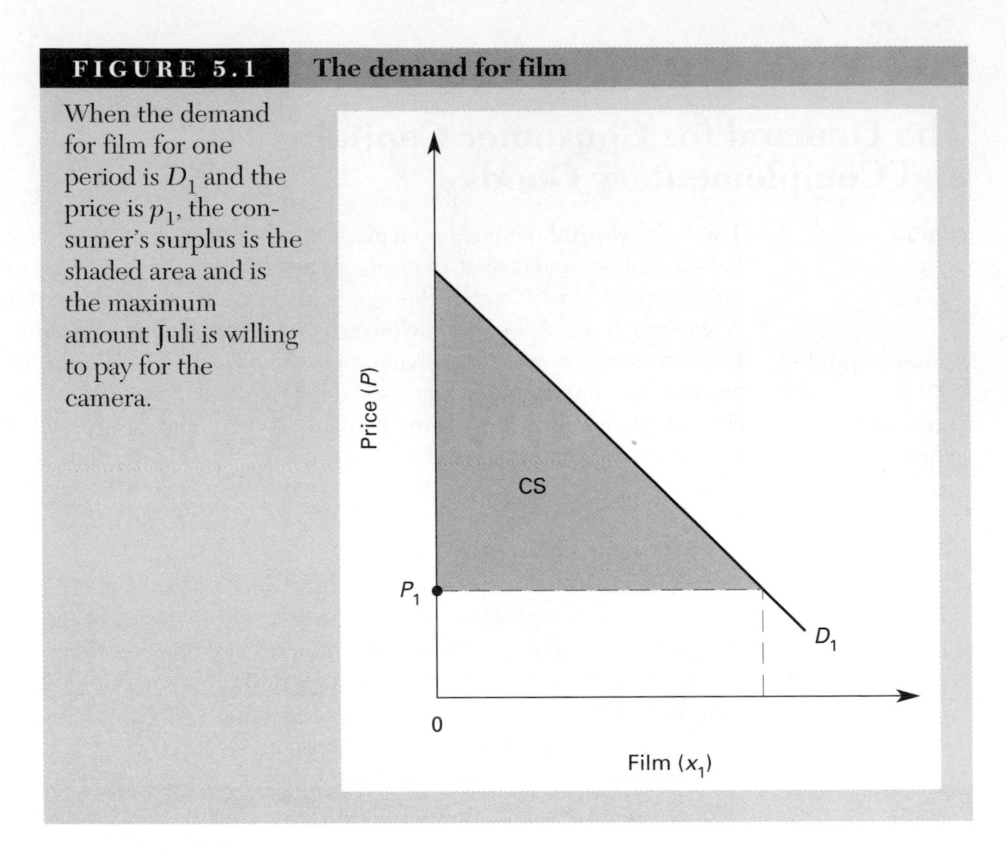

When the demand for film for one period is D_1 and the price is p_1, the consumer's surplus is the shaded area and is the maximum amount Juli is willing to pay for the camera.

$250 because the consumer surplus generated in the future is worth less than the current consumer's surplus. If the interest rate were 10 percent and the camera were expected to last 10 years, the maximum Juli would pay for the camera is $153.50 — the present value of a 10-year $25 annuity at 10 percent.

Figure 5.2 graphs the demand for the camera. The demand for the camera has this peculiar shape because only one camera is required to take photographs. The maximum price of $153.50 is what is called a **reservation price**. We will denote this price by p_c^r. If the price of the camera is lower than Juli's reservation price she buys it, and if the price is higher than the reservation price she does not buy it. Because owning a camera effectively confers the privilege of buying photographs (film) at price p_1, we see that p_c^r is the *maximum price* that Juli is willing to pay for the right to buy photographs at price p_1.

reservation price

Since p_c^r is simply Juli's CV, we know that it is inversely related to p_1. In Figure 5.3, the line RR', which gives the reservation price for the camera associated with any price of film, is therefore downward sloping. If the market prices for film and a camera are in the blue area above this downward-sloping line, Juli will not buy a camera. If prices are on or below the line in the grey area, she will buy a camera.

A great many consumer decisions conform to the structure of our camera and photographs problem. Most decisions about consumer durables — items such as VCRs, personal computers, electric crêpe makers, waterbeds, or backpacks — can be interpreted in this framework.

FIGURE 5.2 **The demand for a camera**

The demand for the camera is simply the discounted consumer's surplus that is derived over the film. Because one camera is sufficient to take all of the photographs, only one is demanded, and the demand curve has a rectangular shape.

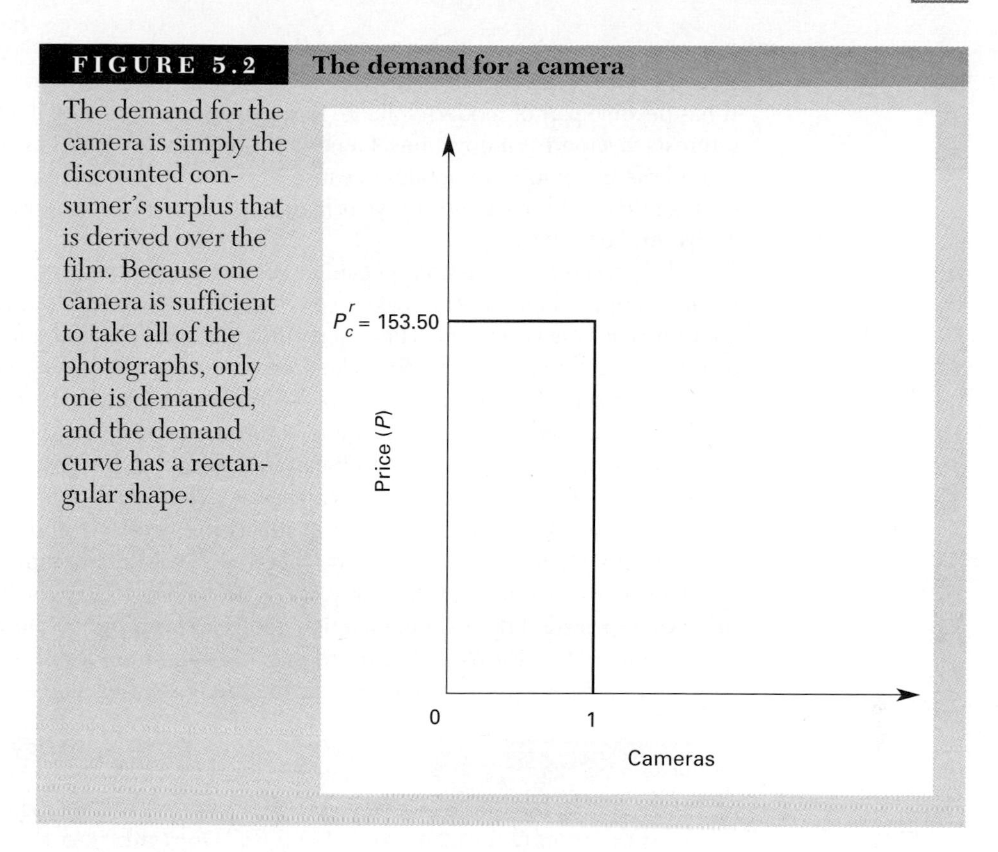

FIGURE 5.3 **Reservation prices**

The line RR' gives Juli's reservation price for the camera, given any price p_1 for film. For combinations of the price of film p_1 and the price of a camera p_c in the area on or below RR', Juli will buy a camera. But for combinations in the blue area above RR' she will not buy a camera.

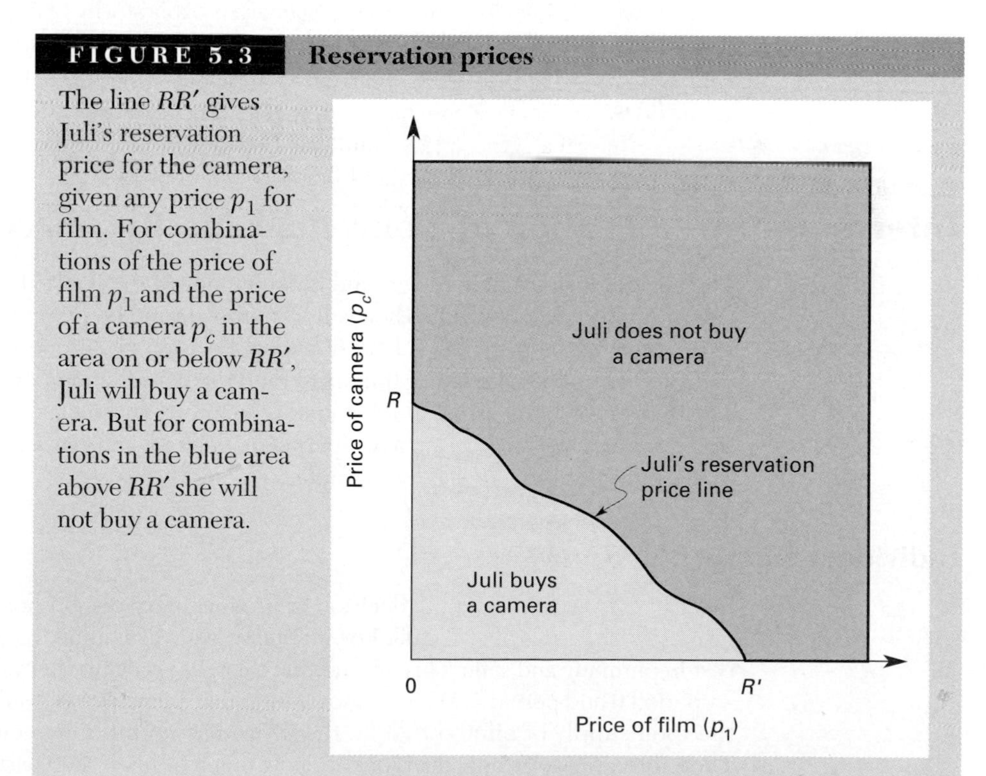

Application: Built-In Low Quality?

It has become part of modern folklore that powerful multinational firms find it in their interests to suppress innovations. General Motors, so it is said, sits on plans that could extend the life of its automobiles because it wants to sell more cars. General Electric, so it is said, could make a thirty-year light bulb, but would rather sell more one-year bulbs. And on it goes.

The preceding discussion on capital goods should make you leery of such sentiments. Suppose Polaroid can make two types of cameras: one that lasts one year, and another that lasts two years. The reservation price for the first camera, assuming all consumers are like Juli, will be $25. The reservation price for the second camera, assuming an interest rate of 10 percent, will be $47.72 = 25 + 25/1.1. The reservation price of the camera is based on the present value of the stream of services the camera provides. Which camera is more profitable to Polaroid depends on the cost of each camera. If it costs the same to produce a one-year camera as it does a two-year camera, then clearly Polaroid makes the camera that lasts longer. If the two-year camera costs disproportionately more than a one-year camera, then the lower-quality camera is made.

Hence, due to the fact that consumers are willing to pay for the future streams of services provided by consumer capital goods, firms produce those goods that maximize their profits. Firms do not try to maximize the number of items sold and, as a result, firms do not suppress innovations that increase the value of the firm.

PROBLEM 5.3

When you buy this textbook you have the option of reselling it at the end of the term — in fact, most of you do! Does this hurt the publisher's income? How does the preceding analysis explain why textbooks are not disposable; that is, why are textbooks not made of cheaper paper and ink, with tear-outs and poor bindings, such that the book falls apart after one term?

5.3 Intertemporal Allocation of Nonrenewable Resources

The old aphorism, "Oil in the ground is like money in the bank," brings up an important intertemporal question: When will oil in the ground be pumped, sold, and turned into money in the bank? This kind of supply decision clearly depends on the prices that suppliers anticipate today, tomorrow, and the day after, and on the interest rate i. To discover the basic principles that guide the intertemporal allocation of nonrenewable resources, we will develop a two-period model for a nonrenewable natural resource that is in fixed supply — oil, for example.

Individual Supply Behaviour

Let us begin with the supply decision of an imaginary person named Bagwell, who owns 10 000 barrels of crude oil. For simplicity, we will assume that Bagwell incurs no cost in pumping and selling his oil, and that there are only two periods in this economy — period 0 and period 1. We will also assume that Bagwell owns only a tiny portion of the total supply of oil and that he therefore has no influence on the price of oil. Therefore, Bagwell's only decisions are how much of his 10 000 barrels of oil to pump and sell (or supply) in period 0, z_0, and how much in period 1, z_1.

Suppose that the market for loanable funds is perfect. From the separation theorem we know that Bagwell will then choose z_0 and z_1 to maximize the present value of his oil income. If we let w_0 and w_1 denote the prices of oil in periods 0 and 1 respectively, the present value of his oil income is

$$PV = w_0 z_0 + w_1 z_1/(1 + i)$$

Of course, since Bagwell has just 10 000 barrels of oil,

$$z_1 = 10\,000 - z_0$$

If we then substitute this expression for z_1 in the expression for the present value of Bagwell's oil income and rearrange it, we get

$$PV = 10\,000 w_1/(1 + i) + z_0[w_0 - w_1/(1 + i)]$$

The first term is Bagwell's wealth if he sells all of his oil in period 1. The second term is the crucial one: notice that in the second term $(w_0 - w_1/(1 + i))$ is the rate of change of Bagwell's wealth as he sells one more unit of oil in period 0 and therefore one less unit in period 1. If this term is positive — that is, if w_0 exceeds $w_1/(1 + i)$ — then his wealth increases as z_0 increases (and z_1 correspondingly decreases). Therefore, Bagwell will sell all 10 000 barrels of his oil in period 0 and none of it in period 1 if w_0 exceeds $w_1/(1 + i)$.

To understand this result, suppose that Bagwell initially sells, say, 9000 barrels in period 0. Now suppose that he considers selling one more unit in period 0, and therefore one less unit in period 1. The increase in the present value of Bagwell's oil income from selling one more unit of oil in period 0 is w_0, and the decrease in the present value of his income from selling one less unit in period 1 is $w_1/(1 + i)$. If w_0 exceeds $w_1/(1 + i)$, the net change in the present value of his income, $w_0 - w_1/(1 + i)$, is positive, and Bagwell therefore will sell his whole supply of oil in period 0.

This sort of reasoning also reveals that if w_0 is less than $w_1/(1 + i)$, he will sell all his oil in period 1. Finally, if w_0 is equal to $w_1/(1 + i)$, the present value of Bagwell's income is independent of how much oil he sells in each period. Obviously, the rules we have just derived for Bagwell describe the supply behaviour of any owner of oil:

If $w_0 > w_1/(1 + i)$, all oil is sold in period 0.
If $w_0 < w_1/(1 + i)$, all oil is sold in period 1.
If $w_0 = w_1/(1 + i)$, some oil may be sold in each period.

Hotelling's Law

We will assume that each of a great many people owns a small portion of a fixed total supply of oil. We will denote the fixed total supply by z', and the quantities allocated to the two periods by z_0 and z_1. Clearly,

$$z_0 + z_1 = z'$$

We will look at the normal case in which some portion of the oil is allocated to each of the two periods — that is, the case in which the equilibrium values of both z_0 and z_1 are positive. From what we just learned about the supply behaviour of individuals like

Bagwell, when z_0 and z_1 are both positive, the following relationship between w_0 and w_1 must hold:

$$w_0 = w_1/(1+i)$$

If w_0 were less than $w_1/(1+i)$, then no one would supply any oil in period 0, and if w_0 were larger than $w_1/(1+i)$, then no one would supply any oil in period 1. Let us rewrite this equation as

$$w_1 = w_0(1+i)$$

We can express this result in words:[3]

The price of oil rises from one period to the next at the rate of interest.

Hotelling's law

This statement is an expression of **Hotelling's law,** which applies to more than just oil. This result is closely related to the material we looked at earlier in the chapter, which argued that different assets had to have rates of return equal to one another and equal to the market rate of interest.

As with the case of different assets having the same rate of return, we might ask the question: Has the price of oil grown at the rate of interest? Not at all. The price of oil, adjusted for inflation, fell throughout the twentieth century, with the exception being the two OPEC-induced price rises in the 1970s. What is going on?

One of the most interesting explanations is that oil is not a fixed resource. Doomsayers have predicted the end of the oil supply given that at any time, known reserves have been equivalent to between 10 and 20 years of consumption. However, when oil prices have risen, efforts in exploration and research into better ways of using oil have led to expanded reserves of oil. As the cost of finding oil has fallen over time, the price has fallen with it. There is nothing wrong with Hotelling's law; it is just that oil is not the best example of it.

PROBLEM 5.4

Land is fixed in terms of area, yet land values bounce all over the place. Why does Hotelling's law not apply here?

Application: When to Harvest

Many goods improve with age. Forests, wines, and many animals increase in value over time. When is the optimal time to harvest such goods? Before we answer this question, let's consider it intuitively in light of Hotelling's law. Suppose you own a bottle of wine that is increasing in value at 25 percent per year. If you can invest your money in a bank at 10 percent per year, you are clearly better off keeping your investment in the bottle of wine. If the growth in the value of the wine starts to slow down to, say, 5 percent, then you would be better off selling the wine and putting your money in the bank. The time to harvest, then, would be when the rate of growth in the bottle of wine is just equal to the rate of interest.

3. Hotelling's law was developed in Hotelling (1931).

Consider Figure 5.4, in which time in terms of years is on the horizontal axis, and price is on the vertical axis. The price at which a bottle of wine might sell if consumed at the point of sale is given by the hypothetical function $y(t)$. As it is drawn, the value at consumption initially grows at an increasing rate, then grows at a decreasing rate, and eventually the wine begins to turn bad and the value at consumption begins to fall. One might think that the best time to consume the wine is in the ninth year when the value is maximized. However, this ignores the fact that you have to wait nine years to get to this point, and in the seventh and eighth years the growth in value is quite slow.

The correct time to harvest is when the present value of the wine is maximized. In Figure 5.4, the curves P^1 and P^2 are constant present-value curves and show the combinations of prices and times of receiving these prices that yield constant present values. At point A the bottle is consumed at five years and in that year fetches a price of P_5, and this price has a present value of PV_5. If the bottle of wine were consumed in the eleventh year at point C, it would sell at that time for a price P_{11}, but it would still have a present value of PV_5. Clearly the present value of consumption is maximized at point B where the wine is consumed in the seventh year. At this point the rate of growth of the value of the wine is just equal to the rate of interest.

PROBLEM 5.5

Using a graph like the one in Figure 5.4, show what happens to the optimal time of harvest when

a. the interest rate is zero;
b. the interest rate is infinite.

FIGURE 5.4 **The optimal time to harvest**

The value of the bottle of wine at consumption is a function of time and is given by $y(t)$. The optimal harvest time is not when the value in consumption is maximized at point D, but when the present value of the wine is maximized at point B.

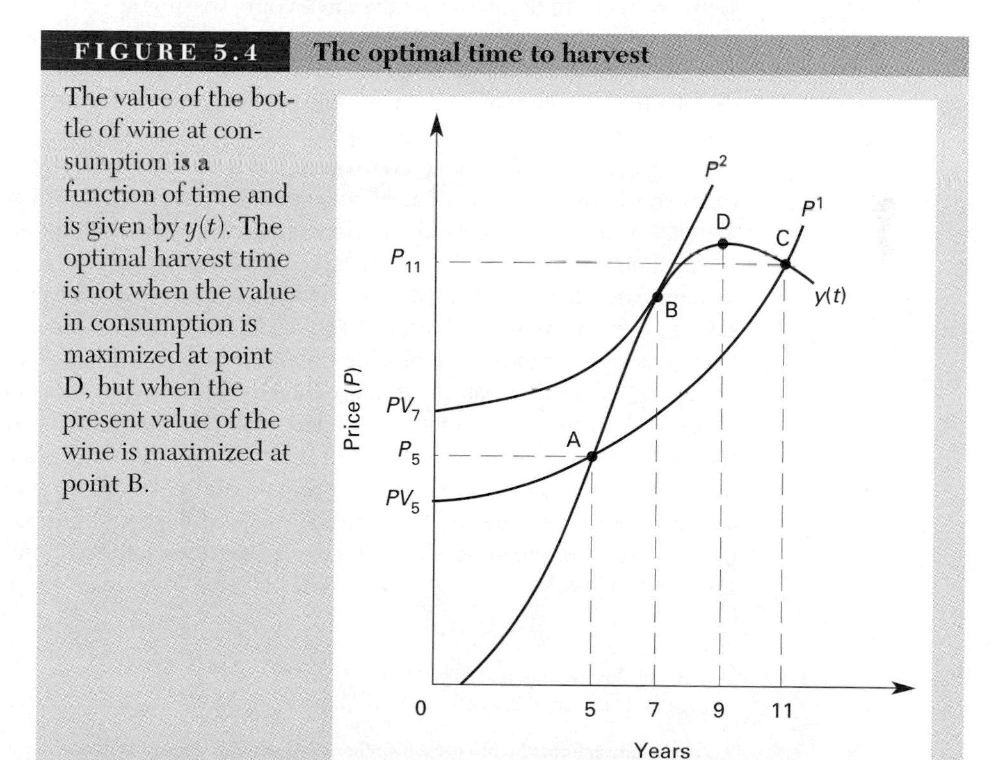

Application: The Rate of Return on a Stradivarius

The most famous of all violins are the ones made by Antonio Stradivari, who built close to 1100 instruments in his lifetime. Of these, close to 700 are still in existence. Since these violins were made from 1680–1736, and since they have been sold at public auction several times, a relatively long time series of prices for these instruments exists. Economists Ross and Zondervan (1989) have estimated the rate of return to average around 2.17 percent over this period, which is very close to the long-term real rate of interest of approximately 2.5 percent over the same period. Interestingly, violins made over different periods of Stradivari's life have different qualities and sell for different prices. Those made in the golden period (1701–1725) sell for much more than violins made in the beginning or end of his productive life. However, as Hotelling's law predicts, even though the prices are different, the rates of growth turn out to be the same.

Given the estimates of Ross and Zondervan, a Stradivarius violin would not have been a great financial investment in 1700. At best it appears you would have earned approximately the going rate of interest. Why would this be the case? The answer is the same as why dentists earn more than drama instructors. A violin provides benefits to the user, and these benefits lower the financial rate of return.

5.4 The Life-Cycle Model

Understanding present values and how future income streams are capitalized into current prices is important in understanding how individuals make decisions over time. In the next section we carefully examine how individuals allocate their income across periods. In doing so we take the income streams as given, and apply the model developed in Chapters 2 and 3. Although the model is modified by the role of interest and the act of discounting, consider carefully the similarities between this model and the one for allocating income in a single period across different goods. In Section 5.5 we extend this model by considering human capital investments in detail.

A freshly minted college graduate is likely to have a substantial student loan to repay in the first few years out of college — it is not unusual for students to borrow $30 000 or more to finance their education. A thirty-something married couple who "own" their own home will typically have a sizable mortgage debt — $200 000 or more in many cases. In contrast, a sixty-something married couple will typically have substantial savings — perhaps as much as $2 000 000. These stylized facts about the representative consumer are indicative of a life cycle in which individuals incur debt when they are young so that they can spend more than they earn, repay that debt and accumulate savings when they are middle-aged, and consume their accumulated savings when they are old. In Chapter 2 we saw that this behaviour resulted from people substituting income across time in order to maximize utility. In this section, we examine this example more carefully and focus on the role of the interest rate as we develop a two-period version of the life-cycle model to explore these intertemporal consumption and saving decisions.[4]

---

4. In its modern form, the life-cycle hypothesis is due to Modigliani and Brumberg (1954) and Friedman (1957). M. R. Fisher's entry "Life Cycle Hypothesis" in *The New Palgrave* is a useful survey of work in this area.

We begin our analysis of the consumption possibilities open to ordinary people by exploring the highly simplified choices available to an imaginary person named Harold. Imagine that Harold is alive for just two periods and that he has income M_0 in the initial period and income M_1 in the next period. We can think of the two periods as the two halves of Harold's life. We will call the first half of Harold's life period 0 and the second half period 1. Since each period is half a lifetime, the incomes M_0 and M_1 will be a great deal larger than a typical annual income. Harold's income per period will be on the order of $1 000 000. Similarly, the interest rate i will be a great deal higher than the usual annual rates of interest. These interest rates will be in the range of 100 percent to 400 percent per period.

The Budget Line

The amounts Harold spends on consumption in period 0 and in period 1 are denoted by C_0 and C_1 respectively. What combinations of C_0 and C_1 can Harold achieve, given that his income is M_0 in period 0 and M_1 in period 1, and given interest rate i? In other words, what is Harold's budget line?

If Harold spends less than his full income in period 0 — that is, if C_0 is less than M_0 — he will earn interest at rate i on his savings, equal to $(M_0 - C_0)$. The amount saved plus interest — equal to $(1 + i)(M_0 - C_0)$ — will then be available for consumption in period 1. The total amount available for consumption in period 1 is then $M_1 + (1 + i)(M_0 - C_0)$. That is,

$$C_1 = M_1 + (1 + i)(M_0 - C_0)$$

In other words, period 1 consumption C_1 is equal to period 1 income M_1 plus the *future value* of period 0 savings $(1 + i)(M_0 - C_0)$. Rearranging this expression, we get

$$C_0(1 + i) + C_1 = M_0(1 + i) + M_1$$

This is Harold's budget line.

The expression on the right side of the equality is the *future value* of the income stream M_0 in period 0 and M_1 in period 1. It is, in other words, the future value of Harold's lifetime income. Analogously, the expression on the left is the *future value* of the consumption bundle (C_0,C_1). The budget line tells us that the future value of Harold's consumption bundle is equal to the future value of his lifetime income.

The slope of this budget line, shown in Figure 5.5, is $-(1 + i)$, a reflection of the fact that the opportunity cost of a dollar consumed in period 0 is $(1 + i)$ dollars of consumption in period 1. Put another way, the *opportunity cost* of a dollar spent in period 0 is the future value of that dollar in period 1.

If we divide both sides of the budget line equation by $(1 + i)$, we get a second version of Harold's budget line:

$$C_0 + C_1/(1 + i) = M_0 + M_1/(1 + i)$$

Now the expression on the right is the *present value* of Harold's lifetime income, and the expression on the left is the *present value* of the consumption bundle (C_0,C_1). This version of the budget line tells us that the present value of Harold's consumption bundle is equal to the present value of his lifetime income. Of course, the two versions of Harold's budget line are equivalent.

FIGURE 5.5 **An intertemporal budget line**

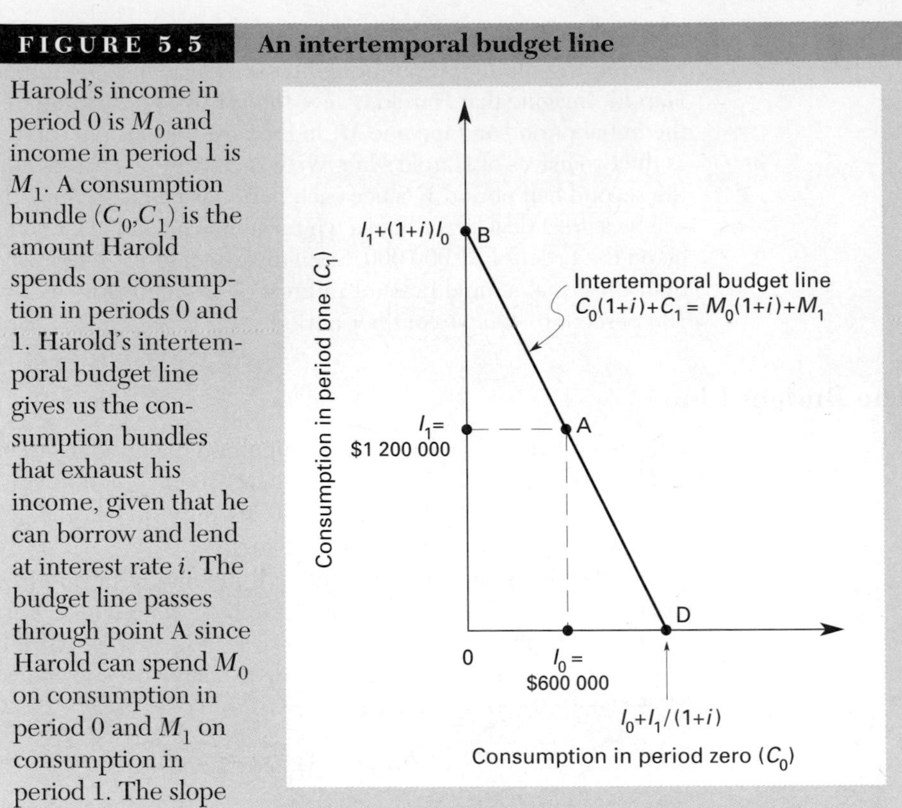

Harold's income in period 0 is M_0 and income in period 1 is M_1. A consumption bundle (C_0, C_1) is the amount Harold spends on consumption in periods 0 and 1. Harold's intertemporal budget line gives us the consumption bundles that exhaust his income, given that he can borrow and lend at interest rate i. The budget line passes through point A since Harold can spend M_0 on consumption in period 0 and M_1 on consumption in period 1. The slope of the budget line is $-(1 + i)$ since the opportunity cost of a dollar spent on consumption in period 0 is $(1 + i)$ dollars not spent on consumption in period 1.

PROBLEM 5.6

In deriving this budget line, we assumed that Harold consumed less than his full income in period 0 and more than his full income in period 1. Let us make the opposite assumption and see if we get the same budget line. If C_1 is less than M_1, then, in period 0, Harold can borrow the present value of savings in period 1 for consumption in period 0. Therefore, in period 0, he can consume the present value of $M_1 - C_1$ plus period 0 income M_0. That is,

$$C_0 = M_0 + \text{present value of } (M_1 - C_1)$$

What is the present value of $(M_1 - C_1)$? Use this present value to rewrite the above equation, and then show that it is equivalent to the budget line above.

Three points on Harold's budget line deserve special attention. Notice first that C_0 equal to M_0 and C_1 equal to M_1 correspond to point A on the budget line — that is, Harold can always spend what he earns in each period. This is his endowment. Notice, too, that if he spends nothing in period 0, he can achieve point B in Figure 5.5 where C_1 is equal to period 1 income plus the future value of period 0 income or

$M_1 + (1 + i)M_0$. Finally, notice that if he consumes nothing in period 1, Harold can achieve point D in Figure 5.5 where C_0 is equal to period 0 income plus the present value of period 1 income or $M_0 + M_1/(1 + i)$.

PROBLEM 5.7

Suppose the interest rate is 300 percent per period and that M_0 = \$600 000 and M_1 = \$1 200 000. Construct Harold's budget line. What is the maximum amount he could consume in period 1? In period 0? What is the opportunity cost of a dollar of consumption in period 0? What is the opportunity cost of a dollar of consumption in period 1? What is the slope of his budget line?

In Figure 5.6 we have shown how Harold's budget line rotates as the interest rate i increases. Since the opportunity cost of a dollar consumed in period 0 is $(1 + i)$ dollars of consumption in period 1, when i increases the budget line gets steeper. And since Harold can always spend M_0 on consumption in period 0 and M_1 in period 1, the budget line always passes thorough point A in Figure 5.6. We see then that when the interest rate i increases, the budget line pivots clockwise around point A. Hence the

FIGURE 5.6 **The rate of interest and the intertemporal budget line**

As the rate of interest i increases, Harold's budget line pivots in the clockwise direction around point A. This reflects the fact that as i increases, the opportunity cost of consumption in period 0 — equal to $(1 + i)$ — increases.

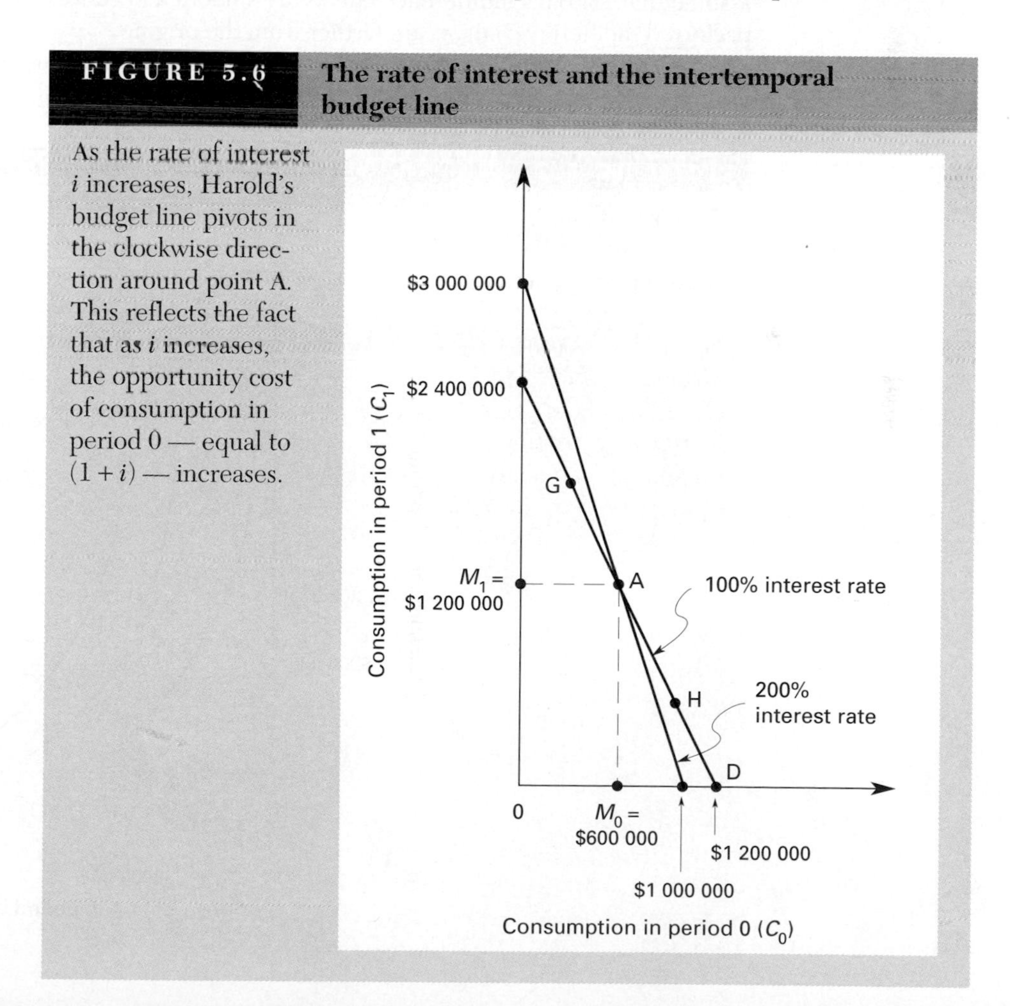

intertemporal budget constraint is another example of endowment, which was examined in Section 3.2.

PROBLEM 5.8

In what circumstances is Harold made better off, and in what circumstances is he made worse off, by an increase in the interest rate? (*Hint*: Suppose that prior to the increase in i, Harold's preferred bundle is at a point like G in Figure 5.6, where C_0 is less than M_0; now ask, given the increase in i, can he still achieve the consumption bundle he preferred prior to that increase?) Now suppose that prior to the increase in i, his preferred bundle is at a point like H where C_0 exceeds M_0, and ask the same question.

The Intertemporal Allocation of Lifetime Income

To complete the picture of Harold's life-cycle consumption decision, we can use the composite commodity theorem to represent Harold's preferences in terms of the amount spent on consumption in the two periods; that is, in terms of C_0 and C_1. We will assume that Harold's indifference curves are smooth and convex, and, naturally, that preferred indifference curves are farther from the origin.

To maximize utility, Harold will choose a bundle (C_0^*, C_1^*) in Figure 5.7 where an indifference curve is tangent to his budget line, or where the marginal rate of substitution

FIGURE 5.7 Choosing an intertemporal consumption bundle

To maximize utility Harold chooses the consumption bundle on his intertemporal budget line where *MRS* is equal to $(1 + i)$, or where the *marginal rate of time preference* is equal to $(1 + i)$.

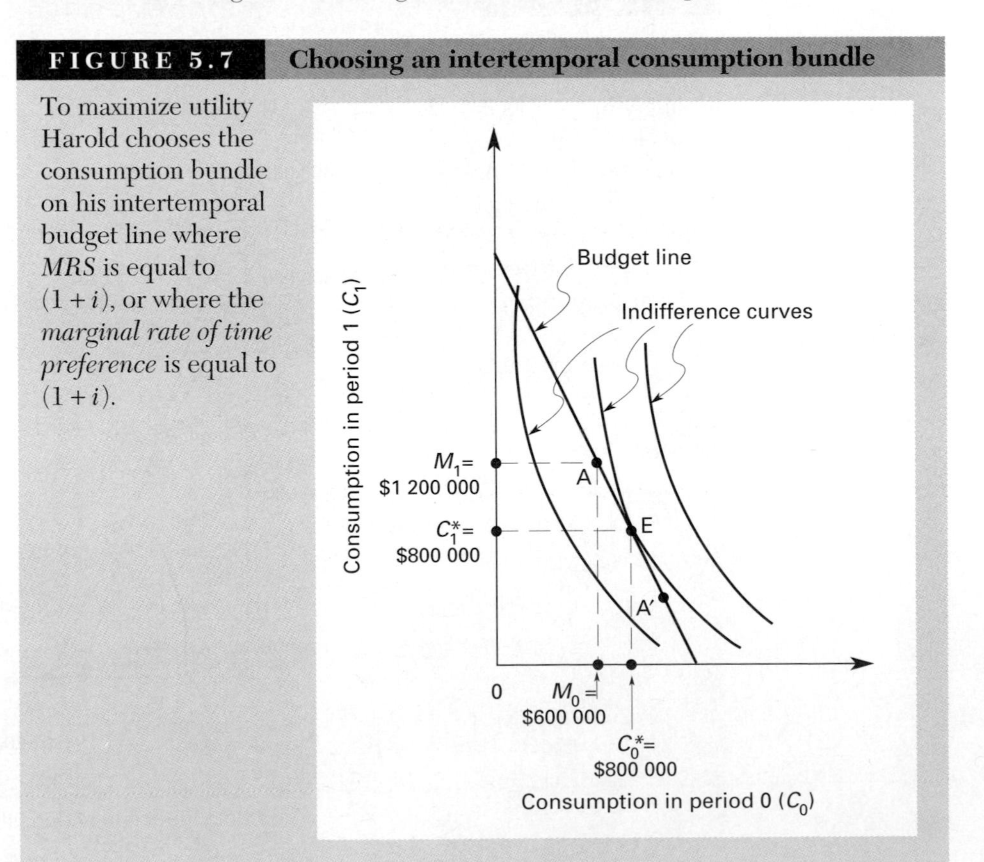

of consumption in period 1 for consumption in period 0 is equal to $(1+i)$. In the current context, the marginal rate of substitution is the marginal value of current consumption. If the interest rate is greater than zero, in equilibrium the *MV* of current consumption must be greater than one. This means that at the margin Harold (and everyone else) prefers current to future consumption. Another way of putting this is that Harold is impatient, or more formally, that his **marginal rate of time preference** is greater than zero.

marginal rate of time preference

In Figure 5.7, Harold's income is \$600 000 in period 0 and \$1 200 000 in period 1, and the interest rate is 100 percent per half a lifetime. In equilibrium, Harold spends \$800 000 in each period. In the equilibrium shown in Figure 5.7, Harold therefore borrows against period 1 income in order to consume more than his income in period 0. Because the interest rate is 100 percent, the opportunity cost of an added dollar of consumption in period 0 is two dollars of consumption in period 1. Accordingly, starting at the income endowment point A, as he increases period-0 consumption from \$600 000 to \$800 000, Harold is forced to reduce period-1 consumption from \$1 200 000 to \$800 000. We see that Harold borrows \$200 000 in period 0 and pays back \$400 000 in period 1 — the \$200 000 borrowed in period 1 plus \$200 000 in interest.

In the case shown in Figure 5.7, Harold consumes more than his income in period 0 and less than his income in period 1. Clearly, this is just one of three possibilities. If Harold's income endowment had been at point A′ instead of at point A, for example, he would have consumed less than his income in period 0 and more than his income in period 1. And if his income endowment had been at point E, his consumption would have been equal to his income in both periods.

PROBLEM 5.9

It is usually assumed that people are "impatient." A person is *impatient* if, when C_0 is equal to C_1, his or her marginal rate of time preference is greater than 1. And a person is *patient* if, when C_0 is equal to C_1, his or her marginal rate of time preference is less than 1. From Figure 5.7, is Harold patient or impatient? Show that an impatient person will always spend more on consumption in the first period than in the second period if the interest rate is zero.

Comparative Statics

The *exogenous variables* in the life-cycle model are income and the interest rate in each of the two periods, and the *endogenous variables* are consumption in the two periods. We can develop a deeper understanding of the model by conducting a series of comparative statics exercises in which we change an exogenous variable and then analyze how the change in the exogenous variable affects the endogenous variables.

We will begin by looking at the effects of an increase in M_0 or M_1. As income in either period increases, the budget line shifts up and to the right, but its slope, equal to $-(1+i)$, does not change. In Figure 5.8, for example, the initial income endowment is at point A on the initial budget line. By holding M_1 fixed, and increasing income in period 0 by ΔM_0 we get the new income endowment at point A′ on the subsequent budget line, which is parallel to the initial budget line. Notice that we get the same subsequent budget line by holding M_0 constant and increasing M_1 by ΔM_1. Notice, too, that ΔM_1 is equal to the future value of ΔM_0.

In the case shown in Figure 5.8, the initial equilibrium is at point E and the subsequent equilibrium is at point E′. Notice that in moving from E to E′ consumption in both periods increases. In this case, consumption in period 0 and consumption in

FIGURE 5.8 **Comparative statics of a change in income**

As income in either period increases the budget line shifts up and to the right, but its slope does not change. Because, in this case, consumption in both periods increases as income increases, both C_0 and C_1 are normal goods.

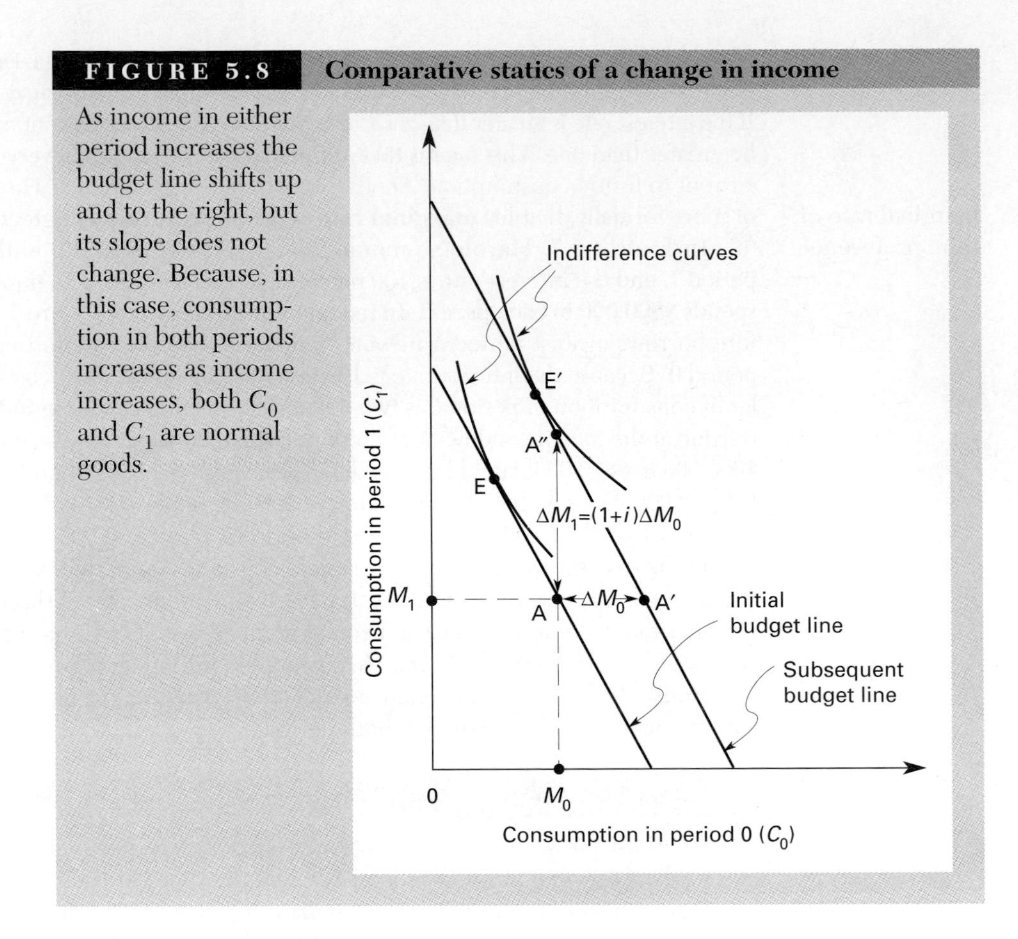

period 1 are therefore both *normal* goods. Although it is possible that consumption in one period or the other is an inferior good, this seems to be an unlikely case. We will therefore adopt the following assumption:

ASSUMPTION

Both C_0 and C_1 are normal goods.

Now let us turn to the more interesting effects associated with a *change* in the interest rate. We will begin with an equilibrium based on a relatively low rate of interest, and then increase the interest rate, and we will ask: What happens to consumption in each period? As you saw from Problem 5.7, an increase in i makes someone who saves in period 0 better off, and it makes someone who borrows in period 0 worse off. In assessing the impact of an increase in i on consumption in the two periods, we will have to consider these two cases separately.

The case of someone who saves in period 0 is shown in Figure 5.9. Given the relatively low interest rate, the initial equilibrium is at point E where this person saves in period 0 — that is, consumes less than his or her income M_0. When the interest rate increases, the budget line pivots clockwise around the income endowment at point A. The new budget line is steeper than the original budget line, reflecting the fact that the opportunity cost of consumption in period 0 increases when the interest rate rises. Given the higher interest rate, the subsequent equilibrium is at point E′ in Figure 5.9. Notice that in this case, consumption in both periods increases.

FIGURE 5.9 Comparative statics of an increase in i — part 1

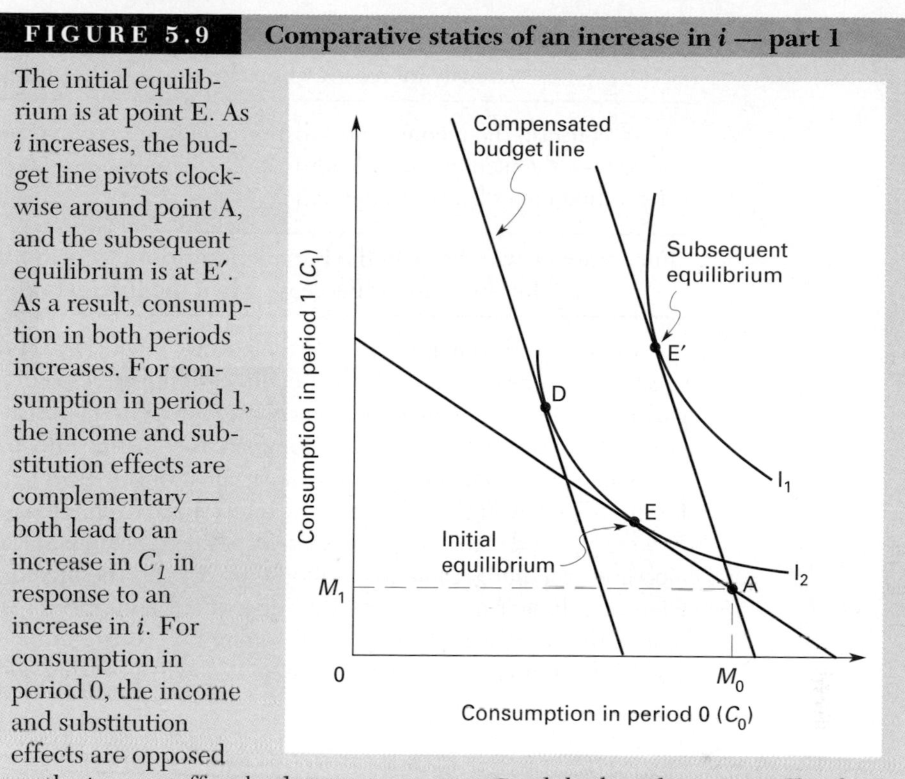

The initial equilibrium is at point E. As i increases, the budget line pivots clockwise around point A, and the subsequent equilibrium is at E′. As a result, consumption in both periods increases. For consumption in period 1, the income and substitution effects are complementary — both lead to an increase in C_1 in response to an increase in i. For consumption in period 0, the income and substitution effects are opposed — the income effect leads to an increase in C_0 while the substitution effect leads to a decrease.

By looking at income and substitution effects for both goods, we will show that consumption in period 1 must increase when the interest rate increases, and that consumption in period 0 may either increase or decrease. Notice that in identifying income and substitution effects for *both goods* we are doing something new here. And keep in mind the assumption that both C_0 and C_1 are normal goods.

To identify the income effects, we have constructed the compensated budget line, parallel to the subsequent budget line and tangent to the lower indifference curve. Since the increase in i makes the saver in Figure 5.9 better off, the compensated budget line lies below the subsequent budget line. And since both goods are normal, in the move from the equilibrium point at D on the compensated budget line to the equilibrium point at E′ on the subsequent budget line, both C_0 and C_1 necessarily increase.

For a person who saves in the initial equilibrium, the income effects associated with an increase in i lead to an increase in consumption in both periods.

To isolate the substitution effects, notice what happens in moving from point E to point D. Since indifference curves are smooth and convex, consumption in period 1 necessarily increases while consumption in period 0 necessarily decreases. Thus, the substitution effect of an increase in the interest rate leads to a decrease in consumption in period 0 and an increase in consumption in period 1.

Notice that the income and substitution effects are complementary for consumption in period 1 — both lead to an increase in consumption.

For someone who saves in the initial equilibrium, consumption in period 1 necessarily increases when the interest rate increases.

In contrast, the income and substitution effects are opposed for consumption in period 0 — the income effect leads to an increase in period 0 consumption while the substitution effect leads to a decrease.

For someone who saves in the initial equilibrium, consumption in period 0 may either increase or decrease when the interest rate increases.

In the case shown in Figure 5.9, the positive income effect dominates the negative substitution effect. Therefore, the net effect of the increase in the interest rate in this particular case is an increase in consumption in period 0. It is entirely possible, however, for the substitution effect to dominate the income effect.

The case of someone who borrows against future income in period 0 is shown in Figure 5.10. Given the relatively low interest rate, the initial equilibrium is at point E, where period 0 consumption exceeds period 0 income M_0. When the interest rate increases, the budget line pivots clockwise around the income endowment point A. Given the higher interest rate, the subsequent equilibrium is at E′ in Figure 5.10. Notice that in moving from point E to point E′ consumption in period 0 decreases and consumption in period 1 increases. We will show that consumption in period 0

FIGURE 5.10 Comparative statics of an increase in *i* — part 2

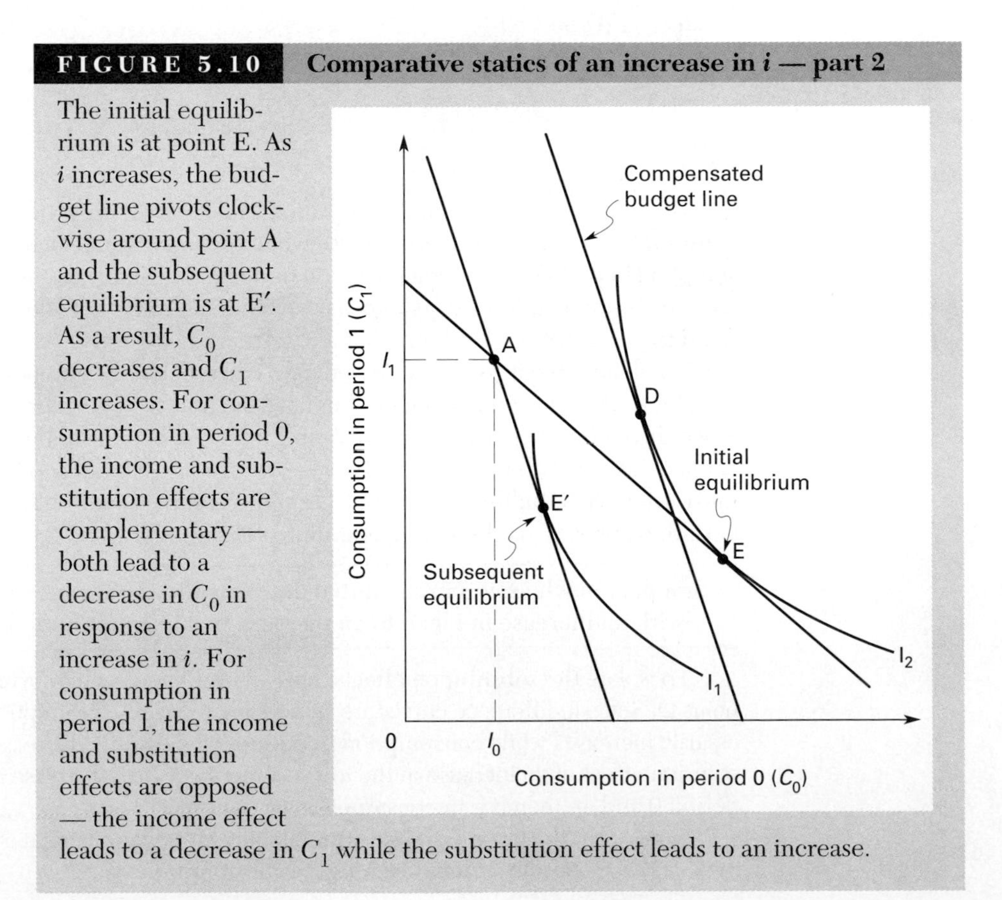

The initial equilibrium is at point E. As i increases, the budget line pivots clockwise around point A and the subsequent equilibrium is at E′. As a result, C_0 decreases and C_1 increases. For consumption in period 0, the income and substitution effects are complementary — both lead to a decrease in C_0 in response to an increase in i. For consumption in period 1, the income and substitution effects are opposed — the income effect leads to a decrease in C_1 while the substitution effect leads to an increase.

must decrease when the interest rate increases, and that consumption in period 1 may either increase or decrease.

To identify the income effects, we have constructed the compensated budget line, which is parallel to the subsequent budget line and tangent to the higher indifference curve in Figure 5.10. Since an increase in i makes the borrower in Figure 5.10 worse off, the compensated budget line lies above the subsequent budget line. And since both goods are normal, in the move from the equilibrium at point D on the compensated budget line to the equilibrium at point E′ on the subsequent budget line, both C_0 and C_1 necessarily decrease:

For someone who borrows in the initial equilibrium, the income effects associated with an increase in *i* lead to a decrease in consumption in both periods.

To isolate the substitution effects we observe what happens in the move from point E to point D. Since indifference curves are smooth and convex, consumption in period 1 necessarily increases while consumption in period 0 necessarily decreases. Thus, the substitution effect of an increase in the interest rate leads to a decrease in consumption in period 0 and an increase in consumption in period 1.

Notice that the income and substitution effects are complementary for consumption in period 0 — both lead to a decrease in period 0 consumption.

For someone who borrows in the initial equilibrium, consumption in period 0 necessarily decreases when the interest rate increases.

In contrast, the income and substitution effects are opposed for consumption in period 1 — the income effect leads to a decrease in period 1 consumption while the substitution effect leads to an increase:

For someone who borrows in the initial equilibrium, consumption in period 1 may either increase or decrease when the interest rate increases.

In the case shown in Figure 5.10, the net effect is an increase in consumption in period 1 because the positive substitution effect dominates the negative income effect.

To check your understanding of the life-cycle model, try the following problem.

PROBLEM 5.10

1. Given the current interest rate, it is known that Reena would consume less than her income in period 0. Indicate whether the following statements are true, false, or uncertain.
   a. Given an increase in the interest rate, Reena would consume less than her income in period 0.
   b. Given a decrease in the interest rate, Reena would consume less than her income in period 0.
2. Given the current interest rate, it is known that Rodrigo would consume more than his income in period 0. Indicate whether the following statements are true, false, or uncertain.
   a. Given an increase in the interest rate, Rodrigo would consume more than his income in period 0.
   b. Given a decrease in the interest rate, Rodrigo would consume more than his income in period 0.

SUMMARY

We began this chapter with a very simple choice problem: given a choice between two windfall gains — $1000 today or $1100 one year from today — which should you choose? We saw that when the borrowing and deposit rates of interest are identical, there is an unambiguous best choice. You should always choose the windfall gain with the larger present value.

This is one application of what is known as the *separation theorem*. The theorem says that in an intertemporal context, an individual's utility maximization problem can be separated into two parts: the choice of an income stream and the choice of a consumption bundle. We saw that (i) given a number of possible income streams, the individual will choose the income stream with the largest present value of income, and that (ii) the individual will choose a consumption bundle to maximize utility, subject to the constraint that the present value of expenditures on consumption is equal to the present value of the individual's income. This separation is achievable only when the borrowing and lending rates of interest are identical, or when the market for loanable funds is perfect. Virtually all of the analysis in the chapter is built on the foundation of the separation theorem.

We used the separation theorem in conjunction with tools developed earlier to analyze the intertemporal allocation of a nonrenewable resource like oil. We saw that the price of the nonrenewable resource will rise from one period to the next at the rate of interest — *Hotelling's law*.

EXERCISES

1. Howard can borrow against future income at a 10 percent rate of interest, and he can earn 10 percent on his savings. His rich uncle has given him the choice between $50 000 now or $72 000 in four years. If he put it all in his savings account, how much would the original $50 000 be worth in four years? What is the present value of the $72 000? Which option should Howard choose?

2. Sarah has been given the following choice of inheritance packages by her parents: Package A is composed of $50 000 today and $100 000 one year from today. Package B is composed of $100 000 today and $44 000 one year from today.
   a. Assuming that the borrowing and deposit rates of interest are identical, identify the conditions under which Sarah should take package A, and the conditions under which she should take package B.
   b. Still assuming that the two rates of interest are identical, identify the conditions under which Sarah is better off when the interest rate changes from 10 percent to 12 percent.
   c. Assuming that the deposit rate is 0 percent and that the borrowing rate is 100 percent, construct the budget lines associated with both of these packages and show that it is impossible to say which package Sarah should choose without information regarding her preferences.
   d. Assuming that the borrowing rate exceeds the deposit rate, identify the circumstances under which Sarah should choose package A, the circumstances under which she should choose package B, and the circumstances under which you need information regarding her preferences to determine which package she should choose.

3. To borrow money from the public, firms sell bonds. A *bond* is just a piece of paper that obligates the firm to pay the holder of the piece of paper a fixed sum of money in each of a fixed number of periods.
   a. What is the maximum amount you would pay today for a bond that promised to pay you $1000 at the end of each of the next three

years, assuming that the interest rate is 5 percent? Assuming that the interest rate is 10 percent? Assuming that the interest rate is 15 percent?

b. If this bond is sold at auction, and if the interest rate is 10 percent, what is your prediction with respect to its price? Explain. What sort of relationship would you expect to see between the price of bonds and the interest rate?

4. You own both stocks and bonds issued by Natural Fruits, Inc., an apple-growing corporation. Explain the effects on: (i) the price of apples now and in the future; (ii) the value of your shares of stock; and (iii) the value of your bonds, of the following events:

   a. an increase in the real rate of interest.
   b. an increase in the nominal rate of interest, due to anticipated higher inflation.
   c. the announcement by the government of an available new hybrid that will increase the number of apples per tree, when these new trees reach maturity in 10 years.

5. Suppose you own some stock in a software company. Last week the *Financial Post* published a front-page article indicating that this company was late on delivery of certain software. (The price of the stock fell substantially, the same day.) How does this article (and the drop in price) affect your decision to sell your stock, to maintain your current holdings, or to buy additional shares?

6. Why is the separation theorem important? What would happen if it did not hold?

7. Fran runs a small delivery service. The borrowing and deposit rates of interest are identical for her. Her only inputs are her time, gasoline, and a very specialized delivery truck. The truck is so specialized to her needs that it has no scrap value. The price of a new truck is \$25 000. As one of these trucks ages, maintenance gets more expensive. The required maintenance at the end of year one costs \$2000, and the maintenance cost increases each year by \$2000: at the end of year two it is \$4000, at the end of year three it is \$6000, and so on. She plans to stay in business for just five more years. Because her current truck is now exactly four years old, if she wants to use it for another year she must now spend \$8000 on maintenance. She is considering two options: option A, using her current truck for the next five years; and option B, buying a new truck today, and using it for the next five years.

   a. What is the present value of costs under option A? Under option B? Which is the better option?
   b. Given that she is going to stay in business for another five years, should she be considering other options?

8. Jerry has just discovered a cache of 100 000 returnable pop cans in an old barn on a property he recently bought. Currently, such cans can be returned for 10¢ per can. However, there has been pressure on politicians to substantially increase the deposit on cans to ensure that they are recycled instead of being discarded by the roadside. Consequently, Jerry (and everybody else) anticipates that he will get 20¢ per can if he holds on to his cans for a year.

   a. Should Jerry sell the cans now, or should he wait a year?
   b. Now take a broader perspective, and look at the decisions of all citizens. What is your prediction about the number of cans that will be returned in each of the next 13 months?

9. Currently in Canada the interest on a home mortgage is not deducted from your income when calculating income taxes. How would reversing this policy affect the wealth of:

   a. Current home owners?
   b. Prospective home owners?
   c. People in the construction business?

10. "The great thing about owning a farm in British Columbia is that you don't have to pay property tax on farms." Assuming the tax part of the statement is true, why isn't it such a great thing for new farmers?

11. What effect would you expect the rate of technological innovation in a society to have on the level of interest rates?

12. Here is a question to ponder and have fun with: If everyone lived forever, what would the rate of interest be?

13. You just got married, and you and your spouse are purchasing appliances for your new home.

You have a choice of two vacuum cleaners. The "Super Sucker" costs $400 to purchase and $100/year to operate. The "Dirt Machine" costs $340 to purchase but $120/year to operate. Both machines last ten years.

a. Which is the cheaper source of clean rugs over ten years?
b. Write out an equation you could use to solve for the interest rate that would make you indifferent between the two machines.

14. In Problem 5.3 you realized that the profit maximizing strategy for a textbook publisher is not to make a book that lasts only one term. Suppose a publisher printed a book and promised never to publish another edition. What would happen to the price of the book? Would you believe a textbook publisher who made such a promise? Given your beliefs, what is the optimal strategy for a publisher? Would publishers gain by a law that forced them to keep such promises?

15. The Not-So-Smart company is trying to get rid of some of its workers. Due to union rules, each worker is entitled to 25 annual payments of $5000. NSS has offered the employees a $30 000 lump-sum payment to quit. At what interest rate would these two income streams be equal? Given the interest rates at the moment, do you think they will be successful?

16. In the 1960s many people had 25-year fixed-rate mortgages. That is, their mortgage had a fixed rate of interest for the full 25 years. As the inflation rate increased, the nominal rate of interest increased as well. Show on a utility space graph how this increased the wealth of those holding these low-interest mortgages.

17. "A higher interest rate will cause borrowers to increase their borrowing and will cause lenders to increase their lending." Is this statement true or false, and explain why.

18. Suppose you buy a new stove for your kitchen at a cost of $1000. You can either pay for the stove with cash drawn from your bank account, or you can pay with your credit card.
    a. If the interest rate on your bank account is the same as the rate charged by the credit card company, show that you'd be indifferent between paying cash and paying with credit with no intention of ever paying more than the yearly interest charges.
    b. Most people don't carry charges on their credit cards forever. Why would this be so?

19. What impact on artist incomes might be expected if artists received a share of future resales of their work?

*20. You're born with no tangible wealth. You work for three periods and retire for one period before you die. You plan to leave nothing for your heirs, and you expect your working income to be $20 000, $60 000, and $80 000 in years 1, 2, and 3. You can borrow and lend at 8% per period. You prefer to consume the same amount every year. You will be paid and will consume at the end of each period.
    a. What is your wealth at the beginning of your life?
    b. What is the largest constant consumption stream you can afford?
    c. What borrowing/lending strategy will you use to accomplish (b)?
    d. What is your wealth at the beginning of each period?

*21. Timothy owns a honey fruit plant. The fruit from this plant gets sweeter over time, but when the fruit is harvested, the plant dies. The market value of the plant in period t is $V(t) = 21(\ln t)$ and the rate of interest is 5 percent.
    a. When should the honey fruit be harvested?
    b. Some honey fruit connoisseurs want to buy Timothy's plant. What is the highest price that he could charge for the plant right now (period 0)?

*22. Sammy Smooth has preferences over consumption in period 0 and 1 of the form $U(C_0,C_1) = \min\{ C_0,C_1 \}$. The price of a unit of consumption in both periods is $1. He has $6000 in the bank now and is trying to decide between two different investment opportunities, A and B.

    A: invest $5000 in period 0 and receive $12 000 in period 1

    B: invest $1000 in period 0 and receive $3000 in period 1

    a. If Sammy can borrow and lend at a rate of interest of 50 percent, which investment opportunity will he choose?

b. Given your answer in (a), how much will he consume in each period?
c. Now suppose that Sammy can lend at a rate of 50 percent but has to borrow at a rate i. What borrowing rate of interest would make Sammy indifferent between the two investment opportunities?

REFERENCES

Fisher, M. R. 1987. "Life Cycle Hypothesis," in *The New Palgrave: A Dictionary of Economics*, J. Eatwell, M. Milgate, and P. Newman (eds.), London: Macmillan.

Friedman, M. 1957. *A Theory of the Consumption Function*, Princeton, N.J.: Princeton University Press.

Hotelling, H. 1931. "The Economics of Exhaustible Resources," *Journal of Political Economy*, 39:137–75.

Modigliani, F. and R. Brumberg. 1954. "Utility Analysis and the Consumption Function: An Interpretation of Cross-Section Data," in *Post-Keynesian Economics*, K. K. Kurihara (ed.), New Brunswick, N.J.: Rutgers University Press.

Ross, M. and S. Zondervan. July 1989. "Capital Gains and the Rate of Return on a Stradivarius," *Economic Inquiry*, 27(3):529–40.

PART III

Production and Cost

In Part III, the focus is on the firms that transform the natural resources owned and supplied by individuals into the goods and services these individuals demand. In Chapters 6 and 7, we take a standard approach to the firm by viewing it as an organization described by its production function (by the terms on which it can transform inputs into outputs) and motivated by its desire to maximize profit. In Chapter 6, we construct the theory of production when only one input is variable, and then we build the corresponding theory of cost. In Chapter 7, we extend the theory of production and cost to the more realistic environment of many variable inputs.

Firms are entities created by and for human beings, to organize economic activity. The natural question arises: Why do firms come into being? Why do they take the particular organizational forms that we see? We address these questions in Part VI of the book. There we see how firms resolve the contradiction between collective interests and individual self-interest through their organizational forms. For the moment, however, we only consider the organization of the firm as a black box.

CHAPTER 6

Production and Cost: One Variable Input

Consumer theory, which helped us to understand the decisions of individual consumers in the marketplace, is complemented by another branch of microeconomics, the *theory of production*. We are now setting out on an extended journey as we create the tools needed to analyze the decisions of individual firms. We can use these tools to answer several important questions: How will a firm decide which industry to enter in the first place? How will a firm decide how much to produce of whatever goods and services it sells? What inputs will a firm buy to make its products and how much of each will it buy? How much will it charge for its products? Finding ways to answer these questions will occupy us in Chapters 6 through 12. Along the way, we will see that these tools can be applied to a number of interesting problems outside the confines of standard firms and markets.

The material is arranged in steps, with each section building on the foundations laid in the last. If you follow through the next few chapters slowly and carefully, checking your understanding at each step, you will arrive at the end with a solid grounding in production, cost, and supply analysis — a grounding that will allow you to think clearly about a whole range of important and interesting economic problems.

We begin by defining and illustrating the concept of a production function. We then discuss the concept of opportunity cost and define a number of cost-minimization problems, ranging from the long run down to the shortest possible short run. We explore the production function when quantities of all inputs but one are held constant. Next, we turn from production to cost considerations as we develop the theory of cost when only one input is variable. Finally, we apply the tools of short-run production and cost to an all-too-familiar traffic congestion problem, to multi-plant firms, and to some curious facts of life.

6.1 The Production Function

Economists think of the firm as an organization that buys inputs and then transforms them into marketable goods or services. This abstraction allows us to see the features common to all firms — from sidewalk hot dog vendors to General Motors. Imagine a manufacturing company that buys inputs such as milk, sugar, sticks, packaging materials, natural and artificial flavouring, moulds, labour, and refrigeration and then processes them to make various types of packaged ice cream. If we suppose for simplicity that the firm produces only one good (say, ice cream bars), we can imagine a function that tells us the maximum quantity of that good the firm can produce from any bundle of inputs. Thus, an ice-cream-bar production function might tell us that if we had 24 hours of labour, 25 kilograms of sugar, 20 litres of milk powder, 80 litres of water, 20 litres of chocolate mixture, 2 kilowatt-hours of electricity, and 10 standard bar moulds, we could, at most, produce 500 dozen ice cream bars.

Defining the Production Function

However, we need to expand on this intuitive definition of a *production function*. Let us begin by considering some product, which we will call good Y, made from two inputs, which we will call input 1 and input 2. (For simplicity, we will concentrate on the two-input case.) We will denote the quantity of good Y by y, the quantities of inputs 1 and 2 by z_1 and z_2, and an **input bundle** by (z_1, z_2). Thus, the input bundle (10,97) is composed of 10 units of input 1 and 97 units of input 2.

input bundle

Of course, these inputs can be combined by using any of a number of technologies, some of which may be more productive than others. For example, if the input bundle is composed of 1 hectare of wheatland (input 1) and 40 kilograms of wheat seed (input 2), these inputs can be combined in many different ways to produce wheat (good Y). The entire hectare can be uniformly seeded at a rate of 40 kilograms of seed per hectare; 1/3 of a hectare can be seeded at a rate of 120 kilograms of seed per acre; and the seed can be sown at any depth. We will assume that among these possible technologies, one is **technically efficient**; that is, it maximizes the quantity of output that can be produced from a particular bundle of inputs. The technically efficient technology is used to define the production function, $F(z_1, z_2)$. Thus, the **production function**

technically efficient

production function

$$y = F(z_1, z_2)$$

tells us the *maximum quantity* of good Y that can be produced from any input bundle (z_1, z_2).

We can describe a firm's activities by this production function if we assume that the technically efficient production process is both known and used. In so doing, we are making the sweeping assumption that the firm has resolved complex informational, organizational, incentive, and engineering problems. For example, we are assuming that the Albertan farmer knows which technology will yield the most wheat from 1 hectare of land and 40 kilograms of seed. Yet this is not always the case. For instance, when Millar Western Pulp Ltd. decided to go into pulp and paper production, it opted for the environmentally cleaner but more energy-intensive chemothermomechanical pulp-mill technology used extensively in Europe rather than the standard chemical technology common in North American pulp mills. Yet the company made its decision without knowing for certain just what this unfamiliar technology involved. These sorts of decisions are made all the time, but for now we put them aside.

To help you understand just what a production function is, we will begin by looking at two types of production functions — fixed and variable proportions.

Fixed-Proportions Production Function

fixed-proportions production function

In a **fixed-proportions production function**, the ratio in which the inputs are used never varies. We need one nut and one bolt to make one fastener; one right shoe and one left shoe to make a pair of shoes; one piano and one pianist to make music. A fixed-proportions production function is analogous to the case of perfect complements in consumer theory.

However, the fixed proportion need not be a one-to-one ratio. For example, 150 millilitres of apple juice and 100 millilitres of cranberry juice are needed to make the perfect cranapple drink. This recipe gives rise to the following fixed-proportions production function:

$$y = \min(z_1/150, z_2/100)$$

where y is the number of cranapple drinks, z_1 is millilitres of apple juice, and z_2 is millilitres of cranberry juice. If you had 600 millilitres of apple juice and 500 millilitres of cranberry juice, how many cranapple drinks could you make? There is enough apple juice for four drinks (4 = 600/150) and enough cranberry juice for 5 drinks (5 = 500/100), so you could make just four drinks (4 = min(5,4)) and you would have 100 millilitres of cranberry juice left over. In fact, as you will see in the following problem, the recipe for any food or drink gives rise to a fixed-proportions production function.

PROBLEM 6.1

A good recipe for seviche calls for 500 grams of red snapper fillet, 125 millilitres of lime juice, 30 grams of cilantro, and 250 grams of Bermuda onion.

a. If a restaurant has 1 kilogram of snapper, 275 millilitres of lime juice, 150 grams of cilantro, and 1500 grams of onion, what is the maximum quantity of seviche the restaurant can make?
b. What is the production function for seviche?

These production functions are useful as illustrations not only because they are so simple, but also because they are economically important. For example, fixed-proportions production functions (also known as **Leontief production functions** in this context) are the basis of *input-output analysis*, a tool widely used for economic planning.

Leontief production functions

Variable-Proportions Production Functions

variable-proportions production functions

In most production functions, however, the proportions of the inputs can be varied. In **variable-proportions production functions**, increased amounts of one input can be substituted for decreased amounts of another. For example, let us imagine a firm — Mr. Tipple's Courier Service — that produces the output, courier services, measured in kilometres. Tipple owns a truck around which he has built his courier service. In addition to the truck itself, he uses two inputs: a driver's time (input 1) and gasoline (input 2). Tipple can combine time and gasoline in varying proportions to produce the courier services he provides. For example, if he tells his employee to drive at 140 kilometres per hour, he uses less time and more gas to produce each mile of courier services than if he tells his employee to drive at 80 kilometres per hour.

Let us suppose that Tipple has an input bundle composed of z_1 hours of a driver's time and z_2 litres of gasoline. The maximum number of kilometres of courier services, y, that he can produce given z_1 hours of time is determined by how fast the truck is driven. Letting s denote speed in kph, we see that

$$y \leq sz_1$$

For example, if z_1 is 10 and s is 50, a driver cannot drive more than 500 kilometres. To determine how many kilometres z_2 litres of gas will produce at speed s, we need the technological relationship between kilometres per litre (kpl) and speed. For Tipple's truck, kpl is inversely proportional to s, and the factor of proportionality is 1200. That is,

$$\text{kpl} = 1200/s$$

For example, if the truck is driven at 80 kph, it gets 15 kpl, and if it is driven at 120 kph, it gets 10 kpl. This relationship between kpl and s tells us that

$$y \leq 1200z_2/s$$

For instance, if the truck is driven at 120 kph, it is impossible to go more than 200 kilometres on 20 litres of gas.

Given the constraints embodied in these two inequalities, we can find the production function for Tipple's Courier Service by choosing speed s to maximize distance y. The two inequalities are plotted in Figure 6.1 for fixed values of z_1 and z_2. The solution to this maximization problem must be *on* or *below* both of these lines. The blue area represents all combinations of s and y that satisfy both constraints by requiring no more than z_1 hours of time or z_2 litres of gas. In this blue area, s^* — the

FIGURE 6.1 **Finding a production function**

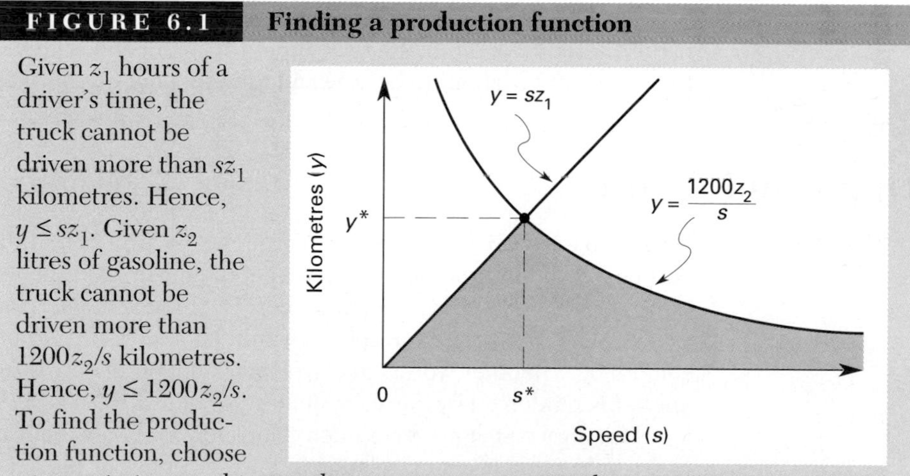

Given z_1 hours of a driver's time, the truck cannot be driven more than sz_1 kilometres. Hence, $y \leq sz_1$. Given z_2 litres of gasoline, the truck cannot be driven more than $1200z_2/s$ kilometres. Hence, $y \leq 1200z_2/s$. To find the production function, choose s to maximize y, subject to these two constraints. Both constraints are satisfied only in the blue area. The solution is to drive at speed s^*, which means that the truck can be driven y^* kilometres.

speed that maximizes distance y — is determined by the point at which the two constraints intersect. As you can easily determine, the speed that maximizes y is just

$$s^* = (1200z_2/z_1)^{1/2}$$

and the distance travelled y^* is

$$y^* = (1200z_1z_2)^{1/2}$$

To underscore the fact that this is the production function, we can rewrite this result:

$$F(z_1, z_2) = (1200z_1z_2)^{1/2}$$

How do we know that this is the production function? Because it tells us the *maximum* number of kilometres that any input bundle composed of time and gasoline will produce. Furthermore, we have also identified the technologically efficient method for combining any bundle of time and gasoline. Driving the truck at speed s^* will make the most of any such input bundle.

PROBLEM 6.2

Suppose that Tipple has an input bundle composed of 10 hours and 120 litres of gas. What is the maximum number of kilometres his truck can be driven? What speed is required to achieve this result? Given the same input bundle, how far can the truck be driven at 80 kph? At 160 kph?

Cobb-Douglas production function

This production function is an illustration of the historically important **Cobb-Douglas production function**. The general form of this function in the two-input case is

$$y = Az_1^u z_2^v$$

where A, u, and v are positive constants. Cobb and Douglas (the latter of whom later became a US senator from Illinois) used this form to estimate a relationship between national product and the aggregate inputs of labour and capital (1948). Douglas found the exponent on labour to be 0.63 and the exponent on capital to be 0.34.

6.2 Opportunity Costs

In this chapter we are going to explore how the production function influences the cost curves of the firm, but before we get too involved in the mechanics of cost functions, let's pause and consider what cost is. If you stopped people on the street and asked "What is cost?" the response would be almost unanimous: "What you pay for something." In other words, the layperson's notion of cost is the *historical cost*. This answer is reinforced by the accountant's use of historical cost as a measure of cost.

Historical cost, however, is often completely irrelevant in measuring actual *costs* and, as a result, often bears no relation to current prices or behaviour. Your parents may have paid a low price for their home 30 years ago, but it might be worth a small fortune today. Perhaps you've purchased a car for $10 000, only to find out that it is rusted out and needs major repairs. The $10 000 you paid is irrelevant to what the car is worth and irrelevant to how you will behave with respect to the car. A firm may own an asset that has long been fully depreciated on the accountant's books, but is still a valuable piece of equipment. In all of these examples, the historical cost is irrelevant.

opportunity cost

Economists use the term **opportunity cost** to avoid confusion with historical costs. Opportunity cost is *the value of the next best alternative*, and is often independent of historical cost. To begin with, opportunity cost always refers to an action. In our casual speech we say things like "How much does the book cost?", but such a statement does not make sense literally. What we should say is, "How much does it cost to *buy* the book? *read* the book? *write* the book?" and so on. Actions imply that there is a forgone alternative, and therefore a cost. If there is no action taken or no choice among alternatives, then there is no cost.

Opportunity cost is the value of the highest forsaken alternative.

The most common linguistic mistake made in this regard is with respect to time. We say things like, "Time is money," or "My time is valuable," or even "I'm a high time-cost person." These are examples of sloppy language; time is not a cost! Time marches on and there is nothing we can do about it. What is costly is what we do with our time. If I sleep in, I forgo having breakfast. It is the value of the lost breakfast that is the cost of using my time between 7:00 and 8:00 AM for sleeping. When we say that an individual is a high time-cost person, what we really mean is that the value of the alternative uses of this person's time is high.

Adding Up Costs

Opportunity cost critically hinges on the value of the *next best* alternative, not the value of all the alternatives. At this moment, what is the cost to you of reading this chapter? Perhaps you could be working right now for $10 per hour. Perhaps you could be at a party, or eating lunch with friends. If you think about it, the set of things you could be doing right now is very large. The cost of reading this chapter is **not** the sum value of all these activities; rather it is the value of the single alternative activity you value the most.

This is not to say that several values are never added up to arrive at the cost of an activity. Suppose the final exam for this course is only three days away — on a Friday. On the Tuesday night before the exam there are three mutually exclusive things you can do besides study. Ranking them from most to least preferred, you can (i) go to a party, (ii) go to a movie, or (iii) watch an old *Star Trek* episode. On Wednesday night you could (i) go to a party, (ii) visit your mom, or (iii) get some sleep. On Thursday night you could (i) go visit your priest, (ii) do the laundry, or (iii) go to yet another party. If you decide to study all three nights, what is the cost? It is not merely the value of the single highest-ranked activity, nor the total value of all nine possible activities; it is the value of two parties and one visit to the priest. Cost is the value of the highest forsaken alternative, and the key to understanding it is to determine the true alternative.

For example, suppose you buy a hot dog from a sidewalk vendor for $1.50. Is the $1.50 a cost? Absolutely, since the money could have been spent on anything else, including the most valuable alternative. Suppose that in addition to the money, you had to wait for ten minutes, and what you could do with this time was worth $2. Is this part of the cost of the hot dog? Absolutely, because in deciding to purchase the hot dog, you are deciding to forgo the time as well as the money.

As a final example, consider the cost of your education. The tuition is an obvious sacrifice, but so is your forgone income. By being in school you are out of the workforce, and this constitutes a major cost of education. What about your textbooks; are they part of your education cost? If you wouldn't have bought them otherwise (which is probably true for all your books but this one!), then, yes, they are a cost. What about the rent for your apartment; is it a cost of your education? This is a little trickier. If, by going to school, you had to move and increase your rent, then this *increase* in rent is a cost of education. Presumably, you would have been renting something had you not gone to school, so if your rent does not change, then it is not part of the cost of your education.

Application: Who Is the Better Economist: The Poet or the Critic?

One of Robert Frost's most famous poems is "The Road Not Taken." In it a traveller comes upon a fork in the road, pauses, and considers which to take, knowing that a different adventure lies along each. In the end he says, "I shall be telling this with a sigh/ Somewhere ages and ages hence:/ Two roads diverged in a wood, and I —/ I took the one less traveled by, / And that has made all the difference."

In a running commentary one critic wrote, "The poet's 'difference' is in him from the beginning, long before he sets out on his career. The road that Robert Frost took was not only the 'different' road, the right road for him, but the only road he could have taken."[1]

From an economic point of view the critic has it all wrong. Frost was lamenting the fact that decisions in life have an opportunity cost. Taking the road more travelled would have led to a different life for Frost, with different values. This sacrificed life is the cost of taking the road less travelled. To say that Frost had no choice is to say that there was no cost. If there was no cost then it makes little sense to lament taking one road over the other. The poet wins, hands down.

Costs and Bads

It is a common mistake to always think of costs as bads. Every decision brings good things and bad things. The bad things, however, are not the costs of the decision. Hence, sweat, toil, and pain, unless they affect the value of alternatives, are not costs. For example, suppose there are two mutually exclusive choices: you can purchase a swimming pool for your home or purchase a new car. There are good things about the swimming pool — you can exercise, cool off, etc., and these may be worth $15 000 to you. However, there are also some bad things — the neighbour kids are always over, your heating bill is higher, etc., and perhaps these "bads" are worth –$2000 to you. The difference of $13 000 is the value of the pool, namely the amount you would be willing to pay to have one. Suppose the car also has good and bad features, and the difference of $9000 is the value of the car. What is the cost of having the pool? It is not the value of the bads ($2000), it is the forgone value of the car ($9000).

PROBLEM 6.3

Roger hates doing his income tax, but his wife Rita loves doing it for him. Is it more costly for Roger to do his income tax, or his wife?

When we think of costs always as bads, we miss the fact that increasing costs can sometimes be a good thing. Suppose Taddeus is working for Microsoft in Seattle and has a salary of $60 000. Would he be worse off if the cost of staying in Seattle increased? If Corel offered him a job for $100 000 in Ottawa, he would clearly be better off, but

1. Frost, R. *The Road Not Taken*, with running commentary by Louis Untermeyer. p. 270.

the cost of staying in Seattle has gone up. Any increase in outside opportunities is an increase in cost, but this type of increased cost is a good thing because it represents an increase in wealth. The employee who has zero opportunity costs of staying at his or her job is not exactly in a strong bargaining position!

PROBLEM 6.4

Suppose at a conference on global warming countries agreed to have quotas for greenhouse gas emissions. That is, countries agreed to, say, a 15 percent reduction in emissions. If these rights were tradable (that is, a country like Canada might pay Mexico some amount of money to reduce its emissions by 20 percent so that Canada could only reduce emissions by 10 percent), would this raise or lower the cost of the quota?

Sunk, Avoidable, Fixed, and Variable Costs

sunk costs
avoidable costs

For economists there are two critical distinctions among different types of costs. The first is the difference between ordinary costs of production and transaction costs. This distinction is central to Part VI of the book, but is ignored for now. The second central distinction is between **sunk** (unavoidable) **costs** and **avoidable costs**.

Sunk costs have no bearing on economic decisions because there is nothing that can be done about them. When your mother told you not to cry over spilled milk, she was recognizing that the lost milk was sunk, gone ... history. Avoidable costs, on the other hand, are costs that need not occur and can be avoided. If you buy an ugly lamp and later lament your decision, the cost is not sunk if you can resell the lamp for what you paid for it. People base their decisions on avoidable costs, not sunk costs.

Sunk costs are costs that, once incurred, cannot be recovered. Avoidable costs are costs that need not be incurred.

PROBLEM 6.5

Suppose a fishing equipment retailer buys 30 new lobster traps that have the special feature that they collapse and are therefore easy to store on dock. Suppose he pays $2000 for the traps, but after one month he has sold no traps, and suspects it is because of a news release that the traps are also collapsing under water and releasing the lobsters. The only good news is that a local school has offered to buy the lot for $2100 for holding class supplies. The retailer has checked out the scrap yard and discovered that the traps are worth $560 as junk metal. In order to make his decision, the retailer calculates his costs.

Wholesale costs	$2000
Interest charges	20
Handling and Advertising	230
Display Space	110
Total Cost	$2360

Since it is bad business to sell below cost, our retailer decides to turn down the offer from the school. Did he make the right decision?

fixed costs
variable costs

There is another distinction made among costs, namely the difference between **fixed costs** and **variable costs**. A fixed cost is a cost that does not vary with output, while a variable cost is one that changes when the level of output changes. Costs can be sunk and either fixed or variable, or they can be avoidable and either fixed or variable. Table 6.1 provides some examples.

Fixed costs do not vary with output, variable costs do change with output.

Suppose you own a factory that makes a special auto part for the engines in General Motors cars. Let us consider some of the costs in your factory. The cost of lighting the factory space is a fixed cost, since it does not change with the number of parts produced. The light bill is also avoidable because you can shut the lights off at any time. Your parts may be partially made of wire. The wire is a variable cost because the more parts you make, the more wire you use. The wire is also an avoidable cost because if you stop producing parts, you don't have to use any wire. Any advertising already done is a sunk fixed cost. You cannot get the investment back, and the advertiser doesn't charge based on output. Finally, there may be a special stamp or press that is used in producing the part, and this stamp may wear out the more you produce. Because it wears out it is a variable cost, and because it is only used by this firm it is a sunk cost.

TABLE 6.1 Classification of costs

	Avoidable Cost	Sunk Cost
Fixed Costs	lighting costs	advertising costs
Variable Costs	wire input	firm-specific stamp

Although any combination is possible, for the remainder of the book, unless otherwise stated, we will make the standard assumptions that all fixed costs are sunk and that all variable costs are avoidable. These are strong assumptions, and they are made only to make the presentation simpler and easier to understand.

As you work through the cost functions in this and the next chapter, keep in mind that the costs referred to are opportunity costs. When a competitive firm pays workers \$10 per hour, it does so because these workers could earn \$10 per hour at some other activity — they must pay them their opportunity cost. When you read about marginal costs and supply curves, keep in mind that the cost of producing an additional unit ultimately reflects the value of the inputs in their next best use. Hence, though the term "opportunity" will be dropped, the costs relevant to a cost function are still opportunity costs.

6.3 Cost-Minimization Problems

Before we further explore the production function, we will put it in perspective by seeing just how it fits into the standard theory of the firm. We will assume that the firm's objective is to maximize its profit. A firm's profit is simply its revenue from selling its product minus the cost of producing that product. We begin that analysis with an important result:

Profit maximization implies cost minimization.

That is, a profit-maximizing firm will produce its output at minimum cost. We will defer analysis of the firm's revenue until later chapters. In this chapter and the next we will focus on the firm's costs.

The Long-Run Cost-Minimization Problem

long-run cost minimization

Let us begin with the problem of **long-run cost minimization**. By the long run, we mean a planning horizon long enough that a firm can vary all its inputs. In the two-input case, the long run is the planning horizon in which the firm can choose quantities of both inputs 1 and 2. Let us suppose that a particular firm wants to produce y units of output per period. It will minimize its cost by finding the least expensive input bundle that will produce y units of output. If the prices of its inputs are w_1 and w_2, then the cost of any input bundle the firm buys is simply the sum of the amounts spent on inputs 1 and 2, or

$$w_1z_1 + w_2z_2$$

The firm's long-run cost-minimizing problem, then, is to choose the input quantities z_1 and z_2 that minimize its total costs, subject to the constraint that it can actually produce y units of output. Symbolically, we can write the long-run cost-minimization problem as

$$\begin{aligned}&\text{minimize } w_1z_1 + w_2z_2\\&\text{choosing } z_1 \text{ and } z_2\\&\text{subject to the constraint } y = F(z_1, z_2)\end{aligned}$$

Remember that the cost-minimization problem is formulated in terms of *one period*. Therefore, we are considering input quantities and prices in terms of one period — and this can be a subtle qualifier. We must be careful to measure quantities of all inputs and all input prices in terms of the same period. No real problem is associated with *hired inputs*, such as labour, or *rented inputs*, such as temporary office space. If the period is a year and if input 1 is labour, for instance, then the unit of measure for input 1 is one worker for one year, and the price of input 1 — w_1 — is a worker's annual wage. In contrast, if the period is instead a week and if input 1 is once again labour, then the unit of measure for input 1 is one worker for one week, and the price of input 1 — w_1 — is a worker's weekly wage.

But some confusion is possible if *capital inputs* such as trucks or buildings are *bought* rather than rented. Let us suppose, for example, that a firm hires labour (input 1) and buys trucks (input 2) to produce transportation services. If the firm buys trucks that last for five years, it is convenient to take the unit of time, or the period, to be five years. The unit of measure for input 2 is then *a truck*, the price of input 2 is the price of a truck, and quantity of input 2 is number of trucks bought. The unit of measure for input 1 (labour) is then one worker for five years, the price of input 1 is the present value of a worker's earnings over a five-year period, and quantity of input 1 is number of workers hired for five years.

Alternatively we can take a shorter unit of time, with the price of input 2 being the implicit *rental price* of the truck. If the truck sells for $20 000, the annual interest rate is 10 percent, and we set aside any capital gains, depreciation, or uncertainty, the annual rental price of the truck is $2000. The cost of any input can be adjusted to fit the appropriate time dimension. The key is that both input costs must be measured for the same unit of time.

Short-Run Cost-Minimization Problems

As we have seen, a firm's long-run planning horizon is long enough to vary the quantities of all its inputs. Yet firms are not always in this fortunate position of complete flexibility. If Ford Motor Company wants to produce more Mustangs this year, its options are distinctly limited. It can run its assembly lines around the clock by hiring and training more workers, and it may be able to accelerate the assembly process itself, provided that its body-stamping plants, engine plants, and other facilities can produce enough parts. However, it does not have the necessary lead time in the space of a year to create new assembly lines (or body-stamping or engine plants).

If the firm's planning horizon is such that the firm can vary *some*, but not all, of its inputs, it faces the problem of short-run cost minimization. There are many short runs corresponding to planning horizons in which the firm can vary the quantity of just one, just two, or just three inputs, and so on. Each of these planning horizons defines its own short-run cost-minimization problem.

In the two-input case, if the quantity of input 2 is fixed, we have a short run in which input 1 is the only variable input. The short-run cost-minimization problem is then to choose z_1 to minimize the cost of producing y units of output. We consider this short-run cost-minimization problem later in this chapter, and we take up long-run cost minimization in the next chapter. But first we must see what the production function looks like when the quantity of one input is fixed.

6.4 Production: One Variable Input

We know what a production function is, what two simple production functions look like, and where the production function fits into the firm's profit and cost calculations. The next step is to ask: What happens to output as we vary the quantity of one input, holding the quantities of all other inputs fixed? For example, how does a wheat farmer's harvest change if the quantity of wheat seed is varied, holding the quantities of land and all other inputs fixed?

Total Product

total product function

By fixing, or holding constant, the quantity of all inputs except one, we can write the production function as a function of one variable — the quantity of the single variable input. Written this way, the production function is called the **total product function**. It tells us what the output — or *total product* — will be for any quantity of the variable input (given the fixed quantities of the other inputs). To see how a total product function is derived from a production function, let us look at the case in which there are only two inputs. If we fix z_2 at 105 units, then the total product function, denoted by $TP(z_1)$, is defined as follows:

$$TP(z_1) = F(z_1, 105)$$

In other words, the total product function $TP(z_1)$ is derived from the production function simply by fixing the value of z_2 in the production function $F(z_1, z_2)$.

PROBLEM 6.6

We have already derived the following production function for Tipple's Courier Service on p. 192:

$$F(z_1, z_2) = (1200 z_1 z_2)^{1/2}$$

Find the total product function when z_2 is 12; when z_2 is 27; when z_2 is 48. Graph these total product functions with z_1 on the horizontal axis and y on the vertical axis.

In Figure 6.2, we have constructed the typical, or standard, total product function. The quantity of the variable input z_1 is plotted on the horizontal axis, and output y is on the vertical axis. Notice that the slope of this total product function — which indicates the rate at which output changes as z_1 increases — is different at different values of z_1. For instance, the slope is steep near point G, while it is not so steep near the origin and near point C. This rate of change has a special name and a special role in the theory of the firm.

Marginal Product

marginal product

The rate at which output changes as the quantity of the variable input increases (given fixed quantities of all other inputs) is called the **marginal product** of the input and is denoted by $MP(z_1)$.[2] Because this rate of change is just the slope of the total product function, we see that

$$MP(z_1) = \text{slope of } TP(z_1)$$

FIGURE 6.2 **A total product function**

The curve 0GCE is the standard stylization of a total product function. It gives us the maximum quantity of output y that can be produced for any given quantity of input 1.

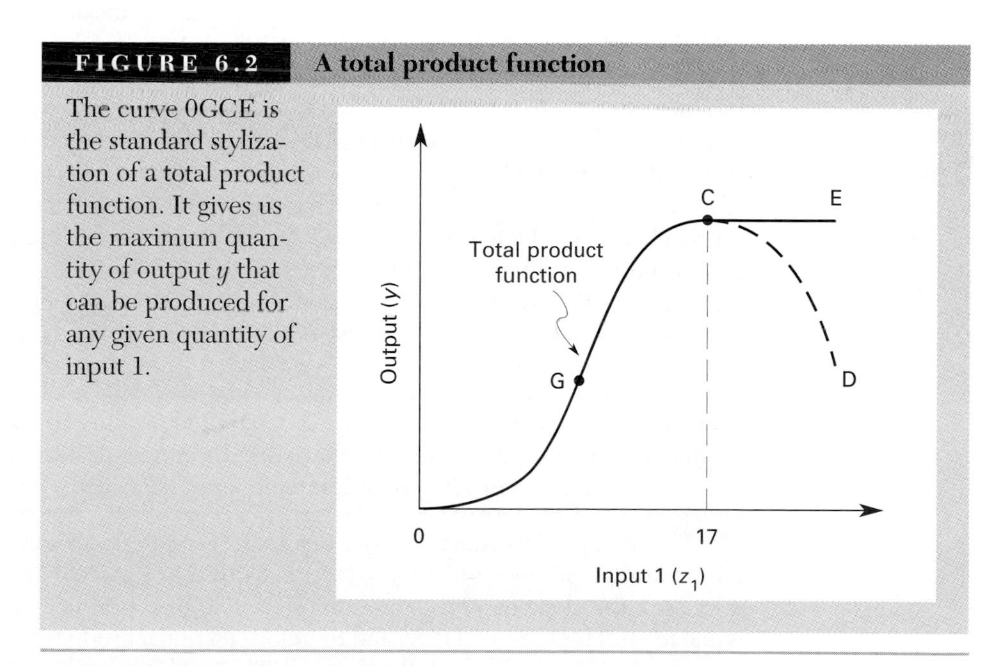

2. In mathematical terms, the marginal product is the derivative of the production function with respect to one of the inputs:

$$MP(z_1) = \partial F(z_1, z_2)/\partial z_1$$

In Figure 6.2, if you consider the curve that includes the dashed segment CD rather than the solid segment CE, perhaps you will recognize it from an introductory economics course. You have probably noticed, too, that the general shape of this curve is different from the total product functions you graphed in Problem 6.6. In a moment, we will look more closely at the reasons for constructing the standard total product function in this way and consider, too, alternative stylized functions.

Notice that because the slope of the dashed segment CD in Figure 6.2 is negative, marginal product is also negative when z_1 exceeds 17. In this region, more of the variable input actually reduces the total product. Cows and common pasture can be combined to produce milk, but too many cows on the pasture land can cause milk production to decrease.

Although these possibilities are real, they are *not* consistent with our definition of a production function — if we assume that firms have the option of using all or part of any input bundle. Because a production function gives the maximum output producible from any bundle of inputs, if the firm in Figure 6.2 has more than 17 units of input 1, it will decide to use precisely 17 units of input 1 and no more. In other words, if too many cooks spoil the broth, some of the cooks will be kept out of the kitchen.

free-disposal assumption

This is sometimes called the **free-disposal assumption**. In the common-property problem, there is no central authority — that is, no firm — to keep the counterproductive cows off the common pasture. Taken together, the definitions of the production function and the free-disposal assumption imply that marginal product cannot be negative — that is, CE rather than CD is the relevant total product function when z_1 exceeds 17.

Now let us consider a related question: Can the marginal products of all inputs simultaneously be zero? Imagine that input 1 is farm labour (measured in worker-hours), input 2 is a strawberry patch (measured in hectares), and good Y is strawberries (measured in litres). If the input of land is fixed at 1 hectare and if units of farm labour are continually added to it, eventually the point of maximum total product, corresponding to point C in Figure 6.2, will be reached. As more labour is added to the one-hectare patch beyond that point, an excess of farm labour will occur, and its marginal product will be zero.

What is the marginal product of land when the marginal product of labour is zero? Notice that in posing this question, we are assuming that farm labour is now the fixed input and the size of the strawberry patch is the variable input. If another hectare of land is brought into production and the excess farm labour is used to cultivate it, more litres of strawberries will be produced. In other words, when the marginal product of farm labour is zero, the marginal product of land is positive. More generally, although the marginal product of one input may be zero, the marginal products of all inputs cannot simultaneously be zero:

Given the free-disposal assumption, the marginal product of any input is always greater than or equal to zero; furthermore, for any input bundle, the marginal product of at least one input is positive.

The total product function from Figure 6.2 is plotted in Figure 6.3a. The associated marginal product function $MP(z_1)$ is plotted in Figure 6.3b. Notice that as z_1 increases, the slope of $TP(z_1)$, and therefore marginal product, increases until z_1 is equal to 10. The slope of $TP(z_1)$ and therefore marginal product, then decreases until z_1 is equal to 17. Finally, both the slope of $TP(z_1)$ and marginal product are zero when z_1 exceeds 17. Because marginal product begins to decline at 10, this point is called the

FIGURE 6.3 From total product to marginal product

The marginal product associated with any value of z_1 is the slope of the total product function at that value of z_1. For $z_1 < 10$, marginal product increases as z_1 increases because the total product function gets steeper as z_1 gets larger. For $z_1 > 10$, marginal product decreases as z_1 increases because the total product function gets flatter as z_1 gets larger. For $z_1 > 17$, marginal product is zero because the slope of the total product function is zero.

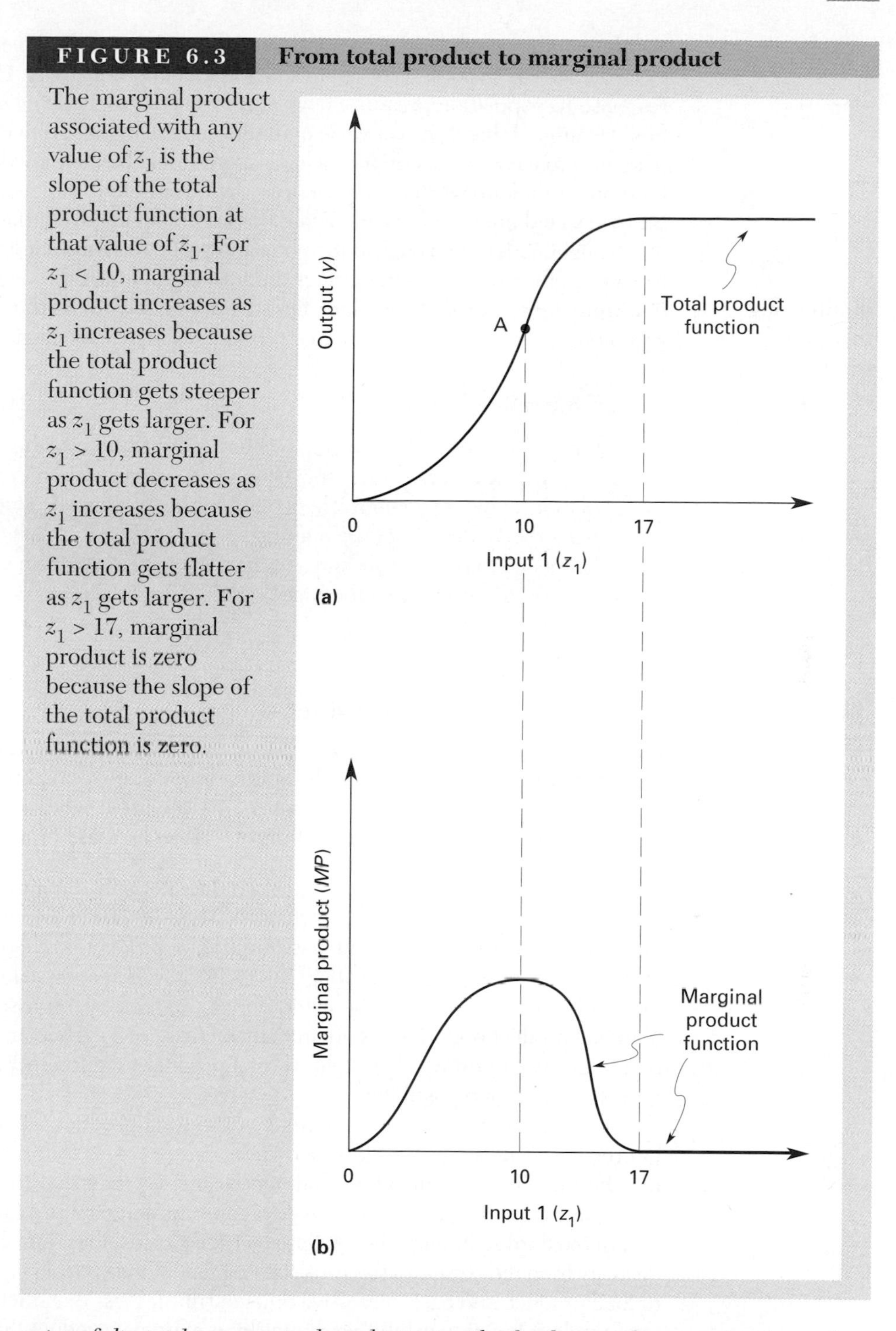

point of *diminishing marginal productivity*. The fundamental assumption in production theory is that such a point of diminishing marginal productivity always exists.

Diminishing Marginal Productivity

The idea of diminishing marginal productivity is not only significant in the theory of production but also fundamental to the history of economic thought. Reverend Thomas

Malthus, a prominent English economist of the early nineteenth century, was the first to formulate the hypothesis of diminishing marginal productivity. He observed that in response to population pressure, new land was continually being opened for cultivation. He argued that if the converse of diminishing marginal productivity — increasing marginal productivity — were true, added labour would be more productive on cultivated than on virgin land. If that were the case, we would have no economic incentive to bring raw land under cultivation. From this argument and from the fact that new land was brought under the plough as the population grew, he concluded that labour devoted to food production necessarily brings diminishing marginal product. The assumption of **diminishing marginal product**, linked historically with Malthus's name, reflects his argument that at some point marginal product will inevitably begin to diminish.

diminishing marginal product assumption

PROBLEM 6.7

One of the greatest demographic shocks in history was the Black Death in fourteenth-century Europe, which killed up to 30 percent of the population. What do you think happened to the marginal products of labour from this? What about the marginal product of land? What do you think happened to the rent on land and the wages of labour? Can you use these answers to explain why the standard of living for the survivors increased after the plague?

Assumption: Diminishing Marginal Product

Suppose that the quantities of all inputs except one — say, input 1 — are fixed. There is a quantity of input 1 — say, z_1'' — such that whenever z_1 exceeds z_1'', the marginal product of input 1 decreases as z_1 increases.[3]

Notice that in Figure 6.3b, marginal product not only diminishes when z_1 exceeds 10 but also increases when z_1 is less than 10. The Malthusian hypothesis of a declining marginal product is a fundamental assumption in production theory, and the empirical evidence that supports it is strong. But an initially increasing marginal product is neither an inevitable feature of the world nor guaranteed by our assumptions. Whether marginal product does or does not initially increase in a particular production process is an empirical question. The stylized total product function in Figure 6.3 therefore represents only one possibility.

At least two alternative stylizations of the total product function are useful and interesting. One such possibility, shown in Figure 6.4, is that marginal productivity may be initially constant rather than increasing. (Notice that the linear segment of $TP(z_1)$ in Figure 6.4a is associated with a constant marginal product in Figure 6.4b.)

In the third stylization, the total product function exhibits diminishing marginal productivity from the outset. In this case, the first unit of the variable input contributes most to total product, and each successive unit contributes less than the one preceding it. A total product function exhibiting diminishing marginal product throughout looks like

3. Diminishing marginal product is an assumption about a second partial derivative of the production function. For $z_1 > z_1''$, we assume that the partial derivative of marginal product with respect to z_1 is negative. That is,

$$MP'(z_1) = \partial[\partial F(z_1, z_2)/\partial z_1]/\partial z_1 < 0 \quad \text{for } z_1 > z_1''$$

FIGURE 6.4 **From total product to marginal product: Another illustration**

The slope of the total product function in (a) is constant for $z_1 < 29$; marginal product in (b) is therefore constant for $z_1 < 29$. For $z_1 > 29$, the slope of the total product function gets smaller as z_1 gets larger; marginal product therefore decreases as z_1 increases for $z_1 > 29$.

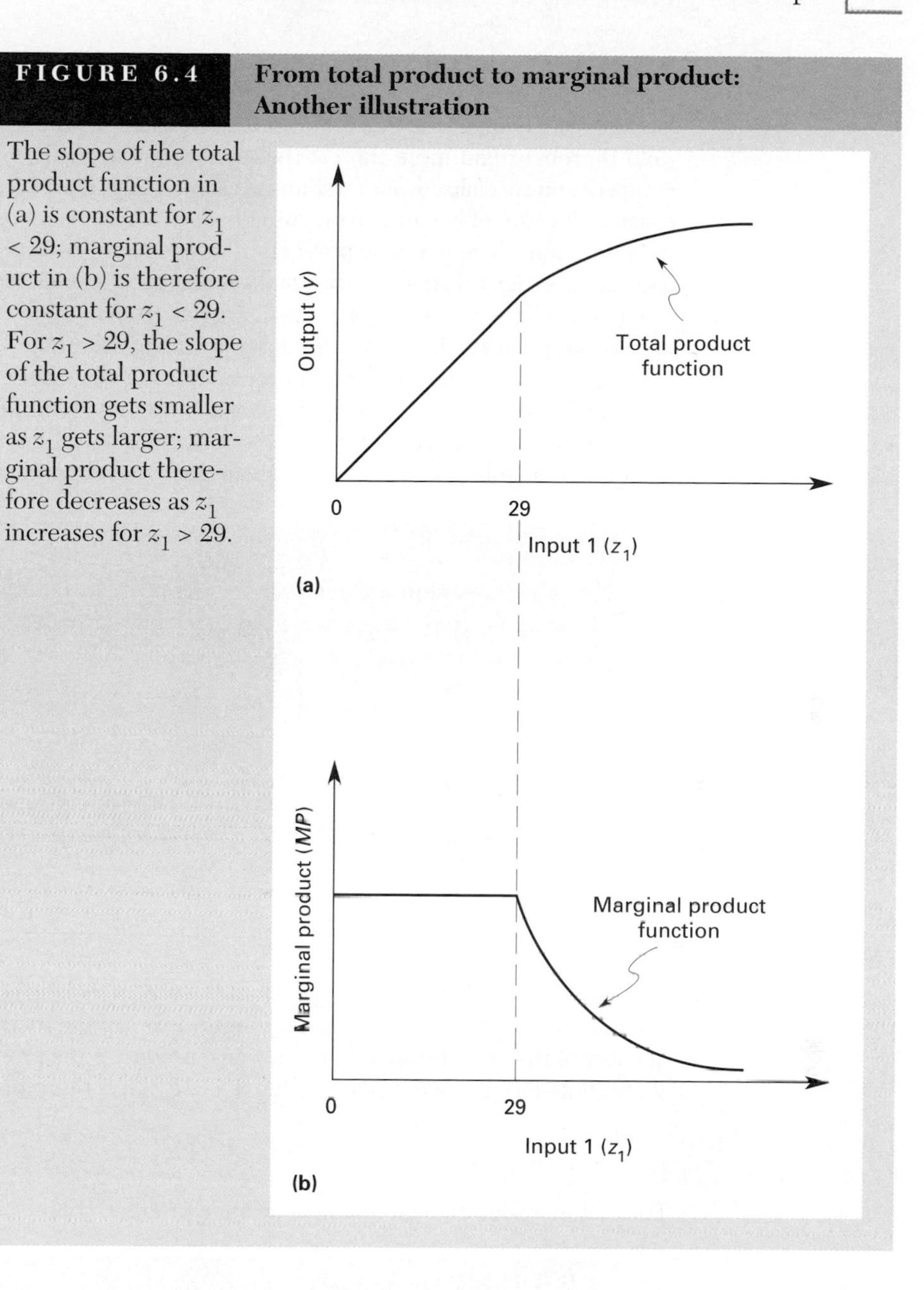

those you constructed in answering Problem 6.6. The slopes of those total product functions became progressively less steep as z_1 increased, reflecting diminishing marginal productivity of the variable input for all values of z_1.

These alternative stylizations of the total product function are conceivable and relevant. However, $TP(z_1)$ is usually drawn to indicate that as the quantity of the variable input increases, the marginal product rises at first and only later begins to diminish. The rationale is that increasing the amount of the variable input at first increases the productivity of all the units of that input. Imagine the kitchen of a major downtown hotel. The dinner shift begins with only a few kitchen workers, but as more and more help is added, the number of dinners the kitchen can produce increases at a rapid rate. Why? One reason is that the workers can specialize. Some prepare only vegetables; others make only sauces; still others wash dishes. Another reason is that the kitchen can be organized more efficiently. For example, the workers can all save steps (and thereby spend more time at their individual tasks) by preparing food at more compact and specialized work stations. At some point, however, the gains from a more efficient division of labour and organizational structure begin to diminish. Beyond this point of diminishing marginal product, $TP(z_1)$ gets progressively flatter as z_1 increases. As even more help is added to the hotel kitchen, food production continues to increase, but at a declining rate until, perhaps, marginal product finally reaches zero.

Although this rationale seems most convincing when the variable input is labour, whether any particular production process does or does not exhibit initially increasing marginal product is a question we can answer only by empirical investigation. It is therefore useful to have all three of the stylized total product functions at your fingertips. In the following problem, you can discover yet another possibility.

PROBLEM 6.8

We can think of producing fasteners (good Y) by combining nuts (input 1) and bolts (input 2). If z_2 is fixed at 10 units ($z_2 = 10$), the total product function is

$$TP(z_1) = \begin{cases} z_1 & \text{if } z_1 \leq 10 \\ 10 & \text{if } z_1 > 10 \end{cases}$$

In one diagram, carefully graph this total product function. In another diagram directly below the first, graph the associated marginal product function.

Average Product

average product

Like marginal product, **average product** is a way of looking at how output varies with changes in the quantity of the variable input. It is just the total product divided by the quantity of the variable input; that is, average product is the product per unit of the variable input. The average product of input 1, $AP(z_1)$, is therefore

$$AP(z_1) = TP(z_1)/z_1$$

To reinforce your understanding of average product, try the following problem.

PROBLEM 6.9

In the production function for Tipple's Courier Service, suppose that z_2 is 12. Then, from Problem 6.6, the total product function is

$$TP(z_1) = 120(z_1)^{1/2}$$

Find the average product function.

FIGURE 6.5 From total product to average product

Average product at point A is the slope of the dashed line 0A because DA is total product and 0D is quantity of input 1. Similarly, average product at point B is the slope of the dashed line 0B. Notice that at point B average product is at its maximum, and average product is equal to marginal product.

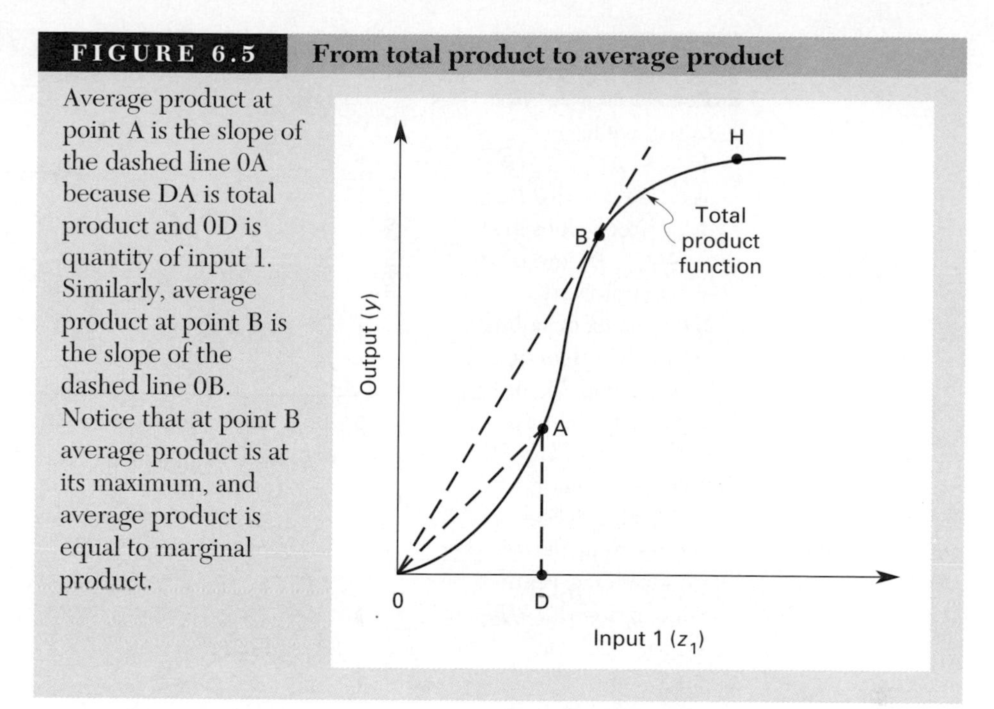

Let us see how to derive the average product function from the total product function in Figure 6.5. First, choose any point on the total product function and, from the origin, draw a ray that passes through that point. The slope of this ray is equal to the average product at the point where the ray intersects the total product function. At point A, for instance, the average product is the slope of the ray 0A. Why? The slope of the ray is equal to distance DA divided by distance 0D. But DA is the total product at point A, and 0D is equal to quantity of input 1 at point A. Therefore, the slope of the ray 0A is the total product divided by the quantity of input 1, or the average product. Similarly, the slope of the ray 0B is the average product at point B.

Let us now compare $MP(z_1)$ and $AP(z_1)$. At point A in Figure 6.5, for instance, $MP(z_1)$ exceeds $AP(z_1)$. At point H, however, $AP(z_1)$ exceeds $MP(z_1)$. To see why, simply construct the line tangent to the total product function at point A and notice that the slope of the tangent line, which is the marginal product at point A, exceeds the slope of the ray through point A. The opposite is true at point H.

Point B is of special interest. At this point, average product and marginal product are identical because the ray through the origin to point B is tangent to $TP(z_1)$ at B. It is also a point of special interest for another reason: average product is at a maximum at B. To see why B is the point of maximum average product, try drawing another ray through the origin that intersects or is tangent to the total product function and that is steeper than 0B. It cannot be done.

In Figure 6.6a, we have constructed the standard stylization of the total product function and in Figure 6.6b, we have derived both measures of productivity — average

FIGURE 6.6 Comparing the average and marginal product functions

In (b), we have derived *AP* and *MP* associated with *TP* in (a). Three values of z_1 — 23, 38, and 67 — are noteworthy: 1. *MP* is rising or falling as z_1 is less than or greater than 23, and *MP* attains its maximum value at $z_1 = 23$; 2. *AP* is rising or falling as z_1 is less or greater than 38, *AP* attains its maximum value at $z_1 = 38$, *MP* is equal to *AP* at $z_1 = 38$, and *MP* is greater or less than *AP* as z_1 is less or greater than 38; 3. *MP* is zero when z_1 exceeds 67.

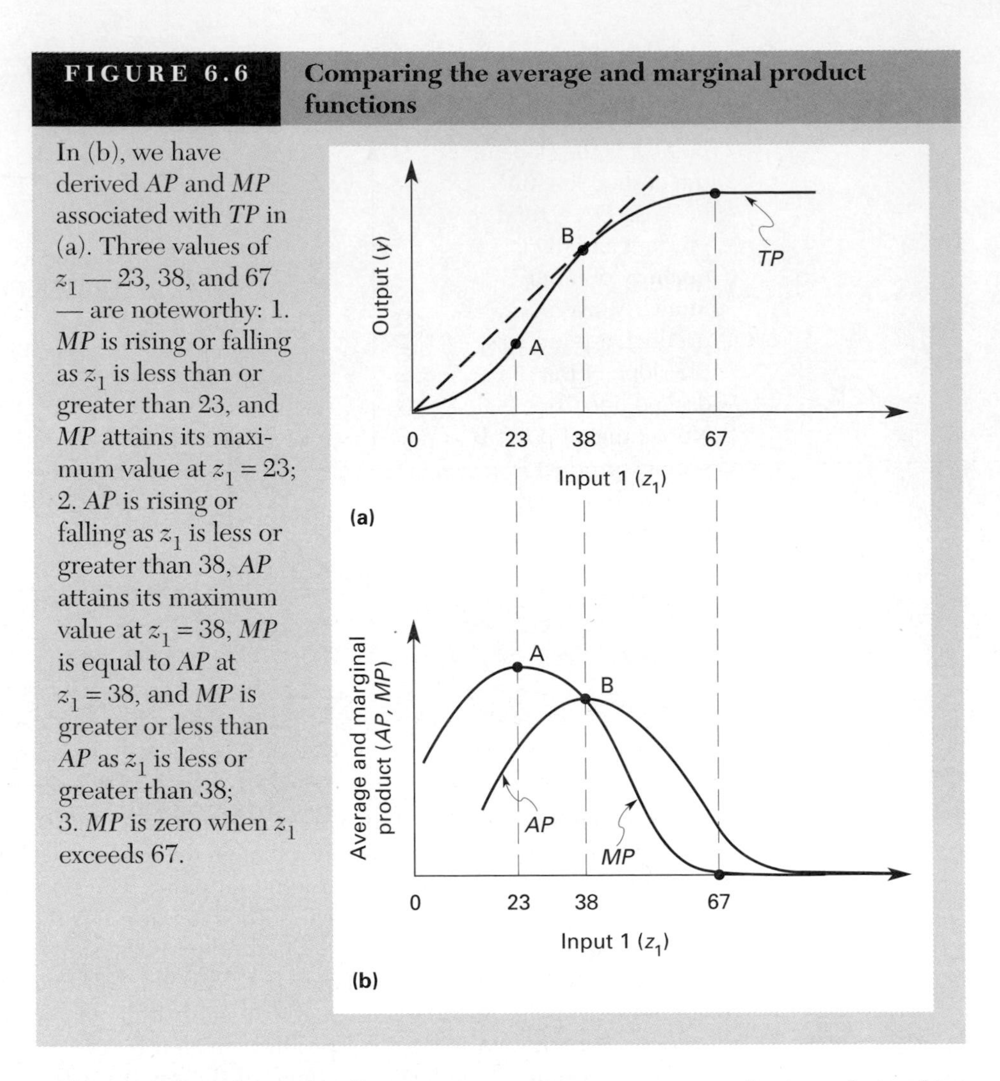

and marginal product. This figure presents some important qualitative relationships between marginal product and average product.[4]

4. Because we will encounter these sorts of relationships at several points in this and the following chapters, it is useful to explore them more carefully. Consider any function $f(x)$ with domain $x \geq 0$ and the implied marginal function

$$M(x) = f'(x)$$

and average function

$$A(x) = f(x)/x$$

Differentiating $A(x)$, we have

$$A'(x) = (xf'(x) - f(x))/x^2$$

or, equivalently,

$$A'(x) = (f'(x) - f(x)/x)/x$$

But this can be written as

$$A'(x) = (M(x) - A(x))/x$$

Therefore $A(x)$ is increasing, decreasing, or stationary as $M(x)$ is greater than, less than, or equal to $A(x)$.

1. When marginal product is greater than average product, average product is increasing.

2. When marginal product is less than average product, average product is decreasing.

3. When marginal product is equal to average product, average product is neither increasing nor decreasing; it is constant.

A simple analogy may help you to see the common sense of these relationships. Imagine a kindergarten room. If the average weight of the assembled children is a (for average pounds) and if another small person whose weight is m (for marginal pounds) joins the group, what will happen to the average weight of any child now in the schoolroom? If m exceeds a, the average weight of the children in the now larger group will rise; if m is less than a, it will fall; if m is equal to a, it will not change.

As you will discover in Problem 6.10, these curves will be different for different stylizations of the total product function.

PROBLEM 6.10

Construct a total product function like the one shown in Figure 6.4a. Below the graph of the total product function, derive the corresponding average and marginal product functions. Compare these curves with those in Figures 6.6a and 6.6b. Check to see that the curves you have drawn are consistent with the three observations above concerning the relationships between average and marginal products.

6.5 Costs of Production: One Variable Input

Now let us consider the short-run cost-minimization problem that arises when just one input is allowed to vary. If input 2 is the fixed input and input 1 the variable input, then the cost-minimization problem can be stated as

$$\text{minimize } w_1 z_1 \text{ by choice of } z_1$$

$$\text{subject to the constraint } y = TP(z_1)$$

That is, choose z_1 to minimize the expenditure on the variable input ($w_1 z_1$), subject to the constraint that the firm produces y units of output [$y = TP(z_1)$].

Because this problem is so simple, in the space of a few pages we can learn everything there is to know about how various cost functions relate to their corresponding total product functions. This elementary grounding in the relationship between production functions and the cost of production will be very useful in the next chapter, where we will reconsider production and cost in the more complex, realistic cases in which more than one input is variable.

We begin with the variable cost function, define average variable cost and short-run marginal cost, explore the fixed cost of production, and conclude with definitions of short-run total cost and short-run average cost.

The Variable Cost Function Illustrated

Once we know what quantity of output a particular firm wants to produce, we can discover from the total product function the minimum quantity of the variable input required to produce that output. This minimum quantity is the solution to our simple cost-minimization problem. We can then determine what the *minimum variable cost* of the output will be by multiplying this quantity by the price of the input w_1. We will assume throughout that the firm can buy any amount of the variable input at a fixed price w_1 per unit. We can thus derive from the total product function the **variable cost function**, written as $VC(y)$:

variable cost function

$$VC(y) = \text{the minimum variable cost of producing } y \text{ units of output}$$

Let us use Tipple's Courier Service to develop an algebraic illustration. Suppose that Tipple has just 48 litres of gas on hand and that he cannot buy any more in this period. In this case, gasoline is the fixed input and his driver's time is the variable input. From Problem 6.6, the total product function is

$$TP(z_1) = 240(z_1)^{1/2}$$

where z_1 is hours of time. Since this function describes the relationship between kilometres driven (y) and hours of the driver's time (z_1), we have

$$y = 240(z_1)^{1/2}$$

For example, if Tipple wants the truck driven 480 kilometres, the minimum amount of a driver's time that he needs is 4 hours. Although a driver could take more than 4 hours to drive 480 kilometres on 48 litres of gas, 4 hours is the minimum time required. Letting w_1 denote the hourly wage of Tipple's driver, we see that $4w_1$ is the variable cost of driving 480 kilometres or $VC(480) = 4w_1$. Similarly, if Tipple wants the truck driven 720 kilometres, he needs 9 hours. In this case, we see that $VC(720) = 9w_1$.

More generally, if we invert the total product function by solving for z_1 in terms of y, we have the minimum time needed to drive the truck y kilometres. If we let z_1^* represent this minimum time, we have

$$z_1^* = y^2/(57\ 600)$$

Now, simply by multiplying by w_1 we have the variable cost function for Tipple's Courier Service when he has 48 litres of gas:

$$VC(y) = w_1 y^2/(57\ 600)$$

This gives us the minimum cost of driving the truck y kilometres when Tipple pays his driver w_1 per hour and has just 48 litres of gas on hand.

PROBLEM 6.11

Suppose that Tipple has 27 litres of gasoline on hand. First find z_1^*, the minimum number of hours needed to drive y kilometres. Then find the corresponding variable cost function, $VC(y)$.

Deriving the Variable Cost Function

To this point, we have explored two variable cost functions for Tipple's Courier Service. Now we will develop a graphic technique that can be applied to any cost-minimization problem when only one input is variable. The series of four interlinked diagrams in Figure 6.7 shows just how the variable cost function $VC(y)$ can be derived from the total product function $TP(z_1)$ and the cost of input 1, w_1. We have plotted the standard total product function in Figure 6.7a, and we have then used the diagrams in Figure 6.7b and 6.7c to derive the variable cost function in Figure 6.7d.

Let us see how that derivation is accomplished. Suppose that the firm wanted to produce 768 units of good Y. Consulting $TP(z_1)$ in Figure 6.7a (top right panel), we see that 16 units of input 1 is the least costly way of doing so because 16 is the smallest quantity of input 1 that will produce 768 units. From the ray in Figure 6.7b, we see that 16 units of input 1 will cost $16w_1$. Because the minimum cost of producing 768 units of Y is $16w_1$, $(768,16w_1)$ is one point on the variable cost function $VC(y)$ in Figure 6.7d.

To identify this point in Figure 6.7d, we have (horizontally) projected the cost $16w_1$ from Figure 6.7b into Figure 6.7d. Using the 45° line in Figure 6.7c, we have also projected output 768 from Figure 6.7a into Figure 6.7d. The intersection of these two projections at $(768,16w_1)$ in Figure 6.7d is one point on $VC(y)$. All other points on $VC(y)$ have been constructed in the corresponding way. For example, 22 units of input 1 are needed to produce 2971 units of good Y, and $(2971,22w_1)$ is therefore another point on $VC(y)$.[5]

Average Variable Cost and Short-Run Marginal Cost

We defined the concepts of average product and marginal product when we looked at the total product function. Now we will define the corresponding concepts of average variable cost and short-run marginal cost in relation to the variable cost function. Although their labels are a bit of a mouthful, the concepts themselves are straightforward. As you may have guessed, **average variable cost**, written $AVC(y)$, is just the variable cost per unit of output:

average variable cost

$$AVC(y) = VC(y)/y$$

The **short-run marginal cost**, $SMC(y)$, as you may also have guessed, is the rate at which cost increases in the short run as output increases. Because the only variable cost in the short run is the cost associated with the variable input, the short-run marginal cost of output is simply the slope of the variable cost function:[6]

short-run marginal cost

$$SMC(y) = \text{slope of } VC(y)$$

5. What we accomplish in Figure 6.7 is, in essence, the inversion of the function $y = TP(z_1)$. Write the inverse of this function as $z_1 = H(y)$. This function tells how much z_1 is required to produce any given y. The variable cost function is then just w_1 multiplied by $H(y)$:

$$VC(y) = w_1H(y)$$

6. Mathematically, we see that $SMC(y)$ is simply the derivative of $VC(y)$:

$$SMC(y) = VC'(y)$$

FIGURE 6.7 Deriving the variable cost function

VC in (d) is derived from *TP* in (a). From (a), we see that $z_1 = 16$ is necessary to produce output $y = 768$; from (b), we see that 16 units of input 1 cost $16w_1$. Projecting $y = 768$ into (d), through the 45° line in (c), and projecting $16w_1$ into (d), we have one point on *VC*, the point $(768, 16w_1)$.

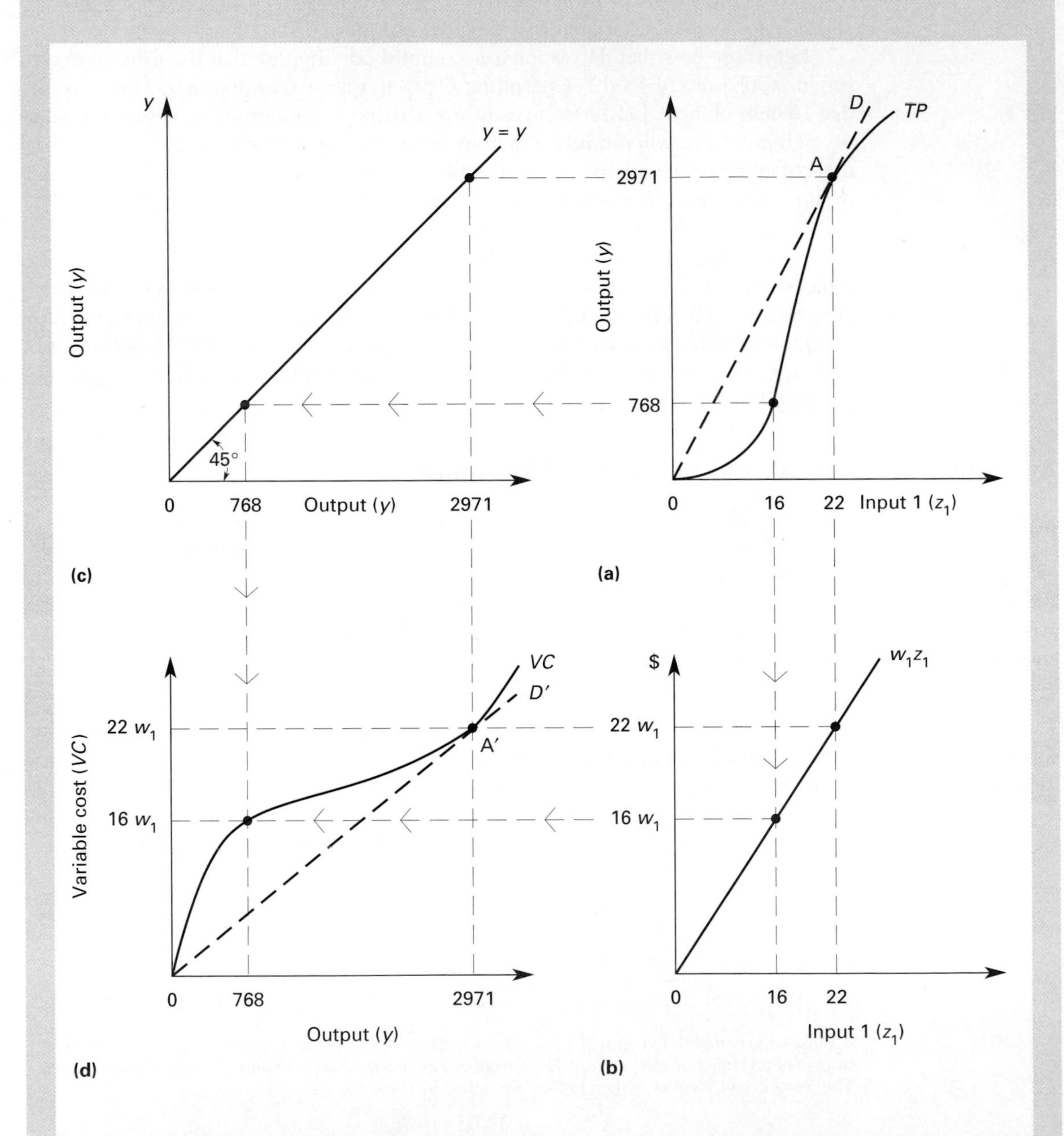

In Figure 6.8, we have illustrated the graphic techniques used to derive the average variable cost and the short-run marginal cost. We have constructed the ray through the origin to point A on $VC(y)$ and the line TT that is tangent to $VC(y)$ at point A. Because the slope of the ray is average variable cost at A and the slope of the tangent line is marginal cost at A, we see that $AVC(y)$ is less than $MC(y)$ at point A.

We can use these graphic techniques to derive and compare the average variable cost and short-run marginal cost functions implied by any variable cost function. The variable cost function $VC(y)$ from Figure 6.7d is reproduced in Figure 6.9a. The average variable cost function $AVC(y)$ and the short-run marginal cost function $SMC(y)$ derived from $VC(y)$ are shown in Figure 6.9b. You need to understand why both curves in Figure 6.9b are U-shaped and why they intersect at output level 2971. If you are unsure, pick up a pencil and paper and derive $SMC(y)$ and $AVC(y)$ from $VC(y)$, using the technique described in Figure 6.8.

What does Figure 6.9 tell us about the relationship between average variable cost and short-run marginal cost? We see three perhaps familiar relationships:

1. When *SMC* lies below *AVC*, *AVC* decreases as *y* increases.

2. When *SMC* is equal to *AVC*, *AVC* is neither increasing nor decreasing: its slope is zero.

3. When *SMC* lies above *AVC*, *AVC* increases as *y* increases.[7]

These relationships follow from the same arithmetic truisms that predict your grade point average: if your grades this term are lower than your previous average,

FIGURE 6.8 **Deriving average variable cost and short-run marginal cost**

AVC at point A is equal to the slope of the dashed line 0A. *SMC* at point A is the slope of the tangent line *TT*. At point A, *AVC* is less than *SMC*.

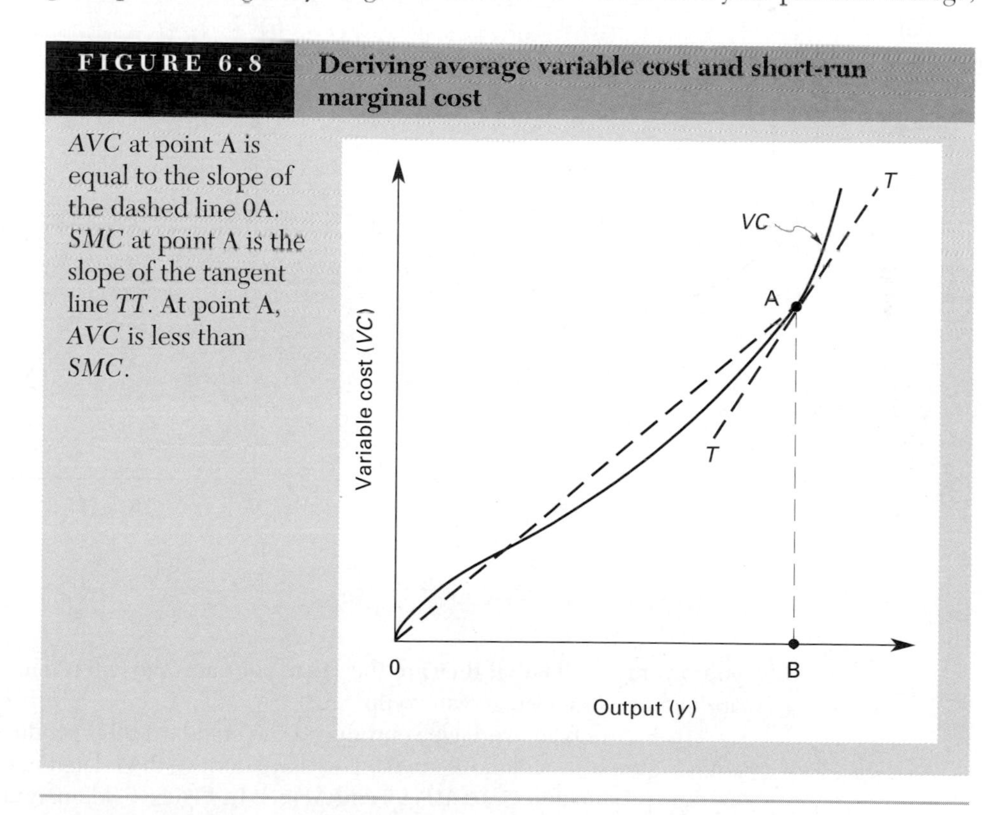

7. These results are another application of the general relationship between averages and marginals developed in footnote 3.

FIGURE 6.9 Comparing cost and product functions

In (b), we have derived *SMC* and *AVC* from *VC* in (a). The slope of *VC* is smallest at $y = 768$; therefore, *SMC* attains its minimum value at $y = 768$. At $y = 2971$, the ray 0A is tangent to *VC*; therefore, *SMC* is equal to *AVC*, and *AVC* attains its minimum value at $y = 2971$. Similarly, in (d), we have derived *MP* and *AP* from *TP* in (c). In comparing (b) and (d), notice that *SMC* and *AVC* are inverted images of *MP* and *AP*.

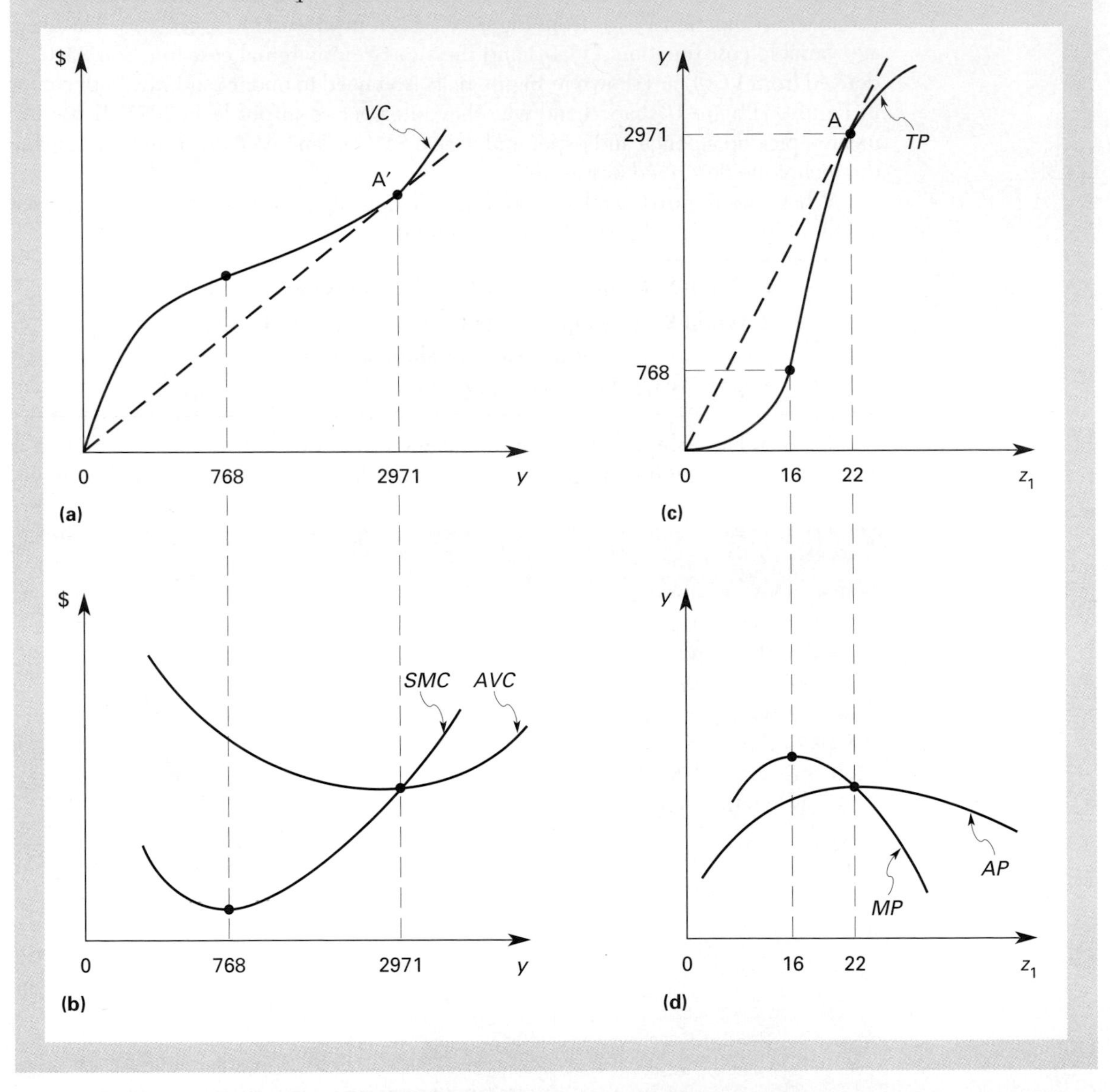

your average will fall; if they are the same, your average will remain the same; if they are higher, your average will go up.

In Figure 6.9c, we have reproduced the standard total product function $TP(z_1)$ from Figure 6.7a, and in Figure 6.9d, we have derived the related marginal product and average product functions $MP(z_1)$ and $AP(z_1)$. In Figure 6.9d, marginal product is at its peak when the quantity of the variable input is 16 or when the output is 768, and it diminishes thereafter. Correspondingly, in Figure 6.9b, short-run marginal cost is at its lowest point when the output is 768, and it increases thereafter. Increasing short-run marginal cost, then, seems to be a direct implication of diminishing marginal product. Similarly, decreasing short-run marginal cost seems to be a direct implication of increasing marginal product. It is almost as if we could generate the marginal cost curve in Figure 6.9b by inverting the image of the marginal product curve in Figure 6.9d.

The average product and average variable cost curves in Figures 6.9b and 6.9d show the same kind of strikingly similar, but inverse, relationship. At input levels below 22 (or output levels below 2971), average product is increasing and average variable cost is decreasing. At input levels above 22 (or output levels above 2971), average product is falling, and average variable cost is rising. Once again, we could almost generate the average variable cost function by inverting the image of the average product function.

Average Product and Average Cost

Doing two simple algebraic exercises will help you to see why these relationships hold. We will look at an arbitrary point on the total product function:

$$y' = TP(z_1')$$

Average product at this point is just the output $TP(z_1')$ divided by the quantity of the variable input z_1':

$$AP(z_1') = TP(z_1')/z_1'$$

Average variable cost at this point is just the expenditure on input 1 divided by the output:

$$AVC(y') = w_1 z_1'/TP(z_1')$$

We can rewrite this expression as

$$AVC(y') = w_1/[TP(z_1')/z_1']$$

But the denominator here is just average product. Thus, average variable cost is equal to the price of the variable input divided by average product:

$$AVC(y') = w_1/AP(z_1')$$

In this sense, the average variable cost function is the inverted image of the average product function.

Marginal Product and Marginal Cost

Let us turn now to the relationship between the marginal product function and the short-run marginal cost function. Again, imagine choosing some arbitrary level of the variable input z_1' and then increasing that level by some very small amount Δz_1. The corresponding increase in the variable cost Δc will be just the additional quantity of the input multiplied by the price of the input:

$$\Delta c = w_1 \Delta z_1$$

The amount by which output increases, Δy, will be (approximately) the marginal product of the variable input at level z_1' multiplied by the additional quantity of the variable input:

$$\Delta y = MP(z_1')\Delta z_1$$

By definition, short-run marginal cost is simply the rate of increase of variable cost as output increases; that is, it is approximately $\Delta c / \Delta y$. Substituting the results from above,

$$SMC(y') = [w_1 \Delta z_1]/[MP(z_1')\Delta z_1]$$

Dividing out Δz_1, we see that the short-run marginal cost at output y' is simply the price of the variable input divided by the marginal product of the variable input at level z_1':

$$SMC(y') = w_1/MP(z_1')$$

In this sense, the short-run marginal cost function is the inverted image of the marginal product function.[8]

Fixed Cost

fixed cost

By specifying the price of the variable input w_1, we have been able to derive from the total product function the associated variable cost function. But what about the cost associated with the fixed input? The cost of the fixed input, which is called a **fixed cost**, is simply the price of the input multiplied by its quantity:

$$FC = w_2 z_2$$

where z_2 is quantity of the fixed input.

average fixed cost

We can express fixed costs on a per-unit basis by dividing the fixed cost by output. This is called the **average fixed cost** of production, denoted by $AFC(y)$:

$$AFC(y) = FC/y$$

To understand the relationship implied by this statement, try the following problem.

PROBLEM 6.12

Plot the horizontal line FC on a graph in which y is on the horizontal axis and dollars are on the vertical axis. Now graph $AFC(y)$. What happens to $AFC(y)$ as y gets arbitrarily large? As y gets arbitrarily small?

Short-Run Total Cost and Short-Run Average Cost

short-run total cost

The **short-run total cost** of output, written $STC(y)$, can be calculated simply by adding up the variable cost and the fixed cost:

$$STC(y) = VC(y) + FC$$

---

8. We noted in footnote 5 that

$$VC(y) = w_1 H(y)$$

where $H(y)$ is the inverse of $y = TP(z_1)$. Differentiating this expression, we see that

$$SMC(y) = w_1 H'(y)$$

But $H'(y)$ is $1/[TP'(z_1)]$, or $1/[MP(z_1)]$. Hence,

$$SMC(y) = \frac{w_1}{MP(z_1)}.$$

short-run average cost

Short-run total cost can also be expressed on a per-unit basis, called **short-run average cost** and written $SAC(y)$, by dividing the short-run cost by the number of units of output:

$$SAC(y) = STC(y)/y$$

PROBLEM 6.13

$SMC(y)$ is defined as the slope of $VC(y)$. Show that $SMC(y)$ is also equal to the slope of $STC(y)$. In other words, show that for any value of y, the slope of $STC(y)$ is equal to the slope of $VC(y)$.

Short-run average cost can also be calculated by adding up the average variable cost and the average fixed cost:

$$SAC(y) = AVC(y) + AFC(y)$$

Figure 6.10 shows all of these cost functions. FC, $STC(y)$, and $VC(y)$ are shown in Figure 6.10a, and $AFC(y)$, $AVC(y)$, $SAC(y)$, and $SMC(y)$ are shown in Figure 6.10b. Because $SMC(y)$ is the marginal function associated with $STC(y)$ and because $SAC(y)$ is the average function associated with $STC(y)$, we immediately know a great deal about the relationship between $SMC(y)$ and $SAC(y)$:

***SAC* is increasing or decreasing as *SMC* lies above or below it, and the slope of *SAC* is zero when *SMC* is equal to *SAC*.**

Application: Traffic Congestion and Multi-Plant Firms

Let us use these tools to do some problem solving. The number of cars entering and leaving every major city in the world has grown dramatically over the past three decades. Bumper-to-bumper traffic is a daily frustration for millions of commuters. Although the problem of traffic congestion does not involve a firm, we can generate some interesting insights into the problem using the production and cost concepts developed in this chapter. Conversely, much of what we learn about the congestion problem can easily be applied to firms.

Imagine a suburb called Surrey that is connected to the nearby city of Wetvan by two roads: route 1 and route 2. Route 1 is the shorter road, but route 2 is the wider; having many lanes, it does not become congested. Imagine, too, that every weekday morning 5000 residents of Surrey hop into their cars and drive to work in Wetvan. What principles determine how many commuters will choose each route? What are the costs of commuting for the Surrey commuters? Do these commuters make the most effective use of the two available roads? Throughout the analysis we will ignore the money these commuters spend on gasoline and automobiles so that we can isolate the *time costs* of commuting.

As you undoubtedly know, commuting time on most roads depends on traffic density. If the number of commuters who pick a particular road is small, the trip is relatively quick. As more and more cars converge on a road, however, traffic builds up until, beyond some point, the larger the number of commuters, the longer it takes each commuter to get to work.

FIGURE 6.10 Seven cost functions

In (a), *STC* is derived from *VC* by adding *FC*. Each of the cost functions in (b) can be derived from the cost functions in (a): $AFC = FC/y$, $AVC = VC/y$, and $SAC = STC/y$. Finally, SMC = slope of VC, and SMC = slope of STC.

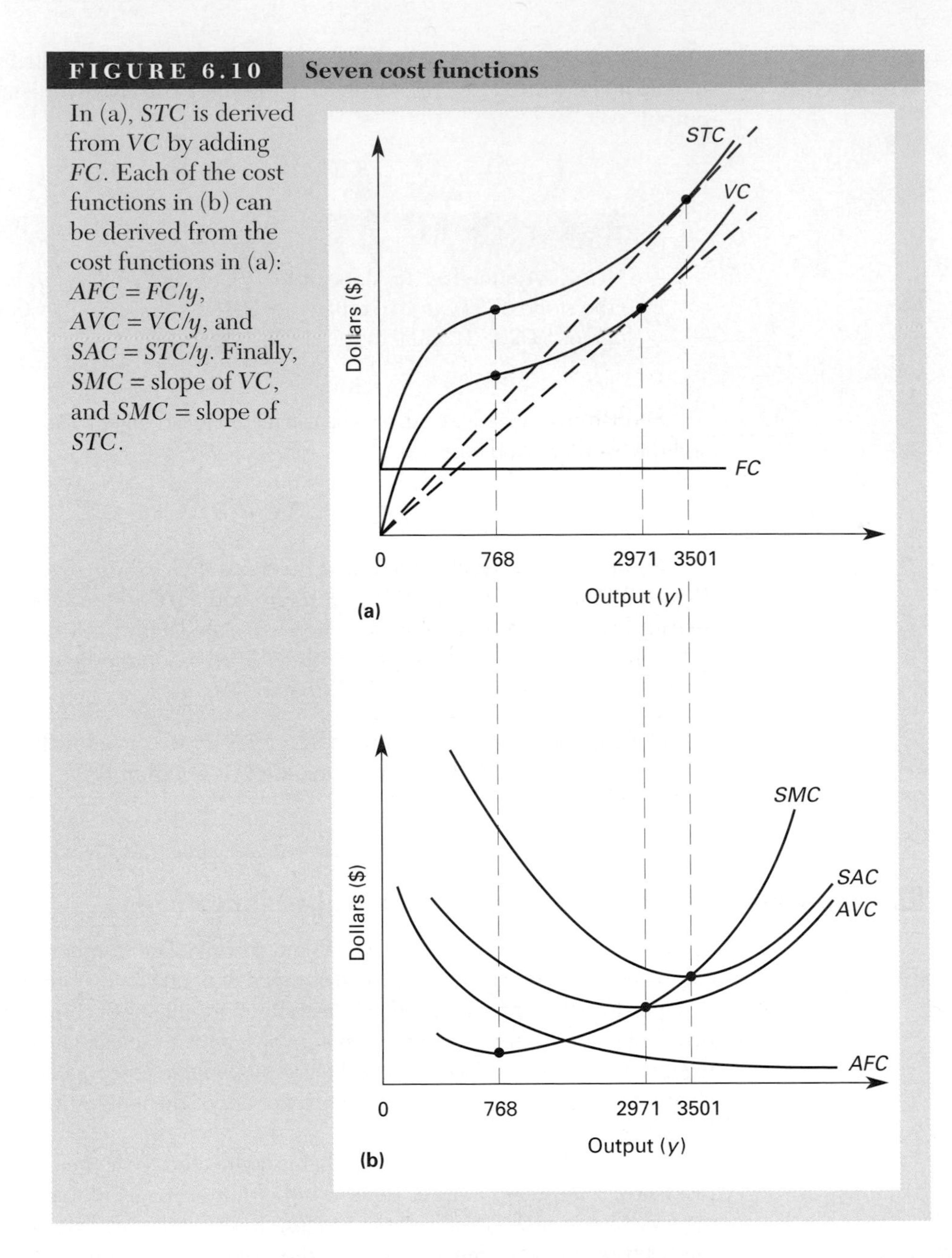

The precise relationship between average commuting time and numbers of commuters on route 1 is presented in Figure 6.11. Our model will ignore the complexities of real commuting situations (such as the possibility of rising early to beat the rush hour) to concentrate on the relationship between traffic density and commuting time. We are supposing that every commuter on route 1 spends the same amount of time commuting.

The time per commuter is measured on the vertical axis and the number of commuters using route 1, N_1, is measured on the horizontal axis. Notice that when N_1 is less than 1200, route 1 is congestion-free and each commuter spends 18 minutes travelling

FIGURE 6.11 **The costs of commuting**

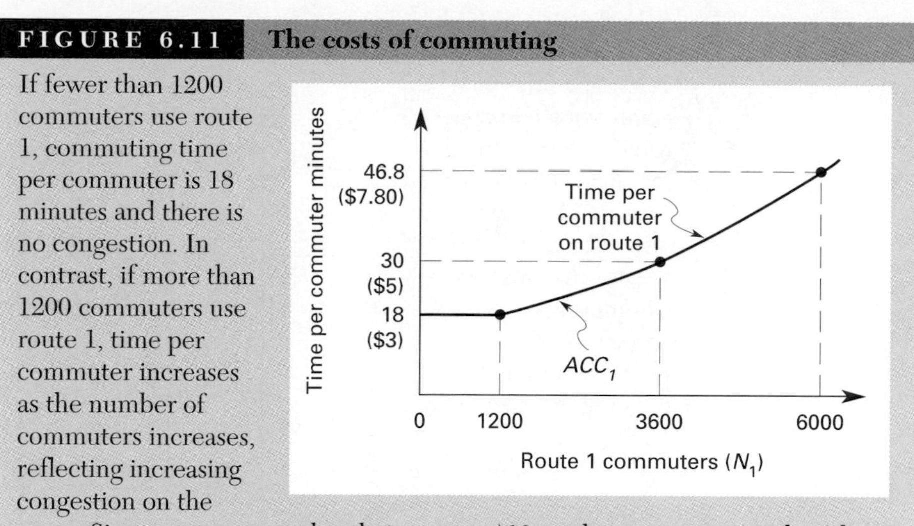

If fewer than 1200 commuters use route 1, commuting time per commuter is 18 minutes and there is no congestion. In contrast, if more than 1200 commuters use route 1, time per commuter increases as the number of commuters increases, reflecting increasing congestion on the route. Since commuters value their time at $10 per hour, we can translate the time costs of commuting into money costs. For example, if 3600 commuters use the route, the money cost is $5 per commuter, equal to half an hour (30 minutes) × $10 per hour. ACC_1 gives the average cost per commuter on route 1.

from Surrey to Wetvan. When more than 1200 commuters use route 1, commuting time increases as N_1 increases. For example, if 3600 commuters use route 1, the time per commuter rises to 30 minutes.

For many purposes, it is useful to express this time cost in monetary terms. We will assume that these commuters can earn $10 an hour and value their time at this rate. An 18-minute commute then costs $3 — since 18 minutes is three-tenths of an hour — and a 60-minute commute costs $10. On the vertical axis in Figure 6.11, we have given dollar as well as time values for commuting costs.

Notice that the dollar cost per commuter is, in effect, an average cost function, where the output is the number of trips to Wetvan from Surrey N_1, and the total cost is the total value of the time spent by the N_1 Surrey commuters in travelling to Wetvan. To reflect this fact, we have used the label ACC_1 in Figure 6.11 for *average commuting cost* on route 1. What are the corresponding total and marginal cost functions?

To derive the total cost function, we just need to observe that the total commuting cost is equal to the number of commuters N_1 multiplied by the average commuting cost ACC_1. In Figure 6.12, we have constructed the *total commuting cost* function for route 1 and labelled it TCC_1. When N_1 is less than 1200, TCC_1 rises at a constant rate. When N_1 exceeds 1200, however, the ever-increasing congestion means that TCC_1 rises at an ever-increasing rate. For any point such as point A on TCC_1, the average commuter cost ACC_1 is equal to the slope of the ray from the origin to A, and what we will call the *marginal commuter cost* — or MCC_1 — is equal to the slope of TCC_1. Notice that MCC_1 exceeds ACC_1 when N_1 exceeds 1200.

Because it is not subject to congestion, commuting on route 2 is easy to model. A Surrey commuter on route 2 will arrive in Wetvan in 30 minutes, *regardless* of how many other commuters are also using this route. In other words, route 2 is slow but sure. The average cost of the 30-minute commute on route 2 is $5 ($10/hour × 0.5 hours); $ACC_2 = \$5$. The total commuting cost on route 2 is then $TCC_2 = 5N_2$. And finally, the marginal commuting cost is also $5, or $MCC_2 = 5$.

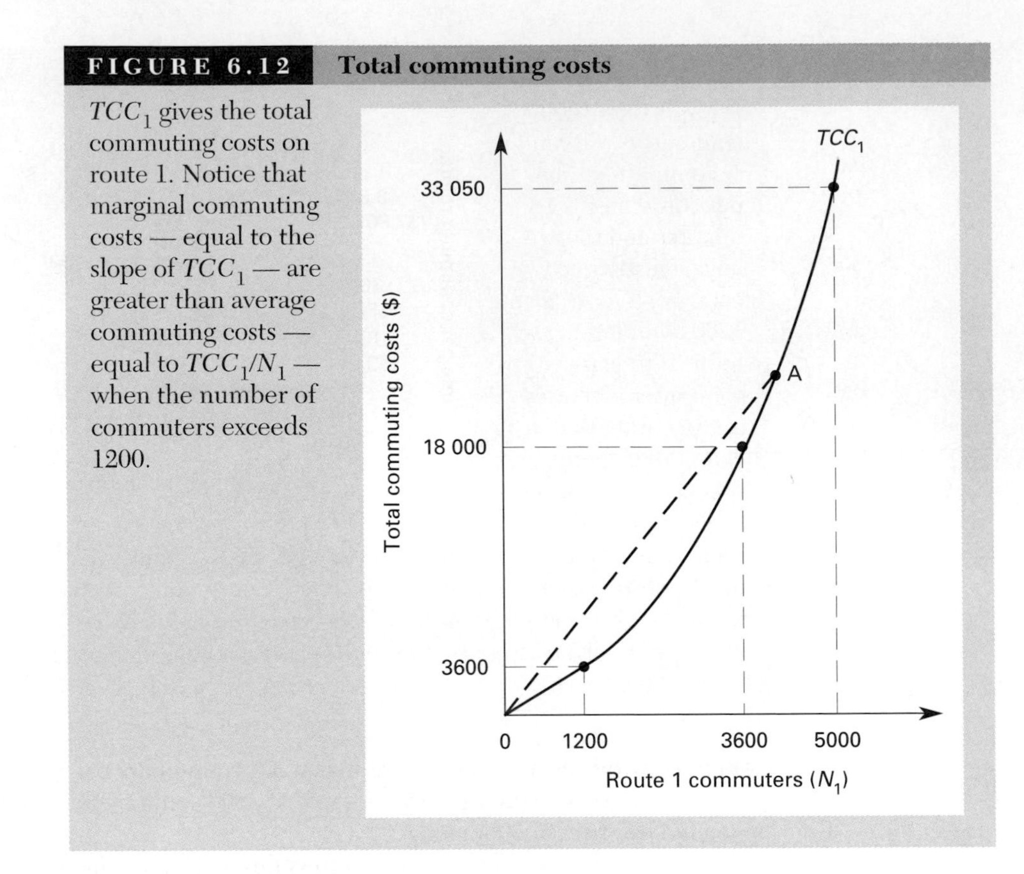

FIGURE 6.12 **Total commuting costs**

TCC_1 gives the total commuting costs on route 1. Notice that marginal commuting costs — equal to the slope of TCC_1 — are greater than average commuting costs — equal to TCC_1/N_1 — when the number of commuters exceeds 1200.

Now, how many of Surrey's 5000 commuters will choose route 1 and how many will choose route 2? We will assume that every commuter wants to minimize the cost in time spent commuting. Because each commuter is free to choose either route, the average commuting cost in equilibrium must be the same on both routes. Why? Suppose that on Monday, 1200 commuters choose route 1 and 3800 choose route 2. Then the average commuting cost on route 1 is only $3 but the average commuting costs on route 2 is $5. Some of the commuters who took route 2 on Monday will then decide to switch to route 1 on Tuesday. As a result, ACC_1 will increase on Tuesday. This process will end only when enough commuters have switched from route 2 to route 1 so that ACC_1 is equal to ACC_2. Therefore, in equilibrium, 3600 commuters will use route 1, and the remaining 1400 commuters will use route 2.

PROBLEM 6.14

What will the equilibrium allocation be if there are 6000 commuters? If there are 4000 commuters? If there are 3000 commuters?

Are these Surrey commuters making effective use of their roads? To find out, let us turn to Figure 6.13a, where we have plotted both TCC_1 and TCC_2. Notice that TCC_1 has been plotted relative to 0_1 in the standard way, and the values for N_1, which are set out just below the horizontal axis, increase from left to right beginning at 0_1. However, TCC_2 has been plotted relative to the second origin at 0_2, and the values

FIGURE 6.13 The allocation of commuters to routes

In (a), total commuting costs on route 1 and route 2, TCC_1 and TCC_2, are plotted relative to 0_1 and 0_2, respectively. Since any point on the horizontal axis corresponds to an allocation of commuters to routes, we get total commuting costs for any allocation by vertically summing TCC_1 and TCC_2 to get TCC. Total commuting costs TCC are minimized when 2000 commuters are allocated to route 1 and 3000 to route 2. In (b), we see that marginal commutin costs on the two routes — MCC_1 and MCC_2 — are equal when TCC is at minimum. Further, if commuters have common access to the two routes, average commuting costs on the two routes — ACC_1 and ACC_2 — are equalized in the equilibrium at E. The equilibrium allocation is 3600 commuters to route 1 and 1400 to route 2.

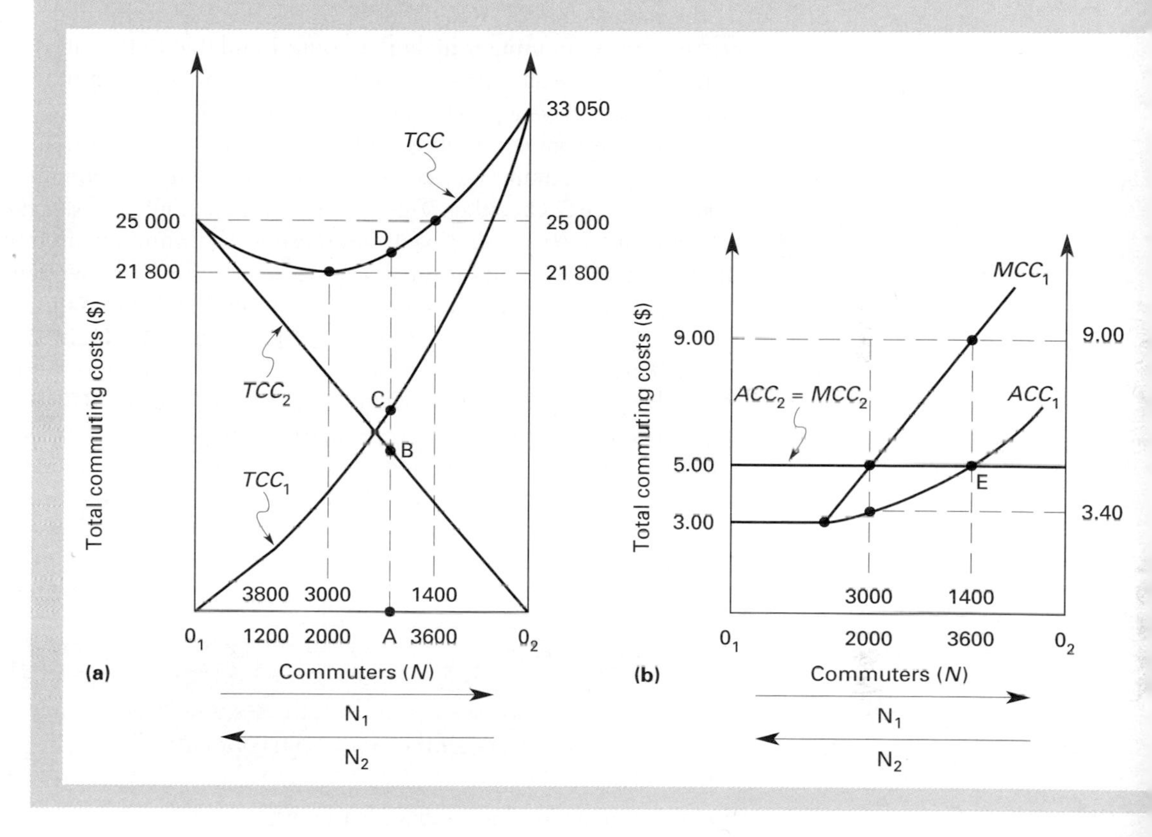

for N_2, which are set out just above the horizontal axis, increase from right to left, beginning at 0_2. The distance from 0_1 to 0_2 is exactly 5000, reflecting the fact that 5000 Surrey commuters travel to Wetvan. Therefore, any point along the horizontal axis in Figure 6.13a corresponds to an allocation of commuters to the two routes. For example, at the equilibrium allocation, 3600 commuters take route 1 and 1400 take route 2.

Now consider the allocation at point A. Distance AC is the total cost of commuting on route 1, TCC_1, and distance AB is the total cost of commuting on route 2, TCC_2. Adding up the two distances gives us distance AD, the total cost of commuting for this allocation. Using this method, we have computed the total commuting cost for all possible allocations and have labelled the resulting curve TCC. Notice that TCC is smallest when 2000 commuters take route 1 and 3000 take route 2. The total commuting costs associated with this allocation are just $21 800. By contrast, at the equilibrium allocation (where 3600 take route 1 and 1400 take route 2), the total commuting costs are $25 000. Notice that if all 5000 commuters travelled along route 2, the total commuting costs would likewise be $25 000. In this equilibrium, then, it is as if route 1 simply did not exist.

Using the cost-benefit criterion, we then see that the Surrey commuters are not making effective use of their roads. According to the cost-benefit criterion, one allocation is preferred to another if it is associated with smaller total commuting costs. The cost-benefit-optimal allocation — the one with the smallest total commuting costs — occurs when 2000 commuters use route 1 and 3000 use route 2.

To better understand these results, let us turn to Figure 6.13b. We have drawn the two sets of average and marginal cost curves and identified the equilibrium at point E at the intersection of ACC_1 and ACC_2. Notice that to the right of point E the average cost of commuting is higher on route 1 and that to the left it is higher on route 2. Therefore, if the allocation of commuters were at any point other than E, some commuters would have a private incentive to switch routes.

The marginal commuting cost curves reveal why the equilibrium is suboptimal and why total commuting costs are minimized when 2000 commuters use route 1 and 3000 use route 2. On either route, the marginal commuting cost is the rate at which total commuting costs on that route increase as the number of commuters increases. Beginning at the equilibrium allocation, let us ask: What happens to the total commuting costs if we force one commuter off route 1 and onto route 2? Since MCC_1 is $9, TCC_1 will decrease by (approximately) $9, and since MCC_2 is $5, TCC_2 will increase by $5. Thus, total commuting costs TCC will decrease by approximately $4. More generally, beginning at any point where MCC_1 is not equal to MCC_2, TCC can be reduced by shifting a commuter from the route where marginal cost is larger to the route where marginal cost is smaller. Therefore, we know that total commuting costs are smallest at the allocation where the marginal costs of commuting on the two routes are identical. The allocation where $MCC_1 = MCC_2$ in Figure 6.13b (and where TCC is lowest in Figure 6.13a) is at $N_1 = 2000$ and $N_2 = 3000$. More generally, to minimize total commuting costs TCC, allocate commuters to the two routes so that $MCC_1 = MCC_2$.

PROBLEM 6.15

What is the optimal allocation if there are 6000 commuters? If there are 3000 commuters? If there are 1000 commuters?

Let us summarize what we have learned:

In equilibrium, commuters allocate themselves to routes so as to equalize the average commuting cost on the two routes. Yet optimality demands that the commuters are allocated so as to equalize marginal costs on the two routes. Because route 1 is subject to congestion, marginal cost exceeds average cost. Therefore, in equilibrium, too many commuters use route 1.

The suboptimal equilibrium in this model arises because commuters have unrestricted, or common, access to a road that is subject to congestion. Taking this perspective, you can see that the traffic congestion problem is yet another type of *common-property problem*. Like some of the other common-property problems you already encountered, solutions are possible. For example, one solution is to charge a *toll* on route 1. What toll can be levied on route 1 that will be large enough that commuters on route 2 have no incentive to switch to route 1 at the optimal allocation, when 3000 commuters use route 2 and 2000 commuters use route 1? From Figure 6.13b, we see that the optimal toll is \$1.60 (\$5.00 – \$3.40).

This toll will raise \$3200 per day — \$1.60 from each of the 2000 commuters using route 1. If this toll revenue were distributed to the 5000 commuters, each commuter would receive \$0.64 per day. The net effect of this optimal toll is then to make each commuter better off by \$0.64 per day than in the initial, common-property equilibrium.

On route 1, the input called "commuters' time" is used to produce an output called "trips to Wetvan." Notice from this perspective that TCC_1 is just a variable cost function. What is the associated total product function that translates the input "commuters' time" into the output "trips to Wetvan"? To find out, we could begin with the variable cost function TCC_1 and derive the total product function by reversing the procedure used in Figure 6.7. Yet without doing so, we can readily see two important properties of that total product function. First, it exhibits a constant marginal product for any amount of time less than 18 minutes per commuter. Second, it exhibits a diminishing marginal product for any amount of time greater than 18 minutes per commuter. Therefore, it has the same general shape as the total product function in Figure 6.4a. Of course, the point at which marginal product begins to diminish is just the point at which additional commuters begin to create congestion. In other words, *congestion* is a specialized name for *diminishing marginal product* on a road. Although Malthus never encountered this sort of congestion problem, he certainly would have recognized it as a case of diminishing marginal product.

Application: The Allocation of Output Among Different Plants

multi-plant firms

Now let us reinterpret what we learned about congestion to solve an interesting problem that all **multi-plant firms** face. A firm with more than one production facility or plant faces the problem of allocating output to its various plants. For example, if a firm wants to produce 5000 units of output at minimal cost, what principles govern the amount that is produced in each of its plants? To answer this question, all we need to do is to reinterpret Figure 6.13.

Let us suppose for the moment that the firm has just two plants. We can then think of TCC_1 and TCC_2 in Figure 6.13a as the variable cost functions associated with the two plants, and MCC_1 and MCC_2 in Figure 6.13b as the corresponding short-run marginal cost functions. In both parts of the figure, the length of the axis connecting 0_1 and 0_2 can be reinterpreted as the output of 5000 units. The firm's problem is to allocate the output to its two plants so as to minimize its total variable cost.

The curve TCC in Figure 6.13a tells us the firm's total variable cost for any allocation of the 5000 units of output to the two plants. The firm's optimal solution is to allocate 2000 units to the first plant and 3000 to the second plant. More important, using the logic of Figure 6.13b, we can derive the general rule that governs the cost-minimizing allocation of *any* quantity of output to *any* number of plants. Consider any allocation of output to two plants in which short-run marginal cost is not the same for both plants. Total cost can be reduced by allocating output from the high-marginal-cost plant to the low-marginal-cost plant.

To minimize the total variable cost of producing a given output in two or more plants, a firm allocates output to the plants so that short-run marginal cost is the same in all plants.

Application: Sports Stars, Submarines, Triage, and Book Publishing

By now you should be getting accustomed to thinking about life using marginal analysis. In the last two applications we saw that optimality occurs when marginal costs are equated. Let us briefly consider four more examples to test our economic intuition. We will analyze these cases using marginal products rather than marginal costs. To test yourself, see if you can also reframe the discussion in terms of marginal costs. Keep in mind that marginal products and marginal costs are inversely related.

In the early 1990s the Toronto Blue Jays achieved the remarkable feat of winning back-to-back World Series. They were unable, however, to win three times in a row. Professional sports dynasties are rare and short-lived. What prevents a wealthy team owner from accumulating all of the stars on one team and winning year in, year out?

Before we answer that question, consider an analogous one. In World War II, submarines sank almost 90 percent of all boats sunk in the war. They were by far the most important weapon in a navy's arsenal. Why, then, would navies invest in other types of vessels? Why not have just submarines?

To answer both questions, consider the relevant production functions and marginal products. The marginal product of a single star to a given club is quite large. When Wayne Gretzky was traded to the Los Angeles Kings, he almost single-handedly turned the team around, and within a couple of years they made it to the Stanley Cup finals. However, given diminishing marginal products, the marginal product of a second star player of the same quality is lower than the first. The same is true for the third, fourth, and fifth star. The more stars on a team, the lower is their marginal contribution. For teams without a star, the marginal product is very high. As a result, poor teams without stars are able (and willing) to pay more for the marginal star player on the good team, and this draws some star players to the poor team. In the process, the marginal products of the various quality sports stars are equalized across teams, and, usually, no single team dominates.[9]

The same answer applies to the submarines. Submarines were very effective in total, but at the margin their product could be quite low. If the navy must make a decision between the thousandth submarine and the first battleship, it is quite possible that the marginal product of the latter is higher than the former. When the marginal products of the different weapons are equalized, there are necessarily larger numbers of those weapons with the higher total product.

The great power of economics is that you don't have to learn a new theory every time a different situation arises. Can you use the notion of diminishing marginal products to explain the practice of triage by medical doctors in wartime? Or the practice of textbook publishers printing small runs of expensive graduate texts? Under battle conditions, when doctors are in short supply, wounded soldiers are sorted, or "triaged," into three categories: those who will get better without attention; those who will get better with attention; and those who will die no matter what is done. Although it is a crude system, battlefield triage is an attempt to equalize marginal products across patients. The marginal product of the first and third categories is close to zero and, as a result, the doctors concentrate on the second group of patients. Likewise with textbook publishing. Pearson Education Canada publishes books at all levels: first-year books to graduate books. The market for first-year books is huge compared to graduate books, and the average profit is higher as well. However, Pearson doesn't focus just on the introductory market, because total profits are

9. One possible exception is the Montreal Canadiens that has won almost 1 out of 4 Stanley Cup championships for close to a century. Given that Montreal has always had a preference for hockey players from Quebec, and vice versa, can you think of an explanation?

higher when they equate the marginal product across all of the markets. Sure, they sell more introductory books but, at the margin, each market is equally important.

PROBLEM 6.16

Canada and the United States both are major producers of oil, and have enough reserves to supply their own demands. However, in both countries oil is produced and imported. Why?

Application: Slavery

To show just how general our theory of production is, consider its application to the area of slavery. In the 1960s, historians studying slavery in the American South came across several puzzling facts: slaves ate more than poor but free whites; slaves had lower birth mortality than poor free whites; and slave owners required their slaves to take part in activities that today we would consider healthy living styles (e.g., no excessive drinking, the practice of good personal hygiene, etc.). Amazingly, some researchers came to the conclusion that slave owners were either altruistic or felt sorry for the slaves, and as a result fed them better and provided better medical attention. This view seemed to be supported when it was also learned that slaves, as a general practice, were not beaten regularly. Our economic model, on the other hand, not only explains why slaves were treated this way but also demonstrates that this behaviour was certainly not the result of any fond feelings that slave owners had for their slaves.

Slavery is a situation where the labour inputs are owned not by the labourerd but by the slave owners. The slave owners decide how much slave labour to use in production, just as they would decide how much land to put into cotton or how many mules to use at harvest. The slaves must do as they're told.

FIGURE 6.14 **Labour choice for free people and slaves**

Free people work until the marginal product of labour equals the marginal value of output, but slaves are forced to work until their marginal products are zero. Slaves, therefore, worked longer than free people.

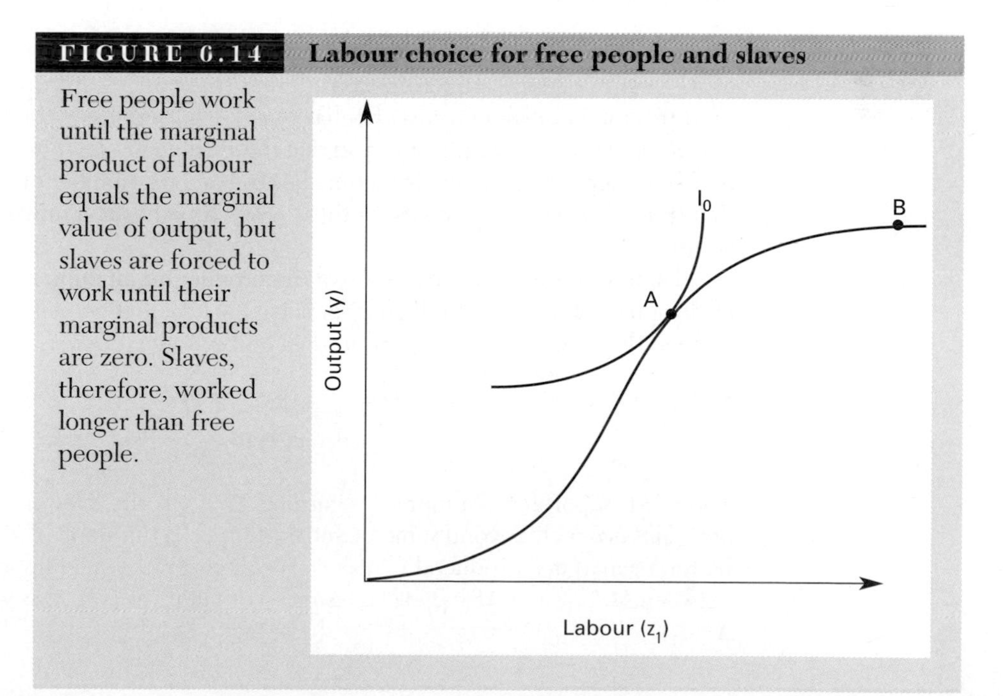

Consider Figure 6.14, which shows a production function for, say, cotton. As with all production functions, this one experiences diminishing marginal products. In this figure we've also shown the indifference curve I_0 for a free person. The indifference curve is upward sloping because working is a bad (that's why people have to be paid for it). Utility is also increasing as the output/labour combination moves up and to the left. A free person who grows cotton will maximize his or her utility by working at point A. At this point the marginal product of working just equals the marginal value of the output. The free person could work harder but doesn't want to.

Now consider the work effort of slaves. Because slaves don't get to decide how many hours they work, and because slave owners don't care about the leisure time of slaves, the owners will force the slaves to work until their marginal product is zero. This means that the slaves work until they reach point B. The slaves, because they work longer, will produce more than free white people.

This explains the puzzling historical fact of higher caloric intake by slaves. Since slaves worked longer (and harder) than poor free people, they simply required more food. If they didn't receive this food, they would have died, and no slave owners want their assets destroyed. Consistent with this, slaves were fed the cheapest food, not necessarily tasty, more valuable food. Slavery in agriculture always took place in warm climates where they could work all year long. Since slaves produced more over their lives than free people, slave owners were willing to pay more to keep them alive in case of injury or disease. As a result, owners would provide medical treatments that poor white families could not afford. In order to minimize medical expenses, slave owners often required slaves to stay away from lifestyles that were detrimental to their health. Some treatment of slaves by slave owners may look altruistic, but our production model shows that this behaviour was simply profit-maximizing on the part of the owners.

SUMMARY

We began this chapter by defining a *production function* and providing illustrations of it. Next, we spent some time considering that cost means opportunity cost, and what this might mean in terms of behaviour. Then we defined the *long-run cost-minimization problem* and then observed that there are many *short-run cost-minimization problems*, depending on the firm's time horizon and the number of variable inputs over that time horizon. The simplest of these is the time horizon in which only one input is variable.

Then we began our exploration of the production function by fixing the quantity of all inputs but one, input 1, thereby defining the *total product function* $TP(z_1)$. We then defined the concepts of *marginal product* and *average product*:

$$MP(z_1) = \text{slope of } TP(z_1)$$
$$AP(z_1) = TP(z_1)/z_1$$

The most important assumption regarding $TP(z_1)$ is the *assumption of diminishing marginal product*: beyond some quantity of input 1, the slope of $TP(z_1)$ begins to get flatter, or marginal product diminishes. We discovered some important interrelations between $MP(z_1)$ and $AP(z_1)$: $AP(z_1)$ is rising or falling as $MP(z_1)$ is greater or less than $AP(z_1)$.

We then learned virtually everything there is to know about costs in the simple one-variable-input case. Indeed, we developed a total of seven cost concepts, beginning with the variable cost function $VC(y)$:

$$VC(y) = \text{minimum expenditure on the variable input necessary to produce y units of output}$$

The expenditure on the fixed input, or the fixed cost FC, is held constant by definition and is therefore unrelated to the quantity of output.

All the other cost functions can be constructed from these two. First, by adding them up, we can define the *short-run total cost function*, $STC(y)$:

$$STC(y) = VC(y) + FC$$

Associated with each of these is an *average function*, which is derived simply by dividing by the quantity of output:

$$AVC(y) = VC(y)/y$$
$$SAC(y) = STC(y)/y$$
$$AFC(y) = FC/y$$

The *average fixed cost function* $AFC(y)$ is negatively sloped and asymptotic to both axes (that is, as y goes to zero, $AFC(y)$ goes to infinity, and as y goes to infinity, $AFC(y)$ goes to zero). In the standard case, both *average variable cost* $AVC(y)$ and *short-run average cost* $SAC(y)$ are U-shaped, and $SAC(y)$ lies above $AVC(y)$. Indeed, we can generate $SAC(y)$ from $AVC(y)$ by adding (vertically) $AFC(y)$ to $AVC(y)$:

$$SAC(y) = AVC(y) + AFC(y)$$

The most interesting cost concept is *short-run marginal cost*: the rate at which cost increases as output increases, or the added cost required to produce an additional unit of output. $SMC(y)$ can be derived from either $VC(y)$ or $STC(y)$ as follows:

$$SMC(y) = \text{slope of } VC(y) = \text{slope of } STC(y)$$

We also developed some important interrelationships: $SMC(y)$ intersects $AVC(y)$ at the point where $AVC(y)$ attains its minimum value. To the left of this point, where $SMC(y)$ is less than $AVC(y)$, $AVC(y)$ is falling as y increases; to the right of this point, where $SMC(y)$ exceeds $AVC(y)$, $AVC(y)$ is rising as y increases. The interrelationships between $SMC(y)$ and $SAC(y)$ are qualitatively the same as those between $SMC(y)$ and $AVC(y)$.

Finally, we considered a series of applications. In the traffic congestion problem, we discovered that to minimize total commuting costs, commuters travelling on two different routes should be allocated so that the marginal commuting costs on the two routes are identical. However, when commuters have unrestricted access to all routes, the equilibrium will be suboptimal because *average*, rather than *marginal*, commuting costs are equalized. We then saw how to find a toll that would shift the equilibrium to the optimum. Secondly, we reinterpreted these results in the context of a multi-plant firm that wanted to produce a fixed output at minimum variable cost. The firm must allocate its output so that the short-run marginal costs in all its plants are identical. Finally, we saw how the practice of equalizing marginal products could explain why sports dynasties are often short-lived, why submarines were not the only naval weapon during World War II, even though they were the most effective in total, why doctors in battle practise triage, and why textbook publishers print books across such different markets.

EXERCISES

In Exercises 1, 2, and 3, y is quantity of output and z is quantity of the variable input. In all three exercises, the total product function has the standard shape shown in Figure 6.3.

1. Suppose that the following statement is true: "When z increases from 10 to 11, average product increases from 45 to 48." Indicate whether each of the following statements is true, false, or uncertain; explain your answers.
   a. Output y is 450 when z is 10.
   b. When y is 450, *SMC* is upward sloping.
   c. When y is 450, *AVC* is downward sloping.
   d. When y is 450, *SAC* is downward sloping.
   e. When z is 10, *MP* is upward sloping.
   f. When z is 10, *MP* exceeds 45.
   g. When y is 450, *SMC* is less than *AVC*.
   h. When y is 450, *SMC* is less than *SAC*.
   i. *SAC* is greater when y is 450 than it is when y is 528.

2. Suppose that the following statement is true: "When y is 300, *SMC* is \$75, *SAC* is \$65, and *AP* is 30." Indicate whether each of the following statements is true, false, or uncertain; explain your answers.
   a. When y is 300, z is 10.
   b. When z is 10, *MP* is less than 30.
   c. When y is 300, *AVC* exceeds *SMC*.
   d. The point of diminishing returns to the variable input occurs where z is greater than 10.
   e. The price of the variable input is less than \$2000.
   f. The price of the variable input is greater than \$500.
   g. *VC* at y equal to 300 is less than \$20 000.

3. Suppose that the following statement is true: "When y is 100 units, *SMC* is \$100, *SMC* is upward sloping, *MP* is 10, and *AP* is 20." Indicate whether each of the following statements is true, false, or uncertain; explain your answers.
   a. The price of the variable input is \$1000.
   b. The price of the fixed input is \$1000.
   c. When z is 10, *MP* is downward sloping.
   d. When y is 100, *AVC* is less than *SMC*.
   e. When y is 100, *AVC* is \$50.
   f. When y is 100, *SAC* is upward sloping.
   g. When y is 100, *SAC* is greater than \$49.

4. "It's time to quit; we've all reached the point of diminishing returns." Does this comment make sense?

5. Consider the production function

$$y = \min(z_1, z_2)$$

   First, supposing that the quantity of input 2 is fixed at 100 units, derive and plot $TP(z_1)$, $MP(z_1)$, and $AP(z_1)$. Then, supposing that w_1 and w_2 are both \$1, derive all seven cost functions and plot them in a graph analogous to Figure 6.10.

6. Consider the following production function:

$$y = (z_1)^{1/3}(z_2)^{2/3}$$

   Input prices are $w_1 = \$2$ and $w_2 = \$3$.
   a. Suppose that z_2 is fixed at 1 unit: $z_2 = 1$. Derive the total product function, the variable cost function, the average variable cost function, and the short-run total cost function. (*Hint*: To find the variable cost function, first observe that y^3 units of z_1 are needed to produce y units of output when $z_2 = 1$, and then compute the cost of y^3 units of input 1.)
   b. Now suppose that z_2 is fixed at 8 units; repeat the same exercises.
   c. Using the cost functions from (a) and (b), compute and compare the variable and short-run total cost of producing 1, 2, 3, and 4 units of output.

7. A firm owns two plants that produce the same good. The marginal cost functions for the two plants are

$$SMC_1 = 10y_1$$
$$SMC_2 = 5y_2$$

where y_1 and y_2 are quantities of output produced in each plant.

a. If the firm wants to produce fifteen units of output at minimum cost, how much should it produce in each plant?
b. Now consider an arbitrary quantity of output y. To minimize costs, what fraction of the total output should the firm produce in each plant?

8. If a firm has two plants and can vary just one input, then to minimize cost it should allocate output to the plants so that the marginal product of the variable input is the same in the two plants. Explain.

9. Examination writing poses an interesting economic problem. For simplicity, think of a three-hour final examination with two 50-point essay questions. The student has 180 minutes to allocate to the two questions. What principles should guide the student's allocation of time if the student's objective is to maximize the mark received on the examination? How does this argument extend to studying for different courses during the exam week? Will students study the courses they enjoy more if they are only interested in maximizing their grade point average?

10. Hank works for his dad, producing widgets by tending his dad's magic widget maker. (His dad does not allow anyone else to touch the machine.) For every hour he tends the machine, Hank produces ten widgets. His dad pays Hank $10 per hour for the first eight hours in any day, $20 per hour for the next eight hours, and $40 per hour for the last eight hours of the day.

a. Find *VC*, *AVC*, and *SMC*.
b. Now suppose that Hank's dad can sell each widget for $2.50 and that he wants to maximize his profit. How many widgets should he ask Hank to produce, and how many hours per day will Hank have to work?

11. "I currently have a job, and I hope the cost of staying at the job will rise dramatically." Does this make any sense? Explain.

12. Ralph is a surgeon and, like his neighbour Tim (a teacher), he enjoys woodwork. Ralph had recently purchased a special saw to save some time, but later decided it was too dangerous and sold it to Tim. Tim is like the Three Stooges when it comes to safety, but he uses the saw all the time. Why would he do this when his careful neighbour thought it was too dangerous?

13. Airlines always try to overbook their flights. If a situation arises where enough seats are not available, the airline bids for passengers to be bumped to another flight. For compensation, the airline supplies an additional ticket for any flight over the next year. Suppose an average airfare is worth $300. It seems likely that many passengers would be willing to wait for $300 (quite often the wait is only one or two hours, and many times passengers argue over who will be bumped). Why would the airline pay so much when it could pay less?

14. What happens to the cost of completing high school if the minimum driving age is raised to 18?

15. How long will you wait for an elevator if you value the ride at $10 and the value of your time is $5 per 15 minutes? Suppose you know that the elevator is working, but you have no idea what floor it is currently on. (*Hint*: Is your waiting time a sunk cost?)

16. Suppose the front right brake on your car starts to make a grinding noise and you decide to replace the right brake pads (each wheel has two brake pads). However, when you go to your local auto-parts store, you find that you cannot buy one set of brake pads, since they come in sets of four. Hence, after you replace the right side, you've got a pair of pads left over. You cannot take the extra pads back to the store for a refund, but you do have a left wheel on your car that also uses brakes. Suppose the complete set of pads cost you $25. To replace the left brake pads is going to take you one half-hour, and you value your time at $20 per hour. The value you place on having new left brake pads in place is $15. Should you replace the left brake pads?

17. When Emily takes a nap, she always gets a cramp in her leg. Her sister Alison never gets a cramp when she takes a nap. Is it more costly for Emily to take a nap than for Alison?

18. On a certain section of the Trans-Canada highway, 3000 cars can travel without impeding each other's speed between points T and H. When

the highway is uncongested, the trip takes one hour. Travel on the side roads always takes 2 hours for the same trip regardless of the number of cars. Each car beyond the 3000 increases the trip time by 6 minutes.

a, If there are no tolls on the highway, how many cars will use the highway? Is this an efficient use of the highway?
b. If the highway was owned by Conrad Brown, a private individual, what toll would be charged, assuming all drivers value their time at $10 per hour? Does this lead to an efficient use of the highway?
c. What would happen if the value of time was $6 per hour? What would happen to the number of people using the highway?

19. Everyone who gets a speeding ticket mumbles to themselves, "Why can't the police spend their time catching real criminals?" Why don't the police spend all their time preventing murders and rapes?

20. Why are public swimming pools more crowded than private ones run for public use? What can you say about the respective marginal and average products at each of the pools?

21. On every sports team there is the star scorer. In hockey, basketball, football, rugby — you name it — there is a person who is most likely to score if given the puck or ball. Why is it that this person does not take all of the shots?

22. Different types of cars are stolen at different rates: sports cars and trucks are stolen often, while Ford Escort station wagons are not stolen often at all. It is not sufficient to say that thieves only go after the most valuable vehicles, because these are also the vehicles that are better protected. Some vehicles are clearly overprotected. Using the notion of declining fixed costs of production, can you explain this?

23. Along the same line of reasoning as Exercise 22, why do drive-through bank machines have Braille lettering on the buttons?

24. Studies have shown that mandatory attendance to university classes increases an average student's grade by 6.7 percent This evidence has been used to suggest that students who skip classes are not acting rationally. One study stated, "A mandatory class attendance policy would help students make rational intertemporal tradeoff choices." What very simple economic fact is missing from this argument?

The following production function is used in problems 25, 26, and 27.

$$y = (z_1)^{1/3}(z_2)^{2/3}$$

where z_1 is the fixed input and z_2 the variable input. There are two plants using this technology: in plant 1, quantity of the fixed input is $z_1 = 1$, and in plant 2, quantity of the fixed input is $z_1 = 2$. The price of the variable input is $w_2 = \$5$.

25. Find the total, average, and marginal product functions for the two plants. Then find the variable cost, the average variable cost, and the marginal cost functions for the two plants.

26. What allocation of output to the two plants minimizes the total variable cost of producing 120 units of output? What is the minimized variable cost of producing 120 units? What is marginal product in plant 1 and in plant 2 when total variable cost is minimized?

27. Now consider the production of an arbitrary quantity y of output.

a. What allocation of output y to the two plants minimizes total variable cost?
b. Write down the function that gives minimized total variable cost as a function of the quantity of output y.

28. A firm has the production function $f(Z_1,Z_2) = Z_1^{1/2} + Z_2^{1/2}$. If the prices of Z_1 and Z_2 are W_1 and W_2 and Z_2 are fixed at 4,

a. Find this firm's *TP* and *MP* functions.
b. What are the firm's variable cost, total cost and marginal cost functions?

REFERENCES

Douglas, P. H. 1948. "Are There Laws of Production?" *American Economic Review*, 67:297–308.

Frost, R. 1973. *The Road Not Taken*, commentary by L. Untermeyer. New York: Holt, Rinehart and Winston.

CHAPTER 7

Production and Cost: Many Variable Inputs

In Chapter 6, we concentrated on the simple case in which only one input in a production process was variable. In this chapter, we use the understanding developed in Chapter 6 to explore cost and production in the more complicated, realistic environment in which more than one input is variable. In most real situations, firms do have the flexibility to vary more than one input during the relevant period. For example, if the Canadian Pacific Railroad wants to increase the amount of coal it hauls out of northern British Columbia, it can usually acquire new rolling stock and hire more train crews within six weeks. If it wants to double its existing track, it can acquire the additional quantities of inputs such as tracks, ties, and signalling equipment, but it needs much more lead time. If it wants to add whole new lines, it can again alter the quantities of the inputs it uses, but it needs an even longer lead time. These lead times themselves are not fixed, since faster adjustment times can be accomplished with higher costs.

7.1 Isoquants and Input Substitution

In Chapter 6, we defined the production function, $y = F(z_1, z_2)$, and began to explore it by fixing the quantity of one input to define the total product function. This allowed us to see how output changed as the quantity of the variable input changed. In this section, we resume our exploration of the production function by fixing the quantity of output. This procedure allows us to investigate input substitution — that is, how one input can be substituted for another. Our goal is to understand the many ways in which a fixed quantity of output can be produced.

isoquant

An **isoquant** is a curve composed of all the input bundles that produce some fixed quantity of output. Isoquants are to production theory what indifference curves are to consumer theory. Just as indifference curves in consumer theory represent all the consumption bundles that a person ranks as equally attractive, an isoquant in production theory represents all the input bundles that can produce the same quantity of output.

To get a sense of what isoquants are, let us return to Tipple's production function for courier services,

$$y = (1200z_1z_2)^{1/2}$$

Recall that y is the quantity of courier services measured in kilometres, z_1 is hours of a driver's time, and z_2 is gallons of gas. By fixing y, we define an isoquant. For example, suppose we fix y at 120 kilometres. Then, setting y equal to 120 in the expression above gives us the following algebraic description of the isoquant:

$$120 = (1200 z_1 z_2)^{1/2}$$

Now, squaring both sides of this expression and dividing by 1200 gives us a simpler expression for the isoquant:

$$12 = z_1 z_2$$

This expression tells us every input bundle combination that produces 120 kilometres of courier services. For example, the input bundle might be composed of 2 hours of a driver's time and 6 litres of gasoline, or 3 hours of a driver's time and 4 litres of gasoline, or 4 hours of a driver's time and 3 litres of gasoline. In Figure 7.1, we have constructed both this isoquant and the isoquant for 240 kilometres. As you can verify, the 240-kilometre isoquant can be described by the following equation: $48 = z_1 z_2$.

Just as any indifference map is filled with indifference curves, any isoquant map is filled with isoquants. And just as the farther an indifference curve is from the origin, the higher its utility number, so, too, the farther an isoquant is from the origin, the higher the level of output associated with it.

The Shape of Isoquants

Notice that both isoquants in Figure 7.1 are smooth and that their slopes decrease from left to right. But do all isoquants look like this? Are other general shapes possible? Try the following problem to find out.

FIGURE 7.1 **Isoquants for courier services**

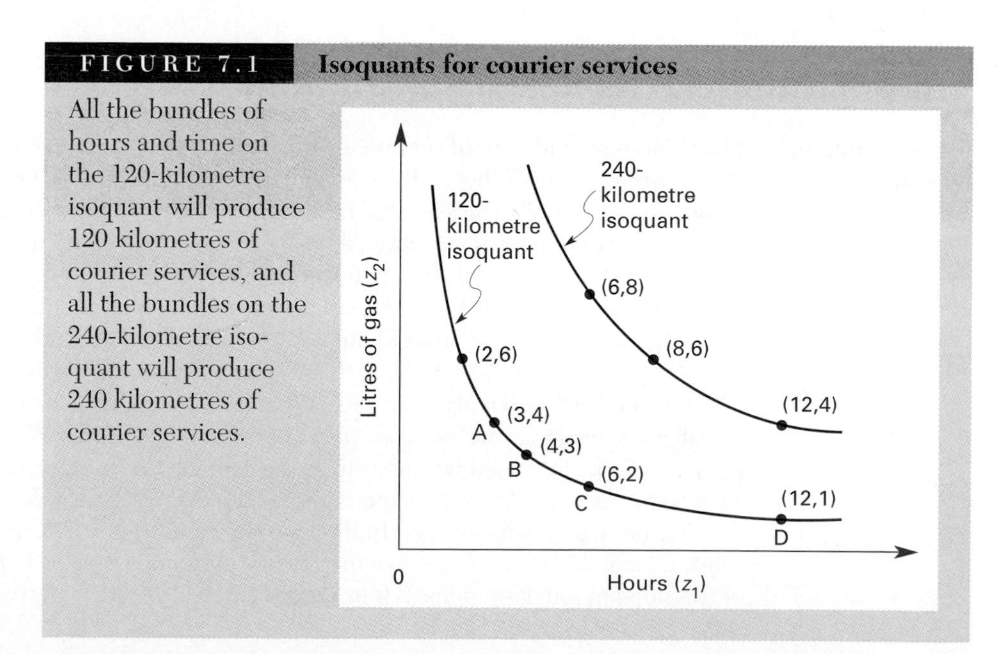

All the bundles of hours and time on the 120-kilometre isoquant will produce 120 kilometres of courier services, and all the bundles on the 240-kilometre isoquant will produce 240 kilometres of courier services.

PROBLEM 7.1

1. John Henry uses a furnace and fuel to produce heat. The furnace can use either coal or wood for fuel. One tonne of coal produces 5 kilojoules of heat, and one tonne of wood produces 2 kilojoules. Given the furnace, the production function for heat is

$$y = 5z_1 + 2z_2$$

where y is kilojoules of heat, z_1 is tonnes of coal, and z_2 is tonnes of wood. Construct the isoquant for 20 kilojoules.

2. The standard bartender's recipe for rum-and-Coke calls for 10 millilitres of rum and 30 millilitres of Coke. The implied production function is

$$y = \min(z_1/10, z_2/30)$$

where y is number of drinks, z_1 is millilitres of rum, and z_2 is millilitres of Coke. Construct the isoquant for two drinks.

As you discovered in Problem 7.1, isoquants may take different forms. But what can we learn from the shapes of isoquants? For example, what is the economic meaning of the differences between the isoquants in Figures 7.2a and 7.2b? (These are the isoquants you constructed in Problem 7.1.) Notice that the shape of each is distinctive. In Figure 7.2a, the slope of the isoquant is constant throughout. In Figure 7.2b, the slope of the isoquant is infinite above the kink and zero to the right of the kink. At the kink itself, the isoquant has no well-defined slope. What does the slope of an isoquant tell us? And what is the significance of the fact that the isoquant in Figure 7.2b is kinked? Before we can answer these questions, we need a new tool — a measure called the marginal rate of technical substitution.

7.2 Marginal Rate of Technical Substitution

marginal rate of technical substitution

The term **marginal rate of technical substitution** deliberately echoes another familiar one from consumer theory: the marginal rate of substitution (*MRS*). In consumption theory, we used *MRS* to measure the rate at which one good was substituted for another, holding utility constant. The marginal rate of technical substitution (*MRTS*) measures the rate at which one input can be substituted for the other, holding output constant.

To begin, we will pick an arbitrary input bundle — say, bundle A in Figure 7.3 — on the isoquant for 100 units of output. Our objective is to find *MRTS* at bundle A. Imagine that the firm is initially at A and consider a nonmarginal reduction in the quantity of input 1 by 5 units — $\Delta z_1 = 5$. What increase in the quantity of input 2 — Δz_2 — will compensate for the reduction in quantity of input 1? From Figure 7.3 we see that input 2 must be increased by 3 units to get back to the isoquant for 100 units of output. That is, the increase $\Delta z_2 = 3$ compensates for the decrease $\Delta z_1 = 5$. The ratio $\Delta z_2/\Delta z_1$ is a discrete rate of substitution. In the case shown in Figure 7.3, this discrete rate of substitution is 3/5 or 0.6. Notice that this rate of substitution is equal to the absolute value of the slope of the dashed line AB in Figure 7.3.

FIGURE 7.2 Some illustrative isoquants

In (a), where inputs 1 and 2 are perfect substitutes, any bundle on the isoquant will produce 20 kilojoules (thermal units) of heat. In (b), where inputs 1 and 2 are perfect complements, any bundle on the isoquant will produce two drinks.

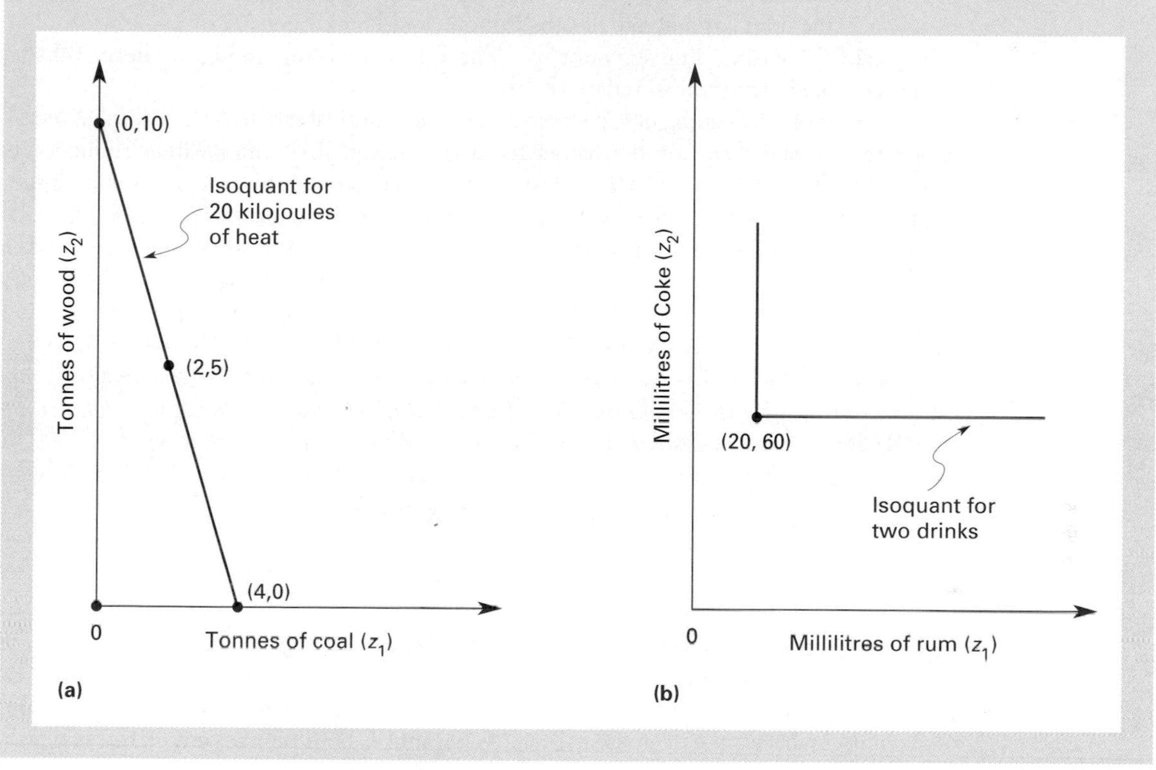

FIGURE 7.3 The marginal rate of technical substitution, *MRTS*

The marginal rate of technical substitution *MRTS* at point A is the absolute value of the slope of the line *TT*, which is tangent to the isoquant at A.

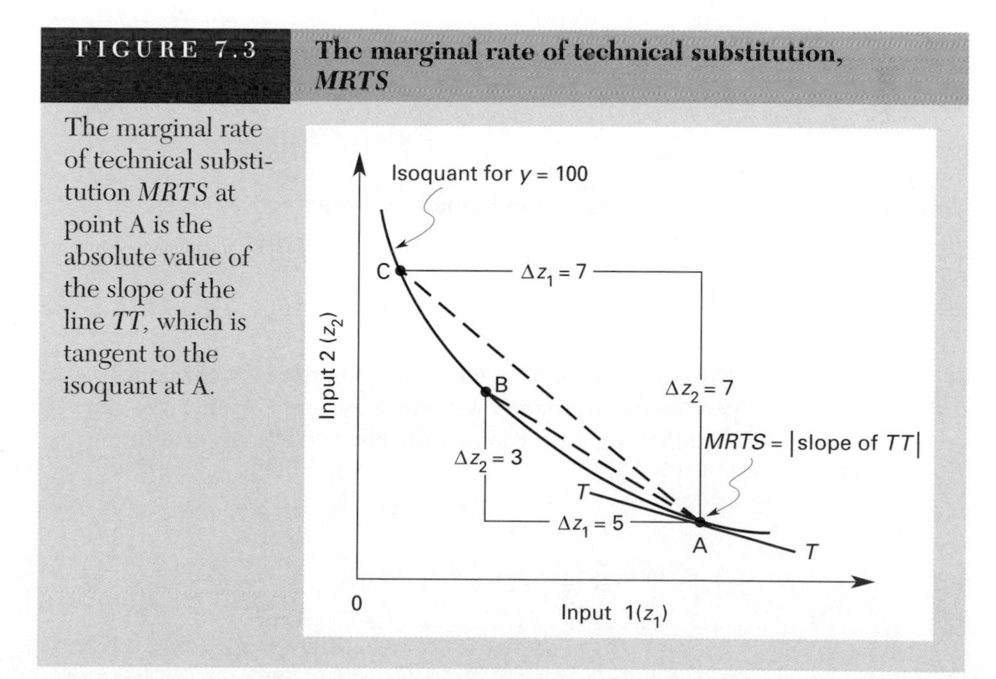

The ratio $\Delta z_2/\Delta z_1$ is called a *rate of substitution* because it tells us the rate at which we must increase quantity of input 2 per unit reduction in quantity of input 1. It is *discrete* because the initial reduction in quantity of input 1 is a *measurable change*. The ratio $\Delta z_2/\Delta z_1$ is an ambiguous and therefore an unsatisfactory measure because it depends on the magnitude of Δz_1. As you can see from Figure 7.3, had we chosen $\Delta z_1 = 7$, the nonmarginal rate of substitution would have been 7/7 or 1 — the absolute value of the dashed line segment AC. There is a troubling ambiguity here. What is the rate of substitution — 0.6 or 1?

To resolve this ambiguity, economists use the marginal rate of technical substitution, *MRTS*: the rate of substitution associated with a marginal, or infinitesimal, reduction in quantity of input 1. To find *MRTS*, just imagine what happens to the discrete rate of substitution as Δz_1 gets smaller and smaller, eventually approaching zero. For $\Delta z_1 = 7$, the discrete rate of substitution is determined by the slope of the dashed line segment AC. For $\Delta z_1 = 5$, the discrete rate of substitution is determined by the slope of the dashed line segment AB. Notice that as Δz_1 approaches zero, the dashed line segment approaches the line labelled *TT* tangent to the isoquant at input bundle A. Therefore, *MRTS* at bundle A is the absolute value of the slope of *TT*. Or, more formally: *the marginal rate of technical substitution of input 2 for input 1 at any input bundle (z_1, z_2), denoted by $MRTS(z_1, z_2)$, is the absolute value of the slope of the isoquant at that point.*

To get a better working knowledge of *MRTS*, let us find out what *MRTS* is for Tipple's Courier Service. The production function is

$$y = (1200 z_1 z_2)^{1/2}$$

Our objective is to find *MRTS* at an arbitrary bundle (z_1, z_2). If we reduce quantity of input 1 by Δz_1 and compensate for the reduction by increasing quantity of input 2 by Δz_2, we get input bundle: $(z_1 - \Delta z_1, z_2 + \Delta z_2)$. Since the increase in quantity of input 2 compensates for the decrease in quantity of input 1, both bundles are on the same isoquant. Alternatively, both bundles produce the same output y. This last statement gives us the following equations:

$$y = (1200 z_1 z_2)^{1/2}$$
$$y = [1200(z_1 - \Delta z_1)(z_2 + \Delta z_2)]^{1/2}$$

Setting the right sides of these equations equal to each other and solving explicitly for Δz_2, we get

$$\Delta z_2 = (z_2 \Delta z_1)/(z_1 - \Delta z_1)$$

This equation gives us the increase in quantity of input 2 — Δz_2 — needed to compensate for an arbitrary decrease in quantity of input 1 — Δz_1. Using this result, we get the following expression for the discrete rate of substitution:

$$\Delta z_2/\Delta z_1 = z_2/(z_1 - \Delta z_1)$$

Then, letting Δz_1 approach 0, we get

$$MRTS = z_2/z_1$$

In Figure 7.1 we plotted two isoquants for Tipple's Courier Service. Using this formula, you can calculate *MRTS* for any point on these isoquants. At input bundle (2,6) for example, *MRTS* is 3. Notice that as we move from left to right along either of these isoquants, *MRTS* continually decreases.

PROBLEM 7.2

The following isoquant for heat produced from coal (input 1) and wood (input 2) as fuels is plotted in Figure 7.2a:

$$20 = 5z_1 + 2z_2$$

Determine the *MRTS* of wood for coal for all points along this isoquant.

Perfect Substitutes and Perfect Complements

There are two extreme cases of input substitutability — *perfect substitutes* and *perfect complements*. You saw in Problem 7.2 that wood can be substituted for coal in the production of heat at a constant rate of 5/2. If the quantity of coal is reduced by 2 tonnes, for example, then the quantity of wood must be increased by 5 tonnes (2 tonnes × 5/2) to maintain heat output. Or, if the product is denim jeans, and if input 1 is cotton thread and input 2 is polyester thread, polyester thread can be substituted for cotton thread at the constant rate 1/1. When inputs are **perfect substitutes**, one input can always be substituted for the other on fixed terms and *MRTS* is constant.

perfect substitutes

PROBLEM 7.3

The following isoquant for two rum (z_2) and Coke (z_1) cocktails is plotted in Figure 7.2b.

$$2 = \min(z_1/10,\ z_2/30)$$

Now determine the *MRTS* of Coke for rum for all points along the horizontal and vertical segments of the isoquant. Is *MRTS* defined at input bundle (20,60)?

As you saw in answering Problem 7.3, when mixing standard rum-and-Cokes, more Coke is *not* a substitute for less rum: a bartender who has only 20 millilitres of rum cannot make more than two rum-and-Cokes no matter how much Coke is on hand. So, too, in producing fasteners from nuts and bolts, more bolts cannot be substituted for fewer nuts. When inputs are **perfect complements**, substitution is impossible, and *MRTS* cannot be defined for the bundle at the kink in the isoquant.

perfect complements

Diminishing Marginal Rate of Technical Substitution

Most interesting economic cases fall somewhere in between perfect substitutes and perfect complements: one input can be substituted for the other, but the *MRTS* is not a constant. This intermediate case is represented by the isoquants for Tipple's Courier Service in Figure 7.1. In such intermediate cases, it becomes progressively more difficult to substitute one input for the other. To see why, let us substitute input 1 for input 2 on the 120-kilometre isoquant in Figure 7.1. In the move from A to B, 1 added hour of time substitutes for 1 less litre of gas, while in the move from B to C, 2 added hours are needed to substitute for 1 less litre, and in the move from C to D, 6 added hours are needed to substitute for 1 less litre. This diminishing capacity to substitute one input for another seems to make intuitively good sense. Notice, too, it means that *MRTS* gets smaller and smaller, or diminishes, from left to right along an isoquant. A diminishing *MRTS* is an assumption that is commonly adopted in production theory.

MRTS as a Ratio of Marginal Products

Now we want to establish an important relationship between *MRTS* and the *marginal products* of the two inputs. The marginal rate of technical substitution of input 2 for input 1 is equal to the marginal product of input 1 divided by the marginal product of input 2.

To understand why this is true, notice first that when the quantity of input 1 is decreased by Δz_1, the change in total output y is (approximately) the marginal product of input 1 multiplied by the change in quantity of input 1:

$$\Delta y = MP_1 \Delta z_1$$

Since Δz_2 compensates for this reduction in z_1, it must produce an identical change in output, Δy. Thus,

$$\Delta y = MP_2 \Delta z_2$$

Of course, when Δz_1 is very small, *MRTS* is approximately $\Delta z_2/\Delta z_1$. Solving the first of these approximations for Δz_1 and the second for Δz_2 and then forming the substitution ratio $\Delta z_2/\Delta z_1$ yields

$$MRTS = (\Delta y/MP_2)/(\Delta y/MP_1)$$

But this expression reduces to

$$MRTS = MP_1/MP_2$$

Or, to restate this expression in words:

MRTS is equal to the marginal product of input 1 divided by the marginal product of input 2.[1]

1. We can use the implicit function theorem to express *MRTS* in terms of the partial derivatives of $F(\bullet)$. The isoquant for y^0 units of output can be written as

$$y^0 = F(z_1, z_2)$$

where y^0 is fixed and z_1 and z_2 are free to vary. Since the isoquant defines z_2 as an implicit function of z_1, we can use the implicit function theorem to express this isoquant as

$$z_2 = g(z_1)$$

MRTS is, of course, just $-g'(z_1)$, where $g'(z_1)$ is the derivative of $g(z_1)$. Combining these equations, we have the following identity

$$y^0 \equiv F[z_1, g(z_1)]$$

Differentiating the identity with respect to z_1 gives us

$$\partial F[z_1, g(z_1)]/\partial z_1 + \partial F[z_1, g(z_1)]/\partial z_2 = 0$$

The partial derivative $\partial F(z_1, z_2)/\partial z_i$ is, of course, the marginal product of input i. Rearranging this equation, we get

$$-g'(z_1) = \frac{\partial F(z_1, z_2)/\partial z_1}{\partial F(z_1, z_2)/\partial z_2}$$

But the left side of this equation is just *MRTS*. Hence,

$$MRTS\ (z_1, z_2) = \frac{\partial F(z_1, z_2)/\partial z_1}{\partial F(z_1, z_2)/\partial z_2}$$

Thus, for example, for the production function $F(z_1, z_2) = z_1 z_2$, $MRTS(z_1, z_2) = z_2/z_1$.

Application: Religious Inputs and Church Growth

The theory of production is very general, and has applications well beyond an imaginary firm producing widgets. One can think of churches as firms that convert (pardon the pun) inputs like labour, buildings, and literature into outputs like more believers. Iannaccone, et al. (1995) analyze growth in church membership in light of two inputs: time and money. To study this relationship they employ the Cobb-Douglas production function that was introduced in Chapter 6. In particular, they suggest that:

$$G = T^u M^v$$

where G is the growth rate of the church, T is the amount of time devoted by church members, M is the amount of money given to the church, and u and v are parameters.

Iannaccone, et al. find some very interesting things. First, not surprisingly, the marginal products of time and money are both positive. That is, if church members devote more time and/or more money to their church, the church grows. For the past hundred years mainstream churches such as the Methodists, Episcopalians, and Lutherans have been losing memberships, while the more fundamentalist churches, like the Baptists, Evangelicals, and Pentecostals, have been growing. These latter churches, it turns out, put more demands on their memberships to give both time and money. As a result, they experience an increased output in terms of membership.

A second, and more interesting result, is that time and money are substitutes in production. A membership can reduce the amount of financial giving and still achieve high growth rates if the time input is increased enough. The most striking example of this comes from the differences in inputs between the Mormons and Jehovah's Witnesses. As was mentioned in Chapter 4, Jehovah's Witnesses devote a great deal of time to their religion, but are not large financial givers. The Mormons, on the other hand, give a great deal of money, but devote little time to their religion. Both have high growth rates. In other words, despite using strikingly different input bundles, they are both able to reach high isoquant levels.

7.3 Returns to Scale

So far we have used two strategies to explore the production function. In the last chapter we held quantity of one input constant so that we could look at the relationship between quantity of the variable input and quantity of output. In the preceding two sections of this chapter, we held output constant so that we could look at the way in which one input can be substituted for another. In this section, we will hold the *input mix* constant so that we can look at the relationship between the *scale of production* and *quantity of output*.

Once again Tipple's Courier Service provides a convenient example. Notice that input mix is *constant* along any ray through the origin in Figure 7.4. For all input bundles on ray 0A in Figure 7.4, for example, the ratio of z_1 to z_2 is 3. Therefore, as we move along the ray, the **scale of production** — but not the input mix — changes. How does output respond to a change in scale of production along ray 0A? Suppose we start at bundle (6,2) on the 120-kilometre isoquant. If we were to double the scale of production, we would get input bundle (12,4) on the 240-kilometre isoquant. If we were to triple the scale of production, we would get input bundle (18,6) on the 360-kilometre isoquant. And, finally, if we were to quadruple the scale of production, we would get input bundle (24,8) on the 480-kilometre isoquant. Notice that when we doubled the

scale of production

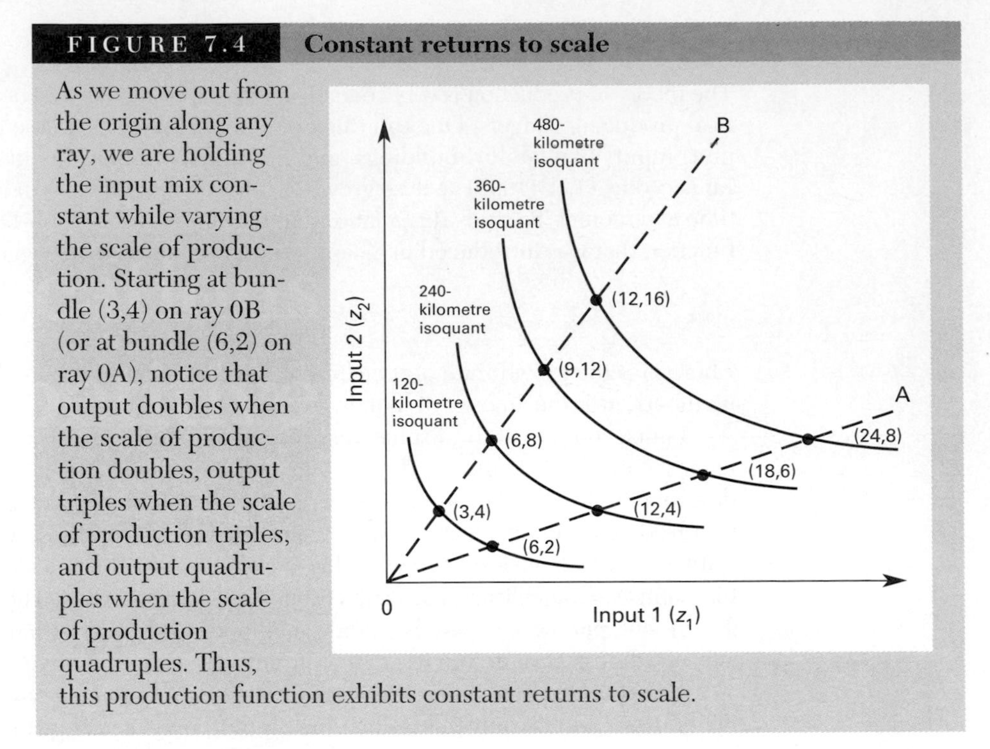

FIGURE 7.4 Constant returns to scale

As we move out from the origin along any ray, we are holding the input mix constant while varying the scale of production. Starting at bundle (3,4) on ray 0B (or at bundle (6,2) on ray 0A), notice that output doubles when the scale of production doubles, output triples when the scale of production triples, and output quadruples when the scale of production quadruples. Thus, this production function exhibits constant returns to scale.

scale of production, output doubled; when we tripled the scale of production, output tripled; when we quadrupled the scale of production, output quadrupled. Notice also that there is nothing special about ray 0A. Had we chosen ray 0B instead, we would have arrived at the same conclusion: when we increase the scale of production by some factor a, output increases by the same factor a. These observations reflect the fact that Tipple's production function exhibits *constant returns to scale*.

It is useful to define constant returns to scale more carefully. Beginning at bundle (z_1, z_2), if we increase the scale of production by factor $a > 1$, we get bundle (az_1, az_2). Of course, output at the initial bundle is $F(z_1, z_2)$, and output at the scaled-up bundle is $F(az_1, az_2)$. A firm experiences **constant returns to scale** if

constant returns to scale

$$F(az_1, az_2) = aF(z_1, z_2) \quad \text{for } a > 1$$

To get a better understanding of this definition, let us use it to verify what we learned from Figure 7.4 — that Tipple's production function has constant returns to scale. For Tipple, $F(z_1, z_2)$ is $(1200z_1z_2)^{1/2}$. To get an expression for $F(az_1, az_2)$, simply substitute az_1 for z_1 and az_2 for z_2 in this production function to get $(1200az_1az_2)^{1/2}$. But this can be rewritten as $a(1200z_1z_2)^{1/2}$, which is just $aF(z_1, z_2)$. And we see that Tipple's production does exhibit constant returns to scale.

Constant returns to scale is thought by many economists to characterize many actual production processes, but it is definitely not the only possible case. In particular, increasing returns to scale is important in many production processes. A firm experiences **increasing returns to scale** if

increasing returns to scale

$$F(az_1, az_2) > aF(z_1, z_2) \quad \text{for } a > 1$$

For example, if a firm doubles its scale of production and its output triples, then this is a case of increasing returns to scale. The following problem allows you to begin the exploration of the geometric foundations of increasing returns to scale.

PROBLEM 7.4

Galina's product is "fenced pasture land," measured in square metres. She produces it with two inputs. Input 1 is land (measured in square metres) and input 2 is barbed wire (measured in metres). The barbed wire is used to fence the land. Galina's pastures are square, and she needs a metre of barbed wire to produce a metre of fencing. Her production function is

$$y = \min[z_1, (z_2/4)^2]$$

That is, given z_1 square metres of land, Galina can produce a pasture no larger than z_1 square metres, and given z_2 metres of barbed wire, she can fence a pasture no larger than $(z_2/4)^2$ square metres since each side uses $z_2/4$ metres of barbed wire.

a. Suppose that Galina's initial input bundle is (20,8). She can then produce just 4 square metres of fenced pasture. Show that her output more than doubles as she doubles the scale of production, or that there are increasing returns to scale.

b. Suppose that Galina's initial bundle is (120,48). She can then produce 120 square metres of fenced pasture. Show that her output doubles as she doubles the scale of production, or that there are constant returns to scale.

Most examples of increasing returns to scale result from the fact that we live in a world of one, two, and three dimensions. This mixture of dimensions means that various components of production change in such a way that yield increasing returns to scale. Problem 7.4 demonstrated this: doubling the length of fencing results in a quadratic increase in the amount of pasture fenced. This effect of geometry can be found everywhere. Increases in the surface area of containers by some factor x leads to a cubing of the volume of the container (x^3). Hence, containers for oil, grains, and other bulk goods tend to be quite large. Blast furnaces, steam engines, and ships all experience increasing returns to scale due to the multiple dimensions involved.[2]

decreasing returns to scale

We can complete this classification of returns to scale by defining decreasing returns to scale. A firm experiences **decreasing returns to scale** if

$$F(az_1, az_2) < aF(z_1, z_2) \quad \text{for } a > 1$$

With decreasing returns to scale, if a firm doubles its scale of production, its output increases by less than double. If the production function includes all relevant inputs, it is difficult to imagine decreasing returns to scale. After all, by exactly replicating what was done with the initial input bundle, a firm can double output when the scale

2. See Lipsey (2000) for a discussion of these issues.

of production is doubled. For this reason, decreasing returns to scale are usually attributed to unmeasured or hidden inputs.[3]

From Problem 7.4 it is clear that mixed cases of returns to scale are possible. It is perfectly possible, for example, that there are initial increasing returns to scale and eventual decreasing returns to scale.

PROBLEM 7.5

Consider the following general form of the Cobb-Douglas production function:

$$y = Az_1^u z_2^v$$

where A, u, and v are positive constants. Show that there are increasing, constant, or decreasing returns to scale as $u + v$ exceeds, is equal to, or is less than 1.

Application: Centres of Excellence

In Chapter 6 we noted that sports dynasties were quite rare, due to the diminishing marginal product of individual sports superstars. In academia the opposite often happens: dynasties are quite common, and are often called centres of excellence. Princeton, for example, has the Center for Advanced Studies (originally designed for economists!), where Albert Einstein spent the last years of his life. The University of Chicago, another private university, has won more Nobel prizes than any other university in the world and has been consistently in the top 5 percent of universities for almost a century.

One explanation for this observation is that the "synergy" of collecting a group of high-quality minds creates an academic production function that has increasing returns to scale. Suppose y is a composite good called "academic output," and suppose it is produced with three academics according to the following production function:

$$y = 3z_1z_2z_3,$$

where z_i (i =1, 2, 3) is the skill level of the three academics. Note that output is higher the higher the skill of the academics.

Now suppose there are two universities: Joe Blow University and the University of Toronto. Suppose the U of T has two academics with a skill level of 0.8 and assume that JBU also has two academics but each with a skill level of 0.5. Assume that both universities are competing for a third faculty member, of which there are only two available: one with a skill level of 0.8 (academic A) and the other with a skill level of 0.6 (academic B). Obviously each university prefers A to B. Each university is guaranteed B if it is unable to get A.

The output of U of T with academic B is 3(0.8)(0.8)(0.6) = 1.152, while the output of JBU with B is 3(0.5)(0.5)(0.6) = 0.45. The output of U of T with A is 3(0.8)(0.8)(0.8) = 1.536, and the output for JBU is 3(0.5)(0.5)(0.8) = 0.6. Hence U of T is willing to pay

3. Returns to scale for homogeneous production functions deserve special attention. A production function is homogeneous of degree $h > 0$ if

$$F(az_1, az_2) = a^hF(z_1, z_2) \text{ for all } a > 0$$

As you can easily show, for a homogeneous production function there are decreasing, constant, or increasing returns to scale as the degree of homogeneity h is less than, equal to, or greater than 1.

a premium amount of 1.536 – 1.152 = 0.384 to attract academic A and JBU is only willing to pay a premium of 0.6 – 0.45 = 0.15 to attract academic A.

Clearly the better academics at the University of Toronto allow it to attract better academics because of the increasing returns to scale. This effect is self-perpetuating. Low-quality schools are unable to attract high-quality faculty because of the interactive effects (sometimes called network effects) that generate higher output at the high-quality schools. In 1999 the economist Robert Barro made headlines when Columbia University offered him \$400 000 per year to leave Harvard. No economist at an average school is paid even close to this sum. When academics are characterized by economies of scale, better academics are attracted to better schools, even when there is just a marginal difference in skill levels. Hence small differences in skills can lead to large differences in incomes.

7.4 The Cost-Minimization Problem: A Perspective

Now we are ready to define the long-run cost-minimization problem and to use the solution — a system of input demand functions that identifies the least costly input bundle for any level of output — to form the cost function. The *cost function* tells us the minimum cost of producing any level of output in the long run. Before plunging into a detailed analysis of cost minimization, however, let us put the **long-run cost-minimization problem** and its solution into perspective. From Section 6.3, we know that the long-run cost-minimization problem will take this form:

long-run cost-minimization problem

$$\begin{aligned}&\text{minimize } w_1 z_1 + w_2 z_2\\&\text{choosing } z_1 \text{ and } z_2\\&\text{subject to the constraint } y = F(z_1, z_2)\end{aligned}$$

Before we solve this problem, we must distinguish between the variables being chosen, or determined (the *endogenous* variables), and the variables that are givens (the *exogenous* variables).

In this problem, the endogenous variables are the quantities of the two inputs, z_1 and z_2. The exogenous variables are the prices of the two inputs w_1 and w_2 and the level of output y. The input prices are, we assume, genuinely outside the firm's control; from the firm's point of view, they are fixed. The fact that output is exogenous in this problem simply reflects the fact that we are analyzing the firm's problem in stages. In the next stage (considered in later chapters), we will combine the cost function developed in this chapter with revenue considerations to analyze the firm's choice of output. For now, however, we assume that the level of output is fixed.

The solution to the cost-minimization problem gives us the cost-minimizing values of the endogenous variables, written as z_1^* and z_2^*, as functions of the exogenous variables y, w_1, and w_2. These functions are simply the rules prescribing the quantity of each input that minimizes the cost of producing y units of output when the prices of the inputs are w_1 and w_2. Because the quantity demanded of each input is so clearly dependent, or *conditional*, on the level of output y, these input demand functions are usually called **conditional input demand functions**.

conditional input demand functions

Once we know these demand functions, determining the **long-run cost function** is a simple accounting step. This function — written $TC(y, w_1, w_2)$ to remind you that the total cost of production depends on the quantity of output and on the

long-run cost function

prices of the inputs — is just the sum of the quantities demanded of the inputs multiplied by the respective prices of those inputs:

$$TC(y, w_1, w_2) = w_1 z_1^* + w_2 z_2^*$$

To help you understand just what the terms *conditional input demand function* and *long-run cost function* mean, we will derive these functions for the standard rum-and-Coke production function introduced in Problem 7.1. We have chosen this simple example because we can readily identify the cost-minimizing input bundles. The production function is

$$y = \min(z_1/10, z_2/30)$$

where y is number of drinks, z_1 is millilitres of rum, and z_2 is millilitres of Coke.

To minimize costs for this fixed-proportions production function, for every drink, simply use 10 millilitres of rum and 30 millilitres of Coke. If y is 2, use exactly 20 millilitres of rum and 60 millilitres of Coke; if y is 7, use exactly 70 millilitres of rum and 210 millilitres of Coke; and so on. More generally, the following rules tell us how much rum and how much Coke a bartender needs to mix y standard rum-and-Cokes:

$$z_1^* = 10y$$
$$z_2^* = 30y$$

These are the conditional input demand functions for this production function. Because the input proportions are fixed in this production function, the conditional input demand functions do not depend on prices of the inputs: if we want five standard rum-and-Cokes, we need 50 millilitres of rum regardless of how expensive rum may be or how inexpensive Coke may be.

When we move from the conditional input demand functions to the long-run cost function, however, input prices necessarily enter the picture because the total cost is calculated by multiplying the price of each input by quantity demanded and then totalling the results. The long-run cost function for rum-and-Cokes is

$$TC(y, z_1, z_2) = y(10w_1 + 30w_2)$$

where w_1 is the price of a millilitre of rum and w_2 is the price of a millilitre of Coke.

In the following problem, you can find conditional input demand functions and a long-run cost function for another simple case.

PROBLEM 7.6

From Problem 7.1, we know that John Henry produces heat from coal and wood according to the following production function:

$$y = 5z_1 + 2z_2$$

where z_1 is tonnes of coal and z_2 is tonnes of wood. Find the conditional input demand functions and the long-run cost function for this production function. Begin by assuming that $2w_1 < 5w_2$ and show that John Henry should buy only coal to minimize his costs; then show that he needs $y/5$ tonnes of coal to produce y kilojoules of heat; then calculate the cost of producing y kilojoules of heat using coal as the only input. Now suppose that $2w_1 > 5w_2$. Which input should John Henry use? How much of it does he need to produce y kilojoules of heat? How much must he spend to produce y kilojoules of heat?

7.5 Solving Cost-Minimization Problems

To solve more complex cost-minimization problems, we can use graphic techniques like those used to solve the consumer's utility-maximization problem in Chapter 3. Here we limit our attention to cases where there is a diminishing *MRTS* and where the quantity of both inputs in the cost-minimizing input bundle is positive. As you know from Chapter 3, this type of solution is called an *interior solution.*

feasible input bundles

For any level of output y, the set of feasible input bundles is composed of all the input bundles that produce at least y units of output. In Figure 7.5, we have used Tipple's Courier Service to illustrate the feasible input bundles for 120 kilometres of courier service. The blue area is the set of bundles of time and gasoline that allow Tipple to produce at least 120 kilometres of courier service. More generally, the set of **feasible input bundles** for y units of output is composed of all the input bundles on or above the isoquant for y units of output.

FIGURE 7.5 The cost-minimizing bundle

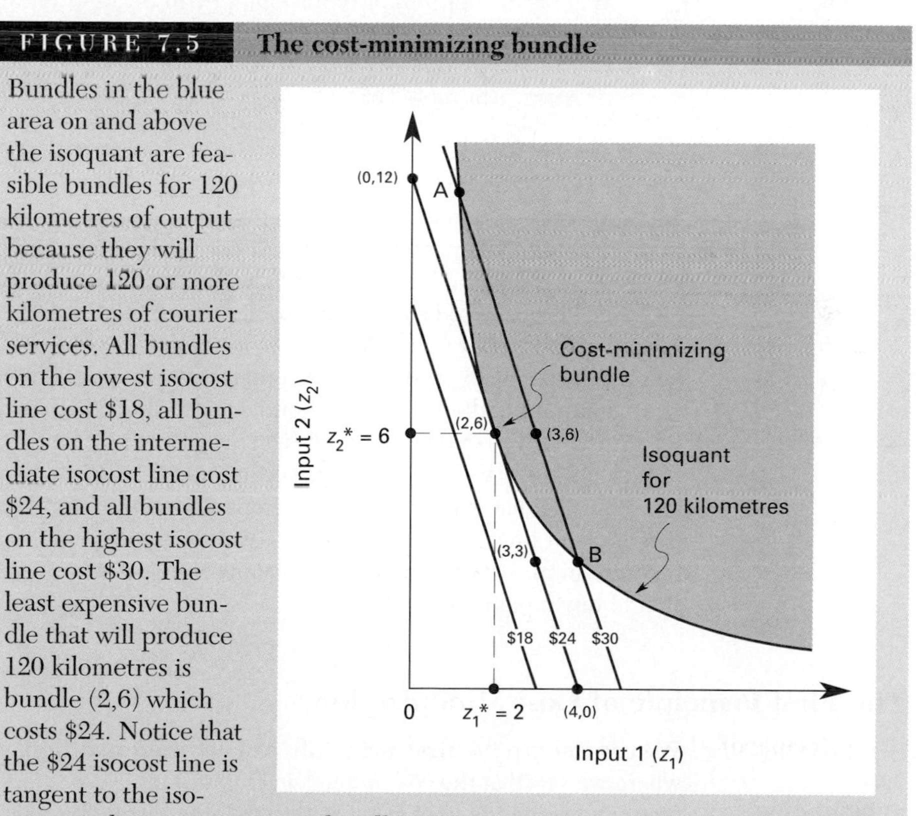

Bundles in the blue area on and above the isoquant are feasible bundles for 120 kilometres of output because they will produce 120 or more kilometres of courier services. All bundles on the lowest isocost line cost $18, all bundles on the intermediate isocost line cost $24, and all bundles on the highest isocost line cost $30. The least expensive bundle that will produce 120 kilometres is bundle (2,6) which costs $24. Notice that the $24 isocost line is tangent to the isoquant at the cost-minimizing bundle (2,6). Alternatively, *MRTS* is equal to w_1/w_2 at the cost-minimizing bundle.

To solve the cost-minimization problem, we must find the least costly feasible input bundle. But how can we represent the cost of various input bundles in Figure 7.5? Let us look first at an example. Suppose an hour of a driver's time costs \$6 ($w_1 = 6$) and a litre of gas costs \$2 ($w_2 = 2$). Then, as you can easily verify, all the following input bundles cost \$24: (4,0), (0,12), (2,6), (3,3). Indeed, any input bundle on the line

$$24 = 6z_1 + 2z_2$$

costs exactly \$24. This line is an isocost line because all the input bundles on it cost the same amount, namely \$24. In Figure 7.5, we have constructed this isocost line and two other isocost lines associated with \$18 and \$30. Notice that the isocost line for \$30 is further from the origin than the isocost line for \$24, which in turn is further from the origin than the isocost line for \$18.

isocost line

More generally, an **isocost line** is *a line along which all bundles cost the same, and is described by the following equation:* $c = w_1z_1 + w_2z_2$.

Notice that the absolute value of the slope of the isocost line is w_1/w_2. This slope reflects the fact that a firm must give up w_1/w_2 units of input 2 to get an additional unit of input 1. In other words, the *opportunity cost* of input 1 in terms of input 2 is w_1/w_2.

PROBLEM 7.7

What is the opportunity cost of input 2 in terms of input 1? Where does the isocost line intersect the z_1 axis? The z_2 axis? What happens to the isocost line as w_1 approaches 0. As w_2 approaches 0? As c approaches 0? As c gets arbitrarily large?

We now have the tools necessary to solve the cost-minimization problem. Figure 7.5 shows the solution to Tipple's cost-minimizing problem — assuming that he wants to produce 120 kilometres of courier services, that the price of a driver's time is \$6 per hour, and that the price of gas is \$2 per gallon. Because Tipple wants to minimize his costs, his goal is to be on the isocost line associated with the smallest possible total expenditure. In other words, he wants to be on the isocost line closest to the origin. But, because he wants to produce 120 kilometres of service, he is constrained to choose a feasible input bundle — an input bundle in the shaded area on or above the isoquant for 120 kilometres. No input bundles on the \$18 isocost line are feasible because none of these bundles will actually produce an output of 120 kilometres. The least costly input bundle that will produce 120 kilometres is input bundle (2,6) — a combination of 2 hours of time and 6 litres of gas — which lies on the \$24 isocost line. In this case, the minimum cost of producing 120 kilometres of courier services is \$24, and Tipple should buy input bundle (2,6).

The First Principle of Cost Minimization

first principle of cost minimization

We can deduce the **first principle of cost minimization** from Tipple's problem, where we saw that the cost-minimizing input bundle (z_1^*, z_2^*) for y units of output lies on or above the isoquant. That is, the cost-minimizing bundle is a feasible input bundle. But as long as input prices are not zero, the cost-minimizing bundle lies *on* the isoquant, not above it. Why? Because for any bundle above the isoquant, there are cheaper bundles on the isoquant. Consider, for example, input bundle (3,6) in Figure 7.5, which lies above the isoquant for 120 kilometres. Any bundle between points A and B on that isoquant is cheaper.

The first principle of cost minimization is that the cost-minimizing input bundle is on the isoquant:

$$y \equiv F(z_1^*, z_2^*)$$

where z_1^* and z_2^* are the cost-minimizing choices.

The Second Principle of Cost Minimization

We can also deduce the second principle of cost minimization from Tipple's problem in Figure 7.5. Since the cost-minimizing bundle must be *feasible*, it cannot be on an isocost line that lies below the isoquant for 120 kilometres. And since it must be the *cheapest* feasible bundle, it cannot be on an isocost line that intersects the isoquant. We know, then, that the cost-minimizing bundle must be at the point where the isocost line is tangent to the isoquant in Figure 7.5. Recall that absolute value of the slope of the isoquant is *MRTS* and that the absolute value of the slope of the isocost line is w_1/w_2.

The second principle of cost minimization is that *MRTS* is equal to w_1/w_2 at the cost-minimizing bundle:

$$MRTS(z_1^*, z_2^*) \equiv w_1/w_2$$

We can provide a more intuitive understanding of the second principle by making use of the fact that *MRTS* is the ratio of MP_1 to MP_2.[4] The second principle can then be written as

$$MP_1/MP_2 = w_1/w_2$$

Manipulating this expression yields

$$MP_1/w_1 = MP_2/w_2$$

---

4. We can use the method of Lagrange to obtain these two principles. The Lagrange function is

$$L(z_1, z_2, \lambda) = w_1 z_1 + w_1 z_2 + \lambda[y - F(z_1, z_2)]$$

Setting the partial derivatives of L(•) with respect to z_1, z_2, and λ equal to zero, we obtain

$$w_1 - \lambda \partial F(z_1, z_2)/\partial z_1 = 0$$
$$w_2 - \lambda \partial F(z_1, z_2)/\partial z_2 = 0$$
$$y - F(z_1, z_2) = 0$$

The third condition is, of course, the first principle of cost minimization. Combining the first two conditions to eliminate λ yields.

$$\frac{\partial F(z_1, z_2)/\partial z_1}{\partial F(z_1, z_2)/\partial z_2} = \frac{w_1}{w_2}$$

But from footnote 1, the left side is $MRTS(z_1, z_2)$, and we then have the second principle of cost minimization:

$$MRTS(z_1, z_2) = \frac{w_1}{w_2}$$

In other words, at the cost-minimizing input bundle, the marginal product per dollar for input 1, MP_1/w_1, is equal to the marginal product per dollar for input 2, MP_2/w_2. To see why, let us consider some other input bundle on the isoquant where the marginal product per dollar of input 1 is less than the marginal product per dollar of input 2. Let us suppose, for example, that MP_2 is 6 and w_2 is \$2 and that MP_1 is 2 and w_1 is \$1. Then

$$MP_1/w_1 = 2/1 < 6/2 = MP_2/w_2$$

Because at the margin, a dollar spent on input 1 is less productive than a dollar spent on input 2, the firm ought to be able to reduce its costs by substituting input 2 for input 1. To see why, suppose that the firm reduces the quantity of input 1 by 1 unit. Its output will fall by approximately 2 units since MP_1 is 2. To compensate for this decrease in output, the firm must increase the quantity of input 2 by approximately 1/3 of a unit since MP_2 is 6. Has the firm succeeded in reducing costs? The answer is yes. Since w_1 is \$1, as the firm reduces the quantity of input 1 by 1 unit, its costs dropped by \$1. Since w_2 is \$2, as the firm increases the quantity of input 2 by 1/3 of a unit, its costs rise by \$2/3 (1/3 multiplied by \$2). The reduction in costs is (\$1 – \$2/3) or \$1/3. Thus, by substituting input 2 for input 1, the firm is able to reduce costs by one-third of a dollar, while maintaining its output. More generally, if MP_1/w_1 is less than MP_2/w_2, the input bundle cannot be the cost-minimizing input bundle because cost can be reduced and output maintained by substituting input 2 for input 1.

Using this line of reasoning, we can generalize the second principle of cost minimization to the case in which there are many inputs:

To minimize costs, the marginal product per dollar must be identical for all inputs.

Now let us use the production function for Tipple's Courier Service to provide a concrete example. The first principle of cost minimization in the context of Tipple's Courier Service is

$$y \equiv (1200 z_1^* z_2^*)^{1/2}$$

Above we showed that *MRTS* for Tipple's Courier Service is z_2/z_1. The second principle of cost minimization then gives us

$$z_2^*/z_1^* \equiv w_1/w_2$$

We now have two equations with two unknowns, z_1^* and z_2^*. We can solve these equations for the conditional input demand functions

$$z_1^* = y[w_2/(1200 w_1)]^{1/2}$$
$$z_2^* = y[w_1/(1200 w_2)]^{1/2}$$

Notice that z_1^* increases as w_2 increases and decreases as w_1 increases, and that z_2^* increases as w_1 increases and decreases as w_2 increases. That is, as our intuition suggests, the cost-minimizing quantity of either input is positively related to the price of the other input and negatively related to its own price. Notice, too, that *both* z_1^* and z_2^* increase as y increases — that is, the cost-minimizing quantities of both inputs increase as the quantity of output increases. This result also makes sense intuitively.

If we now multiply z_1^* by w_1 and z_2^* by w_2 and add the results, we will have the long-run cost function for Tipple's Courier Service:

$$TC(y, w_1, w_2) = y(w_1 w_2/300)^{1/2}$$

Notice that cost increases as output increases and as either input price increases. These results, too, are intuitive. In subsequent sections, we will see which of them can be generalized. But first, try the following problem.

PROBLEM 7.8

1. First solve the two simultaneous equations above to verify that they are indeed the conditional input demand functions for this production function.
2. If w_1 = \$6 and w_2 = \$2, what is the cost-minimizing input bundle for 120 kilometres and what is the total cost? For 240 kilometres? For 360 kilometres?
3. Now suppose that input prices double so that w_1 = \$12 and w_2 = \$4. Show that the cost-minimizing input bundle for 120 kilometres is the same as it was in (2) and that total cost is double what it was in (2).

Application: Tin Cans and Cardboard Boxes

The next time you visit your local grocery store, take a walk down the canned goods section. You'll notice that most of the cans have a particular shape — the relationship between the height and diameter of the can is relatively constant. This turns out to be an implication of cost minimization. A little thought on the matter might help your intuition of production.

Let's suppose a tin can has the general shape of Figure 7.6a, where D is the diameter of the can and h is its height. Let's also suppose there is no wastage in making the side piece of tin, but the top and bottom must be cut from a square piece of tin and this leaves wasted tin, shown as the shaded area in Figure 7.6b. It is a simple mechanical problem to show that the cost minimizing amount of tin for a given volume is $h = 1.27D$. That is, in order to use the minimum amount of tin for a given volume, the height of the tin is required to be about 25 percent bigger than the diameter.[5]

A walk down the canned goods aisle shows that about 90 percent of the cans satisfy this relationship. Soup, beans, vegetables, fruit, and spaghetti seem to satisfy this rule. There are two big exceptions: pop cans are too tall and tuna cans are too short. This means there must be some aspect to these cans other than size that matters to consumers in order for producers to make a more expensive can. For pop cans, the answer is obvious. Many times people drink straight from the can. A can with the relative dimensions of a soup can is too thick to comfortably hold in the hand, so the can is made thinner and taller to accommodate this. Why would tuna cans, though, be so short? Consider the contents of these short tins: tuna, salmon, cat food, and other meat products. The problem with putting meat in a can is that the bacteria are not killed by simple canning procedures. It is necessary to can meat under 10 to 15 pounds of pressure per square inch. When the meat cools inside the can, pressure is placed on

5. Gene Silberberg was the first economist to notice this implication of cost minimization.

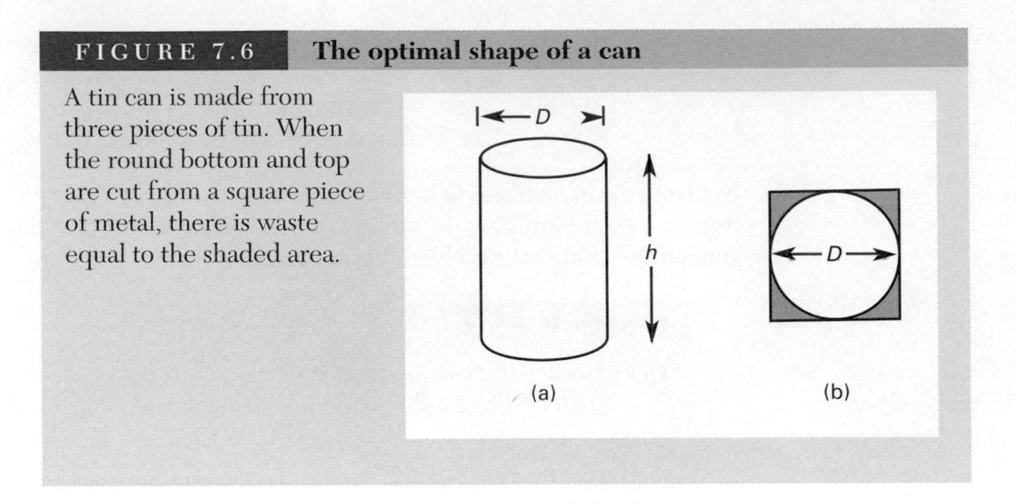

FIGURE 7.6 The optimal shape of a can

A tin can is made from three pieces of tin. When the round bottom and top are cut from a square piece of metal, there is waste equal to the shaded area.

the walls of the can. A can shaped like a soup can would likely collapse under this pressure, so the can is made shorter and stronger. Interestingly, cat food comes in short cans, while dog food generally comes in tall cans. It turns out that cat food is mostly made of meat but dog food is mostly cereal-based.

If you walk down the cereal aisle in any grocery store, you'll notice cereal is never sold in cans or cylindrical containers. The shape of the container often depends on the method used to pack the contents. Contents under pressure or packed under heat often require a cylindrical container for strength. For a given volume of content, a cylindrical container also minimizes the cost of container material. However, a cylindrical container wastes shelf space, while rectangular boxes can utilize shelf space more effectively. Here again we see predictable tradeoffs by firms trying to minimize costs. When the value of the contents and the cost of the container material fall relative to the value of shelf space, the goods are more likely to be sold in boxed form. Cereals (such as corn flakes and Cheerios), dish soap, and items sold close to the checkout stand seem to conform to this pattern. Exceptions abound at every turn in a grocery store, of course, because of the huge variety of items being sold, but our simple understanding of cost minimization and tradeoffs between different inputs seems to explain a great deal of packaging at the local store.

7.6 Comparative Statics for Input Prices

In this section, we will look at some comparative statics properties of the conditional input demand functions and the long-run cost function. First we will look at the effects of a uniform percentage change in the prices of *all* inputs. Then we will look at the effects of a change in the price of just *one* input.

Suppose that Tipple initially has to pay \$6 per hour for labour and \$2 per litre for gas, and that subsequently both input prices double. What effects do these price changes have on the amount of labour and gas that Tipple will use and on the cost of producing a given quantity of courier services? First, by looking at Tipple's conditional input demand functions, we see that the cost-minimizing input bundle does not change: for each kilometre of service produced, Tipple will use 1/60 of an hour of labour and 1/20 of a litre of gas. Then, by looking at the long-run cost function, we see that long-run costs double. At the initial prices, Tipple's costs are $0.20 per kilometre and, at the higher prices, his costs are $0.40 per kilometre.

We can show that these are very general results. Suppose that for output y we have one set of input prices, (w_1, w_2), and the corresponding cost-minimizing input bundle (z_1^*, z_2^*). We will denote the cost of this bundle by c^*. Given these input prices, we know that there is an isocost curve tangent to the isoquant for y units of output at bundle (z_1^*, z_2^*). Now let us generate another set of input prices by multiplying the original prices by a positive number a, to get prices (aw_1, aw_2). Since both input prices have changed by the same factor of proportionality, the slope of the isocost lines has not changed. Therefore, given the new input prices, it is still true that an isocost curve is tangent to the isoquant for y units of output at bundle (z_1^*, z_2^*). This means that the cost-minimizing input bundle has not changed. What *has* changed is the cost of that bundle. At the original prices, its cost was c^*; at the new prices, its cost is ac^*.

If all input prices change by the same factor of proportionality a, (i) the cost-minimizing input bundle for y units of output does not change, and (ii) the minimum cost of producing y units of output changes by the factor of proportionality a.

Next let us look at the effects of an increase in the price of one input, holding the price of the other input and the level of output constant at y. Suppose that the price of labour quadruples, so that Tipple has to pay $24 per hour for labour, while the price of gas remains at $2 per litre. What effects does this change have on the amount of labour and gas Tipple will use and on the cost of producing a given quantity of courier services? First, by looking at Tipple's conditional input demand functions, we see that the cost-minimizing quantity of labour drops from 1/60 to 1/120 of an hour for each kilometre of service produced, and that the cost-minimizing quantity of gas rises from 1/20 to 1/10 of a litre for each kilometre of service produced. Then, looking at the long-run cost function we see that long-run costs increase from $0.20 per kilometre to $0.40 per kilometre.

Now we will show that these are also very general results. We will assume that there is a diminishing $MRTS$ and that a positive quantity of both inputs is demanded prior to an increase in the price of input 1. The initial equilibrium in Figure 7.7 is at bundle (z_1', z_2'). The increase in the price of input 1 means that isocost curves necessarily get steeper since the slope of an isocost line is the absolute value of w_1/w_2. Then, given a diminishing $MRTS$, the second principle of cost minimization dictates that the new cost-minimizing bundle (z_1'', z_2'') is on the steeper portion of the isoquant above and to the left of the initial equilibrium as shown in Figure 7.7. Notice that quantity of input 1 necessarily decreases and quantity of input 2 necessarily increases. To summarize this result:

Supposing that the cost-minimizing quantity of both inputs is positive and that there is a diminishing $MRTS$, if the price of input i increases and the price of input j does not change, the cost-minimizing quantity of input i decreases and the cost-minimizing quantity of input j increases.

Now let us show that in response to the increase in the price of input 1 in Figure 7.7, the cost of producing y' units of output necessarily increases. The key is to notice that — even before the increase in the price of input 1 — bundle (z_1'', z_2''), which is the cost-minimizing bundle *after* the price of input 1 increases, is more expensive than bundle (z_1', z_2'), the cost-minimizing bundle *before* the price of input 1 increases. To see why, try drawing an isocost line through bundle (z_1'', z_2'') in Figure 7.7 that is parallel to the initial isocost line. It will be further from the origin than the initial isocost line,

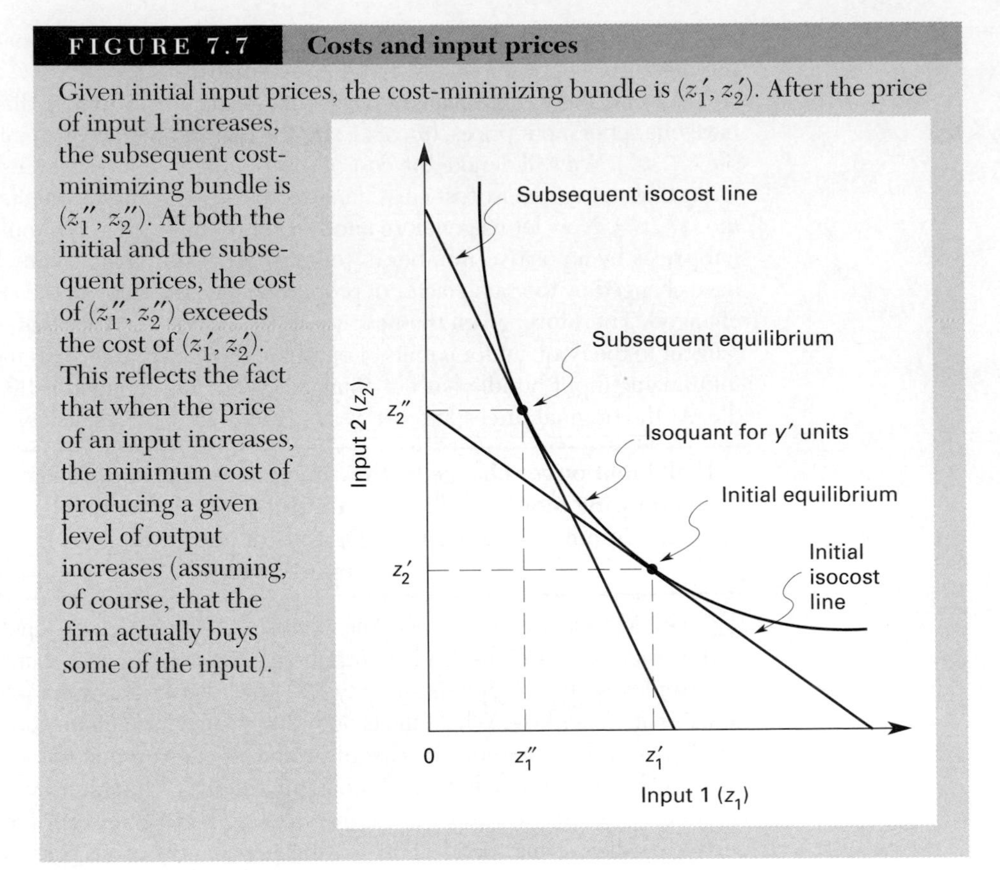

FIGURE 7.7 Costs and input prices

Given initial input prices, the cost-minimizing bundle is (z_1', z_2'). After the price of input 1 increases, the subsequent cost-minimizing bundle is (z_1'', z_2''). At both the initial and the subsequent prices, the cost of (z_1'', z_2'') exceeds the cost of (z_1', z_2'). This reflects the fact that when the price of an input increases, the minimum cost of producing a given level of output increases (assuming, of course, that the firm actually buys some of the input).

indicating that at the initial prices, bundle (z_1'', z_2'') is more expensive than bundle (z_1', z_2'). To summarize this result:

If the price of an input increases and if the quantity demanded of that input is positive, then the minimum cost of producing any given level of output increases.

To see why the *opportunity cost of an input* is key in determining which combination of inputs minimizes costs, try the following problem.

PROBLEM 7.9

In determining the cost-minimizing input bundle, it is really the opportunity cost of an input that matters. The opportunity cost of input 1 is just w_1/w_2. Suppose there is a diminishing *MRTS* and that a positive quantity of input 1 is initially demanded. Show that an increase in the opportunity cost of input 1 leads to a decrease in quantity demanded of input 1 and an increase in quantity demanded of input 2.

Now let us look briefly at the implications of an increase in the price of just one input — say input i — in the more general context in which there are many inputs. We will assume that there is a diminishing *MRTS* between input i and every other input, and that quantity demanded of input i is positive. In response to an increase in w_i, two things necessarily occur:

When the price of one input increases, (1) the cost of producing any given level of output increases, and (2) the cost-minimizing quantity of input i decreases. In other words, the firm substitutes away from an input when its relative price increases.

This seemingly obvious insight is important because many noneconomists overlook or underestimate this substitution response. The input substitution in the shrimp-packing industry on the Gulf of Mexico, discussed in Chapter 1, is just one international example of input substitution. Instances of input substitution appear regularly in the headlines. For example, increases in the price of oil in the 1970s resulted in a massive, economy-wide substitution away from oil and from energy use in general. When aluminum sheet prices jumped in the late 1980s, most US beverage-can makers switched to sheet steel, which was selling at 15 percent less per pound than sheet aluminum.

PROBLEM 7.10

Earlier we derived the following conditional input demand functions for the rum-and-Coke production function:

$$z_1^* = 10y \qquad z_2^* = 30y$$

Notice that when the price of input 1 increases, the bartender does not substitute away from input 1. Yet we just argued that firms substitute away from inputs when their price increases. Explain this discrepancy.

7.7 Comparative Statics for the Level of Output

In this section, we want to explore two questions. First, how does quantity demanded of an input respond to a change in the level of output? Does quantity demanded necessarily increase when the level of output increases? Second, what happens to long-run total cost as output increases? Does long-run cost necessarily increase linearly with output?

Normal and Inferior Inputs

To explore the first of these questions we have constructed an output expansion path in Figure 7.8. Notice that line *EE* in Figure 7.8 runs through each of the three isoquants at the cost-minimizing input bundle. The path is called an **output expansion path** because it connects the cost-minimizing input bundles that are generated as output is increased, or expanded. Because input prices are held constant in this comparative exercise — w_1 is \$10 and w_2 is \$20 — the isocost lines in Figure 7.8 are parallel.

output expansion path

The output expansion path in the theory of the firm is analogous to the income-consumption path in consumer theory. We can therefore draw on consumer theory for analogies as we classify and compare types of inputs. An input is said to be a **normal input** if the quantity demanded increases as output increases; it is an **inferior input** if quantity demanded decreases as output increases. For example, if you use a shovel to dig one small ditch but a machine to dig big ditches, then shovels are an inferior input in ditch-digging. In Figure 7.8, input 2 is a normal input — at least in the

normal input

inferior input

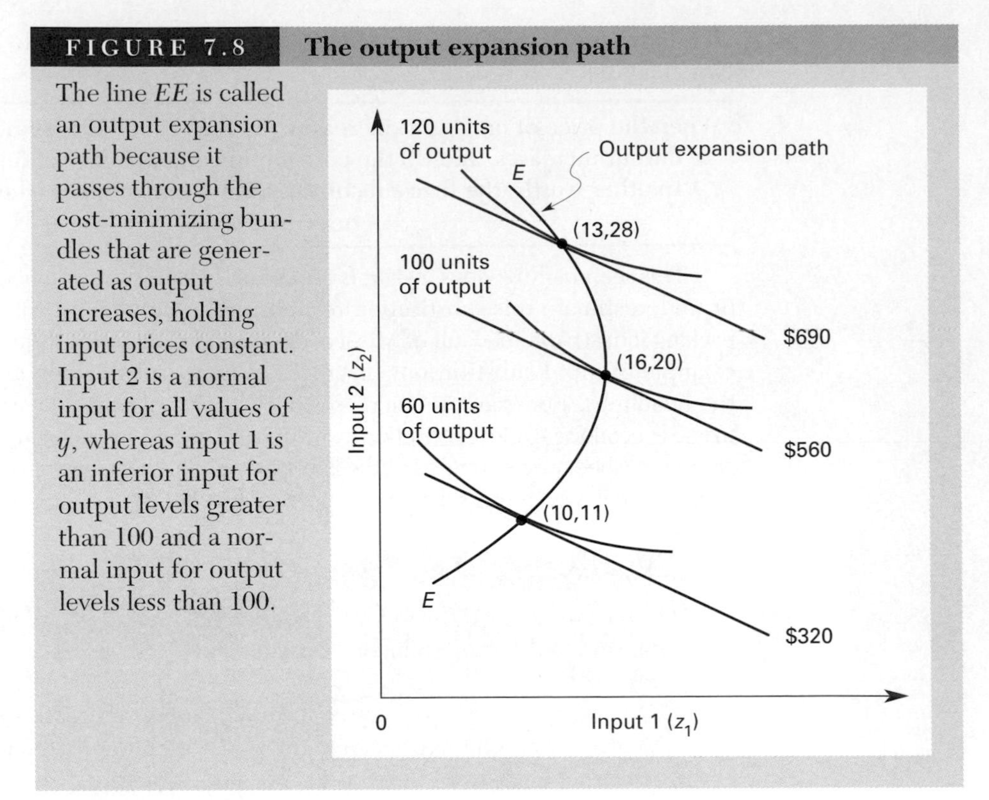

FIGURE 7.8 The output expansion path

The line *EE* is called an output expansion path because it passes through the cost-minimizing bundles that are generated as output increases, holding input prices constant. Input 2 is a normal input for all values of y, whereas input 1 is an inferior input for output levels greater than 100 and a normal input for output levels less than 100.

range of output levels represented in the figure — because as output increases, so does the quantity demanded of input 2. On the other hand, input 1 is a normal input at output levels up to 100. At levels beyond 100, however, input 1 is an inferior input because as output increases beyond 100, the quantity demanded of input 1 decreases. It is clear that as output increases, quantity demanded of an input may increase or decrease. Just as normal and inferior goods were possible in consumer theory, so, too, normal and inferior inputs are possible in production theory.

We can easily derive the output expansion path for Tipple's Courier service. From the second principle of cost minimization we know that along the output expansion path, *MRTS* is equal to w_1/w_2. In other words, along the output expansion path, an isoquant is tangent to an isocost line. Recall that *MRTS* for the courier service is just z_2/z_1. We then see that along Tipple's output expansion path

$$z_2^*/z_1^* = w_1/w_2$$

But this can be rewritten as

$$z_2^* = (w_1/w_2)z_1^*$$

So, Tipple's output expansion path is just a ray through the origin with slope w_1/w_2. When w_1 is \$6 and w_2 is \$2, for example, the output expansion path is $z_2 = 3z_1$.

homothetic production functions

Tipple's production function exemplifies an important class of production functions, called **homothetic production functions,** in which the expansion path is a ray through the origin. For a homothetic production function, *MRTS* is constant along any ray through the origin in (z_1, z_2) space, and the output expansion path of a homothetic production function is therefore a ray through the origin.[6] Keep in mind, however, that not all production functions are homothetic. For example, because its output expansion path in not a ray through the origin, the production function shown in Figure 7.8 is not homothetic.

PROBLEM 7.11

Can either input 1 or input 2 be an inferior input when the production function is homothetic?

Long-Run Costs and Output

long-run average cost

By focusing on homothetic production functions it is easy to develop some important relationships between long-run costs and returns to scale. Let us begin with **long-run average cost** (*LAC*). *LAC* is equal to total cost of output divided by quantity of output:

$$LAC(y) = TC(y)/y$$

We want to show that as output y increases, *LAC* is constant, decreasing, or increasing as there are constant, increasing, or decreasing returns to scale. These results are intuitive. When all quantities in the input bundle double, costs double. In the case of constant returns to scale, output also doubles, and, as a result, average cost does not change. In contrast, in the case of increasing (decreasing) returns to scale, output more (less) than doubles, and, as a result, average cost falls (rises).

To begin, let us pick an input bundle on the output expansion path — say, bundle (z_1', z_2') on the isoquant for y' units of output in Figure 7.9. Because this bundle is on the expansion path, an isocost curve is tangent to the isoquant at this initial bundle. Let c' denote the cost of this bundle. Clearly,

$$c' = w_1 z_1' + w_2 z_2'$$

Then, the long-run average cost of y' units of output is just

$$LAC(y') = c'/y'$$

Now let us increase both inputs by factor $a > 1$ to get input bundle (az_1', az_2'). Because the production function is homothetic, this new bundle is also on the output expansion path, and it is associated with y'' units of output. Since this new bundle contains a times as much of each input, its cost is ac'. The long-run average cost of y'' units of output is then

$$LAC(y'') = ac'/y''$$

Now, suppose that the production function exhibits constant returns to scale. Then y'' is equal to ay'; that is, increasing quantities of all inputs by factor of proportional-

---

6. A differentiable production function is homothetic if $MRTS(z_1, z_2)$ can be written as a function of z_2/z_1. This property ensures that $MRTS(z_1, z_2)$ is constant along any ray through the origin and therefore that expansion paths are rays through the origin.

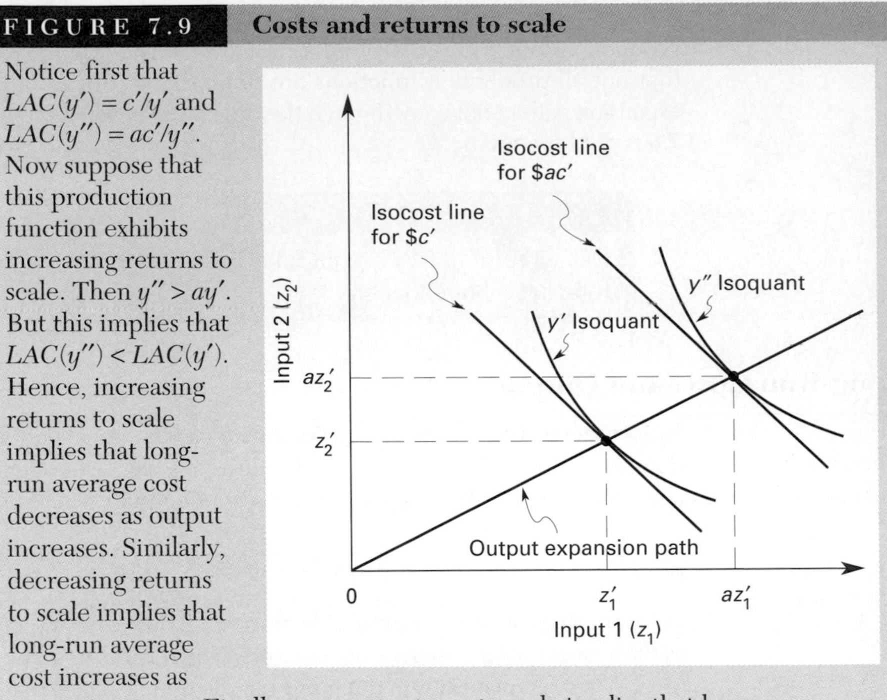

FIGURE 7.9 **Costs and returns to scale**

Notice first that $LAC(y') = c'/y'$ and $LAC(y'') = ac'/y''$. Now suppose that this production function exhibits increasing returns to scale. Then $y'' > ay'$. But this implies that $LAC(y'') < LAC(y')$. Hence, increasing returns to scale implies that long-run average cost decreases as output increases. Similarly, decreasing returns to scale implies that long-run average cost increases as output increases. Finally, constant returns to scale implies that long-run average cost does not change as output increases.

ity a results in an increase in output by factor of proportionality a as well. Using this result, we see that $LAC(y'')$ is equal to $LAC(y')$. When there are *constant returns to scale*, average cost remains constant as output increases.

Next, suppose that the production function exhibits increasing returns to scale. Then y'' exceeds ay', and we see that $LAC(y'')$ is less than $LAC(y')$. When there are *increasing returns to scale*, average cost decreases as output increases.

Finally, suppose that the production function exhibits decreasing returns to scale. Then y'' is less than ay', and we see that $LAC(y'')$ exceeds $LAC(y')$. When there are *decreasing returns to scale*, average cost increases as output increases.

PROBLEM 7.12

As you know, Tipple's production function exhibits constant returns to scale. Find Tipple's $LAC(y)$ and verify that long-run average cost does not change as output changes.

In Figure 7.10, we have shown TC and LAC for the three pure cases. In Figure 7.10a and 7.10b, there are constant returns to scale at all levels of output; in Figure 7.10c and 7.10d, there are increasing returns to scale; and in Figure 7.10e and 7.10f, there are decreasing returns to scale.

In Figure 7.11a (page 256), we have shown a mixed case. Up to 19 units of output, there are increasing returns to scale and LAC is therefore decreasing. Beyond 19 units of output, however, there are decreasing returns to scale and LAC is therefore increas-

FIGURE 7.10 More on costs and returns to scale

Because in (a) and (b) there are constant returns to scale, *TC* is a linear function of output, and *LAC* is constant. Because in (c) and (d) there are increasing returns to scale, *TC* increases at a decreasing rate as output increases, and *LAC* decreases as output increases. And because in (e) and (f) there are decreasing returns to scale, *TC* increases at an increasing rate as output increases, and *LAC* increases as output increases.

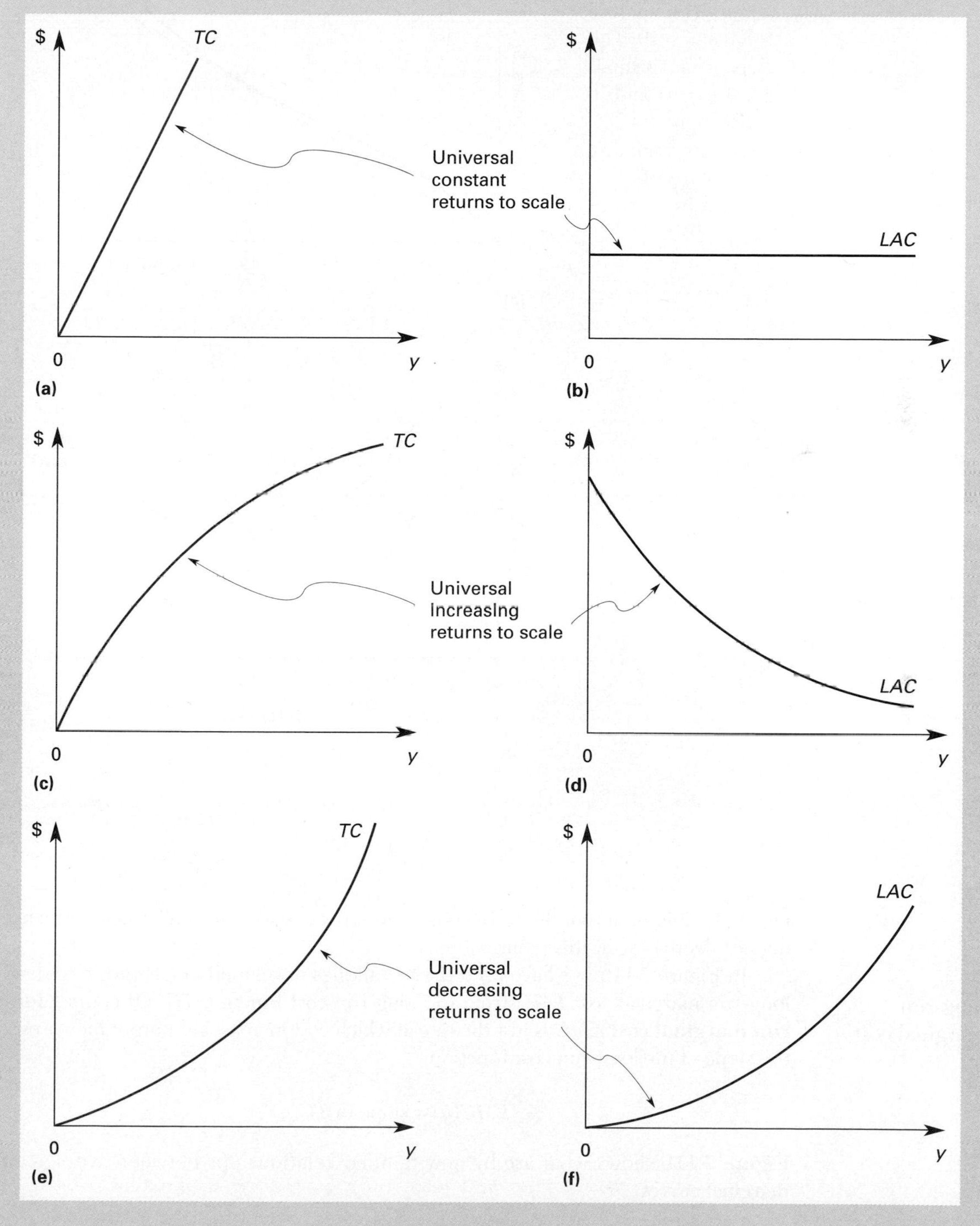

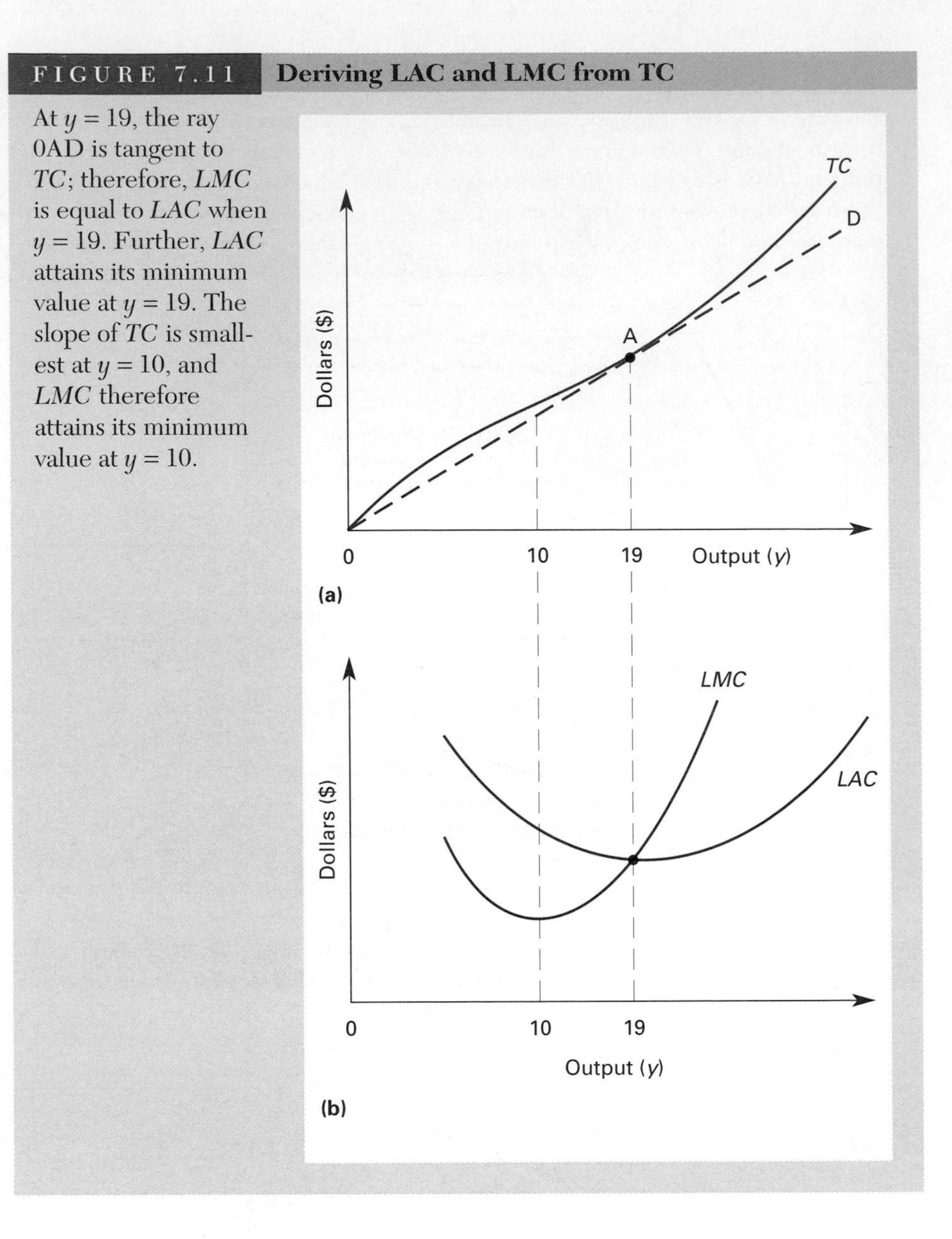

FIGURE 7.11 Deriving LAC and LMC from TC

At $y = 19$, the ray 0AD is tangent to TC; therefore, LMC is equal to LAC when $y = 19$. Further, LAC attains its minimum value at $y = 19$. The slope of TC is smallest at $y = 10$, and LMC therefore attains its minimum value at $y = 10$.

ing. At 19 units of output there are constant returns to scale and LAC is neither increasing nor decreasing at this point.

long-run marginal cost

In Figure 7.11b, we have used the techniques developed in Chapter 6 to derive long-run marginal cost LMC from the long-run cost function TC. Of course, **long-run marginal cost** LMC is just the rate at which cost increases as output increases, or the slope of the long-run cost function:

$$LMC(y) = \text{slope of } TC(y)$$

Figure 7.11b shows what are by now familiar relationships between average and marginal curves.

When *LMC* lies below *LAC*, *LAC* is decreasing; when *LMC* lies above *LAC*, *LAC* is increasing; *LMC* intersects *LAC* where *LAC* is at a minimum.

And we can interpret these relationships in a different way:

With increasing returns to scale, long-run marginal cost is less than long-run average cost; with decreasing returns to scale, long-run marginal cost exceeds long-run average cost; and with constant returns to scale, long-run marginal cost equals long-run average cost.

7.8 Comparing Long-Run and Short-Run Costs

One final topic remains: identifying the relationships between long-run and short-run costs of production. Although only one long run exists, many short runs are possible, depending on the number of inputs that are variable. To further complicate matters, each of these short runs can have any number of cost functions, depending on the quantities of the fixed inputs. We can learn most of what there is to know about the relationship between short- and long-run costs, however, by limiting our discussion to the two-input case.

All the relationships between long-run and short-run costs spring from two basic relationships between the single long-run cost function and any of the short-run cost functions:

The long-run cost of production is less than or equal to the short-run cost of production for all levels of output:

$$TC(y) \leq STC(y) \text{ for all values of } y$$

In addition, the long-run and short-run costs of production are identical at one level of output:

$$TC(y) = STC(y) \text{ for one value of } y$$

These two assertions are illustrated in Figure 7.12. $STC(y)$ lies above $TC(y)$ at all values of y other than $y = 100$, where $TC(y) = STC(y)$. How do we know that these assertions are true? Suppose, for example, that the input bundle (10,35) is cost-minimizing for 100 units of output. Then the long-run minimum cost of 100 units of output can be easily calculated:

$$TC(100) = 10w_1 + 35w_2$$

Now let us fix the quantity of input 2 at 35, thereby defining a total product function. What will be the minimum cost of producing 100 units of output in this particular short run with this total product function? Clearly, 10 units of input 1 are cost-minimizing in this short run. In turn, this implies that

$$STC(100) = 10w_1 + 35w_2$$

In other words, the minimum cost of producing 100 units of output is identical in this particular short run and in the long run. Thus, the two cost functions have one point in

FIGURE 7.12 Comparing TC and STC

STC is a short-run cost function. When $y = 100$, $STC = TC$, and the two functions are tangent at $y = 100$. For all other values of y, STC exceeds TC.

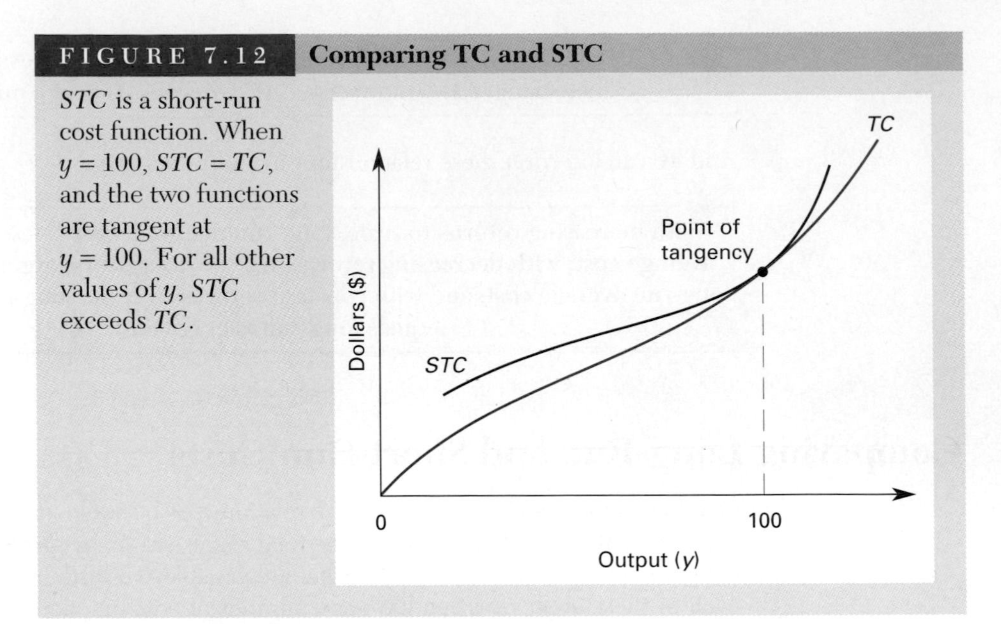

common. For any other level of output, the cost of production in the short run cannot be less than in the long run. Why not? Because the firm has more flexibility in the long run, it can choose the quantities of all its inputs in the long run, but it cannot do so in the short run. And, except in very odd cases, the short-run cost of production will exceed the long-run cost of production for any output level other than the point in common. This standard case is presented in Figure 7.12.

We can draw a number of implications from this standard case. The long-run cost function in Figure 7.13a is derived from a production function characterized by increasing returns to scale up to 78 units of output and by decreasing returns to scale thereafter. Figure 7.13a also includes two short-run cost functions STC_1 and STC_2. STC_1 is tangent to TC at 45 units of output, where there are increasing returns to scale. And STC_2 is tangent to TC at 93 units of output, where there are decreasing returns to scale. The corresponding average and marginal cost functions are presented in Figure 7.13b.

Let us concentrate first on the relationship between the two short-run average cost functions and the long-run average cost function. SAC_1 is tangent to LAC when y is equal to 45, the output at which STC_1 is tangent to TC. At all other output levels, SAC_1 lies above LAC. Similarly, SAC_2 is tangent to LAC at 93 units of output and lies above it elsewhere.

Now let us turn to the relationships between the two short-run marginal cost functions and the long-run marginal cost function. Notice that at output 45, SMC_1 is equal to LMC and that at output 93, SMC_2 is equal to LMC. To understand why these relationships must hold, look for a moment at SMC_1 and LMC. Each is just the slope of the corresponding total cost function. Because the two total cost functions are tangent at output level 45, they have the same slope at this point. Notice, too, that both SMC_1 and SMC_2 intersect LMC from below.

Finally, notice the following relationships: the output at which SAC_1 attains its minimum value is greater than 45, and the output at which SAC_2 attains its minimum value is less than 93. These relationships are a bit surprising. The first implies that to produce 45 units of output at minimum cost in the long run, in the corresponding

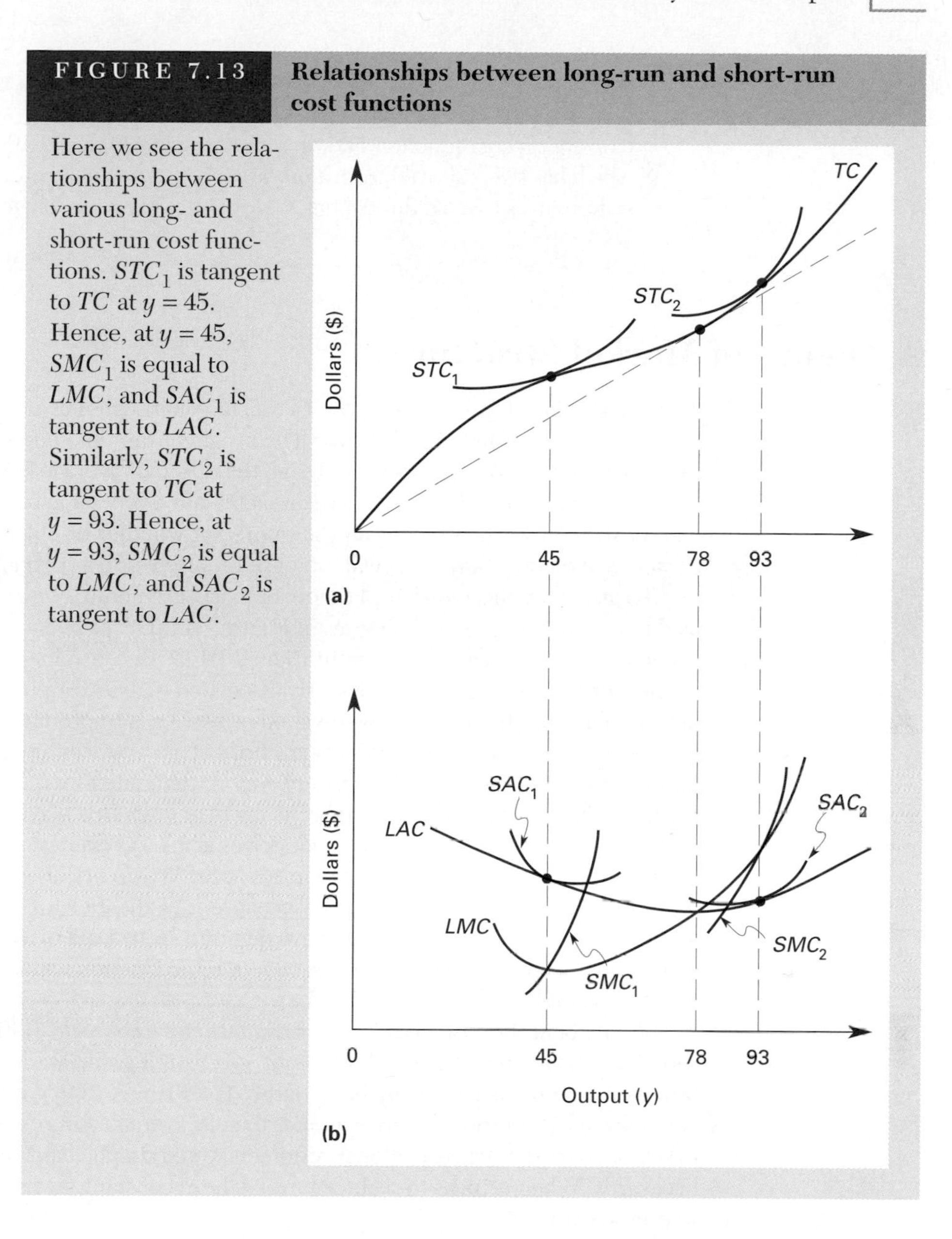

FIGURE 7.13 **Relationships between long-run and short-run cost functions**

Here we see the relationships between various long- and short-run cost functions. STC_1 is tangent to TC at $y = 45$. Hence, at $y = 45$, SMC_1 is equal to LMC, and SAC_1 is tangent to LAC. Similarly, STC_2 is tangent to TC at $y = 93$. Hence, at $y = 93$, SMC_2 is equal to LMC, and SAC_2 is tangent to LAC.

short run, the firm will be producing at a point where SAC_1 is still decreasing. Conversely, the second implies that to produce 93 units at minimum cost in the long run, in the corresponding short run, the firm must be producing at a point where SAC_2 is increasing.

How can we understand these results? Let us look more closely at 45 units of output. LMC is less than LAC at this level of output, and LAC therefore must be falling at 45. Since STC_1 is tangent to TC at 45, SMC_1 must also be less than SAC_1 at 45. Therefore, SAC_1 must also be falling at 45 units. You may want to construct an analogous argument to explain why SAC_2 must be increasing at 93 units.

Because these relationships can be slippery and practice is needed to master them, try your hand at the following problem.

PROBLEM 7.13

Consider a cost function like the one shown in Figure 7.10a and 7.10b, which has been derived from a production function characterized by constant returns to scale throughout. Construct a diagram analogous to Figure 7.13.

7.9 A Theory of Market Structure

At the beginning of this Part, we posed a fundamental economic question: Why do markets have different numbers of firms? The insights from this chapter allow us to tackle that question from one perspective. Using the different average cost functions that we have encountered in this chapter, we can sketch out a very basic but insightful theory of market structure: a theory we can use to predict whether or not firms will come into existence and how many firms will establish themselves in a particular market.

To articulate this cost-based theory of market structure, we will use the four stylized long-run average cost functions in Figure 7.14. Let us begin with the case of *universal decreasing returns to scale* in Figure 7.14a. Because long-run average cost is everywhere increasing, size is obviously associated with a cost penalty. The bigger the output of a firm, the more costly the good or service is to produce. In fact, goods and services will not be supplied in this case by firms at all — at least not by firms as we know them. Why? Suppose a firm tries to serve more than one buyer. To cover its costs, its price will have to be no smaller than its average cost. But because potential buyers can produce the good or service for themselves at a lower average cost, they will not pay the higher price needed to cover the firm's costs. We do not know of any firms selling tooth brushing services, for example, because it is cheaper for us to brush our own teeth. We can think of the case of decreasing returns to scale as a case where a market will be characterized by *household production*: production will be conducted on the smallest possible scale.

What about the case of *universal constant returns to scale* in Figure 7.14b? When returns to scale are constant throughout, size is not associated with a cost penalty; however, nothing is gained by being large. If a firm were to come into existence, it could not sell its output at a price greater than its average cost of production. If it tried to sell at a higher price, its potential customers would simply make the good in their own backyards. When returns to scale are everywhere constant, firms have no compelling reason to exist.

In the remaining two cases in Figure 7.14, firms will come into being. Because in certain ranges of output there are *increasing returns to scale*, the potential do-it-yourselfer must labour under the cost disadvantage associated with a relatively small scale of production.

Only in these two cases, then, do firms serve an economic purpose. When long-run average cost of production is everywhere downward-sloping, as in Figure 7.14c, there are *universal increasing returns to scale*, and a cost advantage is always associated with a still larger output. As we will discover in Chapter 10, in this circumstance, a small number of relatively large firms will supply the good or service in question. Public utilities such as electricity and telephone service are industries in which being big pays off. We have an important understanding, then, of the elementary force that generates markets characterized by *monopolies* or *oligopolies*.

FIGURE 7.14 A cost-based theory of market structure

With decreasing returns to scale, as in (a), *LAC* is everywhere upward-sloping. Thus, a cost penalty is associated with large size, and we expect this sort of good to be produced on the smallest possible scale. With constant returns to scale, as in (b), neither a cost penalty nor a cost advantage is associated with size, and this sort of good could be produced on any scale. With increasing returns to scale, as in (c), a cost advantage is associated with size, and this sort of good will be produced by one or a few firms. In the mixed case, as in (d), the initial increasing returns to scale guarantee that production will be done by firms. Whether it will be done by a few relatively large firms or by many relatively small firms depends on the output level at which *LAC* attains its minimum value.

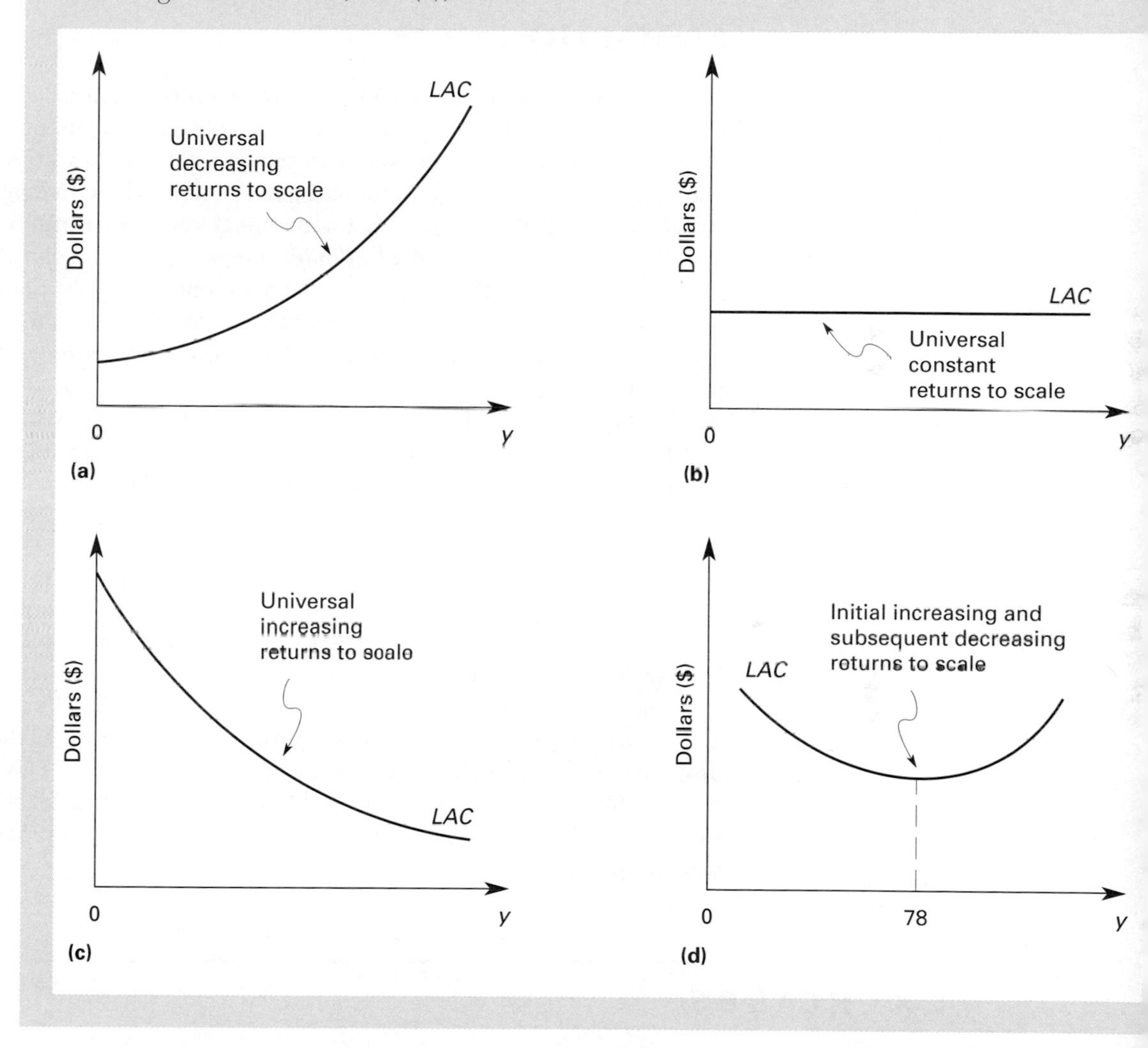

We know that a U-shaped average cost curve reflects *initial increasing and subsequent decreasing returns to scale*, as in Figure 7.14d. Broadly speaking, *two possible market structures* arise in this case. If the output level at which $LAC(y)$ attains its minimum value (78 units in Figure 7.13d) is relatively large, we again expect to see a market characterized by *monopoly* or *oligopoly*. On the other hand, if the output level at which the long-run average cost curve attains its minimum value is relatively small, then a large number of relatively small firms will supply the good or service. The initial increasing returns to scale guarantee that production will be done by firms, and the subsequent decreasing returns to scale guarantee that a large number of firms will do the job. Since there will be a large number of competing firms, we will have a *competitive market*.

In this section, we have laid the groundwork for understanding market structure. In Chapters 8 and 9, we take a closer look at competitive markets typified by a relatively large number of firms, while in Chapter 10 we turn to the problem of monopoly. In Part VI we examine the case of industries characterized by relatively few firms.

SUMMARY

This chapter continued the exploration of a firm's production function begun in Chapter 6 by extending the analysis to cases in which more than one input is variable. We drew on correspondences between consumer theory and the theory of the firm as we looked at *isoquants* (analogous to indifference curves), defined the marginal rate of technical substitution *MRTS* (analogous to the marginal rate of substitution in consumption), and discussed the *assumption of a diminishing marginal rate of technical substitution*.

We then defined the important concept of returns to scale. Suppose we double the quantities of all inputs. We have *constant returns to scale* if output also doubles, *increasing returns to scale* if output more than doubles, and *decreasing returns to scale* if output less than doubles.

Turning from the theory of production to the theory of cost, we solved the firm's *cost-minimization problem* for y units of output by identifying the input bundle on the isoquant for y units of output where *MRTS* is equal to w_1/w_2, or where the marginal product per dollar is identical for all the inputs in the input bundle.

We then took up several comparative statics exercises. One of the resulting propositions — that firms substitute away from inputs as those inputs become relatively more expensive — is extremely useful in understanding economic reality. We then turned to the important relationship between returns to scale and costs of production. We saw that as output increased, the average cost of production increased, decreased, or remained unchanged as returns to scale were decreasing, increasing, or constant.

We then compared costs in the short run and the long run. All the comparisons were driven by two fundamental points: the short-run cost function *STC* is tangent to the long-run cost function *TC* at one point, and *STC* lies above *TC* at all other points. Finally, we presented a cost-based *theory of market structure* that prepares the way for the analysis in Part IV.

EXERCISES

1. Suppose that a cost-minimizing firm, faced with constant input prices, recently increased the quantity of each of its inputs by 10 percent. As a result, its output increased from 100 units to 120 units. Indicate whether each of the following statements is true, false, or uncertain, and explain your answer.
   a. When y is 100, there are increasing returns to scale.
   b. The firm's production function is not homothetic.
   c. When y is 100, *LAC* is downward sloping.
   d. When y is 100, *LMC* exceeds *LAC*.
   e. When y is 100, *LMC* is downward sloping.

f. If the firm had increased the quantity of each input by 5 percent, output would increase from 100 to 110 units.

2. Suppose that when $w_1 = w_2 = \$10$, the cost-minimizing bundle for 100 units of output is $z_1 = z_2 = 20$. When $w_1 = \$8$ and $w_2 = \$10$, the cost-minimizing bundle for 110 units of output is $z_1 = 28$ and $z_2 = 19$. Indicate whether each of the following statements is true, false, or uncertain, and explain your answer.
   a. When $w_1 = w_2 = \$10$, *LAC* for $y = 100$ is \$4.
   b. Input 2 is an inferior input.
   c. Input 1 is a normal input.
   d. The firm's output expansion path is downward sloping.
   e. The production function is not homothetic.
   f. When $w_1 = w_2 = \$5$, *LAC* for $y = 100$ is \$2.
   g. When $w_1 = \$16$ and $w_2 = \$20$, the minimum cost of producing $y = 110$ is \$828.
   h. When $w_1 = \$8$ and $w_2 = \$10$, the minimum cost of producing $y = 100$ is no greater than \$360.
   i. The bundle with 22 units of both inputs will not produce $y = 110$.
   j. When $w_1 = \$20$ and $w_2 = \$20$, the minimum cost of producing $y = 110$ is no greater than \$940.

3. Indicate whether the following statements are true, false, or uncertain, and explain your answer.
   a. Increasing returns to scale and diminishing marginal product are incompatible.
   b. When the firm's output expansion path has a negative slope, input 2 is inferior.
   c. When the firm's output expansion path has a negative slope, both inputs are inferior.
   d. A cost-minimizing firm would never use an input bundle where the isoquant was upward sloping.
   e. At Fomoco, the marginal products of inputs 1 and 2 are 5 and 10, respectively, and their prices are \$30 and \$15; hence, Fomoco is using a cost-minimizing input bundle.
   f. The production function $F(z_1, z_2) = \min(z_1, 2z_2)$ is homothetic.

4. Indicate whether each of the following statements is possibly true or certainly false, and explain your answer.
   a. The cost-minimizing bundle for $y = 50$ is $z_1 = 10$ and $z_2 = 40$ when $w_1 = w_2$, and it is $z_1 = 12$ and $z_2 = 37$ when $w_1 = \$20$ and $w_2 = \$15$.
   b. The cost-minimizing bundle for $y = 50$ is $z_1 = 10$ and $z_2 = 40$ when $w_1 = w_2$, and it is $z_1 = 7$ and $z_2 = 42$ when $w_1 = \$20$ and $w_2 = \$15$.
   c. The cost-minimizing bundle for $y = 50$ is $z_1 = 10$ and $z_2 = 40$ when $w_1 = w_2$, and it is $z_1 = 6$ and $z_2 = 45$ when $w_1 = \$20$ and $w_2 = \$15$.

5. Complete the following table (note that the values in the MC column lie in between the values in the Q^s column):

Q^s	FC	VC	AVC	TC	MC	ATC
					250	
10			100	2500		
20						
					145	
30						195
40		5500				
50		6500				
60		7500				
70		8650				
80		10 100				
90		12 000				
100		14 500				

6. Jeff runs a roadside stand where he sells soft drinks. One of his creations, Razapple Juice, is concocted by mixing raspberry juice with apple juice. Long experience has taught Jeff that he must use at least 30 percent apple juice and at least 30 percent raspberry juice when mixing a batch of Razapple. If he does not, his customers demand a refund, claiming that the mix is not Razapple. If he does, they are perfectly satisfied with the product.
   a Considering only the costs associated with buying apple and raspberry juice, what is the minimum cost of producing a litre of Razapple Juice when raspberry juice costs \$2.50 per litre and apple juice costs \$5 per litre? When raspberry juice costs \$5 per litre and apple juice costs \$2.50 per litre? When raspberry juice

costs \$2.50 per litre and apple juice costs \$2.50 per litre?

b. Construct the isoquant for 1 litre of Razapple Juice and for y litres of Razapple Juice.
c. Find the cost-minimizing bundle for y litres of Razapple Juice when the price of a litre of apple juice is less than the price of a litre of raspberry juice and when the price of a litre of apple juice is greater than the price of a litre of raspberry juice.
d. Find the cost function for Razapple Juice.

7. A young entrepreneur, Liz, is considering going into the lawn-mowing business for the summer. Since she can work as many hours as she chooses in the family business at w_1 per hour, her time is worth w_1 per hour. The price per litre of the gasoline that she needs to buy for her lawn-mower is w_2. She can rent a mower that cuts a 30-centimetre swath and uses 1 litre of a gallon of gas per hour for w_3 per hour. Using this mower, she can cut 1000 square metres of lawn in an hour. For convenience, let 1000 square metres be the unit in which output is measured. She can rent a larger mower, for w_4 per hour, that uses 3 litres of gas per hour and cuts 3 units of lawn per hour.

   a. Find the production functions for the smaller and the larger mowers. Note that each production function has three inputs: hours of Liz's time, litres of gas, and hours of the smaller or the larger mower.
   b. Derive the conditional input demand functions and the cost functions.
   c. Show that using the smaller mower is a cheaper way to cut grass if $2w_1 < w_4 - 3w_3$. Why is this result independent of the price of gasoline?
   d. What price must she get for cutting a unit of lawn to induce her to choose to cut grass rather than to work in the family business?

8. Leigh's Fashions, a ladies' clothing plant, rents all of its capital and hires local labour by the day.

   a. Is this firm always on its long-run cost curve?
   b. Morgan Fashions is another plant that hires its workers, but owns all of its own capital outright. Is it true that Morgan Fashions has lower costs of business than Leigh's Fashions?

9. "If you can do something once, you should be able to do it twice. Hence all we can ever have is constant returns to scale." Comment.

10. If you are travelling through a remote small town, you may notice that vending machines are uncommon. The local bowling alley has an attendant to sell chips and pop, as does the gas station. In large urban centres, on the other hand, vending machines are much more common. Explain this using the notion of relative input prices and isoquants.

11. When more musical instruments playing each part are added to a symphony orchestra, the music is not only louder but "richer." Is this an example of increasing returns to scale?

12. Lindsay and Zane love to play squash. On average Zane wins more points with his forehand shot than with his backhand. Unfortunately, the more times he uses it, the less likely he is to catch Lindsay off guard. Suppose the percentage of shots won with a forehand for Zane is given by $100 - 10f$, where f is the proportion of forehand shots. The percentage of shots won with a backhand for Zane is given by $2 + 4f$. What is the optimal fraction of forehand shots for Zane to use?

13. "The production of y is a function of two inputs, z_1 and z_2, and the production function is $y = z_1 z_2^2$. If the input price for z_1 is equal to the input price for z_2, then to minimize costs, the firm will use equal quantities of both inputs." Indicate if this comment is true or false, and explain your answer.

14. "To minimize the cost of producing a given quantity of output, the input bundle must be chosen so that the marginal products of all inputs are identical." Indicate if this comment is true or false, and explain your answer.

15. Can all inputs be inferior?

*16. The following is a general case of the Cobb-Douglas production function:

$$F(z_1, z_2) = z_1^u z_2^v$$

where u and v are positive constants.

   a. What is the marginal product of input 1? Of input 2?

b. Show that, for this production function,

$$MRTS(z_1, z_2) = (uz_2/vz_1)$$

c. What do the first and second principles of cost minimization imply about the cost-minimizing input bundle for this production function?
d. Let $u = 1/3$ and $v = 2/3$, and then find the conditional input demand functions, the cost function, and the average cost function.
e. Then, for arbitrary u and v, find the conditional input demand functions, the cost function, and the average cost function.
f. Show that this production function is homothetic.
g. When does this production function exhibit increasing returns to scale? Decreasing returns to scale? Constant returns to scale?
h. Show that $MRTS(z_1, z_2)$ diminishes as input 1 is substituted for input 2 along any isoquant.

*17. Consider the following production functions:

$$(1) \quad F(z_1, z_2) = [(z_1)^2 + (z_2)^2]^{1/2}$$

$$(2) \quad F(z_1, z_2) = z_1 + z_2$$

a. On one diagram, draw the isoquants associated with one unit of output for both production functions, paying special attention to the points where the isoquants intersect the axes.
b. Keeping the shapes of these isoquants in mind, explain why the Lagrangian method for solving cost minimization problems is not appropriate for these production functions.
c. Find the marginal products and the marginal rates of technical substitution for these two production functions.
d. Does $MRTS(z_1, z_2)$ diminish as input 1 is substituted for input 2 along any isoquant of production function number 1? Along any isoquant of production function number 2?
e. What can you say about returns to scale for these production functions?
f. Now suppose that $w_1 < w_2$, and find the cost-minimizing bundles on each isoquant. Then find the cost-minimizing bundles when $w_1 > w_2$.
g. Find the cost functions associated with these production functions.

h. "The concave portion of any isoquant is economically irrelevant." Do you agree? Carefully explain your answer.

*18. Consider the following production function:

$$F(z_1, z_2) = (z_1 - 5)^{1/3}(z_2 - 7)^{2/3} \quad \text{if } z_1 \geq 5 \text{ and } z_2 \geq 7$$

$$F(z_1, z_2) = 0 \quad \text{if } z_1 < 5 \text{ or } z_2 < 7$$

a. Is there anything unusual about this production function?
b. What can you say about returns to scale for this production function?
c. What is the marginal product of input 1? Of input 2?
d. What is the marginal rate of technical substitution?
e. Suppose that the input prices are identical. Carefully draw the output expansion path.
f. Is this production function homothetic?
g. Find the conditional input demand functions and the cost function.

*19. Acme Hunting Supplies makes roadrunner traps for coyotes using labour and capital according to the following production function:

$$\text{Traps} = L^{1/2} + K^{1/3}.$$

a. What are the marginal products? The marginal rate of technical substitution?
b. Is there anything unusual about this production function? What are the shapes of the isoquants?
c. If Acme has orders for 3000 traps, what is the least costly combination of labour and capital to use if labour costs \$10 per hour and capital costs \$15 per hour?
d. What can you say about returns to scale for this production function?

20. An input is *essential* for a particular good if the good cannot be produced without the input. For each of the production functions in Exercises 11 through 14, indicate whether the inputs are essential or not.

*21. Output produced by a firm using inputs Z_1 and Z_2 with the production function $f(Z_1,Z_2) = Z_1Z_2$. The prices of the inputs are W_1 and W_2, respectively.

a. If Z_2 is fixed at Z_2^0, derive the short-run total cost function for the firm as a function of y, W_1,W_2, and Z_2^0.
b. Now suppose that Z_2 is free to vary. Using the first and second principles of cost minimization, derive the conditional input demand functions and the long-run total cost function.
c. What value of Z_2^0 would make the cost functions you found in (a) and (b) equal?
d. If Z_2^0 does not equal this value, which is larger, the cost function in (a) or (b)? Explain your answer using a diagram in Z_1, Z_2 space.

*22. Original Ray's makes "mystery meals" using two secret ingredients, Z_1 and Z_2. Its production function is homothetic and the prices of both inputs are the same. Last week, Original Ray's served 70 meals using the cost-minimizing bundle of $(Z_1, Z_2) = (20{,}50)$.

a. If Ray's produces 120, 150, or 200 meals using 90, 100, and 125 units of Z_2, respectively, what are the corresponding cost-minimizing values of Z_1?
b. Can we determine Ray's output expansion path from the given information? If yes, what is it? If no, explain why not.
c. Can we determine Ray's *MRTS* function from the given information? If yes, and Ray's makes "mystery meals" using two secret ingredients, Z_1 and Z_2, what is it? If no, explain why not.
d. Can either Z_1 or Z_2 be inferior? Explain.

23. In 1882, Thomas Edison built the first small-scale power plant in Manhattan. As the use of electricity increased, large-scale, centralized power plants were built and the electricity was shipped to customers along wire grids. Within the past few years firms have again developed small power plants which fit on office rooftops and generate electricity for the building alone, independent of an electrical grid. Suppose the twentieth century was dominated by power plants with economies of scale, but now those economies no longer exist. What changes do you think this difference will make to the structure of the electricity industry?

REFERENCES

Iannaccone, L., D. Olson and R. Stark. 1995. "Religious Resources and Church Growth," *Social Forces*, 74(2):705–31.

Lipsey, R. 2000. "Economies of Scale in Theory and Practice," unpublished manuscript.

Markets for Goods

In Part IV, we combine the theories of consumer choice and of the firm into a larger picture of the interaction of consumers and firms in markets for goods. Our objective is to learn about the forces that determine equilibrium price and quantity in any goods market and about the properties of equilibrium in such markets. We look at competitive markets for goods in Chapters 8 and 9 and monopoly markets for goods in Chapter 10. These chapters contain the core of the economists' tool kit.

CHAPTER 8

The Theory of Perfect Competition

At the end of the last chapter, we noted that one type of market structure — competition — is characterized by a large number of relatively small firms. In this chapter, we explore *perfect competition* in detail and define the kinds of markets to which the model of perfect competition applies. Much of the theory of perfect competition was developed by Alfred Marshall, a turn-of-the-century British economist. The classic reference is Book V of Marshall's *Principles of Economics* (1920).

In the first two sections, we focus on conceptual issues: What is a competitive equilibrium? What are its properties? In what circumstances is the model of perfect competition appropriate? In the remainder of the chapter, we look at technical issues: Where do the demand and supply functions used to identify a competitive equilibrium come from? How does short-run equilibrium differ from long-run equilibrium?

8.1 A Competitive Model of Exchange

By creating an extremely simple competitive model, we can highlight the essential features of competitive market transactions in the ordinary world. We will set aside production questions until Section 8.4 and focus on a simple **exchange economy**. In this very basic market, goods are exchanged but not produced.

exchange economy

The goods in our simple competitive model are five tickets to a rock concert and the participants are ten students. All ten students would like to see the concert but only five tickets are available. For simplicity, we will suppose that potential buyers are male and potential sellers are female. Each of the five female students has a ticket; none of the five male students do, nor can they buy a ticket elsewhere. The students can potentially enter into market exchanges among themselves. Which five students will ultimately hold the concert tickets and at what price will the tickets be exchanged?

Assuming that each student wants only one ticket to the concert, we can completely describe the preferences of a student by a **reservation price**. If the student does not have a ticket, what is the maximum price he will pay to buy one? Or, if the student does have a ticket, what is the minimum price she will accept to sell it? In either case, the answer is the student's reservation price.

reservation price

A male student will buy a ticket if he is offered one at a price less than or equal to his reservation price, and will not buy one offered at a price greater than his reservation price. A female student will sell her ticket if she is offered a price higher than her reservation price but will not sell it if the price is less than or equal to her reservation price.

We can then describe the preferences of these ten students by ten reservation prices, R_A through R_J, which we will list in descending order. Let us suppose that the highest reservation price is \$100 and that reservation prices fall by \$10 decrements as we move down the list. Thus,

$$R_A = \$100, R_B = \$90, \ldots, R_J = \$10$$

Suppose that the five tickets are initially allocated to the five students whose reservation prices are $R_B = \$90$, $R_C = \$80$, $R_F = \$50$, $R_H = \$30$, and $R_I = \$20$. We will give each of these students a name that begins with the letter of the subscript identifying her reservation price. (Beatriz is the student whose reservation price is R_B, Cathy is the one whose reservation price is R_C, and so on.) These students are the *potential suppliers* of tickets. We will use the same system to identify the male students without tickets — the *potential demanders* — whose reservation prices are $R_A = \$100$, $R_D = \$70$, $R_E = \$60$, $R_G = \$40$, and $R_J = \$10$.

Market Demand

market demand function

We know the individual demand functions of each male student. For example, Dan is willing to buy one ticket at any price less than or equal to \$70, but he will not buy one at any higher price. We can use individual demand information of this kind to construct a **market demand function** that gives the total number of tickets demanded by the five male students at any given price. First, let us consider relatively high prices. Because Ahmed's reservation price, $R_A = \$100$, is the highest of the five demanders, we know that if the price of a ticket exceeds \$100, the demand for tickets will be zero. At slightly lower prices — prices below $R_A = \$100$ but above $R_D = \$70$ — Ahmed is willing to buy a ticket, but Dan and the other three demanders are not. At such moderately high prices, the market demand is one ticket. At any price less than $R_D = \$70$ but greater than $R_E = \$60$, Ahmed and Dan are willing to buy tickets, but Earl and the remaining two demanders are not. At any price in this range, the market demand is two tickets. By simply repeating this procedure, we can construct the entire market demand function for the group of five demanders.

That market demand function is plotted in Figure 8.1a, where p is price and y is quantity. The six vertical line segments labelled *dd* represent the market demand function. (The horizontal dashed lines have been added to visually complete the shape of the demand function.) To read the quantity demanded at any given price from Figure 8.1a, first locate the price on the vertical axis, move horizontally to the demand function, and then move vertically downward to identify quantity demanded on the horizontal axis. For instance, at a price of \$25, the quantity demanded is four.

Market Supply

market supply function

Now let us construct a **market supply function**. Whether or not the suppliers will be willing to sell their tickets is determined by their individual reservation prices. For instance, Cathy will offer her ticket for sale at any price greater than $R_C = \$80$, but she will keep it at any price less than or equal to \$80. Using this kind of information, we can construct the market supply function just as we constructed the market demand function.

FIGURE 8.1 Demand and supply

In (a), we have constructed the market demand function implied by the five reservation prices of students without tickets: \$100, \$70, \$60, \$40, and \$10. In (b), we have constructed the market supply function implied by the five reservation prices of students with tickets: \$20, \$30, \$50, \$80, and \$90.

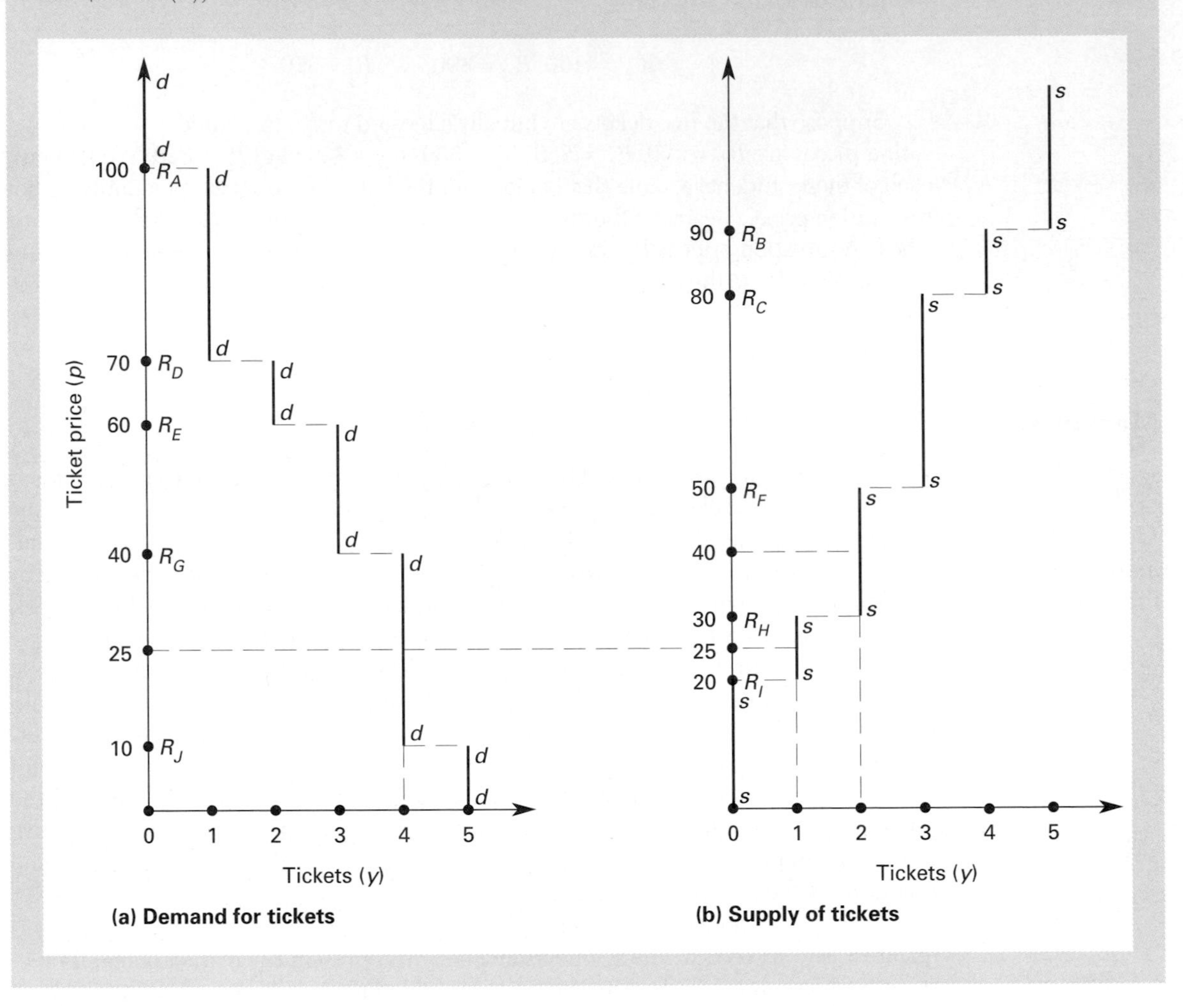

The market supply function in Figure 8.1b is composed of five vertical segments labelled *ss* and connected by dashed lines. Figure 8.1b is read in exactly the same way as Figure 8.1a. For example, if the price is \$40, two tickets will be supplied: Helen and Irina will each offer a ticket for sale because \$40 exceeds their reservation prices (\$30 and \$20), but the remaining three suppliers will not because \$40 is less than their reservation prices (\$50, \$80, and \$90).

Notice that in Figure 8.1 all individuals supply or demand only one unit of the good, and their individual demand and supply curves are given by their reservation willingness to pay for that good. In such a case everyone is either "in" or "out" of the market. This in-or-out decision is called the **extensive margin**. In this situation all demanders are out of the market when the price is very high. As the price falls, demanders start to enter the market, but they never increase their quantity demanded as the price

extensive margin

falls. Likewise, at a very high price every supplier is in the market, and as price falls they leave. In Chapter 3 we mostly examined the case where an individual demanded more than one unit at a time. When the price of the good fell, they demanded more of that good. Thus, in Chapter 3 we were examining the **intensive margin**. As Figure 8.1 shows, even when demanders and suppliers are only on the extensive margin, the market demand curve is downward sloping, and the market supply is upward sloping.

intensive margin

The Walrasian Auctioneer

Now that both the market supply and the market demand functions are in place, how many tickets will ultimately be exchanged and at what price? In other words, what will be the equilibrium in this market for concert tickets?

As you will see later, all participants in competitive markets are assumed to be *price takers*, not *price setters*; that is, to take the price as given. In our imaginary simple market, we will imagine that there is an auctioneer who acts as a *price setter* in the market. The auctioneer is called the **Walrasian auctioneer** (pronounced "Valrasian") after the nineteenth-century French economist Léon Walras (pronounced "Val-russ"), who invented this useful analytical device to study competitive equilibrium.

Walrasian auctioneer

Suppose the Walrasian auctioneer begins by announcing a price for a ticket. Each demander then writes "*X*" on a slip of paper if he is willing to buy a ticket at that price and "*O*" if he is not. At the same time, each supplier writes down "*Y*" if she is willing to sell a ticket at that price and "*O*" if she is not.

The auctioneer then collects the slips from all ten students and compares the number of *X*'s — quantity demanded at the announced price — and the number of *Y*'s — quantity supplied at the announced price. If quantity demanded at the announced price exceeds quantity supplied — that is, if there is **excess demand** — then the auctioneer announces a higher price and repeats the procedure. If, instead, quantity supplied exceeds quantity demanded — that is, if there is **excess supply** — then the auctioneer announces a lower price and repeats the procedure.

excess demand

excess supply

If the auctioneer announces the price $25, for example, Ahmed, Dan, Earl, and George will mark down *X*'s, but only Irina will write down a *Y*. Because there is excess demand, the auctioneer will announce a higher price and then tabulate the results at that new and higher price. If the auctioneer announces the price $95 only Ahmed will be willing to buy a ticket, but all five ticket holders will be willing to sell their tickets. Because there is excess supply, the auctioneer will announce a new, lower price and again tabulate the results.

The auction ends — and the market is in *competitive equilibrium* — only when quantity demanded is equal to quantity supplied. When this happens, the auctioneer collects money from each demander willing to buy at the announced price, gives the appropriate amount of money to each of the sellers, and transfers the tickets from sellers to buyers.

Competitive Equilibrium

How many tickets will be exchanged once this point of equilibrium has been reached, and what will the competitive equilibrium price be? In Figure 8.2, both the demand and supply functions have been plotted in one diagram. The demand function is labelled *DD* and the supply function *SS*. From Figure 8.2, we see that the auction will end only when the auctioneer announces a price that lies somewhere in the interval $50 to $60.

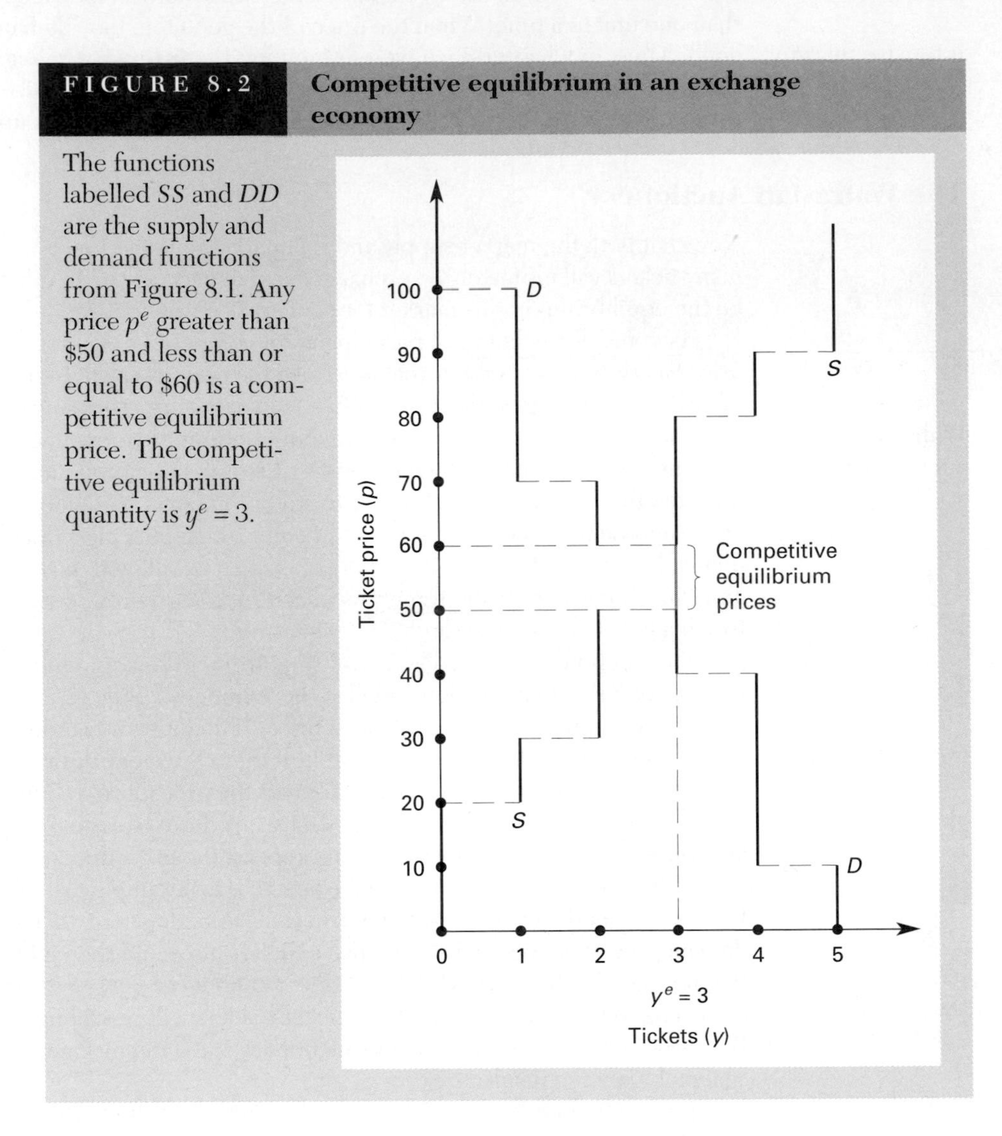

FIGURE 8.2 Competitive equilibrium in an exchange economy

The functions labelled SS and DD are the supply and demand functions from Figure 8.1. Any price p^e greater than \$50 and less than or equal to \$60 is a competitive equilibrium price. The competitive equilibrium quantity is $y^e = 3$.

At higher prices, there is excess supply; at lower prices, excess demand. At any price in this interval, however, three tickets will be demanded and three supplied.

competitive equilibrium

Any point at which quantity demanded is equal to quantity supplied is a **competitive equilibrium**. In this case, there are many competitive equilibrium prices. Denoting an equilibrium price by p^e, we see that $\$50 < p^e \leq \$60$. (We have used the weak inequality sign because we assume that at \$60, Earl — whose reservation price is \$60 — will buy a ticket.) Denoting an equilibrium quantity by y^e, we see that in each of these competitive equilibria $y^e = 3$; that is, three tickets are exchanged.

This market-clearing process thus determines both equilibrium price and equilibrium quantity. In our ticket model, although the equilibrium quantity is unique, the equilibrium price is not: the auction will stop when the auctioneer announces any price between \$50 and \$60. The equilibrium price that actually emerges from the auction will depend on the precise rules used by the auctioneer. Yet, equilibrium price and quantity are simply by-products of a more fundamental process in this competitive market: the allocation of tickets and of wealth to students. By allocation, we mean two things: (1) which students finally do and do not have a ticket to the concert, and (2) how much money is in each student's pocket at the end of the process. The competitive equilibrium therefore determines how both tickets and wealth (or command over all other goods) are allocated to students.

Pareto Optimality, or Efficiency

One feature of the *competitive equilibrium allocation* in this market deserves careful attention. The students with the five highest reservation prices, R_A through R_E, have tickets, and the five students with the lower reservation prices, R_F through R_J, do not; that is, the five students who value the tickets most highly are the ones who have them. An implication of this feature is that no further exchange of tickets for money between any two of the ten students can keep both students as well off and make at least one of them better off. Why is this true?

The highest reservation price among those without tickets is Fran's, $R_F = \$50$, and the lowest among those with tickets is Earl's, $R_E = \$60$. Since R_E exceeds R_F, there is no sum of money that Fran will be willing to offer Earl for a ticket and that Earl will also be willing to accept. We have then established an important result: the competitive equilibrium allocation is **Pareto-optimal**, since no student can be made better off while leaving the other students at least as well off. This illustrates an important, even fundamental, result:

Pareto-optimal

Provided that certain conditions are met, a competitive equilibrium allocation is Pareto-optimal, or efficient.

PROBLEM 8.1

Suppose that the reservation prices for the tickets to our rock concert increased in variance, but that the ranking remained the same. That is, suppose $R_A = 200$, $R_B = 180$, ... $R_J = 20$. What would happen to the allocation of tickets? What would happen to gains from trade? Will competitive markets be of more or less value as the differences among people increases?

We will consider the conditions under which competitive equilibrium is Pareto-optimal at various points in this and later chapters. Before we move on, however, see if you can spot the relevance of this well-known economics joke. Three men were golfing: an economist, a counsellor, and a priest. Ahead of them was a pathetic twosome, who were hitting balls all over the place and taking forever to make their shots. The three men started to make rude remarks, and by the sixth hole they were getting nasty. Finally the twosome's caddie came back and said, "Gentlemen, please don't be so mean. The men in front of you are ex-firefighters who lost their sight in a fire rescuing little children." "Oh, this is terrible," remarked the counsellor. "I've spent my whole life trying to make people feel good about themselves, and look what I've done." "Oh, this is terrible," said the priest. "I've spent my whole life working to improve the lot of man, and look what I've said." "Oh, this is terrible," said the economist. "These men should be golfing at night."

Politicians and business leaders often talk about "win-win" situations. If both parties to the transaction come out better than when they went in, is the exchange Pareto-optimal? Not if there is a third party who is made worse off. For example, consider native land claims. It may well be that settling a claim makes both the provincial government and the natives better off; but the taxpayers or those who previously held the land might be worse off. When something is not Pareto-optimal it does not necessarily mean that the total costs are greater than the total benefits, nor that it is a bad choice; it only means that *someone* was made worse off. Settling the land claim may well be the best thing to do even though it is not a Pareto-optimal outcome. Pareto-optimality is a very high standard, and few things in life are truly "win-win" all the way around.

One of the features of the Pareto equilibrium condition we just observed is that it maximizes the gains from trade. No other allocation of the tickets leads to a larger level of consumer and seller surplus. This also means that the competitive equilibrium maximizes the average value of goods and that the average value of goods must be greater than the price — which equals the marginal value. Randomly allocating goods among people can only lower the value of those goods because individuals with low reservation values are more likely to acquire them.

▶ Application: Why Everyone Loves Britney Spears

Another way of thinking about competitive equilibriums maximizing the gains from trade is to realize who ends up consuming goods. Those people with the highest valuations consume the goods. This means, when we observe consumption behaviour, that we're not seeing a random sample but a biased one.

Consider the case of a Britney Spears concert. None of the authors has ever been to such a concert, and none of us likely ever will ... it's just not our cup of tea. But check out those lined up to get into the concert, or listen to the reviews of those coming out afterwards. Everyone loves Britney! Why is this? It's because only someone who loves her music and performances would be willing to stand in line for several hours for the right to buy a $100 ticket. Britney could come out on stage and play checkers and these people would still be happy.

As another example, have you ever heard people say things like, "Hot dogs taste better at a baseball game?" If anything, a hot dog tastes better when it's made fresh at home, but few at home ever boast about a hot dog. Hot dogs at a ballpark cost about $5 each. Only someone who really likes hot dogs will be willing to pay such a price. Again, it could be a poor hot dog, and the person might still rave about it. If we were to randomly allocate Britney Spears tickets or randomly allocate hot dogs at the ball park, the opinions about quality would change dramatically. A competitive market allocates goods in a very special way.

The Role of Initial Allocation

What would happen with a different initial allocation of tickets to students? Would the equilibrium price and quantity also be different? Would the tickets still be allocated to those with the highest reservation prices? Would the equilibrium allocation again be Pareto-optimal? To find out, try the following problem.

PROBLEM 8.2

Suppose that the students who were given the tickets in the initial allocation were those with the reservation prices \$100, \$90, \$70, \$40, and \$10. Construct a diagram analogous to Figure 8.2. What is the range of equilibrium prices and the equilibrium quantity in this case? What is the allocation of tickets in this competitive equilibrium? Identify the students who are better off and those who are worse off in the new equilibrium than in the original equilibrium.

This problem illustrates some important points about this particular economy. First, the competitive equilibrium quantity depends on the *initial allocation*. In the case analyzed in the text, the quantity exchanged in the competitive equilibrium was 3. However, in Problem 8.2 — where the initial allocation of tickets to students was different — the quantity exchanged was 2. To cite another example of the dependence of equilibrium quantity on the initial allocation: first, if tickets were initially given to the students with the five highest reservation prices, equilibrium quantity would be zero. Second, a student is better off when he or she initially has a ticket. Third, although equilibrium quantity and the welfare of individual students depend on the initial allocation, the competitive equilibrium allocation is always the same. In the competitive equilibrium, the tickets go to the five students, male or female, with the five highest reservation prices.

The Function of Price

Finally, notice that the range of competitive equilibrium prices does not depend on the initial allocation in this model. This reflects the fact that price is a signal that serves to allocate tickets to the students who place the highest value on them. The imaginary device of a Walrasian auctioneer highlights the allocational role of price, since each demander responds to the announced price by indicating whether he wants to buy a ticket at that price and each supplier responds by indicating whether she wants to sell her ticket at that price. Thus, we see the fundamental role that price plays in an unfettered market economy — that is, in an economy free of impediments to the voluntary exchange of goods or services between suppliers and demanders.

In a market economy, prices are the signals that guide and direct allocation.

In our ticket model, price performs this allocative function well, since the equilibrium is Pareto-optimal. As we will see in subsequent chapters, however, the Pareto optimality of competitive equilibrium is a result that requires careful qualification and interpretation. For example, in Chapter 18, we will look at some important qualifications under the general heading of *externalities*. In the meantime, you can discover the general nature of such qualifications in the following problem.

PROBLEM 8.3

Consider a ticket model with just four people and two tickets. Harry and Sarah have ordinary reservation prices, each equal to \$10. However, because Jane and Bob are dating, their reservation prices are interrelated. If Jane has a ticket, then Bob's reservation price is \$20; if she does not, his reservation price is \$0. Similarly, if Bob has a ticket, Jane's reservation price is \$20; if he does not, her reservation price is \$0. Show that there are two competitive equilibrium allocations. In one allocation, the price is less than or equal to \$10, and Harry and Sarah have the tickets. In the other, the price is greater than \$10 and less than \$20, and Jane and Bob have the tickets. Show that the first of these allocations is not Pareto-optimal.

8.2 Potential Difficulties with the Competitive Model

Our ticket model is founded on two crucial assumptions that are analytical trouble spots. Because these two troublesome assumptions are at the core of all models of perfect competition, we will look at both very carefully.

Price Taking or Price Manipulating

First, let us consider the implicit assumption that all the students behaved as if they were price takers. We assumed that in responding to the auctioneer's announced price, the students simply consulted their preferences and honestly reported the action that was in their own self-interest at the announced price.

Yet any of these students might have *misrepresented* their preferences in an attempt to influence the market-clearing price. Indeed, we can easily identify real-world situations in which demanders or suppliers intentionally misrepresent their positions. In the residential real estate market, for instance, homeowners regularly quote a selling price higher than their real reservation price to agents or to prospective buyers in an attempt to increase the price at which the house is finally sold. Their behaviour indicates that they do not see themselves as mere price takers, unable to affect the market price of a good. On the other side of the real estate coin, potential home buyers typically negotiate by underrepresenting their real reservation price for buying a home in an attempt to lower the price at which the house is sold. Again, these potential home buyers do not see themselves as price takers.

Individuals do have the incentive and, as we will see, some power to manipulate prices. Suppose that nine students in our ticket model are ingenuous souls who view themselves as price takers but that one student is a fox among the chickens: a price manipulator. Now, suppose that the manipulator is a supplier, Fran. How can she increase the market-clearing price? By responding to the auctioneer's announced prices as if her reservation price were higher than $R_F = \$50$, or, loosely speaking, by reporting a false reservation price R_F' higher than \$50. Will her manipulative behaviour pay off? Suppose that her false reservation price R_F' is \$55, which is less than Earl's reservation price, $R_E = \$60$, but greater than her true reservation price, $R_F = \$50$.

Fran's price manipulation in this case gives rise to a (false) supply function that shifts from two to three tickets at \$55 rather than at \$50. As you can easily verify, the range of market-clearing prices is now reduced from the interval \$50 to \$60 to the interval \$55 to \$60. In this instance, Fran's deliberate misrepresentation works to her advantage (and, incidentally, to the advantage of Helen and Irina as well) because the market-clearing price may increase but will not decrease as a result of her manipulations.

What will happen if Fran decides to report an even higher false reservation price, \$65, which is larger than R_E = \$60 but less than R_D = \$70? Now the (false) supply function, $S'S'$ in Figure 8.3, shifts from two to three tickets at \$65. In this situation, the auction will not close at a competitive equilibrium price. Instead, as Figure 8.3 reveals, the market-clearing price will be in the interval \$60 to \$65, and only two units will be traded. Ahmed and Dan will each buy a ticket, and Helen and Irina will each sell one. In this case, Fran's misrepresentation works to her disadvantage, since she ends up keeping a ticket she otherwise would have sold.

If she does not overdo it, then, Fran can manipulate the price of the tickets to her own advantage by misrepresenting her true position — and she may be tempted to do so. Of course, any of the demanders or suppliers could choose to play the role of the fox among the chickens. If one of the demanders — Earl, for example — is the price manip-

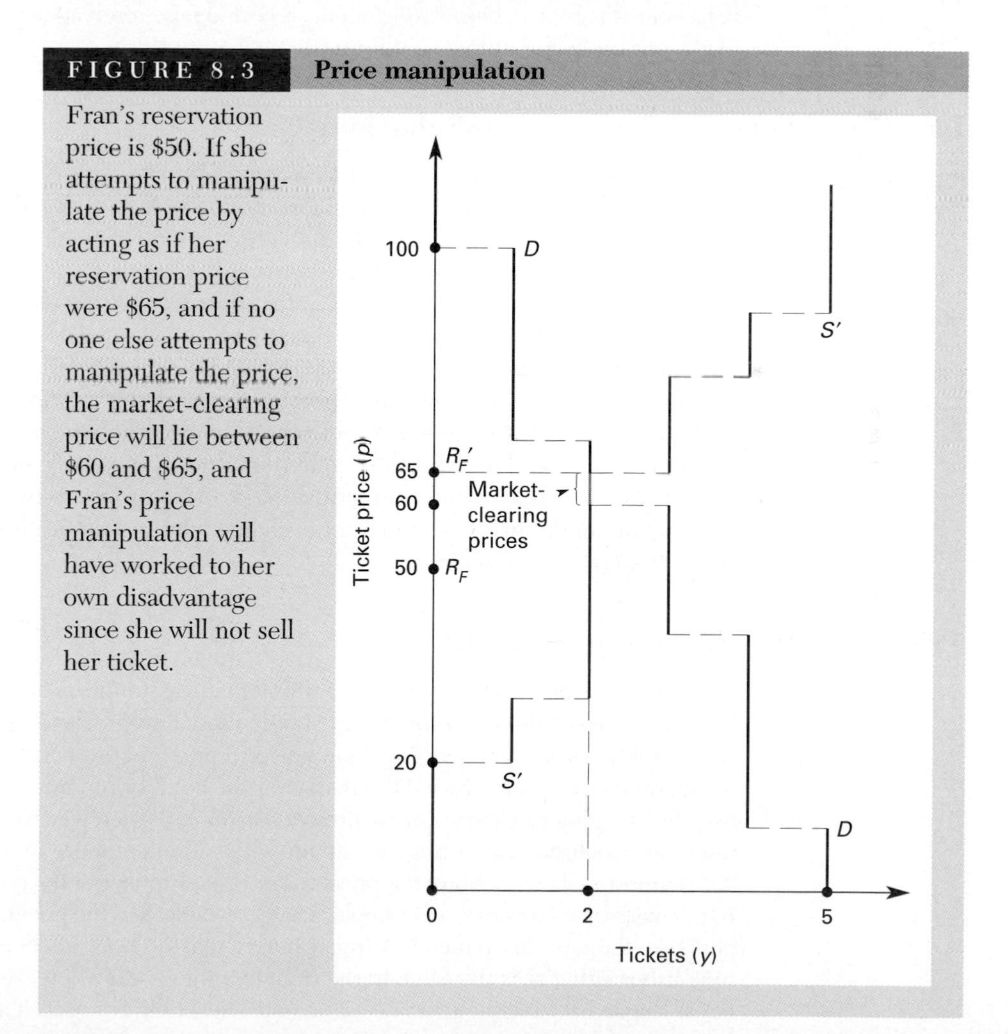

FIGURE 8.3 Price manipulation

Fran's reservation price is \$50. If she attempts to manipulate the price by acting as if her reservation price were \$65, and if no one else attempts to manipulate the price, the market-clearing price will lie between \$60 and \$65, and Fran's price manipulation will have worked to her own disadvantage since she will not sell her ticket.

ulator instead of Fran, and if the nine other students all represent their positions honestly, he could reduce the range of market-clearing prices from the interval \$50 to \$60 to the interval \$50 to \$52 by reporting the false reservation price $R_E' = \$52$. If Earl is the only price manipulator, reporting $R_E' = \$52$ would clearly be in his own best interest.

PROBLEM 8.4

Suppose that Earl chooses to report an even lower false reservation price, $R_E' = \$45$. What would be the range of market-clearing prices? How many tickets would be traded? Who would gain and who would lose as a result of this misrepresentation?

Why would any of the students then choose to be chickens (or price takers) rather than foxes (or price manipulators)? By misrepresenting their true reservation prices rather than reporting them honestly, all the students could potentially manipulate the market-clearing price to their own advantage. Yet if any of them chose to do so, the result might or might not be a competitive equilibrium. And, of course, the manipulator might or might not gain from the misrepresentation. The assumption of price-taking behaviour is necessary because if students reported false reservation prices, the outcome might not be a competitive equilibrium.

Large Numbers and Price-Taking Behaviour

One way out of this dilemma is to restrict our model to situations in which there are large numbers of both demanders and suppliers, none of whom demands or supplies a significant percentage of the quantity traded in a competitive equilibrium. In this case, it is reasonable to suppose that the gaps between reservation prices will be small. As a result, since no individual can significantly affect the market-clearing price by misrepresenting his or her true position, no individual has any incentive to try to manipulate price. If, for instance, out of 100 000 wheat farmers, one farmer chooses to report a false reservation price, the likely consequences are that the price will not be significantly affected, and the lone manipulator will end up holding wheat that he or she would have preferred to sell at the equilibrium price. Given large numbers of insignificant buyers and sellers, the competitive model is appropriate because all potential participants in the process of market exchange will see themselves as price takers rather than price manipulators.

Price Making: The Walrasian Auctioneer

We have now come to terms with one problematic assumption only to be confronted by another, more difficult one. In our simple model, we invoked the convenient artifice of a Walrasian auctioneer, who announced a price, adjusted it in response to excess demand or supply, and cleared the market at the equilibrium price. This artifice functions like the dramatic device of the *deus ex machina*, the god who brings a play to a harmonious conclusion by sorting out the muddled affairs of mere human beings.

In most real transactions, the price maker is the supplier or the demander (or both). In the market for groceries, for example, a Safeway outlet sets the prices, and grocery shoppers take them (or leave them). A tuna cannery sets the price it will pay for tuna, and a tuna fisher either sells the catch to the cannery or goes elsewhere. A ticket scalper at a major league ballpark quotes a price; a potential ticket buyer rejects it and offers another;

the scalper rejects the buyer's price and makes another. The process continues until either the two strike a bargain or the potential buyer goes off to find another scalper.

In all these cases, price makers are constrained by the prices their competitors offer, because their potential customers (or suppliers) typically have the option of approaching someone else. Safeway cannot set prices higher than those their customers think they can get at the A&P, for example, without losing potential buyers to the A&P. The point remains, however, that individual suppliers or demanders are the price makers in most actual market transactions.

Once we eliminate the assumption of the auctioneer, does any other assumption guarantee that a competitive equilibrium will result from the more characteristic real-world process of offer and counter-offer?

Perfect Information

Economists sometimes invoke the assumption of perfect information to fill the void. The argument is that if all buyers and sellers are sufficiently well informed, the process of offer and counter-offer will result in a competitive equilibrium price. Suppose that all the participants in the process of exchange set prices: buyers make bids to buy and sellers make offers to sell. Suppose, too, that every buyer knows the offer prices of all sellers and that every seller knows the bid prices of all buyers. All the buyers will approach the seller with the lowest offer price; the seller then raises it. Conversely, all the sellers will approach the buyer with the highest bid price; the buyer then lowers it. This process continues until all the bid and offer prices converge to the same price.

Will the price at the point of convergence necessarily be a competitive equilibrium price? If it were not, there would be either excess demand or excess supply. If there were excess demand, some buyer or buyers, unable to buy anything at the common price, would raise their bid prices, and sellers would respond by raising their offer prices. At a common price, then, there can be neither excess demand nor excess supply; that is, a competitive equilibrium price has been reached.

The bedrock assumptions of the theory of competitive markets are thus large numbers (or price taking) and perfect information. But are either or both assumptions necessary? Economists debate whether or not a competitive equilibrium will result from voluntary market exchange even in the absence of large numbers of inconsequential buyers and sellers or of perfect information.

8.3 The Assumptions of Perfect Competition

Having looked at perfect competition in a simple exchange economy, we can now present a comparatively more complex treatment of the theory in markets where firms produce the goods demanded by consumers. We will begin by setting out the traditional assumptions on which the theory is built: the two assumptions described in the last section, and three new ones.

ASSUMPTION: LARGE NUMBERS

No individual demander buys and no individual supplier produces a significant proportion of the total output.

As we saw in considering a simplified market environment, this assumption implies that all demanders and suppliers will be price takers. Here, we will broaden the assumption somewhat to apply to more complex market environments in which goods are also produced.

ASSUMPTION: PERFECT INFORMATION

All participants have perfect knowledge of all relevant prices and of all relevant technological information.

That is, on one hand, firms know the prices of all the goods they could possibly produce, the technology for producing those goods, and the prices at which they could buy the required inputs. On the other hand, all individuals know both the prices at which they can buy all goods and the prices at which they can sell their resources in general and their labour in particular.

The third assumption concerns the nature of the products made for sale in a competitive market.

ASSUMPTION: PRODUCT HOMOGENEITY

In any given market, the products of all firms are identical.

This assumption limits the applicability of the competitive model to markets in which the products made by competing firms are the same, or *homogeneous.* The model applies to the market for corn, for instance, because the corn produced by thousands of farmers is virtually indistinguishable. But it does not apply to the automotive industry, because no two firms' cars or trucks are identical.

The fourth assumption concerns the possibility of switching resources from one use to another.

ASSUMPTION: PERFECT MOBILITY OF RESOURCES

All inputs are perfectly mobile.

If firms can freely allocate resources to different uses, they are then able both to expand (or to contract) their scale of production in a particular market and to enter (or to leave) the industry itself. As we will see later on in the chapter, this flexibility, or *mobility*, plays an important role in the theory of perfect competition.

The fifth assumption rules out a variety of externalities. It rules out, for example, the interdependent preferences you encountered in Problem 8.3. This assumption is not necessary for the competitive model, but it makes the analysis easier.

ASSUMPTION: INDEPENDENCE

The preferences of each individual are independent of the consumption decisions of other individuals and the production decisions of firms. The production functions of all firms are independent of the consumption decisions of individuals and the production decisions of other firms.

Instances of interdependent preferences abound in everyday life. For example, people who are sensitive to second-hand smoke often base their own decisions about where to work or sit in a restaurant on the behaviour of smokers in their vicinity. Technologies, too, are often interdependent. In Chapter 1, for example, you saw that how much oil a particular oil company could pump from a common pool depended on the decisions of other oil companies with wells in the same reservoir: the more oil that other firms pumped from the common pool, the less a particular firm could pump out of it. The independence assumption, however, rules out the complications of interdependent preferences and technologies. In Chapter 18, we consider these problems, known as externality problems.

8.4 The Firm's Short-Run Supply Decision

As we saw in the ticket exchange model, competitive equilibrium price and quantity are determined by the intersection of a demand and a supply function. Before we can implement this approach in a situation where firms supply goods and consumers demand them, we need the firm's short-run supply function.

What exactly is a short-run supply function? Just as an individual consumer's demand function for good y tells us how much the consumer will demand at any given price p, so the individual firm's short-run supply function for good y tells us how much the firm will supply at any given price p. Just as we found the consumer's demand function by solving the consumer's utility-maximizing problem, we can find the firm's short-run supply function by solving its profit-maximizing problem.

A firm's profit is simply the firm's revenue minus its cost:

$$\text{profit} = \text{revenue} - \text{cost}$$

total revenue function

Since the competitive firm is a price taker, its revenue is just price multiplied by the quantity produced, or py. It is convenient to call this expression the competitive firm's **total revenue function**, $TR(y)$. Thus,

$$TR(y) = py$$

In the short run, the competitive firm's cost is given by the short-run cost function $STC(y)$ from Chapter 7. We can therefore express the firm's profit as a function of its output y in the following way:

$$\pi(y) = TR(y) - STC(y)$$

profit function

We will call $\pi(y)$ the firm's **profit function** because this function gives us the firm's profit as a function of its output y.

Notice that profit depends on both price p and output y. But, since the competitive firm is a price taker, price is an exogenous variable — one that the firm cannot choose. It can choose its own output, however, and y is therefore the endogenous variable in this profit-maximizing problem. The problem we want to solve is then

$$\text{maximize profit } \pi(y) \text{ by choice of output } y$$

short-run supply function

The solution to this problem will give us the profit-maximizing output, which we will denote by y^*, as a function of the exogenous variable p. This function is called the firm's **short-run supply function**. Keep in mind that all relevant prices are held constant in this exercise — the price of the firm's output p is constant, and the prices of all the inputs the firm uses are also held constant.

In Figure 8.4a, the firm's total revenue function is the line py, and its short-run cost function is the curve STC. Because p is fixed, the total revenue function is a straight line whose slope is p: each additional unit of output adds p to the firm's total revenue. The short-run cost function is the standard stylization from Section 7.4.

The profit function $\pi(y)$ in Figure 8.4b is derived from the two functions in Figure 8.4a by subtracting cost $STC(y)$ from revenue py for every value of y. For example, when output is 33, profit is the distance CD in Figure 8.4a. Therefore, the distance C′D′ in

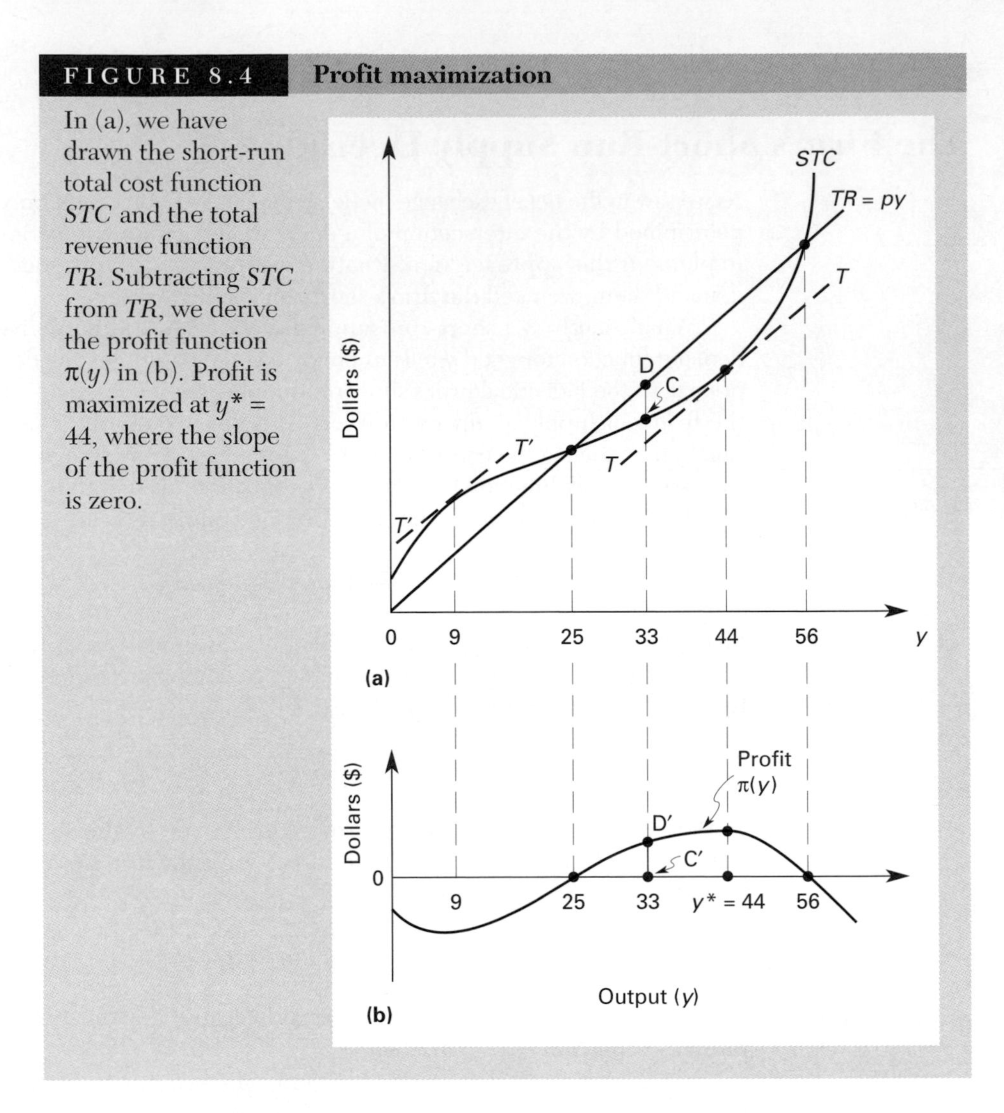

FIGURE 8.4 **Profit maximization**

In (a), we have drawn the short-run total cost function *STC* and the total revenue function *TR*. Subtracting *STC* from *TR*, we derive the profit function $\pi(y)$ in (b). Profit is maximized at $y^* = 44$, where the slope of the profit function is zero.

Figure 8.4b is equal to the distance CD in Figure 8.4a. Notice, too, that in Figure 8.4a, revenue is equal to cost at two levels of output — at 25 and at 56. Therefore, in Figure 8.4b, profit is equal to zero at these output levels. Finally, notice that profit is negative when output is less than 25 or when it is greater than 56.

The profit-maximizing output in Figure 8.4 is clearly $y^* = 44$. What can we say about this level of output that will help us to identify the firm's profit-maximizing rule and, therefore, its supply function? The crucial observation is that the slope of the profit function is zero at $y^* = 44$ or, putting the same observation differently, that the rate of change of profit with respect to output is zero at the point where profit is a maximum. To see why, notice that if the slope of the profit function is positive (as it is to the left of 44 units of output in Figure 8.4b), the firm can increase profit by increasing output. Conversely, if the slope of $\pi(y)$ is negative (as it is to the right of 44 units of output), the firm can increase profit by decreasing output. We can summarize this result:

The rate of change of profit with respect to output is zero at the point where profit is a maximum.

marginal revenue

short-run marginal cost

But the rate of change of profit with respect to output is simply the rate of change of total revenue with respect to output — **marginal revenue** MR — minus the rate of change of cost with respect to output — **short-run marginal cost** SMC. So, to maximize profit, the firm chooses the quantity of output where MR minus SMC is equal to zero, or where SMC is equal to MR. For a price-taking firm, MR is constant and equal to price p, since each unit of output contributes p to the firm's revenue. To maximize profit, therefore, the firm will choose the level of output y^* at which $SMC(y^*)$ is equal to MR, which itself is equal to price p. That is,

$$SMC(y^*) = MR = p$$

To understand this result, let us return to Figure 8.4a. Line TT, which is tangent to $SC(y)$ at $y^* = 44$, has the same slope as the total revenue function. This means that SMC is equal to MR at 44 units of output. As a result, the slope of the profit function is zero at $y^* = 44$.

We seem to have found a simple rule of thumb:

To maximize profit, produce the level of output at which marginal revenue (or price) is equal to marginal cost.

This rule requires qualification, however, because SMC is equal to MR at two levels of output in Figure 8.4 — at 44 units, where profit is a maximum, and at 9 units, where profit is a minimum. And as we will see, the firm's profit-maximizing rule requires yet another qualification.

Although the diagram in Figure 8.4 is fine for finding the profit-maximizing output for one price, it is not useful for finding the profit-maximizing output for many different prices. The "marginal revenue equals marginal cost" rule suggests that to find the firm's supply function, we need a diagram that includes MR and SMC. In Figure 8.5, we have also included the average variable cost function $AVC(y)$ to illustrate an additional qualification. We will show that the firm's short-run supply function is composed of the two segments labelled ss in Figure 8.5.

Let us begin by identifying the profit-maximizing output when price is \$36 in Figure 8.5. We know that the horizontal line running through \$36 and labelled MR is marginal revenue when price is \$36, since marginal revenue is equal to price. Notice that marginal cost is equal to marginal revenue, or $SMC = MR$, at two levels of output: 7 and 40. From Figure 8.4 we know that one of these levels of output maximizes profit and the other minimizes it. Which is which?

Profit is at a maximum at 40 units because $SMC(y)$ intersects MR from below. To see why, suppose that the firm is producing 40 units. What will happen to its profit if the firm produces an additional unit? The added cost of the extra unit is given by SMC and the added revenue by MR. Because SMC exceeds MR to the right of 40 units, the added unit of output adds more to cost than to revenue, and profit falls. Beginning again at 40, what will happen to the firm's profit if it produces one less unit of output? The reduction in revenue is given by MR and the reduction in cost by SMC. Since MR exceeds SMC to the left of 40 units, the decrease in revenue exceeds the decrease in cost, and profit falls once again. Profit is therefore at a maximum at 40 units.

FIGURE 8.5 The competitive firm's supply function

The competitive firm's supply function is composed of the two segments labelled *ss*. When p is less than \$23, the firm supplies nothing because it cannot cover the variable costs associated with any positive quantity. When p exceeds \$23, the firm chooses the level of output where $p = SMC$. Thus, the second segment of the firm's supply function is *SMC* above the point where *SMC* intersects *AVC*.

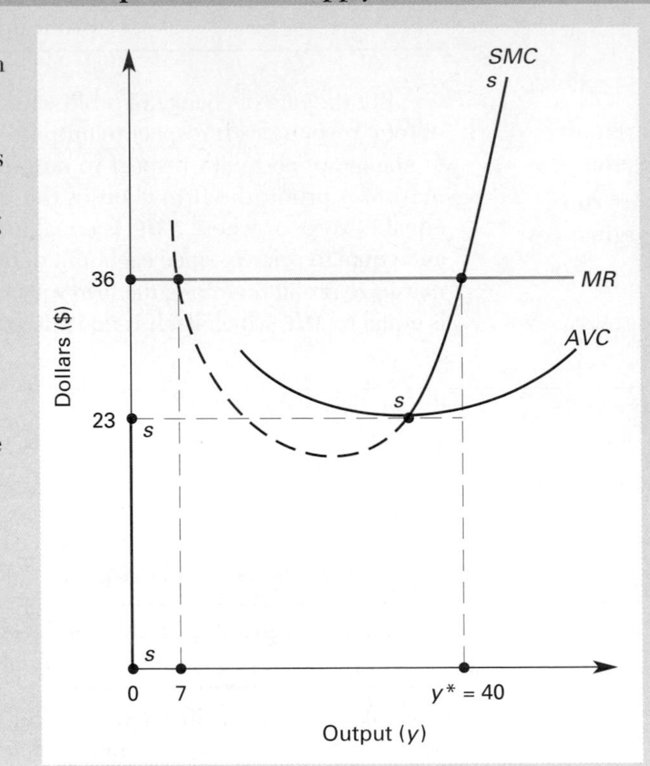

On the other hand, profit is at a minimum at 7 units because *SMC* intersects *MR* from above. To see why, let us suppose that the firm is producing 7 units. What will happen to its profit if the firm produces an additional unit? The added cost of the extra unit is given by *SMC*, and the added revenue by *MR*. Because *SMC* is less than *MR* to the right of 7 units, the increase in cost resulting from an additional unit of output is less than the increase in revenue, and profit rises. Beginning again at 7 units, what will happen to the firm's profit if it produces one less unit of output? The reduction in revenue is given by *MR* and the reduction in cost by *SMC*. Since *MR* is less than *SMC* to the left of 7 units, the decrease in revenue is less than the decrease in cost, and profit rises once again. Profit is therefore at a minimum at 7 units.

These results suggest a rule that can be used to identify the profit-maximizing output for any price: move horizontally from the price to the rising portion of *SMC* and then vertically down to the quantity axis. The firm's supply function therefore seems to be the rising, or positively sloped, portion of *SMC*.

This rule, however, needs a final qualification. Notice that in Figure 8.5, average variable cost is never less than \$23 since the minimum value of *AVC* is \$23. This means that at any price less than \$23, the firm cannot cover its variable costs of production if it produces a positive quantity of output. Because it can avoid these variable costs of production altogether by shutting down production, when price is less than \$23, the firm will maximize profit by producing nothing at all. The firm's supply curve in Figure 8.5 is then composed of the two segments labelled *ss*. These results are easily generalized:

When price is less than the minimum value of *AVC*, there is no positive level of output at which the firm can cover its variable costs of production, and it will therefore produce nothing. When price is greater than the minimum value of *AVC*, the firm's supply function is the rising portion of *SMC* that lies above *AVC*.[1]

Now let us find a way to represent the firm's profit using a similar diagram. Profit is simply total revenue py^* minus short-run total cost $STC(y^*)$. $STC(y^*)$ is equal to output multiplied by short-run average cost, or $y^*SAC(y^*)$. The firm's profit can therefore be expressed as

$$\pi(y^*) = y^*[p - SAC(y^*)]$$

By adding *SAC* to the diagram, we can identify the firm's profit as well as its supply function. In Figure 8.6 (on page 287), the firm's profit when p is \$36 can be identified by the area labelled *profit rectangle.* The vertical side of the profit rectangle is price minus short-run average cost, $p - SAC$. The horizontal side is the profit-maximizing output y^*. The area of the profit rectangle is then $y^*(p - SAC)$, or the firm's profit.

PROBLEM 8.5

Construct your own diagram of Figure 8.6, and suppose that p is \$24. In your diagram, identify the quantity that the firm will supply at this price. Notice that short-run average cost at this level of output is greater than $p = \$24$, so the firm's profit is negative. Construct a rectangle in your diagram with area equal to the firm's negative profit. Why would a firm ever produce a positive output when it makes a negative profit by doing so?

8.5 Short-Run Competitive Equilibrium

Graphically, a competitive equilibrium is determined by the intersection of a market demand function and a market supply function. To get the market demand function we need to add up or aggregate demand over individual demanders, and to get the market supply function we need to aggregate supply over individual firms.

---

1. The firm's supply function is derived by solving its profit-maximization problem: maximize $\pi(y)$ by choice of y. Differential calculus tells us two useful things about the profit-maximizing value of y, y^*, in the event that $y^* > 0$.

   1. If $\pi(y)$ is differentiable, then $\pi'(y^*) \equiv 0$. That is, a necessary condition for $y^* > 0$ to be the profit-maximizing value of y is that $\pi'(y)$ be equal to zero at y^*.
   2. If $\pi'(y^*) = 0$ and $\pi''(y^*) < 0$, then $\pi(y)$ attains a (local) maximum at y^*. That is, $\pi'(y^*) = 0$ and $\pi''(y^*) < 0$ are sufficient conditions for $\pi(y)$ to attain a (local) maximum at y^*.

These two statements allow us to find the firm's supply function. Application of the first yields

$$p - STC'(y^*) \equiv 0$$

or

$$p \equiv MC(y^*)$$

because $STC'(y)$ is $MC(y)$. The second statement is satisfied at y^* if $STC''(y^*) > 0$ or, equivalently, if $MC'(y^*) > 0$. $MC'(y^*) > 0$ simply means that the marginal cost function is rising at y^*. That is, $\pi''(y^*) < 0$ tells us that only the rising portion of the marginal cost function is relevant. Of course, y^* will be zero if p is less than the minimum value of $AVC(y)$, because in this case there is no positive output that will allow the firm to recover its variable costs.

Aggregating Demand

First, we will examine the *market demand function*. We have assumed that all demanders are price takers, and in Chapter 3 we used the same price-taking assumption to derive individual demand functions. To find the market demand function for any particular good, we need a way to aggregate individual demand functions. Figure 8.7 (page 286) illustrates the process of aggregation for two demanders. The individual demand functions for good Y are labelled AA′ and BB′, and the line labelled *BCD* represents the aggregation of these two individual demand functions, or the market demand curve, when there are just two consumers in the market. This market demand curve is constructed by choosing a price, finding the quantities of good Y demanded by each of the individuals at that price, summing the quantities to locate one point on the aggregate demand function, and then repeating the process for all other possible prices. When the price is \$4, for instance, the buyer whose demand function is AA′ will demand 5 units; the buyer whose demand function is BB′ will demand 11 units; and their aggregate demand is 16 units. The point (16,4), is therefore one point on the market demand function.[2]

Implicit in this aggregation procedure is the assumption that quantity demanded by one individual is independent of quantity demanded by other individuals. This independence follows from the independence assumption — which guarantees that the preferences of any individual are independent of the consumption decisions of other individuals.

PROBLEM 8.6

Why is the aggregate demand function coincident with BB′ when price exceeds \$12 in Figure 8.7? What is distance 0D in Figure 8.7?

---

2. Let us consider an algebraic example. Suppose the two individual demand functions are

$$p_1 = \frac{1}{y_1} \quad \text{for the first individual}$$

$$p_2 = \frac{10}{y_2} \quad \text{for the second individual}$$

The aggregation question is this: Given a common price, say $p = p_1 = p_2$, what is the aggregate quantity demanded? To answer the question, we first write y_1 and y_2 as functions of the common price p (that is, $y_1 = 1/p$, $y_2 = 10/p$) and then add to obtain

$$y_1 + y_2 = \frac{1}{p} + \frac{10}{p} = \frac{11}{p}$$

In aggregating the supply functions of individual firms, the same procedure is necessary. Since we are interested in obtaining the aggregate quantity supplied at any price, we must write the quantity supplied by any firm as a function of the common price before adding.

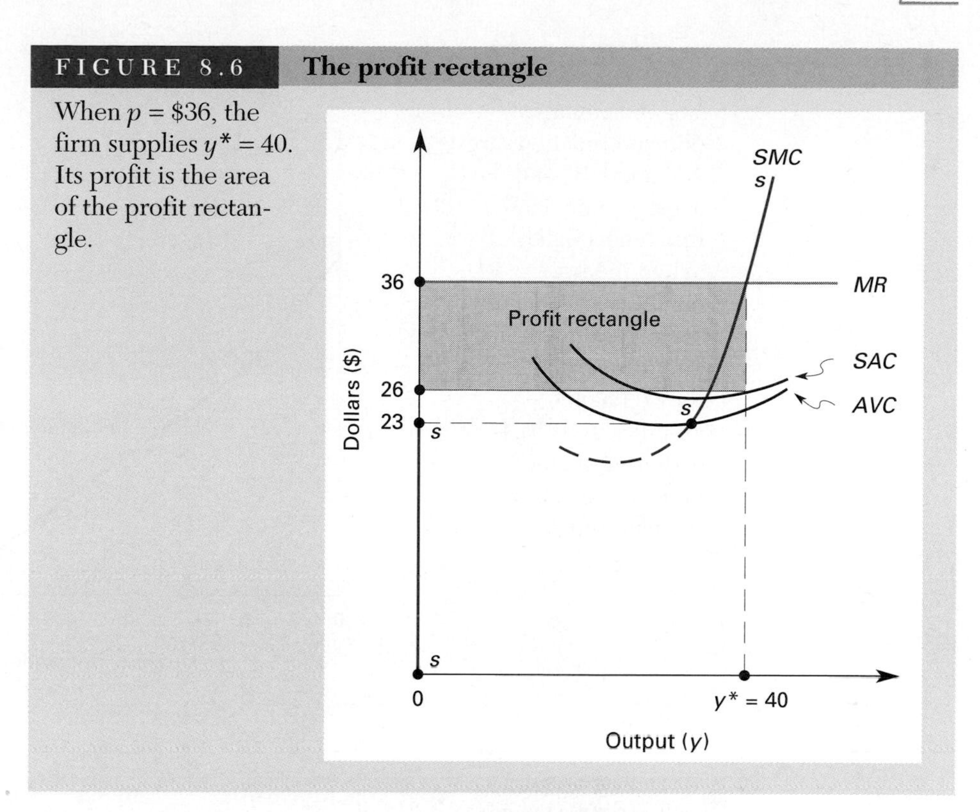

FIGURE 8.6 The profit rectangle

When $p = \$36$, the firm supplies $y^* = 40$. Its profit is the area of the profit rectangle.

PROBLEM 8.7

Suppose there are 1000 individuals with the following demand function for good Y:

$$\text{Quantity demanded} = 1 - 0.001p$$

Show that the market demand function is $y = 1000 - p$, or that the market demand curve is $p = 1000 - y$.

Aggregating Short-Run Supply

It is now a simple matter to calculate the short-run market supply function by aggregating the short-run supply functions of all firms in the market. To illustrate the aggregation procedure, we have constructed the market supply function in Figure 8.8 for a case in which there are two firms in a market. One firm's supply function is represented by the two segments 0A and BC, and the other firm's by the two segments 0A′ and B′C′. The aggregate, or market supply function, is composed of the three segments labelled *SS* in Figure 8.8.

Like the demand aggregation procedure, the supply aggregation procedure is based on an implicit assumption — that the quantity supplied by any firm is independent of quantity supplied by other firms. The independence assumption guarantees that the production function of any firm, and therefore its short-run marginal cost function, is independent of the production decisions of other firms. In the following problem, you can check your understanding of this aggregation procedure.

FIGURE 8.7 **Aggregating demand**

The individual demand functions are AA′ and BB′, and the aggregate demand function is BCD. When the price is $4, one person demands 5 units and the other 11 units. Together they demand 16 units, and (16,4) is therefore one point on the market demand function.

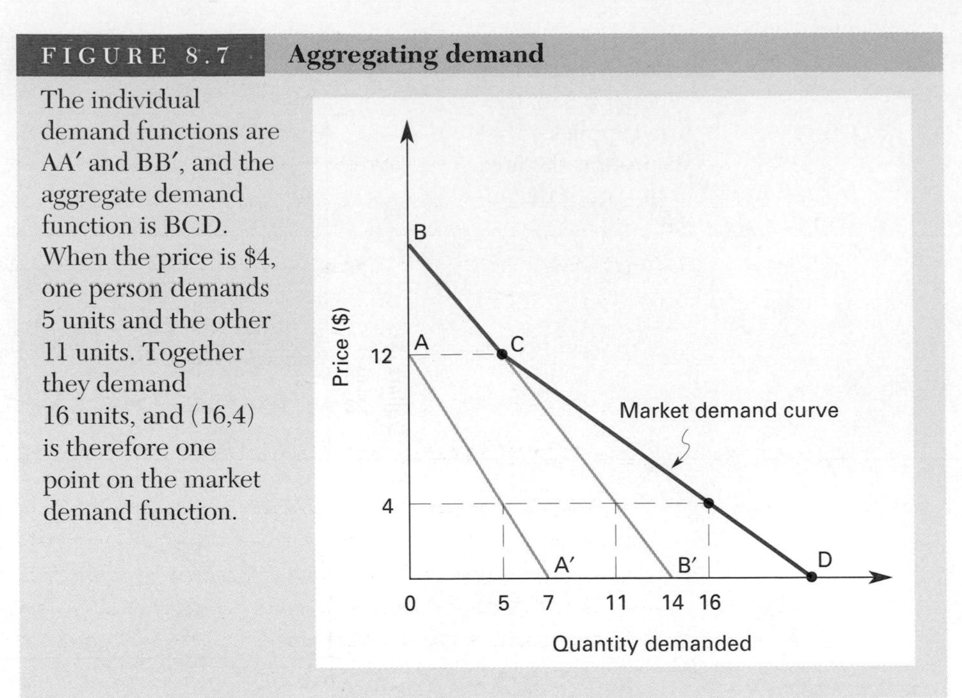

FIGURE 8.8 **Aggregating supply**

The supply function for one firm is composed of segments 0A and BC; the supply function for the other is composed of segments 0A′ and B′C′. The aggregate supply function is composed of the three segments labelled *SS*.

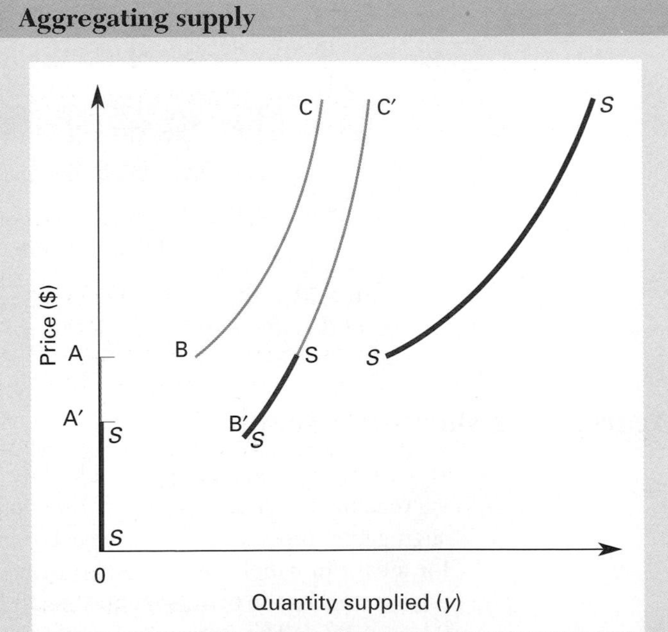

PROBLEM 8.8

Suppose that 100 firms — each with the following short-run supply function for good Y — are in a particular market:

$$\text{quantity supplied} = 0.01p$$

Show that the market supply function is

$$y = p$$

Short-Run Competitive Equilibrium

We can now identify the short-run competitive equilibrium by finding the price at which quantity demanded equals quantity supplied. This equilibrium is represented in Figure 8.9b by the intersection of the market supply and market demand functions at point (y^e, p^e). The competitive equilibrium price is p^e, and the quantity exchanged at this price is y^e. The position of a representative firm in this market is illustrated in Figure 8.9a. Because the scales on the two (vertical) price axes are identical, we can project the market price p^e from Figure 8.9b into Figure 8.9a. Notice, however, that the

FIGURE 8.9 Short-run competitive equilibrium

In (b), the competitive equilibrium price is p^e and quantity is y^e. In (a), the representative firm supplies 15 units at the equilibrium price p^e. The light blue area in (b) is aggregate consumers' surplus, and the dark blue area is aggregate producers' surplus.

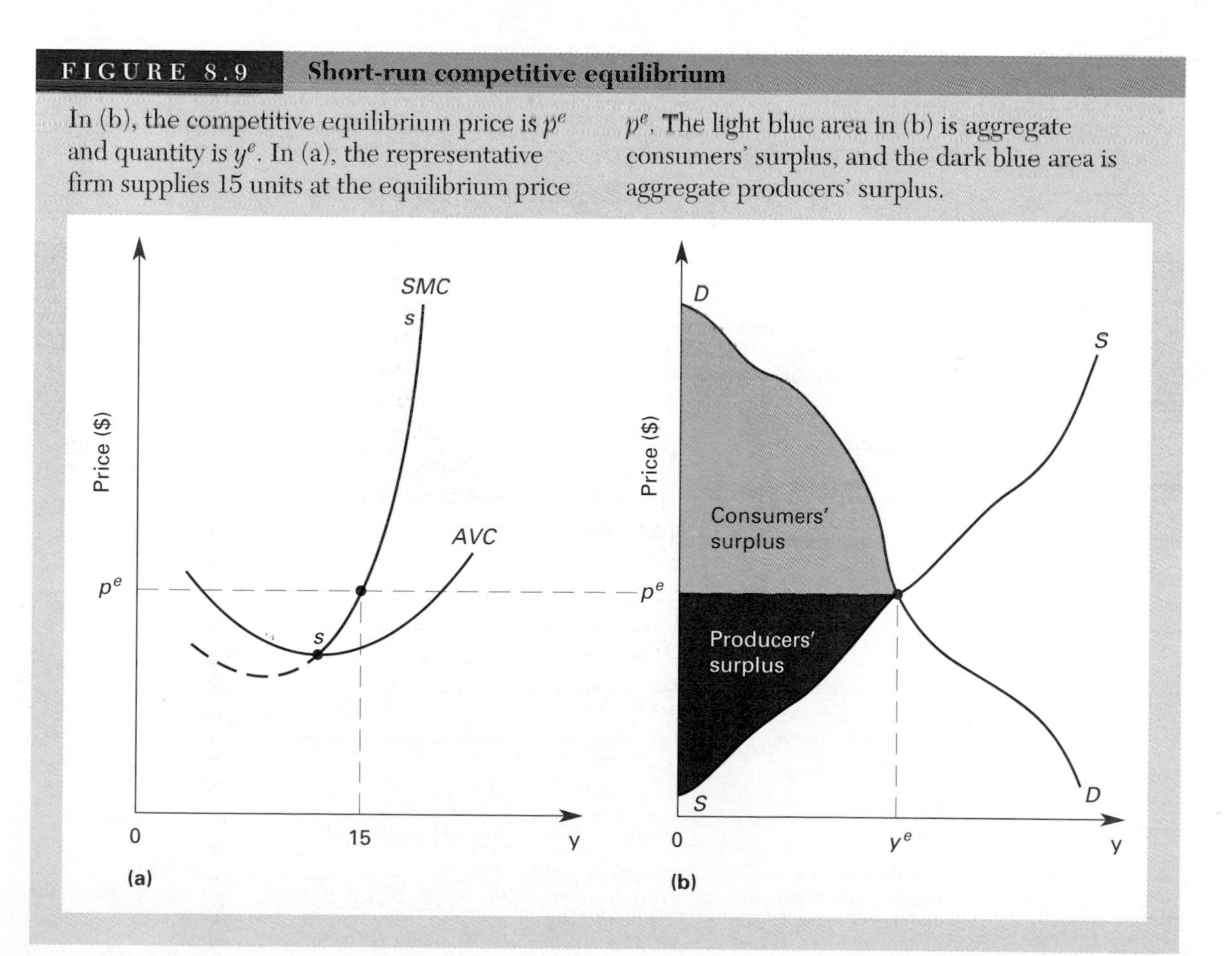

scales on the two (horizontal) quantity axes are not the same because the representative firm's output, 15 units, is only a small fraction of the total market output y^e.

Notice that once again the independence assumption plays a role in the analysis. The equilibrium in Figure 8.9b makes sense only if (1) the market demand function is independent of quantity supplied and (2) the market supply function is independent of quantity demanded. The first assumption is satisfied if the preferences of individuals are independent of the production decisions of firms, and the second is satisfied if the production functions (and therefore supply functions) of firms are independent of the consumption decisions of individuals. The independence assumption guarantees that these conditions are met. To get some practice with short-run competitive equilibrium, try the following comparative statics exercise.[3]

PROBLEM 8.9

Suppose that firms are forced to pay an excise tax of \$10 per unit on every unit of output they sell. Show that this tax shifts each firm's supply curve vertically upward by \$10. What happens to the market supply curve? If the demand curve is vertical — that is, if demand is perfectly price-inelastic — what happens to equilibrium price when this tax is imposed? If the demand curve is not perfectly price-inelastic, show that the price increases will be less than \$10.

8.6 Efficiency of the Short-Run Competitive Equilibrium

At the beginning of this chapter, we saw that the competitive equilibrium of the exchange economy model was Pareto-optimal, or efficient. Is the equilibrium in Figure

---

3. We can use differential calculus to see the precise nature of this sort of comparative statics question. For example, suppose that we are interested in the effect that a change in the price of mangoes p_M will have on the equilibrium price of apples p_A. Write the demand for apples as

$$y = D(p_A, p_M)$$

to reflect the possibility that the demand for apples is affected by the price of mangoes. Because different soil conditions and climates are needed to produce mangoes and apples, the supply of apples will not depend on the price of mangoes; so we write the supply of apples as

$$y = S(p_A)$$

In equilibrium, we have

$$D(p_A^e, p_M) = S(p_A^e)$$

where p_A^e is the equilibrium price of apples. Now, totally differentiate this equilibrium condition to obtain

$$[\partial D(p_A^e, p_M)/\partial p_M]dp_M = [S'(p_A^e) - \partial D(p_A^e, p_M)/\partial p_A]dp_A^e$$

and solve for dp_A^e/dp_M: the rate of change of the equilibrium price of apples with respect to the price of mangoes:

$$\frac{dp_A^e}{dp_M} = \frac{\partial D(p_A^e, p_M)/\partial p_M}{[S'(p_A^e) - \partial D(p_A^e, p_M)/\partial p_A{}^e]}$$

The denominator on the right is ordinarily positive since $S'(p_A)$ is likely to be positive and $\partial D(p_A, p_M)/\partial p_A$ negative. Therefore, the sign of dp_A^e/dp_M turns on the sign of $\partial D(p_A{}^e, p_M)/\partial p_M$. For example, if apples and mangoes are substitutes, then $\partial D(p_A{}^e, p_M)/\partial p_M > 0$ and therefore $dp_A^e/dp_M > 0$. Chapters 9 and 10 of Samuelson (1947) are devoted to the method of comparative statics analysis in economics.

8.9 similarly efficient? Because every firm in this competitive equilibrium is producing at the point where price equals short-run marginal cost, no firm can sell an additional unit of output at a price that will cover its short-run marginal cost of producing that additional unit. Remember, too, that the short-run marginal cost of a unit of output is just the market value of the variable inputs needed to produce the unit. If we think of firms in the short run as trading variable inputs (processed into good Y) for consumers' dollars, we recognize that the potential gains from trade are fully realized in this equilibrium. Once the competitive equilibrium is attained, it is impossible to sell an additional unit of output at a price that will cover the market value of the added resources needed to produce it. In this sense, the short-run competitive equilibrium is efficient.

Having an economic measure of the gains from trade is useful in many circumstances. (We will be using such a measure in this and subsequent chapters.) In Figure 8.9, we can identify gains to both consumers and firms. The aggregate measures of these gains are known, respectively, as **consumers' surplus** — indicated by the light blue area of Figure 8.9b — and producers' surplus — indicated by the dark blue area. But where do these measures come from and what do they mean?

consumers' surplus

We introduced the notion of one consumer's surplus in Section 4.5. (You may want to review that discussion briefly.) Consumers' surplus in competitive equilibrium is just the sum of the surplus enjoyed by all consumers at the competitive equilibrium price. As we noted in Section 4.5, however, consumers' surplus is a theoretically well-grounded benefit measure only in the special case in which the consumer's indifference curves are vertically parallel — the case in which quantity demanded of Y is unresponsive to the consumer's income. If the indifference maps of all consumers are characterized by such parallel indifference curves, then consumers' surplus can be used without hesitation as a measure of aggregate consumers' benefit. If consumer demand for Y is responsive to income, however, we can use CS as long as we recognize that it is just a rough-and-ready approximation of consumers' benefits.

Producers' surplus is a measure of benefits to the owners of firms. The measure of benefit to any one owner would seem to be a profit measure. In the short run, the appropriate measure is revenue minus variable cost since the firm's fixed cost is just that — fixed. **Producers' surplus** is calculated by subtracting aggregate variable cost from aggregate revenue. Aggregate revenue is the rectangle in Figure 8.9b with sides p^e and y^e. Since the supply curve is the marginal cost of output, aggregate variable cost is the area under the supply curve SS from the origin to y^e. Thus, producers' surplus, calculated by subtracting aggregate variable cost from aggregate revenue, is indicated by the dark blue area in Figure 8.9b.[4] The sum of consumers' surplus and producer's surplus — called **total surplus** — is a measure of the aggregate gains from trade realized in this market.

producers' surplus

total surplus

4. It is important to keep in mind that the calculation of producers' surplus is based on the assumption that input prices are constant. If there are substantial changes in input prices as industry output expands, then the producers' surplus calculation is misleading.

PROBLEM 8.10

In Problems 8.7 and 8.8, you found the following market demand and supply functions

$$\text{market demand} = 1000 - p$$
$$\text{market supply} = p$$

First, find the competitive equilibrium and draw a diagram to illustrate it. Then compute consumers' and producers' surplus in this equilibrium. (Remember that the area of a triangle is 1/2 its base multiplied by its height.)

Because the aggregation procedures used to define these measures of benefit are simply to add up the benefits accruing to all individuals without any regard to the distribution of those benefits, they are *cost-benefit measures*. Wherever we use them, we are implicitly invoking the assumption discussed in Section 1.6 that a dollar of benefit is a dollar of benefit — regardless of who gets it.

8.7 Long-Run Competitive Equilibrium

Although new firms cannot enter or leave the industry in the short run, they can *enter* or *exit* in the long run. Therefore, in the long-run analysis we need to distinguish between established firms (those already in the market) and potential firms or entrants (those not yet in existence). If, for instance, the market is house painting, the established firms are the commercial house painters currently in business. The potential entrants are house-painting firms that have not yet been established — firms, for example, that are just a gleam in some entrepreneurial student's eye.

No-Exit, No-Entry, and Long-Run Equilibrium

There are two requirements, or conditions, of long-run equilibrium:

1. No-exit condition: In long-run equilibrium, no established firm wants to exit the industry.
2. No-entry condition: In long-run equilibrium, no potential firm wants to enter the industry.

The no-exit condition implies that the long-run equilibrium price p^e must be high enough that each established firm makes at least zero profit. The no-entry condition implies that p^e must be low enough that no potential entrant could earn positive profit.

Notice the economic role of profit as a signal guiding the allocation of resources in the long run.

Positive profit is a signal that induces entry, or the allocation of additional resources to the industry. On the other hand, negative profit (loss) is a signal that induces exit, or the allocation of fewer resources to the industry.

To put the allocation role of profit in proper perspective, bear in mind that profit and cost — as we use the terms — are economic, not accounting, concepts. In the economic calculation of cost, all inputs that are used by the firm are valued at their opportunity cost. To produce its output in any period, say a year, a firm uses variable inputs, like labour and electricity, and capital inputs, like buildings and machines. The opportunity cost calculation for variable inputs is straightforward — they are valued at market prices. If the market wage of a tool-and-die maker is $40 per hour, this price is used to value the labour services of tool-and-die makers used by the firm during the year. For capital inputs, however, the opportunity cost calculation is more subtle. Capital inputs are valued at the maximum price they would fetch in some other use. Consider a firm's warehouse, for example. The opportunity cost of the warehouse is the maximum amount that another user would pay to rent the warehouse for the year. In contrast, accountants value capital inputs based on their historical cost and on somewhat arbitrary rates of depreciation.

Two factors determine the menu of long-run production choices open to established firms: the long-run average cost function *LAC* and the possibility of exiting the industry. (We will use the U-shaped stylization of *LAC* in Figure 8.10 throughout the analysis, even though other stylizations are possible.) Established firms can decide to produce at any point on *LAC* in Figure 8.10, or they can decide to exit — to buy no inputs. The choices open to entrants are much the same. They can enter the market by producing at some point on *LAC*, or they can stay out of the industry.

To talk more easily about the position of any particular firm in the long-run competitive equilibrium, we need some terminological shorthand. We will call the level of output at which long-run average cost attains its minimum value the **efficient scale of production**. In Figure 8.10, the efficient scale of production is y' units of output. And we will call the average cost at the efficient scale of production the **minimum average cost**. In Figure 8.10, minimum average cost is c'.

efficient scale of production

minimum average cost

Price Equal to Minimum Average Cost

The no-exit and no-entry conditions imply that the long-run competitive equilibrium price is equal to the minimum average cost. To see why, suppose the price were higher than c' — say, p_1 in Figure 8.10. Because p_1 exceeds *LAC* for any level of output larger than y_1 but smaller than y_2, potential entrants anticipate making a positive profit at any such level of output. In the long run, then, new firms will enter the industry when the price is p_1. That is, because the no-entry condition is not satisfied, price p_1 cannot be the long-run equilibrium price. Because an analogous argument applies to any other price higher than c', we see that the no-entry condition implies that the long-run equilibrium price cannot exceed the minimum average cost.

Now suppose that the price were less than c' — say, p_2 — in Figure 8.10. Because *LAC* now exceeds p_2 at all levels of output, all established firms will incur losses. In the long run, profit-maximizing firms will leave the industry. That is, because the no-exit condition is not satisfied, p_2 cannot be the long-run equilibrium price. Because an analogous argument applies to any other price less than c', we see that the no-exit condition implies that the long-run equilibrium price cannot be less than the minimum average cost.

Since p^e cannot exceed c' and cannot be less than c'; it must equal c'. That is:

In long-run equilibrium, price is equal to the minimum average cost.

FIGURE 8.10 Exit, entry, and long-run competitive equilibrium

The no-exit condition is violated for any price less than c', the minimum average cost. And the no-entry condition is violated for any price larger than c'. The only price that satisfies both conditions is c'. Therefore, the long-run competitive equilibrium price p^e is equal to the minimum average cost c'.

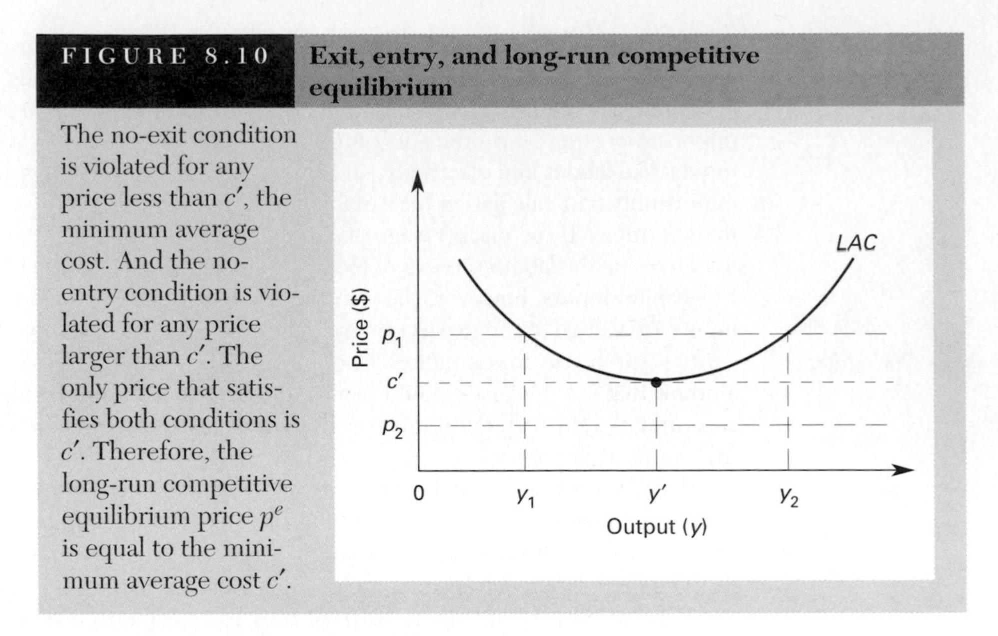

The Individual Firm in Long-Run Equilibrium

Knowing that price equals minimum average cost, we also know the position of every firm in the long-run equilibrium. In Figure 8.11, y' is the only output level at which an established firm can cover its cost of production when price is equal to c'. To avoid losses at the equilibrium price, each must be producing at the efficient scale of production y'. This, in turn, means that each firm will be on the short-run average cost function *SAC* tangent to *LAC* at y' in Figure 8.11. From the relationship between marginals and averages developed in Chapters 7 and 8, we also know that both long-run and short-run marginal cost functions will pass through the point (y', c'). We can summarize these results by the following series of equalities:

In long-run equilibrium, marginal revenue is equal to price, which is equal to the minimum average cost of production, which in turn is equal to long-run average cost, short-run average cost, long-run marginal cost, and short-run marginal cost:

$$MR = p^e = LAC(y') = SAC(y')$$
$$= LMC(y') = SMC(y')$$

Long-Run Supply Function

long-run supply function

We can use the properties of equilibrium to develop what is called the **long-run supply function** (*LRS*). The long-run competitive equilibrium is then determined by the intersection of *LRS* and the demand function. We will consider three cases: industries characterized by *constant costs,* by *increasing costs,* and by *decreasing costs.* In the short run, we assumed that all input prices were constant. As we derive *LRS*, we will incorporate changes in input prices that arise as industry-wide output expands or contracts. These changes in input prices determine whether any particular industry is a constant-cost, increasing-cost, or decreasing-cost industry.

As the aggregate output of a certain industry expands or contracts, the aggregate quantities of the inputs used in that industry will correspondingly expand or contract.

FIGURE 8.11 **The firm in long-run competitive equilibrium**

In long-run competitive equilibrium, each firm produces at the efficient scale of production y', and price is equal to the minimum average cost c'. As a consequence, $p^e = c' = LAC = LMC = SMC = SAC$.

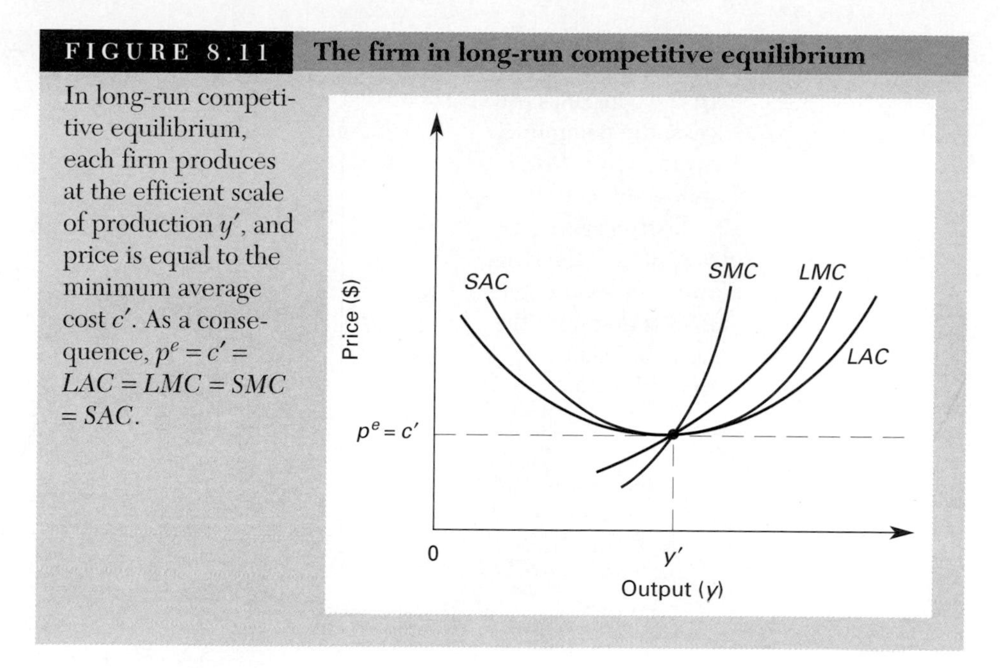

And as input requirements increase, the price of any particular input will either remain constant, increase, or decrease.

The Constant-Cost Case

In the constant-cost case, as the aggregate quantity of output produced changes, the prices of all inputs remain constant, and the various cost functions for individual firms will not change. In particular, neither the efficient scale of production nor the minimum average cost will change as aggregate industry output expands or contracts. The position of a representative firm in long-run equilibrium will always be exactly as shown in Figure 8.11, and the long-run competitive equilibrium price will always be c'. This means that *LRS* must be a horizontal line through c', as in Figure 8.12, because this is the only possible shape such that any market demand function will intersect *LRS* at price c'. If the market demand function in Figure 8.12 is *DD*, for instance, the long-run equilibrium quantity will be y_1; if it is *D′D′*, the long-run equilibrium quantity will be y_2. In both cases, the long-run equilibrium price is c'.

The Increasing-Cost Case

In many industries, as the industry-wide output expands and as the quantities of inputs demanded therefore increase, the prices of some or all of those inputs will also increase. This input-price response is almost universally true for natural resources. Mining firms that supply ore, for example, naturally exploit the richest and most accessible ore bodies first. As more ore is demanded, they move on to poorer, less accessible ore bodies, and the cost per unit of ore rises.

In industries where inputs are characterized by increasing costs, what will the long-run supply curve look like? As aggregate industry output increases and as the prices of at least some inputs also increase, the minimum average cost of production must rise. Therefore, as industry-wide output increases, the long-run equilibrium price — which is equal to the minimum average cost of production — must also increase. This

FIGURE 8.12 ***LRS* in the constant-cost case**

In the constant-cost case, the minimum average cost c' is independent of the industry's aggregate output, and the long-run supply function *LRS* is therefore the horizontal line through c'.

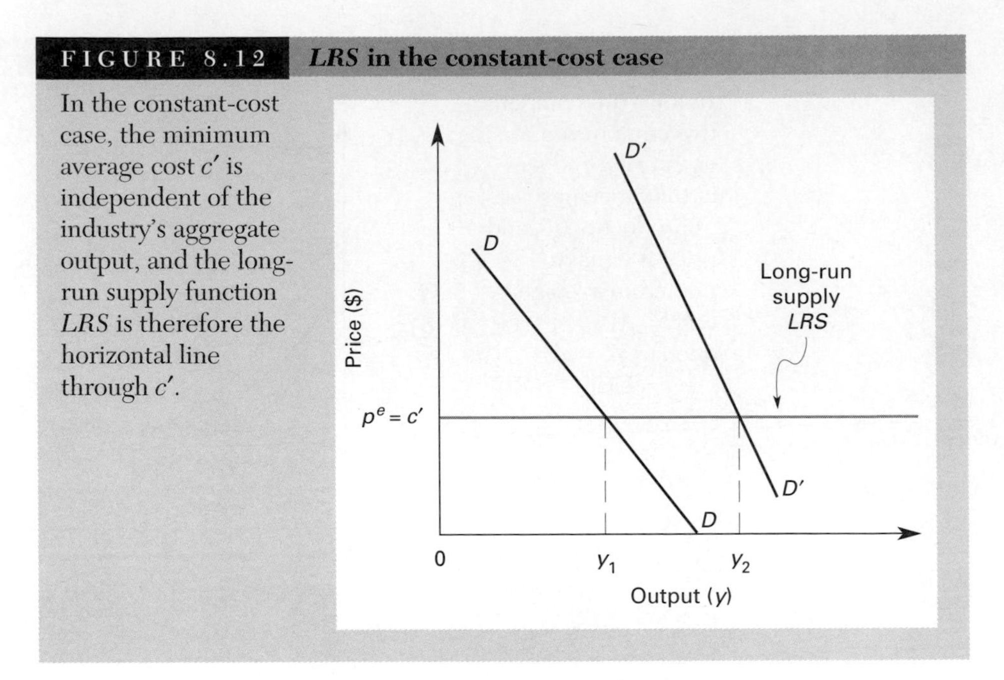

means that the *LRS* must be upward sloping. The increasing-cost case is illustrated in Figure 8.13. Given the demand function *DD*, the long-run equilibrium price is p_1 and quantity is y_1. Given $D'D'$, the long-run equilibrium price is p_2 and quantity is y_2.

FIGURE 8.13 ***LRS* in the increasing-cost case**

In the increasing-cost case, efficient average cost increases as industry output increases. Thus, *LRS* is upward sloping. In response to a shift of the demand function from *DD* to $D'D'$, output in long-run equilibrium increases from y_1 to y_2, and equilibrium price increases from p_1 (the minimum average cost in the initial equilibrium) to p_2 (the minimum average cost in the subsequent equilibrium).

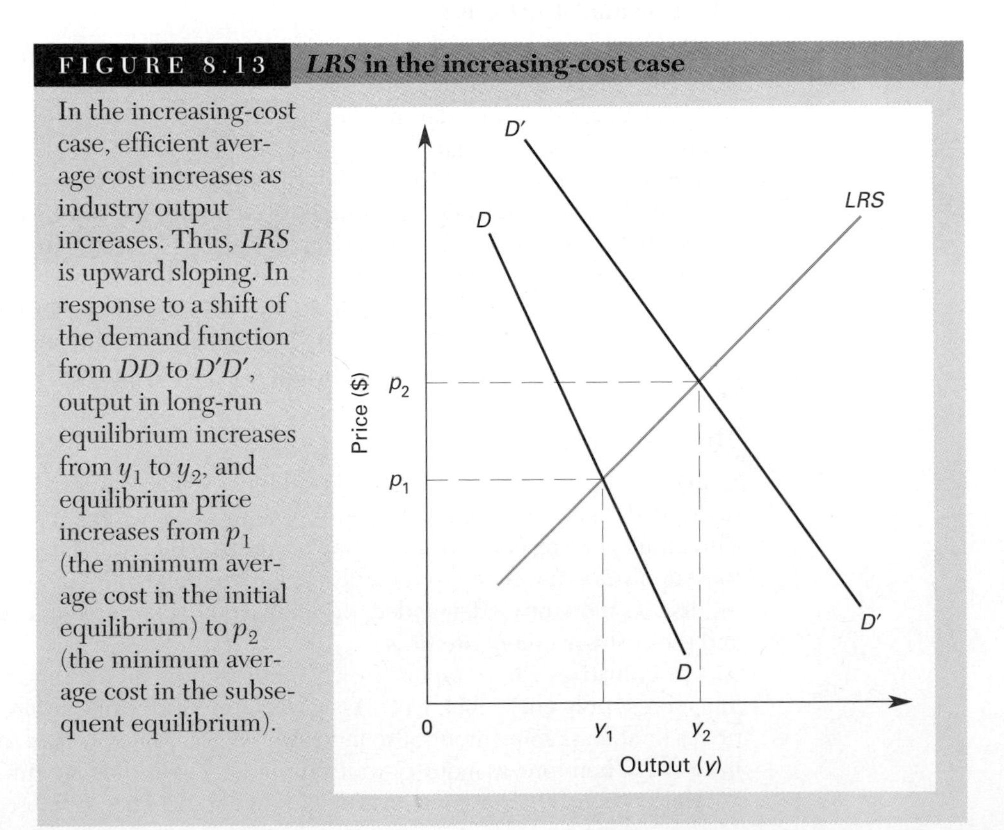

The Decreasing-Cost Case

It is also possible — though quite unusual — that the prices of some inputs might decrease as industry demand for them increases. As you can verify easily, if the prices of some or all inputs decrease (and if the prices of the remaining inputs are constant) as the aggregate quantity of inputs demanded increases, the *LRS* will be downward sloping.

SUMMARY

A *market demand function* tells us the aggregate quantity of a good demanded by all consumers at any given price, and a *market supply function* tells us the aggregate quantity supplied by all suppliers at any given price. A *competitive equilibrium price* — determined by the intersection of market demand and market supply functions — is the price at which the quantity demanded exactly equals the quantity supplied. Although both a price and a quantity are determined in any competitive equilibrium, both are symptomatic of the more fundamental function served by any market: the *allocation of goods* to individual consumers.

We began the chapter with an elementary exchange-economy model that allowed us to concentrate on the properties of a competitive market allocation and examine two crucial (and problematical) assumptions of the competitive model. The most important property is that the allocation of goods in competitive equilibrium is Pareto-optimal: all the gains from trade are realized in the competitive equilibrium. However, this result requires careful qualification — a task we will take up in Chapter 17.

We used the device of the *Walrasian auctioneer* to find the competitive equilibrium in this exchange economy. In so doing, we implicitly assumed that all the economic actors behaved as price takers in responding to the prices announced by the auctioneer. This *price-taking assumption* raised an important conceptual difficulty: In what circumstances will individuals act as price takers rather than price manipulators? We found that individuals act as price takers when there are large numbers of insignificant buyers and sellers. This is the basis of the large-numbers, or price-taking, assumption, which is included in most models of perfect competition.

The presence of the Walrasian auctioneer raises yet another conceptual problem: In the absence of this device, is the competitive model still applicable? We found that it does apply if all buyers and sellers are perfectly informed. This is the basis of the *perfect-information assumption*, which models of perfect competition also include.

Because the world so rarely conforms to the conditions of large numbers and perfect information, we naturally are led to ask if something less will do. This is the question at the heart of a great deal of recent work in experimental economics. The results to date suggest that the competitive model seems to yield fairly good predictions even when numbers are small and information quite imperfect.

When we replaced the exchange model with a more complex competitive model incorporating both production and exchange, the supply function became more complicated. We discovered that (with suitable qualifications) a firm's *marginal cost function* is its *short-run supply function*. Then, by aggregating short-run supply functions over firms and demand functions over individuals, we were able to identify the *short-run competitive equilibrium*.

In the long run, the competitive model is driven by *exit* and *entry*. Taken together, these two processes imply that in long-run equilibrium, each firm will operate at the minimum point on its long-run average cost function and that price, marginal revenue, long-run average cost, short-run average cost, long-run marginal cost, and short-run marginal cost will be identical.

The *long-run competitive equilibrium* is determined by the intersection of the *long-run supply function* and the market demand function. The slope of a long-run supply function, *LRS*, depends on the nature of the response of input prices to an industry's demand for those inputs. *LRS* may be upward sloping, horizontal, or downward sloping, depending on whether the industry is characterized by increasing costs, constant costs, or decreasing costs.

Because in any competitive equilibrium with production, the competitive price is equal to the short-run marginal cost of each firm (and in any long-run equilibrium, price is equal to long-run marginal cost), no further gains from trade are possible. No customer is willing to pay what it costs any firm to produce an additional unit of output. This result is a reflection of the *Pareto optimality or efficiency of competitive equilibrium*.

EXERCISES

1. Indicate whether each of the following statements is true, false, or uncertain, and explain your answer.
   a. In the short run, a competitive firm would never produce where *AVC* is downward sloping.
   b. A competitive firm in long-run equilibrium in an increasing-cost industry will produce at a point where *LAC* is rising.
   c. If *LAC* is U-shaped, the number of firms in a constant-cost industry will decrease in response to a decrease in demand.
   d. In the short run, a competitive firm would never produce where *SAC* is downward sloping and *AVC* is upward sloping.
   e. If a competitive firm is currently producing where *SAC* is upward sloping, then other firms will enter the industry.
   f. If *LAC* is U-shaped, the number of firms in an increasing-cost industry will increase in response to an increase in demand.
   g. A competitive firm in long-run equilibrium in a constant-cost industry will produce at a point where *LAC* is at a minimum.
   h. In the short run, a competitive firm would never produce where *SMC* is downward sloping.
   i. A competitive firm in long-run equilibrium in a decreasing-cost industry will produce at a point where *SMC* exceeds *LMC*.
   j. If a competitive firm is currently producing where *SAC* is downward sloping, then no other firms will enter the industry.
   k. In long-run competitive equilibrium, all firms produce at a point where there are constant returns to scale in production.
   l. If a competitive firm in short-run equilibrium is currently making zero profit, then no other firms will enter the industry.

2. Gizmos are produced in a constant-cost industry by firms that have a U-shaped *LAC*. Minimum average cost is $2 and the efficient scale of production is 50 gizmos. The demand for gismos is

$$p = 12 - 0.001y$$

   where p is price and y is quantity of gizmos.
   a. In the long run, what are the equilibrium price and quantity of gizmos? How many firms will produce gizmos, and how much will each produce in equilibrium? What profit will each firm earn in equilibrium?
   b. Now suppose the demand for gizmos changes to

$$p = 16 - 0.001y$$

   What are the equilibrium price and quantity of gizmos? How many firms will produce gizmos, and how much will each produce in equilibrium?

c. Suppose now that the market for gizmos is initially in the long-run equilibrium you described in (a) and that demand again shifts as in (b). What could you say about the new long-run equilibrium if the gizmo industry is an increasing-cost industry instead of a constant-cost industry?

3. In this chapter we've shown the price-taking firm facing a flat demand curve, but in fact, it has the same slope as the market demand curve. The relative elasticities, however, are:

$$E_m = (\Delta Q/\Delta P) \times (P/Q_m)$$

$$E_f = (\Delta Q/\Delta P) \times (P/Q_f)$$

where Q_m is the market level of output and Q_f is the individual firm level of output.

a. Show that if there are N identical firms, that $E_f = N \times E_m$.
b. Suppose there are 1 000 000 firms, that the elasticity of the market demand curve is −1, and that each firm currently produces 10 000 units of output at a price of $5/unit. What would happen to the revenue of firm 1, if it alone increased output to 15 000 units?
c. Is this firm going to worry about the slope of its demand function?

4. If everyone takes the price as given in a price-taker model, who sets it?

5. Suppose that the strawberry industry is perfectly competitive, and the cost function of a typical firm is

$$TC(y) = 100 + y^2$$

where y is crates of strawberries per day. The corresponding marginal cost function is

$$LMC(y) = 2y$$

What is $LAC(y)$? What is the efficient scale of production? (*Hint*: LMC intersects LAC at the efficient scale of production.) What is the minimum average cost? What is the long-run equilibrium price of strawberries?

6. In Chapter 7 we derived the following cost function for Tipple's Courier Service

$$TC(y, w_1, w_2) = y(w_1 w_2/300)^{1/2}$$

This cost function is associated with the following constant-returns-to-scale production function,

$$y = (1200 z_1 z_2)^{1/2}$$

The associated average and marginal cost functions are

$$LMC(y) = LAC(y) = (w_1 w_2/300)^{1/2}$$

a. Given these cost functions, what is the long-run competitive equilibrium price?
b. *Claim*: The number and sizes of firms in long-run competitive equilibrium are indeterminate even though long-run equilibrium price and quantity are perfectly well defined. Explain. What accounts for these curious results?

7. Firm F's short-run cost function is

$$STC(y) = 30y + y^2 + 400$$

and its short-run marginal cost function is

$$SMC(y) = 30 + 2y$$

a. If $p = \$50$, how much will this firm produce? What will its profit be? Is $p = \$50$ a long-run equilibrium price?
b. What is this firm's short-run supply function? Graph the supply function.
c. Find the price at which this firm would earn zero profit in the short run. Is this price a long-run equilibrium price?

8. Consider an industry in which there are 10 identical firms and 1000 identical demanders. Each demander has the following demand function:

$$y = 1 - 0.005p$$

Each firm has the following short-run cost function:

$$STC(y) = 10y + y^2$$

The associated marginal cost function is

$$SMC(y) = 10 + 2y$$

a. What is the market demand function?
b. What is one firm's supply function?
c. What is the market supply function?
d. Construct a graph illustrating one firm's supply function, the market supply function, and the market demand function. What are short-run equilibrium price and quantity?

9. With the mounting evidence on the relationship between smoking and health, the demand for cigarettes is expected to fall. Some people fear, however, that because of the fall in demand, the price of cigarettes will be lowered, and at the lower price people will smoke as many cigarettes as they did before. Are these fears justified?

10. The production of gasoline in the United States is an increasing-cost industry because the price of crude oil increases as gasoline producers demand more crude oil. Suppose that the supply of crude oil to the United States from the Middle East is cut off. What impact will this have on *LRS* for gasoline? On the equilibrium price and quantity of gasoline in the US market? In response to this disruption in the supply of crude oil, imagine that an effective ceiling is imposed on the price of gasoline. Write a short essay on the probable impacts of the price ceiling. Address the following questions. How will the available supply of gasoline be allocated? Will the allocation be Pareto-optimal? Will the allocation process needlessly use real resources? Will a black market for gasoline emerge? Relative to the free-market equilibrium, who will benefit from the price ceiling and who will be hurt by it? What sorts of enforcement issues are likely to arise?

11. What's wrong with the statement, "If the price rose to $100 000 then no one could afford to purchase the good"? (*Hint*: How are prices determined? How does the market demand curve depend on income?)

12. When two sets of identical individuals begin trading with each other, individuals in both groups gain from trade. Will allowing a third group to trade be Pareto-improving? Will it increase the total gains from trade?

13. Forty years ago colour photographs were more expensive than black and white photographs. Now the opposite occurs even though the process for colour is more complex. Which model in this chapter best explains this?

14. A paint-ball operator charges $12 for each patron to enter his facility and shoot at other customers. His variable costs are $11 per person and he has fixed costs of $10 000 per year. He expects about 5000 patrons per year. Should he remain open in the short run?

15. Can the "long run" happen sooner than the "short run"?

*16. A perfectly competitive industry has a large number of potential entrants. Each firm has an identical cost structure such that long-run average cost is minimized at an output of 20 units. The minimum average cost is $10 per unit. Total market demand is given by $Y = 1500 - 50p$.
   a. What is the industry's long-run supply curve?
   b. What is the long-run equilibrium price? The total industry output? The output of each firm?
   c. The short-run total cost curve for each firm's long run equilibrium output is

   $$C = 0.5y^2 - 10y + 200.$$

   Calculate the short-run average and marginal cost curves. At what output level does short-run average cost reach a minimum?
   d. Calculate the short-run supply curve for each firm and the industry short-run supply curve.
   e. Suppose the market demand curve shifts up to $Y = 2500 - 50p$. Redo (b).

*17. A representative firm in a constant-cost industry has a cost function equal to $TC = 2y^2 + 50y + 50$.
   a. What is the marginal and average cost of this firm?
   b. What is the equilibrium price in the market?
   c. If the market demand is $y = 3000 - p$, how many firms will exist in equilibrium?

*18. A perfectly competitive market has demand curve $P = 30 - 0.03Y$. If every firm in the industry has an average cost function $AC = 36/y + y$,
   a. what is the equilibrium price and quantity in the market?
   b. what is the long-run equilibrium number of firms?
   c. find the market supply function.
   d. calculate the producer and consumer surplus for this competitive equilibrium.

*19. A perfectly competitive, constant cost industry has a market demand curve $P = 100 - (1/5)Y$. Each firm has a U-shaped long-run average cost function with a minimum of \$20. The efficient scale of production for these firms is 10 units.

a. What is the long-run equilibrium market price and quantity?

b. What is the long-run number of firms in the industry? How much does each produce? What are their profits?

c. Suppose that market demand drops so that the new demand curve is $P = 90 - (1/5)Y$. If the short run marginal cost of firms is $SMC = 4y - 20$, what is the short-run equilibrium price and quantity in the market? What is the output of each firm in the short run?

d. Now find the new long-run equilibrium market price and quantity. What is the new equilibrium number of firms?

REFERENCES

Marshall, A. 1920. *Principles of Economics*, 8th ed. New York: Macmillan.

Samuelson, P. A. 1947. *Foundations of Economic Analysis*. Cambridge, Mass.: Harvard University Press.

CHAPTER 9

Applications of the Competitive Model

We have come a long way. We have developed a model of consumer behaviour that began by examining preferences and budget constraints and culminated in the individual's demand function and the market demand curve. We have developed a model of production, which began with notions of opportunity costs and technical production functions, and culminated in the firm's marginal cost curve and market supply functions.

In the last chapter we brought the concepts of market demand and supply together and argued that in the context of a perfectly competitive market structure, equilibrium was reached when the market supply was equal to the market demand. We argued that this equilibrium was Pareto-efficient because it maximized the gains from trade. That is, it maximized the sum of the consumer's surplus (the difference between what consumers would have been willing to pay and what they had to pay), and producer's surplus (the difference between what producers received and their opportunity costs).

In this chapter we pause for a moment to use this model and exploit some of its power by using it with a series of examples. Work through the examples with us to fully appreciate what a remarkable model you have added to your human capital. We begin with a discussion of basic comparative statics. Next we analyze why homes in cold climates are warmer inside than homes in warmer climates. Then we examine the effect of quotas in agriculture, the long- and short-run effects of rent control for apartments, the impact of taxes and tariffs, and the market for loanable funds. Finally we apply our model to issues of crime.

9.1 Comparative Statics in the Basic Supply and Demand Model

Figure 9.1 summarizes the basic short-run supply and demand model. The market demand curve for good Y, first and foremost, is a function of the price of good Y. When the price of good Y changes there is a change in the *quantity demanded*, and the demand curve itself does not shift. When there is a change in any of the other parameters, namely the price of other goods, incomes, or tastes, the demand curve shifts either in or out. The market supply curve for good Y is also a function of the price of good Y. When the price of good Y changes there is a change in the quantity supplied, but the supply curve itself does not shift. When any of the other parameters in the supply curve change, namely the price of an input, or technology, the supply curve shifts either in or out.

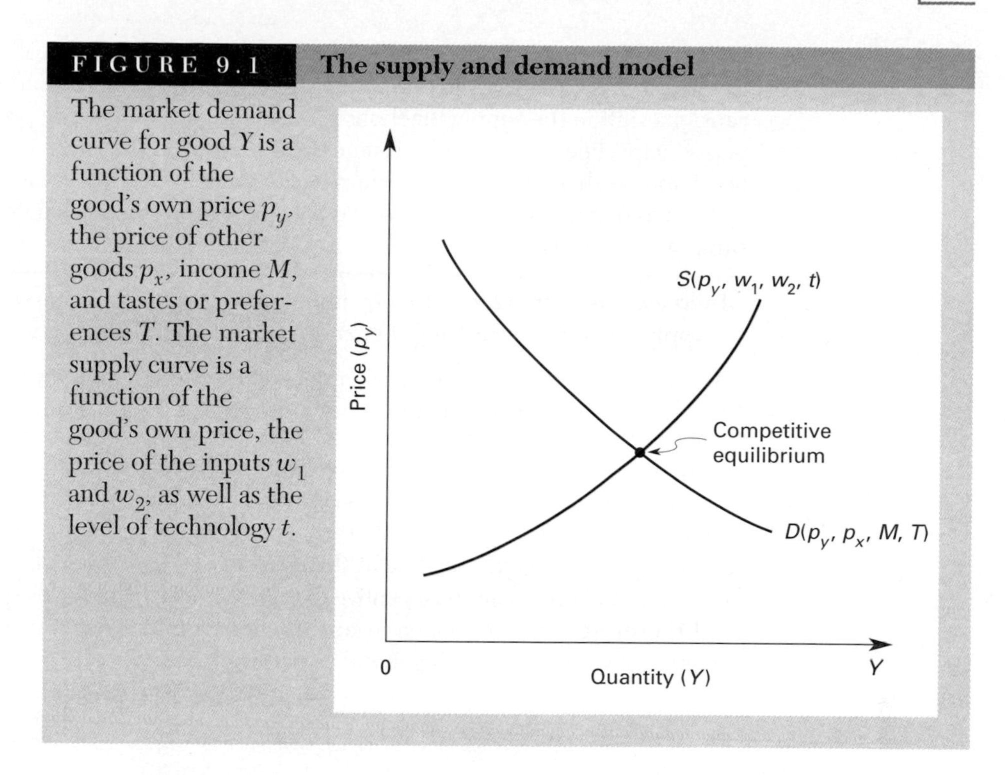

FIGURE 9.1 The supply and demand model

The market demand curve for good Y is a function of the good's own price p_y, the price of other goods p_x, income M, and tastes or preferences T. The market supply curve is a function of the good's own price, the price of the inputs w_1 and w_2, as well as the level of technology t.

Let us consider what happens to the equilibrium price and quantity when market demand shifts and when market supply shifts. You should be able to verify the following results by constructing the relevant demand and supply diagrams. Simply start with a graph like Figure 9.1 and shift the relevant curve.

As mentioned, the market demand function for a good can shift for a number of reasons. Tastes may change, causing a shift in market demand. For example, in the 1980s, there was apparently no demand for "grunge" clothing, "stair-climber" exercise machines, or piercing body parts that seldom see the sun. So, too, the price of either a substitute or a complement for the good may change, causing the market demand for that good to shift accordingly. If the price of a substitute for good Y goes up, then the market demand function for good y will shift upward and to the right. For example, if coffee becomes more expensive, the demand for tea will shift upward and to the right. If the price of a complement goes up, the opposite will occur. For example, if a ski-lift ticket becomes more expensive, the demand for ski-equipment rentals will shift down and to the left.

Suppose that for some reason the demand function for good Y does shift up and to the right. In all three cases — constant costs, increasing costs, and decreasing costs — both short-run equilibrium price and quantity will increase. In the constant-cost case, however, the long-run equilibrium quantity will increase, but long-run equilibrium price will remain unchanged. In the increasing-cost case, both long-run equilibrium price and quantity will increase. In the decreasing-cost case, long-run equilibrium price will decrease, but long-run equilibrium quantity will increase.

Let us turn now to changes in market supply. Again, a number of factors can cause a shift in the market supply function. Technological change — the development of more efficient production processes, for example — can cause shifts in market supply functions. So can changes in the prices of inputs. If the price of a variable input goes up, both the short-run and the long-run market supply functions will shift upward and to the left. For instance, the dramatic increases in the price of crude oil in the 1970s caused a shift in the supply functions for a whole range of plastic products, including plastic cups, because crude oil is an essential input in the production of many plastics. Suppose, then, that either the short-run or the long-run market supply function does shift up and to the left. In all three cases, equilibrium price will increase and equilibrium quantity will decrease.

Increases in demand lead to movements along the supply curve and, when the supply curve is upward sloping, an increased equilibrium price and quantity.

Increases in supply lead to movements along the demand curve, an increased equilibrium quantity, but a decreased equilibrium price.

As we saw earlier, these kinds of price and quantity responses to changes in market demand and market supply are merely symptomatic of a more fundamental market process: the competitive allocation of resources. An equilibrium occurs where "supply equals demand" because at that quantity all consumers have equal marginal values (and therefore have no incentive to trade), and all firms have equal marginal costs (and therefore have no incentive to shift production). We return to this topic in Chapter 12 when we discuss general equilibrium.

PROBLEM 9.1

Throughout the nineteenth century North Americans faced vast supplies of timber. At the same time, England had small supplies of wood.

a. Assuming the demand for wood products was the same across countries, what would you predict was true about the price of wood in England and in North America? Draw a graph to show your answer.

b. What would you predict about the relative uses of wood in the two countries? For example, which country would be more likely to use wood for fuel? For roads and bridges? For construction?

PROBLEM 9.2

In the winter of 1998 Quebec suffered a disastrous ice storm that knocked out power lines and electricity for weeks. In 1996 Hurricane Fran hit North Carolina and caused a similar amount of destruction. Generally speaking, there is much less interprovincial trade than interstate trade because of poorer trade routes in Canada and government restrictions on trade between provinces. In which situation do you think there would be larger changes in prices and in which case do you think there would be larger quantity responses for the shortages caused by the tragedies?

9.2 Reading the Newspaper and Other Stories

In 1972 a group of social and physical scientists published a book called *The Limits to Growth,* based on a conference in Rome. Later this group became known as The Club of Rome. The book sold over 9 million copies in almost 30 different languages. The book had, and continues to have, a tremendous impact on the way many people think about the future and natural resources, even though it contains a flawed analysis of the way markets work.

The Limits to Growth made many bold predictions. Tin and silver were to be completely exhausted by the mid-1980s, other precious metals were to be depleted by the 1990s, and population and pollution were to grow unchecked — eventually terminating life as we know it. The basic reason for these calamities was that our industrialized world uses up resources that are presumably fixed, and so eventually we must run out. An example of the argument found in *The Limits to Growth* is contained in Figure 9.2. You've seen pictures like Figure 9.2 in newspaper articles and perhaps some textbooks. The argument that accompanies it usually goes something as follows. "For years the demand for (some resource) has just happened to equal its supply, but in the near future, the demand will outstrip the supply and there will be a habitual shortage." This line of reasoning has been going on since the time of Malthus in the nineteenth century. What is wrong with it? Why have none of the catastrophic predictions of the Club of Rome come true?

Part of the reason, as you now know, is that prices and quantities are *endogenously* determined in the competitive model. When the demand for a resource like tin increases, there is a movement along the supply of tin, and the quantity of tin demanded and supplied both increase. At the new equilibrium, supply *still* equals demand. Had the price not increased, more tin would have been demanded and less would have been supplied, and there would have been a shortage. However, the rise in the price acts to equilibrate the quantity demanded and supplied. It is not a fluke, in diagrams like Figure 9.2, that the quantities supplied and demanded just happened to be equal until the present. The fact that quantity supplied is equal to quantity demanded is, to an economist, a theorem: price always adjusts so that supply equals demand.

When people like the Club of Rome or Paul Ehrlich, author of *The Population Bomb*, predict shortages for our limited planet, they make several fundamental mistakes. The first is the one just mentioned: they ignore the role of the price mechanism in directing consumption and production. The second is that they often ignore long-run

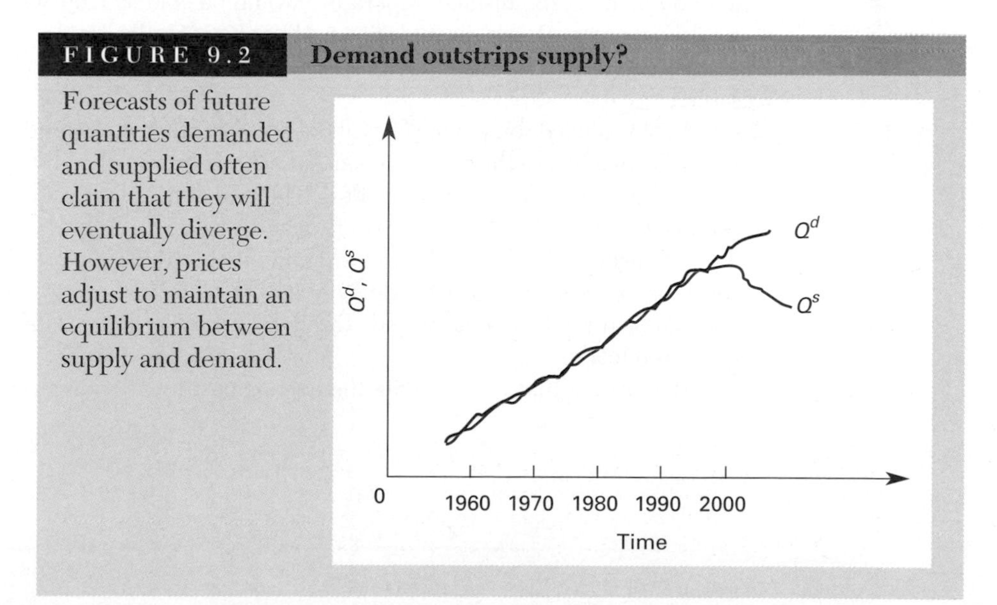

FIGURE 9.2 Demand outstrips supply?

Forecasts of future quantities demanded and supplied often claim that they will eventually diverge. However, prices adjust to maintain an equilibrium between supply and demand.

impacts. Over time, demand curves tend to become more elastic as a result of improved knowledge of substitutes—the **second law of demand**. When the oil embargo drastically raised oil prices in the early 1970s, few North Americans had ever heard of solar energy, power cells, double-paned windows, or even Honda automobiles. With high oil prices, individuals begin to explore new substitutes for goods mitigating the initial price increase, and, in essence, reducing the scarcity problem.

second law of demand

There are long-run effects on the supply side as well. At high prices firms seek new methods of production and new sources of inputs. In the nineteenth century the great social scientist Stanley Jevons predicted that England's growth would soon terminate because the reserves of coal would soon be exhausted. As the price of coal increased, however, new reserves were found, better extraction and transportation methods were developed, and eventually oil replaced most uses of coal. This process of innovation tends to increase the elasticity of supply over time, which tends to mitigate the initial rise in price. Human history provides one example after another of exogenous shocks resulting in high prices, followed by the development of new substitutes, new methods of production, and new sources of supply. Necessity may be the mother of invention, but it is the equilibrating movement of prices that signals individuals to move into action. Our equilibrium model suggests that we should be optimistic about the future of the planet, not doomsayers.

9.3 Warm Houses in Cold Climates[1]

One of the advantages of the competitive model is that it often yields surprising solutions to puzzling observations. Take, for example, the case of home heating. Anyone who has lived in Ottawa in the winter knows the meaning of the word cold! Winter temperatures are often 30° below zero, which is cold in both Fahrenheit and Celsius. In comparison, winters in Vancouver are very mild. Seldom does the temperature fall below freezing. Given the differences in outside temperatures, what would you expect to be the inside temperatures of the homes?

Common sense might tell you that in cold locations where people have to spend a lot on heating, the inside temperature would be colder. However, just the opposite tends to happen. Homes in cold climates have hotter indoor temperatures, other things equal, than homes in warmer climates. This is a puzzle that is easily explained by our model.

First you need some basic facts about home heating. Heat inside a house flows, like water down a hill, to the cooler outside air. The better insulated the walls of the house are, the more they slow down this flow. The rate of heat flow also depends on the difference between the temperature outside and inside. Anyone who has ever camped in a poorly insulated cabin in the winter knows that as the temperature outside falls the cabin becomes more drafty inside. Often, as the difference in temperature increases, you can hear the heated air whistle through the cracks in the doors and windows as it escapes outside.

It turns out that we can write the heating cost function in a very simple form:

$$TC = p_h \times B(T_i - T_o)$$

1. This application is taken from David Friedman, 1987.

where p_h is the price of heat, T_i is the temperature inside, T_o is the temperature outside, and B is the "barrier" to heat loss. The size of B depends on how well the home is insulated as well as the shape and size of the home. This is a good spot to stop and test your economic understanding of cost functions. This cost function looks different than those discussed in earlier chapters because it is linear. Don't be alarmed. This is a simplification that characterizes the actual heating cost function. This cost function must still obey all the properties discussed earlier.

Figure 9.3 draws three different cost functions representing three different homes. TC_1 is a poorly insulated home that has an outside temperature of 0°. Note that if you want an inside temperature of 0 degrees it costs nothing — you just open the window. TC_2 is the *identical* house but the outside temperature is now 20 degrees. Notice for a given inside temperature that house 2 will have a lower *total* cost of heating because nature is "adding" 20°s to the home's heat. TC_3 is a better insulated home which has an outside temperature of 0°. Compared to house 2, house 3 starts heating sooner, but the marginal cost of an additional unit of heat is lower due to the better insulation. For high inside temperatures, it is possible that house 3 has the lowest total heating bill.

Now let's see if we can resolve the paradox of warm houses in cold climates. Let a house in Ottawa be house 1 and an identical house in Vancouver be house 2. Furthermore, let's suppose that the demand for heat is identical for both homes. Figure 9.4 shows the

FIGURE 9.3 Heating cost functions

Heating costs are linear with respect to inside temperatures, and costs are not incurred until the inside temperature rises above the outside temperature. The marginal costs of heating depend on the design of the house and how well it is insulated. House 3 is better insulated, while house 2 is identical to house 1 but in a warmer climate. B^p is the insulation factor for the poorly insulated house, while B^w is the insulation factor for the well-insulated house.

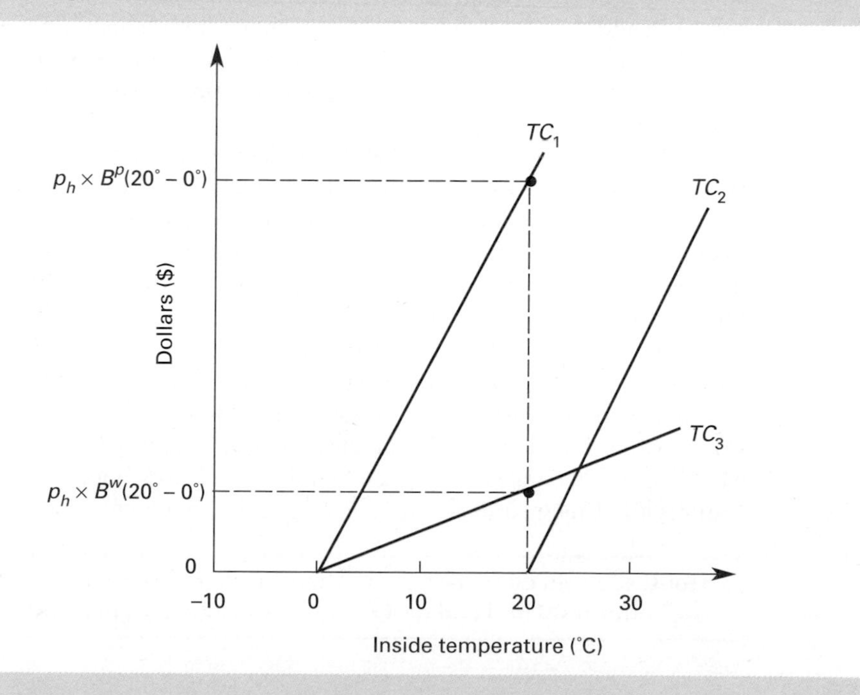

FIGURE 9.4 **Optimal heating in identical homes**

When homes are identical in terms of their marginal costs, they heat to the same temperature.

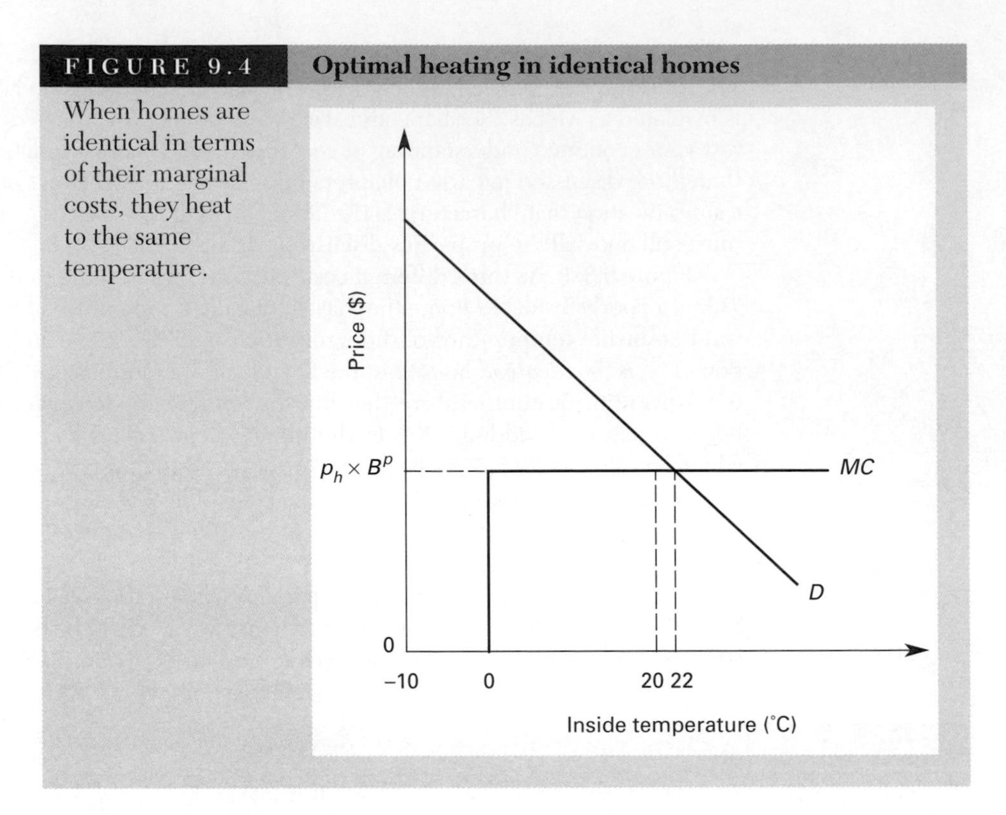

optimal heat for each house. The two houses have identical marginal costs of heat. Notice that the marginal cost curves are flat because the total cost curves are linear. Each additional unit of heat costs the same for both homes. Since each home has the same marginal cost of heat, both homes heat their homes to the same temperature. The only difference is that the home in Ottawa heats sooner and has a higher total heating bill.

But why should we assume that the homes in Vancouver and Ottawa are identical? What would be true for the demand for insulation in Ottawa versus Vancouver? In Ottawa a little insulation saves a lot of money because more heating is being done. Likewise, homes in Ottawa will more likely be designed to lower the value of *B* because the benefits are greater. In other words, homes in Ottawa are more likely to have cost functions like house 3 in Figure 9.3.

Figure 9.5 shows the heating situation for homes number 2 and 3. The home in Vancouver is cooler because at the margin it is more expensive to heat. In Ottawa homes are not only better insulated, they are made of brick rather than wood, they are two stories with basements rather than ranch bungalows and split-levels, they have smaller windows, no cathedral ceilings, and often share walls with homes next door. All of these features lower the marginal cost of heating and lead to higher inside temperatures.

Houses in cold climates have warmer inside temperatures because they are better insulated and designed to lower the marginal cost of heating.

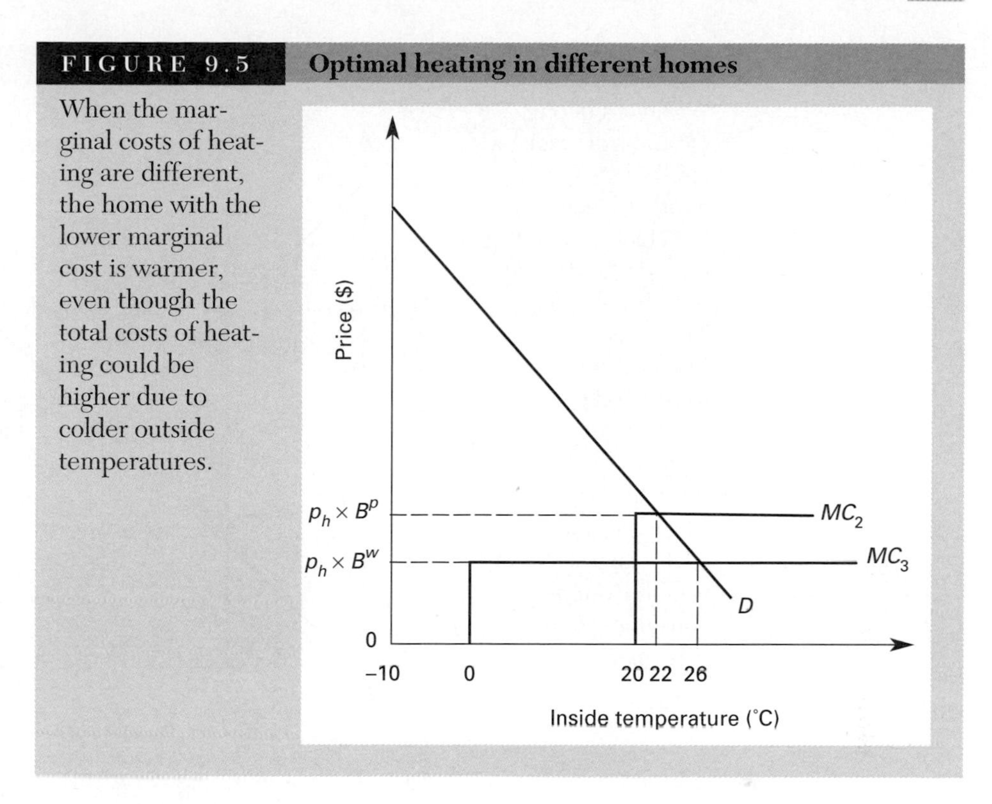

FIGURE 9.5 **Optimal heating in different homes**

When the marginal costs of heating are different, the home with the lower marginal cost is warmer, even though the total costs of heating could be higher due to colder outside temperatures.

PROBLEM 9.3

For a given home that is being heated, will individuals be constantly adjusting their thermostat based on the temperature outside?

9.4 Quotas in Agriculture

A great number of agricultural policies can be analyzed with our simple supply and demand model. For example, farmers have been very successful in lobbying governments to establish farm programs. In Canada only about 4 percent of the population live on farms, yet in 1986 about $8 billion were transferred from governments to farmers. These transfers accounted for almost 43 percent of agricultural income. Do these farm income policies simply amount to transfers of wealth from non-farmers to farmers, or are there economic losses that result from them?

One type of agricultural policy is the farm quota, largely introduced in Canada during the 1970s. A government-issued quota is essentially a licence for a particular farmer to raise a specified amount of some crop or animal. Quotas are common for chicken, turkey, egg, and milk production.

Figure 9.6 shows the effect of a quota on chickens. Prior to the quota, a price of p^* existed. At this price, each individual chicken farm was earning zero profits, and there was no incentive to leave or enter the industry. At the price p^*, there are Q^* chickens supplied, which amounts to Q^*/n chickens per farm on average. When the quota is introduced, only those farmers who have a quota can supply the market. The entire pur-

FIGURE 9.6 **The economics of a quota**

Without a quota, Q^* units of chicken are traded. When a quota is placed on the chicken market, the number traded is reduced to Q'. This causes the price to consumers to rise and creates a deadweight loss equal to the blue triangle. The grey rectangle represents the transfer of wealth from the consumers to the producers.

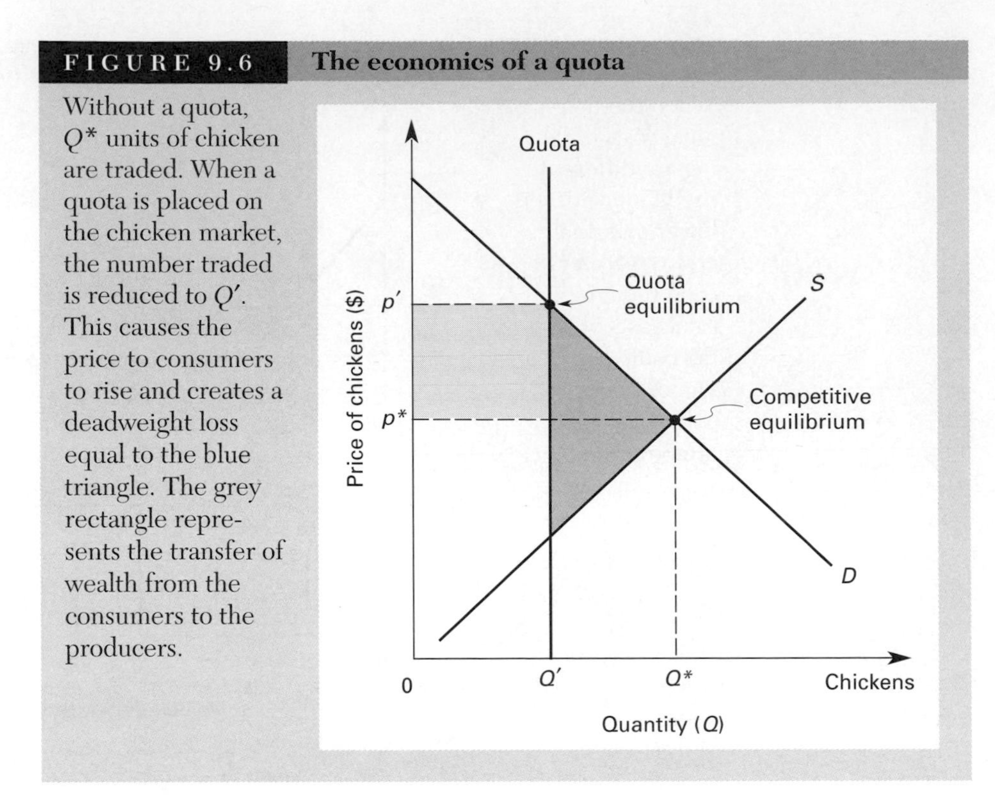

pose of a quota is to raise the price of chickens, and so the total supply must fall below Q^*. Suppose that quota allows for Q' chickens in total, or Q'/n per farm on average. At that supply, the market clearing price is p'.

An effective quota reduces the quantity supplied and raises the price to consumers.

At the new price the marginal value of chickens is greater than its marginal cost. As a result the quota leads to a deadweight loss equal to the blue shaded triangle. This loss is made up of a loss of consumer surplus and a loss of producer's surplus, resulting from the reduction in chickens produced. But there is also a transfer of wealth from consumers to producers equal to the grey shaded area. This transfer results from the higher price that consumers now face for purchasing chickens. Hence consumers are unambiguously hurt by the quota. On the other hand, the farmers benefit from the quota because presumably the transfer from the higher price is greater than the loss from reduced output.

Quotas introduce a number of distributional problems for farmers. Under perfect competition, price is the basis for the farmers' decision to enter the industry and their decision about how many chickens to produce. At the higher price p′ more farmers want to enter the industry than the quota will allow, and for individual farmers with a quota there is an incentive to produce more than their individual quotas allow. Since the price mechanism is ruled out as a solution to this problem, farmers must decide how to allocate the smaller output Q' to the farmers who are still producing and how to keep new farmers from entering. Fortunately for the farmers, the problem of preventing entry is taken care of by the government, which enforces the quota. However, the problem of allocating the reduced output to the existing farmers remains.

An additional problem is deciding whether or not some farmers with quotas should leave the industry. Given that output has been reduced, only the lowest-cost producers should remain. However, if the quotas are allocated evenly among all existing producers, then the high-cost producers remain in the industry. Our model does not indicate how these distribution problems are solved, but to the extent the solution is costly, the net benefit of the quota is reduced.

As a method of raising incomes to farmers, quotas have an additional drawback. Suppose that the quota is introduced as a complete surprise to a group of farmers. Overnight they find that if they obey their quota and reduce their production the price will rise and their incomes will increase. To these farmers, the quota is like a gift from heaven. The quota allows them to earn, year-in, year-out, an **economic rent** — that is, a return over and above their opportunity cost.[2] If the farmer wished to sell the quota, however, what price would he or she set for it? Clearly he or she would charge what it is worth, the present value of the stream of rents. But if he or she charges this amount, this means that the farmer who purchases this quota is now earning a zero profit return. The quota has simply increased the costs of entering the business; in fact, the quota is now necessary to avoid losses. Hence, when a quota is sold to another farmer, the value of the quota is transferred completely to the original farmer. This problem is called the **transitional gains trap**, and points to how difficult it is to actually improve the incomes of farmers with quotas.

economic rent

transitional gains trap

PROBLEM 9.4

Suppose the demand and supply of turkeys is given by:

$$Q^d = 20\,500 - 250p$$

$$Q^s = 5000 + 100p$$

a. Graph the demand and supply curves and determine the equilibrium price and quantity.
b. Suppose a quota of 4000 turkeys is imposed. What will be the new equilibrium price? What is the loss to consumers? What is the net gain, if any, to producers?

9.5 Rent Control

A quota is a restriction on the quantity that is allowed to be traded. Our model just as easily handles restrictions on the price at which individuals are allowed to trade. In this section we look at a case in which a **price ceiling** is imposed in a competitive market. Specifically, we will consider a market for rental housing in which the price ceiling is popularly known as *rent control*. Although the rental market is characterized by significant variation among rental units, we will assume that all rental units are identical.

price ceiling

2. An economic rent should not be confused with economic profit. Economic profit is the difference between revenue and cost; economic rent is the difference between revenues and opportunity costs. The difference between the two is the level of sunk costs.

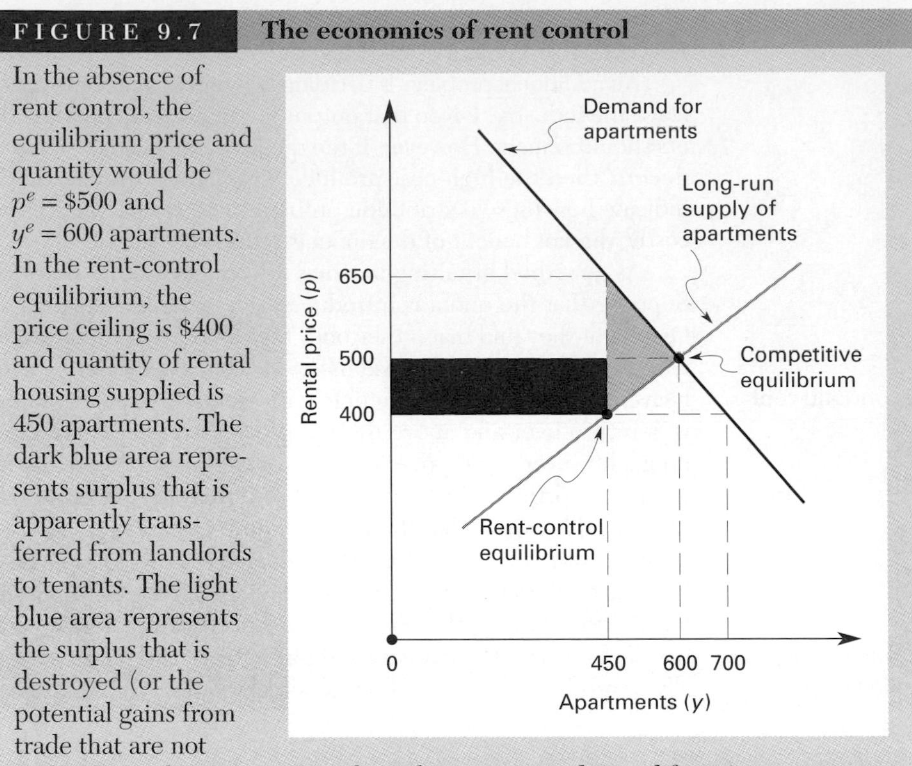

FIGURE 9.7 The economics of rent control

In the absence of rent control, the equilibrium price and quantity would be $p^e = \$500$ and $y^e = 600$ apartments. In the rent-control equilibrium, the price ceiling is \$400 and quantity of rental housing supplied is 450 apartments. The dark blue area represents surplus that is apparently transferred from landlords to tenants. The light blue area represents the surplus that is destroyed (or the potential gains from trade that are not realized). At the \$400 price ceiling, there is excess demand for 250 apartments (700 – 450).

The Rent Control Model

Suppose that in any month there are 1000 demanders of rental housing units. We will call all these people renters, the rental units apartments, the renters who are looking for an apartment searchers, and the renters who occupy an apartment tenants. Each renter's demand can be described by a *reservation price*, and, as we learned in Chapter 8, the market demand curve is then composed of 1000 vertical segments. For simplicity, we have approximated this segmented curve in Figure 9.7 by a smooth market demand curve.

Because real rental markets cater to the housing needs of people, such as students, who move frequently, *rental turnover* is an important feature of any such market. To capture turnover in this model, we will assume that each month 2 percent of the 1000 renters leave this market and are replaced by other renters with identical reservation prices. As a result, the market demand curve remains the same, but the population of renters changes from month to month as renters enter and leave the market.

Like the market demand curve, the long-run supply curve is composed of a large number of vertical segments reflecting a reservation supply price for each apartment. (Shortly, we will consider more carefully the factors that determine reservation supply price.) Once again, we have approximated this segmented curve in Figure 9.7 by a smooth long-run supply curve.

Since the decisions to replace and maintain rental units are important in real rental markets, we will assume that apartments last for a finite period of time and that they require periodic maintenance. Specifically, we will adopt the following assumptions. Each apartment is owned by one landlord and accommodates one renter. Maintenance entails the expenditure of $50 per month. Each new apartment lasts for 120 months (10 years) if it is maintained every month. If maintenance is not done in a given month, the apartment becomes uninhabitable. In any event, it becomes uninhabitable after 120 months.

In a competitive equilibrium, it makes no difference who actually pays the monthly maintenance. If the tenant pays the maintenance cost, the equilibrium rental price for an apartment is lower by $50 than if the landlord pays. For simplicity, we will assume that the landlord pays for maintenance.

Let us suppose that this market is initially in the long-run equilibrium shown in Figure 9.7, where the rental rate is $500 per month and 600 apartments are supplied. Now suppose that a rent ceiling of $400 per month is imposed in this market. What are the effects of this rental ceiling in the short run? In the long run? Who gains and who loses from rent control?

Apparent Effects of Rent Control

Assuming that this price ceiling is enforced, its impact seems to be straightforward. There is an apparent distributional effect, since each tenant seems to be better off by $100 per month and the owner of each apartment seems to be worse off by $100. When the $400 ceiling is imposed, income or surplus is then transferred from landlords to tenants. There are apparently no *short-run* allocational effects, since the initial allocation is Pareto-optimal, and no tenant has an incentive to move once the rental price falls to $400 per month. Yet the actual distributional and allocational effects may not be so clear-cut as the model initially suggests. Let us see what we might be overlooking.

Short-Run Effects

We can begin by looking at the allocation of the 600 existing apartments. To capture one important feature of real rental markets, we assumed a 2 percent turnover rate in this market. As some renters move on and others replace them, an average of 12 apartments are vacated and reallocated to new tenants in each month. What principles govern this reallocation of apartments? If the landlord gets only $400 per month, then price no longer guides allocation because from Figure 9.7 we know that there is excess demand at the $400 rental rate. Seven hundred renters want an apartment, but only 600 can be accommodated in the 600 existing apartments. If price does not perform the allocational role, what does?

Let us suppose for a moment that the addresses of all vacant apartments are published in the local newspaper and that the first searcher to get to a vacant apartment rents it. Rent control thus creates a game, apartment hunting, played each month by a large number of searchers trying to rent just 12 apartments. It is this game that replaces price as the allocative mechanism.

If you have ever hunted for an apartment in a tight rental market, you will know how this game is played. The minute the local paper hits the streets, searchers thumb through the "for rent" section of the classified ads and then speed off to the closest advertised vacancy, hoping to be the first on the scene. Any more leisurely strategy is bound to fail when excess demand is significant at the rent-controlled price. Of course, the success rate will be small, meaning that a searcher who is new to the market must expect to spend a great deal of time and energy before finally finding an apartment. The costs of this search activity — gas, time, and wear and tear on the car and nerves — mean that the effective price of an apartment will be considerably more than the $400 paid to the landlord each month.

Viewed from another perspective, these search costs mean that some of the surplus available from the original 600 apartments is destroyed in the game of apartment hunting, which replaces price as the allocative mechanism under rent control. That is, attempting to use a rent ceiling to transfer surplus from landlords to tenants creates forces that tend to destroy some of that surplus. Because effective rent control confers a valuable monthly bonus on tenants, searchers willingly expend time, energy, and money to get access to this bonus, thereby dissipating its value.

The situation is closely analogous to the problem of allocating squash courts on a first-come-first-served basis in Section 4.4. Real resources are used to achieve an allocation that could have been achieved at lower cost by a price mechanism. We can draw a general conclusion:

The real costs of allocating a fixed quantity of some good or service are higher when a non-price allocative mechanism is substituted for a price mechanism.

The next question is this: Who gets the vacant apartments? So far we have assumed that landlords advertise vacant apartments and rent to the first searcher who shows up. In reality, the landlord may not be willing to rent to the first searcher. Because there is excess demand, the landlord can afford to pick and choose among searchers based on his or her personal likes and dislikes. It is also possible, and even likely, that if excess demand is large enough, vacant apartments won't be advertised at all. The landlord (or the last tenant) may already know one or more searchers and may find it attractive to rely on these informal contacts rather than to deal with the large numbers of searchers who will respond to a formal ad.

Thus blind chance, the personal preferences of landlords, and personal contacts will all play some role in reallocating apartments as they become vacant. As a consequence, the allocation of apartments will not be Pareto-optimal because the 600 available apartments will not be allocated to the 600 renters with reservation prices greater than or equal to the long-run equilibrium price of $500. Instead, some of the 100 renters with reservation prices between $400 and $500 will inevitably manage to rent apartments because they are lucky enough to spot an ad first, or because some landlord likes their looks, or because they know the vacating tenant. Again, we can draw a general conclusion:

When the allocation of a fixed quantity of some good or service is not guided by price signals, the allocation need not be Pareto-optimal.

To this point, we have assumed implicitly that the tenant pays and the landlord receives just $400 per month for any apartment. Even the most casual observation of real markets with rent control reveals that more money is likely to change hands. In New York City, "key money" means a bribe that a searcher pays a landlord for the privilege of signing an initial lease. In Toronto, during the period of rent control, a "sublet fee" meant a bribe that a searcher paid a tenant to sublet a rent-controlled apartment. These bribes were so much a part of apartment hunting that often no attempt was made to be discreet about them. For example, the following advertisement appeared on a bulletin board in a convenience store located in a large rent-controlled apartment complex: "Wanted: one-bedroom apartment. Willing to pay $500 sublet fee."

Rent control can also be circumvented in more subtle ways. In this model, maintenance is the landlord's responsibility. Given the excess demand caused by rent control, the landlord has an incentive to pass the $50 per month maintenance cost to the tenant, while maintaining the rent-controlled price of $400. And the landlord can always find a tenant willing to pay the additional $50. If it is possible to do so, then, landlords will shift maintenance responsibilities to tenants. Alternatively, the landlord may be able to tie the lease of the apartment to the lease of furniture — charging just $400 to rent the apartment while overcharging for the furniture — thereby increasing the effective rental rate for the apartment.

These are just a few of the many possibilities for circumventing the intent of rent control. These can be thought of as informal and incomplete price mechanisms that emerge to fill the void created when the real price mechanism is suspended. They clearly work to reduce the extent of income redistribution and to increase the price of rent-controlled accommodations.

The actual extent of redistribution of income from landlords to tenants will be less than it initially appears to be.

Long-Run Effects

Before we can consider the effects of rent control in the long run, we need to think about what the *long-run reservation supply price* for an apartment actually means. Once an apartment becomes uninhabitable at the end of 120 months, the landlord faces a long-run investment decision: whether to build a new apartment or to convert the land to its next best use. For example, let us suppose that it will cost some landlord $60 000 to rebuild the apartment and that the landlord's next best option is to sell the land to a 7-Eleven convenience store for $50 000. The landlord's reservation supply price is a monthly rental price for the apartment such that he or she is indifferent between rebuilding the apartment and selling the land to 7-Eleven. If the rental price is $\$p$ per month, the landlord's net monthly return is $\$(p - 50)$, since maintenance is the landlord's responsibility. The reservation supply price is then the value of $\$p$ such that the discounted present value of the net monthly return over 120 months, less the $60 000 rebuilding cost, is just equal to the $50 000 that 7-Eleven is willing to pay for the property. If the real rental rate is larger than this value, then the landlord will rebuild the apartment; if it is less than this value, he or she will sell the land to 7-Eleven.

To the extent that rent control reduces the net monthly return of landlords, the supply of apartments in the long run will diminish as some landlords decide to convert their land to alternative uses at the end of the 120 months. If we suppose for purposes of illustration that the $400 rent ceiling is effective, then we see from Figure 9.7 that just 450 apartments will be supplied in the long run. Thus, 150 potential landlords and potential tenants will be frozen out of the market by rent control. The surplus that is destroyed as a result is represented by the triangular shaded area in Figure 9.7. Notice, too, that in the long run, apartment hunting becomes a grim affair. Again assuming a turnover rate of 2 percent per month, many searchers will be looking and only nine apartments will be vacant each month.

Although we have learned that in the long run, the supply of rental housing will shrink under rent-control legislation, it is entirely possible that the supply may shrink even more quickly. For instance, one obvious response that landlords can and do make to rent control is to convert their rental units to owner-occupied units, which they then sell off to individual buyers. Renters in apartments and townhouses are sometimes evicted; their vacated apartments are then converted into condominium units and sold within a matter of months. Not surprisingly, in many rent-controlled jurisdictions, it is illegal to convert apartments into condominiums. Indeed, in some places it is illegal to demolish rental accommodation.

Let us briefly summarize what we have learned about the potential effects of rent control in this model. Some lucky tenants will clearly be better off under rent control. In particular, tenants who occupy apartments when rent-control legislation is imposed will benefit. All landlords will be worse off, and some will be induced to convert their land to alternative uses, thereby reducing the supply of apartments. As a consequence of that reduced supply, some renters will be worse off. Under rent control, the ways in which available apartments are allocated both impose costs on searchers — thereby increasing the effective price of rental housing — and produce an allocation that is not Pareto-optimal.

price floor

Rent control is just one example of a market impediment. In the following problem, you can explore some implications of another market impediment — a **price floor**.

PROBLEM 9.5

In Section 1.2, we briefly considered two schemes for supporting the price of agricultural goods, the *price subsidy program* and the *buy-and-store program*. Identify the surplus destroyed and the implications for the public purse for each of these programs.

9.6 Taxes and Tariffs

In Chapter 3, we analyzed the difference between a lump sum and an excise tax in terms of the preferences and budget constraints of a consumer. We can analyze the effect of these taxes again, but now in the context of our supply and demand model. Once again we will see that our model provides different answers than our common sense might first suggest. For example, we might think that in terms of tax revenue, it does not matter what goods get taxed. After all, if the government is faced with two goods to tax that each has a current volume of trade of 10 000 units, and if a $1 tax per unit is placed on either good, then $10 000 of revenue should be raised. However, this is not the case. We might also think that if the government puts a tax of $1 per unit on a good that the price of the good must rise by $1, but this is not the case either. Finally, we might think that it matters a great deal whether or not the consumer is taxed at the point of consumption or the firm is taxed at the point of production. Yet again, our model suggests otherwise.

Let us begin by considering only the effect of a $1 per unit tax on a group of firms in a particular industry. A per-unit tax means that for every unit of output produced, the cost of production is increased by the amount of the tax. Hence the marginal costs of production increase by the amount of the tax, in this case by $1. If every firm in the industry is taxed by the same amount, then the market supply curve must also shift up by the amount of the tax.

Figure 9.8 shows the effect of an imposition of a $1 per unit tax on all firms. Before the tax the equilibrium is at E, with an equilibrium price and quantity of p^* and Q^*. Since the tax shifts the supply curve up by $1, the new equilibrium is at E', with a new equilibrium price and quantity of p' and Q'. Several things are immediately apparent from Figure 9.8. First, it is clear that as long as the demand curve is not perfectly inelastic, the price will not increase by the full amount of the tax. As firms raise the price, consumers substitute out of the good being taxed and into goods that have become relatively cheaper. This substitution hinders the ability of firms to pass the tax on to consumers; as a result, prices rise, but by less than the amount of the tax.

Thus, the consumer does not pay all of the tax revenue. The relative tax burdens are shown by the shaded regions. Consumers pay an amount of taxes equal to the blue shaded area in Figure 9.8. The area is defined by the increase in price they face $(p' - p^*)$ multiplied by the amount of the good they purchase, Q'. On the other hand, firms do not receive the price p′, but rather receive $(p' - 1)$. Therefore the amount of the tax that the firms pay is given by $(p^* - 1) \times Q'$, which is equal to the grey shaded area.

deadweight loss

Moreover, the level of output traded has been reduced from Q^* to Q'. This fall in the amount of trade causes a deadweight loss to result. A **deadweight loss** is the lost gains from trade that results from movements away from the equilibrium quantity of trade, and is made up of lost consumer's and producer's surplus. The total deadweight loss is given by the triangle *EE′E″*, which could be considered the cost of taxation.

A per-unit tax increases the equilibrium price by less than the amount of the tax, and creates a deadweight loss.

The amount of tax collected and who pays the tax depend critically on the elasticity of demand. Figure 9.9 shows two markets that have each had an identical per-unit tax placed on the firms. In part (a) we see that the demand curve is very inelastic. This good has very few substitutes and as a result, the bulk of the tax is passed on to the consumer in the form of a higher price. If the demand curve were perfectly inelastic,

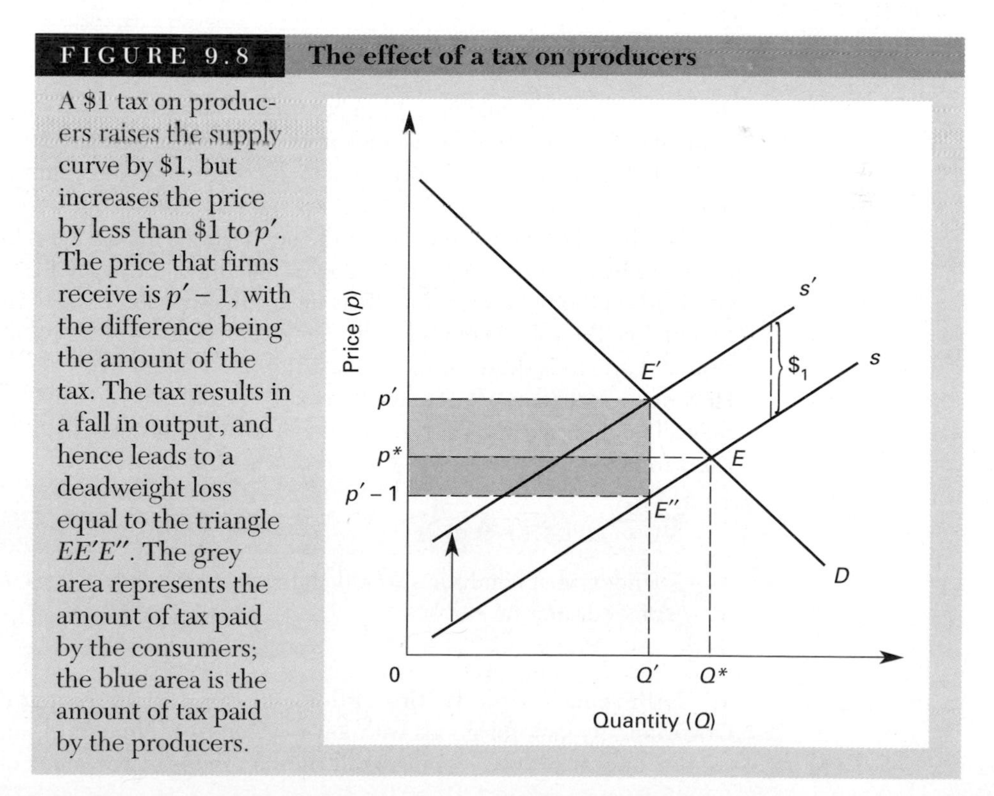

FIGURE 9.8 The effect of a tax on producers

A $1 tax on producers raises the supply curve by $1, but increases the price by less than $1 to p'. The price that firms receive is $p' - 1$, with the difference being the amount of the tax. The tax results in a fall in output, and hence leads to a deadweight loss equal to the triangle *EE′E″*. The grey area represents the amount of tax paid by the consumers; the blue area is the amount of tax paid by the producers.

FIGURE 9.9 Elasticity of demand and per-unit taxes

The effect of a tax on the price to consumers, price to producers, and the quantity traded depends on the elasticity of demand. In part (a) the demand curve is highly inelastic and, as a result, there is a large increase in the price to consumers and a small deadweight loss. In part (b) the demand curve is highly elastic and, as a result, there is a small rise in the price to consumers and a relatively large deadweight loss.

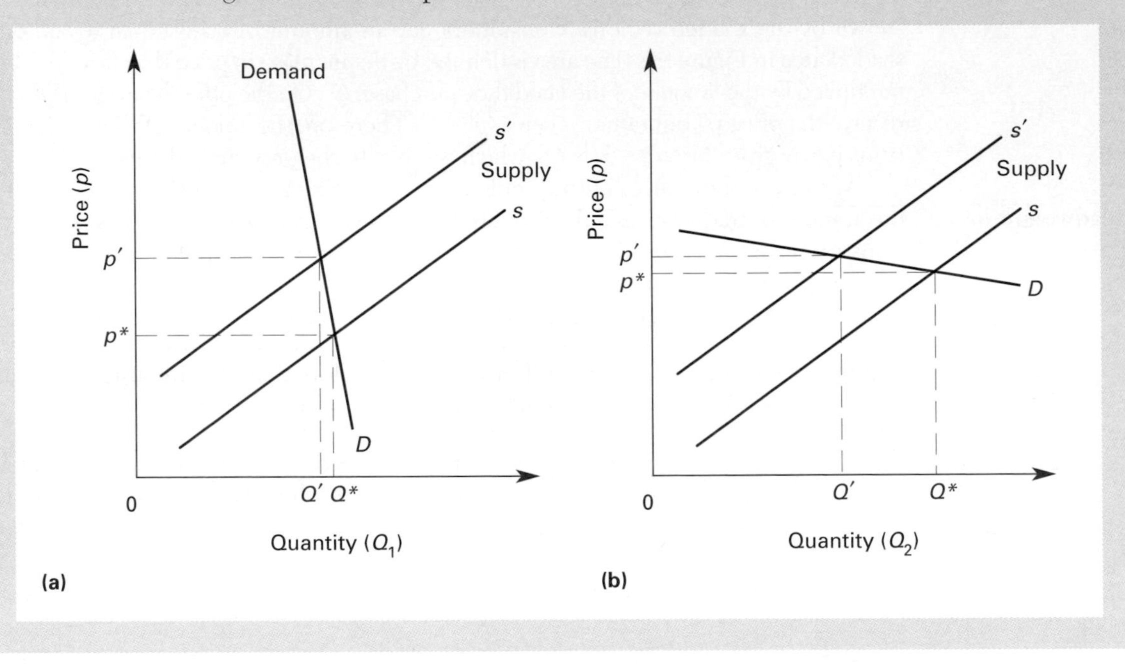

then the entire tax would have been passed on. There is also very little reduction in the amount of the good traded. As a result there is only a trivial deadweight loss, and the amount of tax revenue is almost equal to the original traded volume times the amount of the tax.

On the other hand, demand for the good shown in part (b) is highly elastic. Since there are many substitutes for this good, consumers are quick to substitute into other goods when the price increases. This means that consumers pay very little of the tax. In addition, the volume of trade falls significantly, and a relatively large deadweight loss results. Part (b) is drawn under the assumption that all firms remain in the industry. However, a secondary effect of the tax could be that firms leave the industry. At the limit, they all might leave and the deadweight costs of the tax would be the loss of the entire gains from trade.

PROBLEM 9.6

Under what conditions would all firms in an industry leave as the result of a per unit tax?

Differences in elasticities of demand can explain a great deal of tax policy. Governments look for goods with low elasticities of demand to tax, because if consumers and/or producers can avoid the tax, then tax revenues obviously fall. This explains why consumers firmly believe that if a good gets taxed, they're likely to pay. Historically, one of the most commonly taxed goods was salt. Before refrigeration, salt was used for more important things than flavouring food. Not surprisingly, throughout the centuries, salt had a very low elasticity of demand. In modern times it is fashionable to tax gasoline, alcohol, and tobacco. All of these goods have relatively low elasticities of demand. What we never see is the taxation of a particular brand of gasoline, beer, or cigarette. If the government suddenly decided that it wanted to tax Molson Canadian it would quickly find itself with zero revenue. Not only would consumers switch immediately to other beers, but Molson would cease to produce that particular brand.

Who pays the tax depends on the elasticity of demand. Lower elasticities lead to consumers paying a larger fraction.

Taxing Consumers

We have been examining taxes in the context of a tax on the firms at the point of production. An alternative form of taxation would be a tax placed not on the firm at the point of production, but on the consumer as a sales tax. One question we might ask is: Will the same tax per unit placed on the consumer lead to a different equilibrium price and quantity than what we just observed with producers?

Consider Figure 9.10, which shows the effect of a sales tax on the demand curve. The demand curve tells us the *maximum* consumers are willing to pay for the good. When a tax is put on, consumers are still only willing to pay at most the height of their demand curve. As a result, the demand curve that the firm *perceives* shifts down by an amount equal to the tax. For example, if a consumer is willing to pay $10 for the first unit and the tax is $1, then the most that the firm can receive is $9. Hence, a sales tax has the result of lowering the demand for the good by the amount of the tax.

As with the case of the producers, however, the price received by the firm does not fall by the amount of the tax. Rather, as is shown in Figure 9.10, the price to the consumer rises to p', and the price to the firm falls to $(p' - 1)$. The difference between the two prices is the amount of the tax. Since the demand curve falls by the amount of a tax when consumers are taxed directly, and the supply curve shifts up by the amount of a tax when firms are taxed directly, the impact on price and quantity is identical. In other words, it does not matter if consumers are taxed or producers are, the outcome is the same. In addition, the relative share of tax burden is the same, and in either case depends on the elasticities of demand and supply.

PROBLEM 9.7

Who bears the cost of shoplifting, the consumer or the producer? Likewise, when a firm is forced to offer its employees medical and dental coverage, who bears these costs?

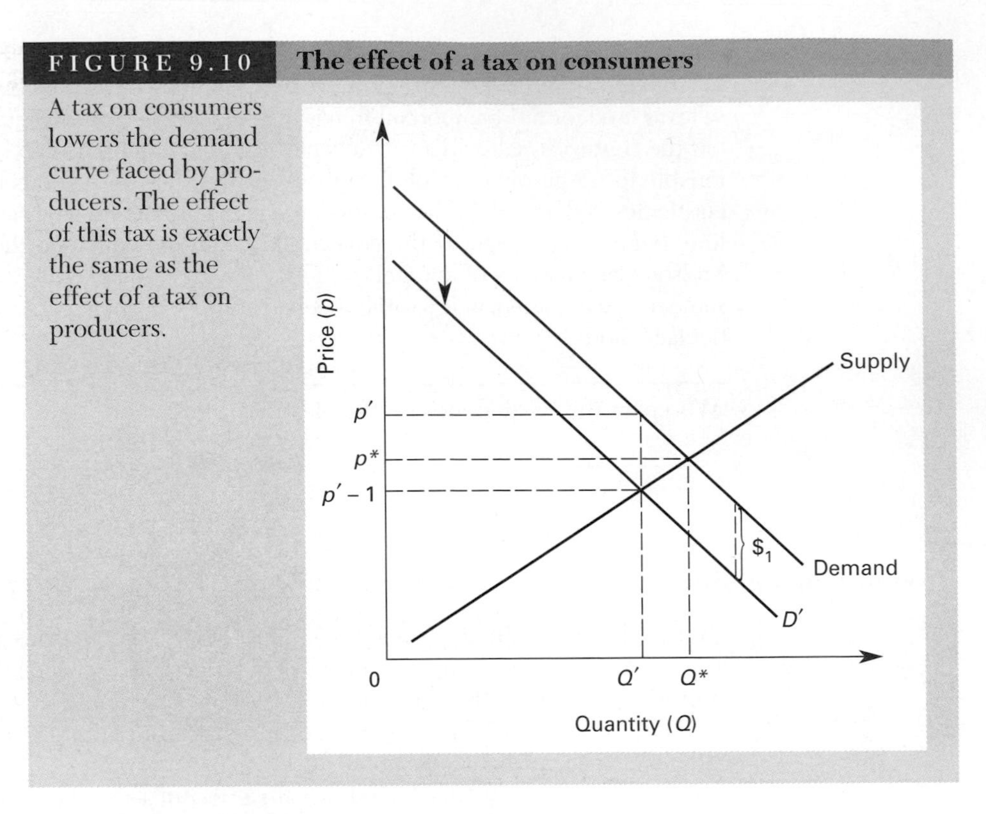

FIGURE 9.10 The effect of a tax on consumers

A tax on consumers lowers the demand curve faced by producers. The effect of this tax is exactly the same as the effect of a tax on producers.

Tariffs

One particular type of taxation that has been common throughout history is a tariff on imported goods. A tariff is nothing more than a per unit tax on goods that cross a border. With the advent of the *General Agreement on Tariffs and Trade* (GATT) in 1944, there has been pressure on countries throughout the world to reduce tariffs. In this regard GATT has been quite successful and general tariffs on manufactured goods fell from 40 percent in 1947 to less than 10 percent in the mid-seventies. Since then, tariffs have fallen even further, and with the *North America Free Trade Agreement*, tariffs will be eliminated between the participating countries.

The analysis of a tariff is quite straightforward now that we have analyzed the effect of a tax in general. In Figure 9.11, we have a supply and demand graph for a product that is produced and consumed domestically, say, shoes. Had this country only produced and consumed shoes domestically, the equilibrium price would have been p'. When the country trades on the world market it faces a price, p^w, which is assumed to be lower than the domestic price. At this lower price, several things are clear. First, domestic consumers increase the quantity demanded to q_d^w, and domestic producers reduce the amount supplied to q_s^w. The difference between these two quantities is the amount of imports. Second, the gains from trade are increased by the triangle ABC. This increase in surplus comes to the consumers in part at the expense of the domestic producers. Domestic producers cannot be expected to support free trade agreements when it means that cheaper foreign goods will be imported. Finally, we see that there is still some domestic production. It is not true that if a country imports a good, it should only import. Some domestic producers will have low enough costs to be able to weather the arrival of new imports.

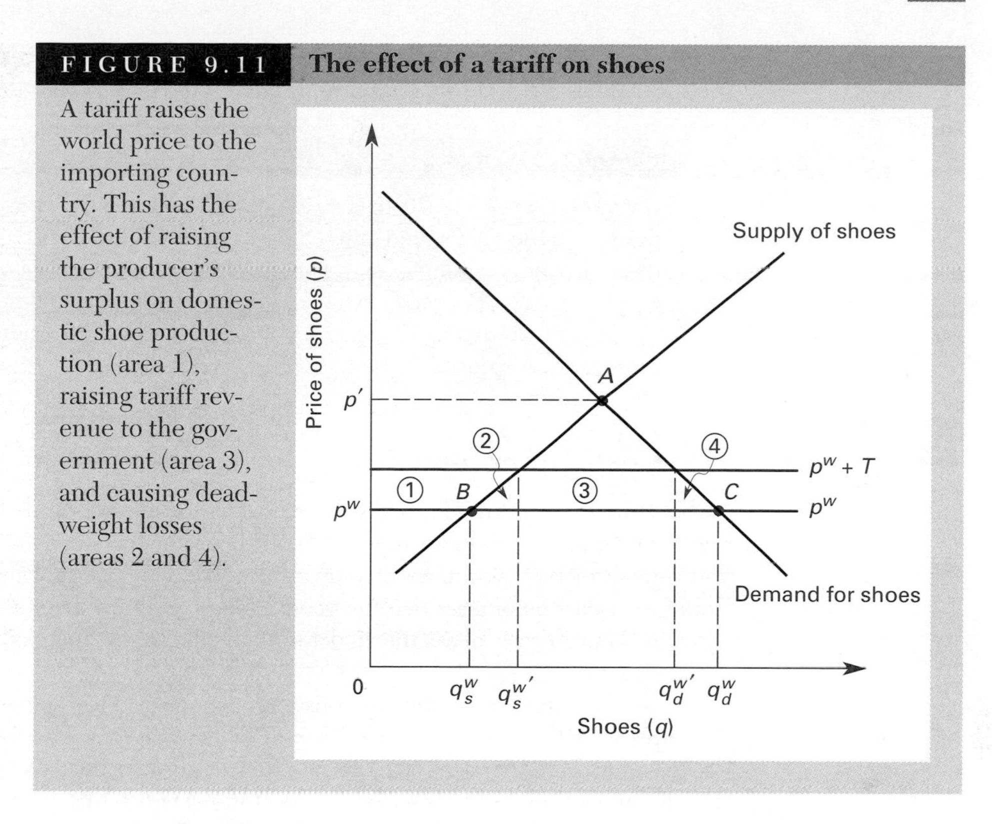

FIGURE 9.11 The effect of a tariff on shoes

A tariff raises the world price to the importing country. This has the effect of raising the producer's surplus on domestic shoe production (area 1), raising tariff revenue to the government (area 3), and causing deadweight losses (areas 2 and 4).

When a tariff is placed on the shoes, the world price line shifts up by the amount of the tariff. As a result, domestic producers now increase the amount that they supply the domestic market to $q_s^{w'}$. Similarly, domestic consumers reduce the quantity of shoes demanded to $q_d^{w'}$. As a result, the amount of imports is also reduced. Consumers are clearly worse off, and we can divide the lost consumer surplus into four sections, as shown in Figure 9.11. Section 1 is an increase in producers' surplus caused by the increased price. As a result we would predict that domestic suppliers will support import tariffs. Section 3 is the quantity of imports times the tariff, or the tariff revenue to the government. Both sections 1 and 3 represent transfers of wealth from consumers to either producers or the government. The other two sections, however, represent deadweight losses caused by the tariff. Section 2 is the increased costs that this economy incurs by producing expensive domestic output, rather than purchasing cheaper imports. The fourth section is the loss of consumer's surplus resulting from the reduced domestic consumption. Hence overall, tariffs lower wealth.

It might be thought that tariffs are necessary to protect domestic producers; however, this conclusion appears plausible only because we tend to have a narrow view of what "domestic producer" means. Suppose that Canada was interested in producing a Honda automobile. One production method would be to set up a domestic Honda plant in Oshawa, Ontario and build them directly. Another method would be to plant wheat in Saskatchewan. When the wheat grows and is harvested, it is put into a rail car and shipped to a magical place called Japan. A week after shipping a boat full of wheat to Japan it returns home full of Hondas! In fact, there are many ways to produce Honda cars, or any other commodity that gets imported. When we impose a tariff to protect the Honda plant in Ontario, we must keep in mind that we are hurting the wheat-growing plant in Saskatchewan. The farmer in Saskatchewan, or the logger in British

Columbia, *is* the competition of the plant worker in Oshawa. To help one domestic producer is, always, to hurt another domestic producer.

PROBLEM 9.8

Rather than use a tariff to restrict imports, countries often use import quotas. In the 1980s the United States imposed "voluntary" import quotas on Japanese automobiles. Using your knowledge of how a quota works, graph a quota that would have the same impact on the volume of imports as the tariff drawn in Figure 9.11. Does the importing country benefit more from the quota or the tariff?

Application: Do Costs Determine Prices?

Perhaps the most common mistake the average person makes about economic matters regards how prices are determined. The average person is convinced that prices are determined by cost. When costs go up, prices go up by an equal amount. We can see from the discussion of taxes that this is incorrect. Prices are determined by supply and demand. Though costs play a role in determining the supply function, they are only half of the equation.

In a competitive market many consumer actions lead to changes in costs that give the impression that costs influence prices. For example, suppose that the demand for hockey equipment increases. Parents and their eager kids head off to their local sports store to buy hockey sticks and pads. The local stores notice this increase in demand and, in turn, increase their demand to their suppliers. These suppliers must increase production, which involves increasing their costs at the margin. Higher production then leads to higher prices which in turn leads to higher prices to the consumer. The consumer might ask, "Why are prices going up?" To which the reply might be, "I don't know; my costs have just increased." However, the increase in cost came about through an increase in consumer demand in the first place. One of the most common examples of this is pure inflation. Prices increase in times of inflation, not because costs are increasing, but because large changes in the money supply allow consumers to chase the existing stock of goods around with more dollars in their pockets.

**Prices are determined by the intersection of demand and supply.
Prices are not determined by costs.**

9.7 The Marriage Market

Marriage is a complex institution which legally regulates the terms of formation and dissolution of a union between a man and woman.[3] Though there can be marriages without children, most people marry for the purpose of raising their own children. Marriages involve the state, family members, often the church, and even friends and larger social

3. At the time of writing, three provincial Courts of Appeal have ruled that banning same-sex marriage is unconstitutional. The federal government is now trying to find a solution, either by declaring marriage open to homosexual couples or by creating a special type of civil union for them. In the United States, only Vermont recognizes a civil union for homosexuals.

groups. Marriage is mostly about *how* production in the household is organized, and as such is a topic better left for the last section of this book. However, if we're willing to make some very strong assumptions and think about the entire marriage market as opposed to specific relationships, we can see that our current model can tell us a few things regarding the volume of marriages and the (implicit) terms of trade.

To begin with, let's assume individuals are free to marry whomever they wish, and that all benefits and costs from marriage accrue to the couple. Historically, this was not always true. Four hundred years ago, children in Western countries were the property of their fathers. Once men reached the age of majority they were able to achieve legal status as citizens, but for women who married, their ownership transferred to their husbands under the legal doctrine of coveture. Under this system, it was quite common for marriages to be arranged. Under such circumstances the benefits and costs of marriage do not necessarily rest with the individuals marrying. Though only a few rituals of coveture remain today,[4] it is unlikely for a husband or wife to receive all the benefits or costs of marriage. For example, marriage is the chief vehicle through which humans procreate. Married individuals, however, are never compensated for providing this fundamental benefit to society. Despite these issues, we'll make this simplifying assumption anyway.

Second, let's assume every marriage is monogamous, and everyone is homogeneous. That is, all males are the same and all females are the same. We'll also assume it is possible for a price for a spouse to exist. This price is either negative or positive. In a Western society we don't have explicit prices for a spouse, but we do have implicit ones. When a couple gets married, they bring assets, human capital, and expected future earnings with them. To the extent that one person brings more than the other, that person is paying the other spouse. If a wife pays a positive price to obtain a husband, then by definition the husband pays a negative price to obtain a bride. To keep matters simple, we'll assume there is an explicit price for a spouse.

Third, let's assume that everyone wants to get married in order to engage in some type of household production. This production might be the raising of children or simply producing the mundane daily goods of food, shelter and clothing. Under these circumstances we might expect a market situation as shown in Figure 9.12. In this graph we've drawn the demand and supply curves for wives such that at equilibrium A, the price of the spouse is zero. Keep in mind that there would be a symmetrical graph for the market for husbands, since the supply of wives is the mirror image of the demand for husbands.

Now let's consider what happens in such a market when there are shocks to either the supply or demand for wives. Suppose a large war breaks out and most of the eligible men in a town leave to fight. The effect would be a fall in the demand for wives, and is shown as a movement to equilibrium B. This fall in demand means the price of wives becomes negative, or, which is the same thing, the price of husbands becomes positive. In a Western culture where prices are implicit, how might this fall in price manifest? Women would find they would have to promise men more things in order for them to agree to marriage. Perhaps more of the household duties would be assigned to the wife; perhaps the husband would have more say in the number of children, where the couple lives, and what the relative shares in the marriage would be. One form of competition women might engage in when the terms of trade go against them is premarital sex. Historically sex was much more costly for women to engage in than men. Even

4. For example, it is still the case that most women assume the last name of their husbands.

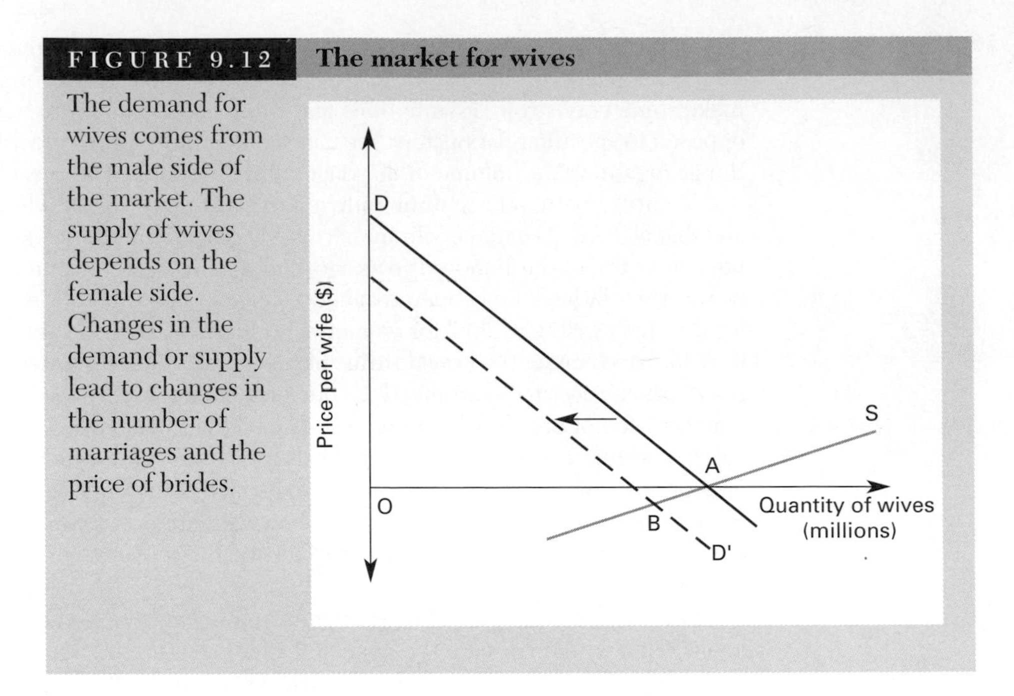

FIGURE 9.12 The market for wives

The demand for wives comes from the male side of the market. The supply of wives depends on the female side. Changes in the demand or supply lead to changes in the number of marriages and the price of brides.

today women bear most of the costs of sex when a pregnancy arises. As a result women tend to be less willing to engage in premarital sex than men. When the price of a wife falls, however, one form of payment to men might be to engage in sex before marriage.

What would happen to this market if instead of a war, the number of eligible females in society fell? Since women often marry men a few years older than they are, this can happen when age cohorts are not the same. For example, if a large birth rate is followed by a small one, by the time the women of the small group are of age to marry, they will be in relatively small numbers to those men in the large group slightly older than them. Such situations happened in North America during the 1930s and the 1980s. According to the simple model, the supply of wives is reduced, and the price of wives increases. Now potential husbands must pay more for a spouse than previously. This might arise in terms of commitments to allow the wife more say in the marriage. It might also manifest in more commitment from the male prior to the marriage. Under such circumstances, males are more likely to commit to marriage and less likely to pressure the woman to engage in premarital sex. Both the 1930s and 1980s were conservative times in the popular culture.

Our simple little marriage market model cannot explain much about marriage. However, it does tell us how changes in the sex ratio in the population of men and women of marrying age affects the terms of trade in marriage. To test your intuition, consider what would happen if polygamy were made legal. Polygamy is where a husband is allowed to legally have more than one wife. Our intuition might suggest this would make women worse off; after all, who would want to share a husband? But consider the model. Polygamy increases the demand for wives, and this raises the price of wives. Some wives will accept being the second wife because the price paid to them compensates for the reduced attention they get from sharing. Wives in a monogamous marriage are much better off because they too receive the higher price. Those males with only one wife are made worse off.

There are only a few examples of widespread voluntary polygamy in history. One important case was the Mormon experience in Utah during the nineteenth century. Studies have shown that opposition to polygamy at the time did not come from women in Utah or the rest of the US, but from unmarried men in Utah and males outside the state. When Utah was granted statehood, one of the conditions was that polygamy be made illegal. This restriction was placed by Congress, whose members were made up of and elected by men from states other than Utah. An interesting question is: Had women been allowed to vote in the nineteenth century, would polygamy have been made illegal?

9.8 The Economics of Crime

Although there are many aspects of crime that are beyond our simple model of supply and demand, there is a great deal that can still be understood. The use of economics to understand criminal behaviour and the criminal law strikes many as incongruous. After all, aren't criminals irrational, acting on impulse and upbringing? This may be the common view of the criminal, but economists always assume that human activities are the result of self-interest. Ultimately the proof of the pudding is in the eating. To the extent that an economic explanation can account for criminal behaviour, it supports the assumption of rational criminals.

When we say that crime is subject to economic analysis, we are saying that the quantity of crime depends on costs and benefits, and that criminal behaviour takes place when the benefits are greater than the costs. Criminals, like everyone else, participate in a particular type of "employment" because they earn more than they can in other types of employment. When the costs of crime increase, the amount of crime should fall. When the benefits of crime increase, the amount of crime should increase. As economists, we do not claim that *everyone* will engage in rational criminal behaviour. We only claim that as the cost of crime is reduced, those committing crime will commit more, and that some individuals will find it in their interests to become criminals.

Figure 9.13 shows a simple supply and demand model, where the horizontal axis measures the quantity of crime committed. The demand curve for crime is not an ordinary demand curve since criminals do not "purchase" crime. This demand curve gives us the marginal benefit of crime as a function of the number of crimes. It is downward sloping because the marginal benefit of crime decreases as the number of crimes increases. The supply of crimes is upward sloping, demonstrating the rising marginal costs of production. One of the major costs of crime is the forgone income from legitimate employment. People with low alternative earnings are the first to engage in crime. As the returns to crime increase, others are induced into the industry, but these people naturally have higher opportunity costs. In equilibrium, the amount of crime is where the marginal benefits equal the marginal costs.

This simple model suggests two methods of reducing crime. The first is to reduce the net benefits. Societies attempt in many ways to achieve this goal. One of the most common is to impose penalties for crimes and to try to catch criminals. A criminal considering a crime will compare the expected penalty (the amount of the penalty times the probability of getting caught) with the expected benefit. If the expected penalty is too high, then the crime is not committed.

The other method of reducing crime is to raise the opportunity cost of crime. If employment opportunities improve, or if one is eligible for social services given no criminal record, then the costs of crime increase, and again there will be less crime. Here

FIGURE 9.13 The equilibrium amount of crime

The demand and supply for crime obey the same principles as in any other market. The equilibrium amount of crime is the point at which the marginal benefits equal the marginal costs.

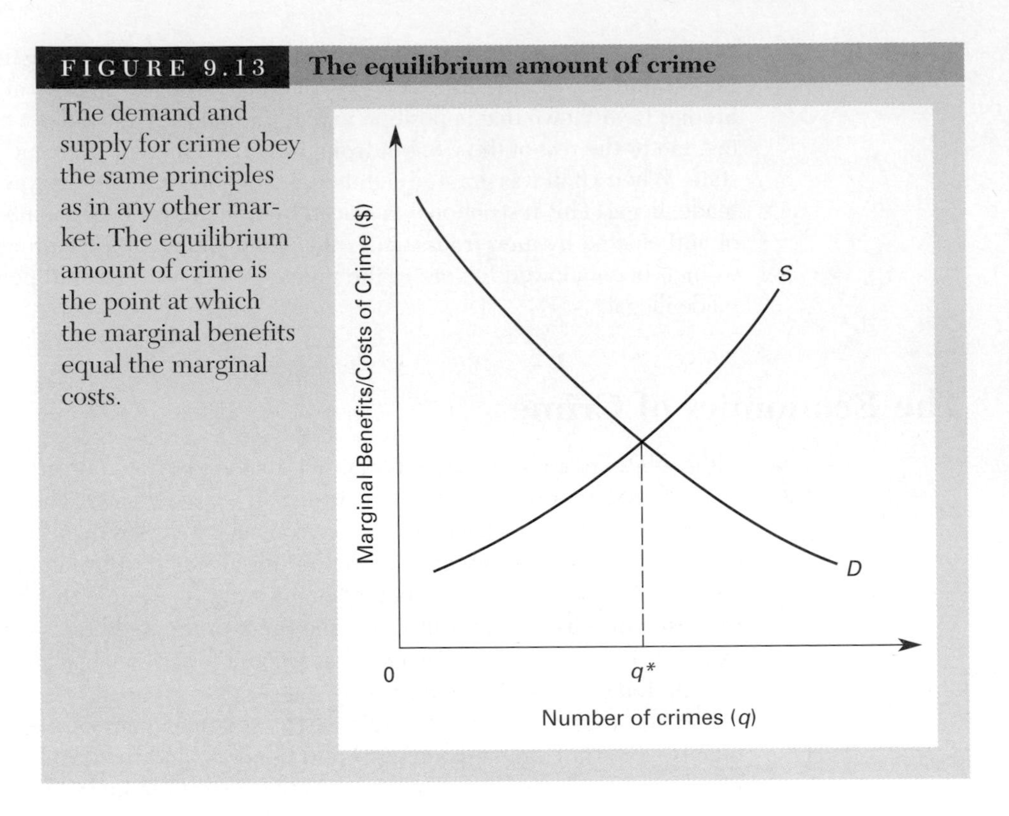

again, most societies have social safety nets designed in part to discourage low-income individuals from engaging in crime.

It is important to note that both the severity of the penalty and the chance of detection are under social control. Penalties can always be made more severe, and more police and detection devices can be employed. In situations where the chance of detection is very small, as in cattle rustling in the old west or late-night muggings in large cities, the penalties tend to be high to compensate for the low probability of getting caught. It may seem that the rational thing to do is to spend very little on detection and simply make penalties enormous. For example, we could have the death penalty for all crimes. However, there are a number of problems with this type of penal system. First, since mistakes are occasionally made in detection, we wouldn't want to have only extreme penalties. Second, having only one penalty ignores the principle of substitution. If the penalty of a crime is always death, then anyone about to be caught goes to extreme lengths to get away. Kidnappers are more likely to kill their victims and robbers to kill any witnesses if it reduces the likelihood of getting caught at no cost to them. An example of this lack of marginal deterrence is found in prisons with inmates who have no chance of ever being released. They often become extremely violent and difficult to control because the maximum penalty has already been imposed.

An example of how increasing the penalty of crime can reduce the amount of crime is found in the recent fascinating work of Lott and Mustard (1997), who have been studying the "right to carry" gun laws of the United States. The murder rate in the United States has been in the news for many years because it is so high compared to other countries. During most of the twentieth century, it was illegal for a private citizen to carry a concealed handgun. However, in the 1970s a number of states passed laws that allowed ordinary citizens to carry concealed weapons, and to use them in self-defence. The percentage of individuals in any given state who actually applied for a weapon was quite small, between 2 percent and 4 percent. However, even with this low take-up rate the effects were quite large. Lott and Mustard have found that all violent crime rates fell with the introduction of right-to-carry laws. Murder rates fell by 8 percent, rape by 5 percent, robbery by 3 percent, and aggravated assault by 7 percent. Interestingly, for crimes that involved stealth, such as burglary, crime rates increased.

The reasoning is pretty straightforward, given our model. If a criminal is going to engage in an activity where he or she now stands a slight chance of running into a weapon, the cost of crime increases dramatically. Given the small number of individuals who actually carry a weapon, it might seem unreasonable that there should be such a large effect on crime. However, what if you knew that the chance of a serious car accident was 2 percent? That is, in the next fifty times behind the wheel, you would be probably be involved in a serious accident that might kill you. No doubt, you would stop driving. Unlike driving, most crimes do not bring great benefits. Hence it is not unreasonable that the effect of the law should be so large. Note, too, that the fact that criminals substitute into crimes of stealth where they are less likely to run into people suggests that criminals do indeed behave rationally.[5]

One additional finding is worth noting. Concealed weapon laws had a much larger protective effect for women than for men. When an additional woman carries a concealed handgun it reduces the murder rate by about 3 to 4 times more than when an additional man carries a concealed handgun. This no doubt reflects the larger marginal gain of a handgun to a woman than to a man. Criminals prey on those they think will be the easiest victims. Robbing an elderly woman is much easier than taking on a large adult male. The marginal benefit of women carrying weapons, then, is much greater.

Now, when it comes to guns, Canadian (and Western European) culture is quite different from US culture. Many citizens of Canada abhor the idea of guns, and the point of this application is not to say that a country would be better off if it allowed any citizen to carry a hidden weapon. Lott and Mustard's work simply shows that in a society where guns are common, allowing ordinary citizens the right to carry weapons reduces violent crime. As such, it provides a nice example of using the economic model to understand crime. This application also gives evidence that many criminals do behave in ways that are consistent with our general model. As a society, we design our laws in light of this model. Laws are planned to ensure marginal deterrence: repeat offenders get larger sentences, and young offenders get lighter sentences (in order to raise the cost of future crime by not destroying their future earning ability).

SUMMARY

The competitive model is the fundamental tool in an economist's tool kit. Its usefulness stems from its relative intuitiveness and its applicability to a vast number of situations. The model assumes that there are many consumers and producers engaged in efforts to maximize utility or profit, and in this process the gains from trade are also maximized. The competitive model does not depend on the type of good we happen to place on the horizontal axis. As long as competitive conditions exist, anything that is valued can be analyzed with this model. This means that we can apply the model not

5. The standard argument against ordinary citizens carrying a weapon is that they are likely to be injured with it by accident or by the criminal. Lott finds that incidences of both types of injury are virtually nil.

only to market situations, like the effect of a tax on the price of orange juice, but also to non-market transactions like marriage, religion, or crime.

This chapter has applied the competitive model to a wide variety of applications from the analysis of instruments that restrict output, like a quota, to those that restrict price, like a rent control. We've seen how the competitive model can resolve puzzling behaviour, as in the case of home heating, as well as how it can point to flawed thinking, as in the case of doomsday forecasts. In all of these cases, the same basic framework was applied.

In addition to mere applications, however, we also observed that more subtle behaviour emerged from our analysis. For example, rent control and quotas were seen to be noncompetitive institutions that are intended to redistribute income or wealth. The appeal of all such institutions lies largely in their redistributionary impact. Yet they all result in an equilibrium that is not Pareto-optimal. The rent-control case thus serves to highlight a troubling issue in economics: the tension that often arises between the objectives of economic efficiency, or Pareto optimality, and distributional equity. In Chapter 13, we will analyze this problem of efficiency versus equity in more detail.

EXERCISES

1. Many people turn the heat down when they go to bed. How would you explain this pattern using the model outlined in this chapter?

2. Describe how the Japanese "manufacture" coal.

3. "A tax on the logs cut down by 38-year-old loggers with brown hair will mostly fall on the consumers of logs if the demand for logs is highly inelastic." True or false?

4. "A tax reduces efficiency. Since a subsidy is the opposite of a tax, it should increase efficiency." True or false?

5. Canada has a balance-of-trade deficit with Japan. That means that we import more goods from Japan than we export, and the Japanese accept Canadian dollars to make up the difference. Are Canadians made better off by this deficit?

6. An industry consisting of 1000 firms produces a standardized product. Each firm owns and operates one plant, and no other size of plant can be built. The variable costs of each firm are identical and are given in the following table; the fixed costs of each firm are $100.

Output	*TVC*	*Output*	*TVC*
1	10	13	101
2	19	14	113
3	27	15	126
4	34	16	140
5	40	17	155
6	45	18	171
7	50	19	188
8	56	20	206
9	63	21	225
10	71	22	245
11	80	23	266
12	90	24	288

The industry demand curve is $p = \$255\ 000/q$.

a. Calculate the marginal and average costs of a firm, and the demand schedule of the industry for prices from $10 to $20 (The MC equation is $MC = q - 2$.)

b. Draw the industry supply curve (that is, the sum of the marginal cost curves) and the industry demand curve on the same graph. Read off the equilibrium price and quantity. Calculate the same price and quantity algebraically.

c. Draw the cost and demand curves of the individual firms on another graph. Explain their construction.

The government now unexpectedly imposes a tax of $4 per unit on the manufacture of this commodity. The tax becomes effective immediately and remains in effect indefinitely.

d. Draw the new supply curve and the demand curve of the industry. What is the new equilibrium price?

e. Draw the new cost curve and demand curve of the individual firm.

7. Suppose you are a price taker and there is an increase in the amount of theft of your inventory, thus raising your costs of doing business. Will you be able to charge a higher price than before?

8. In the United States many property rights are legislated at the state level, which has led to considerable variation across states. For example, the rights of women have historically not been equal across the states. Can you explain why the western frontier states were the first to grant women the rights to hold property, divorce, vote, and enter contracts?

9. The government of Terabithia is thinking about paying every milk producer a $100 000 annual subsidy. Supposing that milk production is a constant-cost industry in Terabithia and that milk producers have U-shaped average cost curves, what effect will this subsidy have on:

   a. the long-run equilibrium price and quantity of milk?

   b. the quantity of milk produced by each firm?

   c. the number of firms producing milk?

10. The government of Xanadu is going to impose one of two taxes on the widget industry, which is a perfectly competitive, constant-cost industry in which firms have U-shaped average cost curves. One is a $2 per unit excise tax on widgets, and the other is a $1000 lump-sum tax on each firm in the industry. The Secretary of Commerce has determined that the two taxes will raise the same tax revenue from each firm in the long-run equilibrium associated with each tax.

    a. Which tax will widget consumers prefer?

    b. What effect will the excise tax have on output per firm? What effect will the lump-sum tax have on output per firm?

11. Suppose that egg production is a constant-cost industry initially in long-run competitive equilibrium, that LAC is U-shaped, and that each farmer currently produces 5000 eggs per day. Now suppose that each farmer is given a quota allowing the farmer to produce up to 4000 eggs per day and that quotas can be bought and sold.

    a. What impact will this quota system have on the price of eggs in the short run and in the long run?

    b. What impact will it have on the number of eggs produced by a typical firm in the short run and the long run?

    c. What impact will it have on the number of firms in the long run?

    d. Who benefits and who is harmed by this quota system? In particular, do future egg farmers benefit from this quota system?

    e. What sort of enforcement problems do you think the quota system might raise?

    f. Will this quota system be more attractive to established egg farmers when the demand for eggs is inelastic with respect to price or when the demand is elastic with respect to price?

12. Recently a representative of a large publishing house visited the economics department at Simon Fraser University to demonstrate the new interactive software that went along with the intermediate textbook he was selling. One of the advantages of the software, he said, was that it contained a lot of real data that could be graphed. The rep then plotted the price and quantity data for some commodity (say coal) over time, and he got something that looked a lot like a demand curve. In fact, the rep even said this was a real demand curve. Someone in the audience then asked him to do the same thing for another commodity, but this time the picture was just a random plot of numbers. Why was the first graph a fluke, and even if the plot was downward sloping, why was it not a demand curve?

13. The demand for fruits and vegetables is relatively constant throughout the year, but the supply varies depending on when the item is harvested.

a. Explain what the pattern of prices throughout the year would look like for raspberries, which are harvested in July.
b. Turnips are also harvested in the summer, but store much better than raspberries. What would you predict the pattern of turnip prices would look like, and how would it compare to the pattern of raspberry prices?

14. Why might most criminal behaviour take place among males below the age of eighteen? Can you explain why males are more apt to engage in criminal behaviour than females?

15. "Robbery involves a simple transfer of wealth; it does not reduce the wealth of society." Why is this statement not true? That is, why does theft involve more than simple transfers of wealth?

16. Employers often pay partial or full benefits to workers, including sharing some taxes such as pension or social security taxes. For example, in the United States, employers pay 50 percent of the social security taxes for employees. Would such a system really result in employers paying 50 percent? Who do you think pays a larger fraction of such a tax: secretaries or economists? If employers had to pay all of such a tax, how would your answers to the first two questions change?

17. Ballard Energy is a company in Vancouver that is developing a fuel cell, which creates energy without having to ignite a fossil fuel. Supposing they are successful, show on a supply and demand graph what would happen to the prices and quantities of gasoline.

18. Abortion became legal in Canada in 1988 after the Morgentaler Supreme Court case. Using a supply and demand graph, show what this change does to: the number of abortions; the number of other medical services; the price of adoption.

19. In the United States, the ratio of males to females at birth is slightly lower for blacks than for whites. The incarceration rate for black males between the ages of 15 and 30 is much higher than for whites of the same age. Finally, the fatality rate among young black males is much higher than for young white males. All of these facts lead to a lower male-to-female ratio for blacks than for whites. What implication might this have for births out of wedlock between the two groups?

20. Suppose that the demand for carrots is given by $y = 1000 - 5p$. The long-run supply curve for carrots is given by $y = 4p - 80$.
a. Find the equilibrium quantity and price. What is the total expenditure on carrots? What are the consumer and producer surpluses?
b. If $y = 300$, what would be the deadweight loss?

21. Supposing the demand for carrots from Question 20 increases to $y = 1270 - 5p$, what is the new equilibrium price and quantity and the new levels of surpluses? If the government created a price ceiling at the old price, what would be the new surpluses? What would be the deadweight loss?

REFERENCES

Friedman, D. 1987. "Cold Houses in Warm Climates and Vice Versa: A Paradox of Rational Heating," *Journal of Political Economy* 95:1089–98.

Lott, J. Jr. and D. Mustard. 1997. "Crime, Deterrence and Right-to-Carry Concealed Handguns," *Journal of Legal Studies* 26:1–69.

CHAPTER 10

Monopoly

Now we turn from the competitive market to its extreme opposite: monopoly. Imaginatively, this is a shift from the Toronto Stock Exchange (a market characterized by many buyers and sellers) to local telephone service (a market served by a single firm). We begin by defining monopoly and analyzing how a monopolist chooses price and quantity. Next, we identify the sources of monopoly power and consider a number of public policy responses to monopoly. In Chapter 14 we return to the problem of monopoly pricing and examine the extremely clever pricing strategies monopolists can and do use.

10.1 Monopoly Defined

monopoly

A firm is a **monopoly** if no other firm produces either the same good or a close substitute for it. This definition of monopoly is unavoidably ambiguous because we cannot define "close substitute" with perfect precision. For example, we might decide to call General Motors (GM) a monopolist in Corvettes because only GM makes Chevrolet Corvettes. But are any (or all) of the sports cars produced by Jaguar, BMW, Mercedes-Benz, or Nissan close substitutes for a Corvette? So, too, the Toronto Blue Jays are the only major-league baseball team in Toronto. But are the Blue Jays a monopolist in the Toronto market? Or are the Argos football team or the Raptors basketball team close substitutes? Is a television all-sports network a close substitute? Whether either GM or the Blue Jays is technically a monopolist is unclear.

This point was brought home in the recent Senate hearings over the Microsoft case. At issue was whether Microsoft was a monopoly provider of software, and many news commentators were aghast when Bill Gates calmly pointed out that it was not clear what the Microsoft market was nor who their competitors were. How could the wealthiest man in the world not know what his market was? Where you draw the line between the end of one market and the beginning of another is a fuzzy business, and not as easy as it might first appear.

How can we be certain that a conceivable substitute is a close substitute? One test is *cross-price elasticity:*[1] Does a change in the price of any substitute substantially change the demand for the good or service in question? If the demand for one good (steel or cellophane, for example) does not change significantly with a change in the price of another good (aluminum or waxed paper, for example) then none of the potential substitutes is close enough. The firm can then be regarded as a monopoly.

1. You may want to review the definition of cross-price elasticity in Section 3.9.

Why is this qualification about close substitutes so important? Suppose that two firms produce two distinct products but that these products are close substitutes. For example, the New York City Opera and the Metropolitan Opera Company offer similar kinds of musical entertainment to New Yorkers. How much profit each company makes depends both on its own pricing decisions and on its competitor's pricing decisions. When the Met thinks about cutting the price of a season ticket, for example, it must also anticipate the New York City Opera's reaction to the price cut. Pricing decisions are *interdependent*. We will look further at these complex pricing scenarios in Part V, in the two chapters on oligopoly. By contrast, the theory of monopoly is simpler because a monopolist does not need to concern itself with how other firms will react to its decision.

In Chapter 8, we thought of the competitive firm as choosing quantity to maximize profit, which is total revenue minus total cost. Once again in this chapter we will think of the firm — in this case, a monopolist — as choosing quantity to maximize profit. The analysis is similar in important respects. In particular, in both cases the profit-maximizing problem is solved by finding the output where marginal revenue MR is equal to marginal cost MC. Nevertheless, the monopolist's problem is more complex because, for a monopolist, price and marginal revenue are endogenous variables — chosen by the monopolist — while for the competitive firm they are exogenous variables — determined by impersonal market forces. Before turning to the monopolist's profit-maximizing decision we must sort out the relationships among a number of revenue concepts.

10.2 The Monopolist's Revenue Functions

market demand curve

For the monopolist, the relationship between price p and output y is determined by the **market demand curve**; that is,

$$p = D(y)$$

Thus, given any quantity y, price p is determined by the demand curve $D(y)$. This market demand curve is the aggregation of quantity demanded over all the monopolist's consumers. We will suppose that the market demand curve is downward sloping — the more the monopolist wants to sell, the lower its price must be.

average revenue

total revenue

We assume that the monopolist sells all the units it produces at the same price. Price can then be interpreted as **average revenue** AR. Since all units are sold at the same price, the average amount any unit contributes to the firm's revenue is the price at which it is sold. Then, for any quantity of output y the market demand curve $D(y)$ determines both price p and average revenue AR. **Total revenue** $TR(y)$ is then just quantity y multiplied by average revenue or price $D(y)$.

$$TR(y) = yD(y)$$

Marginal Revenue

Recall that for a competitive firm both price and marginal revenue are exogenous variables. Indeed, because a competitive firm has no control over price, marginal revenue is equal to price. For the monopolist, both price and marginal revenue are endogenous variables, determined by the monopolist's choice of output. This is the fundamental difference between a monopolist and a competitive firm.

marginal revenue

Marginal revenue $MR(y)$ is, of course, the rate at which total revenue $TR(y)$ changes as output y changes. What is the relationship between price (or average revenue) and marginal revenue for a monopolist? When the monopolist's output is *positive*, marginal revenue is *less than price.*

To understand this important result, keep in mind that the monopolist sells all units at the same price and has a downward-sloping demand curve. Because the demand curve is downward sloping, to sell an additional unit the monopolist must lower price. Therefore, its marginal revenue is less than the price at which the additional unit is sold by an amount equal to the quantity originally sold multiplied by the price reduction. Suppose that the monopolist in Figure 10.1 is initially at point A, where it is selling 3 units at price \$82. To sell one additional unit — or 4 units in total — it must reduce its price by \$6 from \$82 to \$76. The resulting change in total revenue, approximately equal to marginal revenue, is \$58 — or \$304 (4 multiplied by \$76) minus \$246 (3 multiplied by \$82). This change is \$18 less than \$76, the price at which the fourth unit sold. The \$18 difference between price and marginal revenue is equal to the original 3 units sold multiplied by the \$6 price reduction. In Figure 10.1, the shaded area represents the revenue gained by selling the fourth unit at \$76, and the hatched area represents the revenue lost by reducing the price on the original three units by \$6.

For a more precise understanding of the relationship between marginal revenue and price or average revenue, let us consider a more general experiment. Suppose initially that the monopolist is on its market demand curve, selling y units at price p and generating total revenue equal to py. Now suppose it reduces price by amount Δp

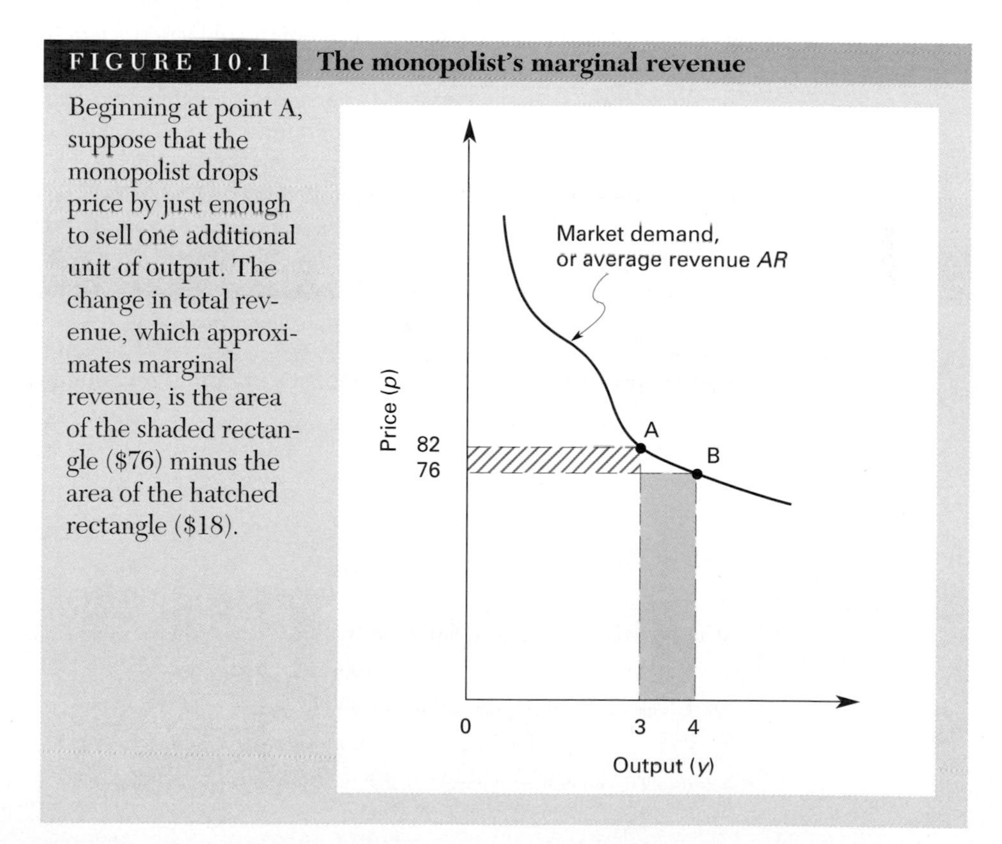

FIGURE 10.1 **The monopolist's marginal revenue**

Beginning at point A, suppose that the monopolist drops price by just enough to sell one additional unit of output. The change in total revenue, which approximates marginal revenue, is the area of the shaded rectangle (\$76) minus the area of the hatched rectangle (\$18).

and that quantity demanded increases by amount Δy, generating total revenue $(p - \Delta p)(y + \Delta y)$. The resulting change in total revenue is then

$$p\Delta y - y\Delta p - \Delta p\Delta y = (p - \Delta p)(y + \Delta y) - py$$

Now divide the left-hand side of this expression by Δy to express this relationship as a rate of change with respect to output:

$$[p - \Delta p] + y[-\Delta p/\Delta y]$$

To find marginal revenue, we let Δp approach zero. As Δp approaches zero, the first term in square brackets approaches p. The second term in brackets — $[-\Delta p/\Delta y]$ — is approximately the slope of the demand curve at the initial point. As the price change Δp gets smaller and smaller, the approximation gets better and better, and in the limit as Δp approaches zero, the approximation is perfect. Thus, as Δp approaches zero, we get the following expression for marginal revenue:

$$MR(y) = p + y \times \text{(slope of the demand curve)}$$

In other words:

Marginal revenue (MR) is equal to price p plus quantity y multiplied by the slope of the demand curve.

In this expression, p captures the rate at which revenue increases as an infinitesimal additional amount is sold at price p. This term is analogous to the added revenue generated in Figure 10.1 when a fourth unit is sold at a price of $76. The rate at which price must be decreased in order to sell an infinitesimal additional amount is given by the slope of the demand curve. Of course, it is negative because the demand curve is downward sloping. Therefore, the second term — $y \times$ (slope of the demand curve) — captures the rate at which revenue on the original y units drops as price is decreased to sell an infinitesimal additional amount. This second term is analogous to the reduction in the revenue from the original three units in Figure 10.1 when price is reduced from $82 to $76 to sell a fourth unit.

Since the slope of the demand curve is negative, we get an important relationship between price and marginal revenue for a monopolist:

For any positive output, the monopolist's marginal revenue is less than its price.[2]

2. Letting $D(y)$ be the demand function, we have

$$TR(y) = yD(y)$$

Marginal revenue is, of course, just the derivative of $TR(y)$. Differentiating $TR(y)$, we have

$$MR(y) = D(y) + yD'(y)$$

which is clearly less than price as long as y is positive; that is,

$$D(y) + yD'(y) < D(y)$$

because $D'(y)$ is negative. Notice, too, that the demand and marginal revenue functions must intersect the price axis at the same point since, when y is zero, marginal revenue is equal to price.

Marginal Revenue and the Price Elasticity of Demand

Economists sometimes find it convenient to express marginal revenue in terms of the *price elasticity of demand,* introduced in Chapter 3. Price elasticity of demand at a point (y, p) on the demand curve can be written as

$$E = p/[y \times (\text{slope of the demand curve})]$$

Combining this expression with the earlier expression for marginal revenue yields

$$MR(y) = p[1 + 1/E]$$

Price elasticity E is, of course, a negative number since the slope of the demand curve is negative. It is instructive to rewrite the relationship between marginal revenue and the price elasticity of demand in terms of the absolute value of price elasticity — $|E|$.

$$MR(y) = p[1 - 1/|E|]$$

Notice that marginal revenue is positive if $|E|$ exceeds 1 and negative if $|E|$ is less than 1. In other words:

Marginal revenue is positive if demand is elastic with respect to price, and it is negative if demand is inelastic with respect to price.

These results are intuitive. Suppose, for example, that demand is elastic with respect to price. Then, for a marginal decrease in price, the proportionate increase in quantity is larger than the proportionate decrease in price, and total revenue increases or, equivalently, marginal revenue is positive. In contrast, if demand is inelastic with respect to price, for a marginal decrease in price, the proportionate increase in quantity is smaller than the proportionate decrease in price, and total revenue decreases or, equivalently, marginal revenue is negative.

Linear Demand Curve

So far, we have formed the total revenue function, defined marginal and average revenue, and discovered that marginal revenue is less than price, or average revenue, for any positive quantity of output. To give you a better sense of what these relationships mean, we will explore in some detail the special (and simpler) case in which the demand curve is a straight line. We will be using such linear demand curves at several points in this and subsequent chapters.

The linear demand curve in Figure 10.2a can be written algebraically as

$$p = a - by$$

where a and b are positive constants. The total revenue function for this market demand function is y multiplied by $a - by$, or

$$TR(y) = ay - by^2$$

This total revenue function is plotted in Figure 10.2b and labelled TR.

FIGURE 10.2 A linear demand function and the associated total and marginal revenue functions

The linear demand function $p = a - by$ intersects the price axis in (a) at a and the quantity axis at a/b. The associated marginal revenue function MR is also linear. It, too, intersects the price axis at a, but it is twice as steep as the demand function and therefore intersects the quantity axis at $a/2b$. Comparing TR and MR, we see that when marginal revenue is positive (negative), total revenue increases (decreases) as more output is sold and that when marginal revenue is zero, total revenue is at a maximum.

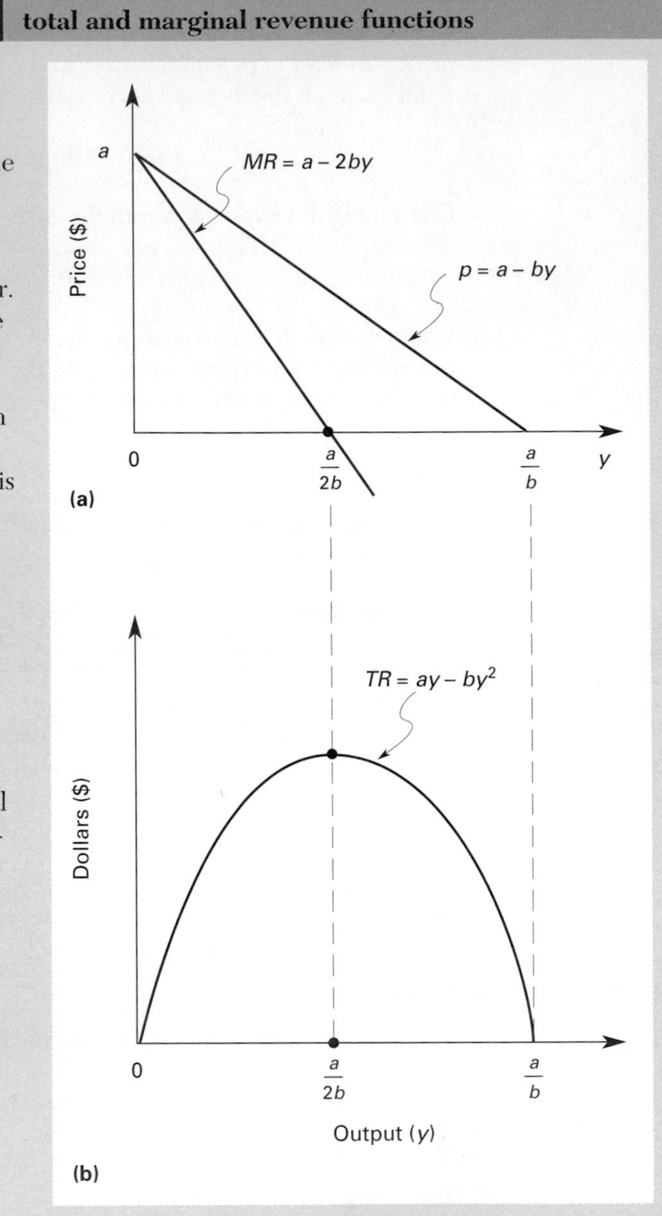

Two features of this TR function are immediately apparent. First, when output is zero, total revenue must also be zero. Second, when output is equal to a/b, total revenue must again be zero because the quantity a/b can be sold only at a price equal to zero. Of course, for any quantity of output greater than zero and less than a/b, total revenue will be positive because price exceeds zero for any such quantity. In Figure 10.2b, total revenue increases as y increases until it reaches a maximum when y is $a/2b$. Thereafter, as y increases, total revenue decreases until it is again zero when y is a/b.

Now let us find the marginal revenue function $MR(y)$. We know that marginal revenue is equal to price p plus quantity y multiplied by the slope of the demand curve. But, for this linear demand curve, p is equal to $a - by$ and the slope of the demand curve is equal to $-b$, so marginal revenue is equal to $a - by - by$, or

$$MR(y) = a - 2by$$

This marginal revenue function is also plotted in Figure 10.2a. It intersects the vertical axis at a, just as the market demand curve does, but it is twice as steep as the market demand curve. The demand curve intersects the quantity axis at a/b. Because the marginal revenue function is twice as steep, it intersects the quantity axis at $a/2b$.

Notice especially the following relationships between $TR(y)$ and $MR(y)$:

---

1. When the total revenue function is positively sloped, marginal revenue is positive.

2. When total revenue is at a maximum, marginal revenue is zero.

3. When the total revenue function is negatively sloped, marginal revenue is negative.

These relationships are obvious once we translate the original definition of marginal revenue. Above we said that marginal revenue $MR(y)$ is the rate at which total revenue $TR(y)$ changes as output y changes. Equivalently, we could have said that $MR(y)$ is the slope of $TR(y)$. In the following problem, you can establish similar relationships between marginal revenue and the price elasticity of demand.

PROBLEM 10.1

First show that for a linear demand curve

$$|E(y)| = (a - by)/(by) = a/(by) - 1$$

Then establish the following relationships:

1. When marginal revenue is positive, demand is elastic with respect to price.
2. When marginal revenue is negative, demand is inelastic with respect to price.
3. When marginal revenue is zero, the price elasticity of demand is 1.

10.3 Maximizing Profit

Let us turn now to the monopolist's profit-maximizing decision. Because the principles that guide the monopolist's choice in the short run and in the long run are virtually identical, we will consider them together. The monopolist's cost function $TC(y)$ can therefore be interpreted as either the long-run cost function or the short-run variable cost function. (We will soon see why we use the variable cost function in the short run.)

We can then write profit $\pi(y)$ as a function of output y as follows:

$$\pi(y) = TR(y) - TC(y)$$

Alternatively, we can write profit in terms of average revenue $AR(y)$ and average cost $AC(y)$:

$$\pi(y) = y[AR(y) - AC(y)]$$

The monopolist's profit-maximizing problem is then to *maximize profit* $\pi(y)$ *by choice of output* y.

In Figure 10.3 we have plotted the average and marginal revenue curves, AR and MR, and the average and marginal cost curves, AC and MC. First, notice that average revenue AR is equal to average cost AC at two levels of output: $y = 30$, and $y = 95$. Consequently, profit π is equal to zero at these output levels. Profit π is positive in the range of output between 30 and 95 because AR exceeds AC. Conversely, it is negative at output levels less than 30 and greater than 95 because AC exceeds AR.

Notice, too, that marginal revenue MR is equal to marginal cost MC at two levels of output: $y = 8$, and $y = 58$. Because MC intersects MR from above at 8 units of output, profit is at a minimum at 8 units of output. In contrast, because MC intersects MR from below at 58 units of output, profit is at a maximum at 58 units of output. That is, the profit-maximizing quantity y^* is 58.

To show that profit is maximized at $y^* = 58$, let us suppose that the monopolist is initially producing $y^* = 58$ and ask: What will happen to its profit if it produces one more unit of output? The addition to its revenue is given by MR and the addition to its cost by MC. Because MC exceeds MR to the right of $y^* = 58$, the increase in its cost exceeds the increase in its revenue, and profit therefore falls as the monopolist produces one more unit. Now, beginning again at $y^* = 58$, let us ask: What happens to its profit if the monopolist produces one less unit? The reduction in its revenue is given by MR and the reduction in its cost by MC. Because MR exceeds MC to the left of $y^* = 58$, the reduction in revenue exceeds the reduction in cost, and profit therefore falls as the monop-

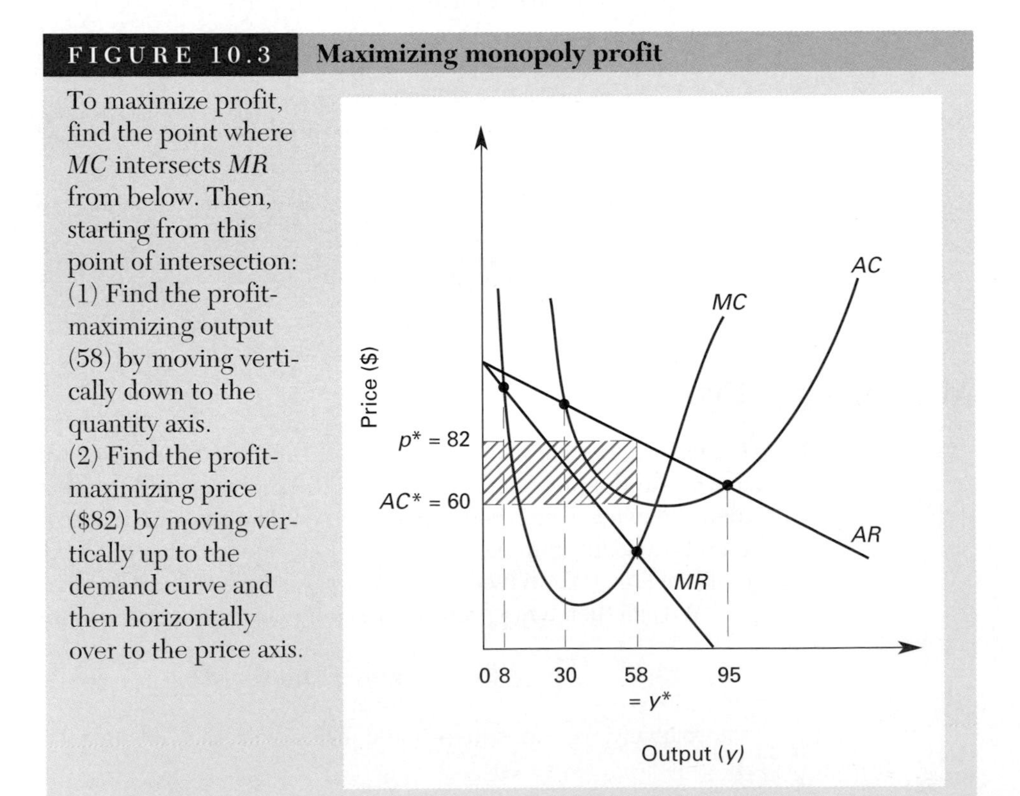

FIGURE 10.3 **Maximizing monopoly profit**

To maximize profit, find the point where MC intersects MR from below. Then, starting from this point of intersection: (1) Find the profit-maximizing output (58) by moving vertically down to the quantity axis. (2) Find the profit-maximizing price ($82) by moving vertically up to the demand curve and then horizontally over to the price axis.

olist produces one less unit. Since profit falls as the monopolist produces either more than or less than $y^* = 58$, profit is a maximum at $y^* = 58$.[3]

The hatched rectangular area in Figure 10.3 is the monopolist's *profit rectangle*: its vertical side is profit per unit sold, equal to price ($82) minus average cost ($60); its horizontal side is the profit-maximizing output (58 units); the area of the rectangle is the monopolist's profit.

PROBLEM 10.2

Show that profit is at a minimum when $MR = MC$ and MC intersects MR from above.

If the average cost function AC lies above the average revenue function AR at all levels of output, there is no positive output level at which the monopolist can cover its costs. However, it can achieve zero profit by producing nothing, incurring no costs and receiving no revenue. Therefore, if AC lies entirely above AR, the monopolist will shut down production. Because the monopolist's profit is *zero* if it produces nothing but is *negative* if it produces some output, it will produce nothing. This line of reasoning is obviously true in the long run, when AC is the long-run average cost function. It is also true in the short run — if AC is the short-run average variable cost function. It is for this reason that we defined $TC(y)$ at the outset of this section as either the long-run cost function or the short-run variable cost function.

One last detail requires attention. Notice when MC and MR are both positive, they intersect one another to the left of where MR equals zero. Since the elasticity of demand is –1 when $MR = 0$, this must mean the monopolist produces in the elastic region of the demand curve. Notably, a monopolist would never produce where the demand curve is inelastic. If the demand curve was inelastic, the firm could reduce output, reduce costs, increase revenues, and therefore increase profit. The firm would do this until it reached the elastic portion of the demand curve.

Let us summarize what we have learned about the monopolist's profit-maximizing problem in the case where AC intersects AR:

First find the point where MC intersects MR from below. Then, to identify the profit-maximizing level of output, move vertically downward from the point of intersection to the horizontal axis. To identify the profit-maximizing price p^*, move vertically upward from the point of intersection to the average revenue AR curve and then horizontally over to the price axis. Finally, to identify the monopolist's profit, construct the profit rectangle with horizontal side equal to y^* and vertical side equal to $p^* - AC^*$.

3. All this can be said more simply using a little calculus. We know (1) that $\pi'(y^*) \equiv 0$ is necessary for $y^* > 0$ to be a profit-maximizing level of y and (2) that $\pi(y)$ attains a (local) maximum at y^* if, in addition, $\pi''(y^*) < 0$. By definition,

$$\pi(y) = TR(y) - TC(y)$$

Differentiating with respect to y and setting the result equal to zero, we obtain the following first-order condition for profit maximization:

$$MR(y^*) \equiv MC(y^*)$$

The second-order condition, $\pi''(y^*) < 0$, is just

$$MR'(y^*) < MC'(y^*)$$

That is, the slope of the marginal revenue function is less than the slope of the marginal cost function at the profit-maximizing quantity.

Application: Are Artists and Authors Altruists?

We have seen that a profit-maximizing monopolist chooses that quantity which equates the MC and MR. As long as MC is positive, this quantity *is not* the quantity that maximizes total revenue. In Section 10.2 we saw that total revenue is maximized when MR is zero, which is at a lower price and higher quantity than the monopoly solution. This fact explains the behaviour of many artists with respect to the price of their products.

A few years ago Bono, the lead singer of the rock group U2, complained in an interview that his record company charged a price for CDs that he thought was too high. He was not alone. Musicians, authors, and actors often complain that the prices of their music, books, and plays are set too high. Are these people altruists or are they actually acting in their own self-interest?

The key to resolving this puzzle is to note that performers and authors are usually paid a royalty based on the revenue generated from gross sales, not on profits. Thus, their income is maximized when revenues are maximized, and their interests are at odds with the firm selling the product. Artists, or authors, or singers, will personally benefit from a lower price and a larger volume. Since they do not bear the costs of production, they do not care that profits are not maximized when revenues are. Bono and company are not altruists — after all, he didn't make the case that records should be given away!

PROBLEM 10.3

Suppose that the average revenue function is

$$p = 100 - y$$

and that the cost function is

$$TC(y) = 40y$$

On one diagram, carefully construct the average revenue, marginal revenue, average cost, and marginal cost functions. Then show that y^* is 30 and p^* is \$70. Construct the profit rectangle and show that profit is equal to \$900.

PROBLEM 10.4

First, draw a linear AR curve, like the one in Problem 10.3, and the associated MR curve. Then draw a U-shaped MC curve that is tangent to the MR curve at one point and lies above it at all other levels of output. Beginning at the point where $MR = MC$, what happens to profit as the monopolist produces one more unit? One less unit? What is the profit-maximizing level of output? What can you say about the relationship between the AC and AR curves?

Application: "Big Tobacco Monopolies?"

Over the past few years tobacco companies have been sued by state governments for health care costs attributed to cigarette smoke. As the companies began losing cases, many wondered where the money would come from to pay out large sums to comply with court-imposed damage awards, to reach private out-of-court settlements, or to buy immunity sanctioned by the US Congress.

It would appear that most of the increase in costs have been passed on to smokers in the form of higher cigarette prices. Worse, there's some indication that profits are even higher with these higher prices. This has lead to a number of outcries in letters to editors, TV slots, and other public forums. The consensus seems to be that an injustice is being committed. These companies are supposed to be paying damages for their wrongdoings, and instead, due to their monopoly power, they are simply passing the costs back on to the smokers and making more money at the same time.

But the analysis must be wrong, and the facts suggest that big tobacco companies could not be monopolies. If increases in prices lead to increased revenue, then the tobacco market must be selling cigarettes in the inelastic region of the market demand curve. As we've seen, a monopolist firm would never do this. A monopolist tobacco company wouldn't need an adverse court case to help it maximize profits. On its own it would have raised prices and made more money. The fact that it took large settlements to increase prices and profitability is evidence the market is not monopolistic.

10.4 The Inefficiency of Monopoly

As we saw in the last chapter, in a competitive equilibrium all the gains from trade are realized. Recall that in a competitive equilibrium, each competitor chooses a level of output such that marginal cost is equal to price. Furthermore, if any firm were to produce a bit more output, marginal cost would exceed price. Therefore, in a competitive equilibrium, it is impossible to sell an additional unit of a good at a price that covers the marginal cost of producing the extra unit.

By contrast, the gains from trade are *not* fully realized in the monopoly equilibrium. In the monopoly equilibrium, marginal cost — which is equal to marginal revenue — is less than price. Therefore, beginning at the profit-maximizing output, an additional unit could possibly be sold at a price that covers its marginal cost. (We will soon see why a monopolist may not be able to take advantage of this opportunity.) Consequently, the gains from trade are not fully exploited in monopoly equilibrium. For example, the profit-maximizing output in Figure 10.4 is $y^* = 6$, and the profit-maximizing price is $p^* = \$50$, which is greater than $MC^* = \$25$.

Because p^* exceeds MC in the monopoly equilibrium, some potential gains from trade are not realized.

To better understand this result, we can perform a thought experiment. Let us begin by reinterpreting the average revenue, or market demand, function as the aggregation of individual reservation prices for one unit of the monopolist's good. (You encountered this type of demand curve in the discussion of the exchange model in Section 8.1.) Although such a market demand curve is actually a series of descending vertical segments rather than a smooth line, if the number of individual demanders is large enough, their aggregated demand function can be approximated by a smooth market demand function. Imagine that a monopolist first announces a "take-it-or-leave-it" price of $p^* = \$50$ and that all potential buyers take the monopolist's announcement at face value. The result is just the standard monopoly equilibrium in Figure 10.4: the six buyers with reservation prices greater than \$50 buy the good and buyers with lower reservation prices do not. Now suppose the clever monopolist considers making and selling one additional unit. If it sells that unit at any price greater than distance AB but less than distance AG, both the monopolist and the purchaser of that

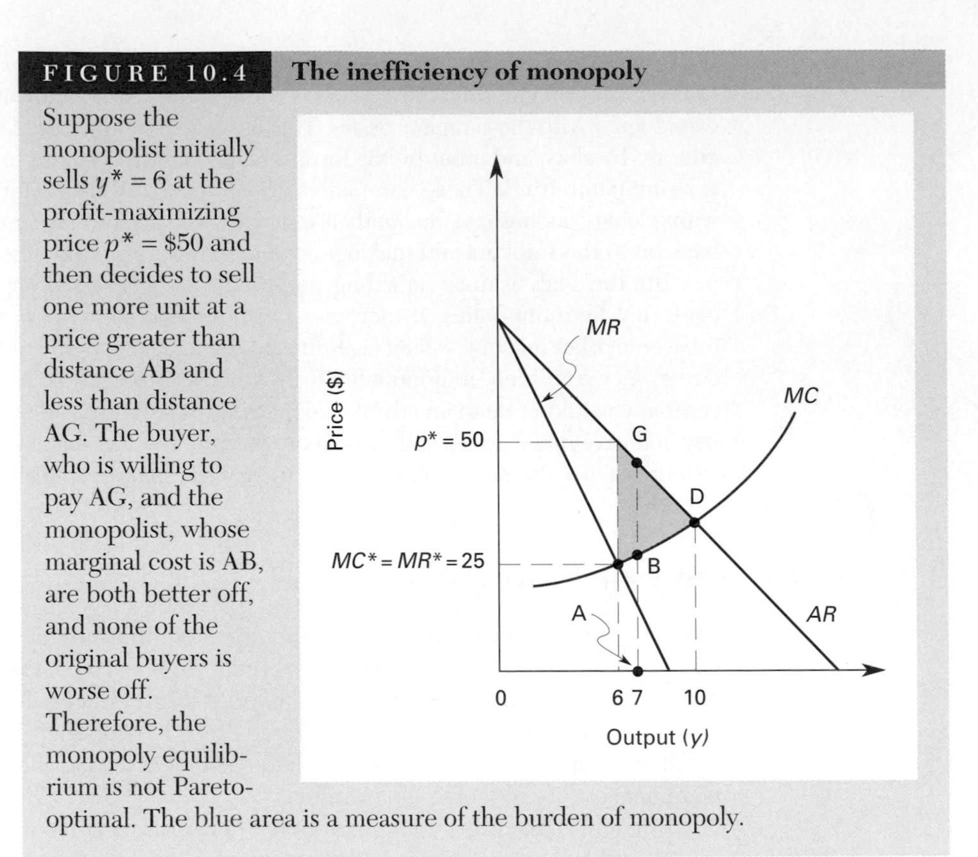

FIGURE 10.4 The inefficiency of monopoly

Suppose the monopolist initially sells $y^* = 6$ at the profit-maximizing price $p^* = \$50$ and then decides to sell one more unit at a price greater than distance AB and less than distance AG. The buyer, who is willing to pay AG, and the monopolist, whose marginal cost is AB, are both better off, and none of the original buyers is worse off. Therefore, the monopoly equilibrium is not Pareto-optimal. The blue area is a measure of the burden of monopoly.

additional unit will be better off — and no purchaser who bought the good at price $p^* = \$50$ will be worse off. Therefore, beginning at the monopoly equilibrium, the sale of the additional unit is Pareto-improving. That is:

The monopoly equilibrium is not Pareto-optimal.

If we pursue this thought experiment to its logical conclusion by imagining that the monopolist continues to sell additional output one unit at a time — at a price greater than or equal to its marginal cost and less than or equal to the corresponding reservation price on the demand function — we see from Figure 10.4 that eventually 10 units will be sold. Relative to the monopoly equilibrium, the additional total surplus realized is indicated by the blue area in Figure 10.4. This is a measure of the **deadweight loss of monopoly** — that is, the potential surplus that is unrealized at the monopoly equilibrium. Because these gains are not fully realized, monopoly is often said to represent a **market failure**.

deadweight loss of monopoly

market failure

This thought experiment also reveals that the gains from trade in Figure 10.4 are fully realized when 10 units are produced and sold. More generally, it reveals the **efficiency criterion** for a market that is monopolized and, indeed, for markets in general:

efficiency criterion

Efficiency requires that the good be produced up to the point where price p is equal to marginal cost MC.

One final, important message comes out of this thought experiment:

The unrealized gains from trade in the monopoly equilibrium signal unrealized monopoly profit.

In other words, at the monopoly equilibrium, the monopolist has failed to extract the maximum profit possible. Indeed, the monopolist's strategy in this thought experiment of first announcing a take-it-or-leave-it price and later announcing a price reduction is a wily attempt to extract a profit greater than the profit it makes in the monopoly equilibrium. In a market characterized by repeated sales over many periods, however, this strategy will not work. What eventually occurs is a slightly altered version of the story of the boy who cried wolf. The buyers with the higher reservation prices soon catch on to the monopolist's stratagem and withhold their demand at the original price in anticipation of being able to buy the good at a lower price in the future. Even though this particular pricing strategy cannot succeed for long, we should nevertheless recognize that a monopolist has a clear incentive to devise strategies that are more profitable and more complex than the simple *MR* equals *MC* strategy.

We will look at such strategies in Chapter 14, under the general rubric of *price discrimination*. In the meantime, the following problem will help you to review the important points arising out of our thought experiment. Because we will be returning to this problem at crucial points later in the chapter, it deserves your careful attention.

PROBLEM 10.5

Suppose that some book vendor can produce a book at a constant marginal cost of $8 and that 11 potential buyers have the following reservation prices: $55, $50, $45, … , $10, $5. Each will buy the book at any price less than or equal to his or her reservation price.

1. If the book vendor must announce a take it-or-leave-it price, what price maximizes profit? What quantity will be sold, and what are the book vendor's profits? Are there unrealized gains from trade? (*Hint*: The only prices you need to consider are the 11 reservation prices, and you can calculate profit for each of these reservation prices.)
2. Suppose that the book vendor knows what each potential buyer's reservation price actually is and that those buyers are completely isolated from each other. The vendor can then set an individual price for each buyer. How many books will it sell? At what price will it sell each book? What are its profits? Show that this solution is Pareto-optimal, or efficient.

Application: Why Is It So Hard to Shop in Holland?

Anyone who has ever visited Holland or stayed there for a while will have noticed that it is often quite difficult to shop. Compared to North America there are relatively few stores, they are more crowded, and open for more limited hours. Often it is difficult to find a store open after 6:00 pm. In Chapter 16 we will discuss in some detail the issue of collusion, but suffice to say for now that a perfect cartel would like to operate as a monopolist, and the point of every monopolist is to raise the price and reduce output in order to maximize profits. Remarkably, in Holland there is a law that requires local store owners to approve the licensing of new stores in their neighbourhood. In effect, the law allows local bakers and candlestick makers to act as monopolists in their community. The result is the limited shopping every tourist notices. A more subtle result may be the extremely low female labour force participation rate in Holland. In an average family, when both the husband and wife are working, shopping becomes a major burden. Couples often substitute a second income for the ability to shop during the limited daytime hours.

10.5 Sources of Monopoly

By now, you know what a monopoly is, how the profit-maximizing monopolist chooses price and quantity, and in what sense the monopoly equilibrium represents a market failure. But what forces bring a monopoly into being in the first place? And what are the possible policy responses to the market failure associated with monopoly? Let us examine each question in turn.

Although the sources of monopoly power are many and varied, we can classify monopolies under five categories: the franchise monopoly; the resource-based monopoly; the patent monopoly; the technological, or natural, monopoly; and what we might call the monopoly by good management.

Government Franchise Monopoly

franchise monopoly

One historic and contemporary source of monopoly power is the franchise. A **franchise monopoly** arises when a government grants the exclusive right to do business in a specified market to some individual or firm. A historic example is King Charles II's granting of the exclusive rights to the North American fur trade to the Hudson's Bay Company in 1670. A contemporary example is the granting of exclusive rights to broadcast at specified frequencies to radio and television stations. Broadcast franchises sometimes give rise to monopoly, and more frequently to oligopoly.

Patent Monopoly

patent monopoly

Another form of monopoly arising from governmental action in many countries is the **patent monopoly**, secured by either patent or copyright. In most countries, including Canada, inventors are granted the exclusive right to their discoveries for a set period. Patents in Canada are granted for a period of twenty years. Patent monopoly is a pervasive phenomenon in the prescription drug trade and has played a central role in a wide range of other industries as well, including the photocopying, computer, and telecommunications industries. Even the shoe machinery industry was at one time significantly affected by patent monopoly.

Resource-Based Monopoly

resource-based monopoly

Another source of monopoly power is the exclusive ownership of a natural resource essential in a particular production process. For example, owning one of the various hot springs scattered throughout Europe and North America conveys monopoly power to its owners in the local or regional markets for water spas. The Aluminum Company of America offered a more powerful example of a **resource-based monopoly** prior to the end of World War II. Alcoa was a virtual monopolist in primary aluminum production from its inception in the late nineteenth century until 1945; its monopoly position arose in part from its control of virtually all domestic sources of bauxite ore.

Technological (or Natural) Monopoly

In Section 7.9, we discussed market structure and argued that if the efficient scale of production in a given industry is large enough, we expect to see only one firm in the market. The source of monopolistic power in this case is technological, the by-product of significant economies of scale. A firm in this category is therefore called a technological or natural monopoly. Because these firms experience declining average cost over a significant range of output, rival firms are unable to produce at these low costs and will fail.

Public utilities such as natural gas, electricity, and telephone services are classic illustrations of technological, or natural, monopolies. In all three cases, the economies of scale are driven by the distribution networks needed to deliver the good or the service to the point of use. We find other, less conspicuous natural monopolies in the many small towns of rural North America that have only one movie theatre or one gas station. Although the economies of scale of showing films are not large in absolute terms, they are large relative to the demand generated by a population of 5000 or fewer. The local movie theatre is to a small town what the Blue Jays baseball club is to Toronto.

natural monopoly

Let us be more precise about what we mean by the term **natural monopoly**. We say that *a firm is a natural monopolist if no other firm will enter the market when the monopolist produces the standard profit-maximizing output.*[4] To use this definition, we need a theory of entry, since a firm is a natural monopolist *only* if no other firm will enter its market when it pursues the profit-maximizing strategy outlined in the previous section. We will use a very simple theory of entry driven by one assumption — often called the **Sylos postulate**, after the Italian economist Paulo Sylos-Labini:

Sylos postulate

ASSUMPTION: THE SYLOS POSTULATE

In deciding whether to enter a market, a potential entrant takes the output of existing firms as given.

Figure 10.5a presents the standard production and pricing decisions of a monopolist. It chooses to produce $y^* = 410$ and to sell each unit of output at a price of $p^* = \$48$. First, we will examine the case in which the firm presented in Figure 10.5a is a natural monopolist. Assuming that the potential entrant regards the monopolist's current output $y^* = 410$ as fixed, it will consult its own **residual demand function** in Figure 10.5b to see if it can expect to cover its costs if it does enter. The market demand function faced by the potential entrant is called *residual* because it represents that portion of the market demand that remains unsupplied by the monopolist. Thus, the origin of the residual demand function in Figure 10.5b, labelled 0_E, corresponds to the output level $y^* = 410$ in Figure 10.5a. The entrant's residual demand function intersects the entrant's price axis at $p^* = \$48$, which means that price will be no higher than \$48 even if the entrant produces nothing. The entrant's average cost curve AC in Figure 10.5b is plotted relative to the entrant's origin 0_E.

residual demand function

4. The term *natural monopoly* is sometimes used in another way by economists. If AC is everywhere downward sloping, then to minimize the total cost of industry output, all the output should be produced by just one firm. Therefore, industries in which AC is everywhere downward sloping are sometimes called natural monopolies.

In general, whether the potential entrant can find a level of output that allows it to cover its costs will depend on the relationship between its average cost function and the residual demand function. Because *AC* lies entirely above the residual demand function in the case shown in Figure 10.5b, the potential entrant will recognize that it cannot cover its production costs at any level of output, and it will decide against entry. The firm presented in Figure 10.5a is therefore a natural monopoly. Interestingly, it is entirely possible that the entrant in Figure 10.5 is more efficient than the established firm (in the sense of having lower *AC* for any level of output). In the following prob-

FIGURE 10.5 Natural monopoly

In (a), the monopoly equilibrium is price $p^* = 48$ and quantity $y^* = 410$. If an entrant took the monopolist's output $y^* = 410$ as fixed, it would perceive the residual demand function in (b). Since *AC* lies above the residual demand function, there is no quantity at which the entrant could make a profit, and this is therefore a case of natural monopoly.

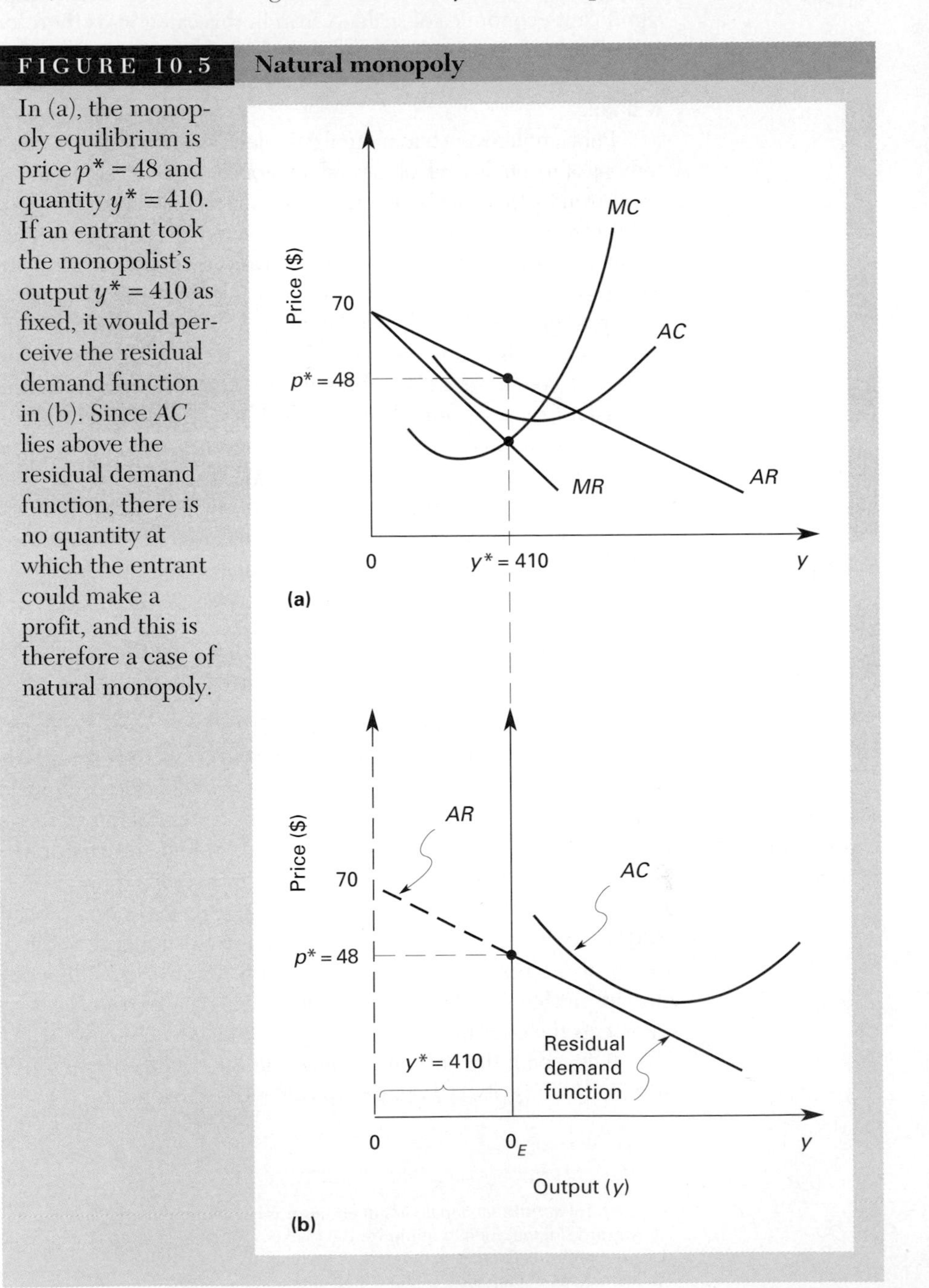

lem, you can construct the case in which there is no natural monopoly in the industry because the potential entrant does see a chance of becoming a viable competitor.

PROBLEM 10.6

In Figure 10.5a, the average revenue function intersects the price axis at $70. Construct a diagram identical to Figure 10.5a in all respects except one. Shift the average and marginal revenue functions up by $30. Then show that there is no natural monopoly in this case.

Monopoly by Good Management

Suppose that a monopolist finds itself in the position you considered in Problem 10.6. If it chooses price and quantity in the ordinary way, a second firm will enter — and the first firm therefore will *not* be a natural monopolist. Some intriguing questions beg to be answered in this case.

First, is there anything the monopolist could do to deter entry of a second firm? If so, would the monopolist find it profitable to deter entry? These are really oligopoly rather than monopoly questions because they involve the interaction between two firms: the established monopolist and a potential entrant. Although we will not consider them until Chapter 14, we can preview the results by noting that in certain circumstances, the answer to both questions is yes. In these circumstances, there will be just one firm in the market, but that firm will not be a natural monopolist. Rather, this is a case of **monopoly by good management**; the firm is a monopolist because it manages its affairs with an eye to deterring entry.

monopoly by good management

In these circumstances, the monopolist will not simply produce the output where marginal revenue is equal to marginal cost. It will instead take a larger view of the profit-maximizing problem, by essentially redefining it as the problem of maximizing profit subject to the constraint that there be no entry. Ordinarily, to deter entry, the solution is to produce an output larger than the standard monopoly output. It is important to realize that this behaviour can result in significantly less unrealized surplus than occurs in the ordinary monopoly equilibrium. The burden of monopoly is dramatically reduced. Monopoly by good management is thus quite a different phenomenon from natural monopoly.

10.6 Regulatory Responses to Monopoly

From whatever sources monopoly power may spring, its very existence poses two closely related problems that seem to demand some kind of governmental regulatory response. The first problem is that the potential gains from trade are not fully realized because price exceeds marginal cost. The problem for governments is that in monopolized industries, the goods or services are *underproduced*. Governments then face an *efficiency dilemma*: Should they step in and attempt to induce greater production?

The second problem stems from the fact that price ordinarily exceeds average cost at the monopoly solution. As a result, monopolists may be able to make a *supranormal* profit — one above the normal or "fair" return on capital investment included among the costs in the cost function. Governments then face a *distributional dilemma*. Who should be the ultimate recipients of the supranormal profit — the owners of the monopoly or someone else? To complicate matters, the current owners of a monopoly may not be earning a supranormal profit. Suppose that the present owners bought the monopoly from its original owners. The selling price of such a firm will have capitalized the discounted present value at the time of sale of all future monopoly profits. In this case, the current owners will be earning only a normal return on their investment. (This effect recalls the transitional gains trap discussed in Chapter 9 in the context of a quota.) In this section, we will largely ignore the distributional questions raised by monopoly and concentrate on the efficiency issue.

What governmental responses will be effective depends on the source of the monopoly power. In resource-based monopolies, regulatory measures that promote competition as an alternative to monopoly are sometimes possible. In the other monopolies, however, competition is not a feasible alternative, and governments must look elsewhere for remedial measures.

Divestiture in a Resource-Based Monopoly

From an economic standpoint, regulating resource-based monopolies is relatively easy because eliminating monopoly power is both feasible and sensible. If exclusive ownership of a resource is the only source of monopoly power, a regulatory body can simply force the monopolist to sell off, or divest itself of, some portion of the essential resource. Such *divestiture* then makes competition a feasible market alternative to monopoly.

Responses to Natural Monopoly

Natural monopoly presents quite a different set of issues for regulatory agencies. Because a natural monopoly arises in response to a technological phenomenon — an efficient scale of production that is large relative to market demand — competition is not a feasible alternative: the industry simply cannot support a large number of competing firms.

Governments have recognized that some industries — local telephone services, electricity, and other public utilities, for instance — are natural monopolies. They typically permit such industries to be monopolized but attempt to limit the monopolist to a "fair" rate of return on its investment. Fixing a precise value on a fair rate of return is a serious accounting problem, and debate on this question periodically flares up between public utilities and regulatory agencies. Nevertheless, a fair rate of return is easy enough to define theoretically as a zero profit rate of return. (Remember that a normal rate of return on investment forms a part of the costs included in the cost functions.) We will look at two regulatory mechanisms aimed at achieving a fair rate-of-return.

Average Cost Pricing

average-cost-pricing policy

To limit monopolies to a fair, or normal, rate of return, regulatory agencies sometimes attempt to implement an **average-cost-pricing policy**. Although this policy (if successful) does eliminate monopoly profit, it does not induce the monopolist to produce the efficient level of output. Figure 10.6a presents one such average-cost-pricing regulatory solution. In this case, the monopoly will, in effect, be ordered to produce 47 units of output and to set the price equal to its average cost of $20. Yet, like the monopoly solution it is intended to replace, the regulatory solution at point A is inefficient. At point A, marginal cost of $30 exceeds price of $20. From the perspective of efficiency, the monopolist produces too much. In this case, the efficient solution is instead at point B, where price equals marginal cost and output is 42 units.

Figure 10.6b presents another possibility. Although the regulatory solution is at point A, where price equals average cost, the efficient solution is instead at point B, where price equals marginal cost. In this case, the regulatory solution induces the monopolist to produce too little output relative to the efficient solution. An even more serious drawback is that average cost pricing gives the monopolist no incentive to minimize its costs of production. If the regulatory authority allows the monopoly to recover all its costs but never permits it to make a profit, why should the firm worry about keeping its costs as low as possible?

Rate-of-Return Regulation

rate-of-return regulation

Closely related to average cost pricing is the predominant form of regulation in Canada and the United States, **rate-of-return regulation**, which is aimed at limiting the rate of return a regulated natural monopoly can earn on its invested capital. Unfortunately, under this type of regulation, a natural monopolist will again fail to minimize its costs of production — in this instance, by choosing to use too much capital relative to the cost-minimizing input bundle. (See Averch and Johnson, 1961, on this point.) To understand why this distortion arises, let us consider a natural monopolist that is using just two inputs: labour (input 1) and capital owned by the firm (input 2). The monopolist's return on its capital is then its total revenue $TR(y)$ minus its expenditure on input 1, w_1z_1:

$$\text{Return on capital} = TR(y) - w_1z_1$$

FIGURE 10.6 **Average cost pricing**

In both (a) and (b), the monopolist is forced to operate where it makes no profit — where AC is equal to price. In (a), the resulting output $y = 47$ is larger than the output $y = 42$ where price is equal to MC, and average cost pricing induces the monopolist to produce too much output. In (b), the resulting output $y = 35$ is less than the output $y = 41$ where price is equal to MC, and average cost pricing induces the monopolist to produce too little output.

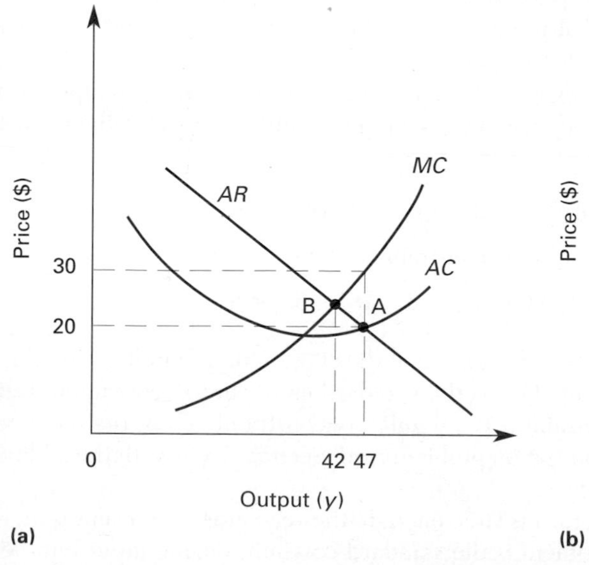

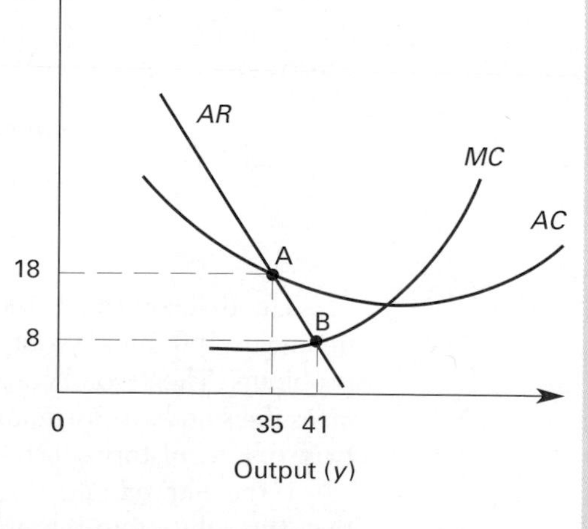

Rate-of-return regulation constrains the firm to choose output y and an input bundle (z_1, z_2) such that

$$TR(y) - w_1 z_1 \leq r z_2$$

where r is the *allowed rate of return* on capital and z_2 is the quantity of capital. Averch and Johnson argue that the sensible regulatory agency will choose an allowed rate of return r greater than the price of capital w_2, because if r is less than w_2, the monopolist will be forced out of business. When r is equal to w_2, rate of return regulation is equivalent to average cost pricing. Therefore, we will assume that the allowed rate of return r is greater than the price of capital w_2.

Why will the monopolist use too much capital? We can develop an intuitive understanding by analogy. Imagine that a monopolist were told that its profit could not exceed \$1 per pound of jelly beans held in the firm's vault. To maximize profit, the firm would fill a huge vault with useless jelly beans. A similar effect occurs when it is the quantity of capital that constrains the firm's ability to earn profit. We can see why by subtracting $w_2 z_2$ from both sides of the rate-of-return constraint:

$$TR(y) - w_1 z_1 - w_2 z_2 \leq (r - w_2) z_2$$

The expression on the left is just the firm's profit, and the entire inequality then means that the profit the firm is allowed to earn is constrained by the quantity of capital it has. As a result, rate-of-return regulation induces the regulated firm to use *too much capital* and *too little labour*.

Let us be more precise about the distorting effect of rate-of-return regulation on the monopolist's choice of an input bundle. Suppose that the quantity of output produced by the monopolist, the prices of the two inputs, and the allowed rate of return on capital are all fixed. Specifically, suppose that output is 100, that the prices w_1 and w_2 are both \$5, and that r is \$8. We will show that if the rate-of-return regulation is effective, the monopolist will produce 100 units of output using an input bundle that has too much capital and too little labour relative to the cost-minimizing input bundle.

Because output is fixed, price and therefore total revenue are also fixed. Again for convenience, suppose that price per unit of output is \$1.85 when the firm sells 100 units. Its total revenue is then \$185. Since output and revenue are fixed, the monopolist's profit-maximizing problem is now reduced to choosing an input bundle that minimizes the cost of producing the fixed level of output, subject to the regulatory constraint:

$$\text{minimize } 5z_1 + 5z_2 \text{ by choice of } z_1 \text{ and } z_2$$

$$\text{subject to the constraint } 100 = F(z_1, z_2)$$

$$\text{subject to the constraint } 185 - 5z_1 < 8z_2$$

The first constraint, $100 = F(z_1, z_2)$, is that the chosen input bundle be on the isoquant for 100 units of output. This is the standard constraint in cost minimization problems. The second constraint is the regulatory constraint. Thus, the monopolist faces the standard cost-minimization problem from Section 7.5 — with the additional twist of a regulatory constraint.

If the allowed rate of return is large enough, the regulatory constraint is ineffective; the solution to the problem is the standard cost-minimizing input bundle for 100 units of output, and the monopolist's behaviour is unaffected.

The interesting case occurs when the regulatory constraint is effective or binding. In Figure 10.7, the standard cost-minimizing input bundle is (10,10) at point E, where the 100-unit isoquant is tangent to the dashed \$100 isocost line. If the firm were to choose this input bundle, its profit would then be \$85 (\$185 – \$100). The rub is that this input bundle fails to satisfy the regulatory constraint because 135 — that is, 185 – (5 × 10) — is greater than 80 (8 × 10). To satisfy the rate-of-return constraint, the monopolist will instead choose an input bundle on or above the regulatory constraint. As Figure 10.7 reveals, the cheapest input bundle on the 100-unit isoquant that satisfies that constraint is (5,20) at point E′. It is this input bundle that the monopolist will choose. Since this bundle is on the \$125 isocost line, the monopolist's profit under rate-of-return regulation is \$60 instead of \$85, and its costs are \$125 instead of \$100. More generally:

The rate-of-return-regulated firm chooses an input bundle that is not cost minimizing, and it uses too much capital and too little labour relative to the cost-minimizing bundle.

Why is this choice a matter of social concern? Suppose that demand for the monopolist's good is independent of income and that the prices of the inputs are independent of the monopolist's demand for them. In this case, point E is clearly Pareto-preferred to point E′. The monopolist's customers are indifferent between the two points because they buy 100 units at \$1.85 per unit in either case. The owners of the inputs are also indifferent because they sell their inputs for \$5 in either case. But the monopolist is better

FIGURE 10.7 **Rate-of-return regulation**

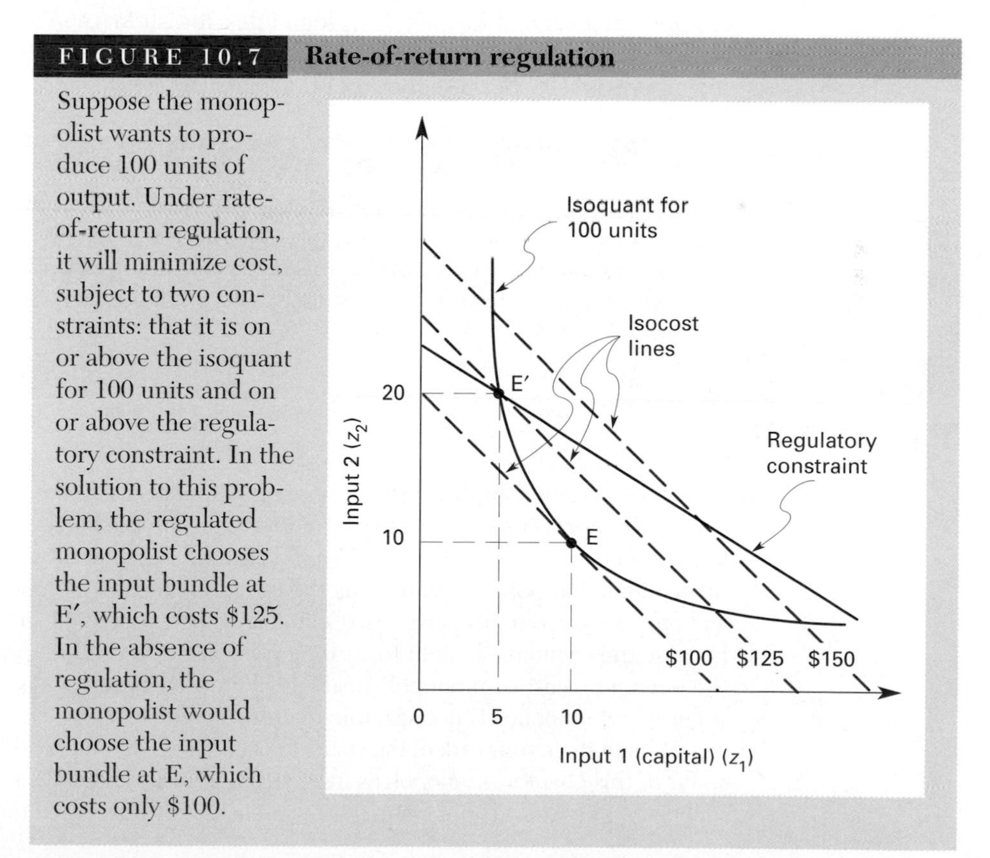

Suppose the monopolist wants to produce 100 units of output. Under rate-of-return regulation, it will minimize cost, subject to two constraints: that it is on or above the isoquant for 100 units and on or above the regulatory constraint. In the solution to this problem, the regulated monopolist chooses the input bundle at E′, which costs \$125. In the absence of regulation, the monopolist would choose the input bundle at E, which costs only \$100.

off at point E because its profit is larger by $25. Thus, rate-of-return regulation creates a social problem because it induces an inefficient equilibrium.

Application: The Plush Carpet Theorem

The notion that regulated firms fail to minimize costs is casually referred to as the *plush carpet theorem* because when the owners of regulated firms operate at higher costs, they direct the excess resources of the firm to those goods and services that provide them with utility directly.

In any firm, the owner has particular tastes for every aspect of the firm, from the architectural style of the building and interior decorating to the characteristics of the employees. In an unregulated firm, however, these preferences are tempered by the forces of competition and the drive to maximize profits. Even in a monopolistic firm the owners wish to maximize profits, and therefore, minimize costs.

As we have seen, though, the cost-minimizing condition is "relaxed" in a regulated firm. As a result the owners spend money within the firm to suit their own preferences. We should not be surprised to find plush carpets, large offices, higher ratios of support staff to managers, more fringe benefits, more job security, excessive computers (with games), and a relaxed working atmosphere. Perhaps the preferences of the owner even extend to forms of discrimination that many may not find acceptable. Unconstrained by a need to hire the most productive employees, for example, managers may decide to hire only members of their own race, sex, religion, or social club (and only good-looking ones as well!). This leads to an interesting implication: we expect more of all types of illegal discrimination among regulated firms than among for-profit firms. For example, Alchian and Kessel (1962) found that Jewish MBA graduates from Harvard were underrepresented in regulated industries. That is, most went into the for-profit sector, presumably because the cost of discrimination is higher there.

PROBLEM 10.7

Harold Demsetz, a famous economist, provided an interesting solution to the regulation of natural monopolies. He suggested that potential providers of the service simply bid in terms of price and output for the right to be the supplying firm. If this was done, what would be the equilibrium bid?

10.7 Patent Policy

Governments could apply a regulatory remedy similar to divestiture to patent monopolies and simply wipe the right to patent inventions off the books; the monopoly power that patents convey would then be disposed of neatly. Yet patents serve a potentially useful economic purpose by stimulating the invention and development of new products and processes. From this perspective, eliminating patenting rights might not be sensible, because the economic benefit to customers of patented products might well outweigh the economic cost of monopolistically exploited innovations. As these observations suggest, patent policy is not a simple matter.

Seen in the framework of the static, unchanging economic world we have modelled so far in this chapter, monopoly is most striking for its allocative inefficiency. Yet the real economic world is not static but dynamic. As we now place monopoly within the very different framework of a dynamic model, it will undergo a striking metamorphosis. The lure of monopoly profit becomes the magnet that attracts new and better products into being, and monopolists become the providers of products for the future.

Step back from monopoly for a moment to appreciate just how rapidly the economic world is changing. First, try to think of ten products available in 1903 that are still on the shelves today. (Once past Arm & Hammer baking soda, we found that it was no easy task.) Now try to list some of the products that are a familiar part of your landscape but that were unavailable, and perhaps even unimaginable, to a university student a hundred years ago. Your list can legitimately include almost any product in transportation or communication; any article of clothing made from a synthetic fabric; any item of frozen food in your local supermarket; all of your audio equipment, tapes, records, and compact discs; almost all prescription drugs; all computer products; and on and on. Now try to imagine the thousands of new products that are on the market: *National Geographic*'s CD-ROM mammal encyclopedia, complete with film clips and sound; a lobster trap with a biodegradable door made of plastics, cobalt, starch, and a fatty acid that rots away, allowing the lobster to escape if the trap is lost; Fuji's palm-sized video projector, which weighs only one pound and fits easily into a camcorder bag; a miniature sewing machine that can be swallowed by patients and used to stitch internal tissues together without surgery; and Internet access through handheld digital phones.

In this dynamic context, monopoly — provided for a time by patent and copyright protection — plays an important role in ensuring that bright, new ideas about potential goods and services are actually transformed into bright, new goods and services. As you know, patents provide exclusive rights to a new product, invention, or process for a specified period of time. Similarly, copyrights provide exclusive rights to art, music, or written material for a specified period of time: in Canada, 50 years from the death of the creator. (We will use the word *patent* to refer to both.) These exclusive, or monopoly, rights are an important policy tool for governments in virtually all market economies. In this section, we will develop a model that will let you see why granting patents can make economic good sense — and see, too, some of the economic pitfalls associated with patents.

The Appropriability Problem

What economic problems do patents solve? When Jonas Salk created the Salk vaccine, his invention conferred real benefits on society at large. Polio was virtually eliminated in developed countries by the early 1960s. So, too, thousands of other inventions — Bell's telephone, Land's camera, Mozart's music, Jobs' and Wozniak's computer, Virginia Woolf's novels, Lear's jet, and so on — have created what we will call social value. We will see shortly how to use the cost-benefit criterion to attach a dollar figure to the social value of an invention. For now, we can simply note that according to this criterion, a bright idea should be developed into a new product if the social value of the new product is greater than the development cost. But will a socially valuable invention always come into being? It is easy to see that if inventors were to bear all the development costs and reap all the benefits, thereby personally capturing, or *appropriating*, all the excess of social value over the cost of development associated with their inventions — every socially useful invention would be produced. Yet inventors are not able to appropriate all the social value created by their inventions. As a result, many potentially valuable ideas never appear as products on market shelves, because their inventors simply do not have the private incentive to pursue them. This is the **appropriability problem**.

appropriability problem

A number of responses to this appropriability problem are possible. Governments may assist directly with the sometimes massive costs of product research and development (R&D). For example, to develop a new microeconomics textbook — to write and edit it, to have it reviewed and to respond to the reviews, to design the book and the graphs, to set the type — costs approximately $500 000. To put a new prescription drug on the market may cost $250 million or more. Governments can and do subsidize new product development by providing a variety of support measures. For instance, scattered across North America are more than 75 joint industry–government research consortiums that are developing generic technologies in everything from cement to semiconductors. Member companies can then hone those technologies for their own specific needs.

We will be focusing instead on another possible response: granting patents that confer monopoly power and, therefore, monopoly profit — to inventors, thereby increasing their private incentive to create new products. For example, the copyright on "Happy Birthday to You" — the four-line verse written by two Louisville teachers as a classroom greeting — generates about $1 million in royalties annually.

A Model of Inventions

Let us begin by supposing that a vast number of individuals or firms — for convenience, we will call them all "developers" — have an equally vast stock of innovative ideas that can be developed into marketable products. Let us suppose, too, that it costs money — a good deal of money — to transform innovative ideas into marketable products.

Suppose, too, that the developer — once having invested in the R&D necessary to create a marketable product — can produce it at a constant marginal cost of $1 per unit, and that in each of a number of years, the market demand for its product is given by a linear market demand function like the one presented in Figure 10.8.[5] The blue area in Figure 10.8 is the annual profit $\$M$ that a monopolist in this market could earn. (We will consider only innovations for which $\$M$ is positive.) Of course, the development cost $\$D$, the annual monopoly profit $\$M$, and the precise shape of the demand curve will vary from one innovation to another.

Initially, the developer of this new product will be a monopolist, and the period over which it will remain the sole firm in its industry will be determined by what we will call an *imitation lag* L. For example, when the IBM personal computer hit the market in 1981, its rival clone manufacturers were in hot pursuit less than a year later. In this case, then, the imitation lag L is a year. The imitation lag for a book is even shorter. Using modern reproduction techniques, book bootleggers can begin to market duplications of a newly released book in a matter of days. And as any experienced software pirate knows, the imitation lag for much computer software can be a matter of minutes.

In other cases, the lag time is apparently large. Thus, we will assume that the developer is a monopolist for a lag period of L, but that once the lag period L has elapsed, anyone can manufacture the developer's product at a marginal cost of $1. Without patents, at this point, the developer becomes just another perfectly competitive producer. (Notice that we are implicitly supposing that imitators incur no development costs.) Clearly, if patent protection is to mean anything, it must extend the monopoly period.

5. Throughout our discussion, we will assume that the demand functions for different products are independent of each other; that is, new products are neither substitutes nor complements for each other. Without this assumption, we could not use consumer surplus to measure the social value of a new product.

FIGURE 10.8 **The inducement to develop**

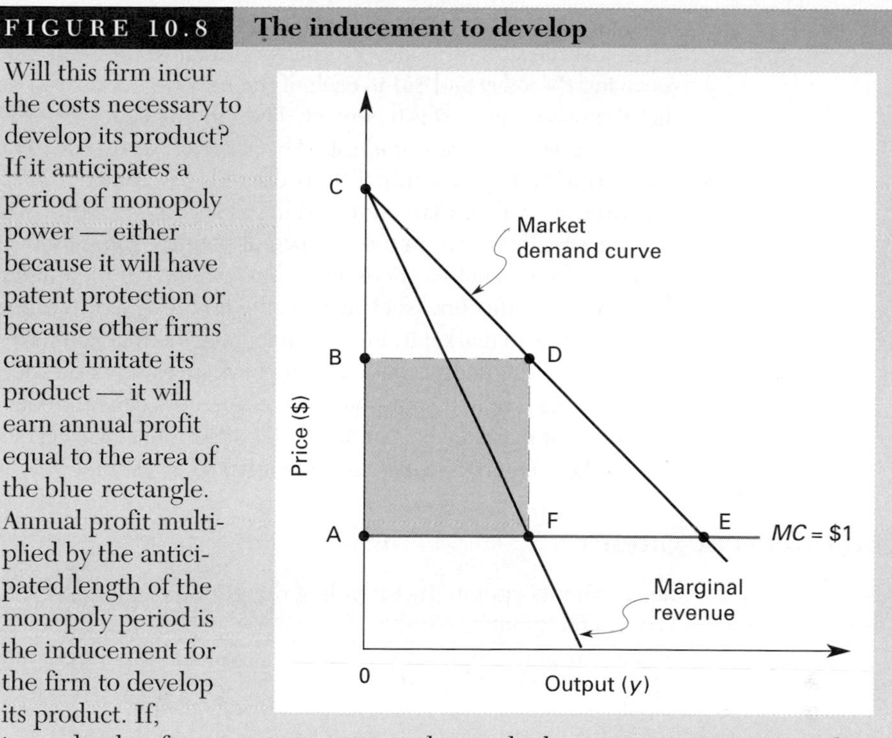

Will this firm incur the costs necessary to develop its product? If it anticipates a period of monopoly power — either because it will have patent protection or because other firms cannot imitate its product — it will earn annual profit equal to the area of the blue rectangle. Annual profit multiplied by the anticipated length of the monopoly period is the inducement for the firm to develop its product. If, instead, other firms can imitate its product and it has no patent protection, the equilibrium price will be $1, the firm will earn zero annual profit, and the inducement to develop its product will also be zero.

Finally, because patents obviously raise intertemporal issues, time considerations must be introduced. For simplicity, let us suppose that every product has a 40-year product cycle. Specifically, suppose that the market demand curve (shown in Figure 10.8) will be stable for 40 years, and thereafter it will evaporate overnight. In addition, suppose that the entire stock of innovative ideas is in place at time zero, that all decisions about product development are made at time zero, and that product development itself requires no time. A patent policy will then shape developers' incentives at time-zero, thereby indirectly determining the products that will be marketed in this miniature economy across the whole 40-year time span.

In this model, each of the multitude of innovative ideas in the minds of developers can be described by its demand curve and three numbers: $*D*, the sum of money needed to develop the idea into a marketable product; $*M* the profit per year that a monopolist could earn by marketing the product; and *L*, the number of years before other firms can imitate the developed product.

We will assume that each developer knows what these three numbers are and that no one else does. In what circumstances will a developer choose to transform an innovative idea into a marketable new product?

Product Development in the Absence of Patents

In deciding whether to go ahead with its product development and marketing plans, a profit-maximizing developer will compare the present value of its monopoly profits with the development cost $\$D$. The present value of monopoly profit $\$M$ over L periods is just the sum of money PV that would make the monopolist indifferent between receiving PV today and $\$M$ in each of the next L periods. For simplicity, let us suppose that the rate of interest is 0 percent. Then the present value of annual monopoly profit $\$M$ over L years is just L multiplied by M, or $\$LM$. A profit-maximizing developer will proceed with its plans only if $\$LM$ exceeds $\$D$. Thus, if L is greater than D/M, the new product will be marketed, and if L is less than D/M, it will not.

We see, then, that in the absence of patents, some innovative ideas will be transformed into marketable goods and others will not. If the imitation lag period L is small enough, no matter how socially valuable an idea might be, the developer has no private incentive to market it. For example, imagine that you have thought up a new computer game. You realize that once you have invested in the R&D necessary to develop a marketable product, your potential competitors can immediately copy and produce it at a constant marginal cost of \$1. In this situation, L will certainly be less than D/M — and neither you nor anyone else will bother to invest in developing the computer game.

The Effects of Patents

Since patents operate by extending the period of monopoly, the next question is this: What is the number of years of monopoly profit J just sufficient that the present value of the annual monopoly profit $\$M$ is just equal to the development cost $\$D$? Since J satisfies $\$JM = \$D$, we see that

$$J = D/M$$

If a developer could count on being a monopolist for J years, then it could just recover its R&D costs. Therefore, if its actual monopoly period exceeds J, the developer will opt for creating its new product. We will suppose that J is shorter than a 40-year product cycle. (Otherwise, the product would never come into being, because it would be obsolete before the developer could recover its R&D costs.)

How will patent protection alter a developer's decision making? A patent law can be described by T, the time period over which patent (or monopoly) rights are granted. For example, in Canada, the copyright period for works of art extends 50 years beyond the artist's death, and the standard patent period is 20 years. How any particular patent law will affect a developer's decision depends on the nature of the relationships among the patent period T, the imitation lag L, and the just-sufficient monopoly period J. Let us look at these relationships systematically:

1. If $T > J > L$, in the absence of patent protection, the potential new product will not be marketed because the just-sufficient period J is longer than the imitation lag period L. Under patent protection, however, it will be marketed, because the patent period T is longer than the just-sufficient period J. In this case, then, a patent law solves the appropriability problem.
2. If $T > L > J$, the new product will be marketed even in the absence of patent protection because the imitation lag time L is longer than the just-sufficient period J. The patent period T simply extends the monopoly period from L years to T years. In this case, a patent law is not required to solve the appropriability problem, yet it does increase the developer's monopoly profit.
3. If $L > T > J$, the new product will be marketed because the imitation lag time L is longer than both the patent period T and the just-sufficient time J. In this case, the patent law is irrelevant.

4. If $J > T$ and $J > L$, the potential new product will not be developed and marketed because the just-sufficient period J is longer than both the patent period T and the imitation lag time L. Once again, the patent law is irrelevant.

Optimal Patent Policy

Now let us turn to patent policy. Our first problem is to define the social value of a new product. If we suppose that the demand for these new products is independent of income, we can use the concepts of consumers' and producers' surplus to define social value.

For any new product in the marketplace, the equilibrium will be in one of two phases: either a monopoly equilibrium (where its developer is still protected from competition by imitation lag or by a patent) or a competitive equilibrium (where neither imitation lag nor a patent remains operative). In the monopoly phase, total surplus in each period is the trapezoidal area $ACDF$ in Figure 10.8. It is composed of producer's surplus (that is, the monopolist's profit), an amount equal to the area of rectangle $ABDF$, and consumers' surplus, an amount equal to the area of triangle BCD. In the competitive phase, total surplus in each period is the area of the triangle ACE. It is composed entirely of consumers' surplus. Notice that total annual surplus is thus larger in the competitive phase than in the monopoly phase by an amount equal to the area of triangle DEF in Figure 10.8. This triangle simply reflects the deadweight loss of monopoly. Of course, if the product is not developed and marketed, then total surplus is zero in each period.

social value

social cost

In general, the cost-benefit criterion defines the social value of a new product as the discounted present value of the total annual surplus over the product's life. In the present context, the **social value** of any new product is then just the sum of total surplus in each period over all 40 periods.[6] In this model, the **social cost** of any new product is its R&D cost $\$D$.

We will consider two cases in analyzing optimal patent policy and begin by making the entirely unrealistic assumption that a product-specific patent law can be devised for each possible new product. Then we will drop this assumption as we take up the more realistic and challenging case in which one patent law applies across the board to all new products.

Given our assumptions, we know that each of the multitude of innovative ideas described in this model is socially desirable. Why? Recall that the just-sufficient time period J for each product is less than 40 years. The social value of each product therefore exceeds its social cost even when its developer is a monopolist over the entire 40-year product cycle. This means that if the patent period T is 40 years, every innovative idea will actually be translated into a marketable product, and both the developer and all the products' consumers will be better off. Of course, this does not mean that the optimal patent period is 40 years.

What is an optimal patent policy in this circumstance? It is one that maximizes a new product's social value less its social (or R&D) cost. First, consider a potential new product that will not come into existence unless it is patent-protected — that is, a potential product for which the just-sufficient period J is longer than the imitation lag time L. The patent period we choose must be long enough that its developer will have a profit incentive to bring the product to market — that is, the patent period T must be longer than or identical to the just-sufficient period J. Once we have hit this target,

6. Here we are ignoring an important question: What is the appropriate social discount rate? This is a complex issue, which we will not address.

our objective then will be to minimize the length of the monopoly phase. Why? Because total surplus in each period in the monopoly phase is smaller than it is in the competitive phase. Therefore, when J is greater than L, the optimal patent period is $T^* = J$. Any shorter patent period would fail to provide the developer with a profit incentive. Any longer patent period would extend the monopoly period needlessly, thereby reducing total surplus for each additional year of monopoly by an amount equal to the area of triangle DEF in Figure 10.8.

Now let us take up the case of a product that will come into being even though it is not patent-protected — that is, a product for which the lag time L is longer than the just-sufficient period J. In this case, no patent is required. The developer already has all the profit incentive it needs to bring the product to market. And that is all there is to optimal patent-policy making — when we can tailor a product-specific patent period for each new product.

This seemingly easy answer has a fatal drawback. The policy maker does not have the information necessary to compute the just-sufficient monopoly period J for each product. This means that policy makers are inevitably forced to apply a single patent period to a whole host of products.

Assuming that a single patent period covers all products, what is the optimal patent policy? To answer that question, we need to aggregate social value and social (or product development) costs over all products. We will call the sum of social value over all products the **aggregate social value** and the sum of social cost over all products **aggregate social cost**. The optimal patent policy maximizes aggregate social value less aggregate social cost.

aggregate social value

aggregate social cost

Unfortunately, when one patent period applies to a multitude of innovations, policy makers confront a tradeoff between creating the necessary incentives to encourage new product development and minimizing the static inefficiency of monopoly. Suppose, for example, that a policy maker is trying to choose between patent periods T of 15 or 20 years. If the shorter period is chosen, some innovative ideas will remain undeveloped that would have come into being if T had been 20 years long instead. If the longer patent period is chosen, the increased profit incentive means that these innovations, for which J is between 15 and 20 years and L is less than J, will come into being — and aggregate social value less aggregate social cost will rise accordingly.

Yet this gain is offset by a loss. If the policy maker settles on the longer, 20-year patent period, the monopoly period of some — but not all — of the products that would have been developed under the shorter patent period is needlessly extended. (If the imitation lag L is shorter than 15 years, then the needless extension of the monopoly period is 5 full years; if L is between 15 and 20 years, then the extension is 15 minus L years; and if L exceeds 20 years, then the monopoly period is unaffected by the increase in T.) The total social value from these products therefore drops under the longer patent period because, for each product, annual surplus in the now-extended monopoly phase is less than in the now-shortened competitive phase. How, then, can policy makers decide on the optimal patent policy?

To find out, let us consider a small, or marginal, increase in the patent period. A marginal increase in T will have two effects. On the one hand, because it will stimulate the development of additional new products, it will tend to increase aggregate social value less aggregate social cost. On the other hand, because it needlessly increases the monopoly period of some products that would have been brought to market in any case, it will tend to decrease aggregate social value less aggregate social cost. If we call the first effect the **marginal social benefit**, and the second effect the **marginal social cost**, we can neatly characterize the optimal patent policy:

marginal social benefit

marginal social cost

At the optimal patent period, the marginal social benefit of increasing the patent period is equal to the marginal social cost.

But to apply this rule, the policy maker would need a list of all the possible products and — for each product — the annual total surplus associated with that new product in both its monopoly and its competitive phases, the product developer's R&D costs and annual monopoly profit, and the imitation lag time. To even begin to approximate this type of information is a major undertaking. As a result, policy makers typically are forced to set patent policy under conditions of very imperfect information.

Time and again, policy makers are caught between a rock and a hard place, trying, with limited information, to find the delicate balance between encouraging innovation and minimizing static inefficiency. Thus, the principles and problems that arise in trying to set an optimal patent policy can serve as a metaphor for the more general principles and problems encountered in a wide spectrum of policy issues.

SUMMARY

From a formal standpoint, what differentiates the monopolist's profit-maximizing problem from the perfect competitor's is that its revenue function is more complex because the monopolist is a price setter. Its *marginal revenue function* lies *below* the demand, or average revenue, function. As a result, at the monopolist's profit-maximizing solution, the output level where marginal revenue equals marginal cost, price exceeds marginal cost, and two important implications follow. First, the monopoly solution is not Pareto-optimal; it is inefficient. Second, at the monopoly solution, the monopolist fails to extract the maximum possible profit.

In considering what should be done about monopoly, we argued that the proper policy response to monopoly depends on the source of monopoly power. If monopoly power springs from the monopoly ownership of some scarce resource, then competition — created by a governmental policy of divestiture — is a feasible alternative. If monopoly power comes from economies of scale — and the monopoly is therefore a natural monopoly — the ideal regulatory response is to induce the monopolist (whether public or private) to behave efficiently. Unfortunately, neither *average-cost pricing* nor *rate-of-return regulations* — both standard governmental responses — is entirely satisfactory because neither regulatory mechanism induces the monopolist to behave efficiently. As we saw, however, if the regulatory agency knows the monopolist's demand curve, it can devise an *efficient regulatory mechanism*.

Finally, in our discussion of *patents* we looked at monopoly as a possible solution to an important social problem, the *appropriability problem*. Because innovators bear most of the development costs of their new ideas, but cannot appropriate most or even a significant portion of the benefits, innovators have no economic incentive to develop many socially valuable ideas. One way to enhance the innovator's economic incentive is to grant the inventor a patent monopoly — the exclusive right to use the new idea for a specified period of time. As we saw, the design of an optimal patent policy involves a troublesome tradeoff between stimulating product development and reducing the inefficiency of monopoly.

EXERCISES

1. The demand function for a very famous introductory economics textbook is

$$p = 100 - 0.005y$$

The publisher must pay \$20 per book in printing and distribution costs and, in addition, it must pay the author a \$20 royalty for each book sold.

a. Your job is to advise the publisher. What price will maximize the publisher's profit? How much profit will the publisher earn? How large will the author's royalty cheque be?

b. A consultant says that the publisher and the author have the wrong sort of agreement. He says that the author and the publisher should tear up their original agreement, in which the author gets \$20 per book sold, and enter a profit-sharing agreement. He recommends that the author get 40 percent of the profit and the publisher 60 percent. What price should the publisher set with this profit-sharing agreement? (*Hint*: Is marginal cost \$40 or only \$20? Will both the author and the publisher prefer the profit-sharing agreement to their original agreement? Which agreement will the students who buy the textbook prefer?)

c. Can you explain why the original royalty agreement is not economically sound?

2. The demand for Wayless, a dietary supplement, is

$$p = 110 - y$$

and the cost function for any firm producing Wayless is

$$C(y) = 10y + F$$

where F is a fixed cost.

a. What is marginal cost? How much Wayless would a monopolist produce? What price would it charge? How much profit would it earn?

b. If the monopolist did produce the profit-maximizing quantity you found in (a), show that an entrant's residual demand function would be

$$p_E = 60 - y_E$$

c. What quantity would maximize an entrant's profit, given this residual demand function? What would the price be? What would the entrant's profit be?

d. For which of the following values of F is the market for Wayless a natural monopoly? $F = \$200$, $F = \$400$, $F = \$600$, $F = \$800$.

3. When Warner-Lambert Company's patent on its anticholesterol drug Lopid was about to expire, it lobbied the US Congress to extend its patent for five more years. If you had been an economic advisor to Congress, what advice would you have offered? What are the implications for the price of Lopid? Is there an economic case for extending this patent? If there is an economic case for offering a patent before the drug is invented, is there a case for extending the patent period after it is invented?

4. Suppose a monopolist must pay an excise tax equal to t per unit sold — if it produces y units, it must pay ty in taxes. To the monopolist, these taxes are just another cost of production, so we can write the monopolist's profit function as

$$\pi(y) = yD(y) - ty - TC(y)$$

The monopolist's profit-maximizing rule is then

$$MR(y^*) = MC(y^*) + t$$

a. Explain this rule.

b. Now, suppose that the monopolist's demand curve is

$$p = 200 - 5y$$

and that the monopolist's marginal cost is \$10 per unit. What are the profit-maximizing price and quantity and the monopolist's profit when t is \$10? When t is \$20? When t is \$30? When t is \$0?

5. Price ceilings offer some interesting possibilities in monopoly markets. Consider the following demand function of some monopolist:

$$p = 200 - 2y$$

The monopolist's marginal cost is \$80.

a. What is MR? Carefully draw both the demand curve and the marginal revenue curve. What is the profit-maximizing price and quantity?
b. Now suppose a price ceiling equal to \$100 is imposed on the monopolist. Show that the monopolist's MR curve is now composed of two segments: MR is \$100 for the first 50 units and is given by the original MR function for larger outputs. Draw this revised MR curve. Notice the gap or discontinuity in MR at $y = 50$.
c. What is the profit-maximizing price and quantity when a \$100 price ceiling is imposed? When a \$160 price ceiling is imposed?
d. What is the efficient level of output? Is there a price ceiling that will induce the monopolist to produce the efficient output?

6. The following are cost and revenue tables for a monopolist:

Q	P	TR	MR	AC	TC	MC
0	10					
1	9			4		
2	8			4		
3	7			4		
⋮	⋮			⋮		
10	0			4		

a. Complete the table.
b. Graph the demand curve, the MR, AC, MC curves all on the same graph and find the monopolist's optimal price, quantity, and profits.
c. What is the value of consumer's surplus?
d. Suppose the monopolist is forced to set the price and quantity to the competitive level. What price and output does this imply? In doing this, what assumptions are you making about the cost function?
e. At this new output level, what is the value of profit? of consumer's surplus?
f. What is the deadweight loss of the monopoly?
g. Suppose (instead of (d)), that the government imposes a profits tax (99 percent) on the monopolist that extracts most of the profits, and later redistributes the money back to the customers. What is the new output level? What is the nominal price paid and the effective price paid (i.e., after the redistribution)? What is the level of consumers' surplus?

7. Suppose a certain monopolist has a flat MC curve at \$5, and faces a straight-line demand curve. Now the MC curve shifts up to \$6. By how much will the firm's optimal price increase?

8. If there is one peanut seller in the park, is he a monopoly? Does he face a downward-sloping demand curve?

9. Suppose that the Nickel Company is the sole producer of nickel in Canada. The demand function for nickel in Canada is

$$p = 100 - y$$

where y is tonnes of nickel sold in Canada. Outside Canada, the market for nickel is perfectly competitive and nickel is priced at \$60 per tonne. Canada sets a tariff on imported nickel equal to \$30 per tonne. Show that Nickel Company's aggregate marginal revenue function is

$$\begin{aligned} MR(y) &= 90 && \text{if } y \le 10 \\ MR(y) &= 100 - 2y && \text{if } 10 < y \le 20 \\ MR(y) &= 60 && \text{if } y > 20 \end{aligned}$$

Nickel Company's marginal cost function is $MC(y) = ay$.

a. Suppose that $a = 2$. How much nickel will the company produce? How much will it sell in Canada and at what price? How much will it sell in the international market? What profit will Nickel Company earn?
b. Now suppose that $a = 14/3$ and repeat these exercises.
c. Finally, suppose that $a = 30$ and repeat these exercises.

10. Let us reconsider one aspect of the efficient regulatory solution in Section 10.6. We will use the following demand function:

$$p = 160 - y$$

Recall that the subsidy associated with any quantity y was identical to consumers' surplus at y, which implies that the firm's marginal revenue function is identical to its demand function. First, compute the subsidy paid for an arbitrary quantity of output y. (Remember that the area of a triangle is 1/2 its base multiplied by its height.) Then compute the firm's total revenue — including the subsidy — as a function of y.

Finally, divide total revenue by y to get the average revenue function associated with this subsidy scheme. Then construct a diagram in which you identify the regulated firm's profit-maximizing output and use the average revenue function to identify its profit.

11. In 1991 the Disney corporation sold the movie *Fantasia* on video, but only for 50 days before Christmas. At the same time it issued a statement that no future sales would ever be made (although the movie would be available on the rental market). Why would Disney do this? How does the durability of a good affect the monopoly pricing problem?

12. In Canada it is not a violation of any law to be a monopoly as long as you are not reducing competition through blocking entry or engaging in some other "bad" practice. Why would the law be so lenient given that monopolies tend to price above marginal costs?

*13. A firm is a monopoly with demand $p = 100 - y$ and total costs $C = y^2 + 900$.
   a. Find the marginal cost and the marginal revenue equations along with the minimum of the AC curve.
   b. What is the profit-maximizing condition for a monopolist?
   c. Draw the AC, MC, MR, and demand curves on a single graph.
   d. Show on the graph and with math what quantity the monopoly will produce and at what price it will sell this quantity. What are the profits of the firm?
   e. Suppose the government imposes a price ceiling of \$65. Draw the new outcome with an emphasis on the MR and demand curves. What are the profits now?

14. Suppose a firm faces two markets for the same product. In market A the inverse demand curve is $p^a = 60 - y^a$, while in market B the inverse demand curve is $p^b = 36 - 0.5y^b$. The total cost function is $TC = 6(y^a + y^b)$.
   a. Find the profit-maximizing price and quantity in each market.
   b. Now suppose consumers can buy the product in market B and sell it in market A, but face a transportation charge of \$6 per unit. What is the new profit-maximizing price and quantity?

*15. A monopolist faces a market demand curve given by $y = 70 - p$.
   a. If the monopolist can produce at constant average and marginal costs of \$6, what output and price will maximize profits? What are the profits?
   b. If instead of the costs in (a), the total costs are described by $C = 0.25Y^2 - 5Y + 300$. What is the new price/quantity combination that will maximize profits? What are the profits?

*16. Suppose a regulated monopoly has the production function $y = f(L,K)$, and purchases labour and capital at constant prices w and v.
   a. Write out the firm's profit function.

   Suppose also that the regulatory agency only allows a fair rate of return s per unit on capital such that $sK + wL - py = 0$.

   b. Write out the Lagrangian equation that this monopoly must solve. What are the first-order conditions?
   c. If $s < v$, what is the profit-maximizing level of output?
   d. If $s = v$, what is the profit-maximizing level of output?
   e. If $s > v$, how will the firm's average costs compare to what they would be if the firm was unconstrained?

*17. Suppose a monopolist has a constant marginal and average cost equal to \$10. That is, $AC = MC = \$10$. Further, suppose that the market demand curve is given by $y = 100 - p$.
   a. Calculate the profit maximizing price and quantity along with the firm's profits.
   b. What output would be produced under perfect competition assuming no change in costs?
   c. Calculate the deadweight loss due to monopoly.
   d. Suppose that costs were to rise under a competitive market. How much higher would they have to be such that the monopoly market would be considered the efficient market structure?

*18. A certain monopolist faces demand $y = 120 - 2p$ and has total costs $c = 12y$.

a. Derive the marginal cost and marginal revenue functions.
b. What is the profit-maximizing output and price for this monopolist?
c. Calculate and illustrate on a graph the monopolist's profits, consumers' surplus, and deadweight loss associated with your answer in (b).
d. Suppose the monopolist can set a minimum purchase requirement specifying that, if you want to consume its product, you must buy at least y^0 units. If the monopolist continues to charge the price you found in (b), what should it set as y^0?
e. Explain using a graph what happens to consumer surplus, monopoly profits, and deadweight loss with the minimum purchase requirement.

*19. A firm is a monopolist with demand $y = 60 - (1/2)p$. Calculate the monopoly output and price; the efficient (competitive) output and price; and explain graphically whether an average cost pricing regulation would ensure that the efficient level of output is produced

a. if the monopolist's total costs are $TC = 20y$.
b. if the monopolist's total costs are $TC = 2y^2$.
c. if the monopolist's total costs are $TC = 20y + 50$.

REFERENCES

Alchian, A. and R. Kessel. 1962. "Competition, Monopoly and the Pursuit of Money," *Aspects of Labor Economics*, Princeton, NJ: Princeton University Press.

Averch, H., and L. L. Johnson. 1961. "Behavior of the Firm Under Regulatory Constraint," *American Economic Review*, 52:1052–69.

PART V

Resource Markets and General Equilibrium

In Part V, we complete our basic study of neoclassical microeconomics by examining input markets, income distribution, and general equilibrium. We take advantage of the analytical similarities between output-market and input-market analysis to treat perfectly competitive and monopsonistic input markets in the space of a single chapter.

Chapter 12 discusses problems in describing the distribution of income and the efficiency problems that arise in trying to alter it. In particular, we examine the problems associated with minimum wages and welfare.

In Chapter 13, we carefully define efficiency in a general equilibrium framework and explore the conditions under which the general competitive equilibrium is, and is not, efficient. Chapter 12 offers an elegant model of the economy, and completes the analysis of markets that was started in Chapter 2. The next half of the book examines more advanced topics, including the issue of monopoly pricing, market structure, and the economics of information.

CHAPTER 11

Input Markets and the Allocation of Resources

It is all too easy to lose sight of the fact that economics is essentially about the allocation of scarce resources to alternative uses. In Chapter 8, we studied the concept of a scarce good by imagining an exchange economy with a limited number of rock concert tickets. Then we created a simple competitive model to analyze the allocation of tickets and money. As you discovered, the price of the tickets served as a signalling device; it guided the allocation of tickets and of money to the ten students. The competitive equilibrium price and quantity were therefore indicative of a more basic allocative process whereby certain people got scarce tickets and others got money (or command over other scarce goods).

We then extended the simple exchange model in Chapter 8 to include production. Looking back at the extended model of a perfectly competitive market in Chapters 8 and 9 and at the models of monopolistic markets in Chapter 10, we can see that all firms serve a similar allocative function. We can loosely regard firms as combining an assortment of scarce resources into a finished product and then offering the resulting resource "package" for sale. This vision of the role of firms allows us to see that the equilibrium price and quantity in *any* market for goods are indicative of a more fundamental allocative process in which scarce resources (packaged as finished goods) are traded by firms for consumers' dollars. For example, labour and iron ore, among other resources, are packaged as automobiles, toasters, and filing cabinets. These "processed resources" then end up in the garages, kitchens, and offices of the nation. In this sense, the price system serves to allocate resources to competing ends.

11.1 The Role of Input Markets

input markets

What we have so far ignored in our analysis is the allocative role played by resource or **input markets**. The time has come to bring input markets to centre stage. For example, how does the input price of steel affect the amount of steel bought, processed, and sold by automobile, small-appliance, and office-equipment manufacturers? How do input prices of sugar and vanilla flavouring affect the amount of these inputs bought, processed, and sold by bakers and ice cream makers? How does the input price of farm labour affect the amount of labour bought by tomato and lettuce producers in Holland Marsh, Ontario?

Notice, however, that in analyzing input markets, output markets cannot completely disappear from view, since an input's value to any firm depends on the price that the firm can charge for its output. In this sense, the demand for an input is said to be *derived* from the demand of the output. For example, demand for the epoxy resins and the assembly-line labour used to make cars depends on the output prices of goods in the automobile industry. Like the output prices in goods markets, the input prices for raw and processed resources and for various kinds of labour signal where more resources are needed in input markets and from where they are to be drawn.

Input markets, like output markets, range all the way from *perfectly competitive markets*, characterized by many insignificant buyers, to *monopsonistic markets*, characterized by a single buyer.

11.2 Perfectly Competitive Input Markets

perfectly competitive input market

Let us begin with a model of equilibrium price and quantity in a **perfectly competitive input market**. A perfectly competitive input market is characterized by firms that are *price takers*, in the sense that they fail to exercise any appreciable control over the price they pay for the input. For instance, if the input market for unskilled labour in the Edmonton area is perfectly competitive, none of the many firms hiring unskilled labour can significantly affect the wage rate.

Notice that this definition says nothing about the position of firms in their output markets, where they may be either perfectly competitive or monopolistic. For example, a lettuce grower is a perfect competitor in both the input and output markets. Lettuce growers have no real control over the prices they pay for inputs like water, seed, fertilizers, or labour, nor do they have control over the price they are paid for their lettuce. On the other hand, a local telephone company is competitive in many of its input markets but monopolistic in its output market. It may have no real control over the price it pays for inputs like secretarial services but, as the only firm selling local telephone service, it can exercise significant control over the price it charges for its service. We will include both types of firms in our analysis.

primary input markets

intermediate input markets

Now let us begin the analysis of supply and demand in input markets. There are two types of input markets: primary and intermediate input markets. Inputs in **primary input markets**, which include resources such as land, oil, and labour, have not been processed by other firms. For convenience, we will assume that all suppliers in primary input markets are individuals. Inputs in **intermediate input markets**, which include inputs such as iron ingots, flour, hog bellies, or cold rolled steel, are the processed output of other firms. Again for convenience, we will assume that all suppliers in intermediate input markets are firms. Then the supply functions in primary input markets (the market for unskilled labour, for example) will reflect the utility-maximizing decisions of individuals. By contrast, the supply function in intermediate input markets (the iron ingot market, for instance), will reflect the profit-maximizing decisions of firms. We will also assume that the demanders in all input markets are firms, and the input demand functions will therefore reflect the profit-maximizing decisions of firms.

Our primary objective in this chapter is to derive these input supply and demand functions. First, however, we need to look quickly at the key assumptions about competitive input markets. Not surprisingly, they closely parallel earlier assumptions about competitive output markets. In particular, the first two assumptions are familiar and important. The first is the assumption of large numbers, which guarantees that all demanders and all suppliers are price takers in the input market.

ASSUMPTION: LARGE NUMBERS

The number of input demanders (suppliers) is large enough and each demander (supplier) is small enough so that no individual buys (sells) a significant portion of the total quantity traded.

The second is the assumption of perfect information, which guarantees that all demanders and all suppliers are perfectly informed. In other words, the demanders (firms, in this case) know the prices of all inputs and outputs as well as the relevant production functions. The suppliers (individuals in primary input markets and firms in intermediate input markets) know the prices of all goods and, in particular, the prices of all relevant inputs.

ASSUMPTION: PERFECT INFORMATION

All demanders and suppliers have perfect knowledge of the relevant prices, and all firms have perfect knowledge of the relevant production functions.

The third assumption is that inputs are homogeneous, or identical: one barrel of bunker-C oil can be substituted for any other barrel and the labour of one systems analyst in the Atlanta labour market is indistinguishable from that of any other systems analyst. This assumption rules out the case of differentiated inputs.

ASSUMPTION: INPUT HOMOGENEITY

In any input market, all units of the input are identical.

The last assumption is that inputs are perfectly mobile. This implies that all units of the same input will command the same price in competitive equilibrium. However, as you will discover in Section 11.9, often this assumption is not satisfied. For example, intermediate goods like cement may not be easy to transport, and individual workers may not want to relocate. When resources are imperfectly mobile, the firms demanding these "immobile" inputs can exercise some control over input prices. The result, known as monopsony, is something very much like monopoly in output markets. For example, a fish-processing plant located in an isolated coastal community will exercise some significant control over the wages it pays its workers.

ASSUMPTION: PERFECT MOBILITY OF RESOURCES

All inputs are perfectly mobile.

If all four assumptions are satisfied, the perfectly competitive model can be applied without hesitation. But if one (or more) of the assumptions is not fulfilled, the model may or may not apply. The question in this case is whether the model continues to yield accurate predictions or not. An answer necessarily comes from empirical and experimental testing.

11.3 The Supply of Non-Labour Inputs

We can think of inputs as falling into two categories: labour and everything else. First, let us look at non-labour inputs like land, steel, cement, or chemicals. As we said, we will think of firms as the suppliers in intermediate input markets and individuals as the suppliers in primary input markets. If the supplier is a firm selling an intermediate input — say, a manufacturer of cold rolled steel — then the analysis of supply decisions is a simple matter. In this case, we can think of these firms as producing and supplying

— not a consumption good — but an intermediate input, and then apply the analysis in Chapter 9 directly to input markets.

renewable resource

If the supplier is an individual selling a primary input that is a **renewable resource** — such as land — a resource that can be used over and over again — we will make the simplifying assumption that the supply is perfectly inelastic with respect to input price: landowners, for example, simply offer their land at the going price in the marketplace. In making this assumption, however, we are ignoring some important questions concerning the improvement of a resource to make it fit for a specific use. If a marshland needs to be drained before it can be used for farming, for example, the supply will not be perfectly price inelastic because the price must be high enough to justify the expense of drainage.

nonrenewable resource

If a supplier is an individual selling a primary input that is a **nonrenewable resource**, like oil or iron ore — a resource that, once used, is gone — we will again make the simplifying assumption that the supply is perfectly price inelastic. In doing so, however, we are ignoring the question of the period in which the resource will be supplied (a question we considered in Section 5.3). In other words, when we assume that supply is perfectly price inelastic, we are analyzing the equilibrium within a single period.

11.4 The Supply of Labour

Analyzing labour supply is necessarily different from the supply of non-labour inputs. Labour supply depends on the decisions that individuals make about how much of their time to apportion to work rather than to other, leisure-time activities. We will suppose that people divide their time between work (uses of time that generate income) and leisure (all other uses of time). We will also suppose that their preferences can be reduced to preferences over consumption bundles composed of two goods — leisure, x_1, and income, x_2. Notice that both goods are composite commodities. Leisure is a composite of time spent in activities like sleeping, eating, watching TV, exercising, reading, and so on. Income is a composite of money spent on items like food, clothing, transportation, housing, entertainment, and so on.

time constraint

In this model, an individual faces two constraints. The **time constraint** dictates that total time devoted to work and to leisure must be equal to total time available. Letting T denote total time available in the period and h denote hours of work, the time constraint is

$$h + x_1 = T$$

income constraint

Hours spent at work (h) plus hours spent at leisure (x_1) add up to total hours available T.

The **income constraint** says that the individual's income is the sum of income earned from work and non-work income. Let w denote the individual's wage rate and A denote his or her non-work income from sources like savings accounts, rental income, stocks and bonds, and so on. The income constraint is

$$x_2 = wh + A$$

leisure-income budget constraint

Income x_2 is equal to income from work wh plus non-work income A.

From the time constraint, we see that $h = T - x_1$. Using this result to eliminate h from the income constraint, we get what we will call the **leisure-income budget constraint**:

$$wx_1 + x_2 = A + wT$$

price of leisure

full income

Two important insights follow from this budget constraint. First, the wage rate w can be interpreted as the **price of leisure**, since $\$w$ of income must be given up to get an additional hour of leisure. Second, $A + wT$ can be interpreted as **full income**, since it is the amount that could be earned by devoting all T hours to work.

We can then think of an individual as choosing a bundle of leisure and income so as to maximize utility, subject to the constraint that the value of leisure (wx_1) plus income (x_2) be equal to full income ($A + wT$). The solution to this problem is shown in Figure 11.1. The budget constraint has slope equal to $-w$ since the price of leisure is w. When T hours are spent working (or, when no time is apportioned to leisure), income is $A + wt$. When T hours are devoted to leisure (or, when no time is spent working) income is just A. The utility-maximizing bundle is at point E, where the indifference curve is tangent to the leisure-income budget constraint: this person chooses to devote x_1^* hours to leisure and to supply h^* hours of work.

In solving this problem, we have determined both this person's demand for leisure (x_1^*) and his or her supply of labour (h^*) since $h^* = T - x_1^*$. This suggests two comparative statics questions. First, how do an individual's supply of labour h^* and demand for leisure x_1^* respond to changes in non-work income A? Second, how do they respond to changes in the wage rate w? Notice that because hours of leisure and hours of work use up the total time available, the labour supply response and demand for leisure response will have opposite signs. For example, if labour supply increases, then the demand for leisure must decrease.

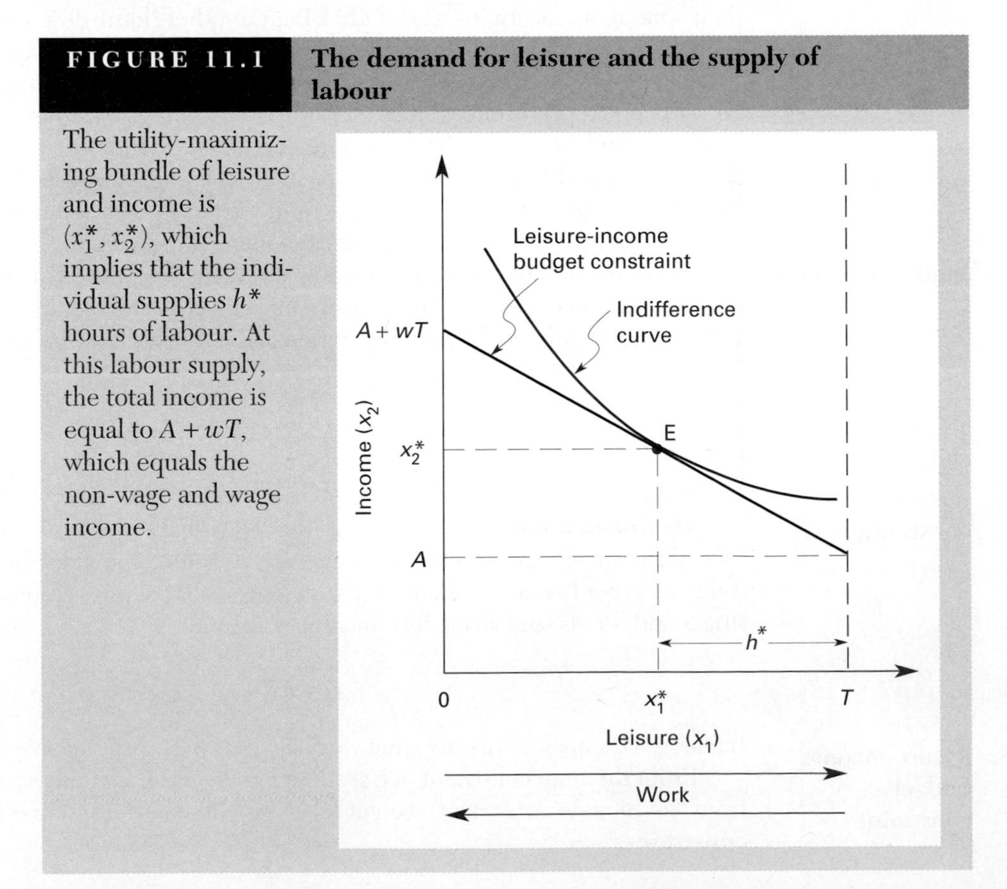

FIGURE 11.1 The demand for leisure and the supply of labour

The utility-maximizing bundle of leisure and income is (x_1^*, x_2^*), which implies that the individual supplies h^* hours of labour. At this labour supply, the total income is equal to $A + wT$, which equals the non-wage and wage income.

Responses to Changes in Non-Work Income

Our theory provides no definitive prediction about the first comparative statics question: What are the supply and demand responses to changes in non-work income A? However, it does yield a useful taxonomy. Leisure is a *normal good* if the response to an increase in non-work income A is an increase in hours of leisure and therefore a decrease in hours of work. This case is shown in Figure 11.2. Non-work income is initially \$500 per week, and in the initial equilibrium, this person chooses to devote 120 of the 168 hours in the week to leisure and the remaining 48 hours to work. Non-work income subsequently rises to \$800 per week, and in the subsequent equilibrium, this person chooses to devote 138 hours to leisure and the remaining 30 hours to work. We see, then, that in response to a \$300 increase in non-work income, this person's demand for leisure rises by 18 hours and his or her supply of labour drops by 18 hours.

In contrast, leisure is an *inferior good* if the response to an increase in non-work income A is a decrease in hours of leisure and, therefore, an increase in hours of work.

PROBLEM 11.1

Construct a diagram similar to Figure 11.2 to illustrate the case in which leisure is an inferior good.

Responses to a Change in the Wage Rate

For most people, non-work income is a relatively small proportion of income. In economies like Canada, about 80 percent of all income is work-generated for the economy as a whole. For typical individuals, the proportion of work-generated income is even higher. Therefore, economists have paid more attention to the second comparative

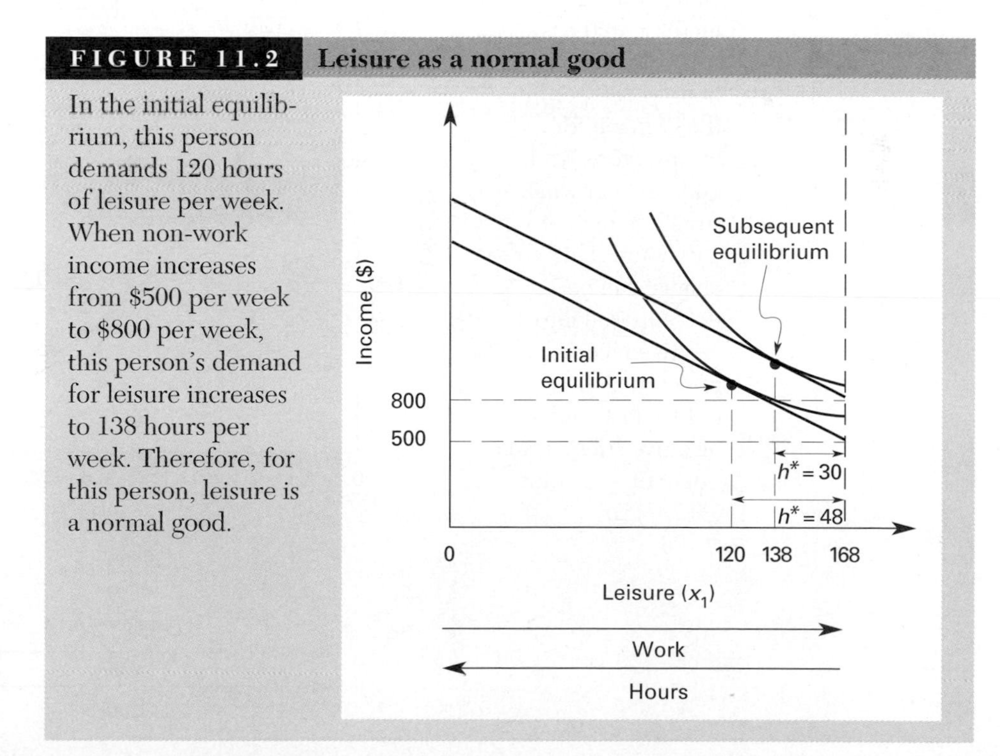

FIGURE 11.2 **Leisure as a normal good**

In the initial equilibrium, this person demands 120 hours of leisure per week. When non-work income increases from \$500 per week to \$800 per week, this person's demand for leisure increases to 138 hours per week. Therefore, for this person, leisure is a normal good.

statics question: How does the supply of labour — and therefore the demand for leisure — change in response to a change in the wage rate? Or, to put it another way: Does the individual's supply of labour increase or decrease as the wage rate increases?

Consider the case in Figure 11.3, where this individual has no non-work income and the wage rate is initially \$10 per hour. This person selects utility-maximizing bundle A, choosing 126 hours of leisure and 42 hours of work per week and earning an income of \$420 per week. What happens if the wage rate increases to \$20 per hour? Given the higher wage rate, this person now selects bundle B, choosing 140 hours of leisure and 28 hours of work per week and earning an income of \$560 per week. We see that in response to the \$10 per hour wage increase, this person's demand for leisure increases — and supply of labour decreases — by 14 hours per week.

For a better understanding of these results, let us decompose the response in Figure 11.3 into income and substitution effects. Beginning at point B, imagine reducing the individual's non-work income by just enough so that he or she could attain the initial (lower) indifference curve in Figure 11.3, given the \$20 per hour wage rate. The result is the compensated budget line in the figure. This person would choose point C on the compensated budget line. We see that the income effect for this wage increase is to increase hours of leisure (and therefore to decrease hours of work) by 27 hours per week. In contrast, the substitution effect for this increase in the wage rate (or price of leisure) is to reduce hours of leisure (and therefore increase hours of work) by 13 hours per week. Because the income effect is larger than the substitution effect, the net effect is an increase in hours of leisure (and a decrease in hours of work) by 14 hours per week.

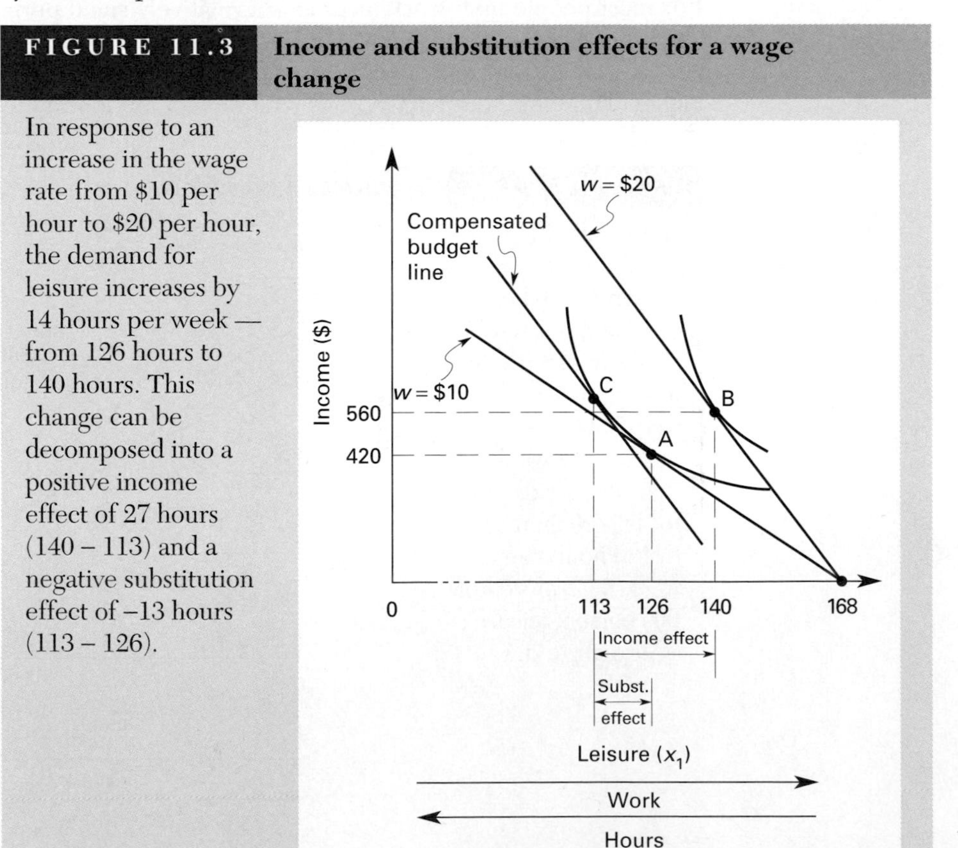

FIGURE 11.3 Income and substitution effects for a wage change

In response to an increase in the wage rate from \$10 per hour to \$20 per hour, the demand for leisure increases by 14 hours per week — from 126 hours to 140 hours. This change can be decomposed into a positive income effect of 27 hours (140 – 113) and a negative substitution effect of –13 hours (113 – 126).

In Figure 11.3, leisure is clearly a normal good. When leisure is a normal good, the income effect of a wage increase invariably leads to an increase in hours of leisure and a decrease in hours of work. But the substitution effect works in just the opposite direction: a wage increase leads to a decrease in hours of leisure and an increase in hours of work:

When leisure is a normal good, the income and substitution effects are at cross purposes, and the results are ambiguous. Whether hours of work increase or decrease in response to an increase in the wage rate depends on whether the income effect is smaller or larger than the substitution effect.

When leisure is an inferior good, however, the income and substitution effects are complementary, and the results are unambiguous:

When leisure is an inferior good, an increase in the wage rate invariably leads to a decrease in hours of leisure and an increase in hours of work.

To check your understanding of the leisure-income model, give the following problem careful attention.

PROBLEM 11.2

Are the following statements true or false? Carefully explain your answer.

1. If in response to an increase in the wage rate, hours of work increase, then leisure is necessarily an inferior good.
2. If in response to an increase in the wage rate, hours of work decrease, then leisure is necessarily a normal good.

Labour Supply Curves

By considering a number of different wage rates, we can easily derive an individual's labour supply curve. In Figure 11.4a, we have solved an individual's utility-maximizing problem for six wage rates. The point labelled E on each of the budget lines indicates the chosen bundle of leisure and income. (For simplicity, we have not shown the indifference curves. You will have to imagine the points of tangency between these budget lines and the implied indifference curves.)

The information from Figure 11.4a has been used to derive this individual's labour supply curve in Figure 11.4b. For example, we see from Figure 11.4a that when the wage rate is $25 per hour, this person demands 138 hours of leisure per week and therefore supplies (168 – 138) or 30 hours of labour per week. In the case shown in Figure 11.4, when the wage rate is low (less than $10 per hour), this person's labour supply increases as the wage rate increases. However, when the wage is higher (more than $10 per hour), this person's labour supply decreases as the wage rate increases. Of course, there is nothing in our theory to suggest that *all* labour supply curves look like the supply curve in Figure 11.4b. This is just one possible labour supply curve.

FIGURE 11.4 The demand for leisure and the supply of labour

The curve EE in (a) passes through the utility-maximizing bundles that are generated as the wage rate increases from $5 to $30 in $5 increments. The information from (a) has been used to construct the labour supply curve in (b).

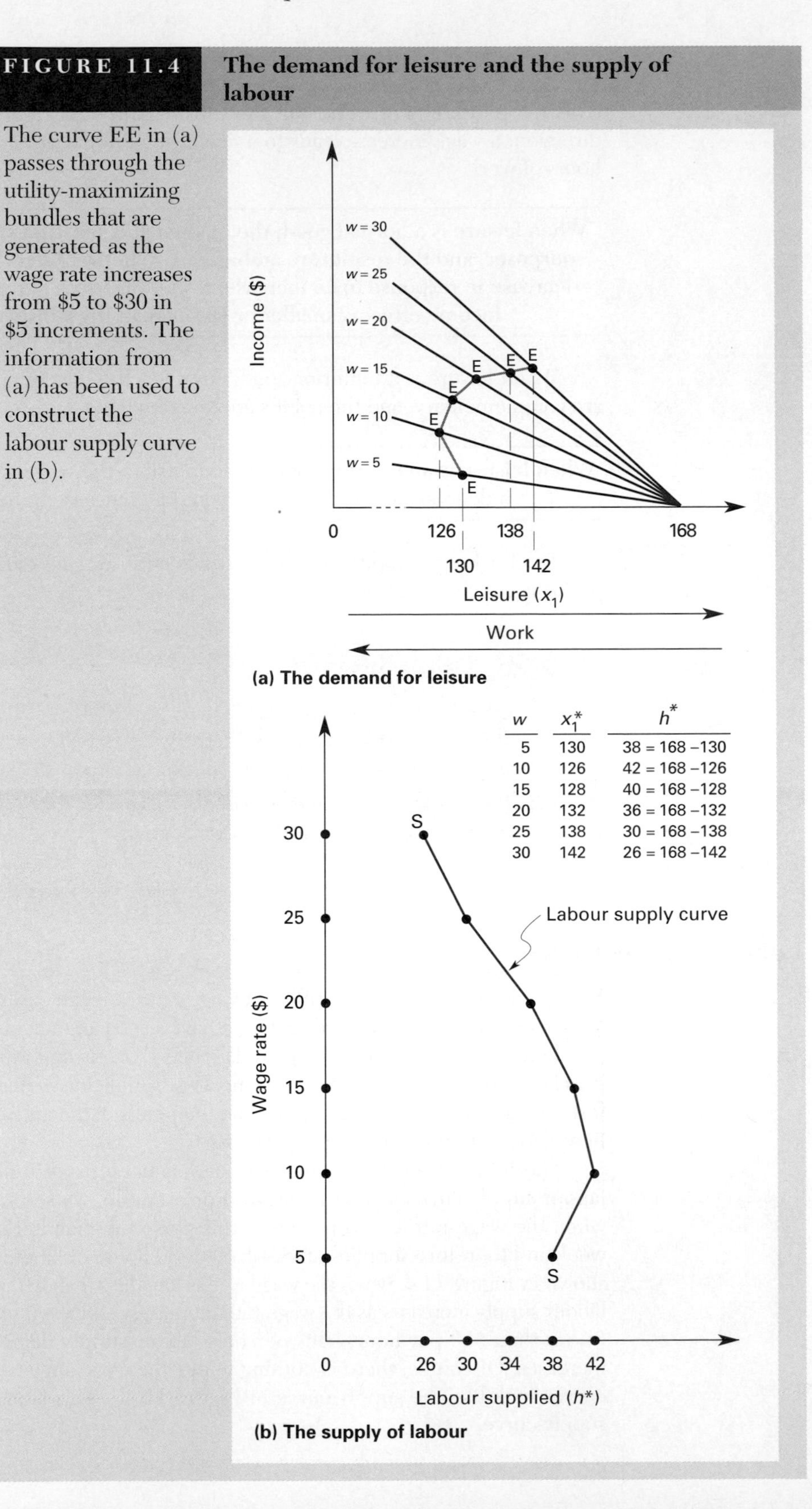

w	x_1^*	h^*
5	130	38 = 168 − 130
10	126	42 = 168 − 126
15	128	40 = 168 − 128
20	132	36 = 168 − 132
25	138	30 = 168 − 138
30	142	26 = 168 − 142

(a) The demand for leisure

(b) The supply of labour

11.5 The Firm's Demand for One Variable Input

short-run input demand function

Now let us turn from the supply of inputs to the demand for inputs. We will begin with what we will call the **short-run input demand function,** where only one input is variable. Specifically, let us imagine a firm — The Fish Company — that hires people to catch fish from a company-owned lake. To keep the analysis simple, we will initially suppose that there is just one good in the economy, namely fish. In this case, The Fish Company's profit will be measured in fish and the workers will be paid "in kind" — that is, in fish instead of dollars. The hourly wage rate, denoted by w, is the number of fish a worker is paid for an hour of fishing. After we find the firm's demand for labour in this case, we can easily generalize results to the more realistic case in which workers are paid in dollars.[1]

Input Demand in a One-Good Economy

The Fish Company's marginal product function $MP(z)$ and its average product function $AP(z)$, where z is hours of labour, are shown in Figure 11.5. Because the unit of measure on the vertical axis is numbers of fish, we can represent the wage rate w on this axis. We will find The Fish Company's demand curve by answering the following question: Given any wage rate (in fish), how many hours of labour will The Fish Company buy to maximize its profit?

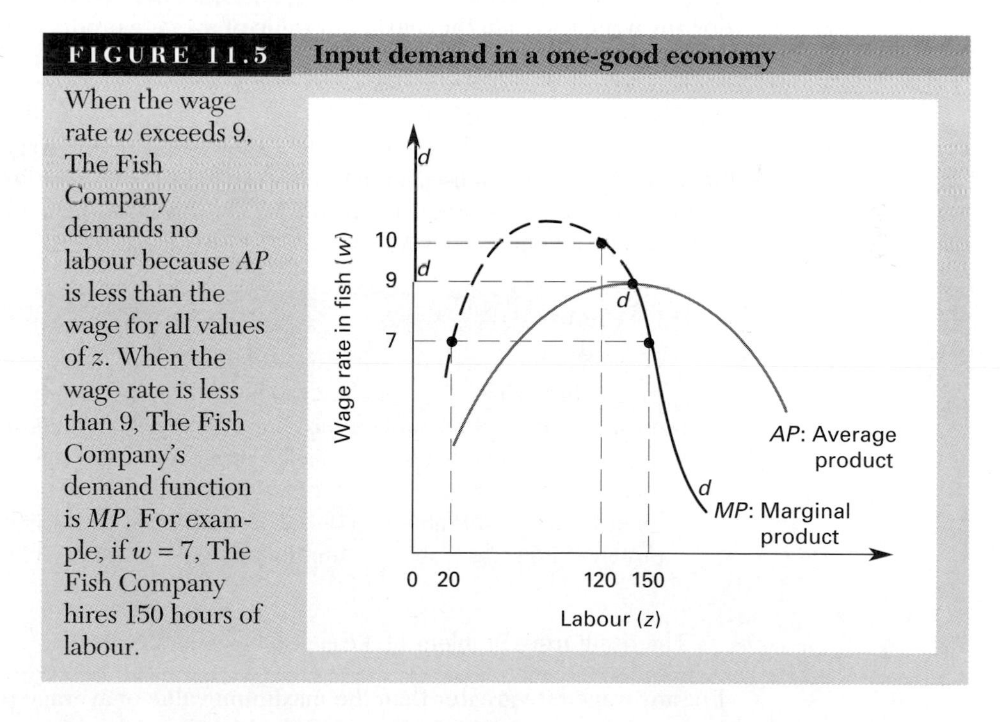

FIGURE 11.5 Input demand in a one-good economy

When the wage rate w exceeds 9, The Fish Company demands no labour because AP is less than the wage for all values of z. When the wage rate is less than 9, The Fish Company's demand function is MP. For example, if $w = 7$, The Fish Company hires 150 hours of labour.

---

1. For a historical perspective on the material covered in the next few sections, see the entry in *The New Palgrave* by Robert Dorfman on "Marginal Productivity Theory."

Marginal product is the number of fish attributable to an additional hour of labour, and the wage rate is the number of fish that The Fish Company must pay to hire an additional hour of labour. Therefore, when marginal product exceeds the wage rate, The Fish Company's profit increases as it hires more labour. When marginal product is less than the wage rate, its profit decreases as it hires more labour. It would seem that to maximize its profit, The Fish Company should hire labour up to the point at which marginal product is equal to the wage rate. In other words, the marginal product function appears to be the firm's demand curve.

With two qualifications, the marginal product function *is* the demand curve. To see why we need the first qualification, suppose that the wage rate is 7 fish in Figure 11.5 — a wage rate less than the maximum value of average product, which is 9 fish. Although marginal product equals 7 fish at both 20 hours of labour and 150 hours of labour, the point of maximum profit is — as you will discover in the following problem — at 150 hours of labour on the downward-sloping portion of the marginal product function.

PROBLEM 11.3

Assuming that the wage rate is 7 fish, show that profit is maximal at 150 hours of labour. To do so, imagine that the firm is currently hiring 150 hours of labour, and then show that profit falls both as the firm hires more labour, and as it hires less labour. Now show that profit is minimal at 20 hours of labour.

The result from Problem 11.3 can be generalized:

For any wage less than the maximum value of average product, the firm's demand function is the downward-sloping portion of its marginal product function.

This segment of the marginal product function is labelled *dd* in Figure 11.5.

To see why we need a second qualification, suppose the wage rate is 10 fish in Figure 11.5. As you will discover in the following problem, since 10 exceeds the maximum value of average product, which is 9, The Fish Company maximizes its profit by deciding not to hire any workers.

PROBLEM 11.4

Given that the wage rate is 10 fish in Figure 11.5, if the company actually were to hire labour, it would hire 120 hours. On the other hand, if it hired no labour, its profit would be zero, since no fish would be caught and no wages paid. Show that the company's profit is larger if it hires no labour than if it hires 120 hours — or equivalently, that its profit is negative if it hires 120 hours of labour. (*Hint*: The company's profit is just average product minus the wage rate multiplied by the number of hours.)

The result from Problem 11.4 can also be generalized:

For any wage rate greater than the maximum value of average product, the firm maximizes profit by hiring no labour.

Thus, for wage rates greater than 9 fish in Figure 11.5, the company's demand function is the vertical axis, also labelled *dd*. At any of these wage rates, the firm will shut down. The Fish Company's demand for labour in this one-good economy is thus composed of the two segments labelled *dd* in Figure 11.5.

Now let us generalize these results to any firm's demand for a variable input. The generalization is surprisingly simple. We need to introduce a money price for the variable input, denoted by w, and we need to transform the two measures of physical productivity, marginal and average product, into monetary units.

First let us transform marginal product MP into what is called marginal revenue product MRP. If a firm buys an additional unit of the variable input, its output will increase by approximately $MP(z)$. When the additional output is sold, the change in the firm's revenue is the additional output $MP(z)$ multiplied by marginal revenue in the firm's output market $MR(y)$. The product of marginal revenue and marginal product is called **marginal revenue product**, or $MRP(z)$:

marginal revenue product

$$MRP(z) = MR(y)MP(z)$$

If $MP(z)$ is 5 and $MR(y)$ is \$5, for example, then $MRP(z)$ is equal to \$25. $MRP(z)$ is the rate at which the firm's revenue changes as the quantity of the variable input, z, increases. Therefore, $MRP(z)$ tells us the monetary value to the firm of an additional unit of the variable input. (Even though y and z both appear on the right side of the equality sign, marginal revenue product is written as a function of z alone because the quantity of output, y, is itself determined by the quantity of input, z.)

average revenue product

Now let us transform average product AP into what is called **average revenue product** ARP. Average revenue product is the price of the firm's output, p, multiplied by the average product of the variable input, $AP(z)$.

$$ARP(z) = pAP(z)$$

In the following problem, you can derive $MRP(z)$ and $ARP(z)$ from $MP(z)$ and $AP(z)$ for a firm that is a perfect competitor in both its input and output markets.

PROBLEM 11.5

First draw the standard stylizations of $MP(z)$ and $AP(z)$ from Figure 11.5. The units on the vertical axis are measures of output. (If the output is fish, the unit might be tonnes of fish.) Now change the label on the vertical axis from units of output to units of money, or dollars. Suppose initially that p is \$1, and construct $MRP(z)$ and $ARP(z)$. Recall that for a perfect competitor in the output market, marginal revenue is equal to price. Next, suppose that p is \$2, and again construct $MRP(z)$ and $ARP(z)$.

The standard stylizations of $MRP(z)$ and $ARP(z)$ are illustrated in Figure 11.6. Generalizing what we learned from the encounter with The Fish Company, we see that the firm's demand function for z is composed of the two segments labelled *dd*.

We will look at each of the two segments of the input demand function in turn. First:

For input prices less than the maximum value of ARP, the firm's demand function is the downward-sloping portion of MRP.

FIGURE 11.6 The firm's demand for one variable input

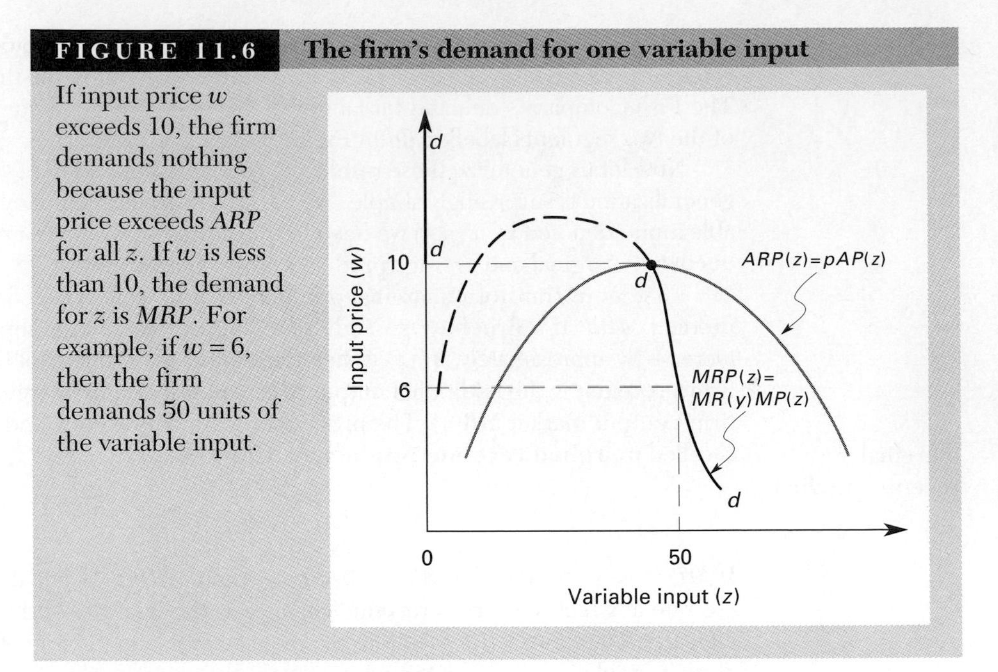

If input price w exceeds 10, the firm demands nothing because the input price exceeds *ARP* for all z. If w is less than 10, the demand for z is *MRP*. For example, if $w = 6$, then the firm demands 50 units of the variable input.

If the input price, w, is \$6, for example, the firm will demand 50 units of the variable input. Why? If the firm were to buy more than 50 units, its profit would fall because, when z exceeds 50 units, the rate at which its revenue increases as z increases *MRP*(z) — is less than the rate at which its cost increases as z increases — w. And if the firm were to buy fewer than 50 units, its profit would fall, because when z is less than 50 units, the rate at which its revenue decreases as z decreases — *MRP*(z) — is greater than the rate at which its cost decreases as z decreases — w. Since profit falls as the firm buys either more or less of the variable input, profit is at a maximum when the firm buys 50 units.[2] Second:

For input prices greater than the maximum value of *ARP*, the firm will demand none of the variable input.

---

2. When there is just one variable input, the firm's profit function is $\pi = yD(y) - wz - FC$, where FC is the firm's fixed cost and $D(\bullet)$ is the firm's price as a function of quantity produced. Of course, $y = TP(z)$. Using this fact, we can write the firm's profit as a function of z:

$$\pi(z) = TP(z)D[TP(z)] - wz - FC$$

If z^*, the profit-maximizing value of z, is positive, then $\pi'(z^*) \equiv 0$, or

$$MP(z^*)\{D[TP(z^*)] + TP(z^*)D'[TP(z^*)]\} \equiv w$$

since $MP(z) = TP'(z)$. The expression in braces is marginal revenue at the profit-maximizing level of output, since

$$p + yD'(y) = D[TP(z)] + TP(z)D'[TP(z)]$$

But $MP(z)MR(y)$ is just $MRP(z)$, and we see that $\pi'(z^*) \equiv 0$ implies that

$$MRP(z^*) \equiv w$$

Why not? The firm's revenue is equal to $zARP(z)$ and its short-run cost is wz. Its variable profit — its revenue minus its variable cost — is therefore just

$$\text{variable profit (rent)} = z[ARP(z) - w]$$

At input prices higher than \$10, w exceeds $ARP(z)$ for all values of z. This means that if the firm were to buy a positive amount of the variable input, its variable profit would be negative. By contrast, if it buys none of the variable input, its revenue, its variable cost, and its variable profit will all be zero. Therefore, when the wage rate exceeds \$10, it will buy none of the variable input — that is, it will shut down. The firm's demand curve is then composed of the two segments labelled *dd* in Figure 11.6.

It is useful to highlight one qualitative property of the firm's input demand function:

In response to an increase in the price of an input, a firm will not demand an increased quantity of the input. If the firm originally demanded a positive quantity of the input, the quantity demanded will decrease.

In short, we know that the firm's short-run demand function is downward sloping when only one input is variable: the lower the input price, the higher the quantity demanded of the input.

We have now looked at the firm's short-run profit-maximizing decision in two ways. In Chapters 9 and 10, we concentrated on the firm's choice in the output market. Here, we have fixed our attention on the firm's choice in the input market. In the following two problems, you can show that the two short-run profit-maximizing rules are equivalent.

PROBLEM 11.6

In Section 8.4, you saw that if the firm produces a positive output, then $SMC = MR$. You just learned that if the firm buys a positive amount of the variable input, then $w = MRP$. From Section 6.5 you know that $SMC = w/MP$. Using this relationship, show that the two profit-maximizing rules are equivalent.

PROBLEM 11.7

You know from Section 8.4 that a perfectly competitive firm will produce no output if the output price p is less than the minimum value of AVC. You have just learned that if the input price w exceeds the maximum value of ARP, the same is true. Can you show that these statements are equivalent?

Value of the Marginal Product

Now let us turn to the question of efficiency in input markets. The key question here is: What is the value to consumers of an additional unit of an input used by a firm? For example, what is the value to consumers who buy Roquefort cheese of an additional litre of sheep's milk used by some Roquefort cheese maker? Knowing that these consumers value the cheese, not sheep's milk, we can break this question into two parts: How much additional cheese can be made from 1 more litre of milk? How much do the consumers value that additional amount of cheese? The answer to the first question is, of course, $MP(z)$. If p is the price of Roquefort, the answer to the second question is just p times $MP(z)$. More generally, the **value of the marginal product** of the variable input $VMP(z)$ is output price multiplied by marginal product:

value of the marginal product

$$VMP(z) = pMP(z)$$

In the following problem you are asked to establish some important results, so give this problem special attention.

PROBLEM 11.8

First, show that if the firm is a perfect competitor in its output market, then $VMP = MRP$. Next, show that if the firm is a monopolist in its output market, then $VMP > MRP$. (*Hint*: If a firm is a perfect competitor in its output market, then p is equal to MR while, if it is a monopolist, MR is less than p.)

VMP can be interpreted as the value to consumers of an additional unit of the variable input in a given production process. *MRP* is, of course, the value to a firm of an additional unit of the variable input. From Problem 11.8, you know that if a firm is a perfect competitor in its output market, its valuation of an additional unit of the variable input is identical to consumers' valuation — that is, for such a firm, $VMP = MRP$. If the firm is a monopolist in its output market, however, its valuation of an additional unit is less than consumers' valuation. That is, for such a firm, $MRP < VMP$. As we will see in Section 11.7, these observations are the keys to understanding why monopoly in the output market is inefficient whereas perfect competition is efficient.

PROBLEM 11.9

In the fall of 1997 the Vancouver Canucks hockey team paid Mark Messier \$20 million to play for the team. Is it true or false to state that at this price Messier was overpaid?

11.6 Input Demand with Many Variable Inputs

In the preceding section, we derived the firm's input demand function when only one input was variable. What will a firm's input demand function look like when more than one input is variable — say, when two inputs are variable? We will denote quantity of input 1 by z_1 and quantity of input 2 by z_2 and their respective input prices by w_1 and w_2. We can interpret the results as either a short run in which only two of any number of inputs are variable or a long run in which there are only two inputs. For convenience, here we will call it the long-run case.

We learned earlier that the short-run input demand function is downward sloping: the lower the input price, the higher the quantity demanded. In this section, we will argue that the long-run demand function is also downward sloping, and we will compare these two input demand functions.

Downward-Sloping, Long-Run Input Demand Curve

substitution effect
output effect

Firms have more flexibility in responding to an input-price change in the long run than in the short run. The added flexibility is reflected in two kinds of decisions the firm makes in response to an input-price change: it can change its mix of inputs by substituting towards the relatively cheaper input, and it can alter its total output. Thus, we will decompose the firm's response to an input-price change into a **substitution effect** and an **output effect**. Then we will argue that *both* effects tend to produce a downward-sloping, long-run input demand curve.

First, let us fix the price of both inputs at, say, $w_1 = \$15$ and $w_2 = \$12$ and then identify the initial long-run equilibrium. When a firm is in long-run equilibrium, its output — say, $y = 100$ units — is, by definition, produced at minimum cost. This means that the point of long-run equilibrium in Figure 11.7 is at E, where the steeper isocost line is tangent to the 100-unit isoquant. At input prices $w_1 = \$15$ and $w_2 = \$12$, then, this firm demands 15 units of input 1 and 30 units of input 2. Now, how will its demand for input 1 change if its price drops from $w_1 = \$15$ to $w_1 = \$10$?

Let us begin with the substitution effect. If we imagine that the firm continues to produce 100 units of output after the price change, it would substitute towards the now-cheaper input 1, moving from point E to point E′ on the 100-unit isoquant in Figure 11.7. The quantity demanded of input 1 would therefore rise from 15 units to 22 units. In this case, the substitution effect produces an *inverse relationship* between the quantity demanded of an input and its price. As we saw in Section 7.6, this inverse

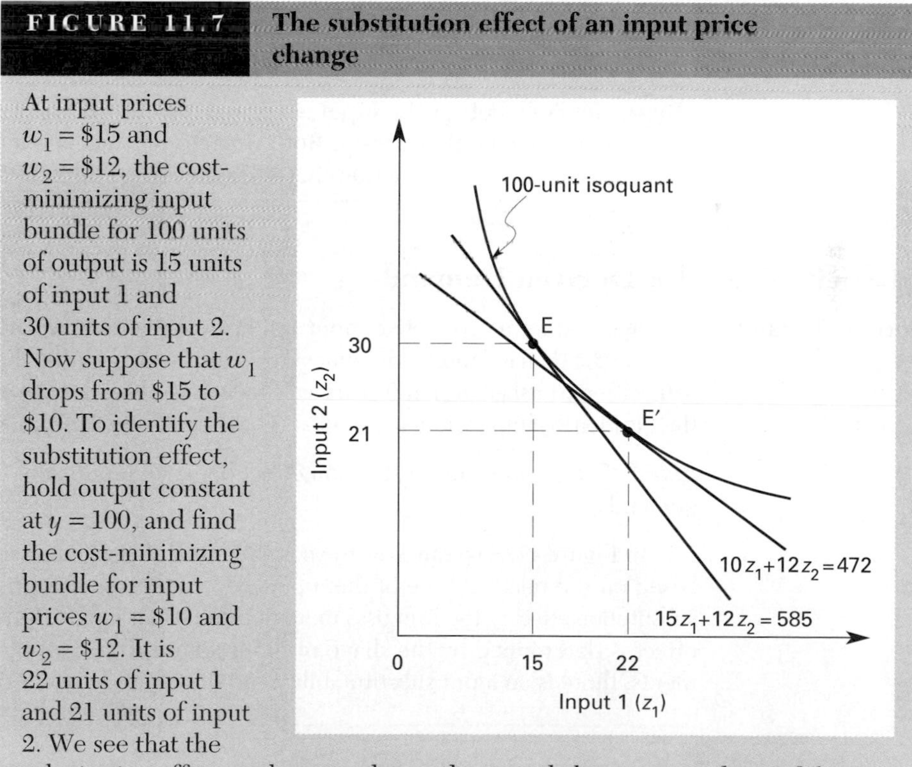

FIGURE 11.7 The substitution effect of an input price change

At input prices $w_1 = \$15$ and $w_2 = \$12$, the cost-minimizing input bundle for 100 units of output is 15 units of input 1 and 30 units of input 2. Now suppose that w_1 drops from \$15 to \$10. To identify the substitution effect, hold output constant at $y = 100$, and find the cost-minimizing bundle for input prices $w_1 = \$10$ and $w_2 = \$12$. It is 22 units of input 1 and 21 units of input 2. We see that the substitution effect works to produce a downward-sloping input demand function — as the price of an input decreases, the firm demands more of it.

relationship is generally true. The substitution effect therefore tends to produce a downward-sloping demand function.

Now let us turn to the output effect. When the input price changes, the firm alters its level of output because its total cost function is now different. We can easily see how the firm's cost function shifts. At the original input prices, the minimum cost of producing 100 units was $585 — ($15 × 15) + ($12 × 30). At the new input prices, it is only $472 — ($10 × 22) + ($12 × 21). The minimum cost of producing 100 units is less after the price decrease. By extension, the cost of producing any level of output has decreased and the firm's cost function has therefore shifted downward. Therefore its choice of output — and its demand for input 1 — will also change.[3]

Just how is the shift in the firm's cost function reflected in its choice of output? If input 1 is a normal rather than an inferior input, the input-price reduction means that not only the firm's total cost function but also its marginal cost function shift downward. As a result, the firm will produce more output. Because input 1 is a normal input, the firm will demand even more of input 1 as it produces more output. Therefore, the output effect reinforces the substitution effect in generating a downward-sloping demand function when input 1 is a normal input.

If input 1 is instead an inferior input, will the two effects still tend to produce a downward-sloping demand curve? The direction of the substitution effect is unchanged: the firm will substitute input 1 for input 2 as w_1 drops. Surprisingly, the direction of the output effect is also unchanged. A reduction in the price of an inferior input causes the marginal cost function to shift upward. As a result, the firm will produce less output and, because input 1 is an inferior input, it will demand more of that inferior input as its output decreases. Again, substitution and output effects complement each other in producing a downward-sloping demand function in the long run.

To summarize:

Regardless of whether the input is normal or inferior, the substitution and output effects are complementary. Both work to produce a long-run input demand function that is downward sloping.

Elasticity Rules for Derived Demand

derived demand

The demand for a productive input has historically been called a **derived demand** because the demand indirectly comes from the demand for the final product. Beginning with Alfred Marshall over 100 years ago, economists have known several rules regulating the elasticity of input demand curves. These rules are quite simple and intuitive.

Rule 1: The greater the substitution effect between inputs, the more elastic the input demand.

In Figure 11.7 we saw how the cost-minimizing firm chooses a given input bundle based on the relative price of the inputs. When the relative price changes, there is a substitution effect as the firm uses more of the cheaper input. The size of this substitution effect is determined by the shape of the isoquant. If the inputs are perfect complements, there is no input substitutability and the input demand will be very inelastic. If

3. In Chapter 8, we analyzed the firm's conditional input demand function, which gives the quantity of the input in the cost-minimizing input bundle when output y is held constant. Since output is held constant, the conditional input demand function captures only the substitution effect. The long-run input demand function that we are now considering captures the output effect as well as the substitution effect.

the inputs are perfect substitutes, then the input demand curve will be perfectly elastic.

Rule 2: The more elastic the demand for the final good, the more elastic the demand for the input.

Suppose there is an equilibrium in the final goods market, and the demand for the good is very elastic. If there is an increase in supply of the final good, this will lead to a large change in the quantity demanded of the good, and a relatively small change in the goods price. This large increase in the demand for the good will translate to a larger quantity demanded for the input used to produce it.

Rule 3: The more elastic the supply of other inputs, the more elastic the demand for the given input.

When the price of one input increases, this increase will be borne either by the buyers of the final good through higher prices or by other input suppliers through lower prices for those inputs. The more elastic are the supplies of other inputs, the less their price will fall for a given reduction in their use. This means there must be a larger fall in the quantity demanded of the input whose price initially increased.

Rule 4: Long-run input demands are more elastic than short-run input demands.

If we compare the steepness of the long-run and the short-run demand functions, we discover that the long-run function is flatter than its short-run counterparts. In other words, the quantity response to an input-price decrease (or increase) is larger in the long run than in the short run — the long-run demand curves are more elastic.

The long-run input demand function in Figure 11.8 is labelled *dd*; the representative short-run function is labelled *MRP*. (We can identify any number of possible

FIGURE 11.8 Comparing long-run and short-run input demand functions

dd is the long-run demand function for input 1, and *MRP* is a short-run input demand function. The two demand functions have one point in common, and *MRP* is steeper than *dd*.

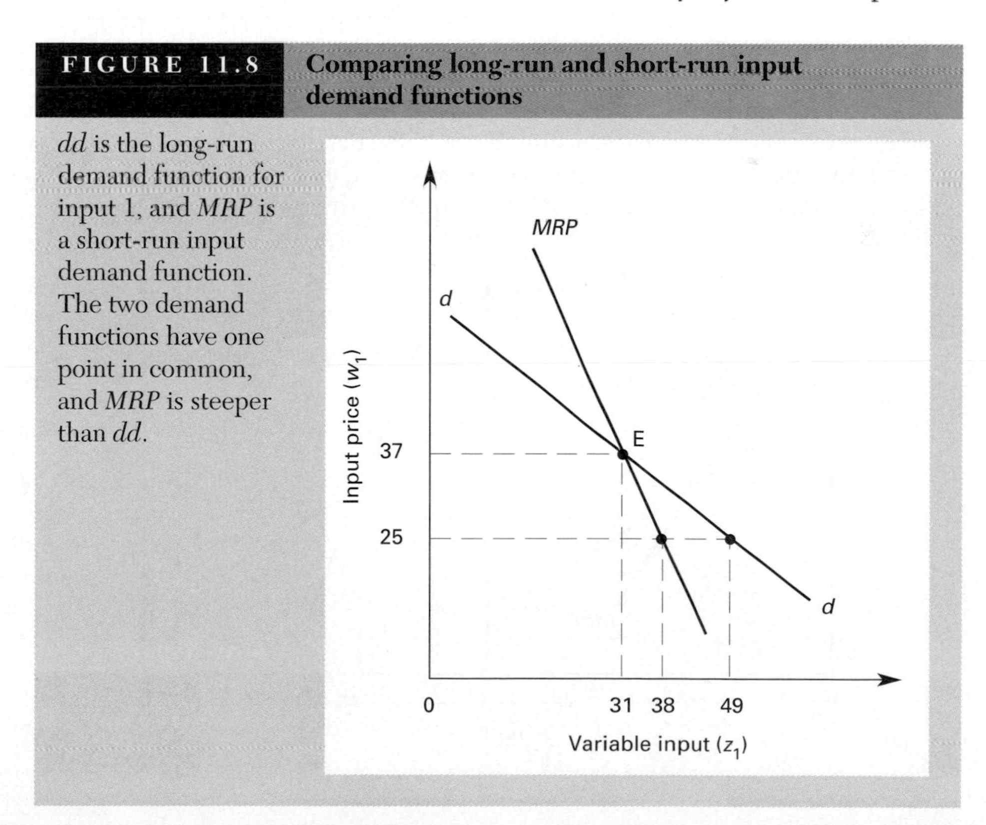

short-run demand functions, depending on the quantity of the fixed input 2.) The long-run input demand function and any short-run demand function will have one point in common because a firm in long-run equilibrium is also in a particular short-run equilibrium. Accordingly, *dd* and *MRP* intersect at point E in Figure 11.8. However, *dd* is flatter than *MRP*, indicating that the response to an input-price change is greater in the long run:

The response to an input price change in both the short and the long run is to demand more (less) of the input as its price falls (rises), and the response to any such price change is greater in the long run than in the short run.

11.7 Competitive Equilibrium in an Input Market

A long-run competitive equilibrium in an input market is presented in Figure 11.9. The market demand and market supply functions, *DD* and *SS*, are shown in Figure 11.9c. To get *DD* we have horizontally summed the demand functions of all firms that demand the input, and to get *SS* we have horizontally summed the supply functions of all suppliers. Recall that we used the same aggregation procedure — horizontal summation — to get the market supply and demand functions in Chapter 8. The competitive equilibrium is identified in the familiar way: at the equilibrium price w^e, quantity supplied equals quantity demanded.

The position of a firm that is a perfect competitor in both its output market and the input market is shown in Figure 11.9b. The position of a firm that is a monopolist in

FIGURE 11.9 Equilibrium in a competitive input market

From (c), we see that w^e is the equilibrium input price. In (b), we see that a firm that is perfectly competitive in its output market buys z_2^* of the input, where *VMP* and *MRP* are equal to the input price w^e. In (a), we see that a firm that is a monopolist in its output market buys z_1^* of the input, where *MRP* is equal to w^e and where *VMP* exceeds w^e.

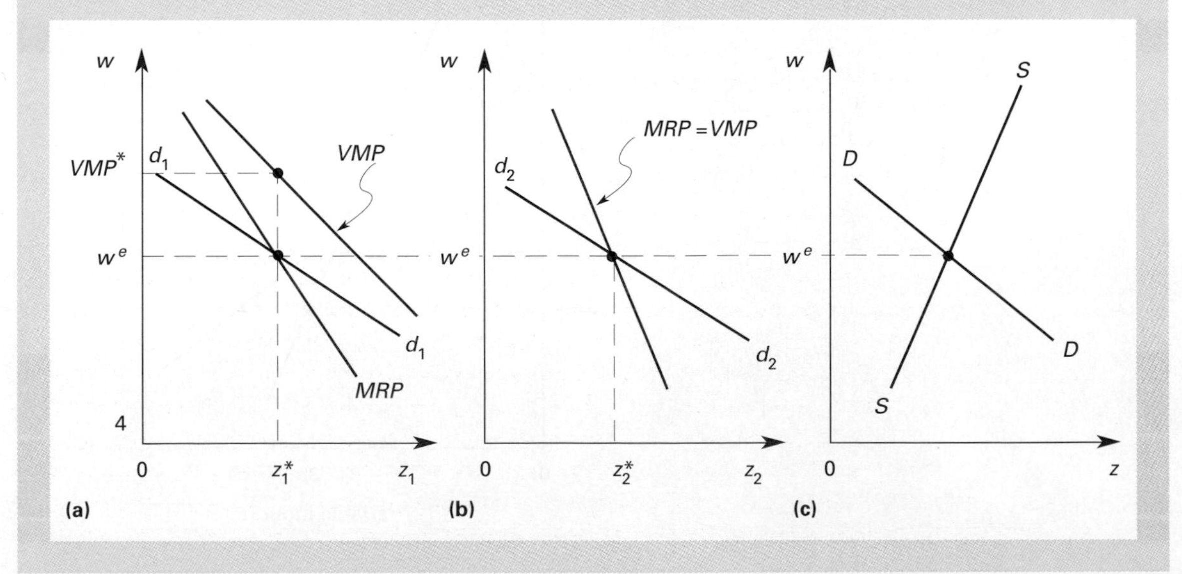

its output market and a perfect competitor in the input market is shown in Figure 11.9a. Recall that we can interpret *MRP* as the value of one more unit of the input to the firm itself. In contrast, *VMP* is the value of one more unit of input to consumers of the firm's product. We can use these interpretations in conjunction with Figure 11.9 to deepen our understanding of the inefficiency of monopoly and the efficiency of perfect competition.

Let us begin with the firm shown in Figure 11.9b. In long-run equilibrium, the firm is on both its long-run demand function d_2 and its short-run demand function *MRP*. Since the firm is a perfect competitor in its output market, *MRP* is coincident with *VMP*. Thus, beginning at the equilibrium position of the firm, we know that if the firm were to use one more unit of the input, the increase in its cost of production w^e would exceed the value it's consumers place on the added output *VMP*. In other words, if these consumers were allowed to make the firm's production decisions, they would decide against buying more than z_2^* units of the input since the additional output that an additional unit of the input would produce is not worth w^e to these consumers. This property reflects the efficiency of perfect competition.

Now consider the firm shown in Figure 11.9a. In equilibrium, the monopolist, like the competitive firm, is on both its long-run demand function d_1 and its short-run demand function *MRP*. But, because this firm is a monopolist in its output market, *MRP* is less than *VMP*. Therefore, *VMP* exceeds w^e at the monopolist's point of equilibrium. If this firm's customers were put in charge, they would opt for buying more of the input because at z_1^* their valuation of the output produced by an additional unit of the input, *VMP** in Figure 11.9a, exceeds the price of the additional unit of the input w^e.

Let us summarize these important results:

In long-run equilibrium, a firm that is a perfect competitor in both its output and its input markets will choose an input bundle such that, for each input,

$$w^e = MRP(z) = pMP(z) = VMP(z)$$

In long-run equilibrium, a firm that is a perfect competitor in its input markets, but a monopolist in its output market, will choose an input bundle such that, for each input,

$$w^e = MRP(z) = MR(y)MP(z) < pMP(z) = VMP(z)$$

Application: The Levitical Curse

In the year 2001, the wage rates of women were still lower on average than those of men occupying the same job. That is, if you took cross-sections of female employees in almost any occupation, from secretaries and clerks to sales workers and painters, you would find that they earned less (as much as 40 percent less) than the men in those jobs. This phenomenon has been observed throughout the ages. In fact, it is often called the Levitical curse, based on the following Biblical passage: "... thy valuation shall be for the male from 20 years old even to sixty years old, even thy valuation shall be fifty shekels of silver ... And if it be a female, then thy valuation shall be thirty shekels" (Lev. 27:1-4). Why would this difference in wages be so pervasive?

There is an ongoing debate in economics over what explains this difference in the pattern of wages. This debate is not settled yet, and we do not resolve it here. However, we will articulate the debate in terms of the competitive supply and demand model for inputs to see what light our model can shed on the issues.

In the competitive labour model, wages are determined by the intersection of the demand and supply for labour, where the demand curve reflects the value of the marginal product of labour, and the supply curve is determined by the tradeoff between work and leisure. Given that the interaction of supply and demand determines wages, there are only two potential general explanations for the wage differences. First, the supply of female labour could be larger for women, and men and women compete in separate labour markets. Second, the demand for female labour could be lower in labour markets where men and women compete together.

The first explanation simply does not fit the facts. Universally, men participate in the workforce at a higher rate than women. So the first explanation should be rejected. Hence, the only general explanation left is that the demand for female labour must be lower. But why would the demand for female labour be lower than for men? Here again, there are a number of explanations. First, there may be widespread discrimination on the part of firm owners (both male and female) to offer lower wages to female workers. Second, consumers may be willing to pay more for products made by men than by women. Finally, women may have lower marginal products than men.

The second explanation would appear to be rejected immediately. Consumers generally have no idea whether men or women were used as inputs in the production of a good, nor is it obvious why they should care. Hence it is unlikely that the lower wages for women are the result of a lower price of their output.[4] A more plausible explanation of the wage difference is widespread discrimination against female workers. However, there are a number of problems with this explanation. First, suppose that this were true, and that the degree of discrimination varied among firms. If there were few women in the labour market, women would work for the firms that discriminated least among them, and female wages would be close to those of men. As the number of women in the market increased, though, more women would be forced to work for firms that discriminated more at the margin, and the wage rate would tend to fall. This pattern, however, does not fit the experience of the last 40 years, which has seen large increases in female labour force participation and the move of female wages a little closer to male wages.

Many economists find a simple discrimination model like this implausible because a firm that indulges in a taste for workers that is not reflected in productivity pays more for labour than a firm that takes advantage of the lower wage rate for women. (See Arrow, 1972 and Becker, 1957.) If women were equally productive on average as men, an owner of a firm would be forgoing huge profits by not hiring them at lower wage rates. Employers tend to keep a close eye on the bottom line, because the discipline of a competitive market stands ready to punish firms with higher costs. Competition among firms forces the wage rate of women up when they are equally productive because employers are more concerned with the tastes of their customers than with their own preferences for workers. Hence, in a competitive model, simple discrimination seems unlikely. It should be mentioned that in models of incomplete information, or in markets where there is a monopsony employer, discrimination is a more viable explanation.

The final explanation for a lower demand for female labour is that women on average have lower marginal products than men. On the surface this seems as silly as some of the other explanations, unless one is talking about purely physical occupations.

---

4. Although an exception might be female sporting events. Viewers of sporting events have traditionally paid more to watch men golf, play tennis, basketball, soccer, etc. This difference in what people are willing to pay for the output is reflected in the prize money that female athletes collect. With the introduction of the WNBA and the popularity of women's tennis and golf, this is changing, and the corresponding difference in prize money is becoming smaller.

However, this argument usually revolves around the fact that women often take time out of the workforce to bear and raise children. This directly handicaps them against men since continuity in the job is a valuable attribute of an employee. In anticipation of being absent from the workforce, women may invest less in their own human capital, which further lowers their productivity. Finally, as an empirical matter, mothers are more likely to stay at home when children are sick, less likely to work late and travel away from home, and more likely to work part time. All of these factors lower the marginal productivity of women on average, and therefore lower the wages of all women — even though any given woman may not behave this way. In occupations where the effects of having children on one's human capital are less severe, the wages of men and women should be closer together.

To sum up, lower wages for woman can best be explained by a lower demand for their labour. This results from either widespread discrimination or widespread lower productivity.

PROBLEM 11.10

Some industries are dominated by women because they are more productive. For example, mushroom pickers tend to be women because their smaller hands don't bruise the mushrooms. Often men are able to compete with women in this market by working for lower wages. What would happen if mushroom workers formed a union and required all workers to be paid the same wage rate?

Application: Who Supports Immigration?

Very few topics in public policy generate as much heat as immigration. Our simple model helps explain why some general groups are in favour of more relaxed immigration policies, while others are opposed. The answer is not always that some groups are more racist or bigoted against foreigners, but rather that their incomes are directly affected.

Suppose an economy is made up of capitalists and labourers, and suppose that these two inputs are complements in production. That is, increases in the quantity of labour increases the marginal product of capital. Under such conditions, increases in the supply of labour will drive down the wage rate but increase the rental rate on capital. Not only is one group hurt by the immigration, but the other group benefits. Hence, labour groups tend to oppose more relaxed immigration laws, while capital owners tend to favour it. It is not a question of preferences, but rather a simple matter of income.

11.8 Monopsony in Input Markets

monopsony

Let us now begin to explore **monopsony** in an input market; that is, a market in which a monopsonist — like its logical cousin, the monopolist — is a price setter. That is, a monopsonist has significant control over the price it pays for an input. For example, the Harlem Globetrotters basketball team is a monopsonist in the market for show-biz basketball players. For basketball players who are entertainers rather than competitors, it is the only game in town. Any company owning a "company town" is likewise a monopsonist in the local labour market because it, too, is the only game in town. A sugar refinery in an isolated, relatively small agricultural region is a monopsonist in the local sugar beet market for precisely the same reason.

Let us look at two closely related questions. How will such a monopsonist choose input price and quantity? What are the sources of a monopsonist's input market power? To determine how a monopsonist will set price and quantity in an input (or "factor") market, we need three new concepts: the firm's total factor cost TFC, its marginal factor cost MFC, and its average factor cost AFC.

The Monopsonist's Factor Cost Functions

For a monopsonist, the relationship between input price w and quantity of the input z is determined by the market supply function for the input:

$$w = S(z)$$

If the monopsonist wants to buy z units of the input, the price w it must pay is determined by the supply function $S(z)$. It is natural to suppose that the supply function is upward sloping. In other words, we are assuming that the more the monopsonist wants to buy, the higher the price it must pay.

average factor cost

Keep in mind that the monopsonist buys all units at the same price. Price can then be interpreted as **average factor cost** AFC. Since all units are bought at the same price, the average amount any unit contributes to the firm's cost is the price at which it is bought. Then, for any quantity of the input z, the supply function $S(z)$ determines both price w and average factor cost AFC.

total factor cost

Total factor cost TFC is then just quantity z multiplied by average factor cost, or price $S(z)$.

$$TFC(z) = zS(z)$$

marginal factor cost

Of course, **marginal factor cost** MFC is the rate at which total factor cost TFC changes as the quantity of the input z changes. What is the relationship between input price w and marginal factor cost MFC for a monopsonist?

When the monopsonist buys a positive quantity of the input, marginal factor cost MFC exceeds price w or average factor cost AFC.

To understand this important result, recall that the monopsonist buys all units at the same price and faces an upward-sloping supply curve. Because the supply curve is upward sloping, to buy an additional unit, the monopsonist must raise the price it pays for the input. Therefore MFC is greater than the price at which the additional unit is bought by an amount equal to the quantity originally bought multiplied by the price increase. Suppose, for example, that the monopsonist in Figure 11.10 is initially at point A, where it is buying three units of an input at a price of \$70. To buy one additional unit — or four units of input in total — it must increase the price it pays per unit by \$10 from \$70 to \$80. The resulting change in total factor cost, which is approximately equal to marginal factor cost, is \$110 — $(4 \times \$80) - (3 \times \$70)$. This change is \$30 more than the \$80 price at which the fourth unit is bought. The \$30 difference between the \$80 price at which the fourth unit is bought and the marginal factor cost is equal to the original three units sold times the \$10 price increase. In Figure 11.10, the shaded area represents the cost of buying the fourth unit at \$80, and the hatched area represents the added cost of buying the original three units at \$80 instead of \$70 per unit.

For a more precise understanding of the relationship between marginal factor cost and input price or average factor cost, we will look at a more general experiment. Suppose initially that the monopsonist is on its supply curve, where it is buying z units at price w for a total factor cost equal to wz. Now suppose that it increases the input price

FIGURE 11.10 Marginal factor cost

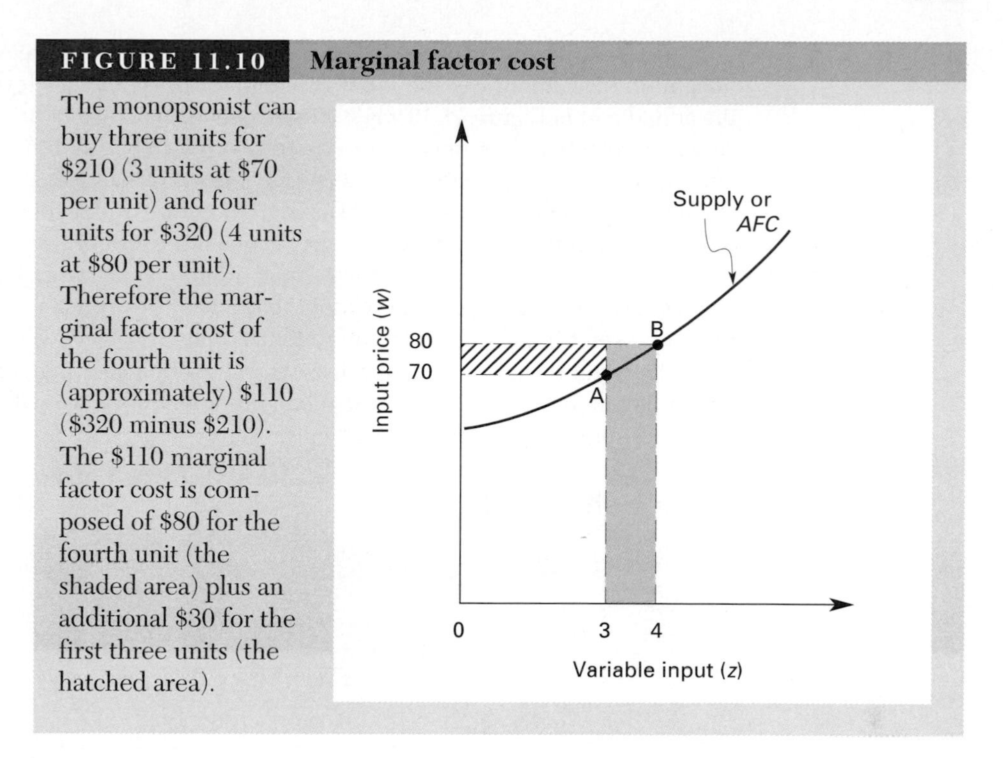

The monopsonist can buy three units for \$210 (3 units at \$70 per unit) and four units for \$320 (4 units at \$80 per unit). Therefore the marginal factor cost of the fourth unit is (approximately) \$110 (\$320 minus \$210). The \$110 marginal factor cost is composed of \$80 for the fourth unit (the shaded area) plus an additional \$30 for the first three units (the hatched area).

by amount Δw and that the quantity supplied increases by amount Δz. Total factor cost is then $(w + \Delta w)(z + \Delta z)$, and the resulting change in total factor cost is

$$w\Delta z + z\Delta w + \Delta w\Delta z = (w + \Delta w)(z + \Delta z) - wz$$

Now, we divide this expression by Δz to get the rate of change of total factor cost with respect to z:

$$w + z[\Delta w/\Delta z] + \Delta w$$

The term in brackets is approximately the slope of the demand curve at the initial point. As the price change Δw gets smaller and smaller, the approximation gets better and better. As Δw approaches zero, the approximation is perfect, and we then have the following result

$$MFC(z) = w + z \times [\text{slope of the supply curve}]$$

In other words, marginal factor cost MFC is equal to input price w plus quantity z multiplied by the slope of the supply curve.[5]

5. Total factor cost is

$$TFC(z) = zS(z)$$

Marginal factor cost is the derivative of $TFC(z)$. Hence,

$$MFC(z) = S(z) + zS'(z)$$

which can be written as

$$MFC(z) = w + zS'(z)$$

because $w = S(z)$. Since $S'(z) > 0$ for a monopsonist, it is clear that when $z > 0$, $MFC(z) > w$. In contrast, $MFC(z) = w$ for a competitor, since the supply curve for a perfect competitor is horizontal.

In this expression, w captures the rate at which revenue increases as an infinitesimal additional amount of the input is bought at price w. This term is analogous to the added cost in Figure 11.10 when a fourth unit is bought at a price of $80. The rate at which the input price must be increased in order to buy an infinitesimal additional amount is given by the slope of the supply curve. Of course, this slope is positive because the supply curve is upward sloping. Therefore, the second term — $z \times$ (slope of the supply curve) — captures the rate at which the cost of the original z units rises as price is increased to buy an infinitesimal additional amount. This second term is analogous to the increase in the cost of the original three units in Figure 11.10 when price is raised from $70 to $80 to buy a fourth unit.

This result is analogous to our discovery in Section 10.2 that a monopolist's marginal revenue function lies below its demand function. As we will see, the resulting efficiency implications are also analogous.

PROBLEM 11.11

Suppose that the supply function is

$$w = 1 + z$$

Show that

$$MFC(z) = 1 + 2z$$

(*Hint*: What is the slope of the supply function?)

We can generalize what you learned in Problem 11.11. If the supply function is linear,

$$w = a + bz \quad \text{where } a > 0 \text{ and } b > 0$$

then MFC is

$$MFC(z) = a + 2bz$$

Notice that the linear supply function and its MFC intersect the input price axis at the same point, and MFC is twice as steep as the supply function.

The Short-Run Monopsony Equilibrium

We can learn the essential features of monopsony equilibrium by concentrating on the monopsonist's short-run decisions. Figure 11.11 presents a monopsonist's supply function for an input, the associated MFC, and the firm's MRP. On the one hand, MRP is the value to the firm of buying an additional unit of the input because it is the rate at which the firm's revenue increases as z increases. On the other hand, MFC is the cost to the firm of each additional unit of the input because it is the rate at which its total factor cost TFC increases as z increases.

To maximize profit, the firm in Figure 11.11 will buy z^* units of the input. Why? As it moves to the right of z^*, buying more of the input, its profit decreases because MFC exceeds MRP. And as it moves to the left of z^*, buying less of the input, profit once again decreases because the rate of decrease of its costs MFC is less than the rate of decrease of its revenues MRP:

FIGURE 11.11 A monopsonist's profit-maximizing decision

A profit-maximizing monopsonist buys any input up to the point where *MFC* is equal to *MRP*. Thus, the monopsonist buys z^* units of the input at price w^*.

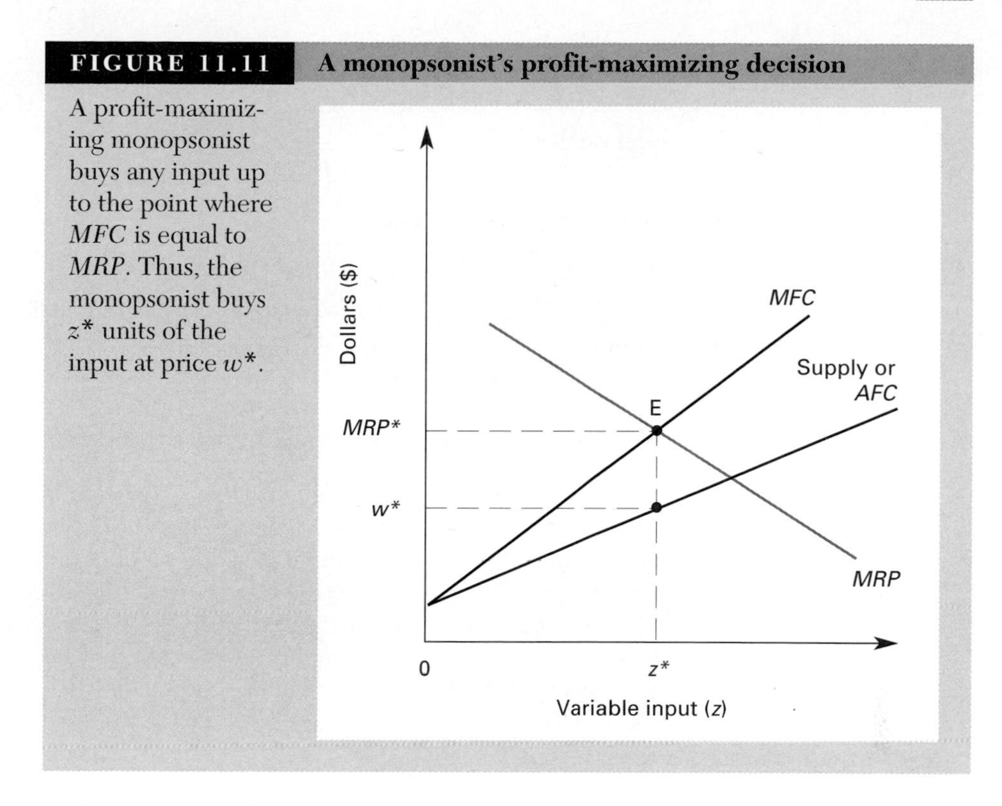

The monopsonist maximizes profit by choosing the quantity of an input where marginal factor cost is equal to marginal revenue product: $MFC(z^*) \equiv MRP(z^*)$.[6]

It is useful to describe mechanically the monopsonist's profit-maximizing rule: to find the profit-maximizing level of the input z^*, first identify the intersection of *MFC* and *MRP* — point E in Figure 11.11. Then move vertically down to the z axis to find the profit-maximizing quantity of the input — z^* in Figure 11.11. To find the associated equilibrium input price w^*, move vertically up from z^* to *AFC*, and then horizontally over to the vertical axis.

The following problems will help you check your understanding of monopsony.

6. When there is just one variable input, the monopsonist's profit function is

$$\pi(z) = TP(z)D[TP(z)] - zS(z) - FC$$

If z^* is the profit maximizing value of z and is positive, then $\pi'(z^*) \equiv 0$, or

$$MP(z^*)\{D[TP(z^*)] + TP(z^*)D'[TP(z^*)]\} \equiv S(z^*) + z^*S'(z^*).$$

We saw in footnote 2 that the left side of this expression is $MRP(z^*)$. The right side is, of course, $MFC(z^*)$. Hence, $\pi'(z^*) \equiv 0$ implies that

$$MRP(z^*) \equiv MFC(z^*)$$

PROBLEM 11.12

Suppose that

$$MRP(z) = 10 - z$$

and that the supply function is

$$w = 1 + z$$

Show that $z^* = 3$ and $w^* = 4$. Carefully construct a diagram illustrating this solution.

PROBLEM 11.13

Ten suppliers of coal are spread out along a railroad line at 50, 150, 250,..., 950 kilometres from the origin in Figure 11.12. The lone demander is located at the origin. Each supplier will supply 1 tonne if the price offered by the demander minus the transport costs incurred by the supplier is greater than or equal to $100. It costs $0.10 to transport 1 tonne of coal 1 kilometre. Derive the supply function faced by the demander. If the demander's *MRP* is $200 per tonne, show that it will buy 5 tonnes at $145 per tonne.

As we saw in Section 11.5, a firm that is competitive in its input markets buys an input up to the point where the input price is equal to *MRP*. Of course, for such a competitive firm, the exogenous input price is its marginal factor cost because it can buy all the labour it wants at the competitive wage rate. From this we get:

The general profit-maximizing rule in an input market is to buy an input up to the point where marginal factor cost is equal to marginal revenue product. For a perfect competitor in the input market,

$$MRP(z^*) = MFC(z^*) = w$$

For a monopsonist,

$$MRP(z^*) = MFC(z^*) > w$$

FIGURE 11.12 Monopsony in a spatial resource market

A railroad line runs from point 0 to 1000. A coal demander is located at point 0, and suppliers are located at the points 50, 150, ... , 950, denoted by Xs. As long as it is costly to transport coal, the demander has monopsony power. That is, it must offer a higher price to get more coal.

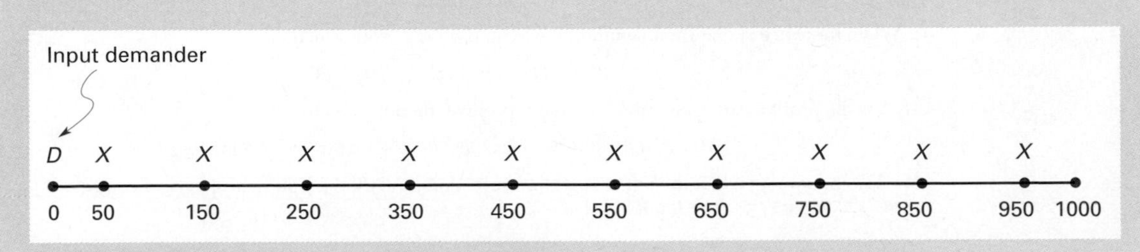

The Inefficiency of Monopsony

Now let us see why monopsony is inefficient. We can eliminate any market failure arising from the monopsonist's output market by assuming that the firm is a perfect competitor in its output market. In this case, $VMP(z)$, is equal to $MRP(z)$, and the value to consumers of the monopsonist's use of an additional unit of the input is identical to the monopsonist's value.

Suppose that the monopsonist in Figure 11.13 follows its maximizing rule by buying z^* at price w^* in a certain period. Now imagine that it "reopens" the market, as it considers buying more units of the input without increasing the price paid for the original z^* units. Can the monopsonist improve its position by buying more of the input? (Notice that this hypothetical experiment corresponds to the exercise used to demonstrate monopoly inefficiency in Section 10.4.) The answer is yes. If the firm buys one more unit at any price less than w'', its profit will increase. Furthermore, the supplier of the additional unit of labour will happily provide it at any price greater than w'. Because at any price less than w'' and greater than w' both the monopsonist and the input supplier are better off, and because no one else is worse off, the original equilibrium clearly was not Pareto-optimal or efficient. Furthermore, we can see from this exercise that in the original equilibrium, the monopsonist fails to extract the maximum possible profit.

The monopsonistic equilibrium identified by picking the point at which MFC intersects MRP is "uninventive" in very much the same way that the monopolistic equilibrium identified by picking the point at which $MR = MC$ is unimaginative. The inventive monopsonist, like the imaginative monopolist who resorts to price discrimination to reap more of its potential harvest of profit, will therefore search for some sort of discriminatory solution. You can discover the theory of the perfectly discriminating

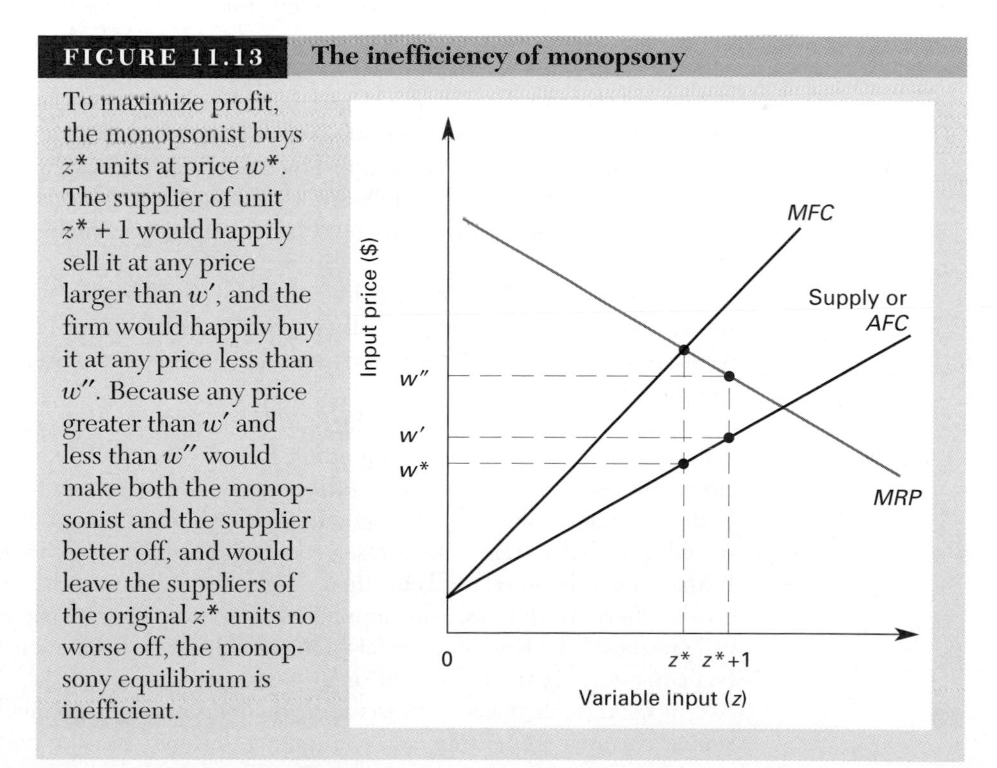

FIGURE 11.13 **The inefficiency of monopsony**

To maximize profit, the monopsonist buys z^* units at price w^*. The supplier of unit $z^* + 1$ would happily sell it at any price larger than w', and the firm would happily buy it at any price less than w''. Because any price greater than w' and less than w'' would make both the monopsonist and the supplier better off, and would leave the suppliers of the original z^* units no worse off, the monopsony equilibrium is inefficient.

monopsonist in the following problem. We will consider monopsonistic discrimination more carefully in Section 11.10.

PROBLEM 11.14

Suppose that the setup is exactly as it was in the previous problem: a demander of coal is at one end of a railroad line, and the suppliers are spread out along the line, as shown in Figure 11.12. But now suppose that the demander buys the coal from each supplier at the mine head and bears the transport cost itself. How much will it buy and how much will it pay for each tonne? (*Hint*: Think back to the perfectly discriminating book vendor in Problem 10.5.)

11.9 Sources of Monopsony Power

monopsony power

The telltale sign of **monopsony power** is an upward-sloping supply function to the individual firm. The extent of monopsony power is determined by the responsiveness of quantity supplied to changes in input price. Let us see what we can discover about one important source of monopsony power by considering the labour supply response to a salary reduction. Imagine that the West Edmonton Mall cuts its security officers' salaries and that the Royal Tyrrell Museum of Palaeontology (dinosaur museum) in Drumheller, Alberta cuts its paleontologists' salaries. How might the supply responses in these two cases differ?

reservation salary

Let us skip over each employee's labour/leisure choice by supposing that the job entails a fixed work week. The supply behaviour of every employee can then be described by his or her **reservation salary**, the lowest possible dollar figure at which the employee will continue to work for the firm. Of course, these reservation salaries will vary from employee to employee, because each places different valuations on such factors as personal relationships on the job, the company's location, and working hours. We can array these different reservation prices from lowest to highest and then use familiar techniques to construct the supply function of current employees shown in Figure 11.14. If the West Edmonton Mall (or the museum) is now paying its seven employees a salary of w'', we know that salary must be higher than the highest reservation salaries of its current employees.

What happens if the West Edmonton Mall (or the museum) decides to cut its security officers' (paleontologists') salary to, say, w', as in Figure 11.14? Every employee whose reservation salary is above the new salary — three employees in this example — will then quit.

What determines exactly how high (or low) any individual's reservation salary will actually be? Perhaps the most important factor is the availability and the salaries of alternative jobs. Because security officers at the West Edmonton Mall are likely to find comparable jobs in the immediate area without too much trouble, we can reasonably expect that most of their reservation salaries will be close to the initial salary w''. If the West Edmonton Mall cuts their salaries by very much, the security officers will go elsewhere. In this case, the supply response to a relatively small salary reduction will presumably be large, and we might think of the West Edmonton Mall as a near-perfect competitor in the market for security officers.

By contrast, the paleontologists at the dinosaur museum are much less likely to find similar research jobs within easy commuting distance. For the paleontologists, a job

FIGURE 11.14 Monopsony and reservation supply prices

Given employees' reservation supply prices, we have constructed the labour supply function by arraying reservation prices from lowest to highest and then aggregating in the familiar way. A firm has some monopsony power with respect to its current employees if, in response to a wage reduction, they do not all quit.

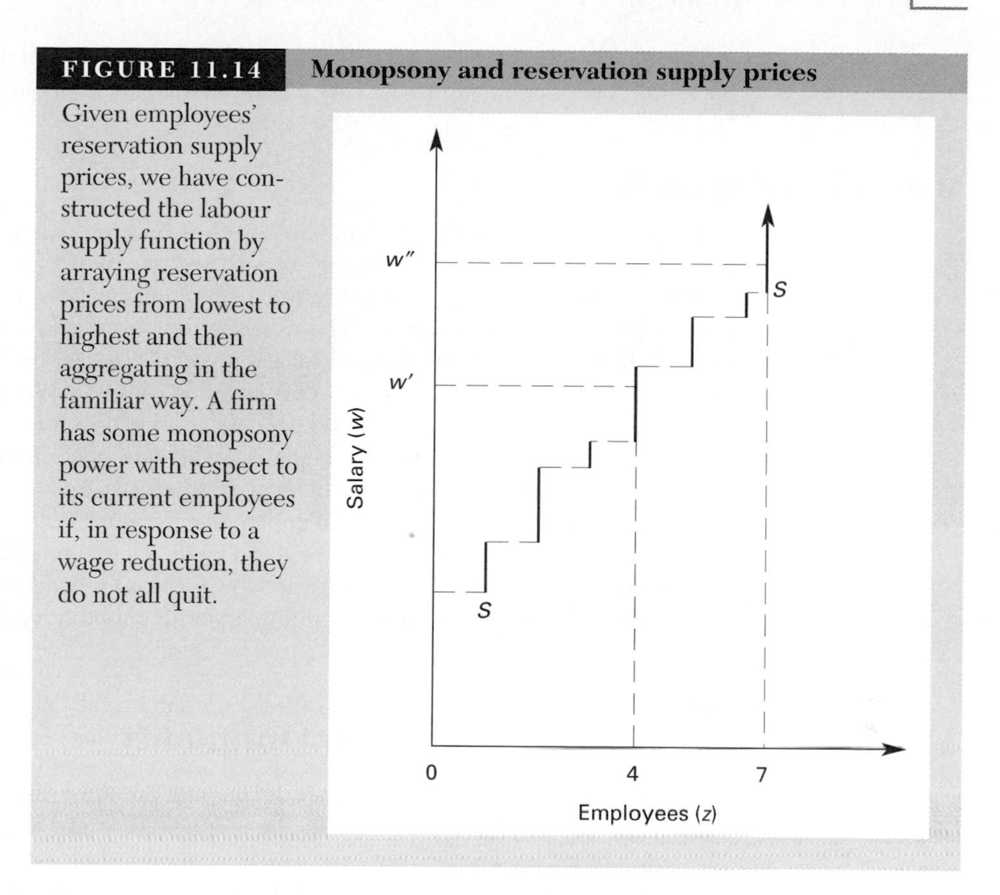

change will probably entail moving and all the attendant social and economic disruption. Even if they are willing to look for non-scientific jobs in the immediate area, a career change is likely to bring a significant salary cut. Thus, the supply response to a significant cut in the paleontologists' salaries will presumably be relatively small. In other words, the museum differs from the West Edmonton Mall in having some significant *monopsony power* with respect to its employees.

Immobility

The general lesson that emerges from this labour-supply discussion and from the earlier coal-supply problems is that immobility of inputs can be an important source of monopsony power. The difficulty for paleontologists is that they are not perfectly mobile: changing jobs is likely to be costly. Therefore, the museum's monopsony power arises from its employees' immobility. The difficulty for the coal suppliers is that coal is not perfectly mobile: transporting coal from the mine to the place where it is needed is expensive. The farther it must be shipped and the higher are the per-mile costs of transporting coal, the more expensive it will be. Therefore coal demanders' monopsony power springs from the immobility of coal.

In both cases, the resource immobility is primarily due to locational considerations. If all the economic activity in the world were concentrated at a single point — which we might call the economist's black hole — this type of monopsony power could not arise. Because economic activity does not take place at a single point, however, monopsony power is an important feature of the input market landscape. Locational issues are therefore at least as important in input markets as in output markets.

Monopoly and Specialized Inputs

For more than 40 years, the Harlem Globetrotters have provided a unique brand of entertainment for children of all ages. As we saw in Section 11.8, the Globetrotters illustrate another (but less central) source of monopsony power: the demand by a monopolist for a specialized input. This organization — a virtual monopolist in show-business basketball — demands a specialized input: the "showboat" basketball player. Organizations like the National Basketball Association (NBA) clubs also demand the services of skilled basketball players, but they look for quite different skills. Because only the Globetrotters' organization wants players who specialize in entertainment, the club is a monopsonist in the market for show-business players.

So, too, Dow Chemical is a virtual monopolist in primary magnesium production in the United States. It demands the specialized input magnesium chloride — a salt with no other important chemical use. Because Dow is the only significant demander, it is also a virtual monopsonist in the magnesium chloride input market.

11.10 Monopoly, Monopsony, and Pareto Optimality

This chapter has focused on one of the fundamental problems in economics: the allocation of resources. The results from the first nine sections are summarized in Figure 11.15, where four types of firms are characterized according to their status as either monopolists or perfect competitors in their output markets, and as either monopsonists or perfect competitors in an input market. We learned that in long-run equilibrium, any profit-maximizing firm uses an input up to the point where *MRP* equals *MFC*. Thus, *MRP* equals *MFC* in each cell of Figure 11.15.

From the perspective of resource allocation, the important differences among firms stem from the following relationships. When a firm is a monopolist in its output market, *VMP* (value of the marginal product) exceeds *MRP* because a monopolist's price is greater than its marginal revenue. When a firm is a perfect competitor in its output market, *VMP* equals *MRP* because the firm's marginal revenue equals its output price. When a firm is a monopsonist in an input market, *MFC* (marginal factor cost) exceeds w^e (the equilibrium wage rate). When a firm is a perfect competitor in an input market, *MFC* equals w^e. These differences arise because perfect competitors are price takers and monopolists and monopsonists are price setters.

The value that consumers place on an additional unit of any input used by a firm is *VMP*. To find out whether too little of an input is allocated to any firm in equilibrium, we can simply ask if *VMP* exceeds w^e. If so, then too little of the input is allocated to the firm. In Figure 11.15, *VMP* does exceed w^e in three of the four types of firms: II, III, and IV. In cell II, $w^e < MFC$ because this type of firm has monopsony power; in cell III, $MRP < VMP$ because this type of firm has monopoly power; and in cell IV, $w^e < MFC$ and $MRP < VMP$ because this type of firm has both monopoly and monopsony power. Only the type of firm in cell I — the case of the perfect competitor in both markets, where $w^e = VMP$ — is consistent with Pareto optimality.

FIGURE 11.15 **Resource allocation summarized**

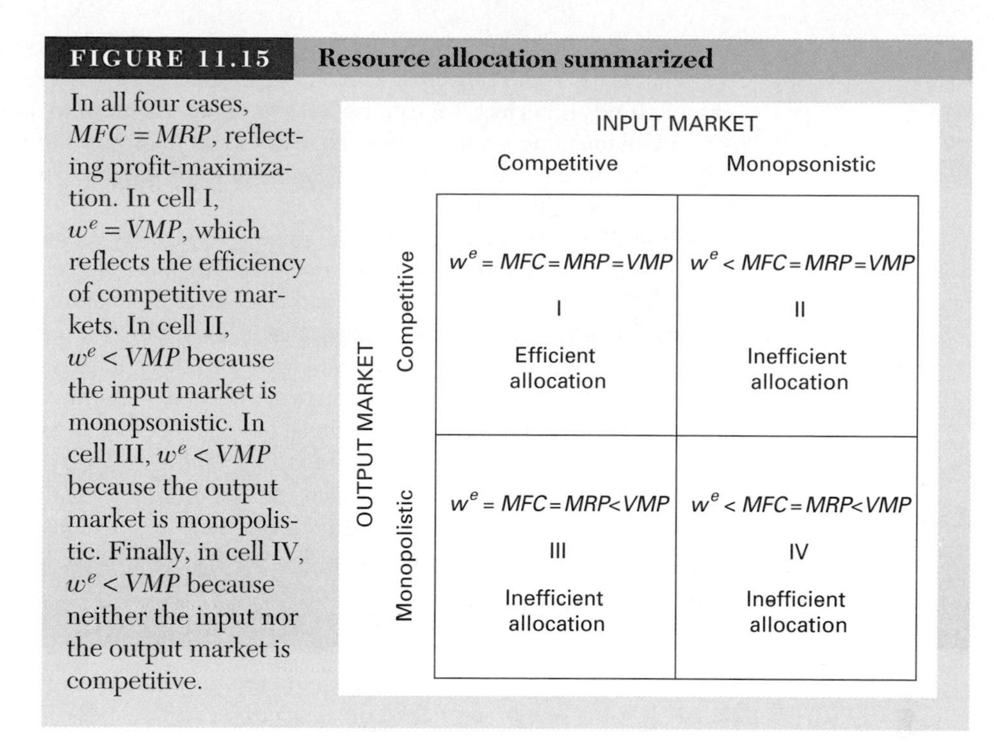

In all four cases, $MFC = MRP$, reflecting profit-maximization. In cell I, $w^e = VMP$, which reflects the efficiency of competitive markets. In cell II, $w^e < VMP$ because the input market is monopsonistic. In cell III, $w^e < VMP$ because the output market is monopolistic. Finally, in cell IV, $w^e < VMP$ because neither the input nor the output market is competitive.

11.11
The Firm's Demand for Capital Inputs

In our discussion of a firm's demand for inputs, we have focused on inputs that were rented or hired on a period-by-period basis. Clearly, firms not only rent and hire inputs, but they also buy inputs that provide productive services over many periods. A railroad, for example, *buys* a variety of different goods that serve as inputs over many periods — locomotives, box cars, signalling equipment, rails, and real estate, to name just a few — and it *hires* other inputs — principally labour. Goods that serve as inputs over many periods are called capital inputs. Here, we extend the analysis of input demand to capital inputs.

Recall that the firm's input demand function for a hired input was, with some qualifications, its marginal revenue product *MRP* function. As you know, *MRP* measures the contribution of an additional unit of the input to the firm's revenue, and input price w measures the contribution of an additional unit of the input to the firm's cost. Accordingly, hiring one more unit of the input results in an increase in the firm's profit when *MRP* exceeds w, and a decrease in the firm's profit when w exceeds *MRP*. Therefore, to maximize profit the firm hires an input up to the point where *MRP* is equal to w. Now we want to find the firm's demand function for capital inputs.

Given a particular capital input, say a truck of some description, the question we want to answer is this: How many trucks will the firm want to have? To answer this question, we need to know what the firm's objective is. In previous chapters, where the firm made decisions for just one period, we took the firm's objective to be profit maximization. We argued that the firm's owners would unanimously agree on this goal because the firm's profit is, in effect, purchasing power for the owners of the firm: by maximizing profit, the firm maximizes the purchasing power of its owners.

What is the firm's objective when there are many periods? When the market for loanable funds is perfect, we can use the separation theorem to argue that the firm's owners will unanimously agree that the firm should maximize the *present value* of the firm's profit: by maximizing the present value of its profit, the firm maximizes the purchasing power of its owners.

We will begin the analysis with a very simple, imaginary capital input, which we call a gadget. Imagine that the purchase price of a gadget is P dollars, the gadget lasts for exactly D years, it has no scrap value, and it requires no maintenance.

Since it lasts for D periods, a gadget that is bought in the current period — period zero — will contribute to the firm's revenue for exactly D periods — period 0, period 1, ..., period $D - 1$. Its contribution to the firm's revenue in period 0 will be MRP_0 — the marginal revenue product of an additional gadget in period 0. Similarly, its contribution to the firm's revenue in period t will be MRP_t, where t is in the range 0 to $D - 1$. If we compute the present value of each of these MRPs and sum them, we have the present value of the gadget's contribution to the firm's revenue. This sum of present values of marginal revenue products is denoted by $\sum MRP$.

$$\sum MRP = MRP_0 + [MRP_1/(1 + i)] + \ldots + [MRP_{D-1}/(1 + i)^{D-1}]$$

The contribution of an additional gadget to the present value of the firm's costs is, of course, just the purchase price of the gadget, P.

Notice that if $\sum MRP$ exceeds P, an additional gadget results in an increase in the present value of the firm's profit. On the other hand, if $\sum MRP$ is less than P, an additional gadget results in a decrease in the present value of the firm's profit. To maximize the present value of its profit, the firm should therefore have enough gadgets so that $\sum MRP$ is equal to P. We see, then, that $\sum MRP$ is the firm's *demand function* for gadgets.

In Figure 11.16 we have drawn the firm's demand function for gadgets for three different rates of interest — 5 percent, 10 percent, and 15 percent. In constructing Figure 11.16, we have assumed a diminishing marginal product for gadgets in all periods; the three $SMRP$ functions therefore are everywhere downward sloping.

Notice that the demand function in Figure 11.16 shifts downward as the interest rate increases. Why? Because, for every period except period 0, the present value of MRP decreases as the interest rate increases. In other words, as the interest rate increases, the contribution of an additional gadget to the present value of the firm's revenue decreases, and the demand function therefore shifts downward. Holding the price of a gadget fixed at $1000, we see from Figure 11.16 that the firm demands 98 gadgets when the interest rate is 5 percent, 71 gadgets when the interest rate is 10 percent, and only 50 gadgets when the interest rate is 15 percent.

We have used the information from Figure 11.16a to construct this inverse relation between quantity of gadgets demanded and the interest rate in Figure 11.16b.

PROBLEM 11.15

Consider a slightly more complex capital input, a widget. The purchase price of a widget is P, a widget lasts for D periods, it has no scrap value, and it requires expenditure on maintenance equal to M at the beginning of each period, excluding period 0. Show that, to maximize its profit, the firm will buy widgets up to the point where

$$\sum MRP = P + [M/(1 + i)] + [M/(1 + i)^2] + \ldots + [M/(1 + i)^{D-1}]$$

FIGURE 11.16 **The demand for a capital input**

To maximize profit, the firm buys gadgets up to the point where ΣMRP is equal to the price of a gadget. As the interest rate i increases, ΣMRP shifts to the left as shown in (a), reducing the firm's demand for gadgets. In (b), we have held the price of gadgets constant at \$1000 and constructed the firm's demand for gadgets as a function of the rate of interest i. Observe that the demand for gadgets is inversely related to the rate of interest.

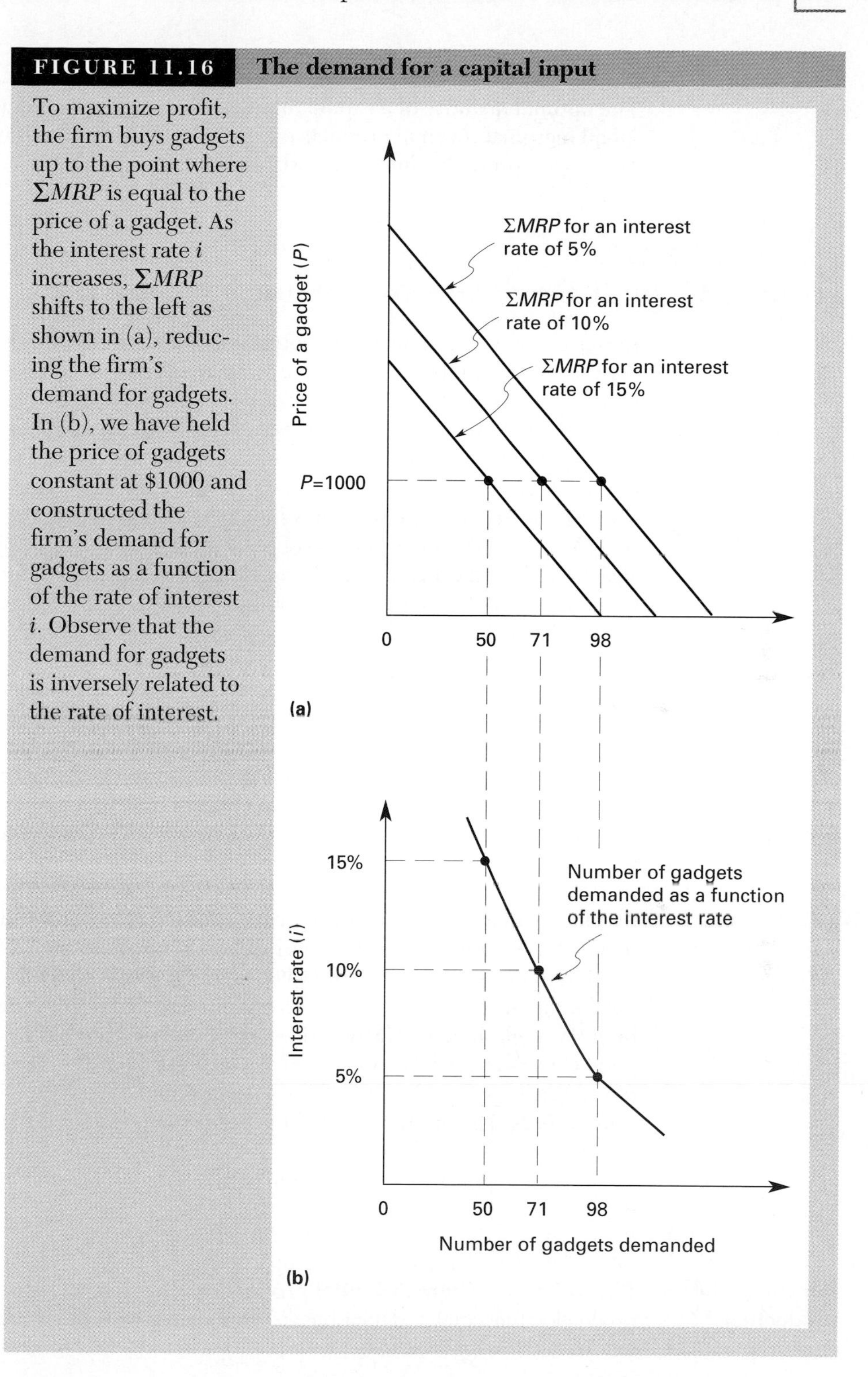

Let us generalize what you learned in this problem:

The optimal quantity of a capital input is the quantity such that the present value of all marginal revenue products over the life of the capital input is equal to the present value of all costs associated with the capital input.

11.12 Human Capital Decisions over Time

In this chapter, and in analyzing intertemporal consumption decisions way back in Chapter 5 we took life-cycle income streams as given. With income in both periods fixed, the only decision was how to allocate fixed lifetime income to consumption in the two periods. Notice, however, that our decisions with respect to schooling and other forms of training allow us to exercise considerable control over our personal life-cycle income stream. When a student chooses to get a bachelor's degree in electrical engineering, for example, the student is simultaneously giving up the *current income* that could be earned by working instead of going to school and enhancing *future income*. Our analysis of the individual's life cycle is seriously incomplete because it ignores the training choices that determine the individual's life-cycle income stream.[7]

In this section, we will use the separation theorem to analyze the training decision of an imaginary person named Harriet, and then we will combine the results of this analysis with results from the life-cycle model for a more complete picture of an individual's economic life cycle.

human capital

Economists call Harriet's investment in training **human capital**, and they measure her investment in human capital by adding up her direct expenditures on training and the income that she gives up by spending time in training as opposed to working, called **forgone income**. Direct expenditures include amounts spent on tuition, books, and lab fees, for example. In most training programs, however, forgone income is the most important component of investment in human capital. Adding the direct costs and the forgone income of training gives us a measure of Harriet's human capital. We will denote this investment, or Harriet's quantity of human capital, by H.

forgone income

Harriet's return on human capital is, of course, additional income that she will earn in the future. We will denote this additional income, or return to human capital, by R. We will think of Harriet's human capital decision in the context of our two-period life-cycle model — she will make the investment H in period 0, and she will get the return R in period 1. Naturally, we will assume that R increases as H increases. The larger is Harriet's investment H in period 0, the larger is the return R she enjoys in period 1.

We will represent the relationship between R and H by the function $F(H)$. That is,

$$R = F(H)$$

human capital production function

$F(H)$ is called the **human capital production function**. We will assume that Harriet's production function has diminishing returns: successive equal increments in human capital, H, add less and less to her return, R. This production function is shown in Figure

7. There has been a great deal of work on human capital in the last thirty years, inspired by the pioneering work of Becker (1964), Mincer (1958), and Schultz (1961). For an overview of this vast body of work, see S. Rosen's entry "Human Capital" in *The New Palgrave*.

marginal product of human capital

11.17. The slope of the production function at any point is, of course, the **marginal product of human capital** *MP*. At point D in Figure 11.17, *MP* is the slope of the tangent line *TT*. *MP* tells us the rate at which Harriet's income in period 1 increases as she invests more in human capital in period 0.

We can use the separation theorem to solve Harriet's investment problem. The separation theorem tells us that Harriet will choose quantity of human capital to maximize the present value of income available for consumption, or what we will call her net income. To begin, suppose that Harriet has invested \$400 000 in human capital — $H = \$400\ 000$ — and then ask: What happens to the present value of Harriet's net income when she invests one additional dollar in human capital? Her net income for period 0 decreases by \$1 because the additional dollar that she invests in human capital is no longer available for consumption. And her net income for period 1 increases by (approximately) $\$MP(H = 400\ 000)$ — equal to the slope of tangent line *TT* in Figure 11.17. But the present value of this increase is just $\$MP(H = 400\ 000)/(1 + i)$, because she does not get the added income until the next period. So, the change in the present value of Harriet's net income stream is

$$\$MP(H = 400\ 000)/(1 + i) - \$1$$

The present value of Harriet's net income increases as she invests one more dollar if this expression is positive, or if

FIGURE 11.17 **Investing in human capital**

The human capital production function *F(H)* gives Harriet's dollar return *R* in period 1 for every level of investment in human capital *H* in period 0. The separation theorem dictates that Harriet should invest in human capital up to the point where the marginal product of human capital is equal to $(1 + i)$. The optimal investment is H^*, which generates return R^*.

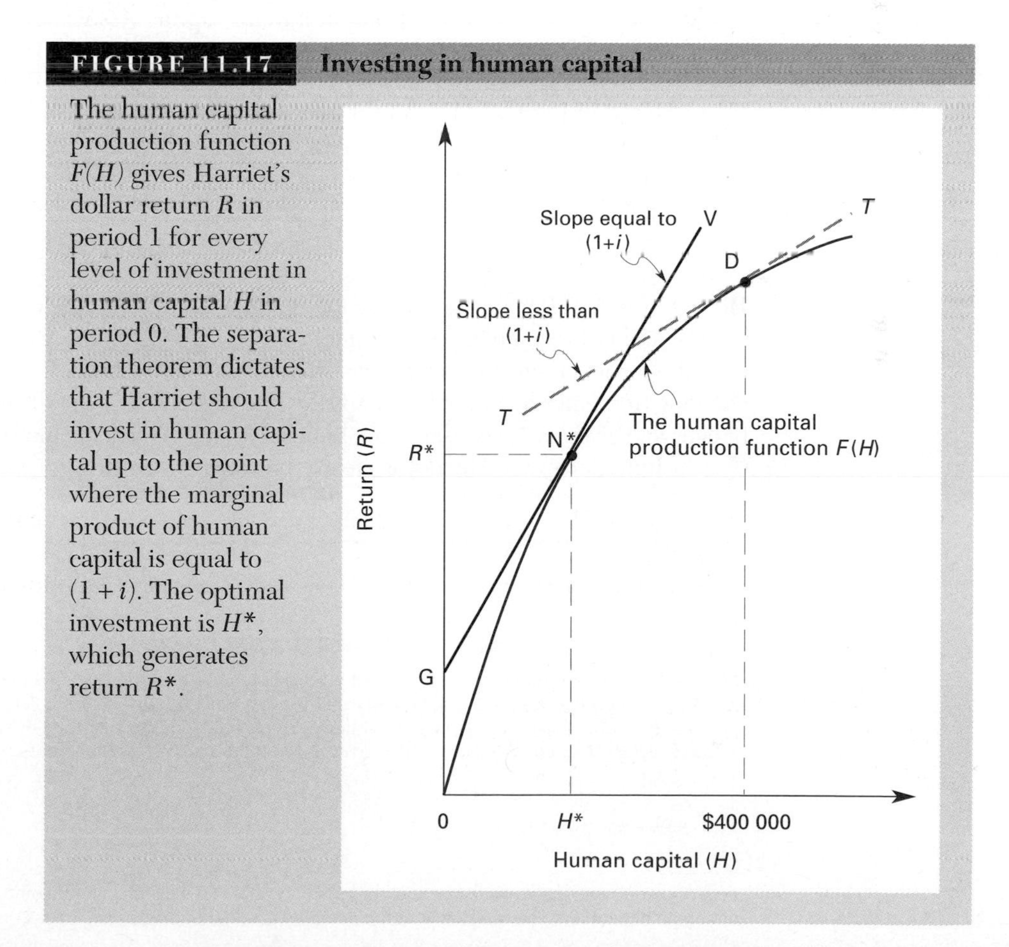

$$MP(H = 400\ 000) > (1 + i)$$

From Figure 11.17 we see that this inequality is not satisfied when H = \$400 000 since the slope of tangent line TT is less than $(1 + i)$, so Harriet definitely should not invest another dollar in human capital.

More generally, we see that Harriet should invest an additional dollar in human capital if MP exceeds $(1 + i)$ and that she should invest one less dollar in human capital if MP is less than $(1 + i)$.[8] That is:

To maximize the present value of net income, invest in human capital up to the point where *MP* is equal to (1 + *i*).

In Figure 11.17, the optimal investment is H^*, since the line GN*V, whose slope is $(1 + i)$, is tangent to the human capital production function at point N*. At point N* Harriet gives up H^* in income in period 0 in return for an increase in income in period 1 equal to R^*. For any point to the left of N* on the human capital production function, the present value of Harriet's net income increases as she invests more in human capital because MP exceeds $(1 + i)$ to the left of N*. Conversely, for any point to the right of N* on the production function, the present value of Harriet's net income decreases as she invests more in human capital because MP is less than $(1 + i)$.

Now let us integrate our understanding of the choice about human capital into the life-cycle model. Point 0′ in Figure 11.18 represents the income stream Harriet would enjoy if she invested nothing in human capital. Associated with this income stream is the budget line of slope $-(1 + i)$ that passes through 0′. This budget line gives us the consumption bundles (C_0,C_1) that Harriet could buy if she invested nothing in human capital. Using point 0′ as an origin, we have plotted Harriet's human capital production function, the line 0′SN*G. Notice that H increases as we move leftward from 0′. The line 0′SN*G traces out the net income streams available to Harriet. We use the adjective *net* because points on 0′SN*G give us Harriet's income stream minus (or net of) her investment in human capital. It is her net income stream that matters here because it is only net income that she can devote to consumption. If Harriet invests $0'H'$ in human capital, for example, her net income in period 0 decreases by $0'H'$ and her income in period 1 increases by H'S. Given this investment in human capital, Harriet attains the net income stream S in Figure 11.18. The budget line associated with the net income stream S is the line of slope $-(1 + i)$ through point S. This budget line gives us the consumption bundles (C_0,C_1) Harriet could buy if she invested $0'H'$ in human capital. Harriet is clearly better off with this investment than she is

---

8. We can derive this result using calculus. The present value of income associated with the investment in human capital, or what we have called net income, is

$$\text{net income} = F(H)/(1 + i) - H$$

$F(H)$ is the return on human capital. Since it is received in period 1, however, its present value is $F(H)/(1 + i)$. H is the investment in human capital, and it must be subtracted to get net income. The problem is then to maximize net income by choice of H. This requires that the derivative of net income with respect to H be equal to zero, which gives us the following first-order condition.

$$F'(H)/(1 + i) - 1 = 0.$$

This can be rewritten as

$$F'(H) = (1 + i)$$

$F'(H)$ is, of course, the marginal product of human capital. To maximize net income, the rule is to invest in human capital up to the point where the marginal product of human capital is equal to $(1 + i)$.

FIGURE 11.18 **Another perspective on the human capital investment**

The human capital production function in this figure specifies the income bundles that Harriet can achieve, and the separation theorem dictates that Harriet chooses the income bundle that generates the budget line farthest from the origin. The optimal income bundle is N*, where the human capital production function is tangent to the budget line for N*. At N* the marginal product of human capital is equal to $(1 + i)$ — the absolute value of the slope of the budget line.

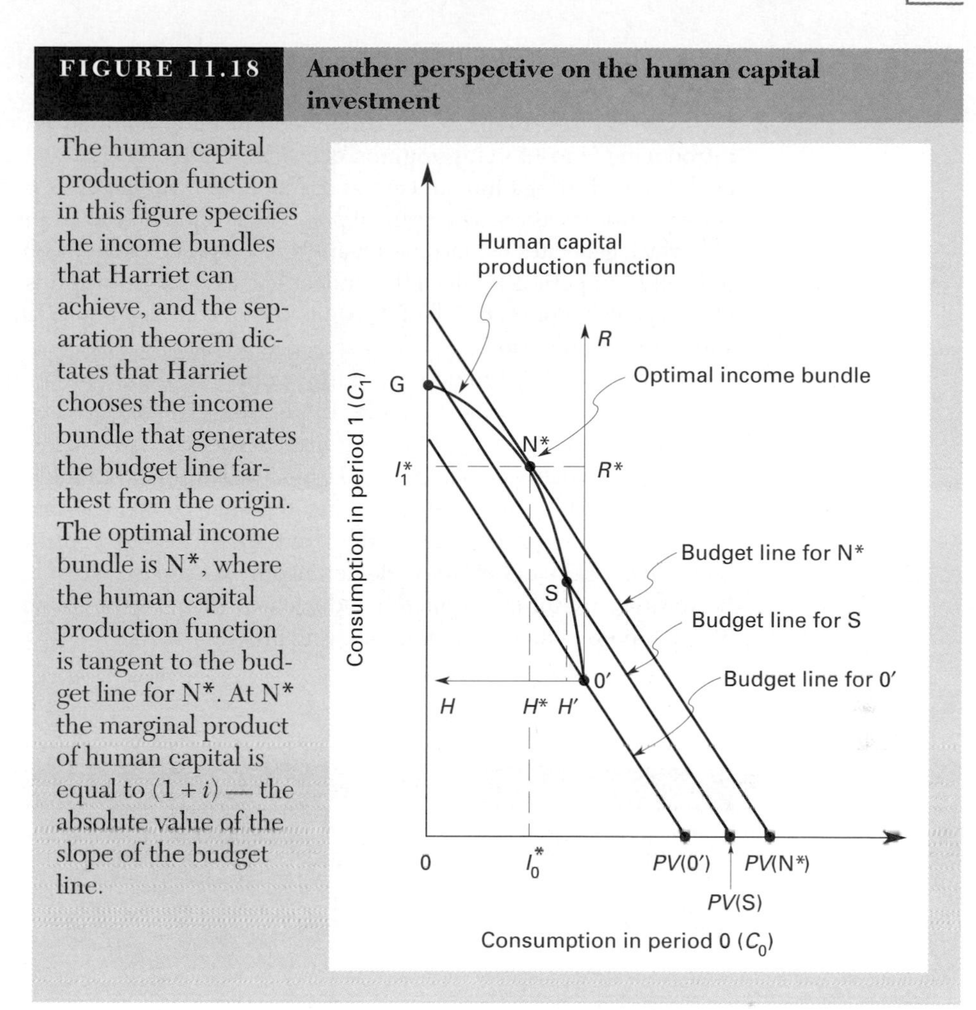

when she invests nothing in human capital. However, she can do better still by investing even more in human capital.

Her optimal investment in human capital is $0'H^*$, which gives her return H^*N*, and the net income stream N*. This result is consistent with the result from Figure 11.17. Notice that at N* in Figure 11.18, Harriet's human capital production function is tangent to the budget line for N*. Even though, relative to the origin at 0, the slope of the budget line is $-(1 + i)$, relative to the origin at 0′, the slope is $(1 + i)$, and Figures 11.17 and 11.18 give us the same result.

Figure 11.18 , however, gives us a more direct perspective on why Harriet should choose to invest in human capital up to the point where *MP* is equal to $(1 + i)$. Notice that the budget line associated with any other investment in human capital lies closer to the origin than the budget line for N*. Therefore, by choosing point N* on her human capital production function, Harriet gets a budget line that is preferred to any other available budget line.

As we saw in the preceding section, we can find the present value of a net income stream by identifying the point where the budget line for the income stream intersects the horizontal axis. Looking at the present values on the horizontal axis in Figure 11.18, we see that by investing $0'H^*$ in human capital, Harriet maximizes the present value of income available for consumption. Of course, this result is dictated by the separation theorem.

Now we can complete this simplified presentation of an economic life-cycle by introducing Harriet's consumption decision. In Figure 11.19 we have combined the analysis of Harriet's human capital decision with the analysis of her intertemporal consumption decision. The optimal point on her human capital production function is N*, which generates net income stream N*, composed of net income I_0^* in period 0 and income I_1^* in period 1. Given the budget line associated with this income stream, she chooses consumption bundle E*, composed of consumption C_0^* in period 0 and consumption C_1^* in period 1.

Figure 11.19 has some interesting features that are true of the life-cycle — not just of Harriet but of most people. In period 0, Harriet invests in human capital to maximize the present value of her net income over her life-cycle. Consequently, the net income she actually earns in period 0 is small relative to both the net income she would earn in period 0 if she invested nothing in human capital and the income she earns in period 1. But her preferences lead her to want a life-cycle consumption bundle that is more *balanced* than her life-cycle net income stream. As a result, in period 0 Harriet borrows against future earnings to indulge in present consumption. To get a firm grasp of this life-cycle model, try the following problems.

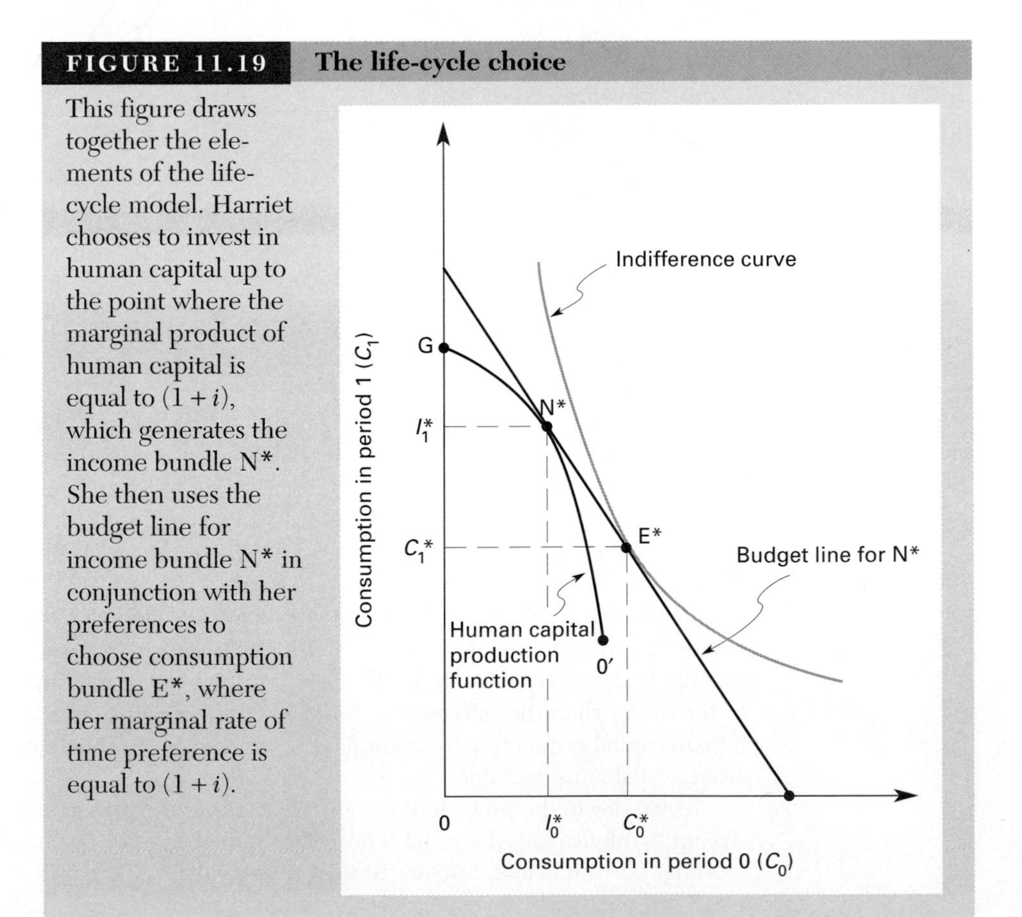

FIGURE 11.19 **The life-cycle choice**

This figure draws together the elements of the life-cycle model. Harriet chooses to invest in human capital up to the point where the marginal product of human capital is equal to $(1 + i)$, which generates the income bundle N*. She then uses the budget line for income bundle N* in conjunction with her preferences to choose consumption bundle E*, where her marginal rate of time preference is equal to $(1 + i)$.

PROBLEM 11.16

Suppose that E* is to the right of N* as in Figure 11.19, and consider a drop in the interest rate. Indicate whether the following statements are true, false, or uncertain.

a. Harriet invests more in human capital.
b. The present value of Harriet's optimal net income stream increases.
c. The future value of Harriet's optimal net income stream increases.
d. Harriet is better off.
e. Harriet consumes more in period 0.
f. Harriet consumes more in period 1.

PROBLEM 11.17

If Harriet has no access to a market for loanable funds — no bank where she can borrow and/or deposit money — then her consumption in each period is equal to her net income in that period. Is she worse off when she has no access to a market for loanable funds than she is when she does have access to such a market? Construct a diagram to support your answer.

In our discussion of human capital, we have assumed that people like Harriet face a perfect market for loanable funds. In particular, we have assumed that, while they are investing in human capital, they can borrow against future income for current consumption. This is the pattern we show in Figure 11.19. In fact, the ability of young people to engage in this sort of borrowing is quite limited. Commercial institutions like banks, trust companies, and credit unions will lend large sums of money only if the loan is secured by a legally enforceable, *conditional claim* against some asset that permits the lender to seize the asset if the borrower defaults on his or her repayment obligations. If you own a home, for example, you can use it as security for a loan from a bank or credit union. The instrument that gives the lender the legally enforceable, conditional claim against the home is, of course, a **mortgage**.

mortgage

Most young people do not own their own homes or any other assets that can be used to secure large loans. Their most valuable asset is their human capital — their future earning potential — and this asset cannot be used as security for a loan. Laws against slavery and other forms of involuntary servitude mean that you cannot "mortgage" your human capital. There is, then, an important imperfection in the market for loanable funds arising from the fact that human capital cannot be used as security. In response to this imperfection, many governments have devised student loan programs. These programs can be seen as attempts to allow young people to borrow against their human capital.

SUMMARY

In this chapter, we applied many of the same principles that we used to examine monopoly and competition in output markets to the markets for resources or inputs. Inputs may be primary, including resources such as land, oil, and labour, or intermediate; that is, the processed output of some other firm. Input markets range from perfectly competitive to monopsonistic, characterized by a single buyer. In a perfectly competitive market, buyers are price takers. The analysis of perfect competition is based on four assumptions, similar to those used in output markets: large numbers, perfect information, input homogeneity, and mobility. In a monopsonistic market, the buyer makes price setting decisions similar to those of the monopolistic seller.

Labour is an important input, and the supply of labour is based on the preferences of individuals for income and leisure; the wage rate may be viewed as the price of leisure. The results of an increase in wages on individual labour supply decisions are ambiguous. When leisure is a normal good, the income effect will lead individuals to prefer more leisure, but the substitution effect will lead them to prefer more hours of labour.

With a single variable input, a firm's input demand curve is its marginal product function, as long as the price of the input is less than the maximum value of average product. For input prices less than the maximum value of average revenue product, the firm's demand function is the downward-sloping portion of marginal revenue product. For input prices greater than the maximum value of average revenue product, the firm will demand none of the variable input.

If a firm is a perfect competitor in its output market, its valuation of an additional unit of variable input will be identical to consumers' valuation of the additional product that can be produced from that unit of input. If the firm is a monopolist in its output market, its valuation of an additional unit will be less than consumers' valuation.

When there are many variable inputs, how will a firm's input demand respond to a change in input price? In both the short run and the long run, the input demand function is downward sloping. Firms will demand more of an input when its price decreases. In long-run equilibrium, a firm that is a perfect competitor in both its output and its input markets will choose an input bundle such that, for each input,

$$w^e = MRP(z) = pMP(z) = VMP(z)$$

In long-run equilibrium, a firm that is a perfect competitor in its input markets, but a monopolist in its output market, will choose an input bundle such that, for each input,

$$w^e = MRP(z) = MR(y)MP(z) < pMP(z) = VMP(z).$$

Monopsony power may arise from immobility of inputs — for example, a natural resource that is expensive to transport or a labour force that is reluctant to move — and from specialized inputs that can be used by only one firm (normally also a monopolist in its output market).

A monopsonist maximizes profit by choosing the quantity of an input where marginal factor cost is equal to marginal revenue product. A monopsony equilibrium is inefficient in the same way and for similar reasons as a monopoly equilibrium; in the absence of competition, the monopsonist fails to extract the maximum possible profit, and monopsony equilibrium is not Pareto-optimal.

We saw how an individual allocates income to consumption over his or her economic life cycle. Then, we used the separation theorem to analyze an individual's choice of human capital. We discovered that to maximize the present value of his or her lifetime income, an individual invests in human capital up to the point where the marginal product of human capital is equal to $(1 + i)$.

We then combined these two pieces of analysis to develop a larger understanding of the typical person's economic life-cycle. A typical individual invests heavily in human capital in the early part of the life-cycle and therefore earns an income considerably smaller than the income that could be earned in the absence of this investment in human capital. Faced with the resulting — and decidedly unbalanced — lifetime income stream, the typical individual borrows in the early part of the life-cycle against his or her future income to finance consumption that exceeds income.

EXERCISES

1. Do the relative salaries of humanities professors and NBA basketball coaches reflect the relative value of basketball and humanities? Do they reflect the number of years that professors and coaches must spend acquiring an education? The number of hours they work? The difficulty or unpleasantness of their work? Why do the basketball coaches usually receive salaries that are so much higher?

2. The Town Council of Podunk has given Wally the exclusive right to sell pop at local baseball games. The operation is very simple. Wally buys pop from the local distributor (who lives next door to him) for $0.40 per can and takes his supply of pop to the ballpark in his picnic cooler. Anyone wanting to buy a can of pop walks down to Wally's seat behind home plate and buys it. Since Wally would go to the ballgames even if he did not have the pop franchise, his only cost in the short run is the $0.40 per can that he pays to buy the pop. The demand for pop at a typical ballgame is

$$p = 1.60 - 0.01y$$

For example, he could sell 100 cans for $0.60 per can, or 150 cans for $0.10 per can.

   a. First, let us focus on the output market. What is Wally's marginal revenue function and what is his marginal cost? What is his profit-maximizing level of output? How much profit does he earn? Construct a graph to illustrate Wally's position in the output market.
   b. Now let us focus on the input market. What is the single costly input? What is the marginal revenue product function? What is the input demand function? How much of the input does Wally buy? If the distributor charged $0.60 per can, how much would he buy? Construct a graph to illustrate Wally's position in the input market.

3. Suppose that the demand function for some nonrenewable resource is

$$w_1 = 200 - 2z_1$$

in period 1 and

$$w_2 = 200 - 2z_2$$

in period 2. There are 100 units of the resource to be allocated for use in the two periods, and the interest rate is 50 percent. Find the competitive equilibrium prices in periods 1 and 2 and the competitive equilibrium allocation to the two periods.

4. A famous economist once remarked: "The economic problem isn't that there are too few jobs, but that there are too many!" Explain what he meant. Does the number of "jobs" depend on the wage rate? If so, what do people really mean when they say "there aren't enough jobs"?

5. In this exercise, you can explore what is called a *bilateral monopoly*. Firm A is the only demander of input Z, and its marginal revenue product function is

$$MRP(z) = 200 - 2z$$

Firm B is the only supplier of input Z, and its reservation price for each unit of input Z, $R(z)$, is

$$R(z) = z$$

You can think of $R(z)$ as firm B's marginal cost of producing input Z.

   a. Suppose first that firm A can choose a price w and that firm B then decides how much input Z to sell to A at A's chosen price. What price maximizes A's profit, and what quantity will B sell to A?
   b. Now reverse the exercise. Suppose that B can choose a price and that A then decides how

much to buy at B's chosen price. What price maximizes B's profit, and what quantity will A buy at this price?

c. Finally, suppose that firm C were to buy both firms A and B. How much input Z would firm C produce?

6. The Fraser River Valley is the breadbasket of British Columbia. The agriculture in the valley uses relatively little labour, except at harvest time. Much of the harvest labour is supplied by recent immigrants to Canada, who live about 80 kilometres away in Vancouver, have little or no facility in English, and do not own cars. The market in harvest labour is mediated by labour brokers. A labour broker typically owns a bus for transporting labourers and speaks both English and the labourers' language. The broker buys labour at one price w_1 and sells it to farmers at a higher price w_2. Assume that the demand for farm labour from a particular broker is linear and downward sloping, that the supply of labour is linear and upward sloping, and that all of the broker's costs are fixed, or independent of the quantity of labour bought and sold. Find the values of w_1 and w_2 and the quantity of labour bought and sold that maximize the labour broker's profit.

7. Historically, as wages rates have increased in western societies, the work week has declined. A hundred years ago in Canada, for instance, the average work week was more than 70 hours. Today it is less than 40. Using the framework developed in this chapter, diagram the case in which the quantity of labour supplied decreases as the wage rate increases. In this case, is leisure a normal or an inferior good?

8. A minimum wage is essentially a price floor.
   a. What types of workers are likely to be most affected by minimum wages (for example, teenagers, skilled craftspeople, handicapped workers)?
   b. Explain the effect on wages, levels of employment, and possible unemployment in the markets most directly affected by this law. Also, what forms of competition among workers might be more prevalent with the higher minimum wage?
   c. Consider that unionized workers generally earn much more than the minimum wage. Unions, however, have always strongly advocated increases in the minimum wage. Are the unionists just interested in the welfare of their poor cousins?

9. Suppose a welfare program offers individuals \$40 per day, with the provision that the grant is reduced \$0.75 for each \$1 of other income the individual earns. Suppose an individual could work as many hours as he or she wished for \$4 per hour.
   a. Draw the individual's budget constraint without the welfare program.
   b. Draw the budget constraint with the program.
   c. What will be the effect of the program?

10. "The hockey players are crazy if they think the NHL can survive free agency for long. Salaries are going through the roof, and teams are bidding so high for a few outstanding players that they will soon be financially ruined!" Comment.

11. Unions commonly bargain for a basic wage rate w and an overtime rate. Assume that the overtime rate is $1.5w$ and that it is paid for hours worked in excess of 40 per week.
    a. Construct the relevant budget line between leisure and a composite good.
    b. Assuming that the union member would choose to work 40 hours per week at wage rate w, will he or she want to work overtime?
    c. Assuming that members are contractually obligated to work at least 40 hours per week, illustrate the conditions under which the union member would prefer no overtime work.

12. Ralph currently has two jobs. His primary job pays well, \$20 per hour, but he can work no more than 40 hours per week at it. In fact, he always chooses to work 40 hours at this job. His secondary job pays only \$15 per hour, but he can work as few or as many hours as he wants. Currently he chooses to work 10 hours at his secondary job. For Ralph, leisure is a normal good. If the wage rate for his primary job increases to \$22 per hour, will Ralph increase or decrease the number of hours he works in the secondary job?

13. Helga currently gets \$1000 weekly in investment income, and she works 10 hours each week at \$50 an hour, thereby earning an additional \$500.

Leisure is neither an inferior nor a normal good for Helga. If offered the choice between a 10 percent increase in her investment income and a 20 percent increase in her hourly wage rate, which would Helga choose? Assume that she is free to choose her hours of work.

14. College and university professors in Canada are represented by faculty associations that negotiate wages for their members. One common feature of these agreements is that faculty be paid similar amounts across disciplines. That is, an English professor is paid the same as an Accounting professor with the same experience.
    a. What types of problems will arise if the demand for professors in different disciplines varies?
    b. Will these problems be more severe at colleges as compared to universities? At good universities as compared to bad universities? (*Hint:* How many "superstar" faculty do you think are at colleges and bad universities?)

15. "Green Capitalism" is a movement that advocates that environmentally friendly groups only borrow from, invest in, and purchase from each other. Does this help or hurt the environmental movement?

16. It can take up to 10 years to become an English professor and only two years to become a CAD technician. Most of the time the technician earns more than the English professor. How can this be?

17 The province of British Columbia has passed a labour law that effectively makes it impossible for children to work before they are 15 (no paper routes, no berry picking, no nothing!). What groups in the economy benefit from such laws?

18. Wages in third world countries are often trivial compared to wages in North America. Why is it that any firms are willing to keep their plants here rather than move to the low-wage locations?

19. What will be the effect on wages in Canada from a massive immigration of people from Sri Lanka? What will be the effect on rental rates on capital in Sri Lanka from a massive immigration of capital from Canada? What will be the effect on wages in Sri Lanka from foreign capital investment from Canada?

20. Does the difference in earnings between the top tennis players of the world (who earn millions of dollars) and the top hundred players in the world (who make enough to cover expenses) reflect the difference in marginal products?

*21. Suppose a fast-food firm operates in a competitive output environment but is a monopsonist in the input market for hired workers.
    a. Draw the input market equilibrium.
    b. Now suppose a minimum wage is placed on the input market, raising the wage. What happens to the level of employment in the market?

*22. Suppose that a firm that is a perfect competitor in its output market can vary only input Z in the short run and that

$$AP(z) = 100 - z$$

and

$$MP(z) = 100 - 2z$$

    a. Suppose that the price of the firm's product is \$10. What are the firm's marginal and average revenue product functions? What is the firm's short-run demand function for input Z? How much input Z will the firm use when its price is \$40? When its price is \$60?
    b. Show that the results in (a) are consistent with the profit-maximizing rule in the firm's output market: Produce the level of output where SMC is equal to output price.
    c. What is the firm's short-run demand function for input Z when the price of the firm's product is \$25? How much input Z will the firm now use when the input price is \$40? When the input price is \$60?

*23. Suppose a good is produced according to the following production function, $Q = K^{0.5}L^{0.5}$. The wage rate is given as w and the rental rate on capital is r.
    a. Suppose w = \$8 and r = \$8. Determine the necessary conditions for the input choices, K and L, to be cost-minimizing. Draw, in a rough fashion. this equilibrium condition, (with K on the vertical axis and L on the horizontal) and explain what it means.
    b. Using the condition found in (a) and the production function, find the demand curves for both inputs.

c. Suppose the government feels the wage rate is too low and decides to impose a minimum wage of $12. Using the demand functions from (b), show what the effect will be of this policy on the equilibrium quantity of labour demanded.

*24. Suppose there is an individual with a utility function $U = C^{0.75}L^{0.25}$ where C is units of a composite consumption good per day and L is hours of leisure per day. Suppose that this individual is endowed daily with 24 hours of potential working time and a non-work income flow of $16 per day.

a. Given that this individual can choose hours of work at a wage of $2 per hour, and purchase units of the consumption good at a price of $4 per unit, determine the optimal consumption bundle of the individual.

b. Determine the supply curve of labour of the individual.

c. Suppose that the individual could not choose hours of work. If the individual was required to work either eight hours a day or not at all, what would be the individual's choice? Why?

*25. Suppose there is a perfectly competitive industry in which each firm produces according to the production function $y = z_1^{0.5}z_2^{0.5}$. Each input is supplied to the industry according to the supply curves $z_1 = w_1$ and $z_2 = 4w_2$.

a. If the industry produces y units of output, find the cost-minimizing demand functions for z_1 and z_2 in terms of y, w_1, and w_2.

b. Using your answer from (a), find the conditions for equilibrium in the two input markets.

c. Show that the long-run supply curve for the industry is $y = p$, where p is the price of the output.

REFERENCES

Arrow, K. 1972. "Models of Job Discrimination," in *Racial Discrimination in Economic Life*, A. H. Pascal (ed.). Lexington, Mass.: D. C. Heath.

Becker, G. 1957. *The Economics of Discrimination*. Chicago: University of Chicago Press.

Becker, G. 1964. *Human Capital*. New York: Columbia University Press.

Dorfman, R. 1987. "Marginal Productivity Theory," in *The New Palgrave: A Dictionary of Economics*, J. Eatwell, M. Milgate, and P. Newman (eds.). London: Macmillan.

Mincer, J. 1958. "Investment in Human Capital and Personal Income Distribution," *Journal of Political Economy*, 66(August):281–302.

Rosen, S. 1987. "Human Capital," in *The New Palgrave: A Dictionary of Economics*, J. Eatwell, M. Milgate, and P. Newman (eds.). London: Macmillan.

Schultz, T. 1961. "Investment in Human Capital," *American Economic Review*, 51(March):1–17.

CHAPTER 12

The Distribution of Income

Chapter 11 explored how well markets performed their allocational function of directing resources to competing uses. In this chapter, we consider how they perform another, equally important function: the distribution of a society's product among its members. By distribution we mean, very loosely, just what share of the national product each person receives. As we turn to the distributional function of markets, we will focus our attention on input markets in a partial equilibrium setting because, in a very real sense, input markets determine the size of everyone's slice of the economic pie.

We all have certain salable input endowments — certain human (labour) resources and nonhuman (property) resources. The input endowments we possess and the prices paid for those inputs in the marketplace, including the prevailing wage rates, are crucial in determining the size of our personal rewards in a market economy. For example, relative incomes in a dental office will vary, depending on the going wage rates for different kinds of training and talents: a dentist might be earning $100 per hour, a dental technician $25 per hour, and a dental receptionist $10 per hour. Prevailing input prices also affect the income of people who are selling resources other than labour. For example, one person we know inherited his grandparents' farm in what is now downtown Houston; he enjoys a relatively large claim to society's product because his land is now prime real estate. Another acquaintance inherited his grandparents' once-elegant estate in the decaying core of Chicago; he has a comparably smaller claim because his property is worth less in the real estate market.

In this chapter we want to address a number of questions regarding the distribution of income. First, although we can casually look around us and observe differences in income, how is this to be measured? For example, how can we determine how many poor people are in an economy? Second, as budding economists, we must ask what determines the distribution of income. If we can understand why income is spread out the way it is, we come to a more troubling question: Is inequality in the distribution of wealth and income right, or just? As you can imagine, our theory is not as useful in addressing this question as the first two. However, it is not completely useless either. Finally, given that since the dawn of time societies have found it in their interests to redistribute income, we must ask what constitutes an efficient redistribution. Here we will discover that all redistributions are a two-edged sword and that equity considerations usually involve a reduction in the wealth of an economy. We consider two specific redistributions: minimum-wage laws and welfare.

12.1 The Lorenz Curve

For the moment, let's suppose that there are no analytical problems in defining an income distribution. How might a person go about describing one? It turns out that economists and other social scientists have developed a number of methods, but perhaps the most common is called the **Lorenz curve**. This measure ranks individuals by income and then plots their cumulative number against the cumulative percentage of income received. For example, we might look at the bottom 10 percent of income earners and the Lorenz curve would tell us what fraction of income they received. If they received 8 percent of the income, the income distribution would be more equal than if they received only 5 percent.

Lorenz curve

Figure 12.1 shows a hypothetical Lorenz curve. If everyone received exactly the same wage, then the Lorenz curve would simply be the straight 45° line. The more unequal is the distribution of income, the more "bowed" out the Lorenz curve becomes. Hence, in Figure 12.1 we see that 15 percent of the earnings are going to 30 percent of the population. This means that a disproportionate share is going to the other 70 percent of the people.

PROBLEM 12.1

Suppose that an economy is made up of 100 people. Draw a Lorenz curve when:

a. One person earns all of the income, and the other 99 earn nothing.

b. The top 25 percent of the people earn 50 percent of the income, and the incomes in the two groups (top 25 percent and bottom 75 percent) are equal.

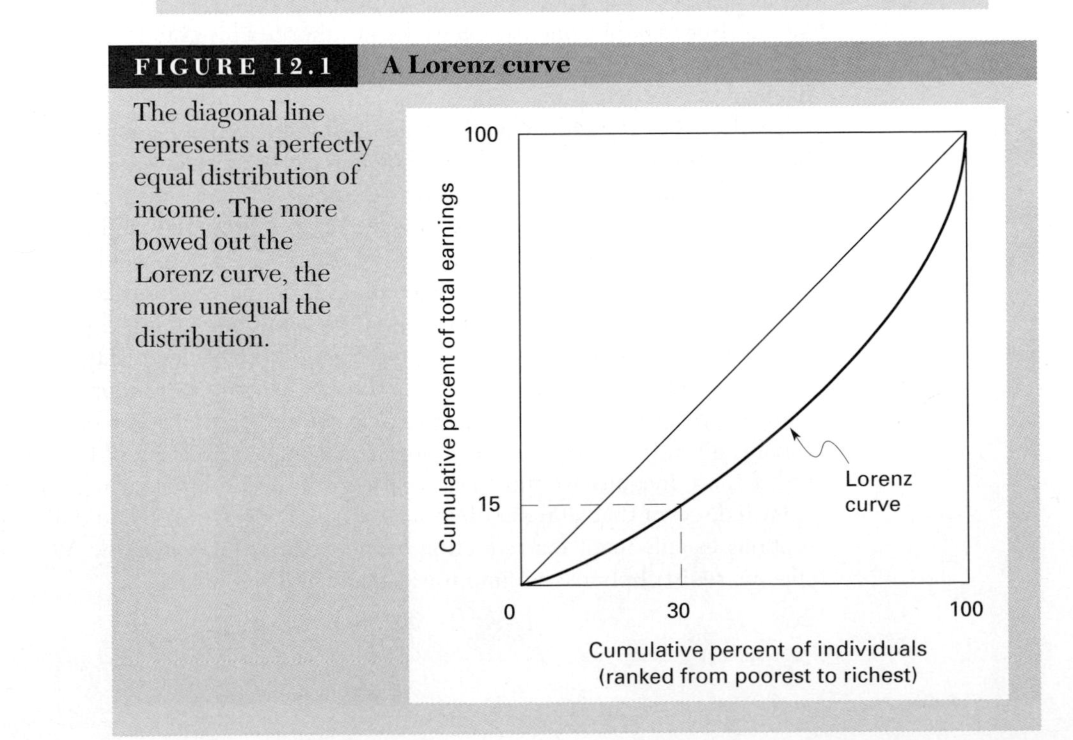

FIGURE 12.1 **A Lorenz curve**

The diagonal line represents a perfectly equal distribution of income. The more bowed out the Lorenz curve, the more unequal the distribution.

Gini coefficient

The **Gini coefficient** is a measure of the inequality of income. The Gini coefficient is defined as the area between the Lorenz curve and the diagonal line, divided by the area under the diagonal line. Hence, for equal income distribution the Gini coefficient is equal to 0. From Problem 12.1a, if one person has all of the income, then the Gini coefficient is equal to 1.

What Does a Distribution of Income Mean?

Depending on your point of view, a Lorenz curve and a Gini coefficient may seem like either an elegant way to describe an income distribution or a trivial exercise in arithmetic. In general, all mechanical descriptions of income distributions are fairly straightforward. However, we must keep in mind that description is only part of the problem. After all, it is quite easy to simply rank incomes and count how many people have incomes of $1 000 000, how many have incomes of $900 000, and so on, all the way down to the bottom. The question is, is this what we're after?

Consider, for starters, the unit of account. Are we to measure the income distribution in terms of individuals, families, or households? If you want to maximize the number of individuals at the bottom end of the income distribution, simply count individuals. It should come as little surprise to you that there are vast numbers of individuals in an economy who have little or no income. Children, students, and spouses working in the home tend to have nominal incomes, and if we count them as separate individuals in the distribution of income, the bottom end gets very large indeed. On the other hand, counting families rather than individuals tends to bias things in the other direction. Family incomes can be quite large, even though many members of the family have no income. This may seem more appropriate, but income distribution within a family is seldom equal, either.

Another problem with simply counting members of an income class was encountered in Chapter 5 in our discussion of wealth versus income. If you will recall, wealth is the present value of your expected lifetime stream of income. As a student you probably have a low income, but your wealth level is high relative to most members in the economy. Is it at all meaningful to count students, and others with low incomes but high wealth, at the bottom of the income distribution? We can do it, certainly, but the point is, does this truly measure the distribution of income?

Consider the additional problem of children. Suppose a couple has a decision to make. They can both remain in the workforce and have professional careers leading to a high family income, or they can start a family, which means that one of them must leave the workforce for an extended period of time, thus reducing their market income. We know that individuals are utility maximizers, and whatever decision they make is the best one for them under the circumstances. Hence if we observe a couple choosing the option of a lower family income but more children, it must be the case that their utility was higher with children than without. In what meaningful sense can we then categorize families by income if the number of children varies across them? Some families decide to have large incomes and consume market goods, while other families decide to have smaller incomes and enjoy children. The incomes are different, but are the individuals with lower incomes worse off than those with higher incomes?

By now your imagination is probably running wild, and you can think of a long list of reasons why a simple ranking of incomes is less than satisfactory for any meaningful measure of income distribution. The problem is more than academic. For example, in any targeted income transfer scheme, such as welfare, it is essential to define a target group. If you want to help the poor, you must know who the poor are and how many of them there are. The Canadian experience in this regard is quite interesting in pointing out the issues.

Believe it or not, and despite constant reference to "poverty lines" and "official numbers of poverty," no government agency in Canada actually calculates any such number. What is calculated is a number called the "Low Income Cut Off" (LICO). This number provides the number of people in a given year spending a certain percentage of their income or more on food, shelter, and clothing. This calculation has a number of problems, many of which have already been mentioned. For example, there is no adjustment made for the type of home. Someone highly mortgaged in a $300 000 house could end up classified as below the "poverty line." It fails to take into account a person's stage in their life-cycle. Hence an elderly couple of modest means, but with little but food and clothing expenses, could be counted as poor. In Canada about half a million seniors are counted as poor, even though most of them own their own homes mortgage-free. Clearly LICOs ignore wealth, and so many students get counted as poor each year. Finally, the cut-off line is completely arbitrary, and Statistics Canada has a habit of lowering the percentage income cut-off number every 10 years. This leads to huge increases in the numbers of reported poverty cases!

As a student of economics, you should be wary of simple statements regarding the distribution of income. Aside from the issues just mentioned, income distributions are always defined in relative terms. Those on the bottom are considered poor. With a relative definition of poverty, the poor, by definition, are always with us. If the lowest end of the income distribution in a country like Canada are compared to the average individuals in a country like Chad or Haiti, then they no longer appear so poor. On the other hand, some have argued for absolute definitions of poverty. On these scales the number of poor in Western countries tends to fall dramatically. For example, Sarlo (1992) estimates that 2.5 percent of Canadians are poor using absolute measures, while using LICOs leads to a poverty rate of 10.1 percent.

12.2 Determinants of the Income Distribution

To begin understanding the determinants of the income distribution we must return to one of the most important points developed in Chapter 11. There we discovered that in a competitive equilibrium, workers receive the value of their marginal products. Not only this, we saw that wage rates were determined by the intersection of the supply and demand for labour, and that in this equilibrium, the wage was equal to the value of the marginal product. As a starting point, then, we might assume that the distribution of income is determined by the endowment of skills we have and the value they have in the market place. This is a good place to start, but we will ignore it at first and assume the opposite; that is, that everyone is identical.

Suppose we begin by assuming that everyone in an economy starts off equal in terms of skills and abilities. Over time, however, we would expect that incomes would differ simply due to luck. As the Bible says, "The race is not to the swift, nor the battle to the strong; neither yet bread to the wise, nor yet riches to men of understanding, nor yet favour to men of skill; but time and chance happeneth to them all." If we recognize that nature plays a role in our life (the role of nature and uncertainty is dealt with in detail in the next section of the book), then we must expect it to play a role in the ultimate distribution of income.

Some luck is purely individual. Some people have a knack at buying and selling at the right time ... others just the opposite. Car accidents, illness, the lucky draw of a good teacher (or a good microeconomics text!), are all factors that can influence a given individual's opportunities to earn income. Some luck may be specific to an industry or just a given firm. If you happen to be a turkey farmer and the government just happens to institute a quota with your name on it, you've just won the lottery. Others may end up investing large amounts of human capital in making buggy whips, only to discover that automobiles have put them out of business.

Luck, however, cannot explain all of the variation in incomes that are observed. A large reason for different incomes simply has to do with differences in human capital investments. Consider two of our identical individuals, Laura and Lana, who are considering careers after high school. Since they are both identical, their wealth levels are equal, and they are equal for a subset of occupations that they are considering. Suppose that Laura ends up taking a six-month course and becomes a dental assistant, while Lana spends seven years becoming a lawyer. Although their wealth levels are still equal, their patterns of income are extremely different. To become a lawyer involves a larger upfront investment and lower earnings while in school, with subsequent larger earnings later on.

Preferences can also play a large role in determining income distributions because ultimately individuals care not just about their financial returns over a time, but about the present value of their lifetime utility. For starters, among our group of identically able people, some might strongly prefer a life of leisure to one of high consumption of market goods. Individuals who prefer leisure will select occupations that provide relatively high amounts of leisure. University professors, for example, have extremely flexible hours and large amounts of time at their disposal. When people compete for jobs with large amounts of leisure, the wage rates fall in compensation. Other on-the-job differences can explain differences in wages. Some jobs have a relatively steady income, while others are more risky. If individuals do not like risk in their life, then risky jobs will have to pay more. Other jobs are dangerous and boring, and have correspondingly higher wages to compensate.

The bottom line is that even if we begin with a population that is equal in terms of ability, the endogenous decisions that these people make throughout their lives based on differences in tastes for income now rather than later, job safety, leisure, etc. will lead to vast differences in the distribution of income. In a world of certainty, however, these decisions do not affect the distribution of wealth at all. Hence differences in the distribution of income do not automatically imply differences in the distribution of wealth.

Now let us consider differences in abilities. Clearly anyone born with greater endowments of capital, whether they be human or physical, will have larger levels of wealth and income. Those born with higher IQ's, great voices, attractive bodies, and a way with words, other things equal, will generate higher incomes than the mentally challenged, tone deaf, ugly, and illiterate. However, keep in mind that people are paid the *value* of their marginal products, and if the value of one's skill is low then the wage will also be low. Before the introduction of Arabic numerals, keeping accounts with Roman numerals was difficult and it required a special talent to remember sums and multiplication. People with this talent could make a substantial living by memorizing sums. Today, we can all multiply (or let a calculator do it), and the returns to this talent are essentially zero.

The one factor we have thus far ignored in the distribution of income is the role of the state. Without the state the distribution of income is determined by the initial endowment, subsequent human capital decisions, and random events. However, the state is both directly and indirectly involved in altering the distribution of income.

12.3 Distributive Justice

Economist Kenneth Arrow (1976) has commented that what Aristotle called "distributive justice" was not seen as an issue in earlier societies. These societies, Arrow claims, tended to view the prevailing distribution of material goods as right, either because they reflected the long-familiar status quo or because earthly rewards were viewed as the workings of divine justice. However, we now recognize that the distribution of wealth and income is, in large part, the handiwork of human beings. In particular, the social and economic institutions we create significantly affect who is rich and who is poor. Just a few of the many institutions affecting distribution in any modern economy are the family, income taxes, inheritance taxes, gift taxes, welfare, social security, collective bargaining, public housing, zoning, public education, minimum wages, rent controls, and agricultural price supports.

Unfortunately, we have no yardstick like the economic concept of Pareto optimality that lets us judge how well the market system (or any other set of institutions) performs the distributional function. That is, we have no way to assess whether the distribution of wealth and income resulting from market forces is in some sense right or just. Indeed, determining what "justice" means is a *philosophical* rather than an economic issue — and even among philosophers, there is no consensus. Broadly speaking, two opposing approaches to this ethical issue have emerged: the *productivity principle* and the *redistributionist principle*.

The Productivity Principle

productivity principle

In a nutshell, the **productivity principle** asserts that each of us ought to receive the monetary equivalent of what we have individually produced from our human resources (or labour) and our nonhuman resources (or property). If we ignore property and look only at labour, the appeal of the productivity principle is clear: it implies that you should reap what you have sown. In other words, the harder you work, the more you will produce — and the larger your market reward ought to be.

Milton Friedman, the 1976 winner of the Nobel Prize in economics, has claimed that the productivity principle is virtually universally held. A major source of evidence for this is that market allocations are generally tolerated throughout history and across different cultures. Experiments with communism aside, most people simply accept the market allocation as the fundamental starting point, and simply argue for minor alterations in its outcome. In fact, arguments against the market-determined distribution of income tend not to reject the productivity principle, but to reject the idea that the market has met it. For example, the Marxian notion that resources should be transferred to the working class is based on the idea that this class of people are exploited; that is, that workers do not receive their marginal products.

product-exhaustion criterion

As economists we can clarify the core concept of the productivity principle: the meaning of productivity itself. If it is to serve as a distributional principle, any definition of productivity must fulfill the **product-exhaustion criterion**. If the owners of all resources receive what their resources produce, then the individual shares of the total product pie must add up to 1. If the sum were less than 1, there would be leftover product that no one had produced; if the sum were greater than 1, there would be too little product to go around.

Surprisingly, a meaning that satisfies the product-exhaustion criterion in any general set of circumstances is not easy to find. However, we can find one set of circumstances (the case in which all production functions exhibit constant returns to scale) and one definition of productivity (the value of the marginal product) that satisfy the criterion. In other words, if all production functions exhibit constant returns to scale, then paying the owners of each input the value of the input's marginal product will exhaust (exactly use up) what we will call the value of the total product: the sum of all (output) prices multiplied by the quantities produced.

Furthermore, there is a set of institutions (the institutions of perfect competition) that guarantees that the owners of each input do, in fact, receive the value of the input's marginal product in these circumstances. Why? Recall that in Chapter 11, we discovered that when every input and output market in an economy is perfectly competitive, the owners of each input are paid the value of the input's marginal product.

Product Exhaustion

Let us see why this pattern of input payments just equals (exhausts) the value of the total product. We will look at a firm in long-run competitive equilibrium that uses just two inputs and is producing y^* units of output. If the firm's input bundle is (z_1^*, z_2^*) and if p and (w_1, w_2) are the competitive equilibrium output and input prices, respectively, we want to show that

$$py^* = w_1 z_1^* + w_2 z_2^*$$

The left side is the value of the firm's output, and the right is the sum of the firm's input payments. If, at the level of the firm, the product is just used up, the two sides must be identical. We can rewrite the product-exhaustion requirement as

$$p = (w_1 z_1^* + w_2 z_2^*)/y^* = LAC(y^*)$$

The second equality follows from the definition of long-run average cost as total cost divided by output. We know from Section 8.7 that price is equal to minimum long-run average cost for any firm in long-run competitive equilibrium. The product-exhaustion criterion is therefore satisfied in a competitive equilibrium.

But just where did the condition of constant returns to scale enter this argument? In long-run competitive equilibrium, each firm is at the bottom of its U-shaped long-run average cost function, operating at the efficient scale of production. As we discovered in Section 7.3, at this level of output the firm experiences constant returns to scale. Therefore, constant returns to scale entered the picture when we observed that p is equal to $LAC(y^*)$ for a firm in long-run competitive equilibrium.

The exhaustion of total product should not be viewed as simply an accident of technology, but rather as an equilibrium condition. Suppose that there are two inputs, labour and capital, and that the capital owner hires the worker and receives the residual as income. Suppose that the residual were greater than the marginal product of capital. Other capital owners would view this favourably and would begin to enter this industry eventually driving down the price of output until the value of the capital's marginal product was equal to the residual. If the opposite were the case, and the residual were less than the value of the marginal product of capital, then this capitalist would leave the industry and rent the capital out at the going rental rate. You will recognize this as simply the equilibrium condition discussed in Chapter 8, namely that competitive firms must earn zero profits. This also means that in a competitive equilibrium, the total product must be exhausted.

Let us view this result from a slightly different perspective. We have found a definition of productivity that can serve as a principle of distribution because this definition satisfies the product-exhaustion criterion. This definition then raises an important normative question: Is payment in accordance with the value of the marginal product an ethically appealing principle of distributive justice? Consider two thought experiments that are useful in trying to answer this question. In both experiments, we will suppose that the economy produces just one good and then examine how output of that good responds to a change in the **endowment** of an input — that is, in the total amount of an input available in an economy.

endowment

Thought Experiments for the Productivity Principle

Imagine an economy in a competitive equilibrium and consider what happens to the total output of the economy if some person — let us call her Rose — simply disappears, taking her resource endowment — including her labour and any other resources she owns — out of the economy. Total output will decrease (approximately) by the amount of Rose's income, since she must have been receiving as income the marginal contribution to the total product of her labour and her other resources. This result follows from the fact that each unit of each input is paid its marginal product in competitive equilibrium. Notice that this exercise, in which there is a *marginal change* in the economy's input endowment, seems to be consistent with the spirit of the productivity principle: Rose seems to have received just what she produced.

Now let us try a second experiment in which there is a *nonmarginal change* in the economy's input endowment. For simplicity, we will assume that the economy has only two resources (or inputs) and produces only one product. We will also assume that the specific production function below describes the entire economy's technology:

$$y = 240(z_1 z_2)^{1/2}$$

(Note, however, that the general nature of the results does not depend on any particular production function.)

The marginal product functions associated with this production function are[1]

$$MP_1 = 120(z_2/z_1)^{1/2}$$
$$MP_2 = 120(z_1/z_2)^{1/2}$$

Suppose that initially this economy's resource endowment consists of 64 units of input 1 and 36 units of input 2. Using this production function, we can calculate that the economy's total output is 11 520 units, and the competitive equilibrium input prices are $w_1 = 90$ and $w_2 = 160$. (Since this economy produces only one product, the unit for input prices is the unit in which output is measured.) Now suppose that the quantity of input 2 increases from 36 to 100, while the quantity of input 1 remains at 64. The total output then rises from 11 520 to 19 200, for an increase of 7680 units. Notice, too, what happens to input prices: w_1 increases from 90 to 150, and w_2 falls from 160 to 96.

---

1. We can use calculus to find these marginal product functions. To get MP_1, partially differentiate $240(z_1 z_2)^{1/2}$ with respect to z_1. To get MP_2, partially differentiate with respect to z_2.

What accounts for (or produces) the 7680-unit increase in output? Because only the quantity of input 2 changed, it seems sensible to attribute the increased output to the 74 additional units of input 2. Notice, however, that these 74 units are paid only 7104 (74 × 96) units — not the 7680 units they apparently have produced. Thus, in this thought experiment, where the change in an economy's resource endowment is a nonmarginal change, marginal product does not seem to be a reasonable measure of productivity, because when the added inputs are paid their marginal product, they do not capture all of the added output.

Notice, too, that once the endowment of input 2 increases, the change in input prices is dramatic. The price paid per unit of input 2 drops sharply, while the price paid per unit of input 1 soars. If we want to argue that marginal productivity actually captures the spirit of the productivity principle — that one should reap what one has sown — we must be prepared to accept that the productivity of each of the original 36 units of input 2 decreased from 160 to 96 and that the productivity of each of the original 64 units of input 1 increased from 90 to 150, solely as a result of the increase in the endowment of input 2.

Input Prices and Scarcity

The changes in input prices in the second thought experiment reflect a fundamental reality of the market system: *markets reward scarcity*. As input 1 became scarcer relative to input 2, the price paid per unit went up. This reward to scarcity serves an allocational function by directing resources to the uses in which their marginal productivity is greatest. Think of tennis great Monica Seles. At least two of her personal characteristics are noteworthy: (1) she is abundantly endowed with athletic talent, and (2) she is a very wealthy person. Most economists would consider her wealth to be a reward for having a scarce natural talent. They are not implying that Seles is rewarded without having worked hard on her game. Rather, they are suggesting that no matter how hard the vast majority of us worked at tennis, we could not put together a game comparable to hers. The size of any individual's claim on the national product therefore depends on how scarce his or her salable talents and resources are relative to the whole society's endowment of resources. If all of us were as talented at tennis as Seles, none of us — including Monica Seles — would receive a large market reward for it.

The productivity principle then, is often used as a normative rule to argue that income should be determined by forces in competitive markets.

The Redistributionist Principle

redistributionist principle

The **redistributionist principle** is at odds with the productivity principle. (See Cowell, 1987.) Redistributionists find significant economic inequalities ethically unacceptable and argue that a more nearly equitable distribution ought to be a social objective. Simply put, they say that wealth and income in the real world should be redistributed from the rich to the poor. The most extreme version of this position is philosopher John Rawls's **difference principle**. Taking equality as a point of reference, Rawls (1971) argues that the only acceptable inequality is one that improves the lot of the worst-off member of society. If we compare all possible distributions of wealth and pinpoint the worst-off member of a society in each distribution, the difference principle asserts that the preferred distribution is the one in which the wealth of the poorest member is largest.

difference principle

But how do redistributionists conclude that distributive justice demands less inequality? They begin by observing the difficulties in thinking objectively about distribution. For example, they note that taking from the rich and giving to the poor is not nearly as popular among wealthy people as it is among the poor. In an attempt to achieve an ethical standard free of personal bias, redistributionists suggest a hypothetical circumstance called the **original position**.

original position

Suppose that a group of individuals had to imagine a distribution of wealth, *ex ante*; that is, they did not know what their actual wealth would be, only what the overall distribution was. To be in such a position is to be in the original position. Those in the redistributionist camp argue that the income distribution agreed upon would be just because it is not biased by individual attempts to protect their own wealth. The main tenet of the redistributionist principle, then, is that the "insurance contract" resulting from the original-position experiment leads to a more equal distribution of income as a moral principle. Try the following problem to check your understanding of this approach to distributive justice.

PROBLEM 12.2

Put yourself into the following original position. Suppose that tomorrow you will be one of two people, A or B, in a very simple two-person economy that has a fixed endowment of one good, manna. You must choose today how the manna is to be apportioned out between A and B tomorrow, but all you know is this: it is equally probable that you will be A or B. A number R greater than 0 but less than 1 is A's share of manna, and $1 - R$ is B's share. What value of R would you choose?

We should underline the fact that this sort of mental experiment does not inevitably lead to the conclusion that equality is necessary for distributive justice. To see why not, let us consider another two-person economy. In the first period, A is alive; in the second period, B is alive. In each period, the endowment of manna is 2 units. In period 1, A can either eat both units of manna or eat one and plant the other. If A eats both, B will have just 2 units of manna in period 2. If A eats just 1 unit, however, the planted manna will triple, so that B will have a total of 5 units in period 2. If you do not know whether you will be A or B, which scheme would you choose in the original position: A gets 1 unit and B gets 5, or A gets 2 units and B gets 2? If you are not too risk-averse, you will choose the first; if you are very risk-averse, you will choose the second. From this, we see that Rawls's difference principle can be justified on the assumption that people hate risk.

An Alternative Hypothesis

Thus far we have considered two grounds for altering the distribution of income. First, some people argue that the market distribution somehow violates the productivity principle. This might happen through monopoly, discrimination, or some other reason. Second, others argue that the distribution of income rests too much on luck, and that if we considered original positions, most would opt for a more equal income distribution.

An alternative explanation, which we only briefly mention here, is that state intervention in the distribution of income has nothing to do with justice, and more to do with bribing members of the lower income distribution to continue to participate in a market economy. One problem of the market is that through different endowments, chance, trade, and specialization, the resulting income distribution can become very skewed. For individuals with low endowments and talents that have little economic value, there is an incentive to opt out of trade and into violence and theft. Countries that ignore the distribution of wealth will end up spending larger amounts on police, military, and prisons, and run the risk of revolutions. By transferring even a small amount of wealth to the lower levels, governments may provide individuals with an incentive to remain within "society" as participants, rather than opt out.

Bruce Johnsen (1986) provides this type of explanation for the Kwakiutl practice of the *potlatch*.[2] The Kwakiutl were a native people who lived on the coast of British Columbia and consumed a diet mostly of salmon. Each clan would have a territory that would include streams in which the salmon would run. A potlatch was a ceremony held at the end of the fishing season in which clans with large catches of salmon would transfer part of the catch to clans with poor catches. Johnsen argues that this was done to avoid bloody battles over the more productive streams. Hence, although the potlatch lowered the immediate wealth of the giving tribe, it raised overall wealth because fewer resources were devoted towards violence and protection.

Regardless of why redistribution takes place, some methods of redistribution are better than others. In the following sections, we will analyze a range of possible redistributive institutions. As you will see, many of these schemes inevitably result in a conflict between the demands of redistribution (or equity) and of efficiency. The challenge, therefore, is to design economic institutions that achieve the desired redistribution while minimizing the adverse consequences in terms of efficiency.

PROBLEM 12.3

In biblical times travellers were allowed, under the law, to glean grain from fields. The amount that could be gleaned depended on whether the harvest had taken place or not, and was limited to specific distances from the path or road. Which explanation provided thus far best explains this law?

12.4 Minimum-Wage Legislation

One of the ever-present features of Western economies is minimum-wage legislation, designed to provide a "living wage" to workers whose wage rate would otherwise be below a legally designated minimum (See Parsons, 1987.) In Canada, for instance, every province has a different minimum wage; these vary between $5 and $7 in specified industries. Supposedly, the objective of minimum wage laws is to redistribute income to less well-paid members of society.

Despite being ubiquitous, the nagging question of all minimum wage laws is, "Do they help the working poor"? In other words, is the objective of redistribution invariably realized under minimum-wage schemes? Are workers in the designated industries actually better off once a minimum wage is put in effect? And whose income falls to make up for the rise in minimum-wage earners' incomes? Is inefficiency invariably an unfortunate side effect of minimum-wage laws?

2. Eaton and White (1991) provide a theoretical model.

As you will see, the answers depend on whether labour markets are perfectly competitive or monopsonistic. In a perfectly competitive labour market, an effective minimum wage creates unemployment or underemployment; redistributes income to workers from the buyers of the goods produced in minimum-wage-designated industries; and invariably creates inefficiency. By contrast, in monopsonistic labour markets, a minimum wage is likely to increase employment, redistribute money from monopsonistic firms to their employees, and offset some of the inefficiency associated with monopsony.

To analyze the implications of a minimum wage in these two market settings — perfectly competitive and monopsonistic — we will think of the labour-supply function as an aggregation of the various reservation wages of workers from lowest to highest. We can then interpret each worker's reservation wage as the value of his or her labour in the best alternative use: work in some other market, work at home, or leisure. For convenience, we will assume that the first of these alternatives — work in some other market — is the best. Although this supply function is actually a series of vertical segments ascending from left to right, we will approximate it by a smooth curve, such as the supply function in Figure 12.2. We will also assume that all other labour markets and all output markets are perfectly competitive. Given this assumption, for any labour market in equilibrium, the wage rate will be equal to the value of the marginal product.

Competitive Labour Markets

Figure 12.2 presents the basic implications of minimum-wage legislation in a competitive labour market. Let us look at what happens before and after a minimum-wage law is introduced. Before the minimum-wage legislation is introduced, the competitive equilibrium in this market is at point E in Figure 12.2, where 270 workers are employed at a wage rate of \$5 per hour. Bringing in a minimum-wage law will change the pre-legislation equilibrium at point E *only* if it is higher than the competitive equilibrium wage of \$5 per hour. If the minimum wage is higher than the competitive equilibrium wage, then the post-legislation equilibrium will shift. If the minimum wage is \$6 per hour, for example, the post-legislation equilibrium shifts to point E′, where just 130 workers are employed.

We can see from Figure 12.2 that one result of the legislation is inefficiency. Why? At the minimum-wage equilibrium at point E′, the value of the marginal product of an additional employee — equal to the minimum wage — is higher than the reservation wage at 130 workers on the supply function, equal to \$3 in Figure 12.2. In other words, some labour that could have been put to its most productive use in this industry will not be hired.

We can also see that labour is in excess supply at the minimum wage equilibrium at point E′ because 370 workers would like to be employed at this wage rate, but only 130 will be hired. It is tempting to interpret this excess supply as unemployment. However, the unemployment created by the minimum wage will almost certainly be less than (370 – 130) or 240 workers. We can decompose the excess supply as follows:

$$370 - 130 = (370 - 270) + (270 - 130)$$

The first term in the decomposition — (370 – 270) or 100 — is the added supply of labour (over and above 270) that would be forthcoming at a wage of \$6 if employment were freely available at this wage. Yet it is unlikely that this component of excess sup-

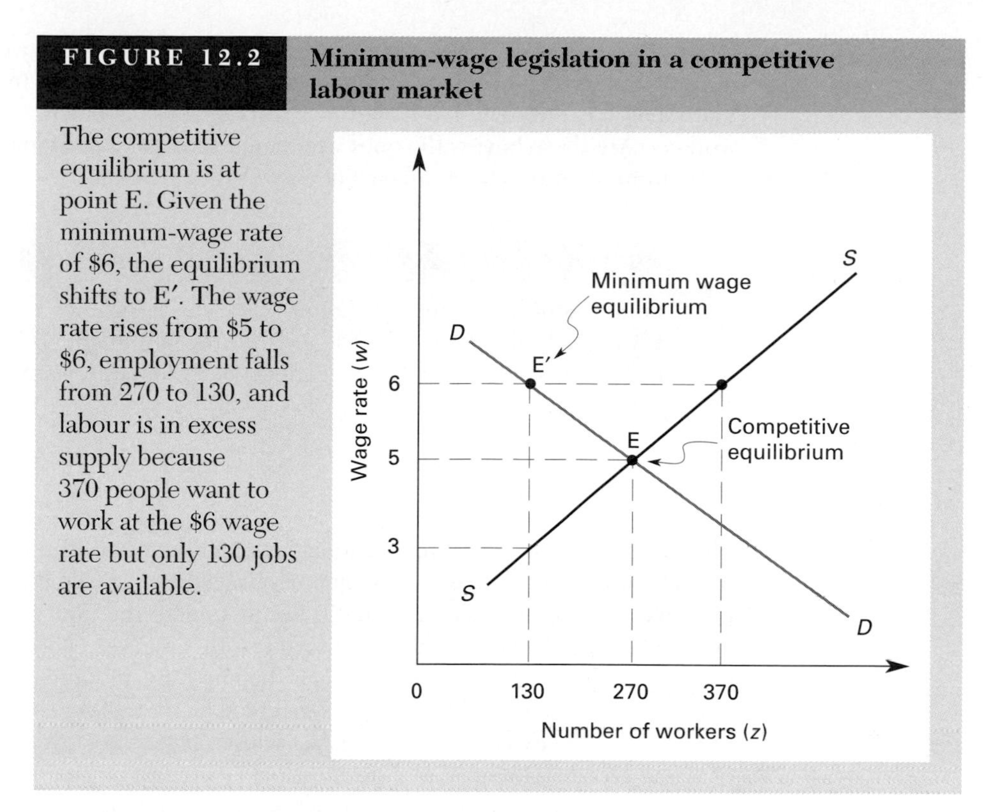

FIGURE 12.2 **Minimum-wage legislation in a competitive labour market**

The competitive equilibrium is at point E. Given the minimum-wage rate of \$6, the equilibrium shifts to E′. The wage rate rises from \$5 to \$6, employment falls from 270 to 130, and labour is in excess supply because 370 people want to work at the \$6 wage rate but only 130 jobs are available.

ply will actually materialize as unemployment. We know that the 100 workers in this group prefer their best alternative option to employment in this market at the \$5 competitive equilibrium wage rate since their reservation wages exceed \$5 per hour. Because job openings are few and far between, these workers are not likely to give up their alternative options to look for jobs in this market once the \$6 minimum wage is introduced. In all likelihood, they will stay put rather than risk unemployment.

The second term in the decomposition — (270 – 130) or 140 — is the number of workers initially employed at the competitive equilibrium who are laid off once the minimum-wage law is introduced. Even these workers may or may not show up among the unemployed. If they have no other options, they may continue to look for jobs at the higher minimum-wage rate of \$6. In this case, they will be unemployed. On the other hand, they may look for less attractive employment in some other industry. In this case, they will instead experience **underemployment**, in the sense that they accept jobs in which the value of their marginal product is less than the competitive equilibrium wage of \$5 per hour. This is just another indication that the minimum-wage equilibrium is inefficient: labour services are not allocated to their most productive uses.

under-employment

In a competitive market, inefficiency is a necessary by-product of an effective minimum-wage law. As labour services are no longer put to their most productive uses, either unemployment or underemployment will signal that inefficiency.

From the perspective of efficiency, then, minimum-wage legislation in competitive markets is unsatisfactory and the legislation is not entirely satisfactory from a redistributional perspective either. Even though the workers who manage to keep their jobs are better off, laid-off workers are clearly worse off. Moreover, the goods produced by firms employing minimum-wage labour will cost more. In effect, this means that income is redistributed from the buyers of those goods to the minimum-wage workers. Are these buyers the ones who ought to bear the burden of redistribution? Without more information, we cannot answer the question.

PROBLEM 12.4

Some people argue that minimum-wage legislation encourages discrimination in hiring. Can you make a supporting argument? (*Hint*: Contrast the employer's costs of discriminating when minimum-wage legislation is and is not in effect.)

Monopsonistic Labour Markets

The implications of minimum-wage legislation are very different in monopsonistic markets. Why? Notice that once a minimum wage law is brought in, the monopsonist's marginal factor cost function changes. Let w' denote the minimum wage rate and z denote the number of workers employed in this market. The monopsonist's pre-legislation marginal factor cost function is the line DBC in Figure 12.3. Once the minimum wage is introduced, however, its marginal factor cost function changes: it is now composed of the two line segments w'A and BC. If this monopsonist hires an amount of labour less than or equal to z', its marginal factor cost is the minimum wage w'. If it hires beyond that point, its marginal factor cost is segment BC of its original marginal

FIGURE 12.3 **Minimum wage and a monopsonist's marginal factor cost**

DAS is the supply function and DBC is the ordinary marginal factor cost function. Given the minimum wage w', the monopsonist's marginal factor cost function is composed of the two blue segments w'A and BC.

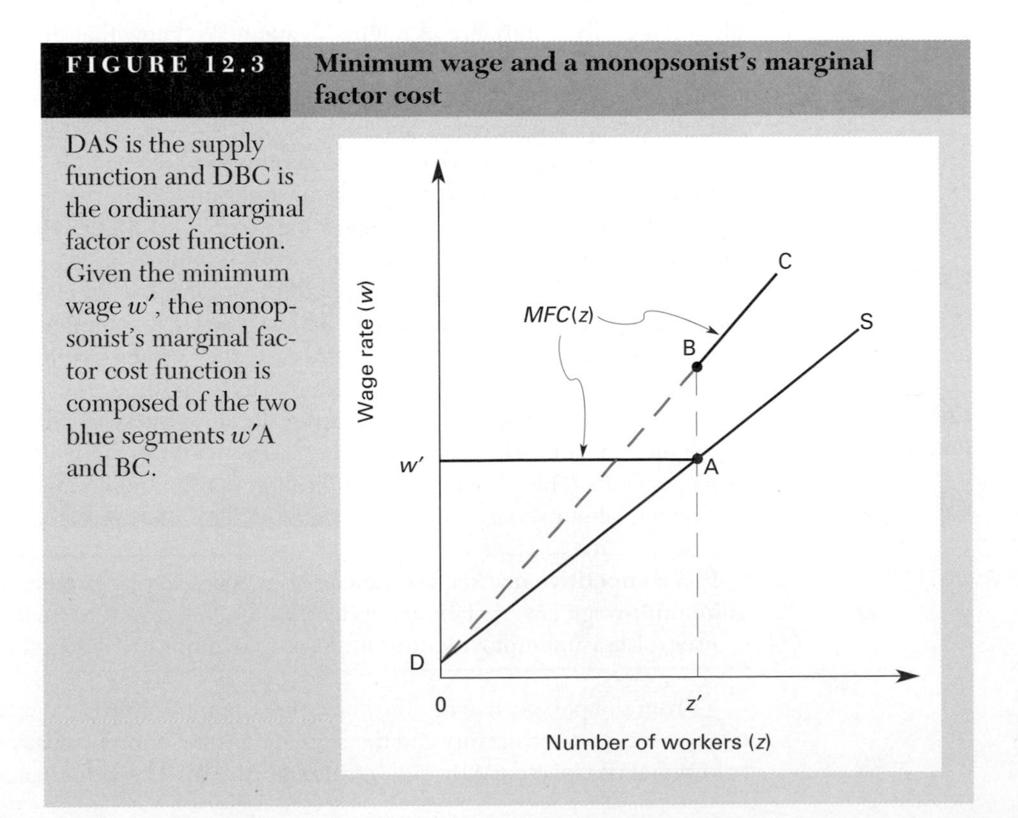

factor cost function because it can hire additional workers only at a wage higher than w'. In Problem 12.5, you can discover the most intriguing implications of a minimum-wage scheme in a monopsonistic labour market.

PROBLEM 12.5

Figure 12.4 illustrates the standard monopsony solution: the monopsonist employs z^* units of labour at a wage rate of w^*. First, show that if the minimum wage is higher than w^* but less than w''' in Figure 12.4, the monopsonist will increase employment. In other words, show that a minimum wage can actually reduce the inefficiency associated with monopsony by inducing the monopsonist to hire more labour. Second, identify the minimum-wage rate in Figure 12.4 that completely eliminates monopsonistic inefficiency. Finally, show that any minimum wage higher than w''' prompts the monopsonist to employ fewer than z^* units of labour. In other words, if the minimum wage is too high, it can increase inefficiency, an increase signalled by reduced employment in the industry.

As you discovered in Problem 12.5, minimum-wage legislation can promote both redistribution and efficiency in a monopsonistic labour market. In fact, if the minimum wage is cleverly chosen, monopsonistic inefficiency can be totally eliminated.

Let us look more closely at the redistributional aspects of the problem in a monopsonistic labour market. Does a minimum wage actually increase workers' incomes? The answer is a carefully qualified yes. As long as the minimum wage is not higher

FIGURE 12.4 **Minimum wage and monopsony**

In the absence of a minimum wage, the monopsonist hires z^* workers at wage w^*. Any minimum wage larger than w^* and smaller than w''' causes the monopsonist to hire more than z^* workers.

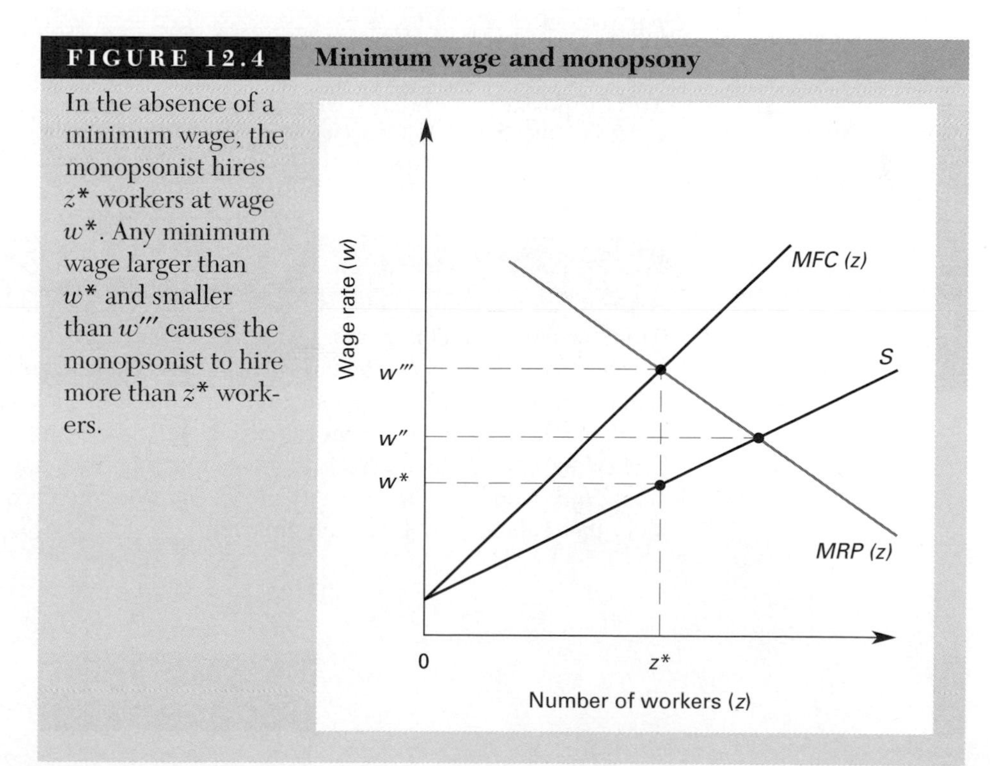

than w''' in Figure 12.4, some workers in the industry will be better off and none worse off. Why? At any minimum wage at or below w^*, the status quo prevails — and legislation is an empty gesture. At any minimum wage rate above w^* but below w''', workers hired before the introduction of the minimum wage will be paid more, and new workers will be hired at the new (minimum) wage rate. If the rate is w''', no new workers will be hired, but existing workers will be paid more. In any of these cases, the workers' increase in income is accomplished largely at the expense of the monopsonist. Is the monopsonist the one who ought to bear the burden of this redistribution? Again, the answer is not obvious.

The attractiveness of minimum-wage legislation thus depends on whether labour markets are competitive or monopsonistic. Empirical evidence suggests that labour markets covered by minimum-wage legislation are essentially competitive. This suggests that such legislation is problematic. Workers who remain employed are better off. It is not clear at whose expense this gain is made, however, because we do not know who is footing the bill. Furthermore, by creating unemployment or underemployment, the legislation will hurt some of the people it was intended to help.

Union Wage Rates: Some Analogous Issues

Many people hold strong opinions about unions: they either hate them or love them. Although analyzing the economic consequences of unionization objectively is not easy, we can make a move in that direction by adapting our minimum-wage analysis to apply to union wage rates. In Problem 12.6, you need only reinterpret the minimum-wage rate as a union wage rate, because — like a minimum wage — a union wage rate is just another **wage floor**. It sets the minimum wage paid in the unionized industry.

wage floor

PROBLEM 12.6

What are the redistributional and efficiency implications of a labour union with the power to negotiate a wage rate in a competitive labour market? In a monopsonistic labour market?

PROBLEM 12.7

A *hiring hall* is common in unionized construction trades and elsewhere. Traditionally, the union member who has been unemployed the longest gets the first available job. The hiring hall thus serves to distribute employment (and unemployment) among union members. If such a union has a fixed membership and (for convenience) a completely wage-inelastic, or vertical, supply function, what is the wage rate that the union would prefer? (*Hint*: Consider the elasticity of demand for labour and also consider the probability of being unemployed.)

PROBLEM 12.8

Under a *seniority rule*, if a unionized job is eliminated, the union member most recently hired is laid off. Will a union with a seniority rule demand a higher wage than one without it? Assume that in the absence of a seniority rule, each member has the same probability of being laid off if the union-negotiated wage dictates a drop in employment. (*Hint*: How does the private interest of a member change as his or her seniority changes?)

Application: Substitution and Union Wages

The effect of rent controls, price floors and ceilings, and union wages are all similar. Constraints placed on prices reduce the volume of trade, create transfers of wealth, and generate deadweight losses to consumers and firms. In Problem 12.6 you saw that under competitive conditions union wages result in a transfer of wealth from the firm to those workers that remain on the job. Jobs, however, are multi-dimensional, and firms are not likely to sit idly by and ignore the transfer of wealth nor the lost gains from trade. Economists have studied the effect of union wages on a number of dimensions and found some interesting forms of substitution taking place.

One of the most obvious forms of substitution is with inputs other than labour. Unionized firms become more capital intensive when union wages are increased. Less obvious forms of substitution relate to the nature of the job itself. Unionized workers are often required to work at a faster pace as firms attempt to get more effort out of the smaller workforce. Unionized workers often have less freedom in determining working hours and holiday time. Often, job safety is sacrificed for the higher wages. Firms with less safe working conditions still obtain workers because individuals are willing to trade it off for the higher wage. All of these substitutions result from firms attempting to recapture the transfer that results from the higher wage. Not surprisingly, many union contract negotiations often focus not on wages, but working conditions. Both the effort to substitute in these dimensions and the effort to negotiate restrictions on this type of substitution demonstrate how powerful the forces of demand and supply are.

12.5 Wage Floors in a Two-Sector Model

We can explore more fully the implications of a wage floor, such as a union wage or a minimum wage, by concentrating on a labour market divided into two sectors — say, a union (or minimum-wage-regulated) sector and a nonunion (or non-minimum-wage-regulated) sector. The market might be the construction industry, in which some workers are unionized and others are not. To keep this model simple, we will assume that a total of 100 workers are looking for jobs in these two sectors and that, in the absence of a wage floor, workers are perfectly mobile between the two sectors.

First, we will identify the competitive equilibrium wage and the allocation of the fixed supply of labour to the two sectors as a point of reference. All four quadrants in Figure 12.5 share an origin at the centre of the figure. The arrows at the ends of the axes indicate the direction in which any variable is increasing. The labour demand functions for sectors 1 and 2 are shown in quadrants I and II. (Notice that in quadrant II,

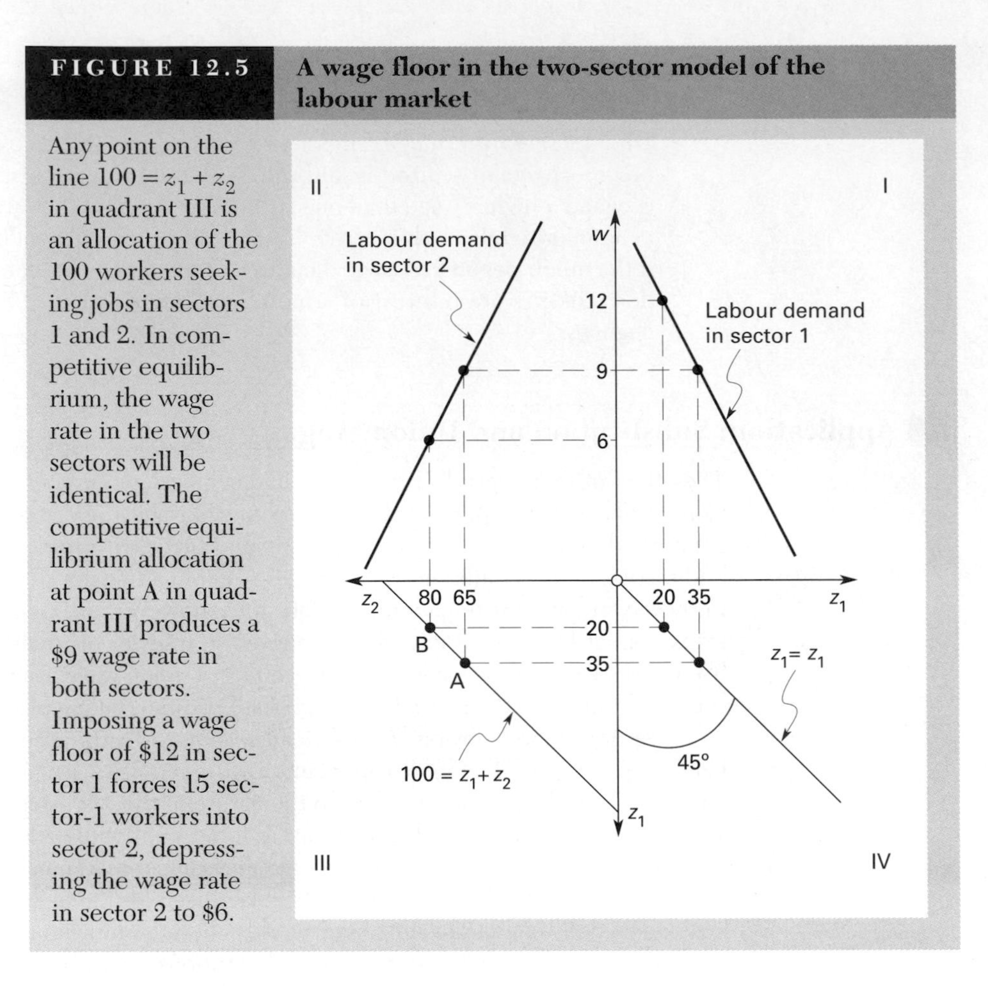

FIGURE 12.5 **A wage floor in the two-sector model of the labour market**

Any point on the line $100 = z_1 + z_2$ in quadrant III is an allocation of the 100 workers seeking jobs in sectors 1 and 2. In competitive equilibrium, the wage rate in the two sectors will be identical. The competitive equilibrium allocation at point A in quadrant III produces a \$9 wage rate in both sectors. Imposing a wage floor of \$12 in sector 1 forces 15 sector-1 workers into sector 2, depressing the wage rate in sector 2 to \$6.

z_2 increases from right to left along the z_2 axis.) The line in quadrant III labelled $100 = z_1 + z_2$ tells us all the possible allocations of the 100 workers to the two sectors. For example, at point A on this line, 35 workers are allocated to sector 1 and 65 workers to sector 2. The line $z_1 = z_1$ in quadrant IV allows us to project values of z_1 from quadrant III into quadrant I, and vice versa.

The competitive equilibrium is the allocation where the wage rates are identical in both sectors. Why? If the wage rates in the two sectors were different, all workers would look for work in the sector with the higher wage rate. The allocation that does the trick is at point A in quadrant III where the wage rate in both sectors is \$9 per hour and where 35 workers are employed in sector 1 and 65 workers in sector 2. (You should check to see that all the allocations to the right of A imply that the wage in sector 1 will be less than the wage in sector 2.)

The Underemployment Equilibrium

Now suppose that a wage floor — a union wage of \$12 per hour — is imposed in sector 1. If we set aside the possibility of unemployment for the moment and concentrate on underemployment, we can easily identify the resulting wage floor equilibrium. At the \$12 wage rate, only 20 workers will find jobs in sector 1. Projecting this value into quadrant III to point B, we discover that 80 workers will be hired in sector 2 and that the wage rate in sector 2 will fall from $9 to $6 per hour. In this two-sector model, then, imposing a wage floor means that some workers are reallocated from sector 1 to sector 2 and that, as a result, the wage rate in sector 2 will fall. Because $6 per hour is less than the competitive equilibrium wage of $9 per hour, we know that workers are not allocated to their most productive jobs: the wage floor results in an equilibrium with underemployment.

The Unemployment Equilibrium

Now let us reintroduce the possibility of unemployment by slightly modifying the wage-floor model in Figure 12.5. The crucial factor in determining the effect of wage floors on unemployment is what kind of institution governs the allocation of employment in the high-wage sector. The following model can be applied to any wage floor, including minimum wages. However, we will talk here in terms of a labour market characterized by unionized and nonunionized sectors, and we will assume that the governing institution is what East Coast dock workers used to call the *shape-up*. In the shape-up, the union members all turned up at a certain time each day, and a union official picked the members who were to work that day from the group.

Let us assume that dock workers were free to seek work in either of two sectors. In other words, they could join the dock workers' union and take part in the union shape-up in sector 1, or they could look for work in the nonunionized sector 2. We will denote the number of dock workers looking for jobs in the union shape-up in sector 1 by z_1 and the number looking for jobs in the nonunionized sector 2 by z_2. The institution of the shape-up (like the hiring hall in Problem 12.7) means that the available employment in sector 1 — or 20 jobs at the union wage of $12 per hour in Figure 12.5 — is shared out among all the union members. If we assume that the work is shared equally, then the proportion of time that any union member will be employed is just the number of jobs divided by the number of union members, $20/z_1$. The expected wage is therefore just the union wage of $12 per hour multiplied by $20/z_1$, or $240/z_1$.

Notice that Figure 12.6 is identical to Figure 12.5 in all but one respect. In quadrant I, we have plotted, not the demand for labour in sector 1, but the expected wage rate in sector 1, $240/z_1$. Notice, too, that the expected wage relationship passes through point G in quadrant I because when 20 union workers are looking for jobs in the shape-up, each worker is employed full-time at the union wage of $12 per hour.

Now let us identify the equilibrium in Figure 12.6. (For purposes of comparison we have included the underemployment equilibrium from Figure 12.5 at point B in quadrant III.) To find the equilibrium allocation, let us suppose that dock workers continue to join the union until the expected wage in unionized sector 1 is equal to the wage in nonunionized sector 2. As you can see by trying out alternative allocations, the equilibrium allocation is at point C in quadrant III, where the expected wage in both sectors is $8 per hour.

In the equilibrium at point C, 30 unionized workers in sector 1 are chasing 20 union jobs paying $12 an hour. As we said, because these unionized workers split the available work equally, the expected wage in sector 1 is 240/30 or $8 an hour. As you can see from Figure 12.6, there is unemployment in sector 1 equal to the distance marked u in quadrant I — the equivalent of 10 full-time workers. And again in the equilibrium at point C, 70 nonunion workers in sector 2 are employed full-time at $8 an hour. By comparison, in the equilibrium in the underemployment model of Figure 12.5 (reproduced at point B in Figure 12.6), 80 nonunion workers in sector 2 are

FIGURE 12.6 **Wage floors and search unemployment in a two-sector model**

When a $12 wage floor is imposed in sector 1, 20 workers are hired. The expected wage of a job searcher in this sector is plotted in quadrant I. In equilibrium, the expected wage is identical in the two sectors. The equilibrium allocation at point C in quadrant III produces an $8 wage rate in sector 2 and an $8 expected wage rate in sector 1. With 30 searchers in sector 1 and only 20 jobs, the $12 wage floor creates search unemployment u equal to 10 workers.

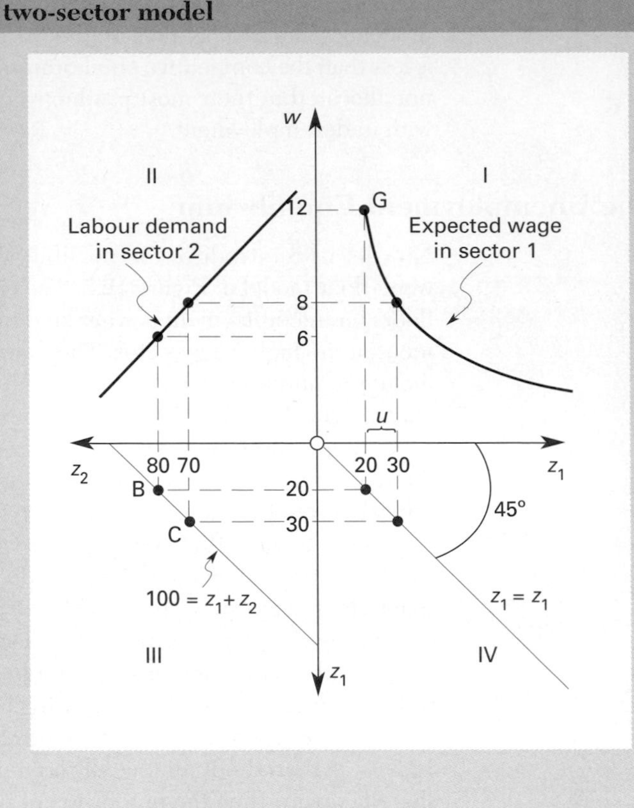

employed at $6 an hour. It is necessarily the case that the equilibrium wage rate in sector 2 of the preceding underemployment model is lower than the equilibrium wage rate in sector 2 of this unemployment model. Why? Because in this unemployment model some nonunionized workers will leave sector 2 to chase union jobs in the sector-1 shape-up, and, as a result, the smaller number of nonunionized workers remaining in sector 2 will earn a higher wage.

Notice that the equilibrium wage of $8 in this unemployment model happens to be less than the competitive equilibrium wage rate of $9 at point A in Figure 12.6. However, this is not always the case. As you may want to show, under different market conditions the equilibrium wage rate in this unemployment model may be either lower or higher than the competitive equilibrium wage rate. If it is higher, all workers are better off with the union wage floor; if it is lower, all workers are worse off with the union wage floor.

Two sources of inefficiency arise in this unemployment equilibrium. First, there is unemployment equal to the distance u in quadrant I of Figure 12.6. Second, the allocation of workers who are employed is inefficient because the union wage floor exceeds the equilibrium wage rate. In other words, the equilibrium in the unemployment model is characterized by both unemployment and underemployment.

PROBLEM 12.9

Michael Todaro (1969) used a two-sector model very much like this one to explain the shantytowns that lie around the perimeters of most large African cities. These cities are peopled by migrants from the agricultural sector who hope to find high-wage employment in the urban economy. Reinterpret our two-sector model to discover Todaro's explanation.

12.6 Income Maintenance

Despite serious disagreement among people living in economically developed societies about how income and wealth should be distributed, most agree that no one should have to live in abject poverty. Given that providing some minimum standard of living for everyone is a widely accepted social objective, what institutional arrangement can best achieve it? In other words, what institution is best for transferring income to the poorer members of society?

In the last section, we saw that there were difficulties associated with using a minimum-wage law as a way to ensure everyone a "living wage." In this section, we will explore three institutions designed to transfer income directly to the poor. The first of these transfer mechanisms is an ideal (but impracticable) income-maintenance institution that is compatible with both redistributional and efficiency objectives. We will call it the **efficient transfer mechanism**. It serves as a benchmark against which to assess the following two more practical but problematic transfer mechanisms. The first of these is a stylized version of the standard welfare system in developed countries that we will call the **topping-up mechanism**. As you will discover, this transfer mechanism is seriously incompatible with efficiency. The second is a combination of the efficient transfer mechanism and the topping-up mechanism, sometimes called a **negative income tax**. As you will see, it at least moderates the gross inefficiency associated with the standard welfare system.

efficient transfer mechanism

topping-up mechanism

negative income tax

The Efficient Transfer Mechanism

To an economist, the words "minimum standard of living" can be directly translated into economic terms as "minimum level of utility." The first transfer mechanism we will explore is concerned, then, not with an income-maintenance program but with a **utility-maintenance mechanism**. This transfer of income allows someone who is below a socially designated minimum level of utility to attain that target indifference curve. Consider the target indifference curve in Figure 12.7, where x_1 is hours of leisure and x_2 is income (a composite commodity). Suppose, too, that the person who is a potential recipient of the income transfer has no access to income other than the opportunity to work at wage rate w. So that we can interpret w as the value of the recipient's marginal product, we will assume that the economy is perfectly competitive.

utility-maintenance mechanism

When there is no income transfer, the potential recipient's opportunities are determined by the budget line $x_2 + wx_1 = wT$, where T is the total time available. Notice that here we can interpret w as the price of leisure, just as we did in Chapter 11. Because this budget line lies below the target indifference curve in Figure 12.7, some social action is needed to boost this person onto the target indifference curve.

FIGURE 12.7 An efficient income-transfer mechanism

In the absence of any income transfer, this person's budget line does not permit him or her to reach the target indifference curve. The unconditional income transfer S^* both allows this person to attain the target indifference curve and is efficient because *MRS* in the equilibrium at point E is equal to the wage rate.

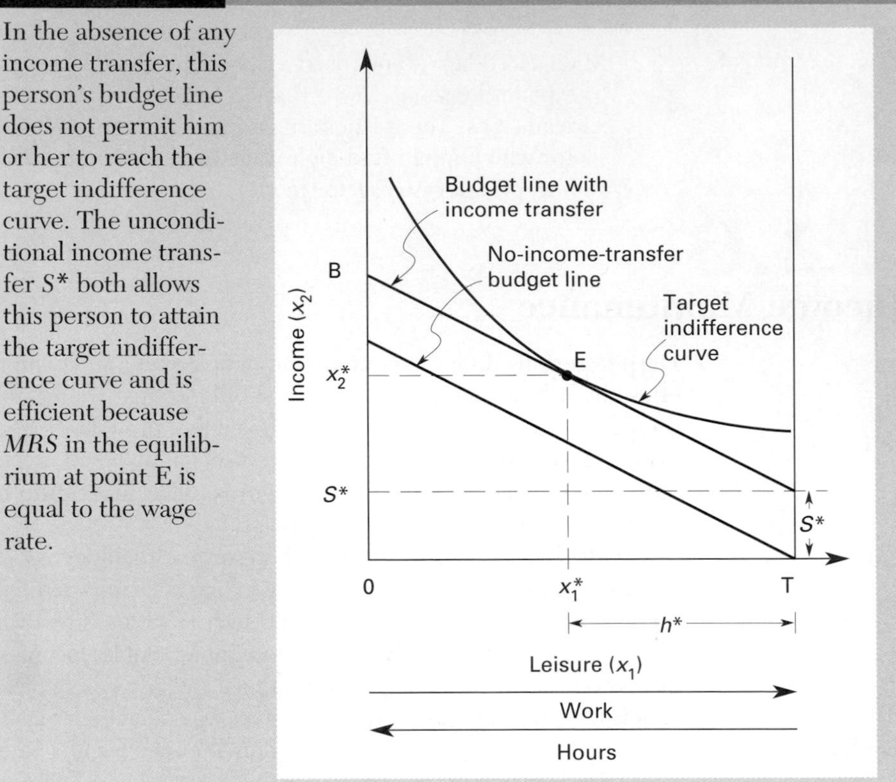

Let us look at a scheme that is ideal, in the sense that it both achieves the necessary redistribution and is consistent with efficiency. The single point on the target indifference curve consistent with efficiency is at point E in Figure 12.7, where *MRS* is equal to w. If this person is given an unconditional transfer of income (a no-strings-attached gift) just large enough to attain the target indifference curve, then he or she will choose the Pareto-optimal combination of income and leisure. Point E will then be the recipient's utility-maximizing combination. Given the appropriate transfer — equal to S^* in Figure 12.7 — the recipient will work h^* hours, enjoy x_1^* hours of leisure, and have income x_2^*. An unconditional lump-sum transfer of income therefore both accomplishes the mandated redistribution and is efficient.

The lump-sum transfer mechanism is ideal in yet another sense. As you will see in Problem 12.10, the transfer S^* is the smallest possible transfer that will allow this person to achieve the target indifference curve.

PROBLEM 12.10

To show that S^* is the minimum transfer, first reproduce Figure 12.7 on the top half of a sheet of paper. Next, construct a diagram on the bottom half in which you calculate for every value of x_1 the amount of income needed in addition to earned income to attain the target indifference curve.

Unfortunately, even though the lump-sum mechanism is efficient, it is not practical. First, we have no systematic way of choosing a target indifference curve for each person. Second, even if we had a way to do it, we would still face the overwhelming task of identifying everyone's individual preferences and everyone's budget line in order to pinpoint subsidy recipients.

income-maintenance program

As a result, maintenance policies are usually formulated in terms of target levels of income rather than utility: they are **income-maintenance programs**, and their object is to raise the income of anyone below a targeted level up to that level. In all practical income-maintenance schemes, the amount of the income transfer is conditional upon the amount of the recipient's earned income. As you will see, the conditional nature of these transfers creates a conflict between efficiency and distribution (or equity).

Topping Up and Welfare

The most pervasive conditional transfer mechanism is the familiar welfare system. Although real-world welfare systems are many and diverse, an essential feature of many is a *topping-up mechanism*, where the subsidy is just large enough to put the recipient at the mandated income level. The result is that potential recipients can affect the amount of income transferred to them by choosing how much (or how little) income they earn. In fact, they cannot avoid making such a choice. And that is the problem.

To see why, let us suppose that the target level of income is S' and that the potential recipient can work at wage rate w and has no wealth. Let S denote the size of the subsidy actually paid out. If the potential recipient earns as much as or more than the target level of income, S', then he or she will not be given any subsidy:

$$\text{If } wh \geq S' \text{ then } S = 0$$

If his or her earned income is below S', however, the amount of the subsidy will be just large enough that the earned income and the subsidy together equal the targeted income level:

$$\text{If } wh < S' \text{ then } S = S' - wh$$

We can translate this topping-up mechanism into the kinked budget line BGDE in Figure 12.8. Segment BG corresponds to the case in which earned income exceeds S' and no subsidy is paid. Segment GDE corresponds to the case in which this person earns an income that is less than S' and receives a subsidy just large enough to top his or her income up to S'.

Given this topping-up scheme, two solutions to the potential recipient's utility-maximization problem are possible. In one solution, which is not shown in Figure 12.8, this person picks some point on segment BG of the kinked budget line BGDE where earned income exceeds S'. In this case, he or she gets no income subsidy. In the other solution, this person picks point E in Figure 12.8. In this case, the recipient does not work, and all of his or her income S' comes instead from the public purse.

What the topping-up mechanism actually does, then, is to encourage potential recipients to give up all income from work (or to conceal any income actually earned). As long as earned income is less than S', the implicit marginal tax rate on that income is 100 percent because all work-generated income is immediately deducted from the subsidy. If the potential recipient in Figure 12.8 considered working h' hours instead

FIGURE 12.8 An inefficient income-transfer mechanism

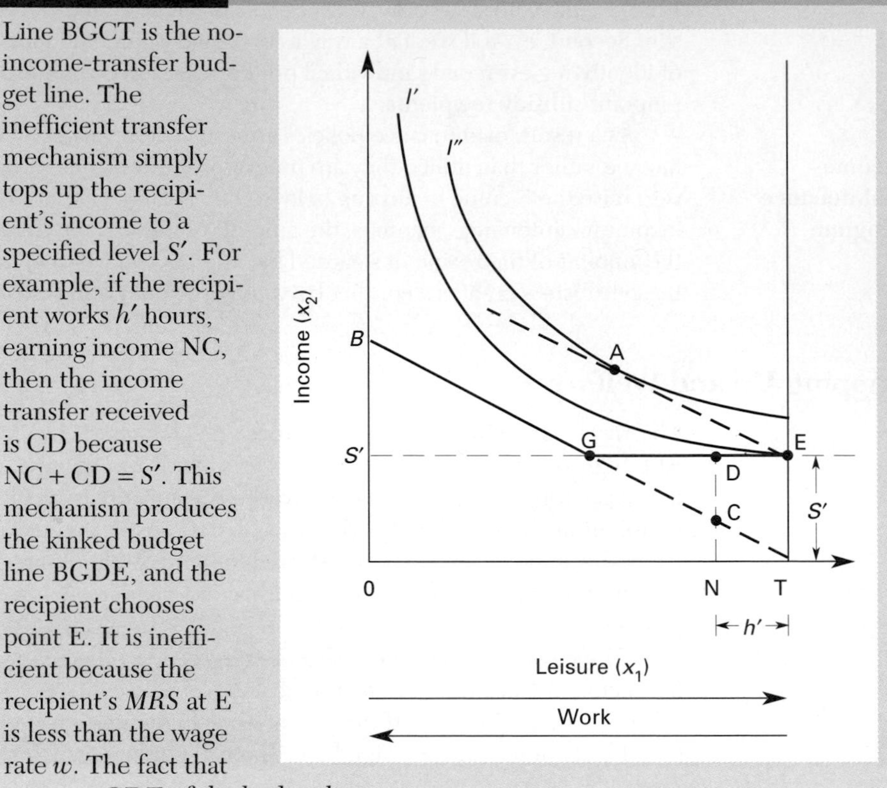

Line BGCT is the no-income-transfer budget line. The inefficient transfer mechanism simply tops up the recipient's income to a specified level S'. For example, if the recipient works h' hours, earning income NC, then the income transfer received is CD because $NC + CD = S'$. This mechanism produces the kinked budget line BGDE, and the recipient chooses point E. It is inefficient because the recipient's *MRS* at E is less than the wage rate w. The fact that segment GDE of the budget line is horizontal reflects an implicit 100 percent tax rate on earned income.

of zero hours, for instance, his or her earned income would rise from zero to distance NC. But the income transfer would fall by precisely the same amount, from S' to the distance CD, reflecting an implicit tax on earned income at a rate of 100 percent. The welfare scheme is thus associated with perverse incentives: it fails to provide recipients with any incentive to work. The topping-up mechanism is clearly inconsistent with Pareto optimality as well because at point E, *MRS* is less than w. We know that the potential recipient could attain point A in Figure 12.8 by receiving the transfer S' and working at the same time. Because he or she would be better off than at point E and because no one else would be worse off, we know that the equilibrium at point E is not efficient. Considerations like these have led to proposals for an alternative to the welfare system known as the negative income tax.

The Negative Income Tax

We will consider a scheme equivalent to one version of the *negative income tax* (NIT). It combines elements of the efficient lump-sum transfer mechanism and the topping-up mechanism. Though not problem-free, this combined scheme redistributes income to poorer members of society without the gross inefficiency and the perverse lack of work incentives associated with the welfare system. (See Watts, 1987.)

This version of the NIT combines an unconditional income transfer for everyone, equal to, say, S'', and a proportional (but moderate) income tax t on earned income—in the range of a 10 percent to 25 percent tax rate rather than the welfare scheme's implicit tax rate of 100 percent. Under this combined scheme, everyone receives the subsidy S'', pays twh in taxes, keeps $(1 - t)wh$ from his or her earned income, and therefore receives a net income of

$$x_2 = S'' + (1 - t)wh$$

(The proposed NIT would use a slightly different mechanism: the government would subtract the income tax due on earned income from S'' and pay only the net subsidy, distance DE in Figure 12.9.)

We can translate this combined scheme into the budget line HES'' in Figure 12.9. To compare this NIT mechanism with the welfare topping-up mechanism, we have chosen S'' and t so that this person reaches indifference curve I' under either transfer scheme. The budget line HES'' is therefore tangent to the indifference curve at point E in Figure 12.9 and this person is indifferent between the two schemes. Nevertheless, under the combined mechanism, this person now works h^* hours and earns income equal to wh^*. (This person's disposable income, including the income subsidy and subtracting taxes payable on earned income, is the larger sum x_2^* in Figure 12.9.) You can see that point E is not an efficient equilibrium because MRS is less than w. Nevertheless, the NIT mechanism offsets at least some of the inefficiency associated with the topping-up mechanism and avoids the disincentive to work. Furthermore, the NIT mechanism makes a smaller demand on the public purse. Once the taxes paid on earned income are deducted from the unconditional sub-

FIGURE 12.9 **A negative income tax**

Think of the NIT as offering an unconditional subsidy S'' combined with a proportional tax on earned income, producing the budget line HES''. This individual chooses point E, working h^* hours and receiving the net subsidy DE. The negative income tax avoids the extreme work disincentive inherent in the topping-up mechanism.

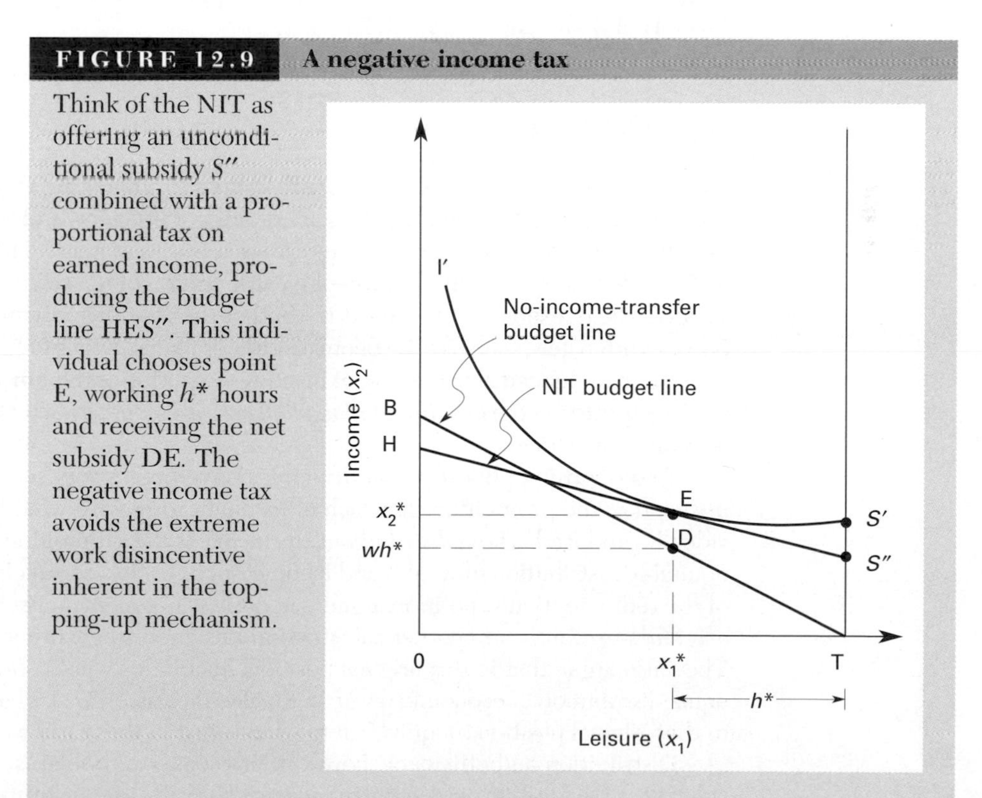

sidy, the net subsidy is just the distance DE in Figure 12.9. This amount is much smaller than S', the transfer under the topping-up welfare mechanism. As you will discover in Problem 12.11, however, these results are not the invariable outcome of a negative income tax.

PROBLEM 12.11

On a single diagram, draw the budget lines associated with the topping-up and NIT schemes. Let the target income under the topping-up mechanism, S', be greater than the unconditional transfer under the NIT, S''. Show that a person who will not receive a subsidy under the topping-up scheme might decide to work less and to receive a subsidy under NIT.

As this problem illustrates, once we leave behind the ideal world of the efficient transfer mechanism, there are no easy answers about how best to redistribute income to poorer members of society. In reality, any income-transfer mechanism that has desirable personal and social effects when applied to one person may have just the opposite effects when applied to someone else. Furthermore, conflicts between efficiency and redistributional objectives are unavoidable.

These difficulties do not suggest that we should throw up our hands in despair, merely that theory can carry us only so far. Theory identifies the potential problems that accompany any income-transfer mechanism; empirical evidence tells us how serious these potential problems are in reality. To design a real income-transfer mechanism that successfully minimizes the tension between efficiency and redistribution, good hard evidence is required, and such evidence is being provided. (See, for example, Cogan, 1983; Hall, 1975; and Keely, 1977.)

SUMMARY

One major task of markets is to allocate resources to competing ends. The question in this context is whether input markets are or are not efficient, and the Pareto criterion provides a precise answer. Another task of markets — and particularly of input markets — is to determine the distribution of wealth and income among the members of a society. The question in this context is whether the resulting distribution is the "right" one. Unfortunately, there is no economic indicator that allows us to say whether the market system, or indeed any other set of institutions, performs the function of distribution well. Determining the *just distribution of income* is essentially an ethical rather than an economic question.

Two opposing philosophical principles have been proposed. The *productivity principle* is the proposition that each of us ought to receive what he or she has individually produced. The *redistributionist principle* is the proposition that a more nearly equitable distribution of wealth and income ought to be a social objective. Advocates of the redistributionist position argue that ethical judgments must be impersonal: the *original position* is a hypothetical situation designed to ensure such impersonality. They also argue that in this original position, each of us would choose a more or less equal distribution of economic rewards. Finally, they assert that what we would choose in this original position is equivalent to what is just in the world we actually inhabit.

Distribution and efficiency, however, are separate problems. As we saw in considering a range of *income-maintenance mechanisms*, the institutions that solve one problem regrettably do not solve the other. This presents us with a fundamental social quandary. Once we realize that the efficient income-transfer institutions are not practicable, we must conclude that any institution or set of institutions that effectively redistributes income or wealth will be inconsistent with economic efficiency, at least to some degree. Thus, a conflict between *efficiency* and *distribution* is inevitable.

The problem for economists is to design redistributionary institutions that minimize the conflict between equity and efficiency. Yet economic theory alone cannot solve this problem. It can only highlight the problems that we expect to arise in any particular institutional context. To take any further step requires empirical work to determine how serious the potential problems identified by economic theory are in reality.

EXERCISES

1. Suppose that in an economy composed of three people we can measure each person's utility cardinally. Suppose, too, that we can use three possible institutions — A, B, and C — to organize economic activity in this economy. The problem is to choose one of the three institutions. The utility of each person under each institution is given below.

Institution	*Person 1's Utility*	*Person 2's Utility*	*Person 3's Utility*
A	45	45	45
B	75	60	30
C	78	63	21

   a. According to Rawls's difference principle, which institution is preferred?
   b. Suppose that you would be one of the three people in this economy, but you don't know which one. Which institution would you choose? If each person maximizes expected utility and if each attaches probability 1/3 to being any one person, which is the preferred institution?
   c. Now suppose that each of the three does know which person he or she will be. If the institution is chosen by majority rule, which one will be chosen by self-interested individuals?

2. Zuzana hires labour to make fancy fishing lures in a small village. She is a profit maximizer. Her marginal revenue product function is

$$MRP(z) = 130 - z$$

and the supply of labour to her firm is

$$w = 10 + z/2$$

where z is the number of workers she hires and w is the daily wage rate.

   a. What wage rate does she pay and how much labour does she hire?
   b. Her workers are forming a union and need advice on what wage rate they should seek. Their advisor has told them that they should ask for a wage no lower than $50. Explain why this is good advice.
   c. The workers have said that they want to ensure that employment does not fall. Given this objective, what is the maximum wage they should bargain for?

3. Recall the two-sector model developed in Section 12.5. Now suppose labour demand functions in the two sectors are $w_1 = 149 - z_1/2$ and $w_2 = 100 - z_2/2$. There are 200 workers to be allocated to the two sectors.

   a. Find the competitive equilibrium allocation and wage rate.
   b. Now suppose that a union wage equal to $100 is established in sector 1 and that available jobs are allocated permanently to a lucky group of 98 workers. Find the underemployment equilibrium.
   c. Finally, suppose once again that a union wage equal to $100 is established in sector 1 but that jobs in this sector are now allocated by the shape-up described in Section 12.5. Find the unemployment equilibrium. What is the level of unemployment? What is the wage in sector 2? What is the expected wage of a worker looking for work in sector 1?

d. Illustrate all three equilibria on one carefully constructed graph.

4. Explain (i) why lump-sum, or unconditional, income transfers and taxes are consistent with Pareto optimality; (ii) why they are impractical as a means of achieving significant redistribution; and (iii) why income transfers and taxes that are conditional on earned income are not consistent with Pareto optimality.

5. Professional associations, such as the Upper Canada Law Society, have considerable leeway in determining both the standards that new entrants must meet and the prices of professional services.

   a. First, suppose that the professional association can set prices but cannot control entry standards. What are the implications of a price increase when the demand for professional services is price-inelastic? In particular, what will happen to the earnings and hours worked of an individual professional in the short run and the long run? What are the implications when demand is price-elastic?
   b. Second, suppose that the association can control entry standards but not prices. What are the implications of increasing the entry standard—say, by requiring entrants to spend an additional term in a training program? In particular, do the established practitioners have private incentives to increase the entry standard?

6. Suppose there are two welfare programs. The first pays $50/day to anyone who was poor last year. The second pays an income supplement of 30 percent of the wage earned this year to anyone classified as poor.

   a. Which program reduces the hours worked the most?
   b. If the wage for poor individuals is $7 per hour, show the effects of each program on the individual's budget constraint.

7. An experiment was once run in British Columbia and New Brunswick (true story). Six thousand single parents on welfare were told that if they worked full time then their wage would be doubled. Another six thousand single parents on welfare were followed as well, but they were not given the wage supplement. After three years 30 percent of the first group were working, but 23 percent of the second group were working. In other words, the doubling of the income only led to a 7 percent difference in participation. Why do you think this was so? If you were to devise a scheme like this, what would be one minor change you would make that might increase the work force participation more?

8. A "closed shop" means that a firm can only hire workers who belong to a union, while a "union shop" means that a firm can hire anyone; they just have to join the union once hired. In which type of firm would you expect more discrimination based on race, religion, and the like?

9. An employment catch word of the past 15 years has been "comparable worth" which attempts to determine the worth of various jobs and whether the wages in those jobs match. Does this make any sense? (*Hint:* How does the wage of a job vary with the number of individuals that perform it?)

10. Human capital depreciates at different rates. It has been estimated that for academics, knowledge in the physical sciences depreciates faster than knowledge in the humanities. How might this explain the higher fraction of women in humanities than in the physical sciences?

11. Over the past decade the stock market has soared. Those in the top 10 percent of wealth hold the lion's share of stock. What has this bull market done to the Lorenz curve over time?

12. Suppose Ransom and Divine are trapped on an island with only 100 kilograms of food. Their utility functions for the food are given by: $U^R = \sqrt{F}$ and $U^D = 1/3\sqrt{F}$, where F is the amount of food each eats.

    a. If they each eat the same amount of food, what is their utility level?
    b. If they have the same level of utility, what amount of food do they consume?
    c. How should the food be allocated to maximize the sum of the utilities?
    d. Suppose the two agree that total welfare results from the following function

    $$W = \sqrt{U^R} \times \sqrt{U^D}$$

    How should the food be distributed to maximize total welfare?

13. It has been suggested that rather than patents, governments should purchase innovations and place them in the public domain. What is the logic behind this suggestion? Assuming the value of the innovation is known, will this improve social welfare above a patent system? What might be some practical problems with such a scheme?

*14. Ross has 24 hours a day to devote to work or leisure. His utility function between income (X_2) and leisure (X_1) is $U(X_1, X_2) = X_1 X_2$ and his wage rate is \$4. For each of the following four cases, calculate Ross's utility-maximizing choice of income and leisure and illustrate your answer using a graph in (X_1,X_2) space.
   a. There is no income-transfer mechanism.
   b. Ross receives an unconditional lump-sum transfer of \$8 per day.
   c. There is a welfare system ("topping-up mechanism") that ensures that Ross's daily income can never fall below \$30.
   d. There is a negative income tax system that provides an unconditional transfer of \$15 per day with an income tax of 25 percent.

*15. A certain market for labour is monopsonistic. The labour supply curve in this market is $W_s = 2 + 1/4\, Z$, where W is the wage rate and Z is the amount of labour. The monopsonist's marginal revenue product of labour is $MRP = 22 - 3/4\, Z$.
   a. How many units of labour will the monopsonist employ? What will be the wage rate?
   b. Explain clearly why the equilibrium in (a) is inefficient.
   c. Suppose a minimum wage policy were to be implemented in this market. Over what range of W would the minimum wage be efficiency-improving? Why?
   d. At what level should the minimum wage be set to completely eliminate the monopsonistic inefficiency?

REFERENCES

Arrow, K. 1976. "The Viability and Equity of Capitalism," E. S. Woodward Lectures in Economics. Department of Economics, University of British Columbia.

Cogan, J. F. 1983. "Labor Supply and Negative Income Taxation: New Evidence from the New Jersey–Pennsylvania Experiment," *Economic Inquiry*, 21:465–83.

Cowell, F. A. 1987. "Redistribution of Income and Wealth," in *The New Palgrave: A Dictionary of Economics*, J. Eatwell, M. Milgate, and P. Newman (eds.). London: Macmillan.

Eaton, B.C. and W.D. White. 1991. "The Distribution of Wealth and the Efficiency of Institutions," *Economic Inquiry*, 29(2):336–50.

Hall, R. 1975. "Effects of the Experimental Negative Income Tax on Labor Supply," in *Work Incentives and Income Guarantees*, J. Peckman and P. M. Timpane (eds.), Brookings Institute.

Johnsen, D. B. 1986. "The Formation and Protection of Property Rights among the Southern Kwakiutl Indians," *Journal of Legal Studies*, 15(1):41–67.

Keely, M., et al. 1977. "The Labor Supply Effects and Costs of Alternative Negative Income Tax Programs: Evidence from the Seattle and Denver Income Maintenance Experiments," Stanford Research Institute.

Parsons, D. O. 1987. "Minimum Wages," in *The New Palgrave: A Dictionary of Economics*, J. Eatwell, M. Milgate, and P. Newman (eds.), London: Macmillan.

Rawls, J. 1971. *A Theory of Justice*. Boston: Belknap Press of Harvard University.

Sarlo, C. 1992. *Poverty in Canada*, 2nd ed. Vancouver: Fraser Institute.

Todaro, M. 1969. "A Model for Labor Migration and Urban Unemployment in Less Developed Countries," *American Economic Review*, 59:138–48.

Watts, H. 1987. "Negative Income Tax," in *The New Palgrave: A Dictionary of Economics*, J. Eatwell, M. Milgate, and P. Newman (eds.). London: Macmillan.

CHAPTER 13

Competitive General Equilibrium

We looked at the question of distribution in Chapter 12. In this chapter, we take up the allocation question once again as we finally fit all the analytical pieces of earlier chapters into one large picture of efficiency in an economy-wide context. We are now widening our perspective from the earlier partial equilibrium framework, characterized by a market-by-market analysis, to a **general equilibrium** framework, in which we simultaneously consider all markets in the economy. At every turn, we will be drawing on what we learned in earlier chapters. If at any point you are uncertain about the earlier material, briefly review it before proceeding.

general equilibrium

A recurring theme in economics concerns the extent to which the interactions of self-interested individuals yield results that are in some sense socially desirable. Adam Smith, the father of the doctrine of **natural identity of interests**, argued that every person, in pursuing his or her own self-interest, would be led as by an "invisible hand" to behave in ways that ultimately contributed to the welfare of society as a whole. But, as George Stigler has observed, Smith's doctrine of the natural identity of interests is "not really a doctrine at all: it is a problem."[1] Smith's doctrine raises this question: What kinds of social arrangements promote an identity between public and private interests? In this chapter, we will rise to the challenge posed by Smith's doctrine as we look for a set of institutions consistent with the natural identity of interests. As you will discover, when certain restrictive conditions are satisfied, the institutions of perfect competition promote Pareto optimality, or efficiency.

natural identity of interests

To an economist, the overriding purpose of the economic system is to transform the scarce resources belonging to individuals into consumption goods that benefit those same individuals. Individual people are therefore the leading actors in the economic drama. From them (and from nature) comes the wherewithal to produce goods, and goods are produced for their benefit. In this larger, general equilibrium drama, then, firms are the minor players. Their only role is to facilitate the process of transforming resources into consumption goods. Questions of efficiency are therefore concerned not with the profit of firms but exclusively with the well-being of individual people.

Using the Pareto criterion as our yardstick for measuring individual well-being, we can see that the general equilibrium of an economy is efficient if no person can be made better off without making another person worse off.

1. See Stigler's (1957) introductory remarks. His *Selections from The Wealth of Nations* is an excellent introduction to Smith's great work.

13.1 Efficiency in an Exchange Economy

Let us begin our analysis by focusing on a simple *exchange economy* in which goods are exchanged and consumed but not produced. We will then introduce production into the model and generalize the understanding developed in the simpler context of an exchange economy.[2]

The Edgeworth Box Diagram

Imagine that two people — Marvin and Shelly — are living on some isolated island where there are 102 units of good 1 and 66 units of good 2. We can use a box diagram to describe all possible allocations of goods in this island exchange economy. The dimensions of the box diagram in Figure 13.1 reflect the available quantities of goods 1 and 2: the horizontal sides are 102 units long because there are 102 units of good 1 in this economy; the vertical sides are 66 units long because there are 66 units of good 2 in this economy. Possible consumption bundles for Shelly — or, to put it another way, possible allocations of goods to Shelly, are plotted relative to the origin 0_S at the lower left-hand corner of the box. Similarly, possible allocations of goods to Marvin are plotted relative to the origin 0_M at the upper right-hand corner of the box diagram.

The important thing to recognize is that any point in the box is an allocation of the available quantities of the two goods to Marvin and to Shelly. Conversely, any allocation of the 102 units of good 1 and 66 units of good 2 to Marvin and Shelly is described by some point in the box.

PROBLEM 13.1

How much of each good does Marvin have, and how much does Shelly have at each of the following points in Figure 13.1, point A; Marvin's origin 0_M; point B? Suppose that all 66 units of good 2 are allocated to Shelly and all 102 units of good 1 to Marvin. What point in Figure 13.1 describes this allocation?

Edgeworth box diagram

Notice, too, that we can plot Shelly's and Marvin's indifference curves in the box diagram. When we include indifference curves, the diagram is called an **Edgeworth box diagram**, after F. Y. Edgeworth, a late-nineteenth-century British economist who was the first to use this type of diagram although some claim that Pareto was the originator of the diagram. Since Shelly's indifference curves, labelled S_1 and S_2, are plotted relative to the origin 0_S, they have the familiar convex-to-the-origin shape. Marvin's indifference curves, labelled M_1 and M_2, are also standard convex-to-the-origin indifference curves, but they look odd because they are plotted relative to Marvin's origin 0_M. To see that they are convex to Marvin's origin, pick your book up and reorient it so that 0_M is at the lower left-hand corner of the box. Marvin's indifference curves will then

2. Walras (1874, 1877) is the founder of general equilibrium theory. Jaffe (1954) is the English translator. Arrow and Hahn (1971) present a comprehensive treatment of general equilibrium theory and (in Chapter 1) an interesting history of it.

FIGURE 13.1 The Edgeworth box diagram

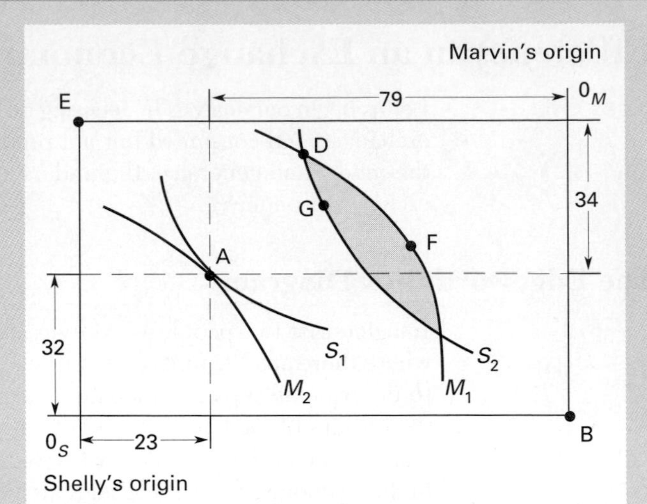

Shelly's consumption bundles and indifference curves are plotted relative to 0_S; Marvin's are plotted relative to 0_M. Because Shelly's and Marvin's indifference curves are tangent at allocation A, the allocation is Pareto-optimal. In contrast, because Shelly's and Marvin's indifference curves intersect at allocation D, the allocation is not Pareto-optimal: allocations in the shaded area are Pareto-preferred to allocation D.

appear in their familiar shape. To be sure that you understand the Edgeworth box diagram, try the following problem.

PROBLEM 13.2

What is Shelly's preference ordering of the four allocations A, D, G, and F in Figure 13.1? What is Marvin's?

PREFERENCE ASSUMPTIONS

To keep our discussion as simple as possible, we will use four assumptions about preferences throughout the chapter:

1. Indifference curves are convex to the appropriate origin.
2. Indifference curves are smooth.
3. Both goods are essential for all consumers.
4. The only variables that affect an individual's economic well-being are the quantities of the two goods consumed by that person.

In Problem 13.3, you will have a chance to discover for yourself the role played by the convexity assumption. The second assumption allows us to use the marginal rate of substitution *MRS* in analyzing Pareto optimality, and the third allows us to concentrate on allocations in the interior of the Edgeworth box. (See Section 2.4 for the definition of *MRS*, and Section 3.4 for a discussion of essential and inessential goods.)

The fourth assumption rules out externalities involving consumption — in essence, it means that the only things that people care about are their own consumption bundles. In Chapter 18, which centres on externalities, you will see that consumption externalities raise some very interesting and difficult questions.

Now let us look at some specific allocations and ask if they are Pareto-optimal. Is the allocation at D in Figure 13.1, which puts Shelly on indifference curve S_2 and

Marvin on indifference curve M_1, Pareto-optimal? Shelly prefers any allocation above and to the right of S_2 to D, and Marvin prefers any allocation below and to the left of M_1 to D. Therefore, any allocation in the shaded area above S_2 and below M_1 is preferred by both Marvin and Shelly to D; that is, any allocation in the shaded area is Pareto-preferred to D. We know, then, that the allocation at D is not Pareto-optimal.

Now let us consider the allocation at A, which puts Shelly on S_1 and Marvin on M_2. Take your pencil and first shade in the allocations above and to the right of S_1 which make Shelly better off than she is at A, and then shade in the allocations on M_2, or below and to the left of M_2, which make Marvin no worse off than he is at A. Since these two shaded areas have no points in common, it is impossible to make Shelly better off without making Marvin worse off. Similarly, given the allocation at A, it is impossible to make Marvin better off without making Shelly worse off. We know, then, that the allocation at A is Pareto-optimal.

What distinguishes allocation D from allocation A is that indifference curve M_1 intersects (or crosses) indifference curve S_2 at D, while indifference curve M_2 is tangent to indifference curve S_1 at A. As you can easily verify, any allocation in the interior of an Edgeworth box where two indifference curves intersect is not Pareto-optimal. Furthermore, the following is true:

When indifference curves are smooth and convex, if two indifference curves are tangent at a point in an Edgeworth box, then that point is a Pareto-optimal allocation.

PROBLEM 13.3

In an Edgeworth box, construct an indifference curve for Shelly that has a concave portion in the middle. Now construct an indifference curve for Marvin, convex to Marvin's origin, that is tangent to Shelly's indifference curve at one point and intersects her indifference curve at two other points. Show that the point of tangency is not a Pareto-optimal allocation, and identify the allocations that are Pareto-preferred to it.

Notice that at the Pareto-optimal allocation at A in Figure 13.1, the marginal rate of substitution *MRS* is identical for Marvin and Shelly. This follows from the definition of *MRS* as the absolute value of the slope of the indifference curve and from the fact that the indifference curves S_1 and M_2 are tangent at point A. This observation lets us restate our understanding of Pareto optimality in an exchange economy:

Given smooth and convex indifference curves, if *MRS* at some allocation is identical for Marvin and Shelly, then that allocation is Pareto-optimal.

Efficiency in Consumption

More generally, let us see what we can say about Pareto optimality (or efficiency) in an exchange economy composed of many people. Suppose that we have a many-person exchange economy and, for purposes of argument, that *MRS* at the current allocation is identical for everyone in that exchange economy. We could isolate any two people — with their consumption bundles in hand — to form an exchange economy very much like the one shown in Figure 13.1. In that two-person exchange economy, the initial allocation would be Pareto-optimal since *MRS* is identical for these two people. Therefore, if *MRS* is identical for every person in a many-person exchange economy, there are no bilateral (two-person) trades that are Pareto-preferred. Although we will not attempt a proof, there are also no multilateral (many-person) trades that are Pareto-preferred. Therefore, we can state the following general result:

Efficiency in Consumption:
Given the assumptions we have made, an allocation of goods is Pareto-optimal in a many-person exchange economy if *MRS* is identical for all individuals.[3]

The Contract Curve

Given our assumptions, we know that any point in an Edgeworth box where the indifference curves of the two individuals are tangent is a Pareto-optimal allocation. By finding all the points in the Edgeworth box where the indifference curves are tangent, we can describe the entire set of Pareto-optimal allocations. This set, called the

contract curve

contract curve, is the line connecting all these points of tangency.

Line *CC* in Figure 13.2 is the contract curve for Marvin and Shelly. Even though we have drawn only three indifference curves for each, the box is filled with indifference curves. At any point on *CC*, two indifference curves, one for Marvin and one for Shelly, are tangent.

3. We can use the technique of constrained maximization to show this result. Pick any two consumers with utility functions $U^1(x_1^1, x_2^1)$ and $U^2(x_1^2, x_2^2)$, and any bundle of the two goods to be allocated to the two individuals— say, the bundle (x_1', x_2'). If we fix the utility level of the first individual at, say, u^1, then efficiency in consumption—Pareto optimality—clearly demands that we allocate the available bundle of goods to the two individuals so as to maximize $U^2(x_1^2, x_2^2)$, subject to the constraint that $u^1 = U^1(x_1^1, x_2^1)$. This is a standard constrained-maximization problem, and we will show that its solution implies that *MRS* is identical for the two consumers. The Lagrangian is

$$L(x_1^2, x_2^2, \lambda) = U^2(x_1^2, x_2^2) + \lambda[u^1 - U^1(x_1' - x_1^2, x_2' - x_2^2)]$$

where (x_1^2, x_2^2) is the second individual's consumption bundle and $(x_1' - x_1^2, x_2' - x_2^2)$ is the first individual's bundle. Setting the partial derivatives of $L(\bullet)$ with respect to x_1^2 and x_2^2 equal to zero, we have

$$\partial U^2(x_1^2, x_2^2)/\partial x_1^2 - \lambda \partial U^1(x_1' - x_1^2, x_2' - x_2^2)/\partial x_1^1 = 0$$
$$\partial U^2(x_1^2, x_2^2)/\partial x_2^2 - \lambda \partial U^1(x_1' - x_1^2, x_2' - x_2^2)/\partial x_2^1 = 0$$

Manipulating these two expressions, we have

$$\lambda = \frac{\partial U^2(x_1^2, x_2^2)/\partial x_1^2}{\partial U^1(x_1' - x_1^2, x_2' - x_2^2)/\partial x_1^1} = \frac{\partial U^2(x_1^2, x_2^2)/\partial x_2^2}{\partial U^1(x_1' - x_1^2, x_2' - x_2^2)/\partial x_2^1}$$

This result implies equality of the marginal rates of substitution:

$$\frac{\partial U^2(x_1^2, x_2^2)/\partial x_1^2}{\partial U^2(x_1^2, x_2^2)/\partial x_2^2} = \frac{\partial U^1(x_1' - x_1^2, x_2' - x_2^2)/\partial x_1^1}{\partial U^1(x_1' - x_1^2, x_2' - x_2^2)/\partial x_2^1}$$

Let us see why this set of allocations is called the contract curve. Any allocation that is not on CC — point A, for example — is not Pareto-optimal. If Marvin and Shelly are initially at A, any point in the shaded area on or above S_1 and on or below M_2 *Pareto-dominates* A. In other words, mutually beneficial exchanges relative to point A are available to them. Segment DE of CC represents the set of Pareto-optimal allocations that are Pareto-preferred to allocation A.[4]

Imagine that Marvin and Shelly agree to an exchange that moves them from point A to some point inside the shaded area. If that agreement, or *contract*, moves them to a point that is not on DE, then both have an incentive to recontract for another mutually beneficial exchange. Because their recontracting activity will end only when they have achieved an allocation on DE, the set of Pareto-optimal allocations is called the *contract curve*. Once on the contract curve, there is no further exchange to which both Marvin and Shelly would willingly agree.

13.2 Competitive Equilibrium in an Exchange Economy

Now let us give Marvin and Shelly an initial endowment of goods at some point in their Edgeworth box, create markets in which they can buy and sell goods 1 and 2, and give them a Walrasian auctioneer to help them find the competitive equilibrium. (Recall the Walrasian auctioneer who coordinated trading in the ticket model in Section 8.1.) We will suppose that Shelly's initial allocation is 22 units of good 1 and 56 units of good 2 and that Marvin's allocation is 80 units of good 1 and 10 units of good 2.

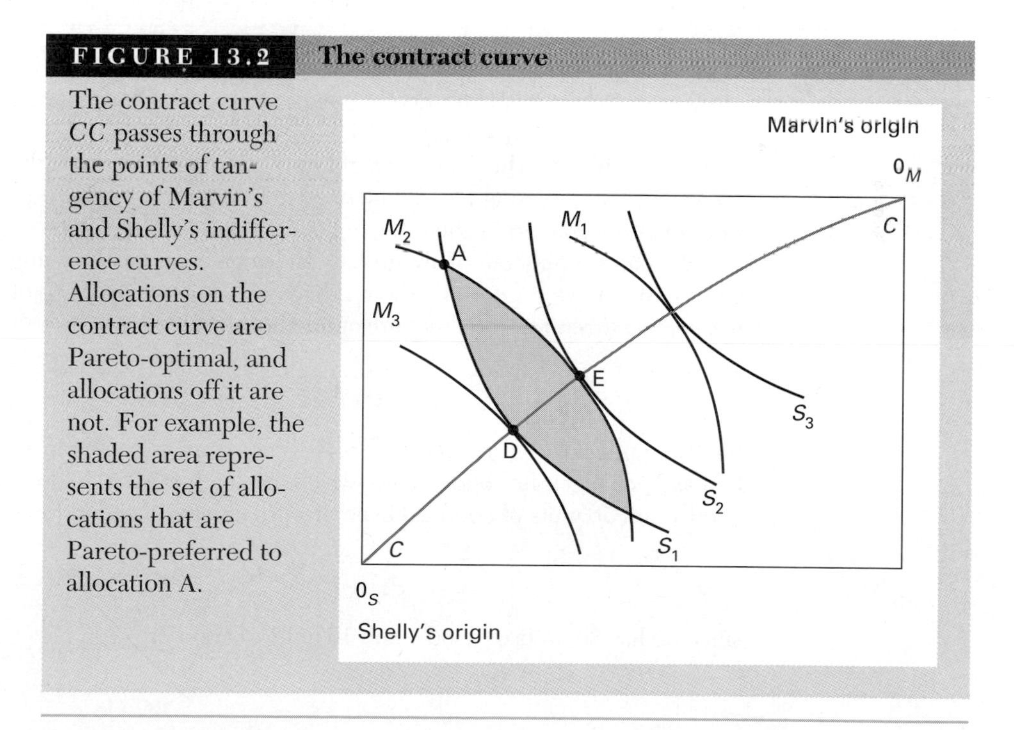

FIGURE 13.2 **The contract curve**

The contract curve CC passes through the points of tangency of Marvin's and Shelly's indifference curves. Allocations on the contract curve are Pareto-optimal, and allocations off it are not. For example, the shaded area represents the set of allocations that are Pareto-preferred to allocation A.

4. The set of Pareto-optimal allocations that are Pareto-preferred to an allocation like A in Figure 13.2 is called the *core*. Therefore, relative to initial allocation A, segment DE of the contract curve is the core.

Budget Lines in an Exchange Economy

The first thing to notice about an exchange economy is that the prices of goods not only determine what consumption bundles a person can buy, given his or her income, but also determine what that income is. Suppose, for example, that the auctioneer announced the following prices: $p_1 = \$2$, and $p_2 = \$1$. In effect, Shelly's income is then equal to \$100 [(\$2 × 22) + (\$1 × 56)] since she could generate that amount of income by selling her initial endowment of 22 units of good 1 and 56 units of good 2. Given these prices, her budget line is

$$2x_1^S + x_2^S = 100$$

Here x_1^S is Shelly's consumption of good 1 and x_2^S is her consumption of good 2. More generally, for arbitrary prices p_1 and p_2, we have

$$\text{Shelly's income} = 22p_1 + 56p_2$$

since she has 22 units of good 1 and 56 units of good 2. Shelly's budget line is then

$$p_1x_1^S + p_2x_2^S = 22p_1 + 56p_2$$

The second thing to notice about an exchange economy with two goods is that there is really only one price to be determined in equilibrium: the price of good 1 relative to good 2, or the relative price of good 1. Notice in Figure 13.3 that Shelly's budget line always passes through her initial endowment; that is, the consumption bundle (22 units of good 1, 56 units of good 2) is always on Shelly's budget line. The budget line will be steeper if p_1 is large relative to p_2, and it will be flatter if p_1 is small relative to p_2, but it will always pass through her initial endowment of 22 units of good 1 and 56 units of good 2. Therefore, the price of good 1 relative to the price of good 2 — or the ratio of p_1 to p_2, or the relative price of good 1 — is what really matters to Shelly. From her point of view, ($p_1 = \$2$, $p_2 = \$1$), ($p_1 = \$4$, $p_2 = \$2$), and ($p_1 = \$6$, $p_2 = \$3$) are equivalent since all three price pairs imply a budget line through her initial endowment, with slope equal to −2, and a relative price of good 1 equal to 2. Similarly, Marvin's only concern is the price of good 1 relative to the price of good 2.

We can simplify our analysis of an exchange economy by fixing the price of good 2 at \$1. When we set $p_2 = \$1$, then p_1 becomes the relative price of good 1. With this *price normalization*,[5] Shelly's budget line becomes

$$p_1x_1^S + x_2^S = 22p_1 + 56$$

Shelly's budget line for three different values of p_1 is shown in Figure 13.3. Notice that as p_1 changes, her budget line swivels around her initial endowment of 22 units of good 1 and 56 units of good 2. Given this price normalization, Marvin's budget line is

$$p_1x_1^M + x_2^M = 80p_1 + 10$$

since he has 80 units of good 1 and 10 units of good 2.

5. We are free to choose any price normalization. Another commonly used normalization is $p_2 = 1 - p_1$.

FIGURE 13.3 **Budget lines in an exchange economy**

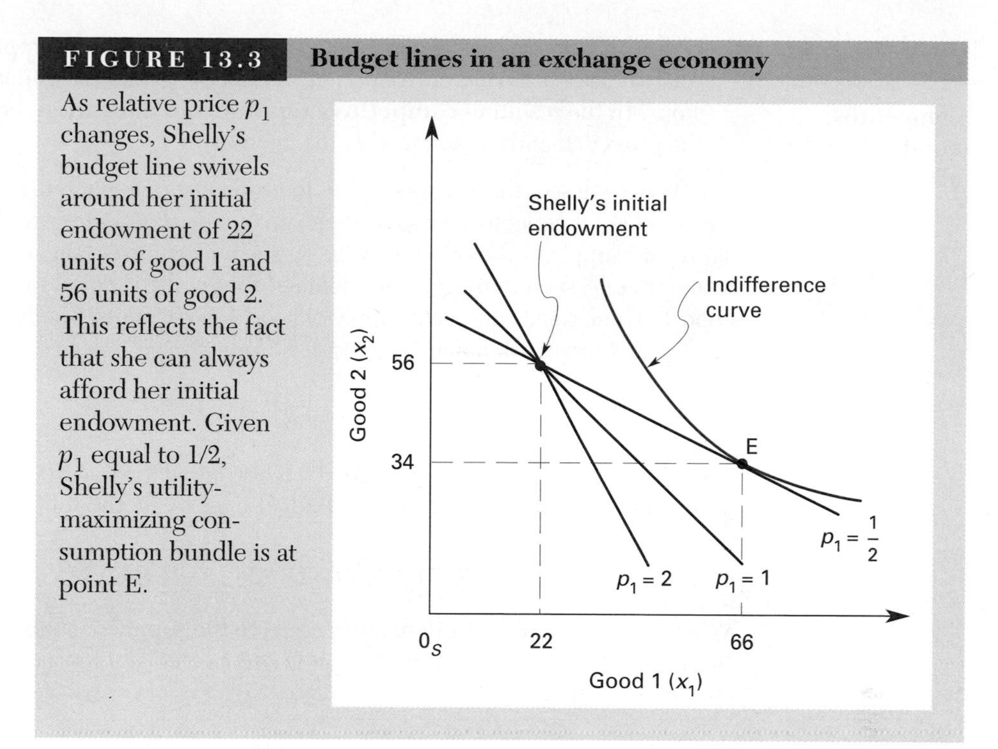

As relative price p_1 changes, Shelly's budget line swivels around her initial endowment of 22 units of good 1 and 56 units of good 2. This reflects the fact that she can always afford her initial endowment. Given p_1 equal to 1/2, Shelly's utility-maximizing consumption bundle is at point E.

Finding the Competitive Equilibrium

net demand

net supply

To find the competitive equilibrium, we will use the Walrasian auctioneer, who begins the bidding process by announcing a relative price p_1. Marvin and Shelly could respond to the auctioneer by announcing a **net demand**, or supply, for each good. For example, if the auctioneer announced $p_1 = 1/2$, we see from Figure 13.3 that Shelly could respond with a *net demand* for good 1 equal to 44 units — since she wants to consume 66 units of good 1 and has 22 units — and a **net supply** of good 2 equal to 22 units — since she has 56 units of good 2 but wants to consume only 34 units.

gross supply

gross demand

Alternatively, Marvin and Shelly could respond to the auctioneer by reporting their **gross supply** of each good and their **gross demand** for each good. In the preceding example, if the auctioneer announced $p_1 = 1/2$, Shelly would respond by offering to supply 22 units of good 1 and 56 units of good 2 — her entire endowment of each good — and to demand 66 units of good 1 and 34 units of good 2.

In either case, at the utility-maximizing bundle, Shelly's *MRS* will be equal to the announced price p_1, since p_1 is the relative price of good 1. Similarly, at his utility-maximizing bundle, Marvin's *MRS* will be equal to the announced price p_1.

aggregate supply

aggregate demand

For clarity, we will suppose that Marvin and Shelly respond by reporting their gross supply of each good and their gross demand for each good. To find the competitive equilibrium, the auctioneer begins by announcing a price p_1. Given that price, Marvin and Shelly then report to the auctioneer the gross *quantity supplied* of each good and the gross *quantity demanded* of each good. The auctioneer first adds their responses to get **aggregate supply** and **aggregate demand**, and then compares aggregate supply and aggregate demand for each good.

1. If aggregate demand is not equal to aggregate supply for both goods, no trading takes place. Instead, the auctioneer announces another price, and the process is repeated.

competitive equilibrium allocation

2. If, for both goods, aggregate demand is equal to aggregate supply, the announced relative price is a competitive equilibrium price, goods are traded, and the auction stops. In the resulting **competitive equilibrium allocation**, both individuals get the gross demands announced to the auctioneer.

As we will see, the auctioneer can focus on just one market because when aggregate demand is equal to aggregate supply in one market, aggregate demand is equal to aggregate supply in the other as well. To see why, suppose the auctioneer has found some price p_1^e such that aggregate demand for good 1 is equal to aggregate supply of good 1. Then, since aggregate supply of good 1 is 102 units, Shelly's demand for good 1, x_1^S, plus Marvin's demand for good 1, x_1^M, must satisfy

$$x_1^S + x_1^M = 102$$

To see that aggregate demand for good 2 is also equal to its aggregate supply (66 units), let us first add Marvin's and Shelly's budget lines to get the following equation:

$$p_1(x_1^S + x_1^M) + (x_2^S + x_2^M) = 102p_1 + 66$$

When price is equal to p_1^e, demand is equal to the supply of good 1, or $x_1^S + x_1^M = 102$; therefore, the first terms on the left and right cancel, and this combined budget constraint reduces to

$$x_2^S + x_2^M = 66$$

Walras' law

Recalling that the aggregate supply of good 2 is 66 units, we see that the demand for good 2 is equal to its supply. This result is known as **Walras' law**:[6]

If at price p_1^e demand is equal to supply in one market, then demand is equal to supply in the other market as well, and p_1^e is therefore a competitive equilibrium price.

We can use the Edgeworth box diagram to illustrate the competitive equilibrium in this two-person exchange economy. In Figure 13.4, the initial endowment is at point A, point E* is the competitive equilibrium allocation, and the grey line is a common budget line whose slope reflects the competitive equilibrium price. Relative to Shelly's origin 0_S, the grey line can be seen as Shelly's budget line, and relative to Marvin's origin 0_M, it can be seen as Marvin's budget line. The utility-maximizing bundles are both at point E*, which is the competitive equilibrium allocation in this exchange economy.

PROBLEM 13.4

In the competitive equilibrium in Figure 13.4, Shelly is a net demander of one good and Marvin a net supplier of that good. Which is the good, and what is her net demand and his net supply? Similarly, Marvin is a net demander of one good and Shelly a net supplier of that good. Which is the good, and what is his net demand and her net supply? What trade will implement the competitive equilibrium allocation?

6. More generally, when there are n markets in a general equilibrium model, Walras' law says that if demand is equal to supply in $n - 1$ markets, then demand is equal to supply in the nth market as well.

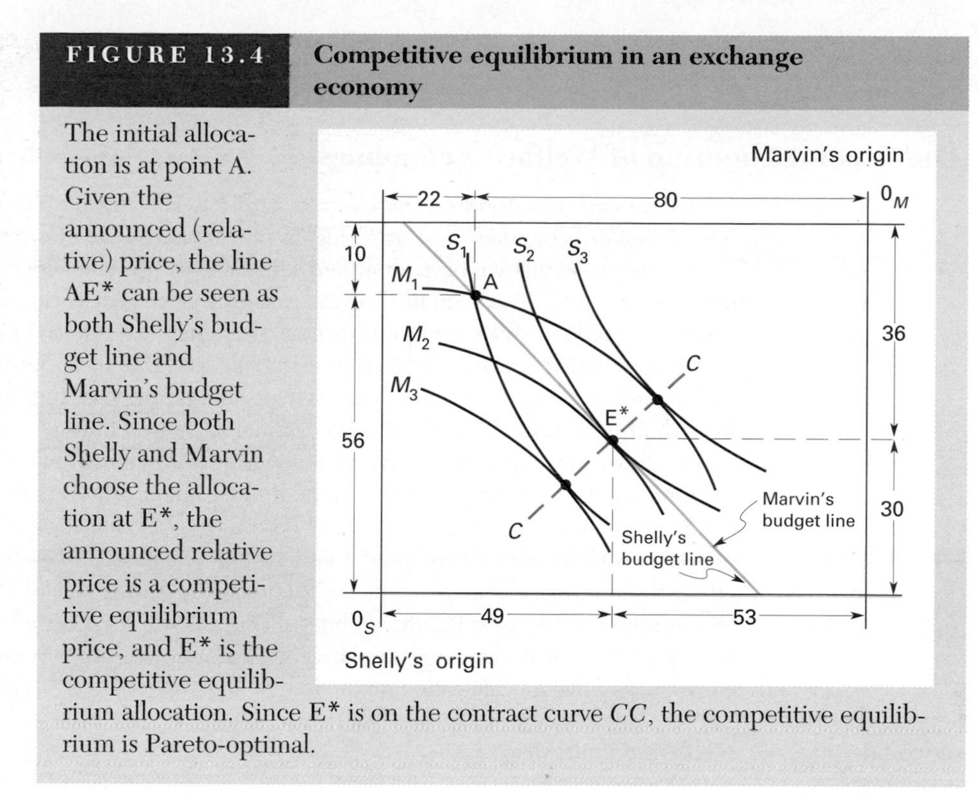

FIGURE 13.4 Competitive equilibrium in an exchange economy

The initial allocation is at point A. Given the announced (relative) price, the line AE* can be seen as both Shelly's budget line and Marvin's budget line. Since both Shelly and Marvin choose the allocation at E*, the announced relative price is a competitive equilibrium price, and E* is the competitive equilibrium allocation. Since E* is on the contract curve *CC*, the competitive equilibrium is Pareto-optimal.

Notice that the competitive equilibrium allocation is on the contract curve in the diagram. This is a general and important result, so let us take time to examine it. In responding to the auctioneer, Shelly and Marvin solve a standard utility-maximizing problem. Each finds a bundle where *MRS* is equal to the announced relative price p_1. That is, every time they respond to the auctioneer, each plans to consume a bundle where *MRS* is equal to the price p_1 announced by the auctioneer. They cannot, and therefore do not, implement these consumption plans until their plans are mutually consistent, or until aggregate demand is equal to aggregate supply in both markets — that is, until the auctioneer has announced the equilibrium price. At the equilibrium price, their consumption plans are consistent; therefore, trades are made to implement the competitive equilibrium allocation where *MRS* is equal to the equilibrium price p_1^e for each of them. Shelly's *MRS* is therefore identical to Marvin's. Of course, this means that the equilibrium allocation is on the contract curve, or is Pareto-optimal.

The First Theorem of Welfare Economics

In a many-person exchange economy, there is an analogous result. In the competitive equilibrium of such an economy, each person consumes a bundle where *MRS* is equal to the equilibrium relative price for good 1. Therefore, *MRS* is identical for all consumers, and the competitive equilibrium allocation is Pareto-optimal. We then have what is called the **first theorem of welfare economics**:

first theorem of welfare economics

Given the assumptions we have made, the competitive equilibrium allocation of a many-person exchange economy is Pareto-optimal.

This theorem says, in effect, that all gains from trade are realized in competitive equilibrium.[7]

The Second Theorem of Welfare Economics

Of course, any allocation on the contract curve is Pareto-optimal. The second theorem of welfare economics concerns a means of attaining any of these Pareto-optimal allocations. Suppose that we have identified some Pareto-optimal allocation that we would like to implement. The second theorem tells us first to redistribute the initial endowment and then to rely on competitive markets to achieve Pareto optimality.

To see how this works, let us reinterpret Figure 13.4 by supposing that the initial endowment is at 0_M, where Shelly owns everything. Suppose, too, that we have somehow identified point E* as the Pareto-optimal allocation that we would like to implement. How can we achieve it? We do so by first redistributing the initial endowment to attain an endowment anywhere on the budget line in Figure 13.4, and then using a competitive market to attain the desired Pareto-optimal allocation at E*. For example, we could transfer 80 units of good 1 and 10 units of good 2 from Shelly to Marvin to attain the endowment at point A, confident in the knowledge that this endowment will produce the desired Pareto-optimal allocation at E*. (After all, we initially found the equilibrium at E* by supposing that the allocation was at A.) A little thought should convince you that any allocation on the budget line, including E* itself, will produce E* as the competitive equilibrium allocation. Thus, we have the **second theorem of welfare economics**:

second theorem of welfare economics

If preferences satisfy the assumptions we have made, given any Pareto-optimal allocation POA, there is an initial allocation IA such that, given the initial allocation IA, POA is a competitive equilibrium allocation.

13.3 Efficiency in General Equilibrium with Production

Now it is time to introduce production into our model and to see how these two theorems of welfare economics can be extended once production is included in the model. After we have concluded this extension, we will try to put the results into perspective. Let us suppose that the number of firms producing good 1 and good 2 is fixed. Therefore, firms do not enter or exit in this general equilibrium model; they simply choose how much of the good to produce. Suppose, too, that the number of people in the economy is fixed and that their preferences satisfy the assumptions laid out in the previous section.

We will also assume that all firms producing the same good have the same constant-returns-to-scale production function. To produce their goods, firms use two primary inputs, input 1 and input 2. And we will assume that there is a fixed supply of each input. Therefore, the quantity supplied is not responsive to input price.

7. Given the assumptions we have made, it is entirely possible that there are many competitive equilibria. If there are many equilibria, the first theorem says that they are all Pareto-optimal. You can easily construct an Edgeworth box with two competitive equilibria. Begin by drawing two budget lines through the same initial endowment, and then construct indifference curves so that there is a competitive equilibrium on both budget lines.

PRODUCTION ASSUMPTIONS

To keep our discussion as simple as possible, we will use five assumptions about production (or technology) throughout the chapter.

1. Isoquants are convex.
2. Isoquants are smooth.
3. Both inputs are essential in the production of both goods.
4. Production functions exhibit constant returns to scale.
5. Production involves no externalities.

The first assumption is standard. The second assumption implies that the marginal rate of technical substitution *MRTS* is well defined, and the third that all firms will use a positive quantity of both inputs. We will explain the role of the fourth assumption when we define the marginal rate of transformation. In Chapter 18, we will see how production externalities like air and water pollution, which are ruled out here by our fifth assumption, fit into the analysis.

Before plunging into the analysis, let us quickly preview this approach to efficiency in this general equilibrium model. Given the assumptions we have made, three conditions are *necessary* and *sufficient* to achieve efficiency in this model. One familiar condition concerns efficiency in consumption; a second, similar condition concerns efficiency in production; and the third condition concerns efficiency of product mix. By *necessary* we mean that if any of the three conditions is *not* satisfied, then the allocation of resources is not Pareto-optimal. By *sufficient* we mean that if *all* three conditions are satisfied, then the allocation of resources is Pareto-optimal. Our discussion will be somewhat incomplete, focusing almost exclusively on showing that these are necessary conditions.

Efficiency in Consumption

efficiency in consumption

Efficiency in consumption means that the allocation to individual consumers of the goods actually produced in the economy must be Pareto-optimal. Therefore, the condition for efficiency in consumption for an exchange economy is directly applicable to an economy with production.

Efficiency in Consumption Condition:
Efficiency in consumption requires that *MRS* is identical for all individuals.

Production Possibilities Set

production possibilities set

The shaded area in Figure 13.5 represents the economy's **production possibilities set** — all the combinations of goods 1 and 2 that can be produced. The upper boundary of the production possibilities set *PP* is the production possibilities frontier. Given the economy's technology and input endowment, any combination of goods on or below *PP* can be produced and any combination above *PP* cannot be produced.

An obvious efficiency requirement is that the combination of good 1 and good 2 actually produced must be on *PP* rather than below it. Point B, for example, is inconsistent with efficiency. By moving upward and to the right from point B, the output of each good increases. And by giving each person some share of that increased output, everyone can be made better off. Point B is therefore inconsistent with efficiency: if the economy

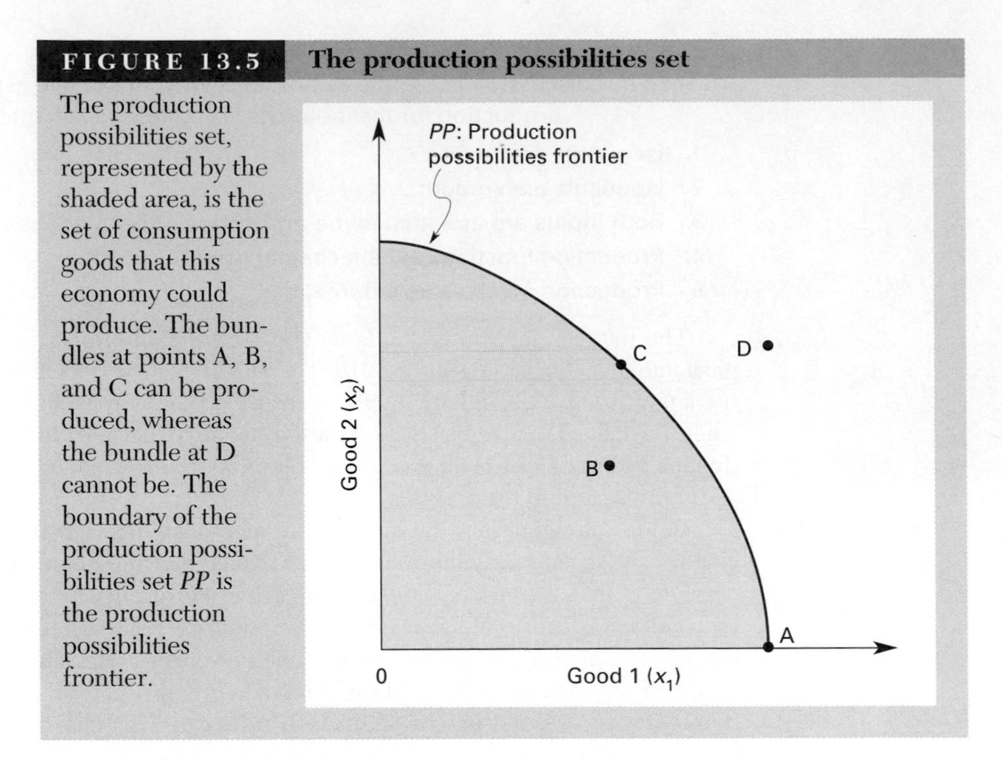

FIGURE 13.5 The production possibilities set

The production possibilities set, represented by the shaded area, is the set of consumption goods that this economy could produce. The bundles at points A, B, and C can be produced, whereas the bundle at D cannot be. The boundary of the production possibilities set *PP* is the production possibilities frontier.

were at point B, Pareto-improving moves would be possible. Thus the second efficiency condition in general equilibrium, called **efficiency in production**, is that the combination of goods actually produced must be on the production possibilities frontier.

efficiency in production

Application: Heading Down the Home Stretch

The theory of general equilibrium can be quite dry and unrealistic, but it is not too hard to find examples of a production possibility curve. Often firms produce more than one good, or face a tradeoff between current and future outputs. For example, consider a baseball team like the Toronto Blue Jays. In any given season they have a choice between winning this year or winning next year. The inputs they use influence the percentage of games they win now versus the future. When the Blue Jays invest heavily in junior players, they in effect make a tradeoff of current game wins for future game wins. The opposite is true when they use more veteran players. Every team probably dreams during spring training of winning the world series, but by late August most of those dreams are shattered. Other teams are well on their way or in a heated pennant race. Late in the season losing teams often let some of their better players go, while winning teams often pick them up. The winning teams pay for these players with junior players in their farm system.

These various teams are moving up and down their production possibility curves. Losing teams put more emphasis on winning in the future and so acquire future players in the form of young junior players. Winning teams substitute future games to ensure winning now. The fact that teams have to make a sacrifice is evidence that they are on the production possibility curve. Were they not, they could increase the games won now and in the future with no cost.

Efficiency in Production

An economy could become "stuck" at an inefficient point such as B in Figure 13.5 in two ways. If any inputs are unemployed, then the economy is inevitably inside *PP*. We will ignore this possibility. There is, however, a more subtle way in which the economy could end up at a point such as B. To understand this more subtle source of inefficiency, we can adapt the Edgeworth box analysis to a new purpose.

Suppose that *MRTS* is different for some pair of firms, given their current input bundles. (See Section 7.2 for the definition of *MRTS*.) Both firms might be producing the same good, or they might be producing different goods. We will show that, because *MRTS* is not identical for the two firms, the output of both firms can be increased by reallocating inputs and that the current allocation of inputs to firms is therefore not efficient.

Suppose, for example, that *MRTS* for the first firm exceeds *MRTS* for the second firm and that the first firm currently has 7 units of input 1 and 17 units of input 2, while the second firm currently has 18 units of input 1 and 3 units of input 2. Now let us put these two firms into an Edgeworth box diagram. The dimensions of the Edgeworth box in Figure 13.6 are determined by the total quantities of inputs 1 and 2 in the two input bundles — its horizontal sides are therefore 25 units long, and its vertical sides are 20 units long. The first firm's isoquants, I_1' and I_1'', are plotted relative to 0_1; the second firm's isoquants, I_2' and I_2'', are plotted relative to 0_2. The current allocation of inputs to the two firms is at point A in Figure 13.6, where *MRTS* is larger for the first firm than for the second. The first firm is currently on isoquant I_1' and the second is on I_2'. Notice that any reallocation of inputs in the interior of the shaded area allows both firms to produce more. Therefore, the input allocation at A is not efficient.

Let us see what these reallocations mean in terms of Figure 13.5. If one firm produces good 1 and the other good 2, then any reallocation from point A to the interior of the shaded area in Figure 13.6 moves the economy shown in Figure 13.5 upward and to the right from a point such as B. If both firms in Figure 13.6 produce the same good — say, good 2 — then the movement in Figure 13.5 is directly upward. If the initial allocation had instead been on the contract curve in Figure 13.6 — that is, if *MRTS* had been identical for the two firms — then increasing the output of one firm would have meant decreasing the output of the other firm. *MRTS* therefore must be identical for all firms if the allocation of inputs is to be efficient.

Efficiency in Production Condition:
Efficiency in production requires that *MRTS* be identical for all firms.[8]

Why is this is a necessary condition for efficiency? If the condition were not satisfied, we could increase the output of one good while maintaining the output of the other, which would allow us to make some consumers better off while leaving all others no worse off.

---

8. The calculus argument in footnote 3 is easily adapted to show that efficiency in production requires that *MRTS* be identical for all firms. Pick any two firms with production functions $F^1(z_1^1, z_2^1)$ and $F^2(z_1^2, z_2^2)$, and any bundle of the two inputs to be allocated to the two firms — say, the bundle (z_1', z_2'). If we fix the output of the first firm at x^1, then efficiency in production clearly demands that we allocate the available bundle of inputs to the two firms so as to maximize $F^2(z_1^2, z_2^2)$, subject to the constraint that $x^1 = F^1(z_1^1, z_2^1)$. From this point, the argument exactly parallels that in footnote 3.

FIGURE 13.6 An Edgeworth box for production

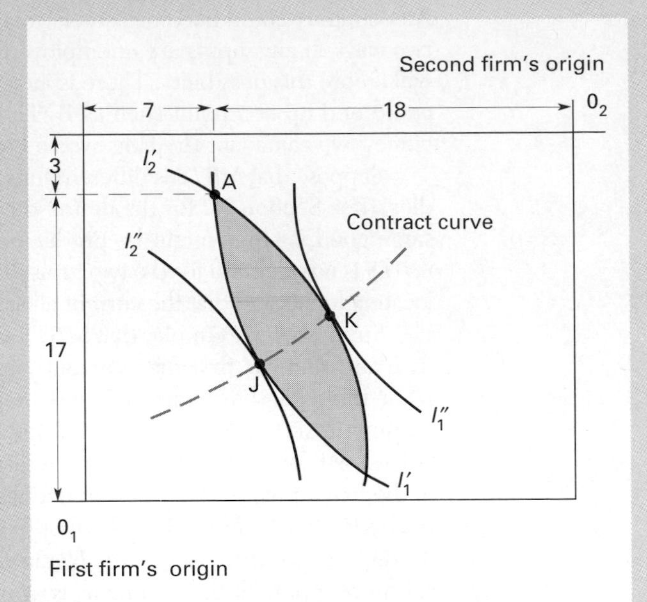

Here we consider the allocation of a fixed quantity of two inputs to two firms. The first firm's input bundle and isoquants are measured relative to 0_1 and the second firm's relative to 0_2. An allocation such as A, which is not on the contract curve, is inefficient. The shaded area is the set of allocations that allow both firms to produce more than they do at A. Allocations such as J and K, where *MRTS* is identical for the two firms, are on the contract curve. Efficiency in production demands that the *MRTS* be identical for all firms.

PROBLEM 13.5

Suppose that *MRTS* for all producers of good 1 exceeds *MRTS* for all producers of good 2. What sort of reallocation of inputs is necessary to achieve efficiency in production? Is it possible to achieve efficiency in production while holding the output of good 1 constant?

Notice that each of these efficiency conditions concerns one side of the economy in isolation from the other. The first proposition concerns consumption and the second concerns production. The third condition for efficiency in general equilibrium concerns the interface between consumption and production. It is called **efficiency of product mix**.

efficiency of product mix

To understand the nature of the product-mix problem, suppose that good 1 is food and good 2 shelter and that 99.9 percent of all inputs go to the production of just one good — say, shelter. If *MRS* is identical for all consumers, the economy will be efficient in consumption. If all firms have the identical *MRTS*, the economy will be efficient in production. But because we humans cannot live by shelter alone, the right product mix has not been produced. In other words, there is more to Pareto optimality in an entire economy than efficiency in production and efficiency in consumption. Before we can confront the product-mix problem head on, we need to understand a little more about the production possibilities frontier.

The Marginal Rate of Transformation

marginal rate of transformation

The absolute value of the slope of the production possibilities frontier at any point is called the **marginal rate of transformation** at that point and is denoted by *MRT*.

$$MRT = |\text{slope of } PP|$$

MRT is the *opportunity cost* for the economy as a whole of a small increase in the amount of good 1 relative to good 2. In Figure 13.7, for example, the absolute value of the slope of the tangent line *TT* is the rate at which production of good 2 must be decreased as production of good 1 is increased when the economy is at point C.

PROBLEM 13.6

Approximately how much of good 2 must be given up to get an additional unit of good 1 if *MRT* is 2? If *MRT* is 1/5? Approximately how much of good 1 must be given up to get an additional unit of good 2 if *MRT* is 3? If *MRT* is 1/3?

We have assumed in this section that all firms experience constant returns to scale in production. This assumption guarantees that *PP* will not be convex to the origin. (We will, in fact, draw *PP* as concave to the origin, as shown in Figure 13.7.) Therefore, in moving from left to right along *PP* in Figures 13.7 and 13.8, the opportunity cost of

FIGURE 13.7 The marginal rate of transformation

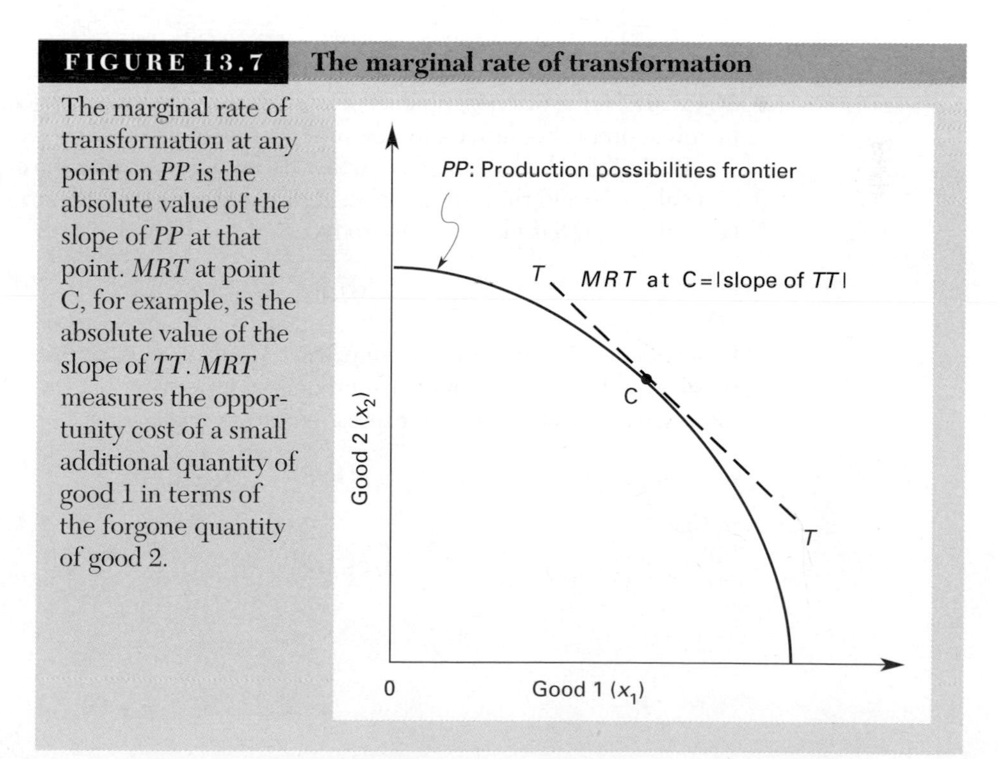

The marginal rate of transformation at any point on *PP* is the absolute value of the slope of *PP* at that point. *MRT* at point C, for example, is the absolute value of the slope of *TT*. *MRT* measures the opportunity cost of a small additional quantity of good 1 in terms of the forgone quantity of good 2.

each additional unit of good 1 in terms of forgone good 2 is progressively larger; that is, MRT becomes progressively larger. If there were significant increasing returns to scale in the production of good 1, however, MRT could decrease in moving from left to right along PP.

We can express MRT in terms of the marginal product of input 1 for a representative producer of good 1 — MP_1^1 — and the marginal product of input 1 for a representative producer of good 2 — MP_1^2. To see how this is accomplished, suppose that we wanted to produce a small additional amount of good 1 — say, Δx_1. We can do it by transferring a small additional amount of input 1 — say, Δz_1 — from the representative producer of good 2 to the representative producer of good 1. The necessary transfer of input 1, Δz_1, (approximately) satisfies

$$\Delta x_1 = \Delta z_1 MP_1^1$$

This implies that Δx_2, the decrease in production of good 2, is (approximately)

$$\Delta x_2 = \Delta z_1 MP_1^2$$

Dividing Δx_2 by Δx_1 gives us the absolute value of the slope of PP, or MRT:

$$MRT = MP_1^2/MP_1^1$$

You may be wondering why we could not achieve this increase in the production of good 1 by transferring input 2 instead of input 1 or by transferring a small additional amount of both input 2 and input 1. The answer is that we could have done so. Suppose that we had transferred input 2 instead of input 1: by replicating the argument of the previous paragraph, we would conclude that

$$MRT = MP_2^2/MP_2^1$$

where MP_2^2 is the marginal product of input 2 for the producer of good 2 and MP_2^1 is the marginal product of input 2 for the producer of good 1.

If MRT is to be meaningful in either of these expressions, the expressions must be equivalent — and they are equivalent. Since we have efficiency in production, we know that $MRTS$ is identical for producers of good 1 and good 2:

$$MRTS_1 = MRTS_2$$

From Section 7.2, we know that any firm's $MRTS$ is equal to the ratio of the marginal product of input 1 to the marginal product of input 2 in that firm. By combining this information with the previous expression, we see that

$$MP_1^1/MP_2^1 = MP_1^2/MP_2^2$$

or that

$$MP_2^2/MP_2^1 = MP_1^2/MP_1^1$$

The two measures of MRT are therefore equivalent.[9] Thus:

The marginal rate of transformation can be expressed in terms of marginal products in two different but equivalent ways:

$$MRT = MP_1^2/MP_1^1 = MP_2^2/MP_2^1$$

These results will be quite useful in subsequent sections.

PROBLEM 13.7

Suppose that $MRTS = 1/2$ for all firms, that $MP_1^1 = 1$, and that $MP_2^2 = 2$. What is MRT?

Efficiency in Product Mix

We can now return to the problem of efficiency in product mix. Imagine that we have picked an arbitrary person, Ms C, and devised a mechanism that (1) allows her to control the allocation of resources in the whole economy by choosing a point on the production possibilities frontier, PP, and that (2) constrains her to leave everyone else in his or her initial position. Imagine, too, that the economy Ms C is about to take charge of is initially at some point on PP — say, at point A in Figure 13.8 — where 30 units of good 1 and 34 units of good 2 are being produced. Imagine, too, that Ms C's current consumption bundle contains 10 units of good 1 and 12 units of good 2. Taken together, the remaining individuals in this economy therefore have 20 units of good 1 (30 – 10) and 22 units of good 2 (34 – 12).

We will show that if this economy is efficient, then Ms C's MRS must be equal to the economy's MRT. To do so, we will suppose that her MRS instead exceeds MRT, and then show that when she takes over, she can make herself better off without making anyone else worse off.

Now let us put Ms C in charge of this economy and allow her to choose a point on PP that is in her own self-interest. Of course, she is constrained to keep all other consumers in their original positions. In Figure 13.8, we see how this constraint works. Point A represents the original position for the economy where there are 30 units of good

9. Suppose that we transfer a small amount of each input from the production of good 2 to the production of good 1. We want to show that this exercise yields an equivalent measure for MRT. To get Δx_1 additional units of good 1, we require

$$\Delta x_1 = \Delta z_1 MP_1^1 + \Delta z_2 MP_2^1$$

which means that the reduction in output of good 2 is

$$\Delta x_2 = \Delta z_1 MP_1^2 + \Delta z_2 MP_2^2$$

Dividing Δx_2 by Δx_1 and rearranging, we get

$$MRT = \frac{MP_1^2(\Delta z_1 + \Delta z_2 MP_2^2/MP_1^2)}{MP_1^1(\Delta z_1 + \Delta z_2 MP_2^1/MP_1^1)}$$

but, since we have efficiency in production, MP_2^2/MP_1^2 is equal to MP_2^1/MP_1^1. But this implies that the terms in parentheses are identical. Hence,

$$MRT = \frac{MP_1^2}{MP_1^1}$$

FIGURE 13.8 Efficiency in product mix

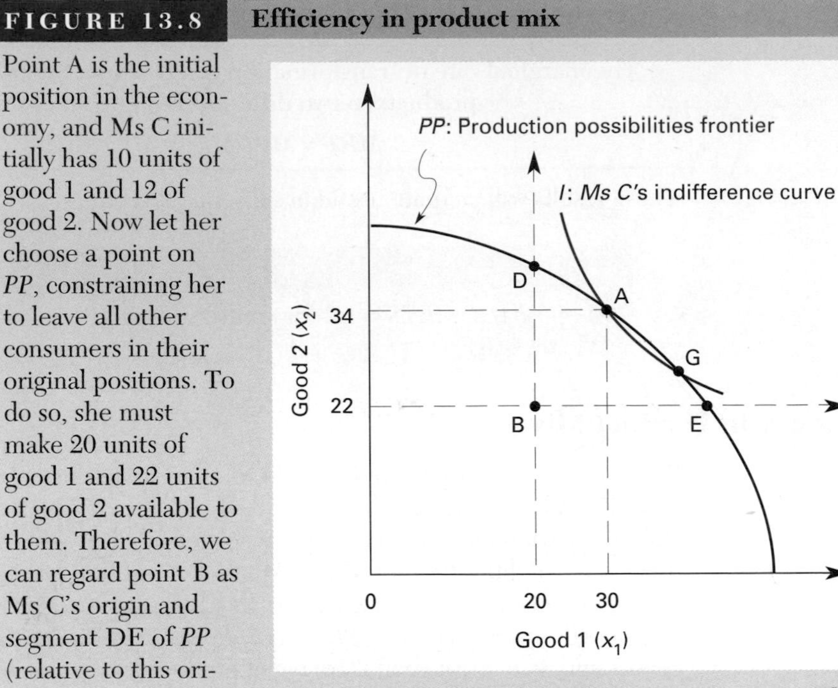

Point A is the initial position in the economy, and Ms C initially has 10 units of good 1 and 12 of good 2. Now let her choose a point on *PP*, constraining her to leave all other consumers in their original positions. To do so, she must make 20 units of good 1 and 22 units of good 2 available to them. Therefore, we can regard point B as Ms C's origin and segment DE of *PP* (relative to this origin) as the consumption choices open to her. She will choose some point other than A because her indifference curve through A intersects *PP*.

1 and 34 units of good 2. If we subtract Ms C's consumption bundle from point A, we get point B in Figure 13.8, where there are 20 units of good 1 and 22 units of good 2. This point represents the initial consumption of everyone else in the economy. Recall that Ms C is constrained to make this combination available to them. This implies that she cannot choose any point on *PP* to the left of point D or to the right of point E, but she can choose any point on segment DE of *PP*.

Analyzing Ms C's problem of choosing a point on segment DE is now a simple matter. We can regard point B as an origin for her private consumption bundle. Segment DE of *PP*, relative to the origin at B, then represents the consumption choices open to her. Now we can simply plot her indifference map relative to the origin at B in Figure 13.8. Remember that we assumed that her *MRS* exceeds *MRT* at point A. She is therefore initially on an indifference curve like *I* in Figure 13.8, that is steeper than *PP* at point A. She will obviously choose some point on *PP* that is to the right of A and to the left of G, a point where some indifference curve not shown in the diagram is tangent to *PP*. When she does, she is better off, and everyone else is just as well off. Therefore, we know that if her *MRS* (or any consumer's *MRS*) is not equal to *MRT*, the allocation of resources to the production of good 1 and good 2 is inefficient.

Efficiency in Product Mix Condition:
Efficiency in product mix requires that each consumer's *MRS* be identical to the economy's *MRT*.

Notice how we have approached each of these efficiency conditions. We have shown that when any of these conditions is not satisfied, a Pareto-improving move is possible and the allocation is therefore inefficient. In other words, we have shown that each of these three conditions is *necessary* for an efficient allocation of resources. Although we will not show it, these three conditions are also *sufficient*: if they are satisfied, then the allocation is efficient. These three conditions thus tell us clearly what **efficiency in general equilibrium** means in our general equilibrium model.

efficiency in general equilibrium

PROBLEM 13.8

Suppose that *MRT* exceeds each consumer's *MRS*. To achieve efficiency in product mix, must the economy be producing more or less of good 1?

13.4 Efficiency and General Competitive Equilibrium

What institutions and circumstances are and are not conducive to efficiency? We will begin this inquiry by recasting the first theorem of welfare economics and then showing that it is true in this general equilibrium model with production.

First Theorem of Welfare Economics:
Given the assumptions we have made, the competitive equilibrium of this general equilibrium model with production is efficient.

The first theorem emphasizes the power of self-interest in directing the allocation of resources. In the perfectly competitive setting envisioned in the theorem, the pursuit of self-interest allows the collectivity of individuals to extract all the gains possible from their economic union. The theorem is, in essence, the embodiment of Smith's doctrine of the natural identity of interests, discussed at the beginning of this chapter.

We can be confident that the theorem is true if we can assure ourselves that an economy in competitive general equilibrium is efficient in production, in consumption, and in product mix. We will not consider how competitive equilibrium is attained in the model. Rather, we will suppose that we have competitive equilibrium prices for goods 1 and 2 and for inputs 1 and 2 — that is, prices such that aggregate demand is equal to aggregate supply for both goods and both inputs. Then we will use our understanding of consumer and producer behaviour to show that the three conditions for efficiency are fulfilled.

Let p_1^e and p_2^e denote the competitive equilibrium prices for goods 1 and 2, and let w_1^e and w_2^e denote the competitive equilibrium prices for inputs 1 and 2. You can easily see that an economy in this competitive equilibrium is efficient in production and in consumption. From Section 7.5, we know that each firm chooses an input bundle at which its *MRTS* is equal to w_1^e/w_2^e. *MRTS* is therefore identical for all firms, and the economy is efficient in production. Similarly, from Section 3.4, we know that each consumer chooses a consumption bundle at which *MRS* is equal to p_1^e/p_2^e. *MRS* is therefore identical for all consumers, and the economy is efficient in consumption.[10]

Showing that an economy in competitive general equilibrium is also efficient in product mix is only slightly more complicated. To do so, we need to use what we know from Section 11.7 about a profit-maximizing firm that is a perfect competitor in its input markets and in its output market. Figure 13.9 illustrates the position of two rep-

---

10. Since there are only three independent relative prices in this model, we could eliminate one price by choosing a convenient normalization. We could, for example, set p_2 equal to 1.

FIGURE 13.9 Efficiency in product mix for general competitive equilibrium

In competitive equilibrium, we see that any producer of good 1 uses input 1 up to the point where $w_1^e = p_1^e MP_1^1$, and that any producer of good 2 uses input 1 up to the point where $w_1^e = p_2^e MP_1^2$. Therefore, $p_1^e/p_2^e = MP_1^2/MP_1^1$. But the right side of the equality is, by definition, MRT. Every consumer chooses a consumption bundle such that $MRS = p_1^e/p_2^e$. Therefore, $MRT = MRS$ for every consumer, and the economy exhibits efficiency in product mix in competitive equilibrium.

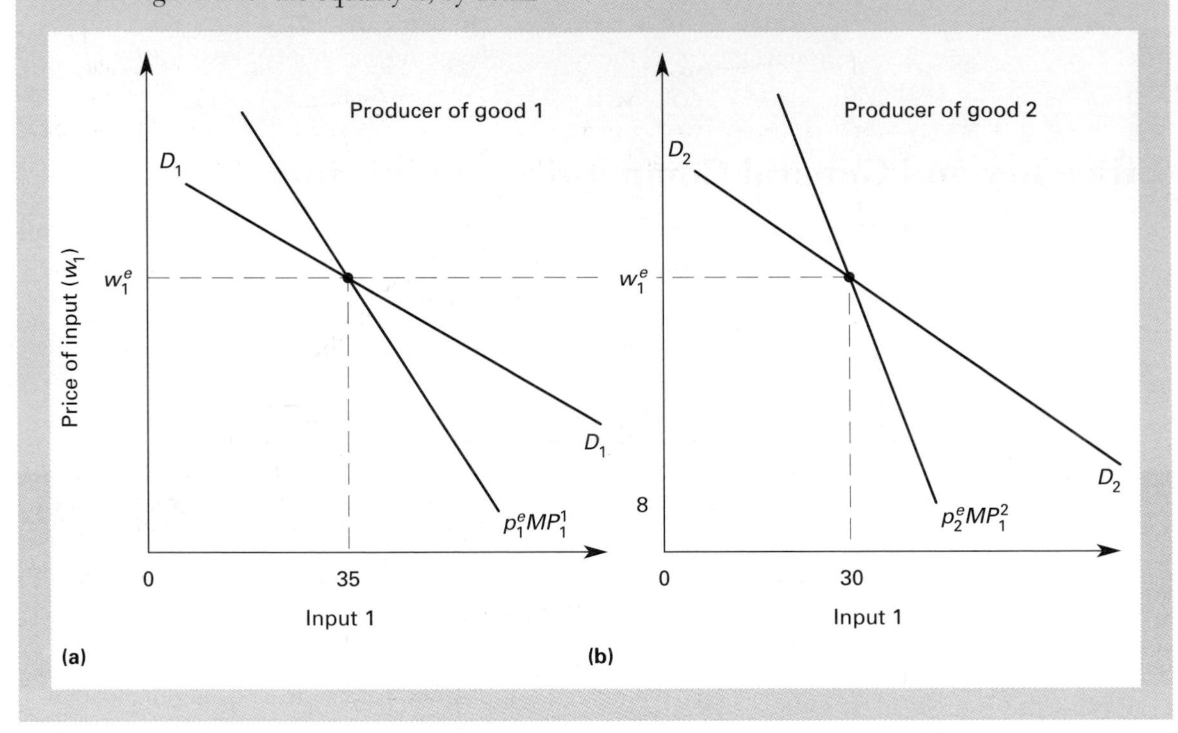

resentative producers — one of good 1 and the other of good 2 — in the market for input 1. The producer of good 1 uses 35 units of input 1 at the equilibrium price w_1^e, and the producer of good 2 uses 30 units. Both firms are in long-run equilibrium and, therefore, in short-run equilibrium as well. Accordingly,

$$w_1^e = p_1^e MP_1^1 = p_2^e MP_1^2$$

Rearranging, we have

$$p_1^e/p_2^e = MP_1^2/MP_1^1$$

As we showed in Section 13.3, the right side of this expression is just the economy's MRT. Because every consumer chooses a bundle at which his or her MRS is equal to the left side, p_1^e/p_2^e we see that every consumer's MRS is equal to the economy's MRT; that is, for every consumer $MRS = MRT$. Therefore, the economy produces an efficient product mix.

Although we will not consider it in great detail, the second theorem of welfare economics also holds in our model of general equilibrium with production. Recall that the second theorem concerns a two-stage procedure for attaining any Pareto-optimal allocation. In the exchange economy, the first stage of this procedure involves the redistribution of goods. In the current model with production, individuals are endowed not with goods but with inputs, which they sell in input markets to earn the incomes that they spend on goods. Therefore, in this model the second theorem relies, in effect, on the redistribution of the ownership of inputs — instead of the redistribution of goods — to redistribute purchasing power. For example, a redistribution of labour (or land), as opposed to some consumption good, might be required to achieve the given Pareto optimum as a competitive equilibrium.

Suppose, then, that we have identified an efficient allocation of goods that we would like to achieve. In the background there is, of course, a corresponding allocation of inputs to firms. But here we are interested in the allocation of goods to individuals. The second theorem is concerned with a two-stage procedure to achieve this allocation. In the first stage, the ownership of inputs is reallocated among individuals. In the second stage, the theorem tells us to rely on competitive markets to achieve efficiency.

Second Theorem of Welfare Economics:
With the assumptions we have made, given any Pareto-optimal allocation of goods POA that is attainable in the model, there is a distribution of ownership of inputs DOI such that POA is a competitive equilibrium allocation associated with DOI.

The beauty of the second theorem is the neat separation of distribution and efficiency that it envisages. In effect, the second theorem tells us:

To achieve equity, redistribute the ownership of inputs; to achieve efficiency, use competitive markets.

A moment's reflection will reveal that the redistribution envisaged in the second theorem involves lump-sum taxes for some individuals and lump-sum subsidies for others. What is being redistributed in a lump-sum fashion is, of course, the ownership of inputs, not money. As we saw in a partial equilibrium context in Chapter 3, these lump-sum taxes and subsidies have some very attractive features. The second theorem reveals the source of their beauty — lump-sum taxes and subsidies do not interfere with the allocative function that competitive markets do so well, whereas other forms of tax and subsidy do.

As we also saw in Chapter 3, it is almost impossible to find a lump-sum tax or subsidy in the real world. It is clear, then, that the second theorem does not dominate the thinking of the people who design taxes and subsidies. Why not? Some economists argue that such taxes and subsidies are a near impossibility. The argument is that a tax always has to be defined in terms of *something*, which always makes it per unit on some margin. A tax per firm, for example, would appear to be a lump sum because it is independent of output, but because it is "per firm," the tax may lead to mergers. In a democratic society, it is extremely difficult to imagine significant lump-sum taxes on the labour of individuals, which, from the point of view of generating income, is the most important input that most people have to offer. Such a tax would lead to substitution in labour force participation. Even a head tax is per head, and could lead to fewer births, more emigration ... and possibly revolution. The real message of the second theorem, then, is that redistribution almost inevitably involves a potentially serious conflict between equity and efficiency.[11] We examined this conflict in Section 12.5 and 12.6.

---

11. The first essay in Koopmans' (1957) book is an excellent exposition of the relationship between efficiency and competitive equilibrium.

Application: International Trade

One of the classic and most important applications of general equilibrium theory is to international trade. Economists use these models to measure the gains from trade, especially when countries enter trade agreements like the FTA or NAFTA. International trade is an enormous subject matter, and so in this little application we only want to show how increases from free trade are represented in this general equilibrium framework.

Consider Figure 13.10a, where a home country's production possibility curve is drawn along with several indifference curves for the economy. If the home country is not trading, it produces at the domestic equilibrium point E. At E, the marginal costs of producing wheat and computers is equal to the marginal costs, and these are equal to the marginal rates of substitution for the economy. The domestic relative price without trade is p_1. When international trade opens up, the world price is assumed to be p_2. On the international scene, wheat is considerably more expensive relative to computers, than in the home economy. Because of the difference in relative prices, free trade encourages the home country to produce more wheat and less computers: a move from point E to point A. However, at these new prices, the most desired consumption level for the home economy is at point B. Thus the country exports DA of its wheat in exchange for DB computers from the foreign country. The area DBA is often called the trade triangle.

FIGURE 13.10 Trade between Two Countries

When the home country in (a) does not trade, production and consumption take place at point E. Trade with the foreign country in (b) increases the wealth of the home country through changes in production to point A and changes in consumption to point B.

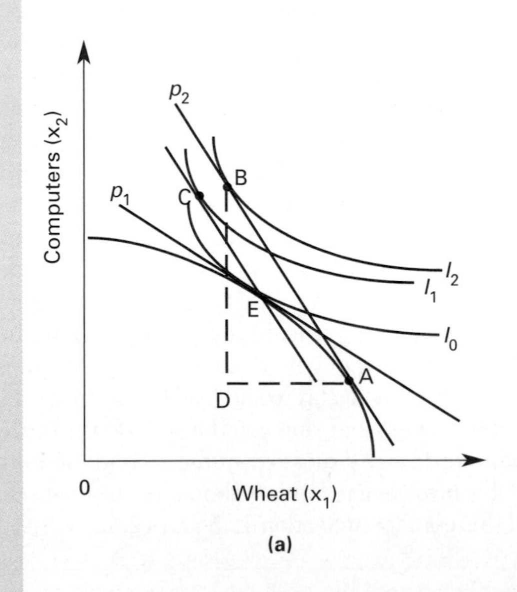

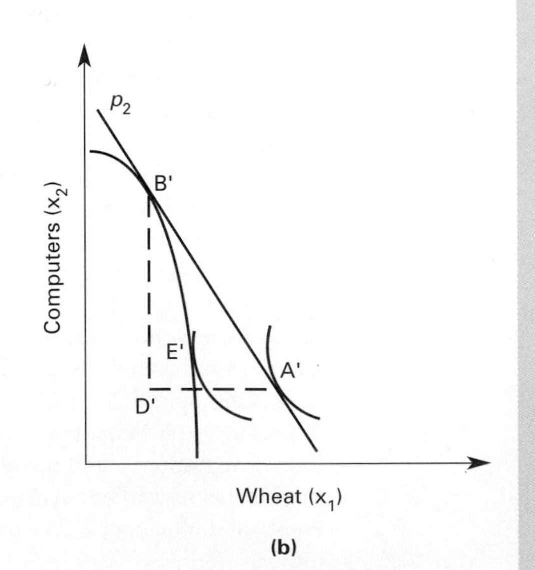

Has the home country become better off through trade? Yes, it has. The increase in real income from I_0 to I_2 represents the improvement in welfare resulting from trade. This improvement is made up of two components. Had the home country not changed its production at all and had remained at point E, it still would have been able to reach point C in terms of consumption. At point C welfare increases to I_1. Thus the total improvement in wealth can be broken into two components: increases caused by changes in consumption and increases caused by changes in production.

In a general equilibrium it must be the case that the exports of the home country are demanded by the foreign country's import demand. We see this in Figure 13.10b. The foreign country was producing at point E′ before free trade was introduced. When the foreign country faces the world price of p_2, it responds by producing more computers, and consuming more wheat. The general equilibrium price p_2 occurs when the trade triangles are equal. Clearly, as we've seen before, free trade benefits both trading parties.

13.5 Sources of Inefficiency

What can go wrong? What produces an inefficient allocation of resources? Although there are many sources of inefficiency, we will look at just two of the major ones in this section: monopoly and taxation.

The Inefficiency of Monopoly

We can begin with monopoly. Suppose that there is only one producer of good 1 and that all other markets are perfectly competitive. To see why resources are inefficiently allocated in general equilibrium, let p_1^e, p_2^e, w_1^e, and w_2^e again represent general equilibrium prices. The equilibrium price of good 1 — p_1^e — is, of course, a monopoly price. The first two efficiency conditions still hold: because all firms face the same input prices, each chooses an input bundle at which *MRTS* is equal to w_1^e/w_2^e. Similarly, because all consumers face the same product prices, each chooses a bundle at which *MRS* is equal to p_1^e/p_2^e. The economy is therefore efficient in production and in consumption in this general equilibrium.

The monopoly inefficiency arises from a distortion of product mix. This becomes apparent when considering the positions of the monopoly producer of good 1 and of any producer of good 2 in an input market. In the market for input 1, for example, both firms use the input up to the point at which marginal revenue product is equal to the price of the input:

$$w_1^e = MRP_1^1 = MRP_1^2$$

where MRP_1^1 and MRP_1^2 are the respective marginal revenue products of input 1 for the monopolist and the representative producer of good 2. But MRP_1^1 is equal to $MR_1MP_1^1$, where MR_1 is the monopolist's marginal revenue in its output market, and MRP_1^2 is equal to $p_2^eMP_1^2$. Therefore,

$$w_1^e = MR_1MP_1^1 = p_2^eMP_1^2$$

Furthermore, as we discovered in Section 10.2, MR_1 is less than p_1^e because a monopolist is producing good 1; that is, a profit-maximizing monopolist always produces at a point where its marginal revenue is less than its price. Combining this knowledge with knowledge from the input market, we see that

$$p_1^e/p_2^e > MP_1^2/MP_1^1$$

However, the right side of this expression is *MRT*, and the left side is equal to each consumer's *MRS*. Each consumer's *MRS* therefore exceeds the economy's *MRT*: for all consumers,

$$MRS > MRT$$

In the presence of monopoly, then, the product mix is wrong; accordingly, the allocation of resources is inefficient:

If we have only one producer of good 1 and if all other markets are perfectly competitive, resources will be inefficiently allocated in general equilibrium.

market power

These inefficiencies arise not just in the case of a monopolist, but in any case in which there is **market power** — any case in which the firm's demand curve is downward sloping. A firm will have some degree of market power whenever it plays a significant role in the market and therefore does not face a horizontal demand curve. In the following problem, you can see more clearly the distortions (inefficiencies) associated with market power.

PROBLEM 13.9

Taking the general equilibrium in the presence of a monopoly producer as an initial condition, construct a diagram in which you show that

1. Ms C could make herself better off, and no one else worse off, if she could directly control the allocation of resources; and that
2. The monopolist produces too little.

Taxation and Efficiency

Taxes not only are painful but also are a source of inefficiency in the allocation of resources. Now that you have some facility in determining whether a particular general equilibrium is efficient, you can discover in Problem 13.10 some inefficiencies associated with taxes.

PROBLEM 13.10

Suppose that some government authority imposes a tax equal to $\$t$ on the sale of each unit of good 2 but not on the sale of good 1. Assuming that all markets are competitive, show that competitive general equilibrium in the presence of this tax is inconsistent with efficiency. (*Hint*: The product mix is not efficient. Is too little or too much of good 2 produced in equilibrium?) Now suppose instead that a subsidy is imposed on the consumption of good 2 and repeat the exercise.

One of the major impediments to trade around the world are taxes in the form of tariffs. We examined the effect of a tariff on a domestic country in Chapter 9, and perhaps you should review that now. Across the world tariff rates differ between countries. As of 2000 Canada had an average tariff rate of 7.1 percent overall, but only an average tariff rate of about 1.0 percent with the United States. In contrast Morocco had an average tariff rate of 23.5 percent and Thailand had an average tariff rate of 30 percent. Not surprisingly, the amount of trade varies inversely with the size of the tariff.

Although tariffs around the world averaged close to 40 percent at the end of the Second World War, GATT (the General Agreement on Tariffs and Trade) encouraged lower tariff barriers until they now hover around 8 percent. Many economists attribute the huge increase in international trade over the past 50 years to the work of GATT, which also mediates trade disputes. In 1995 the WTO (the World Trade Organization) was formed, which has the purpose of further increasing trade internationally. One of the goals of the WTO is the elimination of "non-tariff" barriers to trade. In Canada there are many non-tariff barriers to trade in the form of import quotas, price supports, and other forms of supply management. It has been estimated that the Canadian import restrictions on milk, along with milk quotas, amount to a tariff of 300 percent!

Despite the clear efficiency gains to increased trade, not everyone is in favour of more trade. The riots that took place in Seattle in 2000 when the WTO tried to hold its meetings there are testimony to much of the hostility towards increased trade. As we've discussed in Chapter 9, trade is not neutral with respect to all parties. Although consumers and producers gain on average, there are losers. Countries that succeed in compensating the losers and therefore achieve the gains from trade without violence are the clear winners.

SUMMARY

In this chapter, we have drawn together in a more rigorous *general equilibrium framework* much of what we have already learned about economic efficiency and about the conditions that interfere with it or promote it. In this general equilibrium context, the allocation of resources is *efficient* when no changes of any kind will make some person better off without making someone else worse off.

This correct but imprecise definition of *economic efficiency* is equivalent to the following precise statement: Given the assumptions we made in this chapter, an economy is efficient if (1) *MRTS* is identical for all producers, (2) *MRS* is identical for all consumers, and (3) the common *MRS* is equal to the economy's *MRT*. These three conditions concern *efficiency in production*, *consumption*, and *product mix*, respectively.

We showed that when certain assumptions are satisfied, an economy in general competitive equilibrium satisfies these three conditions: it is efficient. This result, the *first theorem of welfare economics*, is the modern equivalent of Adam Smith's doctrine of the natural identity of interests. Loosely speaking, the institutions that permit individuals to realize all the gains possible from their economic union are the institutions of perfect competition.

We also considered the *second theorem of welfare economics*, which outlines a two-stage procedure for attaining any Pareto-optimal allocation that is possible in the economy. In the first stage, ownership is redistributed among individuals by a set of lump-sum taxes and transfers; in the second stage, efficiency is achieved by relying on perfectly competitive markets. Unfortunately, the lump-sum taxes and transfers envisaged in the first stage are impractical in most real situations.

We found that many things could upset the efficiency applecart. Market power of any sort — monopoly, oligopoly, monopsony — creates inefficiency. As you saw in Problem 13.10, taxes and subsidies also tend to produce inefficiency. And, as we will see in Chapter 18, externalities in consumption and production also mean that competitive general equilibrium is not efficient.

From the perspective of efficiency, the economic world we inhabit is obviously imperfect. Market power is unavoidable in many markets. In addition, externalities such as air and water pollution (which we ignored in this chapter) are an all-too-familiar part of the economic world in which we live. Furthermore, governments are not about to eliminate their taxing and spending activities, and most of us would not want them to do so. Thus, some form of inefficiency seems to be inevitable.

This predictable inefficiency presents the economist, particularly the policy-making economist, with a real challenge. How do we measure inefficiency? How can we minimize inefficiency? One recent approach — called applied general equilibrium analysis — uses data to build general equilibrium models of the economy and extends the surplus measures familiar from earlier chapters to quantify inefficiency in a general equilibrium framework.[12] These models are one step towards meeting that challenge.

EXERCISES

1. If a monopolist produces good 1 while the markets for good 2 and both inputs are perfectly competitive, then general equilibrium is inefficient because *MRS* exceeds *MRT* for all consumers. Show that a tax on the production of good 2 or a subsidy on the production of good 1 can eliminate the inefficiency of monopoly.

2. Suppose that there are immobile producers of goods 1 and 2 in each of two regions and that both inputs are completely mobile. Suppose too that input 1 is taxed in one region but not in the other. What sort of distortion (inefficiency) in the allocation of resources does this produce? Which of the efficiency conditions is violated?

3. Suppose that each firm has monopsony power with respect to input 1 and that no firm has monopoly power. What sort of distortions do these conditions produce? Which of the efficiency conditions is violated? What sort of taxes or subsidies would offset these distortions?

4. Suppose the government passes a law that places a $0.20 / unit tax on boxes of cereal and then redistributes the tax by giving everyone $10 on his or her birthday. Would this be Pareto optimal? How would your answer depend on whether people were identical or not?

5. Was NAFTA Pareto-improving? If not, why would voters elect governments to pursue it?

6. In a general equilibrium, can we have an excess supply of all goods?

7. What would be the nature of production if the production possibility curve were a straight line?

*8. Jonathan Swift, the eighteenth-century writer, often employed satire, irony, and parody in his great prose writings, to superb effect. In *A Modest Proposal,* Jonathan Swift employed these literary devices to vilify the treatment of the Irish at the hands of England's absentee landlords. The subtitle of the essay reads, "For Preventing the Children of Poor People in Ireland From Being a Burden to Their Parents or Country, and for Making Them Beneficial to the Public." In this satire, Swift's "humanitarian" proposer states that "a young healthy child, well nursed, is at a year old a most delicious, nourishing, and wholesome food, whether stewed, roasted, baked or boiled … " The proposer goes to great lengths to suggest the benefits of eating poor children. Would his proposal be Pareto-optimal?

9. Avi (A) and Bindi (B) have the following utility functions:

$$U^A = (X_A)^{0.5} Y_A$$
$$U^B = X_B (Y_B)^2$$

where their endowments of X and Y are as follows:

$$X_A = 16 \quad Y_A = 16 \quad X_B = 4 \quad Y_B = 144$$

12. See Shoven and Whalley (1987) for a survey of work in applied general equilibrium.

a. At the endowment point, what are the marginal rates of substitutions between X and Y for Avi? For Bindi?
b. If they could engage in voluntary exchange would they? If so, which goods would each offer to trade? Explain.
c. Find the competitive equilibrium price.
d. Is the allocation of resources achieved in (c) Pareto-optimal? Explain.

*10. Assume there are two countries living next door to one another in which labour is not mobile. That is, the workers in one country cannot move to the other. Each country produces the same goods X and Y, however. Suppose the production functions for country A are as follows:

$$X_A = (L_{x_A})^{1/3}$$
$$Y_A = (L_{y_A})^{1/3}$$

where L_{x_A} and L_{y_A} are the amounts of labour used to produced the goods. The total amount of labour available in country A is 300 units. That is, $L_{x_A} + L_{y_A} = 300$. Likewise for country B there are the following production functions:

$$X_B = 0.5(L_{x_A})^{1/3}$$
$$Y_B = 0.5(L_{y_B})^{1/3}$$

and in country B there are also 300 units of labour in total.

a. Calculate the production possibility curves for each country.
b. Given that labour cannot move between the countries, what condition must hold for production to be efficient between the two countries?
c. Suppose that a free trade agreement is struck between the two countries and that as a result, labour becomes completely mobile. How will labour be allocated to increase output? Calculate the new production possibility for the "supra" country. How much X can be produced if the total output of Y is 5?

*11. There are two individuals represented by the utility functions

$$U_1 = \ln(x_1) + y_1$$
$$U_2 = x_2^2 y_2$$

The individuals have the following endowments:

$$X_1 = 38 \quad X_2 = 0 \quad Y_1 = 3 \quad Y_2 = 27$$

a. Find the MRS for each individual and show that each of these is diminishing.
b. Draw a box diagram in x and y space representing the endowments of the two.
c. Find the price-consumption path for individual 2, that is, a function $y_2 = f(x_2)$ for varying prices of x.
d. State the conditions for efficient allocations of x and y between the two and calculate the efficient allocation on 2's price-consumption path.

*12. There are two individuals:

Mr. A with a utility function $U_A = x_A y_A$
Ms B with a utility function $U_B = (x_B)^{0.5}(y_B)^{0.5}$

who are endowed as follows:

$$X_A = 30 \quad X_B = 30 \quad Y_A = 30 \quad Y_B = 90.$$

a. Calculate the equilibrium price that you would obtain if Mr. A and Ms B were to trade under perfectly competitive conditions.
b. Check your results by calculating the amounts of x and y traded by one of the two individuals and showing these quantities to be consistent with the price found in part (a).
c. Calculate Mr. A's gain from trade, at the perfectly competitive price, measured in units of Y.
d. Concisely describe how your solution to (c) can be interpreted as a benefit to Mr. A.

*13. Caroline lives on an island where she can produce and consume two goods, X_1 and X_2. She is endowed with 100 units of labour, L, which she can use to produce either of the goods according to the following production functions:

$$X_1 = 10(L_1)^{1/2}$$
$$X_2 = L_2$$

Where L_1 and L_2 are units of labour devoted to production of X_1 and X_2, respectively. Her utility function is $U(X_1, X_x) = (X_1 X_2)^{1/2}$.

a. What is her production possibility curve?
b. What is her utility-maximizing production and consumption of X_1 and X_2?

c. Suppose her island is on a trade route and she is able to buy or sell units of X_1 at a price of 2 units of X_2. Calculate her new utility-maximizing production and consumption of X_1 and X_2.

*14. A small island produces and consumes two goods, clothing (X_1) and fruit (X_2). The aggregate utility function for these goods is

$$U(X_1, X_2) = X_1^{3/5}X_2^{2/5}.$$

Product and factor markets are perfectly competitive, and the production functions for X_1 and X_2 are

$$X_1 = L_1$$
$$X_2 = (R_2L_2)^{1/2}$$

Where L is units of labour and R is units of land. The island has 100 units of both labour and land.

a. If the island can trade at international prices P_1 = \$2 and P_2 = \$3, how much of each good will it produce? How much of each good will it consume?

b. Suppose that trade sanctions are placed on the island and it is no longer able to trade at world prices. How will its production and consumption change?

13A Appendix: Efficiency

In this appendix, we will use differential calculus and the tools of constrained maximization to develop the conditions for economic efficiency for a very simple economy. We have two goods, goods 1 and 2, each produced by one firm, and two individuals, One and Two. We denote One's consumption bundle by (x_1^1, x_2^1) and Two's by (x_1^2, x_2^2). Notice that subscripts index goods and superscripts index individuals. The two utility functions are $U^1(x_1^1, x_2^1)$ and $U^2(x_1^2, x_2^2)$. We have two inputs, inputs 1 and 2, and a fixed supply of each, denoted by z_1' and z_2'. The input bundle used to produce good 1 is (z_1^1, z_2^1); the bundle used to produce good 2 is (z_1^2, z_2^2). In these input bundles, superscripts index goods; subscripts index inputs. The two production functions are $F^1(z_1^1, z_2^1)$ and $F^2(z_1^2, z_2^2)$.

First, let us simply write down the three conditions for efficiency.

1. Efficiency in consumption requires that

$$MRS^1(x_1^1, x_2^1) = MRS^2(x_1^2, x_2^2)$$

or that

$$\frac{\partial U^1(x_1^1, x_2^1)/\partial x_1^1}{\partial U^1(x_1^1, x_2^1)/\partial x_2^1} = \frac{\partial U^2(x_1^2, x_2^2)/\partial x_1^2}{\partial U^2(x_1^2, x_2^2)/\partial x_2^2}$$

2. Efficiency in production requires that

$$MRTS^1(z_1^1, z_2^1) = MRTS^2(z_1^2, z_2^2)$$

or that

$$\frac{\partial F^1(z_1^1, z_2^1)/\partial z_1^1}{\partial F^1(z_1^1, z_2^1)/\partial z_2^1} = \frac{\partial F^2(z_1^2, z_2^2)/\partial z_1^2}{\partial F^2(z_1^2, z_2^2)/\partial z_2^2}$$

3. Efficiency in product mix requires that

$$MRT(x_1, x_2) = MRS^1(x_1^1, x_2^1) = MRS^2(x_1^2, x_2^2)$$

or that

$$\frac{\partial F^2(z_1^2, z_2^2)/\partial z_1^2}{\partial F^1(z_1^1, z_2^1)/\partial z_1^1} = MRS^1(x_1^1, x_2^1) = MRS^2(x_1^2, x_2^2)$$

Alternatively, since the economy's marginal rate of transformation can be expressed in terms of the marginal products of input 1 or of input 2, efficiency in product mix requires that

$$\frac{\partial F^2(z_1^2, z_2^2)/\partial z_2^2}{\partial F^1(z_1^1, z_2^1)/\partial z_2^1} = MRS^1(x_1^1, x_2^1) = MRS^2(x_1^2, x_2^2)$$

Our task is to show that these three conditions are indeed implied by Pareto optimality. Let us fix the utility level of individual One at, say, u^1. Pareto optimality then demands that we allocate the fixed supplies of the two inputs to the production of the two goods and allocate the resulting quantities of the two goods to the two individuals, so that we maximize Two's utility subject to the constraint that One's utility is equal to u^1. That is, Pareto optimality, or economic efficiency, defines a somewhat complex constrained-maximization problem. We wIll see that the solution to this problem implies the three efficiency conditions we set down earlier.

The constrained-maximization problem is this: choose two consumption bundles — (x_1^1, x_2^1) and (x_1^2, x_2^2) — and two input bundles — (z_1^1, z_2^1) and (z_1^2, z_2^2) — to maximize $U^2(x_1^2, x_2^2)$ subject to the following constraints:

$$u^1 = U^1(x_1^1, x_2^1) \tag{1}$$
$$z_1^1 + z_1^2 = z_1{}' \tag{2}$$
$$z_2^1 + z_2^2 = z_2{}' \tag{3}$$
$$x_1^1 + x_1^2 = F^1(z_1^1, z_2^1) \tag{4}$$
$$x_2^1 + x_2^2 = F^2(z_1^2, z_2^2) \tag{5}$$

The first constraint is that the bundle allocated to One yields u^1 utility. The second and third constraints are the economy's resource constraints. The fourth and fifth constraints reflect the fact that the two individuals can consume only what the economy produces.

We can simplify the problem by combining constraints to eliminate some of the endogenous variables. First, in equation (5), use equation (2) to eliminate z_1^2 and equation (3) to eliminate z_2^2:

$$x_2^1 + x_2^2 = F^2(z_1{}' - z_1^1, z_2{}' - z_2^1) \tag{6}$$

Then write equations (4) and (6) as

$$x_1^1 = F^1(z_1^1, z_2^1) - x_1^2 \tag{7}$$
$$x_2^1 = F^2(z_1{}' - z_1^1, z_2{}' - z_2^1) - x_2^2 \tag{8}$$

Now, in equation (1), use equation (7) to eliminate x_1^1 and equation (8) to eliminate x_2^1:

$$u^1 = U^1[F^1(z_1^1, z_2^1) - x_1^2, F^2(z_1{}' - z_1^1, z_2{}' - z_2^1) - x_2^2] \tag{9}$$

We are left with just one constraint, equation (9), and only four endogenous variables: Two's consumption bundle, (x_1^2, x_2^2), and the input bundle to be devoted to good 1, (z_1^1, z_2^1).

We have reduced the original problem to this: choose (x_1^2, x_2^2) and (z_1^1, z_2^1) to maximize $U^2(x_1^2, x_2^2)$ subject to one constraint, equation (9). The Lagrangian is

$$L(x_1^2, x_2^2, z_1^1, z_2^1, \lambda) = U^2(x_1^2, x_2^2) + \lambda\{U^1[F^1(z_1^1, z_2^1) - x_1^2, F^2(z_1{}' - z_1^1, z_2{}' - z_2^1) - x_2^2] - u^1\}$$

Setting each of the partial derivatives of the Lagrangian equal to zero yields the following characterization of the solution, in which we have suppressed the endogenous variables.

$$\partial U^2/\partial x_1^2 - \lambda \partial U^1/\partial x_1^1 = 0 \tag{10}$$

$$\partial U^2/\partial x_2^2 - \lambda \partial U^1/\partial x_2^1 = 0 \tag{11}$$

$$\lambda(\partial F^1/\partial z_1^1 - \partial F^2/\partial z_1^2) = 0 \tag{12}$$

$$\lambda(\partial F^1/\partial z_2^1 - \partial F^2/\partial z_2^2) = 0 \tag{13}$$

$$U^1 - u^1 = 0 \tag{14}$$

Conditions (10) and (11) imply that

$$\frac{\partial U^1/\partial x_1^1}{\partial U^1/\partial x_2^1} = \frac{\partial U^2/\partial x_1^2}{\partial U^2/\partial x_2^2} \tag{15}$$

which is the condition for *efficiency in consumption*. Conditions (12) and (13) imply that

$$\frac{\partial F^1/\partial z_1^1}{\partial F^1/\partial z_2^1} = \frac{\partial F^2/\partial z_1^2}{\partial F^2/\partial z_2^2} \tag{16}$$

$$\frac{\partial U^1/\partial x_1^1}{\partial U^1/\partial x_2^1} = \frac{\partial F^1/\partial z_2^1}{\partial F^1/\partial z_1^1} \tag{17}$$

$$\frac{\partial U^1/\partial x_1^1}{\partial U^1/\partial x_2^1} = \frac{\partial F^2/\partial z_2^2}{\partial F^1/\partial z_2^1} \tag{18}$$

Condition (16) is the condition for *efficiency in production*. Condition (17) or (18), in combination with condition (15), yields the condition for *efficiency in product mix*.

REFERENCES

Arrow, K. J. and F. H. Hahn. 1971. *General Competitive Analysis*. San Francisco: Holden-Day.

Koopmans, T. C. 1957. *Three Essays on the State of Economic Science*. New York: McGraw-Hill.

Shoven, J. B. and J. Whalley. 1987. *Applying General Equilibrium*. Cambridge, England: Cambridge University Press.

Stigler, G. (ed.). 1957. *Selections from The Wealth of Nations*. New York: Appleton-Century-Crofts.

Walras, L. [1874, 1877] 1954. *Éléments d'économie politique pure (Elements of Pure Economics)*. Translated by W. Jaffe. London: Allen and Unwin.

PART VI

Imperfect Competition

In Part IV we examined the allocation of goods in the case of perfect competition and monopoly; that is, in cases where there were large numbers of competitors acting as price takers, and cases where one single firm faced the market demand curve.

In this section we return to the case where a market is supplied by firms with market power—firms that face a downward-sloping demand curve. In Chapter 14 we examine the case of monopoly once more, but in more detail. Rather than just looking at the case where a monopolist firm is constrained to charge one price to everyone, we now consider the pricing strategies of such a firm. We introduce you to the concepts of price discrimination, two-part pricing, and tie-in sales in the process.

Chapters 15 and 16 examine problems where the number of firms is small and strategic behaviour is likely. Chapter 15 introduces the concepts of game theory, and analyzes many different applications. Chapter 16 applies these methods to a specific problem: namely to a small set of firms that sell identical goods.

CHAPTER 14

Price Discrimination and Monopoly Practices

Recall from Chapter 10 that a profit-maximizing monopolist simultaneously chooses price and output. This is contrasted with the price-taking competitive firm, which takes the market price as given and chooses only the level of output to produce. In Chapter 10 we also saw that a monopolist firm *constrained to charge one price to everybody* set $MR = MC$ in determining the profit maximizing level of output. This level of output was Pareto-inferior because the price was greater than the marginal cost.

Figure 14.1 shows these results. Because the monopolist charges all consumers the same price, the marginal revenue from an additional sale is lower than the average revenue, which always equals the price. As a result, when the monopolist determines output using the profit maximizing rule, $MR = MC$, output is y^* and the deadweight loss is equal to the area ABC. At y^* units of output the MV of consumption exceeds the MC of output, because the price is greater than MC.

FIGURE 14.1 **The simple monopoly problem**

A monopolist that can charge only one price chooses a profit-maximizing level of output equal to y^* where marginal revenue equals marginal costs. At this level of output the firm sets a price equal to p^*.

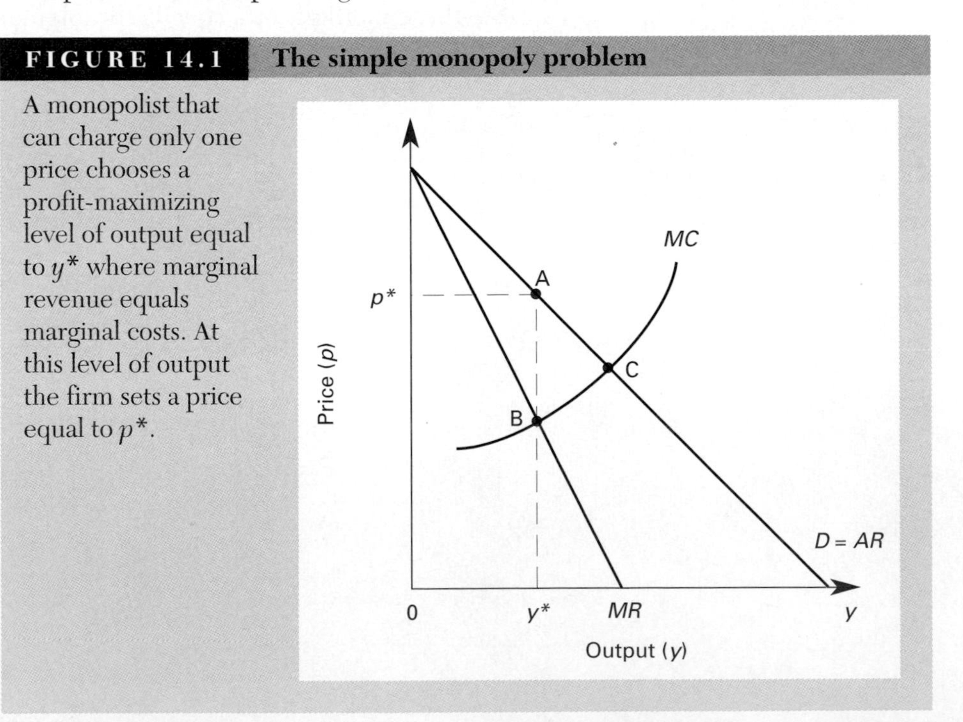

Consider this deadweight loss for a moment. This area represents a loss of wealth to the firm, and results only because our model has constrained the firm to charge one price to every customer. It does not take a genius to figure out that an alternative method of pricing can increase the profits of the firm. In fact, an imaginative monopolist will take dead aim at the as-yet-unrealized profit by trying to devise more sophisticated pricing schemes. These sophisticated strategies aimed at extracting unrealized profit take many forms. In this chapter we examine price discrimination, two-part tariffs, tie-in sales, and all-or-nothing pricing. These different strategies not only allow the firm to capture some or all of the deadweight loss, they also allow the firm to extract some or all of the consumer's surplus.

As you take a closer look at these practices, you will recognize that this behaviour is too pervasive to apply only to monopolists, given our restrictive definition of monopoly. Price-discriminating activities are attractive to any firm with some degree of market power — that is, to any firm with some ability to set its own price. In fact, many economists believe that some of these practices, such as tie-in sales, are so common that they may not even be methods of extracting consumer surplus because they also occur in markets that are extremely competitive. These economists offer what are called "efficiency" explanations for these practices that are independent of the existence of monopoly firms. Although we will occasionally touch on these alternative explanations for this pricing behaviour, in most of the chapter we concentrate on the monopoly explanation.

What we say here about price discrimination and monopoly practices will also apply to *oligopolies*, or markets dominated by a few firms. As you will discover in following chapters, however, the theory of oligopoly is complicated enough in the absence of price discrimination. We will therefore take up price discrimination and monopoly practices in the simpler context of monopoly.

14.1 Price Discrimination and Market Segmentation

All price discrimination schemes share an underlying strategy: to segment the market and to charge each segment a different price relative to cost. You discovered the monopolist's ideal **market segmentation** scheme in the book vendor's pricing strategy in Problem 10.5. There, the monopolist appropriated all the surplus as profit by extracting from every consumer the largest sum of money each was willing to pay. Recall the conditions that made this most profitable strategy possible: the monopolist was able to isolate its potential customers from one another, and it knew the individual reservation prices of each customer. These conditions will rarely, if ever, be satisfied. Nevertheless, the market segmentation that makes this scheme effective can be realized and exploited to a lesser extent by other means.

market segmentation

Economists usually view cases of price discrimination as falling into three broad theoretical categories. The first category is **perfect price discrimination**, the "ideal" but usually unrealizable case exemplified by the book vendor. The monopolist successfully extracts the maximum possible profit from each customer and therefore from the whole market.

perfect price discrimination

The second category is **ordinary price discrimination**. This is the familiar case in which the monopolist identifies potential customers by groups and charges each group a separate price. For example, the pervasive phenomenon of charging different admission prices for groups called "seniors," "adults," "students," and "children" is one instance of ordinary price discrimination.

ordinary price discrimination

multipart pricing or block pricing

The third category, **multipart** or **block pricing**, is the case in which the monopolist charges different rates for different amounts, or "blocks," of a good or service. For instance, it is common practice to charge one rate for the first block of so many kilowatt-hours of electricity in a period and lower rates for subsequent blocks.

Perfect Price Discrimination

Perfect price discrimination results when every consumer pays his or her reservation price. Consider the market demand curve in Table 14.1. For simplicity it is assumed that each individual only demands one unit of the good. Hence when the price is $14, one unit is sold, and when the price falls to $13 two units are sold to two individuals. The demand curve is downward sloping because lower prices induce more people to enter the market.

TABLE 14.1 A market demand curve

Aggregate Quantity	Reservation Price	Total Revenue	*MR*	*AR*
0	15	0		
1	14	14	14	14
2	13	27	13	13.5
3	12	39	12	13
etc.				

Assume for the moment that the monopolist firm facing this demand curve knows each individual's reservation price *and*, through perfect market segmentation, can prevent the resale of the product. Furthermore, assume that the firm exploits this knowledge by price discriminating perfectly. What becomes of the marginal revenue curve? From Table 14.1 it is clear that *MR* begins to approach *AR*. As the size of the market increases, or as demand becomes more continuous, the *MR* curve gets closer to *AR*. In the simple monopoly case, *MR* was less than *AR* because a reduction in price at the margin meant that all the intramarginal units were reduced in price as well. This is no longer the case. With perfect price discrimination the firm can lower the price to the marginal customer, while those already purchasing continue to pay their reservation prices.

Figure 14.2 shows the new equilibrium. As long as $MR > MC$, profit increases as the firm produces more output. When $MR = MC$, as always, the firm reaches the profit maximizing level of output. Note that, since *MR* is equal to the reservation price of the marginal buyer, the perfectly price-discriminating monopolist produces a Pareto-efficient level of output. At this level of output, however, the consumer's surplus is zero, since each consumer pays his or her reservation price. Notice as well that in a market like this there is no single price; every consumer pays a different amount.

The ability to extract the maximum amount of surplus through perfect price discrimination probably has no precise real-world counterpart because the conditions necessary for it are too extreme. Seldom do firms have perfect knowledge of their customers' individual demands, and seldom can they perfectly segment the market to prevent resale. However, there may be examples that come close. For example, some people have interpreted Dutch auctions as a method of perfect price discrimination. Unlike an English (or ordinary) auction where the price starts out low and is bid higher, in a Dutch auction the price starts out high and then falls. The first person to bid takes the lot for sale at that price. Because there is only one bid, there is an incentive to bid

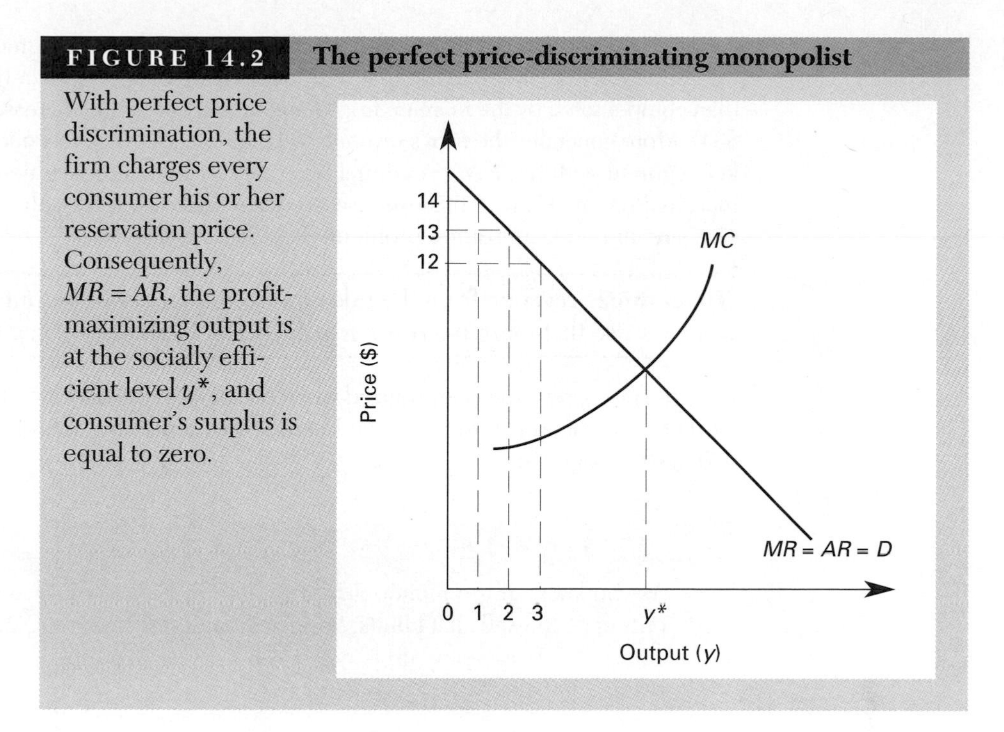

FIGURE 14.2 The perfect price-discriminating monopolist

With perfect price discrimination, the firm charges every consumer his or her reservation price. Consequently, $MR = AR$, the profit-maximizing output is at the socially efficient level y^*, and consumer's surplus is equal to zero.

close to the reservation price, and because the high-marginal-value users bid first, there is a built-in mechanism to prevent resale.[1]

Another example of perfect price discrimination might occur in the provision of accounting services by small firms. Accountants routinely charge their clients different prices for the same service. Given their unique knowledge of their clients' books, the professional restrictions on advertising prices, and the inability of a client to resell the accounting service, this type of industry appears to meet the requirements for perfect price discrimination. Accounting firms are not monopolists, but restrictions on advertising and the nature of the business give each firm some market power.

Ordinary Price Discrimination

Now let us look at ordinary price discrimination by considering first the theory and then the circumstances in which this strategy is feasible. To keep matters simple, we will ask how a monopolist sets price in a market divided into just two segments.

Let us begin with a simplifying assumption, which we will later change: the monopolist has produced a certain quantity of output — say, 44 units — and wants to maximize the profit from selling it. Its problem is to decide how much of the output to sell in each market segment and at what prices. Note that we have assumed away all production questions and reduced the problem to one of maximizing revenue.

The two parts of Figure 14.3 represent the two market segments. Suppose that the monopolist begins by considering selling 21 units in the first market segment and 23 in the second. At this allocation, the marginal revenue of $5 in the first market segment is less than the marginal revenue of $34 in the second segment. Beginning at this allo-

1. Chris Hall (1989) examines the Dutch auction market for the sale of flowers and concludes that it is not a mechanism for price discrimination but a method for producers to exchange information.

cation, if the monopolist transfers 1 unit from the first market segment to the second, the reduction in revenue in the first segment (a drop of approximately $5) will be more than compensated by the increase in revenue in the second (an increase of approximately $34). More generally, the firm's revenue will increase as it transfers output from the market segment with the lower marginal revenue to the market segment with the higher marginal revenue. From this exercise, we have discovered the solution to the monopolist's revenue-maximization problem:

To maximize revenue from the sale of a fixed quantity of output, allocate output so that marginal revenue is identical in all market segments.

In Figure 14.3, revenue is maximized when the monopolist allocates 14 units to the first market segment and 30 to the second market segment, since marginal revenue is then $20 in each segment.

PROBLEM 14.1

As you know, if the monopolist presented in Figure 14.3 has 44 units of output, it will sell all 44 units. Suppose that it has 100 units. Will it sell all 100 units? How many units will it sell in each market segment? Is this result consistent with the rule for maximizing revenue?

Let us expand the problem to include production. Now the monopolist's profit is

$$\pi(y_1, y_2) = TR_1(y_1) + TR_2(y_2) - TC(y_1 + y_2)$$

Here $TR_1(y_1)$ is total revenue from market segment 1, $TR_2(y_2)$ is total revenue from market segment 2, and $TC(y_1 + y_2)$ is the total cost of producing y_1 units for market segment 1 and y_2 units for market segment 2. The monopolist's problem is to choose the two outputs y_1 and y_2 so as to maximize its profit $\pi(y_1, y_2)$.

This problem is more complex than the standard monopoly problem. However, if we think of it in a different way, we can easily use familiar concepts to solve it. Think of the monopolist's decision as occurring in two stages. First, it chooses an aggregate output; then it allocates that aggregate output to the two market segments. From what you just learned, you know that in the second stage the aggregate output will be allocated so that *marginal revenue is identical in the two market segments.* And from what you know from your initial encounter with monopoly, it makes sense that in the first stage, the monopolist will choose aggregate output so that *marginal cost is equal to aggregate marginal revenue.* But exactly what is aggregate marginal revenue?

To find out, let us turn to the aggregate marginal revenue curve presented in Figure 14.4c. It has been constructed by horizontally summing MR_1 and MR_2 from Figures 14.4a and 14.4b. To see its significance, suppose that the monopolist decides to produce 46 units and that it originally allocates 17 units to the first market segment and 29 to the second. As Figures 14.4a and 14.4b reveal, marginal revenue in each market segment is then $4. Therefore, this allocation — 17 units to the first market segment and 29 to the second — maximizes the monopolist's revenue from the 46 units. As Figure 14.4c reveals, the monopolist's marginal revenue is also $4. That is, the aggregate marginal revenue curve in Figure 14.4c gives us the monopolist's marginal revenue when it allocates output to market segments so as to maximize revenue. We can

FIGURE 14.3 Price discrimination: equality of marginal revenue

The monopolist has 44 units of output that it wants to allocate to the two market segments so as to maximize its revenue. To do so, it allocates the fixed quantity to the two market segments so that marginal revenue is identical in the two segments. The optimal allocation is 14 units to segment 1 and 30 units to segment 2.

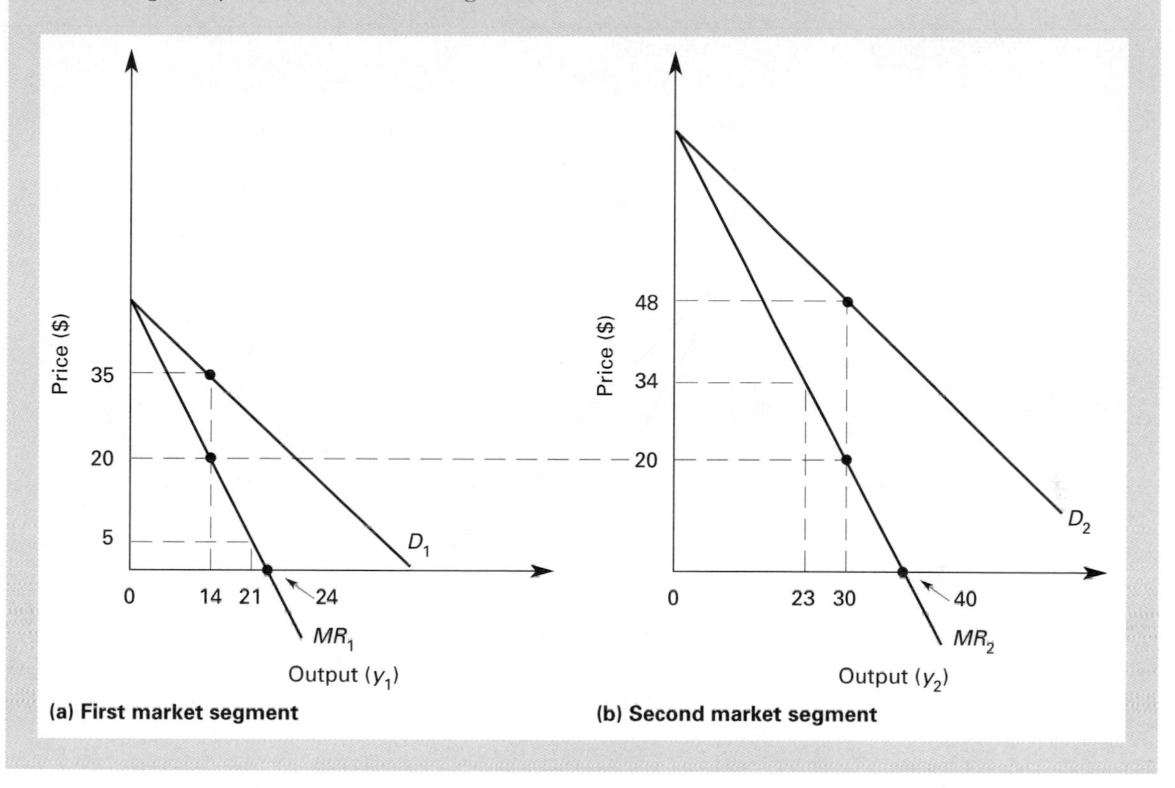

therefore use this curve — in conjunction with the marginal cost curve — to determine the monopolist's profit-maximizing aggregate output.

The profit-maximizing aggregate output is determined by the intersection of the aggregate marginal revenue and marginal cost curves at $y^* = 31$ units in Figure 14.4c. At this output level, aggregate marginal revenue and marginal cost are each \$20. As Figure 14.4 reveals, the monopolist will then allocate $y_1^* = 10$ units to the first market segment and $y_2^* = 21$ to the second, and the corresponding profit-maximizing prices will be $p_1^* = \$30$ and $p_2^* = \$40$. We have learned the following:[2]

---

2. The firm will choose y_1 and y_2 to maximize profit:

$$\pi(y_1, y_2) = TR_1(y_1) + TR_2(y_2) - TC(y_1 + y_2)$$

The partial derivatives of profit with respect to y_1 and y_2 will be equal to zero at the profit-maximizing solution. That is,

$$d[TR_1(y_1)]/dy_1 - \partial TC(y_1 + y_2)/\partial y_1 = 0$$
$$d[TR_2(y_2)]/dy_2 - \partial TC(y_1 + y_2)/\partial y_2 = 0$$

But $d[TR_i(y_i)]/dy_i$ is just $MR_i(y_i)$ and $\partial TC(y_1 + y_2)/\partial y_i$ is just $MC(y_1 + y_2)$. Hence, at the profit maximizing solution,

$$MR_1(y_1) = MR_2(y_2) = MC(y_1 + y_2)$$

FIGURE 14.4 Price discrimination: profit maximization

To find the profit-maximizing set of prices and quantities, first horizontally aggregate the marginal revenue functions in (a) and (b) to obtain the aggregate marginal revenue function in (c). Then find the aggregate profit-maximizing quantity, $y^* = 31$, where aggregate marginal revenue is equal to marginal cost. Finally, allocate the 31 units to the two market segments so as to equalize marginal revenue; that is, sell 10 units at price \$30 in segment 1 and 21 units at price \$40 in segment 2.

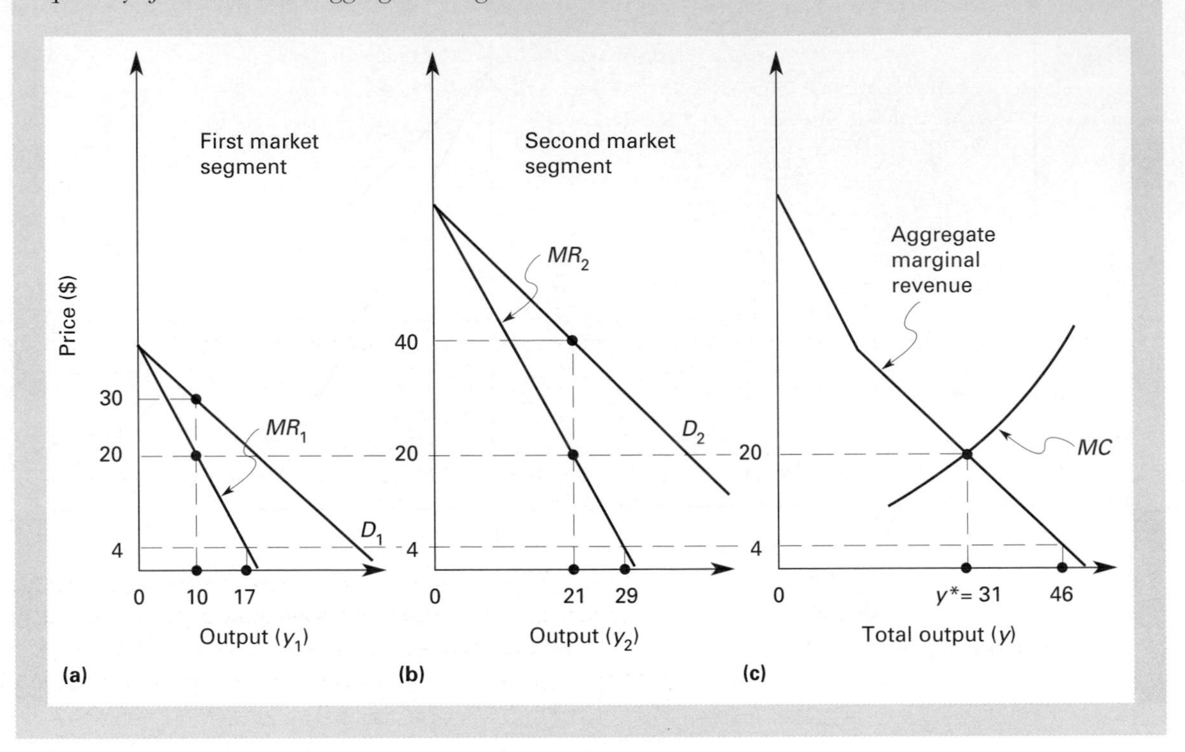

A profit-maximizing monopolist who is able to engage in ordinary price discrimination will choose an aggregate output where aggregate marginal revenue is equal to marginal cost, and it will allocate the profit-maximizing output so that marginal revenue is identical in all market segments.

To get a better sense of what actually determines relative prices in the two market segments, think of the price elasticities of demand in the two market segments. As we saw in Section 10.2, marginal revenue at a point on any demand curve can be expressed in terms of the absolute value of the price elasticity of demand

$$MR(y) = p[1 - 1/|E(y)|]$$

Using this expression for marginal revenue — and keeping in mind that equilibrium marginal revenue is the same in both segments — we see the following:

$$p_1^*[1 - 1/|E_1(y_1^*)|] = p_2^*[1 - 1/|E_2(y_2^*)|]$$

Now let us ask: When will p_2^* exceed p_1^*? Working with this equality, we see that if p_2^* exceeds p_1^*, then

$$[1 - 1/|E_1(y_1^*)|] > [1 - 1/|E_2(y_2^*)|]$$

This inequality can be rewritten as

$$|E_1(y_1^*)| > |E_2(y_2^*)|$$

Therefore, p_2^* will exceed p_1^* if — at the equilibrium — price elasticity of demand in the second market segment is less than price elasticity of demand in the first. Or, putting the result differently:

Price is higher in the market segment with the lower price elasticity of demand.

This result makes good sense of ordinary observations. If one of your parents falls desperately ill in Orlando or if your branch plant in London is threatening to close, you will catch the next flight out almost regardless of the fare. Your demand for airline travel is relatively price-inelastic. By contrast, if you have decided to treat yourself to a holiday next spring but do not care if you go to Orlando or Mazatlan or London or Zermatt, you can pick and choose. Accordingly, your demand on any of these routes is relatively price-elastic. Airline companies respond to these differing elasticities by discriminating — by charging the traveller who wants to depart tomorrow one price and the traveller who wants to depart sometime in the next month or two another, much lower price.

PROBLEM 14.2

The firm in Figure 14.5 has monopoly power in the first market segment but none in the second. First, find the aggregate marginal revenue curve. Then solve the monopolist's profit-maximizing problem for the conditions presented in Figure 14.5.

Application: Why Are Home-Delivered Newspapers so Cheap?

Most newspapers can be acquired by readers either through purchasing them from a street vendor or machine or by direct subscription. Think about the last time you bought a paper that you did not regularly subscribe to. Was it *The Wall Street Journal* because you wanted to read a particular story about a firm you had invested in? Or *The Globe and Mail* because you'd heard that the editorial page had something relevant for your upcoming economics exam? Whatever; you probably had a particular reason, and that reason was probably quite inelastic with respect to price. On the other hand, perhaps you live in a city with several daily papers, all of which provide similar coverage of local and national events. If so, you are probably more sensitive to price with this subscription. In other words the demand for subscriptions is more elastic than the demand for one-time copies of a newspaper.

What would our model of price discrimination say? Newspapers that face these two types of demands should price the same newspapers differently, and the price should be higher at the newsstand than for papers delivered at home. In Vancouver, subscribers of *The Vancouver Sun* pay $13.50 per month (56 cents per copy). The daily rate

FIGURE 14.5 A price-discrimination problem

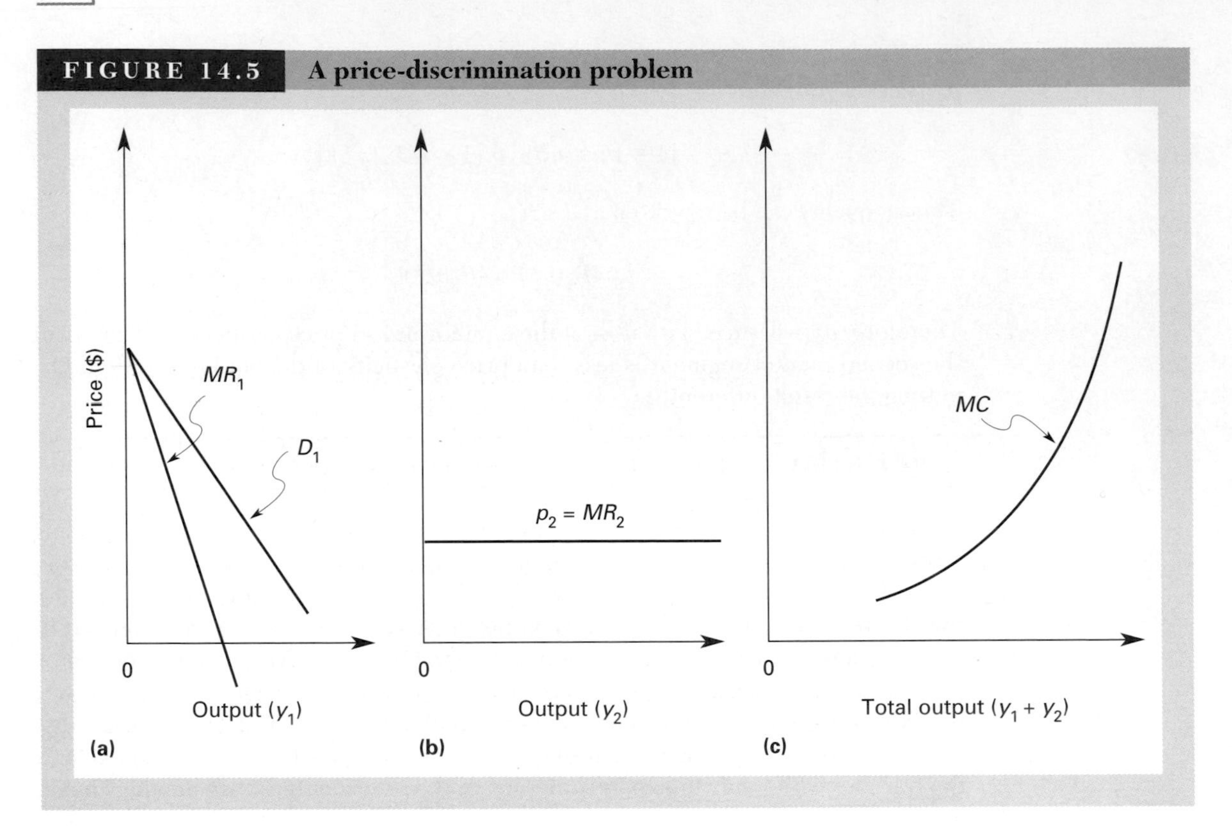

is 75 cents (Monday to Thursday); $1.35 (Friday/Saturday). This pricing is consistent with our model of ordinary price discrimination.

Market Segmentation Revisited

To establish a successful scheme of ordinary price discrimination, the monopolist must be able to *identify different price elasticities of demand* and to segment its market accordingly; it must be able to *isolate* one portion of the market from the other in order to prevent resale. This objective can be undermined by an entrepreneurial activity called **arbitrage,** which consists of buying a good in a low-priced market and reselling it in a high-priced market.

arbitrage

In some markets, however, arbitrage is impossible, and, in other markets, it is unprofitable. For example, arbitrage of personal services is generally impossible. Although seniors get a discount on movie admission prices, for example, they cannot arbitrage in this market because they cannot transfer the good — a movie they have seen — to someone else. Similarly, children cannot arbitrage in the market for haircuts — even though they can buy them more cheaply than adults — because haircuts are not transferable. All sorts of personal services, from massage therapy and fitness classes to dental and medical services, are markets in which arbitrage cannot occur.

In other cases, arbitrage is possible but unprofitable. For example, the retail price of a new car in Oshawa, Ontario, is sometimes lower than the price of the identical model in Regina, Saskatchewan. But, relative to the price differential, the cost of transporting a car from Oshawa to Regina is high enough to discourage significant arbitrage. If a price differential is large enough, however, arbitrage will occur. Thus, the possibility of arbitrage limits the degree to which prices can diverge in the two markets. In general, where **arbitrage costs** — the costs of buying, selling, and transporting — are significant, arbitrage will be unprofitable.

arbitrage costs

In still other cases, arbitrage may be both possible and potentially profitable, but the price discriminator may be able to subvert it effectively. A classic example is the case in which the duopolists Du Pont and Rohm and Haas sold the plastic moulding powder methyl methacrylate to general industrial users for $0.85 per pound and to dental manufacturers for $22 per pound. When arbitrageurs began buying methyl methacrylate at the industrial price and reselling it to denture manufacturers at a price below $22 per pound, Rohm and Haas considered cutting the ground out from under the arbitrageurs by mixing arsenic with the plastic powder sold for industrial use so that it could not be used for denture work. Although the firm ultimately rejected the idea, it did circulate rumours suggesting that the industrial methyl methacrylate had been adulterated (Stocking and Watkins, 1946, 402–4).

The contamination of products is actually not that uncommon. For example, grain intended for seed use only is often poisoned to prevent its use in consumption. An unusual example involved Alcoa, the monopolist aluminum company of America. Alcoa was selling aluminum to aircraft manufacturers at a very high price, and was selling aluminum to electrical cable companies and household appliance companies at a significantly lower price. Alcoa quickly found out that the latter group were reselling their inventories of raw aluminum. To counteract this trade, Alcoa began its own production of cable and pots and pans. Alcoa even had to go to the extreme lengths of adding plastic handles, steel rivets, and copper bottoms to its pots in an effort to stop firms from melting them down to resell the aluminum.

A final example of product tampering to prevent resale is purple gas. Most Canadians are unaware that farmers pay lower gasoline taxes and are thus able to purchase gasoline for their farm vehicles (and trucks) at a price well below the market level. Farmers could not only exploit this by using this gas in the family car, but could clearly set up a "Farmer Joe's resale gas station" behind the barn to sell gas to their urban cousins. One method used to police this practice is to dye the gas purple. Police occasionally set up roadblocks in rural areas and test the gas in the tank. People found driving a non-farm vehicle with purple gas face a fine. The threat of the fine segments the market and reduces the amount of resale.

In cases where arbitrage is either impossible or not profitable, how can the monopolist achieve market segmentation? The most obvious way to isolate market segments from one another is to require direct identification. For example, seniors must somehow certify their age to receive lower prices on prescription drugs or movie tickets. Clients obviously need to hand their books over to their accountants, thereby revealing their financial status.

self-selection

Another method is to rely on **self-selection**; that is, to induce individuals to sort themselves voluntarily into the appropriate market niche. In the Dutch auction case, the high demanders sort themselves by bidding first. A more commonplace example is the two-segment market for airline travel. In the business travel segment of the market, demand is likely to arise on relatively short notice and to be relatively price-inelastic. In the holiday travel segment, demand is usually anticipated well in advance and is likely to be relatively price-elastic. A standard discriminatory mechanism is the "advanced booking discount," often hedged by such other restrictions as requiring the traveller to stay at least a week or to stay over at least one Saturday night. Because only holiday travellers are able to plan well ahead and stay for at least a week, the airline's customers reveal their identity as business people or vacationers simply by their response to its price structure.

Annual or semiannual department store sales are another rather puzzling feature of economic life that we can better understand in the context of price discrimination through self-selection. In these sales, the items are sold at prices substantially below their everyday prices, and the sales are often predictable events. The January white sales are a regular feature of the North American department store landscape, for example. What is puzzling is how stores can still manage to sell a good portion of their merchandise at everyday prices. A form of market segmentation through self-selection is part of the answer. Going to these sales usually means putting up with crowds and long lines at the cash register. To some shoppers, the package of crowds and lower prices is preferred to more elbow room and regular prices. To other shoppers, the opposite is true. Because the two kinds of shoppers select themselves by going to sales or staying away, the retailing strategy effectively segments the market. We cannot regard this strategy as a pure form of ordinary price discrimination, however, because the cost of retailing during such sales, in which volume is considerably heavier, is lower than usual.

Another form of market segmentation is intertemporal. Many individuals love to acquire the newest and latest models of everything from cars and stereos to books and movies. Firms that have some market power over their commodities can price-discriminate over time by charging a high price at the product's launch and then lowering the price over time. Books are first printed in hardcover versions, and then sold as paperbacks. Movies are first sold through theatres, and then through videos. New products in general, whether they are calculators, computers, or waterbeds, often have prices that fall over time. As with the case of sales, the market is segmented through time, with those willing to pay the highest prices purchasing first.

PROBLEM 14.3

Canadian Tire offers a 2.5 percent discount for cash payments. Instead of taking 2.5 percent off the total bill, however, the firm gives customers the equivalent in Canadian Tire money. This "money" then can be presented in lieu of cash the next time customers make a purchase at a Canadian Tire store. Can you identify the two forms of price discrimination through self-selection at work here?

Price Discrimination and the Law

Both Canada and the United States have laws presumably intended to protect consumers against monopoly practices. In Canada the *Combines Investigation Act* was enacted in 1889, while in the US the *Sherman Antitrust Act* was enacted in 1890. In both cases the wording of the law was less than precise. In Canada the law stated that it was a "criminal offence to conspire to unduly lessen competition." Making monopoly practices criminal meant that a strong burden of proof was required; the word "conspire" put the onus on the prosecution to show intent; and no one has ever figured out what "unduly" actually means. In any event, courts in both countries have wrestled with the interpretation of the law, and legislatures have added additional practices over time. In Canada, price discrimination became an offence under the *Act* in 1935.

It turns out, however, that price discrimination is not as easy to prosecute as it is to observe. The problem is one of taking proper account of costs. If a firm charges two separate prices to different customers, but this difference in price is completely the result of differences in the cost of servicing the customers, then under the law this is not price discrimination. For example, one can purchase a perpetuity that pays an annual income until the time of death. Firms charge women higher prices than men; but this is not price discrimination, merely a reflection of women's longer life expectancy. Allowing differences in costs to legitimize differences in prices is like opening up Pandora's box. In most instances of price discrimination, it is relatively easy to come up with a cost difference justification.

For example, when airlines offer lower fares to customers who book in advance, they could be passing the savings of advanced planning on to their customers. If airlines could only book customers on the spot, they would be required to hold larger inventories of planes, flights might leave either half-full or with passengers left on the ground. In effect, by booking early the passengers are providing the airline information about the demands for different routes and times. This information lowers costs, and this saving is reflected in the price. But is this cost difference worth five-sixths of the business fare? The answer is not obvious and what makes price discrimination cases so difficult.

PROBLEM 14.4

Pizza Joe is in trouble, and he needs your help. One of his customers has complained to the Competition Bureau that two of Pizza Joe's pricing tactics amount to price discrimination. The first complaint is that Pizza Joe charges less for his salad bar if you buy a pizza than if you don't. The second complaint is that Pizza Joe offers free delivery of his pizzas. The irate customer says that because customers farther away pay a lower price net of transportation costs than do closer customers, this is price discrimination. You've been hired by Joe's defence team. What might you argue in each case to help him out?

Multipart or Block Pricing

Finally, let us consider *multipart* or *block pricing*. We will not attempt a complete or rigorous analysis of multipart pricing. Rather, we will concentrate on understanding what it is, the circumstances in which it is feasible, and why it is even more profitable than ordinary price discrimination.

price schedule

To understand multipart pricing we need the concept of a **price schedule**. You are already familiar with a one-part price schedule. When your grocer posts a sign indicating that the (single) price of mushrooms is $5 per kilogram, the price schedule that you face is a one-part price schedule since you can buy any quantity you want at a single price. A multipart price schedule associates different prices with different quantity blocks. For example, your grocer might post the following two-part price schedule for mushrooms: $5 per kilogram for the first 5 kilograms and $4 for each additional kilogram. Or the grocer might post a three-part price schedule: $5 per kilogram for the first 5 kilograms, $4 per kilogram for the next 5 kilograms, and $2.50 per kilogram for any amount greater than 10 kilograms.

Why is a multipart price schedule more profitable than ordinary price discrimination? Figure 14.6 presents two individual demand curves. The demand curve for Betty is on the right. The demand curve for Sam is on the left. For reasons that will soon be apparent, we will assume that Sam's demand curve is independent of his income. And to keep the analysis simple, we will also assume that the monopoly supplier of this good incurs no costs in producing it and that Betty and Sam are its only customers.

FIGURE 14.6 Multipart pricing

With the multipart pricing scheme, the firm charges any consumer $12 for the first 18 units and $8 for any units in excess of 18. Betty buys 5 units at $12 and none at $8, while Sam buys 18 units at $12 and 6 units at $8.

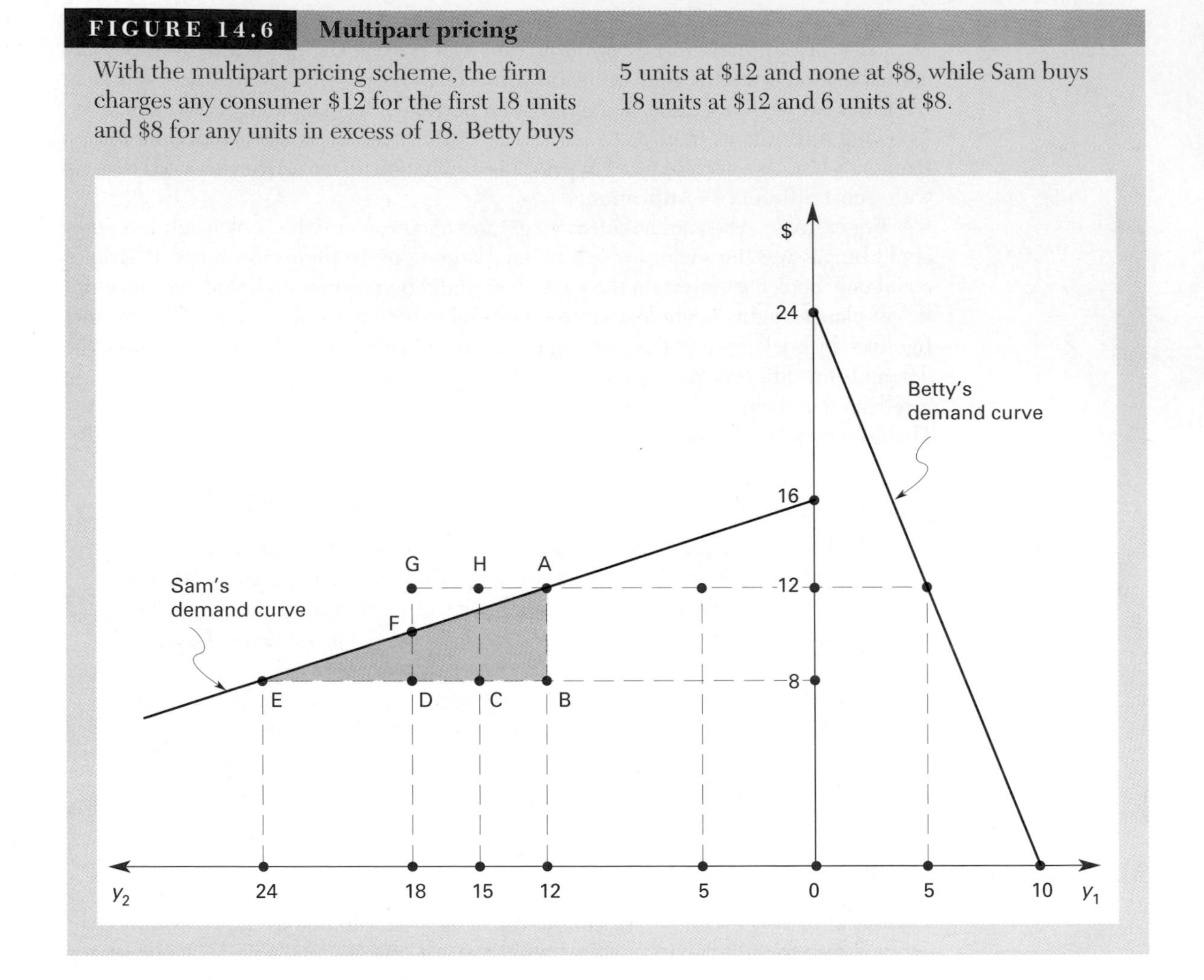

As a point of reference, we can identify what the monopolist's pricing strategy will be if it engages in ordinary price discrimination. Since the monopolist's marginal cost is 0, it will choose the point on each demand curve where marginal revenue is equal to 0. As you can easily verify, it will charge $12 per unit in the first market segment, and Betty will buy 5 units; it will charge $8 per unit in the second market segment, and Sam will buy 24 units. The monopolist's profit and revenue will then be $252.

Now consider a two-part price schedule in which the monopolist charges a price of $12 per unit for the initial quantity block and a lower price of $8 per unit for each unit in excess of the initial block limit. The monopolist's problem is then to choose the block limit in the two-part price schedule — but not the two prices — that maximizes its profit. Clearly, the monopolist will choose a block limit of at least 12. What will happen if the monopolist actually sets a block limit of 12 units? Both Betty and Sam would face this two-part price schedule: a price of $12 per unit for the first 12 units and a price of $8 for every unit in excess of 12. Given this price schedule, Betty will again buy 5 units at $12 per unit. On the other hand, Sam will again buy 24 units, but he will pay $12 instead of $8 for the first 12 units. Relative to the ordinary price discrimination case, then, the monopolist will sell exactly the same amount. Yet its revenue will rise by $48 since Sam will have paid an extra $4 per unit on the first 12 units. The monopolist's profit under this two-part price schedule is $300 rather than $252. Clearly, multipart pricing is more profitable than ordinary price discrimination.

Yet the monopolist can do even better by choosing a *larger* block limit. Suppose, for example, that it increases its block limit to 15. Once again, Betty will buy 5 units at $12 per unit. The interesting question concerns Sam, who has two courses of action open to him. He will either buy just 12 units at $12 per unit, ending up at point A on his demand curve, or he will buy the entire 15-unit block at the $12 price and an additional 9 units at the $8 price, ending up at point E on his demand curve.

To see which course of action Sam will choose, suppose that he is at point A in Figure 14.6, where he has bought just 12 units at $12 apiece. First, what would Sam be willing to pay for the privilege of buying additional units at the $8 price? Second, what is the *implicit price* of this privilege under the 15-unit block limit?

To answer the first question, note that Sam's demand curve is independent of his income; therefore, we can use the concept of consumer surplus to measure his willingness to pay for this privilege. Beginning at point A, if he could buy additional units at the $8 price, he would buy 12 more units (moving from point A to point E on his demand curve). The added consumer surplus would then be $24, equal to the area of shaded triangle EBA in Figure 14.6. Therefore, Sam would be willing to pay up to $24 for this privilege.

Now for the second question. Under the 15-unit block limit, he must pay not $8 but $12 for the first three additional units (units 13, 14, and 15). The implicit price of the privilege is therefore $12. Because $12 is less than $24, he will choose the option represented by point E, where he buys 15 units at $12 per unit and 9 more units at $8 per unit — and the monopolist's profit will therefore rise by an additional $12 to $312.

Which block limit *maximizes* the monopolist's profit? The monopolist will continue to increase the block limit until the implicit price of the privilege of buying additional units at the $8 price is equal to the $24 maximum price Sam is willing to pay for that privilege. The block limit that maximizes the firm's profit is therefore 18 units, since the implicit price of the privilege is then $24, equal to $4 per unit multiplied by 6 units. Under this 18-unit block limit, the monopolist's profit is $324.

Our purpose is not to present a complete analysis of the monopolist's choice of a multipart price schedule, but to indicate how this pricing strategy works. As you will discover in the following problem, the monopolist who institutes such a strategy will not simply mimic the prices it would otherwise have charged under ordinary price discrimination, as we have so far assumed.

PROBLEM 14.5

Notice that for every $1 drop in the price per unit, Sam buys 3 more units.

a. Consider a two-part price schedule with prices of $12 and $6. What block limit maximizes profit? Is the monopolist's profit larger than it is with the $12 and $8 prices and the 18-unit block limit? Is Sam any better off?

b. Consider a two-part price schedule with prices of $12 and $0. What block limit now maximizes profit? Is the monopolist's profit now larger than in (a)? Is Sam any better off?

You may be wondering why ordinary discrimination exists if multipart pricing is so much more profitable. The answer is that the monopolist must be able to meter or otherwise monitor the consumption of specific consumers like Betty and Sam. The reason your grocer does not post a multipart pricing schedule for mushrooms, for example, is that it can neither prevent arbitrage nor monitor the consumption of individual consumers. However, this kind of pricing scheme is common in the sale of electricity, natural gas, and water, because consumption is metered and arbitrage is costly. Cable television service is another, less obvious, example of a market in which multipart pricing schemes are used. For example, Shaw Cable Company offers a limited number of television channels for $15.95 per month; a full range of television channels for $24.95. If you want to add Internet services to your cable, you can get "high-speed lite" for $39.94, "high speed" for $55.95, and "high speed with full cable" for just $74.95! Another example is the common banking practice of charging a higher rate for cashing the first block of so many cheques, a lower rate for the next block, and so on. Whenever it is feasible, then, monopolists do appear to use multipart pricing.

PROBLEM 14.6

Which of the following is price discrimination? What type?

a. The wealthy pay more for medical services.

b. Pay by the frame in bowling.

c. Better students get more valuable scholarships.

14.2 Monopsonistic Price Discrimination

Let us turn to price discrimination in a monopsonistic market. Perfect price discrimination is similar in monopoly and monopsony. Essentially the firm offers the holder of each input his or her reservation price, and in the process extracts all of the rent. In this section, we will exploit the similarity between monopolistic and monopsonistic price discrimination as we do a quick treatment of **ordinary monopsonistic price discrimination**.

ordinary monopsonistic price discrimination

Suppose that a monopsonist can buy an input from two identifiable groups of suppliers — say, labour from women and men, or from whites and nonwhites. Suppose, too, that the supply functions of these groups are different. How will a profit-maximizing monopsonist exploit this chance to price-discriminate? Let us defer the firm's profit-maximizing problem until we have answered a simpler question: What combination of labour from the first group, z_1, and the second group, z_2, will minimize the cost of hiring a fixed amount of labour, say z'?

Recall that we used a similar strategy to solve the monopolist's price-discrimination problem in Section 14.1. The monopsonist in Figure 14.7 will choose z_1 and z_2 so that $MFC_1(z_1)$ and $MFC_2(z_2)$ are equal and so that the sum of z_1 and z_2 is z'. In the solution presented in Figure 14.7, the monopsonist buys z_1^* from the first group at the price w_1^*, and z_2^* from the second group at the price w_2^*. We can see why this is the cost-minimizing solution by considering a departure from it. If the monopsonist were to buy 1 unit less from the first group and 1 unit more from the second, for example, its cost would increase because MFC_1 at $z_1^* - 1$ units in the first market (equal to AB in Figure 14.7a) is less than MFC_2 at $z_2^* + 1$ units in the second market (equal to A′B′ in Figure 14.7b).

Again exploiting the obvious correspondence with the discriminating monopolist's profit-maximizing rule, we have solved the discriminating monopsonist's profit-

FIGURE 14.7 Discriminatory hiring to minimize costs

To minimize the cost of buying a fixed quantity of the input from two market segments, the firm chooses the two quantities so that *MFC* is identical in the two market segments. It buys z_1^* at price w_1^* in the first market segment and z_2^* at price w_2^* in the second.

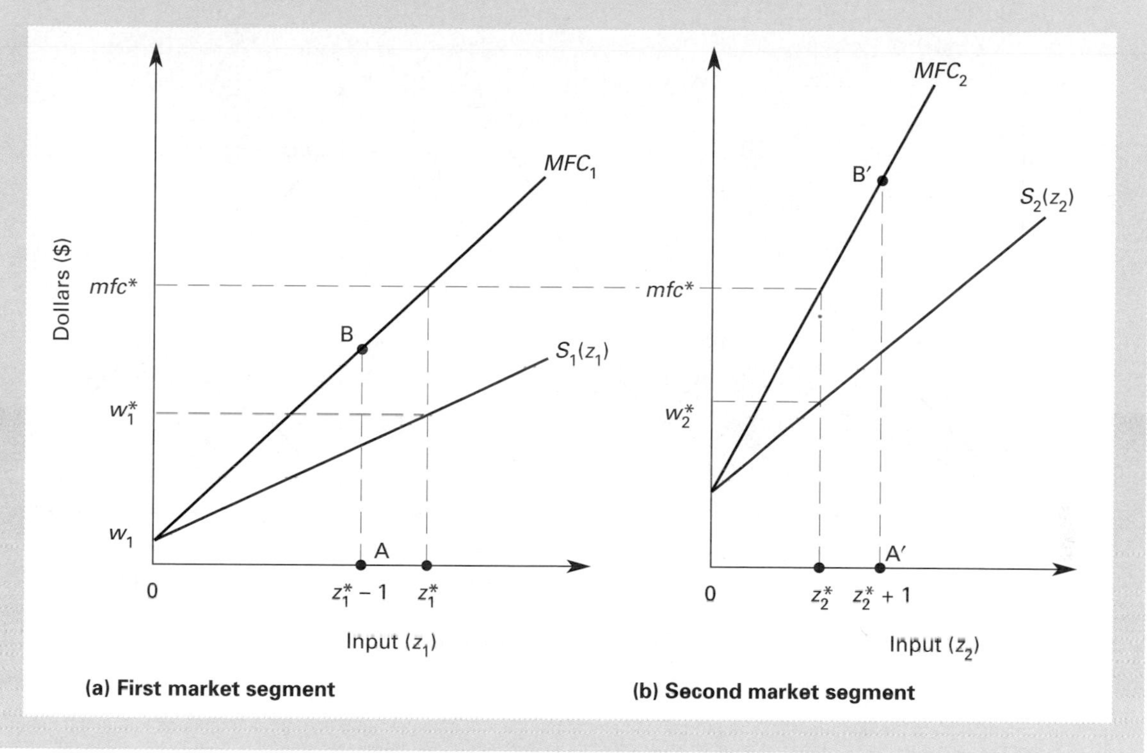

maximizing problem in Figure 14.8. The two marginal factor cost functions in Figures 14.8a and 14.8b have been horizontally summed to obtain the function labelled ΣMFC in Figure 14.8c, which gives the marginal cost of the input when the monopsonist follows its cost-minimizing rule. To maximize its profit, the monopsonist will buy the input up to the point where ΣMFC intersects *MRP* at z^* units in Figure 14.8c. We can identify the corresponding prices and quantities in the component submarkets simply by projecting mfc^* from Figure 14.8c into Figures 14.8a and 14.8b. To summarize:

A profit-maximizing monopsonist will choose aggregate quantity of the input so that aggregate marginal factor cost is equal to marginal revenue product, and it will allocate purchases so that marginal factor cost is identical in all input markets.

In discussing monopoly price discrimination in goods markets, we discovered that the possibility of arbitrage significantly limited the monopolist's ability to price-discriminate. For example, if the price of a new car in Vancouver exceeds the price of the same model in Seattle by more than the combined costs of transportation and import duty, arbitrageurs will begin buying cars in Seattle and selling them in Vancouver. Yet we also found that when the goods are personal services, arbitrage is not possible: parents cannot have their kids buy haircuts for them at the children's price, for example. So, too, when the inputs in resource markets are labour services, arbitrage is once

FIGURE 14.8 Discriminatory hiring to maximize profit

To find the profit-maximizing solution, horizontally aggregate MFC_1 and MFC_2 to obtain ΣMFC in (c). The profit-maximizing quantity z^* is the quantity such that ΣMFC is equal to MRP. Allocate the z^* units to the two market segments so as to equalize MFC in the two segments. That is, buy z_1^* in the first market segment and z_2^* in the second.

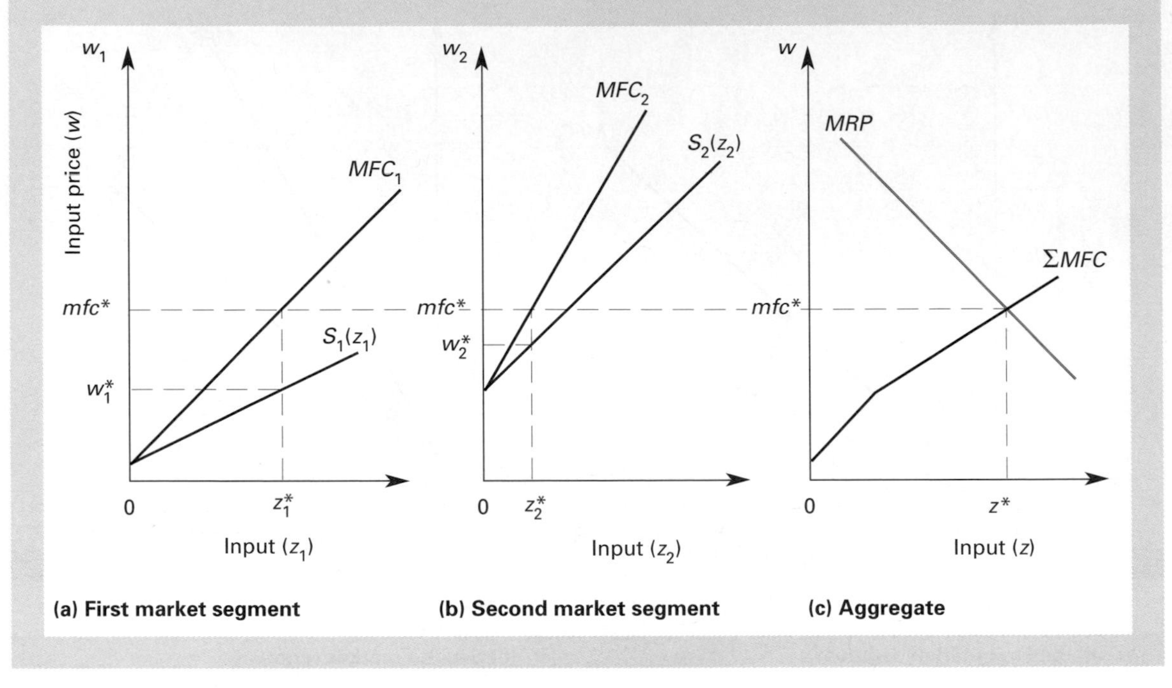

again impossible because employment contracts involve the employer and specific employees: women cannot have men obtain employment for them at the male worker's wage rate. Because arbitrage is difficult in labour markets, we might expect to see significant monopsonistic discrimination.

Certain conditions must prevail, however, before monopsonistic discrimination in labour markets can occur. First, the market must be characterized by monopsony power. Second, the degree of monopsony power must be different for identifiable groups of workers within that market. Although we will not examine this sort of discrimination in any detail, we can outline the important questions to be asked. First, is the labour market characterized by significant job immobility? For example, are accountants or hair stylists fairly immobile? Second, is one segment of the labour force significantly less mobile than another? For example, are female accountants or hair stylists less mobile than their male counterparts? If the answer to both questions is yes and if the less mobile group is paid less, we can tentatively ascribe that differential in wage rates to ordinary monopsonistic discrimination.

The whole question of discrimination is a hotly debated issue as well as a complex economic problem. Comparable pay for comparable work and affirmative action programs for identifiable minorities are just two of the many policy issues related to labour market discrimination that regularly appear in the headlines. We saw in Chapter 11 that in competitive markets, differences in wages are most plausibly explained by differences in productivity. Discrimination in wages, as we have just seen, however, can result from monopsony power. However, it seems implausible to suggest that economy-wide differences in wages can be explained by monopsony power. Monopsony may be present in one-firm towns or within specialized labour markets, but most firms are price takers in input markets.

14.3 Two-Part Tariff Pricing

In Chapter 4, we introduced you to the problem of two-part tariffs as a general strategy for extracting maximum profit from one consumer when the monopolist knows that consumer's preferences. If you will recall, the two-part tariff strategy is to price the good at marginal cost and then charge an "entry fee" equal to the consumer's surplus to extract maximum profit. Figure 14.9 shows the two-part tariff solution for a single consumer. If the firm charges a price higher than p^*, the consumer's surplus is lower, which results in a lower entry fee. The firm can do no better than to sell y^* at a price p^*, and charge an entry fee equal to the shaded region. As we work through two-part tariffs and other pricing strategies, we will be using the concept of a representative consumer developed in Chapter 4.

The major advantage of this type of pricing is that the firm does not have to worry about market segmentation and the problem of resale. Here everyone pays the same price. This type of pricing strategy explains the pricing at such firms as Disneyland and Polaroid, which you encountered in Chapter 4. Other examples include golf courses that charge a membership fee and green fees, car rental firms that charge a daily fee and a charge per kilometre, night clubs that charge a cover charge and prices for food and drinks inside, and telephone and cable TV companies that charge a hookup fee and a monthly rental fee. In the pure case (not necessarily found in these examples), the solution is efficient because the product is sold at marginal cost, and all the potential gains from trade are therefore realized.

FIGURE 14.9 Two-part tariff pricing

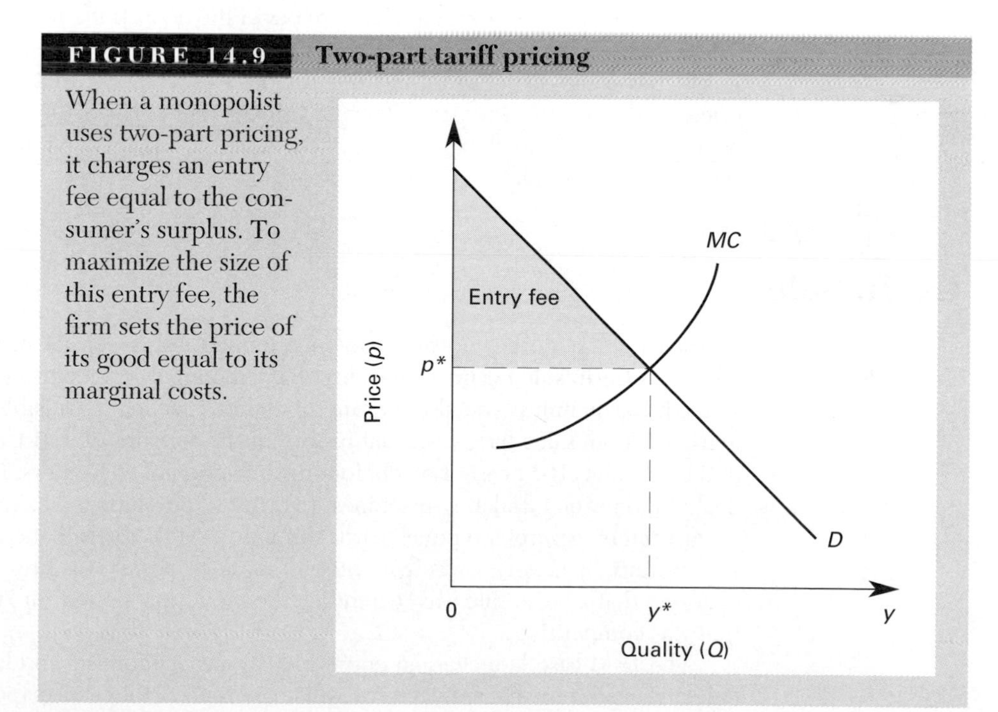

When a monopolist uses two-part pricing, it charges an entry fee equal to the consumer's surplus. To maximize the size of this entry fee, the firm sets the price of its good equal to its marginal costs.

The optimal two-part tariff strategy is to set $P = MC$, and charge an entry fee equal to the consumer's surplus.

Two-part tariffs are clearly more profitable than ordinary price discrimination because all of the consumer's surplus is transferred to the firm. Why, then, would firms ever bother with price discrimination? Why wouldn't two-part tariffs be even more popular? As with all monopoly practices, two-part tariffs have their costs. The problem is that one entry price is charged to everyone, and not everyone is necessarily willing to pay that price. In other words, our assumption of a representative consumer is often violated. Suppose there are two types of customers: high-demand types and low-demand types. If the firm charges the same per-unit price to both types of customers, then the high-demand types generate a higher consumer's surplus. If the firm decides to extract this surplus through the use of an entry charge, then clearly the low demanders drop out of the market. If there are enough low-demand types in the market, the firm may find it more profitable to price-discriminate between the two types.

Two-part tariffs work best when the consumers are homogeneous, or tend to be similar in the demand for the product. As the consumers become more heterogeneous, it will become more profitable to price-discriminate. Hence we observe the wholesale distributor Costco charging an entry fee, while ordinary grocery stores do not. Costco caters to large families and small businesses, and has a more homogeneous set of customers than does a store like Safeway. Night clubs charge entry fees because individual clubs create atmospheres that cater to similar types of people. Neighbourhood pubs, on the other hand, do not charge fees because their clientele is quite varied.

In economic circles, the most famous example of two-part pricing is popcorn at the movies. The example is famous because the price of popcorn is apparently too high. Before you took this course, you might have explained this high price as follows. "Once you enter the theatre, the theater owner is a monopolist popcorn seller, so he sets a high price." But you know now that this does not make sense. Setting a high popcorn price lowers the price moviegoers are willing to pay at the door. If the movie house is engaged in simple two-part tariff pricing in an effort to extract more surplus from moviegoers, surely they could do better by lowering the price of the popcorn and charging a higher price for the movie. One possible explanation is that perhaps the marginal cost of the popcorn is $4 for a small bag. Hardly likely. A better explanation might be that popcorn is used as a tie-in sale.

14.4 Tie-In Sales

tie-in sales

Tie-in sales are another possible way for a monopolist to extract surplus from its customers. A **tie-in sale** occurs when a firm has a monopoly over some good X, but refuses to sell it to you unless you also buy another good Y, which is available in a competitive market. Tie-in sales have a special history in the folklore of anti-trust cases because of the infamous IBM case. Long before the invention of computers, IBM made a great deal of money on tabulating machines. In order to purchase a machine, IBM required its customers to purchase punch cards through IBM — cards that could be purchased at substantially lower prices from other suppliers. A suit was brought against IBM, charging that a tie-in sale was "extending the monopoly power" of IBM into a market that was competitive.

The IBM case launched an entire industry as economists and lawyers developed defences against the charge. Here we will not consider other explanations for tie-in sales, but simply consider how it could be a method of extracting surplus, again using the assumpton of the representative consumer. Suppose we have a firm that has a monopoly on an adding machine (good x), and that the demand for this machine is given in Figure 14.10a. For simplicity we can assume that the marginal cost and average cost of producing these machines is zero, and that it is not profitable to price-discriminate or use a two-part tariff. If the firm acted as a simple monopoly, it would maximize total revenue and charge a price p_x^1 and sell x_1, generating consumer's surplus equal to the shaded region.

Now suppose there is another good, paper (y), that sells in the competitive market. For simplicity, assume the marginal costs of paper are also zero, and therefore, that its price in the market is also zero. The demand for paper is given in Figure 14.10b, and at the market price, y_0 is the amount consumed. One strategy for the monopolist firm is to tie the sale of paper to its adding machines and charge a price of paper above marginal costs. If the firm sets its price for adding machines equal to p_x^1, then it can charge a price of paper equal to $p_y^1 > 0$. The entire shaded area in Figure 14.10b must equal the shaded area in 14.10a. That is, the loss of consumer's surplus from paying more for the paper will just equal the gain in consumer's surplus from consuming the adding machines.

By tying in the paper, the monopolist firm is able to extract the consumer's surplus; however, it is unable to extract all of it. The revenue from paper is equal to the blue rectangle defined by $p_y^1 \times y_1$, which is smaller than the entire shaded area. That is, the tie-in sale creates a deadweight loss, equal to the grey triangle in Figure 14.10b, by charging above marginal cost for the tied good.

The situations in parts (a) and (b), however, do not represent the equilibrium prices. The monopolist firm can still do better. We will not show the full equilibrium, but the general idea can be found in parts (c) and (d). If the monopolist lowers the price of the adding machines, it increases the consumer's surplus. This means that there is more surplus to extract, and as a result the firm can charge more for the paper. As the price of the paper increases, though, the deadweight loss increases. Hence it will never pay for the firm to give its own good away and try to extract all of the surplus away through a tied-in good.

With a tie-in sale, the firm lowers the price of the monopoly good and raises the price of the tied good.

So why is popcorn so expensive at the movies? One explanation is that popcorn is used as a tie-in sale in order to extract the surplus from people who really like movies. In order for this argument to work, there must be different tastes for movies and popcorn among the population. Suppose there are two types: movie lovers and marginal moviegoers, equally distributed in the population. Further, let's suppose that the movie lovers also love popcorn, but the moviegoers just watch the movie.

Perhaps the movie lovers are willing to pay \$12 to see a movie, while the moviegoers are only willing to pay \$7. What are some pricing strategies that the theatre can charge? Once again, we see that a two-part tariff probably won't work because there is too much heterogeneity in the population. Setting a large entrance fee at \$12 will lose half of the customers. Straight price discrimination is unlikely because the movie lovers and moviegoers may not be part of an identifiable group, and so market segmentation is too costly. A tie-in sale might work, however. By setting a low \$7 price of admission, the theatre extracts the maximum willingness to pay from the marginal moviegoers, but leaves a \$5 surplus to the movie lovers. Once inside, however, the movie theatre charges an above-marginal-cost price for its popcorn in an effort to extract the \$5 from the movie lovers. Notice that, in this context, a tie-in sale is a subtle form of price discrimination.

FIGURE 14.10 Tie-in sales

In part (a) the monopolist maximizes profits by charging a price such that $MR = MC$. At this price the consumer's surplus is equal to the shaded area. In part (b) the firm is able to extract most of the surplus by charging a price above marginal cost for the paper. In part (c) the firm raises the surplus on the monopoly good in order to raise the price of the tied-in good in part (d).

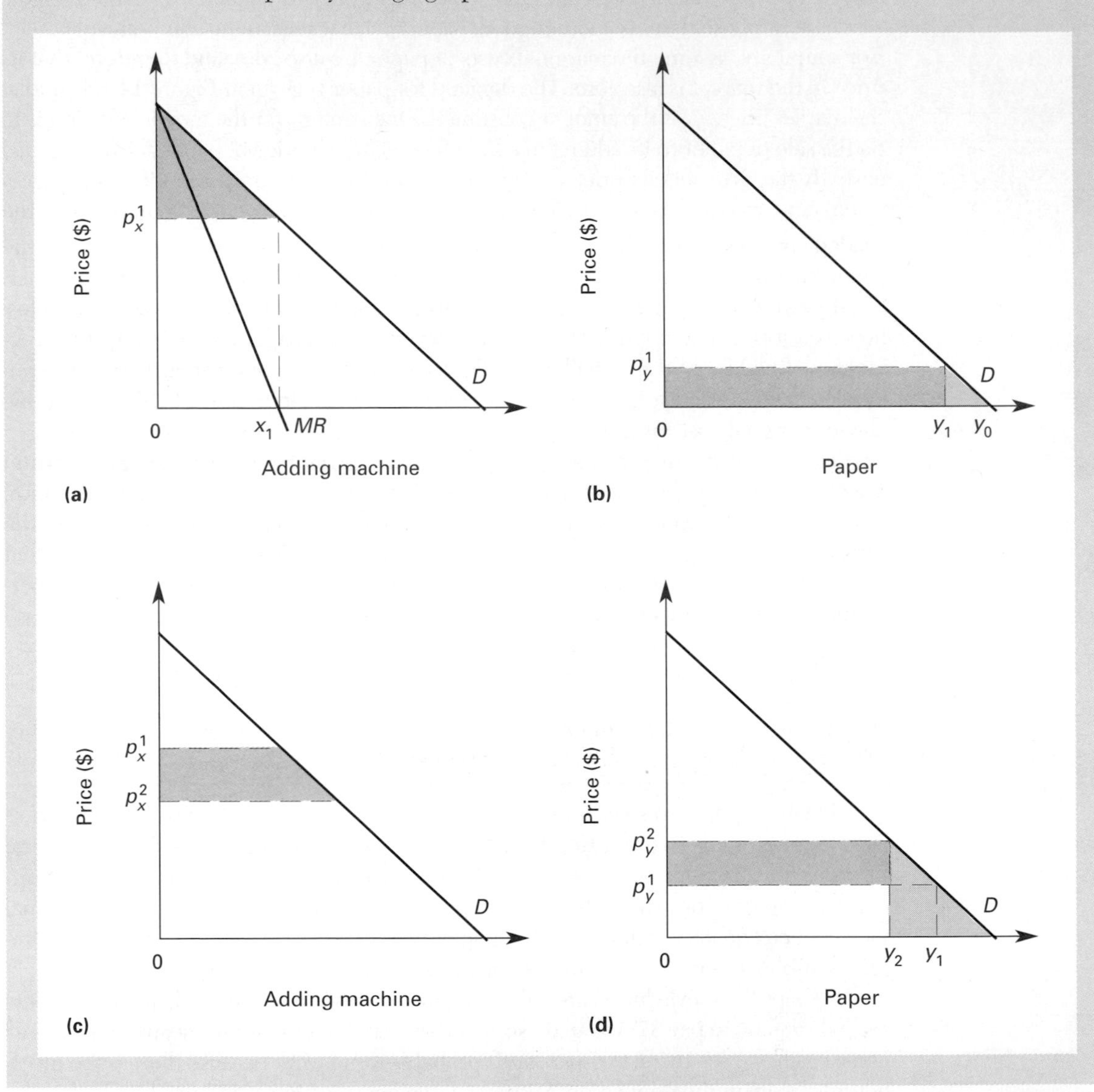

PROBLEM 14.7

What would the theatre company do if the movie lovers didn't snack while watching movies, and it was the marginal moviegoers who had the high demand for popcorn?

14.5

All-or-Nothing Demands and the Exploitation of Affection

all-or-nothing pricing

All-or-nothing pricing may be regarded as a special instance of multi-part pricing. Here we will explore it more fully, and use it to explain a number of interesting personal interactions between friends, family members, and lovers, again assuming consumers are identical in their demands.

all-or-nothing demand curve

An **all-or-nothing demand curve** is different from an ordinary demand curve. An ordinary demand curve tells us the marginal value of a given quantity, while an all-or-nothing demand curve tells us the *average value* of a given quantity. Another way of putting this is that an all-or-nothing demand curve tells us the maximum amount per unit a customer would be willing to pay for a given amount of some good, *rather than have nothing at all*. When a consumer pays the average value for a good, rather than the marginal value, then the consumer's surplus is zero. If a monopolist can charge an all-or-nothing price, then, it is able to extract the entire consumer's surplus.

In Figure 14.11 we have drawn an ordinary demand curve, labelled *MV*, and an all-or-nothing demand curve, labelled *AV*, for good *Y*, assuming that the income effect is zero. Under normal circumstances, at a price p_1, the consumer would set price equal to marginal value in order to maximize utility and would consume y_1 units. At this level of consumption the consumer would earn a consumer's surplus equal to the triangle above the price p_1 and below the *MV* curve. However, a monopolist firm could offer the following deal to the consumer: pay price p_2 for the quantity y_1, or receive nothing at all. Even at the price p_2, the consumer receives surplus for the first units consumed; however, for the last units consumed the level of surplus is negative. The shaded triangle above p_2 is the positive consumer's surplus, while the shaded triangle below p_2 is the negative surplus. When these two triangles are equal the firm has found the maximum average price the consumer is willing to pay for y_1 units, and this price

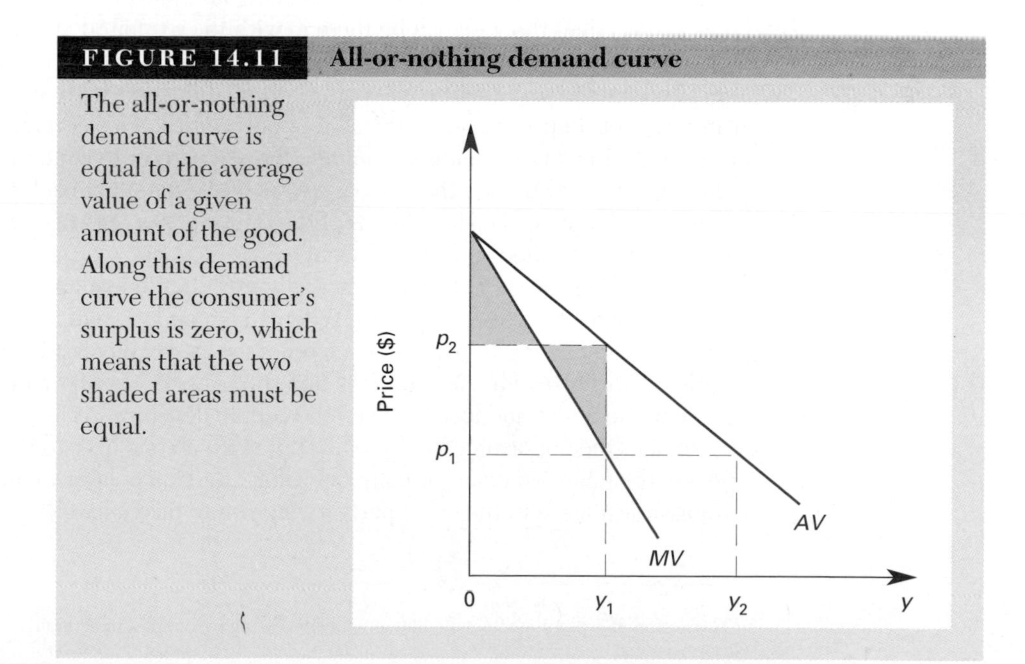

FIGURE 14.11 All-or-nothing demand curve

The all-or-nothing demand curve is equal to the average value of a given amount of the good. Along this demand curve the consumer's surplus is zero, which means that the two shaded areas must be equal.

exhausts the surplus. If we calculate this price for every potential level of output, then we get the average value curve AV, which is the all-or-nothing demand curve.

Another way of interpreting the all-or-nothing demand curve is that it tells us the maximum amount a consumer will purchase at a given price rather than have nothing at all. For example, at price p_1, the consumer, if free to choose, would maximize utility at quantity y_1. However, the firm could force the consumer to purchase y_2 units rather than have nothing at all. Again, at this higher quantity, the consumer's surplus is completely transferred to the firm. All-or-nothing pricing, then, is yet another form of perfect price discrimination, and as such can only exist when there is knowledge of the demand curve and perfect market segmentation.

All-or-nothing pricing may not seem very common, but it is often seen in personal relationships where people generate affection towards one another.[3] Consider a fictitious couple, Pat and Heidi. Suppose Heidi loves Pat, and loves doing little favours for him. She buys him clothes, cooks his favourite meals, and even scratches his balding head every now and then. She does these things because they generate utility for her, but her marginal value for head scratches, like all marginal values, diminishes the more she does it. To keep matters simple, call all of these acts of kindness "gifts." The marginal value of gifts to Pat by Heidi is given in Figure 14.12, along with the marginal costs.

As a maximizing gift giver, Heidi would like to supply Pat with G* gifts. In doing so, she would generate a consumer's surplus equal to the shaded area. However, Pat is a monopolist with respect to Heidi — it is only his head she likes to scratch. What can Pat do? He can exploit Heidi's affection by demanding G** gifts or none at all. Heidi may only want to scratch Pat's head three nights a week, but Pat may be able to extract six nights by threats of not participating at all.

Several things are apparent from this example. The more inelastic is the marginal value of gift giving, the more affection can be exploited. In any interpersonal relationship it is never a good idea to be too dependent on any one person. If you have only one friend in the whole world, that friend will be able to extract great rents from you. In a marriage, if the wife is homebound, without a car, and has few contacts with the outside world, while the husband is out working and playing golf with his buddies on the weekend, then the wife will be the one with the exploited affection. Since asymmetries in a relationship may lead to one party being exploited to the advantage of the other, we might expect that people enter into relationships with others that are similar in terms of their outside relationship opportunities. This certainly seems to hold for marriage. In a marriage it is uncommon for one partner to continue to have friends of the opposite sex. In fact, the marriage vows often state that each partner promises to "forsake all others." Having friends of the opposite sex puts one at an advantage in bargaining for gifts, and so will be discouraged.

Recognizing that affection is potentially exploitable explains why couples fight more as their relationship progresses. When a man and woman first meet, their marginal value curves for gift giving to each other are perfectly elastic, because each has countless substitutes for the other. As time progresses, each person becomes more specific to the other, and love between the couple develops. As affection grows, however, so does the opportunity to exploit it. But since no one likes to be exploited, fights arise. On the other hand, any attempt to exploit affection on a first date doesn't lead to fighting; it just leads to the other party telling you to take a hike!

---

3. The notion of exploiting affection, like so many provocative examples in economics, is attributed to Gordon Tullock.

FIGURE 14.12 **The exploitation of affection**

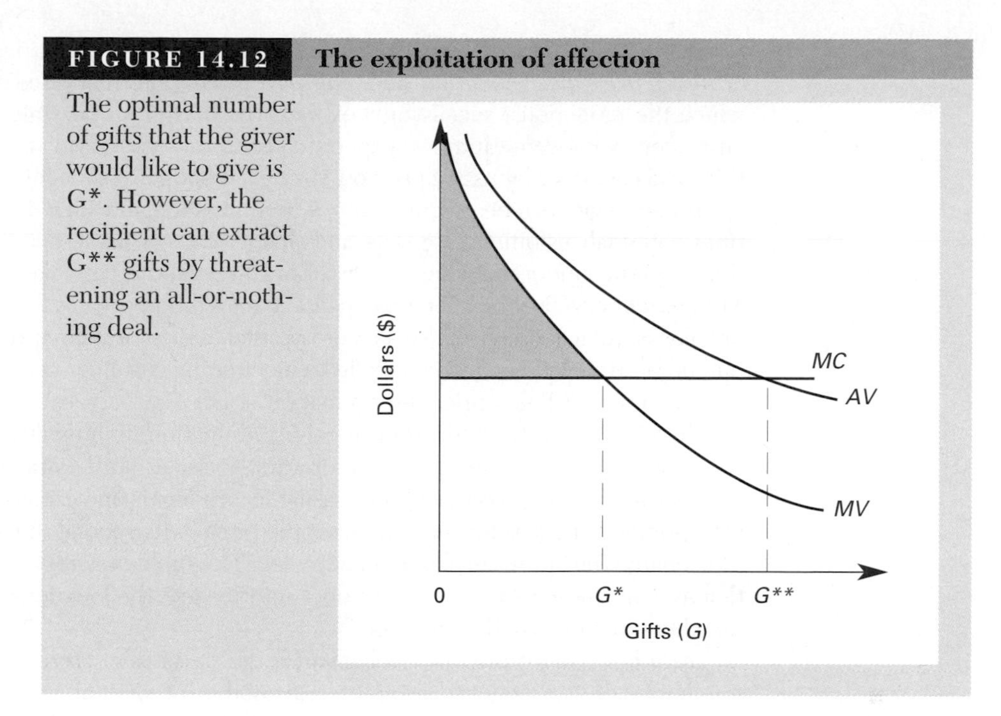

The optimal number of gifts that the giver would like to give is G*. However, the recipient can extract G** gifts by threatening an all-or-nothing deal.

The exploitation of affection also explains some aspects of sibling rivalry. Anyone who has ever seen a proud parent of a first-born child has met someone with an extremely inelastic demand for affection. For a first-time parent, there is no substitute for the child. As a result, the only child is in a unique monopoly position, and can exploit the affection of the parent by making statements like, "If I can't have a pony, I won't love you anymore!" The solution to this problem is to introduce competition in the market for affection. By having more children, parents create rivalry for their attention, which increases the elasticity of demand. When a child threatens to withhold affection, the parent can now reply, "Fine; I'll go play with your sister." The model presented would predict that only children would tend to be more spoiled than children from large families.

PROBLEM 14.8

Using Figure 14.12, under what circumstances would a divorce occur? How would the feminist movement have affected the exploitation of affection in a marriage? Given this, what effect on the divorce rate would the feminist movement have had? What do you think are common characteristics of the partner who *files* for divorce compared to the one who doesn't file?

SUMMARY

In considering the monopolist's response to the "unimaginative" monopoly solution, we analyzed the more sophisticated strategies of *price discrimination* that are based on the monopolist's ability to segment its market. Two types of such market segmentation are common: *direct identification* (as in various discounts for senior citizens and students) and *self-selection* (as in different fares for airline tickets).

We considered three types of price discrimination: *perfect price discrimination*, *ordinary price discrimination*, and *multipart pricing*. Perfect price discrimination, in which the monopolist successfully extracts the maximum possible profit from each customer, is not something we expect to see in the real world very often; however, this ideal case does let us see just how strong a monopolist's incentive to devise clever pricing strategies can be. Ordinary price discrimination, in which the monopolist identifies potential customers by groups and charges each group a separate price, is something we encounter almost every day of our lives, and it can take very subtle forms. Multipart pricing, in which the monopolist charges different rates for different amounts, or "blocks," of a good or service, is more profitable than ordinary price discrimination, but, because it requires the monopolist to monitor the customer's consumption, it is not as common as ordinary price discrimination.

In addition to these forms of price discrimination, monopolist firms can extract consumer's surplus in a number of other ways. Two-part tariffs, where the firm charges an entry fee for the privilege of purchasing its product is one example. As was shown, the optimal strategy is for the firm to set the price of its good at the marginal cost and then charge the entire surplus as an entry fee. The problem with this type of pricing is that as consumer's tastes for the product start to vary, the low-demand types become unwilling to purchase the entry fee.

Another type of pricing mechanism is the tie-in sale. Here a firm requires the purchasers of its product to also purchase another product at a price above marginal costs. The problem with this form of pricing is that it creates a deadweight loss, as the revenue captured from the tie-in sale does not match the full loss of surplus to the consumer. We argued that the tie-in sales model explained why popcorn was so expensive at the movies. Finally, we looked at the case of all-or-nothing pricing, in which the firm again tries to extract the full surplus. This form of pricing seems to explain a number of observations of individual behaviour.

These pricing strategies are not the only ones that monopolists can and do use to avoid the trap of charging only one price. We present these only to provide you with a sample, and to whet your appetite for further study in the field of industrial organization.

EXERCISES

1. Many firms issue coupons in newspapers and flyers that are required in order to receive a lower price. Explain how a coupon could be used as a method of price discrimination.

2. In school cafeterias it is not uncommon to see the following words on the side of condiment packages: "Not for resale to the general public." Why would a manufacturer print this message?

3. Pure grain alcohol is used in many parts of the world as an automobile fuel. However, gasoline is almost always added to the alcohol. Why would this be done, given that the slight amount of gasoline doesn't add to the performance of the fuel?

4. Rogers Cable company has several packages for its consumers. The basic package allows access to about 35 channels. Why does Rogers Cable not allow you to buy one channel at a time?

5. One way for children to exploit affection from parents is to threaten personal harm. Young children may hold their breath; teenagers may threaten not to finish high school, to have a baby, or to get a garish tattoo. Are these types of threats credible? How does their credibility affect their value in exploiting parental affection? Can this explain why teenagers often nurture a reputation for behaving irrationally?

6. The managers of Vancouver's international exposition, Expo '86, considered selling two types of admission tickets: one for $20 and another for $100. The more expensive ticket would have allowed its holder to move to the head of the lineup entering Expo grounds. The Monterey Bay Aquarium in California uses a similar strategy. Customers who take out a year's membership are allowed to enter the aquarium at any time. Non-members must buy day passes good for the next available time slot — ordinarily an hour or two after they buy their tickets. Explain the conditions necessary for this sort of pricing strategy to be profitable.

7. In the book trade, it is common practice to publish a novel in hardcover and sell it for $30 and then to bring out a paperback edition about six months later and sell it for $10. The motion picture industry uses a similar strategy. A good, new movie might be screened at first-run movie theatres for about three months. About the time the first run closes, the movie becomes available on DVD. Explain these curious practices.

8. When you buy a pair of shoes, they always come with shoelaces. Is this an example of a tie-in sale?

9. Night clubs often charge a cover charge to get in, but then they put huge mark-ups on the drinks they serve. Why would they do this when they could charge a larger entry fee if they lowered the price of the drinks?

10. Why is it that cover charges tend to occur in clubs that have dancing, but not in local bars and pubs where only drinking takes place? How is this consistent with the answer to Exercise 9?

11. Firm A has no costs of production and sells its product to just two buyers. Buyer 1's demand function is

$$p_1 = 90 - 10y_1$$

and Buyer 2's demand function is

$$p_2 = 60 - 5y_2$$

a. Assuming that the firm can engage in ordinary price discrimination, find the profit-maximizing prices. What is firm A's profit?
b. Now, suppose that the monopolist can engage in multipart pricing. Find a two-part price schedule that generates more profit than the firm gets in (a). How much additional profit does it earn?
c. Finally, suppose that the firm cannot price-discriminate. First find the firm's aggregate demand function. (It is composed of two linear segments, like the demand function in Figure 14.7.) Then find its marginal revenue function. (It is composed of two linear segments, with a gap or discontinuity.) Find its profit-maximizing price, and compute its profit.

12. Many countries, states, and provinces have passed "equal pay for equal work" legislation, which is intended to discourage discrimination by forcing firms to pay the same wage to all employees who do the same job. Some jurisdictions have gone even further by passing "equal pay for work of equal value" legislation, which is intended to force firms to pay the same wage to all employees whose work is of equal value, regardless of the job.
a. Using the model of monopsony discrimination developed in this chapter, discuss the implications of equal pay for equal work.
b. Using the productivity concepts developed in this chapter, discuss the difficulties involved in implementing "equal pay for work of equal value."
c. Would either kind of legislation serve a useful economic purpose if all labour markets were competitive?

13. Consider a world with only two types of workers, A and B. For example, type A might be Asians (or men) and type B Caucasians (or women). Assume that types A and B both prefer to work with others of their own type, and that there is no difference in productivity across groups. Show that this sort of preference is likely to produce firms in which all workers are of the same type. Will it produce wage differentials?

14. Dress retailers often throw away garments that have not sold after a sale. Often these items are actually torn to prevent them from being worn. Why would they do this?

15. When you go to buy a car, the dealer often asks you, "How much were you planning on spending?" Why does he ask such a thing? Why is it unlikely to work?

16 The Holiday Inn lets children stay free with their parents. Why would they do this?

17. When you buy a new car from General Motors you must get the car serviced by a Mr. Goodwrench mechanic in order for the warranty to be honoured. This is a tie-in sale. Can you offer a non-price-discriminating explanation for this restriction?

18. Chapters is a large retail bookstore where customers can sit, drink a cup of coffee, and look at books before they purchase them. Amazon.com is an on-line discount store that sells the same books for around 20 percent less than Chapters. What type of strategy might a consumer employ to receive the services of Chapters but the prices of Amazon? Might this strategy lead to stores like Chapters going out of business? Would this be socially efficient? What might Chapters do to combat this type of behaviour on the part of consumers?

19. Restaurant dinner meals are often more expensive than identical meals served at lunchtime. If dinnertime patrons stay longer at the restaurant, is this necessarily an example of price discrimination?

20. Suppose an airline has some market power, and is able to engage in third-degree price discrimination between its business and economy customers. In the following questions, assume that the marginal cost of servicing each group is constant and the same; that is, $MC_B = MC_E = k$.
    a. Assuming there is no capacity constraint on how many people in each group can fly, and that the demand for business class is more inelastic than the economy class, draw the equilibrium prices on a graph.
    b. Now assume the size of the plane on a given flight is fixed, and that the sum of business and economy tickets must add up to the number of seats on the plane. Assume this capacity constraint is binding. Now draw a graph showing the equilibrium prices for the two classes. (*Hint:* Draw the horizontal axis with a length equal to the capacity, and then draw the mirror image of one market on top of the other market.)
    c. Under what condition would the airline choose to fly with unsold seats?
    d. What would be the optimal size of plane to use on a given flight for a given set of demands for business and economy passengers?

*21. A monopolist has constant marginal costs of $2. He faces two types of customers: Type I consists of 200 buyers, each with demands $p = 16 - y$. Type II consists of 100 buyers each with demands $p = 10 - y/2$.
    a. What are the profits and price with ordinary monopoly pricing?
    b. What are the profits and prices with ordinary price discrimination?
    c. What are the profits and prices with the optimal two-part pricing scheme?

*22. One simple explanation for the high price of popcorn is that movie theatre owners have to share the movie revenue with large theatre companies, but they get to keep the popcorn revenue for themselves. Suppose the demand for popcorn is given by $p = a/b - (1/b)y$ and the profit to the theatre is equal to the fee charged to get in, the revenue from the price of the movie minus the marginal cost of the popcorn. That is, profit $= 0.5[a/b - p]y + [a/b - y/b]y - ky$ (where k is the marginal cost of the popcorn).
    a. Suppose that the theatre gets to keep all of the movie revenue. What is the optimal price for the popcorn and price for the movie?
    b. Suppose now that the theatre must share the movie revenue by a fraction q. What is the quantity of popcorn to sell, and the price for the movie and popcorn?
    c. Suppose that the theatre gets to keep none of the movie revenue and only gets to keep the revenue from popcorn. What is the price of the popcorn now?

*23. Suppose the market demand can be separated into two distinct markets, where $p_1 = 80 - 5y_1$, $p_2 = 180 - 20y_2$, and the common cost function is $C = 50 + 40(y_1 + y_2)$.
    a. Determine the equilibrium prices and quantities in each market and the overall profits that result from the actions of a price-discriminating monopolist.
    b. Determine the price elasticities of demand in each market, evaluated at the equilibrium

prices and quantities.

c. What is the relationship between the price elasticities of demand in each market and the prices prevailing in each market?

*24. The Edmond Theatre is contemplating charging a different price for a ticket to an afternoon show than for the same film that evening. In adopting a price strategy, the Edmond must consider that fixed costs are $15 per week, and variable (maintenance, ticket-taking, etc.) costs are $0.20 per customer. Furthermore, a study of weekly demand for afternoon and evening shows has revealed:

$$P_A = 10.2 - 0.5Q_A$$
$$P_B = 5.2 - 0.25Q_B$$

a. Which demand curve do you think describes the afternoon market, A or B?

b. Calculate the Edmond's prices, output, and profit, with and without price discrimination.

REFERENCES

Hall, C. 1989. "A Dutch Auction Information Exchange," *The Journal of Law and Economics*, 32:195–214.

Stocking, G. W. and M. W. Watkins. 1946. *Cartels in Action*. New York: Twentieth Century Fund.

CHAPTER 15

Introduction to Game Theory

oligopoly
game theory

Before we analyze the theories of **oligopoly** in Chapter 16, we will take some time in this current chapter to develop some important tools of **game theory**. Although these tools are used in the next chapter to explore a number of models of oligopoly, they are tools which help us understand strategic behaviour generally. Thus in the current chapter you will find a number of applications of these methods to everyday life because every day each of us runs into situations where we must worry about the actions of other people. Game theory, then, is a set of general principles which help us understand situations where the interaction between players cannot be ignored. Our underlying aim in this chapter is to give you an understanding of game theoretic problems and their solutions.

As just mentioned, our ultimate aim is to examine markets where there are small numbers of firms. To this point we have examined two pieces of the theory of market structure: perfect competition and monopoly. We can think of these two market structures as extreme cases. The theory of oligopoly, or competition among the few, fits less neatly into an overall picture of market structure. Indeed, to speak of the theory of oligopoly, as if only one existed, is misleading. Unlike monopoly and perfect competition, oligopoly has no single theory. Instead, a variety of models yield different insights into the conduct of real oligopolies.

15.1 Interactions with Others

Have you ever been watching a baseball game when an announcer starts to say something like this: "Ricky is at the plate, he's got a man on second, the count is three and one … you just know he's going to get a slider to the outside." Perhaps that's what the batter Ricky is actually thinking. He's saying to himself, "When there's a man on second, and the count is three and one, there's only one obvious pitch to do … the slider to the outside of the plate!" But perhaps our batter thinks a little harder. If the batter knows a slider to the outside is the best pitch, and the announcer knows a slider to the outside is the best pitch, then it isn't too much of a stretch of the imagination to believe that the pitcher also knows a slider to the outside of the plate is the best pitch. If the pitcher knows this, thinks the batter, and if the pitcher knows the batter knows this, then perhaps the pitcher will throw a fastball instead. As you can imagine, this type of thinking could go on forever. At the very least, unlike our announcer, we have to admit the solution over which pitch to throw is not so obvious.

Whenever there are a few players interacting with one another, the behaviour of other players cannot be ignored because their actions affect the outcome. With perfect competition every firm and consumer were assumed to be so insignificant relative to the market that everyone could ignore the effect their behaviour had on others. With the case of monopoly the actions of others could be ignored because there were no other players! But life is often characterized by situations where the interactions cannot be ignored. If you play squash, tennis, or badminton you cannot ignore the strengths of your opponent. Perhaps your forehand is your best shot, but you might never use it because your opponent knows this and keeps the ball away from your forehand. If you are in a sailing race you try to find the best point of sail for the wind conditions, but you must also watch what the boats behind and ahead of you are doing. Quite often boats in the lead of a race simply copy the tactics of the boat behind them, not because the second-place boat chooses a better point of sail, but because by copying them there is no way for the following boat to catch them. And, of course, for many firms changing the price of their product or changing the volume of sales cannot be done without considering how other firms in the industry will respond.

Whether we are talking about the decisions of Ford, Honda, and Toyota, or the decisions of a husband and wife, the interactions of decision makers can be important. Game theory provides a language for articulating the issues of such cases. Game theory also provides a number of solution concepts to resolve these issues. If you watched the Academy Award-winning movie *A Beautiful Mind*, you'll know something about the exploits of John Nash and the concept of Nash equilibrium. Hopefully this chapter will provide a better explanation of this concept than the movie without being any less entertaining.

Game Theory: Basic Definitions

Before plunging into the analysis of games, we need to look quickly at some important concepts from game theory. These concepts will have become old friends by the time you have worked through the entire chapter. The actors or "choosers" in games are usually called **players**: they are entities like firms, or individuals, or governments that make choices in the game. In this chapter the players could be anything from pigs to spouses. In the next chapter all of the players are firms.

players

The things players choose — like quantity of output, price, go to the store, get married, ... whatever — are called **strategies**. If firms choose quantity of output, then a strategy for a firm is just a quantity of output for that firm. If instead firms choose price, then a strategy for a firm is just a price for that firm's product. If a soldier in battle has to choose whether or not to shoot, hide, or run, then a strategy for the soldier is one of these actions. A list of strategies, one for each player in the game, is called a **strategy combination**. The central problem in game theory is to predict the choices that players make. Or, using game theoretic terminology, the central problem of game theory is to predict the strategy combination that will be chosen.

strategies

strategy combination

In the eyes of a player, what distinguishes one strategy combination from another? If the player is a firm, and if the firm is a profit maximizer, then strategy combination A is preferred to strategy combination B if the firm's *profit* or **payoff** from strategy combination A is larger than its profit or payoff from strategy combination B. If the player is an ordinary person, then one strategy combination will be preferred to another if the utility payoff to that strategy combination is higher. Payoff is the technical term that game theorists use, but we will use the terms profit, utility, and payoff interchangeably, depending on the context of the example.

payoff

The distinguishing feature of choice problems in game theory is that a player's payoff depends not just on his or her own strategy but also on the strategies of other players in the game. That is, each player's payoff is determined by the entire strategy combination. In this situation, each player must be concerned with the strategy choices made by other players in the game.

How do players go about choosing a strategy in this awkward situation where their payoff is determined jointly by their own choice of a strategy and by the choices of all other players? To many game theorists, the natural answer is that *each player chooses his or her own strategy to maximize his or her own payoff, given the strategies chosen by the other players*. The mapping from the strategies of other players to the strategy that maximizes the player's own payoff is called the player's **best response function**: it specifies the player's best response to the given strategies of the other players.

best response function

A strategy combination is an **equilibrium strategy combination** if every player's strategy is a best response to the strategies of all other players. Given such a strategy combination, there is nothing any individual player can independently do that will increase that player's payoff. In this equilibrium, each player's own strategy maximizes that player's own payoff. This is the notion of **Nash equilibrium** formulated by the American Nobel Prize-winning game theorist John Nash in 1950 (Nash, 1950, 1951). It is really a generalization of ideas developed more than a century earlier by the French economist August Cournot, and for this reason a Nash equilibrium is often called a **Cournot-Nash equilibrium**. We have already used this notion of equilibrium at a number of points in the book — for example, in our discussion of common property problems in Chapter 1, in our discussion of traffic congestion in Chapter 7, and, indeed, in our analysis of competitive equilibrium in Chapter 8.

equilibrium strategy combination

Nash equilibrium

Cournot-Nash equilibrium

Finally, we should mention how games are visually represented. There are two basic types of methods for describing a game: **normal forms** and **extensive forms**. An extensive form game is often referred to as a game tree. Each decision point, or node, has a number of branches stemming from it, each one indicating a specific decision. At the end of a branch there is either another node, or a payoff. Economists use extensive form descriptions of games when there is a sequence of moves, when information sets are complicated, and when actions are not automatically observed by other players. Since none of the games we consider in this chapter are of this type, we will not use the extensive form to describe games. A normal form description of a game simply represents the outcomes in a payoff matrix. Such a mapping connects the strategy combinations to payoffs in an obvious way. But before we are get too far ahead of ourselves, let's look at a series of famous games and see how these concepts manifest themselves.

normal forms

extensive forms

Dominated and Dominant Strategies

Some games are extremely simple because they contain dominated strategies. These are strategy combinations which are worse than others, *no matter what the other players in the game are doing*. Suppose you're playing baseball and you've made it to first base. There are two outs, and there's a full count on the batter. In this situation everyone knows the runner on first will run, no matter what. If the batter swings and strikes out, running doesn't hurt. If the batter walks, then running doesn't hurt. If the batter hits the ball, then running helps the situation because a jump start might prevent being put out on second. When you're on first base in this situation, running is the **dominant strategy**, and every other strategy you might have (staying put, waiting to see what the batter does, etc.) is *dominated* by this one. Not only that; it doesn't matter what the actions of the other team are; running is always the dominant strategy in this situation.

dominant strategy

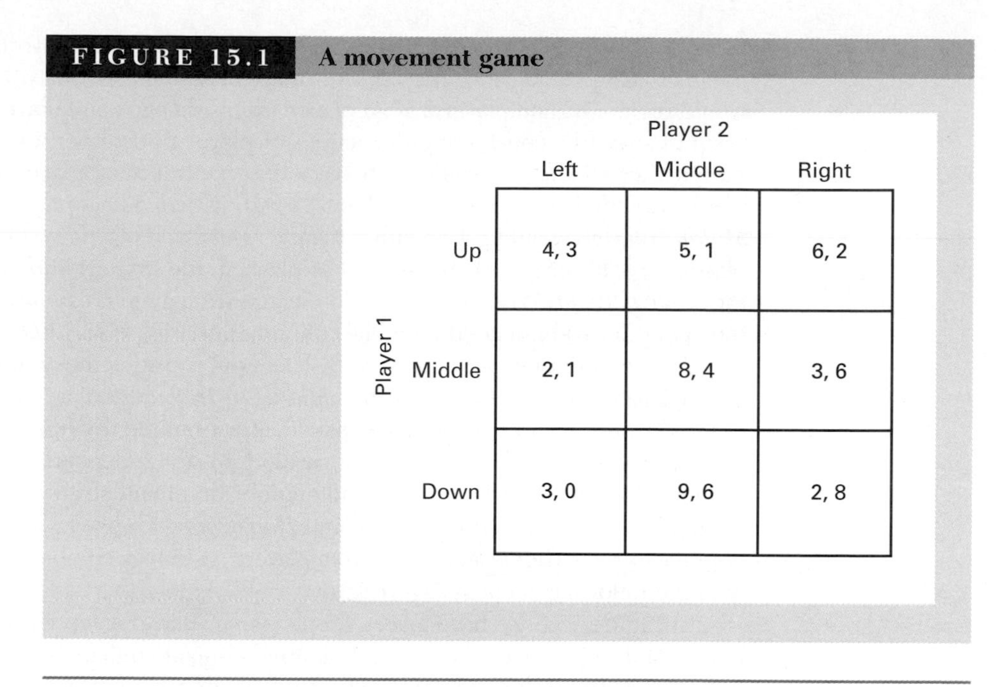

Player 1 \ Player 2	Left	Middle	Right
Up	4, 3	5, 1	6, 2
Middle	2, 1	8, 4	3, 6
Down	3, 0	9, 6	2, 8

FIGURE 15.1 A movement game

A strategy better than all others, regardless of the actions of other players, is a dominant strategy. If one strategy is worse than another for some player, regardless of the actions of other players, then that strategy is a dominated strategy.

Let's consider the game in Figure 15.1. This game, on purpose, has no economic meaning at all. By convention, player 1 is always put on the side, while player 2 is always placed on the top. The strategies of each player are listed along the edge of the matrix. Thus the strategies for player 1 are *Up, Middle, Down*, and the strategies for player 2 are *Left, Middle, and Right*. Also by convention the payoffs to each player are listed in the matrix. The first number is always the payoff to player 1. The second number is the

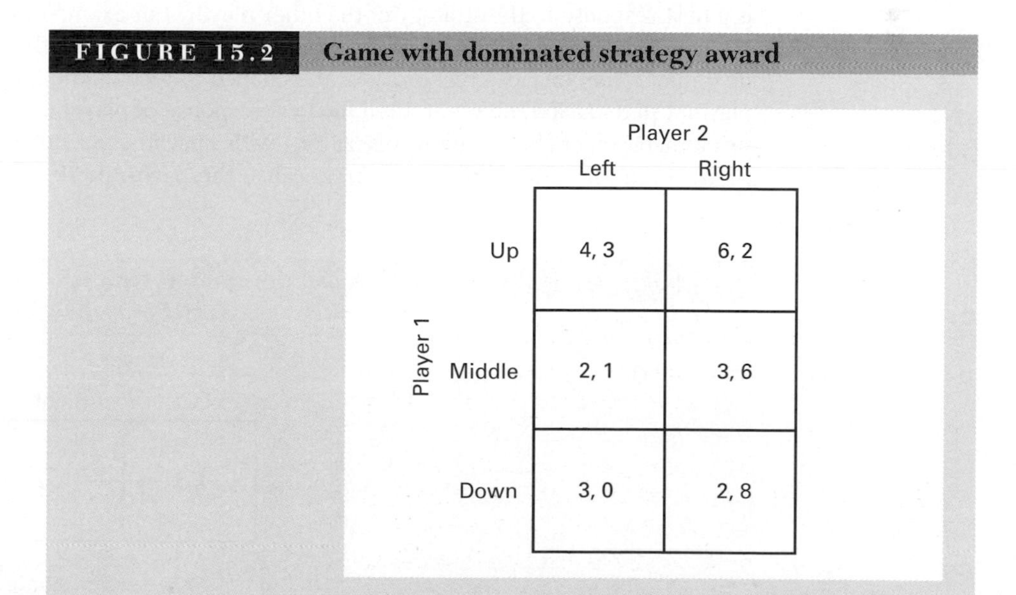

Player 1 \ Player 2	Left	Right
Up	4, 3	6, 2
Middle	2, 1	3, 6
Down	3, 0	2, 8

FIGURE 15.2 Game with dominated strategy award

payoff to player 2. To keep matters simple, we'll consider the payoffs as dollars. This means that if we consider the bottom right corner cell with payoff (2, 8), player 1 would receive $2 and player 2 $8, if player 1 moved *Down* and player 2 moved *Right*.

Let's start by considering the actions of player 2. If player 2 were to play *Right* rather than *Middle*, he would be better off no matter what player 1 did. If player 1 were to move *Up*, player 2 would get $2 rather than $1. If player 1 were to move *Middle*, player 2 would get $6 rather than $4. Finally, if player 1 were to move *Down*, player 2 would get $8 rather than $6. For player 2, the strategy *Middle* is dominated by the strategy *Right*. When you find a dominated strategy, you can just eliminate it from the game. If we eliminate the middle column, then Figure 15.1 becomes Figure 15.2.

With this simpler table of payoffs, let's now consider the actions of player 1. If player 1 were to move *Up* rather than *Middle* or *Down*, then no matter what player 2 does, player 1 would have a higher payoff. For example, by moving *Up* rather than *Down*, player 1 would get $4 or $6 instead of $3 or $2, depending on the actions of player 2. In other words, we've found another dominant strategy. For player 1, the strategy *Up* dominates both *Middle* and *Down*. As with player 2, let's eliminate the dominated rows *Middle* and *Down* from player 1's strategy combination. This leaves us with the following game in Figure 15.3.

In Figure 15.3 we have a very simple game. Player 1 now has no choice but to move *Up*. For player 2, it is obvious that the dominant strategy is to move *Left*. Rather than eliminate another column, we have simply drawn a horizontal arrow pointing in the direction of player 2's preference. Quite often this is easier than eliminating rows, and in subsequent games this is what we will do. We have also placed a star above the payoff (4, 3) to indicate that this is the equilibrium payoff, and we'll do that in subsequent games. The equilibrium strategies of this game are (*Up*, *Left*).

Consider what we have accomplished. Starting with two players, each with three strategies, we've come up with a prediction on how the game will be played. We've assumed each player moves at the same time and does not communicate with the other player. Each player simply looks at the grid of payoffs and figures out what is best for themselves, taking into account the actions of the other player.

The equilibrium we've found is a Nash equilibrium because both players' strategy is a best response to the strategy of the other player. For example, let's consider why (*Down*, *Middle*) would not be a Nash equilibrium. Player 1 might start off thinking he'll play *Down* because this provides the chance to receive the high payoff of $9. If player 1 plays *Down*, however, then the best response of player 2 is to play *Right* and receive a payoff of $8. But this leaves player 1 with a payoff of $2, not $9. If player 2 plays *Right*, then player 1 should play *Up*, because the payoff of $6 is better than $2. If

FIGURE 15.3 Game with last dominated strategy

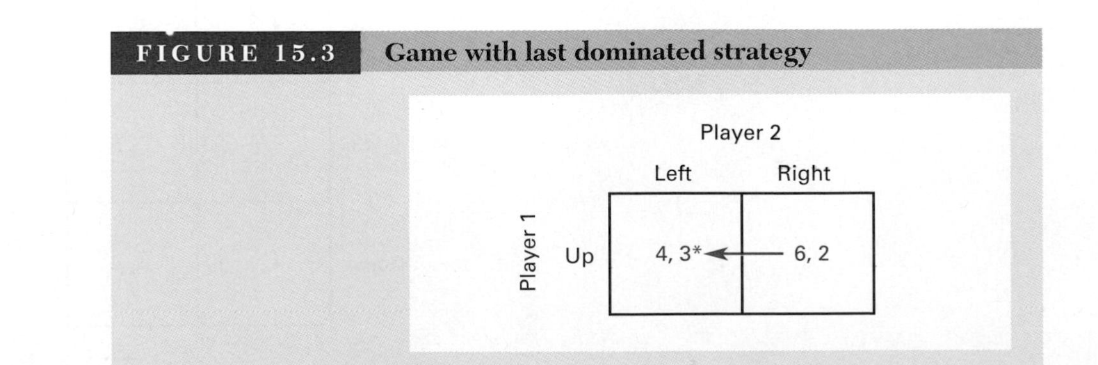

player 1 plays *Up*, though, then player 2 gets only $2 and he should play *Left* for $3. But now look what happens. When player 2 plays *Left*, player 1 still wants to play *Up*. Whenever we are not at a Nash equilibrium there will always be an incentive to move to a new strategy. Only at the Nash equilibrium will both players settle on a strategy and not want to move. This, of course, is what makes it an equilibrium.

Examples of Dominant Strategies

In order to help you understand the notion of a dominant strategy, let's digress for a moment and consider several examples, starting with TV game shows. Everyone has watched the show *The Price is Right* with Bob Barker. Recall that on this show four contestants are called down to the front and are shown a retail item — perhaps a refrigerator — that they must bid on. The person who bids closest to the price without going over wins and gets to stay on the show. Suppose the contestants are Alex, Beverley, Claudia, and Dana, and suppose they bid on the refrigerator alphabetically. Under these conditions, Dana may have a dominant strategy depending on what the other three bid. Suppose Dana believes that Alex, Beverly, and Claudia have all bid too low, with bids of $500, $568, and $589 respectively. In this case Dana should always bid $590, or $1 above the highest bid. That way she wins if the prices are all too low. If she bids anything higher, she only allows the other players an option to win at her expense. On the other hand, if Dana thinks the other bids are all too high, then her dominant strategy is to bid $1. That way she again wins and exposes herself to no risk of losing given her expectation of the other bids. This is a rather aggressive strategy because it effectively rules out other players winning on that round. If Dana was concerned about her public image or what the other contestants thought about her, then this would no longer be a dominant strategy.

A more modern TV game show is *Singled Out* on MTV. This is a cross between *Survivor* and the *Dating Game* wherein 51 contestants start the game and only 2 remain at the end. The game starts with 50 contestants of the same sex (let's suppose they are men), and one member of the opposite sex (Dana again). In the first two rounds of the game 47 men are eliminated from the competition, but three (Peter, Zane, and Clyde) get to move on to the final round. One of these three will win the game and get the prize of a date with Dana. There is no second prize. In the final round the men are asked questions and are required to give an oral answer. Dana has answered the questions earlier, and the first male to match five questions with her wins. The key element here is that the men must answer sequentially. Suppose Peter gets to go first, Zane second, and Clyde third. Because he is last, Clyde gets to hear the other two answers.

In this game there are occasions when a dominant strategy develops. Suppose that Peter can't match an answer with Dana if his life depended on it, and after six questions is still at square 1. Zane, on the other hand, has matched answers four times and feels confident he's about to win. Clyde is still in the game with three matches. Under these circumstances, Clyde has a dominant strategy. Whatever answer Zane gives, Clyde needs to give a different answer. Why is this the dominant strategy? If Zane is correct, then it doesn't matter what Clyde says, he loses anyway. If Zane is wrong, then by giving a different answer Clyde gets a chance to tie Zane with four matches and increase his chance of winning the date. Dominant strategies are quite common; keep your eye out for them.

In most democracies the right to vote in a free election is one of the most treasured rights held by citizens. Yet in many elections as few as 20 to 30 percent of the eligible voters bother to show up to cast their ballot. Recently the city of Vancouver held an election on whether or not to support the bid for the 2010 Olympic games. The voter turnout was around 60 percent of registered voters and this was hailed as a remarkable achievement in civic elections. A 60 percent turnout is a remarkable achievement? What is going on here? If voting is such a sacred right, why do so few individuals bother to exercise it?

The answer comes from dominant strategies. Suppose it costs something to vote. You might have to take time off work, you have to travel to the polling station, and you may want to investigate something about the candidates. On the other hand, if you assume large numbers of other people are going to vote, the benefit to voting is close to zero unless you like voting for its own sake. The benefit is close to zero because your single vote is likely to have no impact on who is elected. Thus, if you vote you incur costs and have no impact on the election. If you do not vote you save on costs and you still have no impact on the election. Thus it is approximately a dominant strategy to not vote in elections.[1] If everyone thinks this way, then very few people will vote, which is what generally happens. Once we understand dominant strategies, perhaps the real question should be, "Why does anyone actually vote?" The answer must be that for some people there is a value to voting. For some it is a patriotic duty, and to not vote causes guilt. Sometimes the margin of victory is almost as important as the victory in an election. When Quebec has a vote on sovereignty, the outcome means much more if 60 percent turn it down rather than just 51 percent turn it down. In such cases there is a benefit to voting, and if this outweighs the cost, one might vote. Finally, some elections are very close, and an individual's vote might be very important.

In 1989 Harrison Ford and Sean Connery teamed up in the movie *Indiana Jones and the Last Crusade*. In the movie, Connery plays father to the adventuresome Indiana Jones as they seek out the Holy Grail. In one of the last scenes Connery has been mortally wounded and is about to die. Indiana realizes he must get his father to drink from the Holy Grail and be healed. He enters a large room where the Grail is located but is confronted with thousands of cups. Which one is the Holy Grail? This is a mighty problem for Indiana because to drink from the wrong cup would mean instant death. He finally selects a cup, but has a second thought: "What if I'm wrong?" "There's only one way to find out," he says, and he dips the cup in water and proceeds to drink from the cup himself! When nothing happens, he realizes he has found the Grail. He gives the cup to his father, his father lives, and they both live happily ever after.

What is wrong with the actions of Indiana Jones? The problem is that he has ignored his dominant strategy! The strategies for Indiana are to either drink first or give the cup first to his father. When Indiana picks the right cup, it doesn't matter what he does; his father lives. But if Indiana had picked the wrong cup, it matters a great deal. If he has the wrong cup and drinks first, then he dies from the drink and his father dies of his wounds. If he gives the bad drink to his father, then his father dies but he lives. Clearly, the dominant strategy is for Indiana to let his father drink first. Failure to follow the dominant strategy ruined the whole movie!

PROBLEM 15.1

Why are public washrooms so dirty and often disgusting? Are there any dominant strategies in using such facilities?

---

1. Strictly speaking, Do Not Vote is not really a dominant strategy since there is always one circumstance where a voter's vote determines the outcome of the election. What is that circumstance? Since this circumstance is highly unlikely, Do Not Vote is approximately a dominant strategy.

15.2
The Prisoner's Dilemma

The most famous game in the world just happens to be a game of dominated strategies. Make sure you pay attention to the mechanics and economics of this game because it will be applied over and over again in the next chapter. The setting of the prisoner's dilemma is a police station. Two suspects have been arrested on charges of a serious crime, and they've been placed in separate rooms. There isn't enough evidence to convict both of the crime, so the police are trying to get a confession out of them. In order to do this, they've offered each prisoner the following deal. Any prisoner who finks on his partner will be let go if the other suspect won't talk and confess. If a prisoner does not confess but his partner does, then the book will be thrown at the silent prisoner. If they both confess they'll spend a lot of time in jail, and if they both remain silent they'll be convicted of a minor charge.

Suppose our two suspects are Ryan and Petra. Ryan and Petra had the great idea to steal Brian's car one night. In the middle of the theft Brian caught them just as they got the car started and drove down the road. The next day the RCMP caught up with Ryan and Petra in possession of the car. They have enough evidence for the charge of possession of stolen property, but they'd really like to convict them of theft as well. Brian got a look at both of them, but he's only 80 percent sure he can make a positive identification, not enough to be assured of a conviction. The police have separated the two and made the standard prisoner's dilemma pitch. The payoffs being offered are given in Figure 15.4.

If Petra remains quiet and Ryan finks, then Petra is going to spend nine months in jail and Ryan is going to walk free. If they both fink, then they will both be convicted of theft and each will spend six months in jail. If neither of them fink, then they will only be charged with possession of stolen property and each will spend only one month in prison. What will Ryan and Petra do? In other words, what is the equilibrium outcome of this game?

As mentioned above, an easy way to find an equilibrium is to draw arrows showing the direction of preferences over strategies for each player. Horizontal arrows show the preferences of Ryan (player 2), while vertical arrows show the preferences of

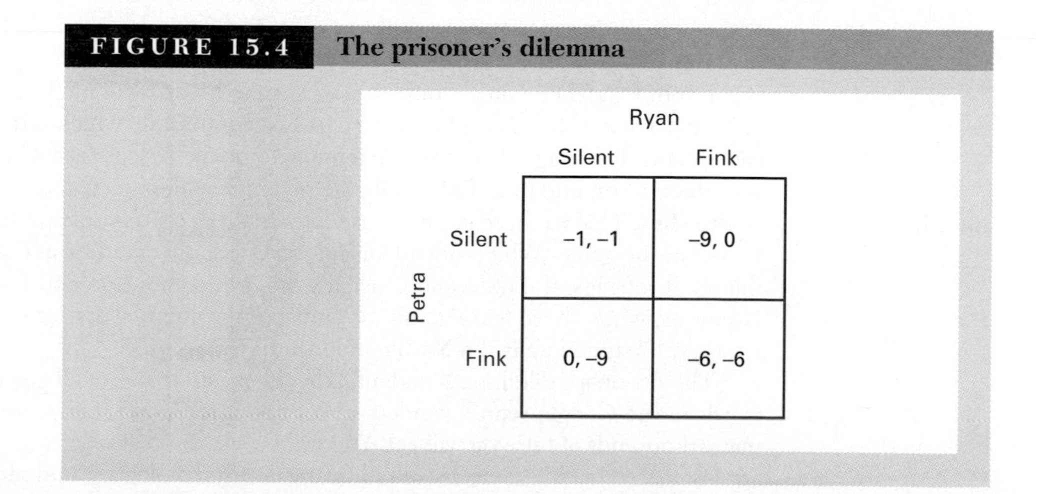

FIGURE 15.4 The prisoner's dilemma

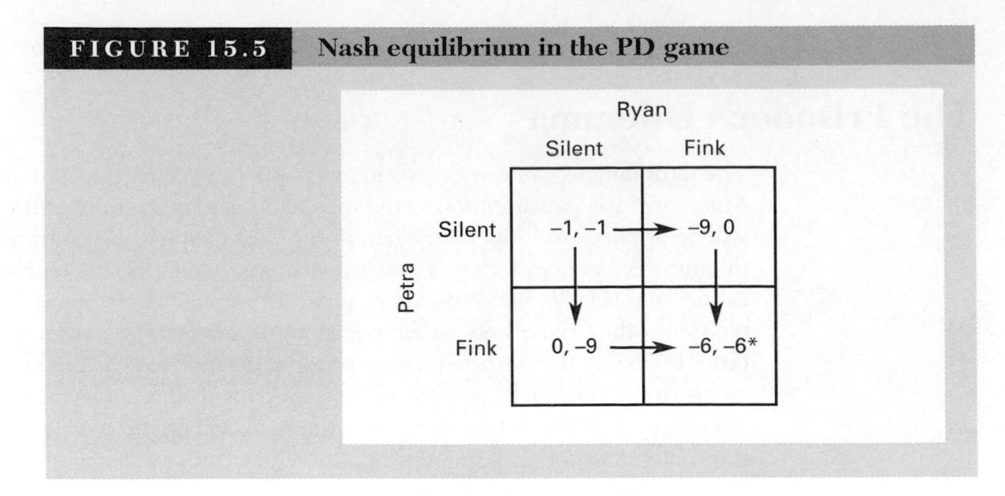

FIGURE 15.5 Nash equilibrium in the PD game

Petra (player 1). When two arrowheads meet, as shown by the asterisk, we have a Nash equilibrium. Figure 15.5 repeats the information of Figure 15.4, except now we have the arrows in place.

Notice that the arrows meet at the cell where both Petra and Ryan fink. (Fink, Fink) then is the equilibrium of the prisoner's dilemma game. There are at least three reasons why this game is so interesting. First, it has many applications in real life. The next chapter demonstrates how much of the oligopoly problem can be thought of as a prisoner's dilemma game, but in the following section we provide a number of other examples as well. Second, the equilibrium results from a dominant strategy for both players. As far as Petra is concerned, it doesn't matter what Ryan has in mind, her dominant strategy is to fink. Likewise for Ryan, he's going to fink no matter what Petra does. Finally, the prisoner's dilemma is interesting because the equilibrium outcome is not Pareto-optimal. Clearly both Ryan and Petra would be better off if they both remained silent.

The Prisoner's Dilemma is a game of dominant strategies where the equilibrium is not Pareto-optimal.

Before we move on it is worthwhile considering why Ryan and Petra are unable to reach the Pareto-optimal result of silence. What would have happened if Ryan and Petra were not in separate rooms? Then, when Ryan was about to fink, Petra might give him a look which said, "If you fink, my big brother Brawn is going to hunt you down and break your legs when you get out." Under such a threat Ryan might think twice about finking. In fact, if Ryan and Petra are part of a community which often interacts with each other, Ryan might know Brawn is going to break his legs for finking, even if Petra isn't there to remind him. Essentially the prisoner's dilemma game assumes the game is **one shot**. That is, there are no consequences to decisions outside the payoffs mentioned in the game. When individuals interact with one another in repeated prisoner dilemma settings, the outcome is usually one of cooperation and Pareto outcomes. However, when there is no ability to punish opposing players for choosing the fink strategy, the outcome is the Nash equilibrium (Fink, Fink).

one shot

The prisoner's dilemma is undoubtedly the most famous of all games. Just type the words in the Google search window of your computer and then sample a few of the many thousands of hits you will get. You will be surprised at what you see. Economists are fascinated by this game as are political scientists, biologists, and philosophers. The reason is that the game serves as a metaphor for myriad social dilemmas, a couple of which we discuss below.

Application: Elite Athletes and Performance-Enhancing Drugs

The prisoner's dilemma captures the essence of a large number of what we might call *social dilemmas*, including the dilemma that high-performance athletes face when they choose whether or not to use some performance-enhancing drug (PED). Surveys of elite athletes reveal a willingness to make almost any sacrifice to win an Olympic gold medal or a world championship, and this willingness has led a number of high-profile athletes to use PEDs.

To see that the essence of the game played among these athletes is captured by the prisoner's dilemma, we need to model the game they are engaged in. For simplicity, consider an athletic contest with just two athletes, and suppose that they are of equal ability. Since they are of equal ability, if neither chooses to use the PED, or if both choose to use the PED, the probability of winning is 1/2 for both athletes. Of course, if one uses the PED and the other does not, the probability of winning is larger than 1/2 for the drug taker and less than 1/2 for the clean athlete — for concreteness, suppose that these probabilities are 2/3 and 1/3. Use of the PED is a problem because, in the long run, it is debilitating. We can capture this by supposing that the athlete incurs a health cost H when he uses the PED. Of course, athletes are tempted to use the PED because they value winning. So let's assign utility $W > 0$ to winning and utility 0 to losing. If we take the surveys alluded to above seriously, then we must assume that W is very large relative to H. We have then a model of the PED game.

The model is encapsulated in the payoff matrix shown in Figure 15.6, in which the strategy set is (Use, Don't Use) for both athletes. If neither athlete uses the PED, the expected utility of each athlete is $W/2$. If both use, the expected utility of each is $W/2 - H$. If one uses and the other does not, the users expected utility is $2W/3 - H$ and the clean athlete's expected utility is $W/3$.

Notice that if $W > 6H$, Use is the dominant strategy for both athletes, and strategy combination (Use, Use) is the Nash equilibrium. Strategy combination (Don't Use, Don't Use) Pareto dominates (Use, Use), because when both athletes use the PED they get no competitive advantage relative to the case in which neither uses, yet they

FIGURE 15.6 Athletes and drugs

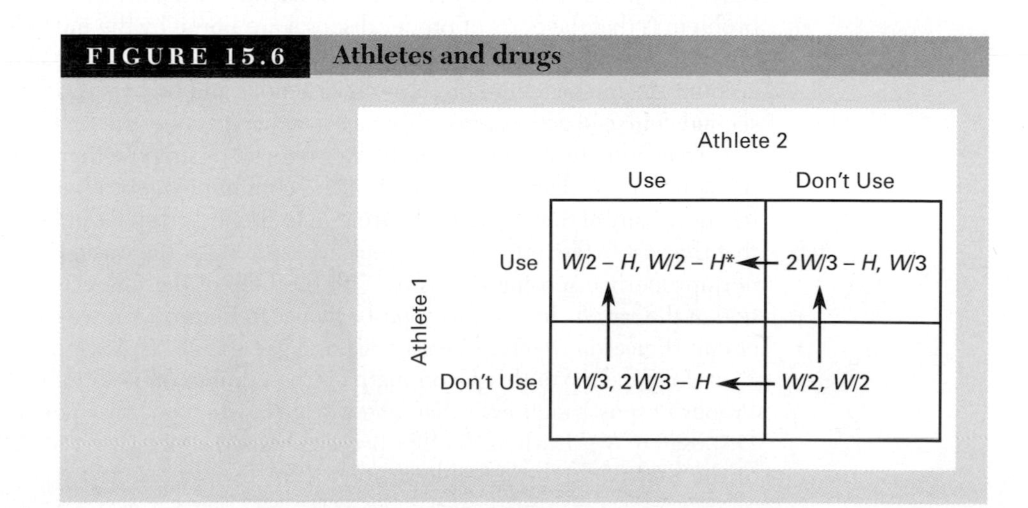

incur the health cost associated with use. So, when $W > 6H$, the PED game is a prisoner's dilemma.

PROBLEM 15.2

Consider an asymmetric athletic context. Let $H_1 > 0$ and $H_2 > 0$ represent the health costs of the two athletes, and let $W_1 > 0$ and $W_2 > 0$ be the utility the two athletes place on winning, and suppose that utility associated with losing is 0 for both athletes. Suppose that the probability that One wins is 6/10 if neither or both athletes use the PED, and that when One uses and Two does not, the probability that One wins is 8/10, and that when Two uses and One does not, the probability that One wins is 4/10. Construct the payoff matrix for this asymmetric contest. Under what circumstances is (Use, Use) a dominant strategy equilibrium? Show that when (Use, Use) is a dominant strategy equilibrium, it is not Pareto-optimal, and indicate which strategy combination or combinations Pareto-dominate it.

Application: Waste Disposal

Curiously, in most cities in North America, household waste is picked up free of charge. Of course, the service is not really free since households pay for it through their property taxes, but within fairly wide bounds, in most towns and cities there is no charge related to the quantity of waste hauled away each week. As we will see, one way of interpreting this curious arrangement is as a solution to a many-person prisoner's dilemma. In order to make this point, we need first to imagine or model what would happen if individuals could not get rid of their waste by putting it in bags in front (or in back) of their home on the appointed trash-collection day.

The individual household would then face the following dilemma: should I expend the time, effort, and money necessary to ensure that my waste is deposited in a proper sanitary landfill, or should I save some time, effort, and money by simply tossing the trash by the side of the road or in the nearest vacant lot? Relative to the second course of action, the first is more costly to the individual but results in a cleaner environment. The problem is that the costs of proper disposal are borne by the individual, but the benefits are spread over the entire community. As a result, the individual does not take into account the full benefit of his or her own actions and may very well choose to take the second course of action when, from a social perspective, the first is preferable.

To capture this common sense in a game, let us suppose there are N individuals in the community, that each member of the community gets a benefit of magnitude B whenever any of them goes to the trouble to properly dispose of her household waste, that the cost to the individual of properly disposing of the waste is C, and that the cost of improperly disposing of it is 0. With the help of the following matrix representation of the payoffs for a *representative player* in Figure 15.7, we can easily discern the circumstances in which this waste disposal game is an N-player prisoner's dilemma.

Along the top of this payoff matrix is the number of other individuals who choose Proper Disposal, a number that ranges from 0, when no other person chooses Proper Disposal, to $N - 1$, when all other people choose Proper Disposal. Along the left side of the matrix are the possible strategies for the representative individual, Proper

FIGURE 15.7 Waste disposal game

	0	1	2	...	$N-1$
Proper Disposal	B – C	2B – C	3B – C	...	NB – C
Improper Disposal	0	B	2B	...	(N – 1)B

Disposal or Improper Disposal, and in the body of the matrix are the representative player's payoffs. If, for example, the representative player chooses Proper Disposal and two other people also choose Proper Disposal, her payoff is 3B – C, since in this case a total of three people choose Proper Disposal, and the representative player bears the cost of properly disposing her own waste. On the other hand, still assuming that two other players choose Proper Disposal, if the representative player chooses Improper Disposal, her payoff is 2B, since in this case a total of two people choose Proper Disposal and the representative player pays nothing to improperly dispose of her waste.

Notice that when C > B, the representative individual has a dominant strategy, Improper Disposal, and there is a dominant strategy equilibrium in which every person chooses Improper Disposal. Each person's payoff in this dominant strategy equilibrium is 0. Notice also that the dominant strategy equilibrium is Pareto-dominated by the strategy combination in which all N players choose Proper Disposal if NB – C > 0. So, when NB > C > B, there is a dominant strategy equilibrium in which everyone disposes of their waste by tossing it on the side of the road or in the nearest vacant lot, and it is Pareto-dominated by the situation in which everyone goes to the trouble of making sure that their waste is deposited in a sanitary landfill. In other words, when NB > C > B the waste disposal game is a N-person prisoner's dilemma.

In the following problem, you can see that this problem is effectively solved when individuals are required to pay amount C in property taxes and offered the opportunity of properly disposing of their waste at no (additional) cost.

PROBLEM 15.3

Assume that NB > C > B. Suppose that the municipal government imposes a lump-sum tax equal to C on all N households, and in return offers to collect household waste for free. Construct a payoff matrix analogous to the one in the text that depicts the payoffs of a representative individual and show that there is now a dominant strategy equilibrium in which everyone chooses Proper Disposal, and that the equilibrium is Pareto-optimal.

There is an important lesson here: it is unwise to ask people to pay large fees for waste disposal if they have inexpensive alternative methods of disposal that impose significant costs on other members of the community.

15.3 Coordination Games

The prisoner's dilemma is an apt description of many situations in life, but it is not the whole picture. Quite often situations may have no equilibrium or they may have multiple equilibria. In these situations, other forms of behaviour will have to arise for a solution to be found.

Consider the case of two academic authors, Dean and Richard. Dean likes to use Microsoft Word software when writing papers, while Richard prefers to use Corel's WordPerfect. Both of them understand and can use the other's favourite program, but they are more comfortable with their preferred package. In their partnership they often discuss an idea at a professional meeting, and then go back to their respective universities to work. They start on the paper and then e-mail the first draft of their work to each other. Although they talk about which program to use, let's suppose they can't tell what the other has used until the draft is received. Figure 15.8 shows the payoffs for Richard and Dean over the various strategies.

When they both use Word for writing their papers, Dean is better off by 2 and Richard is better off by 1. If they both use WordPerfect, these payoffs are reversed, with Richard receiving the higher payoff. It is a minor disaster if one writes in Word and the other in WordPerfect because the files won't fit nicely together and the two authors end up in a big argument. Using our arrow method of finding a Nash equilibrium, we see there are actually two NE. If Dean is going to use Word, then Richard's best response is to also use Word. And if Richard is going to use Word, then of course, Dean's best response is to keep using Word. The same can be said if both use WordPerfect.

coordination problem

battle of the sexes game

Because there are two equilibria in this game, the concept of Nash equilibrium is insufficient to tell us what the actual outcome will be. There is said to be a **coordination problem**. A coordination problem exists when players must somehow decide on which equilibrium to settle on. The game depicted in Figure 15.8 is called the **battle of the sexes game**, based on its first articulation. In the classic battle of the sexes

FIGURE 15.8 **Choosing a word processor**

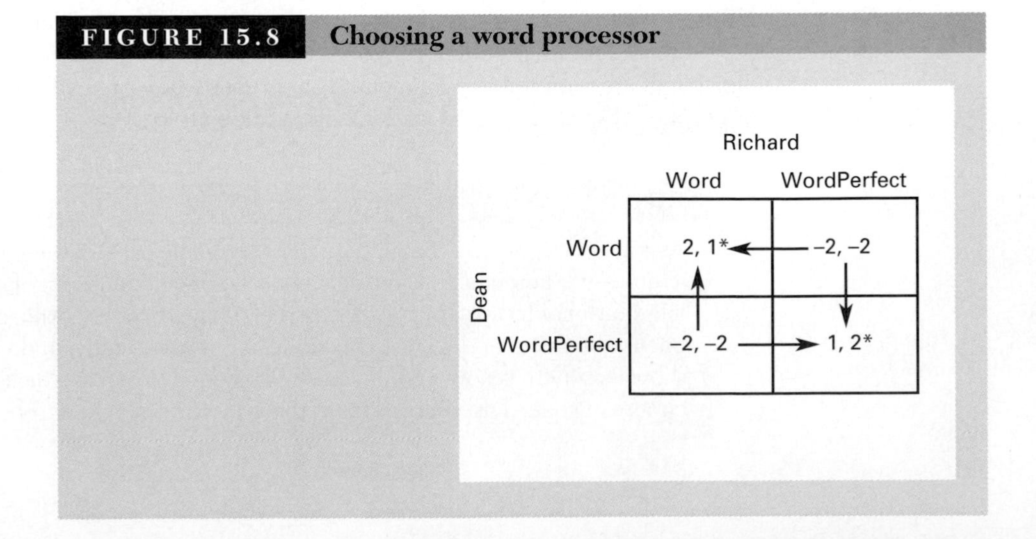

game a man and woman are the players and they are either going to a boxing match or to the ballet. The man prefers the boxing match, the woman prefers the ballet, but they both want to be together. The payoffs are the same as those depicted in Figure 15.8, and again there are two equilibria: both go to the fight, or both go to the ballet. But which one do they choose?

Another famous game of coordination is the game of Chicken. Here we have two teenage drivers in a game of bravery. Each teen is in a car, facing one another on a deserted highway. The cars race towards each other and each player has the choice of staying the course or swerving. If both stay the course, they are both dead from the crash. If both swerve, they live, but are cowards. If only one swerves, he is the coward and the other person is brave. Perhaps our two academic writers, Dean and Richard, try to solve their dispute over which software to use with a game of Chicken, the person who swerves having to use the other's preferred software. The payoffs are given in Figure 15.9.

Unfortunately for Dean and Richard, the game of Chicken is also a game with two equilibria, and so it requires some outside coordination as well.

A game of coordination has multiple Nash equilibria and requires some mechanism for determining the final outcome.

Games of coordination abound, and how we deal with them depends on the context of the game. For example, consider the serious problem of which side of the road to drive on. In Canada, the United States, and France cars drive on the right side of the road. In New Zealand, Australia, and England cars drive on the left side of the road. Although any individual moving from one country to another where the directions are different finds it awkward and unnatural to change, there are no particular advantages to driving on one side or the other. What really matters is for all drivers to be on the same side of the road! If half of the drivers in a city drive on the right side and half the drivers on the left side, all we have are accidents. Coordination in a situation like this is very important and is not left up to individuals to decide upon. In cases such as these we have laws that focus on one equilibrium over another.

In other cases the coordination problem is less serious, but perhaps still annoying. Consider the case of an interrupted phone call. Suppose Dean decides to phone Richard and discuss the issue of which software to use. Just moments after Richard picks up the phone something happens and the connection is broken. Dean's strategy

FIGURE 15.9 Nash equilibrium in word processor game

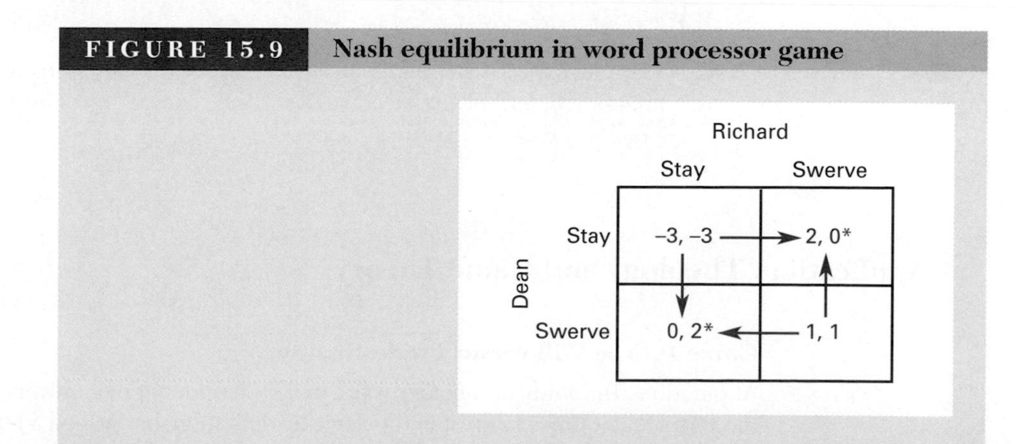

set is to either phone back or wait for Richard to call. Richard's strategy set is the same. If both of them phone back the line just rings busy and they cannot talk. If both of them wait for the other to call, they wait a long time and they still do not talk. The two equilibria in this case are (Call, Wait), and (Wait, Call). Again, it doesn't matter who calls back, but only one person can call; the other must wait. But who does which? In situations like these, social custom often dictates what to do. Although some people feel that the one who is called is obligated to call back, most people feel that the onus is on the original caller to try one more time.

One final method of solving a coordination game is to attempt to pre-empt the game by making some type of first move before the game. For example, in the phoning game, Richard might announce to all of his friends that he never takes note of a phone number, so if in the future a call is interrupted it would be impossible for him to phone back. As another example, one of the authors once moved into a new subdivision where the builder of the homes built wood fencing around each home. The neighbours began meeting informally to discuss what colour they should paint the fence. Although there were a number of opinions on what colour the fence should be, everyone agreed the fence should just be one colour. This, of course, led to a coordination problem, a problem which was solved when the neighbourhood awoke one morning and found someone had gone ahead and painted their share of the fence brown. The others then followed ... although a little peeved!

No Equilibrium

In some games there is no equilibrium. Consider the children's game Rock, Paper, Scissors. In this game two players face each other and bob their closed fists three times. On the third time they simultaneously make one of three hand gestures: an open hand for paper, a closed fist for rock, and two open fingers for scissors. In this game paper always beats rock, rock always beats scissors, but scissors always beats paper. The winner usually gets to hit the loser or do some other such thing. If there is a tie, the game is simply repeated.

The entire point of the game Rock, Paper, Scissors revolves around the fact that there is no Nash equilibrium. Could you imagine playing this game if there were a dominant strategy? Perhaps Rock won over everything else. Both players would endlessly bob their hands three times and each would announce "Rock," and repeat the game. This sounds like a scene from the movie *Dumb and Dumber*!

PROBLEM 15.4

Write out a matrix for the game Rock, Paper, Scissors, using only the numbers 1, 0, and −1 for payoff values. Using arrows, show there is no single cell where two arrowheads meet.

Application: Theology and Game Theory

Game I: Free Will versus Predestination

At one time, the study of theology was a major component of a university education. In modern secular times interest in theology, by definition, has waned a little. Still, it is fun to use our game theory concepts to articulate a few classic theological issues. One of those issues is whether humans have "free will" to choose God or are "predestined" to choose.

Suppose there is a supreme all-knowing God whose primary goal is that he wants a person, Karim, to believe in his existence, and as a secondary goal prefers not to reveal himself. Suppose the primary goal of Karim is to have his belief confirmed by revelation (or his disbelief confirmed by a lack of revelation), and his secondary goal is to prefer to believe in God's existence. Figure 15.10 shows the payoffs of this game, where each outcome is ranked from 1 to 4, with 4 being the best.

Under the assumptions we've made, God has a dominant strategy not to reveal himself. Given this, the Nash equilibrium is clearly for Karim not to believe. This set-up would appear to be refuted by the existence of religions all over the world.

Now let's consider a change in the goals of the players. Let God's primary goal be the same as above, but now let his secondary goal be to prefer revelation. Second, the primary goal of Karim is to not believe, while Karim's secondary goal is to prefer confirmation. Now the payoffs of the game are given in Figure 15.11, where again the outcomes are ranked from 1 to 4.

Now the Nash equilibrium is for God to reveal himself and for Karim to not believe! No one would get to Heaven (assuming you have to believe in order to go) if everyone were like Karim. This situation reminds us of a story about an interaction between God and an atheist. The two meet, and God introduces himself as God. The atheist responds that he doesn't believe in God, and asks for some proof. God immediately turns the bottled water the atheist is holding into a bottle of wine. The atheist then responds, "Hey, what's the trick?"

Finally, let's consider a third game where everything is the same as the second one, but now Karim's primary goal is to prefer to believe. This game's payoffs are shown in Figure 15.12. Clearly in this last game, both players have a dominant strategy, and the outcome is that God reveals himself and Karim believes.

Game theory doesn't provide any of the numbers in these games; they come from particular theologies. According to these games, no one ever goes to Heaven kicking and screaming. One either believes and goes, or does not believe and ... well, goes somewhere else. This is a principle in most major religions of the world. Also consistent with major religions of the world, no one would have any chance at heaven if God never revealed himself. Finally, although the games do not resolve the issue of free will versus predestination, they do allow for a nice articulation of the debate. Those

FIGURE 15.10 **The freewill game**

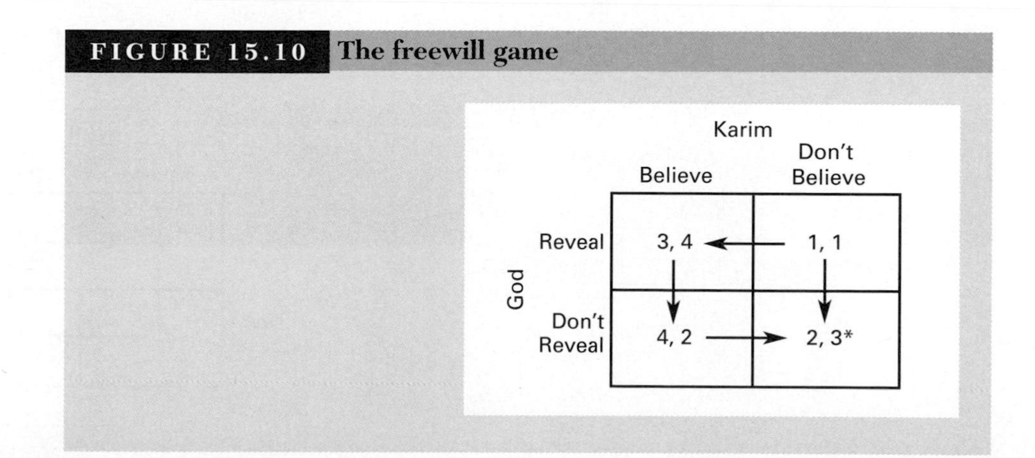

FIGURE 15.11 Nash equilibrium in freewill game

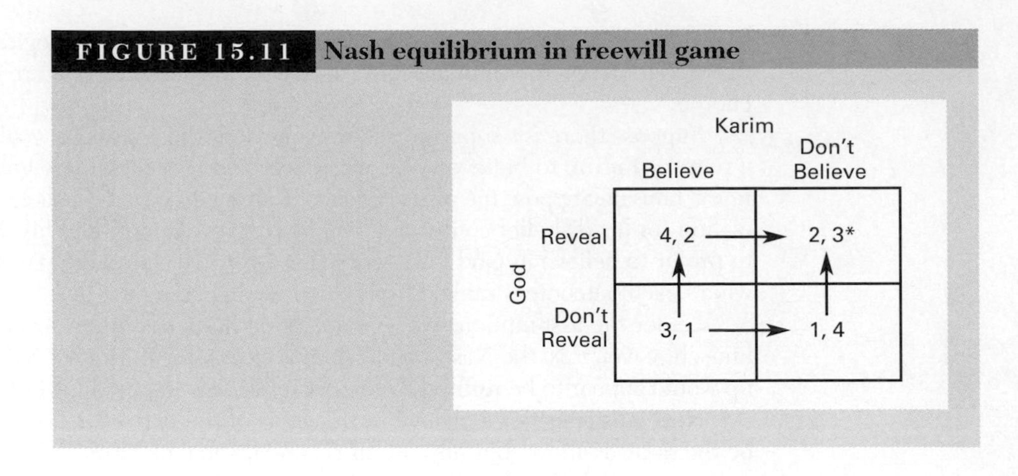

believers who think some people are predestined to go to Heaven would say everyone is born with a nature described in game 15.11, and God works in some lives to change them into natures described by game 15.12. On the other hand, those believers who think there is free will would suggest we get to choose between the games in Figures 15.11 and 15.12.

Game II: If Omniscient, then God Must Be Holy

Most of the religions of the world have a number of characteristics which are similar. For example, their god is omniscient (all-knowing), requires a standard of behaviour or code of conduct, and is capable of exercising mercy at will. So, in the Christian faith, God gave Moses the Ten Commandments, and yet forgave his people over and over again for their transgressions. On the other hand, in almost all religions individuals can either behave according to the rules or disregard the rules. For ease, let's call the actions of both parties Compromise, Not Compromise.

If neither player compromises the outcome is bad for both (say 1, 1). If one compromises but the other doesn't, the stubborn one gets 4 and the other gets 2. If both compromise they each get 3. These payoffs are set out in Figure 15.13.

As you can see, Karim is playing a game of chicken with God. In the game of chicken there are two equilibria, not just one. Interestingly, God's omniscience works against him in a situation like this. By being all-knowing, God knows what Karim will

FIGURE 15.12 Freewill game 2

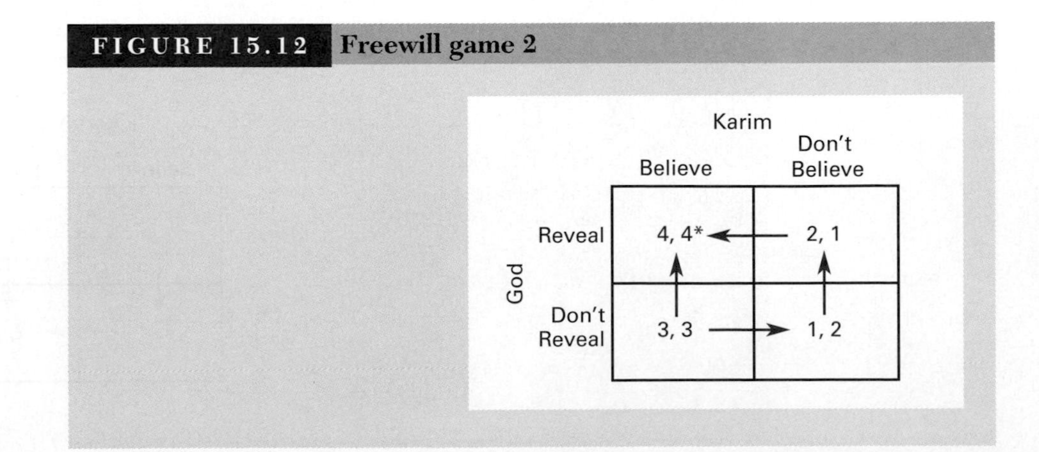

FIGURE 15.13 **Playing chicken with God**

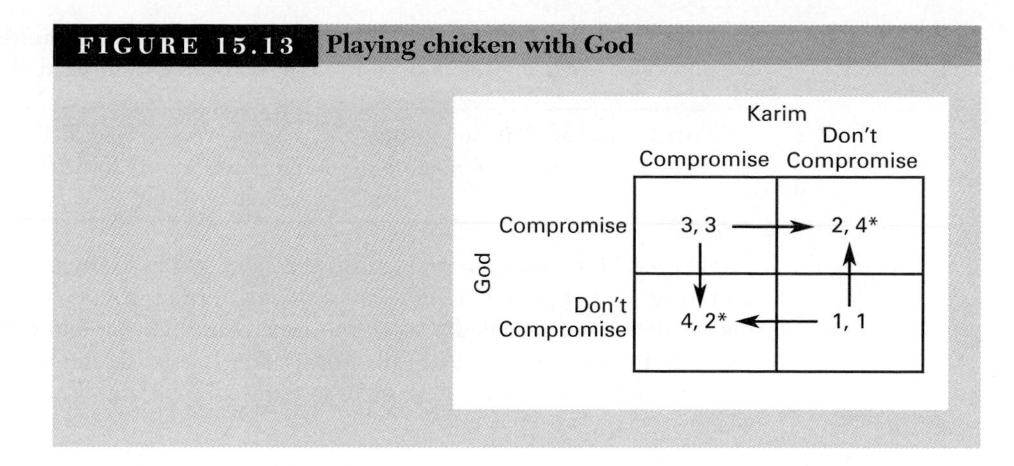

do. But Karim knows God is all-knowing, and knows that if he compromises and goes against the rules, God will compromise and exercise his mercy to Karim. Thus, when God is omniscient, the game of chicken has one unique equilibrium, namely (Compromise, Don't Compromise). From God's point of view, this is a bad equilibrium. A solution for God is to announce he is holy and just, and cannot compromise. If Karim believes this, he may want to avoid testing God and follow the rules.

15.4 Games of Plain Substitutes and Plain Complements

The payoff (measured in utility) to either partner in a personal relationship, a marriage for example, is jointly determined by the effort that each of the two partners puts into the relationship. As you undoubtedly know, one of the more important decisions you will make in your life is how much effort you will put into your relationships. In this relationship game, the strategy space of either of the two partners is continuous. In fact, the strategy space is the set of non-negative real numbers. In all of the games thus far, the strategy space was discrete, but in many instances the number of choices we have are unlimited. For example, if I am thinking about offering a bribe to some government official, or deciding how much effort to devote to a group project, or what quantity of steroids I want to inject in my effort to become the fastest sprinter in the world, I am choosing a strategy from a continuous strategy space. In this section we consider two general classes of games in which each player's strategy space is the set of non-negative real numbers.[2]

In each of these games, the strategies of players One and Two are denoted by y_1 and y_2, and their payoff functions by $\pi_1(y_1, y_2)$ and $\pi_2(y_1, y_2)$. The payoff functions are assumed to satisfy some esoteric mathematical properties: specifically they are assumed to be continuous and quasi-concave. Fortunately, clarity does not require that we dwell on these properties. Throughout we focus on interior Nash equilibria; that is, equilibria in which the equilibrium values of the strategies are strictly positive. First we look at games in which each player's payoff diminishes as the values of the other player's strategy increases, **games of plain substitutes**. Then we look at games in which the opposite is true, games in which each player's payoff increases as the values

games of plain substitutes

2. This section draws heavily on Eaton and Eswaran (2002).

games of plain complements

of the other player's strategy increases, **games of plain complements**. Along the way we introduce the related notions of strategic substitutes and strategic complements.

With a game of plain substitutes the players impose negative externalities on each other, while in a game of plain complements they impose positive externalities on each other.

We establish some powerful and quite general results for games of plain substitutes and for games of plain complements, and we develop some elegant diagrams that encapsulate these results. Because there is an enormous number of interesting and important games in these two categories, there is a considerable personal payoff in understanding the world we live in, to students who make this material their own.

Games of Plain Substitutes with Simultaneous Moves

As a technical matter, games of plain substitutes are distinguished by the fact that player One's (and, respectively, Two's) payoff diminishes as y_2 (respectively y_1) increases. In other words, in a game of plain substitutes, the *cross-effects* in the payoff functions are negative. Alternatively, a game of plain substitutes is a game of *mutual negative externalities*. Two roommates who smoke in their common air space are playing a game of plain substitutes, because each of them is adversely affected by the second-hand smoke their roommate spews out. Two teens who compete for attention by spending money on clothes and accessories to improve their appearance are playing a game of plain substitutes, because the more one teen spends the more difficult is it for the other to get attention. Two firms who produce identical products are playing a game of plain substitutes because the more one firm produces, the lower is the price and hence profit that the other gets. If you put your mind to it, you will see that there are a very large number of games of this sort.

We can quickly establish some important features of the Nash equilibrium of these games. Suppose $y_1{}^*$ and $y_2{}^*$ are the Nash equilibrium values of the strategies. Then, from the definition of Nash equilibrium, $y_1{}^*$ is a best response to $y_2{}^*$. Alternatively, $y_1{}^*$ solves the following constrained maximization problem:

$$\text{maximize by choice of } y_1 \text{ and } y_2 \qquad \pi_1(y_1, y_2) \text{ s.t. } y_2 = y_2{}^*$$

We write the problem this way because we know something about this sort of problem from our encounters with constrained maximization problems earlier in the book. Specifically, we know that an indifference curve, or an iso-payoff contour, of $\pi_1(y_1, y_2)$ is tangent to the constraint at the Nash equilibrium, (y_1^*, y_2^*), as shown in Figure 15.14. In addition, because $\pi_1(y_1,y_2)$ decreases as y_2 increases, this indifference cause must lie below the line $y_2 = y_2{}^*$ elsewhere. Further, and for the same reason, the set of strategy combinations that One prefers to the Nash equilibrium strategy combination lies below this indifference curve, as indicated by the downward-pointing arrows in the figure.

Similar facts hold for Two's indifference curve through the Nash equilibrium. It must be tangent to the line $y_1 = y_1^*$ at (y_1^*,y_2^*). Elsewhere it must lie to the left of the line $y_1 = y_1^*$, and the set of strategy combinations Two prefers to the Nash equilibrium lie to the left of this indifference curve. These facts are also incorporated in Figure 15.14.

Notice that all strategy combinations in the lens-shaped area on the lower left of the Nash equilibrium are preferred by both players to the Nash equilibrium, which

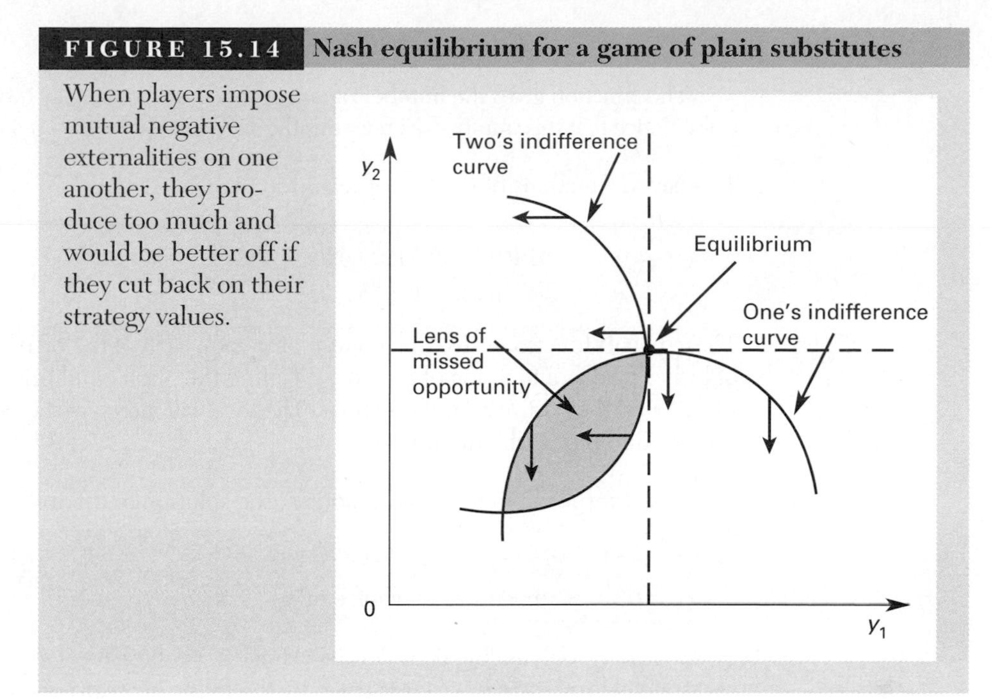

FIGURE 15.14 **Nash equilibrium for a game of plain substitutes**

When players impose mutual negative externalities on one another, they produce too much and would be better off if they cut back on their strategy values.

lens of missed opportunity

explains why we call this the **lens of missed opportunity**. Notice also that in the Nash equilibrium, the players choose strategy values that are in some sense "too large." Thus we have the following interesting and quite general proposition about games of plain substitutes:

Proposition 15.1: Supposing that the Nash equilibrium of a game of plain substitutes is interior, it is not Pareto-optimal; further, relative to the Nash equilibrium, any strategy combination that Pareto-dominates the Nash equilibrium has smaller values of both strategies.

Application: Inefficient Bribe-Taking

As Tullock (1980) observed, in many highly regulated economies, would-be entrepreneurs are forced to bribe a number of government officials in order to get the required permissions to set up a business. As we will show, when there are two (or more) officials who must be bribed, the game the officials are playing among themselves is a game of plain substitutes, and in the equilibrium of the game, the officials demand bribes that are too large (from the narrow perspective of the officials themselves).

Naturally, any entrepreneurs will pay the bribes of the officials only if the profits they anticipate from their entrepreneurial activity are larger than the sums of the bribes demanded by the officials. This, of course, implies that the demand for permissions (and hence bribes) by entrepreneurs is a decreasing function of the sum of the bribes required to get the necessary official permissions. This is the key insight that any model of the bribe-taking game must incorporate.

For simplicity, let us suppose there are just two bribe-taking government officials, and let us denote the bribes they demand by y_1 and y_2. Further, let us suppose that the demand for permissions by entrepreneurs is the following linear function of y_1 and y_2:

$$D(y_1, y_2) = 120 - 2(y_1 + y_2)$$

This function gives the number of entrepreneurs who will pay the bribes to the officials. Notice that this number decreases as the aggregate bribe $(y_1 + y_2)$ required increases.

The payoff functions of the two officials are then

$$\pi_1(y_1, y_2) = y_1 D(y_1, y_2) = y_1(120 - 2y_2) - 2(y_1)^2$$
$$\pi_2(y_1, y_2) = y_2 D(y_1, y_2) = y_2(120 - 2y_1) - 2(y_2)^2$$

These payoff functions give the amount of money each of the official gets in the form of bribes paid as a function of y_1 and y_2. To find the Nash equilibrium of this game, let us first find the best response functions. Then we will intersect the best response functions to find the Nash equilibrium.

One's best response function is, of course, the solution to the following maximization problem

$$\text{maximize by choice of } y_1 \qquad \pi_1(y_1, y_2)$$

To solve this problem, first consider the change in profit that occurs when One changes his strategy form y_1 to $y_1+\Delta$. It is given by the following expression:

$$\pi_1(y_1 + \Delta\, y_2) - \pi_1(y_1, y_2) = \Delta(120 - 2y_2 - 4y_1) - 2\Delta^2$$

(To ensure that you are following the analysis, you should verify this result.) This expression is just the difference in One's payoff when One alters his strategy from y_1 to $y_1 + \Delta$. If we can find a value of y_1 such that this difference is negative for all nonzero values of Δ (both positive and negative), we will have found the solution to this maximization problem. Now notice that, if we choose y_1 so that $120 - 2y_2 - 4y_1 = 0$, then the difference in profit is just

$$\pi_1(y_1 + \Delta\, y_2) - \pi_1(y_1, y_2) = -2\Delta^2$$

which is strictly negative for all $\Delta \neq 0$. So, solving $120 - 2y_2 - 4y_1 = 0$ for y_1, we get the solution to this maximization problem:

$$y_1 = (120 - 2y_2)/(4) = 30 - 0.5y_2$$

Given any y_2, this value of y_1 maximizes One's payoff. This, of course, means that One's best response function, $R_1(y_2)$, is

$$R_1(y_2) = 30 - 0.5y_2$$

In Figure 15.15 we have plotted One's best response function, and two indifference curves (or iso-payoff contours) for One. For reasons discussed above, the indifference curves are horizontal where they intersect the best response function, and they have an inverted U shape. Notice also that the lower is the indifference curve, the higher the associated payoff.

An analogous argument yields Two's best response function, $R_2(y_1)$:

FIGURE 15.15 **Best responses and utility**

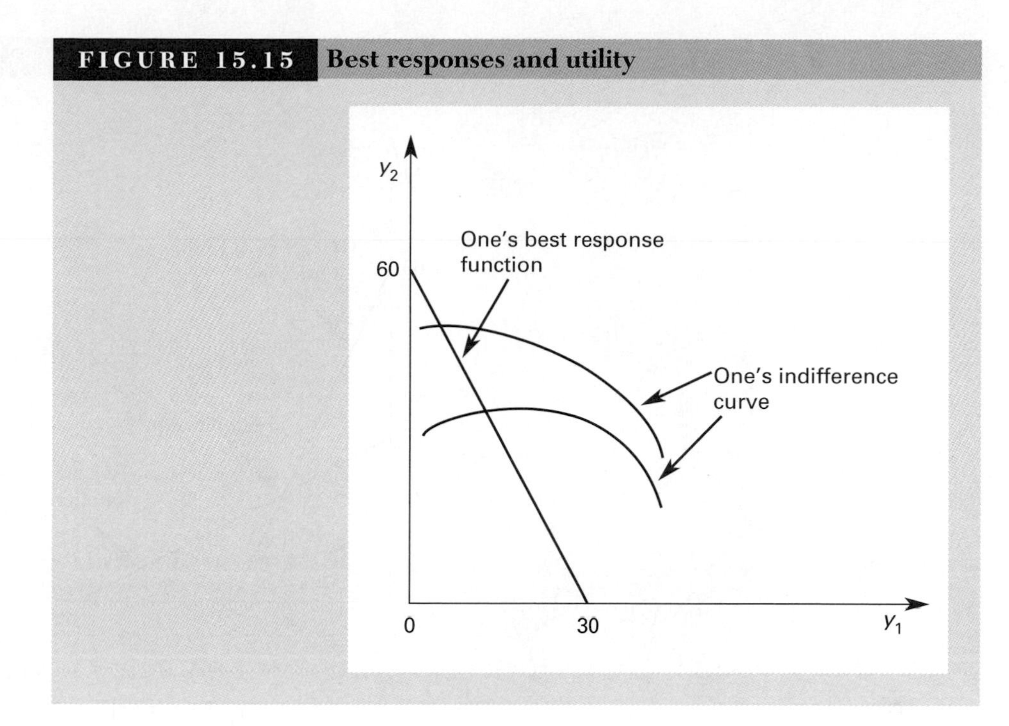

$$R_2(y_1) = (120 - 2y_1)/(4) = 30 - 0.5y_1$$

To find the Nash equilibrium, we must find values of y_1 and y_2 that are mutual best responses. To do so we must intersect the best response functions or, equivalently, solve the following simultaneous equations:

$$y_1 = 30 - 0.5y_2$$
$$y_2 = 30 - 0.5y_1$$

As illustrated in Figure 15.16, the Nash equilibrium values are $y_1^* = y_2^* = 20$. Given these values, 40 entrepreneurs pay the bribes $D(y_1^*, y_2^*) = 40$, and the bribe-taking officials each take home \$800 in bribes ($\pi_1(y_1^*, y_2^*) = 800$).

Since this is a game of plain substitutes, Proposition 15.1 tells us that the bribes are too large. Since we know precisely what the demand for bribes is in this model, we can say more. If the two officials got together and decided on an aggregate bribe, y, their aggregate payoff would be

$$\pi(y) = y(120 - 2y)$$

The value of y that maximizes their aggregate payoff is $y = 120/4 = 30$. (To establish this result, simply find the value of y such that $\pi(y + \Delta) - \pi(y)$ is negative for all $\Delta \neq 0$.)[3] If the aggregate bribe were \$30 instead of \$40, the demand for bribes would be 60 instead of 80, the aggregate amount paid in bribes would be \$1800 instead of \$1600, and each official would pocket \$900 instead of \$800. Thus, the Nash equilibrium bribes are too large, with the result that each corrupt official takes home only \$800

3. If you know calculus, simply take the derivative with respect to x, set it equal to zero and solve for x.

FIGURE 15.16 Equilibrium plain substitutes

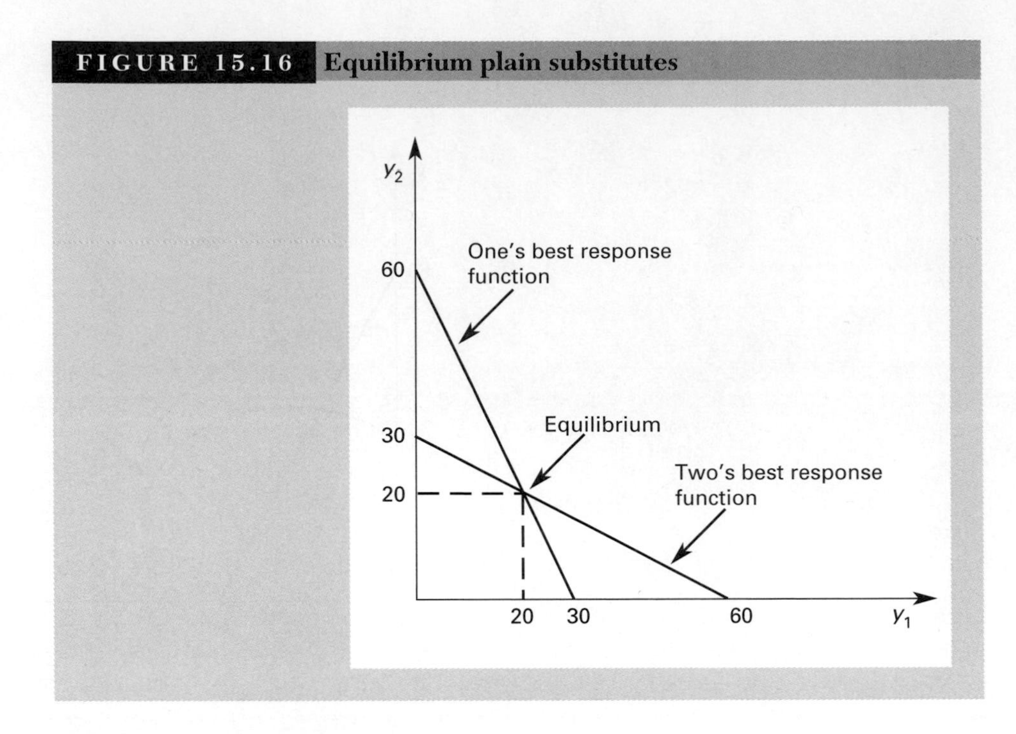

instead of $900. This is the sense in which the Nash equilibrium of this game of plain substitutes is not Pareto-optimal.

Of course, if we think about optimality from the larger societal perspective, we see that the Nash equilibrium of the bribe-taking game is non-optimal, even tragic, in a larger sense, since the number of entrepreneurs who find it attractive to actually enter business is a decreasing function of the aggregate bribe required to get the necessary permissions to enter business. Thus, the real tragedy is that this sort of bribery chokes off entrepreneurial activity, and the more officials who must be bribed, the larger is the number of would-be entrepreneurs who choose not to enter business at all.

Application: Performance-Enhancing Drugs

We have argued that the prisoner's dilemma captures the essence of the game in which individual athletes choose whether or not to take a performance-enhancing drug (PED) in an effort to gain a competitive advantage over their opponents. Of course, the decision that athletes face is not really whether or not to use a PED; rather they must choose how much of the PED they want to use. We can get a deeper understanding of their problem, and of the modeller's art, by recasting the game in continuous strategy spaces.

Seen from the individual athlete's perspective, the upside of PEDs is that they increase the probability of winning, and the downside is that they are costly both because the athlete has to buy them and because they are unhealthy. If we then add the trivial observation that winning is preferred to losing, we have all the elements needed to build a model of this situation.

For simplicity, suppose that there are just two athletes, Ben and Carl, and that y_1 is the quantity of the PED taken by Ben and y_2 the amount taken by Carl. Now let $q_1(y_1, y_2)$ denote the probability that Ben wins. To capture the essential effect of the

PED on performance, we must assume that q_1 is an increasing function of y_1 and a decreasing function of y_2 – that the probability that Ben wins increases as the quantity of drugs he uses increases and decreases as the quantity of drugs used by his opponent increases. To capture the downside of PEDs, we will suppose that the cost to an athlete of using quantity y of the drug is $C(y)$, where C is increasing in y — the more drugs the athletes use, the larger are the costs (both in terms of money and health) borne by the athlete. Finally, to capture the fact that winning is better than losing, we simply assign utilities to winning and losing, W and L, such that $W > L$.

Putting these pieces together, we get the following payoff function for Ben:

$$\pi_1(y_1, y_2) = q_1(y_1, y_2)W + (1 - q_1(y_1, y_2))L - C(y_1) = L + (W - L)q_1(y_1, y_2) - C(y_1)$$

This payoff function is simply the expected utility of the game.[4] Of course, if $q_1(y_1,y_2)$ is the probability that Ben wins, it must also be the probability that Carl loses, and we see that we also have all that is needed to write out Carl's payoff function:

$$\pi_2(y_1, y_2) = (1 - q_1(y_1, y_2))W + q_1(y_1, y_2)L - C(y_2) = W - (W - L)q_1(y_1, y_2) - C(y_2)$$

Notice that Ben's payoff decreases as y_2 increases, since $(W - L) > 0$ and q_1 decreases as y_2 increases. Similarly, Carl's payoff decreases as y_1 increases, since $-(W - L) < 0$ and q_1 increases as y_1 increases. Conclusion: this is a game of plain substitutes, which means that without doing any more work, we know quite a bit about its equilibrium. In particular, Figure 15.14 illustrates the Nash equilibrium, and Proposition 15.1 is applicable to the game. So, we see immediately that the equilibrium is not Pareto-optimal, and that the athletes use too much of the PED.[5]

Games of Plain Complements with Simultaneous Moves

As a technical matter, games of plain complements are distinguished by the fact that player One's (and, respectively, Two's) payoff increases as y_2 (respectively y_1) increases. In other words, in a game of plain complements, the *cross-effects* in the payoff functions are positive. Alternatively, a game of plain complements is a game of *mutual positive externalities*. Two roommates who devote effort to keeping their apartment clean and habitable are playing a game of plain complements because each of them is positively affected by the efforts of the other. Two students who work together in preparation for a final examination are playing a game of plain complements, because the more time one of them spends studying the relevant material, the more knowledge and understanding she can convey to the other. Two firms who produce products that are complements are playing a game of plain complements because the more one firm produces, the higher is the price and hence profit that the other gets.

Adapting what we learned in our consideration of plain substitutes, we see immediately certain key features of the Nash equilibrium of games of plain complements. These key features are illustrated in Figure 15.17. The indifference curve of One through the Nash equilibrium (y_1^*, y_2^*) must be tangent to the line $y_2 = y_2^*$ at (y_1^*, y_2^*). Further, since One's payoff increases as y_2 increases, this indifference curve must lie

4. We discuss expected utility in great detail in Chapter 17. For now it is sufficient to think of expected utility as simply the average utility from taking the PED.

5. To pursue the analysis further, one needs to say more about the functions q_1 and C. If one assumes that $q_1(x_1,x_2) = x_1/(x_1 + x_2)$ and that $C(x) = x$, it is possible to find best response functions, calculate the Nash equilibrium, and demonstrate that $x_1 = x_2 = 0$ is optimal. See the exercises at the end of the chapter.

above the line $y_2 = y_2^*$ elsewhere, and the set of strategy combinations that One prefers to the Nash equilibrium strategy combination lies above this indifference curve. Similarly, the indifference curve of Two through the Nash equilibrium (y_1^*, y_2^*) must be tangent to the line $y_1 = y_1^*$ at (y_1^*, y_2^*), the indifference curve must lie to the right of the line $y_1 = y_1^*$ elsewhere, and the set of strategy combinations that Two prefers to the Nash equilibrium strategy combination lies to the right of this indifference curve.

Notice that the *lens of missed opportunity* in Figure 15.17 lies above and to the right of the Nash equilibrium, indicating that the players choose strategy values that are too small in the Nash equilibrium of this game of plain complements. The figure yields the following interesting, and quite general proposition about games of plain complements:

Proposition 15.2: Supposing the Nash equilibrium of a game of plain complements is interior, it is not Pareto-optimal; further, relative to the Nash equilibrium, any strategy combination that Pareto-dominates the Nash equilibrium has larger values of both strategies.

Application: Team Production

Team production is a good example of a game of plain complements. The essential feature of team production is this: the more effort any one team member exerts, the larger is the payoff of the other team members.

To focus the analysis, think about a term project in some university course that involves a group of students. Instructors in business schools often assign group projects because it is thought that by participating in this sort of team effort, students develop team skills that will be valuable in the workplace. For simplicity, let us imagine a team project with just two team members. To model this situation, it seems sensible to suppose that two things matter to the individual student engaged in such a project: the grade the student gets on the project, and the amount of effort the student devotes to the pro-

FIGURE 15.17 **Nash equilibrium for a game of plain complements**

When the actions of each player exert a benefit to the other player, both players would be better off if they increased their strategy levels.

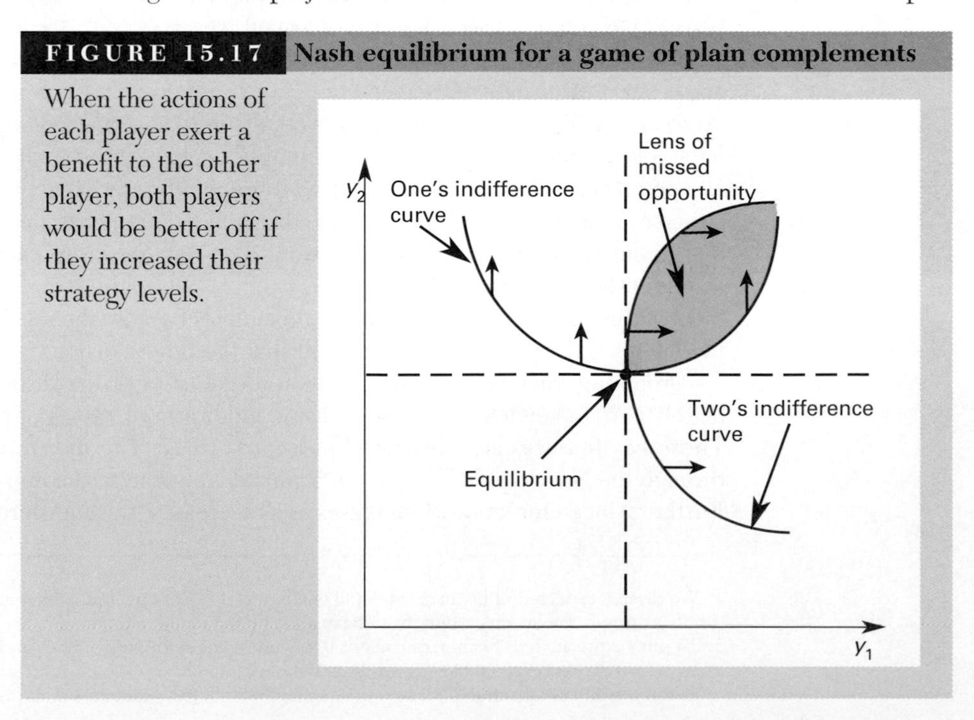

ject. The higher the grade, the better off the student is, and the more effort the student expends, the worse off the student is. Of course, the grade that either student gets on the project is determined by the efforts of both students. In particular, the grade either student gets is an increasing function of the effort exerted by that student and by the other team member. Thus, the team project defines a game in which the students are the players and their effort levels are their strategies. And because the grade that either one of the students gets on the project increases as the amount of effort exerted by the other student increases, it is a game of plain complements.

Proposition 15.2 tells us something about the Nash equilibrium of the game. It is not Pareto-optimal. Further, in the Nash equilibrium, the students expend too little effort. In effect, in the Nash equilibrium, each student is free-riding on the efforts of the other. Of course, if they could freely devise a way of eliminating the free-riding, they could make themselves better off. So, our analysis alerts us to an important problem, one that clever students might be able to overcome. Chapter 19 is devoted to a deeper analysis of this sort of problem in the workplace, and of possible solutions to it.

To develop our modelling skills, it is useful to write out a more detailed model of this team production game. Let us suppose that the grade a student gets for the project is the following function of the efforts of students Iris and James. (To keep the notation simple, we'll let Iris be student 1 and James be student 2.)[6]

$$G(y_1, y_2) = 120y_1 + y_1y_2$$

Notice that the grade for Iris or James is an increasing function of both y_1 and y_2. Further, suppose that from the perspective of student i, the cost of the effort expended on the project is

$$C(y_i) = 2(y_i)^2$$

Then, subtracting the cost of effort from the grade, we get the following payoff functions for the students:

$$\pi_1(y_1, y_2) = 120y_1 + y_1y_2 - 2(y_1)^2$$
$$\pi_2(y_1, y_2) = 120y_2 + y_1y_2 - 2(y_2)^2$$

We can adapt the technique we used to find best response functions for the bribe-taking game to find best response functions for this game. Given y_2, Iris's best response has the property that $\pi_1(y_1 + \Delta y_2) - \pi_1(y_1, y_2) < 0$ for all $\Delta \neq 0$. As you should verify, this expression for the change in Iris's payoff when she chooses strategy $y_1 + \Delta$ instead of strategy y_1 can be written in the following way:

$$\pi_1(y_1 + \Delta y_2) - \pi_1(y_1, y_2) = \Delta(120 + 2y_2 - 4y_1) - 2\Delta^2$$

From this expression, if $120 + y_2 - 4y_1 = 0$, then $\pi_1(y_1 + \Delta\, y_2) - \pi_1(y_1, y_2) = -2\Delta^2$. But $-2\Delta^2$ is less than zero for all $\Delta \neq 0$, so Iris's best response is implicitly defined by the equation $120 + y_2 - 4y_1 = 0$. Solving for y_1 we get

$$R_1(y_2) = (120 + y_2)/4 = 30 + 0.25y_2$$

---

6. You may have noticed that we've chosen numbers similar to those in the case of plain substitutes. There's nothing special about the numbers, and we've maintained them just to keep things simple.

Similarly,

$$R_2(y_1) = (120 + y_1)/4 = 30 + 0.25y_1$$

These best response functions are pictured in Figure 15.18. The Nash equilibrium strategies are

$$y_1^* = y_2^* = 40.$$

PROBLEM 15.5

Set $y_1 = y_2 = y$ in the two payoff functions, and observe that they are identical. Then find the value of y that maximizes the payoff the students get when their effort levels are constrained to be identical. Call these the cooperative effort levels. Show that the cooperative effort levels are larger than the Nash equilibrium effort levels and that the payoffs the students get with the *cooperative effort levels* are larger than the payoffs they get in the Nash equilibrium. Finally, draw a diagram in which you (i) sketch the best response functions, (ii) identify the Nash equilibrium and cooperative effort levels, and (iii) sketch the indifference curves through the Nash equilibrium and cooperative effort levels.

Diagnosing Social Dilemmas

The basic analysis for both games of plain substitutes and games of plain complements embodied in Figures 15.14 and 15.17 is straightforward, powerful, and perhaps dis-

FIGURE 15.18 **Equilibrium of the team production game**

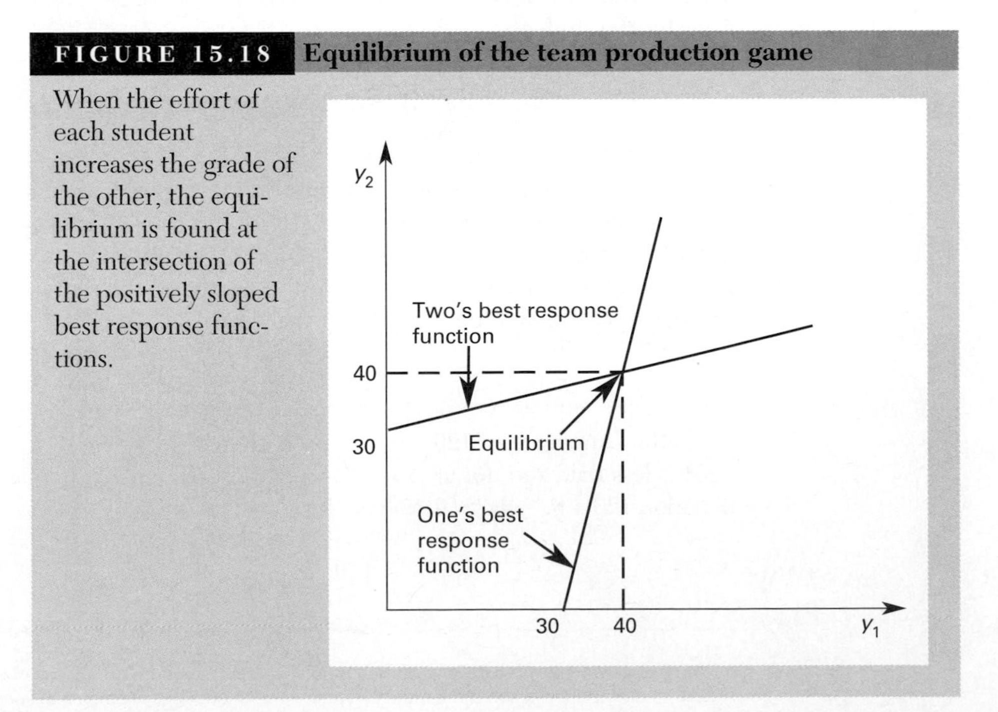

When the effort of each student increases the grade of the other, the equilibrium is found at the intersection of the positively sloped best response functions.

turbing to some. It is powerful in that we get quite general results: the Nash equilibrium of these games is not Pareto-optimal, and equilibrium strategies are too large in games of plain substitutes and too small in games of plain complements. Given that these games serve as a model or metaphor for a large number of important economic and social interactions, the analysis is disturbing because it indicates that when we blindly pursue our own self-interest in situations where interactions are important, we find ourselves in equilibria that are not Pareto-optimal. If, in our many social relations, we blindly pursue our own self-interest without due regard for the implications that our actions have for others, we will find ourselves in unattractive equilibria in which we do not actually achieve the full potential offered by the relationships.

Realizing this, we are naturally led to try to find ways and means of getting more out of these relationships, and perhaps of achieving their full potential. Thus the analysis embodied in these figures is, in essence, a diagnostic tool. The analysis tells us how to spot situations in which the pursuit of self-interest leads to sub-optimal outcomes, and it tells us the direction of the bias of the equilibrium relative to the optimum. If the cross-effects of the actions of the players are negative, equilibrium values are too large, and if the cross-effects are positive, equilibrium values are too small.

Having diagnosed a potential problem, one naturally turns to solutions, and a significant portion of game theory and of economics is devoted to the search for institutions that solve these social dilemmas. At various points in this book we turn our attention to solutions. For example, the whole of Chapter 19 is devoted to the study of team production and possible solutions to the problems identified in our analysis of team production. The Coase Theorem, addressed in Chapter 18, is in essence a property rights approach to the solution of a large class of social and economic dilemmas of the sort considered here.

PROBLEM 15.6

Suppose that One's payoff increases as y_2 increases and that Two's payoff decreases as y_1 increases. Assume that the Nash equilibrium is interior. Construct a figure in which you draw the indifference curves through the Nash equilibrium and identify the lens of missed opportunity.

15.5 Mixed Strategies and Games of Discoordination

Think about the game sometimes called *matching loonies* (when the authors were young[er] the game was called "matching pennies" ... such is one of the many effects of inflation!). For both players the set of pure strategies is (head, tail). If both players choose the same pure strategy, One gets a payoff of \$1 and Two gets a payoff of –\$1, and if they choose different pure strategies, One gets a payoff of –\$1 and Two gets a payoff of \$1. In other words, if player One calls heads and player Two calls heads, then player One gets to keep Two's loonie. Notice that there is no equilibrium in pure strategies for matching loonies. If player One is going to call heads, then player Two will call tails, but if player Two will call tails, then player One will call tails as well, but then ... and on it goes.

How do players typically choose their strategies in this game? They toss a loonie, thus generating their strategy *randomly* (heads with probability 1/2 and tails with probability 1/2). Why do they choose them in this way? If you can answer this question you understand the essence of the equilibrium of a game of mixed strategies.

Think of another game, the party game, in which each of two players chooses to attend 1 of 2 parties. One person (call her Claire) wants to attend the same party as the other (call him Zak), while Zak wants to avoid Claire (that is, Zak wants to attend the party Claire does not attend). The payoff matrix in Figure 15.19 is a model of this game. Do you see why?

game of discoordination

In this matrix, Party A means "go to the party at Anna's house," while Party B means "go to the party at Brett's house." This type of game is called a **game of discoordination**, for obvious reasons.

As you can see from the arrows, there is no Nash equilibrium in pure strategies here. Further, a pure strategy is bound to be unsuccessful. If Claire knew Zak's pure strategy, then Claire would win the game. Similarly, if Zak knew Claire's pure strategy, then Zak would win the game. In this sense, a pure strategy is not a good idea: if one player's pure strategy is known by the other player, then that player will definitely lose the game.

As we'll see, the safe thing to do in a game of this sort is to use a carefully chosen mixed strategy (a strategy chosen randomly). This is one reason for being interested in mixed strategies. In addition, as John Nash showed in one of his early papers, most interesting games have an equilibrium in mixed strategies. So, mixed strategies are a solution to the no- equilibrium-in-pure-strategies problem encountered by Claire and Zak.

To find a mixed strategy equilibrium we follow several steps which are by now fairly familiar. First, we identify the strategy set of each player and the strategy space of the game. Then we use the notion of "expected" or "average" utility again to write down the payoff functions. With these in place we find the best response functions, and finally, we use the best response functions to find the Nash equilibrium of the game.

Let p be the probability that Claire chooses A. Then, $1 - p$ is the probability that Claire chooses B. Probability p is a mixed strategy for Claire. The set of mixed strategies for Claire is then the set of probabilities p, such that $0 \leq p \leq 1$. Similarly, if we let q denote the probability that Zak chooses A, the set of mixed strategies for Zak is the set of probabilities q, such that $0 \leq q \leq 1$.

Plotting p on the horizontal axis and q on the vertical axis, the strategy space of this game, or the set of strategy combinations for this game, is just the box with corners

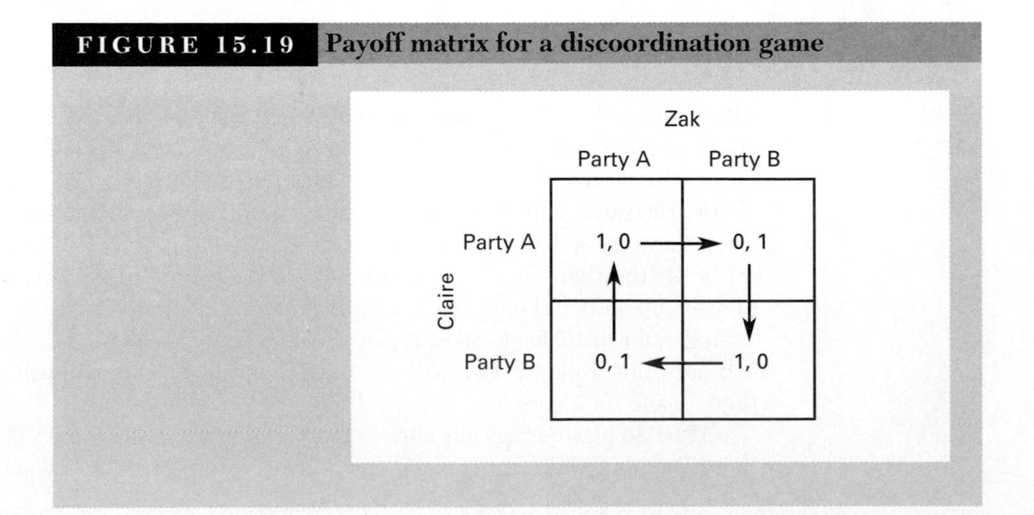

(0, 0), (1, 0), (1, 1), and (0, 1) shown in Figure 15.20. Notice that the set of mixed strategies includes the set of pure strategies — in fact, the set of pure strategy combinations for this game is the four corners of the box. Can you tell what is the pure strategy combination that corresponds to (1, 0) in the box? To (0 ,0)? To (1, 1)? To (0, 1)?

Before we devise payoff functions and find best response functions and the mixed strategy equilibrium, see if you can intuit the best response functions. In particular, how would you answer the following three questions? If $q > 1/2$, what is Claire's best response, given that Claire wants to end up at the same party as Zak? If $q < 1/2$, what is Claire's best response? If $q = 1/2$, what is Claire's best response?

The following table is useful in constructing payoff functions for this game. In fact, any time you see a mixed strategy game it is a good idea to start with this sort of table. If you do, you will find that it is very easy to write down the payoff functions.

TABLE 15.1 Classification of outcomes and payoffs

Possible Outcomes	Claire's Payoff for Each Outcome	Probability of Each Outcome	Zak's Payoff for Each Outcome
(A, A)	1	pq	0
(A, B)	0	$p(1-q)$	1
(B, A)	0	$(1-p)q$	1
(B, B)	1	$(1-p)(1-q)$	0

Claire's payoff is just the *probability weighted average* of the payoffs associated with each outcome.

$$\pi_1(p, q) = 1(pq) + 0(p(1-q)) + 0((1-p)q) + 1((1-p)(1-q))$$

FIGURE 15.20 Mixed strategy space for a discoordination game

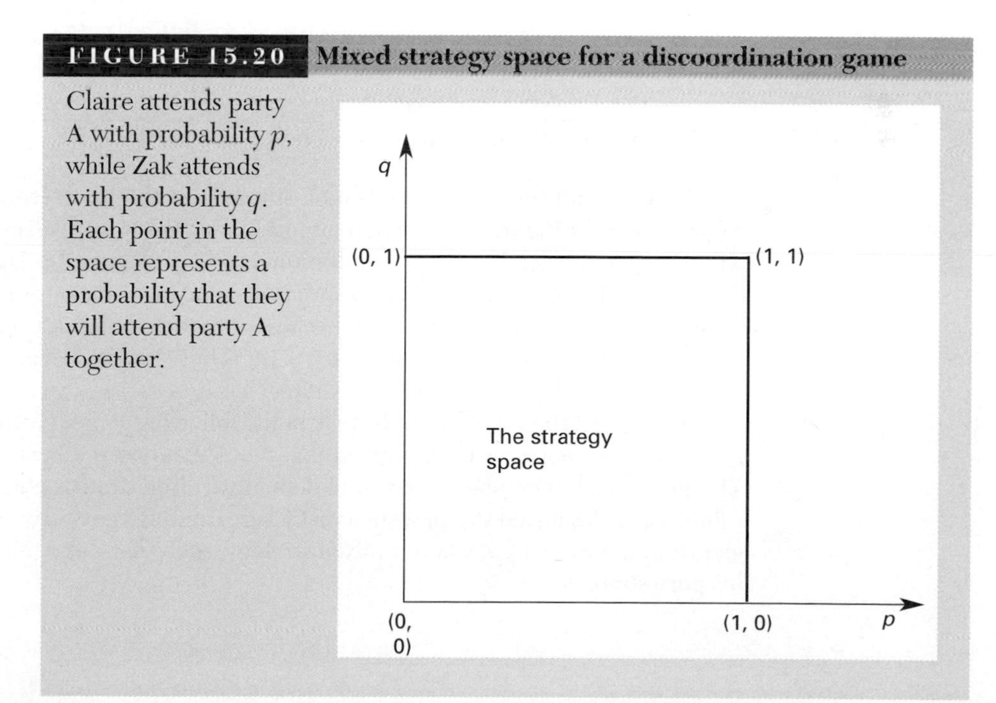

Claire attends party A with probability p, while Zak attends with probability q. Each point in the space represents a probability that they will attend party A together.

To highlight the fact that Claire's payoff is a *linear function* of her strategy, p, let us rewrite her payoff function in the following way:

$$\pi_1(p, q) = (1 - q) + p(2q - 1)$$

Similarly, Zak's payoff function is the following linear function of his strategy, q (Verify this result to ensure that you understand what is going on.)

$$\pi_2(p, q) = p + q(1 - 2p)$$

Notice that the slope of Claire's payoff function, when we plot her payoff on the vertical axis and p on the horizontal axis, is $(2q - 1)$. Clearly, if Claire's payoff increases (respectively, decreases) as p increases, or if the slope of Claire's payoff function is positive (respectively, negative) then her best response is $p = 1$ (respectively, $p = 0$). And if Claire's payoff neither increases or decreases as p increases, or if the slope of her payoff function is 0, then any value of p is a best response for Claire. These observations immediately lead us to Claire's best response function:

1. Claire's payoff increases as p increases if $2q - 1 > 0$, or if $q > 1/2$, and $p = 1$ is Claire's best response.
2. Claire's payoff decreases as p increases if $2q - 1 < 0$, or if $q < 1/2$, and Claire's best response is $p = 0$.
3. Claire's payoff doesn't change as p increases if $2q - 1 = 0$, or if $q = 1/2$, and any value of p is a best response for Claire.

Now notice that when we plot Zak's payoff on the vertical axis and Zak's strategy, q, on the horizontal axis, the slope of his payoff function is $(1 - 2p)$. Replicating the reasoning we used to get Claire's best response function, we get the following best response function for Zak.

1. $q = 0$ is Zak's best response if $(1 - 2p) < 0$ or if $p > 1/2$.
2. $q = 1$ is Zak's best response if $(1 - 2p) > 0$ or if $p < 1/2$.
3. Any q in the interval $[0, 1]$ is a best response if $p = 1/2$.

Now, to find the Nash equilibrium, simply plot the best response functions, as we have done in Figure 15.21 (where unfortunately they look like a swastika) and find where they intersect. The Nash equilibrium is $p^* = 1/2$ and $q^* = 1/2$.

Notice the prevent-exploitation (or cover-your-butt) flavour of this equilibrium. Strategy $p^* = 1/2$ is best for Claire, because it means that Zak cannot exploit information about her strategy. Similarly, $q^* = 1/2$ is best for Zak because it means Claire cannot exploit information about his strategy.

Notice that the equilibrium is weak in the following sense: given that $q = 1/2$, any p is a best response for Claire, given that $p = 1/2$, any q is a best response for Zak. This gives us a less cumbersome way of defining a mixed strategy equilibrium. Find the value of q, Zak's mixed strategy, such that Claire is indifferent between his pure strategies; find the value of p, Claire's mixed strategy, such that Zak is indifferent between his pure strategies.

FIGURE 15.21 Mixed strategy Nash equilibrium

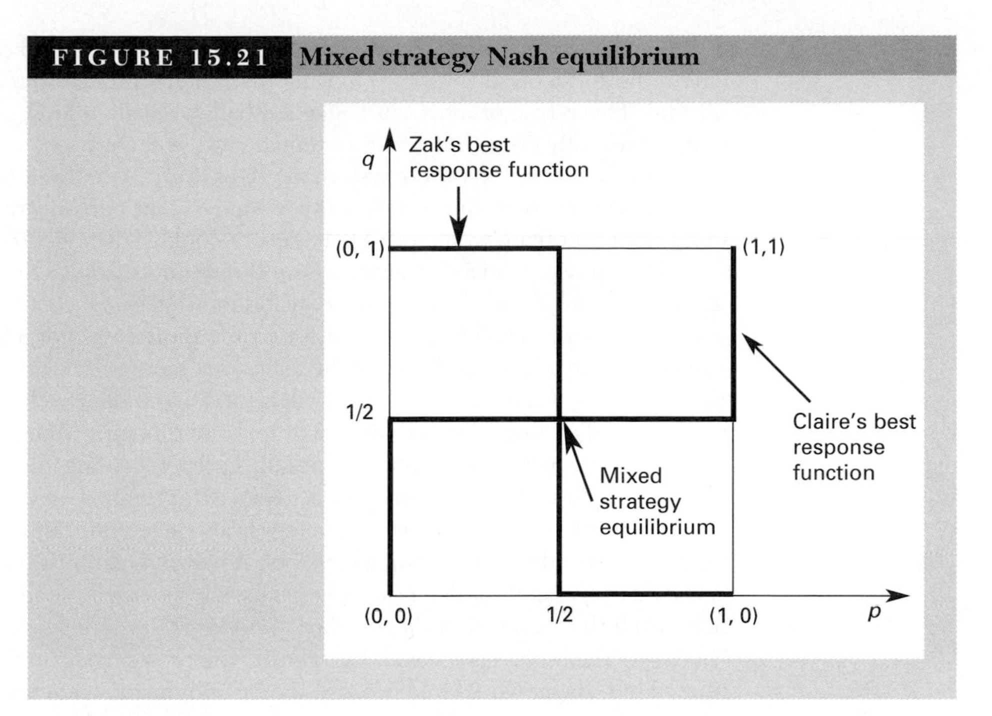

PROBLEM 15.7

Consider the following pure strategy game in which Claire is the row player and Zak the column player. Let p be the probability that Claire chooses pure strategy A and q be the probability that Zak chooses pure strategy A. Write out the payoff functions of the two players, find and plot the best response functions, and then using the diagram find one mixed strategy equilibrium and two pure strategy equilibria.

	A	B
A	1, 2	0, 0
B	0, 0	3, 6

Application: Sports and Preventing Terrorism

Now that you understand the nature of a game of mixed strategies, let's consider some general applications. If you recall, we started this chapter with an imaginary announcer at a baseball game noting the "obvious" pitch forthcoming. In virtually every competitive sporting event, there is no equilibrium in pure strategies. If the batter knows the pitcher will throw a fastball, then he looks for a fastball, but if the pitcher knows the batter is looking for a fastball, he throws a curve ball. The batter knows this, and so he expects a curve ball, and on and on it goes. It is a little bit like the joke of the two travelling salesmen who meet at the airport. "Where are you going, Fred?" asks Joe. "I'm heading to Seattle," is the reply. "You're only saying you're heading to Seattle so I'll think you're actually heading to Portland. But I know you're really heading to Seattle… Fred, why are you lying to me?"

Whenever you are playing a game where one party wins and the other loses, and where there is a disadvantage to moving first, then a mixed strategy will be an equilibrium. This is true of most sports like football, baseball, tennis, or soccer. Any team that consistently does things in a systematic way will always be on the losing end as the other team exploits their systematic behaviour. A football team may have the world's best receiver, but to throw every time to that person would be a great mistake. The other team would be able to devote double coverage to the player and succeed in winning. A mixed strategy where throws are made to the receiver based on the optimal mix of probabilities is the equilibrium strategy. Of course, with a mixed strategy sometimes you still lose. If you listen to any sportscast *after* a big game, the comments will take one of two forms. If the team won, there will be praise at how ingenious the coach was; if the team lost, there will be attacks on the coach's IQ. A coach has to play a mixed strategy. Sometimes going for a long bomb when it is third down and one yard to go works; sometimes it doesn't. The defence for the coach is that he was doing the right thing before the play is made. After the fact, anything is possible.

When you play poker, a mixed strategy is also an equilibrium. A player who never bluffs a bad hand will never win a large pot. A player who bluffs on everything will get called on every hand. Both types of players usually lose their money rather quickly. You may recall the scene from the TV show *M*A*S*H*, where the risk-averse Corporal "Radar" O'Reilly plays poker with the officers. On every single hand, when it became his time to bid, Radar would fold. Finally, on the 50th hand, when the play comes to him he announces "I'm in!" and throws some money in the pot. Everyone at the table immediately folds! The only way to win at poker is to play the optimal mix of bluffing.

Since the terrorist attacks of September 11, 2001, there has been a tremendous increase in the amount of security at the US border and airports. Anyone who travels a reasonable amount, however, notes that the inspections are very systematic. In fact, on November 19, 2001 the US government created the Transportation Security Administration (TSA), which has as part of its mandate to standardize security across airports. Hopefully much of what TSA does is unobservable to any traveller, because what is observable is too systematic. For example, when boarding planes there is a "random" search of passengers as they hand in their boarding pass. This involves being pulled aside, taking your shoes and belt off, having your luggage searched, etc. However, it appears the random person is always one of the first 10 people to approach the gate, and there's never a second person picked! Passengers now hang back and wait for the first person to be picked and then approach the gate. If such behaviour is easy for ordinary passengers to exploit, it is easy for terrorists to exploit as well. Security at the border is similar for car traffic. During an "Orange Alert" drivers pull up, turn their engines off, hand over their keys and have their trunk inspected. It is always the same … every day … every car. Such a strategy, when it is so predictable does nothing to prevent terrorism, since any terrorist will exploit the systematic behaviour (e.g., put the bomb under the hood rather than in the trunk). It is more likely, however, that such procedures are done for public relations, and the real inspections are secret and unpredictable. At least, let's hope so!

SUMMARY

This has been a long and at times difficult chapter. In this chapter, we've dealt with a situation that often doesn't come up in classical economic problems, namely that of strategic behaviour. If you think back to the first 13 chapters of this book, we were constantly looking at problems where any individual could ignore the behaviour of any other individual. We could do this because all relevant information was transmitted through markets via prices. Any given individual was so small relative to the market that their behaviour simply didn't matter. In Chapters 10 and 14 we looked at the opposite case of monopoly, and here again there was no strategic behaviour because there was no competition in the market. As we've seen in this chapter, introducing strategic behaviour creates a certain number of complications, and game theory provides the tools for dealing with these issues. By looking at strategic behaviour we drastically increase the number of applications of our general economic model. We began our study of game theory by looking at dominant and dominated strategies. These are situations where the interaction between people is quite simple: They can ignore the behaviour of others. We examined the Prisoner's Dilemma game, where we saw the dominant strategy was to fink, even though both players would be better off if they could coordinate. We saw how the Prisoner's Dilemma game applied to many situations in life, and how much behaviour can be explained as a reaction to the Pareto inferior outcome. We also saw how a simple game can have multiple equilibria, and that people often behave in ways to force the selection of one equilibria over others. Much of this chapter was spent on more difficult topics: strategic behaviour with complements and substitutes, mixed strategies, and discoordination. Although these situations were more complicated, the bottom line is that game theory provided the tools for making what seemed intractable problems relatively easy to deal with. In the next chapter we use some of the tools from this chapter to analyze how a small number of firms decide on prices and quantities.

EXERCISES

1. The Washington Huskies (football) are down 14 points when they score another touchdown. There is lots of time on the clock for another touchdown, and Don James (the coach) decides to go for the one-point conversion. Later, in the dying seconds of the game, the Huskies pull off a two-point conversion to beat the Bruins by one point. The crowd goes wild. After the game, Coach James explains his strategy: "I decided to go for the safe point first, and then attempt the risky two-point conversion." What do you think about James's strategy? Should he have gone for the two points first?

2. Suppose you were given \$3 on one condition: that you use some of the money to participate in an experiment on competitive bidding. Here is the experiment:

   You are bidding for \$9. There are two bidders: you and another bidder (called "Other") in some other room, who was given \$9 to play the game. If you bid \$$x$ ($0 < x \leq 3$) and Other bids \$$y$ ($0 < y \leq 9$), you will receive \$$9(x/(x + y))$ and Other gets \$$9(y/(x + y))$. In other words, you will divide the \$9 between you and "Other" in proportion to your bids. Thus if both of you bid the same amount, you will each receive \$4.50, regardless of your bid.

   a. Before you do any calculations, what would you bid?
   b. Calculate the Cournot-Nash equilibrium of this game. Note the payoff to Other is:
   $$p = 9 - y + 9(y/(x + y)).$$
   c. Suppose you find out that "other" has only \$3 to bid with. Would this change your answer in (a) or (b)?

   For clarity, think of yourself as Player One and the other player as Player Two. Then, the following are the payoff functions for this game:
   $$\pi_1(x,y) = 9\text{-}y + 9(y/(x+y))$$
   $$\pi_2(x,y) = 3\text{-}x + 9(x/(x+y))$$

3. Linda's utility function is $U_1(x_1, y_1, x_2)$, where x_1 is her expenditure on clothes, y_1 is her expenditure on all other goods, and x_2 is Rosa's expenditure on clothes. Linda's utility is a decreasing function of x_2. Rosa's utility function is $U_2(x_2, y_2, x_1)$, where y_2 is her expenditure on all goods other

than clothing. Rosa's utility is a decreasing unction of x_1. Each has an income of \$100. Use the budget constraints to eliminate y_1 in Linda's utility function and y_2 in Rosa's utility function, thus producing payoff functions for Linda and Rosa that involves just x_1 and x_2. What, if anything, can you say about the equilibrium of this game?

4. Reconsider the game Rock, Paper, Scissors. What is the set of mixed strategies for One and Two? What are the payoff functions for One and Two? What are the best response functions for One and Two? What is the Nash equilibrium of the game?

5. One often hears sports commentators say things like, "When the chips are down, you gotta go with your best stuff." In football they say this when it's third and long and the team absolutely must get a first down if it is to have any hope of winning, and what they mean is that the quarterback should throw a pass to his best receiver. In baseball they say it when the count is three and two and the pitcher must get the batter out if the team is to have a chance of winning, and what they mean is that the pitcher should throw his best pitch. Develop a *simple* model that will allow you to evaluate this advice — to determine when, if ever, it is good advice and when it is bad advice.

6. Consider the game of inefficient bribe-taking in Section 15.4. Suppose the demand curve for permissions was given by $D(y_1, y_2) = A - B(y_1 + y_2)$, where $A > 0$ and $B > 0$ are parameters in the demand function. Everything else about the game is the same as in the chapter. Calculate the best response functions, and find the equilibrium strategies for y_1 and y_2. What happens to the amount of bribes if A increases? What happens to the amount of bribes as B increases? Interpret these results.

7. Consider the game of team production in Section 15.4. Suppose the production function for a team is given by $G(y_1, y_2) = Ay_1 + B(y_1y_2)$, where $A > 0$ and $B > 0$. Suppose also that the cost function is given by $C = N(y_i)^2$. Now calculate the best response functions and the equilibrium strategies. In order to have a solution, what restrictions must be placed on B and N? What happens to the levels of y_1 and y_2 when N increases? What happens to these levels when A or B decrease? Interpret these results.

REFERENCES

Eaton, B. Curtis and Mukesh Eswaran. (2002). "Nooncooperative Equilibria in One-Shot Games: A Synthesis," in *Applied Microeconomic Theory: Selected Essays of B. Curtis Eaton* (author B. Curtis Eaton). Cheltenham, UK: Edward Elgar Press.

Nash, John. (1950). "Equilibrium Points in n-Person Games," Proceedings of the National Academy of Sciences, 36:48–49. (1951). "Non-Cooperative Games," *Annals of Mathematics*, 54:286–95.

Tullock, G. (1980). "Efficient Rent Seeking," in *Toward a Theory of the Rent Seeking Society*, J.M. Buchannan, R.D. Tollison, and G. Tullock (eds). College Station, TX: Texas A&M University Press.

CHAPTER 16

Game Theory and Oligopoly

homogeneous products

In this chapter, we will look at oligopolistic industries in which products are undifferentiated, or *homogeneous*. Some of the more notable oligopolistic industries characterized by **homogeneous products** are steel, crude oil, plywood, sugar, aluminum, and uranium. Ready-mix concrete in a regional market and some pulp and paper products are yet other examples of undifferentiated products. This chapter will apply many of the concepts used in the previous chapter.

16.1 Monopoly Equilibrium

We will develop and examine a number of oligopoly models in this chapter. Because we want to compare the equilibrium of each of these models of oligopoly with the monopoly equilibrium, we will be using a single set of demand and cost conditions throughout. Let us begin by setting out those demand and cost conditions and by computing the monopoly equilibrium.

We will use the following linear market demand function throughout the chapter:

$$p = 100 - y$$

unit cost of production

setup costs

where p is price and y is aggregate, or industry-wide, output. We will also assume that each firm in the industry can make the product at a constant cost of \$40 per unit. Then \$40 is the firm's marginal cost, its average cost, and what we will call its **unit cost of production**. In the first half of the chapter, we will also assume that no additional costs of production are relevant and that the oligopolists are existing, or *established* firms. In the second half, we will add the product development, or **setup costs,** that a potential firm will incur if it decides to enter an industry.

We can begin by computing the standard monopoly solution that will serve as our benchmark throughout the chapter. The standard graphic solution to the monopoly problem is shown in Figure 16.1. The monopolist will produce 30 units, sell them at a price of \$70 per unit, and earn a profit equal to \$900. (Recall that in answering Problem 10.3 you computed this monopoly equilibrium.)

It is useful to find the solution to the monopolist's problem using algebraic techniques as well. Recall that for linear market demand functions, the marginal revenue

FIGURE 16.1 The monopoly equilibrium

The monopoly equilibrium is to produce 30 units and to sell them at price $p^* = \$70$. The resulting monopoly profit is \$900, equal to the shaded area.

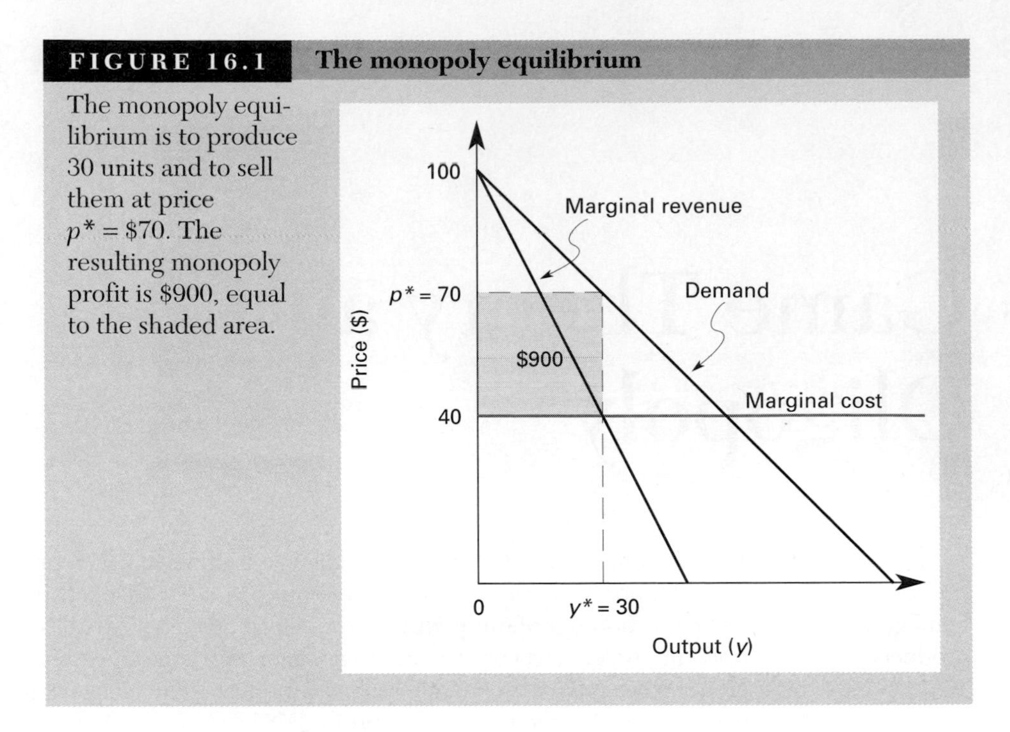

function and the market demand function intersect the price axis at the same point and that the marginal revenue function is twice as steep. Therefore,

$$MR = 100 - 2y$$

To find the profit-maximizing output, simply identify the value of y, written as y^*, at which marginal revenue $(100 - 2y)$ equals marginal cost (40): y^* is equal to 30. Next, using the demand function $(100 - y)$, we can compute price at the profit-maximizing output level (30): p^* is equal to 70. The monopolist's profit is then simply total revenue (p^*y^*) $(70 \times 30 = \$2100)$ minus total cost $(40y^* = \$1200)$: π^* is equal to \$900. The \$900 profit is represented graphically by the shaded area in Figure 16.1.

16.2 Duopoly as a Prisoner's Dilemma

duopoly

To understand the puzzles that arise in oligopolistic settings, we will begin by considering a **duopoly** — an oligopoly in which just two firms are in an industry — and we will suppose that the firms choose quantities. To further simplify the problem, we will artificially restrict the set of strategies to two elements. Specifically, we will suppose that each firm chooses to produce either a small quantity of output S equal to 15 units — or a large quantity of output L equal to 20 units. Notice that 15 units is exactly half the monopoly output of 30 units. Thus, if each firm chose strategy S, their joint output would replicate the monopoly output of 30 units. If they did so, they would also maximize their joint, or total profit. Will the firms actually choose the individual strategies that maximize their joint profit? Or will their rivalry lead them to choose individual strategies that result in a joint profit smaller than the monopoly profit?

TABLE 16.1 Duopoly profit matrix

	Second Firm's Strategy: S	Second Firm's Strategy: L
First Firm's Strategy: S	450/450	375/500
First Firm's Strategy: L	500/375	400/400

To answer this question, we must compute the payoff, or profit functions for the two firms, identify the best response functions, and then look for an equilibrium strategy combination — a strategy combination in which each firm's strategy is a best response to the other firm's strategy. Because each firm will choose either S (15 units) or L (20 units), four strategy combinations are possible in this duopoly game: (S, S) in which both firms choose S; (L, L) in which both firms choose L; (S, L) in which the first firm chooses S and the second, L; (L, S) in which the first firm chooses L and the second, S.

Now let us compute each firm's profit or payoff for each of these strategy combinations. Recall that $p = (100 - y)$. If both choose S, price will be \$70 (100 – (15 + 15)), and profit per unit produced will be \$30 (70 – 40). As a result, each firm's profit will be \$450 (15 × 30) or exactly half the monopoly profit. By contrast, if both choose L, price will be \$60 (100 – (20 + 20)), and profit per unit produced will be \$20 (60 + 40). As a result, each firm's profit will be \$400 (\$20 × 20) or less than half the monopoly profit. If the first firm chooses S and the rival firm chooses L, price will be \$65 (100 – (15 + 20)) and profit per unit produced will be \$25 (65 – 40). As a result, the first firm's profit will be \$375 (15 × 25) and the second firm's will be \$500 (20 × 25). Conversely, if the first firm chooses L and the rival firm chooses S, the first firm's profit will be \$500 and the second's \$375.

We have used these profit functions to construct the profit matrix presented in Table 16.1. The first firm's strategies are represented along the left side of the matrix, and the second firm's along the top of the matrix. Each of the four cells in the matrix corresponds to one of the four possible strategy combinations. In any cell, the entry to the left is the first firm's profit; the entry to the right, the second firm's. The payoffs for strategy combination (S, S) are \$450/\$450; the payoffs for strategy combination (S, L) are \$375/\$500; and so on.

Now let us find the best response functions. Looking at the first column of the profit matrix, we see that if the second firm chooses S, the first firm's best response is to choose L. Why? Because it earns \$500 if it chooses L and only \$450 if it chooses S. Looking at the second column of the profit matrix, we see that if the second firm chooses L, the first firm's best response is again to choose L because it earns \$400 if it chooses L and only \$375 if it chooses S. Thus, no matter which strategy the second firm pursues, the first firm's best response is to choose L. As you should recognize from Chapter 15, L is a dominant strategy for the first firm.

Because the second firm's options are exactly those of the first, its best response is likewise to choose L — regardless of what the first firm chooses. That is, L is a dominant strategy for the second firm as well as for the first. Thus, the Nash-equilibrium strategy combination is (L, L) in which each firm produces 20 units and realizes a profit of $400. Yet, if they could only agree to restrict their individual outputs to 15 units apiece, each could earn $450.

Dominant strategies are quite common, keep your eye out for them.

The Oligopoly Problem

This simplified version of the duopoly game illustrates the fundamental quandary encountered by economic theorists in trying to model oligopoly — and by real oligopolists in trying to play real oligopoly games. As we just saw, the blind pursuit of self-interest leads to an equilibrium in which both oligopolists are worse off than they might otherwise be. This leads us to one important insight:

Oligopolists have a clear incentive to collude or cooperate.

Yet we also discovered that if one firm were to cooperate by producing just 15 units, its rival's best response would be to produce 20 units. This leads us to the second, contradictory insight:

Oligopolists have a clear incentive to cheat on any simple collusive, or cooperative agreement.

We can use these results to put the Nash-equilibrium concept in perspective. Suppose the firms get together before they produce anything and attempt to agree on a strategy combination. A desirable property of any such agreement is that it be **self-enforcing agreement** in the sense that, having reached an agreement, the players have a clear incentive to follow through on the agreement when they actually decide how much output to produce. Strategy combination (S, S) is attractive because it maximizes joint profit, but a joint agreement to pursue this strategy combination is not self-enforcing. To see why not, notice that when the time comes to actually choose output, each firm will be tempted to maximize its own profit by choosing L rather than S. In contrast, the Nash-equilibrium strategy combination (L, L) is clearly self-enforcing. More generally:

self-enforcing agreement

If an agreement is not a Nash equilibrium, it is not self-enforcing.

The Prisoner's Dilemma

Hopefully you recognize the matrix game in Table 16.1 as an example of the *prisoner's dilemma*. The prisoner's dilemma is, in miniature, quite similar to the common property problems faced by common users of a water supply or an oil reservoir, discussed in Chapter 1. The outcome that makes sense for the players collectively cannot be arrived at through each player making a self-interested decision independently.

PROBLEM 16.1

Throughout the twentieth century, soldiers in battle refused to fire their weapons. Some studies in WWII found that up to 80 percent of the weapons were not fired when the enemy was engaged. How is this an example of the prisoner's dilemma?

16.3
The Cournot Duopoly Model

Now that you have some feeling for the oligopoly problem, let us drop the simplifying assumption that the firms have a choice of only two levels of output and replace it with the assumption that they have a free choice of any level of output. In this game, any quantity of output that is positive or zero is a possible strategy for a firm. The resulting game is the oldest and in many ways the most interesting oligopoly model, attributable to the French economist Auguste Cournot and dating from 1838 (Cournot, 1838/1960). Cournot noticed that only two French firms were producing mineral water for sale. He was intrigued by how these two firms would decide just how much to sell of the water that flowed from their mineral springs. In developing his model, he argued that each firm would choose the quantity that would maximize profit, taking the quantity marketed by its competitor as a given. Suppose that the second firm intended to sell 30 bottles of water. Cournot assumed that the first firm would take this quantity as given in deciding how many bottles it should sell.

Cournot model of duopoly

The central features of the **Cournot model of duopoly** are that (1) each firm chooses a quantity of output instead of a price and (2) in choosing its output, each firm takes its rival's output as a given. In Cournot's model, then, strategies are quantities of output. We will denote the first firm's strategy by y_1 and the second's strategy by y_2. A strategy combination is then (y_1, y_2). To find the equilibrium strategy combination, we first need to find the firms' payoff, or profit functions. Then we need to find the best response functions, and, finally, to look for a strategy combination in which each firm's strategy is a best response to the other's strategy.

The first firm's demand function is just

$$p_1 = (100 - y_2) - y_1$$

If the first firm produces nothing, the price will be $100 - y_2$; therefore, the intercept for the first firm's demand function is $100 - y_2$. The first firm's demand function intersects the price axis in Figure 16.2 at $100 - y_2$ and, for every unit the first firm puts on the market, price drops by \$1. (This is another example of a residual demand function, introduced in Section 10.5.) The first firm's payoff function is then

$$\pi_1(y_1, y_2) = y_1(100 - y_2 - y_1) - 40y_1$$

Notice that the larger is y_2, the smaller is the first firm's profit.

If, for each value of y_2, we can find the value of y_1 that maximizes $\pi_1(y_1, y_2)$, we will have found the first firm's best response function. To solve this profit-maximizing problem, we will adapt the techniques used to solve the monopolist's profit-maximizing problem. In Figure 16.2, notice that the first firm's marginal revenue function intersects the price axis at $100 - y_2$ and that, as usual, it is twice as steep as the demand function:

$$MR_1 = (100 - y_2) - 2y_1$$

To maximize its profit, the first firm will choose the output level y_1^* at which marginal revenue equals marginal cost. In other words, y_1^* satisfies

$$(100 - y_2) - 2y_1^* = 40$$

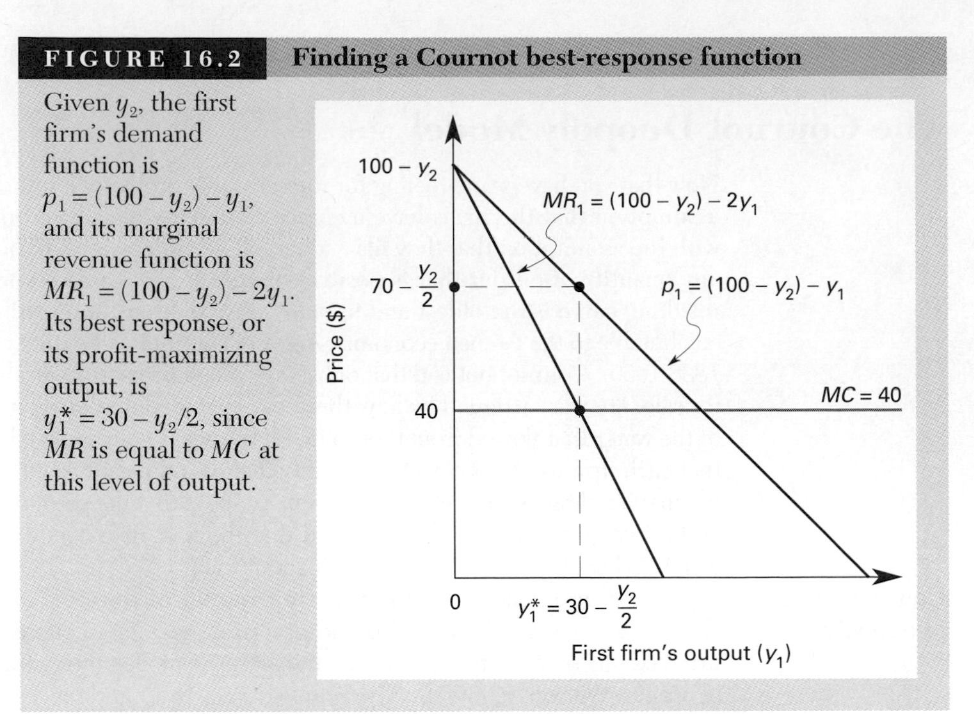

FIGURE 16.2 Finding a Cournot best-response function

Given y_2, the first firm's demand function is $p_1 = (100 - y_2) - y_1$, and its marginal revenue function is $MR_1 = (100 - y_2) - 2y_1$. Its best response, or its profit-maximizing output, is $y_1^* = 30 - y_2/2$, since MR is equal to MC at this level of output.

or, solving this expression for y_1^*,

$$y_1^* = 30 - y_2/2$$

This equation is the first firm's best response function: for any value of y_2, it gives the value of y_1 that maximizes $\pi_1(y_1, y_2)$. For example, if y_1 is zero, the first firm's best response is to produce the monopoly output of 30 units [30 – (0/2)]. If y_2 is 10, the first firm's best response is to produce 25 units [30 – (10/2)], and so on.

Because these two firms produce an undifferentiated product and have the same $40 unit cost of production, the second firm's best response function is a twin to the first firm's:

$$y_2^* = 30 - y_1/2$$

Taken together, these two best response functions can be used to find the *equilibrium strategy combination* for Cournot's model. Both firms' best response functions are shown in Figure 16.3. The equilibrium is at the point where the best response functions intersect: the equilibrium strategy combination is (20, 20). In this equilibrium, each firm produces 20 units, price is $60 (100 – (20 + 20)), profit per unit is $20 (60 – 40), and each firm's profit is $400 (20 × 20).[1]

1. More generally, we can write the duopolists' profit functions as $\pi_1(y_1, y_2) = y_1 D(y_1 + y_2) - TC(y_1)$ and $\pi_2(y_1, y_2) = y_2 D(y_1 + y_2) - TC(y_2)$ where $D(\bullet)$ is the demand function and $TC(\bullet)$ the cost function. The first firm chooses a quantity y_1^*, where the partial derivative of $\pi_1(\bullet)$ with respect to y_1 is equal to zero:

$$\partial\pi_1(y_1^*, y_2)/\partial y_1 = 0$$

Of course, this is an implicit expression for the first firm's best-response function because it determines the profit-maximizing quantity of y_1, y_1^*, for any value of y_2. Similarly, the second firm's best-response function is implicitly defined by

$$\partial\pi_2(y_1, y_2^*)/\partial y_2 = 0$$

The Cournot equilibrium is then a pair of quantities (y_1^c, y_2^c) that satisfies both best-response functions.

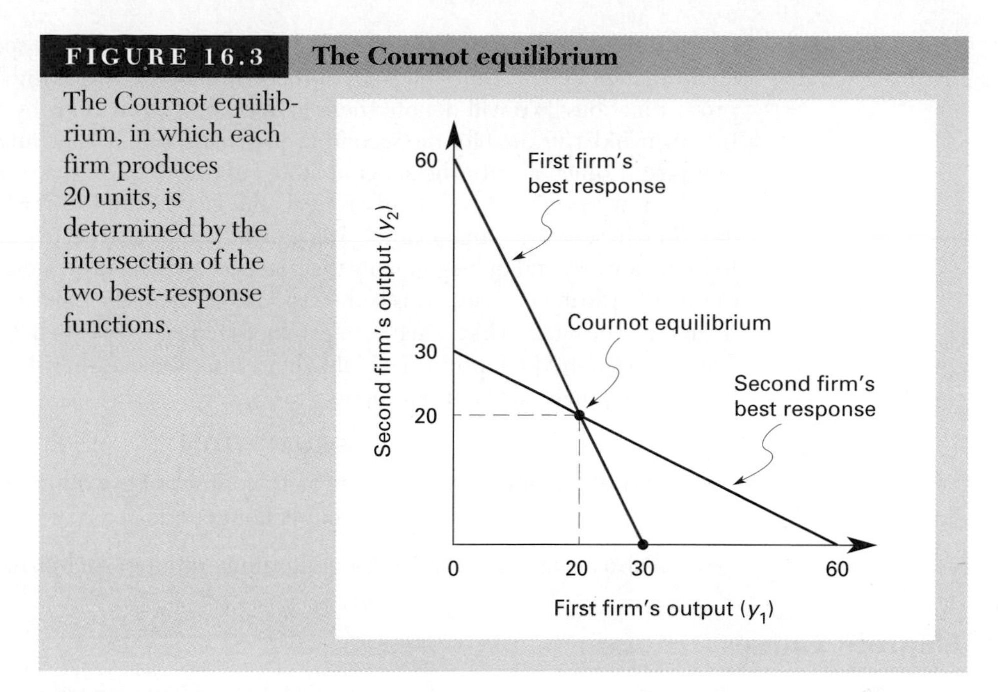

FIGURE 16.3 The Cournot equilibrium

The Cournot equilibrium, in which each firm produces 20 units, is determined by the intersection of the two best-response functions.

In what sense is this strategy combination an equilibrium? From the first firm's best response function in Figure 16.3, we see that when its rival produces 20 units, the output that maximizes the first firm's profit is likewise 20 units. Similarly, from the second firm's best response function, we see that when its rival produces 20 units, the output that maximizes the second firm's profit is also 20 units. At the equilibrium, then, neither firm can increase its profit by choosing some other output.

To find the Cournot-Nash equilibrium algebraically, we could solve the two best response functions for the equilibrium values of y_1 and y_2. However, we can take an even simpler approach. Because the two best response functions are *symmetric*, we know that both firms will produce the same quantity in equilibrium. This means that we can compute the equilibrium by setting both y_1^* and y_2 equal to y' in the first firm's best-response function, reflecting the fact that both will produce the same quantity y' in equilibrium. Then we can simply solve for y'. The resulting number $y' = 20$ is the quantity each will produce in the equilibrium of Cournot's model.[2]

Generalizing Results

Using specific demand and cost functions, we found that (1) in the Nash equilibrium, these two firms failed to maximize their joint profit, and (2) relative to joint profit-maximization, they produced too much output. Just how general are these results? To answer this question we will adapt techniques we used to study the consumer's utility-maximization problem. We will draw curves that are analogous to indifference curves and we will think of these two firms as maximizing profit subject to a constraint, just as we thought of consumers as maximizing utility subject to a budget constraint.

2. If the two firms had different marginal costs, the equilibrium would not be symmetric, and we could not use this approach to find equilibrium quantities.

Instead of working with specific payoff functions derived from specific assumptions about market demand and the costs of the firms, we will work with general payoff or profit functions. We will denote these general profit functions by $\pi_1(y_1, y_2)$ for the first firm and $\pi_2(y_1, y_2)$ for the second firm. What should we assume about these general payoff functions? In the specific model above, we saw that the larger is y_2, the smaller is $\pi_1(y_1, y_2)$. This property reflects the fact that in Cournot's model the firms are vying to serve the same market. Since price falls as aggregate quantity increases, it follows naturally and quite generally that the profit of one firm decreases as the output of the other firm increases. This is the crucial feature of the Cournot model that leads to an equilibrium in which each firm produces more output than it would if the firms were to maximize joint profit. To highlight its importance, we will write this out as the *key assumption* of the Cournot model:

ASSUMPTION

The profit of one firm decreases as the output of the other firm increases, other things being equal.

We will also assume that the Nash-equilibrium output of each firm is positive.

Isoprofit Curves

By choosing the level of profit for one firm in the Cournot model — say, the first firm — and then plotting all the strategy combinations that give the first firm the chosen level of profit, we have an *indifference curve* for that firm. These indifference curves are usually called **isoprofit curves**, but we will use the terms interchangeably. The thing to keep in mind is that the firm is *indifferent* between any two strategy combinations on the same indifference, or isoprofit-curve *because profit is constant on the curve*.

isoprofit curves

Now let us see what we can learn about a specific indifference curve for the first firm — the isoprofit curve that passes through the Nash equilibrium strategy combination. We will denote the equilibrium strategy combination by (y_1^*, y_2^*). We know that y_1^* is the best response to y_2^* — or that y_1^* maximizes the first firm's profit given that the second firm's output is y_2^*. But this suggests that we think of y_1^* as the solution to the following constrained maximization problem:

$$\text{maximize } \pi_1(y_1, y_2) \text{ by choice of } y_1$$

$$\text{subject to the constraint that } y_2 = y_2^*$$

Previous experience with this type of maximization problem helps us here. In solving the consumer's constrained maximization problem, we found that the indifference curve passing through the utility-maximizing bundle was tangent to the budget constraint at the utility-maximizing bundle. Here an indifference (or isoprofit) curve is tangent to the constraint at the solution to the firm's constrained maximization problem.

Figure 16.4 shows the isoprofit curve for the first firm that passes through the Nash equilibrium. Notice that this isoprofit curve is tangent to the constraint at the Nash equilibrium. Notice, too, that it is shaped like an inverted U. To see why, begin at the Nash equilibrium and increase y_1 by a small amount Δy_1, holding the second firm's output constant at y_2^*. As a result, the first firm's profit decreases because y_1^* maximizes the first firm's profit (given that the second firm's output is y_2^*). To compensate the first firm for this decrease in profit (that is, to get it back to the isoprofit curve), we must decrease y_2 because — given our key assumption in the Cournot model — the first firm's profit increases as the second firm's output decreases. In Figure 16.4 the required

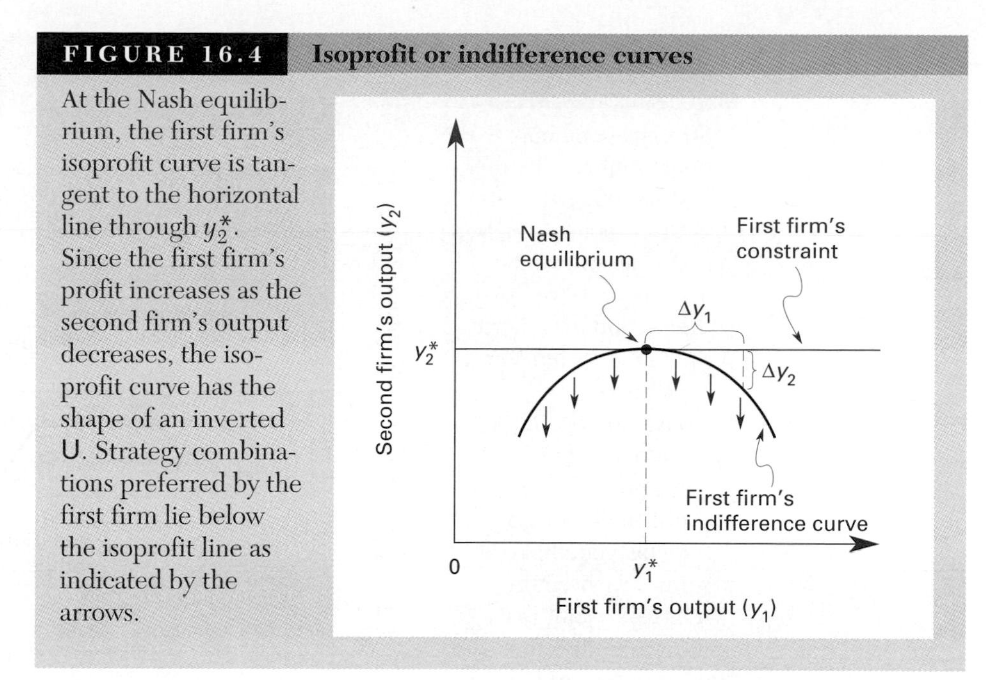

FIGURE 16.4 Isoprofit or indifference curves

At the Nash equilibrium, the first firm's isoprofit curve is tangent to the horizontal line through y_2^*. Since the first firm's profit increases as the second firm's output decreases, the isoprofit curve has the shape of an inverted U. Strategy combinations preferred by the first firm lie below the isoprofit line as indicated by the arrows.

decrease in y_2 is Δy_2. Similarly, starting again at the Nash equilibrium, if we decrease y_1 by a small amount, the first firm's profit will again fall. To compensate the firm for the loss of profit, we will again have to decrease y_2. Therefore, assuming smoothness, the first firm's isoprofit curve through the Nash equilibrium has an inverted U shape as shown in Figure 16.4. The arrows in the figure indicate the direction in which the first firm's profit increases. Any strategy combination below the indifference curve gives the first firm more profit than in the Nash equilibrium: this too follows from the key assumption of the Cournot model.

In Figure 16.5 we have introduced the second firm into the picture. The second firm's indifference curve is tangent to its constraint ($y_1 = y_1^*$) at the Nash equilibrium and has the shape of a backward C. As the arrows indicate, any strategy combination to the left of the second firm's indifference curve gives the second firm more profit than it makes in the Nash equilibrium.

Notice that any strategy combination in the shaded area of Figure 16.5 is both below the first firm's indifference curve and to the left of the second firm's indifference curve. Therefore, strategy combinations in this shaded area offer both firms more profit than they make in the Nash equilibrium. In other words:

In the Nash equilibrium of this general version of Cournot's model, the firms fail to maximize their joint profit.

Furthermore, the output of each firm is smaller for any strategy combination in the shaded area than it is in the Nash equilibrium. In other words:

Relative to joint profit maximization, the firms produce too much output in the Nash equilibrium.

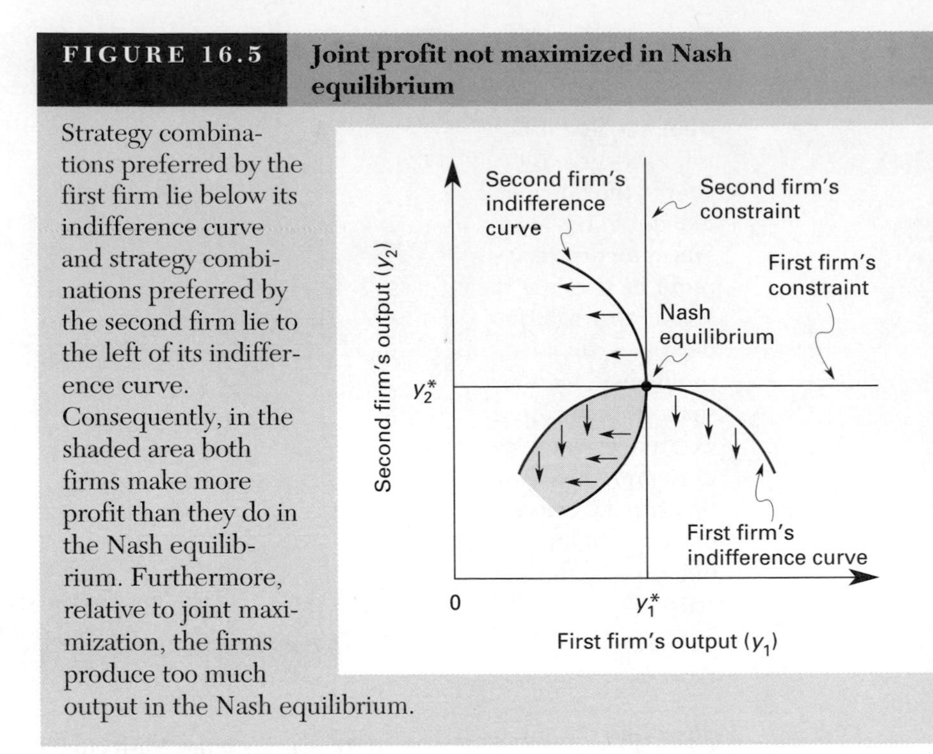

FIGURE 16.5 Joint profit not maximized in Nash equilibrium

Strategy combinations preferred by the first firm lie below its indifference curve and strategy combinations preferred by the second firm lie to the left of its indifference curve. Consequently, in the shaded area both firms make more profit than they do in the Nash equilibrium. Furthermore, relative to joint maximization, the firms produce too much output in the Nash equilibrium.

PROBLEM 16.2

Given the demand and cost conditions used in our specific Cournot model, each firm produces 40 units and gets \$400 profit in the Nash equilibrium. First verify that the first and second firms' isoprofit curves through the Nash equilibrium are

$$400 = y_1(100 - y_2 - y_1) - 40y_1$$
$$400 = y_2(100 - y_2 - y_1) - 40y_2$$

Then carefully construct a diagram analogous to Figure 16.5 for the specific Cournot model. In your diagram, identify the set of strategy combinations that both firms prefer to the Nash equilibrium.

16.4 The Cournot Model with Many Firms

What happens to the Cournot-Nash equilibrium as the number of firms in an industry expands? You can find the answer in the case of three firms in Problem 16.3.

PROBLEM 16.3

Assuming that three firms are in the industry, first show that the first firm's marginal revenue function is

$$MR_1 = (100 - y_2 - y_3) - 2y_1$$

Then show that its best response function is

$$y_1^* = 30 - (y_2 + y_3)/2$$

Finally, show that each of the three firms will produce 15 units in the Cournot-Nash equilibrium and calculate each firm's profit in the three-firm Cournot-Nash equilibrium.

Let us quickly generalize what you discovered in this problem. If n firms are in the market, the demand, marginal revenue, and profit functions of the first firm will be

$$p_1 = (100 - y_2 - y_3 - \dots - y_n) - y_1$$
$$MR_1 = (100 - y_2 - y_3 - \dots - y_n) - 2y_1$$
$$\pi_1(y_1, y_2, \dots, y_n) = y_1(100 - y_1 - y_2 - \dots - y_n) - 40y_1$$

Because the first firm will choose y_1 so that marginal revenue is equal to marginal cost, its best response function is

$$y_1^* = 30 - (y_2 + y_3 + \dots + y_n)/2$$

In this particular model, all n firms will produce the same output in the Cournot-Nash equilibrium. To find the output of one firm in this equilibrium, set $y_1^*, y_2, y_3, \dots, y_n$ all equal to y' in the first firm's best response function. Then solve for y' to obtain

$$y' = 60/(n + 1)$$

This is the output of one firm in the Cournot-Nash equilibrium when there are n firms in the market.

It is useful to compute the aggregate equilibrium output and price in the Cournot model with n firms.

$$\text{aggregate equilibrium output} = 60[n/(n + 1)]$$
$$\text{equilibrium price} = 100/(n + 1) + 40[n/(n + 1)]$$

These formulas yield a number of interesting insights into the Cournot model. First, as n increases, aggregate output increases and equilibrium price decreases. When n is 1, the aggregate output is the monopoly output of 30 units and price is \$70; when n is 2, aggregate output is 40 units and price is \$60; when n is 3, output is 45 and price is \$55; and so on. Second, as n increases without bound, the aggregate output approaches the competitive output, and the price approaches the competitive price. As you can verify, the competitive output is 60 units and the competitive price is \$40. Notice that as n gets arbitrarily large, $n/(n + 1)$ approaches 1. Therefore, in the Cournot-Nash equilibrium, aggregate output approaches 60 units and equilibrium price approaches \$40.

Finally, notice that the Cournot model is appealing because it spans a wide range of market structures. When only one firm is in a market, the Cournot-Nash equilibrium is the monopoly equilibrium. As the number of firms increases, output likewise increases. As a result, price and aggregate oligopoly profit decrease. In the limit, when there are infinitely many firms, the Cournot model is, in effect, a perfectly competitive model, since price is equal to the $40 marginal/average cost and aggregate profit vanishes. None of the other models we will consider has these intuitively appealing properties.

The Cournot Model with Complements

So far we have assumed that the firms in our Cournot model produced goods that were substitutes — in fact, perfect substitutes, since their goods were identical. In this section we examine the case in which two firms produce goods that are complements, and we show that they are playing a game of plain complements. Then we go on to examine public policy with respect to mergers, and we argue that the best policy is quite different when firms produce goods that are complements than it is when they produce goods that are substitutes.

Let y_1 and y_2 denote the quantities produced by firms One and Two respectively, $P_1(y_1, y_2)$ denote the price at which firm One can sell its good, and $P_2(y_1, y_2)$ the price at which firm Two can sell its good. Quite naturally, we suppose that $P_1(y_1, y_2)$ is a decreasing function of y_1 and that $P_2(y_1, y_2)$ is a decreasing function of y_2 – the more either firm produces, the lower is the price it receives for its good.

When the firms produce goods that are complements (DVD players and DVD discs, for example), $P_1(y_1, y_2)$ is an increasing function of y_2, and $P_2(y_1, y_2)$ is an increasing function of y_1 – the more DVD discs (respectively, DVDs) that are sold, the higher is the price at which a DVD player (respectively, DVD discs) can be sold, and vice versa. In other words, when the goods produced are complements, the cross-effects of quantities produced on prices are positive. As we saw in previous sections, when firms produce goods that are substitutes, the cross-effects of quantities on price are negative. In this sense, the nature of competition between firms varies as they produce complements or substitutes.

Let us denote firm One's cost function by $C_1(y_1)$ and Two's by $C_2(y_2)$. We assume, of course, that $C_1(y_1)$ is an increasing function of y_1, and that $C_2(y_2)$ is an increasing function of y_2. Then we can write the firms' profit functions as follows:

$$\pi_1(y_1, y_2) = y_1 P_1(y_1, y_2) - C_1(y_1)$$
$$\pi_2(y_1, y_2) = y_2 P_2(y_1, y_2) - C_2(y_2)$$

What effect does a small increase in y_2 have on One's profit, $\pi_1(y_1, y_2)$? As y_2 increases, $P_1(y_1, y_2)$ increases since the goods are complements, and for y_1 constant, One's profit increases. In other words, $\pi_1(y_1, y_2)$ is an increasing function of y_2. Similarly, $\pi_2(y_1, y_2)$ is an increasing function of y_1.

Drawing on the analysis in Section 15.4, we conclude then that this is a *game of plain complements*, a fact that yields some immediate insights into the Nash equilibrium of this game. First of all, if the firms produce positive quantities in equilibrium, Figure 15.17 is applicable. Looking narrowly at just the interests of the two firms, we see that the Nash equilibrium is not Pareto-optimal, and that they produce too little in the Nash equilibrium since the lens of missed opportunity is above and to the right of the Nash equilibrium.

In previous sections we saw that in the Cournot-Nash equilibrium of the game in which firms produced the same good, the equilibrium was not Pareto-optimal and that they produced too little in the equilibrium. Thus the direction of the distortion of the equilibrium relative to the Pareto optimum is opposite in these two cases: when the goods are complements, the firms produce too little, and when the goods are identical, they produce too much. In the following problem you are asked to generalize this comparison.

PROBLEM 16.4

Assume that the firms produce goods that are substitutes. Given this assumption, $P_1(y_1, y_2)$ is a decreasing function of y_2, and $P_2(y_1, y_2)$ is a decreasing function of y_1. First show that the firms are now playing a game of plain substitutes. Then compare the Cournot-Nash equilibrium of this game of plain substitutes with the game of plain complements that arises when the firms produce goods that are complements.

If we adopt some specific functional forms we can increase our understanding of the game of plain complements. Assume then that

$$P_1(y_1, y_2) = 120 + y_2 - 2y_1$$

$$P_1(y_1, y_2) = 120 + y_1 - 2y_2$$

Assume also that the only cost of production is a constant marginal cost equal to $30. Then the profit functions are

$$\pi_1(y_1, y_2) = y_1(120 + y_2 - 2y_1) - 30y_1$$

$$\pi_2(y_1, y_2) = y_2(120 + y_1 - 2y_2) - 30y_2$$

As you are asked to show in the following problem, the best response functions are

$$BR_1(y_2) = (90 + y_2)/4$$

$$BR_2(y_1) = (90 + y_1)/4$$

The Cournot-Nash equilibrium values are $y_1^\circ = y_2^\circ = 30$. In this equilibrium, the profit of each firm is $1800. For purposes of comparison, we note that the quantities that maximize the sum of profits of the two firms are $y_1 = y_2 = 45$, and that these quantities generate a profit of $2025 for each firm.

PROBLEM 16.5

First verify that the expression in the text for One's best response function is accurate. One way of doing so is to subtract $y_1(120 + y_2 - 2y_1) - 30y_1$ from $(y_1 + \Delta)(102 + y_2 - 2(y_1 + \Delta)) - 30(y_1+\Delta)$ to get an expression for $\pi_1(y_1+\Delta, {}_y2) - \pi_1(y_1,y_2)$. Using this expression, find the value of y_1 as a function of y_2 such that $\pi_1(y_1 + \Delta, y_2) - \pi_1(y_1,y_2)$ is negative for all Δ π 0. This function is, of course, One's best response function. You may want to review Section 15.4, where we first used this technique, to find a best response function. Second, intersect the two best response functions to find the Nash equilibrium.

Application: Merger Policy

In a merger, one firm buys another, with the result that firms that were formerly competitors end up under one roof as one firm. Most developed economies have a public policy with respect to mergers. It is often the case that firms wanting to merge must get permission to do so from a board that reviews mergers. In assessing any merger, the board applies a set of guidelines that indicate the situations in which mergers are permissible.

Does our analysis tell us anything about the reasons firms might want to merge and the way in which merger guidelines ought to be formulated? Regarding the first of these questions, our analysis says quite a lot. Since the Cournot-Nash equilibrium is not Pareto-optimal taking into account only the narrow interests of the firms themselves, the firms have a clear profit incentive to merge regardless of whether the game they are playing is one of plain complements or plain substitutes.

Although not quite so obvious, it also says quite a lot about merger guidelines. Consider first the merger of firms producing the same good. Let us use the example we examined in Section 16.2. If we suppose that prior to the merger the firms are locked in a Cournot-Nash equilibrium, then the profit of each would rise from \$400 to \$450. Other things being equal, from a policy perspective, an increase in profit would seem to be a good thing since it means that the owners of the firm have more income that they can spend on the goods and services that they prefer to consume. The trouble is that other things are not equal. The merger entails a decrease in aggregate quantity produced from 40 units to 30, with a consequent loss of consumers' surplus. As you can easily verify, the loss in consumers' surplus is larger than the gain in profits. Hence, if the maximization of total surplus is the policy objective, this merger is not one that ought to be approved.

Now consider the merger of firms producing goods that are complements. In the example we worked out above, if the firms are initially locked in the Cournot-Nash equilibrium from Problem 16.4, when they merge the profit of each will rise from \$1800 to \$2025. But what happens to the consumers' surplus? The merger would result in an increase in quantity produced of each good from 30 to 45 units, so consumers' surplus also increases. Hence, if the maximization of total surplus is the policy objective, this merger is one that ought to be approved since both the firms and their customers benefit from it.

Real mergers are somewhat more complex than our examples, but we nevertheless get an important and quite robust insight into sensible merger policy from them. Regardless of whether the firms produce goods that are substitutes or complements, a merger tends to increase profit. If the goods they produce are complements, consumers' surplus also increases and there would appear to be no reason to put a policy roadblock in the way of such mergers. On the other hand, if the goods the firms produce are substitutes, merger of the firms will tend to decrease consumers' surplus and the decrease in consumer's surplus may very well outweigh the increase in profit. From a policy perspective, mergers of this sort deserve a careful review. Based on our analysis, in the absence of offsetting efficiencies from the merger, mergers of this sort ought not to be approved.

16.5 The Bertrand Model

Bertrand model

The **Bertrand model** substitutes prices p_1 and p_2 for quantities y_1 and y_2 as the variables to be chosen. Thus, the Cournot and Bertrand equilibria are logical first cousins. Cournot identified what we now call the Nash equilibrium when the firms' strategic decisions centred on a choice of quantities, and Bertrand identified the Nash equilibrium when their strategic decisions centred instead on a choice of prices. We want to find the Nash equilibrium strategy combination — or, more simply, the Bertrand-Nash equilibrium — *when the firms choose prices instead of quantities.*

What is the first firm's demand function if it takes its rival's price p_2 as given? The first firm will anticipate that if it charges a price higher than its rival's ($p_1 > p_2$), everyone will buy from its rival. If the first firm charges a price lower than its rival's ($p_1 < p_2$), however, everyone will buy from it. And if it charges a price equal to its rival's ($p_1 = p_2$), the firms will split the market. For convenience, let us assume that they split the market in half. The resulting — and somewhat peculiar — market demand function is

$$\begin{aligned} y_1 &= 0 && \text{if } p_1 > p_2 \\ y_1 &= 100 - p_1 && \text{if } p_1 < p_2 \\ y_1 &= (100 - p_1)/2 && \text{if } p_1 = p_2 \end{aligned}$$

(Notice that in these equations, the roles of price and quantity have been inverted: quantity is now on the left and price on the right.)

Given this demand function, what will the first firm's profit function look like? If p_1 is greater than p_2, the first firm attracts no business. That is, y_1 is equal to zero, and its profit is also zero:

$$\pi_1(p_1, p_2) = 0 \qquad \text{if } p_1 > p_2$$

On the other hand, if p_1 is less than p_2, the first firm captures the whole market. That is, y_1 is $100 - p_1$, and its profit per unit is $p_1 - 40$. Therefore, its total profit is

$$\pi_1(p_1, p_2) = (p_1 - 40)(100 - p_1) \qquad \text{if } p_1 < p_2$$

If p_1 is equal to p_2, however, the two firms evenly split the market; that is, y_1 is $(100 - p_1)/2$, and profit per unit is $p_1 - 40$. Therefore, the first firm's total profit is

$$\pi_1(p_1, p_2) = (p_1 - 40)(100 - p_1)/2 \qquad \text{if } p_1 = p_2$$

To find the first firm's best-response function, we need to answer the following question: Given p_2, what value of p_1 maximizes the first firm's profit? There are four possible cases to consider. Let us begin with the two easy cases. First, if its rival charges a price greater than the monopoly price of \$70, the first firm can capture the whole market with a lower price, and its best response is obviously to charge the monopoly price of \$70. Second, if its rival charges a price that is less than the \$40 cost per unit produced, the first firm's best response is to charge any price greater than p_2. Why? Because by choosing this price, the first firm will attract no business and will therefore incur a zero profit — an outcome that is clearly better than incurring a negative profit by matching or undercutting its rival's price.

Now let us turn to the more interesting third case, where the second firm's price is greater than the \$40 cost per unit produced and less than or equal to the monopoly price of \$70. The diagram of the profit function for this case is shown in Figure 16.6. The first firm's price is on the horizontal axis and its profit on the vertical axis. The profit function is composed of three segments. First, if the first firm chooses a price lower than its rival's ($p_1 < p_2$), as the first firm's price increases, its profit likewise increases. In this segment of the profit function, the profit-maximizing price is arbitrarily close to — but less than — p_2. Thus, when p_1 is less than p_2, the first firm's maximum

FIGURE 16.6 **Finding a Bertrand best-response function**

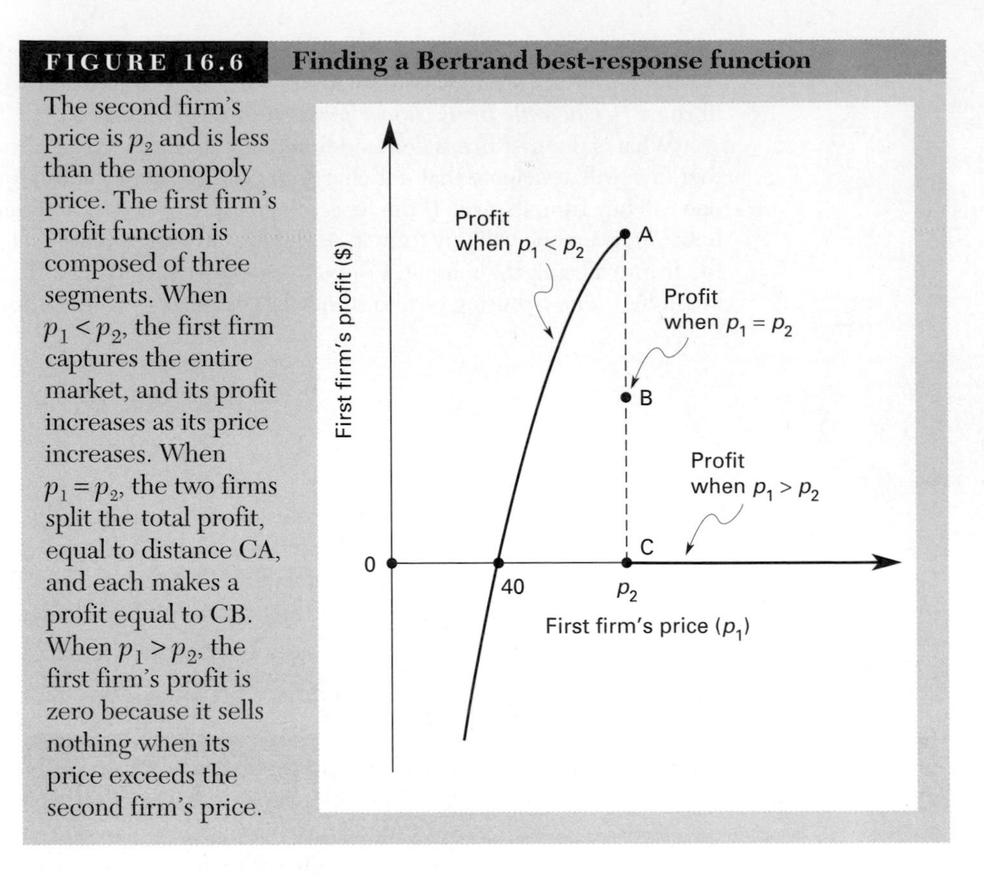

The second firm's price is p_2 and is less than the monopoly price. The first firm's profit function is composed of three segments. When $p_1 < p_2$, the first firm captures the entire market, and its profit increases as its price increases. When $p_1 = p_2$, the two firms split the total profit, equal to distance CA, and each makes a profit equal to CB. When $p_1 > p_2$, the first firm's profit is zero because it sells nothing when its price exceeds the second firm's price.

profit is distance CA, and its best price is a price just less than p_2.[3] Second, if the first firm chooses a price equal to its rival's price ($p_1 = p_2$), its profit drops by a factor of one-half because it now evenly splits the profit with the rival firm. The first firm's profit is therefore just half of the distance CA, or the distance CB. Third, if the first firm chooses a price greater than its rival's price ($p_1 > p_2$), its profit is zero. Graphically, the firm's zero profit is represented by the horizontal axis from point C onward to the right. What have we learned? When its rival's price is greater than the marginal cost of $40 and less than or equal to the monopoly price of $70, the firm's best response is to undercut its rival's price by just a hair's breadth.

Finally, let us take up the fourth case, where the second firm sets a price that is exactly equal to the marginal cost of $40 per unit. If the first firm sets a price lower than $40, it will incur a loss on every unit it sells, and its profit therefore will be negative. On the other hand, if it sets a price greater than or equal to $40, its profit will be equal to zero. Why? If it chooses any price above $40, its profit will be zero because it will attract no business. And if it chooses a price equal to $40, its profit will be zero because it will break even on every unit it sells. Because making a zero profit is better than making a negative profit, the first firm's best response is to charge any price greater than or equal to $40.

Let us summarize the results with respect to the first firm's best response to its rival's price. (The second firm's best-response function is obviously symmetric.)

---

3. Strictly speaking, the best price for the first firm is not well defined here since there is no largest price less than p_2. We will, however, ignore this point.

1. p_1^* is \$70 if $p_2 > 70$
2. p_1^* is any price greater than p_2 if $p_2 < 40$
3. p_1^* is just less than p_2 if $40 < p_2 \leq 70$
4. p_1^* is any price greater than or equal to p_2 if $p_2 = 40$

What is the Bertrand-Nash equilibrium — that is, what is the equilibrium strategy combination — when firms choose prices? From (4), we see that in equilibrium each firm chooses a price equal to \$40. Why? If the second firm sets a price of \$40, then (4) tells us that the first firm's best response is also to set a price of \$40. (Notice, however, that $p_1 = 40$ is not the only best response, since charging any price higher than \$40 also results in zero profit.) Similarly, if the first firm sets a price of \$40, then the second firm's best response is to set a price of \$40. Therefore, the equilibrium strategy combination is $p_1 = 40$ and $p_2 = 40$. Notice that in this equilibrium, each firm's profit is exactly zero.

16.6 The Collusive Model of Oligopoly

Although intuitively appealing, the Cournot model may seem a bit naïve. Its central assumption, after all, is that oligopolists choose their outputs independently, taking the output of rivals as given. And the Bertrand model seems extraordinarily naïve, in that by setting price independently, the oligopolists arrive at an equilibrium in which no one makes any profit whatsoever in a potentially lucrative market. Indeed, in a number of industries dominated by a few firms, *collusive* rather than *independent* behaviour seems to be more likely. For example, the two US companies that control 90 percent of the infant formula market, Ross Laboratories and Mead Johnson, have nearly always raised prices by about the same amounts and at about the same times. The four ready-mix concrete firms in Toronto that control 92 percent of the industry set uniform prices for concrete products for at least five years. In this section, we will set out a **collusive model** of oligopoly to see what happens when oligopolists do decide to collude on a joint strategy. Then we will compare the outcome, or equilibrium, in the collusive model with the monopoly equilibrium on the one hand and with the Cournot and Bertrand equilibria on the other.

collusive model

We can begin with the simplest case of a duopoly. The best equilibrium that the duopolists can jointly come up with is one in which joint output, $y_1 + y_2$, is equal to the monopoly output of 30 units. That is, since each firm's marginal cost is \$40, the two can jointly do no better than the monopoly equilibrium. They might agree, for example, to produce half the monopoly output (15 units) apiece. The price per unit will then be \$70, and each will earn half the monopoly profit, or \$450.

By contrast, each duopolist in the Cournot equilibrium earns only \$400, or \$50 less than in the collusive equilibrium. This means that the Cournot equilibrium, although individually rational, is collectively irrational because each firm earns less profit than it could have earned in the collusive equilibrium. The primary objection to the Cournot model is that if firms do find themselves at the Cournot equilibrium, they have a clear incentive to attempt to form a collusive agreement.

These remarks are even more appropriate to the Bertrand model. Each duopolist in the Bertrand equilibrium earns exactly \$0 profit, or \$450 less than in the collusive equilibrium. Like the Cournot equilibrium, the Bertrand equilibrium is individually rational, but collectively irrational. Again, firms at the Bertrand equilibrium have a clear incentive to collude. Does this mean that the collusive model makes better sense of oligopoly than do the Cournot and Bertrand models?

Not necessarily. To see why not, we will focus on the Cournot model. Suppose that the two rivals agree to split the monopoly output evenly by producing 15 units apiece. Is this agreement self-enforcing? Suppose that the first firm is convinced that its rival will abide by the agreement to produce just 15 units. By consulting the first firm's best-response function, we can infer that its private incentive is to respond by producing 22.5 units [i.e., 30 – (15/2)]. If it actually were to break the agreement by producing 22.5 units — and if its rival kept to the agreement by producing only 15 units — then the total industry output would be 37.5 (i.e., 22.5 + 15), and price would be $62.5 (i.e., 100 – 37.5). The first firm's profit would be $506.25 [i.e., 22.5 × (62.5 – 40)] and its rival's would be $337.50 [i.e., 15 × (62.5 – 40)].

If the first firm could get away with this deceptive strategy, it would earn an additional $56.25 in profit (506.25 – 450) relative to the collusive equilibrium. Again relative to the collusive equilibrium, its rival would lose $112.50 (450 – 337.50) — a loss that exceeds the first firm's gain. Therefore, the collusive strategy is collectively rational because it maximizes joint profit. But, it is individually irrational because each firm's private profit incentive urges it to depart from the collusive equilibrium; that is, the collusive agreement to produce 15 units of output apiece is *not* self-enforcing.

We have once again encountered what we called the oligopoly problem in Section 16.2. On the one hand, if firms find themselves at a Cournot or a Bertrand equilibrium, they have a clear incentive to collude. On the other hand, if firms manage to forge a collusive agreement, there is a clear private incentive for each party to cheat on the collusive agreement.

The history of the OPEC cartel illustrates both sides of the problem. OPEC is a cartel of oil-exporting countries that operates by assigning export quotas to individual member countries in an attempt to reduce the supply of crude oil to the world market. At various times, particularly during the mid-1970s, the cartel has been successful in restricting supply and thereby raising prices. At other times, however, many OPEC member countries have cheated on their collusive agreement by exporting more than their allotted quotas. For instance, in the late 1980s and early 1990s, newspapers often carried reports about individual OPEC countries that were "keeping their spigots wide open" — that is, exceeding their quotas on the sale of crude oil in the international oil market. As you will discover in the following problem, in the Cournot model, the individual incentive to cheat on a collusive agreement increases as the number of parties to the agreement increases, which means that the larger the number of firms in an industry, the less likely is a collusive equilibrium. If the number of firms is large enough, some firm or firms will succumb to the temptation to cheat, thereby destroying the collusive agreement.

PROBLEM 16.6

If three parties form a collusive agreement, the equilibrium is to allocate 10 units to each member at a profit of $300 per member. Show that if one party decides to cheat and the other two do not, the cheater will produce 20 units and enjoy a profit of $400. Therefore, the inducement to cheat is $100 when three firms form a collusive agreement, but only $56.25 when just two firms form the agreement. Now suppose that four firms are party to the agreement and that each firm is allocated 7.5 units. What is the inducement to cheat in this case?

16.7 Experimental Evidence

What are professional economists — and economics students — to make of such a profusion of oligopoly models, all yielding different equilibria? There is no consensus. Indeed, some evidence from experimental economics suggest that there can be *no* general oligopoly model applicable to all situations — at least, not unless the model takes into account the inclinations of the individual economic players.

Let us look briefly at a series of experiments that Fouraker and Siegal (1963) conducted to test the duopoly equilibrium. Two subjects, like the firms in the Cournot model, chose quantities. In the first set of 14 experiments, two subjects played the "duopoly game." Each was given a table specifying his or her individual payoffs (or profits) as functions of the quantities provided by the two players. The two subjects then chose quantities a number of times. In these experiments, each subject knew only the quantities that the other player had chosen in all previous periods — and, of course, his or her own quantities and profits. The equilibrium in the last period of this set of experiments closely approximated the Cournot equilibrium.

In a second set of 14 experiments, both subjects were given more information: both knew their own quantities and profits in all previous periods and those of the other player. Relative to the first set of experiments, they had additional information regarding the other player's profits. In about one-half of these experiments, the equilibrium in the last period closely approximated the Cournot equilibrium; in about one-third, it approximated the collusive equilibrium; and in about one-sixth, it approximated the competitive equilibrium.

In another series of experiments, the subjects were asked to choose price, not quantity. When both subjects knew only the price charged by the other subject in all previous periods, the best approximation was almost invariably the Bertrand equilibrium. When both subjects knew the other subject's profits in all periods as well, in nine cases the best approximation was the Bertrand equilibrium; in four, it was the collusive equilibrium; and in four, it was an intermediate equilibrium.

Taken together, these experiments suggest that no single model is applicable to all oligopoly situations. Perhaps the most economists can hope for is a selection of oligopoly models, each applicable to a particular range of economic circumstances.

16.8 Repeated Play, Supergames, and Richer Strategies

The oligopoly models that we have been looking at do not capture one very important aspect of real-world oligopolies. Because the models are essentially static, or concerned with strategies and payoffs in just one period, they fail to capture the long-term dynamic interplay that characterizes most real-world oligopoly relationships. We have no adequate way to capture in these one-period models the phenomenon of what we might call "repeated play" of similar oligopoly games.

Once we recognize that oligopolists repeatedly play games of strategy and counterstrategy as they jockey for market power — often for extended periods of time — we can imagine that the strategies available to them are potentially far richer than our simpler static models suggest. We will do an intuitive treatment of one strategic possibility developed by James Friedman (1971) that arises under repeated play.

As you know, although collusive agreements are collectively more beneficial to oligopolists, the individual firms nevertheless have strong private incentives to try to grab a larger share of the market for themselves by cheating on the agreement. To induce all members of a collusive agreement to stick to the bargain, Friedman considered **punishment strategies** that oligopolists can devise for breaches of the collusive agreement.

punishment strategies

These punishments must be both *severe* and *credible*. It is obvious that not all punishments satisfy both these criteria. Suppose, for example, that each duopolist threatens to murder the other duopolist for a breach of their agreement. In this case, the punishment is severe enough to deter breach, but it is not credible because carrying it out would surely result in imprisonment or worse for the punisher. We will say that a punishment strategy is credible if it is in the punisher's self-interest to carry out the punishment once a breach of the agreement occurs.

Suppose that two firms play their duopoly game an infinite number of times, in what is sometimes called a **supergame**. Remember that in any particular period, the collusive solution for each is to produce 15 units, and the Cournot solution is for each to produce 20 units. The objective is to devise punishment strategies that will make the collusive solution of 15 units in each period not only the collectively rational but also the individually rational, or profit-maximizing, solution.

supergame

For a possible set of strategies, we will consider the following variant on the fable of the donkey and the carrot and stick. The first firm's carrot is its promise to produce 15 units in any given period, provided that its rival has produced 15 units in all previous periods. Its stick is its threat to provide 20 units in all subsequent periods if it ever discovers that its rival has cheated on the agreement by producing more than 15 units. The second firm's strategy precisely parallels the first firm's. Having devised and announced these carrot-and-stick strategies to each other, the duopolists break off communication and go their separate ways.

Is the threatened punishment severe enough to encourage each duopolist to produce just 15 units in each period? Is it credible? To answer the first question, we need to compare a firm's maximum profit if it abides by the collusive agreement with its maximum profit if it breaches the agreement. Let us focus on the second firm's decision. Given the first firm's announced strategy, if the second firm produces 15 units in all periods, it will earn $450 in each period. As we saw in Section 16.6, if it cheats on the agreement, the best it can do in the present period is to produce 22.5 units (the profit-maximizing quantity, given that the first firm produces 15 units). Its profit is then $506.25 in the present period. If the first firm then carries out its threat by raising its own output to 20 units in all subsequent periods, the best that the second firm can do thereafter is to produce 20 units in each period — thereby inducing the Cournot equilibrium — and its profit will then be $400 in every subsequent period. In contrast to the collusive solution, then, if the second firm breaches the collusive agreement, it gains $56.25 in the present period but loses $50 in all future periods. Whether the punishment is severe enough to be a deterrent then depends on the rate of interest. If a dollar today is not worth significantly more than a dollar tomorrow, then the punishment of losing $50 per period forever will be large enough to offset the temptation of gaining $56.25 today. In other words:

Unless the interest rate is extremely high, the punishment is severe enough to deter cheating.

The other question is whether the punishment is credible. That is, will it be in the first firm's self-interest to carry out its threat by actually producing 20 units in each future period if its rival breaches the collusive agreement? Let us begin with the second firm's strategy. Once it has cheated on the agreement, it will expect the first firm to carry out its threat to produce 20 units. In response, it will decide to produce 20 units as well. Let us see what the first firm's response will be in this situation. Because it will expect the second firm to produce 20 units, the first firm will serve its own self-interest best by producing 20 units as well — thereby producing the Cournot equilibrium in all future periods. The punishment is therefore credible because the first firm will actually make good on its threat to increase its own production when it discovers that its rival has cheated:

If the collusive agreement is breached in some period, the announced punishment strategy will produce the Cournot equilibrium in every subsequent period.

We now know that if either firm breaches the collusive agreement to produce 15 units in each period, the duopolists will be locked into the Cournot solution for all future periods. If the interest rate is not too high, neither firm will ever breach the agreement, and the punishment strategy does make the collectively rational solution individually rational as well.

Repeated oligopoly games open up many more questions and possibilities than our example suggests. We implicitly assumed, for example, that each firm could detect cheating by its rival(s). In an industry in which market demand is subject to significant random variation or in which the number of firms is comparatively large, detection will be a harder task. If detection is too difficult, the punishment strategy simply will not do the job.[4]

PROBLEM 16.7

Salop (1986) has identified an interesting punishment strategy in observing that in some industries, all the firms in the market agree to include in their contracts with buyers a *most-favoured-customer clause*. The clause stipulates that if a firm sells the same product to another customer at a lower price within some specified period of time, then the original customer can claim a rebate equal to the price differential multiplied by the quantity purchased. Explain how such clauses — which are apparently in the individual customer's interest — can be used to support a collusive pricing agreement that is clearly not in the interest of consumers.

16.9 The Limit-Output Model

Because the number of firms has been treated as exogenous, the models we have explored to this point have served only as an introduction to the important and intriguing topic of oligopoly. In the rest of this chapter, we focus on the theory of oligopoly in the long run. In these models, the number of firms — or the market structure — is *endogenous*. The number of firms in any industry is determined by economic considerations, and, in oligopolistic industries, as in competitive industries, the key process in determining the long-run equilibrium is the *possibility of entry*.

We will explore the approach to endogenous market structure pioneered by Joe Bain (1956) and Paolo Sylos-Labini (1962), and we will explore more recent exten-

4. Stigler (1969) presents a good discussion of the conditions that are and are not conducive to collusion. Axelrod's *The Evolution of Cooperation* is a fascinating account of how people often manage to cooperate in repeated games in a variety of economic and noneconomic contexts.

sions of their approach. Bain and Sylos-Labini were the first to recognize the critical role that entry plays in determining the structure of an oligopolistic industry. In particular, they addressed the key question: under what conditions will a potential firm find it *unprofitable* to enter an oligopolistic market? The answer to this question is what we will call a *no-entry condition* — a condition that obviously must be satisfied in any long-run oligopoly equilibrium.

limit-output model

limit-price model

Modigliani (1958) formalized some of the insights of Bain and Sylos-Labini into the **limit-output model**, more commonly called the **limit-price model**. Our objective here is not to produce a general model, but to introduce you to useful ways of thinking about endogenous market structure in oligopolistic industries.

Barriers to Entry

We will continue to use the market demand and cost functions from the first half of the chapter, with one important exception. Given the cost function we have been using, entry will continue until the competitive equilibrium prevails — that is, until price is driven down to marginal cost, or $40. Therefore, the theory of market structure is interesting only when there is some *barrier* to the entry of new firms.

barrier to entry

A natural **barrier to entry** — and the one that we will be using — is a *setup cost*. Such costs are ubiquitous and can be very large indeed. For example, to build a factory, purchase equipment, and set up an assembly line costs millions. Let us suppose that all firms must incur a setup cost equal to $\$S$. In any one period, the rate of interest will determine the fixed cost associated with the setup cost. Denoting the rate of interest by i, the fixed cost is

$$K = iS$$

Adding this fixed cost to previous costs yields the following cost function:

$$C(y) = K + 40y$$

The fixed cost associated with product development — or the barrier to entry — is captured in the first term on the right, K, and what we can now call the variable costs of production are captured in the second term, $40y$.

The key assumption in the limit-output model of market structure — which we introduced as the *Sylos postulate* in Chapter 10 — is that any potential entrant takes the current industry-wide output as a given. For example, if the industry is producing 30 units at present, a potential entrant assumes that if it actually enters the industry, the established firms will continue to produce 30 units. This model is then an extension of the Cournot model, and we can use what we know about that model to develop the limit-output model.

The Inducement to Entry

inducement to entry

If the fixed cost K is the barrier to entry in this model, what is the **inducement to entry** in this market? It is the *excess of revenue over variable costs*. To see what is involved in calculating the inducement to entry, let us suppose that the established firm or firms are currently producing 30 units, and then compute the excess of revenue over variable costs the entrant would earn if it were to enter the market. Figure 16.7 shows the market demand function, the entrant's residual demand function ($p_E = 70 - y_E$), and the entrant's marginal revenue function ($MR_E = 70 - 2y_E$) for this case. The entrant's demand and marginal revenue functions are plotted relative to the origin labelled 0_E, which is 30 units to the right of the origin labelled 0. If the entrant were to enter this market, it would produce 15 units, since its marginal revenue is equal to its marginal cost at this output level. If it did produce 15 units, the price would be $55, its revenue would be $825 (55 × 15), and its variable costs would be $600 (40 × 15). In this case, the inducement to entry is $225 (825 – 600), equal to the shaded area in Figure 16.7. Will a potential entrant actually enter this market or will it stay out? If the barrier to entry $*K* is less than the inducement to entry — that is, if *K* is less than $225 — it will enter. If *K* is greater than or equal to $225, it will stay out. (For simplicity, we are assuming that a potential entrant will not enter if it anticipates zero profit.)

What is the inducement to entry when established firms produce no output? Or 60 units? Or, more generally, *y* units? The first two questions are easily answered. If established firms produce nothing, the inducement to entry is $900 — the excess of revenue over variable costs for a monopolist. If the established firms produce 60 units, the inducement is $0 because the entrant's residual demand curve is then $p_E = 40 - y_E$. As you can see, the inducement to entry shrinks as the output of established firms grows. The third question is harder and more interesting. From the Cournot model, we see that when established firms produce *y* units, the entrant's best response is

$$y_E^* = 30 - y/2$$

The entrant's residual demand function is just

$$p_E = (100 - y) - y_E$$

FIGURE 16.7 **The inducement to entry**

Since the monopolist produces 30 units, the entrant anticipates the residual demand curve in this figure. If it were to enter, it would maximize profit by producing 15 units, and it would anticipate profit per period equal to the shaded area, which is the inducement to entry.

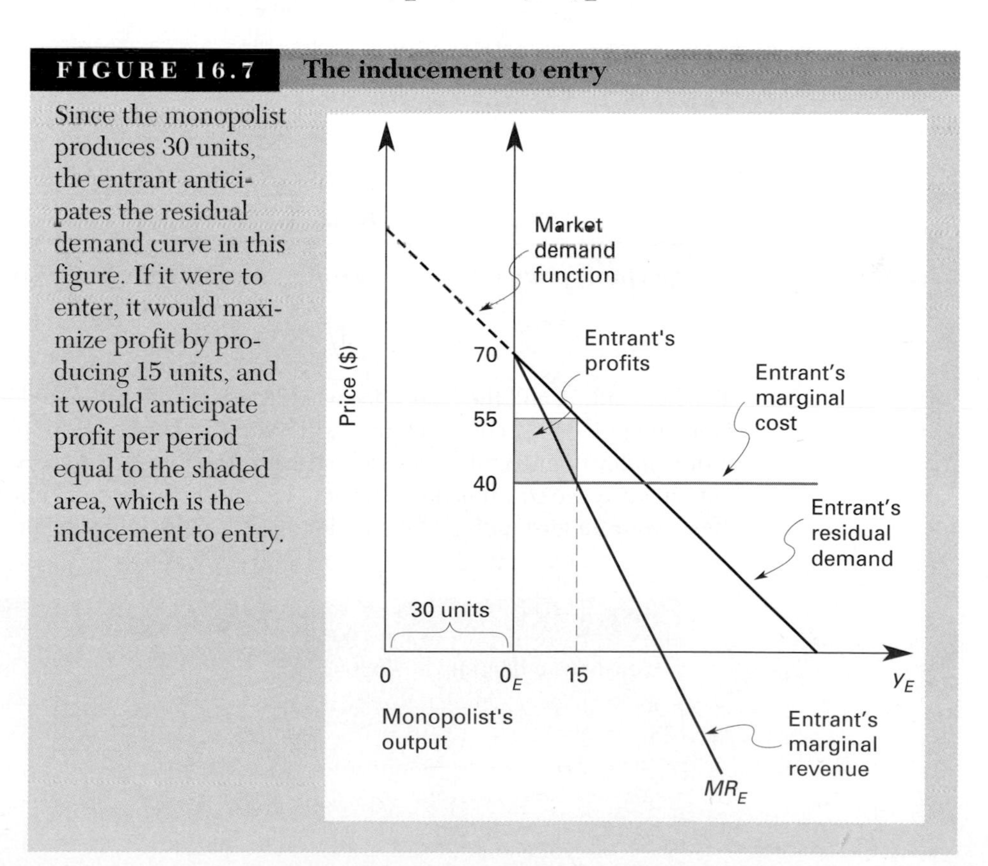

Using this demand function, we can compute the price that will prevail if the entrant produces y_E^* units:

$$p_E^* = 70 - y/2$$

We can compute p_E^* minus the \$40 marginal cost, or profit per unit:

$$p_E^* - 40 = 30 - y/2$$

The inducement to entry, y_E^* multiplied by $(p_E^* - 40)$, is then

$$\text{inducement to entry} = (30 - y/2)^2$$

This expression gives us the excess of revenue over variable costs that an entrant would earn if established firms continued to produce y units after entry. Entry will occur if the inducement to entry exceeds K, but will not occur if it is less than or equal to K. We will call the smallest value of y such that no entry occurs the **limit output**. Alternatively, we can think of the limit output as the value of y such that the inducement to entry is equal to the barrier to entry. Letting y_L denote the limit output, we have

limit output

$$(30 - y_L/2)^2 = K$$

Or, solving for y_L

$$y_L = 60 - 2K^{1/2}$$

For instance, if K is \$100, the limit output is 40 units; if K is \$225, the limit output is 30; and so on. We can use the limit output to write the **no-entry condition** in a different way:

no-entry condition

Entry will not occur if the output of established firms is greater than or equal to the limit output, y_L.

limit price

The **limit price** is just the price associated with the limit output, $100 - y_L$, or

$$p_L = 40 + 2K^{1/2}$$

The limit output and the limit price when K is \$400 are presented in Figure 16.8. The limit output is 20, and the limit price \$80. When established firms produce 20 units, the inducement to entry of \$400 is identical to the barrier to entry K. Therefore, the entrant's average cost function is tangent to its residual demand function at point E. To check your understanding of the limit output, try the following problem.

PROBLEM 16.8

Construct a diagram analogous to Figure 16.8 for the case in which K is \$196.

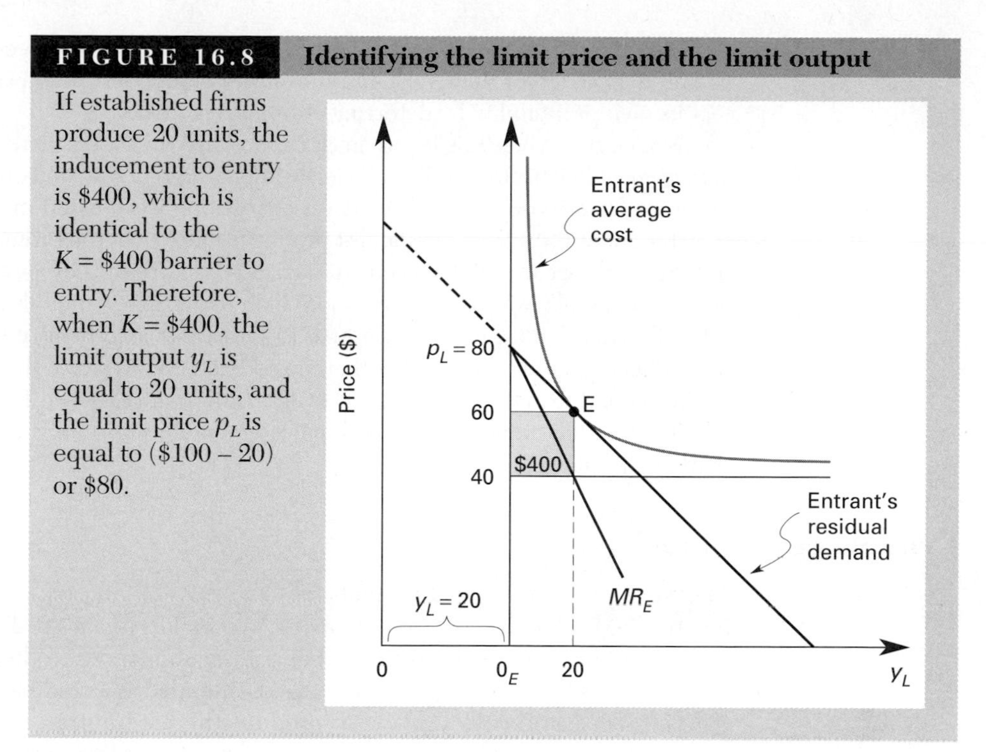

FIGURE 16.8 **Identifying the limit price and the limit output**

If established firms produce 20 units, the inducement to entry is $400, which is identical to the $K = \$400$ barrier to entry. Therefore, when $K = \$400$, the limit output y_L is equal to 20 units, and the limit price p_L is equal to ($100 – 20) or $80.

Strategic Choice of Industry Output

Now let us shift our attention away from entrants and think about the no-entry condition from the perspective of established firms. First, how does the possibility of entry constrain established firms in their ability to earn profit? And how does the possibility of entry affect their strategic decision making — assuming that established firms know that a limit quantity and a limit price will effectively deter such entry? To simplify matters, let us suppose that there is just one established firm, or a *sitting monopolist*.

We already know precisely how the entrant will behave. If y is less than the limit output y_L, it will enter the industry; if y is greater than or equal to y_L, it will stay out. If we presume that the sitting monopolist can also calculate the limit output, how will it make use of this piece of information? We have calculated that if K is $225, then y_L is 30 units — and 30 units is the monopoly output. Thus, if the setup costs in this industry, K, are $225 or higher, the monopoly output of 30 units will successfully deter entry — and the sitting monopolist will remain the only firm in the market. Given the Sylos postulate, if the sitting monopolist is already producing 30 units, an entrant has no profit incentive to enter. When K is $225 or more, then the industry is the case called a *natural monopoly* in Chapter 10.

On the other hand, if K is less than $225, the ordinary monopoly output will not deter entry because the limit output y_L is then larger than 30 units. What action will the sitting monopolist take in this case? It will produce exactly y_L units of output. Why? Because it has already incurred the setup cost, its objective now is to maximize the excess of its revenues over its variable costs, or what we will call **gross profit**; that is, it wants to maximize $y(p - 40)$. If it deters entry by producing the limit output, its gross profit will be $y_L(p_L - 40)$. What would happen to the sitting monopolist's profit if it were to allow entry by producing less than the limit output y_L — say, y'? Because entry would continue until price p' was less than or equal to p_L, its gross profit would

gross profit

then fall to $y'(p' - 40)$ — a sum obviously less than $y_L(p_L - 40)$ because y' is less than y_L and p' is no larger than p_L. Thus, the sitting monopolist will always choose to protect its own profitability by deterring entry in this model.

Notice that when K is less than \$225, we have the case called *monopoly by good management* in Chapter 10. The efficiency implications of this kind of monopoly are very different from those of the other kinds of monopoly discussed in Chapter 10. First, to deter entry, the sitting monopolist produces more than the ordinary monopoly output. Second, because entry is costly — it uses real resources — other things being equal, it is socially wasteful to have more than one firm serving this market. Of course, other things are not necessarily equal. In particular, two firms might produce even more than y_L units of output. Whether the added output is worth the additional expense of the second firm's setup cost, however, is an open question. Indeed, it is entirely possible that the monopoly by good management equilibrium is the best of the free-market alternatives.

Critique of the Model

The Sylos postulate — that entrants take the current industry output as given — is the Achilles heel of the limit-output model. A potential entrant's real concern is not with the present but with the *future output* of a sitting monopolist. When a sitting monopolist produces the limit output, its decision is intended as a credible warning to potential entrants that it will continue to produce the limit output in future periods. If entrants take the warning seriously, they will stay out of the market.

But is the threat credible? If entry does occur, will a sitting monopolist respond by continuing to produce the limit output? The following approach to answering the credibility question raised by the limit-output model was pioneered by Michael Spence (1977).

16.10 Refinements of Limit Output

Let us suppose that the appropriate model of oligopoly is the Cournot model and that every potential entrant knows this. Given n established firms, the entrant can now actually calculate what the industry equilibrium would be if it were to enter and, more to the point, what its own profit would be in that equilibrium.

Notice that this approach neatly finesses the credibility question. Since the entrant knows that the Cournot model is appropriate and can calculate the Cournot equilibrium that will prevail after entry, it knows exactly how much output established firms will actually produce if it does enter. As a result, the credibility question never arises. If established firms are going to produce *more* than the limit output if entry occurs, then the entrant can anticipate that manoeuvre correctly, and it will stay out. On the other hand, if established firms are going to produce *less* than the limit output, the entrant will once again anticipate that manoeuvre correctly, and it will enter. But what if the Cournot model is not appropriate? As you will see in the problems at the end of this section, the same general modelling method can be used with different oligopoly models. To see how this approach works, suppose that the industry is currently a monopoly. If entry occurs, the industry will then be a duopoly. Combining what we learned in sections 16.3 and 16.9, the excess of revenue over variable cost for the entrant — or the inducement to entry — is \$400. Entry will therefore occur if this \$400 inducement exceeds the fixed cost K — the barrier to entry — but it will not occur if K exceeds \$400.

This raises another question: How large must the fixed cost K be so that a third firm will not enter the market? In Problem 16.2, you identified the Cournot equilibrium with three firms: each firm produces 15 units and realizes a gross profit of \$225. If at present only two firms are in the market, the inducement to entry is \$225, and entry will therefore not occur if K is larger than \$225. Thus, if K exceeds \$225 and is less than \$400, only two firms will be in this market. On the other hand, if K is less than \$225, a third firm will enter.

More generally, suppose that n established firms are currently in the industry. What is the inducement to entry? Because the entrant will increase the number of firms to $n + 1$, we can simply reinterpret what we already know about the Cournot model to discover the answer. Each of the $n + 1$ firms will produce $60/(n + 2)$ units in the Cournot equilibrium. As you can easily verify, the price in this equilibrium minus the marginal cost of \$40 is also $60/(n + 2)$. Therefore, when n firms are in the market, the inducement to entry is

$$\text{inducement to entry} = [60/(n + 2)]^2$$

The generalized no-entry condition for the Cournot model is then

$$[60/(n + 2)]^2 \leq K$$

Given K, this condition determines the minimum number of firms that must serve this market if entry is to be unprofitable. If we now suppose that firms enter the industry sequentially, we have a theory of market structure for this example. Given K, the number of firms in the industry will be the smallest value of n such that the generalized no-entry condition is satisfied. These results are presented in Figure 16.9, where K is measured along the horizontal axis. If K is greater than the gross profit of \$900 earned by a monopolist, the market is not a viable one: no firms will serve it. If K is greater than

FIGURE 16.9 Cournot oligopoly and entry equilibrium

The number of firms in entry equilibrium is inversely related to the magnitude of the setup cost, or the barrier to entry K. As K decreases, the number of firms and aggregate output increase, while price and profit decrease. When K is more than \$225 and less than \$400, for example, there are two firms, aggregate output is 40 units, price is \$60, and aggregate profit is $800 - 2K$.

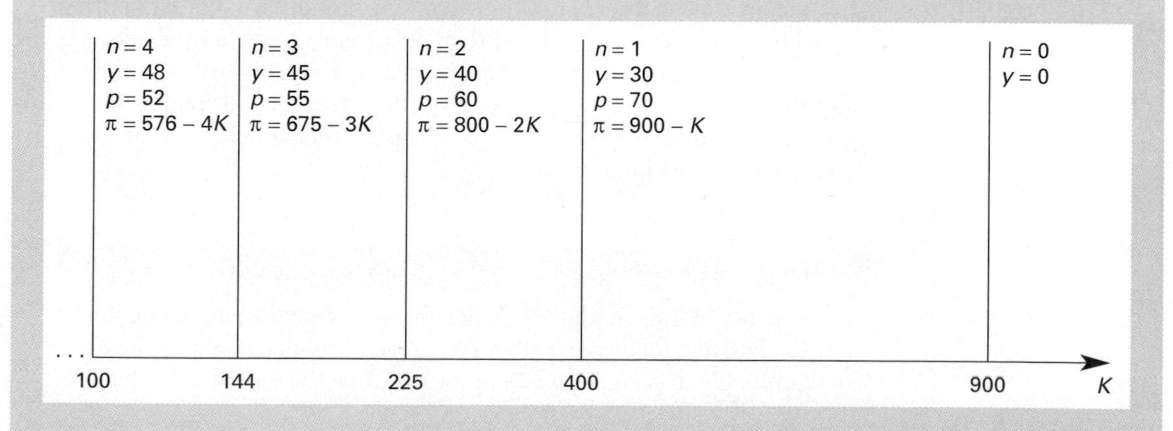

\$400 but less than \$900, the industry is a natural monopoly. A single firm will produce 30 units, sell them at a price equal to \$70, and earn \$900 minus K in profit. If K is greater than \$225 but less than \$400, a duopoly will serve the market. Aggregate output will be 40 units, price will be \$60, and aggregate profit will be \$800 minus $2K$. If K is greater than \$144 but less than \$225, three firms will be in the industry, and so on.

In this model, setup or product development costs K can be interpreted as a barrier to entry; K is the only factor that differentiates established firms from potential entrants. Because established firms have already incurred this cost, they view it as a *sunk cost* — a cost that has no bearing on their profit-maximizing decisions. Because potential entrants have not incurred this cost, however, they see it instead as an *avoidable cost* of production — a cost they will incur only if they opt for entry. When K is large, few firms will opt for entry; when it is small, many firms will opt for entry. Thus, in this model:

The magnitude of the barrier to entry determines the market structure.

In a more elaborate model, however, *demand conditions* will also be factors in determining market structure. For example, if the market demand function is $p = 200 - y$ instead of the demand function used throughout this chapter, $p = 100 - y$, we would expect to see more firms in the industry for any given value of K. Furthermore, as you will soon see, a setup or product development cost is not the *only* barrier to entry. We have used it simply to suggest the role that such barriers play in determining market structure. The precise effect of any particular entry barrier will vary.

As you will discover in the following problems, once the possibility of entry is introduced into the simple oligopoly models of the first half of this chapter, these models appear in a new light. Recall that in the context of a fixed number of firms, the Bertrand model seemed absurd because the cutthroat competition that drives that model ensured that the outcome would be prices equal to marginal cost. When we couple the Bertrand model with entry, however, the result is instead universal monopoly. As long as K is positive, a second firm will never enter the market. By contrast, in the collusive model at the beginning of the chapter, gross profit was maximal for a fixed number of firms. When we couple the collusive model with entry, however, potential entrants find entry enticing. As a result, in the long run, firms continue to enter the market until, in equilibrium, gross profit is minimal.

PROBLEM 16.9

Suppose that cost and demand conditions are identical to those used throughout this chapter. Suppose, too, that the underlying oligopoly model is the Bertrand model and that, at present, a single established firm is in the market. This sitting monopolist is producing the monopoly output and earning the full monopoly profit. Show that as long as K is positive, an entrant who understands oligopoly pricing behaviour in the Bertrand model will never enter.

PROBLEM 16.10

Now suppose that the underlying oligopoly model is the collusive model. In the collusive equilibrium with n firms, each firm makes a gross profit equal to \$900/n in each period. Suppose, too, that the entrant sees that it will be admitted to the collusive club once it incurs the setup cost, thereby becoming an established firm. Show that the no-entry condition is

$$900/(n+1) \leq K$$

Compare industry-wide profit in this model with industry-wide profit in the Cournot and Bertrand models when K is 400; when K is 100.

As you have just discovered, if a sitting monopolist in the Bertrand model can credibly threaten to pursue the post-entry strategy of cutthroat competition implicit in that model, it can continue to monopolize its market regardless of how small K is. By contrast, if the established oligopolists in the collusive model anticipate that their collusive behaviour will simply entice potential entrants to join the collusive club, their pre-entry incentive to act collusively will be seriously eroded. What have we learned?

1. **Setup costs differentiate the real economic position of established firms from the position of potential entrants. Therefore, such costs act as a barrier to entry.**
2. **The precise way in which this differentiation affects an entrant's anticipated profit — or the inducement to entry — depends on the nature of the oligopoly behaviour subsequent to entry. Roughly speaking, the more aggressive (and less cooperative) oligopoly behaviour is subsequent to entry, the more effective setup costs are as a barrier to entry.**
3. **Any firm's decision to incur the setup cost can be seen as a strategic decision to position itself as an established firm. It is strategic because it affects the incentives of other firms.**

This view raises an important question: In what other ways can established firms position themselves to manipulate potential entrants' incentives? The recent literature on long-run equilibrium in oligopolies has examined a whole arsenal of such positioning strategies, discussed in the next section.

16.11 Positioning and Reacting

Because the subject of oligopoly is complex and sometimes confusing, in closing we will attempt to draw together insights from the entire chapter. In doing so, we will be drawing heavily on Spence (1981) — a source that provides an accessible, wide-ranging discussion of the issues raised in this chapter.

Any market in which a firm can earn consistently high profit over a long period of time clearly presents an enticement to potential entrants. What can protect the initial firm's profit from entry? The answer is a combination of *structural features*, such as economies of scale and product development or setup costs, and of *actions designed to inhibit entry*. We have highlighted setup costs, which play a straightforward role as a barrier to entry, as a structural feature in this chapter. More generally, economies of scale are a barrier to entry. A firm producing 3000 widgets a day can take advantage of highly streamlined procedures and high-tech approaches to saving labour costs that would not be cost-effective for a firm producing 300 widgets.

Turning to the actions that established firms undertake to inhibit entry, Spence distinguishes two separate but strategically interrelated sets of activities: positioning and

positioning

reacting

reacting. **Positioning** is concerned with actions taken prior to entry. Accumulating inventory is one possible positioning strategy. Others include advertising, acquiring capital or production capacity, and choosing product durability. Selling durable products today, for example, allows an established firm to capture today's and tomorrow's market today — a strategy that will materially affect a potential entrant's profitability. **Reacting** refers to the actions of established firms subsequent to entry, such as marketing a quantity at least as large as the limit output subsequent to entry.

Reacting and positioning are clearly substitutes, in the sense that if the established firm can credibly threaten to be sufficiently aggressive subsequent to entry, it need not pursue any clever positioning strategy prior to entry. Recall, for example, what you learned from Problem 16.9. If firms behave in accordance with the Bertrand model, as long as K is positive, entry will never occur. Therefore, an established firm might try to substitute the post-entry threat of the ruthless price cutting imagined by Bertrand for the pre-entry positioning strategy of holding inventory. The difficulty is that this post-entry threat may not be credible, because once entry does occur, the established firm would be cutting its own throat (as well as the entrant's) by driving price down to marginal cost.

Where reactive threats may not seem credible in themselves, they sometimes can be made more believable when coupled with a positioning strategy. By actually expanding production capacity, or by actually producing output prior to entry and holding it in inventory, for example, an established firm makes its threat to market that output more credible.

Indeed, in a famous antitrust case, Alcoa was accused of effectively deterring competition by using excess capacity to make more credible its implicit threat to market the limit output if entry occurred. In making a judgment against Alcoa (United States 1945), Judge Hand pointed to Alcoa's deliberate decisions to repeatedly build up its capacity as the market for aluminum expanded:

> It was not inevitable that it should always anticipate increases in the demand for ingot and be prepared to supply them. Nothing compelled it to keep doubling and redoubling its capacity before others entered the field. It insists that it never excluded rivals; but we can think of no more effective exclusion than progressively to embrace each new opportunity as it opened and to face every newcomer with new capacity already geared into a great organization, having the advantage of experience, trade connections and the elite of personnel.

SUMMARY

We began the chapter by using the basic concepts and tools of *game theory* to explore oligopoly when the number of firms is fixed. From the *Cournot* and *Bertrand models*, we learned one very basic lesson about oligopolistic interactions: There is a fundamental contradiction between what is privately rational (or profit-maximizing) and what is collectively rational. In any simple Nash equilibrium, firms have a clear incentive to collude. Yet in exploring the *collusive model* of oligopoly, we discovered that each party to a collusive agreement also has a private incentive to cheat by producing more than the agreed-upon output or by charging less than the agreed-upon price. The *prisoner's dilemma* is the game that illustrates these conflicting forces most clearly. This contradiction arises in Cournot's model of oligopoly, where firms independently choose quantities, and in Bertrand's model, where firms independently choose prices. Evidence from experimental economics and from the history of real collusive agreements supports the view that oligopolists do recognize and act on these conflicting incentives at different times.

We saw, too, that Cournot's model responds in an appealing way to changes in the number of firms. When there is only one firm, Cournot's model is identical to the standard monopoly model. As the number of firms increases, aggregate output increases, and aggregate profit and price decrease. As the number of firms approaches infinity, Cournot's model converges to the competitive equilibrium. Thus, Cournot's model captures a wide range of market structures, from monopoly to perfect competition. Bertrand's model has none of these appealing properties. In that model, price is equal to marginal cost whenever there are two or more firms.

In the second part of the chapter, we arrived at several additional insights as we explored the theory of oligopoly in the long run, when firms are allowed to enter a market. We began with the *limit-output model*, in which established firms produce enough output (the limit output) so that an entrant who takes the output of established firms as given will not enter. As we saw, the weakness of this model lies in the question of credibility: How believable is the threat by established firms to actually produce the limit output after entry occurs? In answering this question, we produced a *theory of market structure* based on Cournot's model.

We closed the chapter by summing up the insights to be drawn from our foray into the fascinating but complicated world of oligopolistic decision making. It is fascinating because it is at heart a game of strategic manoeuvring: a game of *positioning* and *reacting*. Yet it is precisely the business of anticipating and responding to strategic moves of rivals (present and potential) that makes oligopoly so difficult to model.

EXERCISES

1. You can adapt much of the analysis in this chapter to a model with different cost and demand conditions. The market demand function is

$$p = 460 - 0.5y$$

The constant marginal cost for all firms is $100.

a. Find the monopoly output and price, and compute the monopolist's profit.
b. Find the Cournot equilibrium output for each firm and the aggregate output and price in the Cournot equilibrium, and compute the equilibrium profit of a representative firm when there are two firms in the market; when there are three firms in the market; when there are four firms in the market.
c. Suppose that there are two firms in the market. What is the symmetric collusive equilibrium? How much profit does each firm earn in this equilibrium? If one firm honours the collusive agreement, and the other violates the agreement, how much should the violator produce to maximize its profit? What is the magnitude of the inducement to violate the collusive agreement?
d. Now suppose that there is a fixed cost K in addition to the $100 marginal cost. If the fixed cost is $3200, what is the limit output y_L? What is the limit price p_L? Supposing that the limit output effectively deters entry, what profit would a monopolist earn by using the limit-output strategy?
e. Now suppose that K is $20 000, that all firms regard the Cournot model as the correct oligopoly model, and that entry is sequential. How many firms will enter the market? What profit will each firm earn?
f. Now suppose that K is $20 000, that all firms regard the collusive model as the correct oligopoly model, and that entry is sequential. How many firms will enter the market? What profit will each firm earn?
g. Finally, suppose that K is $20 000, that all firms regard the Bertrand model as the correct oligopoly model, and that entry is sequential. How

many firms will enter the market? What profit will each firm earn?

2. In this exercise, you can see that common property creates a prisoner's dilemma. Harry and Sally each have 90 fish in their pens, and each would prefer the highest total number of fish; both are indifferent between fish consumed today and fish consumed tomorrow. Each can choose one of the following two strategies: E denotes the strategy of eating all 90 fish today, and R denotes the strategy of returning all 90 fish to the river. Each fish returned to the river today results in 5/3 fish for consumption tomorrow. Under the common-property institution, Harry and Sally each take half of tomorrow's fish harvest. Construct a matrix analogous to Table 16.1 in which the entries are the total numbers of fish consumed by Harry and by Sally, and show that E is a dominant strategy for both Harry and Sally. Show, too, that they would have been better off had they both chosen R instead of E. Suppose that they are operating under a private-property institution; repeat the exercise.

3. The daily demand for round-trip air travel between cities A and B is

$$p = 2000 - y$$

where y is the number of passengers. There is no demand for one-way travel. Each plane can carry up to 1000 passengers. The cost of flying a plane from A to B and back again is $\$K$, regardless of the number of passengers on the plane. Each firm owns only one plane. Suppose that there is a number of firms in this market and that they can collusively choose and enforce one price. What price will they choose? Now suppose that the price-setting club cannot keep other firms from entering the market. Find the number of firms and the number of seats that will be occupied in each plane in free-entry equilibrium when K is \$600 000; when K is \$300 000; when K is \$150 000.

4. It is sometimes argued that advertising is a barrier to entry. Explain the circumstances in which a large expenditure on advertising by some firm this year may be a barrier to entry for another firm next year.

5. At various times in its history, Dow Chemical, the dominant producer of magnesium in the United States, has held an entire year's production in inventory. Why would the company incur the cost of holding such inventories? Explain how inventories might serve as a barrier to entry.

6. In many high-tech industries, there is considerable "learning by doing." In these industries, the more the firm has produced in the past, the lower its marginal cost of production in the present. Discuss the possible effects of learning by doing on market structure.

7. In Section 16.3 we presented a general argument showing that in the Nash equilibrium, the duopolists (1) failed to maximize joint profit and (2) produced too much output, relative to joint profit maximization. The key assumption we used was that the profit of one firm decreases as the output of the other firm increases. Notice that this assumption is not appropriate when the two firms that between them dominate a market segment produce complementary goods. If one firm produces skis and the other ski boots, for example, it is appropriate to assume that the profit of one firm *increases* as the output of the other firm increases. Using this assumption, show that in the Nash equilibrium such firms (called complementary monopolists) (1) fail to maximize joint profit and (2) produce too little output, relative to joint profit maximization.

8. Cigarette advertising is mostly aimed at brand switching: convincing one smoker to switch brands. Why do you think that cigarette companies were the major lobbying group supporting laws that banned cigarette advertising on television? (*Hint:* Profits increased after the ban.)

9. A company has a monopoly on the production of waterbeds. Demand for these beds is relatively inelastic — at a price of \$1000 per bed, 25 000 will be sold, whereas at a price of \$600, 30 000 will be sold. The only costs of production are the initial costs of building a plant. The company already has a plant that can produce up to 30 000 units. The company has a choice of two strategies — set price equal to \$600 or set price equal to \$1000. Suppose a would-be entrant to this industry could always be assured of half the market share but would have to invest \$10 million in a plant. The entrant has a choice of strategies — enter or don't enter. If the incumbent could lobby for the government to set a maximum price for

waterbeds equal to \$600, would this be a profitable strategy for the incumbent?

10. In many countries it is illegal for competing firms to collude on price. Should this prohibition on price fixing be applied to firms that produce complements?

*11. Milton and Michelle are a married couple who have preferences over leisure and cleanliness (L and C). Suppose that $C = C_1 + C_2$, where C_1 and C_2 are the amounts of time spent in cleaning by Milt (1) and Michelle (2). Each spouse has a total of 1 unit of time per week, so $L_1 + C_1 = 1$ and $L_2 + C_2 = 1$. Suppose that their preferences are given by:

$$U(L_1, C) = L_1 + \ln(C)/2$$
$$U(L_2, C) = L_2 + \ln(C)/2$$

a. Suppose that Milt and Michelle each take the other's clean-up effort as given (i.e., they are like Cournot spouses). What is the optimal effort of Milt as a function of Michelle's clean-up effort? What is the equilibrium? Are there any other equilibria?

b. Suppose that Milt and Michelle agree on a binding schedule of cleaning that maximized the sum of their utilities (now they are collusive spouses). What are the optimal effort levels now? What is the optimal amount of cleanliness C^*? If Milt thinks that Michelle is doing the optimal amount of cleaning, what will he do?

c. Suppose that the total utility of Milt and Michelle over the entire year is the sum of the utilities for each week. Also suppose that Milt and Michelle agree to hire Carla to inspect their apartment every Sunday morning. If the apartment is dirtier than C^* then they both have to babysit Carla's kids for a fraction z of the next K weeks. What fraction z and duration K will enforce the jointly optimal cleanliness in any week (assume this marriage is ongoing)?

d. If, sadly, the marriage is going down the tubes and it looks like it is about to end in five weeks, what would happen to the cleanliness of the apartment in the last week given the punishment figured out in (c)?

*12. Suppose demand for a commodity is given by $y = 100 - p$. There are only two possible factories that can produce this commodity, each with cost function: $c_j = 50 + y_j^2$, where $j = 1, 2$ denotes the factory. The total market output is the sum of the outputs from these two plants.

a. Find the efficient level of output and price for this market. Also, find the total profits of the two firms in this situation.

b. Suppose the two firms form a cartel. Compute the profit maximizing total output, price, profits, and deadweight loss of the cartel in this situation.

c. Instead of a cartel, suppose the two plants are owned by Cournot duopolists. Find the output produced by each firm, the price, and the total profit. Also compute the deadweight loss associated with the Cournot duopoly.

d. Bonus Question: Instead of the Cournot assumption, suppose that firm 1 sets its output before firm 2 does. Firm 2 observes the output choice of firm 1 before it makes its own output choice. Find the output produced by each firm, the price, and total profit. Also compute the deadweight loss in this situation. Compare your results with those in (a), (b), and (c). (The answer to this question is called a "Stackelberg" equilibrium.)

*13. Two courier firms serve a market with the following demand function

$$p = 100 - y$$

where y is aggregate quantity, $y_1 + y_2$. Each firm has the following cost function:

$$C(y_i) = y_i^2/2$$

where y_i is firm i's output. The marginal cost function is

$$MC(y_i) = y_i$$

a. Given y_2, what is the first firm's demand function, and what is its marginal revenue function? Draw the first firm's demand, marginal revenue, and marginal cost functions on the same diagram. What is the first firm's best-response function? What is the second firm's best-response function?

b. How much does each firm produce in the Cournot equilibrium? What is price in the Cournot equilibrium? How much profit does each firm earn in the Cournot equilibrium?

*14. Firms 1 and 2 both produce gizmos, but firm 1 does it at a lower cost than firm 2. Firm 1 has a constant marginal cost of $15, and firm 2 has a constant marginal cost of $30. The demand for gizmos is

$$p = 120 - y$$

where y is aggregate output.

a. Suppose that the firms choose quantities. Find both best-response functions. Remember, marginal costs are different, so the best-response functions will *not* be symmetric. Find the Cournot equilibrium quantities. (*Hint*: Treat the best-response functions as two equations in two unknowns — the Cournot equilibrium quantities — and solve the equations for the unknown quantities. Compute each firm's profit in the Cournot equilibrium.)

b. Suppose that the firms choose prices instead of quantities and that prices must be announced in dollars and cents. (That is, $15.71, and $39.00 are permissible prices, but $45.975 is not.) What are the Bertrand equilibrium prices? How much does each firm earn in the Bertrand equilibrium?

*15. Suppose we have two firms in a market to which entry is restricted. The inverse demand function facing these firms is given by $p = 100 - y$, where $y = y_1 + y_2$. The manager of firm 1 has to decide on what output level to produce, but he holds the expectation that firm 2 will not change its output in response to the output level chosen by this firm. The manager has to decide whether to choose an output level before firm 2 or simultaneously with firm 2. Both firms have the same costs of production: $C = 20q$.

a. Compute the best response functions and find the Cournot equilibrium.

b. Now suppose firm 1 gets to choose y_1 before firm 2 chooses y_2. Suppose also that firm 1 knows the best response function of firm 2. What output should firm 1 produce to maximize profit? What output will firm 2 produce? What profit will each firm make?

c. Draw a diagram to illustrate your answer to (b). In particular, draw the isoprofit curve of firm 1 through the equilibrium.

d. If the manager of firm 1 has the option of choosing output before, simultaneously, or after firm 2, which will he or she choose?

16. Consider two competing firms with the following inverse demand functions:

$$P_1(x_1, x_2) = \alpha + \beta x_2 - \gamma x_1$$

$$P_2(x_1, x_2) = \alpha + \beta x_1 - \gamma x_2$$

where $\alpha > 0$, $\gamma > 0$, and $\gamma > |\beta|$. Notice that β may be either positive or negative. Assume there are no costs of production. For what parameter values is this a game of plain substitutes and for what values is it a game of plain complements? What are the Cournot-Nash equilibrium values? One can think of the game that is defined by this problem as simply an abstract game in which x_1 and x_2 are not quantities but simply strategies. This perspective on the game invites speculation as to the set of other situations for which this game might serve as a model. Can you suggest other interpretations of this game for the case in which $\beta < 0$? For the case in which $\beta > 0$?

REFERENCES

Axelrod, R. 1984. *The Evolution of Cooperation*. New York: Basic Books.

Bain, J. S. 1956. *Barriers to New Competition*. Cambridge, MA.: Harvard University Press.

Cournot, A. A. 1838. *Researches into the Mathematical Principles of the Theory of Wealth*. Trans. Nathaniel T. Bacon, 1960. New York: Augustus M. Keley, chapter 7.

Fouraker, L. and S. Siegal. 1963. *Bargaining Behavior*. New York: McGraw-Hill.

Friedman, J. 1971. "A Non-Cooperative Equilibrium for Supergames," *Review of Economic Studies*, 38:1–12.

Modigliani, F. 1958. "New Developments on the Oligopoly Front," *Journal of Political Economy*, 66:215–32.

Salop, S. C. 1986. "Practices That (Credibly) Facilitate Oligopoly Co-ordination," in *New Developments in the Analysis of Market Structure*, J. E. Stiglitz and G. F. Mathewson (eds.). Cambridge, MA.: MIT Press.

Spence, A. M. 1977. "Entry, Capacity, Investment, and Oligopolistic Pricing," *Bell Journal of Economics*, 8:534–44.

Spence, 1981. "Competition, Entry and Antitrust Policy," in *Strategy, Predation and Antitrust Analysis*, S. Salop (ed.). Washington, D.C.: Federal Trade Commission.

Stigler, G. 1969. "A Theory of Oligopoly," *Journal of Political Economy*, 72:44–61.

Sylos-Labini, P. 1962. *Oligopoly and Technical Progress*. Cambridge, MA.: Harvard University Press.

United States v. *Aluminum Company of America et al.* (1945), 145 F.2d 416, 424.

PART VII

Uncertainty and Asymmetric Information

In Part VII we move into a fascinating field of economics. Throughout the book we have assumed that consumers and producers had complete information. This meant that consumers knew prices of all goods across space and time, that firms knew all demands and costs, and that everyone knew the true equilibrium prices and quantities that maximized the gains from trade. Though this assumption is highly unrealistic, we have seen that it explains a great deal of human behaviour.

However, there is a number of puzzles that cannot be solved with our standard neoclassical model. For example, we observe unemployed resources in our daily experience. Why do prices not fall to eliminate unemployment? Why do lineups form to allocate goods when, again, prices should rise to eliminate the lineup? More fundamentally, prices do not allocate all goods. Firms, families, nonprofit organizations, and the like allocate a tremendous amount of resources without the use of prices. If we look in more detail, even when prices are used, the form in which they are used often varies immensely. Workers are not just paid wages; some are paid by commissions, shares, piece rates, or salaries. Why are different methods of payment used?

The solutions to all of these puzzles hinge on the assumption of complete information. By relaxing this assumption and assuming that the acquisition of information is costly, economic theory can be extended to organizational issues and the discussion of allocation mechanisms other than price. The concept of information costs, however, begins with the notion of uncertainty. Chapter 17 formally introduces uncertainty into our model. Here we use the same tools that were developed in Chapters 2 and 3 to analyze uncertainty. Chapters 18 through 20 examine what happens when, in the face of uncertainty, various individuals hold different information. Chapter 18 introduces the idea of asymmetric information and examines how this affects individual behaviour. Chapter 19 examines organizational questions within the firm. Finally, Chapter 20 looks at how asymmetric information influences market behaviour.

CHAPTER 17

Choice Making Under Uncertainty

Imagine three different card games. In the first game each player is dealt a single card face up. Once the cards have all been dealt out, each player is asked to bet, and the player with the highest card wins. In the second game each player is dealt a single card face down and is asked to bet without looking at the card. In the last game each player is dealt a card face down but is allowed to look at his own card (but not the others!) before a bet is made.

The first card game is a situation of complete information — everyone knows everyone else's card. Such games makes for boring bets, but this is the nature of the information assumption we have developed and explored throughout this book. In our model of consumer behaviour, where consumers decided how to allocate their budget across several goods, each individual knew exactly what his or her income was, as well as the exact prices. Likewise firms, when deciding on what output to produce, knew their production functions, marginal costs, demand curves, and input prices with certainty.

Yet it is clear that the outcomes of everyday decision making are *risky* or *probable* rather than riskless or certain, and are made on the basis of *incomplete information*. Life often resembles the second card game. For example, every time you drop three quarters into a vending machine to buy some gum, there is some probability that you will walk away empty-handed and 75 cents poorer; some other probability that you will get both the gum and the 75 cents back; and some third, larger, probability that you will get the gum but not the 75 cents. Consumers do not always know prices or incomes, and firms spend a great deal of money and effort to discover what the demand for their product is.

asymmetric information

The last game is a situation called **asymmetric information**. Here each person knows something that other people do not know, and they all try to parlay this to their own advantage. In such a world, bluffing and strategic behaviour are very important. This is the nature of the world we will examine in Chapters 18 through 20.

In this chapter, however, we examine the case of game 2. In game 2 each player is uncertain regarding the value of his or her card, and *equally uncertain about the value of all the other cards*. Many aspects of life are like the second card game. In life, blind chance often plays an important role, and we are required to make decisions on the basis of incomplete information. In so doing we must assess the risks associated with alternative courses of action. That is, in a world of uncertainty, a given action can lead to several different outcomes, and we must model our decisions over the distribution of these outcomes.

In the first two sections of this chapter, we extend the theory of consumer choice to incorporate **risk** and **incomplete information**. Using the methodology described in Chapter 1, we first select a familiar situation with a risky outcome — a TV game show. Then we look for an initial hypothesis that explains our observations and carefully restructure the hypothesis to create an economic model, or theory, known as the theory of expected utility. In the following section, we generalize the theory of expected utility and apply it to a range of situations.

risk

incomplete information

17.1 Expected-Utility Theory

We will begin our exploration of the theory of expected utility with simple games of chance because they are so easy to understand. We will then see how to elaborate the theory so that it can be applied in the more complicated environment of the real world.

Let us begin by imagining a TV game show in which a certain player — say, Chauncey — is given the choice between walking away with a fixed sum of money $\$M$ or staking it on a game called Risk. If Chauncey decides to play Risk, the game show host will toss a coin. If a head appears, Chauncey wins \$200; if a tail appears, he wins nothing.

We can think of $\$M$ as the *opportunity cost* of playing Risk. Clearly, if $\$M$ is sufficiently small, Chauncey will choose to play Risk, and if $\$M$ is sufficiently large he will choose to walk away with $\$M$. What more can we say about Chauncey's choice? What principles govern Chauncey's choice in this risky situation?

Calculating Expected Monetary Value

First, let us calculate the expected monetary value of the payoffs to Risk. An **expected monetary value** is simply a weighted average of the payoffs to the possible outcomes, where the weights are the probabilities of occurrence assigned to each of the possible payoffs. In other words, the expected monetary value is just the average payoff. Because in Risk the probability of winning \$200 is 1/2 and the probability of winning nothing is 1/2, the expected monetary value of the payoff to Risk is \$100; $\$100 = (1/2)\$200 + (1/2)\$0$. On any single play of this game, Chauncey would win either \$200 or \$0. However, if he played the game repeatedly, *on average* he would expect to win \$100 per play, winning \$200 half the time and \$0 half the time. The expected monetary value of the other option facing Chauncey is, of course, $\$M$, since if he chooses this option he gets $\$M$ with probability 1.

expected monetary value

Having done these expected monetary value calculations, we are tempted to guess that Chauncey will play Risk in preference to taking $\$M$ if $\$M < \$100$, and will take $\$M$ in preference to playing Risk if $\$M > \$100$. That is, it is tempting to think that in choices involving risk, individuals choose the option with the largest expected monetary value. Let us call this the **expected monetary value hypothesis**. To see why this hypothesis is not necessarily correct, try the following problem.

expected monetary value hypothesis

PROBLEM 17.1

You now have a chance to play Risk — but the stakes are better: you can walk away with $\$M$ dollars, or you can gamble on the outcome of a coin toss. If a head appears, you get \$2 million, but if a tail appears, you get nothing. Calculate the expected monetary value of the game. What value of $\$M$ would make you indifferent between taking $\$M$ or playing this version of Risk? Is it smaller than the expected monetary value of the game?

If past experience is any guide, the number you wrote down in answering Problem 17.1 is certainly less than $1 million — the expected monetary value of Risk in this problem — and it is probably less than $500 000. The expected monetary value hypothesis, then, does not seem to account for our behaviour. It seems that *risk itself plays a role in shaping our behaviour*. Daniel Bernoulli, a contemporary of Adam Smith, proposed the *expected-utility hypothesis* as a replacement for the expected monetary value hypothesis.[1] This hypothesis takes into account the role of risk in shaping our actions. Before you consider the theory of expected utility, however, try the following problem to reinforce your understanding of expected monetary values.

PROBLEM 17.2

Imagine that your rich uncle offers you the chance to toss a die. He promises to pay you $1800 if you toss a 1 or a 3 and $3000 if you toss a 2. On the other hand, if you toss a 4, 5, or 6, you must pay him $300. What is the expected monetary value of your winnings from this die-tossing game?

The Expected-Utility Hypothesis

Bernoulli argued that in evaluating risky prospects, individuals compare not the expected monetary values of prospects but the *expected utilities of prospects*. There is something inherently attractive about this approach because it focuses not on the monetary value of a prize but on just how much the prize means to an individual. Expected utility is calculated in the same way as an expected monetary value, except that the utility associated with a payoff is substituted for its monetary value. To calculate an expected utility, simply compute a weighted average of the utilities associated with the payoffs, using the appropriate probabilities as weights.

What is Chauncey's expected utility for Risk? If we think of wealth (command over goods) as a composite commodity, we can write Chauncey's utility as a function of wealth:

$$u = U(w)$$

where u is Chauncey's utility, w is his wealth, and U is his utility function. For example, let us suppose that Chauncey's wealth before he makes his choice about playing Risk is $0. In other words, he is flat broke. If he decides to play, one of two possible outcomes will occur: (1) He will win $200, his wealth will then be $200, and his utility will be $U(200)$; or (2) He will win $0, his wealth will then be $0, and his utility will be $U(0)$. The probability of each of these outcomes is, of course, 1/2. Taking the probability-weighted average of these utilities gives us Chauncey's **expected utility** of playing Risk.

expected utility

$$\text{Chauncey's expected utility of Risk} = (1/2)U(200) + (1/2)U(0)$$

1. The version by Bernoulli (1954) of this paradox, known as the Saint Petersburg paradox, is treated in Exercise 1 at the end of this chapter.

Of course, his other option is to walk away with $\$M$. If he chooses to take $\$M$ rather than play Risk, his wealth will be $\$M$ with probability 1. The expected utility associated with this option is then $U(M)$.

expected-utility hypothesis

According to the **expected-utility hypothesis**, Chauncey will choose to play Risk in preference to taking $\$M$ if the expected utility of playing Risk is greater than the expected utility of taking $\$M$, or if

$$(1/2)U(200) + (1/2)U(0) > U(M)$$

PROBLEM 17.3

Suppose that Chauncey's utility function is

$$U(w) = 12 - 1200/[100 + w]$$

and that his initial wealth is zero. What is Chauncey's expected utility of playing Risk? If $\$M$ is \$20, will he play Risk or take $\$M$? What value of $\$M$ will make Chauncey indifferent between the two options?

In order to understand Chauncey's position, we need to understand how an expected utility function is actually constructed.

Defining a Prospect

prospect

Throughout the remainder of this chapter we will use the concept of a **prospect**. To keep the discussion relatively simple, we will look at a situation in which any risky prospect has at most three possible outcomes. That is, we will be talking about lotteries — or what we will call *prospects* — which offer *three different prizes*, or *outcomes*. For concreteness, the prizes themselves will be \$10 000, \$6000, or \$1000. Now, suppose that some game offers \$10 000 with probability q_1, \$6000 with probability q_2, and \$1000 with probability q_3. From our understanding of probability, we know that q_1, q_2, and q_3 are numbers greater than or equal to 0 and less than or equal to 1. In addition, since there are only three possible outcomes, these three probabilities must add up to 1: $q_1 + q_2 + q_3 = 1$.

We will use the term prospect to refer to any set of three probabilities — q_1, q_2, and q_3 assigned to their respective outcomes — \$10 000, \$6000, and \$1000. We will denote a prospect by

$$(q_1, q_2, q_3\text{: } 10\,000, 6000, 1000)$$

or, more simply, by

$$(q_1, q_2, q_3)$$

with the understanding that the first probability (q_1) pertains to the first prize (\$10 000), the second probability (q_2) to the second prize (\$6000), and the third probability (q_3) to the third prize (\$1000). For example, the lottery that offers \$10 000 with probability 1/4, \$6000 with probability 1/2, and \$1000 with probability 1/4 is denoted by (0.25, 0.5, 0.25: 10 000, 6000, 1000) or, equivalently, by (0.25, 0.5, 0.25). The notation can also represent riskless, or *assured*, outcomes: outcomes that occur with probability 1.

For example, either (1, 0, 0: 10 000, 6000, 1000) or (1, 0, 0) denotes the assured outcome, \$10 000. To be certain you understand this notation, try the following problem.

PROBLEM 17.4

Describe in words exactly what each of the following prospects is, and calculate its expected monetary value: (0.25, 0.25, 0.50), (0.2, 0.5, 0.3), (0.5, 0.4, 0.1), (0, 1, 0).

17.2 Deriving Expected Utility Functions[2]

Now that we understand prospects, we must ask what assumptions underlie the expected utility function. Our task is to find a utility function such that whenever one prospect is preferred to another, the expected utility of the preferred prospect is larger than the expected utility of the other prospect. The utility function $U(w)$ will assign utility numbers to each of the three outcomes — \$10 000, \$6000, and \$1000. The utility numbers themselves can be written as $U(10\,000)$, $U(6000)$, and $U(1000)$.

To see just what our objective is, let us look at two specific prospects, (0.2, 0.5, 0.3) and (0.3, 0.3, 0.4), and suppose that the person whose preferences we are considering prefers the first prospect to the second one. That is,

(0.2, 0.5, 0.3) is preferred to (0.3, 0.3, 0.4)

We want to find a utility function — the three numbers $U(10\,000)$, $U(6000)$, and $U(1000)$ — such that the expected utility of the first prospect is greater than the expected utility of the second prospect:

$$0.2U(10\,000) + 0.5U(6000) + 0.3U(1000) > 0.3U(10\,000) + 0.3U(6000) + 0.4U(1000)$$

continuity assumption

To find such a function, we will use an assumption that is central to the theory of expected utility: the **continuity assumption**. (Notice that this assumption is different from the *continuity of preferences assumption* in Chapter 2.) To see what our new assumption involves, let us consider another simple game. Suppose that Chauncey is given a choice between the following prospects:

Prospect 1: (0, 1, 0)
Prospect 2: $(e, 0, 1 - e)$

Prospect 1 is the assured prospect \$6000. In Prospect 2, e is the probability of the \$10 000 prize, $1 - e$ is the probability of the \$1000 prize, and the \$6000 prize is impossible (probability 0). Notice that as e increases, Prospect 2 becomes increasingly more attractive. At one extreme, when $e = 0$, both prospects are riskless, or assured, and Prospect 1 is the preferred prospect since it offers \$6000 while Prospect 2 offers only \$1000. At the other extreme, when $e = 1$, both prospects are again assured, but now Prospect 2 is the preferred prospect since it offers \$10 000 while Prospect 1 offers only \$6000. Given these results — Prospect 1 is preferred to Prospect 2 when $e = 0$ and

2. This section is relatively difficult, and may be skipped without loss of continuity.

Prospect 2 is preferred to Prospect 1 when $e = 1$ — it seems plausible to assume that there is some value of e, greater than 0 but less than 1, such that the individual is indifferent between the two prospects. This is the continuity assumption.

CONTINUITY ASSUMPTION

For any individual, there is a unique number e^*, $0 < e^* < 1$, such that he or she is indifferent between the two prospects (0, 1, 0) and (e^*, 0, $1 - e^*$).

Since e^* must be greater than 0 and less than 1, this assumption guarantees that individuals are willing to make *tradeoffs* between risky and assured prospects: they are willing to bear some risk. The probability e^* plays a very significant role in our theory, so you should be certain that you understand the continuity assumption. In particular, notice that for any individual, e^* is a *number* and that *this number will vary from individual to individual.*

PROBLEM 17.5

Jack says that he is indifferent between \$6000 and a lottery that pays \$10 000 with probability 0.75 and \$1000 with probability 0.25. His sister Jane says that she prefers \$6000 to this lottery. What can you say about the number e^* for Jack? For Jane?

We begin to construct the utility function $U(w)$ by assigning the utility number 1 to the \$10 000 prize and the utility number 0 to the \$1000 prize. Thus, $U(10\ 000) = 1$ and $U(1000) = 0$. (We choose utility numbers 1 and 0 as a matter of convenience. We could have assigned arbitrary utility numbers, so long as the number assigned to the \$10 000 prize is larger than the number assigned to the \$1000 prize.) To complete the job, we need to assign a utility number to the \$6000 prize. As you will see, only one number will do: we must choose $U(6000) = e^*$.

From the continuity assumption, we know that in any given individual's eyes there is a risky prospect (e^*, 0, $1 - e^*$) that is equivalent to (0, 1, 0), the assured prospect offering \$6000 with probability 1. In other words, for any individual there is a number e^*, greater than 0 and less than 1, such that (0, 1, 0) is indifferent to (e^*, 0, $1 - e^*$). If the expected-utility result is to hold, the expected utility of the assured prospect (0, 1, 0) must be equal to the expected utility of the equivalent risky prospect (e^*, 0, $1 - e^*$). But the expected utility of the assured prospect is just $U(6000)$. The expected utility of the equivalent risky prospect is $e^*U(10\ 000) + (1 - e^*)U(1000)$, or simply e^*, because $U(10\ 000) = 1$ and $U(1000) = 0$. Therefore, we must choose $U(6000) = e^*$. The expected-utility function is then

$$U(10\ 000) = 1,\ U(6000) = e^*,\ U(1000) = 0$$

To be sure that you know how this utility function has been constructed, try the following problem.[3]

---

3. More generally, given any two numbers a and b with $a > b$, we could let $U(10\ 000) = a$ and $U(1000) = b$. We would then have to assign a utility number to \$6000 as follows:

$$U(6000) = ae^* + b(1 - e^*).$$

PROBLEM 17.6

Using the information from Problem 17.5, construct a utility function for Jack.

von Neumann-Morgenstern utility function

This utility function is often called a **von Neumann-Morgenstern utility function** in honour of the mathematician John von Neumann and the economist Oskar Morgenstern, who developed the modern theory of expected utility in their classic book *The Theory of Games and Economic Behavior*. Notice that this utility function is *not* an ordinal utility function like the utility functions in Chapter 2. If it were an ordinal utility function, we could assign any number larger than $U(1000) = 0$ and smaller than $U(10\ 000) = 1$ to the \$6000 prize. But, as we have seen, we cannot pick an arbitrary utility number for this prize. We must choose $U(6000) = e^*$.

We used the continuity assumption to construct the von Neumann-Morgenstern utility function. Other assumptions are also important in the theory of expected utility. When these assumptions are satisfied, and when the utility function is constructed as described above, we have the following important result:

If an individual prefers one prospect to another, then the preferred prospect will have a larger expected utility. Furthermore, if an individual is indifferent between two prospects, then the two prospects will have the same expected utility.

To see just how powerful this result is, notice that if we have just *one* piece of information for any individual, we can predict that individual's choice in any situation where the prizes are \$10 000, \$6000, or \$1000 — assuming, of course, that the individual's preferences satisfy our assumptions. That crucial piece of information is e^*, the probability that makes the individual indifferent between \$6000 and the risky prospect $(e^*, 0, 1 - e^*)$. The number e^* gives us this powerful predictive capacity because it allows us to construct the individual's utility function and therefore to calculate expected utilities for any prospect involving these three prizes. The following problem will help you check your understanding of this result.

PROBLEM 17.7

Use the utility function you constructed in the previous problem to find Jack's preference ordering for the following prospects: (1/2, 1/4, 1/4); (1/3, 1/3, 1/3); (0, 1, 0); (7/12, 0, 5/12); (1/4, 1/2, 1/4); (3/4, 0, 1/4).

The predictive power of the theory of expected utility means that it is relatively easy to generate experimental evidence to test the theory. In fact, a great deal of experimental testing has already been done. One of the more interesting findings of this research is that, in certain situations, the theory is inadequate. A number of researchers have tried recently to modify the theory so that it does work in these problematical situations. Machina's 1987 article surveys these efforts. Despite its inadequacy in some situations, expected utility theory is by far the most often used theory of decision making in the presence of risk and/or incomplete information. Later in this chapter, we use it to address a number of questions.

Generalizing the Expected-Utility Approach

Obviously, expected-utility theory is not restricted to prospects with the three prizes of \$10 000, \$6000, and \$1000. Clearly, *any* three money prizes would do. Indeed, prizes *other than* money prizes are perfectly possible. For example, the prizes might be cars, houses, training programs, consumption bundles, or virtually anything else that individuals value. As you will see, the expected-utility approach is therefore not limited to financial risk; it can be applied to a whole spectrum of individual choices involving risk.

We can easily extend the theory from the three-outcome case to prospects with any number of possible outcomes. For each additional outcome, we simply need to generate an additional utility number. Suppose, for example, that we added the possibility of a \$3000 prize to the three prizes we have been considering and that Jack is indifferent between this \$3000 prize and a lottery offering \$10 000 with probability 0.4 and \$1000 with probability 0.6. To extend Jack's utility function, we would assign the utility number 0.4 to \$3000. Jack's utility function would then be $U(10\,000) = 1$, $U(6000) = 0.75$, $U(3000) = 0.4$, and $U(1000) = 0$. Using this utility function, we could then predict what his choice would be in any situation in which prospects offer these four prizes. Using this procedure, we can extend the theory to encompass risky prospects with any number of outcomes. In the remainder of this chapter we will write utility as a function of wealth in a given state, $u(w)$. Wealth, in this context, is a composite commodity and effectively allows us to extend expected utility to an unlimited number of outcomes.

Subjective Probabilities

We have been using coin-tossing games as illustrations of risky situations for two reasons. First, these games are clearly risky because their outcomes are random events. Second, in these games, the probability of any outcome is objectively known. Yet, expected-utility theory is often applied to risky situations in which the probability of any outcome is not objectively known. It is also applied to situations that involve not risk, but *incomplete information* — that is, to situations in which the outcome is *certain* but *unknown*. The key to applying expected-utility theory in these latter two cases is to use **subjective probabilities**.

subjective probabilities

First, let us look at buying gum from a vending machine as a risky situation in which the probability of any outcome is not objectively known, and then reconsider it as a situation involving incomplete information. We will see how the expected-utility approach can be applied to both cases with the use of subjective probabilities. Each time you drop 75 cents into a vending machine to get some gum, you think that there is some probability that the gum will not drop. This is a genuinely risky event if and only if the outcome is genuinely random. If, for instance, the machine is built so that it releases gum with probability 19/20 and does not release it with probability 1/20, then there is an objective probability that you will not get the gum; however, in this case you do not know what this probability is.

How do you make rational decisions in this case? Perhaps you could attach a subjective probability to the nonappearance of the gum, based on past experience with this machine or others like it. In this case, the expected-utility approach is applicable — if probabilities are reinterpreted as subjective probabilities.

But what if the outcome is not risky but certain? In other words, what if the vending machine is in one of the two states: working order or out-of-order? In this case, the problem is an informational one: You simply do not know whether the machine is functioning or not. How do you make rational decisions under incomplete information? Perhaps by forming a subjective probability about the state of the machine, again based on past experience with this or similar machines. Here again, the expected-utility approach is applicable if probabilities are interpreted as subjective probabilities.

From the vending-machine user's point of view, then, there is no difference between genuine risk, where outcomes are random, and incomplete information, where outcomes are certain but information is lacking. The outcome is treated as probabilistic in either case.

In fact, many choices involve both risk and incomplete information. For example, consider enrolling in a pre-med program where only three out of every ten applicants are accepted by medical schools. This involves genuine risk if selection procedures by admission officers are random — that is, if candidates are chosen by throwing the names of acceptable applicants into a hat and drawing out the "winners." Enrolling in pre-med also involves incomplete information, however, if students who are unable to meet medical school admission standards nevertheless decide to enroll in the program. In this case, the outcome is certain — these students will *not* be accepted into medical school — but the students themselves do not know it.

Whatever the nature of the choice — a genuinely risky problem, an informational problem, or both — we can still analyze it using the expected-utility approach if we are willing to reinterpret the probabilities as subjective probabilities. The real issue is whether people actually do in fact view outcomes in a particular choice situation as probabilistic.

17.3 The Expected Utility Function

Let us summarize the previous section. Individuals rank prospects not by their expected monetary values but by their expected utility values. We have seen that the probabilities used to calculate the expected utility need not be objective probabilities, but may be the subjective beliefs of the individual choice maker. Furthermore, we have seen that expected utility may be defined over any number of states or outcomes. To this point you may be thinking that the economics of uncertainty is very different from the economic model of choice that you learned in Chapter 2. However, let us now apply the framework that we developed there to help us understand and use expected utility.

First, without loss of generality, let us assume that one of two states of the world will exist tomorrow. These two states could be anything. Perhaps it will either rain or be sunny tomorrow, or your stock portfolio may go up or down in value, or your "significant other" may accept or reject your marriage proposal. Whatever tomorrow's outcomes are, we will represent them as the wealth levels w_1 and w_2, where w_1 is the wealth that occurs in state 1, and w_2 is the wealth that occurs in state 2. These outcomes occur with probabilities q and $1 - q$, and we can write the prospect as $(q, 1 - q\colon w_1, w_2)$. The expected utility function over this prospect of tomorrow is written as:

$$u(q, 1 - q\colon w_1, w_2) = qU(w_1) + (1 - q)U(w_2)$$

Two features of this utility function are worth mentioning. First, the $U(\bullet)$ functions are cardinal, unlike the utility functions you encountered earlier in the book, which were ordinal. This means that the utility values have a specific meaning in relation to one another. It also makes it meaningful to talk about diminishing, constant, and increasing marginal utility. The second feature of this expected utility function is that it is linear in the probabilities. As we will see, this makes the *MRS* simple. We can define an indifference curve as different combinations of w_1 and w_2 that yield the same level of (expected) utility. Figure 17.1 shows an indifference curve for the utility level u. Instead of quantities of different goods, wealth levels in two different states are shown on the axes. Notice also that q and $1 - q$ are fixed in this figure. When tomorrow comes, only one state of the world will exist, but as far as today is concerned, tomorrow is uncertain and either state is possible. We might ask: what is the slope of the indifference curve? As always, the slope of the indifference curve is the marginal rate of substitution (*MRS*). This slope tells us the rate at which an individual is willing to trade wealth in state 1 for wealth in state 2 before either of these states occur. If the indifference curve is steep, then the individual has a high *MRS* for wealth in state 1. As we know, the *MRS* is the ratio of the marginal utilities, which we can write:[4]

$$MRS = \frac{qu'(w_1)}{(1 - q)u'(w_2)}$$

Because of the special additive form of the expected utility function, the *MRS* takes on a very simple form. The slope of the indifference curve is equal to the ratio of probabilities times the ratio of marginal utilities. *Each marginal utility, however, is a function of wealth in only one state.* Since the utility functions themselves are the same in each state, if $w_1 = w_2$ then $U'(w_1) = U'(w_2)$, and the *MRS* just equals the ratio of the probabilities. Hence in Figure 17.1, along the 45° line where wealth in the two states are equal, the slope of the indifference curve is just $q/1 - q$. If q is large relative to $1 - q$,

FIGURE 17.1 **Indifference curves in state space**

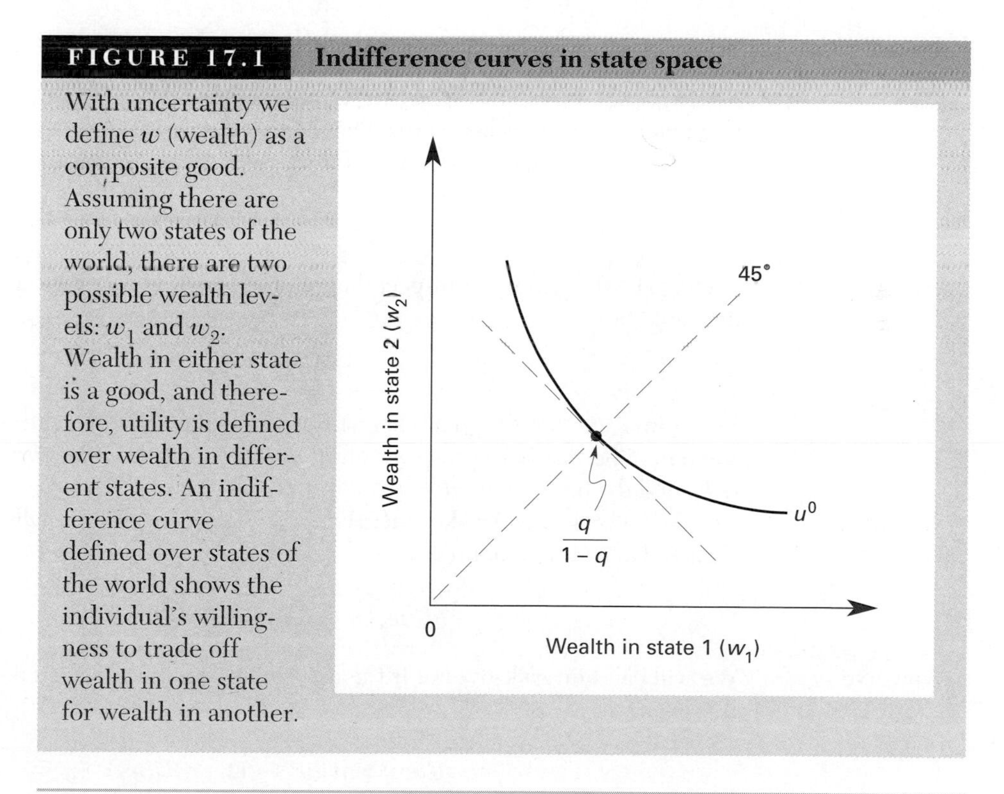

With uncertainty we define w (wealth) as a composite good. Assuming there are only two states of the world, there are two possible wealth levels: w_1 and w_2. Wealth in either state is a good, and therefore, utility is defined over wealth in different states. An indifference curve defined over states of the world shows the individual's willingness to trade off wealth in one state for wealth in another.

4. Taking the derivative of the expected utility function, w_1 yields the marginal utility of wealth in state 1 equal to $qu'(w_1)$. Doing the same for wealth in state 2 yields $(1 - q)u'(w_2)$. Recall from Chapter 2 that *MRS* is equal to MU_1/MU_2, the ratio of marginal utilities.

then the indifference curve is relatively steep, and if it is small relative to $1 - q$, then the indifference curve is relatively flat. What is the intuition behind this? If you believe state 1 is very likely (q is high), then you prefer wealth in state 1 rather than state 2. This also implies that along the 45° line, all of an individual's curves must have the same slope.

PROBLEM 17.8

Suppose the expected utility function is $u = q\ln(w_1) + (1 - q)\ln(w_2)$. The *MRS* for this utility function is $MRS = [q/(1 - q) \times (w_2/w_1)]$. Draw an indifference curve when a. $q = 5$; b. $q = 1$; c. $q = 0$.

Attitudes Towards Risk

Different people have different attitudes towards *risk-taking*: some people are perfectly willing to invest in highly speculative penny stocks, for example, or in a resort development in the heart of the Amazon jungle, whereas others are unwilling to undertake any venture more risky than opening a savings account. A convenient way to think about this variation in attitudes towards risk is to view individual preferences as falling into one of three categories: *risk-averse, risk-neutral,* or *risk-inclined.*

Let us concentrate in this section on attitudes towards financial risk, and continue to express utility as a function of wealth, w. We can write an expected utility for an individual — let us call him Diego — as

$$u(q: w_1, w_2) = qU(w_1) + (1 - q)U(w_2)$$

where q is the probability of getting outcome w_1, and $(1 - q)$ is the probability of getting outcome w_2. In other words, Diego faces the prospect $(q: w_1, w_2)$.

The expected monetary value of this prospect, w_e, is just

$$w_e = qw_1 + (1 - q)w_2$$

If Diego held an assured prospect that offered w_e with probability 1, his expected utility would be

$$U(w_e)$$

Let us imagine that Diego has been offered the choice between these two prospects. Keep in mind that both prospects offer *identical expected monetary values* but one is *risky* and the other *assured.*

risk-neutral

We will call Diego **risk-neutral** if the two prospects are equally attractive to him. That is, Diego is risk-neutral if

$$qU(w_1) + (1 - q)U(w_2) = U(w_e)$$

risk-averse

We will call him **risk-averse** if the assured prospect is preferred. That is, Diego is risk-averse if

$$U(w_e) > qU(w_1) + (1 - q)U(w_2)$$

risk-inclined

Finally, we will call him **risk-inclined** if he prefers the risky prospect. That is, Diego is risk-inclined if

$$qU(w_1) + (1 - q)U(w_2) > U(w_e)$$

The following problem will help you to understand these important distinctions.

PROBLEM 17.9

Melvin's utility function is $U(w) = w^{1/2}$, Jeela's is $U(w) = w$, and Lou's is $U(w) = w^2$. Consider the risky prospect (1/4, 3/4: 100, 0) — a prospect that offers \$100 with probability 1/4 and \$0 with probability 3/4. The expected monetary value of this prospect is \$25 — that is, $w_e = 25$. Show that, if given a choice between \$25 and the risky prospect (1/4, 3/4: 100, 0), Melvin prefers the assured \$25, Jeela is indifferent between the two, and Lou prefers the risky prospect. Now quickly sketch these utility functions. Notice the differences in the curves associated with these risk-averse, risk-neutral, and risk-inclined preferences.

marginal utility of wealth

Attitudes towards risk have specific implications for the shape of indifference curves. In order for someone to be risk-neutral, the slope of the $U(\bullet)$ function must be constant. As wealth, w, increases, utility in a given state increases at a constant rate. Another way of stating this is that the **marginal utility of wealth** is constant.[5] The marginal utility of wealth is simply the rate at which $U(w)$ increases as w increases. If we recall that the *MRS* is

$$MRS = \frac{-qu'(w_1)}{(1-q)u'(w_2)}$$

we see that the *MRS* for a risk-neutral individual is a constant. As w_1 and w_2 change along an indifference curve, the marginal utility of wealth in either state remains constant, and hence their ratio also remains constant (in fact, $U'(w_1)/U'(w_2) = 1$). Figure 17.2a shows indifference curves for a risk-neutral individual. They are straight lines with slopes simply equal to the ratio of probabilities, $q/(1-q)$. Risk-neutral individuals have linear indifference curves.

By comparison, the marginal utility of a risk-averse person *decreases* as wealth increases. This means that the slope of the U function decreases as w increases. Hence $u'(w_1)$ must fall and if w increases, and $u'(w)$ must increase if w decreases. Therefore, as we move down an indifference curve, where w_1 is increasing and w_2 is decreasing, then the *MRS* must be getting smaller, and the indifference curve flatter. Figure 17.2b shows the indifference curves in this case. As you can see, these indifference curves resemble those drawn in Chapters 2 and 3. Risk aversion, therefore, implies a diminishing marginal rate of substitution for wealth in the two states. Notice that the indifference curve drawn in Figure 17.1 assumed that the individual was risk-averse. Risk-averse individuals have indifferent curves convex to the origin.

5. We can use calculus to define marginal utility of wealth, $MU(w)$:

$$MU(w) = U'(w)$$

Then, $U''(w) = 0$ implies risk neutrality, $U''(w) < 0$ implies risk aversion, and $U''(w) > 0$ implies risk inclination.

FIGURE 17.2 Preferences towards risk

In (a), the *MRS* is constant, reflecting constant marginal utility of wealth and risk-neutral preferences. In (b), the *MRS* decreases as w increases, reflecting diminishing marginal utility of wealth and risk-averse preferences. In part (c), the *MRS* increases as w increases, reflecting increasing marginal utility of wealth and risk-inclined preferences.

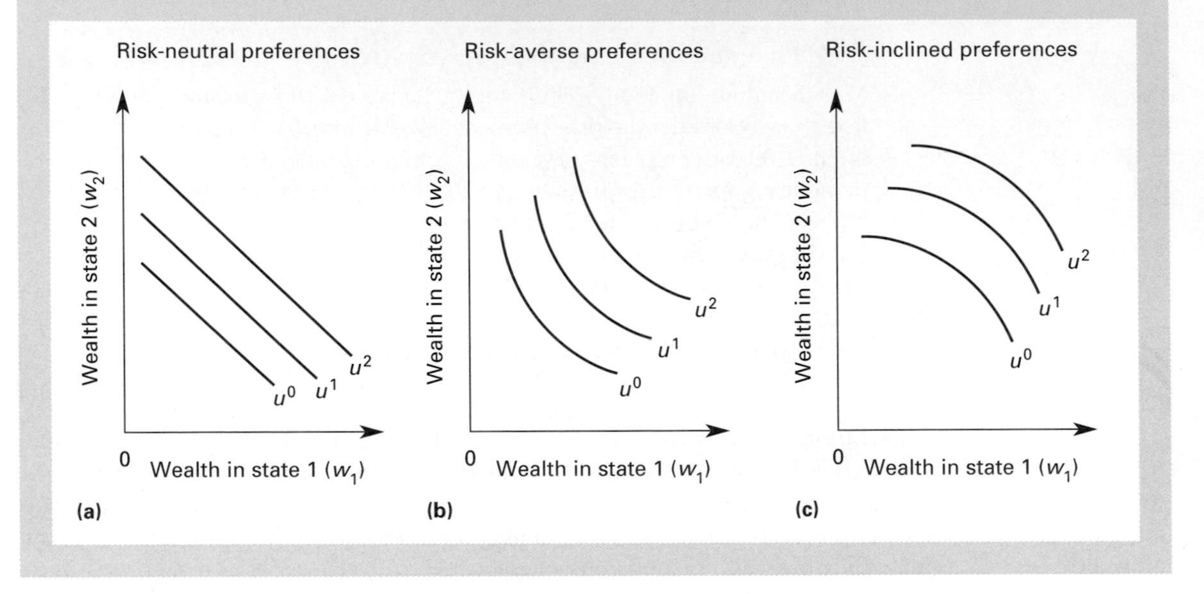

Finally, in the risk-inclined case, the slope of the utility function *increases* as wealth increases. The more wealth the individual has, the more utility it generates at the margin. Now as we move from left to right along an indifference curve, the slope must get steeper. Figure 17.2c shows the indifference curves for a risk-inclined person. These indifference curves look strange to us because we are used to indifference curves being convex to the origin. However, this shape simply reflects the increasing marginal utility of wealth that characterizes individuals who like risk. Risk-inclined individuals have indifferent curves concave to the origin.

Optimal Risk Bearing

Now that we have defined the different attitudes toward risk and shown how these attitudes affect an individual's indifference curves, we can begin to discuss choices over risky prospects. For example, given a choice between a risky prospect and an assured prospect with the same expected monetary value, what will Diego choose and how can we show this in our utility diagram? For that matter, if Diego faced a whole series of prospects, some riskier than others, which one would he choose? In order to answer these questions, we need to graph an expected monetary value line.

Let us begin by supposing that Diego has a wealth level of w_0 for certain tomorrow. No matter what state of the world is realized, Diego is "endowed" with w_0. Figure 17.3 shows w_0 lying along the 45° line at point A. The 45° line contains all of the points at which the level of wealth is equal in either state, that is, where $w_1 = w_2$. As Diego moves away from the origin along this line, his wealth in both states of the world increases in equal proportion.

FIGURE 17.3 The expected monetary value line

Points along the line CC all have the same expected value. The slope of the line CC is equal to $q/(1-q)$: the ratio of the probabilities.

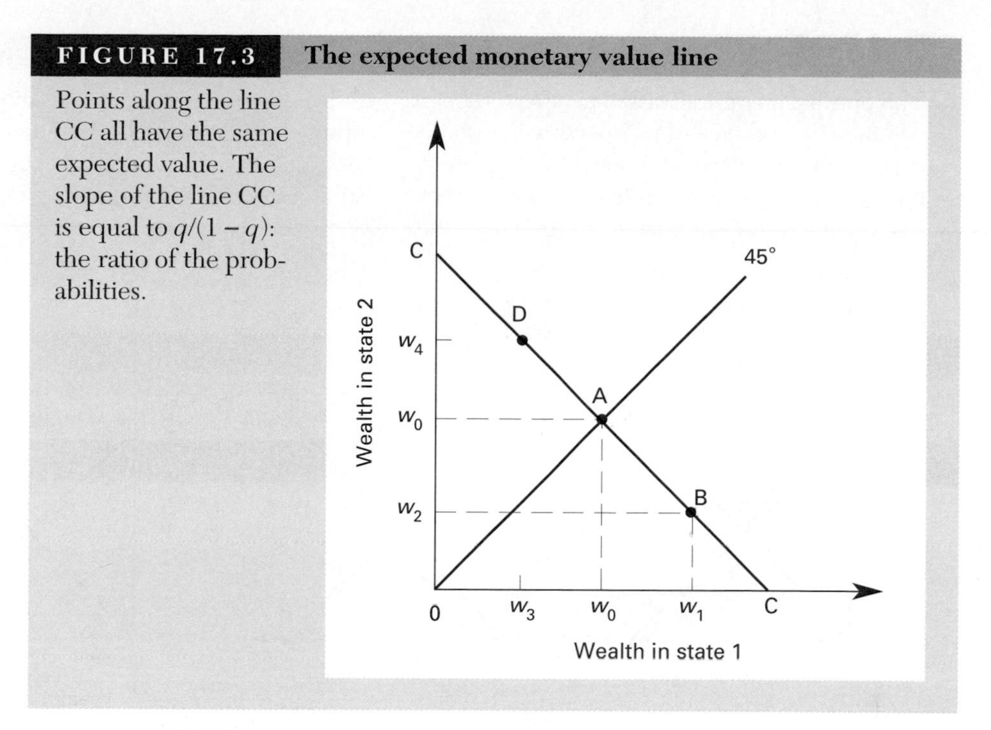

Consider all of the prospects $(q, 1-q: w_1, w_2)$ that might be offered to Diego with an expected value equal to w_0. That is, all prospects such that $w_0 = qw_1 + (1-q)w_2$. If we solve this equation for w_2, we get $w_2 = w_0/(1-q) - q/(1-q)w_1$. This is the famous point slope form, in which the term in front of w_1 $(q/(1-q))$ is the slope of the line. This line is drawn in Figure 17.3 as the line CC. There are an infinite number of prospects along this line that also have an expected monetary value equal to w_0, like $(q, 1-q: w_3, w_4)$, represented as point D in Figure 17.3. In fact, the line CC represents all prospects (or gambles) that have expected monetary values equal to w_0. The line CC is called the **expected value line**. Along this line all of the prospects have the same expected or average value. However, it must also be mentioned that along this line the risk of each prospect varies. There is no risk at point A, and the risk increases as the prospects move away from the 45° line.

expected value line

If we suppose that Diego can choose any prospect along the line CC, then the expected value line is analogous to the budget constraint that was dealt with in Chapter 3. The slope of the expected value line is equal to the ratio of the probabilities, and this slope is analogous to the relative price. When the expected value line shifts out, Diego's wealth increases in both states. When the probability of one state increases, then this changes the rate at which Diego is *able* to trade wealth in one state versus another. The indifference curves, of course, represent Diego's *willingness* to trade wealth in one state for another. Hence, our model of choice under uncertainty provides another opportunity to exploit our fundamental model of choice, since we know that utility will be maximized when Diego's *MRS* is equal to the ratio of probabilities (relative prices).

So, will Diego accept the uncertain prospect at B? This, as always, depends on his preferences. Consider Figure 17.4, which combines Diego's indifference curves and expected value line. In part (a) Diego is risk-averse because his indifference curves are convex to the origin. From Chapter 3 we know that utility is maximized when the indifference curve is tangent to the budget constraint. In this case we can say even

FIGURE 17.4 Optimal risk bearing

The optimal amount of risk that a person bears when facing a choice of prospects with equal expected values depends on his or her preferences. In (a), where the individual is risk-averse, risk is completely eliminated. In (b) where the individual is risk-neutral, any allocation of risk is optimal. Finally in (c), where the individual is risk-inclined, the individual chooses a corner solution where risk is high.

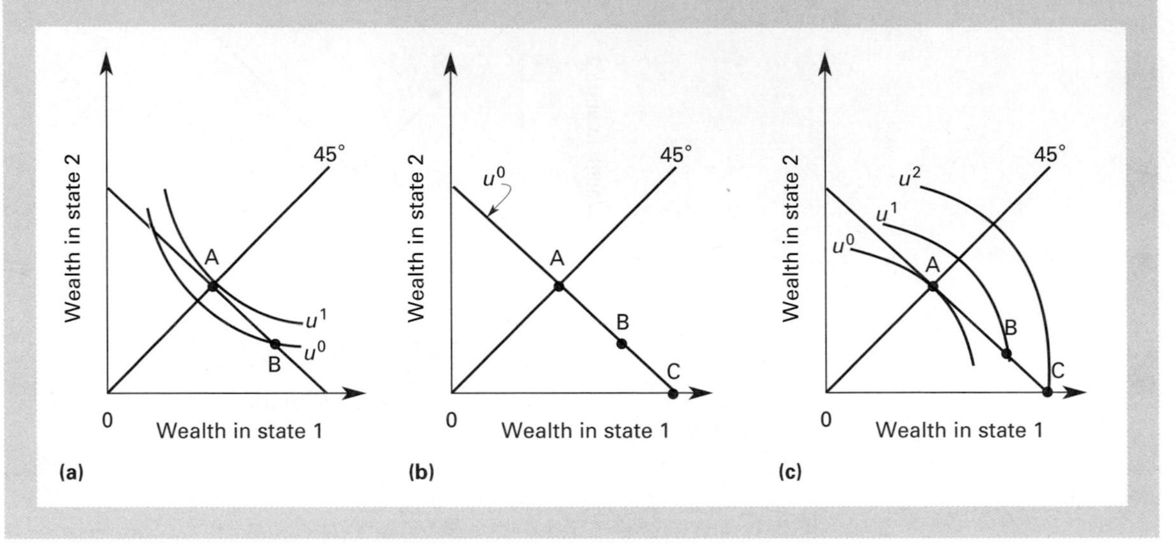

more, however. Recall that the slope of the expected value line is $q/(1-q)$. The slope of the indifference curve is $(q/(1-q)) \times (U'(w_1)/U'(w_2))$. Along the 45° line the levels of wealth are equal in both states, so the slope of the indifference curve simplifies to $q/(1-q)$. This means that Diego's utility is maximized at point A if he is risk-averse.

Before we move on to consider what happens if Diego is risk-neutral or risk-inclined, let us consider this case a little more carefully. Keep in mind that risk aversion means Diego does not like risk; it does not mean that he dislikes all bets. For example, if Diego had an endowment at point B rather than point A, then he would accept a bet that moved him to point A. If a bet reduces the amount of risk while holding the expected wealth constant, then a risk-averse person will accept the bet. (If the concept of a bet reducing risk seems strange, it's because you're thinking of gambles such as horse racing, in which you start with a position of certainty. Insurance, however, is an example of a situation in which you start from an uncertain position and make a bet with the insurance company about the outcome, thus moving to a position of less risk.) The key result is that risk-averse Diego maximizes his utility when he eliminates all risk in his life, which he does at point A.

Now consider part (b) in Figure 17.4. If Diego is risk-neutral it means that he does not care about risk; he only cares about the expected value of a prospect. We have seen that in this case his indifference curves are straight lines with slope $q/(1-q)$. This means that an indifference curve lies on top of the expected value line and there is no single optimum. If Diego were risk-neutral he would be indifferent between points A, B, or C, since they all yield the same expected value.

In part (c) of Figure 17.4 we have the final case where Diego is assumed to be risk-inclined. It is tempting to think that the point of maximum utility is where the slope of the indifference curve is tangent to the slope of the expected value line; however, this is the point where utility is lowest along the expected value line! Since risk lovers have the weird pattern of increasing marginal rates of substitution, the point of maximum utility will be in a corner. Hence, if Diego were risk-inclined and had an endowment at point A, his utility would be higher at point B, but even higher at point C.

The optimal amount of risk that a person bears in life depends critically on his or her degree of risk aversion. The choices of risk-averse individuals tend towards the 45° line where wealth is the same no matter what state of the world arises. Risk-inclined individuals' choices tend away from the 45° line, where they will be much better off if one state occurs and much worse off if the other one arises.

PROBLEM 17.10

In Figure 17.4 it was assumed that the probabilities q and $(1 - q)$ used to define the expected value line were the same as the subjective probabilities in the expected utility function. Suppose that this were not true, and that in fact, Diego thought the probabilities were q' and $(1 - q')$, where $q' > q$.

a. What happens to the slope of Diego's indifference curves?
b. Show what happens to the optimal amount of risk in Diego's life in all three cases of risk-aversion, neutrality, and inclination.

Application: Another Form of Taxation?

Lotteries are often called a form of taxation for people who are bad at arithmetic. When you play a slot machine in an average casino, the machines return about 90 cents for every dollar put in. When you play Bingo the yield is about 75 cents on the dollar. But when you play your average state or provincial lottery, the return is only about 50 cents on the dollar!

Gambling provides a little bit of a puzzle to the economics of uncertainty. If we think that people are generally risk-averse, why would they flock to such unfair bets? In a Florida state lottery that had a jackpot of over $100 million, tickets were selling at a rate of over 1000 tickets per minute! Although a conclusive answer still awaits, it may turn out that the answer is not that people are irrational, love to gamble, or are generally risk-loving. Economists studying state lotteries have discovered that whether the lottery is fair or not depends on a number of factors, especially the fraction of money that is carried over from the past lottery if there was no winner, and the expected elasticity of participants for a given prize. It turns out that quite often a given lottery ends up, after the fact, being better than a fair bet, and as a result it is not inconsistent that risk-averse people participate. In British Columbia the province ran a lottery called "Over and Under" in which the participants had to bet whether the point spread in any particular game would be over or under a number picked by the lottery agency. Apparently the person in charge of picking this number was not a sports fan and picked numbers that made little sense. There was a rush on ticket sales and winnings. One smiling man, leaving the lottery office with a few thousand dollars in his pocket, told a reporter, "This is just like printing money." The lottery was discontinued.

17.4 Pooling Risk

A common institution among people who fish for sport is a share-the-bounty convention. The tacit understanding is that anyone who catches a trophy fish will take it home. Otherwise, the members of the fishing party divide the catch equally, without regard to who actually caught which fish. We can view this institution as a form of insurance against the embarrassment of being "skunked" — coming home empty-handed. Such forms of insurance are arrangements known as **risk pooling**.

risk pooling

Other examples of risk pooling include the understanding among nineteenth-century North American pioneers that if one family lost a home to fire, the whole community would pitch in to help them rebuild, and the tradition among Inuit of sharing their food equally, even in times of famine.

Informal Risk Pooling

In this section, we use our analytical tools to develop an understanding of risk pooling and of the preferences that make such an institution attractive. We begin by considering two householders, Abe and Martha, who face identical but independent risks — the risk that their houses will burn. Can they create any institution that will reduce the burden of risk?

Imagine that the probability that either Abe or Martha will experience a fire is $1 - q$. Further, suppose that the loss associated with a fire is L dollars. (In what follows, we will concentrate on Abe, but it should be clear that the same analysis applies to Martha.) In the absence of a risk-pooling agreement, Abe's expected utility is

$$u(q, L, w_0) = qU(w_0) + (1 - q)U(w_0 - L)$$

where w_0 is his initial wealth. Abe's house will burn with probability $(1 - q)$. If it does, Abe's wealth will be $w_0 - L$, and his utility will be $U(w_0 - L)$. On the other hand, the probability that his house will not burn is q. Abe's wealth will then be w_0, and his utility will be $U(w_0)$. We will call the case where Abe's house does not burn state 1, and the state where his house does burn state 2. Hence $w_1 = w_0$ and $w_2 = w_0 - L$.

Let us now suppose that Abe and Martha agree to *pool* their risks; that is, they agree to share any loss due to fire. We now have three relevant events: both houses burn; one house burns; neither house burns. Because the probabilities of fire are independent, the probability that both will burn is $(1 - q)^2$, the product of the two independent probabilities that either house burns. If both houses do burn, Abe will incur a loss of L. Similarly, the probability that neither burns is q^2. In this event, Abe experiences no loss. Finally, the probability that exactly one house burns is $2q(1 - q)$. In this event, Abe incurs a loss equal to $L/2$.[6] Abe's expected utility associated with this risk-pooling agreement is then

$$(1 - q)^2U(w_0 - L) + 2q(1 - q)U(w_0 - L/2) + q^2U(w_0)$$

6. To calculate this probability, note that the probability that Abe's house burns and Martha's does not is $q(1 - q)$. Similarly, the probability that Martha's burns and Abe's does not is also $q(1 - q)$. Thus, the probability that exactly one house burns is $2q(1 - q)$.

When does this risk-pooling agreement actually enhance Abe's expected utility? More precisely, when is

$$(1-q)^2U(w_0-L)+2q(1-q)U(w_0-L/2)+q^2U(w_0)>(1-q)U(w_0-L)+qU(w_0)$$

The answer is that the risk-pooling agreement enhances Abe's utility if he is *risk-averse*. To see why, first rewrite the inequality from above as follows:

$$2q(1-q)U(w_0-L/2)>q(1-q)U(w_0-L)+q(1-q)U(w_0)$$

Then divide both sides of the expression by $2q(1-q)$ to get

$$U(w_0-L/2)>(1/2)U(w_0-L)+(1/2)U(w_0)$$

Now we can use the graphic tools from the previous section to show that this inequality holds if Abe is risk-averse. To construct Figure 17.5 we assume that Abe is risk-averse. Notice that $U(w_0-L/2)$ is received in each state if risk pooling is done, and so this value is on the 45° line. Without risk pooling, Abe's wealth is higher in state 1 than in state 2, so the non-pooled allocation is off the 45° line — meaning there is risk attached to this allocation. Since the two prospects have equal expected values it is clear from the graph in Figure 17.5 that Abe prefers the risk-pooling agreement to going it alone, because he is risk-averse.

By using the appropriately shaped utility functions, you can check to see that a risk-inclined householder prefers to go it alone and that a risk-neutral householder is indifferent between the two arrangements. An important point emerges from this exercise:

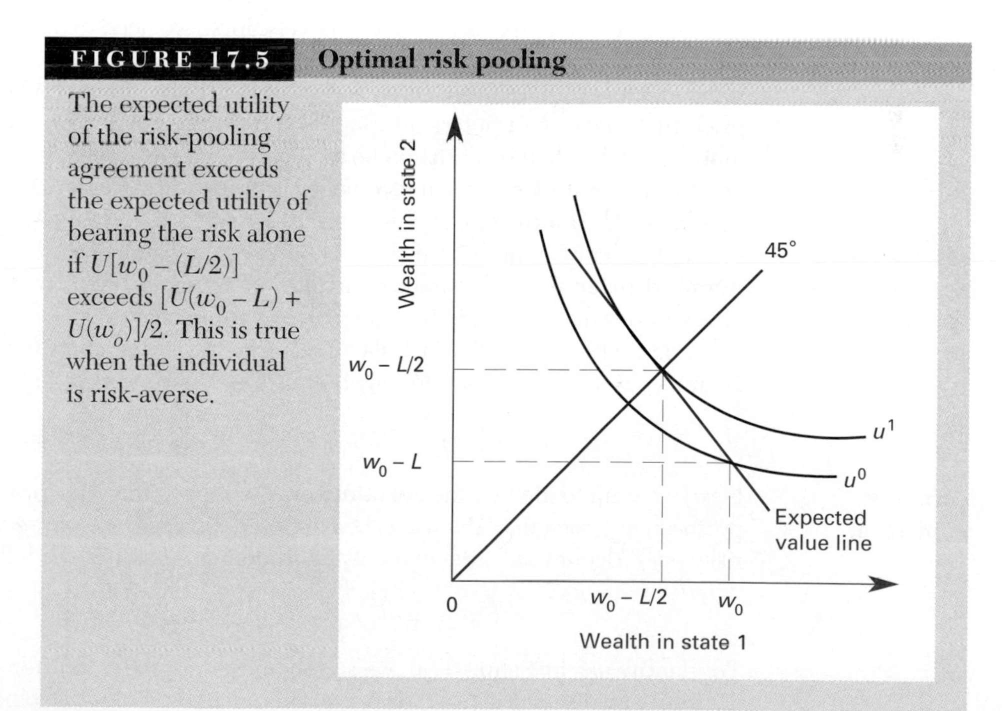

FIGURE 17.5 **Optimal risk pooling**

The expected utility of the risk-pooling agreement exceeds the expected utility of bearing the risk alone if $U[w_0-(L/2)]$ exceeds $[U(w_0-L)+U(w_0)]/2$. This is true when the individual is risk-averse.

When individuals are risk-averse, they have clear incentives to create institutions allowing them to share, or pool, their risks.

Notice that the risk-pooling institution we have considered does nothing to alter the physical environment; that is, it does nothing to reduce the incidence of fire. Yet it does increase the expected utility of the householders in the pool. Just like pure exchange can increase total utility without increasing the amount available for consumption, so trading risk can improve welfare without altering the amount of risk.

PROBLEM 17.11

Consider two identical people fishing for steelhead with expected utility function $u = qw_1^{1/2} + (1 - q)w_2^{1/2}$, where w is the number of fish. Graph this function in w_1 and w_2 space and convince yourself that it represents risk-averse preferences. Assuming that the probability that either will catch one fish is 1/10 and that it is impossible for either to catch two fish, show that if they agree to pool their risks, both will be better off than if they refuse to divide the catch.

In pioneer societies, risk-pooling arrangements such as the community agreement to rebuild homes destroyed by fire were usually informal. Such informal risk-pooling persists today among members of extended families or close-knit communities. In most modern societies, however, the functions these informal institutions used to perform have been largely taken over by insurance markets.

The Market for Insurance

Let us continue to use Abe's risk-of-fire problem as our example and to assume that Abe is risk-averse as we explore insurance markets. First, we need to describe Abe's demand for fire insurance, and then we can look at the supply of insurance. Our objective is to show that in a competitive insurance market he will be able to buy fire insurance at a price that makes him better off than if he bore the burden of risk himself. What's more, he will be better off than if he took part in an informal risk-pooling agreement.

We will consider an insurance policy offering full coverage; that is, one that will reimburse Abe for the full amount of his loss. Such a policy pays Abe L in the event of fire and, of course, nothing if there is no fire. We want to find Abe's **reservation demand price** for such a policy: the *maximum amount* he is willing to pay for the policy rather than having to bear the risk of fire himself.

reservation demand price

Consider Figure 17.6, which shows that Abe's expected utility in the absence of fire insurance is u_0. If Abe does not buy fire insurance, his expected utility is

$$u = qU(w_0) + (1 - q)U(w_0 - L)$$

certainty equivalent

Next, we want to identify the **certainty equivalent** of this risky prospect: the assured prospect, w_{ce}, such that Abe would be indifferent between the assured prospect and the risky one. Algebraically, the certainty equivalent w_{ce} satisfies the following equation:

$$U(w_{ce}) = qU(w_0) + (1 - q)U(w_0 - L) = u^0$$

To identify w_{ce} in Figure 17.6, we simply move along the indifference curve to the 45° line. The distance $w_0 - w_{ce}$ is the maximum amount of money that Abe would pay

FIGURE 17.6 The demand for insurance

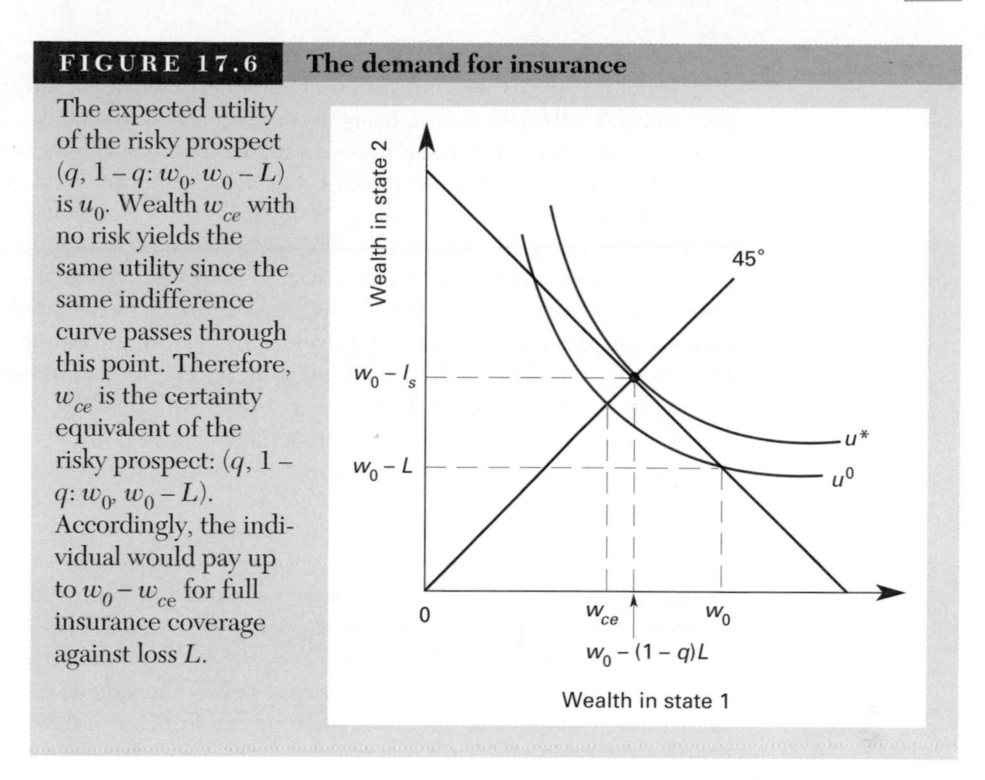

The expected utility of the risky prospect $(q, 1-q\colon w_0, w_0-L)$ is u_0. Wealth w_{ce} with no risk yields the same utility since the same indifference curve passes through this point. Therefore, w_{ce} is the certainty equivalent of the risky prospect: $(q, 1-q\colon w_0, w_0-L)$. Accordingly, the individual would pay up to w_0-w_{ce} for full insurance coverage against loss L.

to avoid the risk of a fire. If Abe has assured prospect w_{ce}, his expected utility is u_0, just as it is in the absence of insurance. (You already have some experience with certainty equivalents. In Problem 17.1, you wrote down your own certainty equivalent of the prospect [1/2, 1/2: 2 000 000, 0], and in Problem 17.3, you calculated Chauncey's certainty equivalent of Risk.) This result is intuitive. If Abe did pay w_0-w_{ce} for insurance, his assured income would be w_{ce}, the certainty equivalent of personally bearing the risk of fire. If the actual price of the insurance is less than w_0-w_{ce}, then Abe's (expected) utility is larger if he buys the policy than if he does not. Conversely, if the price of complete insurance is greater than w_0-w_{ce}, his expected utility is larger if he does not buy the insurance.

Will insurance firms be willing to offer full coverage on terms attractive to Abe? That is, is there a viable market for insurance? Let us begin by making the not-so-satisfactory assumption that insurance companies are risk-neutral.

One way to think about insurance is as a market for state claims. When you buy an insurance policy, you are trading a certain amount of money in all states of the world for a payout in a particular state. In Abe's case, he is saying to the insurance company, "I would like to buy x dollars of wealth in state 1 and y dollars of wealth in state 2 at prices p_1 and p_2." There is no loss of generality in thinking of w_1 and w_2 as simply goods. If the amount of wealth Abe wants is the same in each state, then Abe fully insures himself and receives the same amount of income regardless of whether a fire occurs.

If Abe is endowed with wealth in both states (in Abe's case he has w_0, and w_0-L), and he can trade wealth from one state to another at a set of prices p_1 and p_2, then he faces a budget constraint equal to

$$p_1w_1+p_2w_2=p_1w_0+p_2(w_0-L)$$

This constraint is *exactly* like the endowment budget constraint that we saw in Chapter 3. In order for Abe to consume different amounts of wealth in different states, he simply buys and sells state claims, using his endowment in exchange.

The insurance constraint is drawn in Figure 17.6. As with ordinary constraints, the slope of this line is the relative price of state 1 consumption: p_1/p_2. On the assumption that insurance companies are risk-neutral, what is the lowest price at which such a firm will offer full coverage? In other words, how much state 1 wealth must Abe give up to get equal wealth in both states? The answer to this question is an insurance firm's **reservation supply price**, denoted by I_s. Because the firm is by definition risk-neutral, it will simply compare expected monetary values in deciding whether to offer insurance. Ignoring, for simplicity, any costs it incurs in writing and administering a policy, the firm will pay out L with probability $(1 - q)$ and \$0 with probability q. Its expected costs are therefore $(1 - q)L$. Its revenue from selling a policy is I, and it will write the policy if I exceeds $(1 - q)L$. The insurance firm's reservation supply price is therefore

reservation supply price

$$I_s = (1 - q)L$$

In the case shown in Figure 17.6, there is a viable market for insurance because the reservation supply price I_s (distance $w_0 - [w_0 - (1 - q)L] = (1 - q)L$) is less than the reservation demand price distance $w_0 - w_{ce}$. The straight line that intersects the state endowment has a slope equal to the relative price of insurance claims. When the price of insurance simply reflects the relative probabilities of a state occurring, then the insurance is said to be *fair*.

If we make the standard competitive assumption that many insurance firms compete to write insurance policies, and continue to ignore the costs of writing and administering policies, we can conclude that in equilibrium, the price will be driven down to the zero profit level. (Recall the zero-profit competitive equilibrium from Chapter 9.) This means that the insurance company must offer fair insurance claims; that is, the relative price of insurance must equal $q/(1 - q)$. In this case, Abe trades his risky prospect for the assured prospect $w_0 - (1 - q)L$, and his utility is then $U(w_0 - (1 - q)L)$, and he reaches the indifference curve u^* in Figure 17.6.

In this market equilibrium, Abe's expected wealth is identical to his expected wealth in the absence of an insurance policy — yet he bears no risk. If the insurance company charged prices that were not fair (that is, the slope of the insurance line was not equal to the slope of the expected value line), then Abe would still buy insurance, but he would end up consuming some risk.

As we noted, the analysis is based on the assumption that insurance firms are risk-neutral. In a sense, insurance firms' attitudes towards risk are irrelevant to our analysis because they bear very little risk. If they sell a large number of such policies, they are effectively pooling a large number of independent risks of fire. A fundamental result in statistics — called the *law of large numbers* — then implies that such companies can be quite accurate in projecting their costs. Let us summarize what we have learned:

If no resources are required to write and administer insurance policies and if individuals are risk-averse, there is a viable market for insurance.

Risk Spreading

We have seen that insurance is simply a market mechanism for risk pooling and that it is potentially valuable to risk-averse individuals. The other side of this coin is a phe-

risk spreading

nomenon called **risk spreading**. To see what's involved, imagine that you own some indivisible and risky asset — say a promising two-year-old racehorse. Clearly, risks are entailed. The horse's promise may not materialize: it may break a leg; it may be kidnapped for ransom and disappear; it may fail as a stud horse or brood mare. In this circumstance, someone who is risk-averse might prefer to spread the risk.

For example, as a two-year-old, Devil's Bag was thought to be the latest and greatest American wonder. Its owner chose to sell it to a syndicate — a group of joint shareholders, each of whom owned a fraction of the horse — for \$36 million, rather than to bear the risk alone. In fact, the owner was wise (or lucky) to spread that risk. The racehorse did not fulfill his potential and was retired as a three-year-old.

A syndicate is only one example of a risk-spreading institution. The joint-venture companies that sponsored voyages of discovery (or perhaps, plunder) by men like Sir Francis Drake are illustrations of risk spreading from an earlier time. Today, joint-stock companies spread the risks of a firm among the firm's stockholders. Problem 17.12 conveys the basic insight of risk spreading:

Risk-averse individuals may prefer holding some part of a risky asset to holding the entire asset.

PROBLEM 17.12

Patricia's utility function is $U(w) = w^{1/2}$, and her initial wealth w_0 is \$100. For a price of \$100, she can buy an asset that will yield \$10 000 with probability 1/20 and \$0 with probability 19/20. Observe that the expected monetary value of this asset is \$500 while its price is just \$100. Show that she will not buy this asset alone but will join a syndicate with 10 equal partners.

SUMMARY

In this chapter, we extended the theory of preferences and consumer choice to situations involving *risk* and *incomplete information* and then used this expanded theory to examine a variety of problems in which either risk or incomplete information plays a central role.

We then identified three possible attitudes towards risk — *risk aversion*, *risk neutrality*, and *risk inclination* — and we argued that *risk-pooling* and *risk-spreading* arrangements can be explained by assuming most people are risk-averse. The amount of risk that an individual is willing to bear depends critically on his or her attitude towards risk. When individuals are risk-averse, they seek to find ways to eliminate risk. This led us to a detailed exploration of the market for insurance — an important risk-pooling arrangement.

EXERCISES

1. Consider the following game. Daniel offers to toss a coin until one head appears, and he promises to pay you 2^n dollars, where n is the toss on which the first head appears. If it appears on the first toss, you get \$2; if on the second, \$4; if on the third, \$8; and so on. What is the maximum amount you would pay to play the game? What is the expected monetary value of this game? This is the exercise that led Daniel Bernoulli to propose the expected-utility hypothesis.

2. Show that the expected monetary value hypothesis is a special case of the expected-utility hypothesis. (*Hint*: What attitude towards risk makes an individual indifferent between two prospects if they have the same expected monetary value?)

3. In draw poker, suppose a player is dealt four clubs and a two of hearts. The player may discard the two of hearts in the hope of getting another club to complete a club flush. Does the situation in which the player discards the two of hearts and draws another card involve risk or incomplete information?

4. Guy reveals the following piece of information regarding his preferences for risky prospects with prizes of \$20, \$12, and \$0: He is indifferent between (0, 1, 0: 20, 12, 0) and (0.7, 0, 0.3: 20, 12, 0).
   a. Explain in words the meaning of this preference statement.
   b. Assuming that Guy satisfies the expected-utility assumptions, find a utility function that represents Guy's preferences for prospects with these three prizes.
   c. Is Guy risk-averse, risk-neutral, or risk-inclined? Explain.
   d. Compute Guy's expected utility for the following prospects:
      Prospect A (0.6, 0, 0.4: 20, 12, 0)
      Prospect B (0.4, 0.2, 0.4: 20, 12, 0)
      Prospect C (0, 1, 0: 20, 12, 0)
      Prospect D (0.3, 0.4, 0.3: 20, 12, 0)
      Prospect E (0.5, 0.2, 0.3: 20, 12, 0)
   e. What is Guy's preference ordering for these prospects?

5. Kunuk says that she is indifferent between a lottery that pays either (i) \$100 or \$10 with equal probability and (ii) \$50 with certainty. Which lottery will Kunuk choose in each of the following situations?
   a. (1/4, 3/4: 100, 10) or (1/2, 1/2: 50, 10)
   b. (3/4, 1/4: 100, 10) or (9/10, 1/10: 50, 10)
   c. (1/2, 1/2: 100, 10) or (2/6, 3/6, 1/6: 100, 50, 10)

6. Farmer Ingrid has to decide whether or not to fertilize her field. The decision is a difficult one, because her profit depends not only on her decision with respect to fertilizer, but also on whether it rains or not. Her profit w in each of the four possible cases is as follows:

	Do not fertilize	**Fertilize**
Rain	$w = \$16$	$w = \$25$
No rain	$w = \$\ 9$	$w = \$\ 0$

   Suppose that the probability of rain is 1/2. Will Ingrid fertilize her field if her utility function is $U(w) = w^{1/2}$? If it is $U(w) = w$? If it is $U(w) = w^2$?

7. In looking at insurance markets, we ignored the costs of writing and administering insurance policies. Once we introduce such costs, some of the lessons we learned require amendment. A friend once gave us a piece of advice: even though you are risk-averse, never buy insurance against small losses. Is this good advice?

8. Mike is going to Lake Tahoe and plans to take \$2500. With probability 1/2, he will lose \$1600 on his way to Tahoe. Thus, he will spend \$2500 in Tahoe if he is lucky and only \$900 if he is unlucky. His utility from the trip is given by the following function:

$$U(E) = E^{1/2}$$

   where E is the amount of money he spends in Tahoe.
   a. What is Mike's expected utility from the trip?
   b. Suppose Mike can buy an insurance policy that will cover the entire \$1600 loss. Will he buy it if its price is \$1000? \$900? \$800?
   c. What is Mike's reservation price for this insurance policy?
   d. What is the competitive-equilibrium price of the policy if insurance companies have perfect information and incur no transaction costs?

9. Ms Q, whose \$1000 wealth is invested in a riskless asset, has been offered the chance to buy a firm that produces snake oil. The price of the firm is \$500. Federal regulators are reviewing the snake oil with an eye to banning its sale. She believes that with probability 1/2 the snake oil will be banned and the business will then be worthless and that with probability 1/2 it will be approved and the business will then be worth \$2500. Her utility function is $\ln(w)$, the natural logarithm of her wealth w. Will she buy the business?

10. Lucky Pierre is a risk-averse prospector who has struck it rich. He has $W worth of gold — his only wealth — safely stashed away on his claim. He wants to get his gold from his claim to the big city where he hopes to spend it. His friend Wells Fargo will transport the gold for him free of charge. With probability q, all the gold on any trip will be stolen; with probability $(1 - q)$, none of it will be stolen. Show that Lucky's expected utility is larger if half the gold is transferred in each of two trips than if all the gold is transferred in a single trip.

11. General Motors is one of the world's largest firms and is diversified in many dimensions. For example, GM has plants around the world, produces a large spectrum of products, controls many of its inputs, etc. GM, however, also buys insurance from firms that are much smaller than itself. These smaller firms are less able to diversify risk than is General Motors, and yet insurance is sold. Why do you think GM buys insurance? (*Hint*: This question is intended to motivate you to read the next three chapters.)

12. Show that the reservation price for full coverage of a risk-inclined householder is less than $(1 - q)L$. This result implies that, for such householders, $w_0 - w_{ce} < I_s$. Thus, there is no price at which this householder and a risk-neutral insurance company could engage in a mutually beneficial transfer of risk.

13. Dorothy has a utility function of the form $U = w^{1/2}$, and faces a situation in which income is $36 with probability 0.5 and $100 with probability 0.5.
    a. Dorothy is indifferent between a certain payoff of $$x$ and this gamble. What is x?
    b. What is the risk premium associated with this gamble?
    c. Suppose Dorothy is offered, for $32, full insurance for the $64 (potential) loss. Will she buy it?

*14. "An individual with expected utility function $U(w)$, where w is wealth, will have the same preference over lotteries if her expected utility function is $V(w) = [U(w)]^2$, since this is a simple monotonic transformation." Indicate whether this statement is true or false and explain your answer clearly.

*15. Simon has a comic book collection worth $100. Simon has a dog Rufus and he knows that, with probability 0.1, Rufus will destroy all but $4 of the value of the collection. Simon's utility function is $U(w) = w^{1/2}$.
    a. What is the expected value of the comic book collection? What is Simon's expected utility?
    b. Suppose that there is a company that insures against these "acts of dog." What is the maximum expected revenue that the insurance company could earn from Simon?
    c. Suppose that there is no insurance available but Simon can buy a comic book protection box. If this box fully protects his collection from Rufus, what is the maximum amount Simon would pay for it?

REFERENCES

Bernoulli, D. 1954. "Exposition of a New Theory on the Measurement of Risk," *Econometrica*, 22:23–36.

Machina, M. J. 1987. "Expected-utility Hypothesis," in *The New Palgrave: A Dictionary of Economics*, J. Eatwell, M. Milgate, and P. Newman (eds.). London: Macmillan.

CHAPTER 18

Asymmetric Information, the Rules of the Game, and Externalities

In the last chapter we examined our model of choice with uncertainty. Critical to that discussion was the assumption that information was exogenous and symmetric between all parties entering an exchange. For example, there was nothing Abe could do to influence the probability that his house would burn down, nor did he have any information advantage over the insurance company regarding this probability. The insurance company knew exactly what Abe knew, and neither could affect the outcome.

There are two important lessons from Chapter 17. First, the presence of uncertainty provides an incentive for risk-averse individuals to avoid risk, through risk spreading, informal risk pooling (such as the custom of helping neighbours when disaster strikes), and insurance. According to our model, if individuals faced a perfect insurance market where they could buy fair insurance for any eventuality (that is, insurance where the premium is simply the probability of a loss times the amount insured), they could and would completely eliminate uncertainty in their lives. This led to the second lesson from Chapter 17: adding uncertainty to our neoclassical model does not fundamentally alter the way choices are made. Our standard analysis applies, with attitudes to risk being simply another kind of consumer preference. Adding uncertainty merely generates a demand for insurance. Ultimately the most important purpose of Chapter 17 was to introduce uncertainty to our model, laying the foundation for asymmetric information theory. This theory, which we will introduce in this chapter, helps us understand a vast array of problems not dealt with by our standard neoclassical model.

18.1 Critiques of the Neoclassical Model

If this book has done its job properly, by now you should think the neoclassical model of supply and demand can explain just about anything — in a logical, consistent, and testable fashion. (Well, not the movement of planets, and maybe not why some people prefer to watch *Survivor* and others listen to Bach, but a wide range of human interaction.) Over and over we have used our simple model based on demand, supply, and equilibrium to understand everything from crime to price wars. True enough, from time to time we have made different assumptions regarding the number of firms and the nature of competition, but the essential model has remained the same.

However, there is a number of observations that, if we are honest, we must admit our model cannot explain. First, prices do not always clear markets. If you look around the very spot you are sitting, you will no doubt see great amounts of capital that is currently unemployed: chairs with no one sitting in them, books not read, clothing on shelves, and machines remaining idle. People, too, are often unemployed. Individuals often quit jobs and do not immediately find work for the same pay. When people are laid off they can realistically expect to spend several weeks or months looking for another job. Furthermore, there are parts of every country where unemployment is chronic. For an economist the obvious question is, Why do the prices of these unemployed resources not fall? Unemployment, or excess supply, is always related to the price of the resource. Clearly, the price mechanism is not completely fulfilling its assigned function.

A second problem is similar: chronic shortages. Every night when we leave campus we face the common problem of rush hour: a situation in which too many people demand use of limited road space. Not only do prices fail to allocate space on the road, there are no explicit prices. There is not even a mechanism to try to purchase a spot on the road at which one could travel at 100 km/h during the late afternoon. Other illustrations abound. Grocery shopping on a Friday night may take twice as long as on Friday morning. The store owner knows there is a lineup every Friday night; why does he not raise his prices? The list goes on and on. When the Vancouver Canucks finally made it back to the Stanley Cup finals in the spring of 1994, fans lined up for days to buy tickets. Many were purchased by people who later resold them for hundreds of dollars. Why did the Canucks hockey team, again, not raise prices?

distribution of property rights

Another issue unaddressed by the neoclassical model has to do with what we will call the "rules of the game," or the **distribution of property rights**. That is, until now we have been exclusively concerned with the volume and price of goods traded. We have completely ignored *how* trade is organized. Think for a moment about the "firm" as described in Chapters 6 and 7. There the firm was represented simply by a production function, a mere black box. In those chapters we were concerned with how much output was produced, and at what cost. We were never really concerned with *how* this output was produced. Within some firms the rights and responsibilities assigned to workers look like market transactions, while in other firms they appear bureaucratic.

nonprofit firms

For example, consider the following goods: education, Big Macs, houses, and children. Education is most often provided by local governments, supervised by provincial or state authorities, and funded through taxation. Other times education is provided and paid for privately. In both cases, the schools are almost always what are called **nonprofit firms**. This does not mean that these firms do not earn a profit; it simply means that no individual is allowed to keep the firm's profit. Big Macs are provided by McDonald's restaurants. Most of these restaurants are franchises, which means that a local owner shares the revenue with the parent company, and the parent company exerts a great deal of control over the product line, prices, and marketing. Franchises are used in firms that supply everything from lawn furniture to clothing, and were even used to staff the armies of Europe until the end of the nineteenth century. Houses are most often built by private contractors, who in turn hire subcontractors for particular tasks in construction. Here we have a series of firms using prices to allocate resources for most tasks. Finally, children are produced in "firms" that are called families. In families, a man and woman generally contract for life, often using a formal, standard contract prescribed by their community. Furthermore, in families, the man and woman always agree to share in the output of their firm; neither spouse hires the other.

Here we see four different goods, with four completely different methods of organization to produce them. If we had listed more goods, we could easily have come up with additional ways production is organized. Though there are huge differences, there are also many similarities. For example, just as families share, so do farmers, lawyers, and authors. Just as education is provided by nonprofit firms, so is health care, religion, and humanitarian aid. Can economic theory shed any light on the way production is organized?

In this chapter and the next two, we introduce you to the economics of asymmetric information, which provides answers to these unresolved puzzles. This body of theory is relatively new in economics, only really starting in the 1960s, although threads of it can be found as far back as Adam Smith. In this chapter, we focus on how different rules, laws, or property rights might influence exchange. We discuss these questions in the context of two classic examples: externalities and public goods.

18.2 Externalities and the Coase Theorem

Every nonsmoker who has ever sat at a restaurant table next to the smoking section knows that the behaviour of the smokers influences the enjoyment of a meal. When someone's behaviour increases or decreases another's utility or profit, without compensation, then we say that the agent is imposing an **externality**, either positive or negative, on the person affected.

externality

The smoker's externality is but one example of a large class of similar problems. Consider some recent headlines: "Must Spend Billions to Fight Air Pollution, Report Warns;" "Pulp Mill Effluents Lead to Permanent Ban on Shellfish Harvest;" "Hydro Demands Threaten Grand Canyon;" "World Leaders Meet Over Global Warming." Acid rain, driftnets, dioxins, PCBs, the greenhouse effect, nuclear winter, the ozone layer ... all these words and phrases call to mind important externality problems. Of course, not all externalities are negative. The creation of new public parks and green belts and the reclamation of marshlands for wildlife habitats are just a few examples of activities with positive externalities.

Initially, let us examine the externality problem using the standard neoclassical model developed in this book, excluding uncertainty. Suppose we have two people, Verlyn and Doug, who have to share an office. Doug loves to smoke cigars, and loves to smoke at his desk while working. Unfortunately, Verlyn, finds the smoke distracting and unhealthy. The more smoke there is in the room, the more upset he gets. (Of course, the smoke is unhealthy for Doug, too, but Doug has presumably weighed "bads" against "goods" to arrive at the following values.) Table 18.1 shows the marginal value of cigars to Doug (net of the cigars' cost) and the marginal costs to Verlyn. For simplicity, we are going to assume throughout this chapter that income effects can be ignored.

Let us ask the following question — keeping in mind that there is no uncertainty, and that both people know the rules, prices, true marginal values, and costs: Will the number of cigars that Doug smokes depend on the legal rules for smoking in an office? In other words, if it is perfectly legal to smoke in an office without the permission of other occupants, will there be more smoking than if it is illegal? Another way to phrase this is, will the amount of smoke depend on who has the **property right** over smoke?

property right

TABLE 18.1 Marginal values and costs of cigars

Number of Cigars	Marginal Value	Marginal Cost
1	$30	$2
2	20	10
3	15	15
4	12	20
5	8	40
6	4	100

The obvious answer is that of course it matters. This answer, however, is wrong, because maximizers would choose the level of smoke that maximizes the gains from trade, regardless of who owns the right to smoke.[1] For example, suppose that Verlyn owns the right to smoke, and tells Doug that the office is now a smoke-free environment. Doug would love to have a cigar, and is willing to pay $30 for the first one. Verlyn, on the other hand, does not mind one cigar too much, since the cost to him is only $2. We have a classic situation where there are gains from trade. Doug will pay Verlyn some amount between $2 and $30, and Verlyn will consent to have one cigar smoked. In other words, Verlyn will sell the right to smoke one cigar. Similarly, Doug is willing to pay $20 for the second cigar, while Verlyn is willing to accept a payment higher than $10. With the third cigar both the marginal value and marginal costs are $15. At this price Verlyn and Doug are indifferent to trade. As always, let's assume they make this trade. Thus, when Verlyn owns the right to decide how much smoke is in the room, three cigars are smoked.

Now turn it around, and suppose Doug does have a right to smoke at his desk. He may want to smoke six cigars, but if Doug and Verlyn are maximizers, this is not the equilibrium number. At six cigars Doug's marginal value is only $4, while the sixth cigar causes $100 damage to Verlyn. As before, there are gains from trade, since Verlyn is now willing to pay up to $100 to reduce the number of cigars. As before, Verlyn and Doug will bargain until their marginal values and marginal costs are equal, which occurs at three cigars smoked. When Doug has the right to smoke, he smokes just as much as when Verlyn has the right to stop him. Not only this, but the amount of smoke is the efficient amount as well; that is, Doug smokes until the marginal benefits equal the marginal costs.

On the one hand, this result seems counterintuitive. On the other hand, it is just another example of maximizing the gains from trade, like the rock ticket example in Chapter 8. All of this was pointed out by Nobel prize winner Ronald Coase (pronounced to rhyme with "dose") in his discussion of the allocation of resources in the presence of an externality (Coase, 1960). The result that the allocation of resources does not depend on the distribution of property rights when information is free, is known as the **Coase Theorem**. For reasons that will become clear later, we will call this the Coase Theorem, Part 1.

Coase Theorem

1. For simplicity, throughout this chapter we will refer to the gains from trade (the sum of consumer's and producer's surplus) as wealth.

The Coase Theorem Part 1:
When information is free, the allocation of resources is independent of the distribution of property rights, and the allocation is Pareto-optimal.

As we will see, the Coase Theorem is perfectly general, and applies to much more than simply externalities. When information is symmetric, all distributions of property rights yield the same allocation of resources — the one that maximizes the gains from trade. This means that according to our neoclassical model, laws, organizations (such as firms), customs, and culture do not matter. When information is complete, all individuals maximize the gains from trade independent of any rules. This is the reason why the neoclassical model cannot explain any distribution of property rights, and why, if we are going to pursue this issue, we must consider major alterations to it.

Before we explore this further, let us consider a more realistic example, which will help us understand both the importance and the limitations of the Coase Theorem. This example will introduce a new type of cost into our economic vocabulary, called a **transaction cost**.

transaction cost

Application: No-Fault Divorce

When the three authors of this textbook were in primary school, divorce was relatively unheard of. There may have been the occasional child who came from a divorced family, but it was rare. Now divorce is commonplace, and for certain cohorts of marriages, the probability that a divorce will occur over the life of the marriage approaches 0.5. There are many factors that influence the rate of divorce, and we might suspect that the actual law of divorce is important. In Canada, prior to 1968, the divorce law was "fault"-based. The only grounds for divorce was adultery (except in Nova Scotia, where cruelty was also sufficient grounds). In 1968 the federal government passed the Canada Divorce Act, which, as well as expanding the list of faults, introduced the concept of "no-fault" divorce. "Marital breakdown" became sufficient grounds for divorce. Although a spouse who did not want a divorce could slow down proceedings, since the waiting period lengthened from three to five years if the parties did not agree, it became possible for one of the parties to the marriage to initiate divorce proceedings simply because he or she was dissatisfied with the marriage. The 1985 Divorce Act made this much easier, with marriage breakdown the principal ground for divorce and the waiting period reduced to one year, with or without consent.[2]

In contrast, fault divorce often in practice required the agreement of both parties, because adultery is usually committed in secret and was generally too costly to prove. As a result, couples would often work out a property settlement on their own and then go to court and admit to a fault, perjuring themselves if necessary. When it is critical that both spouses agree to the divorce, the property right — the power to decide whether or not there is a divorce — rests with the spouse who *least* wants the marriage to end.

The opposite applies to no-fault divorce. Since either spouse can leave the marriage and start divorce proceedings, in effect the law becomes unilateral. This means that the

2. Canada was not the only country to switch to no-fault divorce. In the US, California switched in 1969, and was followed by all 50 states by 1985. In fact, almost all Western countries switched to no-fault divorce in the early 1970s. Some US states have begun legislation that would make their divorce laws more "mutual." For example, Louisiana has introduced a new type of marriage called a "covenant" marriage that involves a higher level of commitment and fault grounds for divorce.

property right to divorce is now in the hands of the spouse who *most* wants the divorce. Given our standard neoclassical model, what would we predict should happen to the divorce rate when the divorce law switched from fault to no-fault?

Well, given the Coase Theorem, nothing should have happened. Those marriages that should end in divorce because they are "inefficient" will still end in divorce, while those that are efficient should continue, regardless of the law. Let us consider a simple numerical example. If we assume we can put a dollar value on the net benefits of marriage and divorce, then Table 18.2 shows a possible set of values of being married and divorced for a particular couple.

TABLE 18.2 The value of marriage to a particular couple

	Husband	Wife	Total
Married	$50 000	$50 000	$100 000
Divorced	$60 000	$30 000	$ 90 000

In this example, the total value of being married is $100 000, while the total value of being divorced is only $90 000. This is what we would call an efficient marriage. However, it is also the case that the husband prefers being divorced to be being married, while the wife prefers being married to being divorced. What will happen under the two different legal regimes?

If the couple is married in a fault jurisdiction, then the husband must get his wife's consent to divorce. In effect, he will have to pay her for the divorce. The husband, though, is only willing to pay $10 000 to his wife, while the wife will not accept anything below $20 000. Since the husband is unwilling to compensate his wife for the damage divorce will cause her, she does not consent to the divorce and the divorce does not happen, which is the efficient outcome.

If the couple is married in a no-fault jurisdiction, then the husband can just leave the marriage. In this case the wife must pay him to stay. Since she is willing to pay him up to $20 000 in this example, and since he is willing to accept any payment greater than $10 000, a deal is reached, and again there is no divorce. Just as in the case of the cigars, the rules do not matter for the allocation of resources (in this case whether or not a divorce happens) when information is complete.

What did happen to the divorce rate in Canada after the 1968 Act made no-fault divorce possible? It tripled over the next few years, which obviously suggests that the Coase theorem did not apply. We will find out why shortly, but before we do, we must detour for a moment and better define some terminology.

18.3 Information Costs, Transaction Costs, and Property Rights

When Coase first articulated his ideas, he claimed that his result held when "transaction costs were zero." To understand the economics of asymmetric information, it is important that this term, as well as others, be clearly defined and related to the Coase Theorem. To begin understanding transaction costs we must be explicit about the meaning of property rights.[3]

Economic property rights consist of the ability to exercise choices freely.

3. This section draws heavily on Allen (1991) and Barzel (1985).

Choices over goods can be boiled down to excluding others, deriving income, and transferring goods. The extent of an individual's property rights depends on the extent to which he or she is *able* to make these choices. Economic property rights are seldom all-or-nothing, since our ability to make choices is often circumscribed. For example, we often say things like "My home is my castle; I'm free to do what I want." But on closer inspection, this is not true. You cannot mine for gold in your backyard; you may not be allowed to build a three-metre fence or park six cars on your front lawn. You do not own the airspace above your house; nor can you stop the neighbour's music or barbecue smells from coming into your yard. Just as importantly, you can seldom prevent with certainty a burglar invading your home and making off with "your" property. When you think about it, most of the things you "own" are owned incompletely; that is, your economic property rights are incomplete.

Property rights are often limited by someone else's rights. Hence, you may not own the mineral rights to a parcel of land, but someone else might. At other times, property rights are incomplete simply because it is too costly to enforce them. To "trespass" is to use someone else's legal property without permission. If children take a short cut across your lawn on their way to school, your property rights over the lawn are limited by your reluctance to enforce them. This points to an important distinction. To the lawyer, property rights are always legal rights; that is, one's rights to use property *under the law*. Trespassers have no legal right to the property. But if the trespassers are unhindered, the economist would say they have an economic property right. Most of the time the two definitions overlap, but there are many instances when they do not.

PROBLEM 18.1

Computer software provides many examples where legal and economic property rights diverge. A friend of ours once remarked that when he got a really good research grant he was going to buy a copy of Lotus because it had given him such good service over the years. Can you articulate the economic and legal property rights as they pertain to software use by individuals? Can you come up with other examples?

The distinction between legal and economic property rights raises an important point. When economic property rights are reduced, then wealth is lower, and when economic property rights are eliminated or absent, then wealth is zero. This is true at both an individual level and a social one. Consider a slave. A slave, by definition, has no legal rights, and in practice very few economic ones. A slave has no wealth, has no incentive to increase his or her human capital, and no ability to trade with others. The absence of property rights makes the slave the poorest of all people.

Most often legal property rights are tied closely to economic property rights. If you are the legal owner of your computer, then you are usually the one who knows the password, has access to the room where it is stored, and gets to play the games. If your computer gets stolen, you are still the legal owner, but your economic property rights are eliminated. The value of the computer to the thief, however, is lower than it was to you because the ability to use the computer may be restricted (the thief may not know the password), and the ability to sell the computer is also reduced. For these reasons, stolen property sells for vastly reduced prices on the black market. Once again we see that a reduction in property rights reduces wealth.

A second point, already mentioned indirectly, is that when economic property rights are perfect, wealth is maximized. This is a result of the Coase Theorem. We can conceive of a spectrum of property rights varying from completely absent to perfect, with the level of wealth ranging from zero to some maximum level along this spectrum. Of course, we live in neither extreme. Our property rights are never perfect, but neither are they completely missing. Even slaves had some economic rights, including (sometimes) the right to purchase their freedom. In Roman times, clever slaves sometimes became wealthy and owned slaves themselves. Other things equal, maximizing individuals will always prefer better defined property rights because in this case wealth is higher. These better defined rights, however, are costly to achieve, and in equilibrium we would expect that the optimal level of rights would equate the marginal value of rights with their marginal costs. The costs of establishing and maintaining property rights are what we call transaction costs.

Transaction costs are the costs of establishing and maintaining property rights.

Hence we see that property rights are fundamentally linked to transaction costs. If transaction costs are zero, then economic property rights are complete, wealth is maximized, and the Coase Theorem holds. If transaction costs are positive and significant, then property rights will be incomplete, and the Coase Theorem will not hold. If transaction costs are so large that property rights are absent, then we have a world of anarchy.

PROBLEM 18.2

When goods get stolen, the thief should have an incentive to resell the good back to the original owner since that person clearly has the highest value of the good. Yet very few goods are ever ransomed. Why would this be? Why is it that children are the goods most likely ransomed?

18.4 Asymmetric Information and Transaction Costs

What fundamentally causes transaction costs? That is, why is it necessary to engage in activities that define and protect property rights? Fundamental to these questions is the notion of costly information. As we saw in Chapter 17, when there is costly information, individuals face a risky world. Because none of us is omniscient, not only do we not know whether or not it will rain tomorrow, we do not know if we will be robbed tonight either. Costly information is a necessary condition for transaction costs to exist. If we lived in a world of certainty, then there could be no transaction costs.

Suppose, for example, Betty owns an expensive CD player, with all the nice speakers and other gadgets that go with it. Arnold is a thief who is planning on stealing the sound system tonight. If information were freely available, Betty would know that Arnold is coming, and would be waiting for him with a pit bull and her local police officer. But, of course, information is free, so Arnold knows that Betty is waiting, and therefore, does not show up. Since he will not show up, and Betty knows this, she sleeps soundly. If for some reason Betty sleeps and Arnold does show up and steals the CD player, information is still free, the police arrest Arnold the next day, and all is right with the world again. Of course, Arnold realizes this, and becomes an accountant! When information costs are zero, it is impossible to have theft or any other type of infringement on one's property rights. As a result, no effort is spent protecting property, and transaction costs are zero.

Having costly information is a necessary condition for transaction costs, but it is not sufficient. Recall again the analysis of Chapter 17. With symmetric information costs, the probability of some event is simply given by nature, and there is nothing anyone can do to influence this probability. Individuals in such circumstances will buy insurance to provide them with the optimal amount of risk in their lives, and again transaction costs will be zero. Recall the card game mentioned in Chapter 17 where a card is dealt face down and no one is allowed to look at any cards. In such a game, there is no point in bluffing because all the players know that you have as much information as they do. Only when there is some form of asymmetric information do transaction costs occur.

Asymmetric information means that one individual knows something about the state of the world that others don't, and that the probabilities of different states of the world are endogenous. As a result a person with superior information can choose to behave in a way that benefits himself or herself, and hurts others, and still avoid getting caught by blaming any negative outcome on nature. In this way, it is possible to lie, cheat, steal, shirk, and generally be non-cooperative in order to increase your own wealth at the expense of others. Since other people anticipate this type of behaviour, they engage in costly activities to protect themselves, and these costs are transaction costs. Hence, in order for there to be transaction costs, there must be asymmetric information.

Transaction costs require asymmetric information.

The case of explicit theft is a straightforward example of asymmetric information. For example, let us return to the simple case of Betty and Arnold. Betty knows that there is some chance her home may be robbed; however, information is asymmetric because Arnold knows exactly when he plans to do the deed. Furthermore, Arnold knows how he will do the robbery and plans accordingly. Unfortunately for Arnold, not all of the information advantage is on his side. He does not know Betty's exact schedule, whether a police cruiser is close by, how much the neighbours watch out for one another, nor whether the "beware of man-eating dog" sign in the window is legitimate. It is uncertain that the thief will get caught, and as a result it often pays to protect property. Efforts like Neighbourhood Watch, locks, dogs, police, and the like are used to deter direct theft, and these costs are transaction costs.

Transaction costs exist in any situation involving asymmetric information. For example, suppose Arnold does become an accountant and ends up preparing Betty's books and tax planning. In such a situation there are many asymmetries of information. For example, Arnold may overcharge Betty and explain to her that her particular tax situation is very complicated and required more time than expected. Because Arnold is the accountant, Betty, though suspicious, may have to believe him. Arnold may try to engage in some form of price discrimination, using client knowledge that Betty does not possess. There may be several transaction cost responses to these potential behaviours. First, Betty may shop around for other accountants. Second, the accountants themselves may set up a professional association that handles complaints and disciplines its members. Third, expensive reputations may be put on the line or bonds posted, to guarantee honest performance. Again all of these actions are transaction costs.

One response to an asymmetry problem may be to eliminate the information difference. However, this is seldom done. We have seen throughout this book that there are huge gains from specialization. If we all lived on isolated islands by ourselves we would consume a trivial fraction of what we currently enjoy. In fact, most of us would simply die. Specialized production allows for the vast wealth of our world, but it necessarily entails asymmetric information. To become a brain surgeon requires that the surgeon know more about the operation than the patient. Asymmetric information is a two-edged sword: it allows for large gains from trade, but it also allows for cheating. It is impossible to have the same information as all of the people you trade with. The social problem is to choose a set of rules that optimally hinder the ability to cheat while preserving the incentive to specialize in production and knowledge.

Back to Externalities and the Coase Theorem

Transaction costs are costs that violate the Coase Theorem. This is an important point. If transaction costs were zero, then the distribution of property rights — that is, the set of rules, laws, customs, and organizations — would not matter. If we are going to develop a theory of these things, then it must be based on positive transaction costs.

Let us return to the case of divorce first. It has been well documented that jurisdictions with no-fault divorce laws ended up with higher divorce rates. Using our earlier numerical example, this could happen only if the party that least wanted the divorce was unable to bribe the other party to stay. Although either party might initiate a divorce, let us assume that it is the wife that most wants the marriage to remain together. Empirically speaking, this is an important case and most easily demonstrates how transaction costs can violate the Coase Theorem.

For example, one reason why wives may be unable to compensate husbands who wish to leave is that some of their marital assets are already in the hands of the husband at the time of divorce. In Canada, and in several states in the US, marital property often belonged to the person whose name was on the title. For historical reasons, in the late 1960s and early 1970s, this was almost always the husband. Thus, even though a wife may have contributed to the purchase of a house and other assets through market earnings or an inheritance, at the time of divorce the asset belonged to the husband. Under fault divorce this did not matter since the divorce was negotiated, but under no-fault law the husband could leave the marriage and take most of these assets with him. In effect the husband was able to commit a "theft" under the law.

A second reason why wives may be unable to pay husbands to stay reflects a feature of typical North American marriages. In many marriages wives tend to make large investments early on in the relationship, while husbands tend to make larger ones at the end. There are two major cases of this, each of which is common enough that they have been given their own names among family law experts: the "medical school syndrome" and the "trophy wife divorce."

First, wives often make large financial investments in their husband's human capital. This often takes the form of supporting husbands through college and professional schools. Remarkably, until very recently, courts did not recognize diplomas and degrees as marital property, and hence they were not subject to division at the time of divorce. Once again, husbands were able to "steal" the investment of the wife by simply leaving the marriage after they received the education. Thus, although the total value of the marriage may have been worth more than when the couple is divorced, a divorce occurred nonetheless because the wife was unable to compensate her husband because her wealth was embodied in his human capital.

The second case of large early investments relates to children. Wives, in many marriages, bear most of the cost of having and raising children. Again this puts the wife in jeopardy if the husband does not wish to be an in-house parent. Once the children are born, and once the husband's income has started to grow, he can leave (taking his higher future income with him) and try to obtain a younger wife. To the extent that court-assigned child support payments are not enforced, this problem is exacerbated. As courts have begun to recognize more and more assets as marital property and as they have increased the size of custody support another transaction cost has arisen. Given that men almost always work full time it is very difficult for them to be custodial parents. Recently wives have instigated divorces more often, taking the children and custody supports with them. Bargaining power between husband and wife has been altered by the courts' willingness to provide larger property and support payments. One result of this has been the rise of "Father's Rights" groups that argue that the husband's property rights have been stolen during the divorce.

A final reason why wives may be unable to convince their husbands to stay is that on average husbands are stronger than wives, and may threaten or engage in violence. If the wife tries to bribe her husband to stay, the husband could possibly extort the payment as well as getting the divorce. Violence may also be used to keep wives in marriages that they wish to leave. In either case, it is easy to see that such transaction costs can prevent efficient bargaining.

In all of these cases we see that certain facts of life create situations where transaction costs exist and therefore property rights are not complete. In fact, marriage is a type of exchange that has potential for large transaction costs, which no doubt explains why it has always been so highly regulated. Generally speaking, in most exchanges there are opportunities for some type of behaviour that benefits one party at the expense of others. In these cases property rights are again incomplete, and again, the Coase Theorem *does not apply*. What this means is that the rules of the game *do* matter. But, of course, you knew that already.

18.5 Externalities with Positive Transaction Costs

Externalities are a case of asymmetric information and, therefore, positive transaction costs. When a factory pollutes the air, those who breathe the smoke may not know where it comes from. If they do know, the factory may be in another country. If it is local, there may be too many individuals involved to allow for any practical type of private bargaining. If bargaining is possible, it may be unclear who owns the right to pollute. As a result of positive transaction costs, externalities do matter, and the different rules that are developed to deal with them make a difference in how much gets produced. In this section we wish to analyze externalities more formally, using methods that were developed in earlier chapters.

In Coase's original article, he first discussed a hypothetical externality that involved a rancher and a farmer. In the story, there was no fence, so the rancher's cattle would wander over and eat some of the farmer's grain. The more cattle there were, the more grain was eaten. If transaction costs are zero, then the externality does not matter since the farmer and rancher simply bargain over the optimal number of cattle, with the direction of payment depending on whether cattle are legally allowed to trespass or not. In this section, we start the analysis under the assumption that it is unclear who owns the rights to the range, and that transaction costs are too high to allow bargaining.

Under these circumstances the farmer and the rancher take the other's actions as given in deciding how much crop to plant or how many cattle to raise. That is, the farmer chooses the amount of grain to plant that maximizes his profits, assuming that the rancher will run a given number of cattle. The rancher decides how many cattle to run to maximize his profits, assuming the farmer will plant a certain amount of grain. The structure of this problem should sound familiar to you because it is analogous to the case of oligopoly discussed in Chapter 16.

In the case of homogeneous oligopoly, a firm's output had a negative impact on the demand faced by its competitors and vice versa. Here we have a similar interaction between the farmer and the rancher, except that the interaction is negative for the farmer and positive for the rancher. In other words, we could write the profit function for the farmer and the rancher as:

$$\text{Farmer's profit} = \pi_f(w, c)$$
$$\text{Rancher's profit} = \pi_r(w, c)$$

where w and c are the quantities of wheat and cattle produced. The key to understanding this problem is to recognize that the number of cattle has a negative impact on the profit of the farmer and that the quantity of wheat has a positive impact on the profit of the rancher. That is, the more cattle there are, the lower is the profit of the farmer and the more wheat that is grown, the higher is the profit of the rancher.

Figure 18.1a shows two isoprofit curves for the cattle rancher. These curves are analogous to the ones in Figure 16.5, where we examined oligopoly behaviour, and show the same levels of profit for different combinations of wheat and cattle. For the given amount of wheat, w^*, the optimal number of cattle is c^*. At this number of cattle, the profit to the rancher is \$100. Had the rancher raised c' cattle instead, the profits would have been only \$90 for the given amount of wheat planted. In order to draw the isoprofit curves for the rancher, we must find those points that provide the same amount of profit. If the rancher were to raise c' cattle, then more wheat would need to be planted to increase rancher profits. At c', w', the profits are again \$100. We can repeat this experiment over and over, and we would trace out the U-shaped isoprofit lines shown

FIGURE 18.1 The rancher-farmer externality

The isoprofit lines of the rancher are given in (a). The farmer's isoprofit lines are given in (b). When both are combined in (c) the Nash equilibrium is at point A, where too many cattle and too little wheat is produced.

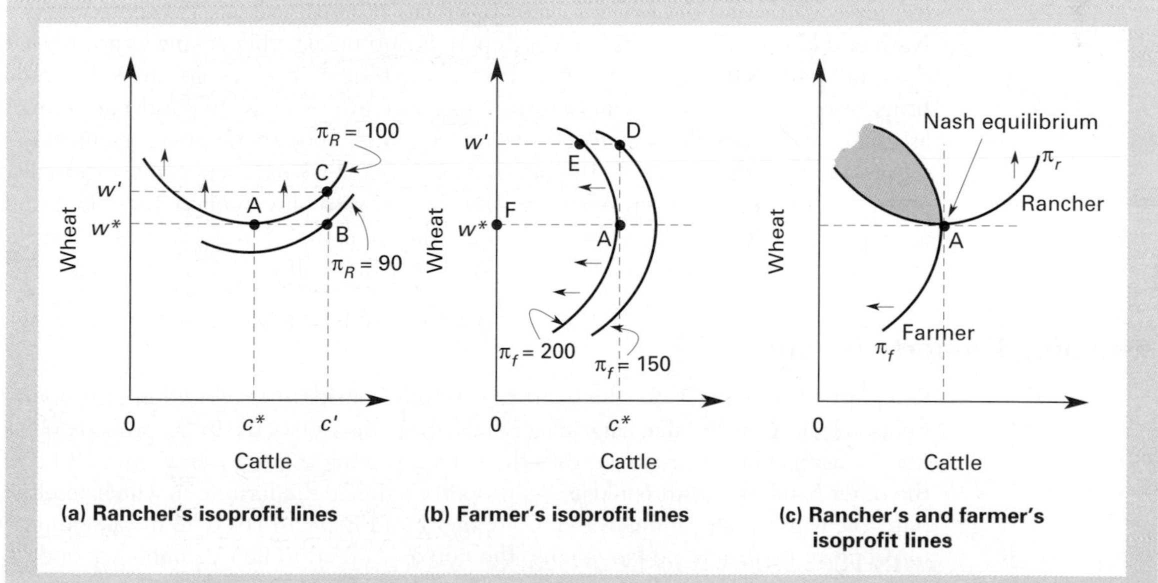

in the graph. As indicated by the arrows, profits to the rancher are clearly increasing as the amount of wheat increases.

In Figure 18.1b we see the isoprofit curves for the wheat farmer. If the cattle rancher is running c^* cattle on the ranch, then the optimal amount of wheat to grow is w^*. If the farmer were to produce any other amount of wheat, his profits would be lower. For example, if he produced w' at point D, his profits would only be $150 instead of $200. In order to find the combination of cattle and wheat that would yield $200 it is necessary to reduce the number of cattle to a point like E. Here profits to the farmer are once again $200. Unlike the rancher, the externality is negative for the farmer. The more cattle there are, the worse off the farmer is. Hence, his profits are increasing to the left of point A.

In part (c) we combine both parts (a) and (b). Point A is now seen as a Nash equilibrium. If you recall, a Nash equilibrium is the point at which the output of each firm is the best response given the output of the other firm. In the rancher-farmer context, c^* is the best output given that the farmer is producing w^*, and w^* is the best output given that the rancher is producing c^*. Clearly point A is not Pareto-optimal since both the rancher and the farmer can earn higher profits by producing more wheat and fewer cattle (indicated by the shaded lens).

However, we must point out that Figure 18.1 is drawn under the conditions of prohibitive transaction costs. By assumption, nothing can be done about the externality caused by the cattle, and as a result there are too many cattle. In order for the rancher and farmer to capture some of the gains from trade shown by the shaded lens, these transaction costs would have to be reduced. Hence we see that the introduction of transaction costs makes Pareto-optimality meaningless. True enough, joint profits would be higher if fewer cattle and more wheat were produced, but given the technology of the situation, it is too costly to negotiate this outcome.

18.6 Responses To Externalities

We have seen that when the rancher is allowed to raise cattle on an open range, he raises too many cattle and the wheat farmer produces too little wheat. This outcome is a Nash equilibrium that results from both parties optimizing while taking as given what the other party is doing. Externalities arise all the time: between consumers, between firms, or between consumers and a firm. When such externalities are positive, resources are *underallocated* to the source of the externality; when they are negative, resources are *overallocated* to the source. In the rancher-farmer case we have a negative externality and a case of overallocation. Whenever there is an externality, though, there is always an opportunity to try to avoid it and increase the gains from trade. We now ask, what kinds of responses to externalities can help rectify these allocational distortions?

Assigning Property Rights

One type of response is for the court to carefully consider the allocation of property rights in light of the fact that bargaining is unlikely. In the case of the cattle, property rights may be assigned to the rancher, with the outcome being at point A in Figure 18.1. On the other hand, the court could assign property rights to the farmer, in which case the outcome with no bargaining would be at point F in Figure 18.1b. With the assignment of property rights and no bargaining, the outcomes tend to be extreme—we end up with either too many or too few cattle.

Coase, and others after him, have argued that courts tend to assign property rights in cases where bargaining is prohibitively costly to those parties that are likely to generate the highest amount of social wealth. Hence, the court would consider the total wealth generated at point A and the amount of wealth when there were zero cattle. The court would then assign property rights to whichever case generated the highest wealth. Coase analyzed a number of famous common law cases, and argued that the decisions struck by the court made sense in terms of wealth generation.

In the nineteenth century a common externality problem involved sparks emitted by steam locomotives, causing crops to catch fire. The courts reasoned that if railroads were held liable for the damage, it would hinder the development of rail, which was so important for commerce. Furthermore, if the railroads were held liable for damage, farmers would plant crops closer to the tracks, and pay no heed to planting crops that were less likely to catch fire. Hence the probability of a fire would increase. On the other hand, if railroads were not made liable, then there would be no incentive for improvements in spark-retarding technology, and farmers would be careful in the type of crop they planted and how close they got to the tracks. The courts found for the railroad, arguing that the costs to farmers were trivial compared to the costs to the railway in mitigating the externality.

If you stop and think for a moment, you will realize that many liability laws are like this. For example, if you move into oncoming traffic while driving, you are held liable no matter what the reason. It would seem efficient to assign ownership to the traffic with the right of way since it is usually easy to keep one's own car on the right side of the road, while the costs of worrying about every other car seem prohibitive.

Notice that the assignment of property rights to the right party does not eliminate the externality, but simply maximizes the gains from trade in light of the externality. In fact, even when transaction costs are zero, there is an optimal level of externality. Recall, in the case of Doug and Verlyn, that the optimal number of cigars was three. In most real-world situations, that the optimal amount of "bad" things is not zero as long as something "good" is being produced with it. Hence, the optimal amount of pollution, garbage, and sewage is not zero. To force them to zero would mean no output and possibly no people!

Second, note that the assignment of property rights is most effective when it is well known who commits the externality. In such cases, the damages are usually also well known and bargaining can take place. Essentially, if a court is capable of trying a case, then the assignment of property rights makes sense. In the 1950s, the Boeing corporation of Seattle developed Innis Arden, a subdivision on the banks of Puget Sound. Over time, trees were planted and invariably some grew to the point of blocking the view of residents higher on the bank. By the 1980s over 30 court cases were pending to decide whether residents had the right to grow tall trees or to enjoy the view. The first case decided in favour of the view, and all other cases were subsequently dropped. If one drives though Innis Arden today, several tall trees can be seen. The owners of these trees simply purchased the right from the owners of the view. Assigning property rights in this case makes sense because all parties are known to one another.

Finally, notice that the assignment of property rights enhances the wealth of some parties, while lowering that of others. This last point is true regardless of whether subsequent negotiations take place or not. In the Fraser Valley of British Columbia, courts have ruled that large mushroom farms are liable for the odours that they cause while composting. The land values of the neighbouring properties immediately increased, while the value of the mushroom farms fell.

From this discussion we see that when transaction costs are positive, the assignment of property rights mitigates the externality problem but does not eliminate it; that simply assigning property rights works best when the parties involved are well known to each other; and that the assignment of property rights enhances the wealth of those in possession of them.

Internalization

internalization

Another remedy for externalities, which requires that property rights already be assigned, is a process called **internalization**, in which a third party, seeing an opportunity to make a private gain, intervenes between the source(s) and the recipient(s) of an externality to bring about an efficient private response. For example, a trend among hotel keepers in the United States is to offer their patrons a choice between smoking and nonsmoking rooms. In this way, they can capture the resulting benefit to nonsmokers by charging commensurately higher prices or, more realistically, by avoiding the loss of nonsmoking patrons to competing hotels.

Another example involves shopping malls containing both department stores and specialized retailers. If we simplify the problem by assuming that the department store is the source of the (positive) externality and the specialized retailers the recipients, then the larger the department store, the more traffic it attracts, and the more benefit it confers on the smaller retailers. We can think of the specialized retailers as **free riders** on the retailing opportunities created by the department store, much as the hobos of the 1930s were free riders on the nation's railroad system.

free riders

Imagine a department store blindly pursuing its own self-interest. If it considers establishing a new branch, it will choose to build a store too small to maximize the joint profits of both that new department store and the specialized retail outlets that almost inevitably spring up to take a free ride on its traffic. Why will the store be too small? Because it cannot capture the benefits conferred on the free riders.

We can even imagine a scenario in which the joint profits from the best possible aggregation of retail activity — the best size for the department store and the best types and sizes for the specialized retailers — might be positive, whereas the profit of the department store itself might be negative. In this case, the department store would never establish its branch, even though it would see potential profits from the retail centre as a whole.

How can we solve this problem of the free rider? We see the answer across the face of post-1950 North America: the shopping centre. We can imagine that the shopping-centre developer first calculates the profit-maximizing configuration of stores and then negotiates a series of contracts with the department store and selected specialized retailers. The contracts must guarantee only that each retailer is at least as well off as it would be in the absence of the shopping centre. By putting all the externality-producing activities under one roof, the developer can extract for itself the maximum profit from the retail agglomerate, profit that otherwise would have gone unrealized. Not surprisingly, large department stores themselves recognize that potential and often become the prime movers in shopping-centre developments.

So, too, Cannell Studios recognized a similar potential in the film industry. When it built its new North Shore Studios in North Vancouver, it designed a facility in which its own studios occupied only a third of the space. All the remaining space was designated for offices to be rented to other film-related companies, including camera, lighting, and catering firms. Likewise, condominium and real estate developers often design housing developments with restrictive covenants that limit individual behaviour, but enhance the overall value of the properties. Perhaps the most common form of internalization is the firm: a collection of contracts in which the owner internalizes various production externalities. This issue will be covered in detail in Chapter 19.

PROBLEM 18.3

Homecoming dances are usually organized (and often subsidized) by a student organization rather than by "leaving it to the market." Are such dances likely to be provided more efficiently through a student organization or through the market?

Governmental Responses

As we have seen, the fact that externalities are pervasive does not necessarily imply that pervasive governmental intervention is necessary or desirable. Private parties always have the incentive (and often the means) to resolve the problems created by the blind pursuit of self-interest. Private negotiations, however, are sometimes unworkable. When problems are not privately resolved, governments may impose **public regulation**, based on cost-benefit analysis, or may take *no action* at all.

public regulation

Public Regulation

Because private negotiations are sometimes unworkable, public regulation based on cost-benefit analysis may be the optimal response to an externality problem. Many governmental agencies concerned with health, resource management, power, education, and recreation use cost-benefit analysis to determine a target level for the source of an externality and then use regulation to achieve these targets. Taxation is one kind of regulation. The heavy taxes imposed on cigars, cigarettes, and liquor are intended, in part, to reduce consumption to more socially desirable levels. Bans on certain offensive activities are another regulatory option. For example, playing radios without earphones is now illegal in some parks in North America; smoking is typically prohibited in public buildings, hospitals, and subways; and factories emitting unacceptably high levels of pollutants are sometimes forced to shut down. Regulatory standards are yet another means of controlling externalities: for example, enforced limits for lead emissions from automobiles and for sulphur emissions from industrial plants are just two of many such governmentally enforced limits. Public regulations are necessarily crude, in the sense that a single solution is imposed on many different problems. Like an off-the-rack pair of jeans, a regulation sometimes fits, but not always.

Public regulation is often an effective means of dealing with an externality when the transaction costs of private contracts are high. Such high costs occur when the number of sources and recipients is relatively large, when direct contact between them is infrequent, when information costs are high, and when large levels of specific investments have been made. For example, the externality problem of smoking in a public elevator or at a bus stop is always changing with the number and identity of the smokers and nonsmokers present at any one time. We simply cannot expect the bus riders waiting at Fifth and Main to negotiate a solution: the costs of negotiation far outweigh the potential benefits. Neither can we anticipate that a third party will internalize the externality: no private person owns these public places. In this kind of circumstance, governmental regulation is often the most feasible option.

Many air and water pollution problems closely resemble the smoker's externality in public places. The number of individuals and firms who contribute to air pollution in Vancouver, for instance, is as large and as continually changing as the number of individuals and firms who suffer from the resulting smog. Moreover, the air pollution changes with the weather. For example, the smog is worse when a temperature inversion occurs or when more sunshine causes chemical reactions in the atmosphere. Thus, the cost of privately negotiating a solution is prohibitive. Moreover, because no one owns the Vancouver airshed, the problem cannot be internalized by a third party.

What first strikes an economist about the regulatory approach is that policy makers need very precise information in order to identify specific regulatory targets. In contrast, the private-property approach requires only that policy makers know the gross features of the problem at hand.

Cost-Benefit Analysis

Economic cost-benefit analysis can be used to generate the information needed to stipulate regulatory targets. We can illustrate this approach by returning once more to the smoking externality. Measuring costs and benefits simply amounts to calculating the demand and marginal cost curves for our representative individuals. Figure 18.2 plots curves based on Doug and Verlyn's costs and benefits, from Table 18.1, still assuming that there are no income effects.

The cost-benefit-optimal quantity of cigars is the quantity that maximizes net social benefit — that is, total benefits minus costs. We know that this occurs where marginal benefits equal marginal costs. This is the allocation that private individuals reach when transaction costs are zero.

We can imagine extending this technique of cost-benefit analysis from our society of two to society at large. At least in principle, we can think either of surveying the costs and benefits of a large number of individual smokers and nonsmokers, or of

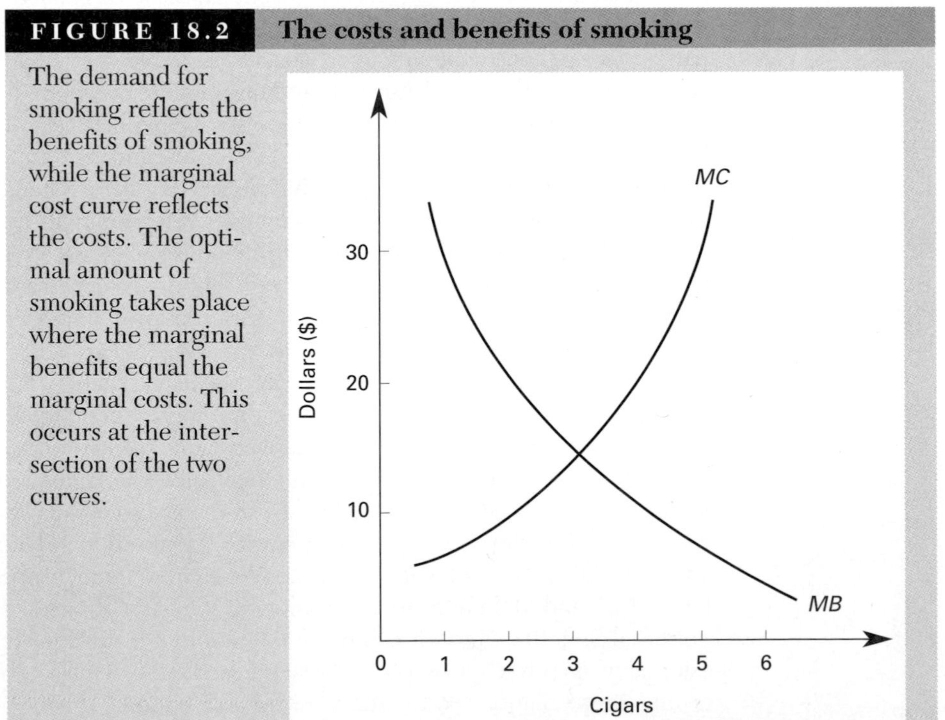

FIGURE 18.2 The costs and benefits of smoking

The demand for smoking reflects the benefits of smoking, while the marginal cost curve reflects the costs. The optimal amount of smoking takes place where the marginal benefits equal the marginal costs. This occurs at the intersection of the two curves.

directly estimating the costs to nonsmokers as a group and the benefits to smokers as a group.

In principle, cost-benefit analysis allows policy makers to determine a target level for some activity that produces an externality. In practice, however, cost-benefit analysis is fraught with difficulty. As we saw in the examples concerning bus-stop smoking and Vancouver smog, what we nominally see as "a problem" is actually a multitude of problems. The cost of gathering the information needed for this sort of cost-benefit analysis is prohibitive.

The best a cost-benefit analyst can do in such cases is to consider a representative problem that captures the average features of the whole gamut of real problems under study. The regulation resulting from the representative cost-benefit analysis is necessarily an umbrella solution: it covers a whole range of problems and is ideally suited to none.

Hitting the Regulatory Target

Suppose that policy makers, using cost-benefit analysis, have identified a *regulatory target* for some externality problem. What kind of regulation will achieve it? We can find no single answer to this question because different problems require different kinds of solutions. Yet economists do have one rule of thumb: they prefer **regulatory mechanisms** based on individual choice to mechanisms proscribing individual behaviour.

regulatory mechanisms

Think of the emissions of sulphur from electricity-generating plants. One regulatory mechanism based on individual choice is to charge an emissions tax of t dollars per unit of sulphur. This regulation leaves the individual electricity-producing firms free to choose any level of emissions they like — as long as they are prepared to pay the price. By contrast, a proscriptive regulatory mechanism is to ban the emission of, say, more than s units of sulphur per kilowatt-hour produced. This ban means that the maximum emissions level applies across the board to every power-generating company.

Assuming that we know the values of s and t that will achieve the target level of sulphur, why is the tax preferable to the ban? If we think of the privilege of emitting sulphur into the atmosphere as an economic resource just like any other, then — in the absence of an externality — the resource is free and requires no regulatory attention. In the presence of an externality, however, only a limited amount of emission will be permitted.

The privilege of emitting sulphur is now a *scarce resource*, and the emissions tax is essentially the price per unit for that privilege. Because all firms face the same price — that is, pay the same emissions tax — the limited amount of sulphur emissions will be allocated to its most productive uses. The tax thus ensures that the limited quantity of emissions will be allocated efficiently, a result we cannot achieve with the blanket proscription.

Some government agencies are experimenting with another mechanism that invokes individual choice to allocate emission rights efficiently. Individual polluters are given marketable emission quotas, or rights. If the firm intends to emit, say, 100 000 tonnes of sulphur and its quota is only 70 000 tonnes, it must buy emission rights for 30 000 tonnes of sulphur from other firms. If the firm anticipates emitting only 40 000 tonnes, it can sell its excess emission rights. For example, such "emissions trading" would let a power plant that plans to emit less than its quota of a pollutant to sell the difference to another utility that plans to emit more than its quota — while the overall target for the region is still met. Like the emissions tax, this marketable emission rights solution ensures that the limited quantity of emissions will be allocated efficiently.

Using this rule of thumb, what kind of regulatory response can you devise to avert a little-publicized tragedy that now threatens much of the United States? The Ogallala Aquifer is a vast underground water reservoir lying beneath much of the Great Plains.

Most of the water pumped through the impressive agricultural sprinkling systems that dot this landscape is drawn from the aquifer. As the sprinkling technology has caught on, the demands on the aquifer have grown at such an alarming rate that it may soon be sucked dry. (The aquifer is so valuable a resource that proposals have been made to drain the Great Lakes to replenish it!)

Any landowner can tap into the aquifer by drilling a well, and the amount of water available to any user of the aquifer next year is virtually independent of how much that person pumps this year, because any individual will use but a tiny fraction of the total. Consequently, no landowner has any incentive to conserve water for future needs. Because access is free to all, the needs of future users of this resource carry no weight in determining its present use.

PROBLEM 18.4

Many of the major oil companies in the world first began oil exploration of the Middle East in the late 1920s through 1930s. When oil was struck, 50-year leases were taken out with the respective governments at very low prices. As the 1970s approached and the leases began to run out, oil companies began to extract huge amounts of oil from the ground for fear that the leases would not be renewed and if they were, then prices would be much higher. What is the property right problem here, and how might it relate to an externality problem? When Saudi Arabia nationalized many of the wells and cut back production, causing the huge oil shortage in the early 1970s, were they acting as an inefficient cartel or efficiently internalizing the externality?

Nonintervention

nonintervention

The final possible governmental response is **nonintervention** — simply to do nothing. Because regulation itself uses up resources, including the costs of information gathering, administration, and enforcement, the best policy may be no policy. For instance, though body odour is a negative externality, it is simply not significant enough to warrant expensive government regulation.

Externalities are just one type of transaction cost problem. However, from the discussion above on how to deal with them a general principle can be reached that we will call the Coase Theorem, Part 2:

Coase Theorem, Part 2:

When transaction costs are positive, economic activities are organized to mazimize the gains from trade net of the transaction costs.

Application: Soldiers for Sale

We've been discussing the fact that rules matter. Let's now consider a very foreign example to push the point to the limit. Most of you have heard of the first Duke of Wellington, Arthur Wellesley, and his military exploits against Napoleon 200 years ago. Did you know, however, that he had no military training? In fact, his military career sounds ridiculous to the modern ear. Wellington's parents first purchased him a commission in the army in 1787 as a lowly ensign. Wellington, not particularly interested in the army, never showed up for work (he wanted to be a politician like his older brother!). Undeterred by this, his family bought him seven further commissions until he was finally a colonel in charge of his own regiment and was forced to take charge. His first encounter with Napoleon was a disaster, but he learned quickly, and the rest ... as they say ... is history.

What is most surprising about this story is the fact that virtually all military commissioned officers *purchased* their positions prior to the nineteenth century. In Britain, the practice did not end until 1871. This seems like an odd way of staffing an army — letting any Tom, Dick, or Arthur with a few thousand pounds lead some troops — but let's consider a few facts first. At the time it was very difficult to monitor a soldier. Battles were small and far away. Soldiers were paid not a salary, but a fraction of the spoils of war. Essentially, an army was run by a franchise owner called a colonel, and his regiment was called a "company." He would bid for the job by purchasing a commission from the King or Queen. This agreement would include an up-front fee, plus an agreement on shares of booty. The colonel would then recruit his own men and go off to do battle. If he was successful, then he got paid. If he was not successful, then ... well, then he was lucky if he survived not to get paid. The entire arrangement was similar to the way Burger King organizes its restaurants. The company leader had a strong incentive to fight, even though he was not monitored, because that was the only way he could earn an income.

As long as battles were small and required little coordination, the system worked reasonably well. As battles became bigger, not all regiments were in a position to capture booty, and so another system of payment was required. Furthermore, as advances in communications, munitions, and technology took place, it became easier to monitor soldiers directly. As a result, the purchase system, which provided an incentive to fight for the King or Queen, was replaced with the current system of a regular army paid through wages. Here we see the Coase Theorem, Part 2 at work. The army was organized in a way to maximize its value net of the costs of monitoring its soldiers.

PROBLEM 18.5

The navies of Europe also paid their officers in terms of prizes; however, the officers were not required to pay for their commissions. Rather there was a system of patronage, exams, and rules on becoming an officer. Can you think of a transaction cost problem that exists in paying ship captains with prizes that does not exist with paying soldiers that way?

18.7 Public Goods

public goods

We now turn from externalities to **public goods** — goods characterized by a perfect positive externality to the whole community. Since public goods are a special case of externality, they are also a special case of asymmetric information and transaction costs. Public goods differ from most of the goods (and services) we have considered, which have been characterized by benefits that flow to a particular consumer. When you buy and eat a Granny Smith apple, for instance, you are the only one who gets to enjoy it. Furthermore, the apple itself is no longer available to anyone. It simply is gone.

rivalrous goods

Such goods are termed **rivalrous goods**: one person's consumption of a unit of a rivalrous good precludes the possibility of anyone else enjoying it.

Other goods and services — those conferring positive externalities, for example — are to some extent nonrivalrous goods. When you enjoy your flower garden, for instance, your neighbours and occasional passersby can also take pleasure in it without lessening your own. (Unless, of course, so many come to gawk that they interfere with your pleasure.) Many other goods and services are similarly nonrivalrous, differing only in degree, and a few are even purely nonrivalrous. For instance, your pleasure in the spectacle of comet Hale-Bopp zinging through the night sky was in no way diminished by the millions of other eyes turned skyward.

Nonrivalrous Goods

Many economists and others take the normative position that, for the sake of efficiency, nonrivalrous goods ought to be provided free of charge. To exclude individuals from the benefit of a nonrivalrous good, they argue, is inefficient, because including them makes them better off and leaves everyone else just as well off. In other words, the number of people who can enjoy the flow of benefits can be increased at virtually no cost.

Indeed, many of the services that governments commonly provide free of charge are, to some degree, nonrivalrous. National defence and navigational safety aids such as channel markers and lighthouses are, in practice, completely nonrivalrous. Roads and bridges, police and fire protection, and many public health programs — such as compulsory immunization against disease — are, to a considerable extent, nonrivalrous. The argument for publicly provided, nonrivalrous goods implies only that access should be free to all. It does not imply that taxes should not be imposed to provide the goods.

Nonexcludable Goods

nonexcludable goods

Many, but certainly not all, goods and services considered in this section are also **nonexcludable goods**, meaning that denial of access to the good or service is very costly. In the nineteenth century, entrepreneurs built fences along the Niagara Falls gorge and charged tourists to look at the falls through peepholes. In this case, the spectacle of Niagara Falls became an excludable good. But even P. T. Barnum, that masterly entrepreneur, could not have denied access to people refusing to pay admission to see Halley's comet. Similarly, the Canadian government can charge a toll for the Trans-Canada Highway, but the same government would find it impossible to deny the benefits of national defence to selected residents without incurring the considerable expense of deporting them. Thus, nonrivalrous goods may or may not be excludable. By contrast, goods that are rivalrous are necessarily excludable. Once the apple is eaten, it is available to no one else.

Pure Public Goods

Goods that are both completely nonrivalrous and nonexcludable are called pure public goods. They tend to be produced by some public authority rather than by profit-seeking firms because firms find it costly to enforce contracts for nonexcludable goods.

However, history provides many examples where there has been the private provision of public goods. For example, one public good that is provided privately is "free" commercial TV broadcasting. At least to the viewers themselves, TV watching is both nonrivalrous and nonexcludable. No matter how many millions of people watch a TV program, the individual viewer's pleasure is unaffected, and the programming is available at no cost to anyone with a TV set. The solution to the public good problem stems from private broadcasting corporations actually being in the business of providing another, both rivalrous and excludable service: a captive audience for advertisers. The programming is merely the bait used to capture the audience. By contrast, ad-free TV programming is produced either by public corporations (such as the BBC in Britain) or by nonprofit organizations (such as PBS in the United States).

PROBLEM 18.6

The invention of cable TV changed forever the face of commercial broadcasting. Viewers can now be excluded from free access to programming if they refuse to pay the installation and monthly charges to private cable TV companies. Is cable TV efficient? Should it be encouraged?

National defence, for several hundred years, was also provided privately. As mentioned above, throughout the medieval period, private armies, staffed by mercenaries and even called "companies," would hire out to local nobles. As the nation-state evolved, national armies began to develop, but the mercenary still played an important role until the Crimean War in the middle of the nineteenth century. Even when the army was staffed by nationals, the officer corps was still mostly made up of individuals who purchased their commissions and shared in the proceeds of war. In England, a completely government-controlled army did not come into existence until 1871.

Nor have navigational aids always been provided publicly. Coase (1974), in another famous paper, has shown how the lighthouse was also privately provided for centuries. Individuals would own a lighthouse and charge local boats a fee for the service. The lighthouse owner would have a schedule for when the paying customers would need the light, and would provide it accordingly. True enough, some individual ships would use the light without paying, but if they landed in the local port they might have some rough company to deal with, and they never knew when the light would be turned out. Until shipping became much more international, this system worked remarkably well.

Today national defence and navigational aids are largely provided by public agencies. This is not because it is impossible for private firms to produce them, but because the technical changes over time have enhanced the public good characteristics and made private provision too costly. Likewise, roads, bridges, police, postal services, and fire protection, all once privately provided, are now mostly provided publicly. Again, this is because governments are better able to solve the transaction cost problems that arise, although they do not solve these problems perfectly.

Are public goods provided at an optimal level? Let's use the method from Section 18.5, which in turn exploited the technique developed in Chapter 16 on oligopoly. Suppose we have two individuals, Velma and Doris, who maximize utility over two goods x and y, where y is a pure public good. As a result, Velma's utility function has the form: $u = U(x_1, y_1 + y_2)$, where the subscript 1 denotes quantity provided by Velma, and the subscript 2 denotes quantity provided by Doris. Because good y is a public good, Velma's utility depends on the total amount of y that is provided, not just her own private provision. Doris has a similar utility function, with the subscripts reversed. Each of these individuals maximizes her utility function subject to a budget constraint of the form: $M = x + y$, where we assume the price of each good is 1. If we substitute for x from the budget constraint into the utility function, then the utility function for Velma becomes:

$$u = U(M - y_1, y_1 + y_2),$$

with an analogous one for Doris as well.

For Velma, it is clear that an increase in Doris's provision leads to an increase in her utility. In other words, Doris exerts a positive externality on Velma. Figure 18.3 plots the indifference curves for Velma and Doris in y_1 and y_2 space. Velma's utility is increasing in y_2, but may be increasing or decreasing in y_1 because more y_1 means less x_1. For a given amount y_2^* that Doris provides, the optimal amount for Velma to provide is y_1^*. Likewise, for a given amount y_1^* that Velma provides, Doris maximizes her utility at y_2^*. Hence point A is the Nash equilibrium of this public good problem.

As we can see, however, the public good is underprovided. Both Doris and Velma would be better off if both y_1 and y_2 were increased. Increasing the amount of y_1 and y_2 moves both of them to the shaded region, which provides a higher level of utility for both.

Public Provision of Nonrivalrous Goods

Governments clearly can use some form of cost-benefit analysis to decide how much of a public good to provide. Our analytical tack in this case must be slightly different, however. We need to imagine that the public good is actually rivalrous rather than nonrivalrous in order to derive an ordinary demand function that answers the question: How much will an individual demand of the public good at any price p?

The ordinary demand functions for two representative citizens, A and B, are labelled AA′ and BB′, respectively, in Figure 18.4. If x' of the public good is supplied, the total value to citizen A is equal to the area under AA′ to the left of x'; the total value to citizen B is the area under BB′ to the left of x'. (To use these consumer surplus measures, we will assume that each person's demand for the public good is independent of his or her income.) More important, the marginal values of x' to citizens A and B are the distances OH and OI, respectively. Because the good is nonrivalrous, the marginal social value is the *vertical summation* of the two individual marginal values,

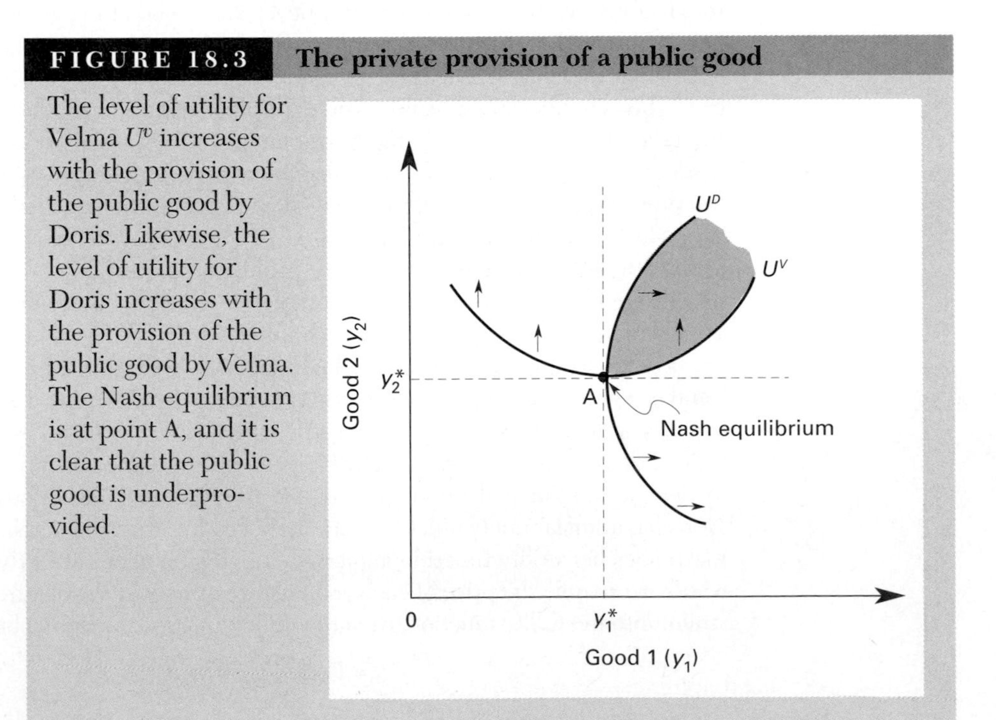

FIGURE 18.3 **The private provision of a public good**

The level of utility for Velma U^v increases with the provision of the public good by Doris. Likewise, the level of utility for Doris increases with the provision of the public good by Velma. The Nash equilibrium is at point A, and it is clear that the public good is underprovided.

FIGURE 18.4 Provision of a pure public good

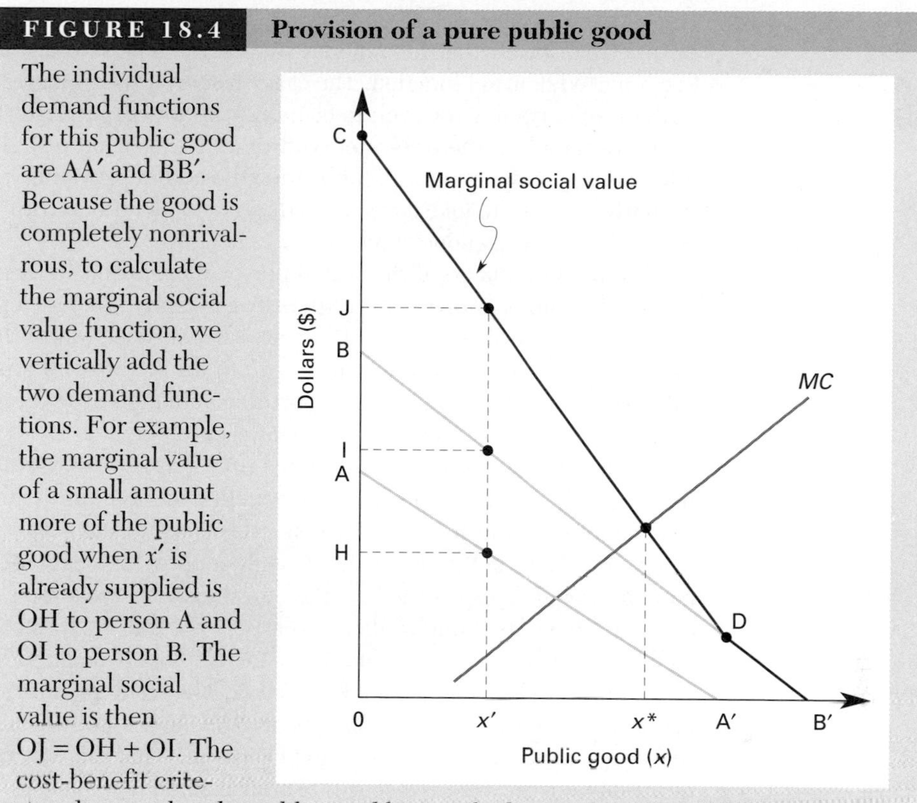

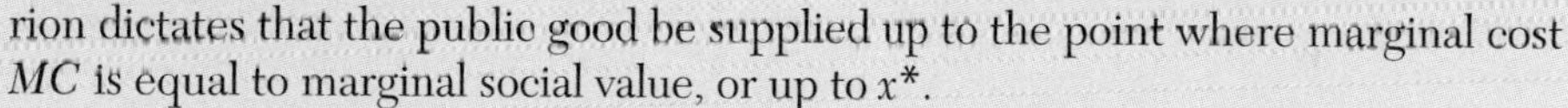

The individual demand functions for this public good are AA′ and BB′. Because the good is completely nonrivalrous, to calculate the marginal social value function, we vertically add the two demand functions. For example, the marginal value of a small amount more of the public good when x' is already supplied is OH to person A and OI to person B. The marginal social value is then OJ = OH + OI. The cost-benefit criterion dictates that the public good be supplied up to the point where marginal cost *MC* is equal to marginal social value, or up to x^*.

OH and OI, or the distance OJ. Notice that the vertical summation associated with public goods is different from the horizontal summation associated with rivalrous goods. Because the public good is consumed in its entirety by everyone, vertically summing marginal valuations is the appropriate aggregation procedure.

By vertically summing the individual marginal values for every quantity, we have derived the function labelled marginal social value in Figure 18.4. This function is sometimes called the demand function for public goods, a potentially confusing term because it does not provide the ordinary information given by a demand function: the quantity demanded of a good for any given price.

From this point on, the cost-benefit analysis is completely straightforward. The optimal amount of the public good is the quantity at which the marginal social value of the good equals the marginal cost of supplying it, or x^* in Figure 18.4.

Asymmetric Information and Revealed Preference

Although applying cost-benefit analysis to public goods is theoretically straightforward, implementing it can be tricky because of asymmetric information problems. The problem is that individual citizens may not reveal their real demand functions for a public good. If the public good is financed by a specially earmarked tax on the citizens who benefit from it and if the more each citizen benefits, the higher his or her tax bill will be, then a self-interested citizen might think twice about reporting personal benefits accurately.

Being only one of a great many who will use the public good, the citizen might assume realistically that the amount supplied will be virtually independent of his or her reported demand function. The cagey response is to underreport the private value of the public good — or even to claim not to value it at all. In this response, we see another example of the free-rider syndrome. The self-interested citizen wants to benefit from the public good without bearing the cost of providing it. If every citizen were similarly tempted to take a free ride, they could all end up with very little of the public good, or perhaps none at all.

On the other hand, if the size of personal tax bills is independent of individually reported benefits, individuals have a clear incentive to overreport benefits. Even if they are not so devious as to distort reported benefits one way or the other, it seems clear that citizens have no particular incentive to think hard and long about the personal value of any public good and to report that valuation accurately, and this makes the whole process of social cost-benefit analysis problematic.

Although this revealed-preference problem is most dramatic in the context of public goods, it also plagues the cost-benefit analysis of any externality. Suppose that a nonsmoker is told that the city council is considering a ban on smoking in public places. If asked whether he or she strongly supports the ban, moderately supports the ban, or strongly opposes the ban, the nonsmoker has no reason to weigh the personal costs and benefits thoughtfully or to report accurately. In fact, the nonsmoker may well be tempted to overestimate the value of smoke-free public places. A parallel distortion occurs if the respondent is a smoker. The resulting information from the smokers and nonsmokers whose opinions are solicited is not necessarily useful to policy makers. A hard-line economist might even argue that the only useful information this questionnaire provides is a census of smokers and nonsmokers.

SUMMARY

This chapter has introduced the notion of asymmetric information into our basic model. We have seen that asymmetric information leads to a special type of costs: transaction costs. These costs have the special feature that they violate the Coase theorem. An interpretation of the Coase theorem is that it essentially tells us that our neoclassical model is incapable of explaining any distribution of property rights, because ownership does not matter when transaction costs are zero.

Given that different rules of the game do matter, the question arises, what set of rules or property rights will be chosen? We have argued in this chapter that those property rights that maximize the gains from trade, taking into account the transaction costs affiliated with those property rights, will be the ones chosen.

In this chapter we have really only examined one particular type of transaction cost problem, namely that of externality. When an externality is present, and transaction costs are positive, there are several methods of dealing with them. First, courts or legislatures may simply assign ownership to one party, and let that person fully exploit the externality. A third party may come along and contract with all of the parties involved. This is called internalizing the externality, and the entrepreneur who does this reaps the benefits. Governments may become directly involved in regulating an externality through taxes, regulations, or tradable permits. Finally, in many cases, nothing is done about the externality because the transaction costs of enforcing a solution are simply too high.

Then, we turned to the related problem of *public goods*. A *pure public good* is both *nonrivalrous* and *nonexcludable*. In modern times such goods tend to be provided publicly because their nonexcludability creates huge costs for profit-seeking firms to produce them. Furthermore, even when a nonrivalrous good is excludable, efficiency requires that it be publicly provided at no cost.

In principle, the provision of public goods is straightforward: the rule is to provide the good up to the point where marginal social benefit is equal to marginal social cost. The problem is to estimate marginal social benefit. Here we encounter the *revealed-preference problem*, a difficulty associated not only with public goods but also with cost-benefit analysis in general, due once again to the ubiquitous problem of asymmetric information.

EXERCISES

1. Interpret the following laws as responses to externalities: Homeowners are required to keep their sidewalks clear of snow and ice. Drivers are required to drive on the right side of the road. Drivers are allowed to enter an intersection only if the traffic light is green. Dog owners are required to have their pets vaccinated for rabies.

2. Two types of firms emit gunk, a nasty pollutant. There are 10 firms of each type. These firms think of "gunk emissions" as a productive input much like any other input. The primary difference is that the price of gunk emissions is currently $0. Their input demand functions for gunk emissions are

$$w_1 = 100 - z_1$$
$$w_2 = 150 - z_2$$

   a. Given the current price of gunk emissions, how much does each firm emit, and what are total emissions?
   b. Suppose that we want to reduce gunk emissions to 1000 units in total and that we must use an emission tax T per unit of gunk emitted. What value of T will induce firms to reduce emissions to the target level? Are the 1000 units of the input gunk emissions allocated efficiently among the 20 firms?
   c. Now suppose that each of the 20 firms is given the right to emit 50 units of gunk and that firms are allowed to buy and sell these rights. What is the aggregate demand for gunk emissions? What is the aggregate supply of emissions? Think of each firm as supplying 50 units. What is the competitive equilibrium price and allocation of gunk emissions? Are the 1000 units allocated efficiently among the 20 firms?
   d. Finally, suppose that each of the 20 firms is allowed to emit no more than 50 units of gunk and that emission rights may not be traded. Are the 1000 units allocated efficiently among the 20 firms?

3. Mosquito control at the local level is a good example of a pure public good. First, suppose that in an economy of two people, the two people are identical and each has the following demand function for mosquito control:

$$p = 20 - y$$

where y is quantity of mosquito control. (We are assuming for convenience that their demands for mosquito control are independent of their incomes.) The cost of mosquito control is $10 per unit.

   a. What is the socially optimal level of mosquito control? (*Hint*: You first need to vertically sum the individual demands.)
   b. Suppose that mosquito control is not publicly provided. If individual 1 provided no mosquito control, how much would individual 2 provide? If individual 1 provided 5 units of mosquito control, how much would individual 2 provide? If individual 1 provided 10 units of mosquito control, how much would individual 2 provide? Building on these results, show that in the Nash equilibrium where each individual takes the quantity of mosquito control provided by

the other as given in choosing how much mosquito control to provide, total quantity provided will be 10 units.

c. Now suppose that we have 100 people with this demand function for mosquito control. What is the socially optimal level of mosquito control? Show that in the Nash equilibrium when there are 100 people, the total quantity provided will again be 10 units.
d. In the Nash equilibria in (b) and (c), there is a free-rider problem. Explain it in detail.

4. Imagine that a public project costs $K and provides benefits to three people: A, B, and C. Let $\$B_A > \$B_B > \$B_C$ be the benefits to the three individuals. Suppose that each must pay one-third of the project's cost. Show that there are circumstances in which two of the three will vote for the project, even though the total benefit from the project is less than its cost. Show that in such circumstances, C will be willing and able to bribe B to vote against the project. Suppose again that only two people will vote for the project but that the project's total benefit exceeds its cost. Is it possible in this case that C will be willing and able to bribe B to vote against the project? Would A be willing to offer B a larger bribe to vote for the project? Do these bribes serve any useful social purpose? Should such bribes be illegal?

5. In the rancher-farmer example, suppose that a barbed-wire fence is installed that allows the cattle and grain to be separated. Is the fence a transaction cost? Using a graph like the one in Figure 18.1c, show where the optimal outcome would be.

6. Consider the following four cases:

   a. A man speeds and wipes out a fence of yours worth $100. The man gets fined.
   b. A man steals $100 from your house, is caught, and thrown in jail.
   c. A man plants a tree on his property that blocks your view and reduces the value of your property by $100. You are told to take him to court.
   d. A man opens a business just like yours and draws $100 worth of customers away. The man gets a pat on the back.

   In each case you lose $100, yet the social rules used to respond to each loss is different.

   i) Why is there no penalty in (d)?
   ii) In (a) and (b) laws were broken. Why is the speeder not thrown in jail? (Do not say that one is more serious or that everyone speeds.)
   iii) Why does the Coase theorem not apply in (c)?

7. Suppose your house is broken into and two items are stolen. One is your collection of rare wines from around the world (valued at $500 000), the other is an old necklace that has been passed down to you by your grandmother, and is known around the world as a special piece. Which one is more likely to be held for ransom and why?

8. Suppose soybean farms have the following production function, where L = labour input and TP = total product (bushels per day). Labour can earn $60 per day in the nonagricultural sector of the economy. Soybeans sell for $10 per bushel.

L:	1	2	3	4	5	6	7	8 or more
TP:	6	14	25	32	38	43	47	48

   Explain what output will be produced on the basis of the self-interest of the owner of the land, under the following systems of property rights. Explain also whether that outcome is economically efficient, and be sure to define that term.

   a. Private property
   b. Common property; the land is farmed by communes, where anyone who wishes may join a commune and each worker shares equally in the output.
   c. Socialist cooperative: the workers decide democratically how many people work on the farm, and share equally in the output.

9. In Robert Frost's poem *Mending Wall*, the narrator wonders why a fence between his property and his neighbour's is necessary, as the trees from his orchard will never cross to the other's property and neither party owns livestock that could wander. However, the narrator's neighbour embraces the old adage, "Good fences make good neighbours." An Internet search (www.google.com) will bring up several college/university sites where you can read the full text of this poem. Why, according to economic theory, would good fences make good neighbours?

*10. On the island of Molo there is a lovely lake that produces fish according to the following total product function:

$$y = 1000z^{1/2}$$

where y is the daily fish take and z is the number of fishermen on the lake. The corresponding marginal and average product functions are

$$MP(z) = 500/z^{1/2}$$
$$AP(z) = 1000/z^{1/2}$$

At the end of the day, each fisherman on the lake has caught the average product, $1000/z^{1/2}$ fish, and the harvest of fish from the lake is therefore equitably distributed among the fishermen. Molo islanders can also fish in the ocean, where they catch 100 fish per fisherman, regardless of the number of fishermen. There are 150 fishermen on the island.

a. What are the total, marginal, and average product functions for the ocean fishery?
b. Currently, 100 fishermen fish on the lake and 50 in the ocean. Verify that all 150 fishermen have 100 fish at the end of each day and that the total harvest is 15 000 fish per day.
c. If all 150 fishermen fished in the ocean, what would the total harvest be? Given the allocation in (b), what is the net value of the lake fishery to the fishermen of Molo?
d. What allocation of fishermen maximizes the total harvest?
e. Given the optimal allocation from (d), what is the total harvest of the fishermen of Molo? What is the net value of the lake fishery with this allocation?
f. Can you devise an institution that would produce the optimal allocation of fishermen? Is there a property-rights solution to this problem?

*11. One and Two are runners competing for a gold medal in the 100-metre dash. Both can take steroids to enhance their speed. Let x and y denote quantities of steroids used by One and Two. The probability that One wins the race is $x/(x + y)$, and the probability that Two wins the race is $y/(x + y)$. The value of winning the race is 100, and the cost, inclusive of adverse effects on the runner's own health, is 1 per unit of steroids consumed. Player One will choose x to maximize $100x/(x + y) - x$, and Two will choose y to maximize $100y/(x + y) - y$,

a. Given y, find the value of x that maximizes One's objective function.
b. Given x, find the value of y that maximizes Two's objective function.
c. Find the equilibrium values of x and y.
d. Explain the nature of the externality problem and show that the equilibrium is not Pareto-optimal.
e. Would these runners embrace an institution that limited their ability to use steroids?

*12. The fish catch C on Nicola lake is a function of aggregate fishing effort E:

$$C = 1000(E - E^2)$$

This equation gives us the total catch as a function of aggregate effort expended. The price of effort is w, and the price of fish is p.

a. Find the value of E that maximizes the commercial value of this fishery.
b. What is the maximized value of the fishery?
c. Now suppose that N independent firms exploit the fishery. The share of the total catch captured by firm i is $E_i/(E_1 + E_2 + \ldots + E_i + \ldots + E_N)$, where E_i is effort supplied by firm i. Supposing the firms independently choose their own effort to maximize their own profit, find the equilibrium values of effort for N firms.
d. Compare the value of the fishery when it is exploited as a common property fishery with the maximized value you calculated in part (b).

REFERENCES

Allen, D. W. 1991. "What Are Transaction Costs?" *Research In Law and Economics*, 14 (Fall):1–18.

Barzel, Y. 1985. "Transaction Costs: Are They Just Costs?" *Journal of Institutional and Theoretical Economics*, 141:4–16.

Coase, R. 1960. "The Problem of Social Cost," *Journal of Law and Economics*, 3:1–44.

Coase, R. 1974. "The Lighthouse in Economics," *Journal of Law and Economics*, 17:357–76.

Frost, Robert. *Complete Poems of Robert Frost* (London: Jonathan Cape, 1959).

CHAPTER 19

The Theory of the Firm

In Chapters 6 and 7 we examined the economics of production. In those chapters we were primarily concerned with *how much* a firm produced. For this purpose it was sufficient to describe the firm by its production function, brushing aside the exact organization of a firm. Such a description of a *black-box* firm is hardly adequate if we are truly interested in its nature.

In order to understand the organization of the firm, we again rely on the theoretical issues raised in the last chapter — in particular, the Coase Theorem. Recall that the Coase Theorem states that if transaction costs are zero, any allocation of property rights leads to the same allocation of resources. In the context of a firm, this means that if transaction costs are zero, any type of organization is capable of producing any level of output — organization is unimportant. This would mean General Motors could be broken into thousands of little manufacturing firms, each selling parts to one another, and the same outcome in terms of number of cars and profitability would exist! As we argued in the last chapter, transaction costs are not zero, and as a result uncertainty and asymmetric information are important features of production within a firm, just as they are across markets. These issues become critical elements of our theory of the firm.

firm

In this chapter we look inside the black box as we raise a number of questions about firms and suggest a general approach to answering them. We begin our analysis by reexamining what the term **firm** means. Of course, a firm can range in size from something as small as a coconut-milk peddler on the beach or a family-run corner grocery store to something as huge as General Motors or Japan's Mitsubishi Corporation. At least as significant as the variation in the size is the variation in organizational forms. The corner grocery and GM differ not only in size but also in organizational structure.

19.1 General Issues in the Theory of the Firm

Who Owns the Firm?

When we ask the question, "Who owns the firm?," we are asking a classic property rights question. By ownership we essentially mean three things: (a) control of decisions within the firm; (b) residual claims in the firm; and (c) the right to sell these two rights.

Control includes deciding what products to make, how much output to produce, how many outlets to use, what pricing structure to adopt and so on. Within a firm, myriad decisions must be made in the process of production, and so control may be spread over a large number of people. For example, in the Ford Motor Company, control is delegated to thousands of individuals.

A residual claimant has the right to take home, as income, the difference between the revenues and costs of the firm. When the firm makes a profit these individuals have positive incomes, but when the firm has a loss then the incomes of these individuals is lower as well. Within a firm there may be many types of residual claimants. For example, stockholders are obvious residual claimants, but so are executives who earn bonuses in good years. More subtly, even workers who earn a fixed wage are partially residual claimants if they are laid off in bad times and given wage increases in good times.

Finally, ownership also involves the right to transfer the assets of a firm. Stockholders may have the right to hire and fire a CEO, but not the right to negotiate capital purchases directly within the firm. Certain types of stocks may have restrictions that prevent resale, while other stocks have the right of resale, but no voting rights in the firm. As we can see, the legal delineation of ownership within a firm can be quite complicated.

In considering the ownership of firms, it is important to keep in mind the difference between legal and economic ownership. You might "own" a firm in the legal sense, and have the authority to tell your wage employee when and how hard to work, but if he is able to shirk his duties, he becomes in part an owner of the firm in an economic sense. The ability to shirk means that the employee is enjoying some amount of the residuals of the firm in the form of leisure, and being a residual claimant is part of what it means to own a firm. One of the objectives of a firm is to match the legal and economic rights within the firm. Hence within firms we observe monitoring of workers, protection of patents and copyrights, and clearly defined claims to the firm's assets in case of bankruptcy.

Another way of looking at who owns the firm is to consider broad classes of groups that might have the rights to control, residuals, and transferability. In Figure 19.1 we see that capital owners (capitalists) combine with labour owners (labourers) in the context of a firm in order to produce output that goes to a group of consumers. Here we can think of the firm as a set of contracts that define who the owners of the firm are: that is, who has the right of control, residuals, and transferability. It is clear from Figure 19.1 that there are four general possibilities for ownership: capitalist firms, labour-owned firms, consumer-owned firms, and "unowned" firms, more commonly known as nonprofit firms.

In a capital-owned firm the owners supply the capital and hire the labour on some type of contract basis (perhaps a fixed wage, for example), in order to produce a good that is then sold to consumers. Most large corporations are owned by capitalists, and

FIGURE 19.1 The pattern of ownership

Firms combine capital and labour to produce output for consumption by consumers. All three participants — capitalists, labourers, and consumers — are potential owners of the firm.

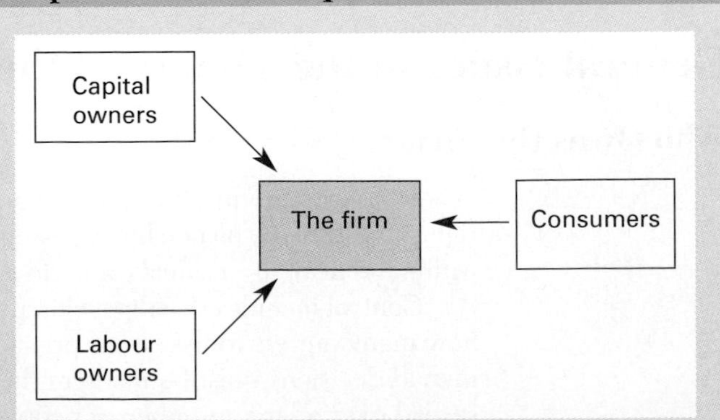

when we think of firms in the stylized sense, this is what comes to mind. These types of firms tend to dominate in manufacturing, and a typical example would be General Motors or General Electric.

In a labour-owned firm the labourers are the owners in the sense that they collect the residuals, exercise control, etc., and they hire capitalists to produce goods for consumers. Partnerships are usually labour-owned firms. For example, in a law office, the lawyers are the owners of the firm and they contract with capitalists, like the owner of their building and photocopy machine, to provide legal services. These types of firms tend to dominate in service industries, but there are a number of exceptions. In the Pacific Northwest, there are plywood firms that are owned by their workers; and in 1994, 53 percent of the stock in United Airlines was purchased by the pilots' and machinists' unions. In effect United Airlines is now a labour-owned firm.

Sometimes the distinction between a labour-owned and a capitalist firm is quite fuzzy. After all, capitalists are still human, and labourers own some capital. In the case of a family farmer, the distinction is almost meaningless. A family farmer typically supplies all of the labour to a farm and all of the capital. In this case the farm is owned by a capitalist who is also the labourer! However, in most cases it is usually pretty clear. For example, with investment banking, it is obvious that the labourers of the firm are also the owners.

It may seem odd to talk about a customer-owned firm. How can that be? Part of this mystery is that there are very few retail consumer-owned firms; most of them are at the wholesale level. In a consumer-owned firm the consumers collectively make the decisions that define ownership. Some easy ones to observe are consumer cooperatives. Anyone who has grown up in the Prairies will be familiar with cooperatives. Across Canada, one of the most popular stores selling outdoor equipment is Mountain Equipment Co-op, which is owned by the customers who shop there. Many condominium developments are organized as cooperatives, where the residents collectively own the entire building and rent from themselves. More common, though less obvious, are the many wholesale supply firms that are consumer-owned. For example, many independent hardware stores own the cooperative wholesale outlet called True Value hardware. Likewise, Sunbeam Bread is a wholesale cooperative owned by the thousands of independent bakeries that are its customers. Other surprising examples include the IGA grocery stores, the Associated Press, MasterCard, and Visa.

The final type of general ownership form is the nonprofit firm. The term "nonprofit" is somewhat of a misnomer. It does not mean that no residuals are earned. It simply means that those who own the right of control must not be the residual claimants. These firms may earn a profit; however, they must legally separate the control of the firm from those that earn the residual. (Ironically, in large corporations where the stockholders are the residual claimants, and the managers are practically in total control, the corporation almost looks like a nonprofit firm!)

There are many examples of nonprofit firms. The university you are studying at is a nonprofit organization. Most hospitals are nonprofit, as are charities, churches, fraternal organizations, and humanitarian groups. The interesting question is, why are some firms nonprofit? Why would anyone deliberately separate control from residual claimancy? More broadly, what explains the overall pattern of ownership? Why is General Motors a capitalist firm, but Welch's, the maker of the well-known grape juice, a farmer-owned cooperative? We will return to these questions, but first we must understand something of the general incentives and tradeoffs associated with different types of ownership.

Three Relationships Between Residual Claimants and Control

Regardless of which class of individual owns the firm, there are three general possible relationships between the residual claimants in the firm and those who control production: residual claimancy and control may be singularly held, shared, or separated. For ease of presentation we can use the more common expressions of "owner-operated firm," "partnership," and "corporation" to represent these three different relationships.

owner-operated firm

In the **owner-operated firm**, the owner-operator is the sole residual claimant. The window cleaning company owned and operated by Will Seymore is one example, and the economics consulting firm run by Marvin Shaffer is another. Both are cases of owner-operated firms because the person who makes the managerial decisions that affect the firm's profit is the same person who lays claim to that profit.

partnership

In the **partnership,** there is no single owner, or residual claimant, and no single manager in control. Instead, the ownership and management functions of the firm are jointly shared by two or more people who work in the firm. Law and accounting firms are commonly organized as partnerships. Many small businesses, such as restaurants, gas stations, meat markets, and clothing stores, are owned and operated by two or more business partners, all of whom work in the business, share in the managerial functions, and receive some share of the firm's profits. A good example of a partnership is a marriage. In a marriage a husband and wife share in the output of the marriage. Neither the husband nor the wife is in complete control, nor is either the sole residual claimant.

The final type of relationship is one in which residual claimancy is almost totally separated from management, or control. For example, in a publicly held corporation, residual claimancy is spread over many individuals, none of whom holds a significant claim on the firm. At the same time, the executives and managers exercise considerable control within the firm, independent of the shareholders.[1]

Most of the firms on the *Fortune 500* list are corporate firms that fit this category. Their owners are their shareholders — all those who hold some of the firm's common stock. The firms themselves, however, are actually run by professional managers who essentially are employees (even though they, too, may hold some of their firm's common stock). These managers are supervised by a board of directors who represent the firm's many shareholders. Although individual shareholders may lay claim to some portion of the firm's profits, they play no significant role in the day-to-day management of the firm. Conversely, the firm's managers can claim relatively little of the firm's profits, even though they are responsible for making the decisions that affect the firm's operation.[2]

---

1. There are really three types of corporations: public, private, and governmental. The common stock of public corporations — the dominant form — is traded on organized markets such as the Toronto Stock Exchange, whereas the common stock of private corporations is not. Because we are concerned in this chapter with private economic activity, government corporations are not a subject of our analysis.

2. These distinctions concern the relationship between ownership and control in firms, not the legal status of firms. By partnerships, then, we mean firms characterized by a small number of residual claimants, each of whom exercises some managerial control. By publicly held firms, we mean not corporations *per se* but rather firms characterized by what Berle and Means (1935) called the "divorce of ownership from control," because ownership is dispersed among a large number of people.

Additional Organizational Complexity

Although we can loosely identify three basic organizational structures, the significant point is that the patterns of ownership across all firms are extremely diverse. Indeed, if we look more deeply into the firm, we see even more organizational diversity. For example, think of the many ways in which workers in a firm are compensated for their labour. Some get hourly wages, some get salaries, and others get piece rates. Compensation can also take other forms: stock options and profit-sharing arrangements for managers and, in some cases, for all employees; Christmas bonuses or productivity-determined bonuses; and all sorts of perquisites ("perks"), ranging from a key to the executive washroom to personal use of the company car or even the corporate airplane.

Think, too, of the diversity of institutional arrangements governing job security. In many firms, seniority determines an employee's job security. The longer an employee has been with a firm, the more secure is his or her position. In other workplaces — in the construction industry, for example — workers are typically hired on a short-term basis and have virtually no job security. In some firms, management is constrained in deciding who is to be terminated by an elaborate set of quasijudicial procedures. In others, management has nearly a free hand in deciding who is to be dismissed and what are acceptable grounds for dismissal.

Once we think in more detail about just what a firm is, we see that the term covers a colossal variety of institutional arrangements. The task of a theory of the firm is to create a systematic way in which to understand the diversity of the entity that we call "the firm." Therefore, a theory of the firm must help us to understand why firms exist and what determines both their size and their particular organizational structures.

Cooperation from Noncooperative Behaviour

Once again, the starting point of this theory is with Coase (1937). While still an undergraduate Coase wrote an honours essay that went on to become the foundation of modern theories of the firm. The basis of this theory centres on the role of transaction costs, which are the costs of establishing and enforcing property rights within the firm. If we think of a firm as a collection of contracts between different parties, a variety of cheating and shirking problems arise. Each type of firm, as we have argued, is simply a different distribution of property rights that solves a particular problem and creates others. Which type of problem is most serious typically determines which organizational structure is chosen.

Coase's theory of the firm begins with a puzzle. If we view the firm from the outside and ignore the details of its operation, we see the firm to be an enterprise fundamentally characterized by cooperation. Two lumberjacks using a double-handled saw work together to produce lumber. Four employees of a small moving company cooperate to get the furniture out of the customer's apartment and into the van. Partners in a law firm specializing in criminal cases may jointly prepare and argue the cases; they may divide the cases between them, each preparing and arguing some of them; or one partner may research all the cases and the other argue them. But, whatever their arrangement, the services their firm provides depend on the partners' joint, or cooperative, effort. In short, the success of any firm ultimately depends on the cooperative efforts of its workers.

Once we abandon this external perspective and look inside the firm, however, a different picture emerges. We see only individuals: owners, managers, secretaries, supervisors, assemblers, receptionists, janitors, sales personnel, and cashiers. What motivates all these individuals? As economists, we assume that they are pursuing their own self-interest. But once we realize that the individuals who compose the firm are motivated by self-interest, a puzzle emerges. How, and to what extent, do the self-interested individuals within the firm actually work to promote the interests of the firm as a whole? Do lumberjacks ever slack off when they are working or spend more time than necessary sharpening the saw? Do the moving company's workers ever take extended coffee breaks or pocket one of the customer's possessions? Does a lawyer ever take office supplies for private use or fail to put in the time needed to track down a key witness?

Such common industrial ailments as slacking off at work, malingering, theft, and sabotage suggest that the behaviour of individuals sometimes does frustrate and even undermine the collective interests of the firm as a whole. For example, a study of phone calls made by employees from the workplace found that about 33 percent of all such calls were personal rather than work-related, costing large companies as much as $1 million per year. In Britain, the former chairman of Guinness was charged with stealing company funds in a multimillion-dollar scandal. Using this internal perspective, we can rephrase our question: how can the firm secure the cooperation of its employees? The answer is that it designs the organization of the firm to mitigate these transaction cost problems. The following questions will help to get you into the spirit of this inquiry.

PROBLEM 19.1

Life insurance salespeople are sometimes paid a large bonus for selling a new policy. For example, a salesperson might receive $1500 today for selling a new policy whose annual premium is only $1000. Of course, the purchaser has the option of cancelling the policy at the end of any year. Given this scheme, how does the self-interest of an unscrupulous salesperson diverge from the insurance company's interest?

PROBLEM 19.2

A stock option allows its holder to buy stock from the firm at a specified price during a specified time period. Suppose that company X's stock is selling today for $10 a share and that the board of directors is thinking of giving Margaret, the Chief Executive Officer (CEO), the following stock option: she can buy up to 10 000 shares at $10 per share any time during the next three years. If you were a shareholder of this company, in what circumstances would you be in favour of giving the CEO this stock option?

The Key: Organizational Solutions to Transaction Cost Problems

As you probably realized from Problems 19.1 and 19.2, the key to answering the question, "How can the firm secure the cooperation of its employees?" lies in the amazing diversity of institutions, or organizational forms, that firms exhibit. The central hypothesis of the theory of the firm is that the institutional structure of a given firm is the structure that best harmonizes the self-interest of individuals within that firm with the wider collective interest of the firm itself. In other words, the firm chooses an organizational form that maximizes its profits net of any transaction costs.

The important point is this: the way in which a firm is internally organized will depend on the nature of its production. Every exchange is different because each involves different transaction costs. For example, a farmer's decision whether to pay rent for land in cash or in kind will depend on the type of crop and the quality of the soil. A garment manufacturer's payment arrangements will be different, depending on whether it makes thousands of cheap dresses or a few hundred very expensive dresses.

Suppose a particular dress manufacturer chooses to pay sewing-machine operators a piece rate (a fixed sum for each dress). What behaviour can it anticipate from its employees? Under this arrangement, operators will try to increase their rate of production by sewing more quickly and paying less attention to detail, because their take-home pay will be greater.

If the manufacturer is in the low-quality, high-volume segment of the garment industry, paying by piece rate serves to harmonize the self-interest of the individual operators with the dress manufacturer's objective. However, if the manufacturer produces an expensive line of dresses in which meticulous attention to detail counts, paying individual workers by piece rate might frustrate the firm's goals. The transaction costs of policing the quality of dresses would be too high. A firm that sells in the high-quality segment of the industry, then, would be increasing its costs by choosing piece-rate payments. We would therefore expect to see such a firm pay its operators an hourly wage.

All institutional arrangements can be analyzed in terms of how nearly they achieve a congruity between individual self-interest and the collective interests of the firm. The work habits of individual sewing-machine operators will vary, for instance, depending on the circumstances in which they can be dismissed or suspended; on how often their work is monitored and on benefit packages and bonus structures. As you saw in answering Problem 19.2, stock options encourage executives to be good managers by allowing them to capture some of the profit their good management creates.

The behaviour of the individuals who make up a firm is moderated by the firm's organizational form — by its institutions:

The central hypothesis of the modern theory of the firm is that the organizational forms that we encounter every day are the ones that achieve the closest possible identity between the objectives of the individuals inside the firm and those of the firm as a whole.

Does cooperation actually arise from noncooperative behavior? We have already seen that people in the workplace sometimes frustrate the interests of the firm as a whole. Problem 19.1, for example, was inspired by a scandal in the sale of life insurance in Ontario. Likewise, Inco's productivity bonuses — characteristic of incentives used throughout much of the hard-rock mining industry — sparked a controversy in the mid-1980s over underground safety. Some miners intentionally shortened the bolts that are critical for underground support because they could install almost three times as many shorter bolts during an eight-hour shift and thus almost triple their bonuses.

The Existence of Multiperson Firms

If we suppose that incidents of this kind are not uncommon — that institutional arrangements resolve the potential conflicts of interest within the firm only imperfectly — then another puzzle arises. If securing the cooperation of individual workers inside a firm is such a tricky business, why bother creating firms of more than one person? In the one-person, owner-operated firm, the firm *is* the individual; its collective goals are therefore identical to the individual's self-interested ones. Because owner-operators of one-person operations need not devise clever institutions to secure their own cooperative behavior, no organizational issues arise. Why, then, do multiperson firms exist? And what determines their size once they come into being?

19.2 Three Models of Organization

A complete theory of the firm which answers these organizational questions does not exist yet. However, we can set out the basic issues and illustrate some of the important research results to date, as well as the method economists use to address these questions. Let us begin with a situation in which we would never expect to see more than one person in a firm. This exercise will help you to understand why multiperson firms create organizational dilemmas.

The Owner-Operator Firm

In our neighbourhood on the third Saturday of every month, the tinker's bell reminds us to bring out our knives for sharpening — at a price, of course. The tinker, whom we will call Roberta, combines her capital equipment (a cart, a foot-powered grinding wheel, and a brass bell); her skill and, most important, her own effort, to sharpen the knives that are brought to her.

How much effort Roberta puts in is entirely up to Roberta. She can work at her wheel either quickly or slowly; she can spend time making small talk or not; she can walk along the sidewalk briskly or at a more leisurely pace; she can work from morning until night or put in only a few hours each day; she can be out on the streets seven days a week or only on weekends. In short, Roberta has a great deal of latitude in the effort she exerts.

In constructing a very simple model, we will ignore other choices Roberta might make, such as location or equipment, and focus on how much effort Roberta chooses to expend. If we assume that the number of knives that Roberta actually sharpens in any period is proportional to the effort she expends and that she charges everyone the same price per knife, then the income her business generates in a period will be directly proportional to the effort she puts into it. For simplicity, we will assume that each unit of effort generates $1 of income. That is,

$$y_R = e_R$$

where y_R is Roberta's income and e_R is her effort. Because this income-effort relationship tells us the terms on which Roberta can convert her effort into command over goods — that is, into income — it effectively describes the technology of tinkering for Roberta.

How much effort will she actually choose to expend? To find the answer, we need to know what Roberta's preferences are. We can capture her preferences in a utility function $U(e_R, y_R)$ in which her utility is a function of the effort she expends, e_R, and the income she earns, y_R. We will assume that income is a "good": holding e_R constant as y_R increases, Roberta is better off. In contrast, we will assume that effort is a "bad": holding y_R constant, as e_R increases, Roberta is worse off. Therefore, as we move upward in Figure 19.2 Roberta gets progressively better off, and as we move to the right she gets progressively worse off.

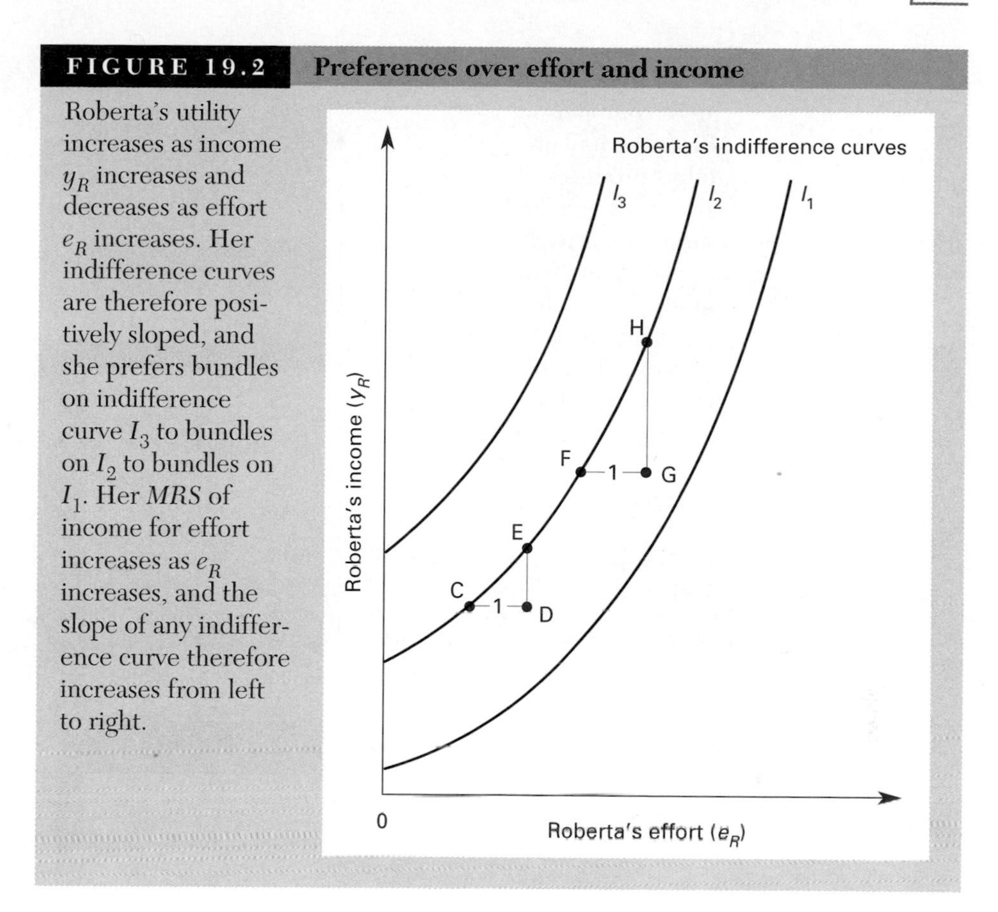

FIGURE 19.2 **Preferences over effort and income**

Roberta's utility increases as income y_R increases and decreases as effort e_R increases. Her indifference curves are therefore positively sloped, and she prefers bundles on indifference curve I_3 to bundles on I_2 to bundles on I_1. Her *MRS* of income for effort increases as e_R increases, and the slope of any indifference curve therefore increases from left to right.

Because income is a good and effort a bad, the indifference curves in Figure 19.2 are upward sloping. We will also assume that the larger the initial level of effort, the greater the increase in income necessary to compensate for a unit increase in effort. In other words, the more effort that Roberta presently puts into her business, the greater must be the increase in her income to compensate for yet more effort on her part. Then, because effort at point F in Figure 19.2 exceeds effort at point C, distance GH exceeds distance DE. The second characteristic of any indifference curve, then, is that its slope increases from left to right.

Seeing how the one-person firm operates is now a simple matter. Roberta will choose the amount of effort e_R that maximizes her utility $U(e_R, y_R)$, knowing that income y_R is proportional to effort: $y_R = e_R$. She must therefore choose a point on the line $y_R = e_R$ in Figure 19.3. The solution to Roberta's choice problem, and therefore the equilibrium for the one-tinker firm, is at point W, where Roberta exerts e^* units of effort and earns income y^* — an amount equal to e^*. Given the constraint that income equals effort, the equilibrium for the one-tinker firm is (e^*, y^*) at point W, because this point is associated with the highest attainable indifference curve:

At the equilibrium of the one-person firm, the slope of the indifference curve, or the marginal rate of substitution of income for effort (*MRS*), is equal to 1, the rate at which additional effort generates additional income.

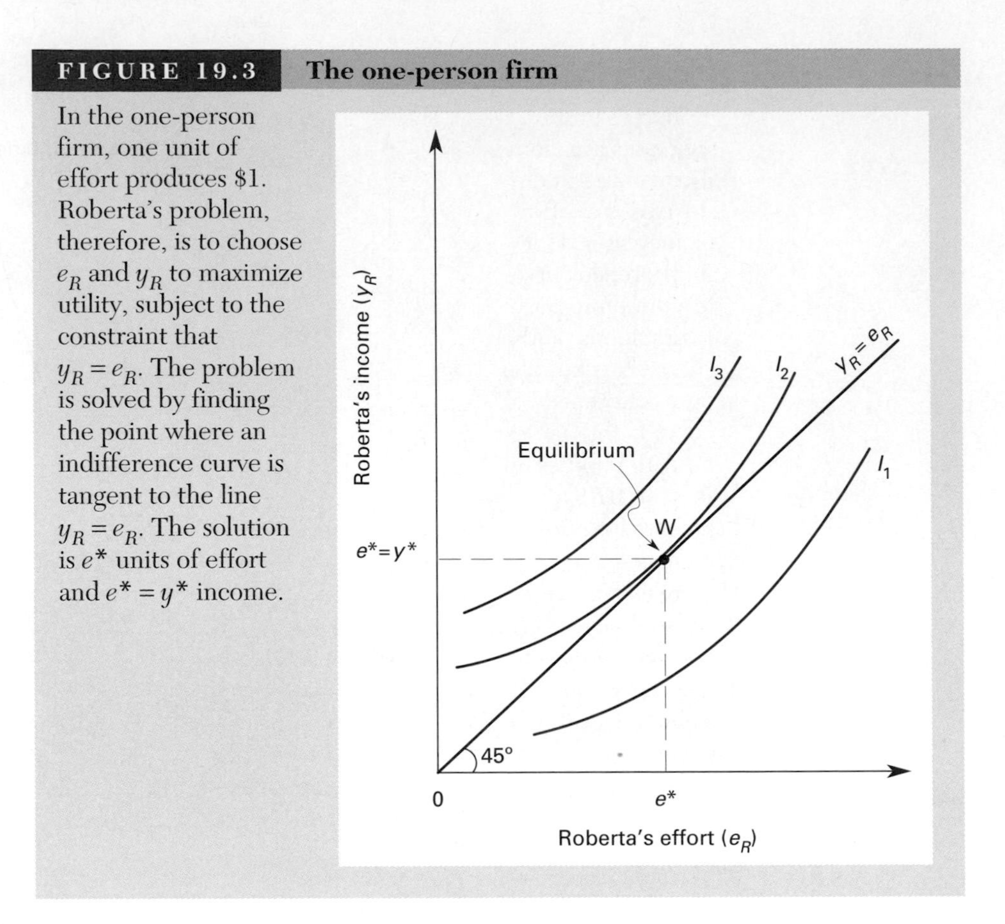

FIGURE 19.3 **The one-person firm**

In the one-person firm, one unit of effort produces \$1. Roberta's problem, therefore, is to choose e_R and y_R to maximize utility, subject to the constraint that $y_R = e_R$. The problem is solved by finding the point where an indifference curve is tangent to the line $y_R = e_R$. The solution is e^* units of effort and $e^* = y^*$ income.

A Partnership Alternative

What would be the comparable equilibrium if Roberta were in a partnership with another tinker? By comparing the one-tinker and two-tinker firms, we can both (a) identify an awkward organizational issue that arises in the two-tinker firm, and (b) see why the one-person firm (at least in this simple model) is the preferred organizational form.

Suppose that two tinkers with identical preferences and identical technologies — we will call them Roberta and Victor — join together to form one firm. We are therefore assuming that the indifference curves in Figures 19.2 and 19.3 describe Victor's preferences as well as Roberta's, and that a unit of his effort produces \$1 of income, just as a unit of her effort does.

The technological constraint faced by the two-tinker firm is that the sum of their incomes must equal the effort that they jointly expend:

$$y_R + y_V = e_R + e_V$$

where y_R and e_R are Roberta's income and effort, and y_V and e_V are Victor's.

We will determine these four quantities — effort and income for Roberta and for Victor— in the context of a partnership form of organization. Let us suppose that Roberta and Victor are *equal partners*: that is, each receives exactly half of their combined earnings. Every day, Roberta and Victor make their rounds, putting their effort into sharpening knives. At the end of the day they meet, pool their earnings, and divide them in half.

What will be the equilibrium in this two-person partnership? In other words, what effort will each put into the business and how much income will each get out of it? Let us suppose that Roberta chooses her own effort to maximize her own utility, *taking Victor's effort as a given*, and that Victor chooses his effort to maximize his own utility, *taking Roberta's effort as a given*. Furthermore, we will look for a *symmetric equilibrium: one* in which Roberta and Victor expend the *same effort* and enjoy the *same income*.

Notice that in this partnership, the aggregate income of the firm is equal to $(e_R + e_V)$, and Roberta's share is exactly half that amount. Therefore, her income is determined by the following income-effort relationship:

$$y_R = (e_R + e_V)/2$$

Notice that if Roberta increases her own effort by one unit, her own income increases by only half of a dollar. Victor's income is determined in an analogous way.

Since their preferences and technologies are identical, we know from our analysis of the single-person firm that by working alone, each partner could have achieved point W in Figure 19.3. Can they manage the same result in their partnership? To find out, let us suppose that initially both tinkers put out e^* units of effort. Assuming that Victor continues to expend e^*, let us see whether or not Roberta will continue to expend e^* as well.

When e_V is equal to e^*, Roberta's income-effort relationship is

$$y_R = (e_R + e^*)/2$$

Given this income-effort relationship, Roberta's private problem is to choose e_R so as to maximize her own utility.

In Figure 19.4, we have constructed this income-effort relationship — the solid line $y_R = (e_R + e^*)/2$. We have also included the analogous income-effort relationship for the one-tinker firm from Figure 19.3 — the dashed line $y_R = e_R$. The dashed line allows us to identify the equilibrium for the one-tinker firm, which is (e^*, y^*) at point W. Notice that the two income-effort relationships intersect at W. In other words, given that Victor puts out e^* units of effort, if Roberta also puts out e^* units of effort, her income would again be y^*.

Yet we see from Figure 19.4 that Roberta will choose point D rather than point W. In other words, even if Victor puts out e^* units of effort, Roberta will decide to put out less effort. Why? Notice that as Roberta reduces her effort by one unit, the total income of the firm declines by \$1, but her personal income declines by only \$0.50. As a result, Roberta chooses the combination of effort and income at D, where her *MRS* is equal to the rate at which her own effort increases her own income (1/2).

Because Roberta and Victor have identical preferences, we also know that if for some reason Roberta were to put out e^* units of effort, Victor would decide to put out less. In sum, the partnership fails to achieve the equilibrium of the one-tinker firm.

The Partnership Equilibrium

How much effort will the tinkers actually put into the partnership? In any symmetric equilibrium, both Roberta and Victor will supply the same effort and earn the same

FIGURE 19.4 **Shirking in a partnership**

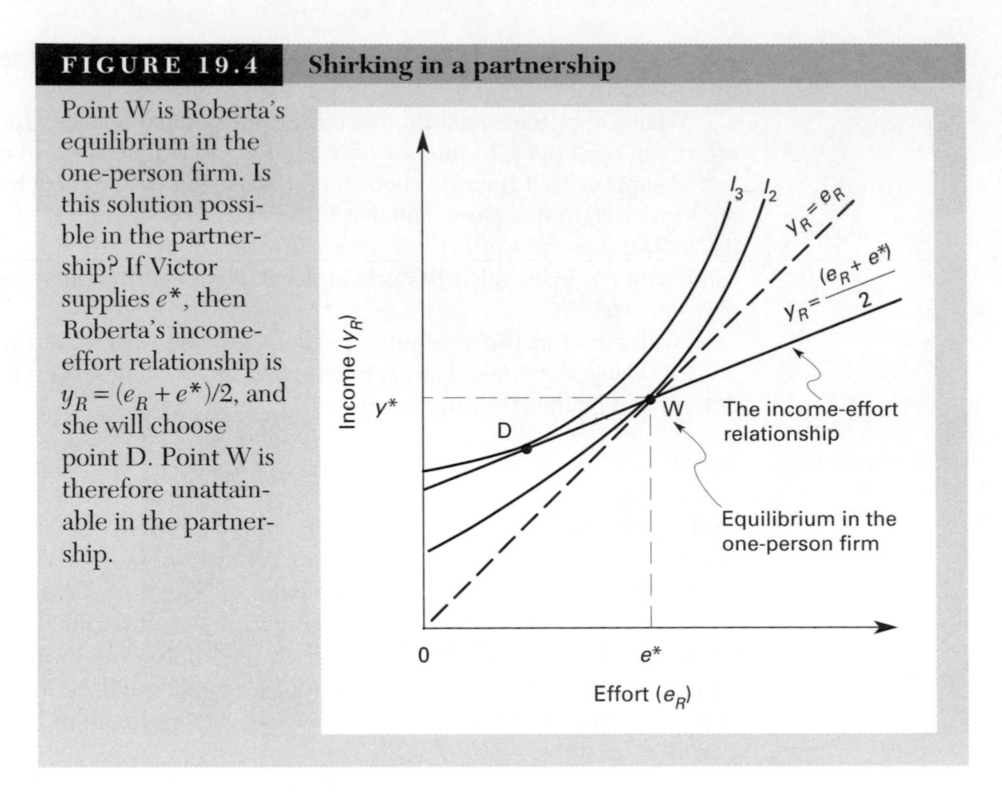

Point W is Roberta's equilibrium in the one-person firm. Is this solution possible in the partnership? If Victor supplies e^*, then Roberta's income-effort relationship is $y_R = (e_R + e^*)/2$, and she will choose point D. Point W is therefore unattainable in the partnership.

income. But this implies that at the equilibrium, Roberta's income will be equal to the effort she supplies, since one unit of effort creates \$1 of income. In other words, the partnership equilibrium will lie on the dashed line $y_R = e_R$ in Figure 19.5. Furthermore, because each will choose the level of effort that maximizes private utility and because the slope of the income-effort relationship is 1/2 for each of them, *MRS* at the equilibrium will be 1/2. Therefore, the equilibrium will be at point F in Figure 19.5 on the line $y_R = e_R$ where *MRS* is equal to 1/2.[3]

Point W in Figure 19.5 is the equilibrium for the one-tinker firm, and point F is the partnership equilibrium. Since W is on a higher indifference curve than F, we see that both Roberta and Victor are worse off in the partnership than if each worked in a one-person firm. Clearly, in this partnership, the pursuit of private self-interest by the two tinkers frustrates their collective interest. If, starting at the partnership equilibrium, the two partners were simultaneously to increase their effort, their personal incomes would increase by \$1 for each additional unit of effort — and they would obviously be better off. For example, Roberta would move upward and to the right from F along the line $y_R = e_R$ in Figure 19.5. The difficulty with their partnership is this: at point F, neither Roberta nor Victor has a *private incentive* to put out more effort, because each receives only half the income generated by an additional unit of personal effort.

The partnership fails to create the right private incentives because neither partner can capture the whole of the added output that his or her personal effort creates.

3. It is possible that there is more than one point on the line $y_R = e_R$ at which *MRS* is equal to 1/2. In this case, there are multiple equilibria in the partnership model. For simplicity, we ignore this possibility.

FIGURE 19.5 The partnership equilibrium

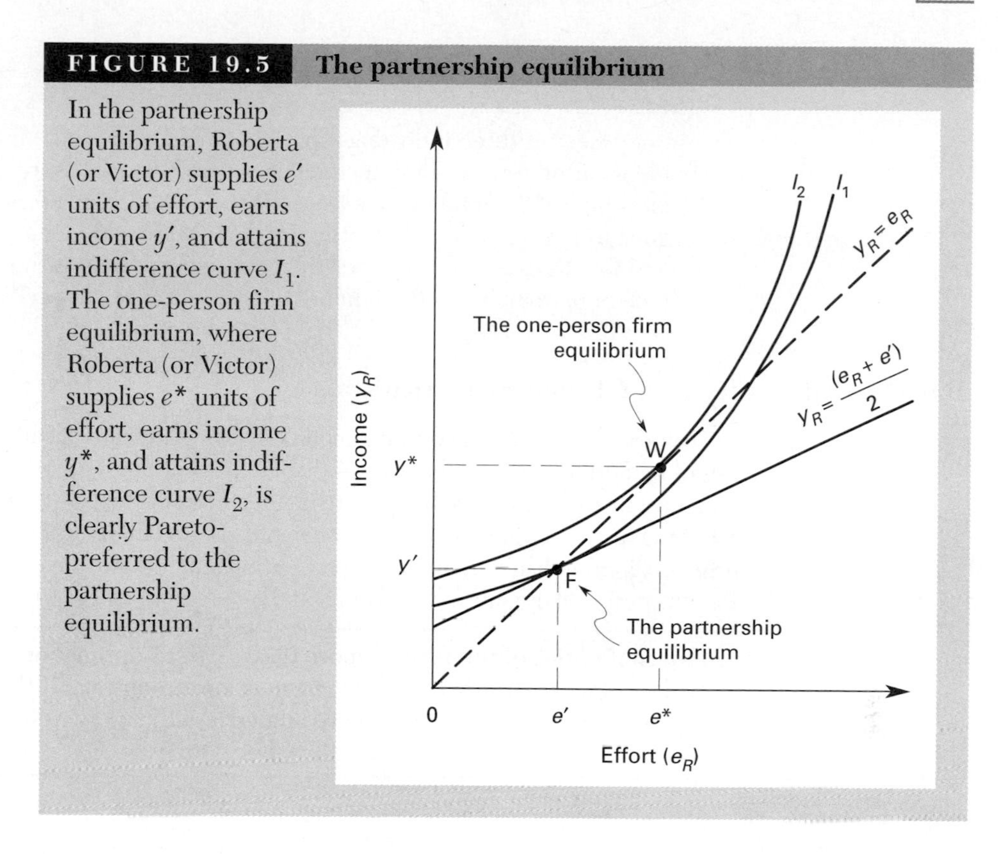

In the partnership equilibrium, Roberta (or Victor) supplies e' units of effort, earns income y', and attains indifference curve I_1. The one-person firm equilibrium, where Roberta (or Victor) supplies e^* units of effort, earns income y^*, and attains indifference curve I_2, is clearly Pareto-preferred to the partnership equilibrium.

residual claimancy

Notice the key role that **residual claimancy** plays as an incentive in this analysis. In both the one and two-person firms, an added unit of effort creates an additional \$1 of income. In the partnership equilibrium, however, each tinker chooses a point where *MRS* is equal to 1/2 because each shares only *half* of the added income generated by additional personal effort. By contrast, in the equilibrium of the owner-operator firm, each tinker chooses a point where *MRS* is equal to 1 because each claims *all* the additional income created by the additional effort. In both cases, the tinker's right as a residual claimant dictates the choice of effort he or she puts into the firm.

We have assumed that Roberta and Victor are not honourable enough simply to agree to the equilibrium at point W in Figure 19.5 and to stick to their bargain by expending e^* effort apiece. This honourable solution is certainly a possibility, particularly in the two-partner case. In Problem 19.3, however, you will have a chance to see why honour might get stretched too thin when a larger number of partners is involved.

The fundamental point is that Roberta and Victor cannot improve on the single-person equilibrium. They have nothing to gain, and — as our analysis reveals — may well have something to lose by forming a partnership. Therefore, the partnership arrangement potentially involves a real cost to the two partners.

The two-tinker firm is preferable only if some real advantage is associated with it — for example, if a unit of effort produced *more income* in a partnership than it does in a one-person firm.

PROBLEM 19.3

Suppose that three individuals are in a partnership, that all three have identical preferences and technologies, and that each partner receives one-third of the total income from the firm. Construct a diagram analogous to Figure 19.5 and identify the equilibria for the one-person firm and for the two- and three-person partnerships. What is the fate of this type of partnership as the number of partners grows larger?

Pareto-Optimality and Choice of Institutions

We can use the one- and two-tinker models to articulate more clearly the basic hypothesis of modern theories of the firm — that the institutions we actually see are the ones that most nearly harmonize the private interest of individuals with the collective interest of the firm as a whole. Because our two tinkers are both better off in the one-person firm equilibrium than they are in the partnership equilibrium, the one-person firm is the Pareto-preferred organizational form and the one we would expect them to choose.

Modern theories of the firm suppose that a Pareto-optimal organizational form will be chosen. An organizational form is Pareto-optimal if there is no other organizational form that will leave all parties at least as well off and at least one party better off.

19.3 Team Production

If multiperson firms create nothing but trouble, why do we encounter so many larger firms in everyday economic life? Multiperson firms come into being only when the advantages that accrue to size outweigh the transaction costs created by organizational difficulties. One such advantage arises from the gains in productivity associated with **team production**, the arrangement in which two or more workers accomplish a productive task through their joint, or team, effort. The idea of team production is simply a variation on the old adage, "Many hands make light work." In team production, the hypothesis is that many hands do *more* work.

team production

We will begin this section, then, by exploring the *productivity gains* associated with team production. We will see that when these gains are large enough, the partnership form of organization is Pareto-preferred to the one-person firm. We will then introduce and analyze another organizational form, the owner-operated team, and determine the circumstances in which each of the three organizational forms — the one-person firm, the partnership, and the owner-operated team — is Pareto-preferred to the other two.

Productivity of Teams

In their pioneering work, Alchian and Demsetz (1972) used the example of workers loading boxes onto a truck to illustrate the productive potential of teams. Imagine two identical workers — each hired for one day only — loading boxes. For the moment, let us fix the effort expended by each worker over the day and compare the output when each labourer works in isolation with the output when the two work as a team.

First, suppose each worker expends his or her fixed effort in loading boxes alone. Let x be the aggregate number of boxes loaded. Then, suppose they work together, lifting one box from opposite sides and expending their fixed effort as a team. Let y be the aggregate number of boxes the team loads. Alchian and Demsetz argue that if the boxes are large and awkward or if they are heavy, y will exceed x. In this case, production in teams is more productive than production in isolation. It is even possible — if the boxes are heavy enough that one worker cannot lift them but not too heavy for two to lift — that x is zero and y is positive.

We can identify a whole array of jobs in which team production is economic. In a large number of construction tasks — installing siding or drywall, for example — in which two pairs of hands are almost essential. Likewise, two surveyors working as a team are vastly more productive than they would be if they worked in isolation.

In creating our own model of team production, we will follow Alchian and Demsetz's lead. Consider again the workers loading boxes onto a truck. Suppose they receive a fixed price for each box they load and that the number of boxes loaded is proportional to effort. We can then describe the technology by a proportional relationship between income and effort. Suppose that when the task is done by individuals working in isolation, each unit of effort produces $1 of income, and when individuals work in two-person teams, each unit of effort produces $$B$ of income. Team production is then more productive than isolated production when B exceeds 1. In this section, we will assume that B is greater than 1.[4]

The superior productivity of teamwork provides an incentive to organize economic activity into multiperson firms. Yet is this sufficient to offset the organizational costs of a two-person firm? If it is, which organizational form should we expect team production to take? To find out, let us return to our two workers, Roberta and Victor, assuming this time that teamwork makes them more productive and continuing to assume that they have identical preferences.

Partnership with Team Production

We already know from the two-tinker model how to find the equilibrium if the team is organized as a partnership. Roberta's equilibrium will lie on the line $y_R = Be_R$ in Figure 19.6 since a unit of effort in the team produces B dollars of income and, at the equilibrium, MRS will be equal to $B/2$ since, in the partnership, an additional unit of effort increases Roberta's income by $B/2$. The partnership equilibrium for Roberta is at point C. (Of course, Victor will also pick a point analogous to point C.) In Problem 19.4, you can discover a key result for yourself:

The partnership is Pareto-preferred to the one-person firm if B is sufficiently large — that is, if the productivity gain associated with team production is sufficiently large.

4. Notice that if one team worker decides not to put out any effort, a difficulty arises with this description of team technology. For example, suppose that Victor decides not to work, and that e_V is therefore equal to zero. This means that Roberta is left loading boxes by herself. In this case, Roberta's effort actually produces only $1 rather than $$B$ per unit. To remedy this difficulty, we assume that the factor of proportionality for team production is B if both e_R and e_V are strictly positive, but is only 1 if either e_R or e_V is zero.

PROBLEM 19.4

Begin by constructing the income-effort relationship for a worker loading boxes alone, and identify the equilibrium for the one-person firm. On the same diagram, identify the point that corresponds to the equilibrium for the partnership at point C in Figure 19.6. In doing so, choose the value of B so that the equilibria of the partnership and the one-person firm are on the same indifference curve. Which organizational form is Pareto-preferred for larger values of B? For smaller values?

The Owner-Operated Team

If Roberta and Victor could overcome the organizational difficulty inherent in the partnership equilibrium at point C in Figure 19.6, however, they could do even better. Specifically, Roberta could attain point D in Figure 19.6, where her effort is e'' and her income y'' — a point clearly preferable to point C. Is there an organizational arrangement that would allow Roberta to attain point D (and Victor to attain the analogous point)? There is, provided that it not too costly to write contracts and to monitor — that is, to observe and verify — the effort of a teammate.

FIGURE 19.6 **The owner-operated firm**

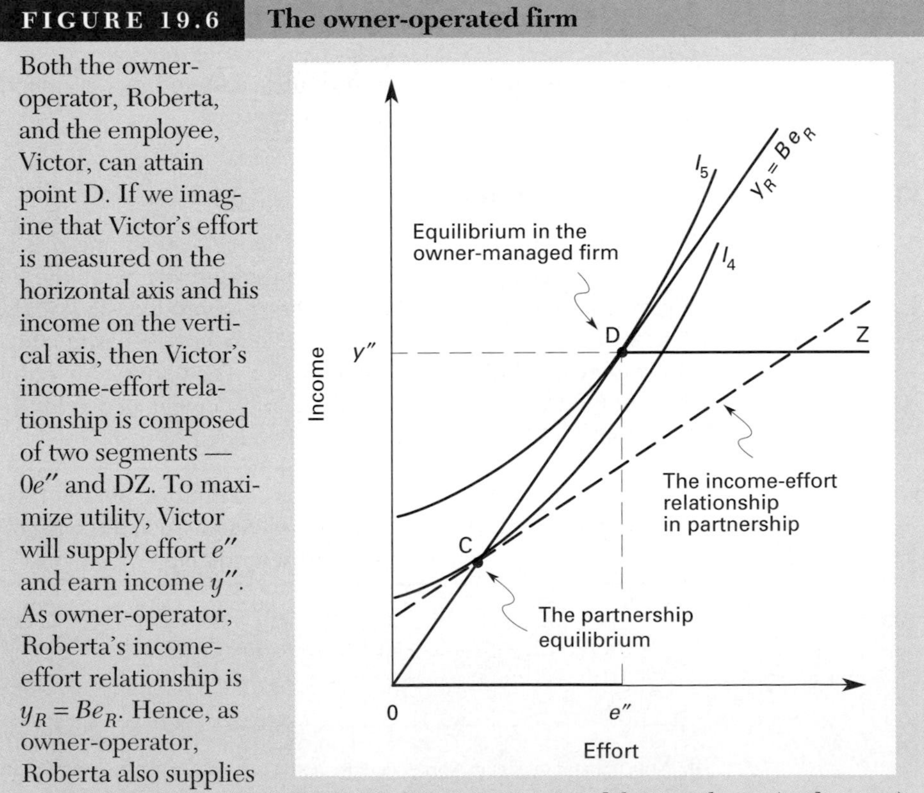

Both the owner-operator, Roberta, and the employee, Victor, can attain point D. If we imagine that Victor's effort is measured on the horizontal axis and his income on the vertical axis, then Victor's income-effort relationship is composed of two segments — $0e''$ and DZ. To maximize utility, Victor will supply effort e'' and earn income y''. As owner-operator, Roberta's income-effort relationship is $y_R = Be_R$. Hence, as owner-operator, Roberta also supplies effort e'' and earns income y''. In the owner-operated firm, Roberta (and Victor) attain an equilibrium that is preferred to the partnership equilibrium.

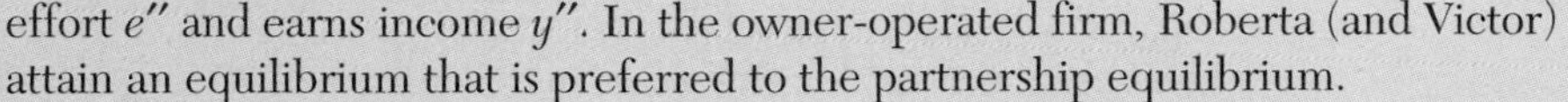

For the moment, let us assume that contracting and monitoring costs are nonexistent. (Later, we will extend the model to include these costs.) Now suppose that Roberta, as the team's owner-operator, offers to employ Victor under this contract: Victor will receive an income of y'' from Roberta if he supplies e'' or more units of effort. If he supplies less than e'' units of effort, however, he will receive no income.

If Victor agrees to these terms, the contract is enforceable, because we have assumed that his effort can be monitored without cost. There are two aspects of enforceability. First, enforceability means that if Victor fails to supply at least e'' units, Roberta can demonstrate to some court, without cost, that Victor did not meet the contractual conditions, and she will not have to pay him y''. On the other hand, it means that if Victor does supply at least e'' units of effort and Roberta fails to meet her end of the deal, then Victor can demonstrate without cost that he has met the contractual conditions, forcing Roberta to pay him y''.

Let us show that this contract allows both parties to attain (e'', y'') at point D in Figure 19.6. First, if we imagine that Victor's effort is measured on the horizontal axis and his income on the vertical axis, then Victor's income-effort relationship is composed of two horizontal line segments. The first is segment $0e''$ of the horizontal axis, because Roberta will pay him nothing if he does not supply at least e'' units of effort. The second is segment DZ of the line $y = y''$, because Roberta will pay him y'' if he supplies at least e'' units. To maximize his own utility, Victor will therefore choose point D on this income-effort relationship where he supplies e'' units of effort and receives y'' in income.

Now let us turn to Roberta. As the owner-operator, she is the exclusive residual claimant for the firm. This means that her income is the amount remaining after Victor has supplied e'' *and* been paid y''. Accordingly, her income-effort relationship is

$$y_R = B(e'' + e_R) - y''$$

But, because y'' is equal to Be'', Roberta's income-effort relationship can be rewritten as

$$y_R = Be_R$$

Given this income-effort relationship, we know that to maximize her own utility, Roberta will also choose point D in Figure 19.6 where she, too, supplies e'' units of effort and receives y'' as income.

The owner-operated team thus allows both team workers to attain the effort-income combination (e'', y''), a combination that is clearly Pareto-preferred to the combination attainable in a partnership at point C. In the following problem, you can show that the owner-operated team is also Pareto-preferred to the one-person firm.

PROBLEM 19.5

Draw a diagram in which you identify the point that corresponds to the equilibrium for an owner-operated team at point D in Figure 19.6. On the same diagram, construct the income-effort relationship for a one-person firm and identify the equilibrium.

To summarize what we have discovered so far:

In the absence of contracting or monitoring costs, the owner-operated team is Pareto-preferred to both the one-person firm and the partnership.

Contracting and Monitoring Costs

We have discovered that when it costs nothing for a firm to enter into contracts with its employees or to monitor their performance, the owner-operated team is Pareto-preferred to both the single-person firm and the partnership. However, entering into such contracts is never free of cost. Even an unwritten agreement — the proverbial handshake — costs the parties to the agreement time and effort. Written contracts are even more expensive because somebody (or several somebodies) must draw them up, type them out, duplicate copies, send the copies to the contracting parties, and so on.

Monitoring workers can also be an expensive business. For example, it costs money — sometimes a great deal of money — to take a case through the courts if an employee does not meet the terms of a contract. It often costs money, too, just to find out whether the terms of a contract have been met. Think of the problem faced by a university president in deciding whether some professor has actually fulfilled his or her contractual obligations. How can the president monitor classroom performance without spending money on regular in-class supervision, student achievement tests, and other assessment methods?

Other types of employee monitoring can also be expensive. For example, more and more businesses of all sizes are investing in costly telecommunications monitoring to generate data to be used to prod workers into higher productivity and to trap workers who abuse the phone system. Depending on the design of a company's telecommunications system, it can cost up to $100 000 to install call-accounting systems used to monitor and report on workers' use of company phones. Alchian and Demsetz (1972) argue that the cost of supervision in the legal profession is also extremely high. For example, if a law firm supervisor wants to determine whether one of its lawyers has prepared a case adequately, he or she may have to replicate the whole of the employee's work. In such cases, the owner-operator's advantage in being the single residual claimant may well be outweighed by the cost disadvantage of monitoring employees.

Let us extend our model to include the costs associated with entering into contracts with employees and monitoring employee productivity. Notice that these costs arise only in the owner-operated team, since neither contracting or monitoring is necessary to enforce the equilibrium in either the partnership or the one-person firm. There, the residual claim in effect monitors the workers.

What is the symmetric equilibrium of the owner-operated team in the presence of these contracting and monitoring costs? To find out, let us begin by identifying the highest indifference curve Roberta can attain if she has to pay for half the monitoring costs, denoted by M, but can keep all the income generated by her own effort. Her income-effort relationship is then

$$y_R = Be_R - M/2$$

Given this relationship, the highest indifference curve that Roberta can attain is the combination of e' units of effort and an income of y' at point V in Figure 19.7.

The following contract will allow both Roberta and Victor to attain the income-effort combination at point V in Figure 19.7. Victor will receive an income of y' from Roberta if he supplies e' or more units of effort. But, if he supplies less than e' units of effort, he will receive no income. To see why, simply adapt the argument used to find the initial equilibrium for the owner-operated team. The following problem will get you started.

FIGURE 19.7 The owner-operated firm with monitoring costs

In any symmetric equilibrium, Roberta's income will be $y_R = Be_R - M/2$. Hence the best symmetric equilibrium is at point V.

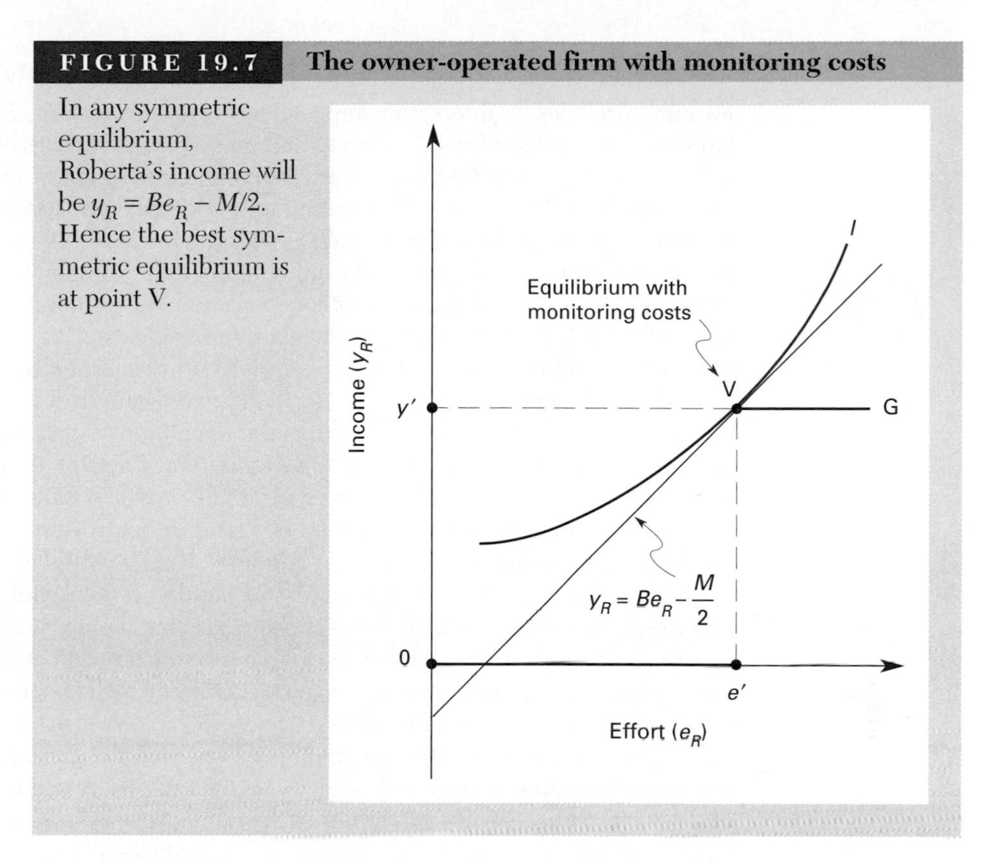

PROBLEM 19.6

Given this contract, what is Victor's income-effort relationship? What is Roberta's?

To reinforce your understanding of the role of monitoring costs, try the following problem.

PROBLEM 19.7

a. First construct a diagram in which you identify the equilibrium of the one-person firm. Then find values for B and M such that the one-person firm and the owner-operated team are equally attractive.
b. Beginning at this position, if you increase M by a small amount, which of the two organizational forms is now Pareto-preferred?
c. Beginning again at the initial position, if you now increase B by a small amount, which is Pareto-preferred?

Application: The Nature of the Farm

Farming provides an interesting application for the ideas we've been discussing. A farm is a firm that takes a series of inputs and converts them to foods like grains and meat (as if you needed to be told that!). Farms are organized in many different ways, however. Traditionally farms were organized around the family, which would do everything from breaking the soil to partially processing the food. Beginning in the middle of the twentieth century, farms started to change their organizational form. Some farms became partnerships, while others became large corporate firms hiring thousands of wage labourers. What brought about these changes?

In terms of our model, farming over the centuries has most often been characterized by small gains from specialization and limited gains from team production. At the same time, in farming it is often difficult to monitor workers. The reason for this is the enormous role that nature plays in production. Farming depends critically on weather and other random elements of nature like pests. A hailstorm can wipe out a crop, and disease can kill large fractions of a herd or flock. Moreover, nature is often random. Farmers can never plan with certainty when a crop will be planted or harvested. On the other hand, some aspects of nature are extremely predictable. For example, spring always follows winter and always comes before summer. The seasonal nature of farming and the biological rhythm of most farm products means that it is often impossible to specialize in any given task. A farmer who is specialized in planting will be unemployed most of the year.

Thus, nature's seasonality has traditionally limited the gains from team production on farming, and nature's random elements limit the ability to monitor workers. Both of these effects have worked in favour of the family farm as the efficient unit of organization. When nature can be removed from the production of farm products, however, the gains from team production increase and the costs of monitoring labour fall. The result is a move towards larger corporate farming.

Nowhere has this change been more prevalent than in the production of meat. The introduction of antibiotics and steroids into cattle and poultry feeds greatly reduced losses from disease and allowed farmers to raise cattle and poultry in confined indoor spaces. Once inside, removed from the seasons of nature, animals can be raised on a continuous cycle and in sizes large enough to allow labour specialization. The result has been a huge increase in the size and structure of farms. For example, in the US, the top three poultry-producing firms account for over 80 percent of the chickens produced in a given year. If wheat could be grown under glass, we'd see the same thing happen.

19.4 The Pareto-Preferred Organizational Forms

We now have a moderately complex model with three possible organizational forms: (a) the single-person firm using the isolated technology, (b) the partnership, or (c) the owner-operated team using the team technology. Because each organizational form has its advantages and disadvantages, choosing the right one can be a complicated and interesting problem. Depending on the productivity advantage associated with teamwork and the costs of monitoring, any one of the three organizational forms we have considered can be Pareto-preferred to the other two forms.

As an example, grain farming offers very few gains from team production but large monitoring costs due to nature's significant role. As a result, single-owner firms dominate. On the other hand, with automobile production there are huge gains from team production, and relatively low monitoring costs due to the repetitive nature and easy task assignment of most jobs. Hence, we tend to observe the owner-operated team, which in most cases takes the form of a corporation.

Clearly, which organizational form will be Pareto-preferred in any given circumstance will depend on the specific values of the parameters B and M. In Figure 19.8, we have indicated the portions of the parameter space in which each of the three organizational forms is Pareto-preferred. Notice that for the sake of completeness, we have also allowed B to be less than 1 in Figure 19.8.[5] (When B is less than 1, team production is less productive than is production in isolation.) Figure 19.8 is essentially a metaphor for the theory of the firm: it conveys both how complex the problem of choosing an appropriate organizational form can be and how economists approach that problem.

FIGURE 19.8 **Pareto-preferred organizational forms**

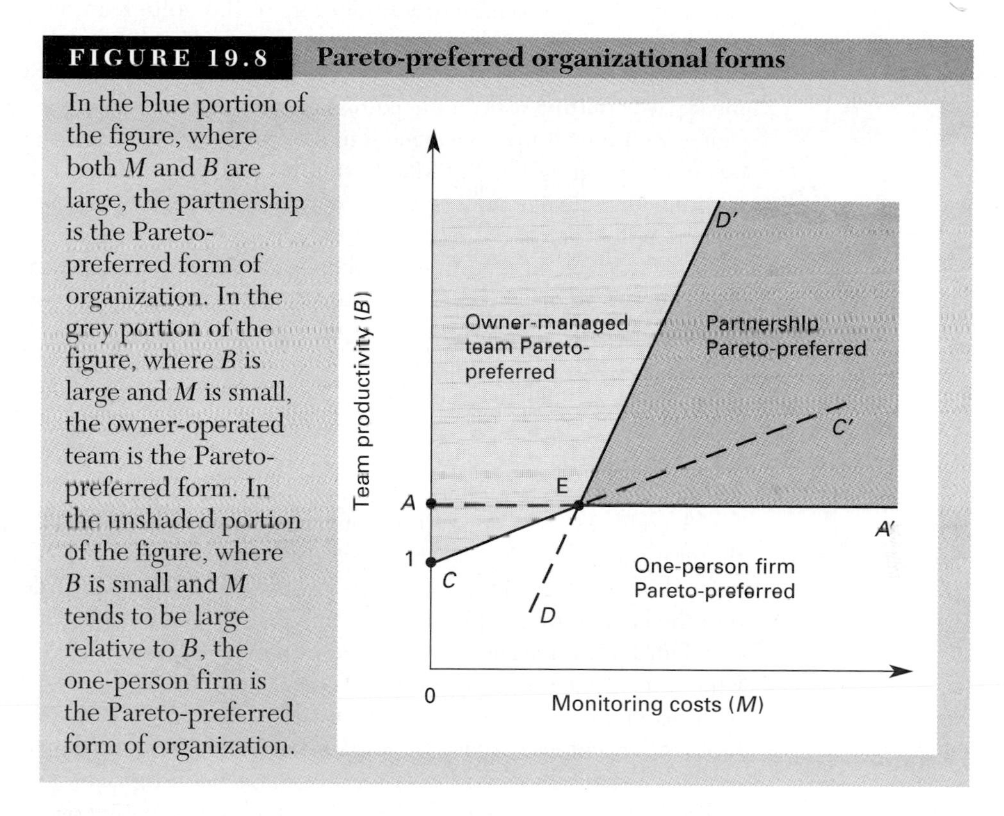

In the blue portion of the figure, where both M and B are large, the partnership is the Pareto-preferred form of organization. In the grey portion of the figure, where B is large and M is small, the owner-operated team is the Pareto-preferred form. In the unshaded portion of the figure, where B is small and M tends to be large relative to B, the one-person firm is the Pareto-preferred form of organization.

5. We can examine Figure 19.8 more closely. Lines CC' and DD' are not necessarily straight, but it is convenient to assume that they are. On the horizontal line AA', the partnership and the one-person firm are equally attractive; above AA' the partnership is Pareto-preferred and below it the one-person firm is Pareto-preferred. On the line CC', the one-person firm and the owner-operated team are equally attractive; above CC' the owner-operated team is Pareto-preferred and below it the one-person firm is Pareto-preferred. Line CC' has two special features: first, the point $M = 0$ and $B = 1$ is on CC'; second, CC' is upward sloping. Notice that all three organizational forms are equally attractive at E, the point where lines AA' and CC' intersect. On the line DD', the partnership and the owner-operated teams are equally attractive; above DD', the owner-operated team is Pareto-preferred and below it the partnership is Pareto-preferred. Line DD' has two special features: first, it passes through point E; second, it is positively sloped and steeper than CC'.

19.5 Specialization and the Division of Labour

specialization
division of labour

Adam Smith was the first to identify **specialization** and the **division of labour** as important sources of the productivity advantages that give rise to the "wealth of nations." (Indeed, most economists date the year of birth of economics as 1776 — the year in which Smith's *Inquiry into the Nature and Causes of the Wealth of Nations* was first published.) In the opening pages of *Wealth of Nations,* Smith argues that the greatest improvement in the productive powers of labour stems from the effects of the division of labour: the breaking up of the productive process into a series of smaller specialized tasks, each performed again and again by a single person.

Smith illustrated this fundamental insight by pointing to the vast productivity gains that specialization offered the eighteenth-century pin factory.We find a modern counterpart of the pin factory under any of the golden arches spread around the globe. In any McDonald's restaurant, the task of making and selling a Big Mac is divided into a number of separate operations: taking the customer's order; cooking the meat patty; putting it in a bun; adding the lettuce, onion, cheese, pickle, and special sauce; wrapping it up; conveying it to the front counter; bagging it; handing it to the customer; pushing the Big Mac button on the cash register; taking the customer's cash; making change; and trying to sell an apple pie as well. No single person ever does all or even most of these jobs. Instead, each McDonald's employee specializes in just one or a few of them. In some outlets, specialization is so extreme that the person who rings up an order is different from the one who takes the customer's money and counts out the change.

According to Smith, three factors explain the increased productivity that arises from specialization and the division of labour. First, specialized workers become more productive simply as a result of practice and repetition. McDonald's employees who wrap the burgers get to be very fast at it. The longer people spend at one task — *learning by doing* — the more proficient they become.

Second, workers do not lose time moving from one task to another. A firm can therefore economize on *aggregate setup costs* — the costs of getting ready to do each task. Think how much time would be lost if each McDonald's order-taker had to walk into the kitchen first to place and then to pick up each order.

Third, Smith argued that specialization encourages *technical progress*. People who concentrate on a small number of tasks are likely to discover more efficient ways to perform them. For example, workers who specialize in a task may be able to design tools and machines to make the work even more efficient. In many McDonald's outlets, for instance, standard cash registers have been replaced by simpler, more specialized ones, in which each key is a pictograph representing one of the items for sale. (Could it be that some clever employee devised this labour-saving cash register?) To see the productivity implications of setup costs, try the following problem.

PROBLEM 19.8

Suppose some manufacturing process involves two separate stages and that the setup times for each stage are 60 and 120 minutes, respectively. It takes 60 minutes for a worker to get ready for stage 1 and 120 minutes to get ready for stage 2. Suppose that the worker, having expended the setup time, takes 10 minutes in each stage to process 1 unit of output. Show that 1 worker could produce 15 units in 8 hours; that 2 workers, each working for 8 hours, could produce 36 units; and that 13 workers, each working for 8 hours, could produce 252 units. Given 13 workers, how many should specialize in stage 1 and how many in stage 2?

Like team production, specialized production offers a productivity improvement that can provide an incentive for the existence of firms. However, unlike team production, in specialized sequential production it is fairly simple to monitor an individual's effort. In a sequential production process, we can watch the semifinished good as it passes from hand to hand. As a result, if something goes amiss, we can assess fairly accurately and relatively costlessly just which worker has let the firm down. For example, at the Western Star assembly plant in Kelowna, British Columbia, where they build large trucks, a worker is sent home for making a mistake that causes the assembly line to stall, and is fired if such a mistake occurs twice. This can only be done because the firm knows exactly who is responsible for every part of the truck.

In team production, however, it may be harder to assess individual effort. Alchian and Demsetz have suggested that clues to each worker's effort might include how rapidly a person loading boxes moves to the next piece to be loaded, or how many coffee breaks are taken. Still, all that we can observe for certain is the output produced by the team as a whole. We cannot see the number of boxes that I lifted, or that you lifted, but only the number that we lifted together.

Moreover, team production must always be carried out within the confines of a single firm. A large, heavy box is indivisible: I cannot first lift and load "my half" of it and then move on while you lift and load "your half." In contrast, specialized production need not be carried out by a single firm. For instance, McDonald's frozen hamburger patties and its sesame-seed buns are both made by other firms; the sesame seeds on top of the buns and the beef that goes into making the meat patties are produced by still other firms.

Specialized production thus permits a choice between coordinating all stages of the process in-house or coordinating some stages through markets. We can see various arrangements in the world around us. A canola oil refinery may buy its canola seeds in the marketplace and have the seed oil extracted by another firm specializing in crushing and extraction, but may carry out the oil refining and product packaging processes in-house. Campbell Soup Company in Canada gets its mushrooms and poultry from its own farms, but it buys the English muffins and precooked fried eggs for its frozen breakfasts from outside suppliers.

Application: Where Have all the .400 Hitters Gone?

As every baseball fan knows, since Ted Williams' .406 batting average in 1941 no one has broken the .400 mark. What many might not know is that Bill Terry hit .401 in

1930, and before him seven players hit over .400 nine times since 1901. In the nineteenth century, hitting over .400 was even more common. What is going on? Baseball players are bigger, paid better, healthier, coached more than the players of the past, so why hasn't hitting improved like the winning times in the 100-metre run?

The pessimist might think that something very bad has happened in baseball. Perhaps today's players just aren't as tough as they used to be. All of the computer games and Little League play that replaced the sandbox games has hurt the sport. However, a better explanation goes back to Adam Smith and his notion of specialization. There is a major factor working against hitting .400: the opposing team. It turns out that with baseball, unlike most sports, there has been a tremendous amount of specialization taking place over the past 100 years in defence, but almost none in offence.

When Ted Williams had his magic season, it was still common to find players that played more than one position. Today this is unheard of. Players who specialize in one position end up playing that position better; that is, they prevent more hits from taking place. One of the most specialized positions, and the one that has seen the most changes over time, is the pitcher. One hundred years ago a pitcher normally pitched an entire game, and may have had two or three pitches to throw. Now there are "starters," "relievers," and "closers," with sliders, changeups, fastballs, and a host of other pitches. One final change has been in the equipment. During the early beginnings of baseball, fielders used their bare hands to catch the ball. This was replaced with a simple glove, and then with a glove with netting between the thumb and index finger. Have you seen a baseball glove lately? They are so large you could catch a football with some of them. Up against specialized positions, pitches, and gloves, what has happened on the batting side of the equation? Nothing! Batters in the major leagues still use wooden bats that are essentially unchanged from the ones used by Babe Ruth. Even though players have improved over time in terms of size and training, the effects of specialization have taken place mostly in terms of the defensive aspects of the game. The result is the dearth of .400-plus hitting for the past 60 years.

Transaction Costs

What determines whether all stages of specialized production will take place within a single firm or will be coordinated by markets? Ronald Coase (1937) argued that the choice of whether to produce within firms or across markets will depend on the relative costs of the two options. Costs include direct production costs as well as transaction costs. When the transaction costs across markets are low and the transaction costs within firms are high, we expect to see a series of small firms interacting in markets for semifinished goods. However, market transactions costs are often high and include the costs of writing and enforcing contracts between firms, the costs of keeping accurate records of transactions, and the time cost of exchanging money for goods, not to mention other costs that will be dealt with in the next chapter.

A firm will expand to the point at which the cost (including transaction cost) of adding another function in-house is just equal to the cost (including transaction cost) of coordinating that function through the marketplace.

Recall that transaction costs are the costs of establishing and enforcing property rights, and can result from a large number of circumstances. To get some feel for Coase's analysis, we can consider a fundamental distinction between two kinds of partly finished goods — *generic* and *specific* — that serve as inputs in other production processes, and we will examine the *transaction costs* associated with each.[6]

Generic Inputs

Think of the relationship between a bakery that makes bread from flour (and other essential ingredients) and a flour manufacturer that makes flour from wheat. We can imagine that a particular baking company might mill its own flour. If the flour it produces in-house is identical to the flour produced elsewhere, the company will be indifferent between using its own flour and using flour produced by a dozen other millers.

generic input

As Gertrude Stein might have said, "Flour is flour is flour." Because flour is a **generic input** — different sources of it are interchangeable — we can imagine a flour market composed of many suppliers (millers) and many demanders (bakeries, etc.). In such a market, we can use Coase's hypothesis to separate the activities coordinated in-house from those coordinated through markets by comparing their respective costs.

Specific Inputs

specific inputs

In some production processes, however, inputs are not generic but specific. For example, N C Machine, a tool-and-die shop in Wichita, Kansas, manufactures a styrofoam container for a McDonald's hamburger, the handle for a Sears Craftsman wrench, and the plastic holder for a Toyota seat belt. Dowty Canada Ltd. builds the nose-wheel and main landing gear for Lockheed's P-7A airplane. These are **specific inputs** because they are of no (or limited) use to any firm except the firm for which they are intended. The plastic holder for a Toyota seat belt, for instance, is of no use to anyone but Toyota.

When an input is highly specific, then, there cannot be a market for that input in the ordinary sense of the word. There might be more than one supplier, but there will be precisely one demander. Furthermore, no supplier will produce firm-specific, partly finished goods simply on speculation that the lone demander will buy them. The demander and its supplier(s) will invariably come to a detailed contractual agreement before any partly finished goods are produced. For example, Campbell Soup Company went through long, delicate negotiations before a small Toronto supplier agreed to buy the equipment it needed to begin producing fried eggs for Campbell's frozen breakfasts. Such agreements are costly.

Let us see what sort of issues specific inputs raise and why costly agreements are necessary if one firm is to produce a specific input for another. Specifically, let us suppose that I want to manufacture a one-of-a-kind customized car for someone whose tastes are so peculiar that the car will be worthless to anyone else. Suppose, too, that we have a verbal agreement in which you agree to make the auto body for me and I agree to pay you $100 000 for it. If you do produce the body to my specifications, will I actually pay you the promised price on delivery day? If I am honest and if I can, I will. But if I am less than honest, I may try to take advantage of you. Ignoring the scrap value of the body, you are now holding an auto body that has value to me alone. Suppose I offered you half the amount we had agreed upon? If I could convince you that I would not offer more, you would accept. In fact, you would accept any positive price rather than keep the body yourself. By producing a highly specific input, then, you have put yourself into a very shaky bargaining position.

6. There are several comprehensive references to the literature on transaction costs. Barzel (1989), Libecap (1989), and Williamson (1985) are all classics.

On the other hand, I may have put myself into an equally awkward position. If I do not have time to get the auto body elsewhere, you may be able to extract more than $100 000 from me. Suppose that I have incurred $100 000 in additional costs and that using the body you have made, I can immediately sell the car for $250 000. Suppose, too, that if I do not deliver the finished product immediately, the deal is off and I will be left with an unmarketable car. What is the maximum I would pay for the body? It is virtually $250 000 — and if you were unscrupulous, you would ask for that amount. Clearly, if you and I are to make a transaction, we must have some form of contractual protection, and that protection will be costly. If it is too costly, our market arrangement simply will not be viable — and all production will be done in-house.

PROBLEM 19.9

The law sometimes attempts to facilitate contracting in the presence of specificity. For example, the Mechanic's Lien Act, on the books in virtually all jurisdictions in North America, permits building tradespeople to register a lien against the real property they are working on. The lien prevents the sale of the property until the tradesperson's bill has been paid. Is such legislation in the self-interest of property owners as well as tradespeople?

Let us summarize the implications of input specificity:

On one hand, firms have an incentive to decentralize their activity; that is, to buy partly finished goods as inputs, because they can thereby avoid the difficulties associated with harmonizing the interests of individuals within the firm. On the other hand, firms have a disincentive to buy specific inputs from other firms, because these inputs are subject to high transaction costs across markets. Whether we will find decentralization (that is, coordination of economic activity by markets) or centralization (that is, coordination of economic activity within firms) depends on whether or not the advantages of decentralization outweigh the resulting contracting costs.

SUMMARY

This exploration of the organization of the firm has been tentative rather than definitive. We wanted to provide you with a sampling of the kinds of intriguing (and sometimes difficult) questions that arise once we look inside the firm itself and to suggest how economists analyze these issues.

We began with the simple question, "Who owns the firm?" and saw that ownership is not a simple matter. Furthermore we pointed out that firms could be owned by capitalists, labourers, or even consumers. The relationship between who owns residual rights and control is important. The goal of the firm is to secure the cooperation of its workers in achieving the firm's collective objective to maximize profit. Broadly speaking, the answer is to mitigate the transaction costs by designing organizational forms that harmonize or identify as closely as possible the collective interests of the firm with the self-interest of the individuals within it.

We then developed a model in which we could explore this problem more fully. We looked at three organizational forms. In a *one-person firm*, the residual claimant is in control. In a *partnership* using team production, residuals and control are shared. In an *owner-operated team* using team production, one person is the residual claimant and in control, but has to monitor worker performance, in a range of environments described by two parameters: the cost of monitoring, M, and the productivity of effort in team production, B. If B is large and M is small, the owner-operated team is Pareto-preferred; if B is small and M is large, the one-person firm is Pareto-preferred, and if both B and M are large, the partnership is Pareto-preferred.

When we considered *specialized production*, we saw that the problem of harmonizing incentives also determines whether certain productive activities will be coordinated *in-house*, in the *marketplace* by means of transactions among vertically interrelated firms, or by a hybrid of the two. The theory of the firm is thus a part of a more general theory of the organization of economic activity as a whole.

Given the diversity of incentive problems and solutions in terms of organizational form, the range of economic questions yet unexplored is enormous. The theory of the firm and the broader theory of economic organization are both wide open to further analysis.

EXERCISES

1. In this problem, we will use the following utility function to illustrate the possible equilibria for the three organizational structures explored in Sections 19.2 through 19.4:

$$U(e, y) = 8(y - e^2/2)$$

where e is the level of effort and y equals income. With this utility function, MRS (or the slope of an indifference curve) is equal to e:

$$MRS = e$$

In the two-person team, each unit of effort produces $\$B$ of income, and in the one-person firm, each unit of effort produces \$1 of income.

   a. Draw two indifference curves.
   b. Derive the following results for the one-person firm and illustrate graphically: (i) utility-maximizing quantity of effort = 1; (ii) utility-maximizing income = 1; (iii) maximized utility = 4. (*Hints*: At the utility-maximizing equilibrium, the slope of the income-effort relationship is equal to MRS. To compute maximized utility, evaluate $U[e, y]$ at the utility-maximizing values of effort and income.)
   c. Derive the following results for the two-person partnership: (i) utility-maximizing quantity of effort = $B/2$; (ii) utility-maximizing income = $B^2/2$; (iii) maximized utility = $3B^2$. (*Hint*: The slope of the income-effort relationship for the partnership is $B/2$.)
   d. Derive the following results for the owner-operated team: (i) utility-maximizing quantity of effort = B; (ii) utility-maximizing income = $B^2 - M/2$; (iii) maximized utility = $4B^2 - 4M$. (*Hint:* In effect, the manager and the employee each pay half of the monitoring cost, M.)
   e. Use the maximized-utility results from above to construct a diagram with M on the horizontal axis and B^2 on the vertical axis, in which you identify values of M and B^2 such that (i) the one-person firm is Pareto-preferred to the other firms, (ii) the owner-operated firm is Pareto-preferred, and (iii) the partnership is Pareto-preferred. (*Hint*: Begin by finding values of M and B^2 such that maximized utility is the same for the one-person firm and the partnership, for the one-person firm and the owner-operated firm, and for the partnership and the owner-operated firm.)

2. Brothers Brett and Bart had a very peculiar argument — each claimed that his horse was slower than his brother's. To resolve their argument, they agreed to bet \$100 on the outcome of a quarter-mile race. At the appointed hour, Brett and

Bart mounted their horses and, when the starter's gun fired, nothing happened — whereupon a bystander, wise in the ways of economic incentives, asked the brothers to dismount and whispered something to them. In a matter of seconds the brothers had remounted and were racing to the finish line, and the question of which horse was the slower was resolved to their satisfaction. What did the wise bystander suggest?

3. Any homeowner will tell you that getting home repairs done satisfactorily by outside tradespeople can be a struggle. The problem is one of *asymmetric information*: although individual tradespeople know whether they are skilled and reliable, it is difficult for the homeowner to know. We pay $50 per year to belong to a homeowners' club that refers us to tradespeople and checks back to see that we are happy with their work. Our cheques for repairs are written to the club, which then pays the tradesperson a specified percentage of the total bill. Is this sort of organization likely to solve the homeowner's asymmetric information problem? If you were the manager of the club, how would you use the information provided by the club members? If you were a homeowner, what sort of management scheme would induce you to join the club? If you were a competent tradesperson, would you work for the club? What quality of work would you provide for club members?

4. Restaurants such as McDonald's and Burger King are typically run as franchises. The parent company teaches the franchisee how to run the establishment (in the case of McDonald's, at an institution called "Hamburger University") and then allows the franchisee to use the product trademark (the golden arches, for example) and to buy specialized packaging materials and ingredients. The terms of the typical franchise contract require the franchisee to pay an initial lump sum and a percentage of its gross revenues to the parent firm. The parent company can and does inspect the franchisee's operation and records from time to time. If the operation is not up to the standards of cleanliness and product quality specified in the contract, the parent company can unilaterally revoke the franchise. In addition, the franchisee must be the exclusive or sole owner of the restaurant and must agree to work full-time in the restaurant. The parent company typically agrees not to franchise another restaurant within a specified radius, say 20 kilometres. This type of contract raises a number of interesting questions. Why does the parent company choose to sell franchises instead of hamburgers? Why does the parent company insist on exclusive ownership of the franchised restaurant? Why does the parent company inspect the operations of its franchisees? Claim: A sensible franchisee would refuse to buy a franchise unless it knew that all other franchise contracts could and would be revoked if the franchisees failed to meet the parent company's standards. Do you agree? Why or why not? Why does one franchisee care about the way in which others run their restaurants? Why does the parent firm agree to the restriction that it cannot sell other franchises within a specified radius of existing franchises?

5. Success in the textbook market requires three things: a good book (the author's responsibility); an attractive book (the designer's responsibility); and an effective sales effort (the responsibility of the sales staff). The author typically is paid a royalty for each book sold, equal to something like 15 percent of the wholesale price of the book; the designer typically is a salaried member of the publisher's staff; and individual salespeople often receive a percentage commission on the sales they make. How do these compensation arrangements influence the incentives of the affected parties? Why are designers paid a salary instead of a commission? Why do publishers not pay authors a fixed sum to produce books? Why are commissions so often used in sales instead of, or in addition to, salaries?

6. A home computer called the Lemon is produced by combining a Pentium chip with specialized equipment designed exclusively for it. Many firms produce identical chips, but only Firm O produces the specialized equipment. The market price for a chip is $\$X$; the cost to Firm O of producing the specialized equipment is $\$Y$; and the market price for the Lemon computer is $\$Z$, which exceeds $\$X + \$Y$. The Lemon computer can be produced and marketed in one of three possible ways. Firm O can buy the chips and then assemble and sell Lemons. Some chip manufacturer can buy the specialized equipment from

Firm O and assemble and sell Lemons. Some third firm can buy both the chips and the specialized equipment produced by Firm O and assemble and sell Lemons. Which of these organizational forms would you expect to see and why?

7. IBM buys many of the specialized parts for its computers from other firms. So, too, General Motors buys many of the specialized parts for its cars and trucks from other companies. Buying a particular specialized part from two or more different firms is common practice for the purchasing firm. Why would a firm like IBM or GM insist on having multiple suppliers for each of its specialized parts?

8. A common practice in the resort business is to pay a substantial bonus to students who stay for the entire season and to refuse to rehire students who quit before the end of the season. Why do resorts use these compensation and hiring schemes? More generally, wages tend to increase with seniority, and firms sometimes establish nonvested pension plans that pay employees a pension only if they stay with the firm for some specified length of time. What purpose do such compensation schemes serve for the firm? (*Hint*: Recall the discussion of specific inputs. How would the concept apply to human capital?)

9. Imagine an extreme case of firm-specific human capital. It takes a new employee one period to learn a job. During that period, he or she is completely unproductive. Having mastered the job in the first period, the employee is productive in the second period. There are only two periods. All potential employees can earn wage w' in some other job in each period. Assuming that the rate of interest is zero, the firm must choose a wage rate for period 1, w_1, and for period 2, w_2, such that

$$w_1 + w_2 \geq 2w'$$

It could choose $w_1 + w_2 > 2w'$ of course, but will not do so. Why not? Will it ever choose $w_1 > w'$ and $w_2 < w'$? Is there any advantage to the firm in choosing $w_2 > w'$ and $w_1 < w'$? Suppose that there are two types of potential employees: the first type is going off to college after one period and the second type is not. Assuming that the firm cannot identify who is college-bound and who is not, show that it should choose $w_1 < w'$ and $w_2 > w'$.

10. In Chapter 17 we argued that insurance was a method of transferring risk from risk-averse individuals to risk-neutral firms. Firms also take out insurance. For example, General Motors buys fire insurance from specialized insurance companies. General Motors is many times larger than the insurance companies it deals with, and in a much better position to diversify any risk resulting from fire. If risk diversification cannot explain why General Motors contracts for insurance, what would?

11. Throughout the twentieth century there was a movement towards incorporation. Firms, in other words, moved to the owner-managed team form of organization to exploit gains from specialization and team production. This has been particularly true in manufacturing. One exception to this has been farming, in which the family unit still dominates as a productive unit. Why do you think corporate farming has not taken over in, say, wheat production?

12. An office building is owned by many people. That is, many people have control over the various attributes of the building, including decorating, heating, interior design, and the like. Large units of equipment, on the other hand, tend to be owned by single individuals. Why might this be?

13. In Chapter 7 we discussed how different cost structures might lead to different types of markets. For example, when an industry is characterized by increasing returns to scale we noted that this would encourage the formation of natural monopolies. One of the puzzles in economics has been the following: As markets grow they specialize more and average costs tend to fall. Hence larger markets should experience more and more monopolization. This, however, has not happened. How can the analysis in this chapter explain this? Why would increases in specialization necessarily increase the amount of transaction costs as well?

REFERENCES

Alchian, A. and H. Demsetz. 1972. "Production, Information Costs, and Economic Organization," *American Economic Review*, 62:777–95.

Barzel, Y. 1989. *Economic Analysis of Property Rights*. Cambridge: Cambridge Press.

Berle, A. and G. C. Means. 1935. *The Modern Corporation and Private Property*. New York: Macmillan.

Coase, R. 1937. "The Nature of the Firm," *Economica*, 4:386–405.

Libecap, G. 1989. *Contracting For Property Rights*, Cambridge: Cambridge Press.

Smith, A. 1937 (orig. 1776). *The Wealth of Nations*, The Cannan Ed. New York: Random House.

Williamson, O. 1985. *The Economic Institutions of Capitalism: Firms, Markets, Relational Contracting*. New York: Free Press.

CHAPTER 20

Asymmetric Information and Market Behaviour

In the last two chapters we have examined two particular instances of asymmetric information where the resulting transaction costs led to organizational solutions that did not exist under our neoclassical model. In Chapter 18 we examined the problem of externalities and public goods, arguing that the presence of transaction costs meant that the allocation of property rights had real economic implications. Contrary to the neoclassical model, when one party is given the right to pollute, it leads to a different level of pollution than if some other party was given the right. In Chapter 19 we examined the problem of the organization of the firm, and argued that when transaction costs were positive, different types of firm organizations led to different levels of profitability for the firm. How much people produced, we saw, depended on how they were paid. Again this analysis was substantially different from the neoclassical model that only treats the firm as a black box.

Two important points were generalized in these two chapters. First, the rules of the game matter. When property rights change hands, we should expect a different allocation of resources to result, whether we're considering the property rights for legal liability or residual claimancy in a firm. Again, this is in direct violation of the neoclassical model, which predicts that the distribution of property rights does not matter. Secondly, it was argued that the rules, or property rights, chosen were those that were Pareto-optimal. This meant that the solution chosen to internalize an externality or to organize a firm will maximize the gains from trade.

In this chapter we continue this line of reasoning by examining cases of asymmetric information in market exchanges. We want to predict how exchanges themselves will be organized to best manage the subsequent transaction cost problems that may arise from buyers and sellers having asymmetric information. There is an enormous body of literature in economics dealing with these questions, and in summarizing a few of these examples we intend mostly to whet your intellectual appetite for more economics.

20.1 Reputations

When you walk up to a vending machine, drop some change into the slot, and then punch the button for an Oh Henry candy bar, what guarantee do you have that it will be fresh and tasty? If the candy bar is old, lacking peanuts, or for some other reason is generally unsatisfactory, what is a consumer to do? You could write to the Hershey company and demand your money back, but this hardly seems worthwhile. How *is* a guarantee guaranteed?

This is a more general problem. My car is valuable enough that if it is defective I will pursue the manufacturer until it is fixed. Because I behave this way I am even willing to purchase a guarantee from the automotive company. But when it comes to minor purchases like a chocolate bar or a T-shirt, why would I believe a seller's guarantee of quality when I know it will never pay me to act on it? Furthermore, if firms know that I will do little or nothing in response to being cheated, and if cheating is more profitable than being honest, then they will always cheat by promising high-quality goods but not delivering them. If consumers anticipate this behaviour then they would never be willing to pay more than a low-quality price for goods and that is all that would get produced. When quality cannot be guaranteed, it would appear that many markets would simply fall apart!

The general market solution to this problem is for the firm to establish a reputation for selling high-quality goods.[1] Reputations, therefore, are a market response to asymmetric information between buyers and sellers. Suppose we have the following asymmetric information situation. A number of price-taking firms are selling refrigerators, with every firm deciding whether to sell high-quality units that will last for ten years or low-quality units that will only last for one year. The problem for the consumer is that he cannot tell them apart, and will not know until one year after the purchase which type he has. The problem for the firms is that a high-quality refrigerator sells for more than a low-quality one, but also costs more to produce.

Figure 20.1 shows the three options available for a given firm. Point A represents the case for a firm that decides to produce the low-quality refrigerator and announce this truthfully. The firm receives the low-quality price p^L, and earns zero profit. Point B is the outcome for a firm that decides to sell a high-quality refrigerator, announces its intentions truthfully, and is believed by its customers. In this case, the firm produces along the higher cost functions and again earns zero profit. Point C represents the case of a firm that produces low quality, lies, and announces that it has produced high quality, and is believed by its customers. In this case the firm receives the high-quality price p^H, but faces the low-quality costs, and so earns a profit equal to the shaded area.

Of these three cases, only one is an equilibrium; can you tell which one? If you picked point A, you are right. Clearly the best thing for any firm to do is to lie and announce it is producing a high-quality product when in fact, it is producing low quality. However, every customer knows that this is the dominant strategy of the firm and therefore never offers to pay a price higher than p^L. If a firm is honest and produces a high-quality refrigerator, no one believes the announcement and the firm loses money because it still receives the low-quality price. Hence the only equilibrium is at point A.

Notice in this situation that punishing a cheating firm by never shopping there again has no effect on its behaviour because the firm is better off cheating than being honest. True, the firm will go out of business if it is discovered to be dishonest, but in the meantime it has earned a rate of return greater than the return to being honest. Since we do observe firms producing high-quality goods, what is the solution? The answer is for the honest firm to be paid a premium for producing high quality. Once this is done, then the punishment of never buying from a cheating firm again has some bite.

1. This solution was first proposed and modelled by Klein and Leffler (1981).

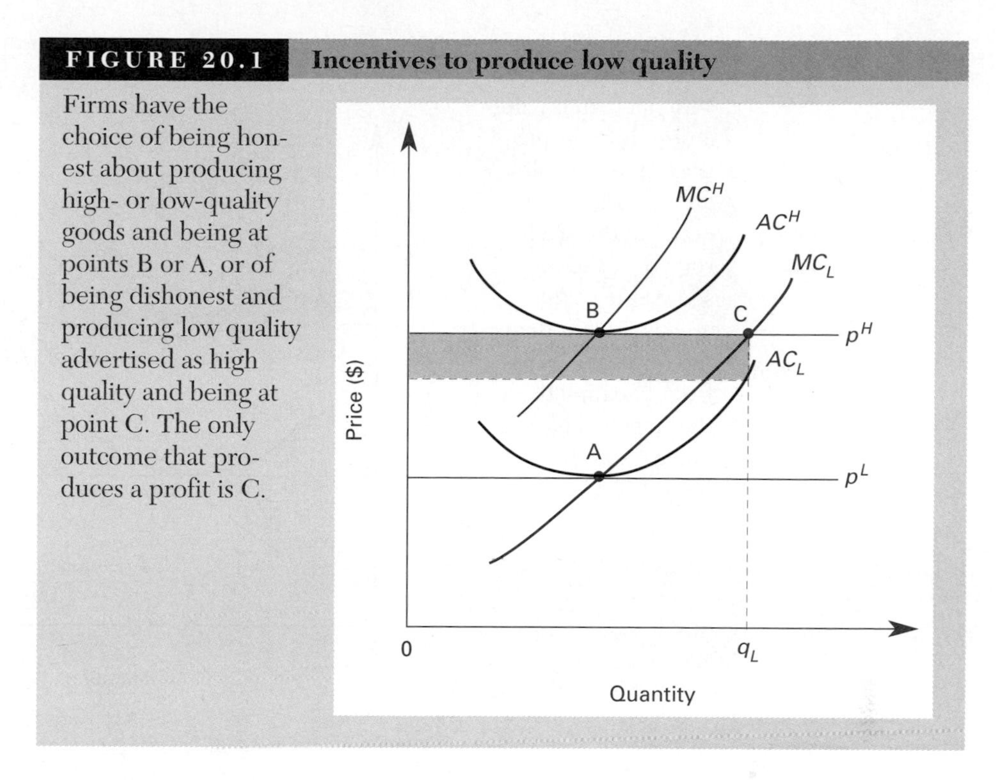

FIGURE 20.1 Incentives to produce low quality

Firms have the choice of being honest about producing high- or low-quality goods and being at points B or A, or of being dishonest and producing low quality advertised as high quality and being at point C. The only outcome that produces a profit is C.

Suppose that customers could pay a higher price for the high-quality good, such that the honest quality producer could now earn a profit. Figure 20.2 shows that if the price of high quality is raised to $p^{H'}$ then the honest firm will earn a profit equal to the shaded region. At this higher price there is an even larger gain to cheating, but when a firm cheats it only gets the gain once and then is "fired" by the consumers. An honest firm gets the shaded region year in and year out. As long as the present value of the shaded region from being honest is greater than the one-time gain from cheating, firms will be honest, and high-quality goods can exist in equilibrium.

The one last thing that needs to be resolved is that at point E the high-quality firm is earning profit, and in equilibrium we know that profits must be driven to zero. Unfortunately, if prices fall, the firms begin to cheat again. The solution is for the firms to invest in sunk capital until profits are zero. Because the capital is sunk, the shaded region is a rent. Profits are zero, but if the firm cheats it loses its sunk investment. In effect, the sunk investment acts as a bond or a guarantee of quality.

Now we can see the role of a reputation. Reputations are not cheap, and they always entail some form of sunk investment. When a firm advertises, spends money in the community, or takes a costly action that informs customers about itself, it incurs sunk costs. If the firm cheats customers, then it loses these investments because it loses its customers, and as a result the existence of a reputation enforces a firm's claims of high quality.

This provides an interesting explanation for several puzzling observations. How many times have you watched an advertisement on TV for some consumer product where there was almost no informational content to the ad? Perhaps the ad showed a beautiful woman on a sailboat in tropical waters, with the camera circling the boat, coming closer and closer. As the picture focuses in on the face of the woman, she turns and utters the name of a large auto company. What information could this possibly

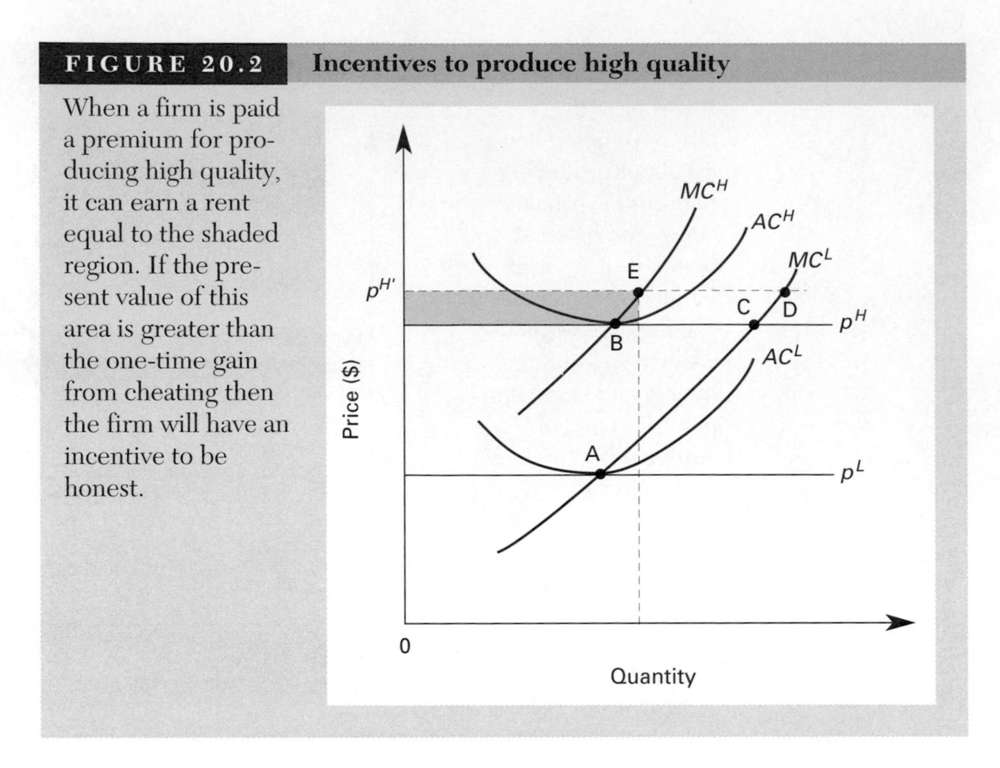

FIGURE 20.2 **Incentives to produce high quality**

When a firm is paid a premium for producing high quality, it can earn a rent equal to the shaded region. If the present value of this area is greater than the one-time gain from cheating then the firm will have an incentive to be honest.

convey? The standard reply is that the auto company is playing with our subconscious. If we buy the advertised car, the story goes, then we will also have a great boat in sunny waters. This model suggests a totally different solution. What the consumer really needs to know is whether they can trust the auto company or not. If the company is willing to "throw" money away on useless advertisements, then they must be earning a rent. If they are earning a rent then they must be planning on staying in business for a while, and that means they must be planning on producing high quality. Hence the company is indirectly advertising that they are honest.

Banks are often chastised for having elaborate buildings and expensive interiors. If you travel from city to city you will find the major local bank often owns the nicest place in town. Why would this be? Suppose that a new bank were set up just outside your university. We could call this bank "The Eaton, Eaton, and Allen Bank." The main feature of this bank would be that it operates out of a motor home (with the motor running). Are you going to put your money in a bank like that? Of course not. Banks, historically, have been required to invest in sunk physical assets in order to guarantee their customers that they will not abscond with their money. Once again, the sunk investment backs up the reputation of the firm and tells customers that they are dealing with an honest firm.

On one occasion one of the authors was walking down Chicago's "miracle mile," a street with extremely expensive stores. He came upon a Rolex store that was unlike any other. The walls were marble, the door handles were gold, the carpet six inches deep (well, not quite, but it was thick!), and inside were watches that cost up to $25 000. Ironically, around the corner was a gentleman in a long overcoat who was selling Rolex watches for $25! To the eye of the author the watches looked the same. Clearly Rolex had to make extreme investments to guarantee that the watches they were selling were not fakes.

PROBLEM 20.1

Mail-order firms send out catalogues and then receive orders from their customers. What is a serious transaction cost problem for a mail-order firm to overcome? Can you think of methods that might be used to overcome this problem?

Sunk Costs

An interesting feature of the role of reputations is that they involve investments in sunk assets. It is the actual commitment of a real resource that demonstrates goodwill. Although this form of commitment often takes the form of a financial bond, we have seen that it can take other forms as well. Posting a bond certainly achieves the purpose of guaranteeing an exchange, but bonds are not productive in and of themselves. If a firm can make a productive investment that is also sunk, then the firm guarantees the exchange at a lower cost. However, the point remains that the "sunk" nature of an investment is in itself productive. Contrast this to the neoclassical treatment of sunk costs, which considers only the costs irrelevant. With asymmetric information, the fact that sunk costs do not affect the level of output makes them the optimal method of developing a reputation.

Although sunk costs may solve some asymmetric information problems, they can create others. Sunk costs are often associated with economic rents. Recall from Chapter 9 that rents are payments over and above opportunity costs. Rents can be taken away, and individuals will not change the level of production. Because of this, when rents exist there is an incentive for others to appropriate them.

Consider the case of a bridge. Suppose a single entrepreneur, Walter, decides to build a small bridge for $1 000 000, with the expectation that each person crossing will pay $2 per trip. Suppose that Walter came up with the $2 number by doing a market survey and asking the commuters what they would be willing to pay. Finally, suppose that at this price Walter would earn a normal rate of return on his investment, and he decides to build the bridge. Once built, however, Walter's investment is sunk. The bridge is not going anywhere, and of course, the commuters know this. If they offer him $1 to cross, it is in Walter's interests to let them cross, assuming that the commuters can make the offer stick. In fact, if the cost of crossing the bridge is zero, then Walter will let them cross if they only offer a penny. Any payment Walter gets is a rent, and by offering next to nothing to cross the bridge, the commuters, in effect can "hold up" Walter because his alternatives are so poor. Whenever there is a large sunk investment involved in an exchange, there is the threat of a **hold-up problem**.

hold-up problem

Walter, and other bridge makers, are generally aware of this type of problem, and if it does not get solved early on, then bridges do not get built. There are two general solutions to the hold-up problem. The first is to vertically integrate and the second is to enter into long-term contracts.

Application: Why Is Sugar Refined in Winnipeg?

Hold-up problems abound, and all of them are usually very interesting in the way certain types of products are sunk at various times in a production process. One of the most interesting is the case of sugar. Have you ever wondered why there are sugar refineries in practically every major city in Canada, even though we don't grow sugar?

Sugar is mostly produced using sugarcane. The cane is grown in hot tropical climates where it is possible to get two crops per year. The cane is cut and taken to a sugar house where it is crushed and the juice extracted. This juice is then boiled and processed into molasses and raw sugar. The raw sugar is then shipped around the world to where it is refined into the various products we consume.

When the sugarcane is cut, the valuable complex sugar (sucrose) that is in its juice immediately starts to break down into less valuable simple sugars (fructose). After as little as 24 hours, most of the value of the cane is lost if it is not processed. Any delays in the initial processing cause huge losses of wealth to farmers. Here we have a classic situation of a hold-up problem. Sugar plants can offer farmers poorer terms for their produce after it is cut, knowing that the farmer's alternative is a worthless pile of cane. As a result, cane farmers almost always jointly own local sugar mills close to their farms. They then coordinate their harvests so that the mill is steadily supplied and no inventory of cut cane builds up. The ironic thing about sugar is that once the cane is converted to raw sugar it is practically indestructible and is very easy to ship anywhere in the world. Sugar farmers who own raw sugar do not face any serious hold-up problems with raw sugar, and as a result do not vertically integrate into ships or special freight cars for carrying their product. The sugar is sold to transporters or directly to refineries. However, once sugar has been refined again into white sugar it again becomes rather fragile. Moisture and mishandling can cause large deterioration in the product. As a result, historically sugar refineries were always located close to the final point of consumption.

vertical integration

horizontal integration

This practice of buying other firms that are "downstream" or "upstream" from an existing firm is called **vertical integration**, in contrast to **horizontal integration,** which is merging with another firm doing exactly the same thing. For example, the oil industry is vulnerable to a double hold-up. The costs of drilling a well are completely sunk and so are the costs of installing a pipeline. Once in place, both the owners of a pipeline and the owners of an oil well would begin to renegotiate the price of transporting the oil. To avoid this problem, oil companies tend to own the pipelines that transport their oil.

PROBLEM 20.2

Newspapers own their own printing presses but magazines generally do not. Why?

long-term contract

When vertical integration would entail considerable losses of output or high transaction costs, a second solution is a **long-term contract** between the two contracting parties. Firms contractually agree to a price for the entire life of the relationship. Such contracts might have clauses that allow for price changes under various circumstances, but in general they are quite rigid.

Long-term contracts are common in the railroad, coal, and electricity industries, but the most extreme form of a long-term contract is in the production of children. Marriage is a contract for life, which is about as long as any one human can handle. Furthermore, marriages usually have an implicit sharing contract of 50-50, which is backed up by most current property-division laws in case of divorce. The lifelong nature of the marriage contract most likely reflects the lifelong cycle of producing a family and the sunk investments involved. Most of the sunk investments made in having children are borne by the mother. These investments come early in the marriage, and as we have discussed already, once they have been made they create an incentive for the husband to leave the relationship. The comment "I gave him the best years of my life" reflects this sentiment. Hence the long-term contract of marriage is designed to protect the sunk investments that husbands and (in particular) wives make. In modern times, as the options and legal rights of women have increased, the transaction costs that arise from these specific investments have fallen and as a result divorce has become easier to obtain.

20.2 Adverse Selection

Young job seekers often complain that they could do jobs they have had no experience with, if only they were given the chance. Implicit in the statement are two presumptions: (1) that the young person in question could indeed do the job, and (2) that he or she cannot successfully convey this fact to the prospective employer. As a result, the employer — who perhaps uses on-the-job experience as the criterion for separating good prospective workers from bad ones — is unwilling to hire the inexperienced youth. Again, we see a problem of asymmetric information. The young person knows that he or she is capable of doing the job, but the employer does not, and the young person may have no effective way to communicate the relevant information to the employer. Furthermore, young people who really are unskilled and incapable of doing the job may make the same claims. Occasionally they may get a job, which lowers the profitability of the employer and makes it more difficult for the truly qualified young person.

A similar phenomenon arises in the market for car insurance. If a driver is under age 25, particularly if that driver is also male and single, collision insurance rates can be astronomical. These rates reflect the fact that, on average, drivers in this category have significantly higher accident rates than do other drivers. But not all young, single males are bad drivers, and some are very good. If we presume that the good drivers know that they are good, they face a problem analogous to that of young job seekers: they cannot easily convey this information to insurance companies.

Young males are not the only ones to experience the ill results of asymmetric information. A great deal of job training takes place at the work site, but firms are reluctant to provide it if they think the employee will leave once the (sunk) investment is made. Firms will often provide training that is specific to their firm and useless at other firms, which lowers the probability of the trained employee leaving. However, one reason employees leave work is to start a family. Women are still more likely to do this than men, and this means that firms are less willing to hire women for jobs that require specific on-site training. The problem for young females entering the workforce is that many have no intention of leaving the workforce to start a family. The problem for firms is that they cannot tell which type of woman is applying to their firm. As a result, women may have to train themselves at their own expense or receive lower wages to compete with men.

adverse selection

This particular asymmetric information problem is called **adverse selection.** The phrase comes from the insurance industry, where it has long been known that the selection of people who purchase insurance is biased in favour of those who need it most. Sick people are more likely to apply for health insurance than healthy people, but this characteristic may be *hidden* from the insurer. In this section, we develop some simple models that let us explore adverse selection problems. We look at a particular **hidden characteristic**: the driving ability of a particular male driver under the age of 25, which is — from the perspective of an insurance company — an unknown, or hidden, factor.

hidden characteristic

Hidden Characteristics

We can extend the insurance model from Chapter 17 to explore problems arising from hidden characteristics. This analysis is complicated from a graphical point of view, however, so we will constrain our discussion to an intuitive level. To begin with we make three assumptions about the particular hidden characteristics.

1. The relevant characteristic of any driver is the *probability of loss from a collision,* and this characteristic is *not* uniform across drivers: some drivers are low-risk and others are high-risk.
2. Each driver is *completely informed* about his or her own characteristic: drivers know whether they are low-risk or high-risk.
3. Drivers cannot communicate their risk characteristic costlessly to insurance companies: the driving characteristic of an individual — high-risk or low-risk — is *hidden* from insurance companies.

We will assume that there are just two types of drivers: a low-risk group and a high-risk group. Let q_1 be the probability that a low-risk driver causes a collision, and q_2 the probability that a high-risk driver causes a collision. The loss from any collision is L, and the cost of the loss is borne by the driver responsible for the collision. Clearly, q_1 is less than q_2. We will also assume that all drivers are risk-averse and that they have identical preferences and identical wealth levels, w_0. In this model, then, the two groups of drivers are differentiated *only* by the probability of collision.

Who is willing to pay more for full insurance, the low- or high-risk group? Clearly the high-risk group is willing to pay more because they will end up using it more often. If insurance companies could identify without cost every driver's risk characteristic, then in a competitive market equilibrium, insurance companies would supply two types of policies: one for low-risk drivers and the other one for high-risk drivers. If we again ignore the costs of writing insurance policies, the competitive prices of the low-risk and high-risk policies would be q_1L and q_2L. These are the prices that would emerge in a **full-information equilibrium** — that is, in a situation where insurance companies were fully informed about each driver's probability of a collision. The full-information equilibrium is, of course, the simple generalization of what we discovered in Chapter 17's model of the insurance market.

full-information equilibrium

In this case, however, a driver's risk characteristic is *hidden* and cannot be *costlessly identified* by insurance companies. What will the equilibrium look like in this situation? Let us begin by assuming that the cost of identifying each driver's risk characteristic is prohibitively high. The market will then offer only one policy. Again assuming a competitive insurance market and ignoring firms' costs of writing and administering policies, the market price for this policy will be determined by the *relative sizes* of the two groups. Let s be the proportion of low-risk drivers in the population and $1 - s$ the proportion of high-risk drivers. The probability that a randomly selected driver will incur loss L is then $sq_1 + (1 - s)q_2$. If they all buy insurance, the market price p will satisfy

$$p = L[sq_1 + (1 - s)q_2]$$

From this equation, we see that

$$q_1L < p < q_2L$$

But q_1L and q_2L are the equilibrium prices for low- and high-risk drivers in the full information equilibrium. These inequalities indicate that when identifying risk characteristics is prohibitively expensive, if all drivers do choose to buy insurance, low-risk drivers pay more than in the full-information equilibrium and high-risk drivers pay less:

In the equilibrium in which all drivers buy insurance, low-risk drivers subsidize the insurance purchases of high-risk drivers.

However, low-risk drivers will buy an insurance policy *only* if p is less than (or equal to) their reservation price. But clearly the average price that the insurance company must charge reduces the consumer's surplus of the low-risk group. Notice, too, that as the proportion of low-risk drivers in the population, s, approaches zero — or equivalently, as the proportion of high-risk drivers, $(1 - s)$, approaches 1 — p approaches q_2L, the price of insurance for the high-risk group. Indeed, if the proportion of high-risk drivers is large enough, the price p may exceed the maximum the low-risk group is willing to pay. In this case, low-risk drivers will refuse to buy an insurance policy, and the market price for insurance will not be p. Instead, the resulting competitive equilibrium will be one in which only high-risk drivers buy insurance, and the market price will be q_2L. To summarize:

If the proportion of high-risk drivers is not too high, then in equilibrium all drivers will buy insurance, and low-risk drivers will subsidize high-risk drivers. But, if the proportion of high-risk drivers is too high, then in equilibrium only high-risk drivers will buy insurance, and low-risk drivers will be forced out of the market.

market failure

Here we have a case where asymmetric information causes the price mechanism to break down. Many economists call this a case of **market failure**: the failure arises in this case because drivers' risk characteristics are hidden from insurance companies. As we saw in Chapter 17, insurance markets perform a valuable function: with perfect information, such markets allow individuals to shed all risk. When drivers' risk characteristics are hidden, the insurance market may fail in the sense that low-risk drivers will personally bear the risk of loss from collision. A single policy causes some low-risk drivers to choose not to insure; rates climb; that rate hike then drives even more low-risk drivers out of the market, causing rates to go even higher. If the proportion of high-risk drivers is large enough, all the low-risk drivers are forced out of the market — an extreme form of adverse selection.[2]

Skimming the Cream

pooling contract

When an insurance company offers a single contract to all types of people, this is called a **pooling contract**. A pooling contract may still not be an equilibrium when competition for the market exists. The problem is that competing firms have an incentive to offer special contracts that only cater to the low-risk types: a practice called "skimming the cream."

In British Columbia, from 1974 until recently, there has been a government monopoly in the provision of car insurance. Since there was a monopoly, and since insurance is mandatory to drive, the government insurance company (ICBC) is able to

2. See Rothschild and Stiglitz (1976) for a more complete analysis of insurance and asymmetric information.

offer a pooling contract that is a great deal for unsafe drivers and not such a great deal for safe drivers. Recently, another company has been allowed to enter the market, but instead of offering another pooling contract, this company has offered lower rates only to drivers who have had no accidents and fit the profile of safe drivers; that is, young males need not apply. Since only the good drivers are attracted to this new company, it has lower costs. Unfortunately for ICBC, it is left with only the high-risk, unsafe drivers, which leads to higher costs and higher insurance rates.

Much of the justification for government-monopoly provision of services centres on this dilemma. If there is a good that, for some reason, we feel should be made available to all citizens, then government-monopoly provision avoids the problem of having the cream skimmed. For example, if private schools are allowed, the public school system ends up being populated by larger percentages of poor students. This raises the costs of providing education to these students. With socialized medicine, the healthy individuals end up subsidizing the sick individuals, but private plans encourage healthy people to opt out, and the costs of public provision rise. In some cases these higher costs result in the service being withdrawn, and then groups of high-risk individuals end up with no service at all. Throughout North America there is a debate raging over this very issue. As government debts increase, the issue of government provision is being challenged. However, adverse selection shows that there are cases where private provision is not always forthcoming.

Adverse Selection: The "Lemons Principle"

The phenomenon of adverse selection has a more colourful tag, the "lemons principle," attributable to George Akerlof (1970). Akerlof was concerned with the market for lemons — the kind you drive, not the kind for making lemonade. Akerlof asked why the market price of a new car drops by $3000 or more the instant the proud owner drives it off the lot. He answered by arguing that (1) anyone who wanted to sell the new car he or she had recently bought might very well have learned in the short period since the car was bought that it was a lemon, and (2) a wary buyer in the second-hand market could figure this out. Therefore, the buyer in the second-hand market will demand a significant discount off the new-car price to compensate for the high subjective probability that the car is a lemon. People who impulsively bought the wrong (for them) new car, or decided that they could not really afford a new car, will be indistinguishable from those who discovered that the car they bought really was a lemon. Those unfortunate people will also be forced to accept a discounted price if they want to sell their car in the second-hand market.

To develop a deeper understanding of the lemons problem, imagine that there are only two types of used cars: "lemons" and "jewels." Imagine, too, that ascertaining whether a particular used car is a lemon or a jewel is prohibitively costly for a potential buyer — but that car sellers do know. That is, the car's characteristic — lemon or jewel — is a hidden characteristic. Imagine also that all car owners who want to sell their cars initially put them on the market. The price of used cars will then reflect the mix of lemons and jewels offered for sale.

Let us assume that buyers form subjective probabilities based on the relative proportions of lemons and jewels offered for sale. The owner of a jewel will then be unable to sell it at a price that reflects its true value, because the owner cannot effectively communicate the car's true worth. (How many lemon owners will honestly say that their car is a lemon?)

Some owners who want to sell their jewels at a "fair" price may decide not to sell at the market price. The proportion of lemons on the market then increases, further depressing the market price and perhaps inducing other owners of jewels to withdraw their cars from the market. In the eventual equilibrium, some owners of jewels — unwilling to accept significantly less than the car's true value — choose not to sell at the market price. If all such owners make this choice, there will be a market for lemons but none for jewels. Because of the hidden characteristic, lemons drive jewels (some or all of them) out of the market — a phenomenon that we might call *the lemons principle*.

PROBLEM 20.3

Suppose that, with perfect information, the market value of a jewel is \$2400 and the market value of a lemon is \$1200. Assume that, in the absence of perfect information, the market price of a car will be $\$2400s + (1 - s)\$1200$, where s is the proportion of jewels on the market. There are three groups of potential sellers: 200 owners of jewels whose reservation prices are \$2000; 400 owners of jewels whose reservation prices are \$1600; and 400 owners of lemons whose reservation prices are less than \$1200. Show that the cars in the last two groups — but not the cars in the first group — will be sold. What is the market failure in this case?

PROBLEM 20.4

Why is it that when interest rates become very high, banks begin to ration credit? For example, when interest rates at banks were in the teens during much of the 1980s, banks would not issue loans to all of those willing to pay the high interest rates. At low interest rates, banks are more willing to lend money on the simple ground that you are willing to pay the rate of interest. Why is this?

20.3 Signalling

Adverse selection is not a hopeless problem. As with other transaction cost problems, people have been extremely clever in finding solutions. As we have seen, when relevant characteristics are hidden, people suffer real economic consequences. Clearly, the individuals who suffer have an incentive to try to find a way out of their dilemma. One response is known as **signalling**.

signalling

Let us modify our model of hidden characteristics in the market for collision insurance to incorporate the possibility that low-risk drivers can *signal* (convincingly identify themselves) to insurance firms. What we need is some form of low-risk certification. If the certificate is to produce a signalling equilibrium, three conditions must hold.

1. Insurance companies must be convinced that the certificate does signal a low-risk driver. Given a convincing certificate, the competitive equilibrium price for insurance for a driver with a certificate will be q_1L.
2. The cost to low-risk drivers of getting a certificate must be small enough so that they have an incentive to acquire it.

3. The cost to high-risk drivers of getting a certificate must be large enough so that they have no incentive to obtain one.

If these conditions are satisfied, two policies will be offered in equilibrium: one for drivers with a certificate at price q_1L, and the other for drivers without a certificate, at price q_2L. Furthermore, all low-risk drivers — but no high-risk drivers — will present a certificate.

Differential costs of acquiring a certificate are central to this signalling model. Let C^1 and C^2 denote the costs of acquiring such a certificate for low- and high-risk drivers respectively, and suppose that C^1 is less than C^2. For the moment, suppose too, that condition 1 is satisfied: insurance firms find the certificate convincing. Then, condition 2 will be satisfied if the following inequality holds:

$$C^1 < p_r^1 - q_1L$$

where p_r^1 is the reservation price of the low-risk drivers. If low-risk individuals choose not to insure when offered full coverage at price q_2L, then the reservation price is the one identified in Chapter 17. Otherwise it is q_2L. Low risk drivers will acquire a certificate if this value is larger than the cost of a certificate. Similarly, condition 3 will be satisfied if the following inequality holds:

$$q_2L - q_1L < C^2$$

The value of the certificate to high-risk drivers would be $q_2L - q_1L$, which must be smaller than C^2 to insure that high-risk drivers do not acquire the certificate. Finally, if both of these inequalities are satisfied, the credibility of the certificate as a signal, specified in condition 1, is also satisfied, and the result is a signalling equilibrium. To summarize:

If it is very costly for high-risk drivers to obtain the signal and not too costly for low-risk drivers, then there will be a signalling equilibrium in which low-risk drivers acquire the signal in order to differentiate themselves from high-risk drivers and obtain a lower insurance rate.

How will this signalling equilibrium differ from equilibrium in the absence of signalling? Let's compare it, first, to the equilibrium in which all drivers buy insurance and low-risk drivers subsidize high-risk drivers. Signalling simply *redistributes wealth* from high-risk drivers to low-risk drivers. However, since low-risk drivers spend money to acquire certificates, the *gains* to low-risk drivers as a group are *smaller* than the losses for high-risk drivers as a group. Now compare the signalling equilibrium to the equilibrium in which low-risk drivers simply do not insure. This change, in effect, *creates wealth* since it facilitates the formation of a new market in which low-risk drivers shed the risk that they otherwise would have borne themselves.

Can we find real-life examples of a signalling equilibrium? In some places, insurance companies offer a discount to any young driver who presents a certificate or diploma from a reputable driver education program. That is, insurance companies accept these certificates as a convincing signal that a young driver is a lower risk than a young driver who does not have a certificate. Why?

One possibility is that drivers with certificates are lower-risk because they learned good driving habits in the driver education program. This is what economists call a *human capital* explanation. By taking the driver education course, the young driver acquires skills — the human capital — that make him or her a better driver. Another possibility is that drivers with certificates are at lower risk because of an inherent low-risk characteristic. This explanation — which presumes that there is an *inherent difference* between young drivers — requires, first, that a high-risk driver's cost of acquiring a certificate is higher than the anticipated benefit in the form of lower insurance rates and, second, that a low-risk driver's cost of acquiring a certificate is lower than the anticipated benefits. Is it true that a significant number of young drivers — knowing that they are inherently high-risk — anticipate that they will have a hard time acquiring a certificate and therefore choose not to even try for it? If so, then this signalling model would seem to provide at least a partial explanation of insurance companies' policies.

If we look a little further afield, we can find clear instances of signalling equilibrium. Imagine, for example, a number of firms that produce competing products, say different CD players. Some produce high-quality players and others produce low-quality players, but consumers are unable to accurately assess quality prior to purchase. Firms that produce high-quality players have a real incentive to signal that high quality because they can sell their products at a higher price. They will therefore look for some kind of "certificate of quality" that they can afford to offer—and that low-quality firms cannot afford to offer. That certificate is a sufficiently comprehensive warranty against defects. Clearly, offering a product warranty costs high-quality firms less for the simple reason that their products have fewer defects. Just consider the extreme case of a firm that produces a product that is 100 percent defect-free. It can offer a comprehensive warranty, secure in the knowledge that the warranty will cost it nothing. Thus, the signalling model leads us to anticipate an equilibrium in which high-quality products are sold at relatively high prices with comprehensive warranties, and low-quality products are sold at relatively low prices with minimal warranties or no warranty at all. This is what we actually see in many markets for consumer durables.

Signalling behaviour is practically ubiquitous. When you go to a party, you dress a certain way and act a certain way to impress other people. When you go for a job interview, you dress and act an entirely different way. The problem with simple signalling like this is that it may be too easy for the other types of people to mimic. The greater the difference in the cost of acquiring the signal for the two groups the better the signal. If the signal is impossible to acquire for the low-quality group, then the signal is a perfect measure of type.

Application: The Veal Signal

As a young boy one of the authors would visit a local cattle auction with his father every Saturday morning. Every week the auctioneer would say something like, "OK, folks, here come the beef cattle," and out from the back barns would come a herd of beef cattle (beef breeds are Herefords, Angus, and the like). Later the auctioneer would say, "OK, here come the dairy cattle," and again another herd would come from the back, but this time they would all be Holsteins (those are the cute black-and-white milk cows). Finally, towards the end of the auction there would be an announcement, "OK, now we've got the veal calves coming," and rather than a herd of beef cattle coming through the door (after all, veal is a form of beef) ... out would come nothing but Holstein calves. Occasionally a beef breed would be included, but then it would receive a price that was often 1/3 that of the Holstein calves. This is a puzzle because beef breeds have a comparative advantage in converting feed to meat. Why use an inefficient animal to produce meat?

Veal is an expensive pale tender meat that comes from young steers that have been fed grain and milk, but not grass.[3] Milk is a very expensive input and grain almost as expensive, but grass is a relatively cheap feed. Because a veal calf fetches a price per pound of up to three times the going beef price there is a large incentive for farmers to feed their steers the cheaper grass and sell the animals as veal. Veal sellers are anonymous at the auction so it is impossible for any of them to establish a reputation for honest sales. Furthermore, it is too costly to determine the quality of the veal meat as long as the calf is alive, and so inspection of the meat at the auction is virtually impossible. Under these conditions, the buyer anticipates that only grass-fed animals are for sale, and pays only the low-quality price — a classic lemons problem. And yet, veal is mostly sold through auctions.

The solution turns out to be a signalling property that is unique to the Holstein breed of cattle. All cattle have four stomachs. Grass goes into one particular stomach called the rumen which basically functions like a septic tank. The grass mixes with gases, is regurgitated and chewed as cud, and then goes back to the rumen. Throughout this process a lot of gas is produced, causing the belly to enlarge. When a cow is fed grain or milk these inputs go to a separate stomach and are digested directly without producing gas. Because Holsteins are tall and lanky, the enlarged "pot-bellied" stomach is easy to see. With stocky beef breeds it is difficult to determine. Hence the Holstein's pot belly (or lack of one) signals to buyers exactly what the animal has been fed. At a glance buyers know if they are buying a true veal animal and as a result veal is sold at the auction ... but only with one breed.

PROBLEM 20.5

The veal sold at the auction is called "pink veal" because the animals are fed grain and milk. When the animals are fed just milk they are called "white veal" and fetch a price almost three times that of pink veal. Since milk and grain enter the same stomach, why is white veal not sold through the auction? When white veal is sold directly from the farmer to the butcher, what would you predict about the breeds used?

Screening

screening

The other side of the coin is **screening**. In the collision insurance model, low-risk drivers acquired a certificate to signal that they were low-risk, and insurance firms used the certificate to *screen* drivers — that is, to divide drivers into different risk groups. Likewise, customers used the warranty to screen CDs for quality. To return to our inexperienced job searcher, we see that employers sometimes use job experience (and, of course, references) to screen applicants — that is, job experience signals an applicant's capability. Frustratingly, this particular screening technique has a Catch-22. If all employers use it, inexperienced workers may find it impossible to break into the market. This is particularly true in times of high unemployment when employers may have no incentive to experiment with other screening techniques, and inexperienced workers may be frozen out of the market.[4]

3. This application comes from Allen (1993).

4. Interested readers are referred to the insightful book by Spence (1974).

Once we grasp the basic insights of signalling/screening equilibria, we can look at familiar events from a new perspective. For example, these ideas suggest that a major function of higher education is to provide relatively gifted individuals with a means of signalling their abilities to the world. A degree from Harvard or Stanford or Oxford or Queen's may be valuable partly because it is seen as a signal of the degree-holder's ability. The following problem, adapted from Stiglitz (1975), will allow you to explore this possibility in a very simple model.

PROBLEM 20.6

Imagine a world populated by superior and inferior workers: a superior worker is worth \$50 per hour to any employer, and an inferior worker is worth only \$20 per hour. These people work for exactly 10 hours and then retire. Let s be the proportion of superior workers, and $1 - s$ the proportion of inferior workers. What will the common wage be if the superior workers do *not* signal their ability? Assume that in the labour-market equilibrium, workers are paid their expected worth. Now suppose that a degree costs superior workers \$200 and that it is simply impossible for an inferior worker to get a degree. For what values of s will superior workers acquire a degree to signal their superior productivity?

Application: Screening and the Duel of Honour

From 1500 to 1900 AD, thousands of aristocrats lost their lives in duels of honour. Duelling had a long history before this time, but earlier duels were nothing like the duel of honour. In medieval times justice was often meted out in a judicial duel. These duels took the place of court actions, with the winner considered judged by God to be innocent of whatever crime was committed. In addition to these duels were chivalrous duels between knights. These contests were public events used to raise the profile of brave fighters.

Unlike judicial and chivalrous duels, duels of honour were held in secret and were illegal. They were not fought over serious crimes but over issues of honour (such as a bad look, a slap to the face, or an accusation of lying). More interestingly, they were conducted with a limited set of lethal weapons (rapiers, sabres, and later pistols), using a specific set of rules. When an aristocrat was caught duelling, no legal action would take place unless the rules were not followed. If someone outside the ruling class was caught duelling, he was charged with attempted murder.

There have been many famous duels of honour. Abraham Lincoln was in a duel, although a rather humorous one. He had been challenged by a short man. As the challenged, Lincoln had the right to choose the weapon. On seeing the stature of his opponent he opted for a set of extremely heavy broadaxes (an unconventional weapon). His opponent was unable to lift the weapon! Another president, Andrew Jackson, was in a duel early in his career, a duel most remembered for Jackson's use of a large overcoat. Normally duellers stripped to the waist to avoid infection caused by dirty cloth. Jackson kept his coat on, and when the bullet passed through the coat where his heart should have been, the witnesses were shocked to see Jackson get up and deliver a fatal shot to his opponent. The slender Jackson had apparently shifted his body to one side inside the large coat. Such behaviour, if caught, was frowned upon.

So here's the question: why would men like the Duke of Wellington or the Duke of Marlborough put their valuable lives at stake for such petty issues? The answer is that the duel of honor was acting as a screen to enter and stay in the ruling class. Bureaucracies are a modern invention, and in the pre-modern era governments were run by aristocrats with good reputations. Reputations were made through sunk investments in the aristocratic society, and the duel was the method by which reputations were tested. If an aristocrat turned down a duel, he became a social outcast. By entering a duel, an aristocrat demonstrated his investment in society and his trustworthiness.

There are many facts about duelling consistent with its role as a screen. However, here we will simply mention one: the randomness of outcome. As mentioned, duels of honour were fought under specific rules. Many of these rules attempted to make the duel mostly a game of chance. This was necessary because a duel based on skill could not act as a screen. Thus, in the weapons known as duelling pistols, the aiming beads were removed and the barrels were shortened and not rifled. Furthermore, the participants could not take much time to aim. These efforts essentially randomized the outcome and better allowed the duel to act as a screen for reputation.

20.4 Moral Hazard Problems: Hidden Actions

The asymmetric information problems we have so far looked at involve hidden characteristics — characteristics such as quality of a product or the probability that a particular driver will cause an accident — that are known by one party to a transaction but not by the other. There is another class of asymmetric information problems, sometimes called **moral hazard problems,** that involve not hidden characteristics, but instead **hidden actions**.

moral hazard problems

hidden actions

The term *moral hazard* again comes from the insurance industry, where it was discovered that the probability of an accident increased when it was insured. Part of this increase was due to outright fraud as people tried to cheat the insurance company, but a large part was due to the simple fact that people are less careful when they are insured than when they are not. There is an old prairie story of the man who owned an old grain elevator, the only one in town. One day he built a brand-new one and decided to burn the other one down for the insurance money. He hired a fellow to do the job, and told him he would have no problem spotting the building — it was on the left side of town. Unfortunately the arsonist arrived from the east instead of the west, and burned down the wrong building. That's moral hazard!

Think of a student who wants to write a final examination early. Imagine that this student's last final is scheduled for December 22, and that all his or her other examinations are over by December 8. Clearly, this student would prefer to write the last final, say, on December 9 or 10 rather than December 22.

Will the instructor cooperate? You already know the answer — probably not — but why not? In most cases, if the instructor could be *certain* that the student would not tell other students about the exam, he or she would be happy to accommodate this student. But there is an obvious moral hazard problem — the instructor has no reliable way of knowing whether or not the student will tell other students about the examination. In other words, the student's action is hidden from the instructor. It is not that instructors assume the worst; it is just that they generally have a *non-zero subjective probability* that the student will talk to others about the examination. Notice that the student who wants to write early is *worse off* than he or she would be if the action were *not* hidden.

We can also adapt our collision insurance model to illustrate a similar moral hazard problem. Let us suppose that all drivers are identical: they have the same wealth, the same preferences, and face the same probabilistic loss L. The new wrinkle is this:

sometime prior to an accident but after the driver has bought insurance, the driver can take an action that reduces the probability of loss L. Specifically, if the driver spends C on accident prevention, the probability of loss L is reduced from q to q'. (C is not necessarily money; it might be the value the driver places on exerting time and effort to drive more slowly and practise defensive driving techniques.) The problem is that spending C on accident prevention cannot be observed by insurance companies: it is a hidden action. To make the problem interesting, we will assume that

$$C < L(q - q')$$

If this inequality did not hold, the reduction in the expected loss, equal to $L(q - q')$, would not be large enough to justify the expenditure on accident prevention, C. If insurance companies could be sure that all their customers would actually spend C to reduce the probability of loss from q to q' once they had bought insurance, then the equilibrium price for full coverage would be $q'L$, customers would have assured wealth level $w_0 - C - q'L$, and each customer would enjoy a higher utility level. But the customer — having already bought full coverage against loss L and knowing that spending C on accident prevention is a hidden action — will choose not to spend C. Anticipating the customer's behaviour, insurance companies will not offer insurance at price $q'L$. Instead, they will offer full coverage only at the higher price qL.

If an individual could credibly promise to spend C on accident prevention, the price of full coverage would be $q'L$, and he or she would clearly be better off. But, since the action is hidden, the promise is not credible, and insurance companies will not offer insurance at this price.

To see that hidden action problems are not uncommon, try the following problem.

PROBLEM 20.7

Explain the hidden action problem in the following situations.

a. A teenager has a drinking problem, and the parents refuse to lend the family car to the teenager.

b. Fires and, therefore, fire insurance claims, have a pronounced countercyclical pattern: insurance claims for fires are relatively low when times are good and relatively high when times are bad.

One way that insurance companies attempt to solve this moral hazard problem is with the use of deductibles. A deductible means that the insured individual must pay some fraction of the cost of the accident. In effect the individual is prevented from obtaining full insurance. This tends to work for insurance because often the cost of good behaviour is trivial, and so people are willing to bear this cost in order to avoid the deductible. For example, consider auto theft. Reducing the probability of having a car stolen can be as simple as turning the car off, taking the keys out of the ignition, locking the car in a safe location, and putting valuables in the trunk. An individual who bears no cost of having his or her car stolen because of full insurance has little incentive to take these actions; forcing individuals to pay $100 in case of a theft encourages them to take minor precautions and thus reduces the probability of theft.

Application: The Good Ol' Mule[5]

Moral hazard occurs because those individuals using an asset or a good are not bearing the full cost of their actions. In this sense moral hazard is much like an externality. Before there were tractors and heavy machinery much farm work and hauling was done by draught animals: horses, oxen, and mules. The use of these animals, however, was never even across regions of North America. For example, in the New England states at the close of the nineteenth century the ratio of mules to horses was only 0.005, while in the southern states it was 0.877. Generally speaking, the southern states counted for the lion's share of the mule population.

Mules are interesting animals. They are a cross between a female horse and a male donkey, and share many of the characteristics of both parents. However, mules have several differences, including the fact that they are sterile. One of the most important differences is that a mule, for reasons not well understood, resists injury. Whereas a horse can overdrink and overeat, and can overwork itself to the point of death if pushed, a mule simply stops before injury takes place. Mules also require less maintenance in terms of grooming and looking after their hooves. In short, a mule is a more robust, tougher animal.

Why were mules used more often in the south? Southern agriculture in the nineteenth century was dominated by plantation farming: large tracts of land that used large amounts of wage and sharecrop labour. These workers were capital poor and so it was the landowner that provided them with their draught animals. Since the animals belonged to the landowner but were used by the workers, the workers lacked the proper incentive to look after the animals. Mules were used in the south, despite the fact that they were more expensive than horses, because they could tolerate the abuse and maltreatment given by workers with little incentive to look after them. In the north, where farms were smaller and family-operated, horses were the draught animal of choice.

An interesting extension of this idea is found in the US Army. The nineteenth-century army was a large user of draught animals. Although the army used horses for its cavalry and for draught work, the preference for mules was overwhelming. There were often 50–90 percent more mules than horses in any given time in the army. This occurred because enlisted soldiers have little incentive to look after the capital of the army.

PROBLEM 20.8

Among the most valuable animals in the army were the horses used by the officers of the cavalry. Who do you think owned those horses: the army or the officers?

SUMMARY

This chapter has very lightly examined several market responses to transaction costs and asymmetric information. We began this journey in Chapter 17 when we first looked at the fact that nature interacts with our world and makes events uncertain. As long as information was symmetric, we saw that markets had no problem doing what they always do

5. This application is taken from Kauffman (1993, 1996).

best — allocating resources. However, we saw in Chapters 18 and 19 that when information is asymmetric, then the distribution of property rights mattered. With asymmetric information it is possible for individuals to cheat one another as well as cooperate, and the way an exchange is organized influences the amount of cheating that can take place. The costs devoted to cheating and its prevention are called transaction costs.

In Chapter 19 we saw how transaction costs played a role in the way a firm was organized. In this chapter we have seen how market exchanges, too, are organized to account for transaction costs. Reputations can be used to guarantee that the right goods are traded at a quality that is expected. Vertical integration and long term contracts can solve hold-up problems in the presence of sunk investments.

We then turned to an exploration of some intriguing problems that arise in insurance markets. First we looked at a number of situations involving a *hidden characteristic* and showed how hidden characteristics can give rise to market failure. For example, if young drivers' risk characteristics are hidden — known to the drivers themselves but not to insurance companies — then low-risk drivers may choose not to insure, and if they do insure they will, in effect, be subsidizing high-risk drivers. We then showed how *signalling* and *screening* might partially resolve the market failures associated with hidden characteristics. Finally, we looked at several situations involving *hidden actions* and showed how to mitigate *moral hazard problems*.

EXERCISES

1. Trevor is planning on proposing to his girlfriend Leanne, and he visits his local jewellery store to purchase a ring. When he picks one out, the woman behind the counter says, "One moment please; I'll just go into the back and get the ring." When she returns, Trevor asks why he can't have the one under the glass, the one he just picked out. "Oh," responds the clerk, "none of these rings have real diamonds in them; they are all zircons. We keep the real diamonds in the back in case of a robbery." If diamonds are so hard to tell from quality zircons that sell for a small fraction of the price, how can Trevor be sure that this new ring is for real?

2. Far fewer babies are currently offered for adoption in Canada and the United States than couples want to adopt. Would you call this a shortage? Why does the price of an adopted baby not rise? By what criteria are the scarce babies rationed to prospective adopters? Why do you think we are not allowed to sell babies?

3. Carla likes to sit by the window when she flies. Once, when she got to her assigned window seat, there was a five-year-old girl sitting there. She asked her to move, but the girl said she liked to look out the window when she flies. Carla asked the child's mother and the attendant to clear the seat. The attendant, in front of the other passengers, asked, "Do you really want to make that poor little child move from the window seat?" Who owns the right to the seat in this case?

4. Sometimes "ransom" demands are legal, as when an employee tells the boss that unless there is a larger salary forthcoming, the firm will soon be less one employee. Other times they are illegal, as in the case of stolen children. Can you suggest an economic reason for this difference in legal treatment?

5. All western societies use police to enforce criminal law (e.g., burglary), but not civil law (e.g., broken contracts). Why might this be so?

6. Cars come in every colour, independent of brand or model. Likewise, street motorcycles also come in any colour regardless of who made them. But tractors do not: Fords are blue, John Deeres are green and yellow, International Harvesters are red and gold, Cases are orange-yellow, etc. Offroad motorcycles also tend to have colours that depend on brand: Hondas are red, Kawasakis are

green, Yamahas are yellow, etc. Can you think of an economic explanation for why this might be?

7. In a certain developing country, wheat farms have the following production function, where L = labour input and TP = total product. Labour can earn $4 per day in the nonagricultural sector of the economy.

L	1	2	3	4	5	6	7	8+
TP	10	18	25	31	35	38	40	40

   a. Suppose the farms are owned by landlords who hire workers to farm the land. How many people will work on each farm? Explain.
   b. Suppose the land is "common property": the land is farmed by communes, where the commune is a closed group that decides its own size and then shares equally among its own members. How many people will work on each farm? Explain.
   c. Suppose that the land is still common property, but the commune cannot prevent anyone from joining and sharing the benefits. How many people will work on each farm? Explain.
   d. If the demand for wheat increased substantially in the economy so that many additional farms entered into wheat production, what would happen to the rents received by the owner of this land?

   Share tenancy is a common form of rental agreement in agriculture. In this contract, the farmer agrees to pay some fraction of his or her output to the landlord as payment for rent. The system has been likened by some to a tax on labour.

   e. Using the numbers derived above, explain why a tax on labour would lead to "too little" labour being used on the land, and why the rent on the land would decrease.
   f. A share contract, however, is not a tax. It is a voluntary contract between the landlord and the tenant. The landlord keeps this "tax." Would landlords enter into a contract which gave less rent than a fixed wage contract as in (a) above?
   g. Why would a landlord and farmer choose a share contract over a wage contract, or a fixed land rent contract?

8. In the United States during the 1980s, there was a severe Savings and Loan crisis, where the federal government had to bail out many banks for making bad loans. How is this an example of moral hazard?

9. Many people in the United States get their health insurance through a group health insurance plan. Typically, *all* employees of the same firm are insured under the group plan. Often the per-person group rate is significantly lower than the rate an individual member could get on the open market. Develop an asymmetric information explanation of this phenomenon.

10. A number of serious diseases, including AIDS and hepatitis, can be transmitted via blood transfusion to an uninfected person. This creates a nasty hidden characteristic problem for the supply of blood for transfusions, particularly in the system used in the United States, where blood is purchased. What is the advantage of the approach used in Canada of relying on charitable blood donations? Is this an example of market failure driven by asymmetric information?

11. Some American states have made it illegal to discriminate on the basis of sex and age in the sale of automobile insurance. Insurance firms must offer the same price to all residents of these states, regardless of age or sex. (An older friend is waiting for the day when the same sort of laws prohibit such discrimination in the sale of life insurance.) Could this sort of legislation be a source of market failure?

12. It has been discovered that people who drive Volvos (a car known for its safety) are more likely to get into accidents at interchanges. Is this a moral hazard or an adverse selection problem?

13. When Benjamin Franklin was 16, he lived with his brother as an apprentice. In his autobiography, he later wrote, "I then proposed to my Brother, that if he would given me Weekly half the Money he paid for my Board I would board my self. He instantly agreed to it, and I presently found that I could save half what he paid me." What type of behaviour do you think Franklin was engaged in before and after the change in arrangements that led to a fourfold fall in

expenses? Would you call this behaviour moral hazard or adverse selection?

14. Duels were fought over almost anything, yet the outcome of the duel (who won or lost) was irrelevant. In fact, most opponents reconciled after their duels. Are these facts consistent with duelling being a screen for reputations?

REFERENCES

Akerlof, G. 1970. "The Market for 'Lemons': Quality, Uncertainty and the Market Mechanisms," *Quarterly Journal of Economics*, 84:488–500.

Allen D. 1993. "Pot-Bellies and Cattle Breeds as ReVealing Signals," *Economic Inquiry*, July: 481– 87.

Kauffman, K. 1993. "Why Was the Mule used in Southern Agriculture? Empirical Evidence of Principal Agent Solutions," *Explorations in Economic History*, 30:336–51.

Kauffman, K. 1996. "The U.S. Army as a Rational Economic Agent: The Choice of Draft Animals During the Civil War," *Eastern Economic Journal*, 22(3).

Klein B. and K. Leffler 1981. "The Role of Market Forces in Assuring Contractual Performance," *Journal of Political Economy*, 89:615-41.

Rothschild, M. and J. E. Stiglitz. 1976. "Equilibrium in Competitive Insurance Markets: An Essay on the Economics of Imperfect Information," *Quarterly Journal of Economics*, 90:630–49.

Spence, A. M. 1974. *Market Signaling: Information Transfer in Hiring and Related Screening Processes.* Cambridge, Mass.: Harvard University Press.

Stiglitz, J. E. 1975. "The Theory of 'Screening,' Education, and the Distribution of Income," *American Economic Review*, 65:283–300.

Answers to Problems

PROBLEM 1.1

If there are N households drawing water from the system, and if all of them want more water than they are currently able to get in August, in August an individual householder can use only $(1/N)^{th}$ of any water conserved by that householder in July. Hence, the larger N is, the smaller the individual householder's incentive to conserve water.

PROBLEM 1.2

1. A player motivated only by private gain would reason as follows: There is nothing I can do to influence the actions of the other three players in this game, so I will concentrate on the implications of my own actions. On the one hand, if I keep the $90, I am richer by $90. On the other hand, if I put the $90 in the envelope, there will be 210 additional dollars in the common pool (the $90 I put in the envelope plus the $120 the host will add to it), of which I will get only $52.50. Clearly, I am better off to keep the $90.
2. A player motivated by self-interest will now want to know whether he or she is richer if all players keep $90 or all put $90 in their envelopes. If all four players keep the $90, each is richer by $90. In contrast, if all four players put their $90 in their envelopes, there will be $840 in the common pool, and each will be richer by $210. Hence, each player will vote to require all players to put their $90 in their envelopes.

PROBLEM 1.3

Notice first that the shift in the demand curve does not affect aggregate quantity supplied — under either scheme 105 million kilograms are supplied. APSA's costs under the buy-and-store program decrease as the demand curve gets steeper since the quantity bought by consumers at the $3 support price increases. Conversely, its costs under the price subsidy program increase as the demand curve gets steeper since the market clearing price for 105 million kilograms decreases, necessitating an increase in the per kilogram subsidy.

PROBLEM 1.4

Just as the price of labour relative to the price of machines varies from country to country, so the price of one packaging material, say aluminum, relative to another, say steel, varies from time to time. The hypothesis that the firm chooses the least costly technique can be applied to the choice of a packaging material, suggesting that steel and aluminum can replace each other, depending on which is cheaper at the time.

PROBLEM 1.5

There is no right or wrong preference ordering. However, in this case, most people rank bundle *d* first (because it contains the most money), bundle *a* second, bundle *c* third, and bundle *b* fourth.

PROBLEM 1.6

This is a dual-purpose institution designed to reduce litter and encourage recycling. It works by creating a private monetary incentive to return pop bottles to the retailer or a recycling depot.

PROBLEM 1.7

Suppose that each glutton cares only about his or her own share. Beginning with any value of X, it is impossible to make one glutton better off by increasing his share of the pie without making the other worse off by reducing her share. Hence, given any X, no other attainable state is Pareto-preferred to it. Because no attainable state is Pareto-preferred to any other, every attainable state is Pareto-optimal.

PROBLEM 1.8

Using the cost-benefit criterion, we conclude that in this situation the price subsidy scheme is preferred to the buy-and-store scheme. We want to argue, however, that some people are made worse off when we move from the buy-and-store scheme to the price subsidy scheme. It is useful to focus on two types of people: a type 1 person does pay taxes but does not consume butter; a type 2 person does consume butter but does not pay taxes. There are, of course, other types of people, but we can make our point by focusing on just these two types. Clearly, individuals of type 1 prefer the buy-and-store scheme, while individuals of type 2 prefer the price support scheme. A move from the buy-and-store scheme to the price support scheme trades off losses for type 1 people against gains for type 2 people.

PROBLEM 1A.1

There are 32 customers between addresses 1/2 and 3/4, 96 between 1/4 and 1, and 16 between 0 and 1/8.

PROBLEM 1A.2

When a is 0, the point of market segmentation is 3/8, 48 customers shop at All-Valu, and All-Valu's profit is $48. When a is 1/4, the corresponding values are 1/2, 64, and $64. When a is 1/2, the corresponding values are 5/8, 80, and $80. So long as $a < b$, the number of All-Valu's customers increases as a increases.

PROBLEM 1A.3

With no loss of generality we can restrict All-Valu's location to the interval [0, 1/2], since any location in the interval [1/2, 1] is symmetric to a location in the interval [0, 1/2]. Given a in [0, 1/2], Bestway will choose to locate just to the right of a, All-Valu's market segment will extend from 0 to a, and its profit will be $(P - C)Na$. Since its profit increases as a increases, All-Valu will locate at 1/2. Bestway will then also locate at 1/2.

PROBLEM 2.1

These statements do violate the transitivity assumption. Look at the first, third, and fourth preference statements. From the first and third we infer that (11, 17) is preferred to (15, 8), contrary to the fourth preference statement.

PROBLEM 2.2

The third and sixth statements violate the nonsatiation assumption.

PROBLEM 2.3

The road close to the city is congested because people prefer to live close to the city. If the building of the new road is a surprise, then upon completion, there will be lighter traffic days. As time passes and people begin to move, the cost of using both roads should again equalize. To the extent that people anticipate the new road, they move earlier and there is no difference in cost between the two roads. Los Angeles is congested for this very reason. Building highways that lower the cost of commuting simply leads to more commuting.

PROBLEM 2.4

1. You'll have to answer this one yourself. The authors cannot think of an example.
2. We have often heard people say "I will never do … blank" and then later do that very thing when avoiding it became expensive.
3. "You can have dessert if you finish your vegetables;" "If you disobey me, you'll get a spanking;" or "You can have two ice creams tomorrow if you stop bugging me about an ice cream today!" All of these are examples of substitution.

PROBLEM 2.5

First observe that all bundles fit one of the following categories: A, bundles such that quantity of good 1 exceeds 2; B, bundles such that quantity of good 1 is less than 2; C, bundles such that quantity of good 1 equals 2. All bundles in A are preferred to (2, 3), and (2, 3) is preferred to all bundles in B. Now subdivide C as follows: C.1, bundles such that quantity of good 2 is less than 3; C.2, bundles such that quantity of good 2 is greater than 3; C.3, bundles such that quantity of good 2 equals 3. Bundle (2, 3) is preferred to any bundle in C.1, and any bundle in C.2 is preferred to bundle (2, 3). Hence, all bundles B that are indifferent to bundle (2, 3) are in C.3. But the only bundle in category C.3 is (2, 3) itself, so we see that bundle (2, 3) is a single-point indifference curve. This argument is easily adapted to show that, for Clem, each conceivable bundle is a single-point indifference curve.

PROBLEM 2.6

a. First, bundles (20, 30) and (40, 10); second, bundle (20, 15); third, bundle (15, 15); fourth, bundles (10, 15) and (25, 0).

b. Each of these indifference curves is a straight line with slope of −1. The indifference curves intersect the x_2 axis at the following points: (0, 25), (0, 50), (0, 35), (0, 40).

PROBLEM 2.7

Pick an arbitrary bundle and draw a straight line of slope −1 through the bundle. The line is one of Anna's indifference curves.

PROBLEM 2.8

1. Anna's *MRS* is 1.
2. To compensate Arno for a one-kilogram reduction in quantity of trout (good 1), we must increase his consumption of salmon (good 2) by 1/2 a kilogram since he believes salmon to be twice as nutritious as trout. Hence, Arno's indifference curves are straight lines of slope −1/2. His *MRS* is therefore 1/2 (the absolute value of −1/2).

PROBLEM 2.9

Suppose that all three bundles were on the same indifference curve. Then, by reordering the bundles, the marginal value of 10 units of meat would always be 20 units of fruit. Hence, this would violate the assumption of diminishing *MRS*.

PROBLEM 2.10

a. The utility numbers are 25, 50, 25, 30, 35, and 50. They reflect the preference ordering for these bundles that you found in answering Problem 2.4.

b. Notice that the utility number assigned by this function to any bundle is the number of kilograms of fish in the bundle. Question 1: Since Amy is indifferent between two bundles if and only if their weight is identical, the function does assign the same utility number to bundles among which Amy is indifferent. Question 2: Since the function assigns larger numbers to heavier bundles, it does assign a larger number to the preferred bundle. Question 3: Any bundle of fish has a weight in kilograms, so the function does assign a utility number to all bundles.

PROBLEM 2.11

Let us first concentrate on the function $1000(x_1 + x_2)$. Since the unit of measure for both goods is the kilogram, and since there are 1000 grams in a kilogram, the utility number assigned by this function to any bundle is the number of grams of fish in the bundle. This function assigns the same utility number to any two bundles if and only if their weight is identical, and since Anna is indifferent between two bundles if and only if their weight is identical, the function does assign the same utility number to bundles among which she is indifferent. This function assigns larger numbers to heavier bundles, so if Anna prefers one bundle to another, this function does assign a larger number to the preferred bundle. Finally, since any bundle of fish has a weight in grams, the function does assign a utility number to all bundles. As regards the remaining three functions, the key things to notice are that each of these functions assigns the same utility number to two bundles if and only if their weight is identical, and that they assign larger utility numbers to heavier bundles.

PROBLEM 2.12

Consider the indifference curve for three pairs of shoes. Clearly, it passes through the bundle with three right shoes and three left shoes, bundle (3, 3), and it has a right-angled kink at this bundle. Above the kink, the indifference curve's slope is infinite, and to the right of the kink, the indifference curve's slope is zero. *MRS* is undefined at the kink, zero to the right of the kink, and infinite above the kink.

PROBLEM 2.13

Your graph should have upward-sloping indifference curves. This reflects the fact that you want more oranges to compensate you for the increased torture. The indifference curves should also be convex to reflect your diminishing *MRS*.

PROBLEM 2.14

With increasing *MRS* we should get nothing but corner solutions. Workers would demand higher wages for the first hours worked (lower wages for overtime), and individuals should consume all of their income on payday.

PROBLEM 2.15

Microwaves lowered the cost of small individual meals and snacks. As a result the supply of things like pizza pops increased. At one time, when store-bought pies were large oven pies, apple was the most common type. Now, with small individual pies available, apple is way down the list. Apple used to be a second or third favourite of everybody, and so when everyone had to eat the same pie, it was the flavour agreed upon. This is no longer the case.

PROBLEM 3.1

The budget line is $p_1x_1 + p_2x_2 = M$. On the x_1 axis, x_2 is zero. Thus, where the budget line intersects this axis,

$p_1x_1 = M$. Hence, $x_1 = M/p_1$ at the intersection. Similarly, on the x_2 axis, x_1 is zero. Hence, $x_2 = M/p_2$ at this point of intersection. The slope of the budget line is $-p_1/p_2$; hence, the individual must give up p_1/p_2 units of good 2 to get an additional unit of good 1. Conversely, he or she must give up p_2/p_1 units of good 1 to get an additional unit of good 2. As p_1 approaches zero, the budget line becomes horizontal; as p_2 approaches zero, it becomes vertical.

PROBLEM 3.2

See Figure A3.1. Changes in income shift out the budget constraint, while a change in one price rotates it. When we double income and prices, the budget line does not shift.

PROBLEM 3.3

See Figure A3.2. As in Problem 3.2, a change in price rotates the budget constraint, while a change in the endowment shifts it.

PROBLEM 3.4

Consider any bundle (x_1, x_2) on the budget line, and suppose that $x_1 < x_2$. The utility associated with the bundle is then $x_1 = \min(x_1, x_2)$. Then, staying on the budget line, if we increase x_1 by some very small amount, utility will increase, and we see that any bundle in which $x_1 < x_2$ cannot be the utility-maximizing bundle. Similarly, any bundle in which $x_2 < x_1$ cannot be the utility-maximizing bundle. Therefore, the quantities of good 1 and good 2 in the utility-maximizing bundle are identical; that is, $x_1^* = x_2^*$. Combining this result with the budget line, we have $p_1x_1^* + p_2x_1^* = M$. Solving for x_1^*, we have $x_1^* = M/(p_1 + p_2)$, which is the demand function for good 1. Finally, since $x_2^* = x_1^*$, this is also the demand function for good 2.

PROBLEM 3.5

First draw the budget line. Then draw a strictly convex indifference curve through the point where the budget line intersects the x_1 axis. At this point of intersection, the indifference curve should be *steeper* than the budget line. The result can be described as follows: If, at the point where the budget line intersects the x_1 axis, the convex indifference curve is steeper than the budget line, the consumer buys only good 1.

PROBLEM 3.6

A \$1 increase in either p_1 or p_2 causes quantity demanded of good 1 to fall from 60 units to 40 units. A \$2 increase in M causes quantity demanded of good 1 to increase from 60 to 61 units.

PROBLEM 3.7

In answering these questions, keep in mind that we are using the nonsatiation assumption, which means that the utility-maximizing consumption bundle is always on the budget line. The first statement is false, since *IC* is negatively sloped if either good is inferior. The second statement is true. The third statement is true — if in response to an increase in income, con-

FIGURE A3.1

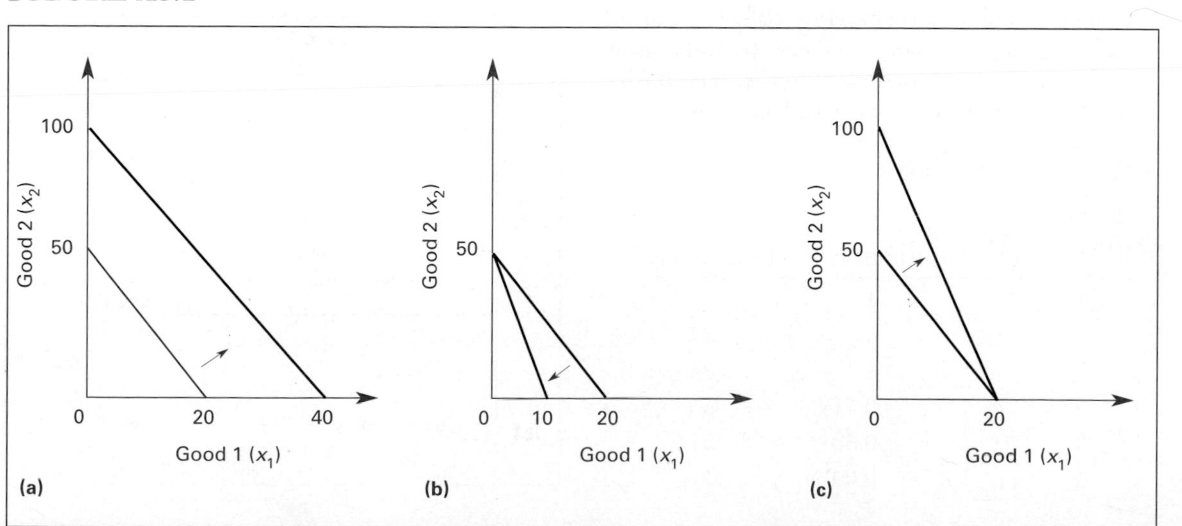

FIGURE A3.2

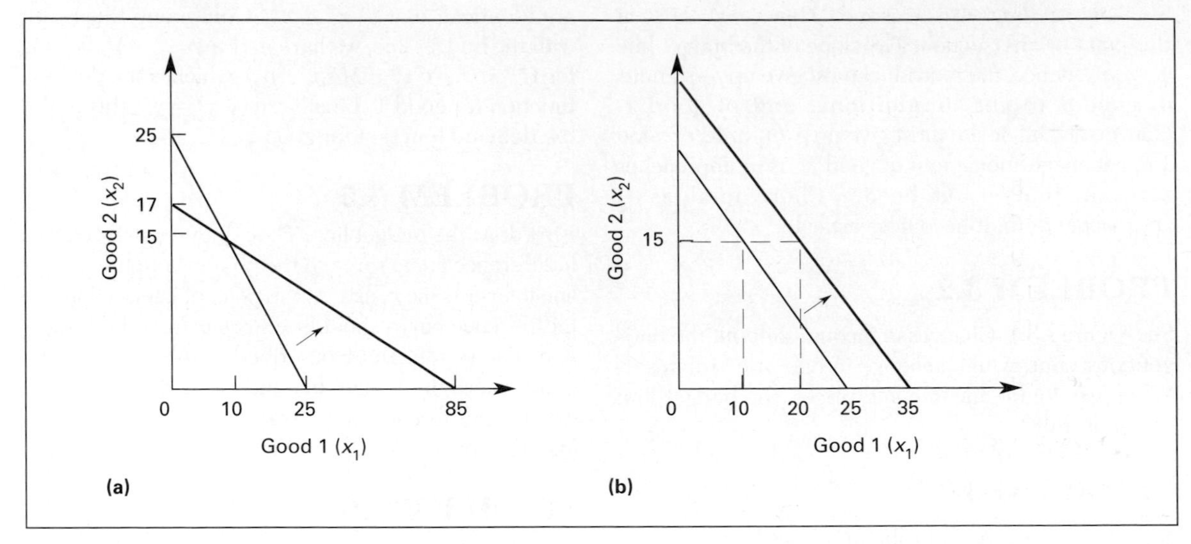

sumption of one good decreases, then consumption of the other necessarily increases, so both goods cannot be inferior. The fourth statement is false.

PROBLEM 3.8

In Figure A3.3a we see that the tangency points lie above one another. Hence a change in income does not lead to any change in the amount of x_1 consumed. The income consumption path is the vertical line passing through the tangency points. In part (b) we see that the Engel curve is flat.

PROBLEM 3.9

At Tradewell, the consumer buys 1 meat, 3 fruit, and 1 canned good for a total of $44. At these quantities the consumer would have spent $46 at Safeway. Starting at Safeway, the consumer would have bought 3 meat, 1 fruit, and 3 canned goods for a total of $58. Buying these quantities at Tradewell would have cost $68.

PROBLEM 3.10

a. Filling out the table gives

P	Q	Elasticity	Total Revenue
11	1	11	11
9	3	3	27
7	5	1.4	35
5	7	0.71	35
3	9	0.33	27
1	11	0.09	11

FIGURE A3.3

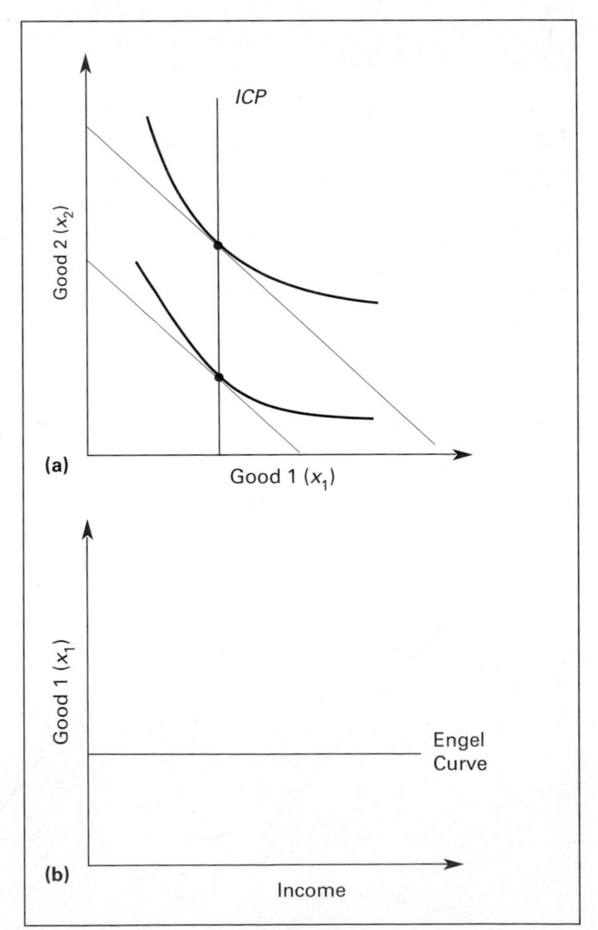

b. When the demand is elastic, then a fall in price raises total revenue. When the demand is inelastic, then a fall in price decreases total revenue.

c.

P	Q	Elasticity	Total Revenue
11	3	3.6	33
9	5	1.8	45
7	7	1	49
5	9	0.55	45
3	11	0.27	33
1	13	0.07	13

The new demand curve is less elastic at every price.

PROBLEM 4.1

The quality of the car should increase. Currently the relative cost of driving a high-quality car is 2 = 1000/500. That is, one sacrifices two low-quality cars for every one high-quality car. After the raise in the fee, however, the relative price falls to 1.7 = 1200/700. With a fall in relative price should come an increase in quantity demanded.

PROBLEM 4.2

The cost of driving faster is lower with ABS brakes, and therefore, more people will drive fast. There may or may not be an increase in the number of accidents, but when there is an accident, there should be more damage and injuries.

PROBLEM 4.3

At point D, expenditure on good 1 is \$66 and expenditure on good 2 is \$44; hence, the income associated with the compensated budget line is \$110. Since prices on the compensated budget line are $p_1 = \$3$ and $p_2 = \$1$, the compensated budget line is $3x_1 + x_2 = 110$. The added income necessary to attain the original indifference curve is \$50.

PROBLEM 4.4

See Figure A4.1. The substitution effect leads to an increase in consumption from 14 to 17 units, while the income effect leads to a decrease in consumption from 17 to 12 units. Since consumption decreased when income increased, good 1 is inferior.

PROBLEM 4.5

In Figure A4.2, notice that the substitution effect is zero and the compensatory income \$45. Since there is no substitution effect, the compensated demand curve is $x_1^* = 15$. Given $p_2 = \$1$ and $M = \$30$, the ordinary demand curve is $x_1^* = 30/(1 + p_1)$.

PROBLEM 4.6

Over the years the value of time for most people has dramatically increased. The increased productivity is what encouraged the innovation of time-saving devices. Hence the rushed lives we lead reflects the increased value of time.

PROBLEM 4.7

Given that there is one concert being held and assuming that each girl can only enter the line once, then if the number of tickets per person is reduced by 1/2, the number of girls in the line doubles. It would look exactly the same, only the actual girls would change. If everyone was identical then a random 5000 get in the line. When the girls are different, those 5000 girls willing to wait the longest enter the line.

PROBLEM 4.8

This is a true story. When parents had to stand in line the line was about 10 hours long. When chairs and umbrellas were allowed it went to about 20 hours and parents slept in the chairs overnight. Tents increased

FIGURE A4.1

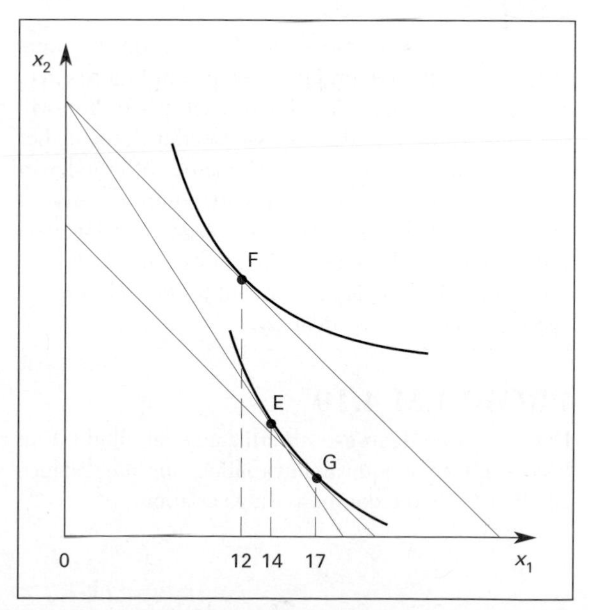

FIGURE A4.2

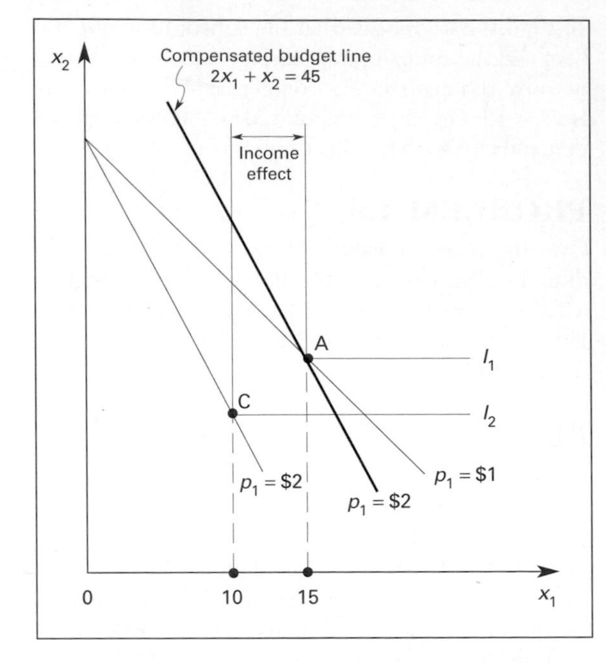

the waiting time to two days, and the line continued to get longer as more services were added. The current wait is now around two weeks as parents essentially take their summer vacation on the school grounds. This does not increase the welfare of those in line. The line must dissipate the value of what is being given away, and making the line easier to stand in only lengthens the line.

PROBLEM 4.9

First pick two prices for good 1. Then, on the same diagram, use the technique developed in Figure 4.8 to identify the *CV* associated with each price. You will see immediately that the *CV* associated with the higher price is smaller than the *CV* associated with the lower price. This result is consistent with common sense: it says that the dollar value of the privilege of buying good 1 at price p_1 decreases as p_1 increases. The *CV* is zero when the price line is just tangent to the indifference curve as it cuts the vertical axis.

PROBLEM 4.10

For this price decrease, the distance labelled *CV* in Figure 4.9 is the equivalent variation, and the distance labelled *EV* is the compensating variation.

PROBLEM 4.11

The benefit of a price decrease from \$60 to \$40 is \$500, and the benefit of being able to buy the good at a price of \$50, as opposed to not being able to buy it at all, is \$625.

PROBLEM 4.12

The consumer's surplus at Tradewell is \$5.5, and at Safeway is \$9.5. Safeway has the lower prices.

PROBLEM 4.13

Because, at the margin, water is not so valuable. These types of remarks confuse the total value with the marginal value.

PROBLEM 4.14

When children ask about a favourite colour, they must be referring to total value. Yet when asked the same type of question, they naturally answer in terms of marginal value. Kids are not the only ones who do this.

PROBLEM 4.15

We simply value them more at the margin, not in total or on average more. If the world were filled with Tiger Woodses, they would receive a much lower income.

PROBLEM 4.16

Figure A4.3 is useful here. If the price of film is equal to its \$1 cost, then the firm's profit is the area of triangle GAF less \$5, because the firm just breaks even on its film sales, the area of triangle GAF is the price of the camera, and the cost of producing the camera is \$5. At the lower price p_1', the price of the camera increases by the area of the trapezoid p_1'GFM, but the firm incurs a loss on sales of film equal to the area of the rectangle p_1'GHM. The net decrease in its profit, relative to the situation in which film is sold at cost, is the area of the triangle FHM.

PROBLEM 4.17

Because B^1 lies above the period-0 budget line, we infer that the expenditure required to purchase B^1 at period-0 prices exceeds actual expenditure or income in period 0. This implies that L exceeds 1. Because B^0 lies above the period-1 budget line, we infer that the expenditure required to purchase B^0 at period-1 prices exceeds actual expenditure or income in period 1. This implies that P is less than 1. To see that it is impossible

FIGURE A4.3

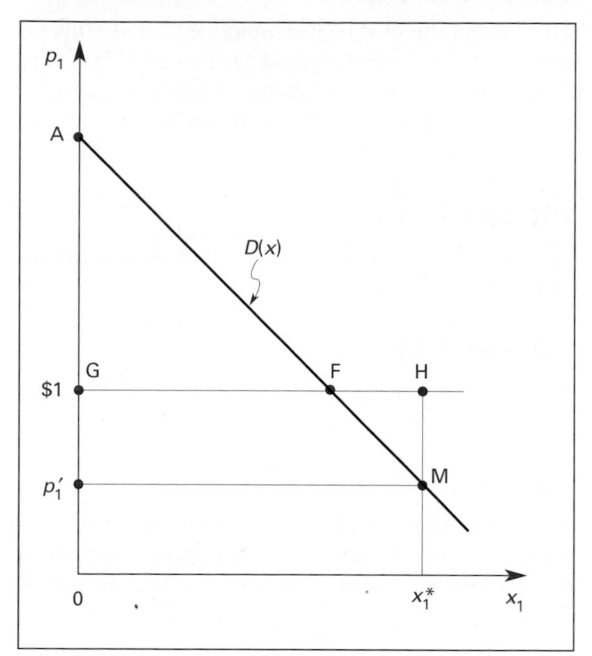

(without further information) to tell which is the preferred bundle, begin by drawing an indifference curve in Figure 4.18 such that the individual is indifferent between bundles B^0 and B^1.

PROBLEM 4.18

The Paasche and Laspeyres quantity indexes are 120/115 and 145/120, respectively. The Paasche and Laspeyres price indexes are 120/145 and 115/120, respectively. Norm is better off in period 1.

PROBLEM 5.1

They are inconsistent. Here the utility one receives depends on the way one's income is generated.

PROBLEM 5.2

The present values are identical when the interest rate is 10 percent. The first income stream has the larger present value for rates of interest lower than 10 percent and the second has the larger present value for rates of interest higher than 10 percent. Relative to each other, the first income stream is back-loaded and the second is front-loaded. The front-loaded income stream has the larger present value when the rate of interest is high, and the back-loaded income stream has the larger present value when the rate of interest is low.

PROBLEM 5.3

The publisher knows that the book will be resold and the future resale value is capitalized into the price of the current book. If students were somehow prevented from reselling the book, the amount they would be willing to pay for it would fall and so would the price of the book. If publishers could somehow commit to not coming out with a new edition every three years, the price of the book would rise to capture the future resales. Books are not made to fall apart after one year because the cost of increasing the quality of the book to last several years is trivial compared to the cost of producing another book. Hence it is more profitable to produce a book that lasts several years (and gets resold) than to produce books that can only be used once (and fetch the one-time-use price).

PROBLEM 5.4

First, the demand for land constantly changes. Second, changes in technology allow for changes in the "land" available. The introduction of steel and concrete in general construction allowed for massive highrises that essentially increased the "amount" of land available.

PROBLEM 5.5

Your graph should have a production function as in Figure 5.4, but the present value lines should have a different shape. In the case of a zero interest rate, they are flat and the optimal harvest time is at point D. When the interest rate is infinite, they are vertical and the optimal harvest time is right now.

PROBLEM 5.6

Note that the present value of $I_1 - C_1$ is $(I_1 - C_1)/(1 + i)$. If we substitute this expression into "$C_0 = I_0$ + present value of $(I_1 - C_1)$" and rearrange, we get the expression we derived in the text for Harold's budget line.

PROBLEM 5.7

Harold's budget line is $C_0 + C_1/4 = 900\ 000$. If he consumed nothing in period 1 he could consume \$900 000 in period 0. If he consumed nothing in period 0, he could consume \$3 600 000 in period 1. The opportunity cost of \$1 of consumption in period 0 is \$4 of consumption in period 1. The opportunity cost of \$1 of consumption in period 1 is \$0.25 of consumption in period 0. The slope of the budget line is −4.

PROBLEM 5.8

If Harold initially chooses to borrow against future income to finance consumption in period 0, he is made worse off by an increase in the interest rate. On the other hand, if Harold initially consumes less than his income in period 0, he is made better off by an increase in the interest rate. In terms of Figure 5.6, Harold is made worse off by an increase in the interest rate if he chooses a bundle on his initial budget line that is to the right of A, and he is made better off if he chooses a bundle on his initial budget line that is to the left of A.

PROBLEM 5.9

Harold is impatient because his marginal rate of time preference is 2 at bundle E, composed of \$800 000 of consumption in each period. When the interest rate is 0 percent, the slope of the budget line is −1 and, in addition, C_1 is equal to C_0 at the midpoint of the budget line. If the individual is impatient, the indifference curve through the midpoint of the budget line is steeper than the budget line, and the utility maximizing bundle is therefore to the right of the midpoint, where C_0 exceeds C_1.

PROBLEM 5.10

Statements 1.a and 2.b are true, and statements 1.b and 2.a are uncertain.

PROBLEM 6.1

Two units of seviche use all the available red snapper, so the restaurant can make just two units of seviche. The production function is

$$y = \min(z_1/500, z_2/125, z_3/30\ z_4/250)$$

PROBLEM 6.2

This bundle will produce at most 1200 kilometres, and the speed required is 120 km/h. If the truck is driven at 80 km/h, it can be driven only 800 kilometres, and if it is driven at 160 km/h, it can be driven only 900 kilometres.

PROBLEM 6.3

Not necessarily! The cost of doing income tax is the value of the next best alternative. Maybe Rita is an expensive lawyer whose time is worth \$300/h, while Roger is unemployed.

PROBLEM 6.4

This lowers the cost of the quota. If Canada finds it costly to lower emissions and Mexico finds it cheap, then a deal can be struck between the two countries that makes both better off and still reduces the overall emissions by the same amount.

PROBLEM 6.5

He made the wrong decision. Most of these costs are sunk and irrelevant.

PROBLEM 6.6

The total product functions are $120(z_1)^{1/2}$ when z_2 is 12, and $180(z_1)^{1/2}$ when z_2 is 27.

PROBLEM 6.7

The marginal product of labour increased and with it the wage to labour. The exact opposite happened to land. Since most people were landless peasants, the average standard of living increased for those who survived.

PROBLEM 6.8

The associated marginal product function is

$$MP(z_1) = 1 \quad \text{if } z_1 \leq 10$$
$$MP(z_1) = 0 \quad \text{if } z_1 > 10$$

PROBLEM 6.9

The average product function is

$$AP(z_1) = 120/(z_1)^{-1/2}$$

PROBLEM 6.10

See Figure 6.6.

PROBLEM 6.11

From Problem 6.5, the total product function is

$$TP(z_1) = 180(z_1)^{1/2}$$

The minimum time necessary to drive y kilometres is then

$$z_1^* = y^2/32\ 400$$

and the variable cost function is

$$VC(y) = w_1 y^2/32\ 400$$

PROBLEM 6.12

See $AFC(y)$ in Figure 6.10b.

PROBLEM 6.13

$STC(y)$ is simply $VC(y) + FC$. Since FC does not depend on y, for any y, the slope of $STC(y)$ is equal to the slope of $VC(y)$.

PROBLEM 6.14

Since ACC_2 is always \$5 and ACC_1 is \$5 when N_1 is 3600, if there are more than 3600 commuters, in equilibrium, 3600 will use route 1 and the rest will use route 2. If there are fewer than 3600 commuters, all of them will use route 1.

PROBLEM 6.15

Since MCC_2 is always \$5 and MCC_1 is \$5 when N_1 is 2000, if there are more than 2000 commuters, in the cost-benefit optimum, 2000 should use route 1 and the rest should use route 2. If there are fewer than 2000 commuters, all of them should use route 1.

PROBLEM 6.16

Oil is produced at rising costs. As long as oil is cheaper to produce domestically, it is produced, but when it can be imported more cheaply, countries import. Hence a country like Canada produces low-cost oil and imports the rest, even though there is still oil in the ground.

PROBLEM 7.1

See Figure 7.2.

PROBLEM 7.2

The $MRTS$ of wood for coal is 2.5. The $MRTS$ of coal for wood is 0.4.

PROBLEM 7.3

The $MRTS$ of Coke for rum is zero on the horizontal segment of the isoquant, and is infinite on the vertical segment. $MRTS$ is not defined at the kink in the isoquant — that is, at input bundle (4, 12).

PROBLEM 7.4

a. Given bundle (20, 8) she can produce just 4 square metres of fenced pasture since she does not have enough wire to fence a larger pasture. Given bundle (40, 16) she can produce 16 square metres of pasture. Since output quadruples as the quantities of both inputs are doubled, there are increasing returns to scale.

b. Given bundle (120, 48) she can produce 120 square metres of fenced pasture and she has excess barbed wire. Given bundle (240, 96) she can produce 240 square metres of pasture. Since output doubles as the quantities of both inputs are doubled, there are constant returns to scale. More generally, for bundles in which there is excess land, there are increasing returns to scale, and for bundles in which there is excess barbed wire, there are constant returns to scale.

PROBLEM 7.5

Notice first that for this production function

$$F(az_1, az_2) = (a^{u+v})F(z_1, z_2)$$

Suppose $a > 1$. If $u + v > 1$, the term a^{u+v} is greater than a, and there are increasing returns to scale. If $u + v < 1$, the term a^{u+v} is less than a, and there are decreasing returns to scale. If $u + v = 1$, the term a^{u+v} is equal to a, and there are constant returns to scale.

PROBLEM 7.6

If $2w_1 < 5w_2$, then $z_1^* = y/5$, $z_2^* = 0$, and $TC(w_1, w_2) = w_1y/5$. And if $2w_1 > 5w_2$, then $z_1^* = 0$, $z_2^* = y/2$, and $TC(w_1, w_2) = w_2y/2$. Finally, if $2w_1 = 5w_2$, any bundle on the y unit isoquant is cost-minimizing and $TC(w_1, w_2) = w_2y/2 = w_1y/5$.

PROBLEM 7.7

The opportunity cost of input 2 in terms of input 1 is w_2/w_1 because, to get an additional unit of input 2, one must give up w_2/w_1 units of input 1. The isocost line intersects the z_1 axis at $z_1 = c/w_1$ and the z_2 axis at $z_2 = c/w_2$. The isocost line becomes horizontal as w_1 approaches 0, and it becomes vertical as w_2 approaches 0. As c gets large, the isocost line shifts out from the origin.

PROBLEM 7.8

When $w_1 = \$6$ and $w_2 = \$2$, or when $w_1 = \$12$ and $w_2 = \$4$, the conditional input demand functions are $z_1^* = y/60$ and $z_2^* = y/20$. In words, for each kilometre, use 1 minute of the driver's time and 1/20 of a litre of gas. When $w_1 = \$6$ and $w_2 = \$2$, the cost function is $y/5$, and each kilometre costs \$0.20. When we double the input prices, the cost function is $2y/5$, so each kilometre costs \$0.40.

PROBLEM 7.9

For concreteness, suppose we want to produce 100 units of output. Initially, the cost-minimizing input bundle is the point on the 100-unit isoquant where *MRTS* is equal to w_1/w_2. Subsequently, after the opportunity cost of input 1 increases, or after w_1/w_2 increases, the cost-minimizing bundle is the point on the 100-unit isoquant where *MRTS* is equal to the now larger value of w_1/w_2. Since there is a diminishing *MRTS*, this cost-minimizing bundle is necessarily above and to the left of the initial cost-minimizing bundle, and therefore contains less of input 1 and more of input 2. In other words, as the opportunity cost of an input increases, the firm substitutes away from that input.

PROBLEM 7.10

Rum and Coke are perfect complements in the rum-and-Coke production function, so it is impossible to substitute one input for the other. As result, the cost-minimizing input bundle is unresponsive to relative input prices.

PROBLEM 7.11

The output expansion path for a homothetic production function is a ray through the origin — that is, a straight line that passes through the origin in input space. If the output expansion path is not coincident with either axis, its slope is positive, and both inputs are normal. On the other hand, if the output expansion path is coincident with one of the axes, then one input is normal and the other is neither normal nor inferior. Therefore, if the production function is homothetic, neither input is inferior.

PROBLEM 7.12

At the end of Section 7.5 we derived Tipple's long-run cost function:

$$TC(y,w_1,w_2) = y(w_1w_2/300)^{1/2}$$

Dividing by y to get $LAC(y)$, we have

$$LAC(y) = (w_1w_2/300)^{1/2}$$

PROBLEM 7.13

See Figure A7.1.

PROBLEM 8.1

The allocation of tickets remains the same, but the gains from trade increase. Increases in differences among people always increase the gains from market exchange. This is why the gains from trading globally have increased wealth so much in the last 50 years, both on the consumption and production sides.

FIGURE A7.1

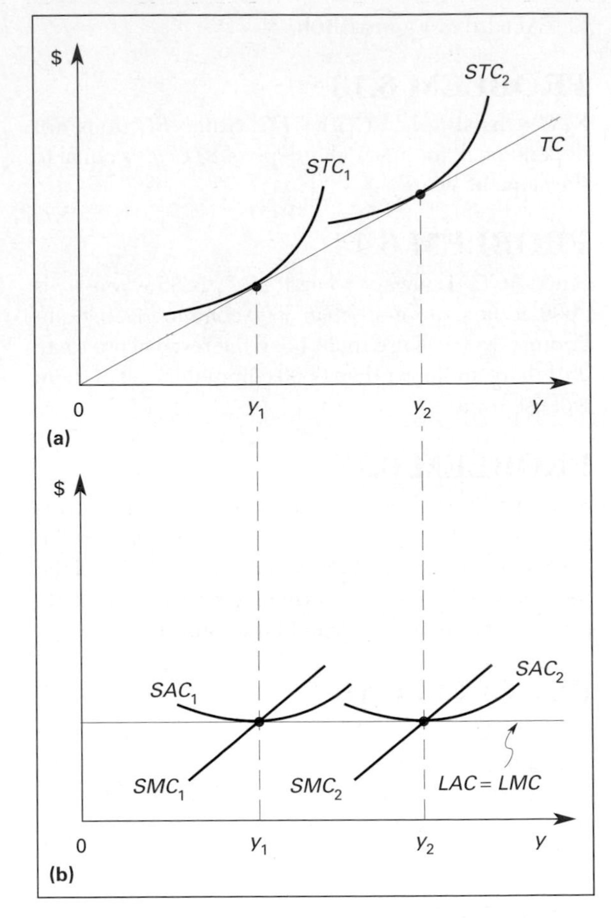

PROBLEM 8.2

The range of equilibrium prices is unchanged. Any price less than or equal to \$60 and greater than \$50 is a competitive equilibrium price. In this case, only two units are traded in the equilibrium: individuals G and J sell and C and E buy. The final allocation of tickets is the same: individuals A, B, C, D, and E end up with tickets. The individuals who are (unambiguously) better off are those who were initially given tickets this time around but not the first time around. Similarly, those who are (unambiguously) worse off are those who were not given a ticket this time but were the first time.

PROBLEM 8.3

There are two competitive equilibria. (1) Consider any price less than or equal to \$10. Harry and Sarah will buy or not sell at any such price. Similarly, Jane and Bob will sell or not buy, given that their mate does not end up with a ticket. Therefore, for any such price, we have a competitive equilibrium, with Harry and Sarah holding tickets. This equilibrium is not Pareto-optimal because Jane and Bob together would be willing to offer more than \$20 to Harry and Sarah for the pair of tickets, and Harry and Sarah would be willing to accept such an offer. (2) Any price greater than \$10 but less than or equal to \$20 is a competitive equilibrium price, and the equilibrium allocation at this price leaves the tickets in the hands of Jane and Bob.

PROBLEM 8.4

In this case, any price between \$45 and \$50 is a market-clearing price; two units are traded; Earl and the suppliers with the three lowest reservation prices lose; the demanders with the two highest reservation prices gain.

PROBLEM 8.5

See Figure A8.1. As we have drawn the diagram, the profit-maximizing output is $y^* = 35$. Why does the firm produce anything when its profit is negative? If it produced nothing, its profit would be $-FC$, which is equal to -1 multiplied by the area of rectangle ABCD. Do you see why? By producing $y^* = 35$, the firm incurs the *smaller loss* equal to -1 multiplied by the area of rectangle GBCE. Thus, by producing 35 units, the firm incurs a smaller loss than it would if it produced nothing.

FIGURE A8.1

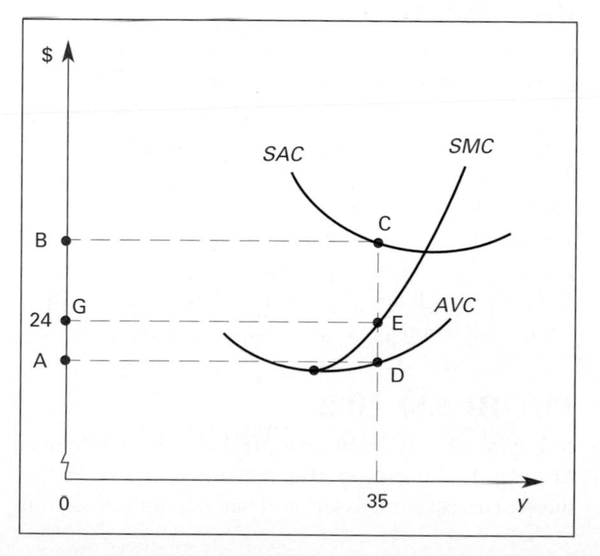

PROBLEM 8.6

It is coincident because, when price exceeds \$12, one individual demands a zero quantity. Distance $0D$ is equal to 21 units.

PROBLEM 8.7

First multiply the right-hand side of the individual demand function by 1000 to get $y = 1000 - p$, and then invert this function to get $p = 1000 - y$.

PROBLEM 8.8

Just multiply quantity supplied by one firm by the number of firms.

PROBLEM 8.9

The \$10 excise tax shifts each firm's supply function and the industry supply function vertically upward by \$10. If industry demand is perfectly inelastic, equilibrium price increases by \$10 and equilibrium quantity does not change. If demand is not perfectly inelastic, equilibrium price increases by less than \$10, and equilibrium quantity decreases.

PROBLEM 8.10

Equilibrium price is \$500 and equilibrium quantity is 500 units. Producers' surplus and consumers' surplus are each \$125 000.

PROBLEM 9.1

The price of wood would be lower in North America. Wood in North America was used much more extensively than in England. Wood was used for heat rather than coal, bridges were made of wood rather than stone, and wood also replaced stone and brick for homes.

PROBLEM 9.2

There were only minor price changes from the hurricane in North Carolina. Almost instantly trucks started moving in supplies of chainsaws and crews for clearing fallen branches. In Quebec, on the other hand, there were shortages of generators for electricity.

PROBLEM 9.3

No. People set the temperature where marginal costs equal marginal benefits, and they keep it there. The outside temperature affects the total costs, not the marginal costs.

PROBLEM 9.4

a. The equilibrium price is \$44.28, with an equilibrium quantity of 9430.

b. The new price is \$66. The total loss to consumers is \$145 849.80, and the potential gain to producers is \$86 880.

PROBLEM 9.5

Figure A9.1 depicts the situation under the price subsidy program. Here, p_s is the support price, and y_s the quantity supplied at that price. The price at which y_s units can be sold is p_1. Therefore, the agency will spend $(p_s - p_1)y_s$ to achieve the support price p_s. The surplus destroyed is the shaded area in the diagram. Relative to the competitive equilibrium, it represents the excess of the cost of producing $y_s - y^e$ additional units over the consumers' willingness to pay for those units. Figure A9.2 depicts the situation under the buy-and-store program. At the support price p_s, a total of y_s units are produced: y_2 are sold in the open market and the agency buys and stores the remaining $y_s - y_2$ units. Under this scheme, the agency spends $p_s(y_s - y_2)$ plus storage costs to achieve the support price p_s. Relative to the competitive equilibrium, the surplus destroyed under this bizarre scheme is the shaded area in Figure A9.2. This is, in essence, the policy that the European Economic Community pursued for many years with respect to butter and other agricultural products.

FIGURE A9.1

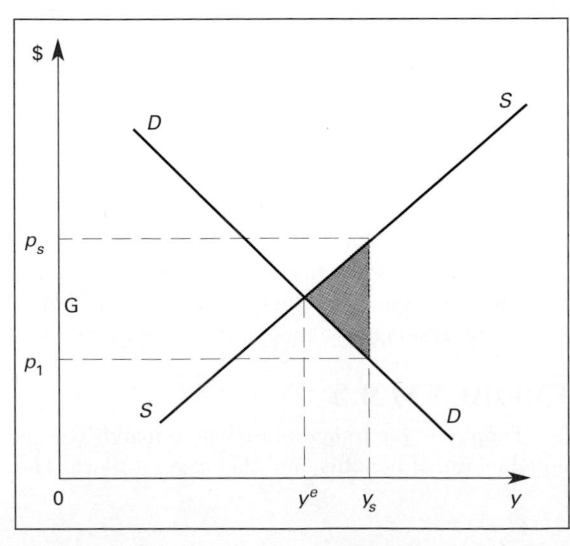

FIGURE A9.2

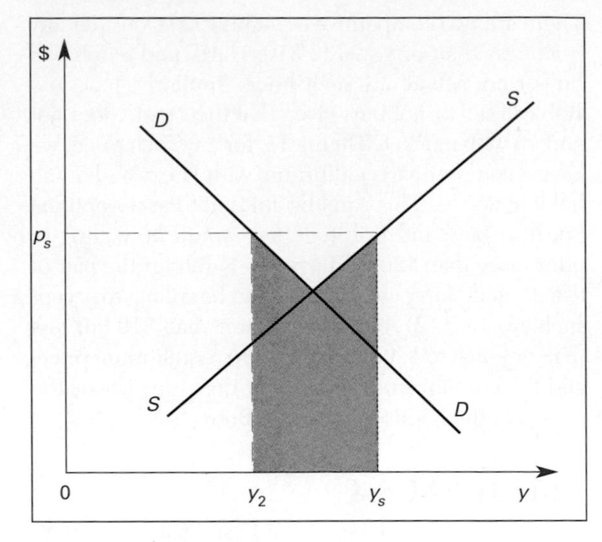

PROBLEM 9.6

One condition would be one in which all firms were identical in every respect, and there were no sunk costs.

PROBLEM 9.7

Both do, with the relative size of the burden depending on the elasticities of demand and supply.

PROBLEM 9.8

The domestic country is worse off with the quota because the lost tariff revenue is transferred to the other country.

PROBLEM 10.1

We know that $E(y) = p/[y(\text{slope of the demand curve})]$. In this equation, substitute $a - by$ for p, and $-b$ for "slope of the demand curve" and then rearrange to get $E(y) = 1 - a/(by)$. Since $y \leq a/b$, price elasticity of demand is negative. Therefore, to get $|E(y)|$, we must multiply by -1. We see then that $|E(y)| = a/(by) - 1$. To establish 1, notice that when $y < a/2b$, $MR(y) > 0$ and $|E(y)| > 1$. To establish 2, notice that when $y > a/2b$, $MR(y) < 0$ and $|E(y)| < 1$. Finally, to establish 3, notice that when $y = a/2b$, $MR(y) = 0$, and $|E(y)| = 1$.

PROBLEM 10.2

In Figure 10.3, MC intersects MR from above at 8 units of output. Beginning at $y = 8$ in Figure 10.3, the increase in revenue associated with an additional unit of output exceeds the increase in cost, since MR exceeds MC to the right of 8 units of output; hence, we see that profit increases as output increases. Beginning again at $y = 8$ in Figure 10.3, the decrease in revenue associated with 1 less unit of output is less than the decrease in cost, since MC exceeds MR to the left of 8 units of output, and we see that profit increases as output decreases. Thus, profit is at a minimum when output is 8 units in Figure 10.3.

PROBLEM 10.3

Let us solve the problem algebraically. The "marginal revenue equals marginal cost" condition is $100 - 2y = 40$, which yields $y^* = 30$. Price is then $p^* = 100 - 30 = 70$, and profit is $30(70 - 40)$, or 900.

PROBLEM 10.4

Beginning at the point where $MR = MC$, profit falls as the firm produces more output, and profit increases as the firm produces less output. Hence, to maximize profit, the firm produces nothing. AC must lie above AR.

PROBLEM 10.5

The answer to part 1 is to sell 5 books at a price equal to \$35. Profit is \$135. There are obviously unrealized gains from trade equal to \$30 – \$8 plus \$25 – \$8 plus \$20 – \$8 plus \$15 – \$8 plus \$10 – \$8. In part 2, the book vendor sells a book to each individual whose reservation price exceeds \$8. The price charged is the individual's reservation price. The solution is efficient because the only demander who does not buy a book has a reservation price of \$5, which is less than the book vendor's marginal cost. Profit is \$245.

PROBLEM 10.6

In your diagram, the residual demand function should intersect the entrant's AC function at two levels of output — say y' and y''— with $y' < y''$. Any level of output for the potential entrant larger than y' and less than y'' offers the entrant a positive profit. Therefore, this is not a case of natural monopoly.

PROBLEM 10.7

Competition among the firms would force the price equal to average costs where the firm earns zero profit. Demsetz was making the claim that there was no need for regulation if you allow for competitive bidding up front.

PROBLEM 11.1

See Figure A11.1.

PROBLEM 11.2

1. False. Suppose leisure is a normal good and that the income effect is dominated by the substitution effect. Then an increase in the wage rate leads to less leisure and more work.
2. True. For hours of work to fall in response to an increase in the wage rate, the income effect must dominate the substitution effect. This is possible if leisure is normal since the two effects are then opposed, but it is impossible if leisure is inferior since the two effects are then complementary.

PROBLEM 11.3

Suppose the firm is currently hiring 150 hours of labour. If it hires one more hour its costs increase by 7 fish (the wage rate) but its revenue increases by less than 7 fish since MP is less than 7 fish to the right of 150 hours of labour; consequently, profit falls as the firm hires more labour. If it hires one less hour, its costs decrease by 7 fish (the wage rate) but its revenue decreases by more than 7 fish since MP is greater than 7 fish to the left of 150 hours of labour; consequently profit falls as the firm hires less labour. Profit is therefore (locally) maximal when the firm hires 150 hours of labour. Using the same logic, we can easily see that 20 is the minimal profit level of labour hours.

PROBLEM 11.4

Given a wage rate of 10 fish, profit at 120 hours of labour is $120[AP(120) - 10]$ fish, which is negative since

FIGURE A11.1

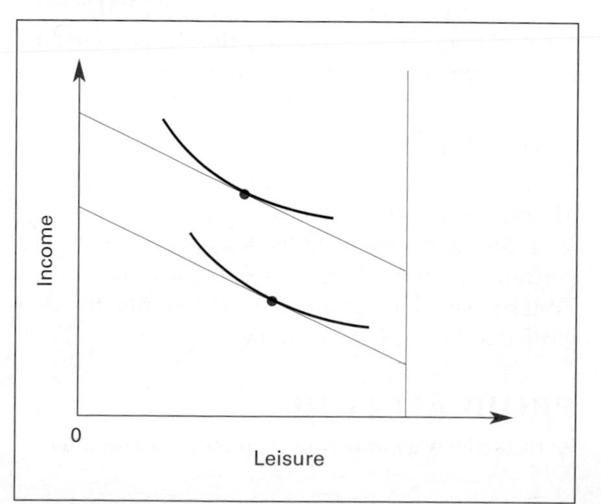

$AP(120)$ is less than 10. Hence, given a wage rate of 10 fish, the firm maximizes profit by hiring no labour and catching no fish.

PROBLEM 11.5

When $p = \$1$, simply relabel MP as MRP and AP as ARP. When $p = \$2$, shift MP and AP vertically up by a factor of 2 and attach the labels MRP and ARP.

PROBLEM 11.6

Because, by definition, $MRP(z) = MR(y)MP(z)$, we can rewrite the input market profit-maximizing rule, $w = MRP(z^*)$, as $w = MR(y^*)MP(z^*)$. Dividing both sides by $MP(z^*)$, we have $w/MP(z^*) = MR(y^*)$. But $w/MP(z^*)$ is $SMC(y^*)$. Therefore, we can again rewrite the input market rule as $SMC(y^*) = MR(y^*)$, which is the output market profit-maximizing rule.

PROBLEM 11.7

Let y^* denote the positive output at which marginal cost is equal to p. The firm will produce no output if $p < AVC(y^*)$. But from Section 7.4, we know that $AVC(y) = w/AP(z)$. Therefore, we can rewrite the shutdown condition for the output market as $p < w/AP(z^*)$ or as $pAP(z^*) < w$. But, by definition, $pAP(z) = ARP(z)$. Therefore, we can rewrite the shutdown condition as $ARP(z^*) < w$, which is the input market shutdown condition we just defined.

PROBLEM 11.8

By definition, $MRP(z) = MR(y)MP(z)$, and $VMP(z) = pMP(z)$. In a competitive output market, $MR(y^*) = p$; therefore, $VMP(z^*) = MRP(z^*)$ for a firm that is a perfect competitor in its output market. In a monopolistic output market, $MR(y^*) < p$; therefore, $VMP(z^*) > MRP(z^*)$ in this case. Be sure that you understand these simple but important relationships.

PROBLEM 11.9

False. The Vancouver Canucks must have thought that Messier would provide services that would generate at least this much income to the team. Given their poor performance in the 97/98 season, this may have been a mistake, but it cannot simply be stated from the facts given that Mark Messier was overpaid.

PROBLEM 11.10

At the same wage rate only women would be hired.

PROBLEM 11.11

The slope of the supply function is 1. Then, since $w = 1 + z$ and $MFC = w + z$[slope of the supply function], $MFC = 1 + z + z = 1 + 2z$.

PROBLEM 11.12

At z^*, MRP is equal to MFC. From Problem 11.11, we know that MFC is $1 + 2z$ in this case. Hence, $10 - z^* = 1 + 2z^*$, or $z^* = 3$, and $w^* = 1 + z^* = 4$.

PROBLEM 11.13

The supply function and the marginal factor cost of each tonne of coal are given below. When marginal revenue product is 200, the firm buys 5 tonnes.

Input Price	Tonnes supplied	*MFC*
$w < 105$	0	
$105 \leq w < 115$	1	105
$115 \leq w < 125$	2	125
$125 \leq w < 135$	3	145
$135 \leq w < 145$	4	165
$145 \leq w < 155$	5	185
$155 \leq w < 165$	6	205
$165 \leq w < 175$	7	225
$175 \leq w < 185$	8	245
$185 \leq w < 195$	9	265
$195 \leq w$	10	285

PROBLEM 11.14

The demander will obviously pay any supplier \$100 per tonne for any coal it buys. It will buy the coal supplied by any supplier if \$100 plus the transport cost the demander must pay is less than the demander's marginal revenue product, \$200. The cost of transporting a tonne of coal from the most distant supplier is \$95 — 950 miles multiplied by \$0.10 per kilometre. The demander therefore will buy all 10 tonnes. It will pay \$1000 in total to the suppliers, and \$5 + \$15 + \$25 + … + \$95 to transport the coal.

PROBLEM 11.15

The firm's objective is to maximize the present value of its profit. To do so, it should acquire widgets up to the point where the contribution of an additional widget to the present value of revenue is equal to its contribution to the present value of costs. The contribution of an additional widget to the present value of the firm's revenue is just ΣMRP, but the contribution of an additional widget to the present value of the firm's costs is no longer just P, since we must also account for the costs needed to maintain the widget in working order. The present value of the maintenance costs is:

$$M/(1+i) + M/(1+i)^2 + \ldots + M/(1+i)^{D-1}.$$

PROBLEM 11.16

a. True. The cost of investing has fallen.

b. True. The future returns on the investment are discounted less.

c. False.

d. True. Since Harriet is a net borrower, the fall in interest makes her better off.

e. Uncertain. This depends on the shape of Harriet's indifference curves. If consumption is normal in both periods, then she consumes more in period 0.

f. True.

PROBLEM 11.17

She is definitely worse off when she has no access to the loanable funds market. In Figure 11.19, she would have access only to bundles of consumption along the human capital production function. All of these bundles lie below her indifference curve.

PROBLEM 12.1

See Figure A12.1.

PROBLEM 12.2

This question has no "correct" answer, since each person's response depends on his or her preferences.

PROBLEM 12.3

This observation seems at odds with both the productivity principle and the redistributive principle. It is more consistent with the notion that redistribution takes place to prevent acts of theft. In biblical times travel was costly and loads were light. Hungry travellers might find it in their interests to steal food along the way. The custom of gleaning provided food for the travellers and relieved the local farmers from overinvestments in protection.

PROBLEM 12.4

An effective minimum wage implies excess supply; employers therefore can choose among applicants on the basis of sex, race, age, or any other characteristic at no cost to themselves. In the absence of a minimum wage, there is no excess supply, and if the employer does not like the applicants, it must pay a higher wage to attract more "acceptable" applicants.

FIGURE A12.1

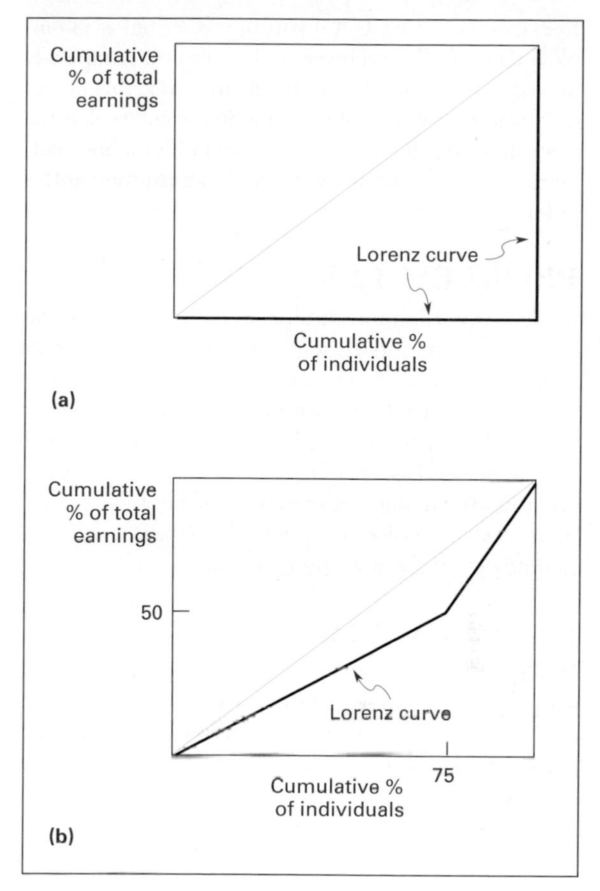

PROBLEM 12.5

You can derive these results by constructing the marginal factor cost function implied by different minimum wages (as in Figure 12.2), and then finding the quantity of labour that maximizes the firm's profit.

PROBLEM 12.6

Under competitive conditions, a union will raise the wage rate and increase the income of those workers who retain a job. This increase in income is a transfer of wealth from the firm owners to the workers. However, the number employed also falls, which results in a loss of efficiency. In a monopsonistic labour market, where one firm is able to pay just the marginal factor cost, there is too little employment. Over a certain wage range, increases in wages result in a transfer from firms to workers and an increase in employment.

PROBLEM 12.7

Because the hiring-hall institution distributes unemployment equally and because the supply is completely inelastic, each member wants to maximize his or her earnings. The wage that such a union would seek is the wage at which the elasticity of demand for labour is 1, because the firm's total wage bill is a maximum at this point.

PROBLEM 12.8

In this case, the more junior members of the union bear all the unemployment associated with a higher wage. If the more senior members do not care about the unemployment of junior members, they will favour a much higher wage rate, knowing that they will not be unemployed as a result. The natural coalition is the coalition involving just over half of the most senior members; this coalition will seek the highest wage such that no one of them is unemployed.

PROBLEM 12.9

In Figure 12.6, interpret $w = 12$ as the high urban wage and interpret "labour demand in sector 2" as the demand for labour in rural areas. Assume a casual labour market in the urban area, one with lots of job turnover, so that each urban worker gets the same share of the available urban employment. Then u is the unemployment rate among urban workers.

FIGURE A12.2

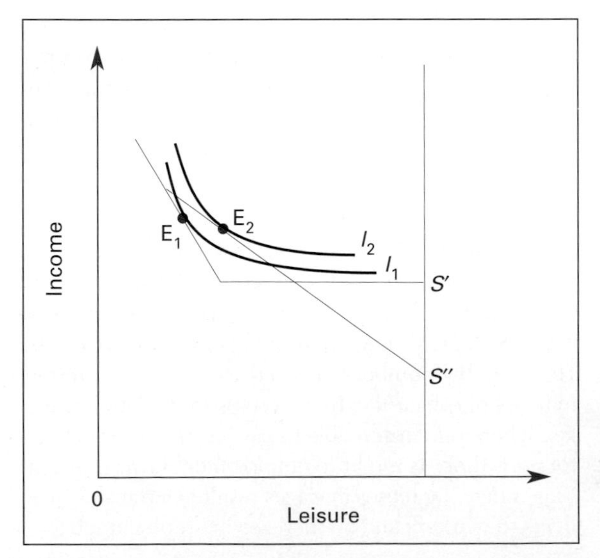

PROBLEM 12.10

In Figure 12.7, for any value of x_1, the subsidy required to put the individual on the target indifference curve is the vertical distance from the "No-income-transfer budget line" to the "Target indifference curve." This distance is minimized at x_1^*.

PROBLEM 12.11

In Figure A12.2 under the topping-up mechanism, the individual chooses E_1 on indifference curve I_1 and chooses not to receive the topping-up transfer S'. Given the NIT budget line, the individual chooses point E_2 on indifference curve I_2 and receives the NIT transfer S''.

PROBLEM 13.1

At point A, Shelly has 23 units of good 1 and 32 of good 2, while Marvin has 79 units of good 1 and 34 of good 2. At point 0_M, Shelly has 102 units of good 1 and 66 of good 2, while Marvin has 0 units of good 1 and 0 of good 2. At point B, Shelly has 102 units of good 1 and 0 of good 2, while Marvin has 0 units of good 1 and 66 of good 2. At point E, Shelly has 66 units of good 1 and 0 of good 2, while Marvin has 102 units of good 1 and 0 of good 2.

PROBLEM 13.2

Shelly's ordering: first, F; second, D and G; third, A. Marvin's ordering: first, A; second, G; third, D and F.

PROBLEM 13.3

All points in the shaded area in Figure A13.1 are Pareto-preferred to point T.

PROBLEM 13.4

Shelly's net demand for good 1 is 27 units, equal to Marvin's net supply. Marvin's net demand for good 2 is 26 units, equal to Shelly's net supply. If Marvin traded 27 units of good 1 for 26 units of good 2, and Shelly traded 26 units of good 2 for 27 units of good 1, the economy would move from the initial allocation at A to the competitive equilibrium at E.

PROBLEM 13.5

Producers of good 1 must use relatively more of input 1 and relatively less of input 2, while producers of good 2 must do the opposite. Yes, it is possible to achieve efficiency in production while maintaining a constant output of good 1.

FIGURE A13.1

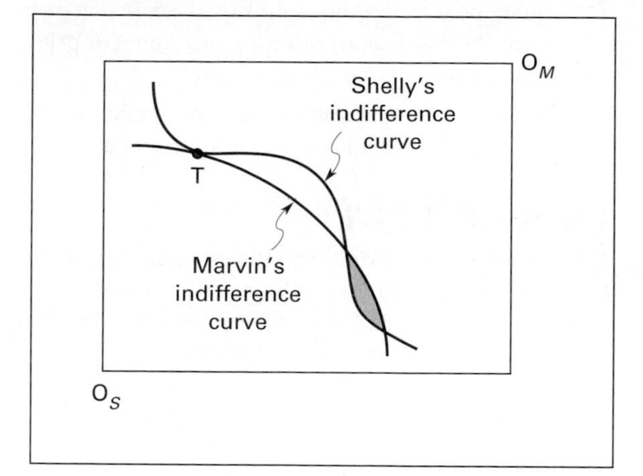

PROBLEM 13.6

2, 1/5, 1/3, 3.

PROBLEM 13.7

MRT is 1.

PROBLEM 13.8

Less.

PROBLEM 13.9

Supposing that the monopolist produces good 1, the relevant diagram is Figure A13.2. Ms C's origin is point B. Initially, she is at a point such as point A in the figure because, as we just discovered, her *MRS* (at the initial equilibrium) necessarily exceeds *MRT* when good 1 is produced by a monopolist. When she takes control, she will choose point Z, a point at which she consumes more good 1 and less good 2. At point Z, she is better off, and no one else, including the owner of the firm producing good 1, is worse off, because their consumption bundles have not changed. Therefore, in the general equilibrium, when good 1 is produced by a monopolist, too little of that good is produced.

PROBLEM 13.10

Let p_1, p_2, w_1, and w_2 denote equilibrium prices. Each consumer will choose a bundle where $MRS = p_1/(p_2 + t)$, and the economy is efficient in consumption. Each producer will use an input bundle where $MRTS = w_1/w_2$, and the economy is efficient in production. Because the prices firms receive are p_1 and p_2, $MRT = p_1/p_2$. *MRT* therefore exceeds the common value of *MRS*, and we do not have efficiency in product mix.

FIGURE A13.2

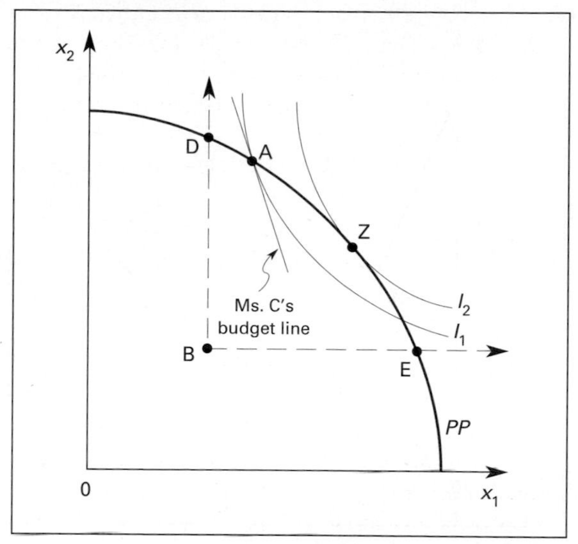

Using a diagram like Figure 13.9, you can show that too little of good 2 is produced in general competitive equilibrium when consumption of good 2 is taxed. Similarly, if consumption of good 2 is subsidized, although we have efficiency in consumption and production, we do not have efficiency in product mix, and too much of good 2 is produced in general competitive equilibrium.

PROBLEM 14.1

In each market, the monopolist will sell the quantity at which marginal revenue is zero. Hence, it will sell 24 units in the first market and 40 in the second; that is, it will sell less than 100 units. This result is consistent with the rule we developed.

PROBLEM 14.2

In Figure A14.1, we have drawn both demand and marginal revenue functions and the marginal cost function. The aggregated marginal revenue function is the heavy line composed of MR_1 for y less than y_1^* and $MR_2 = p_2$ for y greater than y_1^*. The profit-maximizing output is y^*, of which y_1^* is sold in the first market at price p_1^*, and $y^* - y_1^*$ is sold in the second market at price p_2.

PROBLEM 14.3

First, Canadian Tire induces buyers who have ready cash to part with it rather than to use their credit cards; receiving cash is valuable to Canadian Tire because credit card companies charge the retailer for their ser-

FIGURE A14.1

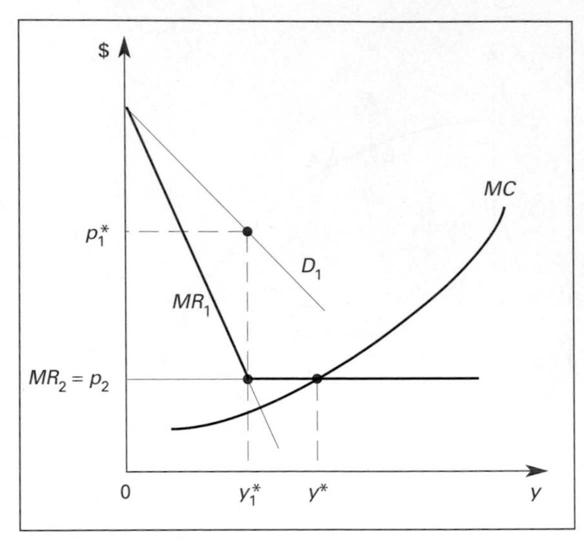

vices. Thus, there is a form of price discrimination between customers with and without ready cash. Second, among those who are entitled to receive the cash discount, some proportion do not take it because they lose the Canadian Tire money or never return to a Canadian Tire store.

PROBLEM 14.4

You might argue in the first case that people who order a pizza eat less salad, and as a result it costs less to serve them. In the second case, you might argue that the pizza gets colder the farther it gets delivered, and so the good is not the same.

PROBLEM 14.5

a. The profit-maximizing block limit is 21 units, the monopolist's profit is \$366 (an increase of \$42), and Sam is neither better off nor worse off.

b. The profit-maximizing block limit is 30 units, the monopolist's profit is \$420, and Sam is neither better off nor worse off.

PROBLEM 14.6

a. This is probably ordinary price discrimination, but the wealthy also tend to buy a lot of medical services (such as private hospital rooms) with their medical care.

b. Better bowlers tend to bowl faster. Hence paying by the frame means that they pay more per hour than poorer bowlers. Since better bowlers also cause less damage to the lane, this looks like price discrimination. This points to one of the problems in defining price discrimination. Equal pricing on one margin (by the frame) often means unequal pricing on another margin (by the hour).

c. The university might argue that better students cost less to educate, so it is not price discrimination.

PROBLEM 14.7

The theatre owner would want to raise his entrance fee for everyone and lower the price of popcorn. In fact, he would want to subsidize popcorn prices to induce the snack lovers to pay the high movie price.

PROBLEM 14.8

A divorce should occur when one party tries to exploit more affection than exists. As women entered the workforce, they gained opportunities outside of marriage, and as a result, their demands for their spouse became more elastic. Since there is less consumer surplus to extract, there should be less exploitation. We can't say what would happen to the divorce rate. Husbands should recognize the better opportunities of their wives and exploit less.

PROBLEM 15.1

When people use public washrooms, they have a dominant strategy to not clean up after themselves. There is a benefit to using the washroom, and of course a cost of cleaning it up. If you use the same washroom more than once, you have an incentive to keep it clean, but in a public washroom you are unlikely to use it again. Hence the dominant strategy is to use the washroom and not clean it.

PROBLEM 15.2

The payoff matrix is given in the table below. The strategy combination (Use, Use) is dominant as long as $W_i > 5H_i$. When this is used, it is not Pareto-optimal because both parties incur the health cost with no change in the probability of winning. (Don't Use, Don't Use) Pareto-dominate this one.

		Athlete 2	
		Use PED	Don't Use PED
Athlete 1	Use PED	$6/10W_1 - H_1$, $4/10W_2 - H_2$	$8/10W_1 - H_1$, $2/10W_2$
	Don't Use PED	$4/10W_1$, $6/10W_2 - H_2$	$6/10W_1$, $4/10W_2$

PROBLEM 15.3

The new payoff matrix is

	0	1	2	$n-1$
Proper Disposal	B	2B	3B	*N*B
Improper Disposal	0	B	2B	$(N-1)$B

Clearly the dominant strategy is for the individual to properly dispose of their own garbage.

PROBLEM 15.4

The payoff matrix is in Figure A15.1. Clearly there is no cell where two arrowheads meet.

PROBLEM 15.5

When $y_1 = y_2 = y$, either player's payoff is given by the following expression

$\pi(y) = 120y - y_2$

Now verify that

$\pi(y + \Delta) - \pi(y) = \Delta(120 - 2y) - \Delta^2$

From this we see that the payoff is maximized when $120 - 2y = 0$ or when $y = 60$. When $y_1 = y_2 = 60$, each player's payoff is 3600, which is larger than the payoff of 3200 that they get when they choose the Nash equilibrium values, $y_1^* = y_2^* = 40$.

See Figure A15.2. Notice that the strategy combination (60, 60) is Pareto-optimal, and that this leads to a situation where the indifference curves are tangent. This is akin to the general equilibrium result found in a standard Edgewoth box diagram.

FIGURE A15.1

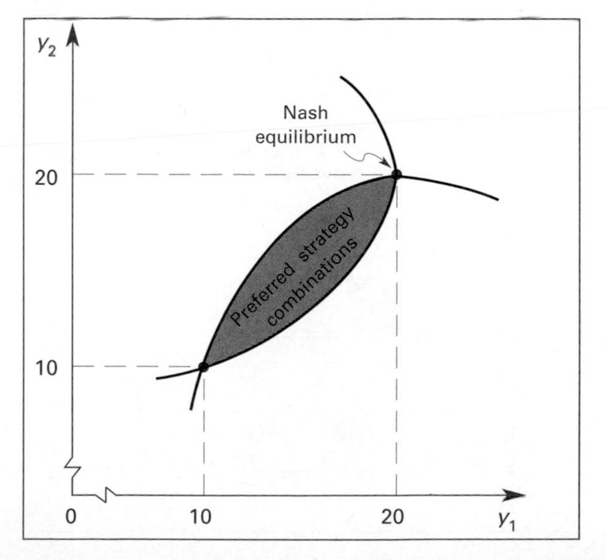

FIGURE A15.2

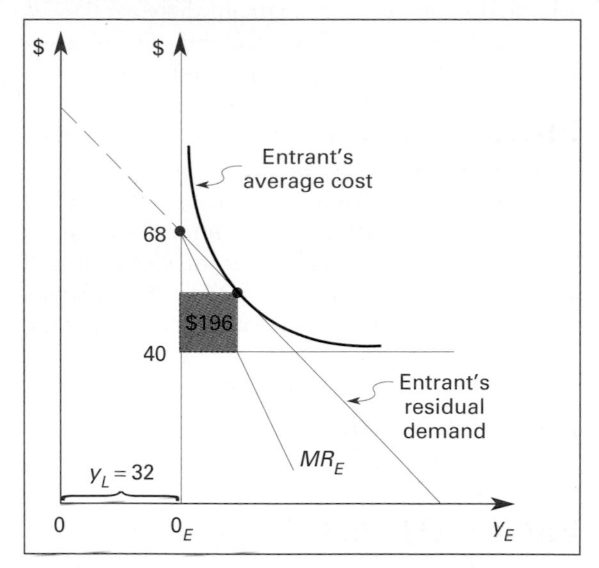

PROBLEM 15.6

See Figure A15.3.

PROBLEM 15.7

Consider a representative player, say player *i* with reservation price R_i. Observe first that in constructing this player's best-response function, the only information about the strategies of other players that is relevant is the maximum bid of the other $N-1$ players, call it x_{max}. Do you see why? Now, to find player *i*'s best-response function, in the paragraph where we found player 1's best-response function, simply substitute x_i for x_1 and x_{max} for x_2, and you will have found player *i*'s best response function, which we can then use to prove that

FIGURE A15.3

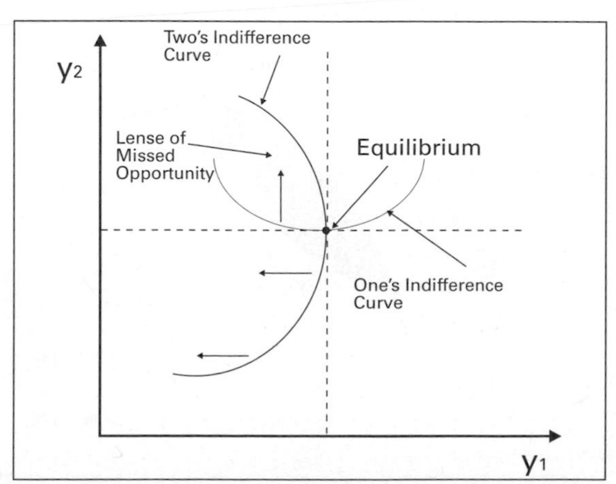

$x_i = R_i$ is a weakly dominant strategy for player i. To achieve this end, in the paragraph where we showed that $x_1 = R_1$ is a weakly dominant strategy for player 1, simply replace R_I by R_i, x_1 by x_i, and x_2 by x_{max}.

PROBLEM 16.1

If a soldier doesn't fire his weapon, he attracts no attention to himself and has an insignificant effect on the outcome of the battle. If the soldier does fire his weapon, he attracts a lot of fire and attention to himself and still has an insignificant effect on the outcome. Hence, the soldier has a dominant strategy to not fire his weapon.

PROBLEM 16.2

See Figure A16.1.

PROBLEM 16.3

The first firm's demand function is $p_1 = (100 - y_2 - y_3) - y_1$, so its marginal revenue function is $MR_1 = (100 - y_2 - y_3) - 2y_1$. Setting marginal revenue equal to marginal cost (40) and solving for y_1^*, we get the first firm's best response function:

$$y_1^* = 30 - (y_2 + y_3)/2$$

Then, using the fact that the output of all three firms will be the same in the equilibrium, we set y_1^*, y_2, and y_3 all equal to y' in this expression and solve for y', the output of each of the three firms in the Cournot equilibrium: $y' = 15$. Aggregate output is then 45 and price 55. Profit of each firm is $225.

PROBLEM 16.4

If we draw the profit functions, we see that they look like Figure 15.14, which means that they are playing a game of plain substitutes.

PROBLEM 16.5

If we subtract the two expressions, we end up with an expression $y_i = 90 + y_i - 4y_i$. If we then solve this for y_i we get the BR function for y_i. We solve the two best response functions by substituting one equation into the other. For example, substitute BR_1 into BR_2 to get $y_2 = 90/4 + 90/16 + y_2/16$. Solving gives $y_2 = 30$. Similarly for y_1.

PROBLEM 16.6

Suppose first that there are just three parties to the agreement. The cheater will produce 20 units, aggregate output will be 40 units, and price will be $60. The cheater's profit will be $400, and the inducement to cheat $100 since each firm gets $300 in the collusive agreement. If there were four parties to the agreement, the cheater would produce 18.75 units, aggregate output would be 41.25 units, and price would be $58.75. The cheater's profit would be $351.56, and the inducement to cheat $126.56, since each firm gets $225 in the collusive agreement. The inducement to cheat gets larger and larger as the number of firms in the collusive agreement increases.

FIGURE A16.1

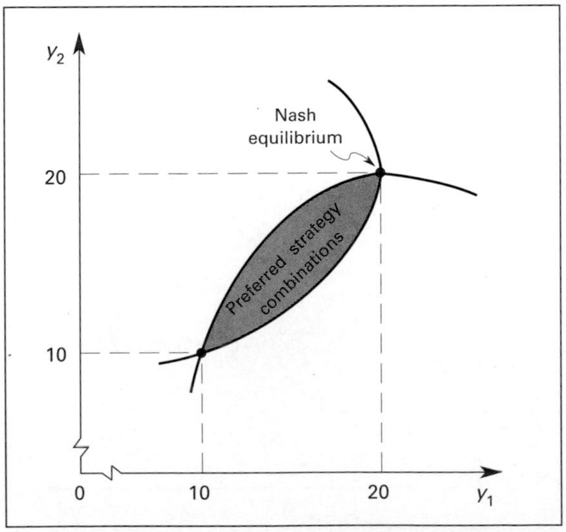

FIGURE A16.2

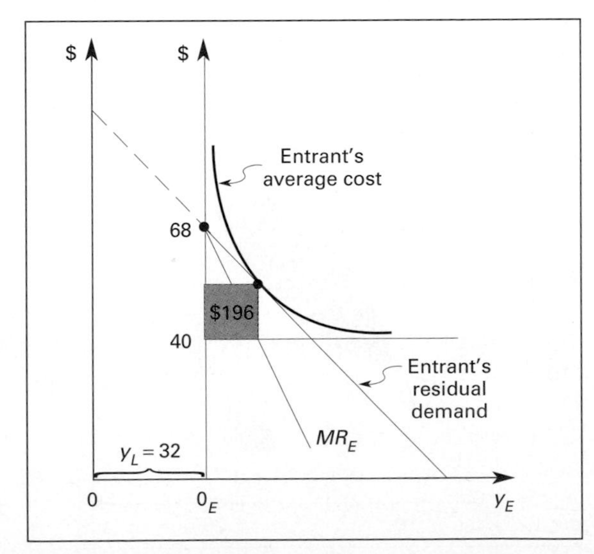

PROBLEM 16.7

Suppose that a collusive solution has been in place for some time and that all sales have included the most-favoured-customer clause. Then, by cheating, the firm gets the standard payoff identified above, but it incurs a loss equal to the difference between the collusive price and the discount price multiplied by the total quantity sold at the collusive price under the most-favoured-customer clause. Therefore, if the most-favoured-customer clause has been in effect long enough, no firm will cheat.

PROBLEM 16.8

See Figure A16.2.

PROBLEM 16.9

In the Bertrand duopoly equilibrium, price is equal to marginal cost. An entrant would therefore anticipate price equal to marginal cost after entry. Hence the inducement to entry is $0. Therefore, if K is positive there will be no entry.

PROBLEM 16.10

Given n established firms, an entrant's profit would be $900/(n+1) - K$. The no-entry condition is then $900/(n+1)$, $K \leq 0$. Industry-wide profit, given collusive behaviour and sequential entry, is $100 when K is $400 and $100 when K is $100. Using Figure 15.9, we see that industry-wide profit, given Cournot behaviour and sequential entry, is $500 when K is $400 and $176 when K is $100. Given Bertrand behaviour and sequential entry, industry-wide profit is $\$900 - K$.

PROBLEM 17.1

The expected monetary value of the game is $1 000 000.

PROBLEM 17.2

$950 = (2/6)$1800 + (1/6)$3000 – (3/6)$300.

PROBLEM 17.3

Chauncey's expected utility from playing Risk is 4. He is indifferent between the two options if M is equal to 50, prefers to play Risk if M is less than 50, and prefers to take M if M exceeds 50.

PROBLEM 17.4

The first prospect pays $10 000 with probability 0.25, $6000 with probability 0.25, and $1000 with probability 0.5, and its expected value is $4500. The expected values of the other prospects are $5300, $7500, and $6000.

PROBLEM 17.5

For Jack, the number e^* is 0.75, and for Jane the number e^* is greater than 0.75.

PROBLEM 17.6

Jack's utility function is $U(10\,000) = 1$, $U(6000) = 0.75$, and $U(1000) = 0$.

PROBLEM 17.7

To find Jack's preference ordering for these prospects, we can compute their expected utilities. For the first prospect, Jack's expected utility is $(1/2 \times 1)$ plus $(1/4 \times 3/4)$ plus $(1/4 \times 0)$, or 33/48. The expected utilities for the remaining prospects are, respectively, 28/48, 36/48, 28/48, 30/48, 36/48. Hence, Jack's preference ordering for these prospects is as follows: first, (0, 1, 0) and (3/4, 0, 1/4); second, (1/2, 1/4, 1/4); third, (1/4, 1/2, 1/4); fourth, (1/3, 1/3, 1/3) and (7/12, 0, 5/12).

PROBLEM 17.8

See Figure A17.1.

PROBLEM 17.9

For Melvin, the expected utility of the risky prospect is 2.5, and the expected utility of $25 is 5; hence, he prefers $25. For Jeela, the expected utility of the risky prospect is 25, and the expected utility of $25 is also

FIGURE A17.1

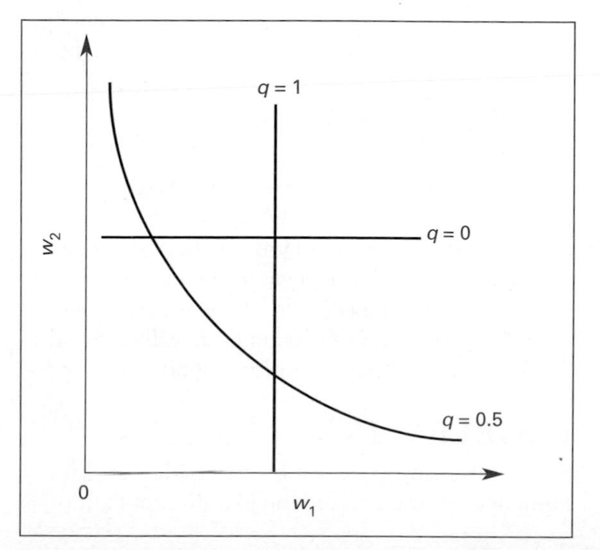

25; hence, she is indifferent. For Lou, the expected utility of the risky prospect is 2500, and the expected utility of $25 is 625; hence, Lou prefers the risky prospect.

PROBLEM 17.10

The slope of Diego's indifference curves all get steeper. When Diego is risk-averse, he now consumes some risk. When he is risk-neutral or risk-inclined, he will consume at a corner.

PROBLEM 17.11

The expected utility of the risk-pooling agreement is $1/100 + (18/100)(1/2)^{1/2}$, while the expected utility with no agreement is 1/10. As you can easily verify, the risk-pooling agreement has the larger expected utility and is therefore preferred.

PROBLEM 17.12

Patricia will not buy this asset alone because $(100)^{1/2}$, her expected utility if she does not buy it, exceeds $(1/20)(10\ 000)^{1/2}$, her expected utility if she does buy it. If she joins a syndicate with 10 equal partners, her expected utility is $(1/20)(1090)^{1/2} + (19/20)(90)^{1/2}$, which exceeds $(100)^{1/2}$, so she would join the syndicate.

PROBLEM 18.1

The legal property rights to a program belong to the developer. For example, Microsoft has the legal rights to its program, Word. However, when you copy a pirated version onto your computer, you essentially own the economic rights to it. There are many examples of this distinction. Behind the property of one of the authors is a creek that his children play in. They have no legal right to be there but go unnoticed most of the time and hence have the economic property right.

PROBLEM 18.2

When a good is stolen, the economic rights and the legal rights are separated. This makes an exchange very difficult between the thief and the original owner because they both know this fact. How can they get together without one still trying to cheat the other? Children are ransomed for the simple fact that there is such a huge difference between what the parents are willing to pay to get them back and what the next best offer is.

PROBLEM 18.3

Such things are plagued by free-rider problems. Student organizations and the like attempt to develop school spirit and monitor one another in an attempt to avoid free riding.

PROBLEM 18.4

The property rights to the well did not match the life of the well. The firms had 50-year leases to wells that had an indefinite lifespan. When the firms began to overextract the oil, they were imposing an externality on the host country. It is quite possible that Saudi Arabia, in cutting back output, was acting in the global interest.

PROBLEM 18.5

The problem of paying with booty is that soldiers simply look for easy takings. With the army this is less of a problem because cities are in fixed locations and one can assign the booty from a particular location. On the high seas, however, the prizes are floating about. It was a constant struggle of the Admiralty to prevent captains from looking for easy merchant prizes when they were supposed to be doing battle with the enemy or patrolling an enemy coast.

PROBLEM 18.6

Subscriber cable TV is clearly not efficient. It is akin to building a fence around Niagara Falls and charging tourists to look through peepholes in the fence. However, it is not obvious that it is worse than the alternatives. In the next section of the text, we will encounter the very thorny problems associated with the public provision of a service such as television. Furthermore, current cable TV channels provide many programs that ordinary commercial television stations do not offer. Both the consumers of these services and the firms that provide them are better off.

PROBLEM 19.1

The salesperson can offer to pay the customer's premium for the first year. If the customer accepts, he or she gets free insurance for one year and the salesperson pockets $500. If the customer then cancels the policy after the first year, the insurance company is an obvious loser.

PROBLEM 19.2

The CEO is (arguably) the person who makes the decisions that affect the company's profit and therefore the value of its stock. The stock option gives the CEO an incentive to make decisions that enhance the value of the company's stock. For example, if the CEO makes a decision that increases the value of the company's stock to \$15, the CEO can make \$50 000 by making the appropriate decision, buying 10 000 shares at \$10 per share, and then selling the 10 000 shares at \$15 per share. If the CEO would fail to make the appropriate decision in the absence of the stock option, then giving that option is clearly of benefit to the company's shareholders — in this case, the stock option means that the value of each share will increase by \$5. It is not, however, always true that a stock option is in the shareholders' interest. Consider, for example, a case in which the CEO can take an action, call it action *W*, that will lead to a \$5 increase in the value of the stock with probability 1/2 and a \$10 reduction with probability 1/2. Since the stock option offers the CEO a \$50 000 gain if the price of the stock increases but does not force a loss on the CEO if the price of the stock decreases, the stock option gives the CEO an incentive to take action *W*, an action that is clearly not in the interest of shareholders.

PROBLEM 19.3

Regardless of the number of individuals in the partnership, the solution lies on the line $y_R = e_R$ in your diagram. Where? Suppose n is the number of individuals. The solution is at the point on this line where *MRS* is equal to $1/n$, because each individual gets this fraction of the total income generated by the partnership. As n increases, these solutions move toward the origin. Further, the larger n is, the smaller each individual's utility at the solution.

PROBLEM 19.4

The appropriate diagram is Figure A19.1. For larger values of B, the partnership is Pareto-preferred, and for smaller values, the one-person firm is Pareto-preferred.

PROBLEM 19.5

In Figure A19.2 the equilibrium for the owner-managed team is at D and the equilibrium for the one-person firm is at W. Clearly, the equilibrium for the owner-managed team is preferred.

PROBLEM 19.6

If in Figure 19.7 we interpret e_R as Victor's effort, Victor's income-effort relationship is composed of the two horizontal segments $0e'$ and VG. Given this income-effort relationship, Victor will supply e' units of effort. Now suppose that Victor supplies e' units of effort, and in Figure 19.7 interpret e_R as Roberta's effort. Then Roberta's income-effort relationship is the line labelled $y_R = Be_R - M/2$. Given this income-effort relationship, she too will supply e' units of effort.

PROBLEM 19.7

Figure A19.3 is the required diagram. The equilibrium for the one-person firm is at W, and the equilibrium for the owner-managed team is at V. If we increase M by a small amount, the one-person firm is Pareto-preferred. And, if we increase B by a small amount, the owner-managed firm is Pareto-preferred.

FIGURE A19.1

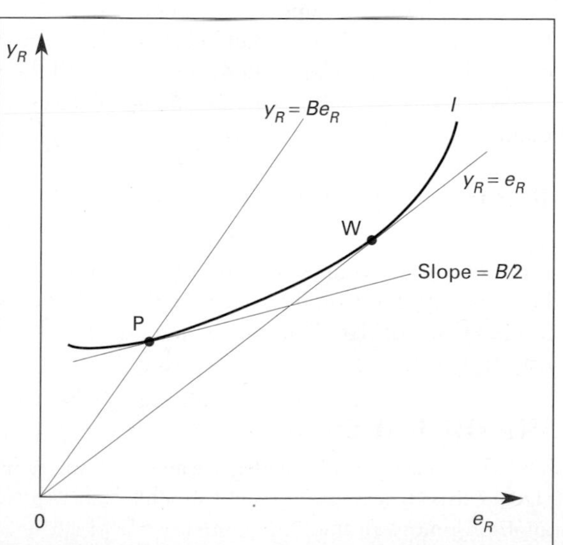

FIGURE A19.2

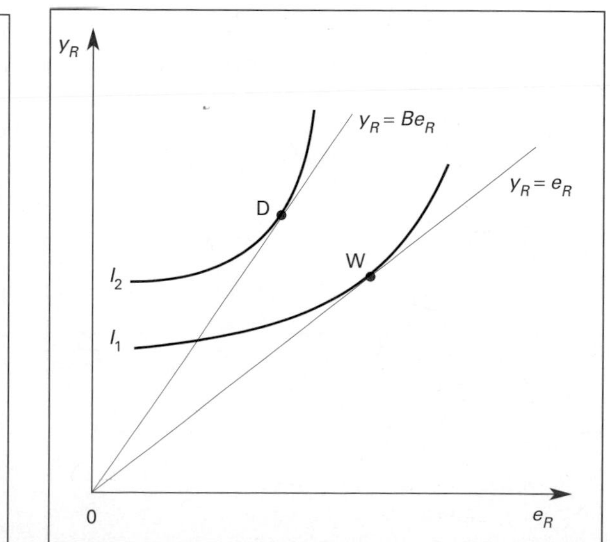

PROBLEM 19.8

If there is just one worker and if he or she has expended 180 minutes in setup time, then he or she has 300 minutes left. Dividing this time equally between the two stages, he or she can produce 15 units. If there are two workers and if one specializes in each stage, then the worker in stage 1 can process 42 units, but the worker in stage 2 can process only 36. Thus, we cannot fully utilize the effort of the stage-1 worker. To maximize productivity per worker, we want each worker to specialize so that he or she incurs only one setup cost, and we want to fully utilize the 8 hours of each worker's time. This means that the number of workers in stage 1 — let us call this number N — multiplied by 42 must be equal to the number of workers in stage 2 — let us call this number M — multiplied by 36. That is, we want two integers — N and M — such that $42N = 36M$, or such that $N/M = 36/42 = 6/7$. Then N equal to 6 and M equal to 7 will do (as will 12 and 14, or 18 and 21, and so on). The 13 workers can produce 252 units.

PROBLEM 19.9

In many cases, it is in the property owner's self-interest. Consider, for example, an owner who is developing a property for resale. The Mechanic's Lien Act assures tradespeople that they will be paid and therefore makes it easier for the property owner to contract with tradespeople. In the absence of such an act, the tradespeople might well demand some other form of assurance that they will be paid, and the assurance is likely to be costly for the property owner.

FIGURE A19.3

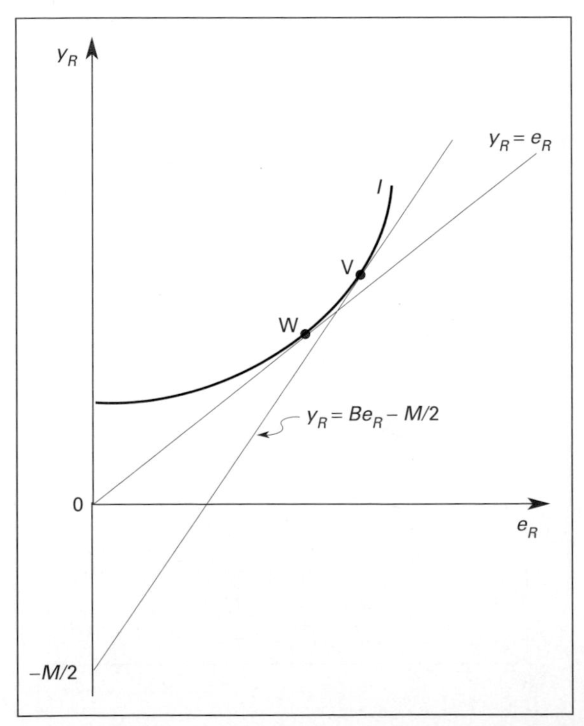

PROBLEM 20.1

The problem is that you may be reluctant to send them your money, fearing that they will just keep it without sending you the goods. Firms that are in the mail-order business spend a lot of money developing a reputation. Sears, for example, built its first warehouse out of bricks with each brick stamped with the word "Sears." A picture of this building appeared on early catalogues, and demonstrated their sincerity in staying in business and not cheating their customers.

PROBLEM 20.2

One reason is that newspapers must get the papers out fast, and are more likely to have hold-up problems with workers and other firms than are magazines, which are not so rushed.

PROBLEM 20.3

If all three groups sold their cars, the market price would be \$1920, equal to 0.6 multiplied by \$2400 plus 0.4 multiplied by \$1200. But this price is not large enough to induce those potential sellers of jewels whose reservation prices are \$2000 to part with them. Hence, in equilibrium, all the cars will not be sold. If the last two groups sold their cars, the market price would be \$1800, equal to 0.5 multiplied by \$2400 plus 0.5 multiplied by \$1200. Since \$1800 exceeds \$1600, in equilibrium, these two groups will sell their cars, but the first group will not. The market failure is that the first group of potential sellers, who would gladly sell their jewels at the \$2400 value of a jewel, do not, in fact, sell them.

PROBLEM 20.4

The only people who are willing to borrow at high interest rates are individuals who are planning on taking huge risks. If they win, they pay back the loan. If they lose they just declare bankruptcy and only lose their existing wealth.

PROBLEM 20. 5

The white veal cannot be sold at the auction because no signal exists to separate it from the pink veal. Hence, another lemons problem. Farmers use beef cattle to produce white veal because it is a more efficient animal in converting milk to meat. These farmers use reputation to police the exchange, and as a result do not have to worry about the lack of signal.

PROBLEM 20.6

With no signallIng, the common hourly wage w is equal to $\$50s + (1 - s)\$20$. If superior workers anticipate getting this hourly wage if they do not get a degree, they will acquire a degree if $10w < 500 - 200$. Substituting for w, this inequality reduces to $s < 1/3$. Hence, superior workers will acquire a degree to signal their superior productivity if s is less than 1/3.

PROBLEM 20.7

a. If the teenager could credibly promise not to drink and drive, the parents might be happy to lend the car to the teenager. But, since the action "drink and drive" is hidden from the parents, they assume the worst and refuse to lend the car.

b. The hidden action problem here is arson. Insurance companies refuse to insure a property for significantly more than its market value because this raises the possibility that the owner of the insured property might profit by intentionally burning the property. In bad economic times, the market value of some properties drops below the insured value, and some owners cannot resist the temptation to profit by burning their own property.

PROBLEM 20.8

The officers owned their own horses. This provided them with the proper incentives to look after them. Even when the army did provide a lesser soldier with a cavalry horse, that soldier always had the same horse. This at least prevented blaming other soldiers for a horse's fall in value.

Glossary

Adverse Selection: the problem of having the wrong group selected given some selection criteria. The term comes from the insurance industry where it was noted that mostly sick people apply for health insurance.

Aggregate Demand: the sum of the individual gross demands.

Aggregate Supply: the sum of the individual gross supplies.

Alchian-Allen Theorem: adding a fixed charge to two qualities of the same good raises the nominal price of each, but lowers the relative price of the high-quality good.

All-or-Nothing Demand Curve: a schedule that gives the consumer's average valuation of a good.

All-or-Nothing Pricing: the practice of offering a specific quantity of a good for sale at a particular price on a take-it or leave-it basis.

Annuity: an income stream with equal payments.

Appropriability Problem: the inability of an inventor to reap all of the rewards of his invention.

Arbitrage: the act of buying a good in a low price market and reselling it in a high price market. The process of arbitrage tends to eliminate differences in prices across markets.

Arbitrage Costs: the costs of selling commodities across segmented markets.

Arc Elasticity: measuring the elasticity between two discrete points along the demand curve.

Asymmetric Information: a situation where some individual holds knowledge not possessed by others.

Attainable Consumption Bundles: those bundles of goods that individuals can afford.

Average Cost Pricing: setting price equal to average costs. Often used by regulators in the context of natural monopoly.

Average Factor Cost: for a monopsonist, this is just equal to the price.

Average Fixed Costs: fixed costs divided by output.

Average Product: total output divided by the total amount of input used.

Average Revenue: total revenue divided by total output.

Average Revenue Product: average revenue times the average product.

Average Total Costs: total costs divided by output.

Average Variable Costs: variable costs divided by the level of output.

Avoidable Costs: true opportunity costs in that you can choose not to incur them.

Barrier to Entry: a cost that new firms must pay to enter a market.

Battle of the Sexes Game: a game with two symmetric Nash equilibria.

Bertrand Model of Duopoly: a model where firms assume that the price of the other firm is constant.

Best-Response Function: the function that yields the maximum payoff to a player's strategies given the strategies of the other players. That is, the function that provides the best thing to do in light of what your opponent is doing.

Borrowing Rate: the rate of interest charged on funds borrowed.

Budget Constraint: an equation that states the sum of expenditures on all goods must not be greater than the total budget available.

Budget Line: an equation that shows the maximum combinations of goods a consumer is able to afford with a given budget.

Capital: any good that yields service or utility over time.

Capital Inputs: inputs that last over many periods.

Capitalization: the process by which future income streams are imputed into the current price of an asset.

Cardinal Utility: the utility function that ranks bundles and the difference in utility number between bundles has a specific cardinal interpretation.

Certainty Equivalent: an assured prospect that makes one indifferent to a risky prospect.

Coase Theorem, Part 1: the allocation of resources is independent of the distribution of property rights when transaction costs are zero. Furthermore, the allocation is Pareto-optimal.

Coase Theorem, Part 2: when transaction costs are positive, property rights are assigned to maximize the gains from trade net of the transaction costs.

Cobb-Douglas Production Function: an historically important production function of the form $y = Az_1^u z_2^v$.

Collusion: when a group of firms get together to raise price by restricting output. The ideal objective of collusion is to restrict output to the monopoly level.

Common Property: a situation where the individual or group of resource owners do not have the right to exclude others from using the resource. This creates a problem due to over-exploitation of the resource.

Comparative Statics: an analysis involving the comparison of one equilibrium with another.

Compensated Budget Line: the budget line that results when the consumer's income is adjusted to place him or her on the original indifference curve after a price change has taken place.

Compensated Demand Curve: a demand curve where the consumer has his or her nominal income adjusted when a price changes such that utility is held constant.

Compensated Demand Function: the demand function derived by holding utility constant. Along this demand function, the individual is given the compensatory income needed to keep him or her on the original indifference curve after a price change.

Compensating Variation: the amount of income that compensates someone for having the right to face a certain set of prices taken away.

Compensatory Income: the minimum income that allows the consumer to attain the original indifference curve after a price change.

Competitive Equilibrium Allocation: an allocation where the quantity demanded equals the quantity supplied.

Competitive Equilibrium Price: the price which clears the market; that is, the price whereby there is no excess demand or supply.

Complements: two goods are complements when an increase in the price of one good leads to a reduction in the quantity demanded of the other. Not to be confused with compliments!

Completeness: the ability to compare any two bundles of goods and rank them according to a preference statement.

Composite Commodity: an aggregation of many commodities into one.

Conditional Input Demands: the demand for inputs holding output constant. These demand functions are analogous to compensated demands for the consumer.

Consol: term used for loans to governments (in the form of the purchase of a bond) which are never repaid. Also called a Perpetuity.

Constant Returns to Scale: the functional property whereby an increase in the level of all inputs leads to the same proportional increase in the output. For example, a doubling of all inputs leads to a doubling of output.

Consumer Capital: goods that are valued for the services they provide.

Consumer's Surplus: the area below a demand curve and above the price of the good. Consumer's surplus is an approximation to EV and CV, and is identically equal to them when income effects are zero.

Consumption Bundle: a combination of a specific quantity of each good.

Continuity Assumption: this applies to cases of uncertainty. There is always some probability that a person would be indifferent between a certainty outcome and a risky prospect.

Continuity of Preferences: indifference curves, unlike political arguments, have no holes in them.

Contract Curve: the locus of allocations at which both trading parties have equal marginal rates of substitution.

Coordination Problem: a situation where more than one equilibrium exists, requiring some type of additional coordination.

Corner Solution: this is the solution to a maximization problem where some choice variables are zero.

Cournot Model of Duopoly: a model where firms assume that the output of the other firm is constant and unresponsive to their own level of output.

Cournot-Nash Equilibrium: see Nash equilibrium.

Cross-Price Elasticity: the percentage change in the quantity demanded of one good, divided by the percentage change in the price of another good.

Deadweight Loss: gains from trade that are destroyed due to some failure to reach the quantity where supply equals demand.

Deadweight Loss of Monopoly: the lost gains from trade that result from the monopoly's reduced level of output.

Decreasing Returns to Scale: the functional property whereby an increase in the level of all inputs leads to a decreased proportional change in the output. For example, a doubling of all inputs leads to a less than doubling of output.

Demand Functions: a function that results from the consumer's maximization problem. This function tells the quantity demanded for a given set of prices and income or utility level.

Deposit Rate: the rate of interest earned on funds saved.

Derived Demand: historical name given to input demand curves to highlight the fact that the demand ultimately depends on the demand for the output.

Difference Principle: the position that the only acceptable inequality in income is the one that improves the lot of the worst-off member of society.

Diminishing Marginal Productivity: adding more of an input, holding other inputs constant, eventually leads to an increase in output at a decreasing rate.

Diminishing *MRS*: Holding utility constant, one is willing to sacrifice less of good y for x the more x one has.

Distribution of Property Rights: the total collection of economic rights.

Division of Labour: the act of having workers specialize according to their comparative advantage.

Dominant Strategy: a strategy better than all others, regardless of the actions of other players. The opposite of a dominated strategy, which is worse than all others regardless of the actions of other players.

Economic Model: a framework for analyzing human behaviour. An economic model contains assumptions about preferences, costs, and market structure.

Economic Rent: a return over and above opportunity costs. This is not the same as economic profit because it ignores sunk costs.

Economics: the study of human behaviour using the principles of economics. Commonly held to be the study of allocating scarce goods among competing ends.

Economy: a metaphor for the place in which all exchange and production takes place.

Edgeworth Box Diagram: a diagram that has the preferences of two individuals in it. Used to determine the general equilibrium of exchange.

Efficiency Criterion: goods must be produced up to the point where price equals marginal cost.

Efficiency in Consumption: all individuals have the same *MRS*.

Efficiency in General Equilibrium: when there is efficiency in consumption, production, and product mix.

Efficiency in Production: the economy is on the production frontier. This means every firm has the same *MRTS*.

Efficiency of Product Mix: every consumer's *MRS* must equal the economy's *MRT*.

Efficient Scale of Production: the level of output at which the long run average cost is at a minimum.

Efficient Transfer Mechanism: a transfer scheme that operates without cost.

Elastic: a large percentage change in quantities for a given percentage change in prices.

Endogenous Variables: variables that are chosen within the model. For example, quantities to consume in the consumer problem or quantities to produce in the producer problem.

Endowment: the total amount of an input, or goods, that is available for use.

Engel Curve: another name for an income consumption path.

Equilibrium: a set of choices for the individual and a corresponding social state such that no individual can make himself better off by making some other choices.

Equilibrium Strategy Combination: a strategy combination where every player's strategy is a best response to the strategies of all other players.

Equivalent Variation: the amount of income one is willing to pay to face a certain price.

Essential Good: one where the indifference curve never crosses an axis.

Excess Demand: the quantity demanded exceeds the quantity supplied at a given price.

Excess Supply: the quantity supplied exceeds the quantity demanded at a given price.

Exchange Economy: a model of an economy where goods are exchanged but not produced.

Excise Tax: a tax that is added to the price of the good being sold.

Exogenous Variables: variables outside the model. For example, income in the consumer model or technology in the producer model.

Expected Monetary Value: the weighted average of the payoffs to a set of possible outcomes. The average winning.

Expected Utility: the probability weighted average of the utilities of a gamble.

Expected Value Line: a line analogous to a budget constraint. It simply identifies those points in the state space that have the same expected value.

Extensive Margin: the margin of either being in or out of a market.

Externality: a situation where an individual does not bear all the costs and/or benefits of their actions.

Feasible Input Bundles: bundles of inputs that can produce a given amount of output, or more.

Firm: an organization that transforms inputs into outputs.

First Theorem of Welfare Economics: the competitive equilibrium is Pareto-optimal.

Fixed Costs: costs that do not vary with output.

Fixed-Proportions Production Function: the property that the optimal input combination is always a constant proportion.

Forgone Income: the income lost due to time spent out of the workforce at some other activity.

Franchise Monopoly: a monopoly founded on a government grant that eliminates competition.

Free Riders: individuals who benefit from some good or service, but who do not pay for it.

Free-Disposal Assumption: the idea that excess inputs (those with negative marginal products) can be avoided or disposed of.

Full Income: the amount of non-wage income plus the wage income.

Full Price: the price of the good both in terms of dollars and time.

Full-Information Equilibrium: the equilibrium reached when information costs are zero.

Future Value: the amount that a sum of dollars today will grow to by a given future time for a given interest rate.

Game of Discoordination: a game with no Nash equilibria.

Game Theory: a branch of mathematics used to find equilibriums in situations where the interaction of players is important.

Games of Plain Substitutes: games where the interactions of players results in a negative externality.

Games of Plain Complements: games where the interactions of players results in a positive externality.

General Equilibrium: a situation where all markets are simultaneously cleared.

Generic Input: an input that is not specialized to any given firm.

Giffen Good: a good for which its price and quantity demanded are positively related. That is, the good has an upward-sloping demand curve.

Gini Coefficient: a measure of income inequality. It is the area between the Lorenz curve and the 45° line, divided by the area under the 45° line. The larger the number, the more unequal the income distribution.

Good: anything a consumer values.

Gross Demand: the amount that individuals demand, ignoring their endowment.

Gross Profit: another word for rent: revenues over variable costs.

Gross Supply: the amount that individuals are endowed with, ignoring what they demand.

Hidden Actions: actions taken by one individual that are hidden from the other individual involved in the transaction.

Hidden Characteristics: attributes of a good or person that are not revealed to the other side of the transaction at the time of exchange.

Hold-up Problem: a situation where someone attempts to extract rents from another that arise out of the existence of sunk costs.

Homogeneous Products: outputs that are identical from one firm to another.

Homothetic Production Functions: production functions that have linear output expansion paths. This means that all of the isoquants are radial blowups of each other.

Horizontal Integration: the merging of firms at the same stage of production.

Hotelling's Law: an asset in fixed supply that yields no utility directly will grow in value at a rate equal to the rate of interest.

Human Capital: a phrase to emphasize that people are capital assets ... our bodies yield services over time.

Human Capital Production Function: a function that relates the amount of human capital to the return.

Income Constraint: essentially a budget constraint, but it takes into account how income is acquired.

Income-Consumption Path: a collection of utility maximizing points derived from changing income while holding prices constant.

Income Effect: the change in quantity demanded that results from the change in real income brought about by a change in the price.

Income Elasticity: the percentage change in the quantity demanded of a good, divided by the percentage change in income.

Income Elasticity of Demand: the percentage change in the quantity demanded, divided by the percentage change in income.

Income-Maintenance Program: a welfare program that targets a level of income as opposed to a level of utility.

Increasing Returns to Scale: the functional property whereby an increase in the level of all inputs leads to an increased proportional change in the output. For example, a doubling of all inputs leads to more than a doubling of output

Indifference Curve: a line connecting all the points which represent the bundles a consumer is indifferent to. When a consumer is indifferent, he or she is willing to allow someone else to choose which bundle he or she consumes. When preferences are represented by a utility function we call an indifference curve a utility curve, where each point on the curve has the same level of utility.

Inducement to Entry: something, like profits, which encourages firms to enter an industry.

Inelastic: a small percentage change in quantities for a given percentage change in prices.

Inessential Good: a good where the indifference curve crosses the axis.

Inferior Good: a good is inferior if its consumption decreases with income.

Inferior Input: an input that decreases in use as output increases.

Inflation: a general rise in the price level.

Input Bundle: the quantities of inputs, like labour and capital, that enter into a production function.

Input Market: a market for capital, labour, or any other input. Inputs are allocated by supply and demand in the same way outputs are.

Institutions: a broad category of rules, laws, customs, and organizations that either substitute or complement exchange and production.

Intensive Margin: the act of changing behaviour at the margin. Thus, when a price changes, a marginal change in the quantity demanded would be an intensive margin adjustment.

Interest Rate: the price of borrowing. The amount paid for early consumption.

Interior Solution: this is a solution to a maximization problem where the choice variables are all positive.

Intermediate Input: an input that is the output of some other firm.

Intermediate Input Markets: markets where the inputs are outputs from other firms.

Internalization: the practice of making the agent responsible for all their actions.

Intertemporal Resource Allocation: the act of spreading income across time in order to consume bundles that may exceed or be smaller than the income in any given period. When people save or borrow, they do this.

Isocost Line: similar to a budget line, it is those combinations of inputs which cost a given amount.

Isoprofit Curves: indifference curves for firms. They show all the strategy combinations that lead to the same level of profit.

Isoquant: a curve composed of all the input bundles that will produce some fixed quantity of output.

Laspeyres Price Index: the period 0 bundle evaluated at the period 1 prices, divided by the period 0 bundle evaluated at the period 0 prices.

Laspeyres Quantity Index: the period 1 bundle evaluated at the period 0 prices, divided by the period 0 bundle evaluated at the period 0 prices.

Law of Demand: there are many definitions of the law of demand. Some consider it just an empirical regularity: when the price of a good increases the quantity demanded falls. Others consider it a statement that ordinary demand curves are always downward sloping in their own price, holding other prices and income constant. This essentially assumes that substitution effects dominate income effects from a price change. Finally, others consider it equivalent to the statement that substitution effects are always negative. This is the same as saying compensated demand curves are downward sloping in their own price.

Leisure-Income Budget Constraint: a budget constraint that takes into account the source of income and the value of time.

Lens of Missed Opportunity: strategy combinations with higher payoffs to all players than the equilibrium strategy.

Leontief Production Function: see Fixed-Proportions Production Function.

Limit Output: the output level that just discourages entry by other firms.

Limit Price: the price that exists when the firm is producing the limit output.

Limit-Price Model: a firm sets its price such that it limits the entry of other firms into the market. Also known as the limit-output model.

Long Run: where all inputs are allowed to vary.

Long-Run Average Costs: the total cost divided by output when all inputs are variable.

Long-Run Cost Function: the minimum cost function when all inputs are variable.

Long-Run Cost Minimization: the process whereby a firm minimizes all costs subject to a level of output by choosing all inputs.

Long-Run Marginal Costs: the rate at which cost increases as output increases when all inputs are variable.

Long-Run Supply Function: the function that gives the quantity supplied for every price when all inputs are allowed to vary.

Long-Term Contract: a contract that lasts for more than one year.

Lorenz Curve: a graphical measure of income distribution that plots the cumulative number of people against the cumulative income. The further the Lorenz curve is from the 45° line, the more skewed the income distribution.

Lump-Sum Tax: a tax that is simply a fixed amount of dollars independent of the quantity sold or the price of the good.

Luxury Good: a good that has an income elasticity greater than 1.

Marginal Change: a small, even infinitesimal, change in some variable.

Marginal Cost: the change in total costs divided by the change in output.

Marginal Factor Cost: the rate at which total factor cost changes as the quantity of the input changes.

Marginal Product: the change in total product divided by the change in the variable input.

Marginal Rate of Substitution: the amount of one good that you are willing to sacrifice to obtain some amount of another good at the margin.

Marginal Rate of Technical Substitution: the rate at which one input can be substituted for the other, holding output constant.

Marginal Rate of Time Preference: a measure of an individual's impatience. When positive it means that individuals prefer current to future consumption at the margin.

Marginal Rate of Transformation: the slope of the production possibility frontier.

Marginal Revenue: the change in total revenue divided by the change in output.

Marginal Revenue Product: the marginal revenue times the marginal product. For a price taking firm in the output market where marginal revenue equals the price, the *MRP* is called the value of the marginal product.

Marginal Value: the maximum amount one is willing to sacrifice at the margin. Marginal value is another name for marginal rate of substitution.

Market Demand: the horizontal summation of individual demands. It gives the total quantity demanded for a given price.

Market Failure: a name given to models that fail to achieve the maximum gains from trade. For example, the monopoly model is often called a case of market failure.

Market for Loanable Funds: a market where individuals borrow and lend money for periods of time.

Market Power: when a firm faces a downward-sloping demand curve.

Market Segmentation: the practice of a monopolist to divide the market into different groups, each of which receives a different price.

Market Supply: the horizontal summation of the individual firm supply curves. It gives the total quantity supplied for a given price.

Maximizing Behaviour: individuals always choose the bundle of goods that yield the highest preference ordering.

Minimum Average Cost: the lowest point on the average cost curve.

Minimum Differentiation: the observation that products and firms often cluster and resemble one another; for example, when gasoline stations locate at the same intersection rather than spread out.

Mixed Strategy: a players' equilibrium strategy consists of a probability distribution over a set of actions.

Money Illusion: the belief that individuals only consider the nominal dollars they own for consumption decisions and not their real purchasing power. The consumer choice model has the property of no money illusion.

Monopoly: the situation where there is only one firm in the market, and the firm faces a downward-sloping demand curve.

Monopoly by Good Management: a firm remains a monopoly by pricing in such a way that it deters entry by other firms.

Monopsony: a market in which there is only one buyer, but many sellers.

Monopsony Power: when a firm faces an upward-sloping supply of labour or other inputs.

Moral Hazard: changes in behaviour brought about because the individual does not face the entire cost of their actions and others cannot observe their behaviour.

Mortgage: a loan that gives the creditor a legal claim against the home on which the loan is based.

Multi-Plant Firms: a firm with more than one production facility.

Nash Equilibrium: same as an equilibrium strategy combination.

Natural Identity of Interests: the doctrine that private vice leads to public virtue.

Natural Monopoly: a monopoly that results from having a declining average cost function over the entire range of the market demand curve.

Necessity Good: a good that has an income elasticity between 0 and 1.

Negative Income Tax: a welfare scheme that includes an unconditional subsidy combined with a proportional tax on earned income. The NIT avoids the extreme work disincentive inherent in the topping-up mechanism but still improves welfare.

Net Demand: the difference between the quantity demanded and the endowment.

Net Supply: the difference between the quantity supplied and the endowment.

No Money Illusion: since a budget constraint is unaffected by a pure inflation, it causes no change in a consumer's behaviour. This is called no money illusion.

No-Entry Condition: no firm will enter the market if the existing firm is producing the limit output or greater.

Nonexcludable Goods: goods that you cannot prevent others from using or enjoying.

Nonintervention: where the state takes no action in trying to solve an externality.

Nonprofit Firms: firms where the directors or controllers are not the residual claimants.

Nonrenewable Resource: an input that can only be used once.

Nonsatiation: there is always one good, that if you had more of it, you would improve your preference ranking.

Normal Good: a good is normal if its consumption increases with income.

Normal Input: an input that increases in use when output increases.

Normative Economics: the subjective study of economic issues. Normative economics attempts to judge between social states.

Oligopoly: competition among a few firms. Each firm faces a downward-sloping demand curve, but the price of the product also depends on the behaviour of other firms.

Opportunity Cost: the highest valued forsaken alternative.

Ordinal Utility: the utility function only ranks bundles. The absolute difference in utility numbers is meaningless.

Ordinary Demand Curves: a relationship between the quantity demanded of one good with its own price, other prices, and income. This relationship is derived from the utility maximizing problem. Also known as Marshallian Demand Curves and Uncompensated Demand Curves.

Ordinary Monopsonistic Price Discrimination: charging different prices based on differences in demand elasticities.

Original Position: the wealth you would have in an imaginary world where all you knew was the total distribution of wealth, not your actual position in it.

Output Effect: when the price of an input goes down, it shifts out the supply curve of output. Thus, the output effect increases the demand for labour.

Output Expansion Path: a path in input space that connects the cost minimizing input bundles that are generated when output increases.

Own-Price Elasticity: the percentage change in the quantity demanded of a good, divided by the percentage change in its own price.

Owner-Operated Firm: a firm where the owner is the labourer and the residual claimant.

Paasche Price Index: the period 1 bundle evaluated at the period 1 prices, divided by the period 1 bundle evaluated at the period 0 prices.

Paasche Quantity Index: the expenditure of the period 1 bundle evaluated at the period 1 prices, divided by the period 0 bundle evaluated at the period 1 prices.

Pareto Criterion: if one person is better off in social state A compared to social state B, and no one is worse off, then by the Pareto Criterion, we would say state A is better.

Pareto-Optimal: an allocation where no rearrangement can make someone better off without making someone else worse off.

Partnership: a firm where the both the control and residual claimancy is shared.

Patent Monopoly: a monopoly that results from a patent or copyright.

Payoff: a term used in game theory to refer to the outcome of a game. Used interchangeably with profit or utility.

Perfect Complements: a situation where the indifference curve is a right angle. The consumer must consume the goods in a fixed proportion.

Perfect Substitutes: a situation where the indifference curve is a straight downward-sloping line. The consumer views both goods as identical.

Perfectly Competitive Input Market: an input market where both the firms and the workers are price takers.

Perfectly Competitive Markets: markets characterized by many firms, many consumers, free exit and entry of firms, and an equilibrium where the quantity demanded equals the quantity supplied.

Perpetuity: an annuity that lasts forever. Also called a Consol.

Players: in game theory the agents in a model are called players.

Pooling Contract: a contract offered to the entire class of customers regardless of their type.

Positioning: actions taken by a firm prior to entering a market.

Positive Economics: the objective study of economic issues. Positive economics attempts to predict or explain social states.

Preferences: individual tastes that influence the choices of goods chosen. Preferences are represented by a utility function.

Preference Ordering: a ranking of all possible bundles.

Preference Statement: either the statement "I prefer bundle A to B" or "I am indifferent to bundles A and B."

Present Value: an amount of future dollars that are discounted by the interest rate to current dollars.

Price Ceiling: a restriction on prices that does not allow the market price to rise higher than some level. For example, a rent control.

Price-Consumption Path: a collection of utility maximizing points arrived at by changing one price and holding income and other prices constant.

Price Discrimination: the price searching practice of selling the same good to different customers at different prices. There are three broad cases: *perfect price discrimination*, where the firm extracts all of the surplus and produces the efficient level of output; *ordinary price discrimination*, where the firm segments the market into two or three groups and charges each group a separate price; and *multipart pricing*, where the firm charges different prices based on the size of "block" of the good purchased.

Price Elasticity of Demand: the percentage change in the quantity demanded, divided by the percentage change in its own price.

Price Floor: a restriction on prices that does not allow the market price to fall below some level. For example, a minimum wage.

Price Index: an indicator of the price level that consumers face in the marketplace.

Price Schedule: when a firm charges multiple prices, each price schedule tells you the blocks of goods that you can buy at a given price.

Primary Inputs: inputs that have not been processed by any other firm. For example, land.

Primary Markets: markets where the inputs have not been processed by other firms (e.g., oil from the ground).

Producer's Surplus: the area above the supply curve and below the market price. It is the difference between total revenue and total variable costs.

Product-Exhaustion Criterion: If the owners of all resources receive what their resources produce, then the individual shares of the total product must add up to 1.

Production Function: A function that reports the maximum amount of output for a given level of inputs.

Productivity Principle: the philosophical position that individuals should receive a share of total income based on the value of what they produce.

Profit Function: total revenue minus total costs.

Property Right: the ability of someone to exercise a choice over a good. These choices usually fall into the categories of consumption, exclusion, and transferability.

Prospect: a term that refers to a gamble; that is, a set of probabilities and their respective outcomes.

Public Goods: goods for which there is no rivalry in consumption.

Public Regulation: the government regulates a price, output, or action of a firm or individual.

Punishment Strategies: strategies that firms use when there has been a breach of contract.

Pure Inflation: a theoretical condition where all prices, including all wages, increase by the same factor.

Quantity Index: an indicator of the amount of real disposable income available to consumers.

Rate of Return: the difference between the future and current price of an asset, divided by the current price.

Real Income: nominal income divided by some price level. In the simple consumer choice model, real income is nominal income divided by one of the prices.

Redistributionist Principle: the philosophical position that the only equitable income distribution is an equal one.

Regulatory Mechanisms: the tools available to the state for enforcing regulations.

Relative Prices: the cost of goods, not in terms of dollars, but in terms of how many other goods must be sacrificed to obtain them.

Renewable Resource: an input that can be used over and over again.

Representative Consumer: the practice of examining one consumer to represent a group of consumers. It assumes income and preferences are the same within the group.

Reservation Price: the maximum value one is willing to pay for a good. The same as Total Value.

Reservation Salary: the lowest salary at which the employee will continue to work.

Residual Claimancy: the distribution of ownership in an economic relationship.

Residual Demand Function: the demand function left over after some fixed level output has been subtracted from it.

Resource Endowment: the list of inputs an individual, firm, or economy has to begin with.

Resource-Based Monopoly: a monopoly that results from owning all of an essential input in a production process.

Resources: inputs used in the production of goods.

Returns to Scale: refers to the effect on the level of output of increasing all inputs by the some proportion. If output doubles when inputs are doubled, then there are constant returns to scale. If output increases by more than double (or less than double) when all inputs are doubled, then there are increasing (decreasing) returns to scale.

Risk Pooling: the practice of reducing risk by spreading it over many individuals.

Risk Spreading: the practice of reducing risk by dividing the ownership of an asset. Similar to risk pooling.

Risk-Averse: an individual who does not like risk. Starting from an endowment of certainty, a risk averse person will turn down a fair bet.

Risk-Inclined: an individual who likes risk. This individual will always accept a fair bet that increases his risk.

Risk-Neutral: an individual who is indifferent to risk.

Rivalrous Goods: goods for which consumption by one person precludes the consumption by another.

Rule of Capture: the legal doctrine whereby ownership is established by the first person who captures or otherwise occupies a resource.

Scarcity: a situation where more of a good is demanded at a zero price than is available.

Screening: a mechanism to filter out the bad types in an adverse selection problem.

Second Law of Demand: the empirical observation that the elasticity of demand increases over time.

Second Theorem of Welfare Economics: given any initial allocation, any Pareto-optimal outcome is a competitive equilibrium.

Self-Enforcing Agreement: an agreement that players have an incentive to carry through on.

Self-Interest: the act of maximizing (either utility or profit) subject to a constraint.

Self-Selection: a process whereby individuals sort themselves voluntarily into the appropriate market.

Separation Theorem: when the borrowing and lending rates of interest are identical, individuals choose income streams that maximize their wealth, independently of how they plan on spending their wealth.

Setup Costs: the costs of establishing an enterprise.

Short Run: where a firm is unable to vary all of its inputs.

Short-Run Average Cost: the total cost divided by the total output when some inputs are held constant.

Short-Run Input Demand Function: the demand function for a variable input when the other inputs are assumed to be constant.

Short-Run Marginal Cost: the change in total cost, divided by the change in output, when some inputs are held constant.

Short-Run Supply Function: a function that gives the quantity supplied for every price when some of the inputs are held constant.

Signal: an action made by an individual to indicate the type of person they are. Signals are used to avoid an adverse selection problem. It is critical that the cost of acquiring the signal be inversely correlated with the high-quality types.

Social Cost: the sum of all the costs of an action.

Social State: the outcome in a given economy.

Social Value: the sum of all the values of an action.

Specialization: the act of performing the task that one is least costly at.

Specific Inputs: inputs that have no (or limited) use to other firms.

Strategies: the things that an agent or player chooses in a model.

Strategy Combination: a list of strategies for every player.

Subjective Probability: the probability of an event that individuals believe. This probability may or may not equal the actual probability of an event.

Substitutes: two goods are substitutes when an increase in the price of one good leads to an increase in the quantity demanded of the other.

Substitution Effect: the change in quantity demanded resulting from a change in the good's own price, holding other prices and utility constant. The substitution effect is always negative. That is, the quantity demanded always falls for a rise in price.

Sunk Costs: costs that have no bearing on behaviour because there is nothing that can be done about them.

Supergame: a model where the firms play a one-period oligopoly game over and over, perhaps an infinite number of times.

Sylos Postulate: in deciding whether to enter a market, a potential entrant takes the output of existing firms as given.

System of Demand Functions: the set of solutions to the consumer maximization problem.

Team Production: the arrangement in which two or more workers accomplish a productive task through their joint effort.

Technically Efficient: a technology that produces the maximum output for a given input bundle.

Technology: the tools used to convert inputs into outputs.

Theory of Self-Interest: the fundamental assumption in economics. The idea that all behaviour is motivated to improve the welfare of the decision maker.

Tie-In Sale: the price-searching practice of selling one good together with another.

Time Constraint: the total hours of work and leisure must add up to 24 h.

Topping-Up Mechanism: the typical welfare scheme of providing non-working individuals with income to meet some minimum standard.

Total Factor Cost: the quantity of an input hired times the price it is hired at.

Total Product Function: a function that tells the total output for a given level of inputs. Also called the Production Function.

Total Revenue: simply price times quantity sold.

Total Surplus: consumer's surplus plus producer's surplus. Also called the gains from trade.

Total Value: the sum of all the marginal values. When income effects are zero, the total value is the area under the demand curve up to the amount consumed. TV is the maximum an individual would be willing to pay for a quantity of goods rather than have none at all.

Transaction Costs: the costs of establishing and maintaining a property right.

Transitional Gains Trap: the problem that results from transfer policies to individuals. The transfers become capitalized in some asset and are sold to others. The new buyers pay a higher price and therefore are no better off because of the transfer.

Transitivity: preferences must be consistent. If A is preferred to B, and B is preferred to C, then A is also preferred to C.

Two-Part Tariff: a form of pricing where an entry fee is charged and then the good is priced separately. Quite often the equilibrium is to price the good at marginal cost.

Two-Term Consistency: if there are only two bundles of goods, A and B, then either A is preferred to B, B is preferred to A, or A is equal to B.

Underemployment: when a person accepts a job in which their value of marginal product is less than the wage rate.

Unit Cost of Production: the cost function for one unit of output.

Unitization: the practice of managing a pool of oil which may span across many private tracts of land as a single unit.

Utility Function: a mathematical function that represents preferences.

Utility-Maintenance Mechanism: an income transfer scheme that targets a minimum level of utility.

Utility Number: a number assigned to a bundle of goods by a utility function.

Value: the maximum amount one is willing to sacrifice.

Variable Cost Function: the minimum variable cost of producing a given level of output.

Variable Costs: costs that change with changes in output.

Variable-Proportions Production Functions: inputs in the production function can be used in different amounts. Essentially the inputs are substitutes for one another.

Vertical Integration: the merging of firms at different stages of production.

Von Neumann-Morgenstern Utility Function: a function that says the utility of a risky prospect is equal to the expected utility of the outcomes.

Wage Floor: another name for minimum wage laws, which place a legal floor on wages.

Walras' Law: If n-1 markets are in equilibrium, then the last market must also be in equilibrium.

Walrasian Auctioneer: an imaginary character who sets the price in a competitive market model.

Water-Diamond Paradox: the puzzle that diamonds, often considered useless, sell for a higher price than water, which is considered essential for life. The resolution is to recognize that the marginal value of diamonds is high, but the total value is low. The opposite holds for water.

Index